D0325787

ROGET'S THESAURUS

BY

PETER MARK ROGET, M.D., F.R.S.

ENLARGED BY

JOHN LEWIS ROGET, M.A.

NEW EDITION REVISED AND ENLARGED BY

SAMUEL ROMILLY ROGET, M.A.

General Reference

MOUNT WASHINGTON PRESS

PLAN OF CLASSIFICATION

Class	Section	Nos.
I. ABSTRACT RELATIONS	I. Existence	1 to 8
	II. Relation	9— 24
	III. Quantity	25— 57
	IV. Order	58— 83
	V. Number	84— 105
	VI. Time	106— 139
	VII. Change	140— 152
	VIII. Causation	153— 179
II. SPACE	I. Generally	180— 191
	II. Dimensions	192— 239
	III. Form	240— 263
	IV. Motion	264— 315
III. MATTER	I. Generally	316— 320
	II. Inorganic	321— 356
	III. Organic	357— 449
	Division	
IV. INTELLECT	(I.) Formation of Ideas	450— 515
	(II.) Communication of Ideas	516— 599
V. VOLITION	(I.) Individual	600— 736
	(II.) Intersocial	737— 819
	Section	
VI. AFFECTIONS	I. Generally	820— 826
	II. Personal	827— 887
	III. Sympathetic	888— 921
	IV. Moral	922— 975
	V. Religious	976—1000

TABULAR SYNOPSIS OF CATEGORIES

CLASS I. ABSTRACT RELATIONS

I. EXISTENCE		
1°. ABSTRACT	1. Existence.	2. Inexistence.
2°. CONCRETE	3. Substantiality.	4. Unsubstantiality.
3°. FORMAL	*Internal.*	*External.*
	5. Intrinsicality.	6. Extrinsicality.
4°. MODAL	*Absolute.*	*Relative.*
	7. State.	8. Circumstance.
II. RELATION		
1°. ABSOLUTE	9. Relation.	10. Irrelation.
	11. Consanguinity.	
	12. Correlation.	
	13. Identity.	14. Contrariety.
	15. Difference.	
2°. CONTINUOUS	16. Uniformity.	16*a*. Non-uniformity.
3°. PARTIAL	17. Similarity.	18. Dissimilarity.
	19. Imitation.	20. Non-imitation.
	20*a*. Variation.	
	21. Copy.	22. Prototype.
4°. GENERAL	23. Agreement.	24. Disagreement.
III. QUANTITY		
1°. SIMPLE	*Absolute.*	*Relative.*
	25. Quantity.	26. Degree.
2°. COMPARATIVE	27. Equality.	28. Inequality.
	29. Mean.	
	30. Compensation.	
	By Comparison with a Standard.	
	31. Greatness.	32. Smallness.
	By Comparison with a similar Object.	
	33. Superiority.	34. Inferiority.
	Changes in Quantity.	
	35. Increase.	36. Decrease.
3°. CONJUNCTIVE	37. Addition.	38. Non-addition. Subduction.
	39. Adjunct.	40. Remainder.
		40*a*. Decrement.
	41. Mixture.	42. Simpleness.
	43. Junction.	44. Disjunction.
	45. Vinculum.	
	46. Coherence.	47. Incoherence.
	48. Combination.	49. Decomposition.

SYNOPSIS OF CATEGORIES

4°. CONCRETE	50. Whole.	51. Part.
	52. Completeness.	53. Incompleteness.
	54. Composition.	55. Exclusion.
	56. Component.	57. Extraneous.
IV. ORDER		
1°. GENERAL	58. Order.	59. Disorder.
	60. Arrangement.	61. Derangement.
2°. CONSECUTIVE	62. Precedence.	63. Sequence.
	64. Precursor.	65. Sequel.
	66. Beginning.	67. End.
	68. Middle.	
	69. Continuity.	70. Discontinuity.
	71. Term.	
3°. COLLECTIVE	72. Assemblage.	73. Non-assemblage. Dispersion.
	74. Focus.	
4°. DISTRIBUTIVE	75. Class.	
	76. Inclusion.	77. Exclusion.
	78. Generality.	79. Speciality.
5°. CATEGORICAL	80. Rule.	81. Multiformity.
	82. Conformity.	83. Unconformity.
V. NUMBER		
1°. ABSTRACT	84. Number.	
	85. Numeration.	
	86. List.	
2°. DETERMINATE	87. Unity.	88. Accompaniment.
	89. Duality.	
	90. Duplication.	91. Bisection.
	92. Triality.	
	93. Triplication.	96. Trisection.
	94. Quadruplication.	
	95. Quaternity.	97. Quadrisection.
	98. Five, &c.	99. Quinquesection, &c.
3°. INDETERMINATE	100. Plurality.	100*a*. Fraction.
		101. Zero.
	102. Multitude.	103. Fewness.
	104. Repetition.	
	105. Infinity.	
VI. TIME		
1°. ABSOLUTE	106. Time.	107. Neverness.
	Definite.	*Indefinite.*
	108. Period.	109. Course.
	108*a*. Contingent Duration.	
	110. Diuturnity.	111. Transientness.
	112. Perpetuity.	113. Instantaneity.
	114. Chronometry.	115. Anachronism.
2°. RELATIVE — 1. *to Succession*	116. Priority.	117. Posteriority.
	118. Present time.	119. Different time.
	120. Synchronism.	
	121. Futurity.	122. Preterition.
2°. RELATIVE — 2. *to a Period*	123. Newness.	124. Oldness.
	125. Morning.	126. Evening.
	127. Youth.	128. Age.
	129. Infant.	130. Veteran.
	131. Adolescence.	
2°. RELATIVE — 3. *to an Effect or purpose*	132. Earliness.	133. Lateness.
	134. Occasion.	135. Intempestivity.
3°. RECURRENT	136. Frequency.	137. Infrequency.
	138. Periodicity.	139. Irregularity.

VII. CHANGE

1°. Simple	140. Change.	141. Permanence.
	142. Cessation.	143. Continuance.
	144. Conversion.	145. Reversion.
	146. Revolution.	
	147. Substitution.	148. Interchange.
2°. Complex	149. Changeableness.	150. Stability.
	Present.	*Future.*
	151. Eventuality.	152. Destiny.

VIII. CAUSATION

1°. Constancy of Sequence	153. *Constant Antecedent.* Cause.	154. *Constant Sequent.* Effect.
	155. *Assignment of Cause.* Attribution.	156. *Absence of Assignment.* Chance.
2°. Connection between Cause and Effect	157. Power.	158. Impotence.
	Degrees of Power.	
	159. Strength.	160. Weakness.
3°. Power in Operation	161. Production.	162. Destruction.
	163. Reproduction.	
	164. Producer.	165. Destroyer.
	166. Paternity.	167. Posterity.
	168. Productiveness.	169. Unproductiveness.
	170. Agency.	
	171. Energy.	172. Inertness.
	173. Violence.	174. Moderation.
4°. Indirect Power	175. Influence.	175*a*. Absence of Influence.
	176. Tendency.	
	177. Liability.	
5°. Combinations of Causes	178. Concurrence.	179. Counteraction.

Class II. SPACE

I. SPACE IN GENERAL

1°. Abstract Space		180*a*. Inextension.
	180. *Indefinite.* Space.	181. *Definite.* Region.
		182. *Limited.* Place.
2°. Relative Space	183. Situation.	
	184. Location.	185. Displacement.
3°. Existence in Space	186. Presence.	187. Absence.
	188. Inhabitant.	189. Abode.
	190. Contents.	191. Receptacle.

II. DIMENSIONS

1°. General	192. Size.	193. Littleness.
	194. Expansion.	195. Contraction.
	196. Distance.	197. Nearness.
	198. Interval.	199. Contiguity.
2°. Linear	200. Length.	201. Shortness.
	202. Breadth. Thickness.	203. Narrowness. Thinness.
	204. Layer.	205. Filament.
	206. Height.	207. Lowness.
	208. Depth.	209. Shallowness.

SYNOPSIS OF CATEGORIES

2°. Linear—*continued*...		210. Summit.	211. Base.
		212. Verticality.	213. Horizontality.
		214. Pendency.	215. Support.
		216. Parallelism.	217. Obliquity.
		218. Inversion.	
		219. Crossing.	
3°. Centrical	1. *General*	220. Exteriority.	221. Interiority.
		222. Centrality.	
		223. Covering.	224. Lining.
		225. Investment.	226. Divestment.
		227. Circumjacence.	228. Interjacence.
		229. Circumscription.	
		230. Outline.	
		231. Edge.	
		232. Inclosure.	
		233. Limit.	
	2. *Special*	234. Front.	235. Rear.
		236. Laterality.	237. Contraposition.
		238. Dextrality.	239. Sinistrality.

III. FORM

1°. General..........	240. Form.	241. Amorphism.
	242. Symmetry.	243. Distortion.
2°. Special...........	244. Angularity.	
	245. Curvature.	246. Straightness.
	247. Circularity.	248. Convolution.
	249. Rotundity.	
3°. Superficial.......	250. Convexity.	252. Concavity.
	251. Flatness.	
	253. Sharpness.	254. Bluntness.
	255. Smoothness.	256. Roughness.
	257. Notch.	
	258. Fold.	
	259. Furrow.	
	260. Opening.	261. Closure.
	262. Perforator.	263. Stopper.

IV. MOTION

1°. Motion in General	264. Motion.	265. Quiescence.
	266. Journey.	267. Navigation.
	268. Traveler.	269. Mariner.
	270. Transference.	
	271. Carrier.	
	272. Vehicle.	273. Ship.
2°. Degrees of Motion	274. Velocity.	275. Slowness.
3°. Conjoined with Force...........	276. Impulse.	277. Recoil.
4°. With Reference to Direction....	278. Direction.	279. Deviation.
	280. Precession.	281. Sequence.
	282. Progression.	283. Regression.
	284. Propulsion.	285. Traction.
	286. Approach.	287. Recession.
	288. Attraction.	289. Repulsion.
	290. Convergence.	291. Divergence.
	292. Arrival.	293. Departure.
	294. Ingress.	295. Egress.
	296. Reception.	297. Ejection.
	298. Food.	299. Excretion.
	300. Insertion.	301. Extraction.
	302. Passage.	
	303. Overstep.	304. Shortcoming.

4°. WITH REFERENCE TO DIRECTION—*cont.*...	305. Ascent.	306. Descent.
	307. Elevation.	308. Depression.
	309. Leap.	310. Plunge.
	311. Circuition.	
	312. Rotation.	313. Evolution.
	314. Oscillation.	
	315. Agitation.	

CLASS III. MATTER

I. MATTER IN GENERAL.......	316. Materiality.	317. Immateriality.
	318. World.	
	319. Gravity.	320. Levity.

II. INORGANIC MATTER

1°. SOLIDS............	321. Density.	322. Rarity.
	323. Hardness.	324. Softness.
	325. Elasticity.	326. Inelasticity.
	327. Tenacity.	328. Brittleness.
	329. Texture.	
	330. Pulverulence.	
	331. Friction.	332. Lubrication.
2°. FLUIDS — 1. *In General*	333. Fluidity.	334. Gaseity.
	335. Liquefaction.	336. Vaporization.
2°. FLUIDS — 2. *Specific*...	337. Water.	338. Air.
	339. Moisture.	340. Dryness.
	341. Ocean.	342. Land.
	343. Gulf. Lake.	344. Plain.
	345. Marsh.	346. Island.
2°. FLUIDS — 3. *In motion*	347. Stream.	
	348. River.	349. Wind.
	350. Conduit.	351. Air-pipe.
3°. IMPERFECT FLUIDS...	352. Semiliquidity.	353. Bubble.
	354. Pulpiness.	355. Unctuousness.
		356. Oil.
		356*a*. Resin.

III. ORGANIC MATTER

1°. VITALITY — 1. *In General*....	357. Organization.	358. Inorganization.
	359. Life.	360. Death.
		361. Killing.
		362. Corpse.
		363. Interment.
1°. VITALITY — 2. *Special*	364. Animality.	365. Vegetability.
	366. Animal.	367. Vegetable.
	368. Zoology.	369. Botany.
	370. Cicuration.	371. Agriculture.
	372. Mankind.	
	373. Man.	374. Woman.

SYNOPSIS OF CATEGORIES

2°. SENSATION

(1) *General*

- 375. Sensibility. — 376. Insensibility.
- 377. Pleasure. — 378. Pain.

(2) *Special*

1. *Touch*

- 379. Touch.
- 380. Sensations of Touch. — 381. Numbness.

2. *Heat*

- 382. Heat. — 383. Cold.
- 384. Calefaction. — 385. Refrigeration.
- 386. Furnace. — 387. Refrigeratory.
- 388. Fuel.
- 389. Thermometer.

3. *Taste*

- 390. Taste. — 391. Insipidity.
- 392. Pungency.
- 393. Condiment.
- 394. Savouriness. — 395. Unsavouriness.
- 396. Sweetness. — 397. Sourness.

4. *Odor*

- 398. Odor. — 399. Inodorousness.
- 400. Fragrance. — 401. Fœtor.

5. *Sound*

(i.) *Sound in General.*

- 402. Sound. — 403. Silence.
- 404. Loudness. — 405. Faintness.

(ii.) *Specific Sounds.*

- 406. Snap. — 407. Roll.
- 408. Resonance. — 408*a*. Non-resonance.
- 409. Sibilation.
- 410. Stridor.
- 411. Cry. — 412. Ululation.

(iii.) *Musical Sounds.*

- 413. Melody. Concord. — 414. Discord.
- 415. Music.
- 416. Musician.
- 417. Musical Instruments.

(iv.) *Perception of Sound.*

- 418. Hearing. — 419. Deafness.

6. *Light*

(i.) *Light in General.*

- 420. Light. — 421. Darkness.
- 422. Dimness.
- 423. Luminary. — 424. Shade.
- 425. Transparency. — 426. Opacity.
- 427. Semitransparency.

(ii.) *Specific Light.*

- 428. Color. — 429. Achromatism.
- 430. Whiteness. — 431. Blackness.
- 432. Gray. — 433. Brown.
- 434. Redness. — 435. Greenness.
- 436. Yellowness. — 437. Purple.
- 438. Blueness. — 439. Orange.
- 440. Variegation.

(iii.) *Perceptions of Light.*

- 441. Vision. — 442. Blindness.
- 443. Dimsightedness.
- 444. Spectator.
- 445. Optical Instruments.
- 446. Visibility. — 447. Invisibility.
- 448. Appearance. — 449. Disappearance.

SYNOPSIS OF CATEGORIES

CLASS IV. INTELLECT

Division (I.). FORMATION OF IDEAS

I. OPERATIONS OF INTELLECT IN GENERAL....	450. Intellect.	450*a*. Absence of Intellect.
	451. Thought.	452. Incogitancy.
	453. Idea.	454. Topic.
II. PRECURSORY CONDITIONS AND OPERATIONS......	455. Curiosity.	456. Incuriosity.
	457. Attention.	458. Inattention.
	459. Care.	460. Neglect.
	461. Inquiry.	462. Answer.
	463. Experiment.	
	464. Comparison.	
	465. Discrimination.	465*a*. Indiscrimination.
	466. Measurement.	
III. MATERIALS FOR REASONING..........	467. Evidence.	468. Counter-evidence.
	469. Qualification.	
	Degrees of Evidence.	
	470. Possibility.	471. Impossibility.
	472. Probability.	473. Improbability.
	474. Certainty.	475. Uncertainty.
IV. REASONING PROCESSES .	476. Reasoning.	477. { Intuition. Sophistry.
	478. Demonstration.	479. Confutation.
V. RESULTS OF REASONING .	480. Judgement.	481. Misjudgement.
	480*a*. Discovery.	
	482. Over-estimation.	483. Under-estimation.
	484. Belief.	485. { Unbelief. Doubt.
	486. Credulity.	487. Incredulity.
	488. Assent.	489. Dissent.
	490. Knowledge.	491. Ignorance.
	492. Scholar.	493. Ignoramus.
	494. Truth.	495. Error.
	496. Maxim.	497. Absurdity.
	Faculties.	
	498. { Intelligence. Wisdom.	499. { Imbecility. Folly.
	500. Sage.	501. Fool.
	502. Sanity.	503. Insanity.
		504. Madman.
VI. EXTENSION OF THOUGHT — 1°. *To the Past*...	505. Memory.	506. Oblivion.
VI. EXTENSION OF THOUGHT — 2°. *To the Future*.	507. Expectation.	508. Inexpectation.
		509. Disappointment.
	510. Foresight.	
	511. Prediction.	
	512. Omen.	
	513. Oracle.	
VII. CREATIVE THOUGHT...	514. Supposition.	
	515. Imagination.	

SYNOPSIS OF CATEGORIES

Division (II.). COMMUNICATION OF IDEAS

I. NATURE OF IDEAS COMMUNICATED	516. Meaning.	517. Unmeaningness.
	518. Intelligibility.	519. Unintelligibility.
	520. Equivocalness.	
	521. Metaphor.	
	522. Interpretation.	523. Misinterpretation.
	524. Interpreter.	
II. MODES OF COMMUNICATION	525. Manifestation.	526. Latency.
	527. Information.	528. Concealment.
	529. Disclosure.	530. Ambush.
	531. Publication.	
	532. News.	533. Secret.
	534. Messenger.	
	535. Affirmation.	536. Negation.
	537. Teaching.	538. Misteaching.
		539. Learning.
	540. Teacher.	541. Learner.
	542. School.	
	543. Veracity.	544. Falsehood.
		545. Deception.
		546. Untruth.
	547. Dupe.	548. Deceiver.
		549. Exaggeration.
III. MEANS OF COMMUNICATION		
1°. *Natural Means*	550. Indication.	
	551. Record.	552. Obliteration.
	553. Recorder.	
	554. Representation.	555. Misrepresentation.
	556. Painting.	
	557. Sculpture.	
	558. Engraving.	
	559. Artist.	
2°. *Conventional Means* — 1. *Language generally*	560. Language.	
	561. Letter.	
	562. Word.	563. Neology.
	564. Nomenclature.	565. Misnomer.
	566. Phrase.	
	567. Grammar.	568. Solecism.
	569. Style.	
	Qualities of Style.	
	570. Perspicuity.	571. Obscurity.
	572. Conciseness.	573. Diffuseness.
	574. Vigour.	575. Feebleness.
	576. Plainness.	577. Ornament.
	578. Elegance.	579. Inelegance.
2. *Spoken Language*	580. Voice.	581. Aphony.
	582. Speech.	583. Stammering.
	584. Loquacity.	585. Taciturnity.
	586. Allocution.	587. Response.
	588. Interlocution.	589. Soliloquy.
3. *Written Language*	590. Writing.	591. Printing.
	592. Correspondence.	593. Book.
	594. Description.	
	595. Dissertation.	
	596. Compendium.	
	597. Poetry.	598. Prose.
	599. The Drama.	

SYNOPSIS OF CATEGORIES

CLASS V. VOLITION

Division (I.). INDIVIDUAL VOLITION

I. VOLITION IN GENERAL	1°. *Acts*	600. Will.	601. Necessity.
		602. Willingness.	603. Unwillingness.
		604. Resolution.	605. Irresolution.
		604*a*. Perseverance. 606. Obstinacy.	607. Tergiversation.
			608. Caprice.
		609. Choice.	609*a*. Absence of Choice. 610. Rejection.
		611. Predetermination.	612. Impulse.
		613. Habit.	614. Desuetude.
	2°. *Causes*	615. Motive.	615*a*. Absence of Motive. 616. Dissuasion.
		617. Plea.	
	3°. *Objects*	618. Good.	619. Evil.
II. PROSPECTIVE VOLITION	1°. *Conceptional*	620. Intention.	621. Chance.
		622. Pursuit.	623. Avoidance.
			624. Relinquishment.
		625. Business.	
		626. Plan.	
		627. Method.	
		628. Mid-Course.	629. Circuit.
		630. Requirement.	
	2°. *Subservience to Ends*	1. *Actual Subservience.*	
		631. Instrumentality.	
		632. Means.	
		633. Instrument.	
		634. Substitute.	
		635. Materials.	
		636. Store.	
		637. Provision.	638. Waste.
		639. Sufficiency.	
		641. Redundance.	640. Insufficiency.
		2. *Degree of Subservience.*	
		642. Importance.	643. Unimportance.
		644. Utility.	645. Inutility.
		646. Expedience.	647. Inexpedience.
		648. Goodness.	649. Badness.
		650. Perfection.	651. Imperfection.
		652. Cleanness.	653. Uncleanness.
		654. Health.	655. Disease.
		656. Salubrity.	657. Insalubrity.
		658. Improvement.	659. Deterioration.
		660. Restoration.	661. Relapse.
		662. Remedy.	663. Bane.
		3. *Contingent Subservience.*	
		664. Safety.	665. Danger.
		666. Refuge.	667. Pitfall.
		668. Warning.	
		669. Alarm.	
		670. Preservation.	
		671. Escape.	
		672. Deliverance.	

SYNOPSIS OF CATEGORIES

II. Prospective Volition—*cont.*	3°. *Precursory Measures*	673. Preparation.	674. Non-preparation.
		675. Essay.	
		676. Undertaking.	
		677. Use.	678. Disuse. 679. Misuse.
III. Action	1°. *Simple*	680. Action.	681. Inaction.
		682. Activity.	683. Inactivity.
		684. Haste.	685. Leisure.
		686. Exertion.	687. Repose.
		688. Fatigue.	689. Refreshment.
		690. Agent.	
		691. Workshop.	
	2°. *Complex*	692. Conduct.	
		693. Direction.	
		694. Director.	
		695. Advice.	
		696. Council.	
		697. Precept.	
		698. Skill.	699. Unskilfulness.
		700. Proficient.	701. Bungler.
		702. Cunning.	703. Artlessness.
IV. Antagonism	1°. *Conditional*	704. Difficulty.	705. Facility.
	2°. *Active*	706. Hindrance.	707. Aid.
		708. Opposition.	709. Co-operation.
		710. Opponent.	711. Auxiliary.
		712. Party.	
		713. Discord.	714. Concord.
		715. Defiance.	
		716. Attack.	717. Defence.
		718. Retaliation.	719. Resistance.
		720. Contention.	721. Peace.
		722. Warfare.	723. Pacification.
		724. Meditation.	
		725. Submission.	
		726. Combatant.	
		727. Arms.	
		728. Arena.	
V. Results of Action		729. Completion.	730. Non-completion.
		731. Success.	732. Failure.
		733. Trophy.	
		734. Prosperity.	735. Adversity.
		736. Mediocrity.	

Division (II.). Intersocial Volition

I. General	737. Authority.	738. Laxity.
	739. Severity.	740. Lenity.
	741. Command.	
	742. Disobedience.	743. Obedience.
	744. Compulsion.	
	745. Master.	746. Servant.
	747. Sceptre.	
	748. Freedom.	749. Subjection.
	750. Liberation.	751. Restraint.
		752. Prison.
	753. Keeper.	754. Prisoner.
	755. Commission.	756. Abrogation.
		757. Resignation.
	758. Consignee.	
	759. Deputy.	

Section		
II. SPECIAL	760. Permission.	761. Prohibition.
	762. Consent.	
	763. Offer.	764. Refusal.
	765. Request.	766. Depreciation.
	767. Petitioner.	
III. CONDITIONAL	768. Promise.	768*a*. Release.
	769. Compact.	
	770. Conditions.	
	771. Security.	
	772. Observance.	773. Non-observance.
	774. Compromise.	

IV. POSSESSIVE RELATIONS

Section		
1°. *Property in General*	775. Acquisition.	776. Loss.
	777. Possession.	777*a*. Exemption.
	778. Participation.	
	779. Possessor.	
	780. Property.	
	781. Retention.	782. Relinquishment.
2°. *Transfer of Property*	783. Transfer.	
	784. Giving.	785. Receiving.
	786. Apportionment.	
	787. Lending.	788. Borrowing.
	789. Taking.	790. Restitution.
	791. Stealing.	
	792. Thief.	
	793. Booty.	
3°. *Interchange of Property*	794. Barter.	
	795. Purchase.	796. Sale.
	797. Merchant.	
	798. Merchandise.	
	799. Mart.	
4°. *Monetary Relations*	800. Money.	
	801. Treasurer.	
	802. Treasury.	
	803. Wealth.	804. Poverty.
	805. Credit.	806. Debt.
	807. Payment.	808. Non-payment.
	809. Expenditure.	810. Receipt.
	811. Accounts.	
	812. Price.	813. Discount.
	814. Dearness.	815. Cheapness.
	816. Liberality.	817. Economy.
	818. Prodigality.	819. Parsimony.

CLASS VI. AFFECTIONS

Section		
I. AFFECTIONS GENERALLY	820. Affections.	
	821. Feeling.	
	822. Sensibility.	823. Insensibility.
	824. Excitation.	
	825. Excitability.	826. Inexcitability.

SYNOPSIS OF CATEGORIES

II. PERSONAL

1°. PASSIVE	827. Pleasure.	828. Pain.
	829. Pleasureableness.	830. Painfulness.
	831. Content.	832. Discontent. 833. Regret.
	834. Relief.	835. Aggravation.
	836. Cheerfulness.	837. Dejection.
	838. Rejoicing.	839. Lamentation.
	840. Amusement.	841. Weariness.
	842. Wit.	843. Dulness.
	844. Humorist.	
2°. DISCRIMINATIVE	845. Beauty.	846. Ugliness.
	847. Ornament.	848. Blemish.
		849. Simplicity.
	850. Taste.	851. Vulgarity.
	852. Fashion.	
		853. Ridiculousness.
		854. Fop.
		855. Affection.
		856. Ridicule.
		857. Laughing-stock.
3°. PROSPECTIVE	858. Hope.	859. Hopelessness. 860. Fear.
	861. Courage.	862. Cowardice.
	863. Rashness.	864. Caution.
	865. Desire.	867. Dislike.
	866. Indifference.	
		868. Fastidiousness.
		869. Satiety.
4°. CONTEMPLATIVE	870. Wonder.	871. Expectance.
	872. Prodigy.	
5°. EXTRINSIC	873. Repute.	874. Disrepute.
	875. Nobility.	876. Commonalty.
	877. Title.	
	878. Pride.	879. Humility.
	880. Vanity.	881. Modesty.
	882. Ostentation.	
	883. Celebration.	
	884. Boasting.	
	885. Insolence.	886. Servility.
	887. Blusterer.	

III. SYMPATHETIC

1°. SOCIAL	888. Friendship.	889. Enmity.
	890. Friend.	891. Enemy.
	892. Sociality.	893. Seclusion.
	894. Courtesy.	895. Discourtesy.
	896. Congratulation.	
	897. Love.	898. Hate.
	899. Favorite.	
		900. Resentment.
		901. Irascibility.
		901*a*. Sullenness.
	902. Endearment.	
	903. Marriage.	904. Celibacy. 905. Divorce.

2°. DIFFUSIVE	906. Benevolence.	907. Malevolence.
		908. Malediction.
		909. Threat.
	910. Philanthropy.	911. Misanthropy.
	912. Benefactor.	913. Evil doer.
3°. SPECIAL	914. Pity.	914*a*. Pitilessness.
	915. Condolence.	
4°. RETROSPECTIVE	916. Gratitude.	917. Ingratitude.
	918. Forgiveness.	919. Revenge.
		920. Jealousy.
		921. Envy.

IV. MORAL

1°. OBLIGATIONS	922. Right.	923. Wrong.
	924. Dueness.	925. Undueness.
	926. Duty.	927. Dereliction.
		927*a*. Exemption.
2°. SENTIMENTS	928. Respect.	929. Disrespect.
		930. Contempt.
	931. Approbation.	932. Disapprobation.
	933. Flattery.	934. Detraction.
	935. Flatterer.	936. Detractor.
	937. Vindication.	938. Accusation.
3°. CONDITIONS	939. Probity.	940. Improbity.
		941. Knave.
	942. Disinterestedness.	943. Selfishness.
	944. Virtue.	945. Vice.
	946. Innocence.	947. Guilt.
	948. Good Man.	949. Bad Man.
	950. Penitence.	951. Impenitence.
	952. Atonement.	
4°. PRACTICE	953. Temperance.	954. Intemperance.
		954*a*. Sensualist.
	955. Asceticism.	
	956. Fasting.	957. Gluttony.
	958. Sobriety.	959. Drunkenness.
	960. Purity.	961. Impurity.
		962. Libertine.
5°. INSTITUTIONS	963. Legality.	964. Illegality.
	965. Jurisprudence.	
	966. Tribunal.	
	967. Judge.	
	968. Lawyer.	
	969. Lawsuit.	
	970. Acquittal.	971. Condemnation.
	973. Reward.	972. Punishment.
		974. Penalty.
		975. Scourge.

V. RELIGIOUS

1°. SUPERHUMAN BEINGS AND REGIONS	976. Deity.	
	977. Angel.	978. Satan.
	979. Jupiter.	980. Demon.
	981. Heaven.	982. Hell.
2°. DOCTRINES	983. Theology.	
	983*a*. Orthodoxy.	984. Heterodoxy.
	985. Revelation.	986. Pseudo-revelation.
3°. SENTIMENTS	987. Piety.	988. Impiety.
		989. Irreligion.

SYNOPSIS OF CATEGORIES

4°. ACTS	990. Worship.	991. Idolatry 992. Sorcery. 993. Spell. 994. Sorcerer.
5°. INSTITUTIONS	995. Churchdom. 996. Clergy. 998. Rite. 999. Canonicals. 1000. Temple.	 997. Laity.

ABBREVIATIONS, &c.

Adj.	*adj.*	Adjectives, Participles, and Words having the power of Adjectives.
Adv.	*adv.*	Adverbs and Adverbial Expressions.
Int.	*int.*	Interjections.
Phr.	*phr.*	Phrases.
V.	*v.*	Verbs.

The numbers are those of the headings, or Categories.

Words in italics within parentheses are not intended to explain the meanings of the words which precede them, but to indicate the nature of allied group of words under the numbers which follow them.

THESAURUS

OF

ENGLISH WORDS AND PHRASES

1. Existence.—N. existence, being, entity, *ens, esse,* subsistence, quiddity.

reality, realness, actuality; positiveness etc. *adj.*; fact, matter of fact, sober reality; truth etc. 494; actual existence.

presence etc. (*existence in space*) 186; coexistence etc. 120.

stubborn fact; not a -dream etc. 515; no joke.

substance, essence, prime constituent, hypostatis.

[Science of existence], ontology.

V. exist, be; have -being etc. *n.*; subsist, live, breathe, stand, obtain, be the case; occur etc. (*event*) 151; have place, rank, prevail, find oneself, pass the time, vegetate.

consist in, lie in, reside in, inhere in.

come into existence etc. *n.*; arise etc. (*begin*) 66; come forth etc. (*appear*) 446.

become etc. (*be converted*) 144; bring into existence etc. 161; coexist, preexist, endure etc. 141.

Adj. existing etc. *v.*; existent, subsistent, under the sun; in -existence etc. *n.*; extant; afloat, on foot, current, prevalent, rife, in force, -vogue; undestroyed.

real, actual, positive, absolute; true etc. 494; substan-tial, -tive; self-existing, -ent.

well-founded, -grounded; un-ideal, -imagined; not -potential etc. 2.

Adv. actually etc. *adj.*; in -fact, – point of fact, – reality; indeed; *de* –, *ipso-facto.*

2. Nonexistence.—N. nonexistence; inexistence, -subsistence; nonentity, *nil*; negativeness etc. *adj.*; nullity; nihil-ity, -ism; *tabula rasa,* blank; abeyance; absence etc. 187; no such thing etc. 4; nothingness, oblivion, *non esse.*

annihilation; extinction etc. (*destruction*) 162.

V. not -exist etc. 1; have no -existence etc. 1; be null and void; cease to -exist etc. 1; pass away, perish; be –, become-extinct etc. *adj.*; die out; disappear etc. 449; melt away, dissolve, leave not a rack behind, leave no trace; go, be no more; die etc. 360.

annihilate, render null, nullify; abrogate etc. 756; destroy etc. 162; take away; remove etc. (*displace*) 185.

Adj. inexistent, non-existent etc. 1; negative, blank, null and void; missing, omitted; absent etc. 187; visionary etc. 515.

unreal, potential, virtual; baseless, *in nubibus*; unsubstantial etc. 4; vain.

un-born, -created, -begotten, -conceived, produced, -made.

perished, annihilated etc. *v.*; extinct, exhausted, gone, lost, departed; defunct etc. (*dead*) 360;

fabulous, ideal etc. (*imaginary*) 515; supposititious etc. 514.

Adv. negatively, virtually, etc. *adj.*

3. Substantiality.—N. substantiality, *hypostasis*; person, thing, object, article; something, a being, an existence; creature, body, substance, flesh and blood, stuff, *substratum*; matter etc. 316; physical nature.

[Totality of existences], world etc. 318; *plenum.*

Adj. substan-tive, -tial, concrete; hypostatic; personal, bodily; tangible etc. (*material*) 316; real, corporeal, evident.

Adv. substantially etc. *adj.*; bodily, essentially.

4. Unsubstantiality.—N. un-, in-substantiality; nothingness, nihility.

nothing, naught, *nil*, nullity, zero, cipher, no one, nobody; never –, ne'er -a one; no such thing, none in the world; nothing -whatever, – at all, – on earth; not a -particle etc. (*smallness*) 32; all - talk, moonshine, – stuff and nonsense, matter of no import.

thing of naught, man of straw, John Doe and Richard Roe; *nominis umbra,* nonentity, figurehead, lay figure; flash in the pan, *vox et praeterea nihil.*

shadow; phantasm, phantom etc. (*fallacy of vision*) 443; dream etc. (*imagination*) 515; *ignis fatuus* etc. (*luminary*) 423; 'such stuff as dreams are made of;' air, thin air; bubble etc. 353; 'baseless fabric of a vision;' mockery.

hollowness, blank; vacuity, void etc. (*absence*) 187.

inanity, fool's paradise, fatuity, stupidity, emptiness of mind.

V. vanish, evaporate, fade, sink, fly –, die –, melt- away, dissolve, disappear etc. 449; become extinct, become invisible.

Adj. unsubstantial; fleeting; base-, ground-less; ungrounded; without –, having no- foundation.

visionary etc. (*imaginary*) 515; immaterial etc. 317; spectral etc. 980; dreamy; shadowy; ethereal, airy, imponderable, tenuous, vague.

vacant, vacuous; empty etc. 187; eviscerated; blank, hollow; nominal; null; inane.

Phr. there's nothing in it.

5. Intrinsicality.—**N.** intrinsicality, inbeing, inherence, inhesion, immanence; subjectiveness; *ego*; essence; essentialness etc. *adj.*; essential part, essential stuff, substance, quintessence, incarnation, quiddity, gist, pith, core, kernel, marrow, sap, lifeblood, backbone, heart, soul, life, flower; important part etc. (*importance*) 642.

principle, nature, constitution, character, ethos, type, quality, crasis, *diathesis*.

habit; temper, -ament; spirit, humor, grain, disposition, streak, tendency etc. 176.

endowment, capacity; capability etc. (*power*) 157; moods, declensions, features, aspects; peculiarities etc. (*specialty*) 79; idiosyncrasy; idiocrasy; diagnostics.

V. be –, run- in the blood; be born so; be - intrinsic etc. *adj.*

Adj. derived from within, subjective; idiocratic, idiosyncratic, intrin-sic, -sical; fundamental, cardinal, normal, inherent, essential, natural; in-nate, -born, -bred, -dwelling, -grained; -wrought; radical, incarnate, thoroughbred, hereditary, inherited, immanent; congen-ital, -ite; connate, running in the blood; coeval with birth, genetic, ingenerate, -genite; indigenous; in the -grain etc. *n.*; bred in the bone, instinctive; inward, internal etc. 221; to the manner born; virtual.

characteristic etc. (*special*) 79, (*indicative*) 550; invariable, incurable, ineradicable, fixed, settled, constant, unchanging.

Adv. intrinsically etc. *adj.*; at bottom, in the main, in effect, essentially, practically, virtually, substantially, *au fond*; fairly.

6. Extrinsicality.—**N.** extrinsicality, objectiveness, *non ego;* extraneousness etc. 57; accident; letter of the law.

Adj. derived from without; objective; extrinsic, -sical; extraneous etc. (*foreign*) 57; modal, adventitious, additional, supervenient, fortuitous; a-, ad-scititious; incidental, casual, accidental, unessential, non-essential, accessory.

implanted, ingrafted; instilled, inculcated.

outward etc. (*external*) 220.

Adv. extrinsically etc. *adj.*

7. State.—**N.** state, condition, category, estate, lot, case, trim, mood, pickle, plight etc. 704; temper; aspect etc. (*appearance*) 448.

constitution, habitude, *diathesis;* frame, fabric etc. 329; stamp, set, fit, mold.

mode, modality, schesis; fettle; form etc. (*shape*) 240.

tone, tenor, turn; trim, guise, fashion, light, complexion, style, character.

V. be in –, possess –, enjoy –, labor under- a -state etc. *n.;* be on a footing, do, fare; come to pass.

Adj. conditional, modal, formal; structural, organic.

Adv. conditionally etc. *adj.;* as -the matter stands, – things are; such being the case etc. 8.

8. Circumstance.—**N.** circumstance, situation, phase, position, posture, attitude, place, point; terms; *régime;* footing, standing, status.

occasion, juncture, conjuncture; contingency etc. (*event*) 151.

predicament; emergen-ce, -cy; exigency, crisis, pinch, pass, push; turning point; crossroads.

bearings, how the land lies.

Adj. circumstantial; given, conditional, provisional; critical; modal; contingent, incidental; adventitious etc. (*extrinsic*) 6.

Adv. in the circumstances etc. *n.*, under the conditions etc. 7; thus, in such wise.

accordingly; that –, such- being the case; that being so, since, seeing that.

as matters stand; as -things, – times- go.

conditionally, provided, if, in case; if -so, – so be, – it be so; if it so -happen, – turn out; in the event of; in such a -contingency, – case, – event; provisionally, unless, without.

according to -circumstances, – the occasion; as it may -happen, – turn out, – be; as the -case may be, – wind blows; *pro re natâ.*

9. Relation.—**N.** relation, bearing, reference, connection, apposition, interconnection, concern, cognation; applicability, appositeness; correlation etc. 12; analogy; similarity etc. 17; affinity, intimacy, friendship; homology, alliance, homogeneity, association, rapport; approximation etc. (*nearness*) 197; filiation etc. (*consanguinity*) 11; interest; relevancy etc. 23; relationship, relative position; relativity; interrelation etc. 12.

comparison etc. 464; ratio, proportion.

link, tie, bond, bond of union.

V. be-related etc. *adj.;* have a relation etc. *n.;* relate –, refer- to; bear upon, regard, concern, touch, affect, have to do with; pertain –, belong –, appertain- to; have respect to; answer to; interest.

bring -into relation with, – to bear upon; connect, associate, draw a parallel; link etc. 43.

Adj. relative; correlative etc. 12; cognate; relating to etc. *v.;* relative to, in relation with, referable *or* referrible to; belonging to etc. *v.;* appurtenant to, in common with.

related, connected; implicated, associated, affiliated, akin, allied to; collateral, cognate, congenial, kindred, affinitive, *en rapport,* in touch with.

approxima-tive, -ting; approaching; proportion-al, -ate, -able; allusive, comparable.

in the same -category etc. 75; like etc. 17; relevant etc. (*apt*) 23.

Adv. relatively etc. *adj.;* pertinently etc. 23.

thereof; as -to, – for, – respects, – re-gards; about; concerning etc. *v.;* anent; relating –, as relates- to; with -relation, – reference, – respect, – regard-to; in respect of; while speaking –, *à propos*-of; in connection with; by the -way, – by; whereas; for –, in -as much as; in point of, as far as; on the -part, – score- of; *quoad hoc; pro re natâ;* under the -head etc. (*class*) 75- of; in the matter of, *in re.*

Phr. 'thereby hangs a tale.'

10. Irrelation. [Want, or absence of relation.]—**N.** irrelation, dissociation; inapplicability; inconnection; multifariousness; disconnection etc. (*disjunction*) 44; inconsequence, independence; incommensurability; irreconcilableness etc. (*disagreement*) 24; heterogeneity;

unconformity etc. 83; irrelevancy, impertinence, *nihil ad rem;* intrusion etc. 24.

V. have no -relation etc. 9 to, – bearing upon, – concern etc. 9 with, – business with; not -concern etc. 9; have -nothing to do with, – no business there; intrude, etc. 24.

bring –, drag –, haul –, lug- in head and shoulders.

Adj. irrelative, irrespective, unrelated, irrelated; arbitrary; independent, unallied; un-, dis-connected; adrift, isolated, insular; extraneous, strange, alien, foreign, outlandish, exotic.

not comparable, incommensurable, heterogeneous; unconformable etc. 83.

irrelevant; rambling etc. 279; inapplicable; not -pertinent, – to the purpose; impertinent, inapposite, beside the mark, *à propos de bottes;* away from –, foreign to –, beside- the -purpose, – question, – transaction, – point; misplaced etc. (*intrusive*) 24.

remote, far fetched, out of the way, forced, neither here nor there, quite another thing; detached, segregated, segregate.

multifarious; discordant etc. 24.

incidental, parenthetical, *obiter dictum,* episodic.

Adv. parenthetically etc. *adj.;* by the -way, – by, *en passant,* incidentally; irrespectively etc. *adj.;* without reference, – regard- to; in the abstract etc. 87, *a se.*

11. Consanguinity. [Relations of kindred.]—**N.** consanguinity, relationship, kindred, blood; parentage etc. (*paternity*) 166; filiation, affiliation; lineage, agnation, connection, cognation, alliance; family -connection, – tie; ties of blood; blood relationship; nepotism.

kins-man, -folk; people; kith and kin; relation, -tive; connection; sib; next of kin; uncle, aunt, nephew, niece; cousin, -german; first –, second- cousin; cousin -once, – twice etc.- removed; near –, distant-relation; brother, sister, one's own flesh and blood.

family, patriarch, matriarch; fraternity; brother-, sister-, cousin-hood.

race, stock, generation; sept etc. 166 ; stirps, side; strain; breed, clan, tribe.

V. be -related etc. *adj.* – to; claim -relationship etc. *n.*- with.

Adj. related, akin, consanguineous, matrilinear, patrilineal, of the blood, family, allied, collateral; cog-, ag-, con-nate; kindred; affiliated, affine; fraternal, avuncular.

intimately –, nearly –, closely –, remotely –, distantly- related, – allied; german.

12. Correlation. [Double or reciprocal relation.]—**N.** reciprocalness etc. *adj.;* recipro-city, -cality, -cation; mutuality, correlation, correspondence, interdependence; interchange etc. 148; exchange, barter; interrelation, interconnection; alternation, see-saw.

V. reciprocate, alternate; interchange etc. 148; exchange; counterchange; interact, correspond, mutualize, give and take.

Adj. reciprocal, mutual, commutual, correlative; alternate; interchangeable; international; correspondent, complementary, analogous.

Adv. *mutatis mutandis; vice versâ;* each other; by turns etc. 148; reciprocally etc. *adj.;* to and fro etc. 314.

13. Identity.—**N.** identity, sameness, oneness, ditto, homogeneity; unity, coincidence, coalescence; convertibility; equality etc. 27; selfness, self, oneself; identification.

monotony, tautology etc. (*repetition*) 104.

synonym.

fac-simile etc. (*copy*) 21; *alter ego* etc. (*similar*) 17; *ipsissima verba* etc. (*exactness*) 494; same; self –, very –, one and the same; very –, actual-thing, no other.

V. be -identical etc. *adj.;* match, coincide, coalesce.

treat as –, render--the same , –identical; identify; recognize the identity of.

Adj. identical; self, ilk; the -same etc. *n.;* self same; synonymous; one and the same.

coincid-, coalesc-ent, -ing; indistinguishable; one; equivalent etc. (*equal*) 27; much -the same, – of a muchness; unaltered.

Adv. identically etc. *adj.;* on all fours; ibid-, -em.

14. Contrariety. [Non-coincidence.]—**N.** contrariety, contrast, foil, antithesis, oppositeness; counterpole; contradiction; antagonism etc. (*opposition*) 708; counteraction etc. 179.

inversion etc. 218; the -opposite, – reverse, – inverse, – converse, – antipodes, – other extreme etc. 237.

antonym.

V. be -contrary etc. *adj.;* contrast with, oppose; differ *toto coelo.*

invert, reverse, turn the tables etc. 218.

contra-dict, -vene; antagonize etc. 708.

Adj. contrar-y, -ious, -iant; opposite, counter, dead against; ad-, con-, reverse; opposed, antithetical, contrasted, antipodean, antagonistic, opposing; conflicting, inconsistent, contradictory, at cross purposes; negative; hostile etc. 708.

differing *toto coelo;* diametrically opposite; as opposite as -black and white, – light and darkness, – fire and water, – the poles, as different as chalk from cheese; 'Hyperion to a satyr;' quite the -contrary, – reverse; no such thing, just the other way, *tout au contraire.*

Adv. contrarily etc. *adj.; contra,* contrariwise, *per contra,* on the contrary, nay rather; topsy-turvy; *vice versâ;* on the other hand etc. (*in compensation*) 30.

15. Difference.—**N.** difference, unlikeness; heterogeneity; vari-ance, -ation, -ety; diversity, dissimilarity etc. 18; disagreement etc. 24; disparity etc. (*inequality*) 28; distinction, contradistinction; distinctness; discrepancy, divergence, contrast etc. 18; nonconformity, incompatibility, antithesis.

discord etc. 713.

modification, moods and tenses.

nice –, fine –, delicate –, subtle- distinction; shade of difference, *nuance;* discrimination etc. 465; *differentia.*

different thing, something else, variant, apple

off another tree, horse of another color, another pair of shoes; this that or the other.

V. be -different etc. *adj.;* differ, vary, ablude, mismatch, contrast; diverge –, depart –, deviate- -from; divaricate; differ -*toto coelo,* — *longo intervallo.*

disagree etc. 713.

vary, modify etc. (*change*) 140.

discriminate etc. 465.

Adj. differing etc. *v.;* different, diverse, divided, heterogeneous; distinguishable; varied, modified; divergent, incongruous, diversified, various; discrepant, dissentient, differential; divers, all manner of; variform etc. 81; discordant etc. 713.

other, another, not the same; unequal etc. 28; unmatched; widely apart.

distinctive, characteristic; discriminative; distinghishing.

Adv. differently etc. *adj.*

Phr. *il y a fagots et fagots; tot nomines tot sententiae;* one man's meat is another man's poison.

16. Uniformity.—**N.** uniformity; homogeneity, -ousness; continuity, stability, consistency; connatural-ity, -ness; homology; accordance; conformity etc. 82; agreement etc. 23.

regularity, constancy, even tenor, routine; monotony, evenness, sameness, dead level; steadiness, equability, unity.

V. be -uniform etc. *adj.;* accord with etc. 23; run through.

become -uniform etc. *adj.;* conform to etc. 82.

render uniform etc. *adj.;* assimilate, level, smooth, dress.

Adj. uniform; homo-geneous, -logous; of a piece, consistent, steady; connatural; monotonous, changeless, dreary, even, invariable, equable, level, regular, stereotyped, unchanged, unvarying; methodical etc. 60; habitual etc. 613.

Adv. uniformly etc. *adj.;* uniformly with etc. (*conformably*) 82; in harmony with etc. (*agreeing*) 23; in a -rut, – groove.

always, ever etc. 112; invariably, without exception, never otherwise; by clock-work; endlessly etc. 112.

Phr. *ab uno disce omnes.*

16a. Non-uniformity. [Absence or want of uniformity.]–**N.** diversity, irregularity, unevenness; multiformity etc. 81; unconformity etc. 83; roughness etc. 256; heterogeneity, heteromorphism.

Adj. diversified, varied, irregular, uneven, rough etc. 256; multifarious; multiform etc. 81; of various kinds; all -manner, – sorts, – kinds- of.

Adv. in all manner of ways, here there and everywhere.

17. Similarity.—**N.** similarity, resemblance, likeness, similitude, semblance; affinity, approximation, parallelism; parity; agreement etc. 23; ana-logy, -logicalness; correspondence, equality etc.

connatural-ness, -ity; brotherhood, family likeness.

alliteration, rhyme, pun.

repetition etc. 104; sameness etc. (*identity*) 13; uniformity etc. 16.

analogue; the like; match, *pendant,* fellow, companion, pair, mate, twin, double, counterpart, brother, sister; one's second self, *alter ego,* chip of the old block, *par nobile fratrum, Arcades ambo,* birds of a feather, *et hoc genus omne.*

parallel; simile; type etc. (*metaphor*) 521; image etc. (*representation*) 554; photograph; close –, striking –, speaking –, faithful etc. *adj.* – likeness, – resemblance.

V. be -similar etc. *adj.;* look like, resemble, bear resemblance, favor; savor –, smack- of; approximate; parallel, match, rhyme with; take after; imitate etc. 19; run in pairs.

Adj. similar; resembling etc. *v.;* like, alike; twin.

analog-ous, -ical; parallel, of a piece; such as, so.

connatural, congeneric, allied to; corresponding, cognate; akin to etc. (*consanguineous*) 11.

approximate, much the same, near, close, something like, such like; a show of; mock, *pseudo,* simulating, representing.

exact etc. (*true*) 494; lifelike, faithful, realistic; true to -nature, – the life; the -very image – picture- of; for all the world like, *comme deux gouttes d'eau;* as like as -two peas, – it can stare; *instar omnium,* case in the same mold, ridiculously like.

Adv. as if, so to speak; as –, as if- it were; *quasi,* just as, *veluti in speculum.*

18. Dissimilarity.—**N.** dissimil-arity, -itude; unlikeness, diversity, disparity, dissemblance; divergence, inequality, difference etc. 15; novelty; variation, variety, originality, disguise.

V. be -unlike etc. *adj.;* vary etc. (*differ*) 15; bear no resemblance to, differ *toto coelo.*

render -unlike etc. *adj.;* vary etc. (*diversify*) 140.

Adj. dissimilar, unlike, disparate; of a different kind etc. (*class*) 75; unmatched, unique; new, novel; unprecedented etc. 83; original.

nothing of the kind; no such –, quite anotherthing; far from it, other than, cast in a different mold, *tertium quid,* as like a dock as a daisy, 'very like a whale;' as different as -chalk from cheese, – Macedon and Monmouth; *lucus a non lucendo.*

diversified etc. 16*a*.

Adv. otherwise, *alias.*

19. Imitation.—**N.** imitation; copying etc. *v.;* transcription; repetition, mimeograph, mimeotype, duplication, reduplication; quotation; reproduction.

mockery, mimicry, mime, simulation, personation; representation etc. 554; semblance, pretence; copy etc. 21; assimilation.

paraphrase, parody etc. 21.

plagiarism; forgery etc. (*falsehood*) 544.

imitator; echo, cuckoo, parrot, ape, monkey, mocking-bird, mimic, impersonator, copyist.

V. imitate, copy, mirror, reflect, reproduce, repeat, borrow; do like, echo, re-echo, catch; transcribe; match, parallel.

mock, take off, mimic, ape, simulate, personate, impersonate; forge; act etc. (*drama*) 599; represent etc. 554; counterfeit, duplicate; portray, parody, travesty, caricature, burlesque.

follow —, tread- in the- -steps, — footsteps, — wake- of; pattern after, take pattern by; follow - suit, — the example of; walk in the shoes of, take a leaf out of another's book, strike in with; take —, model -after; emulate.

Adj. imitated etc. *v.;* mock, mimic; counterfeit, false, pseudo; modelled after, molded on, paraphrastic; literal; imitative, apish; secondhand; imitable; sham etc. 545.

Adv. literally, to the letter, strictly, precisely, *verbatim, literatim, sic, totidem verbis,* word for word, *mot à mot.*

Phr. like master like man.

20. Non-Imitation.—**N.** no imitation, genuineness, originality; creativeness.

Adj. unimitated, uncopied; unmatched, unparalleled; inimitable etc. 33; *unique,* original, primordial, primary, pristine, underived, firsthand, archetypal, prototypal.

20a. Variation.—**N.** variation; alteration etc. (*change*) 140. modification, moods and tenses; modulation.

divergency etc. 291; deviation etc. 279; aberration; innovation.

V. vary etc. (*change*) 140; deviate etc. 279; diverge etc. 291.

Adj. varied etc. *v.;* modified; dissimilar etc. 18; diversified etc. 16*a.*

21. Copy. [Result of imitation.]—**N.** copy, facsimile, counterpart, *effigies,* effigy, symbol, image, form, likeness, similitude, semblance, resemblance, cast, electrotype, stereotype, tracing, ectype; imitation etc. 19; model, representation, adumbration, study; counterfeit presentment, portrait etc. (*representment*) 554.

duplicate; transcript, -ion; reflex, -ion; shadow, echo; chip of the old block; reprint, reproduction, casting, engraving, replica; transfer; second edition etc. (*repetition*) 104; *réchauffé* apograph, fair copy; revise.

parody, caricature, cartoon, burlesque, travesty, paraphrase.

servile -copy, — imitation; counterfeit etc. (*deception*) 545; *pasticcio.*

Adj. faithful; lifelike etc. (*similar*) 17.

22. Prototype. [Thing copied.]—**N.** prototype, original, model, pattern, founding, precedent, standard, scantling, type, arche-, anti-type: protoplast, copy-book, module, exemplar, example, ensample, specimen; paradigm; guide; templet; lay-figure.

text, copy, manuscript, MS., design: fugleman, keynote.

die, mold; matrix, engraving, last, plasm; pro-, proto-plasm; mint; seal, punch, *intaglio,* negative, stamp.

V. be —, set- an example; set a copy; standardize.

23. Agreement.—**N.** agreement; ac-cord, -cordance; unison, harmony, concord etc. 714; concordance, concert, understanding, convention, *entente -cordiale, consortium,* consensus of opinion, pact, mutual understanding, unanimity.

conformity etc. 82; conformance; uniformity etc. 16; consonance, consentaneousness, consistency; congruity, -ence; keeping; congeniality; correspondence, concinnity, parallelism, apposition, union.

fitness, aptness etc. *adj.;* relevancy; pertinence, -cy; sortance; case in point; aptitude, propriety, applicability, admissibility, commensurability, compatibility, suitability; cognation etc (*relation*) 9.

adaptation, adjustment, arrangement, graduation, accommodation; reconcil-iation - ement; assimilation; attunement.

consent etc. (*assent*) 448; concurrence etc. 178; co-operation etc. 709.

right man in the right place, very thing; quite —, just- the thing.

V. be -accordant etc. *adj.;* agree, accord, harmonize; correspond, tally, respond; meet, suit, fit, befit, do, adapt itself to; fall in —, chime in —, square —, quadrate —, consort —, comport- with; dovetail, assimilate; fit like a glove; fit to a -tittle, — T; match etc. 17; become one.

consent etc. (*assent*) 488.

render -accordant etc. *adj.:* fit, suit, adapt, accommodate; graduate; adjust etc. (*render equal*) 27; dress, regulate, readjust; accord, harmonize, reconcile; fadge, dovetail, square.

Adj. agreeing, suiting etc. *v.;* in accord, accordant, concordant, consonant, congruous, consentaneous, correspondent, corresponding, homologous, congenial; becoming; harmonious, reconcilable, conformable; in -accordance, — harminy, — keeping, — unison, etc. *n.;*-with; at one with, of one mind, of a piece; consistent, compatible, proportionate, answerable; commensurate; on all fours.

apt, apposite, pertinent, pat; to the -point, — purpose; happy, felicitous, germane, *ad rem,* in point, bearing upon, applicable, relevant, admissible.

fit, adapted, *in loco, à propos,* appropriate, seasonable, sortable, suitable, idoneous, deft; meet etc. (*expedient*) 646.

at home, in one's proper element.

Adv. *à propos of;* pertinently etc. *adj.; pro rata.*

Phr. *rem acu tetigisti,* the cap fits.

24. Disagreement.—**N.** disagreement, discord, -cordance; disunion, dissonance, dissidence, discrepancy; unconformity etc. 83; incongru-ity, -ence; discongruity, *mésalliance, oxymoron;* jarring etc. *v.;* clash, collision, dissension etc. 713; conflict etc. (*opposition*) 708; controversy etc. 720; falling out, wrangle, argument.

disparity, mismatch, misfit, disproportion; disproportionateness etc. *adj.;* variance, divergence, repugnance.

unfitness etc. *adj.;* inaptitude, impropriety; inapplicability etc. *adj.;* inconsistency, inconcinnity; irrelevancy etc. (*irrelation*) 10.

misjoin-ing, -der; syncretism, intrusion, interference; *concordia discors.*

fish out of water.

V. disagree; clash, quarrel, jar etc. (*discord*) 713; interfere, intrude, come amiss; not concern etc. 10; mismatch; *hymano capiti cervicem jungere equinam.*

Adj. disagreeing etc. *v.;* discordant, discrepant; at -variance, – war; hostile, antagonistic, repugnant, factious, contradictory, dissentious, incompatible, irreconcilable, inconsistent with; unconformable, exceptional etc. 83; intrusive, incongruous; disproportionate, -ed; unharmonious; unconsonant; divergent, repugnant to.

inapt, unapt, inappropriate, inept, infelicitous, improper; unsuit-ed, -able; inapplicable; un-fit, -fitting, -befitting; unbecoming; ill-timed, ill-adapted, unseasonable, *mal â propos,* inadmissible; inapposite etc. (*irrelevant*) 10.

uncongenial; ill-assorted, -sorted, -matched; mis-matched, -mated, -joined, -placed; unaccommodating, irreducible, uncommensurable, unsympathetic.

out of -character, – keeping, – proportion, – joint, – tune, – place, – season, – its element; at -odds, – variance with.

Adv. in -defiance, – contempt, – spite-of; discordantly etc. *adj.; à tort et à travers.*

25. Quantity. [Absolute quantity.]—**N.** quantity, magnitude; size etc. (*dimensions*) 192; amplitude, mass, amount, *quantum,* measure, measurement, substance, strength.

[Science of quantity.] Mathematics, Mathesis.

[Definite or finite quantity] arm-, hand-, mouth-, spoon-, thimble-, capful; stock, batch, lot, dose, ration, quotum, quota, pittance, driblet, part, portion etc. 51.

Adj. quantitative, some, any, more or less.

Adv. to the tune of.

26. Degree. [Relative quantity.]—**N.** degree, grade, extent, measure, proportion, amount, ratio, stint, standard, height, pitch; reach, amplitude, range, scope, size, caliber; gradation, shade; tenor, compass; sphere, station, rank, standing; rate, way, sort.

point, mark, step, stage etc. (*term*) 71; intensity, strength etc. (*greatness*) 31.

V. compare, graduate, calibrate, measure.

Adj. comparative; gradual, shading off, gradational; within the bounds etc. (*limit*), 233.

Adv. by degrees, gradually, inasmuch, *pro tanto*; how-ever, -soever; step by step, bit by bit, little by little, inch by inch, drop by drop, gradatim; by -inches, – slow degrees, – little and little; in some -degree, – measure; to some extent; just a bit.

27. Equality. [Sameness of quantity or degree.]—**N.** equality, parity, co-extension, symmetry, balance, poise; evenness, monotony, level.

equivalence; equi-pollence, -poise, -librium, -ponderance; par, quits; not a pin to choose; distinction without a difference, six of one and half a dozen of the other; identity etc. 13; similarity etc. 17; isotropism; coequality.

equalization, equation, equilibration, coordination, adjustment, readjustment.

drawn -game, -battle, draw, stalemate; neck and neck race; tie, dead heat.

match, peer, compeer, equal, mate, fellow, brother; equivalent.

V. be -equal etc. *adj.;* equal, match, reach, keep pace with, run abreast; come –, amount –, come upto; be –, lie- on a level with; balance; cope with; come to the same thing; level off.

render -equal etc. *adj.;* equalize, level, dress, balance, equate, handicap, give points, trim, adjust, poise; fit, accommodate; adapt etc. (*render accordant*) 23; strike a balance; establish –, restore- equality, – equilibrium; readjust; stretch on the bed of Procrustes.

Adj. equal, even, level, monotonous, coequal, symmetrical, coordinate; on a -par, – level, – footing- with; up to the mark; equiparent.

equivalent, tantamount; quits; homologous; synonymous etc. 522; resolvable into, convertible, much at one, as broad as long, neither more nor less; much the same –, the same thing –, as good- as; all -one, — the same; equi-pollent, -ponderant, -ponderous, -balanced; equalized etc. *v.;* drawn; half and half; isochronous; isoperimetrical.

Adv. equally etc. *adj.; pari passu, ad eundem, caeteris paribus; in equilibrio;* to all intents and purposes.

Phr. it -comes, -adds up, – amounts- to the same thing.

28. Inequality. [Difference of quantity or degree.]—**N.** inequality; dis-, im-parity; odds; difference etc. 15; ill-balanced; unevenness; inclination of the balance, partiality; shortcoming; casting –make- weight; superiority etc. 33; inferiority etc. 34.

V. be -unequal etc. *adj.;* countervail; have –, give- the advantage; turn the scale; kick the beam; topple, -over; over-match etc. 33; not come up to etc. 34.

Adj. unequal, uneven, disparate, partial; un-, over-balanced; top-heavy, lop-sided.

Adv. *haud passibus aequis.*

29. Mean.—**N.** mean, medium, intermedium, average, run of the mill, normal, balance; mediocrity, generality, rule, ordinary -run, -ruck; golden mean etc. (*mid-course*) 628; middle etc. 68; compromise etc. 774; neutrality; middle point, middle course.

V. split the difference; take the -average etc. *n.;* reduce to a -mean etc. *n.;* strike a balance, pair off.

Adj. mean, intermediate; medial; middle etc. 68; average, normal, standard, neutral; middling, moderate.

médiocre, middle-class; *bourgeois,* commonplace etc. (*unimportant*) 643.

Adv. on an average, in the long run; taking -one with another, – all things together, – it for all in all; *communibus annis,* in round numbers.

30. Compensation.—**N.** compensation, equation; commutation; indemnification; compromise etc. 774; neutralization, nullification; counteraction etc. 179; reaction; measure for measure; retaliation etc. 718; equalization etc. 27; redemption, recoupment, recompense.

set-off, offset; make- casting-weight; counterpoise, equipoise, ballast; indemnity, reparation etc. 790; equivalent, *quid pro quo;* bribe, hush-money, tribute etc. 784; amends etc. (*atonement*) 952; counterclaim, counterbalance, equiponderance, countervail, cross demand.

V. make -amends, – compensation; compensate, -pense; indemnify; counter-act, -vail, -poise; equiponderate; balance; out-, over-, counterbalance; set off, offset, cancel; hedge, square, give and take; make up -for, – lee way; cover, fill up, neutralize, nullify; equalize etc. 27; make good; redeem etc. (*atone*) 952; recoup, pay etc. 973.

Adj. compensat-ing, -ory; amendatory, reparative, countervailing etc. *v.;* in the opposite scale; equivalent etc. (*equal*) 27.

Adv. in -return, – consideration; but, however, yet, still, notwithstanding; neverthe-, nathless; although, though; al-, how-beit; in spite of, despite; mauger; at -all events, – any rate; be that as it may, for all that, even so, on the other hand, at the same time, *quoad minus, quand même,* however that may be; after all, – is said and done; taking one thing with another etc. (*average*) 29.

31. Greatness.—**N.** greatness etc. *adj.;* magnitude; size etc. (*dimensions*) 192; multitude etc. (*number*) 102; immensity, enormity, infinity etc. 105; might, strength, intensity, fulness; importance etc. 642; fame etc. 873.

great quantity, quantity, deal, power, sight, pot, volume, world; mass, heap etc. (*assemblage*) 72; stock etc. (*store*) 636; peck, bushel, load, cargo; cart –, wagon –, car –, truck –, shipload; flood, spring tide; abundance etc. (*sufficiency*) 639.

principal –, chief –, main –, greater –, major –, best –, essential- part; bulk, mass etc. (*whole*) 50.

V. be -great etc. *adj.;* run high, soar, loom up, tower, bulk large, transcend; rise –, carry- to a great height; know no bounds; scale, overtop, ascend.

enlarge etc. (*increase*) 35, (*expand*) 194.

Adj. great; greater etc. 33; large, considerable, fair, above par; big, massive, huge etc. (*large in size*) 192; ample; abundant etc. (*enough*) 639; Herculean etc. 159; full, intense, strong, sound, passing, heavy, plenary, deep, high; signal, at its height, in the zenith.

world-wide, wide-spread, extensive; wholesale; many etc. 102.

goodly, noble, precious, mighty; sad, grave, serious, far gone, arrant, downright; utter, -most; crass, gross, arch, profound, intense, consummate; rank, unmitigated, red-hot, desperate; glaring, flagrant, stark staring; thorough-paced, -going; roaring, thumping, thundering, strapping, whacking; extraordinary; important etc. 642; unsurpassed etc. (*supreme*) 33; complete etc. 52.

vast, immense, enormous, extreme; inordinate, excessive, extravagant, exorbitant, outrageous, preposterous, unconscionable, swinging, monstrous, over-grown; towering, stupendous, prodigious, astonishing, incredible; terrific, frightful; marvelous etc. (*wonder*) 870; grand.

unlimited etc. (*infinite*) 105; unapproachable, unutterable, indescribable, ineffable, unspeakable, inexpressible, beyond expression, fabulous.

un-diminished, -abated, -reduced, -restricted.

absolute, positive, stark, decided, unequivocal, essential, perfect, finished.

remarkable, of mark, marked, pointed, veriest; noticeable, uncommon, noteworthy, eminent etc. 873.

Adv. [in a positive degree] truly etc. (*truth*) 494; decidedly, unequivocally, purely, absolutely, seriously, essentially, fundamentally, radically, downright, in all conscience; for the most part, in the main.

[in a complete degree] entirely etc. (*completely*) 52; abundantly, etc. (*sufficiently*) 639; widely, far and wide.

[in a great or high degree] greatly etc. *adj.;* much, muckle, well, indeed, very, very much, a deal, no end of, most not a little; pretty, – well; enough, in a great measure, passing richly; to a -large, – great, – gigantic- extent; on a large scale; so; never –, ever- so; ever so much; by wholesale; mightily, mighty, powerfully; with a witness, *ultra,* in the extreme, extremely, exceedingly, intensely, exquisitely, acutely, indefinitely, immeasurably; beyond -compare, – comparison, – measure, – all bounds; incalculably, infinitely.

[in a supreme degree] pre-eminently, superlatively etc. (*superiority*) 33.

[in a too great degree] immoderately, unduly, monstrously, grossly, preposterously, inordinately, exorbitantly, excessively, enormously, out of all proportion, with a vengeance.

[in a marked degree] particularly, remarkably, singularly, curiously, uncommonly, unusually, peculiarly, notably, signally, strikingly, pointedly, mainly, chiefly; famously, egregiously, prominently, glaringly, emphatically, strangely, wonderfully, amazingly, surprisingly, astonishingly, incredibly, marvelously, awfully, stupendously.

[in an exceptional degree] peculiarly etc. (*unconformity*) 83.

[in a violent degree] furiously etc. (*violence*) 173; severely, desperately, tremendously, extravagantly, confoundedly, deucedly, devilishly, with a vengeance; *à –, à toute- outrance.*

[in a painful degree] painfully, sadly, grossly, sorely, bitterly, piteously, grievously, miserably, cruelly, woefully, lamentably, shockingly, frightfully, dreadfully, fearfully, terribly, horribly, distressingly, balefully.

32. Smallness.—**N.** smallness etc. *adj.;* littleness etc. (*small size*) 193; tenulty; paucity; fewness etc. (*small number*) 103; meanness, insignificance etc. (*unimportance*) 643; mediocrity, moderation.

small quantity, *modicum, minimum;* vanishing point; material point, electron, atom, particle, molecule, corpuscle, point, dab, fleck, speck, dot, mote, jot, iota, ace; *minutiae,* details; look, thought, idea, *soupçon,* whit, tittle, shade, shadow; spark, *scintilla,* gleam; touch, cast; grain, scruple, granule, globule, minim, sup, sip, sop, spice, drop, droplet, sprinkling, dash, smack, tinge, tincture; inch, patch, scantling, dole; scrap, shred, tag, splinter, rag, tatter, cantlet, flitter, gobbet, mite, bit, morsel, crumb, seed, fritter, shive; snip, -pet; snick, snack, snatch, slip, scrag; chip, -ping; shiver, sliver, driblet, clipping, paring, shaving, hair.

nutshell; thimble-, spoon-, hand-, cap-, mouthful; fragment; fraction etc. (*part*)51; drop in the ocean, drop in the bucket.

animalcule etc. 193.

trifle etc. (*unimportant thing*) 643; mere –, next to- nothing; hardly anything; just enough to swear by; the shadow of a shade.

finiteness, finite quantity.

V. be -shall etc. *adj.;* lie in a nutshell.

diminish etc. (*decrease*) 36, (*contract*) 195.

Adj. small, little, tiny, weeny; diminutive etc. (*small in size*) 193; minute; minikin, fine, inconsiderable, dribbling, paltry etc. (*unimportant*) 643; faint etc. (*weak*) 160; slender, light, slight, scanty, scant, limited; meager etc. (*insufficient*) 640; sparing; few etc. 103; low, so-so, middling, tolerable, no great shakes; below –, under-par, – the mark; at a low ebb; halfway; moderate, modest; tender, subtle; petty, shallow, skin-deep.

inappreciable, evanescent, infinite-simal, homeopathic, very small, atomic, molecular, ultra-, -microscopic.

petty, shallow etc. 499.

mere, simple, sheer, stark, bare; near run.

Adv. [in a small degree] to a small extent, on a small scale; a -little, – wee, – tiny bit; slightly etc. *adj.;* imperceptibly; miserably, wretchedly; insufficiently etc. 640; imperfectly; faintly etc. 160; passably, pretty well, well enough.

[in a certain or limited degree] partially, in part; in –, to a certain degree; to a certain extent; comparatively; some, rather; in some -degree, -measure; some-thing, -what; simply, only, purely, merely; at –, at the- -least, – most; ever so little, as little as may be, *tant soit peu,* in ever so small a degree; thus far, *pro tanto;* within bounds, in a manner, after a fashion.

almost, nearly, well nigh, short of, not quite, all but; near –, close- upon; *peu s'en faut,* near the mark; within an -ace, – inch- of; on the brink of; scarcely, hardly, barely, only just, no more than.

[in an uncertain degree] about, therabouts, somewhere about, nearly, say; be the same -more, – little more- or less.

[in no degree] no- ways, – wise; not -at all, – in the least, – a bit, – a bit of it, – a whit, – a jot, – a shadow; in no -wise, – respect; by no -means, – manner of means; on no account, at no hand.

33. Superiority.—**N.** superiority, supremacy, majority; greatness etc. 31; advantage, odds, pull; preponderance, -ation; predominance, vantage ground, coign of vantage, prevalence, partiality; personal superiority; sovereignty etc. 737; nobility etc. (*rank*) 875; Triton among the minnows, *primus inter pares, nulli secundus,* superman; captain etc. 475.

supremacy, pre-eminence; primacy, lead, *maximum;* record; climax, crest, top; culmination etc. (*summit*) 210; transcendence; *ne plus ultra;* lion's share, Benjamin's mess; excess; bisque, surplus etc. (*remainder*) 40, (*redundance*) 641.

V. be -superior etc. *adj.;* exceed, excel, transcend; out-do, -balance, -weigh, -rival, -Herod, outrank, pass, surpass, surmount, get ahead of; over-top, -ride, -pass, -balance, -weigh, -match; top, o'er-top, cap, beat, win out, cut out; beat hollow; outstrip etc. 303; eclipse, throw into the shade, take the shine out of, put one's nose out of joint; have the -upper hand, – whip hand of, – advantage; turn the scale, play first fiddle etc. (*importance*) 642; preponderate, predominate, prevail; precede, take .precedence, come first; come to a head, culminate; beat etc. all others, bear the palm; break the record, take the cake.

become –, render- -larger, etc. (*increase*) 35, (*expand*) 194.

Adj. superior, greater, major, higher; exceeding etc. *v.;* great etc. 31; distinguished, *ultra;* vaulting; more than a match for.

supreme, greatest, maximal, maximum, utmost, paramount, pre-eminent, foremost, crowning; first-rate etc. (important) 642, (*excellent*) 648; unrivalled; peer-, match-less; none such, second to none, *sans pareil;* un-paragoned, -paralleled, -equalled, -approached, -surpassed; superlative, inimitable, *facile princeps,* incomparable, sovereign, without parallel, *nulli secundus, ne plus ultra;* beyond -compare, – comparison; culminating etc. (*topmost*) 210; transcendent, -ental; *plus royaliste que le Roi.*

increased etc. (*added to*) 35; enlarged etc. (*expanded*) 194.

Adv. beyond, more, over; over –, above- the mark; above par; upwards –, in advance- of; over and above; at the top of the scale, on the crest, at it height.

[in a superior or supreme degree] eminently, egregiously, pre-eminently, surpassing, prominently, superlatively, supremely, above all, of all things, the most, to crown all, *par excellence,* principally, especially, particularly, peculiarly, *a fortiori,* even, yea, still more.

Phr. 'we shall not look upon his like again.'

34. Inferiority.—**N.** inferiority, minority, subordinancy; shortcoming, deficiency; handicap; *minimum;* smallness etc. 32; imperfection, shabbiness.

[personal inferiority] commonalty etc. 876; subordinate, substitute, sub.

V. be -inferior etc. *adj.;* fall –, come- short of; not -pass, – come up to; want.

become –, render- smaller etc. (decrease) 36, (*contract*) 195; hide its diminished head, retire into the shade, yield the palm, play second fiddle, take a back seat; bow.

Adj. inferior, smaller; small etc. 32; minor, less, lesser, deficient, minus, lower, subordinate, secondary; second-rate etc. (*imperfect*) 651; sub, subaltern; thrown into the shade; weighed in the balance and found wanting; not fit to hold a candle to.

least, smallest etc. (*see* little, small etc. 193); lowest.

diminished etc. (*decreased*) 36; reduced etc. (*contracted*) 195; unimportant etc. 643.

Adv. less; under –, below- -the mark, – par; at -the bottom of the scale, – a low ebb, – a disadvantage; short of, under.

35. Increase.—**N.** increase; augmentation, addition, enlargement, extension; dilatation etc. (*expansion*) 194; multiplication; increment, accretion; accession etc. 37; production etc. 161; development, growth; aggrandizement, aggravation, intensification; rise; ascent etc. 305; anabasis; ex-aggeration, -acerbation; spread etc. (*dispersion*) 73; flood-, spring-, -tide; gain, produce, profit etc. 618; booty, plunder etc. 793.

V. increase, augment, add to, enlarge; dilate etc. (*expand*) 194; grow, wax, mount, swell, get ahead, gain strength; advance; run –, shoot- up; rise; ascend etc. 305; sprout etc. 194.

aggrandize; raise; exalt; deepen, heighten; lengthen; thicken; strengthen; intensify, enhance, inflate, magnify, double, redouble; multiply; aggravate, exaggerate; ex-asperate, -acerbate; add fuel to the flame, *oleum addere camino*, superadd etc. (*add*) 37; spread etc. (*disperse*) 73.

Adj. increased etc. *v.*; on the increase, undiminished, additional etc. (*added*) 37; increasing etc. *v.*; growing, crescent, intensive, cumulative.

Adv. *crescendo*, increasingly.

Phr. *vires acquirit eundo.*

36. Non-Increase, Decrease.—**N.** decrease, diminution, lessening etc. *v.*; subtraction etc. 38; reduction, abatement, declension; shrinkage etc. (*contraction*) 195; coarctation; abridgment etc (*shortening*) 201; extenuation.

subsidence, catabasis, wane, ebb-, neap-tide, decline; descent etc. 306; decrement, reflux, depreciation; erosion, wear and tear, deterioration etc. 659; anticlimax; mitigation etc. (*moderation*) 174.

V. decrease, diminish, lessen; abridge etc. (*shorten*) 201; shrink etc. (*contract*) 195; drop –, fall –, tail- off; fall away, waste, wear, erode; wane, ebb, decline; descent etc. 306; subside; deliquesce, melt –, die -away; retire into the shade, hide its diminished head, fall to a low ebb, run low, languish, decay, crumble, consume away.

bate, abate, dequantitate; discount; depreciate; extenuate, lower, weaken, attenuate, fritter away; mitigate etc.(*moderate*) 174; belittle, minimize; dwarf, throw into the shade; keep down, reduce etc. 195; shorten etc. 201; subtract etc. 38.

Adj. unincreased etc. (*see* increase etc. 35); decreased etc. *v.*; decreasing etc. *v.*; on the -wane etc. *n.*; deliquescent.

Adv. *diminuendo, decrescendo*, decreasingly.

37. Addition.—**N.** addition, annexation, adjection; junction etc. 43; super-position, -addition, -junction, -fetation; accession, reinforcement; increase etc. 35; increment, supplement; accompaniment etc. 88; interposition etc. 228; insertion etc. 300; summation etc. 85; adjunct etc. 39.

V. add, annex, adject, affix, attach, superadd, subjoin, superpose; clap –, saddle- on; tack to, postfix, append, tag; ingraft; saddle with; sprinkle; introduce etc. (*interpose*) 228; insert etc. 300.

become added, accrue; ad-, supervene; add up etc. 85.

reinforce, strengthen, swell the ranks of; augment etc. 35.

Adj. added etc. *v.*; additional; supplement, -al, -ary; suppletory, subjunctive; adjec-, adsci-, ascititious; additive, extra, spare, further, fresh, more, new, ulterior, other, auxiliary, supernumerary, accessory.

Adv. in addition, more, plus, extra; and, also, likewise, too, furthermore, further, item; and -also, – eke; else, besides, to boot, *et cetera;* etc.; and so -on, – forth; into the bargain, *cum multis aliis*, over and above, moreover.

with, withal; including, inclusive, as well as, not to mention, let alone; together –, along –, coupled –, in conjunction- with; conjointly; jointly etc. 43.

38. Non-Addition. Subduction.—**N.** sub-traction, -duction; deduction, retrenchment; removal; ab-, sub-lation; abstraction etc. (*taking*) 789; garbling etc. *v.*; mutilation, detruncation; amputation, severance; abs-, ex-, re-cision; curtailment etc. 201; minuend, subtrahend; decrease etc. 36; abrasion.

V. sub-tract, -duct; rebate, de-duct, – duce; bate, retrench; remove, withdraw; take – from, – away; detract.

garble, mutilate, amputate, sever, detruncate; cut -off, – away, – out; expurgate; abscind, excise; pare, thin, prune, decimate; abrade, scrape, file; geld, castrate, emasculate, unman, spay, caponize; eliminate.

diminish etc. 36; curtail etc. (*shorten*) 201; deprive of etc. (*take*) 789; weaken.

Adj. subtracted etc. *v.*; subtractive.

tailless, acaudal.

Adv. in -deduction etc. *n.*; less; short of; minus, without, except, excepting, with the exception of, barring, bar, save, exclusive of, save and except, with a reservation.

39. Adjunct. [Thing added.]—**N.** adjunct, addit-ion, -ament; *additum*, affix, appendage, annex; augment, -ation; increment, reinforcement, supernumerary, accessory, item; garnish, sauce; accompaniment etc. 88; adjective, *addendum*, accession, complement, supplement; continuation; extension, subscript, tag, appendix, postscript, interlineation, interpolation, insertion.

rider, codicil, off-shoot, episode, side issue, corollary; piece; flap, lapel, label, tab, strip, fold, lappet, apron, skirt, embroidery, trappings, *cortège*; tail, suffix etc. (*sequel*) 65; wing.

Adj. additional etc. 37.

Adv. in addition etc. 37.

40. Remainder. [Thing remaining.]—**N.** remainder, residue; remains, *remanet*, remnant, rest, relic, relict; leavings, heel-tap, odds and ends, cheese-parings, candle ends, orts; *residuum;* dottle, dregs, etc. (*dirt*) 653; refuse etc. (*useless*) 645; stubble, result, educt; fag-end, stub; ruins, wreck, skeleton, stump; *alluvium.*

surplus, overplus, excess; balance, complement; superfluity etc. (*redundance*) 641; surviv-al, -ance; afterglow.

V. remain; be -left etc. *adj.*; exceed, survive; leave.

Adj. remaining, left; left -behind, – over;

residu-al, -ary; over, odd; unconsumed, sedimentary; surviving; net; exceeding, over and above; outlying, -standing; cast off etc. 782; superfluous etc. (*redundant*) 641.

V. remain; be -left; left -behind, – over; redidual, -ary; over, odd; unconsumed, sedimentary; surviving; net; exceeding, over and above; outlying, -standing; cast off etc. 782; superfluous etc. (*redundant*) 641.

40a. Decrement. [Thing deducted.]—**N.** decrement, discount, rebate, defect, loss, deduction, eduction, tare; drawback; waste, wastage; reprise.

41. Mixture. [Forming a whole without coherence.]—**N.** mix-, admix-, commix-ture, -tion, mingling; commixion, immixture, interfusion, intermixture, alloyage, matrimony; junction etc. 43; combination etc. 48; entanglement, interlacing; miscegenation, interbreeding.

impregnation; in-, dif-, suf-, transfusion; infiltration; seasoning, sprinkling, interlarding; interpolation etc. 228; adulteration, sophistication.

[Thing mixed] tinge, tincture, touch, dash, smack, sprinkling, spice, seasoning, infusion, *soupçon*.

[Compound resulting from mixture] alloy, brass, bronze, pewter etc.; amalgam, *magma*, blend, half-and-half, *mélange, tertium, quid*, miscellany, *ambigu*, medley, mess, hash, hotchpotch, hodgepodge, *pasticcio*, patchwork, odds and ends, all sorts; jumble etc. (*disorder*) 59; salad, sauce, mash, *omnium gatherum*, gallimaufry, ragout, *olla podrida, olio*, salmagundi, *potpourri*, Noah's ark; texture, mingled yarn; mosaic etc. (*variegation*) 440.

half-blood, -caste, -breed, Eurasian; mulatto; terc-, quart-, quinteron etc.; quad-, octo-roon; *griffo, zambo;* cross, hybrid, mongrel etc. 83.

V. mix; join etc. 43; combine etc. 48; com-, im-, inter-mix; mix up with, mingle; com-, inter-, bemingle; shuffle etc. (*derange*) 61; pound together; hash –, stir- up; knead, brew; impregnate with; interlard etc. (*interpolate*) 228; intertwine, -weave etc. 219; associate with, miscegenate, interbreed.

be mixed etc.; get among, be entangled with.

instil, imbue; in-, suf-, trans-fuse; infiltrate, dash, tinge, tincture, season, sprinkle, besprinkle, attemper, medicate, blend, cross; alloy, amalgamate, compound, adulterate, sophisticate, infect.

Adj. mixed etc. *v.;* implex, composite, half-and-half, linsey-wolsey, hybrid, mongrel, heterogeneous; motley etc. (*variegated*) 440; miscellaneous, promiscuous, indiscriminate; miscible.

Adv. among, amongst, amid, amidst, with; in the midst of, in the crowd.

42. Simpleness [Freedom from mixture.]—**N.** simpleness etc. *adj.;* purity, homogeneity.

elimination; sifting etc. *v.;* purification etc. (*cleanness*) 652.

V. render -simple etc. *adj.;* simplify.

sift, winnow, bolt, eliminate; narrow down; get rid of, exclude etc. 55; clear; purify etc. (*clean*) 652; disentangle etc. (*disjoin*) 44.

Adj. simple, uniform, of a piece, homogeneous, single, pure, clear, sheer, neat; Attic.

un-mixed, -mingled, -blended, -combined, -compounded; elementary, undecomposed; unadulterated, -sophisticated, -alloyed, -tinged, -fortified; pure and simple.

free –, exempt- from; exclusive.

Adv. simply etc. *adj.;* only.

43. Junction.—**N.** junction; joining etc. *v.;* joinder, union; con-nection, -junction, -jugation, compendency, annex-ion, -ation, -ment; coalition; astriction, attachment, compagination, vincture, ligation, alligation; accouplement; marriage etc. (*wedlock*) 903; infibulation, inosculation, symphysis, anastomosis, confluence, communication, concatenation; concurrence, meeting, reunion; assemblage etc. 72.

copulation, coition, intercourse.

joint, joining, juncture, chiasma, pivot, hinge, articulation, commissure, seam, suture, gusset, stitch, splice; link etc. 45; miter, mortise.

closeness, tightness etc. *adj.;* coherence etc. 46; combination etc. 48.

V. join, unite; con-join, -nect; associate; put –, lay –, clap –, hang –, lump –, hold –, piece –, tack –, fix –, bind up- together; embody, re-embody; roll into one.

attach, fix, affix, saddle on, fasten, bind, secure, clinch, twist, make -fast etc. *adj.;* tie, pinion, string, strap, sew, lace, stitch, tack, paste, knit, button, buckle, hitch, lash, truss, bandage, braid, splice, swathe, gird, tether, moor, picket, harness, chain; fetter etc. (*restrain*) 751; lock, latch, belay, brace, hook, grapple, leash, couple, accouple, link, yoke, bracket; marry etc. (*wed*) 903; bridge over, span.

pin, nail, bolt, hasp, clasp, clamp, screw, rivet; impact, solder, braze, cement, set; weld –, fuse- together; wedge, rabbet, mortise, miter, jam, dovetail, enchase; graft, ingraft, inosculate; en-, in-twine; inter-link, -lace, -twine, -twist, -weave; entangle; twine round, belay; tighten; trice –, screw-up.

be -joined etc.; hang –, hold- together; cohere etc. 46.

Adj. joined etc. *v.;* joint; con-joint, -junct; corporate, compact; hand in hand.

firm, fast, close, tight, taut, taught, tense, secure, set, intervolved; in-separable, -dissoluble, -secable, -severable.

Adv. jointly etc. *adj.;* in conjunction with etc. (*in addition to*) 37; fast, firmly etc. *adj.;* intimately.

44. Disjunction.—**N.** dis-junction, -connection, -unity, -union, -association, -engagement, -sociation; discontinuity etc. 70; inconnection; abstraction, -edness; isolation; insul-arity, -ation; oasis; separateness etc. *adj.;* severalty; *disjecta membra;* dispersion etc. 73; apportionment etc. 786.

separation; parting etc. *v.;* detachment, segregation; divorce, sejunction, seposition, diduction, diremption, discerption; elision; *caesura*, division, subdivision, break, fracture, rupture; compartition; dis-memberment, -integration, -location; luxation; sever-, dis-severance; scission; re-, ab-scission; circumcision;

lacer-, dilacer-ation; dis-, ab-ruption; avulsion, divulsion; section, resection, cleavage; fission; separability; separatism.

fissure, breach, rent, split, rift, crack, slit, slot, incision.

dissection, anatomy; decomposition etc. 49; cutting instrument etc. (*sharpness*) 253; saw.

V. be -disjoined etc.; come —, fall- -off, — to pieces; peel off; get loose.

dis-join, -connect, -engage, -unite, -sociate, -pair; divorce, part, dispart, detach, uncouple, separate, cut off, rescind, segregate; set —, keep- apart; insulate, isolate; throw out of gear; cut adrift; loose; un-loose, -do, -bind, -tie, -hitch, -chain, -lock etc. (*fix*) 43, -pack, -ravel; disentangle; set free etc. (*liberate*) 750.

sunder, divide, subdivide, sectionalize, sever, dissever, abscind; cut; segment; in-cide, -cise; circumcise; saw, snip, nib, nip, cleave, rive, rend, slit, split, splinter, chip, crack, snap, break, tear, burst; rend etc. -asunder, — in twain; wrench, rupture, shatter, shiver, cranch, crunch, craunch, chop; rip up; hack, hew, slash; whittle; haggle, hackle, discind, lacerate, scamble, mangle, gash, hash, slice.

cut up, carve, quarter, dissect, anatomize; take —, pull —, pick —, tear- to pieces; tear to tatters, — piecemeal; divellicate; skin etc. 226; dis-integrate, -member, -branch, -band; disperse etc. 73; dis-locate, joint; break up; mince; comminute etc. (*pulverize*) 330; distribute, apportion etc. 786.

part, — company; separate, leave; alienate, estrange.

Adj. disjoined etc. *v.;* discontinuous etc. 70; bipartite, multipartite, abstract; digitate; disjunctive; isolated etc. *v.;* insular, separate, disparate, discrete, apart, asunder, far between, loose, free; unattached, -annexed, -associated, -connected; distinct; adrift; straggling; rift, reft, cleft, split.

[capable of being divided] scissile, partible, divisible, separable, severable, detachable.

Adv. separately etc. *adj.;* one by one, severally, apart; adrift, asunder, in twain; in the abstract, abstractedly.

45. Vinculum. [Connecting medium.]—**N.** vinculum, link, *nexus*; connec-tive, -tion; junction etc. 43; bond of union, copula, intermedium, hyphen; bracket; bridge, stepping-stone, isthmus.

bond, tendon, tendril; fiber; cord, -age; riband, ribbon, rope, guy, cable, line, halser, hawser, painter, moorings, wire, chain; string etc. (*filament*) 205.

fastening, tie; liga-ment, -ture; strap; bowline, halliard, tackle, lanyard, rigging, shrouds; standing —, running- rigging; traces, harness; yoke; band, -age; brace, roller, fillet; inkle; with, withe, withy; thong, braid; girder, tie-beam; girt, cinch, girth, girdle, cestus, garter, braces, suspenders, halter, noose, lasso, lariat, surcingle, knot, hitch, running knot, frog.

pin, corking pin, nail, brad, tack, skewer, staple, cleat, clamp; cramp, screw, button, buckle, clasp, hasp, hinge; hank, catch, latch, bolt, ring, latchet, pawl, tag; tooth; stud; hook, — and eye; morse, lock, holdfast, padlock, rivet; anchor, grappling-iron, drawbar, coupler, drawhead, coupling, treenail, trennel, stake, pale, pile, post, bollard.

cement, glue, gum, paste, size, wafer, solder, lute, putty, bird-lime, mortar, stucco, plaster, grout.

shackle, rein etc. (*means of restraint*) 752; suspender etc. 214; prop etc. (*support*) 215.

V. bridge over, span; connect etc. 43; hang etc. 214.

46. Coherence.—**N.** co-, ad-herence, -hesion, -hesiveness; concretion, accretion; con-, agglutination, -glomeration; aggregation; consolidation, set, cementation; sticking, soldering etc. *v.;* connection.

tenacity, toughness; stickiness etc. 352; insepara-bility, -bleness; bur, remora.

conglomerate, concrete etc. (*density*) 321.

V. cohere, adhere, stick, cling, cleave, hold, take hold of, hold fast, close with, embrace, clasp, hug; grow —, hang-together; twine round etc. (*join*) 43.

stick like -a leech, — wax; stick close; cling like -ivy, — a bur; adhere like -a remora, — Dejanira's shirt.

glue; ag-, con-glutinate; cement, lute, paste, gum; solder, weld; cake, coagulate, consolidate etc. (*solidify*) 321; agglomerate.

Adj. co-, ad-hesive, -hering etc. *v.;* tenacious, tough; sticky etc. 352.

united, unseparated, sessile, inseparable, inextricable, infrangible; compact etc. (*dense*) 321.

47. Incoherence. [Want of adhesion, non-adhesion, immiscibility.]—**N.** non-adhesion; immiscibility; incoherence; looseness etc. *adj.;* laxity; relaxation; loosening etc. *v.;* freedom; disjunction etc. 44; rope of sand.

V. make -loose etc. *adj.;* loosen, slacken, relax; un-glue etc. 46; detach etc. (*disjoin*) 44.

Adj. non-adhesive, immiscible; incoherent, detached, loose, slack, baggy, lax, relaxed, flapping, streaming; dishevelled; segregated, like grains of sand; un-consolidated etc. 321; -combined etc. 48; non-cohesive.

48. Combination.—**N.** combination; mixture etc. 41; alloy; junction etc. 43; union, unification, synthesis, incorporation, amalgamation, embodiment, coalescence, crasis, fusion, blend, blending, absorption, centralization, federation.

compound, amalgam, composition, *tertium quid;* resultant, impregnation.

V. combine, unite, incorporate, alloy, intertwine etc. 41; amalgamate, embody, absorb, reembody, blend, merge, fuse, melt into one, consolidate, coalesce, centralize, impregnate; put —, lump- together; federate, associate; fraternize; cement a union, marry, wed, couple, pair, ally.

Adj. combined etc. *v.;* conjunctive, conjugate, conjoint, allied, confederate; impregnated with, ingrained, inoculated.

49. Decomposition.—**N.** decomposition, analysis, diaeresis dissection, resolution, catalysis, electrolysis, hydrolysis, photolysis, dissolution; dispersion etc. 73; disjunction etc. 44;

putrescence, caries, necrosis, corruption etc. (*uncleanness*) 653.

V. decom-pose, -pound; analyze, disembody, dissolve; resolve –, separate- into its elements; electrolyze; dissect, decentralize, break up; disintegrate; disperse etc. 73; unravel etc. (*unroll*) 313; crumble into dust; decay etc. *n.;* deteriorate etc. 659.

Adj. decomposed etc. *v.;* catalytic, analytical.

50. Whole. [Principal part.]—**N.** whole, totality, integrity; totalness etc. *adj.;* entirety, *ensemble,* collectiveness; unity etc. 87; completeness etc. 52; indivisibility, indiscerptibility; integration, embodiment; integer, integral.

all, the whole, total, aggregate, one and all, gross amount, sum, sum-total, *tout ensemble,* length and breadth of, Alpha and Omega, 'be all and end all,' lock, stock and barrel.

bulk, mass, lump, tissue, staple, body, torso, *compages;* truck, bole, hull, hulk, skeleton; greater –, major –, best –, principal –, main-part; essential part etc. (*importance*) 642; lion's share, Benjamin's mess; the long and the short; nearly –, almost- all.

V. form –, constitute- a whole; integrate, embody, amass; aggregate etc. (*assemble*) 72; amount to, come to.

Adj. whole, total, integral, entire; complete etc. 52; one, individual.

un-broken, -cut, -divided, -severed, -clipped, -cropped, -shorn; seamless; undiminished; undemolished, -dissolved, -destroyed, -bruised.

in-divisible, -dissoluble, -dissolvable, -discerptible.

wholesale, sweeping, comprehensive.

Adv. wholly, altogether; totally etc. (*completely*) 52; entirely, all, all in all, considering all things, in a body, collectively, all put together; in the -aggregate, – lump; – mass, – gross, – main, – long run; *en masse,* on the whole, as a whole, bodily, *en bloc, in extenso,* throughout, every inch; substantially.

51. Part.—**N.** part, portion; dose; item, particular; aught, any; division, ward; subdivision, section; chapter, verse; article, clause, count, paragraph, passage; phrase; number, volume, book, fascicule; sector, segment; fraction, fragment; cantle, -t; frustum; detachment, parcel, unit, class etc. 75.

piece, lump, bit; cut, -ting; chip, chunk, collop, slice, scale, shard; lamina etc. 204; moiety; small part; morsel, scrap, crumb; particle etc. (*smallness*) 32; instalment, dividend; share etc. (*allotment*) 786.

débris, odds and ends, oddments, *detritus; excerpta;* member, limb, lobe, lobule, arm, wing, scion, branch, bough, joint, link, offshoot, rami fication, twig, stipule, tendril, bush, spray, sprig; runner; leaf, -let; stump; constituent, ingredient, component part etc. 56.

compartment; department etc. (*class*) 75; county etc. (*region*) 181.

V. part, divide, break etc. (*disjoin*) 44; partition etc. (*apportion*) 786.

Adj. fractional, fragmentary; sectional, aliquot; divided etc. *v.;* in compartments, multifid, incomplete, partial, divided etc. 44.

Adv. partly, in part, partially; piecemeal, part by part; by -instalments, – snatches, – inches, – driblets; bit by bit, inch by inch, foot by foot, drop by drop; in -detail, – lots.

52. Completeness.—**N.** completeness etc. *adj.;* completion etc. 729; integration; integrality.

entirety; universality; totality; perfection etc. 650; solid-ity, -arity; unity; all; *ne plus ultra,* ideal, limit.

complement, supplement, make-weight; filling up etc. *v.*

impletion; satur-ation, -ity; high water; high –, flood –, spring- tide; fill, load, bumper, bellyful; brimmer; sufficiency etc. 639.

V. be -complete etc. *adj.*; come to a head.

render -complete etc. *adj.*; complete etc. (*accomplish*) 729; fill, charge, load, replenish; make-up, – good; piece –, eke- out; supply deficiencies; fill -up, – in, – to the brim, – the measure of; saturate etc. 869.

go the whole -hog, – length, go all lengths.

Adj. complete, entire; whole etc. 50; perfect etc. 650; full, good, absolute, thorough, plenary; solid, undivided; with all its parts.

exhaustive, radical, sweeping, thorough-going; dead.

regular, consummate, unmitigated, sheer, unqualified, unconditional, free; abundant etc. (*sufficient*) 639.

brimming; brim-, top-ful; chock –, choke-full; as full as- an egg is of meat, – a vetch, – a tick; saturated, crammed; replete etc. (*redundant*) 641; fraught, laden; full-laden, -fraught, -charged; heavy laden.

completing etc. *v.;* supplement-al, -ary; ascititious.

Adv. completely etc. *adj.;* altogether, outright, wholly, totally, *in toto,* quite; over head and ears; effectually, for good and all, nicely, fully, through thick and thin, head and shoulders; neck and -heel, – crop; all out; in -all respects, – every respect; at all points, out and out, to all intents and purposes; *toto coelo;* utterly, clean, – as a whistle; to the -full, – utmost, – backbone; hollow, stark; heart and soul, root and branch; down to the ground.

to the top of one's bent, as far as possible, *à outrance.*

throughout; from -first to last, – beginning to end, – end to end, – one end to the other, – Dan to Beersheba, – head to foot, – head to heels, – top to toe, – top to bottom; *de fond en comble; à fond, a capite ad calcem, ab ovo usque ad mala,* fore and aft; every -whit, – inch; *cap-à-pie,* to the end of the chapter; up to the -brim, – ears, – eyes; as ... as can be.

on all accounts; *sous tous les rapports;* with a -vengeance, – witness.

53. Incompleteness.—**N.** incompleteness etc. *adj.;* deficiency, short -measure, – wieght; shortcoming etc. 304; insufficiency etc. 640; imperfection etc. 651; immaturity etc. (*nonpreparation*) 674; half measures.

[part wanting] defect, deficit, shortage, ullage, defalcation, omission, *caret;* interval etc. 198; break etc. (*discontinuity*) 70; non-completion etc. 730; missing link.

V. be -incomplete etc. *adj.;* fall short of etc. 304; lack etc. (*be insufficient*) 640; neglect etc. 460.

Adj. incomplete; imperfect etc. 651; unfinished; uncompleted etc. (*see* complete etc. 729); defective, deficient, wanting; failing; in -default, – arrear; short, – of; hollow, meagre, lame, half-and-half, perfunctory, sketchy; crude etc. (*unprepared*) 674.

mutilated, garbled, mangled, docked, lopped, truncated; bobtailed, cropped, bobbed, shingled.

in -progress, – hand; going on, proceeding.

Adv. incompletely etc. *adj.;* by halves.

Phr. *caetera desunt; caret.*

54. Composition.—**N.** composition, constitution, crasis, synthesis; make-up; combination etc. 48; inclusion, admission, comprehension, reception; embodiment, formation, conformation, production.

compilation etc. 72. (*musical*) composition etc. 415; painting etc. 556; writing etc. 590; typography etc. 591.

V. be -composed, – made, – formed, – made up- of; consist of, be resolved into.

include etc. (*in a class*) 76; subsume; synthesize; contain, hold, comprehend, take in, admit, embrace, embody; involve; implicate, drag into.

compose, constitute, form, make; make –, fill –, build- up; weave, construct, fabricate; compile; write, draw; set up (*printing*); enter into the composition of etc. (*be a component*) 56.

Adj. containing, constituting etc. *v.*

55. Exclusion.—**N.** exclusion, non-admission, omission, exception, rejection, repudiation; exile etc. (*seclusion*) 893; preclusion, lock out, ostracism, prohibition; disbarment, expulsion, ban.

separation, segregation, seposition, elimination, coffer-dam.

V. be excluded from etc.

exclude, bar, ban; leave –, shut –, thrust –, bar- out; reject, repudiate, spurn, blackball; ostracize, boycott; lay –, put –, set-apart, – aside; relegate, segregate; throw overboard; strike -off, – out; neglect etc. 460; banish etc. (*seclude*) 893; separate etc. (*disjoin*) 44.

pass over, omit; garble; eliminate, weed, winnow.

Adj. excluding etc. *v.;* exclusive.

excluded etc. *v.;* unrecounted, not included in; inadmissible; preventive, interdictive.

Adv. exclusive of, barring, except; with the exception of; save, bating.

56. Component.—**N.** component; component –, integral –, integrant-part; element, constituent, ingredient, leaven; part and parcel; contents; appurtenance; feature; member etc. (*part*) 51; personnel.

V. enter into, – the composition of; be a -component etc. *n.;* be –, form- part of; merge –, be merged- in; be implicated in; share in etc. (*participate*) 778; belong –, appertain- to.

form, make, constitute, compose.

Adj. forming etc. *v.;* inclusive; inherent etc. 5.

57. Extraneousness.—**N.** extraneousness etc. *adj.;* extrinsicality etc. 6; exteriority etc. 220; alienism.

foreign -body, – substance, – element; alien, stranger, intruder, interloper, foreigner, tramontane, *novus homo,* new comer, immi-, emi-grant; creole, Afrikander; outsider, outlander, tenderfoot.

Adj. extraneous, foreign, alien, ulterior; exterior, external, outside, outlandish; oversea; tra-, ultra-montane.

excluded etc. 55; inadmissible; exceptional.

Adv. in foreign -parts, – lands; abroad, beyond seas, overseas.

58. Order.—**N.** order, regularity etc. 80; uniformity, symmetry, *lucidus ordo;* harmony, music of the spheres.

gradation, progression; series etc. (*continuity*) 69.

subordination; course, even tenor, routine; method, disposition, arrangement, array, system, economy, discipline; orderliness etc. *adj.*

rank, place etc. (*term*) 71.

V. be –, become- in order etc. *adj.;* form, fall in, draw up; arrange –, range –, place- itself; adjust; fall into –, take- -one's place, – rank; rally round; arrange etc. 60.

Adj. orderly, regular; in -order, – trim, – apple-pie order according to Cocker, – its proper place, neat, neat as a pin, tidy, *en règle,* well regulated, correct, methodical, uniform, symmetrical, ship-shape, business-like, systematic; habitual; unconfused etc. (*see* confuse etc. 61) arranged etc. 60.

Adv. in order; methodically etc. *adj.;* in -turn, – its turn; step by step; by regular -steps, – gradations, – stages, – intervals; *seriatim,* systematically, by clockwork, *gradatim;* at stated periods etc. (*periodically*) 138.

59. Disorder. [Absence, or want of Order, etc.]—**N.** disorder; derangement etc. 61; irregularity; anomaly etc. (*unconformity*) 83; anar-chy, -chism; want of method; dishevelment, untidiness etc. *adj.;* disunion; discord etc. 24.

confusion; confusedness etc. *adj.;* disarray, jumble, mix-up, huddle, litter, lumber; *cahotage;* farrago; mess, muss, mash, muddle, hash; hotchpotch; *imbroglio,* chaos, *omnium gatherum,* medley; mere -mixture etc. 41; fortuitous concourse of atoms, *disjecta membra, rudis indigestaque moles.*

complexity; complexness etc. *adj.;* com-, implication; intri-cacy, -cation; perplexity; network, maze, labyrinth, wilderness, jungle; involution, ravelling, entanglement; coil etc. (*convolution*) 248; sleave, tangled skein, knot, Gordian know, kink, web; wheels within wheels.

turmoil; ferment, etc. (*agitation*) 315; to do, trouble, pudder, pother, row, disturbance, convulsion, tumult, pandemonium, uproar, riot, rumpus, stour, scramble, *fracas,* embroilment, *mêleé,* spill and pelt, rough and tumble; whirlwind etc. 349; bear garden, Babel, Saturnalia, Donnybrook Fair, confusion worse confounded, most admired disorder, *concordia discors;* Bedlam –, hell- broke loose; bull in a china shop;

all the fat in the fire, *diable à quatre,* Devil to pay; pretty kettle of fish; pretty piece of -work, — business.

slattern, slut, sloven; draggle-tail.

V. be -disorderly etc. *adj.;* ferment, play at cross purposes.

put out of order; derange etc. 61; ravel etc. 219; ruffle, rumple; bungle, botch.

Adj. disorderly, orderless; out of -order; — place, — gear, — whack; irregular, desultory; anomalous etc. (*unconformable*) 83; acephalous, disorganized, straggling; un-, im-methodical; unsymmetric; unsystematic; untidy, slovenly, bedraggled, messy; dislocated; out of sorts; promiscuous, indiscriminate; chaotic, anarchical, lawless; unarranged etc. 60; confused, tumultuous, turbulent, tempestuous; deranged etc. 61; topsy turvy etc. (*inverted*) 218; shapeless etc. 241; disjointed, out of joint.

com-plex, -plexed; intricate, complicated, perplexed, involved, ravelled, entangled, knotted, tangled, inextricable; irreducible.

troublous; riotous etc. (*violent*) 173.

Adv. irregularly etc. *adj.;* by fits and -snatches, — starts; pell-mell; higgledy-piggledy; helter-skelter, harum-scarum; in a ferment; at -sixes and sevens, — cross purposes; upside down etc. 218.

Phr. the cart before the horse, chaos is come again.

60. Arrangement. [Reduction to Order.]—**N.** arrangement; plan etc. 626; preparation etc. 673; dispos-al, -ition; col-, al-location; disbribution; sorting etc. *v.;* assortment, allotment; grouping; apportionment, *taxis,* taxonomy, *syn-taxis,* graduation, organization, grading; re-organization, rationalization.

analysis, classification, division, digestion; systematism.

[Result of arrangement] order, orderliness, form, array; digest, synopsis etc. (compendi -um) 596; *syntagma,* table, atlas; register etc. (*record*) 551; score etc. 415; cosmos, organism, architecture.

[Instrument for sorting] sieve etc. 260; file, card index.

V. reduce to —, bring into- order; introduce order into; rally.

arrange, dispose, place, form; put —, set —, place- in order; straighten up, tidy up; set out, collocate, allocate, pack, marshal, range, size, rank, array, group, parcel out, allot, space, distribute, deal; cast —, assign- the parts; dispose of, assign places to; assort, sort; sift, riddle; put —, set- -to rights, — into shape, — in trim, — in array.

class, -ify; divide; file, string together, thread; register etc. (*record*) 551; list, catalogue, tabulate, index, alphabeticize, graduate, digest, grade, codify; orchestrate, score.

methodize, regulate, systematize, standardize, co-ordinate, organize, settle, fix.

unravel, disentangle, ravel, card; disembroil.

Adj. arranged etc. *v.;* embattled, in battle array; cut and dried; methodical, orderly, regular, systematic, tabular.

61. Derangement. [Subversion of Order; bringing into disorder.]—**N.** derangement etc. *v.;* disorder etc. 59; evection, discomposure, disturbance; dis-, de-organization; involvement; dislocation; perturbation, interruption; shuffling etc. *v.;* inversion etc. 218; corrugation etc. (*fold*) 258; insanity etc. 503.

V. derange; dis-, mis-arrange; dis-, mis-place; mislay, discompose, disorder, de-, dis-organize; embroil, unsettle, disturb, confuse, trouble, perturb, jumble, tumble; huddle, shuffle, muddle, toss, hustle, fumble, riot; bring —, put —, throw- into -disorder etc. 59; break the ranks, disconcert, convulse; break in upon.

unhinge, dislocate, put out of joint, throw out of gear.

turn topsy-turvy etc. (*invert*) 218; bedevil; complicate, involve, perplex, confound; im-, embrangle; tangle, en-tangle, ravel, tousle, dishevel, ruffle, rumple etc. (*fold*) 258; dement.

litter, scatter; mix etc. 41.

Adj. deranged etc. *v.;* syncre-tic, -tistic.

62. Precedence.—**N.** precedence; coming before etc. *v.;* the lead, *le pas;* superiority etc. 33; importance etc. 642; anteced-ence, -ency; anteriority etc. (*front*) 234; precursor etc. 64; priority etc. 116; precession etc. 280; anteposition, preference.

V. precede; come -before, — first; forerun, head, lead, take the lead; lead the -way, — dance; introduce, usher in; have the *pas;* set the fashion etc. (*influence*) 175; lead off, kick off, open the ball; take —, have- precedence; outrank; have the start etc. (*get before*) 280.

place before; prefix; premise, prelude, preface.

Adj. preceding etc. *v.;* pre-, antecedent; anterior, prior etc. 116; before; former, foregoing; before-, above-mentioned; aforesaid, said; precurs-ory, -ive; prevenient, preliminary, prefatory, introductory; prelus-ive, -ory; proemial, preparatory.

Adv. before; in advance etc. (*precession*) 280.

Phr. *seniores priores.*

63. Sequence.—**N.** sequence, coming after; going after etc. (*following*) 281; consecution, succession; posteriority etc. 117.

continuation; prolongation, order of succussion; successiveness; Elijah's mantle.

secondariness; subordinancy etc. (*inferiority*) 34.

V. succeed; come -after, — on, — next; follow, ensue, step into the shoes of; alternate.

place after, suffix, append.

Adj. succeeding etc. *v.;* sequent; sub-, consequent; sequacious, proximate, next; consecutive etc. (*continuity*) 69; alternate, amoebaean.

latter; posterior etc. 117.

Adv. after, subsequently; behind etc. (*rear*) 235.

64. Precursor.—**N.** precursor, antecedent, precedent, predecessor; forerunner, van-courier, *avant-coureur,* pioneer, prodrome, *prodromos,* outrider; leader, bell-wether; herald, harbinger; dawn.

prelude, preamble, preface, prologue, foreword, *avant-propos, protasis,* prolusion, proem, *prolepsis, prolegomena,* prefix, introduction;

lead, heading, frontispiece, groundwork; preparation etc. 673; overture, voluntary, *exordium*, symphony, *ritornello;* premises.

prefigurement etc. 511; omen etc. 512.

Adj. precursory; prelu-sive, -sory, -dious; proemial, introductory, prefatory, prodromous, inaugural, preliminary; precedent etc. (*prior*) 116.

65. Sequel.—**N.** sequel, suffix, successor; tail, *queue*, train, wake, trail, rear; retinue, suite; appendix, postscript, subscript; epilogue; conclusion; peroration; codicil; continuation, *sequela;* appendage etc. 39; tail –, heel-piece; tag, more last words; *colophon.*

follower, after-glow, -growth, -crop, -taste, -math.

after-part, -piece, -course, -thought, -game; *arrière pensée*, second thoughts.

66. Beginning.—**N.** beginning, commencement, opening, outset, incipience, inception, inchoation; introduction etc. (*precursor*) 64; *alpha;* initial; foundation; inauguration, *début, le premier pas*, embarcation, rising of the curtain; zero hour; exordium, curtain raiser; maiden speech; prelude; outbreak, onset, brunt; initiative, move, first move; gambit, narrow –, thin- end of the wedge; fresh start, new departure; forefront.

origin etc. (*cause*) 153; source, rise; bud, germ etc. 153; egg, rudiment; genesis, birth, nativity, cradle, infancy, incunabula; start, starting-point etc. 293; dawn etc. (*morning*) 125.

title-page; head, -ing, caption; van etc. (*front*) 234.

en-trance, -try; inlet, orifice, mouth, chops, lips, porch, portal, portico, *propylon*, door; gate, -way; postern, wicket, threshold, vestibule; skirts, border etc. (*edge*) 231; tee.

first -stage, – blush, – glance, – impression, – sight.

rudiments, elements, outlines, *principia*, grammar, *protasis;* alphabet, ABC.

V. begin, commence, inchoate, rise, arise, originate, institute, conceive, initiate, open, dawn, set in, take its rise, enter upon, start; enter; set out etc. (*depart*) 293; embark in.

usher in; lead -off, – the way; take the -lead, – initiative; inaugurate, head; stand -at the head, – first, – for; lay the foundations etc. (*prepare*) 673; found etc. (*cause*) 153; set -up, – on foot, – agoing, – abroach, – the ball in motion; apply the match to a train; launch, broach; open -up, – the door to; set -about, – to work; make a -beginning, – start; handsel; take the first step, lay the first stone, cut the first turf; break -ground, – the ice, – cover; pass –, cross- the Rubicon; open -fire, – the ball; ventilate, air; undertake etc. 676.

come into -existence, – the world; make one's *début*, take birth; burst forth, break out; spring –, crop- up.

begin -at the beginning, – *ab ovo*, – again, – *de novo;* start afresh, make a fresh start, shuffle the cards, resume, recommence.

Adj. beginning etc. *v.;* initi-al, -atory, -ative; inceptive, introductory, incipient; proemial, inaugural; incho-ate, -ative; embryonic, rudimental; primogenial; primeval etc. (*old*) 124; rudimentary, aboriginal; natal, nascent.

first, foremost, front, leading, head; maiden.

begun etc. *v.;* just -begun etc. *v.*

Adv. at –, in- the beginning etc. *n.;* first, in the first place, *imprimis*, first and foremost; *in limine;* in -the bud, – embryo, – its infancy; from -the beginning, — its birth; *ab -initio*, – *ovo*, – *incunabilis*, primarily, originally.

67. End.—**N.** end, close, termination; desinence, conclusion, *finis, finale*, period, term, *terminus*, last, *omega;* extreme, -tremity; gable –, butt –, fagend; tip, nib, point; tail etc. (*rear*) 235; verge etc. (*edge*) 231; tag, epilogue, peroration; *bonne bouche*, bitter end, tail end; terminal; *apodosis;* appendix.

consummation, *dénouement;* finish etc. (*completion*) 729; fate; doom, -sday; crack of doom, day of Judgment, fall of the curtain, wind-up; goal, destination; limit, stoppage, end all, determination; expiration, expiry; death etc. 360; end of all things; finality; eschatology.

break up, *commencement de la fin*, last stage, turning point; *coup de grâce*, death-blow; knock-out.

V. end, close, finish, terminate, conclude, be all over; expire; die etc. 360; come –, draw- to a -close etc. *n.;* have run its course; run out, pass away.

bring to an -end etc. *n.*, put an end to, make an end of; determine; get through; achieve etc. (*complete*) 729; stop etc. (*make to cease*) 142, shut up shop.

Adj. ending etc. *v.;* final, terminal, definitive, conclusive; crowning etc. (*completing*) 729; last, ultimate; hindermost; rear etc. 235; caudal.

contermin-ate, -ous, -able.

ended etc. *v.;* at an end; settled, decided, over, played out, set at rest.

penultimate; last but -one, – two, etc.

unbegun, uncommenced; fresh.

Adv. finally etc. *adj.;* in fine; at the last; once for all.

68. Middle.—**N.** middle, midst, mediety; mean etc. 29; medium, middle term; center etc. 222; mid-course etc. 628; *mezzo termine; juste milieu* etc. 628; half-way house, nave, navel, omphalos; nucle-us, -olus.

equidistance, bisection, half-distance; equator, diaphragm, midriff; interjacence etc. 228.

Adj. middle, medial, mesial, mean, mid; middle-, mid-most; middling; mediate; intermediate etc. (*interjacent*) 228; equidistant; central etc. 222; mediterranean, equatorial.

Adv. in the middle; in the thick; mid-, half-way; midships, *in medias res.*

69. Continuity. [Uninterrupted sequence.]—**N.** continuity; consecu-tion,, -tiveness etc. *adj.;* succession, round, suite, progression, series, train, chain; cat-, concatenation; catena; scale; gradation, course, constant flow, perpetuity.

procession, column; retinue, *cortège*, cavalcade, rank and file, line of battle, array.

pedigree, genealogy, lineage, race etc. 166.

rank, file, line, row, range, tier, string, thread, team; suit; colonnade.

V. follow in –, form- a series etc. *n.;* fall in.

arrange in a -series etc. *n.;* string together, catenate, file, thread, graduate, tabulate.

Adj. continu-ous. -ed; consecutive; progressive, gradual; serial, successive; immediate, unbroken, entire; linear; in a -line, – row etc. *n.;* uninter-rupted, -mitting; unremitting; perennial, evergreen; constant.

Adv. continuously etc. *adj.; seriatim;* in a -line etc. *n.*; in -succession, – turn; running, gradually, step by step, *gradatim,* at a stretch; in -file, – column, – single file, – Indian file.

70. Discontinuity. [Interrupted sequence.]—**N.** discontinuity; disjunction etc. 44; anacoluthon; interruption, break, fracture, flaw, fault, split, crack, cut; gap etc. (*interval*) 198; solution of continuity, *caesura*; broken thread; parenthesis, episode; rhapsody, patchwork; intermission; alternation etc. (*periodicity*) 138; dropping fire.

V. be -discontinuous etc. *adj.;* alternate, intermit.

discontinue, pause, interrupt; intervene; break, – in upon; interpose etc. 228; break –, snap- the thread; disconnect etc. (*disjoin*) 44.

Adj. discontinuous, unsuccessive, broken, interrupted, *décousu;* dis-, un-connected, discrete, disjunctive; fitful etc. (*irregular*) 139; spasmodic, desultory, intermit-ting etc. *v.;* -tent; alternate; recurrent etc. (*periodic*) 138; few and far between.

Adv. at intervals; by -snatches, – jerks, – skips, – catches, – fits and starts; skippingly, *per saltum; longo intervallo.*

71. Term.—**N.** term, rank, station, stage, step; degree etc. 26; scale, remove, grade, link, peg, round –, rung- of the ladder, *status,* position, place, point, mark, *pas,* period, pitch; stand, -ing; footing, range.

V. hold –, occupy –, fall into- a place etc. *n.*

72. Assemblage.—**N.** assemblage; col-lection, location, -ligation; compilation, levy, gathering, ingathering, mobilization, meet, foregathering, muster, *attroupement*; con-course, -flux, -gregation, -tesseration, -vergence etc. 290; meeting, *levée, réunion,* drawing room, at home; conversazione etc. (*social gathering*) 892; assembly, congress, eisteddfod; conven-tion, -ticle; gemote; conclave, etc. (*council*) 696; posse, *posse comitatus;* Noah's ark.

miscellany, *collectanea,* symposium; museum, menagerie, etc. (*store*) 636.

crowd, throng, multitude; flood, rush, deluge; rout, rabble, mob, press, crush, *cohue,* jam, horde, body, tribe; crew, gang, knot, squad, band, party; swarm, shoal, school, covey, flock, herd, drove, kennel; array, bevy, galaxy; *corps,* company, troop, *troupe;* army, force, regiment, etc. (*combatants*) 726; host etc. (*multitude*) 102; populousness.

clan, brotherhood, association etc. (*party*) 712.

volley, shower, storm, cloud.

group, cluster, Pleiades, clump, pencil; set, batch, lot, pack; budget, *dossier,* assortment, bunch; parcel; pack-et, -age; bundle, *fasciculus,* fascine, bale; ser-on, oon; faggot, wisp, truss, tuft; shock, rick, fardel, stack, sheaf, swath, gavel, haycock, stook.

accumulation etc. (*store*) 636; congeries, heap, lump, pile, *rouleau,* tissue, mass, pyramid; drift; snow-ball, -drift; acervation, cumulation; amassment, glom-, agglom-eration; conglobation; conglomeration, -ate; coacervation, coagmentation, aggregation, concentration, congestion, *omnium gatherum, spicilegium,* black hole of Calcutta; quantity etc. (*greatness*) 31.

collector, gatherer; whip, -per in.

V. [be or come together] assemble, collect, muster; meet, unite, join, rejoin; cluster, flock, swarm, surge, stream, herd, crowd, throng, associate; con-gregate, -glomerate, -centrate; center round, *rendezvous,* resort; come –, flock –, get –, pig- together; forgather; huddle; reassemble.

[get or bring together] assemble, muster, mobilize; bring –, get –, put –, draw –, scrape –, lump- together; col-lect, -locate, -ligate; get –, whip- in; gather; hold a meeting; con-vene, -voke, -vocate; rake up, dredge; heap, mass, pile; pack, put up, truss, cram; acervate; ag-glomerate, -gregate; compile; group, aggroup, concentrate, unite; collect –, bring- into a focus; amass, accumulate etc. (*store*) 636; collect in a drag-net; heap Ossa upon Pelion.

Adj. assembled etc. *v.;* closely packed, dense, serried, crowded to suffocation, teeming, swarming, populous; as thick as hops; all of a heap, fasciculated; cumulative.

Phr. the plot thickens.

73. Non-assemblage. Dispersion.—**N.** dispersion; disjunction etc. 44; divergence etc. 291; scattering etc. *v.*; dissemination, broadcasting, diffusion, dissipation, distribution; apportionment etc. 786; spread, respersion, circumfusion, interspersion, spargefaction.

waifs and estrays, flotsam and jetsam, *disjecta membra.*

V. disperse, scatter, sow, disseminate, radiate, diffuse, shed, spread, ted, bestrew, overspread, dispense, disband, disembody, demobilize, dismember, distribute; apportion etc. 786; blow off, let out, dispel, cast forth, draught off; strew, straw, strow; spirtle, cast, sprinkle, shatter; issue, deal out, retail, utter; re-, inter-sperse; set abroach, circumfuse.

turn –, cast- adrift; scatter to the winds; sow broadcast.

spread like wildfire, disperse themselves.

Adj. unassembled etc. (*see* assemble etc. 72); dispersed etc. *v.*; sparse, dispread, broadcast, sporadic, widespread; far-flung; epidemic etc. (*general*) 78; adrift, stray; dishevelled, streaming.

Adv. *sparsim,* here and there, *passim.*

74. Focus. [Place of meeting.]—**N.** focus; point of- convergence etc. 290; corradiation; center etc. 222; gathering-place, resort; haunt; retreat; *venue, rendezvous;* rallying point, head-quarters, home, club; *dépôt* etc. (*store*) 636; tryst, trysting-place; place of -meeting, – resort, – assignation; *point de –, lieu de- réunion;* issue.

V. bring to- a point, – a focus, – an issue; focus.

75. Class.—**N.** class, category, *categorema,* head, order, section; division, subdivision; department, province, domain, sphere.

kind, sort, genus, species, variety, branch, family, race, tribe, caste, sept, clan, breed; *clique, coterie;* type, kit, sect, set; assortment; feather, kidney; suit; range; gender, sex, kin.

manner, description, denomination, persuasion, connection, designation, character, stamp; predicament; conviction etc. 484.

similarity etc. 17.

76. Inclusion. [Comprehension under, or reference to a class.]—**N.** inclusion, admission, incorporation, comprehension, reception.

composition etc. (*inclusion in a compound*) 54.

V. be -included in etc.; come –, fall –, range under; belong –, pertain- to; range with; merge in.

include, compromise, comprehend, contain, admit, embrace, receive; enclose etc. (*circumscribe*) 229; incorporate, cover, embody, encircle.

reckon –, enumerate –, number- among; refer to; place –, arrange-under, – with; take into account.

Adj. includ-ed; -ing etc. *v.;* inclusive; comprehensive, all-embracing; congen-er, -erous; of the same -class etc. 75.

Phr. *et hoc genus omne,* etc.; *et caetera.*

77. Exclusion.*—**N.** exclusion etc. 55.

* The same set of words is used to express *Exclusion from a class* and *Exclusion from a compound.* Reference is therefore made to the former at 55. This identity does not occur with regard to *Inclusion,* which therefore constitutes a separate category.

78. Generality.—**N.** general-ity, -ization; universality; catholic-ity, -ism; miscel-lany, -laneousness; drag-net.

every-one, -body; all hands, all the world and his wife; any body, N or M, all sorts; *tout le monde.*

prevalence, run.

V. be -general etc. *adj.;* prevail, obtain, be going about, stalk abroad.

render -general etc. *adj.;* generalize; spread, broadcast.

Adj. general, usual, current, generic, collective; broad, comprehensive, sweeping; encyclopedical, panoramic, widespread etc. (*dispersed*) 73.

universal; catho-lic, -lical; common, worldwide; e-cumenical; transcendental; prevalent, prevailing, rife, epidemic, besetting; all over, covered with.

every, all; indeterminate, indefinite, unspecified, impersonal.

customary etc. (*habitual*) 613.

Adv. what-ever, -soever; to a man, one and all, without exception.

generally etc. *adj.;* always, for better for worse; in general, generally speaking; speaking generally; for the most part; in the long run etc. (*on an average*) 29.

79. Speciality.—**N.** speciality, *spécialité;* individ-uality, -uity; particularity, peculairity; idiocrasy etc. (*tendency*) 176; personality, characteristic, mannerism, idiosyncrasy, attribute specificness etc. *adj.;* singularity etc. (*unconformity*) 83; reading, version, lection; state; *trait;* distinctive feature; technicality; *differentia.*

particulars, details, minutiae, items, counts.

I, self, I myself, *ego;* my-, him-, her-, it-self.

V. specify, particularize, individualize, realize, specialize, designate, differentiate, determine, define, denote, indicate, itemize, detail.

descend to particulars, enter into detail, come to the point.

Adj. special, particular, individual, specific, proper, personal, intimate, original, private, respective, definite, concrete, determinate, especial, certain, esoteric, endemic, partial, party, peculiar, marked, appropriate, several, characteristic, diagnistic, exact, exclusive; singular etc. (*exceptional*) 83; idiomatic; typical, representative, distinctive.

this, that; yon, -der.

Adv. specially etc. *adj.;* in particular, *in propriâ personâ; ad hominem;* for my part.

each, apiece, one by one; severally, respectively, each to each; *seriatim,* in detail, bit by bit; *pro hac vice, – re natâ.*

namely, that is to say, *videlicet,* viz.; to wit.

80. Rule.—**N.** regularity, uniformity etc. 16; clock-work precision; punctuality etc. (*exactness*) 494; routine etc. (*custom*) 613; formula; system; rut; canon, convention, maxim; rule etc. (*form, regulation*) 697; key-note, standard, model; precedent etc. (*prototype*) 22; conformity etc. 82.

nature, principle; law; order of things; normal –, natural –, ordinary –, model- -state, – condition; standing -dish, – order; normality; Procrustean law; law of the Medes and Persians; hard and fast rule.

Adj. regular, uniform, symmetrical, constant, steady; according to rule etc. (*conformable*) 82; customary etc. 613; orderly etc. 58.

81. Multiformity.—**N.** multi-, omniformity; variety, diversity; multifariousness etc. *adj.*

Adj. multi-form, -fold, -farious, -generous; multiplex, variform, manifold, many-sided, multiplicate; omni-form, -genous, -farious; polymorphic; protean; heterogeneous, motley, mosaic; epicene, indiscriminate, desultory, irregular, diversified, different, divers; all manner of; of -every description, – all sorts and kinds; *et hoc genus omne;* and what not? *de omnibus rebus et quibusdam aliis.*

82. Conformity.—**N.** conform-ity, -ance; observance.

naturalization; conventionality etc. (*custom*) 613; agreement etc. 23.

example, instance, specimen, sample, quotation; exemplification, illustration, case in point; object lesson.

conventionalist, formalist, Philistine.

pattern etc. (*prototype*) 22.

V. conform to, – rule; accommodate –, adapt- oneself to; rub off corners.

be -regular etc. *adj.;* move in a groove; follow –, observe –, go by –, bend to –, obey- -rules, – precedents; comply –, tally –, chime in –, fall in-with; be -guided, – regulated- by; fall into a -custom, – usage; follow the -fashion, – multitude; pass muster, do as others do, *hurler aves les loups;* do at Rome as the Romans do; go –, swim- with the -stream, – current, – tide; tread the beaten track etc. (*habit*) 613; rubber-stamp; keep one in countenance.

exemplify, illustrate, cite, quote, put a case; produce an- instance etc. *n.*

Adj. conformable to rule, adaptable, compliant, consistent, agreeable; regular etc. 80; according to -regulation, – rule, – Cocker; *en règle, selon les règles,* well regulated, orderly; symmetric etc. 242.

conventional commonplace etc. (*customary*) 613; of -daily, – every day- occurrence; in the natural order of things; ordinary, common, – or garden, prosaic, habitual, usual.

in the order of the day; naturalized.

typical, normal, formal; canonical, orthodox, sound, strict, rigid, positive, uncompromising, Procrustean; point device.

secundum artem, ship-shape, technical.

exemplary, illustrative, in point.

Adv. conformably etc. *adj.;* by rule; agreeably to; in -conformity, – accordance, – keeping-with; according to; consistently with; as usual, *ad instar, instar omnium; more -solito, – majorum.*

for the sake of conformity; of –, as a matter of- course; *pro formâ,* for form's sake, by the card; according to plan.

invariably etc. (*uniformly*) 16.

for -example, – instance; *exempli gratiâ; e.g.; inter alia.*

Phr. *cela va sans dire, ex pede Herculem, noscitur a sociis.*

83. Unconformity.—**N.** non-conformity etc. 82; un-, dis-conformity; unconventionality, informality, abnormity, anomaly; anomalousness etc. *adj.;* exception, peculiarity, etc. 79; infraction –, breach –, violation –, infringement- of -law, – custom, – usage; eccentricity, *bizarrerie,* oddity, *je ne sais quoi,* monstrosity, rarity; freak of Nature.

individuality, idiosyncrasy, singularity, oritinality, mannerism.

aberration; irregularity; variety; singularity; exemption; salvo etc. (*qualification*) 469.

nonconformist; nondescript, character, original, nonsuch, monster, prodigy, wonder, miracle, curiosity, missing link, flying fish, black swan, *lusus naturae, rara avis,* queer fish; mongrel; half-caste, -blood, -breed; *métis,* cross breed, hybrid, mule, mulatto, sacatra, marabou; *tertium quid,* hermaphrodite, gynander, androgyn.

phoenix, chimera, hydra, sphinx, minotaur; griff-in, -on; centaur; hippogriff, -centaur; sagittary; kraken; cockatrice, wyvern, roc, liver, dragon, sea-serpent; mermaid; unicorn; Cyclops, 'men whose heads do grown beneath their shoulders:, Teratolgy.

fish out of water; neither -one thing nor another, – fish flesh nor fowl nor good red herring; one in a -way, – thousand; out-cast, -law; Ishmael, pariah; oasis.

V. be -unconformable etc. *adj.;* leave the beaten -track, – path; infringe –, break –, violate- a -law, – habit, – usage, – custom; drive a coach and six through; stretch a point; have no business there; baffle –, beggar- all description.

Adj. unconformable, exceptional; abnorm-al, -ous; anomal-ous, -istic; out of -order, – place, – keeping, – tune, – one's element; irregular, arbitrary; lawless, informal, aberrant, stray, wandering, wanton; peculiar, exclusive, unnatural, eccentric, crotchety, egregious; out of the -beaten track, – common, – common run, – pale of; misplaced; funny.

un-usual, -accustomed, -customary, -wonted, -common; rare, singular, *unique,* curious, odd, extraordinary, strange, monstrous; wonderful etc. 870; unexpected, unaccountable; *outré,* out of the way, remarkable, noteworthy; queer, quaint, nondescript, none such, *sui generis;* original, unconventional, Bohemian, unfashionable; un-described, -precedented, -paralleled, -exampled, -heard of, -familiar; fantastic, newfangled, grotesque, *bizarre;* outlandish, exotic, *tombé de nues,* preternatural; denaturalized.

heterogeneious, heteroclite, amorphous, mongrel, amphibious, epicene, half-blood, hybrid; androgyn-ous, -al; unsymmetric etc. 243.

qualified etc. 469.

Adv. unconformably etc. *adj.;* except, unless, save, barring, beside, without, save and except, let alone.

however, yet, but.

Int. what -on earth! – in the world!

Phr. never was -seen, – heard, – known- the like.

84. Number.—**N.** number, symbol, numeral, figure, cipher, digit, integer; counter; round number; formula; function; series.

sum, total, aggregate, difference, complement, subtrahend; product; multipli-cand, -er, -cator; coefficient, multiple; dividend, divisor, factor, quotient, sub-multiple, fraction; mixed number; numerator, denominator; decimal, circulating decimal, repetend; common measure, aliquot part; reciprocal; prime number; totitive, totient.

permutation, combination, variation; election.

ratio, proportion; progression; arithmetical –, geometrical –, harmonical- progression; percentage.

figurate –, pyramidal –, polygonal- numbers.

power, root, exponent, index, logarithm, antilogarithm; modulus.

differential, integral, fluxion, fluent.

Adj. numeral, complementary, divisible, aliquot, reciprocal, prime, fractional, decimal, figurate, incommensurable.

proportional, exponential, logarithmic, logometric, differential, fluxional, integral.

positive, negative; rational, irrational; surd, radical, real, imaginary, impossible.

85. Numeration.—**N.** numeration, numbering etc. *v.;* pagination; tale, tally, recension, enumeration, summation, reckoning, computation, supputation; calcu-lation, -lus; algorithm, rhabdology, dactylonomy; measurement etc. 466; statistics.

arithmetic, analysis, algebra, fluxions; differential —, integral —, infinitesimal-calculus; calculus of differences.

[Statistics] dead reckoning, muster, poll, census, capitation, roll-call, recapitulation; account etc. (*list*) 86.

[Operations] notation, addition, subtraction, multiplication, division, proportion, rule of three, practice, equations, extraction of roots, reduction, involution, evolution, approximation, interpolation, differentiation, integration.

[Instruments] abacus, swan-pan, logometer, sliding —, slide- rule, tallies, Napier's bones, calculating —, adding- machine, difference engine; cash register.

arithmetician, calculator, abacist; mathematician, actuary, statistician, surveyor, geodesist.

V. number, count, tell; call —, run- over, take an account of, enumerate, call the roll, muster, poll, recite, recapitulate; sum; sum —, cast- up; tell off, score, cipher, compute, calculate, set a price, reckon, — up, estimate, suppute, add, subtract, multiply, divide, extract roots.

check, prove, demonstrate, balance, audit, overhaul, take stock; affix numbers to, page, foliate, paginate.

amount —, come- to.

Adj. numer-al, -ical; arithmetical, analytic, algebraic, statistical, numerable, computable, calculable; commensur-able, -ate; incommensur-able, -ate.

86. List.—**N.** list, catalogue, enumeration, inventory, schedule; register etc. (*record*) 551; account; bill, — of costs, syllabus; terrier, tally, file; almanac, calendar, index, table, atlas, contents, card index; rota, ticket; book, ledger; synopsis, *catalogue raisonné; tableau*, scroll, manifest, invoice, bill of lading; prospectus, *programme;* bill of fare, *menu, carte;* score, census, statistics, returns; Red —, Blue —, Domesday- book; *cadaster;* directory, gazetteer, dictionary, glossary, lexicon, thesaurus, gradus.

roll; check —, chequer —, bead- roll, — of honor; muster -roll, — book; roster, panel; cartulary, diptych.

V. list, enrol, schedule, register etc. *n.;* indent, post, docket; matriculate.

Adj. cadastral, listed etc. *v.*

87. Unity.—**N.** unity; oneness etc. *adj.;* individuality; solitude etc. (*seclusion*) 893; isolation etc. (*disjunction*) 44; unification etc. 48.

one, unit, ace; item; individual; solo, none else, no other, naught beside.

V. be -one, — alone etc. *adj.;* dine with Duke Humphrey.

isolate etc. (*disjoin*) 44.

render one; unite etc. (*join*) 43, (*combine*) 48.

Adj. one, sole, single, solitary, only- begotten; individual, apart, alone; kithless.

un-accompanied, -attended; *solus*, single-handed; singular, odd, unique, unrepeated, azygous, first and last; isolated etc. (*disjoined*) 44; insular; unitary.

lone; lone-ly, -some; desolate, dreary.

in-secable, -severable, -discerptible; compact, irresolvable.

Adv. singly etc. *adj.;* alone, by itself, *per se*, only, apart, in the singular number, in the abstract; one -by one, — at a time; simply; one and a half, *sesqui-*.

Phr. *natura il fece, e poi roppe la stampa.*

88. Accompaniment.—**N.** accompaniment; appurtenance, adjunct etc. 39; context.

coexistence, concomitance, company, association, companionship; part-, copart-nership; coefficiency.

concomitant, accessory, coefficient; companion, attendant, fellow, associate, consort, spouse, colleague, *fidus Achates;* part-, co-partner; satellite, hanger on, shadow; escort, *entourage*, suite, *cortège;* convoy, follower etc. 65; attribute.

V. accompany, coexist, attend, convoy, chaperon; hang —, wait- on; go hand in hand with; synchronize etc. 120; bear —, keep- company; row in the same boat; bring in its train, associate —, couple with.

Adj. accompanying etc. *v.;* concomitant, fellow, twin, joint; associated —, coupled- with; accessory, attendant, *obbligato*.

Adv. with, withal; together —, along —, in company- with; hand in hand, side by side; cheek by -jowl, — jole; arm in arm; there-, here-with; and etc. (*addition*) 37.

together, in a body, collectively.

89. Duality.—**N.** dual-ity, -ism; duplicity; biplicity, -formity; span, polarity.

two, deuce, couple, couplet, doublet, brace, pair, cheeks, twins, Castor and Pollus, *gemini*, Siamese twins; fellows; yoke, conjugation, dyad, distich.

V. [unite in pairs] pair, couple, bracket, yoke; conduplicate, mate.

Adj. two, twain; dual, -istic; binary, binomial; twin, biparous; dyadic; conduplicate; duplex etc. 90; *tête-à-tête;* paired; dihedral.

coupled etc. *v.;* conjugate.

both, — the one and the other.

90. Duplication.—**N.** duplication, doubling etc. *v.;* gemi-, ingemi-nation; reduplication; iteration etc. (*repetition*) 104; renewal.

V. double; re-double, -duplicate; geminate; repeat etc. 104; renew etc. 660; duplicate, copy etc. 21.

Adj. double; doubled etc. *v.;* bicameral, bicapital, bi-fold, -form, -lateral, -farious, -facial; two-fold, -sided, -headed, -edged etc.; duplex; double-faced; twin, duplicate, ingeminate; second; dual etc. 29.

Adv. twice, once more; over again etc. (*repeatedly*) 104; as much again; twofold.

secondly, in the second place, again.

91. Bisection. [Division into two parts.]—**N.** bi-section, -partition; di-, subdi-chotomy; halving etc. *v.;* dimidiation; *hendiadis*.

bifurcation, forking, branching, furcation, ramification, divarication; fork, prong; fold.

half, moiety.
V. bisect, halve, divide, split, cut in two, cleave, dimidiate, dichotomize, divaricate.
go halves, divide with.
separate, fork, bifurcate; branch -off, – out; ramify.
Adj. bisected etc. *v.;* cloven, cleft; bipartite, biconjugate, bicuspid, bifid; bifur-cous, -cate, -cated; semi-, demi- hemi-.

92. Triality.—**N.** triality, trinity,* triplicity.
three, triad, triplet, trey, trio, ternion, trinomial, leash; tierce; triennium; trefoil, triangle, trident, tripod, triumvirate, *troika.*
third power, cube.
Adj. three; tri-form, -nal, -nomial; tertiary; triune.
**Trinity* is hardly ever used except in a theological sense; *see* Deity 976.

93. Triplication.—**N.** tripli-cation, -city; trebleness, trine, trilogy.
V. treble, triple, triplicate, cube.
Adj. treble, triple; tern, -ary; triplex, triplicate, threefold, trilogistic; third; trinal; trihedral.
Adv. three -times, – fold; thrice, in the third place, thirdly; trebly etc. *adj.*

94. Trisection. [Division into three parts.]—**N.** tri-section, -partition, -chotomy; third, – part.
V. trisect, divide into three parts, trifurcate.
Adj. trifid; trisected etc. *v.;* tripartite, -chotomous, -sulcate.

95. Quaternity.—**N.** quaternity, four, tetrad, quartet, quaternion, square, quadrature, quarter, quadruplet; quadrilateral, quadrangle, quatrefoil; *quadriga.*
V. reduce to a square, square.
Adj. four; quat-ernary, -ernal; quadratic; quartile, quartic, tetractic, tetrad, tetrahedral; quadrennial; quadrivalent.

96. Quadruplication.—**N.** quadruplication.
V. multiply by four, quadruplicate, biquadrate.
Adj. fourfold; quad-ruple, -ruplicate, -rible; quadruplex; fourth.
Adv. four times; in the fourth place, fourthly.

97. Quadrisection. [Division into four parts.]—**N.** quadri-section, -partition; quartering etc. *v.;* fourth; quart, -er, -ern; farthing (*i.e.* fourthing); quarto.
V. quarter, divide into four parts, quadrisect.
Adj. quartered etc. *v.;* quadri-fid, -partite.

98. Five, etc.—**N.** five, cinque, quint, quincunx, quintuplet, quintet, pentagon, pentameter, Pentateuch; six, half-a-dozen; sextet, hexagon, hexameter; seven, Heptarchy; eight, octet, octagon, octave; nine, three times three; ten, decade; eleven; twelve, dozen; thirteen; long –, baker's-dozen.
twenty, score; twenty-four, four and twenty, two dozen; twenty-five, five and twenty, quarter of a hundred; forty, two score; fifty, half a hundred; sixty, three score, sexagenarian; seventy, three score and ten, septuagenarian; eighty, four score, octogenarian; ninety, four score and ten, nonagenarian.
hundred, centenary, hecatomb, century; hundredweight, cwt.; one hundred and forty-four, gross; bicentenary, tercentenary etc.
thousand, chiliad; myriad, millennium, ten thousand; lac, lakh, one hundred thousand, plum; million; thousand million, *milliard.*
billion, trillion etc.
V. centuriate.
Adj. five, quinary, quintuple; fifth; senary, sextuple; sixth; seventh; octuple; eighth; ninefold, ninth; tenfold, decimal, denary, decuple, tenth; eleventh; duo-denary, -denal; twelfth; in one's 'teens, thirteenth.
vices-, viges-imal; twentieth; twenty-fourth etc. *n.*
cent-uple, -uplicate, -ennial, -enary, -urial; secular, hundredth; thousandth; millenary etc.

99. Quinquesection, etc.—**N.** division by -five etc. 98; quinquesection etc.; fifth etc.; decimation.
V. decimate, quinquesect.
Adj. quinque-fid, -partite; quinquarticular; octifid; decimal, tenth, tithe, teind; duodecimal, twelfth; sexagesimal, -genary; hundredth, centesimal; millesimal etc.

100. Plurality. [More than one.]—**N.** plurality; a -number, – certain number; one or two, two or three etc.; a few, several; multitude etc. 102.
Adj. plural, more than one, upwards of, some, certain; not -alone etc. 87.
Adv. *et cetera, etc.,* etc.
Phr. *non deficit alter.*

100a. Fraction [Less than one.]—**N.** fraction, fractional part, fragment; part etc. 51.
Adj. fractional, fragmentary, partial.

101. Zero.—**N.** zero, nothing, naught, nought, duck's egg, goose egg; cipher, none, nobody; not a soul; *âme qui vive*; absence etc. 187; unsubstantiality etc. 4.
Adj. not -one, – any.

102. Multitude.—**N.** multitude; numerousness etc. *adj.*; numer-osity, -ality; multiplicity; profusion etc. (*plenty*) 639; legion, host; great –, large –, round –, enormous- number; a quantity, numbers, array, sight, army, sea, galaxy; scores, peck, bushel, school, shoal, swarm, draft, bevy, cloud, flock, herd, drove, flight, covey, hive, brood, litter, farrow, fry, nest; mob, crowd etc. (*assemblage*) 72; lots, loads, heaps; all the world and his wife.
[Increase of number] greater number, majority; multiplication, multiple.
V. be -numerous etc. *adj.*; swarm –, teem –, crawl –, creep -with; crowd, swarm, come thick upon; outnumber, multiply; people; swarm like -locusts, — bees.
Adj. many, several, sundry, divers, various,

not a few; a -hundred, – thousand, – myriad, – million, – thousand and one; some -ten or a dozen, – forty or fifty etc.; half a -dozen, – hundred etc.; very –, full –, ever so- many; numer-ous, -ose; profuse, in profusion; manifold, multiplied, multitudinous, multiferous, multiple, multinomial, teeming, crawling, populous, peopled, crowded, thick, studded; galore.

thick coming, many more, more than one can tell, a world of; no end -of, – to; *cum multis aliis*; thick as -hops, – hail; plenty as blackberries; numerous as the -stars in the firmament, – sands on the sea-shore, – hairs on the head; and -what not, – heaven knows what; endless etc. (*infinite*) 105.

Phr. their name is 'Legion.'

103. Fewness.—**N.** fewness etc. *adj.*; paucity, small number; small quantity etc. 32; scarcity, sparsity; rarity; infrequency etc. 137; handfull; maniple; minority, exiguity.

[Diminution of number] reduction; weeding etc. *v.*; elimination, sarculation, decimation.

V. be -few etc. *adj.*

render -few etc. *adj.*; reduce, diminish the number, weed; eliminate, thin, decimate.

Adj. few; scarce; scant, -y; thin, rare, thinly scattered, few and far between; exiguous, infrequent etc. 137; *rari nantes*; hardly –, scarcely- any; to be counted on one's fingers; reduced etc. *v.*; unrepeated.

Adv. here and there.

104. Repetition.—**N.** repetition, iteration, reiteration, duplication, ding-dong, alliteration; *epistrophe;* harping, recurrence, succession, run; batto-, tauto-logy; monotony, tautophony; rhythm etc. 138; pleonasm, redundancy, diffuseness.

chimes, repetend, echo, *ritornello,* burden of a song, *refrain;* rehearsal; encore; *réchauffé, rifacimento,* recapitulation.

cuckoo etc. (*imitation*) 19; reverberation etc. 408; drumming etc. (*roll*) 407; renewal etc. (*restoration*) 660.

twice-told tale; old -story, – song, chestnut; second –, new- edition; reprint, new impression; return game, return match, reappearance, reproduction; periodicity etc. 138.

V. repeat, iterate, reiterate, reproduce, parrot, echo, re-echo, drum, harp upon, battologize, hammer, redouble.

recur, revert, return, reappear; renew etc. (*restore*) 660.

rehearse; do –, say- over again; ring the changes on; harp on the same string; din –, drum- in the ear; conjugate in all its moods, tenses and inflexions, begin again, go over the same ground, go the same round, never hear the last of; resume, return to, recapitulate, reword.

Adj. repeated etc. *v.*; repetition-al, -ary; recurrent, -ring; ever recurring, thick coming; frequent, incessant, redundant, pleonastic, tautological.

monotonous, harping, iterative; mocking, chiming; retold; aforesaid, -named; above-mentioned, said; habitual etc. 613; another.

Adv. repeatedly, often, again, afresh, anew, over again, once more; ditto, *encore, de novo, bis, da capo.*

again and again; over and over, – again; many times over; time- and again, – after time; year after year; day by day etc.; many –, several –, a number of- times; many –, full many- a time; times out of number, year in and year out, morning, noon and night; frequently etc. 136.

Phr. *ecce iterum Crispinus, toujours perdrix,* cut and come again; 'tomorrow and tomorrow.'

105. Infinity.—**N.** infini-ty, -tude, -teness etc. *adj.;* perpetuity etc. 112.

V. be -infinite etc. *adj.;* know –, have- no -limits, – bounds; go on for ever.

Adj. infinite, immense; number-, count-, sum-, measure-less; innumer-, immeasur-, incalcul-, illimit-, intermin-, unfathom-, unapproach-able; exhaustless, inexhaustible, indefinite; without -number, – measure, – limit, – end; incomprehensible; limit-, end-, bound-, termless; un-told, -numbered, -measured, -bounded, -limited; illimited; perpetual etc. 112.

Adv. infinitely etc. *adj.; ad infinitum.*

106. Time.—**N.** time, duration; period, term, stage, space, span, spell, season; the whole -time, – period; course etc. 109.

intermediate, time, while, *interim,* interval, bit, pendency; inter-vention, -mission, -mittence, -regnum, -lude; respite.

era, epoch, eon, cycle; time of life, age, year, date; decade etc. (*period*) 108; moment, etc. (*instant*) 113; reign etc. 737.

glass –, ravages –, whirligig –, noiseless foot- of time; scythe.

V. continue, last, endure, go on, hold out, remain, stay, persist, abide, run; intervene; elapse etc. 109.

take –, take up –, fill –, occupy- time.

pass –, pass away –, spend –, while away –, consume –, talk against –, kill- time; tide over; use –, employ- time; tarry etc. 110; seize an opportunity etc. 134; waste time etc. (*be inactive*) 683.

Adj. continuing etc. *v.;* on foot; permanent etc. (*durable*) 110.

Adv. while, whilst, during, pending; during the -time, – interval; in the course of; for the time being, day by day; in the time of, when; meantime, -while; in the -meantime, – *interim; ad interim, pendente lite; de die in diem;* from -day to day, – hour to hour etc.; hourly, always; for a -time, – season; till, until, up to, yet; the whole –, all the- time; all along; throughout etc. (*completely*) 52; for good etc. (*diuturnity*) 110.

here-, there-, where-upon; then; *anno,* – *Domini;* A.D.; *ante Christum;* A.C.; before Christ; B.C.; *anno urbis conditae;* A.U.C.; *anno regni,* A.R.; once upon a time, one fine morning.

Phr. time -runs, – runs against; *tempus fugit.*

107. Neverness.—**N.** 'neverness;' absence of time, no time; *dies non;* Tib's eve; Greek Kalends.

Adv. never; at no -time, – period; on no occasion, never in all one's born days, nevermore, *sine die.*

108. Period. [Definite duration, or portion of time.]—**N.** period; second, minute, hour, day, week, sennight, octave, month, moon, quarter, semester, year, *lustrum, quinquennium,* decade, *decennium,* indiction, lifetime, generation, epoch, era, cycle.

century, age, *millennium; annus magnus.*

Adj. horary; hourly, annual etc. (*periodical*) 138.

108a. Contingent Duration.—**Adv.** during -pleasure, – good behavior; *quamdiu se bene gesserit.*

109. Course. [Indefinite duration.]—**N.** course –, progress –, process –, succession –, lapse –, flow –, flux –, effluxion, stream –, tract –, current –, sweep –, tide –, march –, step –, flight- of time; duration etc. 106.

[Indefinite time] aorist.

V. elapse, lapse, flow, run, proceed, advance, pass; roll –, wear –, press –, drag- on; flit, fly, slip, slide, glide, crawl; run -its course.

out; expire; go –, pass- by; be -past etc. 122.

Adj. elapsing etc. *v.;* aoristic; progressive, transient etc. 111.

Adv. in due -time, – season; in -course, – process, – the fulness- of time; in time.

Phr. *labitur et labetur; truditur dies die; fugaces labuntur anni;* 'tomorrow and tomorrow and tomorrow creeps in this petty pace from day to day.'

110. Diuturnity. [Long duration.]—**N.** diuturnity; a -long –, length of -time; an age, a century, an eternity, aeons; slowness etc. 275; perpetuity etc. 112; blue moon.

dura-bleness, -bility; persistence, lastingness etc. *adj.;* continuance, assiduity, endurance, standing; permanence etc. (*stability*) 150; survi-val, -vance; longevity etc. (*age*) 128; distance of time.

protraction –, prolongation –, extension- of time; delay etc. (*lateness*) 133.

V. last, endure, stand, remain, abide, continue, brave a thousand years.

tarry etc. (*be late*) 133; drag -on, – its slow length along, – a lengthening chain; protract, prolong; spin –, eke –, draw –, lengthen- out; temporize; gain –, make –, talk against- time.

out-last, -live; survive; live to fight again.

Adj. durable; perdurable; lasting etc. *v.;* of long -duration, – standing; permanent, chronic, long-standing; intransi-ent, -tive; intransmutable, persistent; life-, live-long; longeval, long-lived, macrobiotic, diuturnal, sempervirent, evergreen, perennial; unin-, ter-, unremitting; perpetual etc. 112.

lingering, protracted, prolonged, spun out etc. *v.;* long-pending, -winded; slow etc. 275.

Adv. long; for -a long time, – an age, – ages, – ever so long, – many a long day; long ago etc. (*in a past time*) 122; *longo intervallo.*

all the -day long, – year round; the livelong day, as the day is long, morning, noon and night; hour after hour, day after day, etc.; for good; permanently etc. *adj.*

111. Transientness. [Short duration.]—**N.** transientness etc. *adj.*; evanescence, impermanence, fugacity, transitoriness, volatility, caducity, mortality, span; flash in the pan, nine days' wonder, bubble, May-fly; spurt; temporary arrangement, interregnum.

velocity etc. 274; suddenness etc. 113; changeableness etc. 149.

V. be -transient etc. *adj.;* flit, pass away, fly, gallop, vanish, fade, fleet, melt away, evaporate; pass away like a -cloud, – summer cloud, – shadow, – dream.

Adj. transi-ent, -tory, -tive; passing, evanescent, fleeting; flying etc. *v.;* fug-acious, -itive; shifting, slippery; spasmodic.

tempor-al, -ary; provis-ional, -ory; cursory, short-lived, ephemeral, deciduous; perishable, mortal, precarious; impermanent.

brief, quick, brisk; cometary, meteoric, extemporaneous, summary; pressed for time etc. (*haste*) 684; sudden, momentary etc. (*instantaneous*) 113.

Adv. temporarily etc. *adj.; pro tempore;* for -the moment, – a time; awhile, *en passant, in transitu;* in a short time; soon etc. (*early*) 132; briefly etc. *adj.;* at short notice; on the -point, – eve -of; *in articulo;* between cup and lip.

Phr. one's days are numbered; the time is up; her to-day and gone tomorrow; *non semper erit aestas; eheu! fugaces labuntur anni; sic transit gloria mundi.*

112. Perpetuity. [Endless duration.]—**N.** perpetuity, eternity, timelessness; everness, aye, sempiternity, immortality, athanasia; everlastingness etc. *adj.;* perpetuation; infinite duration.

V. last –, endure –, go on- for ever; have no end.

eternize, eternify, perpetuate, immortalize.

Adj. perpetual, eternal, eterne; everlasting, -living, -flowing; continual, constant, sempiternal; co-eternal; endless, unending; ceaseless, incessant, uninterrupted, indesinent, unceasing; interminable, having no end; unfading, evergreen, amaranthine; neverending, -dying, -fading; deathless, immortal, undying, imperishable.

Adv. perpetually etc. *adj.;* always, ever, evermore, aye; for -ever, – aye, – evermore, – ever and a day, –, ever and ever; in all ages, from age to age; without end; world –, time- without end; *in saecula saeculorum;* to the -end of time, – crack of doom, – 'last syllable of recorded time;' till doomsday; constantly etc. (*very frequently*) 136.

Phr. *esto perpetuum; labitur et labetur in omne volubilis aevum.*

113. Instantaneity. [Point of time.]—**N.** instantane-ity, -ousness; sudden-, abrupt-ness.

moment, instant, second, minute; twinkling, trice, flash, breath, crack, jiffy, *coup,* burst, flash of lightning, stroke of time.

epoch, time; time of -day, – night; hour, minute; very -minute etc., – time, – hours; present –, right –, true –, exact –, correct-time.

V. be -instantaneous etc. *adj.;* twinkle, flash.

Adj. instantaneous, momentary, extempore, sudden, instant, abrupt; subitaneous, hasty; quick as- thought,* – lightning, – a flash; rapid as electricity.

Adv. instantaneously etc. *adj.*; in – in less than- no time; *presto, subito, instanter,* suddenly, at a stroke, like- a shot, – greased lightning; in a trice, in a moment etc. *n.*; eftsoons, in the twinkling of - an eye, – a bed post; at one jump, in the same breath, *per saltum, uno saltu*; at –, all at- once; in one's tracks; plump, slap; 'at one fell swoop;' at the same -instant etc. *n.*; immediately etc. (*early*) 132; *ex tempore,* on the -spot, – spur of the moment, – dot; just then; slap- dash etc. (*haste*) 684; before you could -turn round, – say -knife, – Jack Robinson.

Phr. touch and go; no sooner said than done.
*See note on 264.

114. Chronometry. [Estimation, measurement, and record of time.]—**N.** chrono-, horo-metry, -logy; date, epoch; style, era.

almanac, calendar, ephemeris; register, -try; chronicle, annals, journal, diary, chronogram.

[Instruments for the measurement of time] clock, watch; chrono-meter, -scope, -graph; repeater, alarum; time-keeper, -piece; dial, sun-dial, *gnomon, pendule,* horologe, pendulum, hourglass, water clock, clepsydra.

mean –, Greenwich –, solar –, sidereal –, local –, summer- time; daylight saving.

chrono-grapher, -loger, -logist; annalist.

V. fix –, mark- the time; date, register, chronicle; measure –, beat –, mark- time; bear date.

Adj. chrono-logical, -metrical, -grammatical; isochronal.

Adv. o'clock; *a.m., p.m.*

115. Anachronism. [False estimate of time.]—**N.** ana-, meta-, para-, prochronism; *prolepsis,* misdate; anticipation, antichronism.

disregard –, neglect –, oblivion- of time.

intempestivity etc. 135.

V. mis-, ante-, post-, over-date; anticipate; take no note of time.

Adj. misdated etc. *v.*; undated; overdue; out of date; anachronous etc. *n.*

116. Priority.—**N.** priority, antecedence, anteriority, pre-existence, precedence etc. 62; precession etc. 280; precursor etc. 64; the past etc. 122; premises.

V. precede, come before; forerun; antecede, go before etc. (*lead*) 280; pre-exist; dawn; premise, presage etc. 511.

be -beforehand etc. (*be early*) 132; steal a march upon, anticipate, forestall; have –, gain- the start.

Adj. prior, previous; preced-ing, -ent; anterior, antecedent; pre-existing, -existent; foresighted; former, foregoing; afore –, before-, above-mentioned; aforesaid, said; introductory etc. (*precursory*) 64; pre-war.

Adv. before, prior to; earlier; previously etc. *adj.*; afore, ere, theretofore, erewhile, ere –, before- -then, – now; erewhile, already, yet, beforehand; aforetime; on the eve of, in anticipation.

117. Posteriority.—**N.** posteriority; succession, sequence; following etc. 281; subsequence, supervention; futurity etc. 121; successor; sequel etc. 65; remainder, reversion.

V. follow etc. 281 –, come –, go- after; ensue, result; succeed, supervene; step into the shoes of.

Adj. subsequent, posterior, following, after, later, succeeding, postliminious, postnate; successive etc. 63; postdiluvial, -an; *puisné;* posthumous; post-war, future etc. 121.

Adv. subsequently, after, afterwards, since, later; at a -subsequent, – later- period; next, in the sequel, close upon, thereafter, thereupon, upon which, eftsoons; from that -time, – moment; after a -while, – time; in process of time.

postcenal, postcibal, postprandial, after-dinner.

118. The Present Time.—**N.** the present -time, – day, – moment, – juncture, – occasion; the times, existing time, time being; twentieth century; nonce, crisis, epoch, day, hour.

age, time of life.

Adj. present, actual, instant, current, latest, existing, that is.

Adv. at this -time, – moment etc. 113; at the - present time etc. *n.*; now, at present.

at this time of day, to-day, now-adays; already; even –, but –, just-now; on the present occasion; for the -time being, – nonce; *pro hâc vice;* on the -nail, – spot, on the spur of the moment, – occasion.

until now; to this, – the present day.

119. Different Time. [Time different from the present.]—**N.** different –, other- time.

[Indefinite time] aorist.

Adj. aoristic.

Adv. at that –, at which- -time, – moment, – instant; then, on that occasion, upon.

when; when-ever, -soever; upon which, on which occasion; at -another, – a different, – some other, – any - time; at various times; some –, one- -of these days, – fine morning, – day; sooner or later; some time or other; once upon a time, once.

120. Synchronism.—**N.** synchronism; coexistence, coincidence; simultaneousness etc. *adj.*; concurrence, concomitance, unity of time, interim.

[Having equal times] isochronism, syntony.

contemporary, coetanian.

V. coexist, concur, accompany, go hand in hand, keep pace with; synchronize, isochronize.

Adj. synchron-ous, -al, -ical, -istical; simultaneous, coexisting, coincident, concomitant, concurrent; coev-al, -ous; contempora-ry, -neous; coetaneous; coterminous, coeternal; isochronous.

Adv. at the same time; simultaneously etc. *adj.*; together, in concert, during the same time; in the same breath; *pari passu;* in the interim.

at the -very moment etc. 113; just as, as soon as; meanwhile etc. (*while*) 106.

121. Futurity. [Prospective time.]—**N.** futurity, -ition; future, hereafter, time to come; approaching –, coming –, after- -time, – age, – days, – hours, – years, – ages, – life;

morrow, to-morrow, bv and bv: millennium, doomsday, day of judgment, crack of doom, remote future.

approach ot tıme, advent, time drawing on, womb of time; destiny etc. 152; eventuality.

heritage, heirs, posterity, descendants.

prospect etc. (*expectation*) 507; foresight etc. 510.

V. look forwards; anticipate etc. (*expect*) 507, (*foresee*) 510; forestall etc. (*be early*) 132.

come –, draw- on; draw near; approach, await, threaten; impend etc. (*be destined*) 152.

Adj. future, to come; coming etc. (*impending*) 152; next, near; near –, close- at hand; eventual, ulterior; expectant, prospective, in prospect etc. (*expectation*) 507.

Adv. prospectively, hereafter, on the knees of the gods, in future; to-morrow, the day after to-morrow; in -course, – process, – the fulness- of time; eventually, ultimately, sooner or later; *proximo; paulo post futurum;* in after time; one of these days; after a -time, – while.

from this time; hence-forth, -forwards; thence; thence-forth, -forward; whereupon, upon which.

soon etc. (*early*) 132; on the -eve, – point, – brink- of; about to; close upon.

122. Preterition. [Retrospective time.]—**N.** preterition, priority etc. 116; the past, past time; days –, times- -of yore, – of old, – past, – gone by; bygone days, good old days; old –, ancient –, former -times; fore time; yesterdays; the olden –, good old- time; auld lang syne; eld.

antiquity, antiqueness, *status quo;* time immemorial; distance of time; remote -age, – time; ancient history; remote past; rust of antiquity; ancientness.

pale-ontology, -ography, -ology; palaetiology,* archaeology; archaism, antiquarianism, mediaevalism, pre- Raphaelitism; retrospection, looking back, memory etc. 505.

laudator temporis acti; mediaevalist, pre-Raphaelite; antiqu-ary, -arian; archaeologist etc.; Oldbuck, Dryasdust.

ancestry etc. (*paternity*) 166.

V. be -past etc. *adj.*;have -expired etc. *adj.*; – run its course, – had its day; pass; pass –, go- -by, – away, – off; lapse, blow over.

look –, trace –, cast the eyes- back; exhume.

Adj. past, gone, gone by, over, passed away, bygone, foregone; elapsed, lapsed, preterlapsed, expired, no more, run out, blown over, that has been, whilom, extinct, never to return, exploded, forgotten, irrecoverable; obsolete etc. (*old*) 124; extinct as the dodo.

former, pristine, *quondam, ci-devant,* late; ancestral.

foregoing; last, latter; recent, overnight; past, preterite, preter-perfect, -pluperfect, past perfect.

looking back etc. *v.;* retro-spective, -active; archaelogical etc. *n.*

Adv. formerly; of -old, –yore; erst, whilom, erewhile, time was, ago, over; in -the olden time etc. *n.;* anciently, long -ago, – since; a long -while, – time- ago; years –, ages-ago; some time -ago, – since, – back.

yesterday, the day before yesterday; last -year, – season, – month etc.; *ultimo,* lately etc. (*newly*) 123.

retrospectively; ere –, before –, till- now; hitherto, heretofore; no longer; once, – upon a time; from time immemorial; in the memory of man; time out of mind; already, yet, up to this time; *ex post facto.*

Phr. time was; the time -has, – hath- been. *Whewell.*

123. Newness.—N. newness etc. *adj.;* neologism, neoterism; novelty, recency; immaturity; youth etc. 127; gloss of novelty.

innovation; renovation etc. (*restoration*) 660.

modernist, neologist, neoteric.

modernism, modernity; mushroom; latest fashion, *dernier cri.*

upstart, *parvenu, nouveau riche.*

V. renew etc. (*restore*) 660; modernize.

Adj. new, novel, recent, fresh, green; young etc. 127; evergreen; raw, immature; virgin; untried, -handseled, -used, -trodden, -beaten; fledgling.

late, modern, neoteric; new-born, -fashioned, -fangled, -fledged; of yesterday; just out, brand –, span-new, up to date, topical; vernal, renovated; innovatory.

fresh as -a rose, – a daisy, – paint; spick and span.

Adv. newly etc. *adj.;* afresh, anew, lately, just now, only yesterday, the other day; latterly, of late.

not long –, a short time- ago.

124. Oldness.—N. oldness etc. *adj.*; age, antiquity; cobwebs of antiquity.

maturity, ripeness; decline, decay; senility etc. 128.

seniority, eldership, primogeniture.

archaism etc. (*the past*) 122; thing –, relic- of the past; megatherium.

tradition, prescription, custom, folklore, immemorial usage, common law.

V. be -old etc. *adj.;* have -had, – seen- its day; become -old etc. *adj.;* age, fade.

Adj. old, olden, ancient, antique; of long standing, time-honored, venerable; eld-er, -est; first-born.

prime; prim-itive, -eval, -igenous; primordi-al, -nate; aboriginal etc. (*beginning*) 66; diluvian, antediluvian; pre-historic; patriarchal, preadamite; paleocrystic; fossil, paleozoic, preglacial, ante-mundane; archaic, classic, mediaeval, pre-Raphaelite, ancestral, black-letter.

immemorial, traditional, prescriptive, customary, whereof the memory of man runneth not to the contrary; inveterate, rooted.

antiquated, of other times, rococo, of the old school, after-age, obsolete; fusty, moth-eaten; out of -date, – fashion; stale, old-fashioned, behind the -age, – times; exploded; gone out, – by; *passé,* outworn, run out; disused; senile etc. 128; time-worn; crumbling etc. (*deteriorated*) 659; second-hand.

old as -the hills, – Methuselah, – Adam, – history.

Adv. since the -world was made, – year one, – days of Methuselah.

125. Morning. [Noon.]—**N.** morning, morn, matins, forenoon, *a.m.,* prime, dawn, daybreak, daylight, sun-up, peep –, break- of day; aurora,

Eos; first blush –, prime- of the morning; twilight, crepuscule, sunrise, cockcrow.
spring; vernal equinox.
noon; mid-, noon-day; noontide, meridian, prime.
summer, midsummer; summer solstice.
Adj. matin, matutinal; vernal, aestival.
Adv. at -sunrise etc. *n.*; with the lark, when the morning dawns.

126. Evening. [Midnight.]—**N.** evening, eve; decline –, fall –, close- of day; eventide, evensong, vespers; candlelight; nightfall, curfew, dusk, twilight, blind man's holiday; eleventh hour; sun-set, -down; going down of the sun, cock-shut, dewy eve, gloaming, bed-time.
afternoon, *post meridiem, p.m.*
autumn; fall, – of the leaf; autumnal equinox, Indian summer, harvest-time.
midnight; dead –, witching time- of night; winter, – solstice.
Adj. vespertine, autumnal, nocturnal, wintry, brumal, hiemal.

127. Youth.—**N.** youth; juven- -ility, -escence; juniority; infancy; baby-, child-, boy-, girl-, youth-hood; *incunabula;* minority, immaturity, nonage, teens, tender age, bloom.
cradle, nursery, leading-strings, pupilage, puberty, *pucelage.*
prime –, flower –, spring-tide –, seedtime –, golden season - of life; heyday of youth, school days; rising generation, younger generation.
Adj. young, youthful, juvenile, green, callow, budding, sappy, *puisné,* beardless, unfledged, unripe, under age, in one's teens; *in statu pupillari;* younger, junior.

128. Age.—**N.** age; oldness etc. *adj.;* old –, advanced- age; sen-ility, -escence; years, anility, grey hairs, climacteric, grand climacteric, declining years, decrepitude, hoary age, caducity, superannuation; second childhood, -ishness; dotage; vale of years, decline of life, 'sear and yellow leaf;' three-score years and ten; green old age, ripe old age; longevity; time of life.
seniority, eldership; elders etc. (*veteran*) 130; firstling; *doyen,* dean, father; primogeniture; nostology.
V. be -aged etc. *adj.;* grow –, get- old etc. *adj.;* age; decline, wane.
Adj. aged; old etc. 124; elderly, senile; matronly, anile; in years; ripe, mellow, run to seed, declining, waning, past one's prime; grey, -headed; hoar, -y; venerable, time-worn, antiquated, *passé,* effete, doddering, decrepit, superannuated; advanced in -life, – years; stricken in years; wrinkled, marked with the crow's foot; having one foot in the grave; doting etc. (*imbecile*) 499.
old-, eld-er, -est; senior; first-born.
turned of, years old; of a certain age, no chicken, old as Methuselah; gerontic; ancestral; patriarchal etc. (*ancient*) 124.

129. Infant.—**N.** infant, babe, baby; nurse-, suck-, year-, wean-ling; *papoose, bambino.*
child, bairn, little- one, – tot, – mite, chick, brat, chit, pickaninny, kid, urchin; bant-, bratling; elf.
youth, boy, lad, slip, sprig, stripling, youngster, cub, unlicked cub, younker, callant, whipster, whipper-snapper, schoolboy, hobbledehoy, hopeful, cadet, minor, master.
scion; sap-, seed-ling; tendril, olive branch, nestling, chicken, duckling; larva, caterpillar, chrysalis, cocoon; tadpole, whelp, cub, pullet, fry, callow; codlin, -g; *foetus,* calf, colt, pup, foal, kitten; lamb, -kin.
girl; lass, -ie; wench, miss, damsel, *demoiselle,* damozel; maid, -en; virgin; nymph; colleen; minx, baggage, school-girl; tomboy, flapper, hoyden.
Adj. infant-ine, -ile; puerile; boy-, girl-, child-, baby-, kitten-ish; baby; new-born, unfledged, new-fledged, callow.
in -the cradle, – swaddling clothes, – long clothes, – arms, – leading strings; at the breast; in one's teens; young etc. 127.

130. Veteran.—**N.** veteran, old man, seer, patriarch, greybeard, dugout, grand-father, -sire; grandam, beldam; gaffer, gammer; hag, crone; pantaloon; sexage-, octoge-, nonage-, centenarian; old stager; dotard etc. 501.
preadamite, Methuselah, Nestor, Rip van Winkle, old Parr; elders; forefathers etc. (*paternity*) 166.

131. Adolescence.—**N.** adolescence, pubescence, majority; adultness etc. *adj.;* manhood, virility, maturity; flower of age; prime –, meridian- of life.
man etc. 373; woman etc. 374; adult, no chicken.
V. come -of age, – to man's estate, – to years of discretion; attain majority, assume the *toga virilis;* have -cut one's eye-teeth, – sown one's wild oats, settle down.
Adj. adolescent, pubescent, of age; of -full, – ripe- age, out of one's teens, grown up, mature, full- blown, – grown, in one's prime, in full bloom, manly, virile, adult; womanly, matronly; marriageable, nubile.

132. Earliness.—**N.** earliness etc. *adj.;* morning etc. 125.
punctuality; promptitude etc. (*activity*) 682; haste etc. (*velocity*) 274; suddenness etc. (*instantaneity*) 113.
prematurity, precocity, precipitation, anticipation; prevenience, a stitch in time.
V. be -early etc. *adj.;* – beforehand etc. *adv.;* keep time, take time by the forelock, anticipate, forestall; have –, gain- the start; steal a march upon; gain time, draw on futurity; bespeak, secure, engage, pre-engage.
accelerate; expedite etc. (*quicken*) 274; make haste etc. (*hurry*) 684.
Adj. early, prime, timely, in time, punctual, forward; prompt etc. (*active*) 682; summary.
premature, precipitate, precocious; prevenient, anticipatory; rathe.
sudden etc. (*instantaneous*) 113; unexpected etc. 508; impending, imminent; near, – at hand; immediate.

Adv. early, soon, anon, betimes, rathe; eft, -soons; ere –, before- long; punctually etc. *adj.;* to the minute; in time; in -good, – military, – pudding, – due- time; time enough.

beforehand; prematurely etc. *adj.;* precipitately etc. (*hastily*) 684; too soon; before -its, – one's- time; in anticipation; unexpectedly etc. 508.

suddenly etc. (*instantaneously*) 113; before one can say 'Jack Robinson,' at short notice, extempore; on the spur of the -moment, – occasion; at once; on the -spot, – instant; at sight; off –, out of- hand; *à vue d'oeil;* straight, -way, -forth; forthwith, incontinently, summarily, instanter, immediately, briefly, shortly, quickly, speedily, apace, before the ink is dry, almost immediately, presently, at the first opportunity, in no long time, by and by, in a while, directly.

Phr. touch and go, no sooner said than done.

133. Lateness.—**N.** lateness etc. *adj.;* tardiness etc. (*slowness*) 275.

de-lay, -lation; cunctation, procrastination; detention; deferring etc. *v.;* filibuster, postponement, adjournment, prorogation, retardation, respite, reprieve, stay; protraction, prolongation, moratorium; contango; demurrage; remand; Fabian policy, *médecine expectante,* chancery suit; leeway; high time.

V. be -late etc. *adj.;* tarry, wait, stay, bide, take time; dawdle etc. (*be inactive*) 683; linger, loiter, saunter, lag behind; bide –, take- one's time; hang -about, – around, – back, – in the balance; gain time; hang fire; stand –, lie-over.

put off, defer, delay, lay over, suspend; shift –, stave- off; waive, retard, remand, postpone, adjourn; procrastinate; dally; prolong, protract; spin –, draw –, lengthen- out; prorogue; keep back; tide over; push –, drive- to the last; let the matter stand over; reserve etc. (*store*) 636; temporize; consult one's pillow, sleep upon it.

shelve, table, lay on the table.

lose an opportunity etc. 135; be kept waiting, dance attendance; kick –, cool- one's heels; *faire antichambre;* wait impatiently; await etc. (*expect*) 507; sit up, – at night.

Adj. late, tardy, slow, behindhand, belated, postliminious, posthumous, backward, unpunctual; dilatory etc. (*slow*), overdue 275; delayed etc. *v.;* in abeyance.

Adv. late; late-, back-ward; late in the day; at -sunset, – the eleventh hour, – length, – last, – long; ultimately; after –, behind- time; too late; too late for etc. 135.

slowly, leisurely, deliberately, at one's leisure; *ex post facto; sine die.*

Phr. *nonum prematur in annum.*

134. Occasion.—**N.** occasion, opportunity, opening, room, scope, field; suitable –, proper- -time, – season; high time; opportuneness etc. *adj.;* tempestivity.

crisis, turn, juncture, emergency, conjuncture; turning point; given time.

nick of time; golden –, well-timed –, fine –, favorable- opportunity; clear stage, fair field; *mollia tempora; fata Morgana;* spare time etc. (*leisure*) 685.

V. seize etc. (*take*) 789 –, use etc. 677 –, give etc. 784- an -opportunity, – occasion; improve the occasion.

suit the occasion etc. (*be expedient*) 646.

strike the iron while it is hot, *battre le fer sur l'enclume,* make hay while the sun shines, take time by the forelock, *prendre la balle au bond.*

Adj. opportune, timely, well-timed, timeous, timeful, seasonable.

providential, lucky, fortunate, happy, favorable, propitious, auspicious, critical; suitable etc. 23; *obiter dicta.*

Adv. opportunely etc. *adj.* ; in -proper, – due- -time, – course, – season; for the nonce; in the -nick, – fulness- of time; all in good time; just in time, at the eleventh hour, now or never.

by the -way, – by; *en passant, à propos; pro -re natâ, – hac vice; par parenthèse,* parenthetically, by way of parenthesis; while -speaking of, – on this subject; *ex tempore;* on the spur of the -moment, – occasion; on the spot etc. (*early*) 132.

Phr. *carpe diem; occasionem cognosce;* one's hour is come, the time is up; that reminds me.

135. Intempestivity.—**N.** intempestivity; unseasonableness; unsuitable –, improper-time; unreasonableness etc. *adj.;* evil hour; *contretemps;* intrusion; anachronism etc. 115.

V. be -ill timed etc. *adj.;* mistime, intrude, come amiss, break in upon; have other fish to fry; be -busy, – engaged, – tied up, – occupied.

lose –, throw away –, waste –, neglect etc. 460- an opportunity; allow –, suffer- the -opportunity, – occasion- to -pass, – slip, – go by, – escape, – lapse; waste time etc. (*be inactive*) 683; let slip through the fingers, lock the stable door when the steed is stolen.

Adj. ill-, mis-timed; untimely, intrusive, unseasonable; out of -date, – season; inopportune, timeless, untoward, *mal à propos,* unlucky, inauspicious, unpropitious, unfortunate, unfavorable; unsuited etc. 24; inexpedient etc. 647.

unpunctual etc. (*late*) 133; too late for; premature etc. (*early*) 132; too soon for; wise after the event.

Adv. inopportunely etc. *adj.;* as ill luck would have it, in an evil hour, the time having gone by, a day after the fair.

Phr. after meat mustard, after death the doctor.

136. Frequency.—**N.** frequency, oftness; repetition, etc. 104.

V. recur etc. 104; do nothing but; keep, – on.

Adj. frequent, many times, not rare, thickcoming, incessant, perpetual, continual, constant, recurrent, repeated etc. 104; habitual etc. 613; hourly, etc. 138.

Adv. often, often to be met with, oft; oft-, often-times; frequently; repeatedly etc. 104; unseldom, not unfrequently; in -quick, – rapid- succession; many a time and oft; daily, hourly etc.; every -day, – hour, – moment etc.

perpetually, continually, constantly, incessantly, without ceasing, at all times, daily and hourly, night and day, day and night, day after day, morning, noon and night, ever and anon.

most often; commonly etc. (*habitually*) 613.

sometimes, occasionally, at times, now and then, from time to time, there being times when, *toties quoties*, often enough, again and again etc. 104.

137. Infrequency.—**N.** infrequency, infrequence, rareness, rarity; fewness etc. 103; seldomness, uncommonness.

V. be -rare etc. *adj.*

Adj. un-, in-frequent; uncommon, sporadic, rare, — as a blue diamond; few etc. 103; scarce; almost unheard of, unprecedented, which has not occurred within the memory of the oldest inhabitant, not within one's previous experience.

Adv. seldom, rarely, scarcely, hardly; not often, unfrequently, infrequently, unoften; scarcely —, hardly- ever; once in a blue moon.

once; once -for all, — in a way; *pro hac vice;* like angels' visits, few and far between.

138. Regularity of recurrence. **Periodicity.**—**N.** periodicity, intermittence; beat; oscillation etc. 314; pulse, pulsation, rhythm; alternation, -nateness, -nativeness, -nity.

bout, round, revolution, rotation, turn.

anniversary, birthday, jubilee, centenary, bi-, ter-centenary.

[Regularity of return] rota, cycle, period, stated time, routine; days of the week; Sunday, Monday etc.; months of the year; January etc.; feast, fast, saint's day etc.; Christmas, Easter, New Year's Day etc. 998; quarter-, Lady-, Midsummer-, Michaelmas-day; May Day, the King's Birthday; leap year, seasons.

punctuality, regularity, steadiness.

V. recur in regular -order, — succession; return, revolve, rotate; come -again, — in its turn; come round, — again; beat, pulsate; alternate; intermit.

Adj. periodic, -al; serial, recurrent, cyclic-, -al, rhythmic-, -al, even; recurring etc. *V.;* inter-, remittent; alternate, every other.

hourly; diurnal, daily; quotidian, tertian, weekly; hebdomad-al, -ary; bi-weekly, fortnightly; monthly, menstrual, catamenial; yearly, annual; biennial, triennial, etc.; bissextile; centennial, secular; paschal, lenten, etc.

regular, steady, punctual, constant, methodical, regular as clockwork.

Adv. periodically etc. *adj.;* at -regular intervals, — stated times; at -fixed, — established-periods; punctually etc. *adj.; de die in diem;* from day to day, day by day.

by turns, in -turn, — rotation; alternately, every other day, off and on, ride and tie, round and round.

139. Irregularity of recurrence.—**N.** irregularity, uncertainty, unpunctuality; fitfulness etc. *adj.*

Adj. irregular, uneven, uncertain, unpunctual, capricious, erratic, desultory, fitful, flickering; rambling, rhapsodical; spasmodic, unsystematic, unequal, variable, halting.

Adv. irregularly etc. *adj.;* by fits and starts etc. (*discontinuously*) 70.

140. Change. [Difference at different times.]—**N.** change, alteration, mutation, permutation, variation, modification, modulation, inflexion, mood, qualification, innovation, *metastasis,* deviation, shift, turn; diversion; break.

transformation, transfiguration; metamorphosis; metabolism; transmutation; transsubstantiation; metagenesis, transanimation, transmigration, metempsychosis; version, metathesis, transmogrification; catalysis; *avatar;* alterative.

conversion etc. (*gradual change*) 144; revolution etc. (*sudden or radical change*) 146; inversion etc. (*reversal*) 218; displacement etc. 185; transference etc. 270.

changeableness etc. 149; tergiversation etc. (*change of mind*) 607.

V. change, alter, vary, wax and wane; modulate, diversify, qualify, tamper with; turn, shift, veer, jibe, tack, chop, shuffle, swerve, dodge, warp, deviate, turn aside, evert, intervert; pass to, take a turn, turn the corner, resume.

work a change, modify, vamp, revamp, superinduce; trans-form, —mute, -ume, -figure etc. *n.;* metamorphose, ring the changes; convert, resolve; revolutionize; chop and change; patch, re-shape.

innovate, introduce new blood, shuffle the cards, spin the wheel; give a -turn, — color- to; influence, turn the scale; shift the scene, turn over a new leaf.

recast etc. 146; reverse etc. 218; disturb etc. 61; convert into etc. 144.

Adj. changed etc. *v.;* new-fangled; changeable etc. 149; transitional; modifiable; alterative.

Adv. *mutatis mutandis.*

Int. *quantum mutatus!*

Phr. 'a change came o'er the spirit of my dream;' *nous avons changé tout cela; tempora mutantur et nos mutamur in illis; non sum qualis eram.*

141. Permanence. [Absence of change.]—**N.** stability etc. 150; quiescence etc. 265; obstinacy etc. 606.

permanence, -cy, persistence, fixity, fixity of purpose, endurance, durability; standing, *status quo;* maintenance, preservation, conservation; conservatism; *laissez-faire;* law of the Medes and Persians; standing dish.

V. let -alone, — be; persist, remain, stay, tarry, rest; hold, — on; last, endure, bide, abide, aby, dwell, maintain, keep; stand, — still, — fast; subsist, live, outlive, survive; hold —, keep- one's ground, — footing; hold good.

Adj. stable etc. 150; persisting etc. *v.;* permanent; established, fixed; durable, unchanged etc. (change etc. 140); unrenewed; intact, inviolate; persistent; monotonous, uncheckered; unfailing.

un-destroyed, -repealed, -suppressed; conservative, *qualis ab incepto;* prescriptive etc. (*old*) 124; stationary etc. 265.

Adv. *in statu quo;* for good, finally; at a stand, -still; *uti possidetis;* without a shadow of turning.

Phr. as you were!; *j'y suis j'y reste; esto perpetua; nolumus leges Angliae mutari;* let sleeping dogs lie.

142. Cessation. [Change from action to

rest.]—**N.** cessation, discontinuance, desistance, desinence.

inter-, re-mission; sus-pense, -pension, interruption, hitch; hartal; stop; stopping etc. *v.;* closure, stoppage, halt; arrival etc. 292.

pause, rest, lull, respite, truce, armistice, drop; interregnum, abeyance.

closure etc. 261.

dead -stop, – stand, – lock; checkmate; comma, colon, semicolon, period, full stop; end etc. 67; death etc. 360; *caesura.*

V. cease, discontinue, desist, stay; break –, leave- off; hold, stop, pull up, stall, stop short, check; stick, deadlock, hand fire; halt; pause, rest.

have done with, give over, surcease, shut up shop; give up etc. (*relinquish*) 624.

hold –, stay- one's hand; rest on one's oars, repose on one's laurels.

come to a -stand, – standstill, – dead lock, – full stop; arrive etc. 292; go out, die away, peter out; wear -away, – off; pass away etc. (*be past*) 122; be at an end.

intromit, interrupt, suspend, interpel; inter-, re-mit; put -an end, – a stop, – a period- to; bring to a stand, -still; stop, cut out, cut short, arrest, avast; stem the -tide, – torrent; pull the check string; switch off.

Int. halt! hold! stop! enough! avast! have done! a truce to! soft! leave off! shut up! give over! chuck it!

143. Continuance in action.—**N.** continu-ance, -ation; run; extension, prolongation; maintenance, perpetuation; persistence etc. (*perseverance*) 604a; repetition etc. 104.

V. continue, persist; go –, jog –, keep –, carry –, run – hold- on; abide, keep, pursue, stick to; endure; take –, maintain- its course; keep up.

sustain, uphold, hold up, keep on foot; follow up, perpetuate. prolong; maintain; preserve etc. 604*a*; harp upon etc. (*repeat*)104.

keep -going, – alive, – at it, – the pot boiling, – the ball rolling, – up the ball; plod-, plug-along; slog on; die in harness; hold on –, pursue- the even tenor of one's way.

let be; *stare super antiquas vias; quieta non movere;* let things take their course.

Adj. continuing etc. *v.;* uninterrupted, unintermitting, unremitting, unvarying, unshifting; unreversed, unstopped, unrevoked, unvaried; sustained; undying etc. (*perpetual*) 112; inconvertible.

follow-up.

Int. carry on! right away!

Phr. *vestigia nulla retrorsum, labitur et labetur.*

144. Conversion. [Gradual change to something different.]—**N.** conversion, reduction, transmutation, transformation, development, resolution, assimilation; assumption; naturalization.

chemistry, alchemy; progress, growth, lapse, flux.

passage; transit, -ion; transmigration, shifting etc. *v.;* conjugation; convertibility.

crucible, alembic, caldron, retort, test tube etc.

convert, neophyte, proselyte, pervert, renegade, deserter, apostate, turncoat.

V. be converted into; become, get, wax; come –, turn- -to, – into; turn out, lapse, shift; run –, fall –, pass –, slide –, glide –, grow –, ripen –, open –, resolve itself –, settle –, merge- into; melt, grow, come round to, mature, mellow; assume the -form, – shape, – state, – nature, – character- of; illapse; assume a new phase, undergo a change.

convert –, resolve- into; make, render; mold, form etc. 240; remodel, new model, refound, reform, reorganize; assimilate –, bring –, reduce- to; transform.

Adj. converted into etc. *v.;* convertible, resolvable into; transitional; naturalized.

Adv. gradually etc. (*slowly*) 275; *in transitu* etc. (*transference*) 270.

145. Reversion.—**N.** reversion, return; revulsion; reaction.

turning point, turn of the tide; *status quo ante bellum;* calm before a storm.

alternation etc. (*periodicity*) 138; inversion etc. 219; recoil etc. 277; regression etc. 283; restoration etc. 660; relapse etc. 661; vicinism, atavism, throwback.

V. revert, turn back, return; relapse etc. 661; recoil etc. 277; retreat etc. 283; restore etc. 660; undo, unmake; turn the -tide, – scale; escheat.

Adj. reverting etc. *v.;* revulsive, reactionary.

Adv. *à rebours,* wrong side out.

146. Revolution. [Sudden or violent change.]—**N.** revolution, *bouleversement,* subversion. break up; destruction etc. 162; sudden –, radical –, sweeping –, organic- change; clean sweep, *coup d'état,* overthrow, *débâcle;* counter-revolution, rebellion etc. 742.

transilience, jump, leap, plunge, jerk, start; explosion; spasm, convulsion, throe, revulsion; storm, earthquake, eruption, upheaval, cataclysm.

legerdemain etc. (*trick*) 545.

V. revolutionize; new model, remodel, recast; strike out something new, break with the past; change the face of, unsex; revert etc. 742.

Adj. unrecognizable.

Revolutionary, Bolshevik etc. 742.

147. Substitution. [Change of one thing for another.]—**N.** substitution, subrogation, commutation; supplanting etc. *v.;* supersession, metonymy etc. (*figure of speech*) 521.

[Thing substituted.] substitute, *succedaneum,* make-shift, temporary expedient, shift, *pis aller,* stop-gap, jury-mast, *locum tenens,* warming-pan, dummy, goat, scape-goat; double; changeling; *quid pro quo,* alternative; remount; representative etc. (*deputy*) 759; palimpsest.

price, purchase-money, consideration, equivalent.

V. substitute, put in the place of, change for; make way for, give place to; supply –, take- the place of; supplant, supersede, replace, cut out, serve as a substitute; step into –, stand in- the shoes of; make a shift –, put up- with; borrow of Peter to pay Paul; commute, redeem, compound for.

Adj. substituted etc. *v.;* vicarious, subdititious; substitutional.
Adv. instead; in -place, – lieu, – the stead, – the room- of; *faute de mieux.*

148. Interchange. [Double or mutual change.]—**N.** inter-, ex-change; com-, per-, intermutation; reciprocation, transposal, transposition, shuffling; reciprocity, castling [at chess]; hocus-pocus.
interchange-ableness, -ability.
barter etc. 794; tit for tat etc. (*retaliation*) 718; cross fire, battledore and shuttlecock; *quid pro quo.*
V. inter-, ex-, counter-change; bandy, transpose, shuffle, change hands, swap, trade, permute, reciprocate, commute; give and take, return the compliment; play at -puss in the corner, – battledore and shuttlecock; retaliate etc. 718; barter etc. 794.
Adj. interchanged etc. *v.;* reciprocal, mutual, commutative, interchanged etc. *v.;* interchangeable, intercurrent.
Adv. in exchange, *vice versâ, mutatis mutandis,* backwards and forwards, by turns, turn and turn about, turn about; each –, every one- in his turn.

149. Changeableness.—**N.** changeableness etc. *adj.*; mutability, inconstancy; versatility, mobility; instability, unstable equilibrium; vacillation etc. (*irresolution*) 605; fluctuation, vicissitude; alternation etc. (*oscillation*) 314.
restlessness etc. *adj.;* fidgets, disquiet; dis-, inquietude; unrest; agitation etc. 315.
moon, Proteus, chameleon, kaleidoscope, quicksilver, shifting sands, weathercock, harlequin, Cynthia of the minute, April showers; wheel of Fortune; transientness etc. 111.
V. fluctuate, vary, waver, flounder, flicker, flitter, flit, flutter, shift, shuffle, shake, totter, tremble, vacillate, wamble, turn and turn about, ring the changes; sway –, shift- to and fro; change and change about; oscillate etc. 314; vibrate –, oscillate- between two extremes; alternate; have as many phases as the moon.
Adj. change-able, -ful; changing etc. 140; mutable, variable, checkered, ever changing, kaleidoscopic, prote-an, -iform; versatile.
unstaid, inconstant; un-steady, -stable, -fixed, -settled; fluctuating etc. *v.;* restless; mercurial; agitated etc. 315; erratic, fickle; irresolute etc. 605; capricious etc. 608; touch-and-go; inconsonant, fitful, spasmodic; vibratory; afloat; alternating; alterable, plastic, mobile; fleeting, transient etc. 111.
Adv. see-saw etc. (*oscillation*) 314; off and on.

150. Stability.—**N.** stability; immutability etc. *adj.;* unchangeableness etc. *adj.;* constancy; stable equilibrium, immobility, soundness, vitality, stabiliment, stabilization, stiffness, ankylosis, solidity, *aplomb.*
establishment, fixture; rock, pillar, tower, foundation, leopard's spots, Ethiopian's skin, law of the Medes and Persians.
stabilimeter, stabilizator.
permanence etc. 141; obstinacy etc. 606.
V. be -firm etc. *adj.;* stick fast; stand –, keep –, remain- firm; weather the storm.
settle, establish, stablish, ascertain, fix, set, stabilitate, stabilize; retain, stet, keep hold; make -good, – sure; fasten etc. (*join*) 43; set on its legs, float; perpetuate.
settle down; strike –, take- root; take up one's abode etc. 184; build one's house on a rock.
Adj. unchangeable, immutable; unalter-ed, -able; not to be changed, constant; permanent etc. 141; invariable, undeviating; stable, durable; perennial etc. (*diuturnal*) 110.
fixed, steadfast, firm, fast, steady, balanced; confirmed, valid, fiducial, immovable, irremovable, riveted, rooted; settled, established etc. *v.;* vested; incontrovertible, stereotyped, indeclinable.
tethered, anchored, moored, at anchor, on a rock, firm as a rock; firmly -seated, – established etc. *v.;* deep-rooted, ineradicable; inveterate; obstinate etc. 606.
transfixed, stuck fast, aground, high and dry, stranded.
indefeasible, irretrievable, intransmutable, incommutable, irresoluble, irrevocable, irreversible, reverseless, inextinguishable, irreducible; indissol-uble, -vable; indestructible, undying, imperishable, indelible, indeciduous; insusceptible, – of change.
Int. *stet.*

151. Eventuality.—**N.** eventuality, event, occurrence, incident, affair, transaction, proceeding, fact; matter of –, naked- fact; phenomenon; advent.
business, concern; circumstance, particular, casualty, happening, accident, adventure, passage, crisis, pass, emergency, contingency, consequence etc. 154.
the world, life, things, doings, affairs, matters; things –, affairs- in general; the times, state of affairs, order of the day; course –, tide –, stream –, current –, run –, march- of -things, – events; ups and downs of life; chapter of accidents etc. (*chance*) 156; situation etc. (*circumstances*) 8.
V. happen, occur; take -place, – effect; come, become of; come -off, – about, – round, – into existence, – forth, – to pass, – on; pass, present itself; fall; fall –, turn- out; run, be on foot, fall in; be-fall, -tide, -chance; prove, eventuate, draw on; turn –, crop –, spring –, cast- up; super-, sur-vene; issue, emanate, arrive, ensue, arise, start, hold, take its course; pass off etc. (*be past*) 122.
meet with; experience; fall to the lot of; be one's -chance, – fortune, – lot; find; encounter, undergo; pass –, go- through; endure etc. (*feel*) 821.
Adj. happening etc. *v.;* going on, doing, current; in the wind, afloat; on -foot, – the *tapis;* at issue, in question; incidental.
eventful, momentous, signal; stirring, bustling, full of incident.
Adv. eventually, ultimately, in -the event of, – case; in the course of things; in the -natural, – ordinary- course of things; as -things, – times- go; as the world -goes, – wags; as the -tree falls, – cat jumps; as it may -turn out, – happen.
Phr. the plot thickens.

152. Destiny.—**N.** destiny etc. (*necessity*) 601; hereafter, future –, post- existence; future state, next world, world to come, after life; futurity etc. 121; everlasting -life, – death; prospect etc. (*expectation*) 507.

V. impend; hang –, lie –, hover- over; threaten, loom, await, come on, approach, stare one in the face; fore-, pre-ordain; predestine, doom, foredoom, foreshadow, have in store for.

Adj. impending etc. *v.;* destined; about to -be, – happen; coming, in store, to come, going to happen, instant, at hand, near; near –, close- at hand; overhanging, hanging over one's head, imminent; brewing, preparing, forthcoming; in the wind, on the cards, in reserve; that -will, – is to-be; in prospect etc. (*expected*) 507; looming in the -distance, – horizon, – future; unborn, in embryo; in the womb of -time; – futurity; on the knees of the gods; pregnant etc. (*producing*) 161.

Adv. in -time, – the long run; all in good time; eventually etc. 151; whatever may happen etc. (*certainly*) 474; as -chance etc. 156- would have it.

153. Cause. [Constant antecedent.]—**N.** cause, origin, source, principle, element; occasioner, prime mover, engine, turbine, motor, *primum mobile; vera causa*; author etc. (*producer*) 164; main-spring, agent; dynamo, generator, battery (electric); leaven; groundwork, foundation etc. (*support*) 215.

spring, fountain, well, font; fountain –, spring- head; *fons et origo,* genesis; descent etc. (*paternity*) 166; remote cause; influence.

pivot, hinge, turning-point, lever; key; kernel, core; proximate cause, *causa causans;* last straw that breaks the camel's back.

ground; reason, – why; why and wherefore, rationale, occasion, derivation; final cause etc. (*intention*) 620; *le dessous des cartes;* undercurrents.

rudiment, egg, germ, embryo, fetus, bud, root, *radix,* radical, etymon, nucleus, seed, stem, stalk, stock, *stirps,* trunk, tap-root; latent organism.

nest, cradle, nursery, womb, *nidus,* birth-, breeding-place, hot-bed.

caus-ality, -ation; origination; production etc. 161.

V. be the -cause etc. *n.*- of; originate; give -origin, – rise, – occasion- to; cause, occasion, sow the seeds of, kindle, suscitate; bring -on, – to pass, – about; produce; create etc. 161; set -up, – afloat, – on foot; found, broach, institute, lay the foundation of, inaugurate; lie at the root of.

procure, induce, draw down, open the door to, superinduce, evoke, entail, operate; elicit, provoke.

conduce to etc. (*tend to*) 176; contribute; promote; have a -hand in, – finger in- the pie; determine, decide, turn the scale, give the casting vote; have a common origin; derive its origin etc. (*effect*) 154.

Adj. caused etc. *v.;* causal, original; prim-ary, -itive, -ordial; aboriginal; radical; inceptive, embry-onic, -otic; *in -embryo, – ovo;* seminal, germinal; formative, productive etc. 168; at the bottom of; connate, having a common origin.

Adv. because etc. 155; behind the scenes.

154. Effect. [Constant sequent.]—**N.** effect, consequence, sequela; derivative, -tion; result; result-ant, -ance; upshot, issue, *dénouement;* outcome; termination, end etc. 67; development, outgrowth, fruit, crop, harvest, product, bud, blossom, florescence, ear.

production, produce, product, finished product, work, handiwork, fabric, performance; creature, creation; offspring, -shoot; first-fruits, -lings; *prémices.*

V. be the -effect etc. *n.*- of; be -due, – owing-to; originate -in, – from; rise –, arise –, take its rise –, spring –, proceed –, emanate –, come –, grow –, bud –, sprout –, germinate –, issue –, flow –, result –, follow –, derive its origin –, accrue- from; come -to, – of, – out of; depend –, hand –, hinge –, turn- upon.

take the consequences, sow the wind and reap the whirlwind.

Adj. owing to; resulting from etc. *v.;* resultant; derivable from; due to; caused etc. by, 153; dependent upon; derived –, evolved- from; derivative; hereditary.

Adv. of course, it follows that, naturally, consequently; as a –, in- consequence; through all, all along of, necessarily, eventually.

Phr. *cela va sans dire,* thereby hangs a tale.

155. Attribution. [Assignment of cause.]—**N.** attribution, theory, etiology, ascription, reference to, rationale; accounting for etc. *v.;* imputation, derivation from.

fil-, affil-iation; pedigree etc. (*paternity*) 166.

explanation etc. (*interpretation*) 522; reason why etc. (*cause*) 153.

V. attribute –, ascribe –, impute –, refer –, lay –, point –, trace –, bring home- to; put –, set- down- to; charge –, ground- on; invest with, assign as cause, charge with, blame, lay at the door of, father upon; saddle with; affiliate; account for, derive from, point out the -reason etc. 153; theorize; tell how it comes; put the saddle on the right horse.

Adj. attributed etc. *v.;* attributable etc. *v.;* refer-able, -rible; due to, derivable from; owing to etc. (*effect*) 154; putative.

Adv. hence, thence, therefore, for, since, on account of, because, owing to; on that account; from -this, – that- cause; thanks to, forasmuch as; whence, *propter hoc.*

why? wherefore? whence? how -comes, – is, – happens- it? how does it happen?

in -some, – some such- way; somehow, – or other.

Phr. that is why; *hinc illae lachrymae; cherchez la femme.*

156. Chance.† [Absence of assignable cause.]—**N.** chance, indetermination, accident, fortune, hazard, hap, haphazard, chance-medley, random, luck, *raccroc,* casualty, fortuity, contingence, coincidence, adventure, hit; fate etc. (*necessity*) 601; equal chance; lottery, raffle, tombola, sweepstake; toss up etc. 621; turn of the -table, – cards; hazard of the die, chapter of accidents; cast –, throw- of the dice; heads or tails, wheel of Fortune, whirligig of chance; *sortes; – Virgilianae.*

probability, possibility, contingency, odds, long odds, run of luck; main- chance.

theory of -probabilities, – chances; bookmaking; assurance; speculation, gamble, gaming etc. 621.

V. chance, hap, turn up; fall to one's lot; be one's -fate etc. 601; stumble on, light –, blunder –, hit- upon; take one's chance etc. 621.

Adj. casual, fortuitous, accidental, haphazard, random, stray, adventitious, adventive, causeless, incidental. contingent, uncaused, undetermined, indeterminate; possible etc. 470; unintentional etc. 621.

Adv. by -chance, – accident; casually; perchance etc. (*possibly*) 470; for aught one knows; as -good, – bad, – ill-luck etc. *n.*- would have it; as it may -be, – chance, – turn up, – happen; as the case may be.

†The word *Chance* has two distinct meanings: the first, the absence of assignable *cause*, as above; and the second, the absence of *design*—for the latter see 621.

157. Power.—**N.** power; poten-cy, -tiality; puissance, might, force; energy etc. 171; dint; right -hand, – arm; ascendency, sway, control; pre-potency, -pollence; almightiness, omnipotence; authority etc. 737; strength etc. 159.

ability; ableness etc. *adj.;* competency; efficiency, -cacy; validity, cogency; enablement; vantage ground; influence etc. 175; horse power; dynamometer.

pressure; elasticity; gravity; attraction, repulsion; *vis inertiae, mortua, – viva;* friction, suction.

electricity, magnetism, galvanism, voltaic electricity, voltaism, electro-magnetism, electrostatics, electrification; electric – current, – power; potential –, dynamic –, kinetic –, electrical –, chemical –, atomic- energy; electric field, circuit, charge, discharge, shock, polarity, pole; amperage, voltage, wattage, resistance, conduction, induction, electrification, electrolysis.

electronics, radionics, electron physics, electrophysics, avionics, radiometry, photoelectronics; electron, negatron, positron, photoelectron, thermion, barytron, electronic effect; electron emission; electron –, cathode –, anode –, positive – ray; electron – current, – flow – stream, – beam, – volt; electronic circuit; conductance; electron tube, tube, vacuum tube, photoelectric tube, call; transistor.

capability, capacity; *quid valeant humeri quid ferre recusent;* faculty, quality, attribute, endowment, virtue, gift, property, qualification, susceptibility.

V. be -powerful etc. *adj.;* gain -power etc. *n.*

belong –, pertain- to; lie –, be- in one's power; can.

electrify, generate, magnetize.

give –, confer –, exercise- power etc. *n.;* empower, enable, invest; in-, en-due; endow, arm; strengthen etc. 159; compel etc. 744.

Adj. powerful, puissant; potent, -ial; capable, able; equal –, up- to; cogent, valid; effect-ive, -ual; efficient, efficacious, adequate, competent; multi-, pleni-, omni-, armi- potent; mighty, ascendent; almighty.

electric, electrical, electronic etc.

forcible etc. *adj.* (*energetic*) 171; influential etc. 175; productive etc. 168.

Adv. powerfully etc. *adj.;* by -virtue, – dint-of.

158. Impotence.—**N.** impotence; in-, dis-ability; disablement, impuissance, imbecility, caducity; incapa-city, -bility; inapt-, inept-itude; indocility; invalidity, inefficiency, incompetence, disqualification.

telum imbelle, brutum fulmen, blank cartridge, flash in the pan, *vox et praeterea nihil,* dead letter, bit of waste paper, dummy; scrap of paper.

inefficacy etc. (*inutility*) 645; failure etc. 732.

helplessness etc. *adj.;* prostration, paralysis, palsy, ataxia, apoplexy, syncope, sideration, *deliquium*, collapse, exhaustion, softening of the brain, emasculation, inanition, senility etc. 128; castrato, eunuch.

cripple, old woman, muff, molly-coddle, milksop.

V. be -impotent etc. *adj.;* not have a leg to stand on.

vouloir -rompre l'anguille au genou, – prendre la lune avec les dents.

collapse, faint, swoon, fall into a swoon, drop; go by the board; end in smoke etc. (*fail*) 732.

render -powerless etc. *adj.;* deprive of power; decontrol; dis-able, -enable; disarm, incapacitate, disqualify, unfit, invalidate, undermine, deaden, cramp, tie the hands; double up, prostrate, paralyze, muzzle, cripple, becripple, maim, lame, hamstring, draw the teeth of; throttle, strangle, *garrotte;* ratten, silence, sprain, clip the wings of, render *hors de combat,* spike the guns; take the wind out of one's sails, scotch the snake, put a spoke in one's wheel; break the -neck, – back; un-hinge, -fit; put out of gear.

unman, unnerve, devitalize, attenuate, enervate; emasculate, spay, caponize, castrate, geld; effeminize.

shatter, exhaust; weaken etc. 160.

Adj. powerless, impotent, unable, incapable, incompetent; ineff-icient, -ective; inept; un-fit, fitted, un-, dis-qualified; unendowed; in-, un-apt; crippled, decrepit; disabled etc. *v.;* armless.

harmless, unarmed, weaponless, defenceless, *sine ictu,* unfortified, indefensible, vincible, pregnable, untenable.

para-lytic, -lyzed; palsied, imbecile; nerve-, sinew-, marrow-, pith-, lust-less; emasculate, disjointed, out of -joint, – gear; un-nerved, -hinged; water-logged, on one's beam ends, rudderless; laid on one's back; done up, dead beat, exhausted, shattered, demoralized; gravelled etc. (*in difficulty*) 704; helpless, unfriended, fatherless; without a leg to stand on, *hors de combat,* laid on the shelf.

null and void, nugatory, imoperative, good for nothing; dud; invertebrate; ineffectual etc. (*failing*) 732; inadequate etc. 640; inefficacious etc. (*useless*) 645.

159. Strength. (Degree of power.]—**N.** strength; power etc. 157; energy etc. 171; vigor, force; main –, physical –, brute- force; spring, elasticity, tone, tension, tonicity.

stoutness etc. *adj.;* lustihood, stamina, nerve,

muscle, sinew, thews and sinews, *physique;* pith, -iness; virility, vitality.

athlet-ics, -icism; gymnastics, feats of strength.

adamant, steel, iron, oak, heart of oak; iron grip; grit, bone.

athlete, gymnast, tumbler, acrobat; Atlas, Hercules, Antaeus, Samson, Cyclops, Goliath, Titan; tower of strength; giant refreshed.

strengthening etc. *v.;* invigoration, refreshment, refocillation.

[Science of forces] dynamics, statics.

V. be -strong etc. *adj.,* — stronger; overmatch.

render -strong etc. *adj.;* give -strength etc. *n.;* strengthen, invigorate, brace, nerve, fortify, buttress, sustain, harden, case-harden, steel; gird; screw —, wind —, set- up; gird —, brace- up one's loins; recruit, set on one's legs; vivify; refresh etc. 689; refect; reinforce etc. (*restore*) 660.

Adj. strong, mighty, vigorous, forcible, hard, adamantine, stout, robust, sturdy, hardy, powerful, potent, puissant, valid.

resistless, irresistible, invincible, proof against, impregnable, unconquerable, indomitable, inextinguishable, unquenchable; incontestable; more than a match for; over-powering, -whelming; all-powerful; sovereign.

able-bodied; athletic, gymnastic; Herculean, Cyclopean, Atlantean; muscular, husky, brawny, wiry, well-knit, broad-shouldered, sinewy, strapping, stalwart, gigantic.

man-ly, -like, -ful; masculine, male, virile, in the prime of manhood.

un-weakened, -allayed, -withered, -shaken, -worn, -exhausted; in full -force, — swing; in the plenitude of power.

stubborn, thick-ribbed, made of iron, deep-rooted; strong as -a lion, — a horse, — brandy; sound as a roach; in -fine, — high- feather; in fine fettle; like a giant refreshed.

Adv. strongly etc. *adj.*; by -force etc. *n.*; by main force etc. (*by compulsion*) 744.

Phr. 'our withers are unwrung.'

160. Weakness.—N. weakness etc. *adj.;* debility, atony, relaxation, languor, enervation; impotence etc. 158; infirmity; effeminancy, feminality; fragility, flaccidity; inactivity etc. 683.

declension —, loss —, failure- of strength; delicacy, invalidation, decrepitude, asthenia, adynamy, cachexy, *cachexia,* anemia, bloodlessness, sprain, strain.

reed, thread, rope of sand, broken reed, house -of cards, — built on sand.

soft-, weak-ling; infant etc. 129; youth etc. 127.

V. be -weak etc. *adj.;* drop, crumble, give way, totter, tremble, shake, halt, limp, fade, languish, decline, flag, fail, have one foot in the grave.

render -weak etc. *adj.;* weaken, enfeeble, debilitate, shake, deprive of strength, relax, enervate; un-brace, -nerve; cripple, unman, etc. (*render powerless*) 158; cramp, reduce, sprain, strain, blunt the edge of; dilute, impoverish; decimate; extenuate; reduce -in strength, — the strength of; invalidate; *mettre de l'eau dans son vin.*

Adj. weak, feeble, debile; impotent etc. 158; relaxed, unnerved etc. *v.*; sap-, strength-, powerless; weakly, unstrung, flaccid, adynamic, asthenic; nervous.

soft, effeminate, feminate, womanish.

frail, fragile, shattery, frangible, brittle etc. 328; flimsy, unsubstantial, gimcrack, gingerbread; rickety, cranky; creachy; drooping, tottering etc. *v.;* broken, lame, halt, game, withered, shattered, shaken, crazy, shaky, tumble-down; palsied etc. 158; decrepit; C3.

lanquid, poor, poorly, infirm; faint, -ish; sickly etc. (*disease*) 655; dull, slack, evanid, spent, short-winded, effete; weatherbeaten; decayed, rotten, worn, seedy, languishing, wasted, washy, wishy-washy, laid low, pulled down, the worse for wear.

un-strengthened etc. 159, -supported, -aided, -assisted; aidless, defenceless etc. 158.

on its last legs; weak as a -child, — baby, — chicken, — cat, — rat; weak as -water, — water gruel, — gingerbread, — milk and water; colorless etc. 429.

Phr. *non sum qualis eram.*

161. Production.—N. production, creation, construction, formation, fabrication, manufacture; building, architecture, erection, edification; coinage; organization; *nisus formativus;* putting togeher etc. *v.;* establishment; workmanship, performance; achievement etc. (*completion*) 729; effect etc. 154.

flowering, fructification fruition.

bringing forth etc. *v.;* parturition, birth, birth-throe, child-birth, delivery, confinement, *accouchement,* travail, labour, midwifery, obstetrics; geniture; gestation etc. (*maturation*) 673; evolution, development, growth; genesis, fertilization, breeding, conception, germination, generation, *epigenesis,* pro-creation, -generation, -pagation; fecundation, impregnation; spontaneous generation; *arche-genesis, -biosis; bio-, abio-, homo-, xeno-genesis.*

authorship, publication; works, *oeuvre, opus.*

edifice, building, structure, fabric, erection, pile, tower, flower, fruit.

V. produce, perform, operate, do, make, gar, form, construct, fabricate, frame, contrive, manufacture; weave, forge, coin, carve, chisel; build, raise, edify, rear, erect, put together; set —, run- up; establish, constitute, compose, organize, institute, get up; achieve, accomplish etc. (*complete*) 729.

flower, sprout, blossom, burgeon, bear fruit, fructify, spawn, teem, ean, yean, farrow, drop, calf, pup, whelp, kitten, kindle; bear, lay, bring forth, give birth to, lie in, be brought to bed of, evolve, pullulate, usher into the world.

make productive etc. 168; create; beget, conceive, get, generate, fecundate, impregnate; procreate, -generate, -pagate; engender; bring —, call- into -being, — existence; breed, hatch, develop, bring up.

induce, superinduce; suscitate; cause etc. 153; acquire etc. 775.

Adj. produc-ed, -ing etc. *v.;* productive of; prolific etc. 168; creative; formative; gen-etic, -ial, -ital; fertile, pregnant; *enceinte,* big —, fraught-with; with child, in the family way, teeming, parturient, in the straw, brought to bed of; puerper-al, -ous.

architectonic; constructive.

162. Destruction. [Non-production.]—**N.** destruction; waste, dissolution, breaking up; di-, dis-ruption; consumption; disorganization.

fall, downfall, ruin, perdition, crash, smash, havoc, *délabrement, débâcle;* break -down, – up; prostration; desolation, *bouleversement*, wreck, crack-up, crash, wrack, shipwreck, cataclysm; Caudine Forks, Sedan.

extinction, annihilation; destruction of life etc. 361; knock-out, knock-down blow; doom, crack of doom.

destroying etc. *v.*; demo-lition, -lishment; biblioclasm; overthrow, subversion, suppression; abolition etc. (*abrogation*) 756; sacrifice; ravage, devastation, *sabotage, razzia*; incendiarism; revolution etc. 146; extirpation etc. (*extraction*) 301; *commencement de la fin,* road to ruin; dilapidation etc. (*deterioration*) 659.

V. be -destroyed etc.; perish; fall, – to the ground; tumble, topple; go –, fall- to pieces; break up; crumble, – to dust; go to -the dogs, – the wall, – smash, – shivers, – wreck, – pot, – wrack and ruin; go -by the board, – all to smash, – to pieces, – under; be all -over, – up- with; totter to its fall.

destroy; do –, make- away with; nullify; annul etc. 756; sacrifice, demolish; tear up; over-turn, -throw, -whelm; upset, subvert, put an end to; seal the doom of, do for, dish, undo; break -, cut- up; break –, cut –, pull –, mow –, blow –, beat- down; suppress, quash, put down; cut short, take off, blot out; dispel, dissipate, dissolve; consume.

smash, – to smithereens, quell, squash, squelch, crumple up, shatter, shiver; batter; tear –, crush –, cut –, shake –, pull –, pick- to pieces; nip; tear to -rags, – tatters; crush –, knock- to atoms; pulverize; ruin; strike out; throw –, knock- -down, – over; lay by the heels; fell, sink, swamp, scuttle, wreck, crash, shipwreck, engulf, submerge; lay in -ashes, – ruins; sweep away, erase, expunge, strike out, delete, efface, raze; level, – with the -ground, – dust.

deal destruction, lay waste, ravage, gut; disorganize; dismantle etc. (*render useless*) 645; devour, swallow up, desolate, devastate, sap, mine, blast, confound; exterminate, extinguish, quench, annihilate; snuff –, put –, stamp –, trample- out; lay –, trample- in the dust; prostrate; tread –, crush –, trample- under foot; lay the axe to the root of; make -short work, – a clean sweep, – mincemeat- of; cut up root and branch; fling –, scatter- to the winds; throw overboard; strike at the root of, sap the foundations of, spring a mine, blow up; ravage with fire and sword; cast to the dogs; eradicate etc. 301.

Adj. destroyed etc. *v.;* perishing etc. *v.;* trembling –, nodding –, tottering- to its fall; in course of destruction etc. *n.;* extinct.

destructive, subversive, ruinous, incendiary, deletory; destroying etc. *v.*; suicidal; deadly etc. (*killing*) 361.

Adv. with -crushing effect, – a sledge-hammer.

Phr. *delenda est Carthago.*

163. Reproduction.—**N.** reproduction, renovation; restoration etc. 660; renewal; new edition, reprint etc. 21; revival, regeneration, palingenesia, revivification; apotheosis; resuscitation, reanimation, resurrection, resurgence, reappearance, atavism; Phoenix; reincarnation.

generation etc. (*production*) 161; multiplication.

V. reproduce; restore etc. 660; revive, renovate, renew, regenerate, revivify, resuscitate, reanimate, refashion, stir the embers, put into the crucible; multiply, repeat, resurge.

crop up, spring up like mushrooms.

Adj. reproduced etc. *v.;* renascent, reappearing; reproductive; resurgent; progenitive; Hydra-headed.

164. Producer.—**N.** producer, creator, deviser, designer, originator, inventor, author, founder, generator, mover, architect; grower, constructor, maker etc. (*agent*) 690.

165. Destroyer.—**N.** destroyer etc. (destroy etc. 162); cankerworm etc. (*bane*) 663; iconoclast; assassin etc. (*killer*) 361; executioner etc. (*punish*) 975, Hun, Vandal, nihilist, anarchist.

166. Paternity.—**N.** paternity; parentage; fatherhood; consanguinity etc. 11.

parent, father, sire, dad, daddy, papa, governor, *pater, paterfamilias, abba;* genitor, progenitor, procreator, begetter; ancestor; grandsire, -father; great-grandfather.

house, stem, truck, tree, stock, *stirps*, pedigree, lineage, line, family, tribe, sept, race, clan; genealogy, descent, extraction, birth, ancestry; forefathers, forbears, patriarchs.

motherhood, maternity; mother, dam, mamma, *materfamilias;* grand-mother; matriarch.

Adj. paternal, parental; maternal; family, ancestral, linear, matrilinear, patrilineal, patriarchal.

167. Posterity.—**N.** posterity, progeny, breed, issue, offspring, brood, litter, seed, farrow, spawn, spat; family, children, grandchildren, heirs; great-grandchild.

child, son, daughter; kid; infant etc. 129; bantling, scion; shoot, sprout, olive branch, sprit, branch; off-shoot, -set; ramification; descendant; heir, -ess; heir -apparent, – presumptive; chip of the old block; heredity; rising generation.

straight descent, sonship, line, lineage, filiation, promogeniture.

Adj. filial.

168. Productiveness.—**N.** productiveness etc. *adj.;* fecundity, fertility, luxuriance, uberty.

pregnancy, pullulation, fructification, multiplication, propagation, procreation; superfetation.

milch cow, rabbit, hydra, warren, seed-plot, land flowing with milk and honey; second crop, after-crop, -growth, -math; fertilization.

V. make -productive etc. *adj.;* fructify; procreate, generate, fertilize, spermatize, impregnate; fecund-ate, -ify; teem, pullulate, multiply; produce etc. 161; conceive.

Adj. productive, prolific; teem-ing, -ful; fertile, fruitful, frugiferous, fruit-bearing; fructiferous; fecund, luxuriant; pregnant, uberous.

procre-ant, -ative; generative, life-giving, spermatic; originative; multiparous; omnific; propagable.

parturient etc. (*producing*) 161; profitable etc. (*useful*) 644.

169. Unproductiveness.—N. unproductiveness etc. *adj.;* infertility, steril; ity, infecundity; impotence etc. 158- unprofitableness etc. (*inutility*) 645.

waste, desert, Sahara, wild, wilderness, howling wilderness.

V. be -unproductive etc. *adj.;* hang fire, flash in the pan, come to nothing.

Adj. unproductive, inoperative, barren, addle, unfertile, unprolific, arid, sterile, unfruitful, acarpous, infecund; *sine prole;* fallow; teem-, issue-, fruitless; unprofitable etc. (*useless*) 645; null and void, of no effect.

170. Agency.—N. agency, operation, force, working, strain, function, office, maintenance, exercise, work, swing, play; inter-working, -action, procuration, procurement.

causation etc. 153; instrumentality etc. 631; influence etc. 175; action etc. (*voluntary*) 680; *modus operandi* etc. 627.

quickening –, maintaining- power; home stroke.

V. be -in action etc. *adj.;* operate, work; act, – upon; perform, play, support, sustain, strain, maintain, take effect, quicken, strike.

come –, bring- into -operation, – play; have -play, – free play; bring to bear upon.

Adj. operative, efficient, efficacious, practical, effectual.

at work, on foot; acting etc. (*doing*) 680; in -operation, – force, – action, – play, – exercise; acted –, wrought- upon.

Adv. by the -agency etc. *n.*- of; through etc. (*instrumentality*) 631; by means of etc. 632.

171. Physical **Energy.—N.** energy, physical energy, force; keenness etc. *adj.;* intensity, vigor, strength, elasticity; go; pep, live wire, high pressure; backbone, mettle, fire, vim.

acri-mony, -tude, -dity; causticity, virulence, poignancy; harshness etc. *adj.;* severity, edge, point; pungency etc. 392.

cantharides; Spanish fly; seasoning etc. (*condiment*) 393, stimulant, excitant.

activity, agitation, effervescence; ferment, -ation; ebullition, splutter, perturbation, stir, bustle; voluntary energy etc. 682; quicksilver.

resolution etc. (*mental energy*) 604; exertion etc. (*effort*) 686; excitation etc. (*mental*) 824.

V. give -energy etc. *n.;* energize, stimulate, kindle, excite, activate, exert; sharpen, pep up, intensify; inflame etc. (*render violent*) 173; wind up etc. (*strengthen*) 159.

strike, – into, – hard, – home; make an impression.

Adj. strong, energetic, forcible, active; strenuous, forceful, mettlesome, enterprising, go ahead; intense, deep-dyed, severe, keen, vivid, sharp, acute, incisive, trenchant, brisk, vigorous, live.

rousing, irritating; poignant; virulent, caustic, corrosive, mordant, harsh, stringent; double-edged, – shotted, – distilled; drastic, escharotic; racy etc. (*pungent*) 392; sarcastic etc. 932.

potent etc. (*powerful*) 157; radio-active.

Adv. strongly etc. *adj.; fortiter in re;* with telling effect.

Phr. the steam is up; *vires acquirit eundo.*

172. Physical **Inertness.—N.** inertness, dulness etc. *adj.;* inertia, *vis inertiae,* inertion, inactivity, torpor, languor; dormancy, quiescence etc. 265; latency, inaction, passivity.

mental inertness; sloth etc. (*inactivity*) 683; inexcitability etc. 826; irresolution etc. 605; obstinacy etc. 606; permanence etc. 141.

V. be -inert etc. *adj.;* hang fire, smoulder.

Adj. inert, inactive, passive, pacific; torpid etc. 683; sluggish, stagnant, dull, heavy, flat, slack, tame, slow, blunt; lifeless, dead, uninfluential.

latent, dormant, smouldering, unexerted.

Adv. inactively etc. *adj.;* in -suspense, -abeyance.

173. Violence.—N. violence, inclemency, vehemence, might, impetuosity; boisterousness etc.; *adj.;* effervescence, ebullition; turbulence, bluster; uproar, riot, row, rumpus, *le diable à quatre,* devil to pay, all the fat in the fire.

severity etc. 739; ferocity, rage, berserk, fury; exacerbation, exasperation, malignity; fit, paroxysm, orgasm; force, brute force; outrage; *coup de main;* strain, shock, shog; spasm, convulsion, throe; hysterics, passion etc. (*state of excitability*) 825.

out-break, -burst; burst, bounce, dissilience, discharge, volley, explosion, blow up, blast, detonation, rush, eruption, displosion, torrent.

turmoil etc. (*disorder*) 59; ferment etc. (*agitation*) 315; storm, tempest, rough weather; squall etc. (*wind*) 349; earthquake, volcano, thunderstorm.

fury, dragon, demon, tiger, beldame, Tisiphone, Megaera, Alecto, madcap, wild beast; fire-eater etc. (*blusterer*) 887.

V. be -violent etc. *adj.*; run high; ferment, effervesce; romp, rampage; run -wild, – riot; break the peace; rush, tear; rush head-long, -foremost; run amuck, raise a storm, make a riot; make –, kick up- a row, – a fuss; bluster, rage, roar, riot, storm; boil, – over; fume, foam, come in like a lion, wreak, bear down, ride roughshod, out-Herod Herod; spread like wildfire.

break –, fly –, burst- out; bounce, shock, strain; break-, pry-, force-, prize- open.

render -violent etc. *adj.;* sharpen, stir up, quicken, excite, incite, urge, lash, stimulate; irritate, inflame, exacerbate, kindle, suscitate, foment; accelerate, aggravate, exasperate, convulse, infuriate, madden, lash into fury; fan –, add fuel to- the flame; *oleum addere camino.*

explode, go off, displode, fly, detonate, thunder, blow up, flash, flare, erupt, burst; let -off, – fly; discharge, detonize, fulminate.

Adj. violent, vehement, forcible; warm; acute, sharp; rough, rude, ungentle, bluff, boisterous, wild, vicious; brusque, abrupt, waspish; impetuous; rampant.

turbulent; disorderly; blustering, raging etc. *v.;* troublous, riotous; tumultu-ary, -ous; obstreperous, uproarious; extravagant; unmitigated; ravening, tameless; frenzied etc. (*insane*) 503; desperate etc. (*rash*) 863; infuriate, towering, furious, outrageous, frantic, hysteric, in hysterics.

fiery, flaming, scorching, hot, red-hot, ebullient.

savage, fierce, ferocious, fierce as a tiger.

excited etc. *v.;* un-quelled, -quenched, -extinguished, -repressed, -bridled, -ruly; headstrong; un-governable, -appeasable, -mitigable; un-, in-controllable; insup-, irre-pressible.

spasmodic, convulsive, explosive; detonating etc. *v.;* volcanic, meteoric; stormy etc. (*wind*) 349.

Adv. violently etc. *adj.;* amain; by -storm, – force, – main force; with might and main; tooth and nail, *vi et armis*, at the point of the -sword, – bayonet; at one fell swoop; with a high hand, through thick and thin; in desperation, with a vengeance; *à* –, *à touteoutrance;* head-long, -foremost, -first; like a bull at a gate.

174. Moderation.—N. moderation; lenity etc. 740; temperance, temperateness, gentleness etc. *adj.;* sobriety; quiet; mental calmness etc. (*inexcitability*) 826.

moderating etc. *v.;* relaxation, remission, mitigation etc. 834; tranquilization, alleviation, assuagement, appeasement, contemporation, pacification.

measure, *juste milieu*, golden mean etc. 29.

moderator; lullaby, sedative, lenitive, demulcent, rose-water, balm, soothing syrup, poppy, opiate, anodyne, milk, opium, laudanum, 'poppy or mandragora;' wet blanket; palliative, calmative.

V. be -moderate etc. *adj.;* keep within -bounds, – compass; sober –, settle- down; keep the pease, remit, relent; take in sail.

moderate, soften, mitigate, temper, accoy; at-, con-temper; mollify, lenify, dull, take off the edge, blunt, obtund, sheathe, subdue, chasten; sober –, tone –, smooth- down; censor, blue-pencil, weaken etc. 160; lessen etc. (*decrease*) 36; check; palliate.

tranquilize, assuage, appease, dulcify, swage, lull, soothe, compose, still, calm, cool, quiet, hush, quell, sober, pacify, tame, damp, lay, allay, rebate, slacken, smooth, alleviate, rock to sleep, deaden, smother; throw -cold water on, – a wet blanket over; slake; curb etc. (*restrain*) 751; tame etc. (*subjugate*) 749; smooth over; pour oil on the -waves, – troubled waters; pour balm into, *mettre de l'eau dans son vin.*

go out like a lamb, 'roar you as gently as any sucking dove.'

Adj. moderate; lenient etc. 740; gentle, mild; cool, sober, temperate, reasonable, measured; tempered etc. *v.;* calm, unruffled, quiet, tranquil, still; slow, smooth, untroubled; tame; peaceful, -able; pacific, halcyon.

un-exciting, -irritating; soft, bland, oily, demulcent, lenitive, anodyne; hypnotic etc. 683; sedative; assuaging.

mild as mother's milk; milk and water; gentle as a lamb.

Adv. moderately etc. *adj.;* gingerly; *piano;* under easy sail, at half speed; within -bounds, – compass; in reason.

Phr. *est modus in rebus.*

175. Influence.—N. influence; importance etc. 642; weight, pressure, preponderance, prevalence, sway, pull; predomi-nance, -nancy; ascendency; control, dominance, reign; authority etc. 737; capability etc. (*power*) 157; interest; spell, magic, magnetism.

footing; purchase etc. (*support*) 215; play, leverage, vantage ground.

tower of strength, host in himself; protection, patronage, auspices.

V. have -influence etc. *n.;* be -influential etc. *adj.*; carry weight, actuate, sway, bias, weigh, tell; have a hold upon, magnetize, bear upon, gain a footing, work upon; take -root, – hold; strike root in.

run through, pervade, prevail, dominate, predominate, subject; out-, over-weigh; over ride, -bear, – come; gain head; rage; be -rife etc. *adj.;* spread like wildfire; have –, get –, gain- -the upper hand, – full play.

be -recognized, – listened to; make one's voice heard, gain a hearing; play a -part, – leading part- in; lead, control, rule, master; get the mastery over; make one's influence felt, cut ice with; take the lead, pull the strings; turn –, throw one's weight into- the scale; set the fashion, lead the dance.

Adj. influential; important etc. 642; weighty; prevailing etc. *v.;* prevalent, rife, rampant; dominant, regnant, predominant, in the ascendant, hegemonical; authoritative, recognized, telling, with authority.

Adv. with telling effect.

175a. Absence of Influence.—N. impotence etc. 158; inertness etc. 172; irrelevancy etc. 10.

V. have no -influence etc. 175.

Adj. uninfluential; unconduc-ing, -ive, -ting to; powerless etc. 158; irrelevant etc. 10.

176. Tendency.—N. tendency; apt-ness, -itude; proneness, proclivity, bent, turn, tone, bias, set, warp, leaning to, predisposition, inclination, conatus, propensity, susceptibility; liability etc. 177; quality, nature, temperament; characteristic, idio-crasy, -syncrasy; cast, vein, grain; humor, mood; drift etc. (*direction*) 278; conduciveness, -ducement; applicability etc. (*utility*) 644; subservience etc. (*instrumentality*) 631.

V. tend, contribute, conduce, lead, dispose, incline, verge, bend to, warp, turn, trend, affect, carry, redound to, bid fair to, gravitate towards; promote etc. (*aid*) 707.

Adj. tending etc. *v.;* conducive, working towards, in a fair way to, calculated to; liable etc. 177; subservient etc. (*instrumental*) 631; useful etc. 644; subsidiary etc. (*helping*) 707.

Adv. for, whither.

177. Liability.—**N.** lia-bility, -bleness; possibility, contingency; suscepti-vity, -bility.

V. be -liable etc. *adj.;* incur, lay oneself open to; run the –, stand a- chance; lie under, expose oneself to, open a door to.

Adj. liable, subject; in danger etc. 665; open –, exposed –, obnoxious- to; answerable, responsible, accountable, amenable; unexempt from; apt to; dependent on; incident to.

contingent, incidental, possible, on the cards, within range of, at the mercy of.

178. Concurrence.—**N.** concurrence, cooperation, coagency; coincidence, consilience; union; agreement etc. 23; consent etc. (*assent*) 488; alliance; concert etc. 709; partnership etc. 712; collaboration, conformity.

V. con-cur, -duce, -spire, -tribute; agree, unite, harmonize; hang –, pull- together etc. (*cooperate*) 709; help to etc. (*aid*) 707.

keep pace with, run parallel to; go –, go along –, go hand in hand- with.

Adj. concurring etc. *v.;* concurrent, conformable, joint, co-operative, concordant, coincident, concomitant, harmonious; in alliance with, banded together, of one mind, at one with; parallel.

Adv. with one consent.

179. Counteraction.—**N.** counteraction, opposition; contrariety etc. 14; antagonism, polarity; clashing etc. *v.;* collision, interference, resistance, renitency, friction; reaction; retroaction; repercussion etc. (*recoil*) 277; counterblast; neutralization etc. (*compensation*) 30; *vis inertiae;* check etc. (*hindrance*) 706.

voluntary -opposition etc. 708, – resistance etc. 719; repression etc. (*restraint*) 751.

V. counteract; run counter, clash, cross; interfere –, conflict- with; jostle; go –, run –, beat –, militate- against; stultify; antagonize, frustrate, oppose etc. 708; withstand etc. (*resist*) 719; hinder etc. 706; repress etc. (*restrain*) 751; react etc. (*recoil*) 277.

undo, neutralize, cancel; counterpoise etc. (*compensate*) 30; overpoise.

Adj. counteracting etc. *v.;* antagonistic, conflicting, retroactive, renitent, reactionary; contrary etc. 14.

Adv. although etc. 30; in spite of etc. 708; *malgré;* against.

180. Space. [Indefinite space.]—**N.** space, extension, extent, superficial extent, expanse, stretch; capacity, volume, room, accommodation, scope, range, latitude, field, way, expansion, compass, sweep, play, swing, spread.

dimension, fourth dimension; relativity, geometry.

spare –, elbow –, house- room; stowage, roomage, margin; opening, sphere, arena; lee-, sea-, head-way.

open –, free- space; wide open spaces, void etc. (*absence*) 187; waste; wild-, wilder-ness; up-, bottom-, moor -land; *campagna, veldt,* prairie, steppe.

abyss etc. (*interval*) 198; unlimited space; infinity etc. 105; world, wide world; ubiquity etc. (*presence*) 186; length and breadth of the land.

proportions, acreage; acres, – roods and perches; square -inches, – yards etc.

V. reach, extend, stretch, sweep, spread, range, cover, thrust out, reach forth.

Adj. spacious, roomy, extensive, expansive, capacious, ample; wide-spread, vast, world-wide, uncircumscribed; boundless etc. (*infinite*) 105; shore-, track-, path-less; large etc. 192.

spatial, dimensional, proportional; two-, three-, four-dimensional; stereoscopic.

Adv. extensively etc. *adj.;* wherever; everywhere; far and -near, – wide; right and left, all over, all the world over; throughout the -world, – length and breadth of the land; under the sun, in every quarter; in all -quarters, – lands; here, there and everywhere; from -pole to pole, – China to Peru, – Indus to the pole, – Dan to Beersheba, – end to end; on the face of the earth, in the wide world, from all points of the compass; to the -four winds, – uttermost parts of the earth.

180a. Inextension.—**N.** in-, non-extension; point; atom etc. (*smallness*) 32; pinprick; limitation etc. 229.

181. Region. [Definite space.]—**N.** region, sphere, sphere of influence, corridor, ground, soil, area, realm, hemisphere, quarter district, beat, orb, orbit, zone, belt, circuit, circle; pale etc. (*limit*) 233; com-, department; domain, tract, territory, terrain, country, canton, county, shire, province, *arrondissement,* diocese, parish, township, borough, constituency, *commune,* ward, wapentake, hundred, riding, lathe, garth, soke, tithing, bailiwick; empire, kingdom, principality, duchy, grand –, arch- duchy, palatinate, republic, commonwealth, dominion, colony, state, island.

arena, precincts, *enceinte,* walk, march; patch, plot, enclosure, etc. 232; close, *enclave,* field, court; street etc. (*abode*) 189.

clime, climate, zone, meridian, latitude.

Adj. territorial, local, parochial, provincial, insular.

182. Place. [Limited space.]—**N.** place, lieu, spot, point, dot; niche, nook, etc. (*corner*) 244; hole; pigeonhole etc. (*receptacle*) 191; compartment; premises, precinct, station, confine; area, court, yard, quadrangle, square, compound; abode etc. 189; locality etc. (*situation*) 183.

ins and outs; every hole and corner.

Adv. somewhere, in some place, wherever it may be, here and there, in various places, *passim.*

183. Situation.—**N.** situation, position, locality, *locale, status,* latitude and longitude; footing, standing, standpoint, post; stage, aspect, attitude, posture, *pose.*

place, site, base, station; seat, *venue,* whereabouts, environment, neighborhood; bearings etc. (*direction*) 278; spot etc. (*limited space*) 182.

top-, ge-, chor-ography; map etc. 554.

V. be -situated, – situate; lie; have its seat in.

Adj. situ-ate, -ated; local, topical, topographical etc. *n.*

Adv. *in -situ, – loco;* here and there, *passim;* here-, there-, whereabouts; in place, here, there.

in –, amidst- such and such- -surroundings, – *environs,* – *entourage.*

184. Location.—**N.** loca-tion, -lization; lodgement; de-, re-position; stow-, pack-age; collocation; packing, lading; establishment, settlement, installation; fixation; insertion etc. 300.

anchorage, roadstead, mooring, mooring mast, encampment, camp, bivouac.

plantation, colony, settlement, cantonment, encampment, reservation; colonization, domestication, situation; habitation etc. (*abode*) 189; cohabitation; 'a local habitation and a name;' indenization, naturalization.

V. place, situate, locate, localize, make a place for, put, lay, set, seat, station, lodge, quarter, post, install, storehouse, stow; extablish, fix, pin, root; graft; plant etc. (*insert*) 300; shelve, pitch, camp, lay down, deposit, reposit; cradle; moor, tether, picket; pack, tuck in; embed; vest, invest in.

billet on, quarter upon, saddle with; load, lade, freight; pocket, put up, bag.

inhabit etc. (*be present*) 186; domesticate, colonize, populate, people; take –, strike-root; anchor; cast –, come to an- anchor; sit –, settle-down; settle; take up one's -abode, – quarters; plant –, establish –, locate- oneself; squat, perch, hive, *se nicher,* bivouac, burrow, get a footing; encamp, pitch one's tent; put up -at, – one's horses at; keep house.

indenizen, naturalize, adopt.

put back, replace etc. (*restore*) 660.

Adj. placed etc. *v.;* situate, posited, ensconced, embedded, embosomed, rooted; domesticated; vested in. unremoved; settled, stationed, established.

moored etc. *v.;* at anchor.

185. Displacement.—**N.** displacement, elocation, transposition.

ejectment etc. 297; exile etc. (*banishment*) 893; removal etc. (*transference*) 270; unshipment.

misplacement, dislocation etc. 61; fish out of water.

V. dis-place, -plant, -lodge, -nest, -establish; misplace, unseat, disturb; exile etc. (*seclude*) 893; ablegate, set aside, remove; take –, cart- away; take –, draft- off; lade etc. 184, unship.

unload, empty etc. (*eject*) 297; transfer etc. 270; dispel.

vacate; depart etc. 293.

Adj. displaced etc. *v.;* un-placed, -housed, -harbored, -established, -settled; house-, homeless; out of -place, – a situation.

misplaced, out of its element.

186. Presence.—**N.** presence; occupancy, -ation; attendance; whereness.

permeation, pervasion; diffusion etc. (*dispersion*) 73.

ubi-ety, -quity, -quitariness; omnipresence.

bystander etc. (*spectator*) 444.

V. exist in space, be -present etc. *adj.;* assist at; make one -of, – at; look on, attend, remain; find –, present- oneself; show one's face; fall in the way of, occur in a place; lie, stand; occupy.

people; inhabit, dwell, reside, stay, sojourn, live, room, abide, bunk, lodge, nestle, roost, perch; take up one's abode etc. (*be located*) 184; tenant, occupy.

resort to, frequent, haunt; revisit.

fill, pervade, permeate; be diffused, – disseminated- through; over-spread, -run; run through; meet one at every turn.

Adj. present; occupying, inhabiting etc. *v.;* moored etc. 184; residential, resi-ant, -dent, -dentiary; domiciled.

ubiquit-ous, -ary; omnipresent.

peopled, populous, full of people, inhabited.

Adv. here; there, where, everywhere, aboard, on board, at home, afield; on the spot; here, there and everywhere etc. (*space*) 180; in presence of, before; under the -eyes, – nose- of; in the face of; *in propriâ personâ.*

187. Absence. [Nullibiety.]—**N.** absence; inexistence etc. 2; non-residence, absenteeism; non-attendance, *alibi.*

emptiness etc. *adj.;* void, *vacuum;* vac-uity, -ancy; *tabula rasa;* exemption; *hiatus* etc. (*interval*) 198; no man's land.

truant, absentee.

nobody, nobody -present, – on earth; no one; not a soul; *âme qui vive.*

V. be -absent etc. *adj.;* keep -away, – out of the way; play truant, absent oneself, stay away.

withdraw, make oneself scarce, vacate; go away, slip out, slip away, retreat etc. 293.

Adj. absent, not present, away, nonresident, gone, from home; missing, lost, wanted, wanting; omitted; nowhere to be found; inexistent etc. 2.

empty, void; blank, vac-ant, -uous; untenanted, -occupied, -inhabited; tenantless; desert, -ed; devoid; un-, uninhabitable.

exempt from, not having.

Adv. without, *minus,* nowhere; elsewhere; neither here nor there; in default of; *sans;* behind one's back.

Phr. the bird has flown, *non est inventus.*

188. Inhabitant.—**N.** inhabitant; habitant, resident, -iary; dweller, in-dweller; occup-ier, -ant, farmer, planter; householder, lodger, boarder, paying guest; inmate, tenant, renter, incumbent, sojourner, *locum tenens,* commorant; settler, squatter, backwoodsman, colonist; islander; denizen, citizen; burgher, oppidan, cockney, cit, townsman, burgess; villager; cottager, -tier, -ter; compatriot.

native, indigene, aboriginal, aborigines, autochthones; Briton, Englishman, John Bull; new comer etc. (*stranger*) 57.

garrison, crew; population; people etc. (*mankind*) 372; colony, settlement; household.

V. inhabit etc. (*be present*) 186; indenizen etc. (*locate oneself*) 184.

Adj. indigenous; enchorial; national, nat-ive, -al; autochthonous; British, English; colonial; domestic, domiciliated, -ed; naturalized, vernacular, domesticated; domiciliary.

in the occupation of; garrisoned –, occupied-by.

189. Abode. [Place of habitation, or resort.]—**N.** abode, dwelling, lodging, -s; diggings, domicile, residence, address, habitation, where one's lot is cast, local habitation, berth, seat, lap, sojourn, housing, quarters, headquarters, resiance, tabernacle, throne, ark.

home, fatherland, mother country, country etc. 181; home-stead, -stall; fireside, chimney corner; hearth, – stone; household gods, *lares et penates*, roof, household, housing, *dulce domum*, paternal domicile; native -soil, – land, blighty.

nest, *nidus*, snuggery; arbor, bower etc. 191; lair, den, cave, hole, hidingplace, cell, *sanctum sanctorum*, aerie, eyry, rookery, hive; *habitat*, haunt, covert, resort, retreat, perch, roost; nidification.

bivouac, camp, encampment, cantonment, castrametation; barrack, casemate, casern.

tent etc. (*covering*) 223; building etc. (*construction*) 161; chamber etc. (*receptacle*) 191.

tenement, messuage, farm, farmhouse, grange, *hacienda*.

cot, cabin, log cabin, shack, hut, *châlet*, croft, shed, booth, stall, hovel, bothy, shanty, igloo, tepee, wigwam; pen etc. (*inclosure*) 232; barn, bawn; kennel, sty, dog-hole, cote, coop, hutch, byre; cowhouse, -shed; stable, dove-cote, shippen.

house, mansion, place, villa, cottage, box, lodge, hermitage, *rus in urbe*, folly, rotunda, tower, *château*, castle, pavilion, hotel, court, manor-house, capital messuage, hall, palace, alcazar; country seat; kiosk, bungalow; temple etc. 1000; home of rest, alms-, poor-, work-house, asylum; boarding-, lodging-house; flat, maisonette, duplex, penthouse, suite of rooms, apartments, rooms, room building etc. 161; Mansion House, town hall, Capitol.

assembly-room, auditorium, coliseum, meeting-house, pump-room, spa, health resort, watering-place; club; theatre etc. 840; drill hall, gymnasium, church etc. 1000; Houses of Parliament etc. 696; school etc. 542; inn; hostel, -ry; hotel, tavern, caravansary, khan, hospice; public-, ale-, pot-, mug-house; gin-palace, gin mill; coffee-, eating-house; canteen, *restaurant, rotisserie*, cafeteria, grill-room, *buffet, café, estaminet, posada, bodega;* bar; saloon, speakeasy, shebeen.

hamlet, village, thorp, dorp, ham, kraal; borough, burgh, town, county-seat, – town, city, capital, metropolis; suburb, quarter, parish etc. 181; ghetto; province, country.

street, place, terrace, parade, esplanade, promenade, pier, embankment, road, villas, row, walk, lane, alley, court, quadrangle, quad, wynd, close, yard, passage, rents, mansions, buildings, mews.

square, polygon, circus, crescent, mall, *piazza*, arcade, colonnade, peristyle, cloister; gardens, grove, residences; block of buildings, market-place, *place*.

anchorage, roadstead, roads; dock, basin, wharf, quay, port, harbor; dry-, graving-, floating-dock.

garden, park, pleasure-ground, pleasance, demesne.

V. take up one's abode etc. (*locate oneself*) 184; inhabit etc. (*be present*) 186.

Adj. urban, oppidan, metropolitan; suburban; provincial, rural, rustic; countrified; regional, parochial, domestic; cosmopolitan; palatial.

190. Contents. [Things contained.]—**N.** contents; cargo, lading, freight, shipment, load, bale, burden; cart-, ship-load; cup –, basket –, etc. (*receptacle*) 191 - of; inside etc. 221; stuffing, ullage.

V. load, lade, ship, charge, fill, stuff.

191. Receptacle.—**N.** receptacle, container; inclosure etc. 232; recipient, receiver, reservatory.

compartment; cell, -ule; follicle; hole, corner, niche, recess, nook; crypt, stall, pigeon-hole, cove, oriel; cave etc. (*concavity*) 252.

capsule, vesicle, cyst, pod, calyx, *cancelli*, utricle, bladder, udder.

stomach, paunch, *venter*, abdomen, ventricle, crop, craw, ingluvies, maw, gizzard, bread-basket, belly, little Mary; mouth.

pocket, pouch, fob, sheath, scabbard, socket, bag, vanity bag, compact, sac, sack, saccule, despatch –, attaché-, tachy- case, wallet, scrip, card-, note-, case, billfold, poke, knit, knap-, haver-, ruck-sack, sachel, satchel, reticule, budget, net; ditty-, -box, -bag, kitbag; portfolio; saddlebags, holster; quiver etc. (*magazine*) 636.

chest, box, coffer, caddy, case, casket, pyx, pix, *caisson*, desk, *bureau*, reliquary, shrine; trunk, portmanteau, band-box, *valise*, suitcase, hand-, traveling-, overnight-, Gladstone-, carpet-bag, brief case; boot, imperial; *vache*; cage, manger, rack.

vessel, vase, bushel, barrel; canister, jar; pottle, basket, punnet, pannier, buck-basket, hopper, maund, creel, cran, crate, cradle, bassinet, wisket, whisket, *jardinière, corbeille*, hamper, wastepaper basket, dosser, dorser, tray, hod, scuttle, utensil, spittoon, cuspidor.

[For liquids] cistern etc. (*store*) 636; vat, caldron, barrel, cask, puncheon, keg, rundlet, tun, butt, firkin, hogshead, kilderkin, carboy, amphora, ampulla, bottle, jar, leather bottle, decanter, ewer, cruse, carafe, crock, kit, canteen, flagon; demijohn; flask, -et; stoup, noggin, vial, phial, ampoulé, cruet, caster; gourd; urn, *épergne*, salver, *patella, tazza, patera*; pig-, big-gin; tea-, coffee-pot, percolator, *samovar*; tyg, nipperkin, pocket-pistol; tub, bucket, pail, skeel, pot, tankard, jug, pitcher, toby, mug, pipkin; gal-, gall-ipot, pannikin; matrass, receiver, retort, alembic, bolthead, can, kettle; bowl, basin, jorum, punch-bowl, cup, goblet, chalice, tumbler, glass, wineglass, rummer, beaker, tass, horn, saucepan, skillet, posnet, tureen, terrine, *casserole*, sauce-, gravy-boat.

plate, platter, paten, dish, vegetable –, *entrée*-dish, trencher, calabash, porringer, potager, saucer, pan, crucible.

shovel, trowel, spoon; table-, dessert-, tea-, egg-,

salt-spoon; spatula, ladle; dipper; baler; watch-glass, thimble.

closet, commode, cupboard, cellaret, *chiffonnière*, locker, bin, bunker, *buffet*, press, safe, sideboard, drawer, chest of drawers, till, *scrutoire*, *secrétaire*, *escritoire*, davenport, book-case, cabinet, canterbury; corner cupboard, wardrobe.

chamber, apartment, room, cabin; office, court, hall, atrium; suite of rooms, flat, story; saloon, *salon*, parlor; presence-chamber; sitting-, drawing-, reception-, state-, living-, work-room; gallery, cabinet, closet, cubicle; pew, box; *boudoir*; *adytum, sanctum*; bed-room, dormitory, dressing-room; refectory, dining-room, *salle-à-manger*; nursery, schoolroom; library, study; *studio*; billiard-, bath-, smoking-room; den, canteen, mess, officers' mess; gun-, ward-, mess-room.

attic, loft, garret, cockloft, clerestory; cellar, vault, hold, cockpit; *entre-sol*; mezzanine floor; ground-floor, *rez-de-chaussée*; basement, kitchen, cook-house, galley, pantry, scullery, offices; store-room etc. (*depository*) 636; lumber-room; dust-hole, -bin; dairy, laundry, coachhouse; *garage*; *hangar*; out-, pent-house; lean-to.

portico, porch, piazza, verandah, lobby, court, hall, vestibule, corridor, passage; ante-room, chamber; lounge; *foyer, loggia*.

conservatory, green-house, glass-house, vinery, bower, arbor, summer-house, alcove, grotto, hermitage, pergola.

lodging etc. (*abode*) 189; bed etc. (*support*) 215; carriage etc. (*vehicle*) 272.

Adj. capsular; saccu-lar, -lated; recipient; ventricular, cystic, vascular, vesicular, cellular, camerated, locular, multilocular, poly-gastric; marsupial; siliqu-ose, -ous.

192. Size.—N. size, magnitude, dimension, bulk, volume; largeness etc. *adj.*; greatness etc. (*of quantity*) 31; expanse etc. (*space*) 180; amplitude, mass; proportions.

capacity; ton-, tun-nage; caliber, scantling.

turgidity etc. (*expansion*) 194; corpulence, obesity; plumpness, etc. *adj.*; *embonpoint*, corporation, flesh and blood, lustihood.

hugeness etc. *adj.*; enormity, immensity, monstrosity.

giant, Brobdingnagian, Antaeus, Goliath, Gog and Magog, Gargantua, monster, mammoth, Cyclops; whale, porpoise, behemoth, leviathan, elephant, hippopotamus; colossus; tun, lump, bulk, block, loaf, mass, clod, nugget, bushel, thumper, whopper, spanker, strapper, Triton among the minnows.

mountain, mound; heap etc. (*assemblage*) 72.

largest portion etc. 50; full-, life-size.

V. ve- large etc. *adj.*; become -large etc. (*expand*) 194.

Adj. large, big; great etc. (*in quantity*) 31; considerable, bulky, voluminous, ample, massive, massy; capacious, comprehensive; spacious etc. 180; mighty, towering, fine, magnificent.

corpulent, stout, fat, plump, squab, full, lusty, strapping, bouncing; portly, burly, well-fed, full-grown; stalwart, brawny, fleshy; goodly; in good -case. – condition; in condition; chopping, jolly; chub-, chubby-faced.

lubberly, hulky, unwieldy, lumpish, gaunt, spanking, whacking, whopping, thumping, thundering, hulking; overgrown; puffy etc. (*swollen*) 194.

huge, immense, enormous, mighty; vast, -y; amplitudinous, stupendous; monst-er, -rous; gigantic, elephantine; giant, -like; colossal, Cyclopean, Brobdingnagian, Garguantuan, Titanic; infinite etc. 105.

large as life; plump as a dumpling, – partridge; fat as -a pig, – a quail, – butter, – brawn, – bacon.

193. Littleness.—N. littleness etc. *adj.*, smallness etc. (*of quantity*) 32; exiguity, inextension; parvi-tude, -ty; duodecimo; Elzevir edition, epitome, microcosm; rudiment; vanishing point; thinness etc. 203.

dwarf, pigmy, atomy, Liliputian, midget, chit, pigwidgeon, urchin, elf; doll, puppet; Tom Thumb, Hop-o'-my thumb, Humpty-dumpty; man-, mannikin; *homunculus*, dapperling, fingerling, dandiprat, cock-sparrow, scalawag.

animalcule, monad, mite, insect, emmet, fly, midge, gnat, shrimp, minnow, worm, maggot, entozoon; *bacillus*, microbe, micro-organism, *bacteria*; *Infusoria*; microbe, grub; tit, tomtit, runt, mouse, small fry; millet, mustard-seed, barleycorn, pebble, grain of sand; mole-hill, button, bubble.

point; atom etc. (*small quantity*) 32; fragment etc. (*small part*) 51; powder etc. 330; point of a pin, mathematical point; *minutiae* etc. (*unimportance*) 643.

micro-graphy, -meter, -scope; vernier; scale.

V. be -little etc. *adj.*; lie in a nutshell; become small etc. (*decrease*) 36, (*contract*) 195.

Adj. little; small etc. (*in quantity*) 32; minute, diminutive, microscopic; inconsiderable etc. (*unimportant*) 643; exiguous, puny, tiny, wee, petty, minikin, miniature, pigmy, elfin; under sized; dwarf, -ed, -ish; spare, stunted, limited; cramp, -ed; pollard, Liliputian, dapper, pocket; port-ative, -able; duodecimo; dumpy, squat; compact, handy; short etc. 201.

impalpable, intangible, evanescent, imperceptible, invisible, inappreciable, infinitesimal, homeopathic; atomic, corpuscular, molecular; rudiment-ary, -al; embryonic.

weazen, scant, scraggy, scrubby; thin etc. (*narrow*) 203; granular etc. (*powdery*) 330; shrunk etc. 195.

Adv. in a -small compass, – nutshell; on a small scale.

194. Expansion.—N. expansion; increase etc. 35 -of size; enlargement, extension, augmentation; ampli-fication, -ation; aggrandizement, spread, increment, growth, development, pullulation, swell, dilation, dilatation, rarefaction; turg-escence, -idness, -idity; obesity etc. (*size*) 192; dropsy, tumefaction, intumescence, swelling, tumor, *diastole*, distension; puff-ing, -iness; inflation; pandiculation.

dilatability, expansibility.

germination, growth, upgrowth; accretion etc. 35.

over-growth, -distension; hypertrophy, tympany.

bulb etc. (*convexity*) 250; plumper; superiority of size.

V. become -larger etc. (large etc. 192); expand, widen, enlarge, extend, grow, increase, incrassate, swell, gather; fill out; deploy, take open order, dilate, stretch, spread; mantle, was; grow –, spring- up; bud, bourgeon, shoot, sprout, germinate, put forth, vegetate, pullulate, open, burst forth, flower, blow etc. 734; gain –, gather- flesh; outgrow; spread like wildfire, overrun.

be larger than; surpass etc. (*be superior*) 33.

render -larger etc. (large etc. 192); expand, spread, extend, aggrandize, distend, develop, amplify, spread out, widen, magnify, rarefy, inflate, puff, puff out, blow up, stuff, pad, cram; exaggerate; fatten.

Adj. expanded etc. *v.*; larger etc. (large etc. 192); swollen; expansive; wide-open, -spread; fan-shaped; flabelliform; overgrown, exaggerated, bloated, fat, turgid, tumid, hypertrophied, dropsical; pot-, swag-bellied; edematous, obese, puffy, pursy, blowzy, distended; patulous; bulbous etc. (*convex*) 250; full-blown, -grown, -formed; big etc. 192.

195. Contraction.—N. contraction, reduction, diminution; decrease etc. 36- of size; defalcation, decrement; lessening, shrinkage; collapse, emaciation, attenuation, tabefaction, comsumption, marasmus, atrophy; systole, neck, hourglass.

condensation, compression, constraint, compactness; compendium etc. 596; squeezing etc. *v.*; strangulation; corrugation; astringency, constringency; astringents, sclerotics; contractility, compressibility; coarctation.

inferiority in size.

V. become -small, – smaller; lessen, decrease etc. 36; grow less, dwindle, shrink, contract, narrow, shrivel, collapse, wither, lose flesh, wizen, fall away, waste, wane, ebb; decat etc. (*deteriorate*) 659.

be smaller than, fall short of; not come up to etc. (*be inferior*) 34.

render smaller, lessen, diminish, contract, draw in, shrink, shrivel, narrow, coarctate; constrict, constringe; condense, compress, boil down, deflate, exhaust, empty; squeeze, corrugate, crush, crumple up, warp, purse up, pack, stow; pinch, tighten, strangle; cramp; dwarf, bedwarf; shorten etc. 201; circumscribe etc. 229; restrain etc. 751; fold etc. 258.

pare, reduce, attenuate, rub down, scrape, file, grind, chip, shave, shear.

Adj. contracting etc. *v.*; astringent; shrunk, contracted etc. *v.*; strangulated, tabid, wizened, stunted, tabescent; marasmic; waning etc. *v.*; neap; compact; shriveled, preshrunk.

unexpanded etc. (expand etc. 194); inswept; contractile; compressible; smaller etc. small etc. 193).

196. Distance.—N. distance; space etc. 180; remoteness, farness; far- cry to; longinquity, elongation; offing, background; removedness; parallax; reach, span, stride; drift.

out-post, -skirt; horizon, sky-line; aphelion; foreign parts, *ultima Thule*, *ne plus ultra*, antipodes; long range, giant's stride.

dispersion etc. 73.

V. be -distant etc. *adj.*; extend –, stretch –, reach –, spread –, go –, get –, stretch away- to; range, outrange, outreach.

remain at a distance; keep –, stand- -away, –off, – aloof, – clear of.

Adj. distant; far -off, away; remote, telescopic, distal, wide of; stretching to etc. *v.*; yon, -der; ulterior; trans-marine, -pontine, -atlantic, -pacific, -continental, -polar, -equatorial, -alpine; tramontane; ultra-montane, -mundane; hyperborean, antihodean; inaccessible, out of the way; unapproached, -able; incontiguous.

Adv. far -off, – away; afar, -off; off; away; a -long, – great, – good- way off; wide away, aloof; wide –, clear- of; out of -the way, – reach; abroad, yonder, farther, further, beyond; *outre mer*, over the border, far and wide, over the hills and far away; from pole to pole etc. (*over great space*) 180; to the -uttermost parts, – ends- of the earth; out of -hearing, – range, nobody knows where, *à perte de vue*, out of the sphere of, wide of the mark; a far cry to.

apart, asunder; wide -apart, – asunder; *longo intervallo*; at arm's length.

197. Nearness.—N. nearness etc. *adj.*; proximity, propinquity; vicinity, -age; neighborhood, adjacency; contiguity etc. 199.

short -distance, – step, – cut; earshot, close quarters, brief span; stone's throw; bow –, gun –, pistol- shot; hair's breadth, span; close-up.

purlieus, neighborhood, vicinage, *environs*, *alentours*, suburbs, confines, *banlieue*, borderland; whereabouts.

bystander; neighbor, borderer.

approach etc. 286; convergence etc. 290; perihelion.

V. be -near etc. *adj.*; adjoin, hang about, trench on; border-, verge upon; stand by, approximate, tread on the heels of, cling to, clasp, hug; cuddle, huddle; hang about the skirts of, hover over; burn; abut.

bring –, draw- -near etc. 286; converge etc. 290; crowd etc. 72; place -side by side etc. *adv.*

Adj. near, nigh; close-, near- at hand; close, neighboring, propinquent, bordering upon; adjacent, adjoining, limitrophe; proxim-ate, -al; at hand, handy; near the mark, near run; home, intimate.

Adv. near, nigh; hard –, fast- by; close -to, upon, – up; at the point of; next door to; within -reach, – call, – hearing, – earshot, – range; within an ace of; but a step, not far from, at no great distance; on the -verge, – brink, – skirts- of; in the -environs etc. *n.*; at one's -door, – feet, – elbow, – finger's end, – side; on the tip of one's tongue; under one's nose; within a -stone's throw etc. *n.*; in -sight, – presence- of; at close quarters; cheek by -jole, – jowl; beside, alongside, side by side, *tête-à-tête*; in juxtaposition etc. (*touching*) 199; yard-arm to yard-arm; at the heels of; on the confines of, at the threshold, bordering upon, verging to; in the way.

about; here-, there-abouts; rougly, in round

numbers; approxim- -ately, – atively; as good as, well nigh.

198. Interval.—N. interval, interspace; separation etc. 44; break gap, opening; hole etc. 260; chasm, *hiatus,* caesura; inter-ruption,-regnum; interstice, *lacuna,* cleft, mesh, crevice, chink, rime, creek, cranny, crack, chap, slit, slot, fissure, scissure, rift, flaw, breach, fracture, rent, gash, cut, leak, dike, ha-ha.

gorge, defile, ravine, canon, *crevasse,* abyss, abysm; gulf; inlet, frith, strait, gully, gulch, nullah; pass; notch; furrow etc. 259; yawning gulf; *hiatus - maxime, – valde- deflendus*; parenthesis etc. (*interjacence*) 228; void etc. (*absence*) 187; incompleteness etc. 530.

V. gape etc. (*open*) 260; part, remove.

Adj. with an interval, far between, separated, spaced, split.

Adv. at intervals etc. (*discontinuously*) 70; *longo intervallo.*

199. Contiguity.—N. contiguity, contact, proximity, apposition, juxtaposition, touching etc. *v.*, abutment, osculation; meeting, appulse, appulsion, *rencontre,* rencounter, syzygy, coincidence, conjunction, coexistence; adhesion . etc. 46.

border-land; frontier etc. (*limit*) 233; tangent.

V. be -contiguous etc. *adj.*; join, adjoin, abut on, march with, border; tick, graze, touch, meet, osculate, kiss, come in contact; coincide; coexist; adhere etc. 46.

Adj. contiguous; touching etc. *v.*; in -contact etc. *n.*, conterminous, end to end, osculatory; pertingent; tangential.

hand to hand; close to etc. (*near*) 197; with no - interval etc. 198.

200. Length.—N. length, longitude, span, extent, mileage.

line, bar, rule, stripe, streak, spoke, radius.

lengthening etc. *v.*; pro-longation, -duction, -traction; ten-sion, -sure; extension.

[Measures of length] line, nail, inch, hand, palm, foot, cubit, yard, ell, fathom, rod, pole, perch, furlong, mile, league; chain, meter, kilo-, centi-, milli- etc meter.

pedometer, perambulator, odometer, odograph, speedometer, cyclometer, log, telemeter, range finder; scale etc. (*measurement*) 466.

V. be -long etc. *adj.*; stretch out, sprawl; extend –, reach –, stretch -to; make a long arm, 'drag its slow length along.'

render -long etc. *adj.*; lengthen, extend, elongate; stretch; pro-long, -duce, -tract; let –, pay –, draw –, spin- out; drawl.

enfilade, look along, view in perspective.

Adj. long, -some; lengthy, lank, wiredrawn, outstretched; stretched, drawn out, lengthened etc. *v.*; sesquipedalian etc. (*words*) 577; interminable, no end of.

line-ar, -al; longitudinal, oblong.

as long as -my arm, —to-day and to-morrow; unshortened etc. (shorten etc. 201).

Adv. lengthwise, at length, longitudinally, endlong, along; *tandem*; in a line etc. (*continuously*) 69; in perspective.

from -end to end; —stem to stern, —head to foot, —the crown of the head to the sole of the foot, —top to toe, —head to heels; fore and aft.

201. Shortness.—N. shortness etc. *adj.*; brevity; littleness etc. 193; a span.

shortening etc. *v.*; abbrevia-tion, -ture; abridgment, concision, retrenchment, curtailment, decurtation; reduction etc. (*contraction*) 195; epitome etc. (*compendium*) 596.

abridger, abstractor, epitomiser.

elision, ellipsis; conciseness etc. (*in style*) 572.

V. be -short etc. *adj.*; render -short etc. *adj.*; shorten, curtail, abridge, abbreviate, take in, reduce; compress etc. (*contract*) 195; epitomize etc. 596.

retrench, cut short, obtruncate; scrimp, cut, chop up, hack, hew; cut –, pare- down; clip, snip, dock, lop, prune; shear, shave, mow, reap, crop; snub; truncate, pollard, stunt, nip, nip in the bud, check the growth of; [in drawing] foreshorten.

Adj. short, brief, curt; compendious, compact; stubby, scrimp; shorn, stubbed, stumpy, thickset, podgy, stocky, pug; squab, -by; squat, dumpy; little etc. 193; curtailed of its fair proportions; short by; oblate; concise etc. 572; summary.

Adv. shortly etc. *adj.*; in short etc. (*concisely*) *572.*

202. Breadth. Thickness.—N. breadth, width, latitude, amplitude; diameter, bore, calibre, radius; superficial extent etc. (*space*) 180.

thickness, crassitude; corpulence etc. (*size*) 192; dilatation etc. (*expansion*) 194.

V. be -broad etc. *adj.*; become –, render- - broad etc. *adj.*; expand etc. 194; thicken, widen.

Adj. broad, wide, ample, extended; discous; fanlike; out-spread, -stretched; wide as a church-door.

thick, dumpy, squab, squat, thickset, tubby; thick as a rope, stubby etc. 201.

203. Narrowness. Thinness.—N. narrowness etc. *adj.*; closeness, exility; exiguity etc. (*little*) 193.

line; hair's –, finger's -breadth; strip, streak, vein.

thinness etc. *adj.*; tenuity; emaciation, slenderness, macilency, *marcor.*

shaving, slip etc. (*filament*) 205; threadpaper, skeleton, shadow, scrag, anatomy, spindle-shanks, barebones, lantern jaws, mere skin and bone.

middle construction, stricture, neck, waist, isthmus, wasp, hour-glass; ridge, *ghaut*, pass; ravine etc. 198.

narrowing, coarctation, angustation, tapering; contraction etc. 195.

V. be-narrow etc. *adj.*; narrow, taper, diminish, contract etc. 195; render -narrow etc. *adj.*

Adj. narrow, close; slender, thin, fine; *svelte;* thread-like etc. (*filament*) 205; finespun, taper, slim, gracile, slight, slight-made; scant, -y; spare, delicate, incapacious; contracted etc. 195; unexpanded etc. (expand etc. 194); slender as a thread, capillary.

emaciated, lean, meager, gaunt, macilent; lank, -y; weedy, skinny, scrawny, scraggy; starv-ed, -eling; attenuated, shrivelled; wizened, pinched, peaky, skeletal, spindling, spindle- -legged, -shanked; extenuated, tabid, marcid, bare-bone, raw-boned; herring-gutted; worn to a shadow, lean as a rake; thin as a -lath,—whipping post,—wafer; hatchet-faced; lantern-jawed.

204. Layer.—N. layer, stratum, course, bed, zone, *substratum*, floor, flag, stage, story, tier, slab, escarpment, table, tablet, panel, plaque; board, plank; trencher, platter.

plate; lam-ina, -ella; sheet, flake, foil, wafer, scale, coat, peel, pellicle, ply, thickness, membrane, film, leaf, slice, shive, cut, rasher, shaving, integument etc. (*covering*) 223.

V. slice, shave, pare, peel; plate, coat, veneer; cover etc. 223.

Adj. lamell-ar, -ated, -iform; laminated, -iferous; micaceous; schist-ose, -ous; scaly; filmy, membranous, flaky, squamous; folia-ted, -ceous; stratified, -form; tabular, discoid, spathic.

205. Filament.—N. filament, line; fiber, fibril; funicle, vein, hair, capillament, *cilium*, tendril, gossamer; hair-stroke; harl.

wire, string, thread, packthread, cotton, sewing-silk, twine, twist, whip-cord, cord, rope, cable, yarn, hemp, oakum, jute, wool, worsted.

strip, shred, slip, spill, list, band, fillet, *fascia*, ribbon, riband, tape, roll, lath, slat, strake, splinter, shiver, shaving.

beard etc. (*roughness*) 256; ramification; strand.

Adj. fil-amentous, -aceous, -iform; fibr-ous, -illous; thread-like, wiry, stringy, ropy; capill-ary, -iform; funicular, wire-drawn; anguilliform; flagelliform; hairy etc. (*rough*) 256; ligulate.

206. Height.—N. height, altitude, elevation, ceiling; eminence. pitch; loftiness etc. *adj.*; sublimity.

tallness etc. *adj.*; stature, procerity; prominence etc. 250.

colossus etc. (*size*) 192; giant, grenadier, giraffe.

mount, -ain; hill, butte, monticle, fell, knap; cape; head-, fore-land; promontory; ridge, hog's back, dune; rising —, vantage- ground; down; moor, -land; Alp; up-, table-, high-lands; heights etc. (*summit*) 210; knoll, hummock, hillock, barrow, mound, mole, *kopje*; steeps, bluff, cliff, craig, tor, peak, pike, clough; escarpment, edge, ledge, brae; dizzy height.

tower, pillar, column, pylon, obelisk, monument, steeple, spire, minaret, *campanile*, belfry, turret, roof, dome, cupola, pagoda, pyramid; sky scraper; Eiffel tower.

pole, pikestaff, maypole, flagstaff; mast, top—, topgallant- mast.

ceiling etc. (*covering*) 223.

high water; high—, flood—, spring-tide.

altimetry etc. (*angle*) 244; altimeter, height-finder, hypsometer, barograph.

V. be -high etc. *adj.*; tower, soar, command; hover; cap, culminate; overhang, hang over, impend, beetle; bestride, ride, mount; perch, surmount; cover etc. 233; overtop etc. (*be superior*) 33; stand on tiptoe.

become -high etc. *adj.*; grow, — higher, — taller; upgrow; rise etc. (*ascend*) 305.

render -high etc. *adj.*; heighten etc. (*elevate*) 307.

Adj. high, elevated, eminent, exalted, lofty, supernal; tall; gigantic etc. (*big*) 192; Patagonian; towering, beetling, soaring, hanging [gardens]; elevated etc. 307; upper; highest etc. (*topmost*) 210; monticulous, perching, hill-dwelling.

up-, moor-land; hilly, mountainous, alpine, subalpine, heaven-kissing; cloud-topt, -capt, -touching; aerial.

overhanging etc. *v.*; incumbent, overlying; super-incumbent, -natant, -imposed; prominent etc. 250.

tall as a -maypole, —poplar,—steeple; lanky etc. (*thin*) 203.

Adv. on high, high up, aloft, up, above, aloof, overhead; up—, above- stairs; in the clouds; on -tiptoe, —stilts,—the shoulders of; over head and ears; breast high.

over, upwards; from top to bottom etc. (*completely*) 52.

207. Lowness.—N. lowness etc. *adj.*; debasement, depression; prostration etc. (*horizontal*) 213; depression etc. (*concave*) 252.

molehill; lowlands; bottomlands; basement-ground-floor; *rez de chaussée* etc. 211; hold; feet, heels.

low water; low—, ebb—, neap—, spring- tide.

V. be -low etc. *adj.*; lie -low, —flat; underlie; crouch, slouch, wallow, grovel; lower etc. (*depress*) 308.

Adj. low, neap, debased; nether, -most; flat, level with the ground; lying low etc. *v.*; crouched, subjacent, squat, prostrate etc. (*horizontal*) 213.

Adv. under; be-, under-neath; below; down, -wards; adown, at the foot of; under-foot, -ground; down—, below-stairs; at a low ebb; below par.

208. Depth.—N. depth; deepness etc. *adj.*; profundity, depression etc. (*concavity*) 252.

hollow, pit, shaft, well, crater, abyss; gulf etc. 198; bowels of the earth, bottomless pit, hell.

soundings, sonar, depth of water, water, draught, submersion; plummet, sound, probe; sounding -rod, — line, — machine; lead; submarine, diving bell, bathysphere; diver.

V. be -deep etc. *adj.*; render -deep etc. *adj.*; deepen.

plunge etc. 310; sound, heave the lead, take soundings; dig etc. (*excavate*) 252.

Adj. deep, -seated; profound, sunk, buried; submerged etc. 310; sub-aqueous, -marine, -terranean, -terrene; underground.

bottom-, sound-, fathom-less; unfathom-ed, -able; abysmal; deep as a well, deep-sea.

knee-, ankle-deep.

Adv. beyond—, out of- one's depth; over head and ears, over one's head.

209. Shallowness.—N. shallowness etc. *adj.*; shoals; mere scratch; veneer, gloss, pinprick.

Adj. shallow, superficial; skin—, ankle—, knee-deep; just enough to wet one's feet; shoal, -y.
V. shallow, shoal, skim— over, —the surface, touch on.

210. Summit.—N. summit, -y; top, vertex, apex, zenith, pinnacle, acme, acropolis, culmination, meridian, utmost height, *ne plus ultra,* height, pitch, maximum, climax, apogee; culminating —, crowning —, turning- point; turn of the tide, fountain head; water-shed, -parting; sky, pole.
tip, -top; crest, crow's nest, cap, truck, peak, nib; end etc. 67; crown, brow; head, nob, noddle, pate, skull, cranium.
high places, heights.
top-, top-gallant mast, sky scraper; quarter —, hurricane- deck.
architrave, frieze, cornice, coping, coping-stone, zoophorus, capital, headpiece, capstone, epistyle, sconce, pediment, entablature; tympanum; ceiling etc. (*covering*) 223.
attic, loft, garret, house-top, upper story, roof.
topping, icing, frosting.
V. culminate, cap, crown, top; overtop etc. (*be superior to*) 33.
Adj. highest etc. (high etc. 206); top; top-, upper-most; tip top; culminating etc. *v.*; meridi-an, -onal; capital, head, polar, supreme, supernal, top-gallant.
Adv. a-top, at the top of — the tree, — the heap.

211. Base.—N. base, -ment; plinth, dado, wainscot, baseboard; foundation etc. (*support*) 215; substructure, *sub · stratum,* sump, ground, earth, pavement, floor, paving, flag, carpet, ground-floor, deck; footing, groundwork, basis; hold, bilge, orlop deck.
bottom, nadir, foot, sole, toe, hoof, keel, kelson, root.
Adj. bottom; under-, nether-most; fundamental; founded —, based —, grounded —, built- on.

212. Verticality.—N. verticality; erectness etc. *adj.*; perpendicularity; right angle, normal; azimuth circle.
wall, palisade, precipice, cliff, steep, bluff.
elevation, erection; square, plumb-line, plummet.
V. be -vertical etc. *adj.*; stand -up, — on end, — erect, — upright; stick —, cock-up.
render -vertical etc. *adj.*; set —, stick —, raise —, cock- up; erect, rear, raise, pitch, raise on its legs.
Adj. vertical, upright, erect, perpendicular, normal, plumb, straight, bolt upright; rampant; straight —, standing- up etc. *v.*; rectangular, orthogonal.
Adv. vertically etc. *adj.*; up, on end; up —, right- on end; *à plomb*, endwise; on one's legs; at right angles.

213. Horizontality.—N. horizontality; flatness; level, plane; stratum etc. 204; dead -level, — flat; level plane.
recumbency; lying down etc. *v.*; reclination, decumbence; de-, discumbency; proneness etc. *adj.*; accubation, supination, resupination, prostration; azimuth.
plain, floor, platform, bowling-green; cricket--ground; court; gridiron; base-ball diamond; hockey rink; tennis-, croquet-ground, — lawn; billiard table; terrace, estrade, esplanade, *parterre,* table-land, *plateau,* ledge.
spirit-, level; T-square.
V. be -horizontal etc. *adj.*; lie, recline, couch; lie -down, — flat, — prostrate; sprawl, loll; sit down.
render -horizontal etc. *adj.*; lay, — down, — out; level, flatten, even, raze, equalize, smooth, align; prostrate, knock down, floor, fell, ground.
Adj. horizontal, level, even, plane; flat etc. 251; flat as a -billiard table, — bowling green; alluvial; calm, — as a mill-pond; smooth, —as glass.
re-, de-, pro-, ac-cumbent; lying etc. *v.*; prone, supine, couchant, jacent, prostrate.
Adv. horizontally etc. *adj.*; on -one's back, —all fours, — its beam ends.

214. Pendency.—N. pend-, dependency; suspension, hanging etc. *v.*
pendant, drop, tippet, tassel, lobe, tail, train, flap, lappet, skirt, pig-tail, queue, pendulum, hanger, suspender, supporter.
peg, knob, button, hook, nail, stud, ring, staple, tenterhook; davit; fastening etc. 45; spar, horse.
chande-, gase-, electro-lier.
V. be -pendent etc. *adj.*; hang, depend, swing, dangle, droop, sag; swag; daggle, flap, trail, flow.
suspend, hang, sling, hook up, hitch, fasten to, append.
Adj. pend-ent, -ulous; pensile; hanging etc. *v.*; dependent; suspended etc. *v.*; lowering, overhanging, beetling, decumbent; loose, flowing.
having a -peduncle etc. *n.*; pedunculate, tailed, caudate.

215. Support.—N. support, backing, ground, foundation, base, basis; *terra firma*; bearing, fulcrum, *point d'appui*, caudex, purchase, footing, hold, *-locus standi*; landing, — stage, — place; stage, platform; block; rest, resting-place; ground--work, *substratum*, sustentation, subvention; floor etc. (*basement*) 211.
supporter; aid etc. 707; prop, stand, anvil, fulciment; hod, stay, shore, skid, rib, sprag, truss, bandage; sleeper; stirrup, stilts, shoe, sole, heel, splint, lap; bar, rod, boom, sprit, outrigger.
staff, stick, crutch, alpenstock, bourdon; *bâton*, maulstick, colstaff, cowlstaff, staddle; stalk, pedicel, -icle, — uncle.
post, pillar, shaft, column, pilaster; pediment, pedestal; plinth, shank, leg, socle, zocle; buttress, jamb, mullion, abutment; pile, baluster, banister, stanchion, king post; balustrade.
frame, -work, body, *chassis*, *fuselage*; scaffold, skeleton, beam, rafter, girder, lintel, joist, cantilever, travis, trave, corner-stone, summer, transom; rung, round, step, sill.
columella, back-bone; key-stone; axle, -tree; axis; arch, ogive, mainstay.
trunnion, pivot, rowlock; peg etc. (*pendency*)

214; tie-beam etc. (*fastening*) 45; thole pin.

board, ledge, shelf, hob, bracket, trevet, trivet, arbor, rack, hatrack; mantel, -piece, -shelf; slab, console; counter, dresser; flange, corbel; table, trestle, teapoy; shoulder; perch; horse; easel, desk; retable, predella.

seat, throne, dais; divan, musnud; chair, bench, form, stool, camp-stool, sofa, settee, davenport, stall, miserere, arm —, easy —, elbow —, rocking-chair; couch, day bed, *fauteuil*, woolsack, ottoman, settle, squab, bench, box, dicky; saddle, pannel, pillion; side —, pack- saddle; pommel.

bed, berth, pallet, tester, crib, cot, bassinet, hammock, shakedown, camp bed, bunk, truckle-bed, cradle, litter, stretcher, bedstead; four-poster, French bed; bedding, mattress, *paillasse;* pillow, bolster; mat, rug, cushion.

stool, footstool, hassock, faldstool, *prie-dieu*; tabouret; tripod.

Atlas, Persides, Atlantes, Caryatides, Hercules.

V. be -supported etc.; lie —, sit —, recline —, lean —, loll —, rest —, stand —, step —, repose —, abut —, beat —, be based etc.- on; have at one's back; be-stride, -straddle.

support, bear, carry, hold, sustain, shoulder; hold —, back —, bolster —, shore- up; up-hold, -bear; prop; under-prop,-pin, -set; bandage, etc. 43; brace, truss; cradle, pillow.

give —, furnish —, afford —, supply —, lend- -support, — foundations; bottom, found, base, ground, embed.

maintain, keep on foot; aid etc. 707.

Adj. support-ing, -ed, etc.*v.*; atlantean, columellar; sustentative, fundamental, basal.

Adv. astride on, astraddle; pick-a-back.

216. Parallelism.—N. parallelism; coextension, concentricity, collimation.

V. be —, lie- parallel to; collimate; equate, match.

Adj. parallel; coextensive, collateral, concentric, concurrent, abreast, aligned.

Adv. alongside, abreast etc. (*laterally*) 236.

217. Obliquity.—N. obliquity, inclination, skew, slope, slant; crookedness etc. *adj.*; slopeness; leaning etc. *v.*; bevel, bezel, ramp, tilt; bias, list, twist, warp, swag, cant, lurch; distortion etc. 243; bend etc. (*curve*) 245; tower of Pisa.

acclivity, rise, ascent, grade, gradient, *glacis*, rising ground, hill, bank, declivity, downhill, dip, fall, devexity; gentle –, rapid- slope; easy -ascent, – descent; shelving beach; *talus; montagne Russe; facilis descensus Averni.*

steepness etc. *adj.*; cliff, precipice etc. (*vertical*) 212; escarpment, scarp.

[Measure of inclination]clinometer, theodolite, level, sextant, quadrant, protractor; angle, sine, cosine, tangent etc. hypothenuse.

diagonal; zigzag, chevron.

V. be -oblique etc. *adj.*; slope, slant, lean, incline, shelve, stoop, decline, descent, bend, heel, careen, sag, swag, seel, slouch, cant, sidle.

render -oblique etc. *adj.*; sway, bias; slope, slant; incline, bend, crook; cant, tilt; distort etc. 243.

Adj. oblique, inclined; sloping etc. *v.*; tilted etc. *v.*; recumbent, clinal, skew, askew, slant, aslant, bias, plagiedral, indirect, wry, awry, ajee, crooked; knock-kneed etc. (*distorted*) 243; bevel, out of the perpendicular.

uphill, rising, ascending, acclivous; downhill, falling, descending; declining, declivous, devex, anticlinal; steep, abrupt, precipitous, breakneck.

diagonal; trans-verse, -versal; athwart, antiparallel; curved etc. 245.

Adv. obliquely etc. *adj.*; on —, all on- one side; askew, askant, askance, aslope, asquint, edgewise, at an angle; side-long, -ways; slope-, slant-wise; by a side wind.

218. Inversion.—N. in-, e-, sub-, re-, retro-, intro-version; contraposition etc. 237; contrariety etc. 14; reversal; turn of the tide.

overturn; upset, capsize; somer-sault, -set; summerset; *culbute*; revulsion; *pirouette*.

transposition, transposal, anastrophy, *metastasis, hyperbaton, anastrophe, hysteron--proteron,* hypallage, *synchysis, tmesis,* parenthesis; *metathesis*; palindrome; Spoonerism.

pronation and supination.

V. be -inverted etc.; turn –, go –, wheel- -round, – about, – to the right about; turn –, go –, tilt –, topple-over; capsize, turn turtle.

in-, sub-, retro-, intro-vert; reverse; up-, overturn, -set; turn -topsy turvy etc. *adj.*; *culbuter*; transpose, put the cart before the horse, turn the tables.

Adj. inverted etc. *v.*; wrong side -out, – up; inside out, upside down; bottom —, keel- upwards; supine, on one's head, topsy turvy, *sens dessus sens dessous.*

inverse; reverse etc. (*contrary*) 14; opposite etc. 237.

topheavy, unstable.

Adv. inversely etc.*adj.*; hirdie-girdie; heels over head, head over heels.

219. Crossing.—N. crossing etc. *v.*; intersection, – lacement, – twinement, -digitation; decussation, transversion; convolution etc. 248.

reticulation, meshwork, network; inosculation, anastomosis, inter-texture, mortise.

net, *plexux*, web, mesh, twill, skein, sleeve, felt, lace; wicker; mat, -ting; plait, trellis, wattle, lattice, grating, *grille*, gridiron, tracery, fretwork, filigree, reticle; tissue, netting, mokes.

cross, crucifix, rood, crisscross, crux; chain, wreath, braid, cat's cradle,knot; entanglement etc. (*disorder*) 59.

[woven fabrics] cloth, linen, muslin, cambric, drill, homespun, tweed, broadcloth etc.

V. cross, decussate; inter-sect, -lace, -twine, -twist, -weave, -digitate, -link.

twine, entwine, weave, inweave, twist, wreathe; anastomose, inosculate, dovetail, splice, link.

mat, plait, plat, braid, felt, twill; tangle, entangle, ravel; net, knot; dishevel, raddle.

Adj. crossing etc.*v.*; crossed, matted etc. *v.*; transverse.

cross, cruciform, crucial; reti-form, -cular, -culated; areolar, cancellated, mullioned, latticed, grated, barred, streaked; textile, secant, plexal; interfretted.

Adv. across, thwart, athwart, transversely, crosswise.

220. Exteriority.—N. exteriority; outside, exterior; surface, superficies: skin etc. (*covering*) 223; *superstratum*; disk, disc; face, facet, external, the open.

excentricity; circumjacence etc. 227.

V. be -exterior etc. *adj.*; lie around etc. 227.

place -exteriorly, — outwardly, — outside; put —, turn- out.

Adj. exter-ior, -nal; extraneous, outer, -most; out-ward, -lying, -side, -door; round about etc. 227; extramural.

superficial, skin-deep; frontal, discoid.

extraregarding; eccentric; outstanding; extrinsic etc. 6.

Adv. externally etc. *adj.*; out, without, over, outwards, *ab extra*, out of doors; *extra muros*.

in the open air; *sub -Jovè, — dio; à la belle étoile, al fresco.*

221. Interiority.—N. interiority; inside, -land, interior, endocrine; interspace, subsoil, *substratum*.

contents etc. 190; substance, pith, marrow; backbone etc. (*center*) 222; heart, bosom, breast, abdomen; vitals, viscera, entrails, bowels, belly, intestines, guts, chitterlings, womb, lap; gland, cell; internal organs, *penetralia*, recesses, innermost recesses; cave etc. (*concavity*) 252.

inhabitant etc. 188.

V. be -inside etc. *adj.*, — within etc. *adv.*

place —, keep- within; enclose etc. (*circumscribe*) 229; intern; embed etc. (*insert*) 300.

Adj. inter-ior, -nal; inner, inside, intimate, inward, intraregarding; in-, inner-most; deep-seated; visceral, intestine, -tinal; inland; subcutaneous; interstitial etc. (*interjacent*) 228; inwrought etc. (*intrinsic*) 5; enclosed etc. *v.*

home, domestic, indoor, intramural, vernacular; endemic.

Adv. internally etc. *adj.*; inwards, within, in, inly; here-, there-, where-in; *ab intra*, withinside; in —, within- doors; at home, in the bosom of one's family.

222. Centrality.—N. centrality, centricalness, center; middle etc. 68; focus etc. 74.

core, kernel; nucleus, nucleolus; heart, pole, axis, pivot, fulcrum, bull's eye; hub, nave, navel; *umbilicus*, spine, backbone, marrow, pith; hot-bed; concentration etc. (*convergence*) 290; centralization; symmetry.

center of -gravity, — pressure, — percussion, — oscillation, — buoyancy etc. metacenter.

V. be -central etc. *adj.*; converge etc. 290.

render central, centralize, concentrate; bring to a focus.

Adj. centr-al, -ical; middle etc. 68; axial, pivotal, focal, umbilical, concentric; middlemost, nuclear, centric, centraidal; spinal, vertebral.

Adv. middle; midst; centrally etc. *adj.*

223. Covering.—N. covering, cover; canopy, tilt, awning, baldachin, tent, marquee, *tente d'abri*, umbrella, parasol, sunshade; veil (*shade*) 424; shield etc. (*defense*) 717; hall.

roof, dome, cupola, mansard roof; ceiling; thatch, tile; pan-, pen-tile; tiling, shingles, slates, slating, leads; shed etc. (*abode*) 189.

top, lid, covercle, door, *operculum*, eyelid, blind, curtain.

bandage, plaster, lint, wrapping, dossil, finger stall.

coverlet, counterpane, sheet, quilt, comforter, eiderdown; tarpaulin, blanket, rug, drugget, linoleum, oilcloth; housing.

in-, tegument; skin, pellicle, fleece, fell, fur, ermine, miniver, sable, sealskin etc.; fabrikoid; leather, morocco, calf, pigskin, elk, kid, cowhide etc.; shagreen, hide; pelt, -ry; cuticle, *dermis*, scarfskin, *epidermis*.

clothing etc. 225; mask etc. (*concealment*) 530.

peel, crust, bark, rind, *cortex*, husk, shell, coat.

capsule; ferrule; sheath, -ing; pod, cod; casing, case, theca; *elytron; involucrum;* wrapp-ing, -er, cellophane; envelope, vesicle; dermatology, conchology.

armor, -plate, armoring; veneer, facing; pavement; scale etc. (*layer*) 204; coating, paint, stain; varnish etc. (*resin*) 356*a*; anointing etc. *v.*; inunction; incrustation, superposition, obduction, ground, enamel, whitewash, plaster, stucco, rough cast, pebble dash, compo; rendering; cerement; ointment etc. (*grease*) 356.

V. cover; super-pose, -impose; over-lay, -spread; wrap etc. 225; incase; face, case, veneer, pave, paper; tip, cap, bind, revet.

coat, paint, varnish, pay, incrust, stucco, cement, dab, plaster, tar; wash; be-, smear; be-, daub; anoint, do over; gild, plate, electroplate, japan, laquer, lacker, enamel, whitewash; lay it on thick.

over-lie, -arch; conceal etc. 528.

Adj. covering etc. *v.*; cutaneous, dermal, cortical, cuticular, tegumentary, skinny, scaly, squamous; covered etc. *v.*; imbricated, loricated, armor-plated, iron-clad; under cover, hooded, cloaked, cowled.

224. Lining.—N. lining, inner coating; coating etc. (*covering*) 223; stalactite, -agmite.

filling, stuffing, wadding, padding, bushing.

wainscot, *parietes*, wall brattice.

V. line, stuff, incrust, wad, pad, fill.

Adj. lined etc. *v.*

225. Investment.—N. investment; covering etc. 223; dress, clothing, raiment, drapery, costume, attire, guise, toilet, *toilette*, trim; habiliment; vesture, -ment; garment, garb, palliament, apparel, wardrobe, wearing apparel, clothes, things.

array; tailoring, millinery; best bib and tucker; finery etc. (*ornament*) 847; full dress etc. (*show*) 882; garniture; theatrical properties.

outfit, equipment, *trousseau*; uniform, khaki, regimentals; academicals, canonicals etc. 999; livery, gear, harness, turn out, accoutrement, caparison, suit, rigging, trappings, traps, slops, togs, toggery; masquerade.

dishabille, morning dress, lounge suit, tea-gown, *kimono*, *négligé*, dressing-gown, *peignoir*, wrapper, undress; shooting-coat; smoking jacket, mufti; rags, tatters, old clothes; mourning, weeds; duds; slippers.

robe, tunic, dolman, *paletot*, habit, gown, coat, coatee, frock, blouse, *pelisse*, middy, sagum, *toga*, smock-frock; frock-, dress-, morning-, tail- coat; dress-suit, — clothes, swallow-tail coat, dinner-, Eton-jacket.

cloak, pall; mantle, mantlet, mantua, shawl, *pelisse*, veil, yashmak; cape, tippet, kirtle, plaid, muffler, comforter, Balaclava helmet, haik, huke, chlamys, mantilla, tabard, housing, horse-cloth, burnous, *roquelaure*, *houppelande*; sur-, top-, over-, great-coat; *surtout*, spencer, cardigan, sweater, blazer; mackintosh, waterproof, slicker, raincoat, oilskin, trench coat, ulster, monkey-, pea-, pilot-jacket, redingote; wraprascal, poncho, cardinal, pelerine, talma.

jacket, jumper, vest, jerkin, waistcoat, doublet, *camisole*, gabardine; stays, *corsage*, corset, corselet, bodice; stomacher; skirt, petticoat, slip, farthingale, kilt, jupe, crinoline, bustle, hobble skirt, *panier*, apron, pinafore; loin cloth.

trousers; breeches, trews, pantaloons, unmentionables, inexpressibles, overalls, pajamas, smalls, small-clothes; tights, pants, shorts, drawers; knickerbockers, knickers, plus fours, bloomers, divided skirt; phil-, fill-ibeg.

head-dress, -gear; cap, *béret*, tam o' shanter, glengarry, topee, sombrero; hat; cocked —, high —, tall —, top —, silk —, opera —, crush - hat, *gibus*, beaver, castor, bonnet, tile, wideawake, billy-cock; bowler; soft felt —, straw —, leghorn- hat, panama; toque; wimple; night-, mob-, skull-cap, biretta; hood, cowl, coif; capote, calach; scull-cap; kerchief, snood; head, *coiffure*; crown etc. (*circle*) 247; *chignon*, pelt, wig, front, peruke, periwig; caftan, turban, fez, *tarboosh*, taj, shako, csako, busby; *képi*, forage cap, bearskin; helmet etc. 717; mask, domino.

body clothes; linen; shirt, sark, smock, shift, *chemise*, *lingerie*; night-gown, -shirt; bed-gown, *sac de nuit*; jersey, guernsey; underclothing, -waistcoat.

neck-erchief, -cloth; tie, ruff, collar, cravat, stock, handkerchief, bandana, scarf; bib, tucker; dicky; boa; girdle etc. (*circle*) 247; cummerbund.

shoe, pump, brogue, boot, slipper, sandal, galoche, galoshes, arctics, rubber boots, overshoes, patten, clog, sabot; high-low; Blucher —, Wellington —, Hessian —, jack —, top- boot; Balmoral; legging, puttee, buskin, greave, galligaskin, moccasin, *gamache*, gambado, gaiter, spatter-dash, spat, antigropeles; stocking, hose, gaskins, trunk-hose, sock, hosiery.

glove, gauntlet, mitten, cuff, muffettee, wristband, sleeve.

swaddling cloth, baby-linen, *layette*; pocket-handkerchief.

shroud, etc. 363.

clothier, tailor, milliner, *costumier*, sempstress, seamstress, snip; dress-, habit-, breeches-, shoemaker; cordwainer, cobbler, Crispin, hosier, hatter; draper, linendraper, haberdasher, mercer.

V. invest; cover etc. 223; envelop, lap, involve; in-, en-wrap; wrap; fold —, wrap —, lap —, muffle-up; overlap; sheathe, swathe, swaddle, roll up in, shroud, circumvest.

vest, clothe, array, dress, dight, drape, robe, enrobe, attire, tire, garb, habilitate, apparel, accouter, rig, fit out; bedizen, deck etc. (*ornament*) 847; perk; equip, harness, caparison; dress up.

wear; don; put —, huddle —, slip- on; mantle.

Adj. invested etc. *v.*; habited; dight, -ed; clad, *costumé*, shod, *chaussé*; *en grande tenue* etc. (*show*) 882.

sartorial.

226. Divestment.—N. divestment; taking off, stripping, removal etc. *v.*

nudity; bareness etc. *adj.*; undress; dishabille etc. 225, altogether; nu-, denu-dation; decortication, depilation, excoriation, desquamation; molting; exfoliation.

baldness, alopecia, acomia.

V. divest; uncover etc. (*cover* etc. 223); denude, bare, strip; undress, unclothe, disrobe etc. (dress, enrobe, etc. 225); uncoif; dismantle; uncase; put —, take —, cast- off; shed, doff; husk, peel, pare, decorticate, desquamate; excoriate, skin, scalp, flay, bark, expose, lay open; exfoliate, molt, mew; cast the skin.

Adj. divested etc. *v.*; bare, naked, nude; undressed, -draped, -clad, -clothed, -appareled; exposed; in dishabille; *décolleté*; bald, threadbare, ragged, callow, roofless.

in -a state of nature, — nature's garb, — buff, — native buff, — birthday suit; *in puris naturalibus*; with nothing on, stark naked; bald as a coot, bare as the back of one's hand; out at elbows; barefoot; bareback; leaf-, nap-, hairless, shaved, clean shaven, tonsured, beardless, bald-headed, acomous.

227. Circumjacence.—N. circumjacence, -ambience; environment, encompassment; atmosphere, medium; surroundings, *entourage*.

outpost; border etc. (*edge*) 231; girdle etc. (*circumference*) 230; outskirts, *boulevards*, suburbs, purlieus, precincts, *faubourgs*, *environs*, *banlieue*, neighborhood, vicinity.

V. lie -around etc. *adv.*; surround, beset, compass, encompass, environ, inclose, enclose, encircle, circle, embrace, circumvent, lap, gird; begird, girdle, engird; skirt, twine round; hem in etc. (*circumscribe*) 229; besiege, invest, blockade.

Adj. circum-jacent, -ambient, -fluent; ambient; surrounding etc. *v.*; circumferential, suburban.

Adv. around, about; without; on -every side, — all sides; right and left, all round, round about; in the neighborhood.

228. Interjacence.—N. inter-jacence, -currence, -venience, -location, -digitation, -penetration; permeation.

inter-jection, -polation, -lineation, -spersion, -calation; embolism.

inter-vention, -ference, -position; in-, ob-trusion; insinuation; insertion etc. 300; dovetailing; infiltration; intromission.

intermedi-um, -ary; go-between, agent, middleman, medium, bodkin, intruder, interloper; parenthesis, episode; fly-leaf.

partition, *septum*, diaphragm, mid-riff; party-wall, panel, vail, bulkhead, brattice, *cloison*; half-way house.

V. lie —, come —, get- between; intervene, slide in, interpenetrate, permeate.

put between, introduce, intromit, import; throw –, wedge –, edge –, jam –, worm –, foist –, run –, plough –, work- in; interpose, -ject, -calate. -polate, -line, -leave, -sperse, -weave, -lard, -digitate; let in, dovetail, splice, mortise; insinuate, smuggle; infiltrate, ingrain.

interfere, put in an oar, thrust one's nose in; intrude, obtrude; have a finger in the pie; introduce the thin end of the wedge; thrust in etc. (*insert*) 300.

Adj. inter-jacent, -current, -venient, -vening etc. *v.*, -mediate, -mediary, -calary, -sitital, -costal, -mural, -planetary, -stellar; embolismal.

parenthetical, episodic: mediterranean; intrusive; embosomed; merged, mean, middle, medium, median.

Adv. between, betwixt; 'twixt; among, -st; amid, st; 'mid, -st; in the thick of; betwixt and between; sandwich-wise; parenthetically, *obiter dictum*.

229. Circumscription.—N. circumscription, limitation, inclosure; confinement etc. (*restraint*) 751; circumvallation, encincture; envelope etc. 232.

V. circumscribe, limit, bound, confine, restrict, enclose; surround etc. 227; compass about; imprision etc. (*restrain*) 751; hedge –, wall –, rail- in; fence –, hedge- round; embar; picket, corral, enfold, bury, incase, pack up, enshrine, inclasp; wrap up etc. (*invest*) 225; embosom.

Adj. circumscribed etc. *v.*; begirt, lapt; circumambient; buried –, immersed- in; embosomed, in the bosom of, imbedded, encysted, mewed up; imprisoned etc. 751; land-locked, in a ring fence.

230. Outline.—N. outline, circumference; perimeter, -phery; ambit, circuit, lines, *tournure*, *contour*, profile, *silhouette*, lineaments; bounds, coastline.

zone, belt, girth, band, baldric, zodiac, girdle, tire, cingle, clasp, girt; *cordon* etc. (*inclosure*) 232; circlet etc. 247.

V. outline, delineate, *silhouette*, circumscribe etc. 229; profile, block out.

Adj. outlined etc. *v.*; circumferential, perimetric, peripheral.

231. Edge.—N. edge, verge, brink, brow, brim. margin, border, confines, skirt, rim, felloe, felly, flange, side, mouth; jaws, chops, chaps, *fauces*; lip, muzzle.

threshold, door, porch; portal etc. (*opening*) 260; coast, shore, strand, beach, bank, wharf, quay, dock.

frame, fringe, flounce, frill, list, trimming, edging, skirting, hem, selvedge, welt; furbelow, valance, exergue.

Adj. border, marginal, skirting; labial; labiated, marginated.

232. Inclosure.—N. inclosure, enclosure, envelope; package, box, crate, case etc. (*receptacle*) 191; wrapper; girdle etc. 230.

pen, fold, croft, sty; pen-, in-, sheep--fold; paddock, pound, corral, kraal; yard, compound; net, seine net.

wall; hedge, -row; *espalier*; fence etc. (*defence*) 717; pale, paling, balustrade, rail, railing, gunwale; quickset hedge, park paling, circumvallation, *enciente*, ring fence.

barrier, barricade; gate; -way; door, hatch, *cordon*; prison etc. 752.

dike, dyke, ditch, fosse, moat, trench.

V. inclose; circumscribe etc. 229.

233. Limit.—N. limit, boundary, bounds, confine, *enclave*, term, bourn, verge, kerb-stone, curbstone, but, pale; termin-ation, -us; stint, frontier, precinct, marches.

boundary line, landmark; line of -demarcation, – circumvallation; pillars of Hercules; Rubicon, turning-point; *ne plus ultra*; sluice, flood-gate.

V. limit, bound, confine, define, circumscribe, demarcate, delimit, encompass.

Adj. definite; contermin-ate, -able, terminable, limitable; terminal, frontier, border, bordering, boundary.

Adv. thus far, – and no further.

234. Front.—N. front; fore, – part; foreground; forefront, face, disk, disc, frontage, *façade*, *proscenium*, facia, frontispiece; priority, anteriority; obverse [of a medal].

fore –, front- rank, first line; van, -guard; advanced guard; outpost, scout.

brow, forehead, visage, physiognomy, phiz, features, countenance, map, mug; rostrum, beak, bow, stem, prow, prore, jib, bowsprit; forecastle.

pioneer etc. (*precursor*) 64; metoposcopy.

V. be –, stand- in front etc. *adj.*; front, face, confront, breast, brave; bend forwards; come to the -front, – fore.

Adj. fore, forward, anterior, front, frontal, head-on, leading, first, primary.

Adv. before; in -front, – the van, – advance; ahead, right ahead; fore-, head-most; in the foreground; before one's -face, – eyes; face to face, *vis-à-vis*.

235. Rear.—N. rear, back, posterior-ity; rear -rank, – guard; background, *hinterland*.

occiput, nape, scruff, chine; heels; tail, rump, croup, buttock, posteriors, bottom, seat, backside, scut, breech, *dorsum*, loin; dorsal –, lumbar-region; hind quarters.

stern poop, after-part, counter; postern, heel-, tail-piece, crupper.

wake; train etc. (*sequence*) 281.

reverse; other side of the shield.

V. be -behind etc. *adv.*; fall astern; bend backwards; bring up the rear; follow etc. 622; tail, shadow.

Adj. back, rear; hind. -er, -most, -ermost; postern, -erior; dorsal, after; caudal, lumbar; mizzen.

Adv. behind; in the -rear, – ruck, – background; behind one's back; at the -heels, – tail, – back- of; back to back.

after, -most, aft, abaft, astern, stern- most, aback, rear-, hind-, back-ward.

236. Laterality.—N. laterality; side, flank, beam, quarter, lee; hand; cheek, jowl, jole, wing; profile; temple, *parietes*, loin, haunch, hip.

gable, -end; broadside; lee side.

points of the compass; East, Orient, Levant; West, occident; orientation.

V. be -on one side etc. *adv.*; flank, outflank; sidle; skirt, border.

Adj. lateral, sidelong; collateral; parietal, flanking, skirting; flanked; sideling.

many-sided; multi-, bi-, tri-, quadri- lateral.

East-ern, -ward, -erly; orient, -al, auroral, Levantine; West-ern, -ward, -erly; occidental, Hesperian; equatorial.

Adv. side-ways, -long; broadside on; on one side, abreast, abeam, alongside, beside, aside; by, – the side of; side by side; cheek by jowl etc. (*near*) 197; to -windward, – leeward; laterally etc. *adj.*; right and left; on her beam ends.

237. Contraposition.—N. contraposition, opposition; polarity; inversion etc. 218; opposite side; antithesis; reverse, inverse; counterpart; antipodes; opposite poles, North and South.

V. be -opposite etc. *adj.*; subtend.

Adj. opposite; reverse, inverse; antipodal, subcontrary; fronting, facing, diametrically opposite.

Northern, Septentrional, Boreal, arctic; Southern, Austral, antarctic, polar.

Adv. over, – the way, – against; against; face to face, vis-à-vis; as poles asunder.

238. Dextrality.—N. dextrality; right, – hand; dexter, offside, starboard.

Adj. dextral, right-handed; ambidextral; dexterous, dextrorsal etc.

239. Sinistrality.—N. sinistrality; left, – hand; *sinister*, nearside, larboard, port.

Adj. sinistral, sinister, sinistrorsal etc., left-handed, sinistromanual, sinistrous.

240. Form.—N. form, figure, shape, physique; con-formation, -figuration; make, formation, frame, construction, design, cut, set, build, trim, cut of one's jib; stamp, type, cast, mold; fashion; contour etc. (*outline*) 230; structure etc. 329.

feature, lineament, outline, turn; phase etc. (*aspect*) 448; posture, attitude, *pose*.

[Science of form] morphology.

[Similarity of form] isomorphism.

forming etc. *v.*; form-, figur-, efform- ation; sculpture.

V. form, shape, figure, fashion, efform, carve, cut, chisel, hew, cast; rough-hew, -cast; sketch; block –, hammer- out; trim; lick –, put- into shape; model, knead, work up into, set, mold, sculpture; cast, stamp; built etc. (*construct*) 161.

Adj. formed etc. *v.*

[Receiving form] plastic, fictile, full- fashioned etc.

[Giving form] plasmic, etc.

[Similar in form] isomorphous etc.

241. Amorphism. [Absence of form.]—**N.** amorphism, informity, uncouthness; unlicked cub, rough diamond; *rudis indigestaque moles*; disorder etc. 59; deformity etc. 243.

disfigure-, deface-ment, deformation; mutilation.

V. [Destroy form] deface, disfigure, deform, mutilate, truncate; derange etc. 61.

Adj. shapeless, amorphous, malformed, formless; un-formed, -hewn, -fashioned, -shapen; rough, rude, Gothic, barbarous, rugged, in the rough; misshapen etc. 243.

242. Symmetry. [Regularity of form.]—**N.** symmetry, shapeliness, finish; beauty etc. 845; proportion, eurythmy, eurythmic, uniformity, parallelism; bi-, tri-, multi-lateral symmetry; centrality etc. 222.

arborescence, branching, ramification.

Adj. symmetrical, shapely, well set, finished; beautiful etc. 845; classic, chaste, severe.

regular, uniform, balanced; equal etc. 27; parallel, coextensive.

arbor-escent, -iform; dendr-iform, -oid; branching; ramous, ramose.

243. Distortion. [Irregularity of form.]—**N.** dis-, de-, con-tortion; knot, mop, warp, buckle, screw, twist; crookedness etc. (*obliquity*) 217; grimmace; deformity; mal-, malcon-formation; monstrosity, misproportion, want of symmetry, *anamorphosis*; ugliness etc. 846; teratology.

V. distort, contort, twist, warp etc. *n.*; wrest, writhe, make faces, deform, misshape.

Adj. distorted etc. *v.*; out of shape, irregular, unsymmetric, awry, wry, askew, crooked, sinuous; anamorphous; not -true, – straight; on one side, crump, deformed; mis-shapen, -begotten; mis-, ill-proportioned; ill-made; grotesque, crooked as a ram's horn; hump-, hunch-, bunch-, crook-backed; bandy; bandy-, bow-legged; bow-, knock-kneed; splay-, club-footed; taliped; round-shouldered; snub-nosed; curtailed of one's fair proportions; scalene, stumpy etc. (*short*) 201; gaunt etc. (*thin*) 203; bloated etc. 194.

Adv. all manner of ways.

244. Angularity.—N. angular-ity, -ness; aduncity; angle, cusp, bend; fold etc. 258; notch etc. 257; fork, bifurcation.

elbow, knee, knuckle, ankle, groin, crotch, crane, fluke, scythe, sickle, zigzag, kimbo.

corner, nook, recess, niche, oriel.

right angle etc. (*perpendicular*) 212; obliquity etc. 217; angle of 45 degrees, miter; acute –, obtuse –, salient –, re-entrant –, spherical –, solid –, dihedral- angle.

angular -measurement, – elevation, – distance, – velocity; trigon-, goni-ometry; altimetry; clin-, graph-, goni-ometer; theodolite; transit circle; sextant, quadrant; dichotomy.

triangle, trigon, wedge; rectangle, square, lozenge, diamond; rhomb, -us; quadr-angle, -ilateral; parallelogram; quadrature; poly-, penta-, hexa-, hepta-, octa-, deca-gon.

Platonic bodies; cube, rhomboid; tetra-, penta-, hexa-, octa-, dodeca-, icosa-hedron; prism, pyramid; parallelopiped.

V. bend, fork, bifurcate, crinkle, divaricate, branch, ramify.

Adj. angular, bent, crooked, aduncous, uncinated, aquiline, jagged, serrated; falc-iform, -ated; furcular, furcated, forked, bifurcate, crotched; zigzag; dovetailed; knock-kneed, crinkled, akimbo, kimbo, geniculated; oblique etc. 217.

fusiform, wedge-shaped, cuneiform; tri-angular, -gonal, -lateral; quadr-angular, -ilateral; rectangular, square, foursquare, multilateral; polygonal etc. *n.*; cubical, rhomboidal, pyramidal.

245. Curvature.—N. curv-ature, -ity, -ation; incurv-ity, -ation; bend; flex- ure, -ion; conflexure; crook, hook, bought, bending; de-, inflexion; arcuation, devexity, turn; deviation, *détour*, sweep; curl, -ing; bough; recurv-ity, -ation; sinuosity etc. 248; aduncity.

curve, arc, arch, arcade, vault, dome, bow, crescent, *meniscus*, half moon, lunule, horse-shoe, loop, crane-neck; para-, hyper-bola; catenary, festoon; conch-, cardi-oid; caustic, instep; tracery.

V. be -curved etc. *adj.*; sweep, swag, sag; deviate etc. 279; turn; re-enter.

render -curved etc. *adj.*; bend, curve, incurvate; de-, in-flect; crook; turn, round, arch, arcuate, arch over, loop the loop, concamerate; bow, coil, curl, recurve, frizzle.

Adj. curved etc. *v.*; curvi-form, -lineal, -linear; devex, devious; recurv-ed, -ous; *retroussé*; crump; bowed etc. *v.*; vaulted; hooked; falc-iform, -ated; semicircular, crescentic; lun-iform, -ular; semilunar, meniscal; conchoidal; cord-iform, -ated; cardioid; heart-, bell-, pear-, fig-shaped; reniform; lenti-form, -cular; bow-legged etc. (*distorted*) 243; oblique etc. 217; circular etc. 247.

246. Straightness.—N. straightness, rectilinearity, directness; inflexibility etc. (*stiffness*) 323; straight –, right –, direct-, bee- line; short cut.

V. be -straight etc. *adj*; have no turning; not -incline, – bend, – turn, – deviate- to either side, go straight; steer for etc. (*direction*) 278.

render straight, straighten, rectify; set –, put- straight; un-bend, -fold, -curl etc. 248, -ravel etc. 219, -wrap.

Adj. straight; rectiline-ar, -al; direct, even, right, true, in a line; unbent etc. *v.*; un-deviating, -turned, -distorted, -swerving; straight as an arrow etc. (*direct*) 278; inflexible etc. 323.

247. Circularity. [Simple circularity.]—**N.** circularity, roundness; rotundity etc. 249.

circle, circlet, ring, washer, areola, hoop, roundlet, *annulus*, annulet, bracelet, armlet, armilla; ringlet; eye, loop, wheel; cycle, orb, orbit, rundle, zone, belt, *cordon*, band; sash, girdle, cestus, cincture, baldric, fillet, *fascia*, wreath, garland; crown, corona, coronet, chaplet, snood, necklace, collar; noose, lasso, lariat.

ellipse, oval, ovule; ellipsoid, cycloid; epicycloid, -cycle; semi-circle; quadrant, sextant, sector.

V. make -round etc. *adj.*; round.

go round; encircle etc. 227; describe -a circle etc. 311.

Adj. round, rounded, circular, annular, orbicular; oval, ovate; elliptic, -al; ovoid, egg-shaped; pear-shaped etc. 245; cycloidal etc. *n.*; spherical etc. 249.

248. Convolution. [Complex circularity.]—**N.** winding etc. *v.*; con-, in-, circum-volution; wave, undulation, tortuosity, anfractuosity; sinu-osity, -ation, sinuousness; meandering, circuit, circumbendibus, twist, twirl, windings and turnings, *ambages*; torsion; inosculation; reticulation etc. (*crossing*) 219.

coil, roll, curl, buckle, spire, spiral, helix, corkscrew, worm, volute, whorl, rundle; tendril; scollop, scallop, escalop; kink.

serpent, snake, eel, maze, labyrinth.

V. be -convoluted etc. *adj.*; wind, twine, turn and twist, twirl; wave, undulate, meander; inosculate; entwine, intwine; twist, coil, roll; wrinkle, curl, crisp, twill; frizz, -le; crimp, crape, indent, scollop, scallop; wring, intort; contort; wreathe etc. (*cross*) 219.

Adj. convoluted; winding, twisted etc. *v.*; tortile, tortive; wavy; und-ated, -ulatory; circling, snaky, snake-like, serpentine; serpent-, anguill-, vermiform; vermicular; mazy, tortuous, anfractuous, sinuous, flexuous, wavy, sigmoidal.

involved, intricate, complicated, perplexed; labyrinth-ic, -ian, -ine; circuitous; peristaltic; daedalian, curly.

wreathy, frizzly, *crêpé*, buckled; ravelled etc. (*in disorder*) 59.

spiral, coiled, helical, turbinated.

Adv. in and out, round and round.

249. Rotundity.—N. rotundity; roundness etc. *adj.*; cyclindricity; spher-icity, -oidity; globosity.

cylin-der, -droid; barrel, drum; roll, -er; *rouleau*, column, rolling-pin, rundle; chimney-pot, drain-pipe.

cone, conoid, pear-, egg-, bell-shape.

sphere, globe, orb, orbit, ball, boulder, bowlder; spher-, ellips-, ge-, glob-oid, oblong –, oblate- spheroid; drop, spherule, globule, vesicle, bulb, bullet, pellet, *pelote*, clew, pill, marble, pea, knob, pommel, knot.

V. render -spherical etc. *adj.*; form into a sphere, sphere, roll into a ball; give -rotundity etc. *n.*; round.

Adj. rotund; round etc. (*circular*) 247; cylindric, -ical, -oid; columnar, lumbriciform; conic, -al; spher-ical, -oidal; glob-ular, -ated, -ous, -ose; egg-, bell-, pear-shaped; ov-oid, -iform; gibbous; campaniform, -ulate, -iliform; fungiform, bead-like, moniliform, pyriform, bulbous; *teres atque rotundus*; round as -an orange, — an apple, — a ball, — a billiard ball, — a cannon ball.

250. Convexity.—N. convexity, prominence, projection, swelling, gibbosity, bilge, bulge, protuberance, protrusion; excrescency, camber.

intumescence; tumor; tubercle, -osity; excrescence; hump, hunch, bunch, gnarl.

tooth, knob, elbow, process, *apophysis*, condyle, bulb, node, nodule, nodosity, tongue, *dorsum*, boss, embossment, bump, clump; sugar-loaf etc. (*sharpness*) 253; bow; mamelon.

pimple, wen, wheal, *papula*, postule, pock, proud flesh, growth, goiter, *sarcoma*, caruncle, corn, bunion, wart, furnuncle, polypus, adenoid, fungus, fungosity, *exostosis*, bleb, blister, blain; boil etc. (*disease*) 655; bubble, blob.

papilla, nipple, teat, pap, breast, dug, mammilla; proboscis, nose, neb, beak, snout, nozzle, snozzle; Adam's apple; belly, paunch, corporation; withers, back, shoulder, lip, flange.

peg, button, stud, ridge, rib, jutty, trunnion, snag.

cupola, dome, bee-hive; arch, balcony, eaves; pilaster.

relief, relievo, *cameo*; *basso-*, *mezzo-*, *alto-rilievo*; low-, bas-, high-relief.

hill etc. (*height*) 206; cape, promontory, mull; fore-, head-land; point of land, naze, ness, mole, jetty, hummock, ledge, spur.

V. be -prominent etc. *adj.*; project, bulge, protrude, bag, belly, pout, bouge, bunch; jut —, stand —, stick —, poke- out; stick —, bristle —, start —, cock —, shoot- up; swell —, hang —, bend-over; beetle.

render -prominent etc. *adj.*; raise 307; emboss, chase.

Adj. convex, prominent, protuberant, underhung, undershot; projecting etc. *v.*; bossed, bossy, nodular, bunchy; clav-ate, -ated; hummocky, *moutonné*, mammiform; papul-ous, -ose; hemispheric, bulbous; bowed, arched; bold; bellied; tuber-ous, -culous; tumorous; cornute, knobby, odontoid; lenti-form, -cular; gibbous.

salient, in relief, raised, *repoussé*; bloated etc. (*expanded*) 194.

251. Flatness.—N. flatness etc. *adj.*; smoothness etc. 255.

plane; level etc. 213; plate, platter, table, tablet, slab.

V. render flat, flatten, squash; level etc. 213.

Adj. flat, plane, even, flush, scutiform, discoid; level etc. (*horizontal*) 213; smooth; flat as -a pancake, — a fluke, — a flounder, — a board, — my hand.

252. Concavity.—N. concavity, depression, dip; hollow, -ness; indentation, *intaglio*, cavity, antrum, dent, dint, dimple, follicle, pit, *sinus*, *alveolus*, *lacuna*; excavation, trench, shaft, sap, mine, tunnel, burrow; trough etc. (*furrow*) 259; honeycomb.

cup, basin, crater, punch-bowl; cell etc. (*receptacle*) 191; socket, faucet.

valley, vale, dale, dell, gap, dingle, combe, bottom, slade, strath, glade, grove, glen, cave, cavern, cove; grot, -to; alcove, *cul-de-sac*, blind alley; gully etc. 198; arch etc. (*curve*) 245; bay etc. (*of the sea*) 343.

excavator, sapper, miner.

V. be -concave etc. *adj.*; retire, cave in.

render -concave etc. *adj.*; depress, hollow; scoop, — out; gouge, dig, delve, excavate, dent, dint, mine, sap, undermine, burrow, tunnel, stave in.

Adj. depressed etc. *v.*; concave, hollow, stove in; dished; spoon-like; retiring; retreating; cavernous; porous etc. (*with holes*) 260; cellular, spongy, spongious; honeycombed, alveolar; infundibul-ar, -iform; funnel-, bell-shaped; campaniform, capsular; vaulted, arched.

253. Sharpness.—N. sharpness etc. *adj.*; acuity, acumination; spinosity.

point, spike, spine, *spiculum*, tine; needle, pin; tack, nail; prick, -le; spur, rowel, barb; spit, cusp; horn, antler; snag; tag; thorn, bristle.

nib, tooth, incisor, tusk; spoke, cog, ratchet.

crag, crest *arête*, cone, peak, sugar-loaf, pike, *aiguille*; spire, pyramid, steeple.

beard, *chevaux de frise*, porcupine, hedgehog, brier, bramble, thistle; comb, awn, bur.

wedge; knife-, cutting- edge; blade, edge-tool, cutlery, knife, penknife, whittle, razor; scalpel, bistoury, lancet; chisel; ploughshare, coulter; hatchet, axe, pick-axe, mattock, pick, adze, bill; bill-hook, cleaver, cutter; skiver; scythe, sickle, scissors, shears; sword etc. (*arms*) 727; bodkin etc. (*perforator*) 262.

sharpener, hone, strop; grind-, whet-stone; steel, emery.

V. be -sharp etc. *adj.*; taper to a point; bristle with.

render -sharp etc. *adj.*; sharpen, point, aculeate, acuminate, whet, barb, spiculate, set, strop, grind.

cut etc. (*sunder*) 44.

Adj. sharp, keen; acute; aci-cular, -form; aculeated, -minated; pointed; tapering; conical, pyramidal; mucron-ate, -ated; spindle-, needle-shaped; spiked, spiky, ensiform, peaked, salient, cusp-ed; -idate, -idated; corn-ute, -uted, -iculate; prickly; spiny, spinous; thorny, bristling, muricated, pectinated, studded, thistly, briery; craggy etc. (*rough*) 256; snaggy; digitated, two-edged, fusiform; denti-form, -culated; toothed; odontoid; star-like; stell-ated, -iform; arrow-headed; arrowy, barbed, spurred, sagittal; spear-shaped, hastate; horned; conical.

cutting; sharp-, knife-edged; sharp —, keen- as a razor; sharp as a needle; sharpened etc. *v.*; set.

254. Bluntness.—N. bluntness etc. *adj.*; abruptness, dullness.

V. be —, render- blunt etc. *adj.*; obtund, dull; take off the -point, — edge; turn.

Adj. blunt, obtuse, dull, bluff.

255. Smoothness.—N. smoothness etc. *adj.*; polish, gloss; lubric-ity, -ation.

down, velvet, silk, satin; slide; bowling green etc. (*level*) 213; glass, ice; asphalt, pavement, flags.

roller, steam-roller; iron, flat-iron, tailor's goose; sand-, emery-paper; burnisher, turpentine and bees-wax.

V. smooth, -en; plane; file; mow, shave; level, roll; macadamize; polish, burnish, planish, levigate, calender, glaze; iron, hot-press, mangle; lubricate etc. (*oil*) 332.

Adj. smooth; polished etc. *v.*; even; level etc. 213; plane etc. (*flat*) 251; sleek, glossy; silken, silky; lanate, downy, velvety; glabrous, slippery, glassy, lubricous, oily, soft; unwrinkled; smooth as -glass, — ice, — velvet, — oil; slippery as an eel; wooly etc. (*feathery*) 256.

256. Roughness.—N. roughness etc. *adj.*; tooth, grain, texture, ripple; asperity, rugosity, salebrosity, corrugation, nodosity, arborescence etc. 242.

brush, hair, beard, shag, mane, whisker, mutton-chops, *moustache*, *mustachio*, imperial, Van Dyke, tress, lock, curl, ringlet, *fimbriae*, *cilia*, *villi*; eye-lashes, eye-brows, love-lock.

plum-age, -osity; plume, *panache*, crest, feather, tuft, tussock, fringe, toupee.

wool, velvet, plush, nap, pile, floss, fluff, fur, down; byssus, moss, bur.

V. be -rough etc. *adj.*; go against the grain.

render -rough etc. *adj.*; roughen, rough cast, knurl; ruffle, crisp, crumple, crinkle, corrugate, engrail; set on edge, stroke —, rub- the wrong way, rumple.

Adj. rough, uneven; scabrous, knotted; nodular; rug-ged, -ose, -ous; asperous, crisp, salebrous, gnarled, unpolished, unsmooth, rough hewn; knurled, cross-grained, crag-gy, -ged; crankling, scraggy, jagged, unkempt, prickly etc. (*sharp*) 253; arborescent etc. 242; leafy, well-wooded; feathery; plum-ose, -igerous; tufted, fimbriated, hairy, bristly, ciliated, filamentous, hirsute; crin-ose, -ite; bushy, hispid, villous, pappous, bearded, pilous, shaggy, shagged; fringed, befringed; set-ous, -ose, -aceous; 'like quills upon the fretful porcupine;' rough as a -nutmeg grater, — bear.

downy, velvety, flocculent, wolly; lan-ate, -ated; lanugin-ous, ose; tomentous.

Adv. against the grain, in the rough, on edge.

257. Notch.—N. notch, dent, nick, cut; indent, -ation; serration; dimple.

embrasure, battlement, machicolation; saw, tooth, crenelle, scallop, scollop, vandyke.

V. notch, nick, cut, pink, mill, score, dent, indent, jag, scarify, scotch, crimp, scollop, crenulate, vandyke.

Adj. notched etc. *v.*; crenate, -d; dentate, -d; denticulate, -d; toothed, palmated, serrated.

258. Fold.—N. fold, plicature, pleat, plait, ply, crease; tuck, gather; flexion, flexure, joint, elbow, doubling, duplicature, wrinkle, rimple, crinkle, crankle, crumple, rumple, rivel, ruck, ruffle, dog's ear, corrugation, frounce, flounce, lapel; pucker, crow's feet.

V. fold, double, plicate, pleat, plait, crease, wrinkle, crinkle, crankle, curl, smock, cockle up, crocker, rimple, rumple, frizzle, frounce, rivel, twill, corrugate, ruffle, crimple, crumple, pucker; turn —, double- -down, — under; tuck, ruck, hem, gather.

Adj. folded etc. *v.*

259. Furrow.—N. furrow, groove, rut, *sulcus*, scratch, streak, *striae*, crack, score, incision, slit; chamfer, fluting.

channel, gutter, trench, ditch, dike, dyke, moat, fosse, trough, kennel; ravine etc. (*interval*) 198.

V. furrow etc. *n.*; flute, groove, carve, corrugate, plough; incise, chase, enchase, grave, engrave, etch, bite in, cross-hatch.

Adj. furrowed etc. *v.*; ribbed, straited, sulcated, fluted, canaliculated; bisculc-ous, -ate; trisulcate; corduroy.

260. Opening.—N. hole, foramen; puncture, blow-out, perforation; pin-, key-, loop-, port-, peep-, mouse-, pigeon hole; eye, — of a needle; eyelet; slot.

opening, apert-ure, -ness; hiation, yawning, oscitancy, dehiscence, patefaction, pandiculation; gap, chasm etc. (*interval*) 198.

embrasure, window, casement, light; sky-, fan-light; lattice; bay-, bow-window; oriel; dormer, lantern.

out-, in-let; vent, vomitory; *embouchure*; orifice, mouth, sucker, muzzle, throat, gullet, placket, weasand, wizen, nozzle, *esophagus*.

portal, porch, gate, ostiary, postern, wicket, trap-door, hatch, door; arcade; gate-, door-, hatch-, gang-way; lych-gate.

way, path etc. 627; thoroughfare; channel, passage, tube, pipe; waterpipe etc. 350; air-pipe etc. 351; vessel, tubule, canal, gut, fistula; adjutage, ajutage; chimney, smoke stack, flue, tap, funnel, gully, tunnel, main; mine, pit, adit, shaft; gallery.

alley, aisle, glade, lane, vista.

bore, caliber; pore; blind orifice.

por-ousness, -osity; sieve, cullender, colander; grater, shredder; cribble, riddle, screen; honeycomb.

apertion, perforation; piercing etc. *v.*; terebration, empalement, pertusion, puncture, acupuncture, penetration.

opener, corkscrew, can opener, key, master-key, *passe-partout*.

V. open, ope, gape, dehisce, yawn, bilge; fly open.

perforate, pierce, empierce, tap, bore, drill; mine etc. (*scoop out*) 252; tunnel; trans-pierce, -fix; enfilade, impale, spike, spear, gore, spit, stab, pink, puncture, lance, trepan, trephine, stick, prick, riddle, punch; stave in.

cut a passage through; make -way, — room- for.

un-cover, -close, -rip; lay —, cut —, rip —, throw-open.

Adj. open; perforated etc. *v.*; perforate; wide open, agape, ajar; un-closed, -stopped; oscitant, gaping, yawning; patent.

tubular, cannular, fistulous; per-vious, -meable; foraminous; vesi-, vas-cular; porous, follicular,

cribriform, honeycombed, infundibular, riddled; tubul-ous, -ated, piped.
opening etc. *v.*; aperient.
Int. *open sesame!*

261. Closure.—N. closure, occlusion, blockade; shutting up etc. *v.*; obstruction etc. (*hindrance*) 706; gag; embolism; contraction etc. 195; infarction; con-, ob-stipation; blind -alley, – corner; *cul-de-sac*, *caecum*; imperforation, -viousness etc. *adj.*; -meability; stopper etc. 263; *operculum*.
V. close, occlude, plug; block –, stop –, fill –, bung –, cork –, button –, stuff –, shut –, dam- up, obturate; blockade; obstruct etc. (*hinder*) 706; bar, bolt, stop, seal, plumb; choke, throttle; ram down, tamp, dam, cram; trap, clinch; put to –, shut- the door; batten down the hatches.
Adj. closed etc. *v.;* shut, operculated; unopened.
unpierced, imporous, caecal; imperforate, -vious, -meable; impenetrable; un-, im-passable; invious; path-, way-less; untrodden.
unventilated; air-, water-tight; hermetically sealed; tight, snug.

262. Perforator.—N. perforator, piercer, borer, auger, gimlet, stylet, drill, wimble, awl, bradawl, scoop, terrier, corkscrew, dibble, trocar, trepan, trephine, probe, bodkin, needle, stiletto, broach, reamer, rimer, warder, lancet; punch, -eon; spikebit, gouge; spear etc. (*weapon*) 727.

263. Stopper.—N. stopper, stopple; plug, cork, bung, spike, spill, stop-cock, tap; rammer; ram, -rod; piston; stopgap; wadding, stuffing, padding, stopping, dossil, pledget, tompion, tourniquet, obturator; wad.
cover etc. 223; valve, slide valve; vent-peg, spigot.
janitor, door –, gate- keeper, porter, commissionaire, *concierge*, warder, beadle, Cerberus, usher, guard, sentry, sentinel; ostiary.

264. Motion. [Successive change of place.*]—**N.** motion, movement, move; motivity, motility, going etc. *v.*; unrest.
stream, current, flow, flux, run, course, stir; conduction, evolution; kinematics.
step, rate, pace, tread, stride, gait, clip, port, footfall, cadence, carriage, velocity, angular velocity; progress, locomotion; journey etc. 266; voyage etc. 267; transit etc. 270.
restlessness etc. (*changeableness*) 149; mobility; movableness, motive power; laws of motion; mobilization.
V. be -in motion etc. *adj.*; move, go, hie, gang, budge, stir, pass, flit; hover -round, – about; shift, slide, slither, glide; roll, – on; flow, stream, run, drift, sweep along; wander etc. (*deviate*) 279; walk etc. 266; change –, shift- one's -place, – quarters; dodge; keep -going, – moving.
put –, set- in motion; move; impel etc. 276; propel etc. 284; render movable, mobilize.
Adj. moving etc. *v.*; in motion; motile, transitional; motory, motive; shifting, movable, mobile, mercurial, unquiet; restless etc. (*changeable*) 149; nomadic etc. 266; erratic etc. 279.
Adv. under way; on the -move, – wing, – tramp, – march.

*A thing cannot be said to *move* from one place to another, unless it passes in succession through every intermediate place; hence motion is only such a change of place as is *successive*. 'Rapid, swift, etc., as thought' are therefore incorrect expressions.

265. Quiescence.—N. rest; stillness etc. *adj.*; quiescence; stag-nation, -nancy; fixity, immobility, catalepsy; indisturbance; quietism.
quiet, tranquillity, calm; repose etc. 687; peace; dead calm, anticyclone; statue-like repose; silence etc. 403; not a -breath of air, – mouse stirring; sleep etc. (*inactivity*) 683.
pause, lull etc. (*cessation*) 142; stand, – still; standing still etc. *v.*; lock; dead -lock, – stop, – stand; full stop; fix; embargo.
resting-place; bivouac; home etc. (*abode*) 189; pillow etc. (*support*) 215; haven etc. (*refuge*) 666; goal etc. (*arrival*) 292.
V. be -quiescent etc. *adj.*; stand –, lie- still; keep quiet, repose, hold the breath.
remain, stay; stand, lie to, ride at anchor, remain *in situ*, mark time, tarry; bring –, heave –, lay- to; pull –, draw- up; hold, halt; stop, – short; rest, pause, anchor; cast –, come to an- anchor; rest on one's oars; repose on one's laurels, take breath; stop etc. (*discontinue*) 142.
stagnate, vegetate; *quieta non movere*; let -alone, – well alone; abide, rest and be thankful; keep within doors, stay at home, go to bed.
dwell etc. (*be present*) 186; settle etc. (*be located*) 184: alight etc. (*arrive*) 292.
stick, – fast; stand, – like a post; not stir a -peg, – step; be at a -stand etc. *n*.
quell, becalm, hush, stay, lull to sleep, lay an embargo on; put the brake on.
Adj. quiescent, still; motion-, move-less; fixed; stationary; at -rest, – a stand, – a stand-still, – anchor; stock-still; immotile; standing still etc. *v.*; sedentary, untravelled, stay-at-home; becalmed, stagnant, quiet; un-moved, -disturbed, -ruffled; calm, restful; cataleptic; immovable etc. (*stable*) 150; sleeping etc. (*inactive*) 683; silent etc. 403; still as -a statue; – a post, – a mouse, – death.
Adv. at a stand etc. *adj.*; *tout court*; at the halt.
Int. stop! stay! avast! halt! hold, – hard! whoa!
Phr. *requiescat in pace*.

266. Journey. [Locomotion by land.]—**N.** travel; traveling etc. *v.*; wayfaring, campaigning.
journey, excursion, expedition, tour, trip, grand tour, circuit, peregrination, discursion, ramble, pilgrimage, *trek*, course, ambulation, march, walk, hike, promenade, constitutional, stroll, saunter, tramp, jog-trot, turn, stalk, perambulation; noctambulation; somnambulism, sleep walking; outing, ride, drive, airing, jaunt.
equitation, horsemanship, riding, *manège*, ride and tie.

roving, vagrancy, pererration; marching and countermarching; nomadism; vagabond-ism, -age; gadding; flit, -ting; migration; e-, im-, de-, intermigration.

plan, itinerary, guide; hand-, road- book; Baedeker, Murray, Bradshaw, time table.

procession, parade, cavalcade, caravan, file, *cortège*, column.

[Organs and instruments of locomotion] vehicle etc. 272; locomotive etc. 271; legs, feet, pegs, pins, trotters.

traveler etc. 268.

V. travel, journey, course; tour; take —, go- a journey, take —, go out for- -a walk etc. *n.*; have a run; take the air.

flit, take wing; migrate, emigrate, *trek*; rove, prowl, roam, range, patrol, pace up and down, traverse; scour —, traverse- the country; peragrate; per-, circum-ambulate; nomadize, wander, ramble, stroll, saunter, hover, go one's rounds, straggle; gad; — about; expatiate.

walk, march, step, tread, pace, plod, wend; promenade; trudge, tramp; stalk, stride, straddle, strut, foot it, stump, bundle, bowl along, toddle; paddle; tread —, follow —, pursue- a path.

take horse, ride, drive, trot, amble, canter, prance, fisk, frisk, *caracoler*; gallop etc. (*move quickly*) 274; motor, cycle, taxi; go by -car, — train, — tram, — bus, — plane.

peg —, jog —, wag —, shuffle- on; stir one's stumps; bend one's -steps, — course; make —, find —, wend —, pick —, thread —, plough one's way; coast, slide, glide, skim, skate, ski; march in procession, file off, defile.

go —, repair —, resort —, hie —, betake oneself- to.

Adj. traveling etc. *v.*; ambulatory, itinerant, peripatetic, perambulatory, roving, rambling, gadding, discursive, vagrant, migratory, nomadic; circumforane-an, -ous; somnambular, nocti-, mundivagant; locomotive, automotive, self-moving.

way-faring, -worn; travel-stained.

Adv. on -foot, — horseback, — Shanks's mare; by the Marrowbone stage; *in transitu* etc. 270; *en route* etc. 282.

Int. come along!

267. Navigation. [Locomotion by water, or air.]—**N.** navigation; aquatics; boating, cruising, yachting; ship etc. 273; oar, scull, sweep, punt pole, paddle, — wheel, screw, propeller, stern wheel, sail, canvas.

natation, swimming; fin, flipper, fish's tail.

aeronautics, aviation, flying, winging, cruising, gliding, ballooning; blind —, instrument — flying, avigation, take-off.

flight, trip, run; solo —, nolo (pilotless) —, supersonic —, test — flight; air -lift, -drop; shuttle, reconnaisence, mission, dry run (coll.), search mission, combat flight, sortie, air raid, bombing mission; air — support, — cover, — umbrella; formation flying, maneuvers, aerobatics, stunt flying (coll.), diving, rolling, barrel roll, spin, tail spin, loop, buzzing.

landing, instrument —, crash — landing.

angle, center, axis, stability, load, pressure, torsion, torque, thrust, propulsion, jet propulsion, pitch, lift, dray, yaw, resistance, drift, flow, wash.

course, heading, altitude; air -route, -lane.

voyage, sail, cruise, passage, circumnavigation, *periplus*; head-, stern-, lee-way.

astro-, cosmo- nautics; space —, interplanetary — travel; space — exploration, — flight.

mariner, aeronaut etc. 269.

V. sail; put to sea etc. (*depart*) 293; take ship, get under way; spread -sail, — canvas; gather way, have way on; make —, carry- sail; plough the -waves, — deep, — main, — ocean; walk the waters.

navigate, warp, luff, scud, boom, kedge; drift, course, cruise, coast; hug the -shore, — land; circumnavigate.

ply the oar, row, paddle, pull, scull, punt, steam.

swim, float; buffet the waves, ride the storm, skim, *effleurer*, dive, wade.

fly, pilot, copilot, astronavigate, solo, take off, taxi, ascend, climb, stunt, spin, loop, roll, dive, buzz, land, descend, level off, bail out, parachute.

Adj. sailing etc. *v.*; seafaring, nautical, maritime, naval; sea-going, coasting; afloat; navigable, aquatic, natatory.

volitant, volant, aerostatic, aerial, aeronautic; alar, alate, pennate.

Adv. under -way, — sail, — canvas, — steam; on the wing.

268. Traveler.—**N.** traveler, wayfarer, voyager, itinerant, passenger.

tourist, excursionist, globe-trotter; explorer, adventurer, mountaineer, Alpine Club; peregrinator, wanderer, rover, straggler, rambler; bird of passage; gad-about, -ling; vagrant, scatterling, landloper, waifs and estrays, wastrel, stray; loafer; tramp, -er, hobo, beachcomber, vagabond, nomad, Bohemian, gipsy, Arab, Wandering Jew, Hadji, pilgrim, palmer; peripatetic; somnambulist; sleep walker, noctambulist; emigrant, fugitive, refugee, *émigré*.

runner, courier, King's messenger; Mercury, Iris, Ariel, comet.

pedestrian, walker, foot-passenger; cyclist; wheelman.

rider, horseman, equestrian, cavalier, jockey, rough rider, trainer, breaker, huntsman.

driver, coachman, whip, Jehu, charioteer, postilion, post-boy, carter, wagoner, drayman, truckman; cab-man, -driver; *voiturier*, *vetturino*, *condottiere*; engine-driver; stoker, fireman, guard, brakeman, conductor; chauffeur, automobilist, motorist, motor —, truck —, taxi- driver.

269. Mariner.—**N.** sailor, mariner, navigator, argonaut; sea-man, -farer, -faring man; yachtsman; tar, jack tar, salt, gob, sea-dog, shellback, able seaman, A.B.; man-of-war's man, bluejacket, marine, jolly; midshipman, middy, reefer; captain, commander, master mariner, skipper, mate; ship-, boat-, ferry-, water-, lighter-, barge-, longshoreman, hoveller; bargee, gondolier; oar-, -sman; rower; boat-, cock-swain; coxswain; steersman, helmsman, pilot; crew; lascar.

aerial navigator, navigator; aero-, astro-, cosmonaut; balloonist, Icarus, aviator, pilot, flyer, copilot, spaceman; fighter —, bomber — pilot; bombardier, gunner; meteorologist; stewardess, aviatrix, aviatress; ground crew, aeromechanic, aeronautical engineer; parachutist, paratrooper.

270. Transference.—N. transfer, -ence; trans-, e-location; displacement; *meta-stasis, -thesis*; removal; re-, a-motion; relegation; de-, asportation; extradition, conveyance, draft; carrying, carriage; convection, -duction, -tagion, infection; transfusion; transfer etc. (*of property*) 783.

transit, transition; passage, ferry, gestation; portage, porterage, carting, cartage; shoveling etc. *v.*; vect-ion, -ure, -itation; shipment, freight, wafture; trans-mission, -port, -portation, -umption, -plantation, -lation; shift-, dodg-ing; dispersion etc. 73; transposition etc. (*interchange*) 148; traction etc. 285.

[Thing transferred] drift, alluvium, detritus, *moraine*; gift, legacy, bequest, lease; freight, mails, cargo, luggage, baggage, goods.

V. trans-fer, -mit, -port, -place, -plant; convey, assign, carry, bear, fetch and carry; carry —, ferry-over; hand, pass, forward; shift; conduct, convoy, bring, fetch, reach.

send, delegate, consign, mail post, relegate, turn over to, pass the buck, deliver; ship, embark; waft; switch, shunt; transpose etc. (*interchange*) 148; displace etc. 185; throw etc. 284; drag etc. 285.

shovel, lade, dip, ladle, bale, decant, draft off, transfuse.

Adj. transferred etc. *v.*; drifted; movable, portable, -ative; conductive; contagious, infectious.

transferable, assignable, conveyable, devisable, negotiable, transmissible.

Adv. from -hand to hand, — pillar to post.

on —, by- the way; on the -road, — wing; as one goes; *in transitu, en route, chemin faisant, en passant*, in mid-progress.

271. Carrier.—N. carrier, porter, red cap, bearer, messenger, postman, tranter, conveyer; stevedore; coolie; conductor, locomotive, tractor, caterpillar tractor, motor.

beast of burden, cattle, horse steed, nag, palfrey, Arab, blood horse, thorough-bred, galloway, charger, courser, racer, hunter, jument, pony, filly, colt, foal, barb, roan, jade, hack, *bidet*, pad, cob, tit, punch, roadster, goer; race-, pack-, draft-, cart-, dray-, post-horse, mount; Shetland pony, sheltie; garran; jennet, genet, bayard, mare, stallion, gelding; stud.

Pegasus, Bucephalus, Rozinante.

ass, donkey, jackass, mule, hinny; sumpter -horse, — mule; reindeer; camel, dromedary, mehari, llama, elephant; carrier pigeon.

carriage etc. (*vehicle*) 272; ship etc. 273.

Adj. equine, asinine.

272. Vehicle.—N. vehicle, conveyance, carriage, car, caravan, van, furniture van, pantechnicon; wagon, wain, dray, cart, lorry.

carriole; sledge, sled, sleigh, bob-sleigh, toboggan, *luge*, truck, tram; limber, tumbrel, pontoon; barrow; wheel-, hand- -barrow, — cart, trolley; perambulator; Bath —, wheel —, sedan-chair, jinriksha, rickshaw; ekka; chaise; palankeen, -quin; litter, horse-litter, brancard, crate, hurdle, stretcher, ambulance; velocipede, hobby-horse, coaster, scooter, go-cart; cycle; bi-, tri-, quadri-cycle; tandem, safety; skate, roller —, ice — skate; sled, sleigh; ski, snow-shoe.

equipage, turn-out; coach, chariot; *quadriga*, chaise, phaëton, break, brake, mail-phaëton, wagonette, drag, curricle, tilbury, whisky, landau, *barouche*, victoria, brougham, clarence, calash, *calèche*, britzska, *arabu*, kibitka; berlin; sulky, *désobligeant*, sociable, *vis-à-vis, dormeuse*; jaunting —, outside- car; *tarantass*; runabout; shay.

post-chaise; diligence, stage; stage —, mail —, hackney —, glass- coach; stage-wagon; car, omnibus, bus, fly, *cabriolet*, cab, hansom, shofle, fourwheeler, growler, *droshki*, drosky.

dog-cart, trap, gig, whitechapel, buggy, four-in-hand, unicorn, random, tandem; shandredhan, *char-á-banc*.

automobile, motor-, auto-, touring-, racing-, cycle-, side-, steam-, electric- car; motor — cycle, — bike; motorized vehicle; bus, minibus; buggy, crate, tub, flivver, jalopy, wreck, clunker, dog, heap (all slang); coupe, coup, sedan, convertible, hard-top; camper, trailer, mobile home; limosine, landaulette, cabriolet, *coupé*, *voiturette*, runabout, electromobile, taxi, -cab.

train; passenger —, express —, freight —, subway —, special —, corridor —, parliamentary —, luggage —, goods- train, *train de luxe*; 1st-, 2nd-, 3rd- class- -train, — carriage, — compartment; Pullman —, sleeping-, club-, observation-, dining-, restaurant-car; mail-, luggage-, brake-van, coach, car, carriage; rolling stock; horse-box, cattle- truck.

273. Ship.—N. ship, vessel, sail; craft, bottom.

navy, marine, fleet, flotilla, squadron; shipping.

man of war etc. (*combatant*) 726; transport, tender, store-ship; merchant ship, merchantman; packet, liner; whaler, slaver, collier, coaster, tanker, freighter, freight steamer, cargo boat, lighter; fishing-, pilot- boat; trawler, drifter; cable ship; hulk; yacht; floating palace, ocean greyhound.

ship, bark, barque, brig, snow, hermaphrodite brig; brigantine, barquentine; schooner; topsail —, fore and aft —, three masted- schooner; *chasse-marée*; sloop, cutter, corvette, clipper, foist, yawl, dandy, ketch, smack, lugger, barge, hoy, cat-, -boat, buss; sail-er, -ing vessel, wind jammer; steamer, -boat, -ship; mail—, paddle —, screw —, stern-wheel- steamer; tug; train-ferry; line of steamers etc.

boat, pinnace, launch, motor-boat, picket-boat; hydroplane; life-, long-, jolly-, bum-, fly-, cock-, ferry-, canal- boat, dory, dugout, galliot; shallop, gig, funny, skiff, dingy, scow, cockleshell, wherry, coble, punt, cog, lerret; eight-, four-, pair- oar; randan; out- rigger; float, raft, pontoon; prame, ice-yacht.

state barge, bucentaur.

catamaran, coracle, gondola, carvel, caravel felucca, caique, canoe; trireme; galley, — foist; bilander, dogger, hooker, howker; argosy, carack; galliass, galleon; galliot, polacca, polacre, corsair, tartane, junk, lorcha, praam, proa, prahu, saick, sampan, xebec, dhow; dahabeah; nuggar, cayak, piroque; trireme.

submarine, submersible.

aircraft (*combatant*) etc. 726; flying machine, air mail, aero-, air-, mono-, bi-, tri-, hydro aeroplane, plane, cabin —, transport —, propeller — plane; *avion*, flying boat, glider; helicopter, rotor —, gyro-plane, whirlybird, autogyro, gyrodine; sea-, hydro-plane; amphibian; jet, — plane; turbo-, ram-, pulse-, subsonic —, supersonic —, strato-jet; rocket — plane, — ship,; space ship; war-, combat — plane; kamikaze, fleet, armada; trainer, fliight simulator; aerostat, dirigible, blimp (coll.), zeppelin; parachute, chute (coll.); kite.

rocket, flying —, ballistic —, guided — missile; projectile; rocket —, robot —, buzz-bomb; multistage —, step —, test — rocket; booster; satellite; flying saucer, unidentified flying object. (UFO).

nacelle, car, gondola, aileron; hangar, airport, landing field, airdrome; catwalk, controls, rudder, tail.

Adj. marine, maritime, naval, nautical, seafaring, sea-, ocean-going, sea-worthy.

aerial, aeronautical, air-worthy, flying etc. *n.*

Adv. afloat, aboard; on -board, — ship board, — board ship.

274. Velocity.—N. velocity, speed, celerity; swiftness etc. *adj.*; rapidity, eagle speed; expedition etc. (*activity*) 682; pernicity; acceleration; haste etc. 684.

spurt, rush, dash, race, steeplechase; smart —, lively —, swift etc. *adj.* —, rattling —, spanking —, strapping- -rate, — pace; round pace; flying, flight.

gallop, canter, trot, round trot, run, scamper; hand —, full- gallop; swoop.

lightning, light, electricity, wind, cannon-ball, rocket, arrow, dart, quicksilver; telegraph, express train; torrent; swallow flight.

eagle, antelope, courser, race-horse, gazelle, greyhound, hare, doe, squirrel.

Mercury, Ariel, Camilla, Harlequin.

[Measurement of velocity.] speedometer, log, -line, tachometer.

air speed, speed of sound, sonic —, subsonic —, supersonic —, ultrasonic —, hypersonic —, transonic — speed.

V. move quickly, trip, fisk; speed, hie, hasten, sprint, spurt, post, spank, scuttle; scud, -dle, scurry; scour, — the plain; scamper, sprint, dash, run, — like mad; fly, race, run a race, cut away, cut and run, shoot, tear, whisk, whiz, sweep, skim, brush; cut —, bowl- along; rush etc. (*be violent*) 173; dash -on, — off, — forward; bolt; trot, gallop, bound, flit, spring, dart, boom; march in -quick, — double-time; ride hard; et over the ground, scorch.

hurry etc. (*hasten*) 684; accelerate, put on; quicken; quicken —, mend- one's pace; clap spurs to one's horse; make-haste, — rapid strides, — forced marches, — the best of one's way; put one's best leg foremost, stir one's stumps, wing one's way, set off at a score; carry —, crowd- sail; go off like a shot, go ahead, gain ground; outstrip the wind, fly on the wings of the wind.

keep -up, — pace- with; outstrip etc. 303.

Adj. fast, speedy, swift, rapid, quick, fleet; nimble, agile, expeditious; express; active etc. 682; flying, galloping etc. *v.*; light- nimble-footed; winged; eagle-winged, mercurial, electric telegraphic; light-legged; light of heel; swift as -an arrow etc. *n.*; quick as -lightning etc. *n.*, — thought.*

Adv. swiftly etc. *adj.*; with -speed etc. *n.*; apace; at -a great rate, — full speed, — railway speed; full - drive, — gallop; post-haste, in full sail, tantivy; trippingly; instantaneously etc. 113; like a shot.

under press of -sale, — canvas, — sail and steam; *velis et remis*, on eagle's wing, in double quick time; with -rapid, — giant- strides; *à pas de géant*; in seven league boots; whip and spur; *ventre à terre*; as fast as one's -legs, — heels- will carry one; as fast on one can lay feet to the ground, at the top of one's speed; by leaps and bounds; with haste etc. 684; in- high — gear, — speed.

Phr. *vires acquirit eundo.*

*See note on *274.*

275. Slowness.—N. slowness etc. *adj.*; languor etc. (*inactivity*) 683; drawl; creeping etc. *v.*, lentor.

retardation; slackening etc. *v.*; delay etc. (*lateness*) 133; claudication.

jog-, dog-trot, walk; mincing steps; slow -march, — time.

slow -goer, — coach, — back; lingerer, loiterer, sluggard, tortoise, snail; dawdle etc. (*inactive*) 683.

V. move -slowly, etc. *adv.*; creep, crawl, lag, slug, walk, drawl, linger, loiter, saunter; plod, trudge, stump along, lumber; trail; drag; dawdle etc. (*be inactive*) 683; grovel, worm one's way, steal along; jog —, rub —, bundle- on; toddle, waddle, wabble, slug; traipse, slouch, shuffle, halt, hobble, limp, claudicate, shamble; flag, falter, totter, stagger; mince, step short; march in -slow time, — funeral procession; take one's time; hang fire etc. (*be late*) 133.

retard, relax; slacken, check, moderate, rein in, curb; reef; strike —, shorten —, take in- sail; put on the drag, apply the brake; clip the wings; reduce the speed, decelerate; slacken -speed, — one's pace, lose ground; back -water, — pedal, put the engines astern, throttle down.

Adj. slow, slack; tardy; dilatory etc. (*inactive*) 683; gentle, easy; leisurely; deliberate, gradual; insensible, imperceptible; languid, sluggish, apathetic, phlegmatic, slow paced, tardigrade, snail-like; creeping etc. *v.*

Adv. slowly etc. *adj.*; leisurely; *piano*, *adagio*; *largo*, *larghetto*; at half speed, under easy sail; at a -foot's, — snail's, — funeral- pace; slower than molasses in January; in slow time; with -mincing steps, — clipped wings; *haud passibus aequis*; in- low —, gear, — speed.

gradually etc. *adj.*; *gradatim*; by -degrees, — slow degrees, — inches, — little and little; step by step; inch by inch, bit by bit, little by little, *seriatim*; consecutively.

276. Impulse.—N. impulse, impulsion, impetus; momentum; push, pulsion, thrust, shove, jog, jolt, brunt, booming, boost, throw; explosion etc. (*violence*) 173; propulsion etc. 284, jet propulsion; firing, launching, projection, trajection.

percussion, concussion, collision, occursion, clash, encounter, cannon, *carambole*, appulse, shock, crash, bump; impact; *élan*; charge etc. (*attack*) 716; beating etc. (*punishment*) 972.

blow, dint, stroke, knock, tap, rap, slap, smack, pat, dab; fillip; slam, bang; hit, whack, thwack, clout; cuff etc. 972; squash, dowse, whap, swap, punch, thump, swipe, jab, pelt, kick, punce, calcitration; *ruade*; arietation; cut, thrust, lunge, yerk.

hammer, sledge-hammer, mall, maul, mallet, flail; ram, -mer; battering-ram, monkey, pile-driver, punch, bat, tamper, tamping iron; cudgel etc. (*weapon*) 727; axe etc. (*sharp*) 253.

[Science of mechanical forces] mechanics, dynamics etc.

V. give an -impetus etc. *n.*; impel, push; start, give a start to, set going; drive, urge, boom; thrust, prod, foin; cant; elbow, shoulder, jostle, justle, hustle, hurtle, shove, jog, jolt, bean, encounter; run –, bump –, butt- against; knock –, run- one's head against; impinge.

fire, launch, project, traject, propel, 284.

strike, knock, hit, bash, tap, rap, bat, slap, flap, dab, pat, thump, beat, bang, slam, dash; punch, thwack, whack; hit –, strike- hard; swap, batter, dowse, baste; pelt, patter, skelter, buffet, belabor, tamp; fetch one a blow, swat; poke at, pink, lunge, yerk; kick, calcitrate; butt; strike at etc. (*attack*) 716; whip etc. (*punish*) 972; propel etc. 284.

come –, enter- into collision; collide; foul; fall –, run- foul of.

throw etc.

Adj. impelling etc. *v.*; im-pulsive, -pellent; booming; dynamic, -al; impelled etc. *v.*

277. Recoil.—N. recoil; re-, retro-action; revulsion; rebound, *ricochet*; re-percussion, -calcitration; kick, *contre-coup*; springing back etc. *v.*; elasticity etc. 325; reflexion, reflex, reflux; reverberation etc. (*resonance*) 408; rebuff, repulse; return.

ducks and drakes; boomerang; spring; reactionist, reactionary.

V. recoil, resile, react; spring –, fly –, bound-back; rebound, reverberate, repercuss, recalcitrate, echo, *ricochet*.

Adj. recoiling etc. *v.*; re-fluent, -percussive, -calcitrant, -actionary; retroactive.

Adv. on the -recoil etc. *n.*

278. Direction.—N. direction, bearing, course, set, drift, tenor; tendency etc. 176; incidence; bending, trending etc. *v.*; dip, tack, aim, collimation; steer-ing, -age.

point of the compass, cardinal –, half –, quarter- points; North, East, South, West; N by E, ENE, NE by N, NE etc; rhumb, azimuth, line of collimation.

line, path, road, range, quarter, line of march; alignment; straight shot, bee-line.

course, bearing, heading, altitude, air -route, -lane, angle, center, axis, torsion, torque, pitch, lift, drift, flow, wash.

V. tend –, bend –, point- towards; conduct –, go- to; point -to, – at; bend, trend, verge, incline, dip, determine.

steer –, make- -for, – towards; aim –, level-at; take aim; keep –, hold- a course; be bound for; bend one's steps towards; direct –, steer –, bend –, shape- one's course; align –, align- one's march; go straight, – to the point; march -on, – on a point.

ascertain one's -direction etc. *n.*; *s'orienter*, see which way the wind blows; box the compass.

Adj. directed etc. *v.*, – towards; pointing towards etc. *v.*; bound for; aligned –, with; direct, straight; un-deviating, -swerving; straightforward; North, -ern, -erly, etc. *n.*

directable etc. *v.*

Adv. towards; on the -road, – high road- to; versus, to; hither, thither, whither; directly; straight, – forwards, – as an arrow; point blank; in a -direct, – straight- line -to, – for, – with; in a line with; full tilt at, as the crow flies.

before –, near –, close to –, against- the wind; windwards, in the wind's eye.

through, *via*, by way of; in all -directions, – manner of ways; *quaqua-versum*, from the four winds.

279. Deviation.—N. deviation; swerving etc. *v.*; obliquation, warp, refraction; flection, flexion; sweep; de-flection, -flexure; declination.

diversion, digression, departure from, aberration, drift, sheer; divergence etc. 291; zigzag; *détour* etc. (*circuit*) 629.

[Desultory motion] wandering etc. *v.*; vagrancy, evagation; by-paths and crooked ways.

[Motion sideways, oblique motion] sidling etc. *v.*; *échelon*, leeway; knight's move (at chess).

V. alter one's course, deviate, depart from, turn, trend; bend, curve, etc. 245; swerve, heel, bear off.

intervert; deflect; divert, – from its course; put on a new scent, shift, shunt, switch, wear, draw aside, crook, warp, short circuit.

stray, straggle; sidle, edge; diverge etc. 291; tralineate, digress, divagate, wander; wind, twist, meander, meander around Robin Hood's barn; veer, tack, sheer; turn -aside, – a corner, – away from; wheel, steer clear of; ramble, rove, drift; go -astray, – adrift; yaw, dodge; step aside, ease off, make way for, shy.

fly off at a tangent; glance off; turn, wheel –, face- about; turn –, face- to the right about; wabble etc. (*oscillate*) 314; go out of one's way etc. (*perform a circuit*) 629; lose one's way.

Adj. deviating etc. *v.*; aberrant, errant; ex-, dis-cursive; devious, desultory, loose; rambling; stray, erratic, vagrant, undirected; circuitous, indirect, zigzag; crab-like.

Adv. astray from, round about, wide of the mark; to the right about; all manner of ways; circuitously etc. 629.

obliquely, sideling, like the move of the knight on a chessboard.

280. Precession. [Going before.]—**N.** precession, leading, heading; precedence etc. 62; priority etc. 116; the lead, *le pas*; van etc. (*front*) 234; precursor etc. 64.

V. go -before, – ahead, – in the van, – in advance; precede, forerun; usher in, introduce, herald, head, take the lead; lead, – the way, – the dance; get –, have- the start; steal a march; get -before, – ahead, – in front of; outstrip etc. 303; take precedence etc. (*first in order*) 62.

Adj. foremost, first, leading etc. *v.*

Adv. in advance, before, ahead, in the van; fore-head-most; in front.

Phr. *seniores priores.*

281. Sequence. [Going after.]—**N.** sequence, run; coming after etc. (*order*) 63; (*time*) 117; following; pursuit etc. 622.

follower, attendant, satellite, shadow, dangler, train.

V. follow; pursue etc. 622; go –, fly- after.

attend, beset, dance attendance on, dog, be-dog; tread -in the steps of, – close upon; be –, go –, follow- in the -wake, – trail, – rear- of; trail, follow as a shadow, hang on the skirts of; tread –, follow- on the heels of, tag after.

lag, get behind.

Adj. following etc. *v.*

Adv. behind; in the -rear etc. 235, – train of, wake of; after etc. (*order*) 63, (*time*) 117.

282. Progression. [Motion forwards; progressive motion.]—**N.** progress, -ion, -iveness; advancing etc. *v.*; advance, -ment; ongoing; flood-tide, headway; march etc. 266; rise; improvement etc. 658.

V. advance; proceed, progress; get -on, – along, – over the ground; gain ground; jog –, rub –, wag- on; go with the stream; keep –, hold on- one's course; go –, move –, come –, get –, pass –, push –, press- -on, – forward, – forwards, – ahead; press onwards, step forward; make –, work –, carve –, push –, force –, edge –, elbow- one's way; make -progress, – head, – way, – headway, – advances, – strides, – rapid strides etc. (*velocity*) 274; go –, shoot- ahead; distance; make up leeway.

Adj. advancing etc. *v.*; pro-gressive, -fluent; advanced.

Adv. forward, onward; forth, on ahead, under way, *en route* for, on -one's way, – the way, – the road, – the high road- to; in -progress, – mid progress; *in transitu* etc. 270.

Phr. *vestigia nulla retrorsum.*

283. Regression. [Motion backwards.]—**N.** regress, -ion; retro-cession, -gression, -gradation, -action; *reculade*; retreat, withdrawal, retirement, remigration; recession etc. (*motion from*) 287; recess; crab-like motion.

re-fluence, -flux; backwater, regurgitation, ebb, return; resilience; reflexion (*recoil*) 277; *volte-face*.

counter -motion, – movement, – march; veering, tergiversation, recidivation, backsliding, fall, relapse; deterioration etc. 659.

turning point etc. (*reversion*) 145.

V. re-cede, -grade, -turn, -vert, -treat, -tire; retro-grade, -cede; back, – down, – out, crawl; withdraw; rebound etc. 277, go –, come –, turn –, hark –, draw –, fall –, get –, put –, run- back; lose ground; fall –, drop- astern; back water, put about; veer, – round; double, wheel, counter-march; ebb, regurgigate; *jib*, shrink, shy.

turn -tail, – round, – upon one's heel, – one's back upon; retrace one's steps, dance the back step; sound –, beat- a retreat; go home.

Adj. receding etc. *v.*; retro-grade, -gressive; regressive, -fluent, -flex, -cidivous, -silient; crab-like; reactionary etc. 277; counter-clockwise.

Adv. back, -wards; reflexively, to the right about; *à reculons*, *à rebours.*

Phr. *revenons à nos moutons*, as you were.

284. Propulsion. [Motion given to an object situated in front.]—**N.** pro-pulsion, -jection; *vis a tergo*; push etc. (*impulse*) 276; e-, jaculation; ejection etc. 297; throw, fling, toss, shot, discharge, shy.

[Science of propulsion] steam –, gas –, diesel –, jet –, rocket – propulsion, gunnery, ballistics, archery.

missile, projectile, ball, *discus*, javelin, hammer, quoit, brickbat, shot, bullet; arrow, shaft, gun etc. (*arms*) 727.

shooter, shot; gunner, gun-layer; archer, toxophilite; bow-, rifle-, marks- man; good –, crack- shot; sharpshooter etc. (*combatant*) 726.

V. propel, project, throw, fling, cast, pitch, chuck, toss, jerk, heave, shy, hurl; flirt, fillip.

dart, lance, tilt; e-, jaculate; fulminate, bolt, drive, sling, pitchfork.

send; send –, let –, fire- off; discharge, shoot; launch, send forth, let fly; dash.

put –, set- in motion; set agoing, start; give -a start, – an impulse- to; push, impel etc. 276; trundle etc. (*set in rotation*) 312; expel etc. 297.

carry one off one's legs; put to flight.

Adj. propelled etc. *v.*; propelling etc. *v.*; propulsive, -jectile.

285. Traction. [Motion given to an object situated behind.]—**N.** traction; drawing etc. *v.*; draft, pull, tug, haul; rake; 'a long pull, a strong pull and a pull all together;' towage, haulage.

V. draw, pull, haul, lug, rake, drag, draggle, tug, tow, trail, trawl, train; take in tow.

wrench, jerk, twitch.

Adj. drawing etc. *v.*; tractive, tractile; ductile, pulling, hauling, tugging, towing.

286. Approach. Motion towards.]—**N.** approach, approximation, appropinquation; access; appulse; afflux, -ion; advent etc. (*approach of time*) 121; pursuit etc. 622; convergence etc. 290.

V. approach, approximate; near; get –, go –, draw- near; come, – near, – to close quarters; move –, set in- towards; drift; make up to; gain upon; pursue etc. 622; tread on the heels of; bear up; make the land; hug the -shore, – land.

Adj. approaching etc. *v.*; approximative; convergent; affluent; impending, imminent etc. (*destined*) 152.

Adv. on the road.

Int. come hither! approach! here! come! come near!

287. Recession. [Motion from.]—**N.** recession, retirement, withdrawal; retreat; retrocession etc. 283; departure etc. 293; recoil etc. 277; flight etc. (*avoidance*) 623.

V. recede, go, move from, retire, ebb, withdraw, shrink; come –, move –, go –, get –, drift- away; depart etc. 293; retreat etc. 283; move –, stand –, sheer- off; swerve from; fall back, stand aside; run away etc. (*avoid*) 623.

remove, shunt, side track, switch off.

Adj. receding etc. *v.*

288. Attraction. [Motion towards, actively.]—**N.** attract-ion, -iveness; pull; drawing to, pulling towards, adduction, magnetism, gravity, attraction of gravitation; lure, bait, decoy.

lode-stone, -star; magnet, siderite, magnetite.

V. attract; draw –, pull –, drag- towards; adduce.

lure, bait, decoy.

Adj. attracting etc. *v.*; attrahent, attractive, adducent, adductive, alluring.

289. Repulsion. [Motion from, actively.]—**N.** repulsion; driving from etc. *v.*; repulse; abduction.

V. repel; push –, drive – etc. 276; from; chase, dispel; retrude; abduce, abduct; send away, repulse, dismiss.

keep at arm's length, turn one's back upon, give the cold shoulder; send packing; send -off, – away- with a flea in one's ear, – about one's business.

Adj. repelling etc. *v.*; repellant, repulsive; abducent, abductive.

290. Convergence. [Motion nearer to.]—**N.** con-vergence, -fluence, -course, -flux, -gress, -currence, -centration; appulse, meeting; corradiation.

assemblage etc. 72; resort etc. (*focus*) 74; asymptote.

V. converge, concur; come together, unite, meet, fall in with; close -with, – in upon; center -round, – in; enter in; pour in.

gather together, unite, concentrate, bring into a focus.

Adj. converging etc. *v.*; con-vergent, -fluent, -current; centripetal; asymptotical.

291. Divergence. [Motion further off.]—**N.** diverg-ence, -ency; divarication, ramification, radiation; separation etc. (*disjunction*) 44; dispersion etc. 73; deviation etc. 279; aberration, declination.

V. diverge, divaricate, radiate; ramify; branch –, glance –, file- off; fly off, – at a tangent; spread, scatter, disperse etc. 73; deviate etc. 279; part etc. (*separate*) 44; splay apart.

Adj. diverging etc. *v.*; divergent, radiant, centrifugal; aberrant.

292. Arrival. [Terminal motion at.]—**N.** arrival, advent; landing; de-, disem-barkation; reception, welcome, *vin d'honneur*.

home, goal, bourn; landing-place, -stage; resting –, stopping -place; destination, harbor, haven, port; terminal, terminus, railway station, depot, airport; halt, halting -place, – ground; anchorage etc. (*refuge*) 666.

return, recursion, remigration; meeting; ren-, encounter.

completion etc. 729.

V. arrive; get to, come to; come; reach, attain; come up, – with, – to; overtake; make, fetch; complete etc. 729; join, rejoin.

light, alight, dismount; land, go ashore; debark, disembark; put -in, – into; visit, cast anchor, pitch one's tent; sit down etc. (*be located*) 184; get to one's journey's end; make the land; be in at the death; come –, get- -back, – home; return; come in etc. (*ingress*) 294; make one's appearance etc. (*appear*) 446; drop in; detrain; outspan.

come to hand; come -at, – across; hit; come –, light –, pop –, bounce –, plump –, burst –, pitch- upon; meet; en- ren-counter; come in contact.

Adj. arriving etc. *v.*; homewardbound; terminal.

Adv. here, hither.

Int. welcome! hail! all hail! good- day, – morrow; greetings! hullo! well!

293. Departure. [Initial motion from.]—**N.** departure, decession, decampment; embarkation; take-off; outset, start; removal; exit etc. (*egress*) 295; exodus, Hejira, flight.

leave-taking, *congé*, valediction, valedictory, adieu, farewell, good-bye, stirrup-cup.

starting -point, – post; point –, place- of -departure, – embarkation; port of embarkation.

V. depart; go, – away; take one's departure, set out; set –, march –, put –, start –, be –, move –, get –, whip –, pack –, go –, take oneself- off; start, issue, march out, debouch; go –, sally- forth; sally, set forward; be gone.

leave a place, quit, vacate, evacuate, abandon; go off the stage, make ones' exit; retire, withdraw, remove; go -one's way, – along, – from home; take -flight, – wing; spring, fly, flit, wing one's flight; fly –, whip- away; take off, hop off; embark; go -on board, – aboard; set sail; put –, go- to sea; sail, take ship; hoist blue Peter; get under way, weigh anchor; strike tents, break camp, decamp; walk one's chalks, make tracks, cut one's stick; cut and run; take leave; say –, bid- -good-bye etc. *n.*; disappear etc. 449; abscond etc. (*avoid*) 623; entrain, embus, emplane; saddle –, harness –, hitch- up; inspan.

Adj. departing etc. *v.*; valedictory; outward bound.

Adv. whence, hence, thence; with a foot in the stirrup; on the -wing, – move.

Int. begone! etc. (*ejection*) 297; to horse! all aboard! farewell! adieu! good-bye, – day! *au revoir! auf wiedersehen!* fare you well! so long! God -bless you, – speed! *bon vayage!*

294. Ingress. [Motion into.]—**N.** ingress; entrance, entry; introgression; influx; intrusion, inroad, incursion, invasion, irruption; pene-, interpene- tration; illapse, import, importation, infiltration; immigration; admission etc. (*reception*) 296; insinuation etc. (*interjacence*) 228; insertion etc. 300.

inlet; way in; mouth, door etc. (*opening*) 260; path etc. (*way*) 627; conduit etc. 350; immigrant, visitor, incomer, newcomer, colonist.

V. have the *entrée*; enter; go –, come –, pour –, flow –, creep –, slip –, pop –, break –, burst- -into, – in; set foot on; burst –, break-in upon; invade, intrude, butt in, horn in, crash; insinuate itself; inter-, penetrate; infiltrate; find one's way –, wriggle –, worm oneself- into.

give entrance to etc. (*receive*) 296; insert etc. 300.

Adj. incoming, ingressive etc. *n.*; inward bound.
Adv. inward.

295. Egress. [Motion out of.]—**N.** egress, exit, issue; emer-sion, -gence; disemboguement; outbreak, -burst; e-, pro-ruption; emanation; evacuation; ex, trans-udation; extravasation, perspiration, sweating, leakage, percolation, distillation, oozing; gush etc. (*water in motion*) 348; outpour, -ing; effluence, effusion; efflux, -ion; drain; dribbling etc. *v.*; defluxion; drainage; outcome, -put; discharge etc. (*excretion*) 299.

export; expatriation; e-, re-migration; *débouche*; exodus etc. (*departure*) 293; emigrant, migrant, *émigré*, colonist.

outlet, vent, spout, tap, sluice, floodgate; pore; vomitory, out-gate, sally-port; way out; mouth, door etc. (*opening*) 260; path etc. (*way*) 627; conduit etc. 350; air-pipe etc. 351.

V. emerge, emanate, issue; go –, come –, move –, pass –, pour –, flow- out of; pass off, evacuate; migrate.

ex-, trans-ude; leak; run, – out, – through; per-, trans-colate; seep; strain, distil; perspire, sweat, drain, ooze; filter, filtrate; dribble, gush, spout, flow out; well, – out; pour, trickle etc. (*water in motion*) 348; effuse, extravasate, disembogue, discharge itself, debouch; come –, break- forth; burst- out, – through; find vent, escape etc. 671.

Adj. effused etc. *v.*; outgoing, outward bound.
Adv. outward.

296. Reception. [Motion into, actively.]—**N.** reception; admission, admittance, *entrée*, importation; initiation; intro-duction, -mission, -ception; immission, ingestion, imbibition, absorption, ingurgitation, inhalation; suction, sucking; eating, drinking etc. (*food*) 298; insertion etc. 300; interjection etc. 228.

V. give -entrance to, – admittance to, – the *entrée*, intro-duce, -mit; usher, admit, receive, import, initiate, bring in, open the door to, throw open, ingest, absorb, imbibe, inhale, infiltrate; let –, take –, suck- in; re-admit, -sorb, -absorb; snuff up; swallow, ingurgitate; enfulf, engorge; gulp; eat, drink etc. (*food*) 298.

Adj. admit-ting etc. *v.*, -ted etc. *v.*; admissible; absorbent; introductory, introceptive, intromittent, initiatory.

297. Ejection. [Motion out of, actively.]—**N.** ejection, emission, effusion, rejection, expulsion, eviction, extrusion, trajection; discharge.

egestion, evacuation, vomition, disgorgement, voidance, eruption, eruptiveness; ruc-, eruc-tation, blood-letting, venesection, phlebotomy, paracentesis; tapping, drainage; clear-ance, -age, voidance; vomiting, excretion etc. 299.

deportation; banishment etc. (*punishment*) 972; rogue's march; relegation, extradition; dislodgment.

V. give -exit, – vent- to; let –, give –, pour –, send- out; des-, dis-patch; exhale, excern, excrete, disembogue, secrete, secern; extravasate, shed, void, evacuate, egest, emit; open the -sluices, – floodgates; turn on the tap; extrude, detrude; effuse, spend, expend; pour forth; squirt, spirt, spill, slop; perspire etc. (*exude*) 295; breathe, blow etc. (*wind*) 349.

tap, draw off; bale –, lade- out; let blood, broach.

eject, reject; expel, discard; cut, send to Coventry, boycott, ostracize; *chasser*; banish etc. (*punish*) 972; throw etc. 284 -out, – up, – off, – away, – aside; push etc. 276 -out, – off, – away, – aside; shovel –, sweep- -out, – away; brush –, whisk –, turn –, send- -off, – away; discharge; send –, turn –, cast- adrift; turn –, bundle- out; throw overboard; give the sack to; send -packing, – about one's business, – to the right about; strike off the roll etc. (*abrogate*) 756; turn out- neck and heels, – head and shoulders, – neck and crop; pack off; send away with a flea in the ear; send to Jericho; bow out, show the door to, dismiss, fire, sack.

turn out of -doors, – house and home; evict, oust; exorcise, un-house, -kennel; dislodge; un-, dis-people; depopulate; relegate, deport.

empty; drain, – to the dregs; sweep off; clear, – off, – out, – away; such, draw off, extract; clean out, make a clean sweep of, clear decks, purge.

em-, dis-, disem-bowel, eviscerate, gut, unearth, root -out, – up; averruncate; weed –, get out; eliminate, get rid of, do away with, shake off; exenterate.

vomit, spew, puke, keck, retch; belch, – out, eruct, eructate; cast –, bring- up; disgorge; expectorate, salivate, clear the throat, hawk, spit, sputter, splutter, slobber, drool, drivel, slaver, slabber.

unpack, unlade, unload, unship; break bulk.
be let out; ooze etc. (*emerge*) 295.

Adj. emitt-ing, -ed etc. *v.*

begone! get you gone! get –, go- away, – along, – along with you! go your way! away, – with! off with you! go, – about your business! be off! avaunt! aroynt! get out!

298. Food. [Eating.]—**N.** eating etc. *v.*; deglutition, gulp, epulation, mastication, manducation, rumination, gastronomy, gastrology; panto-, hippo-, ichthyo-phagy etc.; gluttony etc. 957; carnivorousness, vegetarianism.

mouth, jaws, mandible, mazard, chops.

drinking etc. *v.*; potation, draught, libation; carousal etc. (*amusement*) 840; drunkenness etc. 959.

food, *pabulum*; aliment, nourishment, nutriment; susten-ance, -tation; nurture, subsistence, provender, feed, fodder, provision, ration, keep, commons, board; commissariat etc. (*provision*) 637; prey, forage, pasture, pasturage; fare, cheer; diet, -ary; regimen; belly timber, staff of life; bread, -and cheese; proteins, carbohydrates, vitamines.

comestibles, eatables, victuals, edibles, *ingesta*; grub, prog, tack, hard tack, meat; bread, -stuffs; cereals; viands, cates, delicacy, dainty, creature comforts, contents of the larder, flesh-pots; festal board; ambrosia; good -cheer, – living.

hors-d'oeuvre; soup, pottage, *potage*, broth,

bouillon, *consommé*, *purée*, *borsch*, stock, skilly, gumbo; fish, – cakes, – pie; joint, *rôti*, *pièce de résistance*, *relevé*, hash, *réchauffé*, stew, *ragoût*, fricassee, mince, *salim*, *goulash*, *bouillabaisse*, *remove*, *entrée*, *croquette*, *rissole*, sausage, curry, bubble and squeak; haggis, collops, giblets; poultry, game etc.; biscuit, bun, scone, rusk, pancake, pie, pastry, pasty, patty, *patisseria*, tart, turnover, *vol-au-vent*, *soufflé*, dumpling, pudding, duff, *compote*, fritters, cake, napoleon, *blancmange*, custard, jelly, jam, sweets etc. 396; *entremet*; oatmeal, porridge, hasty pudding, gruel; eggs, omelet, cheese, matzoon, savory; vegetable, salad, *mayonnaise*, fruit; sauce, condiment etc. 393; kickshaws.

table, *cuisine*, bill of fare, *menu*, *table d'hôte*, ordinary, *à la carte*; cover.

meal, repast, feed, spread; mess; dish, plate, course, side dish; regale; regale-, refresh-, entertain-ment; refection, collation, picnic, feast, banquet, junket; breakfast; lunch, -eon, *déjeuner*, bever, tiffin, tea, dinner, supper, snack, whet, bait, dessert; pot-luck, *table d'hôte*, *déjeuner à la fourchette*; hearty –, square –, substantial –, full- - meal; blow out; light refreshment; pemmican.

mouthful, bolus, gobbet, tit-bit, morsel, sop, sippet.

drink, beverage, liquor, broth, soup; potion, dram, draft, drench, swill; nip, peg, sip, sup, gulp.

wine, champagne, spirits, *liqueur* beer, porter, stout, ale, malt liquor, julep, Sir John Barleycorn, stingo, heavy wet, bitter, lager- beer, cider; grog, toddy, flip, purl, punch, negus, cup, bishop, posset, wassail; bitters, *apéritif*, high-ball, cocktail; whisky, rum, absinthe; gin etc. (*intoxicating liquor*) 959; coffee, chocolate, cocoa, tea, *maté*, the cup that cheers but not inebriates.

eating-house etc. 189.

V. eat, feed, fare, devour, swallow, take; gulp, bolt, snap; fall to; despatch, dispatch; discuss; take –, get –, gulp-down; lay –, tuck- in; lick, pick, peck; gormandize etc. 957; bite, champ, munch, cranch, craunch, crunch, chew, masticate, nibble, gnaw, mumble.

live on; feed –, batten –, fatten –, feast- upon; browse, graze, crop, regale; carouse etc. (*make merry*) 840; eat heartily, do justice to, play a good knife and fork, banquet.

break -bread, – one's fast; breakfast; lunch, dine, take tea, sup.

drink, – in, – up, – one's fill; quaff, sip, sup; suck, – up; lap; swig; swill, tipple etc. (*be drunken*) 959; empty one's glass, drain the cup; toss -off, – one's glass; wash down, crack a bottle, wet one's whistle.

cater, purvey etc. 637.

Adj. eatable, edible, esculent, comestible, alimentary; cereal, cibarious; dietetic; culinary; nutri-tive, -tious; succulent; drinkable, pot-able, -ulent; bibulous.

omn-, carn-, herb-, frug-, gran-, gramin-, phytivorous; ichthyophagous.

prandial.

299. Excretion.—N. excretion, discharge, emanation; ejection etc. 297; exhalation, exudation, extrusion, secretion, effusion, extravasation, *ecchymosis*, evacuation, cacation, defecation, dysentery, dejection, *feces*, excrement; perspiration, sweat; sub-, exud-ation; *diaphoresis*; sewage.

saliva, spittle, rheum; ptyalism, salivation, catarrh, distemper; diarrhea; *ejecta*, *egesta*, *sputum*, *sputa*; *excreta*; lava; *exuviae* etc. (*uncleanness*) 653.

hemorrhage, bleeding; catamenia, menses; outpouring etc. (*egress*) 295; leucorrhea.

V. excrete etc. (*eject*) 297; emanate etc. (*come out*) 295.

Adj. excretory, fecal, secretory; ejective, eliminant.

300. Insertion. [Forcible ingress.]—**N.** insertion, implantation, intercalation, embolism, introduction; interpolation, insinuation etc. (*intervention*) 228; planting etc. *v.*; injection, inoculation, importation, infusion; forcible -ingress etc. 294; immersion; submersion, -gence; dip, plunge; bath etc. (*water*) 337; interment etc. 363.

V. insert; intro-duce, -mit; put –, run- into; import; inject; interject etc. 228; infuse, instil, inoculate, impregnate, imbue, imbrue.

graft, ingraft, bud, plant, implant; dovetail.

obtrude; thrust –, stick –, ram –, stuff –, tuck –, press –, drive –, pop –, whip –, drop –, put- in; impact; empierce etc. (*make a hole*) 260.

embed; immerse, immerge, merge; bathe, soak etc. (*water*) 337; dip, plunge etc. 310.

bury etc. (*inter*) 363.

insert etc. -itself; plunge *in medias res*.

Adj. inserted etc. *v.*

301. Extraction. [Forcible egress.]—**N.** extraction; extracting etc. *v.*; removal, elimination, extrication, eradication, evolution.

evulsion, avulsion; wrench; expression, squeezing; extirpation, extermination; ejection etc. 297; export etc. (*egress*) 295; distillation.

extractor, corkscrew, forceps, pliers.

V. extract, draw, pit; take –, draw –, pull –, tear –, pluck –, pick –, get- out; wring from, wrench; extort; root –, weed –, grub –, rake- up, – out; eradicate; pull –, pluck- up by the roots; averruncate; unroot; uproot, pull up, extirpate, dredge.

remove; educe, elicit; evolve, extricate; eliminate etc. (*eject*) 297; eviscerate etc. 297.

express, squeeze –, press- out; distil.

Adj. extracted etc. *v.*

302. Passage. [Motion through.]—**N.** passage, transmission; permeation; pene-, interpene-tration; transudation, infiltration; *osmosis*, osmose, endos-, exos-mose; intercurrence; ingress etc. 294; egress etc. 295; path etc. 627; conduit etc. 350; opening etc. 260; journey etc. 266; voyage etc. 267.

V. pass, – through; perforate etc. (*hole*) 260; penetrate, permeate, thread, thrid, enfilade; go - through, – across; go –, pass- over; cut across; ford, cross; pass and repass, work; make –, thread –, worm –, force- one's way; make –, force- a passage; cut one's way through; find its -way, –

vent; transmit, make way, clear the course; traverse, go over the ground.

Adj. passing etc. *v.*; intercurrent; osmotic etc. *n.*

Adv. *en passant* etc. (*transit*) 270.

303. Overstep. [Motion beyond.]—**N.** transcursion, -ilience, -gression; infraction, intrusion; trespass; encroach-, infringe-ment; extravagation, transcendence; redundance etc. 641; ingress etc. 294.

V. transgress, surpass, pass; go- beyond, – by; show in –, come to the- front; shoot ahead of; steal a march –, gain- upon.

over-step, -pass, -reach, -go, -ride- -leap, -jump, -skip, -lap, -shoot the mark; out-strip, -leap, -jump, -go, -step, -run, -ride, -rival, -do; beat, – hollow; distance; leave in the -lurch, – rear; go one better, throw into the shade; exceed, transcend, surmount; soar etc. (*rise*) 305.

encroach, intrude, trespass, infringe, invade, trench upon, intrench on; strain; stretch – strain- a point; pass the Rubicon.

Adj. surpassing etc. *v.*

Adv. beyond the mark, ahead.

304. Shortcoming. [Motion short of.]—**N.** shortcoming, failure; delinquency; falling short etc. *v.*, de fault, -falcation; leeway; labor in vain, no go.

incompleteness etc. 53; imperfection etc. 651; insufficiency etc. 640; noncompletion etc. 730; failure etc. 732.

V. come –, fall –, stop- short, – short of; not reach; want; keep within -bounds, – the mark, – compass.

break down, stick in the mud, collapse, come to nothing; fall -through, – to the ground, – down; cave in, end in smoke, fizzle out, miss the mark, fail; lose ground, miss stays, slump.

Adj. unreached; deficient; short, – of; *minus*; out of depth; perfunctory etc. (*neglect*) 460.

Adv. within -the mark, – compass, – bounds; behindhand; *re infectâ*; to no purpose; far from it.

Phr. the bubble burst.

305. Ascent. [Motion upwards.]—**N.** ascent, ascension; rising etc. *v.*; rise, upgrowth; leap etc. 309; acclivity, hill etc. 217; stair, stairs, stair-case, -way, flight of -steps, – stairs; ladder, companion, – way; lift, elevator etc. 307.

rocket, lark; sky-rocket, -lark; Alpine Club.

V. ascend, rise, mount, arise, uprise; go –, get –, work one's way –, start –, spring –, shoot- up; zoom; aspire.

climb, clamber, ramp, scramble, swarm, *escalade*, surmount; scale, – the heights.

tower, soar, hover, spire, plane, swim, float, surge; leap etc. 309.

Adj. rising etc. *v.*; scandent, buoyant; supernatant, -fluitant; excelsior.

Adv. uphill.

306. Descent. [Motion downwards.]—**N.** descent, descension, declension, declination; fall; falling etc. *v.*; drop, cadence; subsidence, lapse; come-down, downfall, tumble, slip, tilt, trip, lurch; cropper, *culbute*; titubation, stumble; fate of Icarus; dive, nose-dive, *volpané*.

avalanche, *débâcle*, landslip, slide.

V. descend; go –, drop –, come-down; fall, gravitate, drop, slip, slide, glissade, dive, plunge, settle; decline, slump, set, sink, droop, come down a peg.

dismount, alight, light, get down; swoop; stoop etc. 308; fall prostrate, precipitate oneself; let fall etc. 308.

tumble, trip, stumble, titubate, lurch, pitch, swag, topple; topple –, tumble- -down, – over; tilt, sprawl, plump down, come a cropper.

Adj. descending etc. *v.*; descendent, declivitous; downcast; decur-rent, sive; labent, deciduous; nodding to its fall.

Adv. down, -hill, -wards.

307. Elevation.—**N.** elevation; raising etc. *v.*; erection, lift; sublevation, upheaval; sublimation, exaltation; prominence etc. (*convexity*) 250.

lever etc. 633; crane, derrick, windlass, capstan, winch, dredger, lift, elevator, escalator, dumb waiter.

V. heighten, elevate, raise, lift, erect; set –, stick –, perch –, perk –, tilt- up; rear, hoist, heave; up-lift, -raise, -rear, -bear, -cast, -hoist, heave; buoy, weigh, mount, give a lift; exalt, sublimate; place –, set- on a pedestal.

take –, drag –, fish- up; dredge.

stand –, rise –, get –, jump- up; spring to one's feet; hold -oneself, – one's head- up; draw oneself up to his full height.

Adj. elevated etc. *v.*; standing up; stilted, attollent, rampant.

Adv. on -stilts, – the shoulders of, – one's legs, – one's hind legs.

308. Depression.—**N.** lowering etc. *v.*; depression; dip etc. (*concavity*) 252; abasement; detrusion; reduction.

over-throw, -set, -turn; upset; prostration, subversion, precipitation.

bow; courtesy, curtsy; genuflexion, *kowtow*, obeisance, *salaam*.

V. depress, lower; let –, take- -down, – down a peg; cast; let -drop, – fall; sink, debase, bring low, abase, slash, reduce, detrude, pitch, precipitate.

over-throw, -turn, -set; upset, subvert, prostrate, level, fell; cast –, take –, throw –, fling –, dash –, pull –, cut –, knock –, hew- down; raze, – to the ground; humiliate, trample in the dust, pull about one's ears.

sit, – down; couch, squat, crouch, stoop, bend, bow, courtsey, curtsy; bob, duck, dip, genuflect, kneel; *kowtow*, *salaam*, make obeisance, prostrate oneself; bend, bow- the -head, – knee; incline the head; bow down; cower; recline etc. (*be horizontal*) 213.

Adj. depressed etc. *v.*; at a low ebb; prostrate etc. (*horizontal*) 213; detrusive.

309. Leap.—**N.** leap, jump, hop, spring, bound, vault, saltation.

dance, caper, gambol; curvet, caracole; *gambade, -bado*; capriole, demivolt; buck, – jump; hop, skip and jump.

kangaroo, jerboa, chamois, goat, frog, grasshopper, flea.

V. leap; jump -up, – over the moon; hop, spring, bound, vault, ramp, cut capers, gambol, trip, skip, dance, caper, curvet, *caracole*; foot it, bob, bounce, flounce, start, frisk etc. (*amusement*) 840; jump about etc. (*agitation*) 315; trip it on the light fantastic toe, dance oneself off one's legs.

Adj. leaping etc. *v.*; saltatory, frisky.

Adv. on the light fantastic toe.

310. Plunge.—N. plunge, dip, dive, header; ducking etc. *v.*; submergence, immersion, diver.

V. plunge, dip, souse, duck; dive, plump; take a -plunge, – header, make a plunge; bathe etc. (*water*) 337.

sub-merge, -merse; immerse, douse, sink, engulf, send to -the bottom, – Davy Jones' locker.

get out of one's depth; go -to the bottom, – down like a stone; founder, welter, wallow.

311. Circuition. [Curvilinear motion.]—**N.** circuition, circulation; turn, curvet; excursion; circum-vention, -navigation, -ambulation; north-west passage; ambit, gyre, lap, circuit etc. 629.

turning etc. *v.*; wrench; evolution; coil, helix, spiral; corkscrew.

V. turn, bend, wheel; go –, put- about; heel; go –, turn -round, – to the right about; turn on one's heel; make –, describe- a -circle, – complete circle; encircle; go –, pass- through -180°, – 360°.

circum-navigate, -aviate, -ambulate, -vent; put a girdle round the earth, go the round, make the round of.

turn –, round- a corner; double a point.

wind, circulate, meander; whisk, twirl; twist etc. (*convolution*) 248; make a *détour* etc. (*circuit*) 629.

Adj. turning etc. *v.*; circuitous; circumforaneous, -fluent; devious, roundabout, circumambient, -flex, -navigable.

Adv. round about.

312. Rotation. [Motion in a continued circle.]—**N.** rotation, revolution, gyration, circulation, roll; circum-rotation, -volution, -gyration; volutation, circination, turbination, *pirouette*, convolution.

verticity; whir, whirl, swirl, eddy, vortex, whirlpool, gurge; cyclone, tornado; surge; *vertigo*, dizzy round; Maelstrom, Charybdis; Ixion; wheel of Fortune.

wheel, screw, propeller, whirligig, rolling stone, windmill; top, teetotum, merry-go-round; roller; cog-, fly-wheel, spit; jack; caster.

axis, axle, spindle, spool, pivot, pin, hinge, pole, swivel, gimbals, arbor, bobbin, mandrel, shaft.

[Science of rotatory motion] trochilics, gyrostatics.

V. rotate; roll, – along; revolve, spin; turn, – round; circumvolve; circulate; gyre, gyrate, wheel, whirl, swirl, twirl, trundle, troll, bowl; slew round.

roll up, furl; wallow, welter; box the compass; spin like a -top, – teetotum.

Adj. rotating etc. *v.*; rota-tory, -ry; circumrotatory, trochilic, vertiginous, gyratory; vortic-al, -ose.

Adv. head over heels, round and round, like a horse in a mill.

313. Evolution. [Motion in a reverse circle.]—**N.** evolution, unfolding, development; eversion etc. (*inversion*) 218.

V. evolve; un-fold, -roll, -wind, -coil, -twist, -furl, -twine, -ravel; disentangle; develop.

Adj. evolving etc. *v.*; evolved etc. *v.*

314. Oscillation. [Reciprocating motion, motion to and fro.]—**N.** oscillation; vibration, libration; motion of a pendulum; nutation; undulation; pulsation; pulse; throb; seismic disturbance.

alternation; coming and going etc. *v.*; ebb and flow, flux and reflux, ups and downs; wave, vibratiuncle, swing, beat, shake, wag, see-saw, dance, lurch, dodge; fluctuation; vacillation etc. (*irresolution*) 605.

seismometer, vibroscope, seismograph.

V. oscillate; vi-, li-brate; alternate, undulate, wave; sway, rock, swing; pulsate, beat; wag, -gle; nod, bob, courtesy, curtsy; tick; play; chatter, wamble, wabble; teeter, dangle, swag.

fluctuate, dance, curvet, reel, quake; quiver, quaver, shake, flicker; wriggle; roll, toss, pitch; flounder, stagger, totter, waddle; move –, bob- up and down etc. *adv.*; pass and repass, ebb and flow, come and go, shuttle; vacillate etc. 605.

brandish, shake, flourish.

Adj. oscillating etc. *v.*; oscill-, undul-, puls-, libr-atory; vibrat-ory, -ile; pendulous, shutterwise, seismic.

Adv. to and fro, up and down, backwards and forwards, see-saw, zigzag, wibble-wabble, in and out, from side to side, like buckets in a well.

315. Agitation. [Irregular motion.]—**N.** agitation, stir, tremor, shake, ripple, jog, jolt, jerk, shock, succession, trepidation, quiver, quaver, dance; jactit-ation, -ance; shuffling etc. *v.*; twitter, flicker, flutter.

disquiet, perturbation, commotion, turmoil, turbulence; tumult, -uation; hubbub, rout, bustle, fuss, racket, *subsultus*, staggers, megrims, epilepsy, fits, twitching, vellication, St. Vitus' dance.

spasm, throe, throb, palpitation, convulsion, paroxysm; tetanus.

disturbance etc. (*disorder*) 59; restlessness etc. (*changeableness*) 149.

ferment, -ation; ebullition, effervescence, hurly burly, *cahotage*; tempest, storm, ground swell, heavy sea, whirlpool, vortex etc. 312; whirlwhind etc. (*wind*) 349.

V. be -agitated etc.; shake; tremble, – like an aspen leaf; quiver, quaver, quake, shiver, twitter, twire, dither, dodder; twitch, writhe, toss, shuffle, tumble, stagger, bob, reel, sway; wag , -gle, wiggle; wriggle, – like an eel; squirm; dance, stumble, shamble, flounder, totter, flounce, flop, curvet, prance.

throb, pulsate, beat, palpitate, go pit-a-pat; flutter, flitter, flicker, bicker; bustle.

ferment, effervesce, foam; boil, – over; bubble, – up; simmer.

toss –, jump- about; jump like a parched pea; shake like an aspen leaf; shake to its -center, – foundations; be the sport of the winds and waves; reel to and fro like a drunken man; move –, drive- from post to pillar and from pillar to post; keep between hawk and buzzard.

agitate, shake, convulse, toss, tumble, bandy, wield, brandish, flap, flourish, whisk, jerk, hitch, jolt; jog, -gle; hostle, buffet, hustle, disturb, stir, shake up, churn, jounce, wallop, whip, vellicate.

Adj. shaking etc. *v.*; agitated, tremulous; de-, sub-sultory; shambling; giddy-paced, saltatory, convulsive, jerky, unquiet, restless, all of a twitter.

Adv. by fits and starts; subsultorily etc. *adj.*: *per saltum*; hop, skip and jump; in -convulsions, – fits, pit-a-pat.

316. Materiality.—N. material-ity, -ness; materialization; corpor-eity, -ality; substantiality, material existence, incarnation, flesh and blood, *plenum*; physical condition.

matter, body, substance, brute matter, stuff, element, principle, protoplasm, plasma, *parenchyma*, material, *substratum*, hyle, *corpus*, *pabulum*; frame.

object, article, thing, something; still life; stocks and stones; materials etc. 635.

[Science of matter] physics; somatology, -ics; natural –, experimental- philosophy; physical science, *philosophie positive*, materialism, hylism; applied –, micro-, molecular –, nuclear – physics.

atomics, atomic science, nucleonics, quantum mechanics, radiology.

atom, radical, tracer, isotope, pleiad; atomic – nucleus, – cluster; nuclear particle, neutron, protron, shell, valence electron.

materialist, physicist, atomic scientist, radiologist.

V. materialize, incorporate, incarnate, substantiate, embody.

atomize, split –, smash – the atom; radioactivate.

Adj. material, bodily; corpor-eal, -al; physical; somat-ic, -oscopic; sensible, tangible, ponderable, palpable, substantial; fleshly, incarnate.

physical, bio-, electro-, geo-physical; atomic, nuclear, thermonuclear, radio-active.

objective, impersonal, neuter, unspiritual, materialistic.

317. Immateriality.—N. immaterial-ity, -ness; incorporeity, dematerialization, unsubstantiality, spirituality; inextension; astral plane.

personality; I, myself, me; *ego*, spirit etc. (*soul*) 450; astral body; immaterialism; spiritual-ism, -ist; subliminal –, subconscious- self.

V. disembody, spiritualize, dematerialize.

Adj. immateri-al, -ate; incorpor-eal, -al; asomatous, unextended; un-, dis-embodied; extramundane, supersensible, unearthly; pneumatoscopic; spiritual etc. (*psychical*) 450; aery.

personal, subjective.

318. World.—N. world, creation, nature, universe; earth, globe, wide world; *cosmos*; terraqueous globe, sphere; macro-, mega-cosm; music of the spheres; strato-, tropo-sphere.

heavens, sky, welkin, empyrean; starry -heaven, – host; firmament; vault –, canopy- of heaven; celestial spaces.

heavenly bodies, stars, luminaries, nebulae; galaxy, milky way, galactic circle, *via lactea.*

sun, orb of day, Apollo, Phoebus; photo-, chromo-sphere; solar system; planet, -oid, asteroid; comet; satellite; moon, orb of night, Diana, Luna; aerolite, meteor; falling –, shooting- star; meteorite.

constellation, zodiac, signs of the zodiac, Charles's wain, Great Bear, Southern Cross, Orion's belt, Cassiopeia's chair, Pleiades etc.

colures, equator, ecliptic, orbit.

[Science of heavenly bodies] astronomy; uranography, -logy; cosmo-logy, -graphy, -gony; *eidouranion*, orrery; geography; geodesy etc. (*measurement*) 466; star-gazing, -gazer; astronomer; cosmogonist, geodesist, geographer; observatory.

Adj. cosmic, cosmical, mundane; terr-estrial, -estrious, -aqueous, -ene, -eous; telluric, earthly, geotic, geodetic, cosmogonal, under the sun; sublunary, -astral.

solar, heliacal; lunar; celestial, heavenly, empyreal, sphery; starry, stellar; sider-eal, -al; astral; nebular.

Adv. in all creation, on the face of the globe, here below, under the sun.

319. Gravity.—N. gravi-ty, -tation, weight; heaviness etc. *adj.*; specific gravity; ponderosity, pressure, load; bur-den, -then; ballast, counterpoise; lump –, mass –, weight- of.

lead, millstone, mountain, Ossa on Pelion.

weighing, ponderation, trutination; weights; avoirdupois –, troy –, apothecaries'- weight; grain, scruple, drachm, ounce, pound, lb., load, stone, hundredweight, cwt., ton, quintal, carat, pennyweight, tod, gram, kilogram etc.

[Weighing instrument] balance, scales, steelyard, beam, weighbridge, spring balance, weighing machine.

[Science of gravity] statics.

V. be heavy etc. *adj.*; gravitate, weigh, press, cumber, load.

[Measure the weight of] weigh, poise.

Adj. weighty; weighing etc. *v.*; heavy, – as lead; ponder-ous, -able; lump-ish, -y; cumber-, burden-some; cumbrous, unwieldy, massive.

in-, superin-cumbent.

320. Levity.—N. levity; lightness etc. *adj.*; imponderability, imponderables, buoyancy, volatility.

feather, dust, mote, down, thistledown, flue, cobweb, gossamer, straw, cork, bubble; float, bouy; ether, air.

leaven, ferment, barm, yeast, enzyme.
V. be -light etc. *adj.*; float, swim, be buoyed up.
render -light etc. *adj.*; lighten, levitate; leaven.
Adj. light, subtile, subtle, airy; imponder-ous, -able; astatic, weightless, ethereal, sublimated; uncompressed, volatile; buoyant, floating etc. *v.*; barmy, frothy; portable.
light as -a feather, – thistle down, – air.
fermenting etc. *n.*

321. Density.—N. density, solidity; solidness etc. *adj.*; impenetra-, impermea-bility; incompressibility; imporosity; cohesion etc. 46; constipation, consistence, spissitude.
specific gravity; hydro-, areo-meter.
condensation; solid-ation, -ification; consolidation; concretion, caseation, coagulation; petrifaction etc. (*hardening*) 323; crystallization, precipitation; deposit, precipitate, silt; inspissation; thickening etc. *v.*
indivisibility, indiscerptibility, indissolvableness.
solid body, mass, block, knot, lump; con-cretion, -crete, -glomerate; cake, clot, stone, curd, coagulum, grume; bone, gristle, cartilage.
V. be -dense etc. *adj.*; become –, render- solid etc. *adj.*; solid-ify, -ate; concrete, set, take a set, consolidate, congeal, coagulate; curd, -le; fix, clot, cake, candy, precipitate, deposit, cohere, crystallize; petrify etc. (*harden*) 323.
condense, thicken, inspissate, incrassate; compress, squeeze, ram down, constipate.
Adj. dense, solid, solidified etc. *v.*; cohe-rent, -sive etc. 46; compact, close, serried, thickset; substantial, massive, lumpish; impenetrable, impermeable, imporous; incompressible; constipated; concrete etc. (*hard*) 323; knot-ted, -ty; gnarled; crystal-line, -lizable; thick, grumous, stuffy.
un-dissolved, -melted, -liquified, -thawed.
in-divisible, -discerptible, -frangible, -dissolvable, -dissoluble, -soluble, -fusible.

322. Rarity.—N. rarity; tenuity; absence of -solidity etc. 321; subtility; sponginess, compressibility.
rarefaction, expansion, dilatation, inflation, subtilization.
ether etc. (*gas*) 334.
V. rarefy, expand, dilate, subtilize, attenuate, thin.
Adj. rare, subtile, thin, fine, tenuous, compressible, flimsy, slight; light etc. 320; cavernous, spongy etc. (*hollow*) 252.
rarefied etc. *v.*; unsubstantial; uncom-pact, -pressed.

323. Hardness.—N. hardness etc. *adj.*; rigidity, renitence, inflexibility, temper, callosity, durity.
induration, petrifaction; lapid-ification, -escence; vitri-, ossi-, corni-fication; crystallization.
stone, pebble, flint, marble, rock, fossil, crag, crystal, quartz, granite, adamant; bone, cartilage; heart of oak, block, board, deal board; iron, steel; cast –, wrought- iron; nail; brick, concrete; cement.
V. render -hard etc. *adj.*; harden, stiffen, indurate, petrify, temper, ossify, vitrify.
Adj. hard, rigid, stubborn, stiff, firm; starch, -ed; stark, unbending, unlimber, unyielding; inflexible, tense; indurate, -d; gritty, proof.
adamant-ine, -ean; concrete, stony, rocky, lithic, granitic, vitreous; crystalline; horny, corneous; bony; oss-eous, -ific; cartilaginous; hard as a -stone etc. *n.*; stiff as -buckram, – a poker.

324. Softness.—N. softness, pliableness etc. *adj.*; flexibility; pli-ancy, -ability; sequacity, malleability; flabbiness; duct-, tract-ility; extend-, extensibility; plasticity; inelasticity; flaccidity, laxity.
clay, wax, butter, dough, pudding; cushion, pillow, feather-bed, pad, down, padding, wadding.
mollification; softening etc. *v.*
V. render -soft etc. *adj.*; soften, mollify, mellow, relax, temper; mash, knead, squash, *massage*.
bend, yield, relent, relax, give.
Adj. soft, tender, supple; pli-ant, -able; flex-ible, -ile; lithe, -some; lissom, limber, plastic; duc-tile; tract-ile, -able; malleable, extensile, sequacious, inelastic, mollient.
yielding etc. *v.*; flabby, limp, flimsy.
flaccid, flocculent, downy; spongy, edematous, medullary, doughy, argillaceous, mellow.
soft as -butter, – down, – silk; yielding as wax; tender as a chicken.

325. Elasticity.—N. elasticity, springiness, spring, resilience, renitency, buoyancy.
india-rubber, caoutchouc, gutta-percha, whalebone, gum elastic.
V. be -elastic etc. *adj.*; spring back etc. (*recoil*) 227.
Adj. elastic, tensile, springy, ductile, resilient, renitent, buoyant.

326. Inelasticity.—N. want of –, absence of-elasticity etc. 325; inelasticity etc. (*softness*) 324.
Adj. inelastic etc. (*soft*) 324.

327. Tenacity.—N. tenacity, toughness, strength; cohesion etc. 46; sequacity; stubbornness etc. (*obstinacy*) 606; viscidity etc. 352.
leather; gristle, cartilage.
V. be -tenacious etc. *adj.*; resist fracture.
Adj. tenacious, tough, cohesive, adhesive, strong, resisting, sequacious, stringy, gristly, cartilaginous, leathery, coriaceous, tough as whit-leather; stubborn etc. (*obstinate*) 606.

328. Brittleness.—N. brittleness etc. *adj.*; frag-, friab-, frangib-, fiss-ility; frailty; house of -cards, – glass.
V. be -brittle etc. *adj.*; live in a glass house.
break, crack, snap, split, shiver, splinter, crumble, break short, burst, fly, give way; fall to pieces; crumble -to, – into- dust.

Adj. breakable, brittle, frangible, fragile, frail, friable, delicate, gimcrack, shivery, fissile; splitting etc. *v.*; lacerable, splintery, crisp, crimp, short, brittle as glass.

329. Texture. [Structure.]—**N.** structure, organization, anatomy, frame, mold, fabric, construction; frame-work, carcass, architecture; stratification, cleavage.

substance, stuff, *compages*, *parenchyma*; constitution, staple, organism.

[Science of structures] organ-, oste-, my-, splanchn-, neur-, angi-, aden-ology; angi-, aden-ography.

texture; inter-, con-texture; tissue, grain, web, surface; warp and -woof, – weft; tooth, nap etc. (*roughness*) 256; fineness –, coarseness- of grain.

[Science of textures] histology.

Adj. structural, organic; anatomic, -al.

text-ural, -ile; fine-, coarse-grained; fine, delicate, subtile, gossamery, filmy; coarse; homespun; linsey-woolsey.

330. Pulverulence. [State of powder.]—**N.** pulverulence; sandiness etc. *adj.*; efflorescence; friability.

powder, dust, sand, shingle; sawdust; grit, attrition; meal, bran, flour, *farina*, spore, sporule; crumb, seed, grain; particle etc. (*smallness*) 32; thermion; limature, filings, *débris*, *detritus*, scobs, magistery, fine powder; *flocculi*.

smoke; cloud of -dust, – sand, – smoke; puff –, volume -of smoke; sand –, dust- storm.

[Reduction to powder] pulverization, comminution, attenuation, granulation, disintegration, subaction, contusion, trituration, levigation, abrasion, detrition, multure; limation; filing etc. *v.*

[Instruments for pulverization] mill, millstone, grater, rasp, file, pestle and mortar, nutmeg grater, teeth, molar, grinder, chopper, grindstone, kern, quern, muller.

V. come to dust; be -disintegrated, – reduced to powder etc.

reduce –, grind- to powder; pulverize, comminute, granulate, triturate, levigate; scrape, file, abrade, rub down, grind, grate, rasp, pound, bray, bruise; con-tuse, -tund; beat, crush, cranch, craunch, crunch, muller, scranch, crumble, disintegrate; attenuate etc. 195.

Adj. powdery, pulverulent, granular, mealy, floury, farinaceous, branny, furfuraceous, flocculent, dusty, sandy, sabulous; aren-ose, -arious, -aceous; gritty; efflorescent, impalpable.

pulverizable; friable, crumbly, shivery; pulverized etc. *v.*; attrite; in pieces.

331. Friction.—**N.** friction, attrition; rubbing etc. *v.*; erasure; con-frication, -trition; affriction, abrasion, arrosion, limature, frication, rub; elbow-grease; rosin; *massage*.

V. rub, scratch, abrade, scrape, scrub, fray, rasp, graze, curry, scour, polish, rub out, erase, gnaw; file, grind etc. (*reduce to powder*) 330; *massage*.

set one's teeth on edge; rosin.

Adj. anatriptic, abrasive.

332. Lubrication. [Absence of friction. Prevention of friction.]—**N.** smoothness etc. 255; unctuousness etc. 355.

lubri-cation, -fication; anointment; oiling etc. *v.*

synovia; lubricant, graphite, glycerine, oil etc. 356; saliva; lather.

V. lubri-cate, -citate; oil, grease, lather, soap; wax.

Adj. lubricated etc. *v.*

333. Fluidity.—**N.** fluidity, liquidity; liquidness etc. *adj.*; gaseity etc. 334; liquefaction etc. 334.

fluid, inelastic fluid; liquid, liquor; lymph, humor, juice, sap, serum, blood, serosity, gravy, rheum, ichor, sanies.

solu-bility, -bleness.

[Science of liquids] hydro-logy, -statics, dynamics, hydraulics, etc.

V. be -fluid etc. *adj.*; flow etc. (*water in motion*) 348; liquefy etc. 335.

Adj. liquid, fluid, serous, juicy, succulent, sappy; fluent etc. (*flowing*) 348.

liquefied etc. 335; uncongealed; soluble, hydrostatic etc. *n.*

334. Gaseity.—**N.** gaseity, gaseousness, vapourousness etc. *adj.*; flatulence, -lency; volatility, aeration, gasification.

elastic fluid, gas, air, vapor, ether, steam, fume, reek, *effluvium*, *flatus*; cloud etc. 353.

[Science of elastic fluids] pneumat-ics, -ostatics; aero-statics, -dynamics etc.

gas-, gaso-meter.

V. gassify, aerate, aerify; emit vapor etc. 336.

Adj. gaseous, aeriform, ethereal, aerial, airy, vaporous, volatile, evaporable; flatulent; aerostatic etc. *n.*

335. Liquefaction.—**N.** liquefaction, liquescen-ce, -cy, deliquescence; melting etc. (*heat*) 384; colliqu-ation, -efaction; thaw; de-, liquation; lixiviation, dissolution.

solution, apozem, lixivium, infusion, decoction, flux.

solvent, diluent, menstruum, alkahest, *aqua fortis*.

V. render -liquid etc 333; liquefy, run, deliquesce; melt etc. (*heat*) 384; solve; dissolve, resolve; liquate; hold in solution; leach, lixiviate.

Adj. lique-fied etc. *v.*, -scent, -fiable, deliquescent, soluble, colliquative; solvent.

336. Vaporization.—**N.** vapor-, volatilization; gasification; e-, vaporation; distillation, cohobation, sublimation, exhalation; volatility.

vaporizer, still, retort, spray, atomizer; fumigation, steaming.

V. render -gaseous etc. 334; vaporize, volatilize; distil, sublime; evaporate, exhale, smoke, transpire, emit vapor, fume, reek, steam, fumigate.

Adj. volatilized etc. *v.*; reeking etc. *v.*; volatile; evaporable, vaporizable.

337. Water.—N. water; serum, serosity; lymph; rheum; diluent.

dilution, maceration, lotion; washing etc. *v.*; im-, mersion; humectation, infiltration, spargefaction, affusion, irrigation, *douche*, balneation, bath.

deluge etc. (*water in motion*) 348; high water, flood-, spring-tide.

V. be -watery etc. *adj.*; reek.

add water, water, wet; moisten etc. 339; dilute, dip, immerse; merge; im-, sub-merge; plunge, souse, duck, drown; soak, steep, macerate, pickle, wash, sprinkle, sparge, lave, bathe, affuse, splash, swash, douse, slosh, drench; dabble, slop, slobber, irrigate, inundate, deluge; syringe, inject, gargle; infiltrate, percolate.

Adj. watery, aqueous, aquatic, lymphatic; balneal, diluent; drenching etc. *v.*; diluted etc. *v.*; weak; wet etc. (*moist*) 339.

Phr. the waters are out.

338. Air.—N. air etc. (*gas*) 334; common –, atmospheric- air; atmosphere, stratosphere, isothermal layer, troposphere, Heaviside layer.

open, – air; sky, welkin; blue, – sky; cloud etc. 353.

weather, climate, rise and fall of the barometer, isobar.

[Science of air] pneumatics, aero-logy, -scopy, -graphy; meteorology, climatology; eudio-, baro-, aero-meter; aneroid, baro-graph, -scope; weather-gauge, -glass, -cock.

exposure to the -air, – weather; ventilation; aero-station; -nautics; -naut etc. 265 and 269.

V. air, ventilate; fan etc. (*wind*) 349.

Adj. containing air, flatulent, effervescent; windy etc. 349.

atmospheric, airy; aeri-al, -form; pneumatic; meteorological; weather-wise.

Adv. in the open air, out of doors, *à la belle étoile, al fresco*; *sub -Jove, – dio.*

339. Moisture.—N. moisture; moistness etc. *adj.*; hum-idity, -ectation; madefaction, dew; *serein*; marsh etc. 345; Hygromet-ry, -er.

V. moisten, wet; humect, -ate; sponge, damp, dampen, bedew; imbue, imbrue, infiltrate, saturate; seethe, sop; soak, drench etc. (*water*) 337.

be -moist etc. *adj.*; not have a dry thread; perspire etc. (*exude*) 295.

Adj. moist, damp; watery etc. 337; undried, humid, wet, dank, muggy, dewy; roric; roscid; juicy.

wringing wet; wet -through, – to the skin; saturated etc. *v.*

swashy, soggy, dabbled; reeking, seething, dripping, soaking, soft, sodden, sloppy, muddy; swampy etc. (*marshy*) 345; irriguous.

340. Dryness.—N. dryness etc. *adj.*; siccity, aridity, drought, ebb-, neap-tide, low water.

drying, ex-, de-siccation; evaporation; dehydration; arefaction, dephlegmation, drainage.

drier, desiccator.

V. be -dry etc. *adj.*; render -dry etc. *adj.*; dry; dry –, soak- up; sponge, swab, wipe; ex-, desiccate, dehydrate, anhydrate; drain, parch.

be fine, hold up.

Adj. dry, anhydrous, arid, waterless; dried etc. *v.*; undamped; juice-, sap- less; sear; husky; rainless, without rain, fine; dry as -a bone, – dust, – a stick, – a mummy, – a biscuit; disiccated; dehydrated; water-proof, -tight.

341. Ocean.—N. sea, ocean, main, deep, brine, salt water, waters, waves, billows, high seas, offing, great waters, watery waste, 'vasty deep,' briny ocean, herring pond, steamer track, the seven seas; wave, tide etc. (*water in motion*) 348.

hydrograph-y, -er, oceanography; Neptune, Thetis, Triton, Naiad, Nereid; sea-nymph, Siren, mer-maid, -man; trident, dolphin.

Adj. oceanic; mar-ine, -itime; pleagic, -ian; sea-going, -worthy; hydrographic.

Adv. at –, on- sea; afloat, on the high seas.

342. Land.—N. land, earth, ground, dry land, *terra firma.*

continent, mainland, peninsula, delta; tongue –, neck- of land; isthmus; oasis; promontory etc. (*projection*) 250; highland etc. (*height*) 206.

coast, shore, scar, strand, beach; bank, lea; seaboard, -side, -shore, -bank, -coast, -beach; rock-, iron- bound coast; loom of the land; derelict; innings; *alluvium*, alluvion.

soil, glebe, clay, loam, marl, clodge, chalk, gravel, mold, subsoil, clod, clot; rock, crag, cliff.

acres; real estate etc. (*property*) 780; landsman, land-lubber, farmer.

geography etc. 318; agriculture etc. 371.

V. land, come to land; set foot on -the soil, – dry land; come –, go- ashore.

Adj. earthy; continental, midland; littoral, riparian, ripuarian; alluvial; terrene etc. (*world*) 318; landed, predial, territorial.

Adv. ashore; on -shore, – land.

343. Gulf. Lake.—N. land covered with water, gulf, gulph, bay, inlet, bight, estuary, arm of the sea, fiord, armlet; frith, firth, ostiary, mouth; lagune, lagoon; indraught; cove, creek; natural harbor; roads; strait, narrows; Euripus; sound, belt, gut, kyles.

lake, loch, lough, mere, tarn, plash, broad, pond, pool, lin, puddle, well, artesian well, tank, sump; standing –, dead –, sheet of- water; fish –, mill-pond; race; ditch, dike, dyke, dam; reservoir etc. (*store*) 636.

Adj. lacustrine; land locked.

344. Plain.—N. plain, table land, mesa, face of the country; open –, champaign-country; basin, downs, waste, weary waste, desert, tundra, wild, steppe, pampas, savanna, prairie, champaign, heath, common, wold, veld; moor, -land, uplands, fell; bush; *plateau* etc. (*level*) 213; *campagna.*

meadow, mead, haugh, pasturage, park, field,

lawn, green, plat, plot, grass-plat, greensward, sward, grass, turf, sod, heather; lea, ley, lay; grounds.

Adj. campestrian, champaign, alluvial.

345. Marsh.—N. marsh, swamp, morass, marish, moss, fen, bog, quagmire, slough, sump, wash; mud, squash, slush.

Adj. marsh, -y; swampy, boggy, plashy, poachy, quaggy, soft; muddy, sloppy, squashy, spongy; paludal; moor-ish, -y; fenny.

346. Island.—N. island, isle, islet, eyot, ait, holm, reef, atoll, breaker, archipelago; islander.

Adj. insular, sea-girt.

347. Stream. [Fluid in motion.]—**N.** stream etc. (*of water*) 348, (*of air*) 349.

V. flow etc. 348; blow etc. 349.

348. River. [Water in motion.]—**N.** running water.

jet, spirt, squirt, spout, splash, swash, rush, gush, *jet d'eau*, sluice, chute.

water-spout, -fall; fall, cascade, force, foss; lin, -n, ghyll, Niagara; cata-ract, -dupe, -clysm; *débâcle*, inundation, deluge.

rain, -fall; *serein*; shower, scud; downpour, cloud burst; driving –, pouring –, drenching-rain; hyeto-logy, -graphy; rainy season, monsoon; predominance of Aquarius, reigh of St. Swithin; mizzle, drizzle, *stillicidium*, plash; dropping etc. *v.*

stream, course, flux, flow, profluence; effluence etc. (*egress*) 295; defluxion; flowing etc. *v.*; current, tide, race.

spring; fount, -ain; rill, rivulet, gill, gullet, rillet; stream-, brook-let; runnel, sike, burn, beck, brook, stream, river; reach; tributary.

body of water, torrent, rapids, flush, flood, swash, spate; spring –, high –, full-tide; bore; eagre, *hugre*; fresh, -et; undertow, indraught, reflux, undercurrent, eddy, vortex, gurge, whirlpool, Maelstrom, regurgitation, overflow; confluence, corrivation.

wave, billow, surge, swell, ripple; roller, ground swell, surf, breaker, white horses; comber, beach-comber; rough –, heavy –, cross –, long –, short –, chopping –, choppy- sea, choppiness; tidal wave.

[Science of fluids in motion] Hydrodynamics; Hydraul-ics etc.; raingauge etc.

water-bearer, – carrier, Aquarius.

irrigation etc. (*water*) 337; pump; watering-pot, – cart; hydrant, standpipe, hose, sprinkler, drencher; fire engine, squirt, syringe.

V. flow, run; meander; gush, pour, spout, roll, jet, well, issue; drop, drip, dribble, plash, squirt, spurt, spirtle, trill, trickle, distil, percolate; stream, overflow, inundate, deluge, flow over, splash, swash; guggle, murmur, babble, bubble, purl, gurgle, sputter, regurgitate; ooze, flow out etc. (*egress*) 295.

rain, – hard, – in torrents, – cats and dogs, – pitchforks; come down in sheets; pour with rain, drizzle, mizzle, spit, sprinkle, set in.

flow –, fall –, open –, drain- into; discharge itself, desembogue.

[Cause a flow] pour; pour out etc. (*discharge*) 297; shower down; irrigate, drench etc. (*wet*) 337; spill, splash.

[Stop a flow] stanch; dam, -up etc. (*close*) 261; obstruct etc. 706.

Adj. fluent; dif-, pro-, af-fluent; tidal; flowing etc. *v.*; meand-ering, -ry, -rous; fluvi-al, -atile; streamy, showery, rainy, drizzly, drizzling, pluvial, pluviose, stillicidous.

349. Wind. [Air in motion.]—**N.** wind, draught, *flatus*, *afflatus*, air; breath, – of air; puff, whiff, zephyr; blow, drift; *aura*; stream, current; under-current.

gust, blast, breeze, squall, gale, half a gale, storm, tempest, hurricane, whirlwind, tornado, samiel, cyclone, typhoon; simoon; harmattan, monsoon, trade wind, sirocco, *mistral*, *bise*, *föhn*, tramontane, levanter; capful of wind; fresh –, stiff- breeze; keen blast; blizzard.

windiness etc. *adj.*; ventosity; rough –, dirty –, ugly –, stress of- weather; dirty-, windy-, mackerel- sky; mare's tail; thick –, black –, white squall.

anemography, aerodynamics; windgauge, anemometer, weather-cock, vane.

suf-, insuf-, per-, in-, af-flation; blowing, fanning etc. *v.*; ventilation.

sneezing etc. *v.*; sternutation; hic-cup, -cough; catching of the breath; breathing etc.

Eolus, Eurus, Boreas, Zephyr, cave of Eolus.

air-pump, lungs, bellows, blow-pipe, fan, blower; pulmotor, ventilator, punkah, aspirator, exhauster, ejector.

V. blow, waft; blow -hard, – great guns, – a hurricane etc. *n.*; whistle, roar, howl, ring in the shrouds; stream, issue.

respire, breathe, in-, ex-hale, puff; whif, -fle; gasp, wheeze; snuff, -le; sniff, -le; sneeze, cough, belch.

fan, ventilate; in-, per-flate; blow –, pump- up.

Adj. blowing etc. *v.*; windy, airy, aeolian, flatulent; breezy, gusty, squally; stormy, tempestuous, blustering; boisterous etc. (*violent*) 173.

pulmon-ic, -ary.

350. Conduit. [Channel for the passage of water.]—**N.** conduit, channel, duct, watercourse, race; head –, tail- race; adit, aqueduct, canal, trough, flume, gutter, pantile; dike, canyon, ravine, gorge, hollow, main, gully, moat, ditch, drain, sewer, culvert, *cloaca*, sough, kennel, siphon, *piscina*; pipe etc. (*tube*) 260; funnel; tunnel etc. (*passage*) 627; water –, waste- pipe; emunctory, gully-hole, artery, aorta, vein, blood vessel; lymphatic; throat, alimentary canal, intestine; pore, spout, scupper; ad-, a-jutage; hose; gar-, gurgoyle; penstock, weir; flood-, water-gate; sluice, lock, valve; rose; waterworks.

Adj. vascular etc. (*with holes*) 260.

351. Air-pipe. [Channel for the passage of air.]—**N.** air-pipe, – shaft, – way, – passage, –

tube; shaft, flue, chimney, funnel, vent, blow-hole, nostril, nozzle, throat, weasand, *trachea*; *bronchus*, *-ia*; larynx, tonsils, wind-pipe, spiracle; ventiduct, -lator; louvre, Venetian blinds; blow-pipe etc. (*wind*) 349; pipe etc. (*tube*) 260.

352. Semiliquidity.—N. semiliquidity; stickiness etc. *adj.*; visc-idity, -osity; gumm-, glûtin-, muc-osity; spiss-, crass-itude; lentor; adhesiveness etc. (*cohesion*) 46.

inspiss-, incrass-ation; thickening, coagulation.

jelly, aspic, mucilage, gelatin, isinglass; colloid, mucus, phlegm; pituite, lava; glair, starch, gluten, albumen, milk, cream, protein; syrup, treacle; gum, size, glue, paste; wax, bee's-wax; emulsoid, emulsion, soup; squash, mud, slush, slime, ooze; moisture etc. 339; marsh etc. 345.

V. inspiss-, incrass-ate; coagulate, gelatinize, gelatinify, gel, jell, emulsify, thicken; mash, squash, churn, beat up.

Adj. semi-fluid, -liquid; half-melted, -frozen; milky, muddy etc. *n.*; lact-eal, -ean, -eous, -escent, -iferous; emulsive, curdled, thick, succulent, uliginous.

gelat-, album-, mucilag-, glut-inous; gelatine, mastic, amylaceous, ropy, clammy, clotted; vis-cid, -cous; sticky, tacky; slab, -by; lentous, pituitous; mu-cid, -culent, -cous.

353. Bubble. [Mixture of air and water.] [Cloud.]—**N.** bubble; foam, froth, head, fume, spume, lather, suds, spray, surf, yeast, barm, spindrift.

cloud, vapor, fog, mist, haze, steam; scud, rack, *nimbus*; *cumulus*, woolpack, *cirrus*, *stratus*; *cirro-*, *cumulo-stratus*; *cirro-cumulus*; mackerel sky, mare's tail, dirty sky.

[Science of clouds] nephelognosy, nephology.

effervescence, fermentation; bubbling etc. *v.*

nebula; cloudiness etc. (*opacity*) 426; nebulosity etc. (*dimness*) 422.

V. bubble, boil, foam, froth, spume, mantle, sparkle, guggle, gurgle; effervesce, ferment, fizzle; aerate; cloud, overcast, befog.

Adj. bubbling etc. *v.*; frothy, nappy, effervescent, sparkling, *mousseux*, up, fizzy, with a head on.

cloudy etc. *n.*; vaporous, nebulous, overcast; nubiferous, nephological; foggy, brumous.

354. Pulpiness.—N. pulpiness etc. *adj.*; pulp, paste, dough, sponge, curd, pap, rob, jam, pudding, mush, fool, poultice, grume.

Adj. pulpy etc. *n.*; pultaceous, grumous.

V. pulp, pulpify, mash.

355. Unctuousness.—N. unctuousness etc. *adj.*; unctuosity, lubricity; ointment etc. (*oil*) 356; anointment; lubrication etc. 332.

V. oil etc. (*lubricate*) 332.

Adj. unctuous, oily, oleaginous, adipose, sebaceous; fat, -ty; greasy; waxy, butyraceous, soapy, saponaceous, pinguid, lardaceous; slippery.

356. Oil.—N. oil, fat, butter, cream, grease, tallow, suet, lard, dripping, margarine, oleomargarine, exunge, blubber; glycerine, stearine, elaine, oleagine; soap; soft soap, wax, cerement; paraffin, spermaceti, adipocere; petroleum, mineral –, rock –, crystal- oil, kerosene, vegetable –, colza –, olive –, linseed –, cotton seed –, rape –, nut –, fusel- oil; animal –, neat's foot –, signal –, train- oil; ointment, unguent, liniment, salve, pomade, pomatum, brilliantine, spike –, nard.

356a. Resin.—N. resin, rosin, colophony; gum; lac, shellac, sealing-wax; amber, -gris; bitumen, pitch, tar, asphalt, -e, -um; varnish, copal, mastic, magilp, lacquer, japan.

V. varnish etc. (*overlay*) 223.

Adj. resinous, bituminous, pitchy, tarry.

357. Organization.—N. organized -world, – nature; living –, animated- nature; living beings; organic remains, organism; fossils; animal and vegetable kingdom, *fauna* and *flora*, biota.

prot-oplasm, -ein; albumen; structure etc. 329; organ-ization, -ism.

[Science of living beings] biology; natural history,* organic –, bio-chemistry, anatomy, physiology, embryology, morphology, evolution, Darwinism, Lamarkism, zoology etc. 368; botany etc. 369; naturalist, biologist etc.

Adj. organ-ic, -ized.

*The term *Natural History* is also used as relating to all the objects in Nature whether organic or inorganic, and including therefore *Mineralogy*, *Geology*, *Meteorology*, etc.

358. Inorganization.—N. mineral -world, – kingdom; unorganized –, inorganic –, brute –, inanimate- matter.

[Science of the mineral kingdom] mineralogy; geo-logy, -gnosy, -scopy; metall-urgy, -ography; lithology; orycto-logy, -graphy.

V. turn to dust, pulverize.

Adj. in-organic, -animate; unorganized; azoic; mineral.

359. Life.—N. life; vi-tality, -ability; animation; vital -spark, – flame, – force.

respiration, wind; breath -of life, – of one's nostrils; life-blood; Archeus; existence etc. 1.

vivification, vitalization; revivification etc. 163; Prometheus; life to come etc. (*destiny*) 152.

[Science of life] physiology, etiology, embryology, biology; animal economy.

nourishment, staff of life etc. (*food*) 298.

V. be -alive etc. *adj.*; live, breathe, respire; subsist etc. (*exist*) 1; walk the earth; strut and fret one's hour upon a stage; be spared.

see the light, be born, come into the world; fetch –, draw- -breath, – the breath of life; quicken; revive; come to, – life.

give birth to etc. (*produce*) 161; bring to life, put into life, vitalize; vivi-fy, -ficate; reamimate etc. (*restore*) 660; keep -alive, – body and soul together, – the wolf from the door; support life.

have nine lives like a cat.

Adj. living, alive; in -life, – the flesh, – the land of the living; on this side of the grave, above ground, breathing, quick, animated, viable; lively etc. (*active*) 682; alive and kicking; tenacious of life.

vital; vivi-fying; -fied etc. *v.*; Promethean.

Adv. *vivendi causâ.*

360. Death.—N. death, dying etc. *v.*; de-cease, -mise; dissolution, departure, *obit*, release, rest, *quietus*, fall; loss, bereavement.

end etc. 67 –, cessation etc. 142 –, loss –, extinction –, ebb- of -life etc. 359.

death-warrant, -watch, -rattle, bed; stroke –, agonies –, shades –, valley of the shadow –, jaws –, hand- of death; last -breath, – gasp, – agonies; dying -day, – breath, – agonies; swan song, *chant du cygne*; *rigor mortis*; Stygian shore; crossing the bar, the great adventure.

King -of terrors, – Death; Death, Angel of Death; mortality; doom etc. (*necessity*) 601.

euthanasia; happy release; break up of the system; natural -death, – decay; sudden –, violent- death; untimely end, watery grave; suffocation, *asphyxia*; heart failure; fatal disease etc. (*disease*) 655; death-blow etc. (*killing*) 361.

necrology, bills of mortality, obituary; death-song etc. (*lamentation*) 839.

V. die, expire, perish; meet one's -death, – end; pass away, be taken; yield –, resign- one's breath; resign one's -being, – life; end one's -days, – life, – earthly career; breathe one's last; cease to -live, – breathe; depart this life; be -no more etc. *adj.*; go –, drop –, pop -off; lose –, lay down –, relinquish –, surrender one's life; drop –, sink- into the grave; close one's eyes; fall –, drop- dead, – down dead; break one's neck; give –, yield- up the ghost; be all over with one.

pay the debt to nature, shuffle off this mortal coil, take one's last sleep; go the way of all flesh; join the -greater number, – majority, – choir invisible, to life immortal awake; come –, turn- to dust; cross the Stygian ferry; go to -one's long account, – one's last home, – Davy Jones's locker, – the wall; receive one's death warrant, make one's will, die a natural death, go out like the snuff of a candle; come to an untimely end; catch one's death; go off the hooks, kick the bucket, pet out; go West; hop the twig, turn up one's toes; die a violent death etc. (*be killed*) 361; make the supreme sacrifice.

Adj. dead, lifeless; deceased, demised, departed, defunct; late, gone, no more; ex-, in-animate; out of the world, taken off, released; departed this life etc. *v.*; dead and gone; bereft of life, stone dead, dead as -a door nail, – a door post, – mutton, – a herring, – nits; launched into eternity, gathered to one's fathers, numbered with the dead, gone to a better land, behind the veil, beyond the grave, – mortal ken.

dying etc. *v.*; mori-bund, -ent, Acherontic; hippocratic; *in -articulo*, – *extremis*; in the -jaws, – agony- of death; going, – off; *aux abois*; on one's -last legs, – death bed; at -the point of death, – death's door, – the last gasp; near one's end, given over, booked, fey; with one foot in –, tottering on the brink of- the grave.

still-born; mortuary; deadly etc. (*killing*) 361.

Adv. *post -obit*, – *mortem*.

Phr. life -ebbs, – fails, – hangs by a thread; one's -days are numbered, – hour is come, – race is run, – doom is sealed; Death -knocks at the door, – stares one in the face; the breath is out of the body; the grave closes over one; *sic itur ad astra*.

361. Killing. [Destruction of life; violent death.]—**N.** killing etc. *v.*; homicide, manslaughter, murder, assassination, trucidation, occision; lynching, effusion of blood; blood, -shed; gore, slaughter, carnage, butchery; *battue*, gladiatorial combat.

massacre; *fussillade*, *noyade*, *pogrom*; thuggism; racketeering.

death blow, finishing stroke, *coup de grâce*, *quietus*; execution etc. (*capital punishment*) 972; judicial murder; martyrdom.

butcher, slayer, murderer, Cain, assassin, cutthroat, garrotter, *bravo*, thug, racketeer, gunman, mobster, gangster, Moloch, *matador*, *sabreur*; *guet-à-pens*; gallows, executioner etc. (*punishment*) 975; man-eater.

regicide, parricide, fratricide, infanticide, aborticide etc.

suicide, *felo de se*, *suttee*, *hara kiri*, Juggernaut; immolation, holocaust.

suffocation, strangulation, *garrotte*; hanging etc. *v.*

deadly weapon etc. (*arms*) 727; Aceldama; the potter's field, the field of blood.

fatal accident, violent death, casualty.

[Destruction of animals] slaughtering; phthiozoics;* sport, -ting; the chase, venery; hunting, coursing, shooting, fishing; pig-sticking; sports-, hunts-, fisher-man; hunter, Nimrod; slaughterer, knacker, slaughter-house, shambles, *abattoir*.

V. kill, put to death, slay, shed blood; murder, assassinate, butcher, slaughter; victimize, immolate; massacre; take away –, deprive of- life; make away with, put an end to; despatch, dispatch; burke settle, do, – to death, – for.

strangle, garrotte, hang, lynch, throttle, choke, stifle, suffocate, stop the breath, smother, asphyxiate, drown.

saber; cut -down, – to pieces, – the throat; jugulate; stab, run through the body, bayonet; put to the -sword, – edge of the sword.

shoot, – dead; blow one's brains out; brain, knock on the head; stone, lapidate; give –, deal- a death blow; give a -*quietus*, – *coup de grâce*.

behead, bowstring etc. (*execute*) 972.

hunt, shoot etc. *n.*

cut off, nip in the bud, launch into eternity, send to one's last account, bump off, rub out, sign one's death warrant, strike the death knell of.

give no quarter, pour out blood like water; decimate; run amuck, wade knee-deep –, imbrue one's hands- in blood.

die a violent death, welter in one's blood; dash –, blow- out one's brains; commit suicide; kill – -make away with –, put an end to- oneself.

Adj. killing etc. *v.*; murd-, slaught-erous; sanguin-ary, -olent; blood-stained, -thirsty;

homicidal, red-handed; bloody, -minded; ensanguined, gory, sanguineous.
mortal fatal, lethal; dead-, death-ly; mort-, lethiferous; unhealthy etc. 657; internecine; suicidal.
sporting; piscator-ial, -y.
Adv. in at the death.
*Bentham, 'Chrestomathia.'

362. Corpse.—N. corpse, corse, carcass, bones, skeleton, dry-bones; defunct, relics, *relinquiae*, remains, mortal remains, dust, ashes, earth, clay; mummy; carrion; food for- worms, – fishes; tenement of clay, this mortal coil.
shade, ghost, *manes*, apparition etc. 980.
organic remains, fossils.
Adj. cadaverous, corpse-like; unburied etc. 363.

363. Interment.—N. interment, burial, inhumation, sepulture, entombment; in-, humation; obs-, ex-equies; funeral, wake, pyre, funeral pile; cremation.
funeral -rite, – solemnity; knell, passing bell, tolling; dirge etc. (*lamentation*) 839; cypress; *obit*, dead march, muffled drum; coroner, mortician, undertaker, mute, mourner, professional mourner, pallbearer; elegy; funeral -oration, – sermon; epitaph.
grave clothes, shroud; winding-sheet, cere-cloth; cerement.
coffin, shell, sarcophagus, urn, pall, bier, hearse, catafalque, cinerary urn.
grave, pit, sepulcher, tomb, vault, crypt, catacomb, mausoleum, *Golgotha*, house of death, narrow house, long home; cemetery, necropolis, boneyard; burial-place, -ground; grave-, churchyard; God's acre; mortuary, tope, cromlech, dolmen, menhir, barrow, tumulus, cairn; ossuary; bone-, charnel-, dead-house; *Morgue*; lich-gate; crematorium.
sexton, grave-digger.
monument, memorial, cenotaph, shrine; grave-, head-, tomb-stone; *memento mori*; hatchment, stone, cross.
exhumation, disinterment; necropsy, autopsy, *post mortem* examination.
V. inter, bury, lay in –, consign to- the -grave, – tomb; en-, in-tomb; inhume; lay out, prepare for burial, embalm, mummify; conduct a funeral, hold services; toll the knell; put to bed with a shovel.
exhume, disinter, unearth.
Adj. buried etc. *v.*; burial; fune-real, -brial; mortuary, sepulchral, cinerary; elegiac; necroscopic.
Adv. *in memoriam*; *post-obit*, *-mortem*; beneath –, under- the sod.
Phr. *hic jacet, ci-git, requiescat in pace.*

364. Animality.—N. animal life; anima-tion, -lity, -lization; breath.
flesh, – and blood; corporeal nature; *physique*; strength etc. 159.
V. animalize, incorporate.
Adj. fleshly, incarnate, carnal, corporeal, human.

365. Vegetability.—N. vegetable life; vegetation, -bility; herbage.
V. vegetate, germinate, sprout, shoot; cultivate.
Adj. vegetable etc. 367; rank, lush.

366. Animal.*—N. animal, – kingdom; *fauna*; brute creation.
beast, brute, creature, created being; creeping –, living- thing; dumb -animal, – creature.
flocks and herds, live stock; domestic –, wild-animals; game, *ferae naturae*; beasts of the fields, fowls of the air, denizens of the day.
vertebrate, bi-, quadru-ped, mammal, marsupial, bird, reptile, batrachian, amphibian, fish, crustacean, shell fish, articulate, mollusc, worm, insect, zoophyte; protozoon, animalcule etc. 193.
horse etc. (*beast of burden*) 271; cattle, kine, ox; bull, -ock; steer, stot; cow, milch-cow, calf, heifer, shorthorn; sheep; lamb, -kin; ewe –, pet-lamb; ewe, ram, tup; pig, swine, boar, hog, shoat, sow; tag, teg, wether.
dog, bitch, hound; pup, -py; whelp, cur, mutt, mongrel; house-, watch-, sheep-, shepherd's, sporting-, fancy-, lap-, toy-, bull-, badger-dog; mastiff; blood-, grey-, stag-, deer-, fox-, otter-, hound; harrier, beagle, spaniel, pointer, setter, retriever; Newfoundland; water -dog, – spaniel; pug, poodle; dachshund; Pinscher; turnspit; terrier; fox –, Skye- terrier; Dandie Dinmont; colley.
cat; puss,-y; kitten; grimalkin; gib-, tom-cat; mouser; fox, Reynard, vixen, stag, deer, hart, buck, doe, roe, antelope.
bird; poultry, fowl, cock, hen, chicken, chanticleer, partlet, rooster, dunghill cock, barn-door fowl; feathered -tribes, – songster; singing –, dicky- bird; canary; finch; auk, dodo, moa, roc, phoenix.
snake, serpent, viper, adder; newt, eft; asp, vermin.
Adj. animal, zoological.
equine, bovine, vaccine, canine, feline; fishy; piscator-y, -ial; molluscous, vermicular.
*Extended lists of names of specific varieties of animals, vegetables, etc., are beyond the scope of this work.

367. Vegetable.*—N. vegetable, – kingdom; *flora*, verdure.
plant; tree, shrub, bush; creeper; vine; herb, -age; grass.
annual; per-, bi-, tri-ennial; exotic.
timber; primeval –, virgin- forest; wood, -lands; hurst; frith, holt, weald, park, chase, greenwood, brake, grove, copse, coppice, *bocage*, *tope*, clump of trees, thicket, spinet, spinney; under-, brushwood; boscage, scrub; the oak and the ash and the bonny ivy tree.
bush, jungle, prairie; heath, -er; fern, bracken, furze, gorse, whin, broom; grass, turf, grassland, greensward, green, lawn, meadow; pas-ture, -turage; turbary; sedge, rush, weed; fungus, mushroom, toadstool; lichen, moss, conferva, mold; seaweed etc.; growth, crop.
foliage, leafage, branch, bough, ramage; spray etc. 51; leaf, frond, flag, petal, shoot, tendril.
flower, blossom, bud, bloom, bine; flowering plant; tree, sapling, pollard; timber-, fruit-tree; palm-, gum-tree; pulse, legume.
Adj. veget-able, -ous; herb-aceous, -al; botanic; sylvan, silvan; arbor- ary, -eous, -escent, -ical; den-

dritic, dendriform; woody, grassy; ver-dant, -durous; floral, mossy; lign-ous, -eous; wooden, leguminous; end-, ex-ogenous.

*Extended lists of names of specific varieties of animals, vegetables, etc., are beyond the scope of this work.

368. Zoology. [The science of animals.]—**N.** zoo-logy, -nomy, -graphy, -tomy; anatomy; comparative anatomy; animal –, comparative-physiology; morphology.

anthrop-, ornith-, ichthy-, herpet-, ophi-, malac-, helminth-, entom-, oryct-, paleont-ology; ichthy-etc. -otomy; taxidermy.

zo- etc. -ologist.

Adj. zoological etc. *n.*

369. Botany. [The science of plants.]—**N.** botany; phyto-graphy, -logy, -tomy; vegetable physiology, herborization, dendr-, myc-, fung-, alg-ology; flora, pomona; botanist etc.; botanic garden etc. (*garden*) 371; *hortus siccus*, *herbarium*, herbal.

herb-ist, -arist, -alist, -orist, -arian etc.

V. botanize, herborize.

Adj. botanical etc. *n.*

370. Cicuration. [The economy or management of animals.]—**N.** taming etc. *v.*; cicuration, zoohygiantics; domestication, -ity; *manège*; veterinary art; breeding, pisciculture, apiculture etc.

menagery, vivarium, zoological garden, zoo; bear-pit; aviary, apiary, hive; aquarium, fishery, fish hatchery; duck-, fish-pond; stud-farm; stock farm, dairy.

[Destruction of animals] phthisozoics etc. (*killing*) 361.

neat-, cow-, shep-herd, shepherdess; grazier; drover, cowboy, cowkeeper; trainer, breeder, groom, ostler etc. 746; veterinary surgeon, vet, horse doctor; farrier; keeper; game keeper.

cage etc. (*prison*) 752; hen-coop, bird-cage, cauf; sheep-fold etc. (*inclosure*) 232.

V. tame, domesticate, acclimatize, breed, tend, break in, train, corral, round up; cage, bridle etc. (*restrain*) 751; ride etc. 266.

drive, yoke, harness, hitch; groom, curry-comb; milk; shear; hatch; incubate.

Adj. pastoral, bucolic; tame, domestic, domesticated, broken in, gentle, docile.

371. Agriculture. [The economy or management of plants.]—**N.** agriculture, cultivation, husbandry, farming; georgics, geoponics; tillage, tilth, agronomy, gardening, spade husbandry, vintage; hort-, arbor-, silv-, citr-, vit-, flor-iculture; intensive culture; landscape gardening; forestry, afforestation.

husbandman, horticulturist, citriculturist, gardener, florist; agricult-or, -urist; yeoman, farmer, cultivator, tiller of the soil, ploughman, sower, reaper; woodcutter, backwoodsman, forester; vine grower, vintager; Boer; Triptolemus.

field, meadow, garden; botanic –, winter –, ornamental –, flower –, kitchen –, truck –, market –, hop- garden; nursery; green-, hot-, glass-house; conservatory, cucumber frame, *cloche*, bed, border, seed-plot; grass-plat, lawn; park etc. (*pleasure ground*) 840; *partere*, shrubbery, plantation, avenue, *arboretum*, pinery, *pinetum*, orchard, vineyard, vinery; orangery; farm etc. (*abode*) 189.

V. cultivate; till, – the soil; farm, garden; sow, plant; reap, mow, cut; manure, dress the ground, dig, delve, dibble, hoe, plough, plow, harrow, rake, weed, lop and top, force, transplant, thin out, bed out, prune, graft.

Adj. agr-icultural, -airan, -estic.

arable; predial, rural, rustic, country, bucolic, Boeotian; horticultural.

372. Mankind.—**N.** man, -kind; human -race, – species, – nature; humanity, mortality, flesh, generation.

[Science of man] anthropo-logy, -graphy, sophy; ethno-logy, -graphy; humanitarianism.

human being; person, -age; individual, creature, fellow creature, mortal, body, somebody, one; such a –, someone; soul, living soul; earthling; party, head, hand; *dramatis personae*.

people, persons, folk, public, society, world; community, – at large; general public; nation, -ality, state, realm; common-weal, -wealth; republic, body politic; million etc. (*commonalty*) 876; population etc. (*inhabitant*) 188.

cosmopolite; lords of the creation; ourselves.

Adj. human, mortal, personal, individual, national, civic, public, cosmopolitan; anthropoid.

373. Man.—**N.** man, male, he; manhood etc. (*adolescence*) 131; gentleman, sir, master; yeoman, wight, swain, fellow, guy, blade, *beau*, chap, gaffer, good man; husband etc. (*married man*) 903; Mr., mister, *monsieur*, *sahib*, *Herr*, *señor*, *signor*; boy etc. (*youth*) 129; Adonis.

[Male animal] cock, drake, gander, dog, boar, stag, hart, buck, horse, entire horse, stallion; gib-, tom-cat; he-, Billy-goat; ram, tup; bull, -ock; capon, ox, gelding; steer, stot.

Adj. male, he, masculine; manly, virile; unwomanly, -feminine.

374. Woman.—**N.** woman, she, female, petticoat, skirt, moll, broad.

feminality, feminity, muliebrity; womanhood etc. (*adolescence*) 131; feminism; gynecology, gyniatrics, gynics.

womankind; the -sex, – fair; fair –, softer- sex; weaker vessel; the distaff side.

dame, madam, *madame*, mistress, Mrs., lady, *mem-sahib*, *Frau*, *señora*, *signora*, *donna*, *belle*, matron, dowager, goody, gammer; good -woman, – wife; squaw; wife etc. (*marriage*) 903; matronage, -hood.

Venus, nymph, wench, *grisette*; little bit of fluff; girl etc. (*youth*) 129.

inamorata (love) etc. 897; courtesan etc. 962.

spinster, old maid, virgin, bachelor girl, new woman, amazon.

[Female animal] hen, slut, bitch, sow, doe, roe, mare; she-, Nanny-goat; ewe, cow; lioness, tigress; vixen.

gynecaeum, harem, *seraglio*, *zenana*, *purdah*.

Adj. female, she; feminine, womanly, ladylike, matronly, maidenly; womanish, effeminate, unmanly, gynecic.

375. Physical Sensibility.—N. sensibility; sensitiveness etc. *adj.*; physical sensibility, feeling, perceptivity, anaphylaxis, susceptibility, esthetics; moral sensibility etc. 882.

sensation, impression, effect; consciousness etc. (*knowledge*) 490.

external senses.

V. be -sensible etc. *adj.* -of; feel, perceive.

render, -sensible etc. *adj.*; excite, stir, sharpen, cultivate, tutor.

cause sensation, impress; excite –, produce- an impression.

Adj. sens-ible, -itive, -uous; esthetic, perceptive, sentient; conscious etc. (*aware*) 490; impressionable, responsive, alive to.

acute, sharp, keen, vivid, lively, impressive, thin-skinned.

Adv. to the quick.

376. Physical Insensibility.—N. insensibility, physical insensibility; obtuseness etc. *adj.*; palsy, paralysis, *anesthesia*, *analgesia*, *narcosis*, *hypnosis*, twilight sleep, stupor, coma, trance, catalepsy; sleep etc. (*inactivity*) 683; moral insensibility etc. 823; numbness etc. 381.

anesthetic agent, general –, local- anesthetic, opium, ether, chloroform, cocaine, novocaine, chloral; nitrous oxide, laughing gas; refrigeration.

V. be -insensible etc. *adj.*; have a -thick skin, – rhinoceros hide.

render -insensible etc. *adj.*; blunt, pall, obtund, benumb, deaden, paralyze; anesthetize, drug, dope; put under the influence of -chloroform etc. *n.*; hypnotize; stupefy, stun, narcotize.

Adj. insensible, unfeeling, senseless, comatose, dazed, impercipient, callous, thick-skinned, pachydermatous; hard, -ened; case-hardened; proof; obtuse, dull; anesthetic; paralytic, palsied, numb, dead.

377. Physical Pleasure.—N. pleasure; physical –, sensual –, sensuous- pleasure; bodily enjoyment, animal gratification, sensuality; hedonism, luxuriousness etc. *adj.*; dissipation, round of pleasure; titillation, *gusto*, creature comforts, comfort, ease; pillow etc. (*support*) 215; luxury, lap of luxury; purple and fine linen; bed of -down, – roses; velvet, clover; cup of Circe etc. (*intemperance*) 954.

treat; diversion, divertisement, entertainment; refreshment, regale; feast; *délice*; dainty etc. 394; *bonne bouche*.

source of pleasure etc. 829; happiness etc. (*mental enjoyment*) 827.

V. feel –, experience –, receive- pleasure; enjoy, relish; luxuriate –, revel –, riot –, bask –, swim –, wallow- in; feast on; gloat -over, – on; smack the lips.

live -on the fat of the land, – in comfort etc. *adv.*; bask in the sunshine, *faire ses choux gras.*

give pleasure etc. 829.

Adj. enjoying etc. *v.*; luxurious, voluptuous, sensual, hedonistic, comfortable, cosy, snug, in comfort, at ease.

agreeable etc. 829; grateful, refreshing, comforting, cordial, genial; sensuous; palatable etc. 394; sweet etc. (*sugar*) 396; fragrant etc. 400; melodious etc. 413; lovely etc. (*beautiful*) 845.

Adv. in -comfort etc. *n.*; on -a bed of roses etc. *n.*; at one's ease.

378. Physical Pain.—N. pain; suffering, -ance; bodily – physical -pain, – suffering; mental suffering etc. 828; dolor, ache; aching etc. *v.*; smart; shoot, -ing; twinge, twitch, gripe, head-, ear-, toothache; *migraine*, neuralgia, neuritis, lumbago, gout, sciatica; hurt, cut; sore, -ness; discomfort, *malaise*; *tic douloureux*.

spasm, cramp; nightmare, *ephialtes*; crick, stitch, kink; thrill, convulsion, throe; throb etc. (*agitation*) 315; pang.

sharp –, piercing –, throbbing –, shooting –, gnawing –, burning- pain; anguish, agony.

torment, torture; rack; cruci-ation, -fixion; martyrdom; martyr, toad under a harrow, vivisection.

V. feel –, experience –, suffer –, undergo- pain etc. *n.*; suffer, ache, smart, bleed; tingle, shoot; twinge, twitch, lancinate; writhe, wince, make a wry face; sit on -thorns, – pins and needles.

give –, inflict- pain; pain, hurt, chafe, sting, bite, gnaw, gripe, stab, grind; pinch, tweak; grate, gall, fret, prick, pierce, wring, convulse; torment, torture; rack, agonize; crucify; excruciate; break on the wheel, put to the rack; flag etc. (*punish*) 972: grate on the ear etc. (*harsh sound*) 410.

Adj. in -pain etc. *n.*; – a state of pain; pained etc. *v.*

painful; aching etc. *v.*; biting, poignant; sore, raw, tender, with exposed nerve.

379. Touch. [Sensation of pressure.] **—N.** touch; tact, -ion, -ility; feeling; palp-ation, -ability; manipulation; brush, tick, graze, contact etc. 199.

[Organ of touch] hand, finger, fore-finger, thumb, paw, feeler, *antenna*.

V. touch, feel, handle, finger, thumb, paw, fumble, grope, grabble; twiddle, tweedle; pass –, run- the fingers over, massage, rub, knead; palpate, stroke, manipulate, wield; throw out a feeler.

Adj. tact-ual, -ile; tangible, palpable; lambent.

380. Sensations of Touch.—N. itching etc. *v.*; titillation, formication, *aura*.

V. itch, tingle, creep, thrill, sting; prick, -le; tickle, titillate.

Adj. itching etc. *v.*

381. Numbness. [Insensibility to touch.] **—N.**

numbness etc. (*physical insensibility*) 376; pins and needles.

local anesthetic, cocaine novocaine etc.; morphia.

V. benumb etc. 376; freeze, dull, deaden.

Adj. numb; benumbed etc. *v.*; intangible, impalpable.

382. Heat.—N. heat, caloric; temperature, warmth, fervor, calidity; incal-, incand-, recal-, decal-escence; glow, flush, blush; fever, hectic.

phlogiston; fire, spark, scintillation, flash, flame, blaze; arc; bonfire; firework, pyrotechny; wild-fire; sheet of fire, lambent flame; devouring element; conflagration.

summer, dog-days, canicule; baking etc. 384 –, white –, tropical –, Afric –, Bengal –, summer –, blood- heat; heat wave, sirocco, simoon; broiling sun; isolation; warming etc. 384.

sun etc. (*luminary*) 423; fire worshipper etc. 991; furnace etc. 386.

geyser, hot spring, volcano.

: Science of heat. pyrology; thermology, -otics; thermometer etc. 389.

V. be -hot etc. *adj.*; glow, incandesce, flush, sweat, swelter, bask, smoke, reek, stew, simmer, seethe, boil, burn, singe, scorch, scald, grill, broil, blaze, flame; smoulder; parch, fume, pant.

heat etc. (*make hot*) 384; thaw, fuse, melt, give.

Adj. hot, heated, warm, mild, genial, tepid, lukewarm, unfrozen; therm-al, -ic; calorific; fervent, -id; ardent; aglow.

sunny, torrid, tropical, estival, canicular; close, sultry, stifling, stuffy, suffocating, oppressive; reeking etc. *v.*; baking etc. 384.

red –, white –, smoking –, bruning etc. *v.* –, piping- hot; like -a furnace, – an oven; hot as -fire, – pepper; hot enough to roast an ox.

fiery; incand-, incal-escent; candent, ebullient, glowing, smoking; on fire; blazing etc. *v.*; in -flames, – a blaze; alight, afire, ablaze; unquenched, -extinguished; smouldering; in a -heat, – glow, – fever, – perspiration, – sweat; sudorific; swelter-ing, -ed; blood-hot, -warm; warm as -a toast, – wool; recalescent, thermogenic, pyrotechnic, feverish, febrile, inflamed.

volcanic, plutonic, igneous; isother-mal, -mic, -al.

Phr. Not a breath of air.

383. Cold.—N. cold, -ness etc. *adj.*; frigidity, gelidity, algidity, inclemency, *fresco*..

winter; depth of –, hard- winter; Siberia, Nova Zembla; Ant-, arctic, North –, South- Pole.

ice; snow, – flake, – crystal – drift; sleet; hail, -stone; rime, frost; hoar –, white –, hard –, sharp- frost; icicle, thick-ribbed ice; fall of snow, snow storm, heavy fall, *avalanche*; ice-berg, -floe; floe, berg; *glacier*; *nevée*, *serac*.

[Sensation of cold] chilliness etc. *adj.*; chill shivering etc. *v.*; goose- skin, -flesh; *rigor*, horripilation, chattering of teeth; frostbite, chilblain.

V. be -cold etc. *adj.*; shiver, starve, quake, shake, tremble, shudder, didder, quiver; perish with cold; chill etc. (*render cold*) 385.

Adj. cold, cool; chill, -y; gelid, frigid, algid; fresh, keen, bleak, raw, inclement, bitter, biting, niveous, cutting, nipping, piercing, pinching; clay-cold; starved etc. (*made cold*) 385; shivering etc. *v.*; aguish, *transi de froid*; frost- bitten, -bound, -nipped.

cold as -a stone, – marble, – lead, – iron, – a frog, – charity, – Christmas; cool as -a cucumber, – custard.

icy, glacial, frosty, freezing, wintry, brumal, hibernal, boreal, arctic, antarctic, polar, Siberian, hyemal; hyperbore-an, -al; ice-bound; frozen out.

un-warmed, -thawed, -heated; isocheimal, -chimenal.

Adv. coldly, bitterly etc. *adj.*; *à pierre fendre*.

384. Calefaction.—N. increase of temperature; heating etc. *v.*; cale-, tepe-, torre-faction; melting, fusion; liquefaction etc. 335; burning etc. *v.*; kindling, combustion; in-, ac-censión; con-, cremation; scorification; cauter-y, -ization; ustulation, calcination; in-, cineration; cupellation; carbonization.

ignition, inflammation, adustion, flagration; de-, con-flagration; empyrosis, incendiarism; arson; *auto da fé*; suttee.

boiling etc. *v.*; coction, ebullition, estuation, elixation, decoction.

furnace etc. 386; blanket, flannel, fur, muffler, wrap; wadding etc. (*lining*) 224; clothing etc. 225.

match etc. (*fuel*) 388; incendiary, pryomaniac; *pétroleur, pétroleuse*; cauterant, caustic, lunar caustic, apozem, moxa.

sunstroke, *coup de soliel*; insolation, sunburn.

pottery, ceramics, crockery, porcelain, china; earthen-, stone-ware; pot, mug, *terra-cotta*, brick, clinker; cinder, ash, *scoriae*; embers, dross, slag, products of combustion, coke, carbon, charcoal.

inflamma-, combusti-bility.

[Transmission of heat] diathermancy, transcalency, diathermy.

V. heat, warm, chafe, stive; foment; make -hot etc. 382; sun oneself, bask in the sun.

fire; set -fire to, – on fire; kindle, enkindle, light, ignite, strike a light; apply the -match, – torch- to; re-kindle, -lume; fan –, add fuel to- the flame; poke –, stir –, blow- the fire; make a bonfire of; burn at the stake.

melt, thaw, fuse; liquefy etc. 335.

burn, inflame, roast, toast, fry, grill, singe, parch, bake, torrefy, scorch; brand, cauterize, sear, burn in; corrode, char, carbonize, calcine, incinerate; smelt, cupel, scorify; reduce to ashes; burn to a cinder; commit –, consign- to the flames.

boil, digest, stew, cook, seethe, scald, parboil, simmer; do to rags.

take –, catch- fire; blaze etc. (*flame*) 382.

Adj. heated etc. *v.*; molten, sodden; réchauffe; heating etc. *v.*

inflammable, burnable, inflammatory, combustible; diatherm-al, -anous; burnt etc. *v.*; volcanic.

386. Refrigeration.—N. refrigeration, infrigidation, reduction of temperature; cooling etc. *v.*; con-gelation, -glaciation; ice etc. 383; solidification etc. (*density*) 321; refrigerator etc. 387.

extincteur; fire, – engine, – extinguisher, – annihilator, – brigade, – man; sprinkler, hose, hydrant, standpipe.

incombusti-bility, -bleness etc. *adj.*

V. cool, fan, refrigerate, refresh, ice; congeal, freeze, glaciate; benumb, starve, pinch, chill, petrify, chill to the marrow, nip, cut, pierce, bite, make one's teeth chatter; damp, slack; quench; put –, stamp- out; extinguish.

go –, burn- out.

Adj. cooled etc. *v.*; frozen out; cooling etc. *v.*; frigorific.

incombustible; un-, unin-flammable; fire-proof.

386. Furnace.—N. furnace, blast furnace, fire-box, stove, incinerator, destructor, crematorium, crematory, kiln, oven, oast-house; hot-, bake-, wash-house; laundry; conservatory; hearth, focus; athanor, hypocaust, reverberatory; volcano; forge, fiery furnace; *tuyère*, brasier, salamander, heater, warming-pan, foot-warmer, hot-water bottle; radiator; boiler, geyser, caldron, seething caldron, pot; urn, kettle; chafing-dish; retort, crucible, alembic, still; saggar.

fire-place, -dog, -irons; hearth, ingle, grate, range, kitchener; kitchen range; oil-, gas-, electric, -cooker, -stove; fireless cooker; fire; galley; ca-, cam-boose; poker, tongs, shovel, hob, trivet; and-, grid-iron; frying-, stew-pan etc.

hot –, Turkish –, Russian –, vapor –, shower –, warm- bath; *calidarium*, *tepidarium*, *sudatorium*, sudatory; *hammam*.

387. Refrigerator.—N. refrigerator, -y; *frigidarium*; cold storage; refrigerating-plant, – machine; ice-house, -pail, -bag, -chest, -pack; cooler, damper; wine-cooler, freezing mixture.

388. Fuel.—N. fuel, firing, combustible, coal, wallsend, anthracite, bituminous coal, slack, culm, cannel coal, lignite, briquette, coke, carbon, charcoal; turf, peat, fire-wood, bobbing, faggot, log, yule log, ember, cinder etc. (*products of combustion*) 384; kindling wood, tinder, touch-wood; fumigator, sulphur, brimstone; incense; port-fire; fire-barrel, -ball, -brand.

fuel oil, gas, gasoline, electricity.

brand, torch, fuse; wick; spill, match, safety match, light, lucifer, congreve, vesuvian, vesta, fusee, locofoco; linstock; illuminant.

candle etc. (*luminary*) 423; oil etc. (*grease*) 356; petrol, gasoline, methylated – spirit; gas, acetylene.

Adj. carbonaceous; combustible, inflammable.

V. stoke, fire, feed, add fuel to the flames.

389. Thermometer.—N. thermo-meter, -scope, -stat, -pile, differential thermometer; pyro-, calorimeter; radio micrometer etc.

390. Taste.—N. taste, flavor, gust, *gusto*, relish, savor; sapor, sapidity; twang, smack, smatch; after-taste, tang.

tasting; de-, gustation.

palate, tongue, tooth, stomach.

V. taste, savor, smatch, smack, flavor, twang; tickle the palate etc. (*savory*) 394; smack the lips.

Adj. sapid, saporific; gusta-ble, -tory; strong; flavored, spiced, savory; palatable etc. 394.

391. Insipidity.—N. insipidity; tastlessness etc. *adj.*

V. be -tasteless etc. *adj.*

Adj. void of -taste etc. 390; insipid; jejune; taste-, gust-, savor-less; ingustible, mawkish, milk and water, weak, stale, flat, vapid, *fade*, wishy-washy, mild; untasted.

392. Pungency.—N. pungency, piquancy, poignancy, *haut-goût*, strong taste, twang, race, tang.

sharpness etc. *adj.*; acrimony, acridity; roughness etc. (*sour*) 397; unsavoriness etc. 395.

niter, saltpeter; mustard, cayenne, caviar; seasoning etc. (*condiment*) 393; brine.

dram, cordial, nip, pick-me-up, bracer, potion.

nicotine, tobacco, snuff, quid; segar; cigar, -ette, gasper, fag; cheroot; weed; fragrant –, Indian-weed; pipe, clay pipe, churchwarden, brier, meerschaum, hookah, hubble-bubble.

V. be -pungent etc. *adj.*; bite the tongue.

render -pungent etc. *adj.*; season, spice, salt, pepper, pickle, brine, devil, curry.

smoke, chew, take snuff.

Adj. pungent, strong; high-, full-flavored; high-tasted, -seasoned; gamy; sharp, stinging, rough, *piquant*, racy; biting, mordant; spicy; seasoned etc. *v.*; hot, – as pepper; peppery, vellicating, escharotic, meracious; acrid, acrimonious, bitter; rough etc. (*sour*) 397; unsavory etc. 395.

salt, saline, brackish, briny; salt as -brine, – a herring, – Lot's wife.

393. Condiment.—N. condiment, flavoring, salt, mustard, pepper, cayenne, curry, seasoning, sauce, spice, cinnamon, chillies, relish, *sauce piquante*, caviare, pot-herbs, onion, garlic, pickle, chutney, nutmeg etc.

V. season etc. (*render pungent*) 392.

394. Savoriness.—N. savoriness etc. *adj.*; relish, zest.

tit-bit, dainty, delicacy, ambrosia, nectar, *bonne bouche*; game, turtle, venison.

V. taste good, be -savory etc. *adj.*; tickle the -palate, – appetite; flatter the palate.

render -palatable etc. *adj.*

relish, like, smack the lips.

Adj. savory, well-tasted, to one's taste, tasty, good, palatable, nice, dainty, delectable; tooth-ful, -some; gustful, appetizing, lickerish, delicate, delicious, exquisite, rich, luscious, ambrosial.

Adv. *per amusare la bocca.*

Phr. *cela se laisse manger.*

395. Unsavoriness.—N. unsavoriness etc. *adj.*; amaritude; acri-mony, -tude; roughness etc. (*sour*) 397; acerbity, austerity; gall and worm-wood, rue, quassia, aloes; sickener.

V. be -unpalatable etc. *adj.*; sicken, disgust, nauseate, pall, turn the stomach.

Adj. un-savory, -palatable, -sweet; ill-flavored, un-appetizing, -eatable, inedible; bitter, – as gall; acrid, acrimonious; rough.

offensive, repulsive, nasty; sickening etc. *v.*; nauseous; loath-, ful-some; unpleasant etc. 830.

396. Sweetness.—N. sweetness, dulcitude, saccharinity.

sugar, cane-, beet-sugar; saccharine, glucose, syrup, treacle, molasses, honey, manna; confection, -ary; sweets, grocery, conserve, preserve, *confiture*, jam, marmalade, julep; sugar-candy, -plum; licorice, liquorice, plum, lollipop, *bon bon*, *jujube*, comfit, sweetmeat, caramel, toffee, butterscotch.

nectar; hydromel, mead, metheglin, honeysuckle, *liqueur*, sweet wine.

pastry, pie, tart, puff, pudding, cake.

dulc-ification, -oration.

V. be sweet etc. *adj.*

render -sweet etc. *adj.*; sugar, saccharize, sweeten; edulcorate; dulc-orate, -ify; candy; mull.

Adj. sweet, sugary; sacchar ine, iferous; dulcet, honied, candied, luscious, nectarious, melliferous; sweetened etc. *v.*

sweet as -a nut, – sugar, – honey.

397. Sourness.—N. sourness etc. *adj.*; acid, -ity; acetous fermentation; acerbity.

vinegar, verjuice, crab, alum.

V. be –, turn- -sour etc. *adj.*; set the teeth on edge.

render -sour etc. *adj.*; acid-ify, -ulate.

Adj. sour; acid, -ulous, -ulated; acerb; tart, crabbed; acet-ous, -ose; sour as vinegar, sourish, acescent, sub-acid; styptic, hard, rough; unripe, green.

398. Odor.—N. odor, smell, odorament, scent, effluvium; eman-, exhal-ation; fume, essence, trail, nidor, redolence.

sense of smell; scent; act of -smelling etc. *v.*

V. have an -odor etc. *n.*; smell, – of, – strong of; exhale; give out a -smell etc. *n.*; scent.

smell, scent; snuff, – up, sniff, nose, inhale.

Adj. odor-ous, -iferous; smelling, strong-scented; redolent, graveolent, nidorous, pungent.

[Relating to the sense of smell] olfactory, quick-scented..

399. Inodorousness.—N. inodorousness; absence –, want- of smell.

V. be -inodorous etc. *adj.*; not smell.

deodorize.

Adj. inodor-ous, -ate; scentless; without –, wanting- smell etc. 398.

deodoriz-ed, -ing.

400. Fragrance.—N. fragrance, aroma, redolence, perfume, *bouquet*; sweet smell, aromatic perfume.

perfumery; incense; musk, frankincense; pastil, -le; myrrh, perfumes of Arabia, chypre; otto, ottar, attar; bergamot, balm, civet, *pot-pourri*, pulvil; nosegay, *boutonnière*; scent, -bag; *sachet*, scent-bottle, smelling bottle, *vinaigrette*; toilet water, *eau de Cologne*; thurible, censer, thurification.

perfumer; incense bearer.

V. be -fragrant etc. *adj.*; have a -perfume etc. *n.*; smell sweet, scent, perfume, thurify, embalm.

Adj. fragrant, aromatic, redolent, spicy, balmy, scented; sweet-smelling, -scented; perfum-ed, -atory; thuriferous; fragrant as a rose, muscadine, ambrosial.

401. Fetor.—N. fetor, fetidness; bad etc. *adj.*; smell, – odor; stench, stink; mephitis, foul –, mal- odor; *empyreuma*; mustiness etc. *adj.*; rancidity; foulness etc. (*uncleanness*) 653.

stoat, polecat, skunk; asafetida; fungus, garlic; stink-pot, -bomb.

V. have a -bad smell etc. *n.*; smell; stink, – in the nostrils, – like a polecat; smell -strong etc. *adj.*; – offensively.

Adj. fetid; strong smelling; high, bad, strong, fulsome, offensive, noisome, rank, rancid, reasty, tainted, musty, fusty, frouzy, olid, -ous, nidorous, smelling, stinking; putrid etc. 653; suffocating, mephitic; empyreumatic.

402. Sound.—N. sound, noise, strain; accent, twang, intonation, tone, tune; cadence; sonority, sonorousness etc. *adj.*; audibility; resonance etc. 408; voice etc. 580.

[Science of sound] acou-, acu-stics; catacoustics; cataphonics; phon-ics, -etics, -ology, -ography; diacoustics, -phonics.

telephone, phonograph etc. 418.

V. produce sound; sound, make a noise; give out –, emit- sound; phonetize, phonate; resound etc. 408.

Adj. sounding; soniferous; sonorific; resonant, audible, acoustic, auditory, distinct; stertorous; phonic, sonant; phonetic.

403. Silence.—N. silence; stillness etc. (*quiet*) 265; peace, hush, lull, rest; muteness etc. 581; solemn –, awful –, dead –, deathlike-silence.

V. be -silent etc. *adj.*; hold one's tongue etc. (*not speak*) 585.

render -silent etc. *adj.*; silence, still, hush; stifle, muffle, gag, stop; muzzle, put to silence etc. (*render mute*) 581.

Adj. silent; still, -y; calm, quiet; noise-, sound-, speech-less; hushed etc. *v.*; mute etc. 581; aphonic.

soft, solemn, awful, deathlike, silent as the grave; inaudible etc. (*faint*) 405.

Adv. silently etc. *adj.*; *sub silentio*; in perfect silence.

Int. hush! 'sh! silence! soft! whist! tush! chut! tut! *pax!* mum's the word! hold your tongue! shut up! be

silent! be quiet! stop that noise! hold your row! dry up! peace, be still!
Phr. one might hear a -feather, – pin- drop.

404. Loudness.—N. loudness, power; loud noise, din; clang, -or; clatter, noise, bombilation, roar, uproar, racket, static, grinders, hubbub, *fracas, charivari*, trumpet blast, blare, flourish of trumpets, fanfare, *tintamarre*, peal, swell, blast, alarum, boom; resonance etc. 408.
vociferation; pandemonium, hullaballoo etc. 411; lungs; Stentor; megaphone; siren.
artillery, cannon, gunfire, shellburst, bomb; thunder.
V. be -loud etc. *adj.*; peal, swell, clang, boom, thunder, fulminate, roar; resound etc. 408; speak up, shout etc. (*vociferate*) 411; bellow etc. (*cry as an animal*) 412; give tongue.
rend the -air, – skies; fill the air; din –, ring –, thunder- in the ear; pierce –, split –, rend-the-ears, – head; deafen, stun; *faire le diable a quatre*; make one's windows shake; awaken –, startle- the echoes; make the welkin ring.
Adj. loud, sonorous; high-, big- sounding; blatant; deep, full, powerful, noisy, clangorous, multisonous, *fortisimo*; thundering, deafening etc. *v.*; trumpet-tongued; ear-splitting, -rending, -deafening; piercing; obstreperous, rackety, uproarious; enough to wake the -dead, – seven sleepers.
shrill etc. 410; clamorous etc. (*vociferous*) 411; stentor-ian, -ophonic.
Adv. loudly etc. *adj.*; aloud; at the top of one's voice, lustily, in full cry.
Phr. the air rings with.

405. Faintness.—N. faintness etc. *adj.*; faint sound, whisper, breath; under-tone, -breath; murmur, hum, rustle, buzz, purr; plash; sough, moan, sigh, susurration; tinkle; 'still small voice.'
hoarseness etc. *adj.*; raucity.
silencer, soft pedal, damper, mute, *sourdine.*
V. whisper, breathe, murmur, purl, hum, gurgle, ripple, babble, flow; tinkle; mutter etc. (*speak imperfectly*) 583.
steal on the ear; melt in –, float on- the air.
muffle, mute, deaden, damp, stifle.
Adj. inaudible; scarcely –, just- audible; low, dull; stifled, muffled; hoarse, husky; gentle, soft, faint; floating; purling, flowing etc. *v.*; whispered etc. *v.*; liquid; soothing; dulcet etc. (*melodious*) 413.
Adv. in a whisper, with bated breath, *sotto voce*, between the teeth, aside; *pian-o, -issimo*; *à la sourdine*; *con sourdine*; out of earshot, inaudibly etc. *adj.*

406. Snap. [Sudden and violent sounds.]—**N.** snap etc. *v.*; rapping etc. *v.*; de-, crepitation; smack, clap, report; thud; burst, explosion, discharge, detonation, blow-out, back-fire, firing, salvo, volley, pistol-shot.
squib, cracker, gun, rifle, pop-gun.
V. rap, snap, tap, knock; click; clash; crack, -le; crash; pop; slam, bang, clap, thump, plump; toot; back-fire, explode, burst on the ear.
Adj. rapping etc. *v.*
Int. crash! bang!

407. Roll. [Repeated and protracted sounds.]—**N.** roll etc. *v.*; drumming etc. *v.*; tattoo; ding-dong; tantara; rataplan; whirr; rat-a-tat; rub-a-dub; pit-a-pat; quaver, clutter, *charivari*, racket; cuckoo; repetition etc. 104; peal of bells, devil's tattoo; reverberation etc. 408.
drumfire, barrage.
machine gun.
V. roll, drum, rumble, rattle, clatter, rustle, roar, drone, patter, clack.
hum, trill, shake; chime, peal, toll; tick, beat.
drum –, din- in the ear.
Adj. rolling etc. *v.*; monotonous etc. (*repeated*), 104; like a bee in a bottle.

408. Resonance.—N. resonance; ring etc. *v.*; ringing etc. *v.*; tintinnabulation; reflection, reverberation, clangor.
low –, base –, bass –, flat –, grave –, deep –, pedal- note; bass; *basso*, – *profondo*; bari-, bary-tone; *contralto.*
V. re-sound, -verberate, -echo; ring, ding, sing, jingle, gingle, chink, clink; tink, -le; chime; gurgle etc. 405; plash, guggle, echo, ring in the ear.
Adj. resounding etc. *v.*; resonant, tinnient; tintinnabulary; deep-toned, -sounding, -mouthed; hollow, sepulchral; gruff etc. (*harsh*) 410.

408a. Non-resonance.—N. thud, thump, dead sound; non-resonance; muffled drums, cracked bell; silencer, damper; mute, *sourdine.*
V. sound dead; stop –, damp- the -sound, – reverberations; deaden, muffle.
Adj. non-resonant, dead, muted, muffled.

409. Sibilation. [Hissing sounds.]—**N.** sibilation; hiss etc. *v.*; sternutation; high note etc. 410.
goose, serpent, snake.
V. hiss, buzz, whiz, rustle; fizz, -le, sizzle, swish; wheeze, whistle, snuffle; squash; sneeze.
Adj. sibilant; hissing etc. *v.*; wheezy.

410. Stridor. [Harsh sounds.]—**N.** creak etc. *v.*; creaking etc. *v.*; discord etc. 414; stridor; harshness, roughness, sharpness etc. *adj.*; cacophony.
acute –, high- note; *soprano*, treble, tenor, *alto*, falsetto, *voce di testa*; shriek, cry etc. 411.
piccolo, fife, penny -whistle, – trumpet.
V. creak, grate, jar, burr, pipe, twang, jangle, clank, clink; scream etc. (*cry*) 411; yelp etc. (*animal sound*) 412; buzz etc. (*hiss*) 409.
set the teeth on edge, *écorcher les orielles*; pierce –, split- the -ears, – head; offend –, grate upon –, jar upon- the ear.
Adj. creaking etc. *v.*; strident, stridulous, harsh,

coarse, hoarse, horrisonous, raucous, metallic, rough, gruff, grum, sepulchral.

sharp, high, acute, shrill, high-pitched; trumpet-toned; piercing, ear-piercing; cracked; discordant etc. 414; cacophonous.

411. Cry.—N. cry etc. *v.*; voice etc. (*human*) 580; bark etc. (*animal*) 412.

vociferation, outcry, hullaballoo, chorus, clamor, hue and cry, plaint; lungs; stentor.

V. cry, roar, shout, bawl, brawl, halloo, halloa, hail, hoop, whoop, yell, bellow, howl, scream, screech, screak, shriek, shrill, squeak, squeal, squall, whine, whinny, pule, pipe, yaup.

cheer, hurrah; hoot; grumble, maon, groan.

snore, snort; grunt etc. (*animal sounds*) 412.

vociferate; raise –, lift up- the voice; call –, sing –, cry- out; exclaim; rend the air; thunder –, shout- at the -top of one's voice, – pitch of one's breath; *s'égosiller*; strain the -throat, – voice, – lungs; give a -cry etc.

Adj. crying etc. *v.*; clam-ant, -orous; vociferous; stentorian etc. (*loud*) 404; open-mouthed.

412. Ululation. [Animal sounds.]—**N.** cry etc. *v.*; crying etc. *v.*; ululation, latration, belling; reboation; call, note; bark, howl, yelp; twittering, woodnote; insect cry, fritinancy, drone; screech; cuckoo.

V. cry, ululate, howl, roar, bellow, blare, rebellow, bark, yelp; bay, – the moon; yap, growl, yarr, yawl, snarl, howl; grunt, -le; snort, squeak; neigh, bray; mew, mewl; purr, caterwaul, pule; bleat, low, moo; troat, croak, crow, screech, caw, coo, gobble, quack, cackle, gaggle, guggle; chuck, -le; cluck; clack; cheep, chirp, chirrup, twitter, sing, cuckoo; pout, wail, hum, buzz; hiss, blatter; hoot.

Adj. crying etc. *v.*; blatant, latrant; re-, mugient; deep-, full-mouthed.

Adv. in full cry.

413. Melody. Concord.—N. melody, rhythym, measure; rhyme etc. (*poetry*) 597.

pitch, *timbre*, intonation, tone, overtone.

scale, gamut; diapason; diatonic –, chromatic –, enharmonic- scale; key, clef, chords.

modulation, temperament, syncope, syncopation, preparation, suspension, resolution.

staff, stave, line, space, brace; bar, rest; *appogiato*, *-tura*; *acciaccatura*, shake, *arpeggio*.

note, musical note, notes of a sclae; sharp, flat, natural; high note etc. (*shrillness*) 410; low note etc. 408; interval; semitone; second, third, fourth etc.; diatessaron.

breve, semibreve, minim, crotchet, quaver; semi-, demisemi- quaver; sustained note, drone, burden.

tonic; key-, leading-, fundamental-, note; supertonic, mediant, dominant; sub-mediant, -dominant, organ-, pedal-point; octave, tetrachord; major –, minor- -mode, – scale, – key; Doric mode, passage, phrase.

concord, harmony; unison, -ance; chime, homophony; euphon-y, -ism; tonality; consonance; concent; part.

orchestration; harmonization, – phrasing.

[Science of harmony] harmon-y, -ics; thorough-fundamental- bass; counterpoint; faburden.

piece of music etc. 415; composer, harmonist, contrapuntist.

V. be -harmonious etc. *adj.*; harmonize, chime, symphonize, transpose; put in tune, tune, accord, string; score, arrange, orchestrate.

Adj. harmoni-ous, -cal; in -concord etc. *n.*, – tune, – concert; unisonant, concentual, symphonizing, isotonic, homophonous, assonant, consonant.

measured, rhythmical, diatonic, chromatic, enharmonic.

melodious, musical; tuneful, tunable; sweet, dulcet, canorous; mell-ow, -ifluous; soft; clear, – as a bell; silvery; euphon-ious, -ic, -ical; symphonious; enchanting etc. (*pleasure-giving*) 829; fine-, full-, silver-toned.

Adv. harmoniously etc. *adj.*

414. Discord.—N. discord, -ance; dissonance, cacaphony, caterwauling; harshness etc. 410; consecutive fifths.

[Confused sounds] Babel, pandemonium; Dutch –, cat's- concert; marrow-bones and cleavers.

V. be -discordant etc. *adj.* ; jar etc. (*sound harshly*) 410.

Adj. discordant; dis-, ab-sonant; out of tune, tuneless; un-musical, -tunable; un-, im-melodious; un-, in-harmonious; sing-song; cacophonous; jarring, harsh etc. 410.

415. Music.—N. music, classical –, modern –, descriptive- music; concert, recital; strain, tune, air, *motif*; melody etc. 413; *aria*, *arietta*; piece of music, *sonata*; *rond-o*, *-eau*; *pastorale*, *cavatina*, roulade, *fantasia*, *toccata*, *concerto*, overture, symphony, symphonic poem, tone poem, prelude, voluntary, *intermezzo*, variations, *cadenza*; cadence; fugue, canon, serenade, *nocturne*, *notturno*, rhapsody, romance, *aubade*, dithyramb; opera, operetta; oratorio; composition, movement, stave.

instrumental music; full-, orchestral- score; minstrelsy, tweedledum and tweedledee, band, orchestra etc. 416; concerted piece, *potpourri*, medley, *capriccio*, incidental music; improvisation; peal.

vocal music, vocalism; chaunt, chant; psalm, -ody; hymn; song etc. (*poem*) 597; canticle, canzonet, *cantata*, *bravura*, *coloratura*; lay, ballad, ditty, carol, barcarolle, pastoral, recitative, *recitativo*, *solfeggio*, tonic sol-fa.

Lydian measures; slow -music, – movement; *adagio* etc. *adv.*; minuet; siren strains, soft music, lullaby; *berceuse*, cradle song, dump; dirge etc. (*lament*) 839; pibroch; martial music, march, funeral-, dead- march; dance music; waltz etc. (*dance*) 840; rag-time, syncopation, jazz.

solo, duet, *duo*, *trio*; quartet; quintet, sextet, septet; part song, descant, glee, madrigal, catch, round, chorus, *chorale*; antiphon, -y; accompaniment, second –, alto –, tenor –, bass-part; score, thorough bass; counterpoint.

composer etc. 413; musician etc. 416.
V. compose, perform etc. 416; attune.
Adj. musical; instrumental, orchestral, vocal, choral, lyric, operatic; harmonious etc. 413.
Adv. *adagio*; *largo*, *larghetto*, *andan-te*, *-tino*; *alla capella*; *maestoso*, *moderato*; *allegr-o*, *-etto*; *spiritoso*, *vivace*, *veloce*; *prest-o*, *-issimo*; *pian-o*, *-issimo*, *fort-e*, *-issimo*, *sforzando*; *con brio*; *capriccioso*; *scherz-o*, *-ando*; *legato*, *sostenuto*, *staccato*, *crescendo*, diminuendo, *rallentando*, *affettuoso*, *arioso*; *parlante*, *cantabile*; *obbligato*; *pizzacato*, *tremolo*, *vibrato*.

416. Musician. [Performance of Music.]—**N.** musician, *artiste*, *virtuoso*, performer, player, minstrel; bard etc. (*poet*) 597; instrumental-, organ-, accompan-, pian-, violin-, flaut-, harp-ist; harper, fiddler, fifer, trumpeter, piper, drummer; catgut scraper.
band, orchestra, waits.
vocal-, melod-ist; singer, warbler; songst-, chaunt-er, -ress; *diva*, *cantatrice*, coloratura, soprano, mezzo-soprano, alto, contralto, tenor, baritone, bass, *basso*, *-profundo*.
choir, quire, chorister; chorus, – singer; choral society, festival, *eisteddfod*.
nightingale, philomel, thrush; siren; Orpheus, Apollo, the Muses, Erato, Euterpe, Terpsichore; tuneful -nine, – quire.
composer etc. 413.
performance, virtuosity, execution, touch, expression, solmization.
V. play, pipe, strike –, tune-up, sweep the chords, tickle –, paw- the ivories, vamp, tweedle, fiddle; strike the lyre, beat the drum; blow –, sound –, wind- the horn; grind the organ; touch the -guitar etc. (*instruments*) 417; thrum, strum, twang, drum, beat –, keep- time, conduct.
execute, perform; accompany; sing –, play- a second; compose, write music, set to music, arrange, harmonize, orchestrate.
sing, chaunt, chant, hum, warble, carol, chirp, chirrup, lilt, purl, quaver, trill, shake, twitter, whistle; sol-fa; intone.
have -an ear for music, – a musical ear, – a correct ear, – absolute pitch.
Adj. playing etc. *v.*; musical, lyric.
Adv. *adagio*, *andante* etc. (*music*) 415.

417. Musical Instruments.—N. musical instruments; band; string-, brass-, drum and fife-, military-, bugle-, German-, dance-, jazz-band; orchestra, string quartet; orchestration, orchestrelle.
[Stringed instruments] mono-, poly-chord; harp, lyre, lute, archlute, thearbo; mandol-a, -in, -ine; guitar; *ukulele*; psaltery, zither; bandore, cither, -n; gittern, rebeck, *bandurria*, banjo, zither banjo, *balalaika*, *samisen*; plectrum.
viol, -in, Cremona, Stradivarius; fiddle; kit; *vielle*, *viola*, – *d'amore*, – *di gamba*; tenor, *violoncello*, cello; bass, bass-, bass-viol; double-bass, *contrabasso*, *violone*, hurdy-gurdy; strings, catgut; bow, fiddlestick.
piano, -forte; grand –, concert grand –, baby –, upright –, cottage- piano; pianino, pianette; harpsi-, clavi-, clari-, mani-chord; *clavier*, spinet, virginals; dulcimer, *cymbalo*; Eolian harp; piano-organ, -player, electric piano, player-piano, pianola.
[Wind instruments] organ, church –, pipe –, American- organ; harmoni-um, -phon; accordion, seraphina, concertina; melodeon; barrel- organ; humming top.
flute, fife, piccolo, flageolet, penny-whistle, reed instrument; clari-net, -onet; bass clarionet; saxophone; basset horn, *corno di bassetto*; musette, shawm, oboe, hautboy, *cor Anglais*, *corno Inglese*, bassoon, double bassoon, *contrafagotto*; bag-, union-pipes; ocarina, Pandean pipes; calliope; sirene, pipe, pitch-pipe; sourdet; whistle, catcall.
horn, bugle, key bugle, cornet, *cornet-à-pistons*, cornopean, clarion, trumpet, trombone, ophicleide, serpent; English-, French-, bugle-, sax-, flugel-, alt-, helicon-, post-horn; sackbut, euphonium, bombardon, tuba, bass tuba.
[Vibrating surfaces] cymbal, bell, gong, peal of bells, *carillon*; tambour, -ine; drum, tom-tom, tabor, -ret, -ourine, -orin; *sistrum*, *grand caisse*, bass-, big-, side-, kettle-drum; *tympani*; war drums; tymbal, timbrel, castanet, bones; musical-glasses, -stones; harmonica, sounding– board, rattle; gramophone, phonograph.
[Vibrating bars] reed, tuning-fork, triangle, Jew's harp, musical box, harmonicon, xylophone, marimba, *celeste*.
sord-ine, -et; *sourd-ine, -et;* mute.

418. Hearing. [Sense of sound.]—**N.** hearing etc. *v.*; audition, auscultation; eavesdropping; audibility; acoustics etc. 402.
acute –, nice –, delicate –, quick –, sharp –, correct –, musical -ear; ear for music.
ear, auricle, lug, acoustic organs, auditory apparatus, ear-drum, tympanum; ear-, speaking-trumpet, megaphone; telephone, radiophone, stethoscope, phonograph, gramophone, microphone.
hearer, auditor, listener, eavesdropper; audi-tory, -ence.
V. hear, overhear; hark, -en; list, -en; give –, lend –, bend- an ear; give attention; catch a sound, prick up one's ears; give -a hearing, – audience -to.
hang upon the lips of, be all ear, listen with both ears, monitor.
become audible; meet –, fall upon –, catch –, reach- the ear; be heard; ring in the ear etc. (*resound*) 408.
Adj. hearing etc. *v.*; auditory, auricular, aural, auditive, acoustic.
Adv. *arrectis auribis*.
Int. hark, – ye! hear! list, -en! *Oyez!* attention! lend me your ears!

419. Deafness.—N. deafness, hardness of hearing, surdity; inaudibility.
V. be -deaf etc. *adj.*; have no ear; shut –, stop –, close- one's ears; turn a deaf ear to.
render deaf, stun, deafen.
Adj. deaf, earless, surd; hard –, dull- of hearing; deaf-mute, stunned, deafened; stone deaf; deaf as -a post, – an adder, – a beetle, – a trunk-maker.
inaudible etc. 405; out of hearing.

420. Light.—N. light, ray, beam, stream, gleam, streak, pencil; sun-, moon-beam; dawn, aurora.

day; sunshine; light of -day, – heaven; sun etc. (*luminary*) 432, day-, broad day-, noontide- light; noon-tide, -day; glare.

glow etc. *v.*; afterglow, sunset; glimmering etc. *v.*; glint; play –, flood- of light; phosphorescence, flush, halo, glory, nimbus, aureole, *aureola.*

spark, *scintilla*; *facula*; sparkling etc. *v.*; emication, scintillation, flash, blaze, coruscation, fulguration; flame etc. (*fire*) 382; lightning, *ignis fatuus*, etc. (*luminary*) 423, radio-activity.

luster, sheen, shimmer, reflection; gloss, tinsel, spangle, brightness, brilliancy, splendor; ef-, refulgence; ful-gor, -gidity; dazzlement, resplendence, transplendency; luminousness etc. *adj.*, luminosity; lucidity; renitency; radi-ance, -ation; irradiation, illumination, phosphorescence, luminescence.

radiation, radiant heat, infra-red rays, visible radiation, ultra-violet –, actinic- rays, actinism; X –, Roentgen- rays; phot-, heli-ography; optical instruments etc. 445.

[Science of light] optics; photo-logy, -metry; di-, cat-optrics.

[Distribution of light] *chiaroscuro*, *clair-obscur*, clear obscure, breadth, light and shade, black and white, tonality, half-tone, mezzotint.

reflection, refraction, dispersion, double refraction, polarization, diffraction, interference.

illuminant etc. 423.

V. shine, glow, glitter, phosphoresce; glis-ter, -ten; twinkle, gleam; flare, – up; glare, beam, shimmer, glimmer, flicker, sparkle, scintillate, coruscate, flash, fulgurate, blaze; be -bright etc. *adj.*; reflect light, daze, dazzle, bedazzle, raidate, shoot out beams.

clear up, brighten.

lighten, enlighten; light, – up; irradiate, shine upon; give –, hang out- a light; cast –, throw –, shed- -luster, – light- upon; illum-e, -ine, -inate; relume, strike a light; kindle etc. (*set fire to*) 384.

Adj. shining etc. *v.*; lumin-ous, -iferous; luc-id, -ent, -ulent, -ific, -iferous; illuminating, light, -some; bright, vivid, splendent, nitid, lustrous, shiny, brilliant, beamy, scintillant, radiant, lambent; sheen, -y; glossy, burnished, glassy, sunny, orient, meridian; noon-day, -tide; cloudless, clear; unclouded, -obscured.

garish; re-, tran-splendent; re-, effulgent; ful-gid, -gent; relucent, splendid, blazing, in a blaze, ablaze, rutilant, meteoric, phosphorescent; aglow.

bright as silver; light –, bright- as -day, – noonday, – the sun at noonday.

optical, actinic; photo-genic, -graphic; heliographic, radioactive.

421. Darkness.—N. darkness etc. *adj.*; blackness etc. (*dark color*) 431; obscurity, gloom, murk; dusk etc. (*dimness*) 422; tenebrosity, umbrageousness.

Cimmerian –, Stygian –, Egyptian- darkness; night; midnight; dead of –, witching time of- night; blind man's holiday; darkness -visible; – that can be felt; palpable, obscure; Erebus.

shade, shadow, umbra, penumbra; sciagraphy; *silhouette*; radiograph, skiagraph.

obscuration; ad-, ob-umbration; obtenebration, offuscation, caligation; extinction; eclipse, total eclipse; gathering of the clouds.

shading; distribution of shade; *chiaroscuro* etc. (*light*) 420.

noctivagation, noctograph, noctuary.

obscurantist.

V. be -dark etc. *adj.*

darken, obscure, shade; dim; tone down, lower; over-cast, -shadow; cloud, eclipse; ob-, of-fuscate; ob-, ad-umbrate, cast into the shade; be-cloud, -dim, -darken; cast –, throw –, spread- a -shade, – shadow, – gloom.

extinguish; put –, blow –, snuff- out; doubt.

Adj. dark, -some, -ling; obscure, tenebrous, tenebrious, sombrous, pitch dark, pitchy, caliginous; black etc. (*in color*) 431.

sunless, lightless etc. (*see* sun, light etc. 423); somber, dusky; unilluminated etc. (*see* illuminate etc. 420); nocturnal; dingy, lurid, gloomy; murk-y, -some; shady, umbrageous; overcast etc. (*dim*) 422; cloudy etc. (*opaque*) 426; darkened etc. *v.*

dark as -pitch, – a pit, – Erebus.

benighted; noctivag-ant, -ous.

Adv. in the -dark, – shade; at night.

422. Dimness.—N. dimness etc. *adj.*; darkness etc. 421; paleness etc. (*light color*) 429.

half-light, *demi-jour*; partial -shadow, – eclipse; shadow of a shade; glimmer, -ing; nebulosity; cloud etc. 353; eclipse.

aurora, dusk, twilight, gloaming, blind man's holiday, shades of evening, crepuscule, cockshut time; break of day, daybreak, dawn.

moon-light, -beam, -shine; star- owl's-, candle-, rush-, fire-light; farthing candle.

V. be –, grow- -dim etc. *adj.*; flicker, twinkle, glimmer; loom, lower; fade; darken; pale, – its ineffectual fire.

render -dim etc. *adj.*; dim, bedim, obscure.

Adj. dim, dull, lack-luster, dingy, darkish, shorn of its beams; dark 421.

faint, shadowed forth; glassy; bleary; cloudy; misty etc. (*opaque*) 426; muggy, fuliginous; nebul-ous, -ar; obnubilated, overcast, crepuscular, twilight, muddy, lurid, leaden, dun, dirty; looming etc. *v.*

pale etc. (*colorless*) 429; confused etc. (*invisible*) 447.

423. Luminary. [Source of light.]—**N.** luminary; light etc. 420; flame etc. (*fire*) 382.

spark, *scintilla*; phosphorescence.

sun, orb of day, day star, Phoebus, Apollo, Helios, Phaethon, Hyperion, Ra, Aurora; star, orb, meteor; falling –, shooting- star; blazing –, dog-star; Sirius, canicula, Aldebaran; morning star, Lucifer, Phosphor, evening star; Hesperus, Venus, planet, moon etc. 318; constellation, galaxy; northern light, *aurora -borealis*, – *australis*, zodiacal light; mock sun, parhelion.

lightning; fork –, sheet –, summer- lightning, St. Elmo's fire; phosphorus; *ignis fatuus*; Jack o' – Friar's- lantern; Will o' the wisp, fire-drake, *Fata Morgana.*

glow-worm, fire-fly.

radium, luminous paint.

[Artificial light] gas; gas –, lime –, electric –, head –, search –, spot –, flash –, flood –, footlight; lamp, oil –, gas –, arc –, incandescent-lamp; flare; lant-ern, -horn; dark lantern, bull's eye, projector; candle, *bougie*, tallow –, wax- candle; dip, farthing dip; taper, rush-light; oil etc. (*grease*) 356; wick, burner; Argand, moderator, duplex; torch, *flambeau*, link, brand; cresset; gase-, chande-, electro-lier; candelabrum, *girandole*, sconce, luster, candle-stick.

firework, fizgig; pyrotechnics; Roman candle, Very light, star shell, parachute light; rocket, lighthouse etc. (*signal*) 550.

V. illuminate etc. (*light*) 420.

Adj. self-luminous, incandescent; phosphor-ic, -escent; luminescent, fluorescent, radiant etc. (*light*) 420.

424. Shade.—N. shade; awning etc. (*cover*) 223; parasol, sunshade, umbrella; screen, curtain, shutter, blind, gauze, veil, mantle, mask; cloud, mist, gathering of clouds; smoke screen; smoked glasses, colored spectacles; blinkers, blinders.

umbrage, glade; shadow etc. 421.

V. draw a curtain; put up –, close- a shutter; veil etc. *v.*; cast a shadow etc. (*darken*) 421; screen, obstruct the view.

Adj. shady, umbrageous, bowery.

425. Transparency.—N. transparen-ce, -cy; translucen-ce, -cy; diaphaneity; luc-, pelluc-, limpidity.

transparent medium, glass, crystal, mica; lymph, water.

v. be -transparent etc. *adj.*; transmit light.

Adj. transparent, pellucid, lucid, diaphanous; trans-, tra-lucent; limpid, clear, serene, crystalline, clear as crystal, vitreous, transpicuous, glassy, hyaline.

426. Opacity.—N. opacity; opaqueness etc. *adj.*

film; cloud etc. 353.

V. be -opaque etc. *adj.*; obstruct the passage of light; ob-, of-fuscate.

Adj. opaque, impervious to light.

dim etc. 422; turbid, thick, muddy, opacous, obfuscated, fuliginous, cloudy, hazy, foggy, vaporous, nubiferous, muggy.

smoky, fumid, murky, dirty.

427. Semitransparency.—N. semitransparency, opalescence, milkiness, pearliness; gauze, muslin; film; mist etc. (*cloud*) 353; frosted glass.

Adj. semi-transparent, -pellucid, -diaphanous, -opacous, -opaque; opal-escent, -ine; pearly, milky, frosted, mat; misty.

428. Color.—N. color, hue, tint, tinge, dye, complexion, shade, tincture, cast, livery, coloration, chromatism, glow, flush; tone, key.

pure –, positive –, primary –, primitive –, complementary- color; three primaries; spectrum, chromatic dispersion; broken –, secondary –, tertiary- color.

local color, coloring, keeping, tone, value, aerial perspective.

[Science of color] chromatics, spectrum analysis; prism, spectroscope.

pigment, coloring matter, paint, dye, wash, distemper, stain; medium; mordant; oil-paint etc. (*painting*) 556.

V. color, dye, tinge, stain, tint, tinct, tone, paint, wash, ingrain, grain, illuminate, emblazon, imbue; paint etc. (*fine art*) 556; daub.

Adj. colored etc. *v.*; colorific, tingent, tinctorial; chormatic, prismatic; full-, high-, deep-colored; doubly-dyed; polychromatic.

bright, vivid, intense, deep; fresh, unfaded; rich, gorgeous; highly colored; gay; variegated etc. 440.

gaudy, florid; garish; showy, flaunting, flashy; raw, crude; glaring, flaring; discordant, inharmonious.

mellow, harmonious, pearly, sweet, delicate, tender, refined.

429. Achromatism. [Absence of color.]**—N.** achromatism; de-, dis-coloration; pall-or, -idity; paleness etc. *adj.*; etoilation; neutral tint, monochrome, black-and-white.

V. lose -color etc. 428; fade, fly, go; become -colorless etc. *adj.*; turn pale, pale, whiten.

deprive of color, decolorize, bleach, tarnish, achromatize, blanch, etiolate, wash out, tone down.

Adj. uncolored etc. (*see* color etc. 428); colorless, achromatic, hueless, pale, pallid; pale-, tallow-faced; faint, dull, cold, muddy, leaden, dun, wan, sallow, dead, dingy, ashy, ashen, ghastly, cadaverous, glassy, lack-luster; discolored etc. *v.*

light-colored, fair, *blond*; white etc. 430.

pale as -death, – ashes, – a witch, – a ghost, – a corpse.

430. Whiteness.—N. whiteness etc. *adj.*; argent.

albification, albescence, albinism, etiolation.

snow, paper, chalk, milk, lily, ivory, silver, alabaster; white lead, chinese –, flake –, ivory –, zinc- white, white-wash, -ning, whiting.

V. be -white etc. *adj.*

render -white etc. *adj.*; whiten- bleach, blanch, etiolate, whitewash, silver, frost.

Adj. white; milky, milk-, snow-white; snowy, niveous, candid, chalky; hoar, -y; frosted, silvery; argent, -ine; canescent.

whitish, creamy, pearly, ivory, fair, *blond*, ash-blond, platinum blond; blanched etc. *v.*; high in tone, light.

white as -a sheet, – driven snow, – a lily, – silver; like -ivory etc. *n.*

431. Blackness.—N. blackness etc. *adj.*; darkness etc. (*want of light*) 421; swarthness, lividity, dark color, tone, color; *chiaroscuro* etc. 420.

nigrification, infuscation, denigration.
jet, ink, ebony, coal, pitch, soot, smudge, charcoal, sloe, raven, crow; black.
[Pigments] lamp –, ivory –, blue-black; writing –, printing –, printer's –, Indian- ink.
V. be -black etc. *adj.*
render -black etc. *adj.*; blacken, infuscate, denigrate; blot, -ch; smutch; smirch; darken etc. 421.
Adj. black, sable, swarthy, somber, dark, inky, ebon, atramentous, jetty; coal-, jet-black; fuliginous, pitchy, sooty, swart, dusky, dingy, murky, low-toned, low in tone; of the deepest dye.
black as -jet etc. *n.*, – my hat, – a shoe, – a tinker's pot, – November, – thunder, – midnight; nocturnal etc. (*dark*) 421; nigrescent; gray etc. 432; obscure etc. 421.
Adv. in mourning.

432. Gray.—N. gray etc. *adj.*; neutral tint, silver, pepper and salt, *chiaroscuro*, *grisaille*, grayness.
[Pigments] Payne's gray; black etc. 431.
Adj. gray, grey; steel –, iron- gray, dun, drab, dingy, leaden, livid, somber, sad, pearly; silver, -y, -ed; ash-en, -y; ciner-eous, -itious; grizzl-y, -ed; dove-, slate-, stone-, mouse-, ash-colored; mole; cool.

433. Brown.—N. brown etc. *adj.*
[Pigments] bister, ocher, sepia, Vandyke brown.
Adj. brown, adust, bay, dapple, auburn, chestnut, nutbrown, cinnamon, hazel, fawn, puce, *écru*, russet, tawny, fuscous, chocolate, maroon, foxy, tan, brunette, whitey-brown; snuff-, liver-colored, brown as -a berry, – mahogany; reddish brown; copper-, rust- colored; henna, bronze, khaki; russet, roan, sorrel.
sub-burnt; tanned etc. *v.*
V. render -brown etc. *adj.*; tan, embrown, bronze.

434. Redness.—N. red, scarlet, vermilion, cardinal, Post Office, red, carmine, crimson, pink, lake, *cerise*, cherry red, maroon, carnation, *couleur de rose*, *rose du Barry*; magenta, damask; flesh -color, – tint; color; fresh –, high- color; warmth; gules.
ruby, garnet, carbuncle; rose; rust, iron-mold.
[Dyes and pigments] cinnabar, cochineal; fuchsine; ruddle, madder, redlead; light –, Venetian- red; red ink, annotto.
redness etc. *adj.*; rub-escence, -icundity, -ification; erubescence, blush.
V. be –, become- -red etc. *adj.*; blush, flush, color up, mantle, redden.
render- red etc. *adj.*; redden, rouge; rub-ify, -ricate; incarnadine; ruddle.
Adj. red etc. *n.*; -dish; rufous, ruddy, florid, incarnadine, sanguine, bloody, gory; ros-y, -eate; blowz-y, -ed; brunt; rubi-cund, -form; lurid, stammel, blood-red; russet, murrey, carroty, sorrel, lateritious.
rose-, ruby-, cherry-, claret-, wine-, plum-, flame-, flesh-, peach-, salmon-, brick-, brickdust-colored, reddish brown etc. 433.
red as -fire, – blood, – scarlet, – a turkeycock, – a lobster; warm, hot; foxy.

435. Greenness.—N. green etc. *adj.*; blue and yellow; vert.
emerald, verd antique, verdigris, malachite, beryl, aquamarine, reseda.
[Pigments] *terre verte*, verditer, bice, chlorophyl.
greenness, verdure, verdancy; viridity, -escence.
Adj. green, verdant; glaucous, olive; porraceous; green as grass.
emerald –, pea –, grass –, apple –, sea –, olive –, bottle –, leaf- green.
greenish; vir-ent, -escent.

436. Yellowness.—N. yellow etc. *adj.*; or.
[Pigments] gamboge; cadmium –, chrome –, Indian –, lemon- yellow; orpiment, yellow ocher, Claude tint, aureolin.
crocus, saffron, topaz, gold.
jaundice, London fog; yellowness etc. *adj.*
Adj. yellow, aureate, gold, golden, gilt, gilded, flavous, citrine, fallow; fulv-ous, -id; sallow, luteous, fawny, creamy, sandy; xanth-ic, -ous; jaundiced.
gold-, citron-, saffron-, lemon-, sulphur-, amber- straw-, primrose-, cream-colored; flazen, yellowish, buff.
yellow as a -quince, – guinea, – crow's foot.

437. Purple.—N. purple etc. *adj.*; blue and red, bishop's purple; aniline dyes, gridelin, amethyst; purpure.
livid-ness, -ity.
V. empurple.
Adj. purple, violet, plum-colored, lavender, lilac, puce, *mauve*; livid.

438. Blueness.—N. blue etc. *adj.*; garter-blue; watchet.
[Pigments] ultramarine, smalt, cobalt, cyanogen; Prussian –, syenite- blue; bice, indigo, woad.
lapis lazuli, sapphire, turquoise.
blue-, bluish-ness; bloom
Adj. blue, azure, cerulean; sky-blue, -colored, -dyed; navy-blue, aquamarine, electric blue, royal blue, cyanic; bluish; atmospheric, retiring; cold.

439. Orange.—N. orange, red and yellow; gold; or; flame etc. color, *adj.*
[Pigments] ochre, Mars orange, cadmium.
V. gild, warm.
Adj. orange; ocherous; orange-, gold-, flame-, copper-, brass-, apricot-colored; warm, hot, glowing.

440. Variegation.—N. variegation; di-, trichromism; iridescence, irisation, play of colors, polychrome, maculation, spottiness, striae.

spectrum, rainbow, iris, tulip, peacock, chameleon, butterfly, tortoiseshell; mackerel, – sky; zebra, leopard, mother-of-pearl, nacre, opal, marble, batik.

check, plaid, tartan, patchwork; mar-, parquetry; mosiac, *tesserae*, tesselation, chess-board, checkers, chequers; harlequin; Joseph's coat; tricolor; patches, bands, stripes, spots etc of color.

V. be -variegated etc. *adj.*; variegate, stripe, streak, checker, chequer; be-, speckle, fleck; be-, sprinkle; stipple, maculate, dot, bespot; tattoo, inlay, tesselate, damascene; embroider, braid, quilt.

Adj. variegated etc. *v.*; many-colored, -hued; divers-, parti-colored; di-, poly-chromatic; bi-, tri-, versi-color; of all -the colors of the rainbow, – manner of colors; kaleidoscopic.

iridescent; opal-ine, -escent; prismatic, nacreous, pearly, shot, *gorge de pigeon*, *chatoyant*, irisated.

pied, piebald, skewbald; motley; mottled, marbled; pepper and salt, paned, dappled, clouded, cymophanous.

mosiac, tesselated, chequered, plaid; tortoiseshell etc. *n.*

spott-ed, -y; punctuated, powdered; speckled etc. *v.*; freckled, fleabitten, studded; fleck-ed, -ered; striated, barred, veined; brind-ed, -led; tabby; watered; grizzled; listed; embroidered etc. *v.*; daedal.

441. Vision.—N. vision, sight, optics, eye-sight.

view, look, espial, glance, ken, *coup d'oeil*; glimpse, peep, glint; gaze, stare, leer; perlustration, contemplation; conspect-ion, -uity; regard, survey; in-, intro-spection; *reconnaissance*, speculation, watch, espionage, *espionnage*, autopsy; ocular - inspection, – demonstration; sight-seeing.

macrography, micrography.

point of view; view-, stand- point; gazebo, loophole, *belvedere*, watchtower.

field of view; theater, amphitheater, arena, vista, horizon; commanding –, bird's eye –, panoramic- view; periscope.

visual organ, organ of vision; eye; naked –, unassisted- eye; eye-ball, retina, pupil, iris, cornea, white; optics, orbs; saucer –, goggle –, gooseberry-eyes.

short sight etc. 443; clear –, sharp –, quick –, eagle –, piercing-, –, penetrating- -sight, – glance, – eye; perspicacity, discernment; catopsis.

eagle, hawk; cat, lynx; Argus.

evil eye; basilisk, cockatrice.

spectacles, telescope etc. 445.

V. see, behold, discern, perceive, have in sight, descry, sight, make out, discover, distinguish, recognize, spy, espy, ken; get –, have –, catch- a - sight, – glimpse- of; command of view of; witness, contemplate, speculate; cast –, set- the eyes on; be a -spectator etc. 444- of; look on etc. (*be present*) 186; see sights etc. (*curiosity*) 445; see at a glance etc. (*intelligence*) 498.

look, view, eye; lift up the eyes, open one's eye; look -at, – on, – upon, – over, – about one, – round; survey, scan, inspect; run the eye -over, – through; reconnoiter, glance -round, – on, – over; turn –, bend- one's looks upon; direct the eyes to, turn the eyes on, cast a glance, make eyes at.

observe etc. (*attend to*) 457; watch etc. (*care*) 459; see with one's own eyes; watch for etc. (*expect*) 507; peek, peep, peer, pry, take a peep; play at bo-peep.

look -full in the face, – hard at, – intently; strain one's eyes; fix –, rivet- the eyes upon; stare, gaze; pore over, gloat -over, – on; leer, ogle, glare; goggle; cock the eye, squint, gloat, look askance; give the glad eye.

Adj. seeing etc. *v.*; visual, ocular, -al; ophthalmic.

far-, clear-sighted etc. *n.*; eagle-, hawk-, lynx-, keen-, Argus-eyed.

visible etc. 446.

Adv. visibly etc. 446; in sight of, with one's eyes open.

at -sight, – first sight, – a glance, – the first blush; *primâ facie*.

Int. look! etc. (*attention*) 457.

Phr. the scales falling from one's eyes.

442. Blindness.—N. blindness, anopsia, cecity, excecation, *amaurosis*, cataract, ablepsy, prestriction; dim-sightedness etc. 443.

V. be -blind etc. *adj.*; not see; lose sight of; have the eyes bandaged; grope in the dark.

not look; close –, shut –, turn away –, avert- the eyes; look another way; wink etc. (*limited vision*) 443; shut the eyes –, be blind- to; wink –, blink- at.

render -blind etc. *adj.*; blind, -fold; hoodwink, dazzle; put one's eyes out; throw dust into one's eyes; *jeter de la poudre aux yeux*; screen from sight etc. (*hide*) 528.

Adj. blind; eye-, sight-, vision-less; dark; stone-, sand-, stark-blind; undiscerning; dim-sighted etc. 443.

blind as -a bat, – a buzzard, – a beetle, – a mole, – an owl; wall-eyed.

blinded etc. *v.*

Adv. blind-ly, -fold; darkly.

443. Dim-sightedness. [Imperfect vision.] [Fallacies of vision.]—**N.** dim –, dull –, half –, short –, near –, long –, double –, astigmatic –, failing- sight; dim etc -sightedness; snow blindness; purblindness, lippitude; my-, presby-opia; confusion of vision; astigmatism; nystagmus; color-blindness, dichromism, chromato-pseudo-blepsis, Daltonism; nyctalopy; *strabismus*, strabism, squint, cast in the eye, swivel eye, goggle eyes; obliquity of vision.

winking etc. *v.*; nictitation; blinkard, albino.

dizziness, swimming, scotomy; cataract; ophthalmia.

[Limitation of vision] eye shade, blinker, blinder; screen etc. (*hider*) 530.

[Fallacies of vision] *deceptio visûs*; refraction, distortion, illustion, false light, *anamorphosis*, virtual image, *spectrum*, *mirage*, looming, phasma; phant-asm, -asma, -om; vision; specter, apparition, ghost; *ignis fatuus* etc. (*luminary*) 423; specter of the Brocken; magic mirror; magic lantern etc. (*show*) 448; mirror, lens etc. (*instrument*) 445.

V. be -dim-sighted etc. *n.*; see double; have a -mote in the eye, – mist before the eyes, – film over the eyes; see through a -prism, – glass darkly; wink, blink, nictitate; squint; look ask-ant, -ance; screw up the eyes, glare, glower.

dazzle, glare, blur, swim, loom.

Adj. dim-sighted etc. *n.*; my-, presby-opic; astigmatic; moon-, mope-, blear-, goggle-, gooseberry-, one-eyed; blind of one eye, monoculous; half-, pur-, color-blind; dichromatic.

blind as a bat etc. (*blind*) 442; winking etc. *v.*

444. Spectator.—N. spectator, beholder, observer, inspector, viewer, looker-on, onlooker, witness, eye-witness, bystander, passer by; sight-seer.

spy, scout; sentinel etc. (*warning*) 668.

v. witness, behold etc. (*see*) 441; look on etc. (*be present*) 186.

445. Optical Instruments.—N. optical instruments; lens, meniscus, magnifier, reading –, burning- glass; micro-, mega-, teino-scope; spectacles, glasses, barnacles, goggles, giglamps, eyeglass, *pince-nez*, monocle; periscopic lens; telescope, glass, lorgnette, binocular; spy-, opera-, field-glass, periscope, range finder.

mirror, reflector, speculum; looking-, pier-, cheval-, hand-glass.

prism; camera, *camera-lucida*, *-obscura*; projector, stereopticon, magic lantern etc. (*show*) 448; chro-, thau-matrope; stereo-, pseudo-, poly-, kaleido-scope.

photo-, opto-, erio-, actino-, luci-, radio-, spectro-meter; polari-, polemo-, spectro-scope, diffraction grating.

optics, optician, optometry, optometrist; microscop-y, -ist; photometry, photography; photographer.

446. Visibility.—N. visibility, perceptibility; conspicuousness, distinctness etc. *adj.*; conspicuity; appearance etc. 448; exposure; manifestation etc. 525; ocular -proof, – evidence, – demonstration; field of view etc. (*vision*) 441.

V. be –, become- -visible etc. *adj.*; appear, emerge, open to the view, meet –, catch- the eye, present –, show –, manifest –, produce –, discover –, reveal –, expose –, betray- itself; stand -forth, – out; show; arise; peep –, peer –, crop- out; start –, spring –, show –, turn –, crop- up; glimmer, glitter, glow, loom; glare; burst forth, scintillate; burst upon the -view, – sight; heave in sight; come -in sight, – into view, – out, – forth, – forward; see the light of day; break through the clouds; make its appearance, show its face, materialize, appear to one's eyes, come upon the stage, enter; float before the eyes, speak for itself. etc. (*manifest*) 525; attract the attention etc. 457; reappear; live in a glass house.

expose to view etc. 525.

Adj. visible, perceptible, perceivable, discernible, apparent; in -view, – full view, – sight; exposed to view, *en évidence*; unclouded.

obvious etc. (*manifest*) 525; plain, clear, distinct, definite; well-defined, -marked; in focus; recognizable, palpable, autoptical; glaring, staring, conspicuous; stereoscopic; in -bold, – strong, – high- relief.

periscopic, panoramic.

before –, under- one's eyes; before one, *à vue d'oeil*, in one's eye, *oculis subjecta fidelibus.*

Adv. visibly etc. *adj.*; in sight of; before one's eyes etc. *adj.*; *veluti in speculum.*

447. Invisibility.—N. invisibility, nonappearance, imperceptibility; indistinctness etc. *adj.*; mystery, delitescence.

concealment etc. 528; latency etc. 526.

V. be -invisible etc. *adj.*; be hidden etc. (*hide*) 528; lurk etc. (*lie hidden*) 526; escape notice.

render -invisible etc. *adj.*; conceal etc. 528; put out of sight.

not see etc. (*be blind*) 442; lose sight of.

Adj. invisible, imperceptible; un-, in-discernible; un-, non-apparent; out of –, not in- sight; *à perte de vue*; behind the -scenes, – curtain; view-, sightless; in-, un-conspicuous; unseen etc. (*see* see etc. 441); covert etc. (*latent*) 526; eclipsed, under an eclipse.

dim etc. (*faint*) 422; mysterious, dark, obscure, confused; indistin-ct, -guishable; shadowy, indefinite, undefined; ill-defined, -marked; blurred, fuzzy, out of focus; misty etc. (*opaque*) 426; veiled etc. (*concealed*) 528; delitescent.

448. Appearance.—N. appearance, phenomenon, sight, spectacle, show, premonstration, scene, species, view, *coup d'oeil*; look-out, out-look, prospect, vista, perspective, bird's-eye view, scenery, landscape, picture, *tableau*; display, exposure, *mise en scène*; scenery, *décor*; rising of the curtain.

phant-asm, -om etc. (*fallacy of vision*) 443.

pageant, *spectacle*; peep-, raree-, gallanty-show; *ombres chinoises*; projector, optical –, magic-lantern, phantasmagoria, dissolving views; cinema, -tograph; bio-scope, -graph; moving pictures, movies, film, screen etc.; pan-, di-, cosm-, georama; *coup –*, *jeu- de théâtre*; pageantry etc. (*ostentation*) 882; insignia etc. (*indication*) 550.

aspect, phase, *phasis*, seeming; shape etc. (*form*) 240; guise, look, complexion, color, image, mien, air, cast, carriage, port, demeanor; presence, expression, first blush, face of the thing; point of view, light.

lineament, feature, trait, lines; out-line, -side; contour, *silhouette*, face, countenance, physiognomy, visage, phiz, mug, cast of countenance, profile, *tournure*, cut of one's jib, metoposcopy; outside etc. 220.

V. appear; be –, become- visible etc. 446; seem, look, show; present –, wear –, carry –, have –, bear –, exhibit –, take –, take on –, assume- the -appearance, – semblance- of; look like; cut a figure, figure; present to the view; show etc. (*make manifest*) 525.

Adj. apparent, seeming, ostensible; on view.

Adv. apparently; to all -seeming, – appearance; ostensibly, seemingly, as it seems, on the face of it, *primâ facie*; at the first blush, at first sight; in the eyes of; to the eye.

449. Disappearance.—N. disappearance, evanescence, eclipse, occultation.

departure etc. 293; exit, vanishing point; dissolving views.

V. disappear, vanish, dissolve, fade, melt away, pass, go, avaunt; be -gone etc. *adj.*; leave -no trace, – 'not a rack behind;' go off the stage etc. (*depart*) 293; suffer –, undergo- an eclipse; be lost to –, retire from- -sight, – view.

lose sight of.

efface etc. 552.

Adj. disappearing etc. *v.*; evanescent; missing, lost; lost to -sight, – view; gone; *spurlos versenki.*

Int. vanish! disappear! avaunt! etc. (*ejection*) 297.

450. Intellect.—N. intellect, mind, understanding, reason, thinking principle; rationality; cogitative –, cognitive –, intellectual- faculties; faculties, senses, consciousness, observation, percipience, apperception, mentality, intelligence, intellection, intuition, association of ideas, instinct, flair, conception, judgment, wits, parts, capacity, intellectuality, reasoning power, brains, genius; wit etc. 498; ability etc. (*skill*) 698; wisdom etc. 498.

soul, spirit, ghost, inner man, heart, breast, bosom, ***penetralia mentis, divina particula aurae***, heart's core; ego, psyche, pneuma, subconsciousness, subconscious, subliminal self; dual personality.

organ –, seat- of thought; *sensorium*, sensory, brain, gray matter; head, -piece; pate, noddle, skull, scull, *pericranium, cerebrum, cranium*, brain-pan, -box; sconce, upper story.

[Science of mind] metaphysics; psychics, psycho-logy, -metry, -genesis, -analysis, -physics, psychi-atry, -cal research, thought reading etc. 992; ideology; mental –, moral- philosophy; philosophy of the mind; pneumat-, phren-ology; no –, craniology, -scopy.

ideal-ity, -ism; transcendental-, spiritual-ism; immateriality etc. 317.

metaphysician, psychologist etc.

V. note, notice, mark; take -notice, – cognizance- of; be -aware, – conscious- of; realize; appreciate; ruminate etc. (*think*) 451; fancy etc. (*imagine*) 515; conceive, reason, understand.

Adj. [Relating to intellect] intellectual, mental, rational, subjective, metaphysical, nooscopic, spiritual; ghostly; psych-ical, -ological; cerebral.

immaterial etc. 317; endowed with reason.

Adv. *in petto.*

450a. Absence or want **of Intellect.—N.** absence –, want- of -intellect etc. 450; imbecility etc. 499; brutality; brute -instinct, – force.

Adj. unendowed with reason.

451. Thought.—N. thought; exercitation –, exercise- of the intellect; reflection, cogitation, consideration, meditation, study, lucubration, speculation, deliberation, pondering; head-, brain-work; cerebration; mentation, deep reflection; close study, application etc. (*attention*) 457.

abstract thought, abstraction, contemplation, musing; brown study etc. (*inattention*) 458; reverie, Platonism; depth of thought, workings of the mind, thoughts, inmost thoughts; self-counsel, communing, -consultation.

association –, succession –, flow –, train –, current- of -thought, – ideas.

after –, mature- thought; reconsideration, second thoughts; retrospection etc. (*memory*) 505; excogitation; examination etc. (*inquiry*) 461; invention etc. (*imagination*) 515.

thoughtfulness etc. *adj.*

V. think, reflect, reason, cogitate, excogitate, consider, deliberate; bestow -thought, – consideration- upon; speculate, contemplate, meditate, ponder, muse, dream, ruminate; brood –, con- over; animadvert, study; bend–, apply- the mind etc. (*attend*) 457; digest, discuss, hammer at, weigh, perpend; realize, appreciate; fancy etc. (*imagine*) 515; trow.

take into consideration; take counsel etc. (*be advised*) 695; commune with –, bethink- oneself; collect one's thoughts; revolve –, turn over –, run over- in the mind; chew the cud –, sleep- upon; take counsel of –, advise with- one's pillow.

rack –, ransack –, crack –, beat –, cudgel- one's brains; set one's -brain, – wits- to work.

harbor –, entertain –, cherish –, nurture- an idea etc. 453; take into one's head; bear in mind; reconsider.

occur; present –, suggest- itself; come –, get- into one's head; strike one, flit across the view, come uppermost, run in one's head; enter –, pass in –, cross –, flash on –, flash across –, float in –, fasten itself on –, be uppermost in –, occupy- the mind; have in one's mind.

make an impression; sink –, penetrate- into the mind; engross the thoughts.

Adj. thinking etc. *v.*; thoughtful, pensive, meditative, reflective, cogitative, museful, wistful, contemplative, speculative, deliberative, studious, sedate, introspective, Platonic, philosophical.

lost –, engrossed –, rapt –, absorbed- in thought etc. (*inattentive*) 458; deep musing etc. (*intent*) 457.

in the mind, under consideration, in contemplation.

Adv. all things considered; taking everything into account.

Phr. the mind being on the stretch; the -mind, – head- -turning, – running- upon.

452. Incogitancy. [Absence or want of thought.]**—N.** incogitancy, vacancy, inunderstanding; inanity, fatuity etc. 499; thoughtlessness etc. (*inattention*) 458.

V. not -think etc. 451; not think of; dismiss from the -mind, – thoughts etc. 451.

indulge in reverie etc. (*be inattentive*) 458.

put away thought; unbend –, relax –, divert- the mind.

Adj. vacant, unintellectual, unideal, unoccupied, unthinking, inconsiderate, thoughtless; absent etc. (*inattentive*) 458; diverted; irrational etc. 499; narrow-minded etc. 481.

un-thought of, -dreamt of, -considered; off one's mind; incogitable, not to be thought of, inconceivable.

453. Idea. [Object of thought.]—**N.** idea, notion, conception, thought, apprehension, impression, perception, image, sentiment, reflection, observation, consideration; abstract idea, principle; archetype.

view etc. (*opinion*) 484; theory etc. 514; conceit, fancy; phantasy etc. (*imagination*) 515.

point of view etc. (*aspect*) 448; field of view.

454. Topic. [Subject of thought.]—**N.** subject of –, material for- thought; food for the mind, mental *pabulum*.

subject, -matter; matter, theme, topic, what it is about, *thesis*, text, business, affair, matter in hand, argument; motion, resolution; head, chapter; case, point; proposition, theorem; field of inquiry; moot point, problem, etc. (*question*) 461.

V. float –, pass- in the mind etc. 451.

Adj. thought of; uppermost in the mind; *in petto*.

Adv. under -discussion, – consideration, – advisement; in -question, – the mind; on -foot, – the carpet, – the *tapis*; before the house, relative to etc. 9

455. Curiosity. [The desire of knowledge.]—**N.** interest, thirst for knowledge; curi-osity, -ousness; inquiring mind; inquisitiveness.

sight-seer, quidnunc, newsmonger, Paul Pry, peeping Tom, eavesdropper; gossip etc. (*news*) 532; questioner, *enfant terrible*.

V. be -curious etc. *adj.*; take an interest in, stare, gape; prick up the ears, see sights, lionize; pry, speer; dig up.

Adj. curious, inquisitive, burning with curiosity, overcurious, nosey; inquiring etc. 461; prying; inquisitorial; agape etc. (*expectant*) 507; attentive etc. 457.

Phr. what's the matter? what next?

456. Incuriosity. [Absence of curiosity.]—**N.** incuriosity; incuriousness etc. *adj.*; *insouciance* etc. 866; indifference, apathy.

V. be -incurious etc. *adj.*; have no -curiosity etc. 455; take no interest in etc. 823; mind one's own business.

Adj. incurious, uninquisitive, uninterested, indifferent, bored; impassive etc. 823.

457. Attention.—N. attention; mindfulness etc. *adj.*; intent-ness, -iveness; thought etc. 451; adverten-ce, -cy; observ-ance, -ation; consideration, reflection, perpension; heed; particularity; notice, regard etc. *v.*; circumspection etc. (*care*) 459; study, scrutiny, once-over; in-, intro-spection; revision, -al.

active –, diligent –, exclusive –, minute –, close –, intense –, deep –, profound –, abstract –, labored –, deliberate- -thought, – attention, – application, – study.

minuteness, attention to detail etc. 459.

absorption of mind etc. (*abstraction*) 458.

indication, calling attention to etc. *v.*

V. be -attentive etc. *adj.*; attend, advert to, observe, look, see, view, remark, notice, regard, take notice, mark; give –, pay- -attention, – heedto; listen in, incline –, lend- an ear to; trouble one's head about; give a thought –, animadvert- to; occupy oneself with; contemplate etc. (*think of*) 451; look -at, – to, – after, – into, – over; see to; turn –, bend –, apply –, direct –, give- the -mind, – eye, – attention- to; have -an eye to, – in one's eye; bear in mind; take into -account, – consideration; keep in -sight, – view; have regard to, heed, mind, take cognizance of, be engaged in, entertain, recognize; make –, take- note of; note.

examine cursorily; glance at, – upon, – over; cast –, pass- the eyes over; run over, turn over the leaves, dip into, perstringe; skim etc. (*neglect*) 460; take a cursory view of.

examine, – closely, – intently; scan, scrutinize, consider, give –, bend- one's mind to; overhaul, revise, pore over; inspect, review, pass under review; take stock of; fix –, rivet –, focus –, devote- the - eye, – mind, – thoughts, – attention- on *or* to; hear –, think- out; mind one's business.

revert –, hark back- to; watch etc. (*expect*) 507, (*take care of*) 459; hearken –, listen- to; prick up the ears; have –, keep- the eyes open; come to the point.

meet with attention; fall under one's -notice, – observation; be -under consideration etc. (*topic*) 454.

catch –, strike- the eye; attract notice; catch –, awaken –, wake –, invite –, solicit –, attract –, claim –, excite –, engage –, occupy –, strike –, arrest –, fix –, engross –, absorb –, rivet-the- attention, – mind, – thoughts; be present to, – uppermost in- the mind.

bring under one's notice; point -out, – to, – at, – the finger at; lay the finger on, indigitate, indicate; direct –, call- attention to; show; put a - mark etc. (*sign*) 550- upon; call soldiers to 'attention;' bring forward etc. (*make manifest*) 525.

Adj. attentive, mindful, heedful, observant, regardful; alive –, awake- to, alert; observing etc. *v.*; taken up –, occupied- with; engaged –, engrossed –, interested –, wrapped- in; absorbed, rapt; breathless; pre-occupied etc. (*inattentive*) 458; watchful etc. (*careful*) 459; intent on, open-eyed, breathless, undistracted, upon the stretch; on the watch etc. (*expectant*) 507.

steadfast.

Int. see! look, – here, – out, – alive, – you, – to it! mark! lo! behold! soho! hark, – ye! mind! halloo! observe! lo and behold! attention! *nota bene*; N.B.; *,†; I'd have you to know; notice! take notice! O yes! *Oyez!*

Phr. this is –, these are- to give notice.

458. Inattention.—N. in-attention, -consideration; inconsiderateness etc. *adj.*; oversight; inadverten-ce, -cy; non-observance, disregard.

supineness etc. (*inactivity*) 683; *étourderie*; want of thought; heedlessness etc. (*neglect*) 460; *insouciance* etc. (*indifference*) 866.

abstraction; absence –, absorption- of mind; preoccupation, distraction, reverie, brown study, deep musing, fit of abstraction, woolgathering.

V. be -inattentive etc. *adj.*; overlook, disregard; pass by etc. (*neglect*) 460; not -observe etc. 457; think little of.

close –, shut- one's eyes to; wink at; pay no attention to; dismiss –, discard –, discharge- from one's -thoughts, – mind; drop the subject, think no more of; set –, turn –, put- aside; turn -away from, – one's attention from, – a deaf ear to, – one's back upon.

abstract oneself, dream, indulge in reverie.

escape -notice, – attention; come in at one ear and go out at the other; forget etc. (*have no remembrance*) 506.

call off –, draw off –, call away –, divert –, distract- the -attention, – thoughts, – mind; put out of one's head; dis-concert, -compose; put out, confuse, perplex, bewilder, fluster, muddle, dazzle; throw a sop to Cerberus.

Adj. inattentive; un-observant, -mindful, -heeding, -discerning; inadvertent; mind-, regard-, respect-less; listless etc. (*indifferent*) 866; blind, deaf; flighty, hand over head; cur-, percur-sory; giddy-, scatter-, hare-brained; unreflecting, *écervelé*, inconsiderate, off-hand, thoughtless, dizzy, muzzy, brainsick; giddy, – as a goose; wild, harum-scarum, ranipole, high-flying; heed-, careless etc. (*neglectful*) 460.

absent, absent-minded, abstracted, *distrait*; lost; lost –, wrapped- in thought, woolgathering; rapt, in the clouds, bemused; dreaming –, musing- on other things; pre-occupied; engrossed etc. (*attentive*) 457; in a -reverie etc. *n.*; off one's guard etc. (*inexpectant*) 508; napping; dreamy.

disconcerted, put out etc. *v.*; rattled.

Adv. inattentively, inadvertently etc. *adj.*; *per incuriam, sub silentio.*

Int. stand -at ease, – easy!

Phr. the attention wanders; one's wits gone a -woolgathering, – bird's nesting; it never entered into one's head; the mind running on other things; one's thoughts being elsewhere; had it been a bear it would have bitten you.

459. Care. [Vigilance.]—**N.** care, solicitude, heed; heedfulness etc. *adj.*; scruple etc. (*conscientiousness*) 939.

watchfulness etc. *adj.*; vigilance, *surveillance*, eyes of Argus, watch, vigil, look out, watch and ward, *l'oeil du maître.*

alertness etc. (*activity*) 682; attention etc. 457; prudence etc., circumspection etc. (*caution*) 864; forethought etc. 510; precaution etc. (*preparation*) 673; tidiness etc. (*order*) 58, (*cleanliness*) 652; accuracy etc. (*exactness*) 494; minuteness, attention to detail; meticulousness, nicety, circumstantiality.

V. be -careful etc. *adj.*; reck; take care etc. (*be cautious*) 864; pay attention to etc. 457; take care of; look –, see- -to, – after; keep -an eye, – a sharp eye- upon; keep -watch, – watch and ward; mount guard, set watch, watch; keep in -sight, – view; chaperon, play gooseberry; mind, – one's business.

look -sharp, – about one; look with one's own eyes; keep a -good, – sharp- look-out; have all one's -wits, – eyes- about one; watch for etc. (*expect*) 507; stand to; keep one's eyes –, have the eyes –, sleep with one eye- open.

take precautions etc. 673; protect etc. (*render safe*) 664.

do one's best etc. 682; mind one's Ps and Qs, speak by the card, pick one's steps.

Adj. care-, regard-, heed-ful; taking care etc. *v.*; particular; prudent etc. (*cautious*) 864; considerate; thoughtful etc. (*deliberative*) 451; provident etc. (*prepared*) 673; alert etc. (*active*) 682; sure-footed.

guarded, on one's guard; on the *-qui vive*, – alert, – watch, – look-out; awake, broad awake, vigilant; watch-, wake-, wist-ful; Argus-, lynx-eyed; wide awake etc. (*intelligent*) 498; on the watch for etc. (*expectant*) 507.

tidy etc. (*orderly*) 58, (*clean*) 652; accurate etc. (*exact*) 494; scrupulous etc. (*conscientious*) 939; *cavendo tutus* etc. (*safe*) 664.

Adv. carefully etc. *adj.*; with care, gingerly.

Phr. *quis custodiet ipsos custodes?*

460. Neglect.—**N.** neglect; carelessness etc. *adj.*; trifling etc. *v.*; negligence; omission, laches, default; remissness, slackness, procrastination; supineness etc. (*inactivity*) 683; inattention etc. 458; *nonchalance* etc. (*insensibility*) 823; imprudence, recklessness etc. 863; slovenliness etc. (*disorder*) 59; (*dirt*) 653; improvidence etc. 674; non-completion etc. 730; inexactness etc. (*error*) 495.

paraleipsis [in rhetoric].

trifler, slacker, waster, waiter on Providence; Micawber.

V. be -negligent etc. *adj.*; take no care of etc. (take care of etc. 459); neglect; let -slip, – go; lay –, set –, cast –, put- aside; keep –, leave- out of sight; lose sight of.

overlook, disregard; pass -over, – by; let pass; blink; wink –, connive- at; gloss over; take no -note, – notice, – thought, – account- of; pay no regard to; *laisser aller*; allow to lie on the table.

scamp; trifle, fribble; do by halves; skimp; cut; slight etc. (*despise*) 930; play –, trifle- with; slur; skim, – the surface; *effleurer*; take a cursory view of etc. 457.

slur –, slip –, skip –, jump- over; pretermit, miss, skip, jump, omit, give the go-by to, push aside, throw into the background, shelve, sink; ignore, shut one's eyes to, refuse to hear, turn a deaf ear to; leave out of one's calculation; not -attend to etc. 457, – mind; not trouble -oneself, – one's head- -with, – about; forget etc. 506; be caught napping etc. (*not expect*) 508; leave a loose thread; let the grass grow under one's feet.

render -neglectful etc. *adj.*; put –, throw- off one's guard.

Adj. neglecting etc. *v.*; unmindful, negligent, neglectful; heedless, careless, thoughtless; perfunctory, remiss, slack.

inconsiderate; un-, in-circumspect; off one's guard; un-wary, -watchful, -guarded; offhand.

supine etc. (*inactive*) 683; inattentive etc 458; *insouciant* etc. (*indifferent*) 823; imprudent, reckless etc. 863; slovenly etc. (*disorderly*) 59, (*dirty*) 653; inexact etc. (*erroneous*) 495; improvident etc. 674.

neglected etc. *v.*; un-heeded, -cared for, -

perceived, -seen, -observed, -noticed, -noted, -marked, -attended to, -thought of, -regarded, -remarked, -missed; shunted, shelved.

un-examined, -studied, -searched, -scanned, -weighed, -sifted, -explored.

Adv. negligently etc. *adj.*; hand over head, anyhow; in an unguarded moment etc. (*unexpectedly*) 508; *per incuriam*.

Int. never mind, no matter, let it pass; it will be all the same a hundred years hence.

461. Inquiry. [Subject of Inquiry. Question.]—**N.** inquiry; request etc. 765; search, research, quest; pursuit etc. 622.

examination, review, scrutiny, investigation, indagation; per-quisition, -scrutation, -vestigation; inqu-est, -isition; exploration; *exploitation*, ventilation.

sifting; calculation, analysis, dissection, resolution, induction; Baconian method.

strict —, close —, searching —, exhaustive- inquiry; narrow —, strict- search; study etc. (*consideration*) 451.

scire facias, *ad referendum*; trial.

questioning etc. *v.*; interroga-tion, -tory; third degree; interpellation; challenge, examination, cross-examination, catechism; feeler, Socratic method, zetetic philosophy; leading question; discussion etc. (*reasoning*) 476; questionnaire, questionary.

reconnoitering, *reconnaissance*, prying etc. *v.*, espionage, *espionnage*; domiciliary visit, peep behind the curtain; lantern of Diogenes.

question, query, problem, *desideratum*, point to be solved, porism; subject —, field- of -inquiry, — controversy; point —, matter- in dispute; moot-point; issue, question at issue; bone of contention etc. (*discord*) 713; plain —, fair —, open- question; enigma etc. (*secret*) 533; knotty point etc. (*difficulty*) *704*; *quod-libet*; threshold of an inquiry.

inquirer, investigator, experimenter, inquisitor, inspector, querist, examiner, catechist; scrut-ator, -ineer; analyst; quidnunc etc. (*curiosity*) 455.

V. make -inquiry etc. *n.*; inquire, seek, search, frisk, speer, look -for, — about for, — out for; scan, reconnoiter, explore, sound, rummage, ransack, pry, peer, look round; look —, go- -over, — through; spy, over-haul.

scratch the head, slap the forehead.

look —, peer —, pry- into every hole and corner; look behind the scenes; trace up; hunt —, fish —, dig —, ferret- out; unearth; leave no stone unturned.

seek a -clue, — clew; hunt, track, trail, shadow, mouse, dodge, trace; follow the -trail, — scent; pursue etc. 622; beat up one's quarters; fish for; feel for etc. (*experiment*) 463.

investigate; take up —, institute —, pursue —, follow up —, conduct —, carry on —, prosecute- -an inquiry etc. *n.*; look -at, — into; pre-examine; discuss, canvass, agitate.

examine, study, consider, calculate; dip —, dive —, delve —, go deep- into; make sure of, probe, sound, fathom; probe to the -bottom, — quick; scrutinize, analyze, anatomize, dissect, parse, resolve, sift, winnow; view —, try- in all its phases; thresh out.

bring in question, subject to examination; put to the proof etc. (*experiment*) 463; audit, tax, pass in review; take into consideration etc. (*think over*) 451; take counsel etc. 695.

ask, question, demand; put —, pop —, propose —, propound —, moot —, start —, raise —, stir —, suggsst —, put forth —, ventilate —, grapple with —, go into- a question.

put to the question, interrogate, catechize, pump, grill; cross-question, -examine; dodge; require an answer; pick —, suck- the brains of; feel the pulse.

be -in question etc. *adj.*; undergo examination.

Adj. inquiry etc. *v.*; inquisitive etc. (*curious*) 455; requisit-ive, -ory; catechetical, inquisitorial, analytic; in -search, — quest- of; on the look-out for, interrogative, zetetic; all-searching.

un-determined, -tried, -decided; in -question, — dispute, — issue, — course of inquiry; under -discussion, — consideration, — investigation etc. *n.*, *sub judice*, moot, proposed; doubtful etc. (*uncertain*) 475.

Adv. what? why? wherefore? whence? whither? where? *quaere?* how -comes, — happens, — is- it? what is the reason? what's -the matter, — up, in the wind? what on earth? when? who?

462. Answer.—**N.** answer, response, reply, replication, *riposte*, rejoinder, surrejoinder, rebutter, surrebutter, counter-evidence etc. 468, counter-charge, defence, plea; retort, repartee; contradiction etc. 536; rescript, -ion; antiphon, -y; acknowledgment; password; echo.

discovery etc. 480*a*; solution etc. (*explanation*) 522; rationale etc. (*cause*) 153; clue etc. (*indication*) 550.

Oedipus; oracle, etc. 513; return etc. (*record*) 551.

V. answer, respond, reply, rebut, retort, rejoin; give —, return for- answer; acknowledge, echo.

explain etc. (*interpret*) 522; solve etc. (*unriddle*) 522; discover etc. 480*a*; fathom, hunt out etc. (*inquire*) 461; satisfy, set at rest, determine.

Adj. answering etc. *v.*; respon-sive, -dent; oracular; antiphonal; conclusive.

Adv. because etc. (*cause*) 153; on the -scent, — right scent.

Int. *eureka!*

463. Experiment.—**N.** experiment; essay etc. (*attempt*) 675; research etc. (*investigation*) 461; trial, tentative method, *tâtonnement*.

verification, probation, *experimentum crucis*, proof, criterion, diagnostic test, tryout, crucial test, acid test.

crucible, reagent, check, touchstone, pix; assay, ordeal; ring.

empiricism, rule of thumb.

feeler; pilot —, messenger- balloon, *ballon d'essai*; pilot engine; scout; straw to show the wind.

speculation, random shot, leap in the dark.

analy-zer, -st; adventurer, explorer, sourdough, prospector; experiment-er, -ist, -alist; assayer.

V. experiment; essay etc. (*endeavor*) 675; try, assay, sample; make -an experiment, — trial of; give a trial to; put upon —, subject to- trial; experiment upon; rehearse; put —, bring —, submitto the -test, — proof, prove, verify, test, touch, practise upon, try one's strength.

grope; feel —, grope- -for, — one's way; fumble; *tâttonner, aller à tâtons*; put —, throw- out a feeler; send up a pilot balloon; see how the -land lies, — wind blows; consult the barometer; feel the pulse; fish —, bob- for; cast —, beat- about for; angle, trawl, cast one's net, beat the bushes.

venture, try one's fortune etc. (*adventure*) 675; explore etc. (*inquire*) 461.

Adj. experimental; probat-ive, ory, -ionary; analytic, docimastic; tentative; empirical; speculative, tentive.

under probation, on one's trial, on trial, on approval.

464. Comparison.—N. comparison, collation, contrast; identification.

sim-ile, -ilitude; allegory etc. (*metaphor*) 521.

V. compare -to, — with; collate, confront; place side by side etc. (*near*) 197; set —, pit- against one another; contrast balance.

identify, draw a parallel, parallel.

compare notes; institute a comparison; *parva componere magnis*.

Adj. comparative, relative; metaphorical etc. 521.

compared with etc. *v.*; comparable.

Adv. relatively etc. (*relation*) 9; as compared with etc. *v.*

465. Discrimination.—N. discrimination, distinction, differentiation, diagnosis, diorism; nice perception; perception —, appreciation- of difference; acuteness; estimation etc. 466; nicety, refinement; taste etc. 850; *critique*, judgement, tact; insight, discernment etc. (*intelligence*) 498; *nuances*.

V. discriminate, distinguish, differentiate, severalize; separate; draw the line, sift; separate —, winnow- the chaff from the wheat; split hairs.

estimate etc. (*measure*) 466; know -which is which, — one's stuff, — one's way about, — what is what, — 'a hawk from a handsaw.'

take into -account, — consideration; give —, allow- due weight to; weigh carefully.

Adj. discriminating etc. *v.*; dioristic, discriminative, critical, distinctive; nice.

Phr. *il y a fagots et fagots*; *rem acu tetigisti*.

465a. Indiscrimination.—N. indiscrimination; promiscuity; indistinctness, -ion; uncertainty etc. (*doubt*) 475; obtuseness.

V. not -indiscriminate etc. 465; overlook etc.' (*neglect*) 460- a distinction; con-found, -fuse, jumble; swallow whole.

Adj. indiscriminate, undiscriminating, promiscuous; undistinguish-ed, -able, -ing; unmeasured.

466. Measurement.—N. measurement, admeasurement, mensuration, survey, valuation, appraisment, assessment, assize; estim-ate, -ation; dead reckoning; reckoning etc. (*numeration*) 85; gauging etc. *v.*

metrology, weights and measures, compound arithmetic.

measure, yard measure, standard, rule, foot-rule, chain, tape, staff, compass, callipers; dividers; gage, gauge, planimeter; meter, line, rod, check.

volt, kilowatt, ampere, candle power; horse power; axle load; foot pound.

flood —, high water- mark; Plimsoll mark; index etc. 550.

scale; gradu-ation, -ated scale; nonius; vernier etc. (*minuteness*) 193; pedo (*length*)- 200, sounding line etc. (*depth*) 208, thermo (*heat* etc. 398)-, baro (*air* etc. 338)-, dynamo (*power*)- 276, anemo (*wind* 349)-, gonio (*angle* 244)- meter; landmark etc. (*limit*) 233; balance etc. (*weight*) 310; optical instruments etc. 445.

co-ordinates, ordinate and abscissa, polar co-ordinates, latitude and longitude, declination and right ascension, altitude and azimuth.

geo-, stereo-, hypso-metry; metage; surveying, land surveying; geo-desy, -detics, -desia; ortho-, alti-metry; *cadastre*.

astrolabe, armillary sphere.

land, -surveyor; geometer, topographer, cartographer, hydrographer.

V. measure, meter, mete; value, assess, rate, appraise, estimate, form as estimate, set a value on; appreciate; standardize.

span, pace, step; apply the -compass etc. *n.*; gauge, plumb, probe, calliper, sound, fathom etc. 208; heave the -log, — lead; weigh etc. 319; survey.

take an average etc. 29; graduate.

Adj. measuring etc. *v.*; metric, -al; measurable; geodetical, cadastral, topographical.

467. Evidence. [on one side]**—N.** evidence; facts, premises, *data*, *praecognita*, grounds.

indication etc. 550; criterion etc. (*test*) 463.

testi-mony, -fication; attestation; deposition etc. (*affirmation*) 535; examination.

admission etc. (*assent*) 488; authority, warrant, credential, diploma, voucher, certificate, docket; record etc. 551; document, muniments; *pièce justificative*; deed, warranty etc. (*security*) 771; signature, seal etc. (*identification*) 550; exhibit, citation, reference.

witness, indicator; eye-, ear-witness; deponent; sponsor.

oral —, documentary —, hearsay —, external —, extrinsic —, internal —, intrinsic —, circumstantial —, cumulative —, *ex parte* —, presumptive —, collateral —, constructive- evidence; proof etc. (*demonstration*) 478; evidence in chief; finger prints, dactylogram.

secondary evidence; confirmation, corroboration, adminicle, support; ratification etc. (*assent*) 488; authentication, verification; compurgation, wager of law, comprobation.

citation, reference.

V. be -evidence etc. *n.*; evince, show, betoken, tell of; indicate etc. (*denote*) 550; imply, involve, argue, bespeak, breathe.

have —, carry- weight; tell, speak volumes; speak for itself etc. (*manifest*) 525.

rest –, depend- upon; repose on.

bear -witness etc. *n.*; give -evidence etc. *n.*; testify, depose, witness, vouch for; sign, seal, undersign, set one's hand and seal, sign and seal, deliver as one's act and deed, certify, attest; acknowledge etc. (*assent*) 488.

make absolute, confirm, ratify, corroborate, endorse, countersign, support, bear out, vindicate, uphold, warrant.

adduce, attest, cite, quote; refer –, appeal- to; call, – to witness; bring -forward, – into court; allege, plead; produce –, confront- witnesses; collect –, bring together –, rake up- evidence.

have –, make out- a case; establish, circumstantiate, authenticate, substantiate, verify, make good, quote chapter and verse; bring -home to, – to book.

Adj. showing etc. *v.*; evidential, indica-tive, -tory; deducible etc. 478; grounded –, founded –, based- on; first hand, authentic, verifiable; corroborative, confirmatory; significant, conclusive.

Adv. by inference; according to, witness, *a fortiori*; still -more, – less; *raison de plus*; in corroboration etc. *n.* of; *valeat quantum*; under -seal, – one's hand and seal.

468. Counter-evidence. [Evidence on the other side, on the other hand.]—**N.** counter-evidence; evidence on the other side, hand; disproof; refutation etc. 479; negation etc. 536; conflicting evidence.

plea etc. 617; vindication etc. 937; counter-protest; *tu quoque* argument; other side –, reverse- of the shield.

V. countervail, oppose; run counter; rebut etc. (*refute*) 479; subvert etc. (*destroy*) 162; check, weaken; contravene; contradict etc. (*deny*) 536; tell another story, turn the -tables, – scale; alter the case; cut both ways; prove a negative.

audire alteram partem.

Adj. countervailing etc. *v.*; contradictory, in rebuttal.

un-attested, -authenticated, -supported by evidence; suppositious, trumped up.

Adv. *per contra*, conversely, on the other hand.

469. Qualification.—N. qualification, limitation, modification, coloring.

allowance, grains of allowance, consideration, extenuating circumstances.

condition, proviso, exception; exemption; salvo, saving clause; discount etc. 813.

V. qualify, limit, modify, affect, temper, leaven, give a color to, introduce new conditions.

allow –, make allowance- for; admit exceptions, take into account.

take exception, object.

Adj. qualifying etc. *v.*; conditional; extenuatory; exceptional etc. (*unconformable*) 83.

hypothetical etc. (*supposed*) 514; contingent etc. (*uncertain*) 475.

Adv. provided, – always; if, unless, but, yet; according as; conditionally, admitting, supposing; on the supposition of etc. (*theoretically*) 514; with the understanding, even, although, though, for all that, after all, at all events.

with grains of allowance, *cum grano salis*; *exceptis excipiendis*; wind and weather permitting; if possible etc. 470.

subject to; with this -proviso etc. *n.*

470. Possibility.—N. possibility, potentiality; what -may be, – is possible etc. *adj.*; compatibility etc. (*agreement*) 23.

practicability, feasibility; practicableness etc. *adj.*

contingency, chance etc. 156.

V. be -possible etc. *adj.*; stand a chance, have a leg to stand on; admit of, bear.

render -possible etc. *adj.*; put in the way of.

Adj. possible; on the -cards, – dice; *in posse*, within the bounds of possibility, conceivable, credible, imaginable; compatible etc. 23.

practicable, feasible, workable, performable, achievable; within -reach, – measurable distance; accessible, superable, surmountable; at-, obtainable; contingent etc. (*doubtful*) 475.

Adv. possibly, by possibility; perhaps, -chance, -adventure, may be, haply, mayhap.

if possible, wind and weather permitting, God willing, *Deo volente*, D.V.

471. Impossibility.—N. impossibility etc. *adj.*; what -cannot, – can never- be, sour grapes; infeasibility, impracticability; hopelessness etc. 859.

V. be -impossible etc. *adj.*; have no chance whatever.

attempt impossibilities; square the circle; discover the -philosopher's stone – elixir of life, – secret of perpetual motion; wash a blackamoor white; skin a flint; make -a silk purse out of a sow's ear, – bricks without straw; have nothing to go upon; weave a rope of sand, build castles in the air, *prendre la lune avec les dents*, extract sunbeams from cucumbers, set the Thames on fire, milk a he-goat into a sieve, catch a weasel asleep, *rompre l'anguille au genou*, be in two places at once.

Adj. impossible; not -possible etc. 470; absurd, contrary to reason; unlikely, at variance with facts; unreasonable etc. 477; incredible etc. 485; beyond the bounds of -reason, – possibility; from which reason recoils; visionary; inconceivable etc. (*improbable*) 473; prodigious etc. (*wonderful*) 870; un-, in-imaginable, unthinkable, not a Chinaman's chance.

impracticable, unachievable; un-, in-feasible; insuperable; un-, in-surmountable; unat-, unobtainable; out of -reach, – the question; not to be -had, – thought of; beyond control; desperate etc. (*hopeless*) 859; incompatible etc. 24; inaccessible, uncomeatable, impassable, impervious, innavigable, inextricable.

out of –, beyond- one's -power, – depth, – reach, – grasp; too much for; *ultra crepidam*.

Phr. the grapes are sour; *non possumus*; *non nostrum tantas componere lites*.

472. Probability.—N. probability, likelihood; likeliness etc. *adj.*

vraisemblance, verisimilitude, plausibility;

color, semblance, show of; presumption; presumptive —, circumstantial- evidence; credibility.

reasonable —, fair —, good —, favorable- -chance, — prospect; prospect, well-grounded hope; chance etc. 156.

V. be -probable etc. *adj.*; give —, lend- color to; point to; imply etc. (*evidence*) 467; bid fair etc. (*promise*) 511; stand fair for; stand —, run- a good chance.

presume, infer, suppose, take for granted.

think likely, dare say, flatter oneself; expect etc. 507; count upon etc. (*believe*) 484.

Adj. probable, likely, hopeful, to be expected, in a fair way.

plausible, specious, ostensible, colorable, *ben trovato*, well-founded, reasonable, credible, easy of belief, presumable, presumptive, apparent.

Adv. probably etc. *adj.*; belike; in all -probability, — likelihood; very —, most- likely; as likely as not; like enough; ten etc. to one; apparently, seemingly, according to every reasonable expectation; *primâ facie*; to all appearance etc. (*to the eye*) 448.

Phr. the -chances, — odds- are; appearances —, chances- are in favor of; there is reason to -believe, — think, — expect; I dare say; all Lombard Street to a China orange.

473. Improbability.—N. improbability, unlikelihood; unfavorable —, bad —, little —, small —, poor —, scarcely any —, no —, not a ghost of a- chance; bare possibility; long odds; incredibility etc. 485.

V. be -improbable etc. *adj.*; have a -small chance etc. *n.*

Adj. improbable, unlikely, contrary to all reasonable expectation, implausible.

rare etc. (*infrequent*) 137; unheard of, inconceivable; un-, in-imaginable; incredible etc. 485; more than doubtful.

Int. not likely! no fear!

Phr. the chances are against.

474. Certainty.—N. certainty; necessity etc. 601; certitude, certainness, surety, assurance, sureness; dead —, moral- certainty; infallibleness etc. *adj.*; infallibility, reliability.

gospel, scripture, church, pope, court of final appeal; *res judicata, ultimatum.*

positiveness; dogmat-ism, -ist, -izer; *doctrinaire*, know-all, bigot, -ry; opinionist, Sir Oracle; *ipse dixit*; zealot.

fact; positive —, matter of- fact; *fait accompli.*

V. be -certain etc. *adj.*; stand to reason.

render -certain etc. *adj.*; in-, en-, as-sure; clinch, make sure; determine, decide, set at rest, 'make assurance double sure;' know etc. (*believe*) 484; dismiss all doubt.

dogmatize, lay down the law.

Adj. certain, sure; assured etc. *v.*; solid, well-founded.

unqualified, absolute, positive, determinate, definite, clear, unequivocal, categorical, unmistakable, decisive, decided, ascertained.

inevitable, unavoidable, ineluctable, avoidless.

unerring, infallible; unchangeable etc. 150; to be depended on, trustworthy, reliable, bound.

un-impeachable, -deniable, -questionable; indisputable, -contestable, -controvertible, -defeasible, -dubitable; irrefutable etc. (*proven*) 478; conclusive, without power of appeal, final.

indubious; without —, beyond a —, without a shade or shadow or- -doubt — question; past dispute; beyond all -question, — dispute; undoubted, -contested, -questioned, -disputed; question-, dount-less.

bigoted, fanatical, dogmatic, opinionat-ed, -ive, *doctrinaire.*

authoritative, authentic; official.

sure as -fate, — death and taxes, — a gun.

evident, self-evident, axiomatic; clear, — as day, — as the sun at noonday; obvious.

Adv. certainly etc. *adj.*; for certain, certes, sure, no doubt, doubtless, and no mistake, *flagrante delicto*, sure enough, to be sure, of course, as a matter of course, *à coup sur*, to a certainty, undoubtedly; in truth etc. (*truly*) 494; at -any rate, — all events; without fail; *coûte que coûte*; whatever may happen, if the worst come to the worst; come —, happen- what -may, — will; sink or swim; rain or shine.

Phr. *cela va sans dire*; there is -no question, — not a shadow of doubt; the die is cast etc. (*necessity*) 601.

475. Uncertainty.—N. uncertainty, incertitude, doubt; doubtfulness etc. *adj.*; dubi-ety, -tation, -tancy, -ousness.

hesitation, suspense; perplexity, embarrassment, dilemma, quandary, Morton's fork, bewilderment; timidity etc. (*fear*) 860; indecision, vacillation etc. 605; *diaporesis*, indetermination.

vagueness etc. *adj.*; haze, fog; obscurity etc. (*darkness*) 421; ambiguity etc. (*double meaning*) 520; contingency, double contingency, possibility upon a possibility; conjecture; open question etc. (*question*) 461; *onus probandi*; blind bargain, pig in a poke, leap in the dark, something or other; needle in a bottle of hay; roving commission.

fallibility, unreliability, untrustworthiness, precariousness.

V. be -uncertain etc. *adj.*; wonder whether.

lose the -clue, — clew, — scent; miss one's way.

not know -what to make of etc. (*unintelligibility*) 519, — which way to turn, — whether one stands on one's head or one's heels; float in a sea of doubt, hesitate, flounder; lose -oneself, — one's head, — one's way, wander aimlessly; muddle one's brains.

render -uncertain etc. *adj.*; put out, pose, puzzle, perplex, embarrass; confuse, -found; bewilder, mystify, bother, nonplus, addle the wits, throw off the scent; *ambiguas in vulgus spargere voces*; keep in suspense.

doubt etc. (*disbelieve*) 485; hang —, tremble- in the balance; depend.

Adj. uncertain; casual; random etc. (*aimless*) 621; changeable etc. 149.

doubtful, dubious; indecisive; unsettled, -decided, -determined; in suspense, open to discussion; controvertible; in question etc. (*inquiry*) 461; insecure, unstable.

vague; in-determinate, -definite; ambiguous, equivocal; undefin-ed, -able; confused etc. (*indistinct*) 447; mystic, mysterious, veiled, obscure, cryptic, oracular.

perplexing etc. *v.*; enigmatic, paradoxical; apocryphal, problematical, hypothetical; experimental etc. 463.

fallible, questionable, precarious, slippery, ticklish, debatable, disputable; un-reliable, -trustworthy.

contingent, — on, dependent on; subject to; dependent on circumstances; occasional; provisional.

unauth-entic, -enticated, -oritative; unascertained, -confirmed; undemonstrated; un-told, -counted.

in a -state of uncertainty, — cloud, — maze; ignorant etc. 491; on the horns of a dilemma; afraid to say; out of one's reckoning, astray, adrift; as -sea, — fault, — a loss, — one's wit's end, — a *nonplus*; puzzled etc. *v.*; lost abroad, *désorienté*; dis-tracted, -traught.

Adv. *pendente lite*; *sub spe rati*.

Phr. Heaven knows; who can tell? who shall decide when doctors disagree?

476. Reasoning.—**N.** reasoning; ratio-cination, -nalism; dialectics, induction, generalization.

discussion, comment, ventilation, inquiry etc. 461.

argumentation, controversy, debate; polemics, wrangling; contention etc. 720; logomachy; disputation, -ceptation; paper war.

art of reasoning, logic.

process —, train —, chain- of reasoning; de-, induction; systhesis, analysis.

argument; case, plea, *plaidoyer*, opening; *lemma*, proposition, terms, premises, postulate, *data*, starting point, principle; inference etc. (*judgment*) 480.

pro-, syllogism; enthymeme, sorites, dilemma, *perilepsis*, *a priori* reasoning, *reductio ad absurdum*, horns of a dilemma, *argumentum ad hominem*, comprehensive argument.

reasoner, logician, dialectician; disputant; controver-sialist, -tist; wrangler, arguer, debater, polemic, casuist, rationalist; scientist.

logical sequence; good case; correct —, just —, sound —, valid —, cogent —, logical —, forcible —, persuasive —, persuasory —, consectary —, conclusive etc. 478 —, subtle- reasoning; force of argument; strong -point, — argument.

arguments, reasons, pros and cons.

V. reason, argue, discuss, debate, dispute, wrangle; bandy -words, — arguments; chop logic; hold —, carry on- an argument; controvert etc. (*deny*) 536; canvass; comment —, moralize-upon; consider etc. (*examine*) 461.

open a -discussion, — case; join —, be at- issue; moot; come to the point; stir —, agitate —, ventilate —, torture- a question; try conclusions; take up a -side, — case.

contend, take one's stand upon, insist, lay stress on; infer etc. 480.

follow from etc. (*demonstration*) 478.

Adj. rational; reasoning etc. *v.*; rationalistic; argumentative, controversial, dialectic, polemical; discurs-ory, -ive; disputations.

debatable, controvertible.

logical; in-, de-ductive; synthetic, analytic; relevant etc. 23.

Adv. for, because, hence, whence, seeing that, since, sith, then, thence, so; for -that, — this, — which- reason; for-, inasmuch as; whereas, *ex concesso*, considering, in consideration of; there-, where-fore; consequently, *ergo*, thus, accordingly; *a fortiori*.

in -conclusion, — fine; finally, after all, *au bout du compte*, on the whole, taking one thing with another.

rationally etc. *adj.*

477. Sophistry. [The absence of reasoning.] **Intuition.** [False or vicious reasoning; show of reason.]—**N.** intuition, instinct, association; presentiment; rule of thumb.

sophistry, paralogy, perversion, casuistry, jesuitry, equivocation, evasion, mental reservation; chicane, -ry; quiddit, quiddity; mystification; special pleading; speciousness etc. *adj.*; nonsense etc. 497; word-, tongue-fence.

false —, vicious- reasoning, *petitio principii*, *ignoratio elenchi*; *post hoc ergo propter hoc*; *non sequitur*, *ignotum per ignotius*.

misjudgment etc. 481; false teaching etc. 538.

sophism, solecism, paralogism, quibble, quirk, *elenchus*, elench, fallacy, *quodlibet*, subterfuge, subtlety, quillet; inconsistency, antilogy; 'a mockery, a delusion and a snare;' claptrap, mere words; 'lame and impotent conclusion.'

meshes —, cobwebs- of sophistry; flaw in an argument; weak point, bad case.

over-refinement; hair-splitting etc. *v.*

sophist, casuist, paralogist.

V. judge -intuitively, — by intuition; hazard a proposition, talk at random.

reason -ill, — falsely etc. *adj.*; paralogize; misjudge etc. 481.

pervert, quibble; equivocate, mystify, evade, elude; gloss over, varnish; misteach etc. 538; mislead etc. (*error*) 495; cavil, refine, subtilize, split hairs; misrepresent etc. (*lie*) 544.

beg the question, reason in a circle, cut blocks with a razor, beat about the bush, play fast and loose, blow hot and cold, prove that black is white and white black, travel out of the record, *parler à tort et à travers*, put oneself out of court, not have a leg to stand on.

Adj. intuitive, instinctive, impulsive; independent of —, anterior to- reason; gratuitous; hazarded; unconnected.

unreasonable, illogical, false, unsound, invalid; unwarranted, not following; inconsequent, -ial; inconsistent, incongruous; abson-ous, -ant; unscientific; untenable, inconclusive, incorrect; fall-acious; -ible; groundless, unproved.

deceptive, sophistical, sophisticated, casuistical, jesuitical; illus-ive, -ory; specious, hollow, plausible, *ad captandum*, evasive; irrelevant etc. 10.

weak, feeble, poor, flimsy, loose, vague, irrational; nonsensical etc. (*absurd*) 497; foolish etc. (*imbecile*) 499; frivolous, pettifogging, quibbling; finespun, over-refined.

at the end of one's tether, *au bout de son latin*.

Adv. intuitively etc. *adj.*; by intuition; illogically etc. *adj.*

Phr. *non constat*; that goes for nothing.

478. Demonstration.—N. demonstration, proof; conclusiveness etc. *adj.*; *apodixis*, probation, comprobation.

logic of facts etc. (*evidence*) 467; *experimentum curcis* etc. (*test*) 463; argument etc. 476; irrefragability.

V. demonstrate, prove, establish, make good; show; evince etc. (*be evidence of*) 467; verify etc. 467; settle the question, reduce to demonstration, set the question at rest.

make out, – a case; prove one's point, have the best of the argument; draw a conclusion etc. (*judge*) 480.

follow, – of course; stand to reason; hold -good, – water.

Adj. demonstra-ting etc. *v.*, -tive, -ble; probative, unanswerable, conclusive; apodictic, -al; irre-sistible, -futable, -fragable, undeniable.

categorical, decisive, crucial.

demonstrated etc. *v.*; proven; unconfuted, -answered, -refuted; evident etc. 474.

deducible, consequential, consectary, inferential, following.

Adv. of course, in consequence, consequently, as a matter of course.

Phr. *probatum est*; there is nothing more to be said, Q.E.D., it must follow.

479. Confutation.—N. con-, re-futation; answer, complete answer; disproof, conviction, redargution, invalidation; expos-ure, -ition; clincher; retort; *reductio ad absurdum*; knock down – *tu quoque*- argument.

V. con-, re-fute; parry, negative, disprove, redargue, expose, show the fallacy of, rebut, defeat; demolish etc. (*destroy*) 162; over-throw, -turn; scatter to the winds, explode, invalidate; silence; put –, reduce- to silence; clinch -an argument, – a question; give one a set down, stop the mouth, shut up; have, – on the hip; get the better of; confound, convince.

not leave a leg to stand on, cut the ground from under one's feet.

be confuted etc.; fail; expose –, show- one's weak point.

Adj. confut-ing, -ed etc. *v.*; capable of refutation; re-, con-futable.

condemned -on one's own showing, – out of one's own mouth.

Phr. the argument falls to the ground, *cadit quaestio*, it does not hold water, '*suo sibi gladio hunc jugulo.*'

480. Judgment. [Conclusion.]**—N.** result, conclusion, upshot; deduction, inference, ergotism, illation; corollary, porism; moral.

estimation, valuation, appreciation, judication; di-, ad-judication; arbitr- ament, -ement, -ation; assessment, ponderation.

award, estimate; review, criticism, *critique*, notice, report.

decision, determination, judgment, finding, verdict, sentence, decree, – nisi, – absolute, – interlocutory; dictum; *res judicata.*

plébiscite, referendum, voice, casting vote; vote etc. (*choice*) 609; opinion etc. (*belief*) 484; good judgment etc. (*wisdom*) 498.

judge, jurist, umpire; arbi-ter, -trator; assessor, referee; censor, reviewer, critic; *connoisseur*; commentator etc. 524; inspector, inspecting officer.

V. judge, conclude; come to –, draw –, arrive at- a conclusion; ascertain, determine, make up one's mind.

deduce, derive, gather, collect, draw an inference, make a deduction, weet, ween.

form an estimate, estimate, size up, appreciate, value, count, assess, rate, rank, account; regard, consider, think of; look upon etc. (*believe*) 484.

settle; pass –, give- an opinion; decide, try, pronounce, rule; pass -judgment, – sentence; sentence, doom; find; give –, deliver- judgment; ad-jud-ge, -icate; arbitrate, award, report; bring in a verdict; make absolute, set a question ar rest; confirm etc. (*assent*) 488.

comment, criticize; review, pass under review etc (*examine*) 457; investigate etc. (*inquire*) 461.

hold the scales, sit in judgment; try –, hear- a cause.

Adj. judging etc. *v.*; judicious etc. (*wise*) 498; determinate, conclusive, censorious, critical etc. 932.

Adv. on the whole, all things considered.

480a. Discovery. [Result of search or inquiry.]**—N.** discovery, invention, detection, disenchantment, disclosure, find, ascertainment, revelation.

trover etc. 775.

V. discover, find, determine, evolve; fix upon; find –, trace –, make –, hunt –, fish –, worm –, ferret –, root-out; fathom; bring –, draw-out; educe, elicit, bring to light, invent; dig –, grub –, fish- up; unearth, disinter.

solve, resolve; un-riddle, -ravel, -lock; pick –, open- the lock; find a -clue, – clew- to; interpret etc. 522; disclose etc. 529.

trace, get at; hit it, have it; lay one's -finger, – hands- upon; spot; get –, arrive- at the -turth etc. 494; put the saddle on the right horse, hit the right nail on the head.

be near the truth, burn; smoke, scent, sniff, smell a rat.

open the eyes to; see -through, – daylight, – in its true colors, – the cloven foot; detect; catch, – tripping.

pitch –, fall –, light –, hit –, stumble –, pop- upon; come across; meet –, fall in- with.

recognize, realize, verify, make certain of, identify.

Int. *eureka!*

481. Misjudgment.—N. misjudgment, obliquity of –, warped- judgment; mis-calculation, -computation, -conception etc. (*error*) 495; hasty conclusion.

prejud-gment, -ication, -ice; foregone conclusion; pre-notion, -vention, -conception, -dilection, -possession, -apprehension, -sumption, -sentiment; fixed —, preconceived- idea; *idée fixe*; *mentis gratissimus error*; fool's paradise.

esprit de corps, party spirit, race —, class-prejudice, partisanship, clannishness, *prestige*.

bias, warp, twist; hobby, fad, whim, craze, quirk, crotchet, partiality, infatuation, blind side, mote in the eye.

one-sided —, partial —, narrow —, confined —, superficial- -views, — ideas,— conceptions, — notions; narrow mind; bigotry etc. (*obstinacy*) 606; *odium theologicum*; pedantry; hypercriticism.

doctrinaire etc. (*positive*) 474.

V. mis-judge, -estimate, -think, -conjecture, -conceive etc. (*error*) 495; fly in the face of facts; mis-calculate, -reckon, compute.

overestimate etc. 482; underestimate etc. 483.

pre-, fore-judge; pre-suppose, -sume, -judicate; dogmatize; have a -bias etc. *n.*; have only one idea; *jurare in verba magistri*, run away with the notion; jump —, rush- to a conclusion; look only at one side of the shield; view -with jaundiced eye, — through distorting spectacles; not see beyond one's nose; *dare pondus fumo*; get the wrong sow by the ear etc. (*blunder*) 699.

give a -bias, — twist; bias, warp, twist; prejudice, -possess.

Adj. misjudging etc. *v.*; ill-judging, wrong-headed, prejudiced, prejudicial, etc. *v.*; jaundiced; short-sighted, pur-blind; partial, one-sided, superficial.

narrow-minded; confined, insular, provincial, parochial, illiberal, intolerant, narrow, besotted, infatuated, fanatical, cracked, warped, *entêté*, positive, dogmatic, dictatorial; conceited; opin-, opini-ative; opinion-ed, -ate, -ative, -ated; self-opinioned, wedded to an opinion, *opinâtre*; bigoted etc. (*obstinate*) 606; crotchety, fussy, impracticable; unreason-able, -ing; stupid etc. 499; credulous etc. 486.

misjudged etc. *v.*

Adv. *ex parte*.

Phr. nothing like leather; the wish the father to the thought.

482. Overestimation.—N. overestimation etc. *v.*; exaggeration etc. 549; vanity etc. 880; optim-, pessim-ism, -ist; megalomania.

much -cry and little wool, — ado about nothing; storm in a teacup; fine talking, rodomontade, gush, hot air, gas, bombast.

egotism etc. 880; boasting etc. 884.

V. over-estimate, -rate, -value, -prize, -weigh, -reckon, -strain, -praise; estimate too highly, attach too much importance to, make mountains of molehills, catch at straws; strain, magnify; exaggerate etc. 549; set too high a value upon; think —, make- -much, — too much- of; outreckon.

extol, — to the skies; make the -most, — best, — worst- of, eulogize, panegyrize, gush, puff, boost; make two bites of a cherry.

have too high an opinion of oneself etc. (*vanity*) 880.

Adj. overestimated etc. *v.*; oversensitive etc. (*sensibility*) 822; inflated, puffed up, exaggerated etc. 549.

Phr. all his geese are swans; *parturiunt montes*.

483. Underestimation.—N. underestimation; depreciation etc. (*detraction*) 934; pessim-ism, -ist; undervaluing etc. *v.*; modesty etc. 881.

V. under-rate, -estimate, -value, -reckon; depreciate; disparage etc. (*detract*) 934; not do justice to; mis-, dis-prize; ridicule etc. 856; slight etc. (*despise*) 930; neglect etc. 460; slur over, under-state.

make -light, — little, — nothing, — no account- of; minimize, belittle, run down, think nothing of; set -no store by, — at naught; shake off as dewdrops from the lion's mane.

Adj. depreciat-ing, -ed, -ive, -ory, etc. *v.*; unappreciated, -valued, -prized; pejorative.

484. Belief.—N. belief; credence; credit; assurance; faith, trust, troth, confidence, presumption, sanguine expectation etc. (*hope*) 858; dependence on, reliance on.

persuasion, conviction, convincement, plerophory, self-conviction; certainty etc. 474; opinion, mind, view; conception, thinking; impression etc. (*idea*) 453; surmise etc. 514; conclusion etc. (*judgment*) 480.

tenet, dogma, principle, way of thinking; popular belief etc. (*assent*) 488.

firm —, implicit —, settled —, fixed —, rooted —, deep-rooted —, staunch —, unshaken —, steadfast —, inveterate —, calm —, sober —, dispassionate —, impartial —, well-founded- -belief, — opinion etc.; *uberrima fides*.

system of opinions, school, doctrine, articles, canons; declaration —, profession- of faith; tenets, *credenda*, creed; thirty-nine articles etc. (*orthodoxy*) 983*a*; catechism; assent etc. 488; *propaganda* etc. (*teaching*) 537.

credibility etc. (*probability*) 472.

V. believe, credit; give -faith, — credit, — credence- to; see, realize; assume, receive; set down —, take- for; have —, take- it; consider, esteem, presume.

count —, depend —, calculate —, pin one's faith —, reckon —, lean —, build —, rely —, rest-upon; lay one's account for; make sure of.

make oneself easy -about, — on that score; take on -trust, — credit; take for -granted, — gospel; allow —, attach- some weight to.

know, — for certain; have —, make- no doubt; doubt not; be — rest- -assured etc. *adj.*; persuade —, assure —, satisfy- oneself; make up one's mind.

give one credit for; confide —, believe —, put one's trust- in; place —, repose- implicit confidence in; take -one's word for, — at one's word; place reliance on, rely upon, swear by, regard to.

think, hold; take, — it; opine, be of opinion, conceive, trow, ween, fancy, apprehend; have —, hold —, possess —, entertain —, adopt —, imbibe —, embrace —, get hold of —, hazard —, foster —, nurture —, cherish- -a belief, — an opinion etc. *n.*

view —, consider —, take —, hold —, conceive —, regard —, esteem —, deem —, look upon —, account —, set down- as; surmise etc. 514.

get –, take- it into one's head; come round to an opinion; swallow etc. (*credulity*) 486.

cause to -be believed etc. *v.*; satisfy, persuade, have the ear of, gain the confidence of, assure; convince, -vict, -vert; put across, sell; wean, bring round; bring –, put –, win- over; indoctrinate etc. (*teach*) 537; cram down the throat; produce –, carry- conviction; bring –, drive- home to.

go down, find credence, pass current; be -received etc. *v.*, – current etc. *adj.*; possess –, take hold of –, take possession of- the mind.

Adj. believing etc. *v.*; certain, sure, assured, positive, cocksure, satisfied, confident, unhesitating, convinced, secure.

under the impression; impressed –, imbued –, penetrated- with.

confiding, trustful, suspectless; unsusp-ecting, -icious; void of suspicion; credulous etc. 486; wedded to.

believed etc. *v.*; accredited, putative; unsuspected.

worthy of –, deserving of –, commanding- -belief, – confidence; credible, reliable, trusted, trustworthy, to be depended on, undoubted; satisfactory; probable etc. 472; fiduci-al, -ary; persuasive, impressive.

relating to belief, doctrinal.

Adv. in the -opinion, – eyes- of; *me judice*; me-seems, -thinks; to the best of one's belief; I -dare say, – doubt not, – have no doubt, – am sure; in my opinion; sure enough etc. (*certainty*) 474; depend –, rely- upon it; be –, rest- assured; I'll warrant you etc. (*affirmation*) 535.

485. Unbelief. Doubt.—N. un-, dis-, mis-belief; discredit, miscreance; infidelity etc. (*irreligion*) 989; dissent etc. 489; change of -opinion etc. 484; retraction etc. 607.

doubt etc. (*uncertainty*) 475; skepticism, misgiving, demur; dis-, mis-trust; misdoubt, suspicion, jealousy, scruple, qualm; *onus probandi*.

incredib-ility, -leness; incredulity; unbeliever etc. 487.

V. dis-believe, -credit; not -believe etc. 484; misbelieve; refuse to admit etc. (*dissent*) 489; refuse to believe etc. (*incredulity*) 487.

doubt; be -doubtful etc. (*uncertain*) 475; doubt the truth of; be -skeptical as to etc. *adj.*; diffide; dis-, mis-trust; suspect, smoke, scent, smell a rat; have –, harbor –, entertain- -doubts, – suspicions; have one's doubts.

demur, stick at, pause, hesitate, scruple, waver, stop and consider.

hang in -suspense, – doubt.

throw doubt upon, raise a question; bring –, call- in question; question, challenge, query; dispute; deny etc. 536; cavil; cause –, raise –, start –, suggest –, awake- a -doubt, – suspicion; ergotize.

startle, stagger; shake –, stagger- one's faith, – belief.

Adj. unbelieving; incredulous –, skeptical- as to; distrustful –, shy –, suspicious- of; doubting etc. *v.*

doubtful etc. (*uncertain*) 475; disputable; unworthy –, undeserving- of -belief etc. 484; questionable; sus-pect, -picious; open to -suspicion, – doubt; staggering, hard to believe, incredible, not to be believed, inconceivable.

fallible etc. (*uncertain*) 475; undemonstrable; controvertible etc. (*untrue*) 495.

Adv. *cum grano salis.*

Phr. *fronti nulla fides*; *nimium ne crede colori*; *'timeo Danaos et dona ferentes*;' *credat Judaeus Apella*; let those believe who may.

486. Credulity.—N.. credul-ity, -ousness etc. *adj.*; gull-, cull-ibility; gross credulity, infatuation; self-delusion, -deception; blind reasoning; superstition; one's blind side; bigotry etc. (*obstinacy*) 606; hyper-orthodoxy etc. 984; misjudgment etc. 481.

credulous person etc. (*dupe*) 547.

V. be -credulous etc. *adj.*; *jurare in verba magistri*; follow implicitly; swallow, – whole, gulp down; take on trust; take for -granted, – gospel; run away with -a notion, – an idea; jump –, rush- to a conclusion; think the moon is made of green cheese; take –, grasp- the shadow for the substance; catch at straws.

impose upon etc. (*deceive*) 545.

Adj. credulous, gullible; easily -deceived etc. 545; simple, green, soft, childish, silly, stupid; over-credulous, -confident; infatuated, superstitious; confiding etc. (*believing*) 484.

Phr. the wish the father to the thought; *credo quia impossibile.*

487. Incredulity.—N. incredul-ous-ness, -ity; skepticism, pyrrhonism; want of faith etc. (*irreligion*) 989.

suspiciousness etc. *adj.*; scrupulosity; suspicion etc. (*unbelief*) 485; dissent etc. 489.

unbeliever, skeptic, aporetic; atheist, agnostic, infidel, disbeliever, misbeliever, pyrrhonist etc. 989; heretic etc. (*heterodox*) 984.

v. be -incredulous etc. *adj.*; distrust etc. (*disbelieve*) 485; refuse to believe; shut one's -eyes, – ears- to; turn a deaf ear to; hold aloof; ignore; *nullis jurare in verba magistri.*

Adj. incredulous, skeptical, unbelieving, inconvincible; hard –, shy- of belief; suspicious, scrupulous, distrustful, heterodox etc. 984.

488. Assent.—N. assent, -ment; acquiescence, admission; nod; ac-, con-cord, -cordance; agreement etc. 23; affirm-ance, -ation; recognition, acknowledgment, avowal; confession, – of faith.

unanimity, common consent, *consensus*, acclamation, chorus, *vox populi*; popular –, current- -belief, – opinion; public opinion; concurrence etc. (*of causes*) 178; co-operation etc. (*voluntary*) 709.

ratification, confirmation, corroboration, approval, acceptance, *visa*; indorsement etc. (*record*) 551.

consent etc. (*compliance*) 762.

affirmant, consenter, covenantor, subscriber, endorser, upholder.

V. assent; give –, yield –, nod- assent; acquiesce; agree etc. 23; receive, accept, accede, accord, concur, lend oneself to, consent, coincide, reciprocate, go with; be -at one with etc. *adj.*; go along –, chime in –, strike in –, close- with; echo, enter into one's views, agree in opinion; vote –, give one's voice- for; recognize; subscribe –, conform –, defer- to; say -yes, – ditto, – amen; – aye- to.

acknowledge, own, admit, allow, avow, confess; concede etc. (*yield*) 762; come round to; abide by; permit etc. 760.

come to –, arrive at- -an understanding, – terms, – an agreement.

con-, af-firm; ratify, approve, endorse, countersign; visa; corroborate etc. 467.

go –, swim- with the stream, float with the current; be in the fashion, join in the chorus; be in every mouth.

Adj. assenting etc. *v.*; of one -accord, – mind; of the same mind, at one with, agreed, acquiescent, content; willing etc. 602.

un-contradicted, -challenged, -questioned, -controverted.

carried –, agreed- *-nem. con.* etc. *adv.*; unanimous; agreed on all hands, carried by acclamation.

affirmative etc. 535.

Adv. yes, yea, ay, aye, true; good; well; very -well, – true; well and good; granted; *placet*; even –, just- so; to be sure, surely, 'thou hast said;' truly, exactly, precisely, that's just it, indeed, certainly, certes, *ex concesso*; of course, unquestionably, assuredly, no doubt, doubtless, undoubtedly.

be it so; so -be it, – let it be, so mote it be; amen; with all my heart; willingly etc. 602.

with one -consent, – voice, – accord; unanimously, *unâ voce*, by common consent, in chorus, to a man, *nem. con.*; *nemine -contradicente*, – *dissentiente*; without a dissentient voice; as one man, one and all, on all hands.

489. Dissent.—N. dissent; discordance etc. (*disagreement*) 24; difference –, diversity- of opinion.

non-conformity etc. (*heterodoxy*) 984; protestantism, recusancy, schism; disaffection; secession etc. 624; recantation etc. 607.

dissension etc. (*discord*) 713; discontent etc. 832; cavilling.

protest; contradiction etc. (*denial*) 536; non-compliance etc. (*rejection*) 764; disapprobation etc. 932; hartal.

dissent-ient, -er; non-juror, -content; recusant, sectary, schismatic, protestant, non-conformist, separatist, non-co-operator, conscientious objector, passive resister.

V. dissent, demur; call in question etc. (*doubt*) 485; differ in opinion, disagree; say -no etc. 536; refuse -assent, – to admit; cavil, protest, raise one's voice against, make bold to differ; repudiate; contradict etc. (*deny*) 536; agree to differ.

have no notion of, differ *toto caelo*; revolt -at, – from the idea.

shake the head, shrug the shoulders; look -askance, – askant.

secede; recant etc. 607.

Adj. dissenting etc. *v.*; negative etc. 536; dissident, -entient; unconsenting etc. (*refusing*) 764; non-content, -juring; protestant, recusant; unconvinced, -verted.

unavowed, unacknowledged; out of the question.

discontented etc. 832; unwilling etc. 603; extorted.

sectarian, denominational, schismatic, heterodox, intolerant.

Adv. no etc. 536; at -variance, – issue- with; under protest; *non placet*.

Int. God forbid! not for the world; not on your life; I beg to differ; I'll be hanged if; never tell me; your humble servant, pardon me; tell that to the marines.

Phr. many men many minds; *quot homines tot sententiae*; *tant s'en faut*; *il s'en faut bien*.

490. Knowledge.—N. knowledge; cogn-izance, -ition, -oscence; acquaintance, experience, ken, privity, insight, familiarity; com-, ap-prehension; recognition; appreciation etc. (*judgment*) 480; intuition; consci-ence, -ousness; preception, precognition; acroamatics.

light, enlightenment; glimpse, inkling; side light; glimmer, -ing; dawn; scent, suspicion; impression etc. (*idea*) 453; discovery etc. 480*a*.

system –, body- of knowledge; science, philosophy, pansophy; theory, Etiology; circle of the sciences; pandect, doctrine, body of doctrine; cy , ency-clopedia; school etc. (*system of opinions*) 484.

tree of knowledge; republic of letters etc. (*language*) 560.

erudition, learning, lore, scholarship, reading, letters; literature; booklearning, bookishness; biblio-mania, -latry; information, general information; store of -knowledge etc.; education etc. (*teaching*) 537; culture, attainments; acquirements, -sitions; accomplishments, proficiency; practical knowledge etc. (*skill*) 698; higher education, liberal education; dilettantism; rudiments etc. (*beginning*) 66.

deep –, profound –, solid –, accurate –, acroatic –, acroamatic –, vast –, extensive –, encyclopedical- -knowledge, – learning; omniscience, pantology.

march of intellect; progress –, advance- of -science, – learning; schoolmaster abroad.

V. know, ken, scan, wot; wot –, be aware etc. *adj.*- of; ween, weet, trow, have, possess.

conceive; ap-, com-prehend; take, realize, understand, appreciate; fathom, make out; recognize, discern, perceive, see, get a sight of, experience.

know full well; have –, possess- some knowledge of; be *-au courant* etc. *adj.*; have -in one's head, – at one's fingers' ends; know by -heart, – rote; be master of; *connaître le dessous des cartes*, know what's what etc. 698.

see one's way; learn, discover etc. 480*a*.

come to one's knowledge etc. (*information*) 527.

Adj. knowing etc. *v.*; cognitive; acroamatic.

aware –, cognizant –, conscious- of; acquainted –, made acquainted- with; privy –, no stranger- to; *au -fait*, – *courant*; in the secret; up –, alive- to; sensible of; behind the -scenes, – curtain; let into; apprized –, informed- of; undeceived.

proficient –, versed –, read –, forward –,

strong –, at home- in; conversant –, familiar- with.

erudite, instructed, learned, lettered, educated; high-brow; well-conned, -informed, -read, -grounded, -educated; enlightened, shrewd, insightful, *savant*, blue, bookish, scholastic, solid, profound, deep-read, book-learned; accomplished etc. (*skilful*) 698; omniscient; self-taught, -educated.

known etc. *v.*; ascertained, well-known, recognized, received, notorious, noted; proverbial; familiar, – as household words, to every schoolboy; hackneyed, trite, commonplace.

knowable, cogn-oscible, -izable.

Adv. to –, to the best of- one's knowledge.

Phr. one's eyes being opened etc. (*disclosure*) 529.

491. Ignorance.—N. ignorance, nescience, *tabula rasa*, crass ignorance, *ignorance crasse*; unacquaintance; unconsciousness etc. *adj.*; dark-, blind-ness; incomprehension, inexperience, simplicity.

unknown quantities, *x*, *y*, *z*.

sealed book, *terra incognita*, virgin soil, unexplored ground; dark ages.

[Imperfect knowledge] smattering, superficiality, half-learning, sciolism, glimmering; bewilderment etc. (*uncertainty*) 475; incapacity.

[Affectation of knowledge] pedantry; charlatanry, -ism.

V. be -ignorant etc. *adj.*; not -know etc. 490; know -not, – not what, – nothing of; have no -idea, – notion, – conception; not have the remotest idea; not know chalk from cheese.

ignore, be blind to; keep in ignorance etc. (*conceal*) 528.

see through a glass darkly; have a -film over the eyes, – glimmering etc. *n.*; wonder whether; not know what to make of etc. (*unintelligibility*) 519; not pretend –, not take upon oneself- to say.

Adj. ignorant, nescient; un-knowing, -aware, -acquainted, -apprized, -witting, -weeting, -conscious; wit-, weet-less; a stranger to; unconversant.

un-informed, -cultivated, -versed, -instructed, -taught, -initiated, -tutored, -schooled, -guided, -enlightened; Philistine; behind the age.

shallow, superficial, green, rude, empty, half-learned, illiterate; un-read, -informed, -educated, -learned, -lettered, -bookish; empty-headed; lowbrow; pedantic.

in the dark; be-nighted, -lated; blind-ed, -fold; hoodwinked; misinformed; *au bout de son latin*, at the end of his tether; at fault; at sea etc. (*uncertain*) 475; caught tripping.

un-known, -apprehended, -explained, -ascertained, -investigated, -explored, -heard of, -perceived; concealed etc. 528; novel.

Adv. ignorantly etc. *adj.*; unawares; for -anything, – aught- one knows; not that one knows.

Int. God –, Heaven –, the Lord –, nobody-knows.

Phr. a little learning is a dangerous thing.

492. Scholar.—N. scholar, *connoissuer*, *savant*, pundit, schoolman, professor, graduate, wrangler, moonshee; academ-ician, -ist; fellow, don, post graduate, advanced student; master –, bachelor- of arts; doctor, licentiate, gownsman; philo-sopher, -math; scientist, clerk; soph, -ist, -ister; linguist, classicist; glosso-, etymo-, philologist; philologer; lexico-, glosso-grapher; scholiast, commentator. annotator, grammarian; *littérateur*, *literati*, *dilettanti*, *illuminati*; Mezzofanti, admirable Crichton, Maecenas.

book-worm, *helluo librorum*, biblio-phile, -maniac; blue-stocking, *bas-bleu*; big-wig, learned Theban.

learned –, literary- man; *homo multarum literarum*; man of -learning, – letters, – education; high-brow, intelligentsia.

antiquar-ian, -y; archeologist; sage etc. (*wise man*) 500.

pendant, *doctrinaire*; pedagogue, Dr. Pangloss; pantologist.

teacher etc. 540; schoolboy etc. (*learner*) 541.

Adj. learned etc. 490; brought up at the feet of Gamaliel.

493. Ignoramus.—N. ignoramus, illiterate, moron, dunce, numskull; wooden spoon; no scholar.

sciolist, smatterer, dabbler, half-scholar; *charlatan*; wiseacre.

novice, griffin; greenhorn etc. (*dupe*) 547; tyro etc. (*learner*) 541.

lubber etc. (*bungler) 701; fool etc. 501; pedant etc. 492.*

Adj. bookless, shallow, simple, dense, dumb, thick, dull, ignorant etc. 491.

494. Truth. [Object of knowledge.]**—N.** fact, reality etc. (*existence*) 1; plain matter of fact; nature etc. (*principle*) 5; truth, verity; gospel; orthodoxy etc. 983*a*; authenticity; veracity etc. 543.

accuracy, exactitude; exact-, precise-ness etc. *adj.*; precision, delicacy; rigor, mathematical precision, punctuality; clockwork precision etc. (*regularity*) 80.

orthology; *ipsissima verba*; letter of the law, realism.

plain –, honest –, sober –, naked –, unalloyed –, unqualified –, stern –, exact –, intrinsic- truth; *nuda veritas*; the very thing; not an -illusion etc. 495; real Simon Pure; unvarnished tale; the truth, the whole truth and nothing but the truth; just the thing.

V. be -true etc. *adj.*, – the case; stand the test; have the true ring; hold -good, – true, – water; conform to rule.

render –, prove- -true etc. *adj.*; substantiate etc. (*evidence*) 467.

get at the truth etc. (*discover*) 480*a*.

Adj. real, actual etc. (*existing*) 1; veritable, true; certain etc. 474; substantially –, categorically-true etc; true -to the letter; – to life, – to scale, – the facts, – as gospel; unimpeachable; veracious etc. 543; unre-, uncon-futed; un-ideal -imagined; realistic.

exact, accurate, definite, precise, well defined, just, right, correct, strict, severe; close etc. (*similar*) 17; literal; rigid, rigorous; scrupulous etc. (*con-*

scientious) 939; religiously exact, punctual, mathematical, scientific; faithful, constant, unerring; curious, particular, punctilious, meticulous, nice, delicate, fine.

genuine, authentic, legitimate, pukka; orthodox etc. 983*a*; official, *ex officio*.

pure, natural, sound, sterling; un-sophisticated, -adulterated, -varnished, -colored; in its true colors.

well-grounded, -founded; solid, substantial, tangible, valid; undis-torted, -guised; un-affected, -exaggerated, -romantic, -flattering.

Adv. truly etc.*adj.*; verily, indeed, in reality; as a matter of fact; beyond -doubt, – question; with truth etc. (*veracity*) 543; certainly etc. (*certain*) 474; actually etc. (*existence*) 1; in effect etc. (*intrinsically*) 5.

exactly etc. *adj.* ; *ad amussim*; *verbatim*, – *et literatim*; word for word, literally, *literatim*, *totidem verbis*, *sic*, to the letter, chapter and verse, *ipsissimis verbis*; *ad unguem*; to an inch; to a -nicety, – hair, – tittle, – turn, – T; *au pied de la lettre*; neither more nor less; in -every respect, – all respects; *sous tous les rapports*; at -any rate, – all events; strictly speaking.

Phr. the -truth, – fact- is; *rem acu tetigisti*.

495. Error.—N. error, fallacy; misconception, -apprehension, -understanding; inexactness etc. *adj.*; laxity; misconstruction etc. (*misinterpretation*) 523; miscomputation etc. (*misjudgment*) 481; *non-sequitur* etc. 477; misstatement, -report; anachronism; malapropism.

mistake; miss, fault, blunder, boner, bloomer, howler, *quid pro quo*, cross purposes, oversight, misprint, *erratum*, *corrigendum*, slip, blot, flaw, loose thread; trip, stumble etc. (*failure*) 732; botchery etc. (*want of skill*) 699; slip of the -tongue, – pen; *lapsus -linguae*, – *calami*, clerical error; bull etc. (*absurdity*) 497.

il-, de-lusion; false -impression, – idea; bubble; self-deceit, -deception; warped notion; mists of error; superstition, exploded notion.

heresy etc. (*heterodoxy*) 984; hallucination etc. (*insanity*) 503; false light etc. (*fallacy of vision*) 443; dream etc. (*fancy*) 515; fable etc. (*untruth*) 546; bias etc. (*misjudgment*) 481; misleading etc. *v.*

V. be -erroneous etc. *adj.*

cause error; mis-lead, -guide; lead -astray, – into error; beguile, misinform etc. (*misteach*) 538; delude; give a false -impression, – idea; falsify, garble, misstate; deceive etc. 545; lie etc. 544.

err; be -in error etc. *adj.*; – mistaken etc. *v.*; be deceived etc. (*duped*) 547; mistake, receive a false impression, deceive oneself; fall into –, lie under –, labor under- -an error etc. *n.*; be in the wrong, blunder; mis-apprehend, -conceive, -understand, -reckon, -count, -calculate etc. (*misjudge*) 481.

play –, be- at cross purposes etc. (*misinterpret*) 523.

trip, stumble; lose oneself etc. (*uncertainty*) 475; go astray; fail etc. 732; take the wrong sow by the ear etc. (*mismanage*) 699; put the saddle on the wrong horse; reckon without one's host; take the shadow for the substance etc. (*credulity*) 486; dream etc. (*imagine*) 515.

Adj. erroneous, untrue, false, devoid of truth, fallacious, faulty, apocryphal, unreal, ungrounded, groundless; unsubstantial etc. 4; heretical etc. (*heterodox*) 984; unsound; illogical etc. 477; wrong.

in-, un-exact; in-accurate, -correct; indefinite etc. (*uncertain*) 475.

illus-ive, -ory; delusive; mock; ideal etc. (*imaginary*) 515; spurious etc. 545; deceitful etc. 544; perverted.

controvertible, unsustain-able, -ed; unauthenticated, untrustworthy.

exploded, refuted, discarded.

in –, under an- error etc. *n.*; mistaken etc. *v.*; tripping etc. *v.*; out, – in one's reckoning; aberrant; beside –, wide of the- -mark, – truth; astray etc. (*at fault*) 475; on -a false, – the wrong-scent; in the wrong box; at cross purposes, all in the wrong, all abroad, at sea.

Adv. more or less.

496. Maxim.—N. maxim, aphorism; apo-, apoph-thegm; *dictum*, saying, gnome, adage, saw, proverb, epigram; sentence, *mot*, motto, word, by-word, precept, moral, phylactery, *protasis*, brocard.

axiom, postulate, theorem, *scholium*, truism.

reflection etc. (*idea*) 453; conclusion etc. (*judgment*) 480; golden rule etc. (*precept*) 697; principle, *principia*; profession of faith etc. (*belief*) 484; formula.

wise –, sage –, received –, admitted –, recognized- maxim etc.; true –, common –, hackneyed –, trite –, commonplace- saying etc.

Adj. aphoristic, proverbial, phylacteric; axiomatic, gnomic.

Adv. as -the saying is, – they say.

497. Absurdity.—N. absurd-ity, -ness etc. *adj.*; imbecility etc. 499; alogy, nonsense, paradox, inconsistency; stultiloqu-y, -ence, futility.

blunder, muddle, bull; Irish-, Hibernic-ism; slipslop; anti climax; bathos; sophism etc. 477.

farce, burlesque, *galimatias*, *amphigouri*, rhapsody; farrago etc. (*disorder*) 59; extravagance, romance; sciomachy.

joke, catch, sell, pun, verbal quibble, macaronic.

jargon, fustian, twaddle etc. (*no meaning*) 517; exaggeration etc. 549; moonshine, stuff; mare's nest.

vagary, tomfoolery, mummery, monkey trick, practical joke, *boutade*, *escapade*.

V. play the fool etc. 499; stultify, blunder, muddle; joke; talk nonsense, *parler à tort et à travers*; *battre la campagne*; be -absurd etc. *adj.*

Adj. absurd, nonsensical, preposterous, egregious, senseless, farcical, inconsistent, ridiculous, extravagant, quibbling, futile; macaronic, punning, paradoxical.

foolish etc. 499; sophistical etc. 477; unmeaning etc. 517; without rhyme or reason; fantastic.

Int. fiddle-de-dee! pish! pish and tush! pho! stuff and nonsense! rubbish! !rot! bosh! in the name of the Prophet—figs!

Phr. *credat Judaeus Apella*; tell it to the marines.

498. Intelligence. Wisdom.—N. intelligence, capacity, comprehension, understanding, intellect etc. 450; nous, parts, sagacity, mother wit, wit, *esprit*, gumption, quick parts, grasp of intellect; acuteness etc. *adj.*; acumen, subtlety, penetration; perspica-cy, -city; discernment; long-headedness, due sense of, good judgment; discrimination etc. 465; craftiness, cunning etc. 702; refinement etc. (*taste*) 850.

head, brains, gray matter, headpiece, upper story, long head; eagle -eye, – glance; eye of a -lynx, – hawk.

wisdom, sapience, sense; good –, common –, plain –, horse- sense; clear thinking; rationality, reason; reasonableness etc. *adj.*; judgment; solidity, depth, profundity, caliber; enlarged views; reach –, compass- of thought; enlargement of mind.

genius, inspiration, *geist*, fire of genius, heaven-born genius, soul; talent etc. (*aptitude*) 698.

[Wisdom in action] prudence etc. 864; vigilance etc. 459; tact etc. 698; foresight etc. 510; sobriety, self-possession, *aplomb*, ballast, mental -poise, – balance.

a bright thought, inspiration, brainwave, not a bad idea.

V. be -intelligent etc. *adj.*; have all one's wits about one; understand etc. (*intelligible*) 518; catch –, take in- an idea; take a -joke, – hint.

see -through, – at a glance, – with half an eye, – far into, – through a millstone; penetrate; discern etc. (*descry*) 441; foresee etc. 510.

discriminate etc. 465; know what's what etc. 698; listen to reason.

Adj. [Applied to persons] intelligent, quick of apprehension, keen, acute, alive, brainy, awake, bright, quick, sharp; quick-, keen-, clear-, sharp- -eyed, -sighted, -witted; wide awake; canny, shrewd, astute; clear-headed; far-sighted etc. 510; discerning, perspicacious, penetrating, piercing; argute nimble-, needle-witted; sharp as a needle; alive to etc. (*cognizant*) 490; clever etc. (*apt*) 698; arch etc. (*cunning*) 702; *pas si bête*; acute etc. 682.

wise, sage, sapient, sagacious, reasonable, rational, sound, in one's right mind, sensible, *abnormis sapiens*, judicious, strong-minded.

un-prejudiced, -biassed, -bigoted, -prepossessed; un-dazzled, -perplexed; of unwarped judgment, impartial, equitable, fair, broad-minded.

cool; cool-, long-, hard-, strong-headed; long-sighted, calculating, thoughtful, reflecting; solid, deep, profound.

oracular; heaven-directed, -born.

prudent etc. (*cautious*) 864; sober, staid, solid; considerate, politic, wise in one's generation; watchful etc. 459; provident etc. (*prepared*) 673; in advance of one's age; wise as -a serpent, – Solomon, – Solon.

[Applied to actions] wise, sensible, reasonable, judicious; well-judged, -advised; prudent, politic; expedient etc. 646.

499. Imbecility. Folly.—N. want of -intelligence etc. 498, – intellect etc. 450; shallow-, silli-, foolish-ness etc. *adj.*; imbecility, incapacity, vacancy of mind, poverty of intellect, clouded perception, poor head, apartments to let; stup-, stolidity; hebetude, dull understanding, meanest capacity; short-sightedness; incompetence etc. (*unskilfulness*) 699.

one's weak side; bias etc. 481; infatuation etc. (*insanity*) 503.

simplicity, puerility, babyhood; dotage, anility, second childishness, senile dementia, fatuity; idiocy, -tism; driveling.

folly, frivolity, desipience, irrationality, trifling, ineptitude, nugacity, inconsistency, lip-wisdom, conceit; sophistry etc. 477; giddiness etc. (*inattention*) 458; eccentricity etc. 503; extravagance etc. (*absurdity*) 497; rashness etc. 863.

act of folly etc. 699.

V. be -imbecile etc. *adj.*; have no -brains, – sense etc. 498.

trifle, drivel, *radoter*, dote; ramble etc. (*madness*) 503; play the -fool, – monkey, – goat, take leave of one's senses; not see an inch beyond one's nose; stultify oneself etc. 699; talk nonsense etc. 497.

Adj. [Applied to persons] un-intelligent, -intellectual, -reasoning; mind-, wit-, reason-, brainless; having no -head etc. 498; not -bright etc. 498; inapprehensible.

weak-, addle-, puzzle-, blunder-, muddle-, muddy-, pig-, beetle-, maggotty-, gross-headed; beef-, fat- -witted, -headed.

weak, feeble-minded; dull-, shallow-, rattle-, lack-brained; half-, nit-, short-, dull-, blunt-witted; shallow-, clod-, addle-pated; dim-, short-sighted; thick-skulled; weak in the upper story.

shallow, *borné*, weak, wanting, soft, nutty, sappy, spoony; dull, – as a beetle; stupid, heavy, insulse, obtuse, blunt, stolid, doltish, asinine; inapt etc. 699; prosaic etc. 843.

child-ish, -like; infant-ine, -ile; baby-, bab-ish; puerile; anile; simple etc. (*credulous*) 486.

fatuous, idiotic, imbecile, moronic, driveling; blatant, babbling; vacant; sottish; bewildered etc. 475.

blockish, unteachable; Boeot-ian, -ic; bovine; un-gifted, -discerning, -enlightened, -wise, -philosophical; apish.

foolish, silly, senseless, irrational, insensate, nonsensical, inept; maudlin.

narrow-minded etc. 481; bigoted etc. (*obstinate*) 606; giddy etc. (*thoughtless*) 458; rash etc. 863; eccentric etc. (*crazed*) 503.

[Applied to actions] foolish, unwise, indiscreet, injudicious, improper, unreasonable, without reason, ridiculous, silly, stupid, asinine; ill-imagined, -advised, -judged, -devised; inconsistent, irrational, unphilosophical; extravagant etc. (*nonsensical*) 497; sleeveless, idle; useless etc. 645; inexpedient etc. 647; frivolous etc. (*trivial*) 643; absurd etc. 497.

Phr. *Davis sum non Oedipus.*

500. Sage.—N. sage, wise man; pundit; master -mind, – spirit of the age; longhead, thinker, philosopher.

authority, oracle, mentor, luminary, shining light, *esprit fort*, *magnus Apollo,* Solon, Solomon, Nestor, Magi, 'second Daniel.'

man of learning etc. 492; expert etc. 700; wizard etc. 994.

[Ironically] wiseacre, bigwig.

Adj. wise, learned; authoritative, oracular; erudite etc. 490; venerable, reverenced, revered, *emeritus.*

501. Fool.—N. fool, idiot, tomfool, wiseacre, simpleton, Simple Simon, nit-wit, witling, dizzard, donkey, ass; ninny, -hammer; moron, dolt, booby, Tom Noddy, looby, hoddy-doddy, noddy, nonny, noodle, nizy, owl; goose, -cap; *imbécile*; gaby, *radoteur*, nincompoop, *badaud*, zany; trifler, babbler; pretty fellow; natural, *niais*.

child, baby, infant, innocent, milksop, sop.

oaf, lout, loon, lown, dullard, doodle, calf, colt, buzzard, block, put, stick, stock, numps, tony.

bull-, dunder-, addle-, block-, dull-, logger-, jolt-, jolter-, beetle-, gross-, thick-, giddy-head; num-, thick- skull; lack-, shallow-brain; half-, lack-wit; dunder-pate; fat-head, poor stick.

sawney, gowk; clod, -hopper; clod-, clot-poll, pate; bull-calf; men of Boeotia, wise men of Gotham.

un sot à triple étage, sot; jobbernowl, changeling, mooncalf, *gobemouche*.

dotard, driveller; old -fogey, – woman; crone, grandmother.

greenhorn etc. (*dupe*) 547; dunce etc. (*ignoramus*) 493; lubber etc. (*bungler*) 701; madman etc. 504.

one who -will not set the Thames on fire, – did not invent gunpowder; *qui n'a pas inventé la poudre*; no conjuror.

502. Sanity. N. sanity; soundness etc. *adj.*, rationality, normality, sobriety, lucidity, lucid interval; senses, sober senses, sound mind, *mens sana*.

V. be -sane etc. *adj.*; retain one's senses, – reason.

become -sane etc. *adj.*; come to one's senses, sober down.

render -sane etc. *adj.*; bring to one's senses, sober.

Adj. sane, rational, reasonable, *compos mentis*, of sound mind; sound, -minded.

self-possessed; sober, -minded.

in one's -sober senses, – right mind; in possession of one's faculties.

Adv. sanely etc. *adj.*

503. Insanity.—N. disordered -reason, – intellect; diseased –, unsound –, abnormal- mind; derangement, unsoundness.

insanity, lunacy; madness etc. *adj.*; mania, *rabies*, *furor*, mental aliénation, paranoia, aberration; *amentia*, dementation, -tia, -cy; *dementia praecox*; *morosis*, idiocy, phrenitis, frenzy, raving, incoherence, wandering, delirium, calenture of the brain, delusion, hallucination; lycanthropy, brain storm, *delirium tremens*, D.T.'s.

vertigo, dizziness, swimming; sunstroke, *coup de soleil*, siriasis.

fanatisism, infatuation, craze; oddity, eccentricity, twist, monomania; klepto-, dipso-mania; hypochondriasis etc. (*low spirits*) 837; *melancholia*, hysteria.

screw –, tile –, slate- loose; bee in one's bonnet, rats in the upper story.

dotage etc. (*imbecility*) 499.

V. be –, become- -insane etc. *adj.*; lose one's senses, – reason, – faculties, – wits; go –, run- mad, run amuck; rave, dote, ramble, wander; drivel etc. (*be imbecile*) 499; have a -screw loose etc. *n.*, – devil; *avoir le diable au corps*; lose one's head etc. (*be uncertain*) 475.

derange, render –, drive- -mad etc. *adj.*; madden, dementate, addle the wits, derange the head, infatuate, befool; turn -the brain, – one's head.

Adj. insane, mad, lunatic; crazy, crazed, *aliéné*, *non compos mentis*; not right, cracked, touched; bereft of reason; unhinged, deranged, unsettled in one's mind; insensate, reasonless, beside oneself, demented, daft; phren-, fren-zied, -etic; possessed, – with a devil; far gone, maddened, moonstruck; shatterpated; barmy; mad-, scatter-, shatter-, crack-brained, off one's head; bug-house, *loco*.

maniacal; manic, manic-depressive; delirious, light-headed, incoherent, rambling, doting, wandering; frantic, raving, stark staring mad, amok, amuck.

corybantic, dithyrambic; rabid, giddy, vertiginous, dizzy, wild, haggard, mazed; flighty; distracted, -aught; bewildered etc. (*uncertain*) 475.

mad as a -March hare, – hatter; of -unsound mind etc. *n.* touched –, wrong –, not right- in one's -head, – mind, – wits, – upper story; out of one's -mind, – senses, – wits; not in one's right mind.

fanatical, infatuated, odd, eccentric, hypp-ed, -ish.

imbecile, silly etc. 499.

Adv. like one possessed.

Phr. the mind having lost its balance; the reason under a cloud; *tête -exaltée*, *-montée*.

504. Madman—N. madman, lunatic, maniac, bedlamite, candidate for Bedlam, raver, madcap; energumen; paranoiac; auto-, mono-, pyro-, megalo-, dipso-, klepto-maniac; hypochondriac etc. (low spirit) 837.

dreamer etc. 515; rhapsodist, seer, high-flier, enthusiast, crank, eccentric, nut, fanatic, *fanatico*; *exalté*; knight errant, Don Quixote.

idiot etc. 501.

505. Memory.—N. memory, remembrance; reten-tion, -tiveness; tenacity; *veteris vestigia flammae*; tablets of the memory; readiness.

reminiscence, recognition, recurrence, recollection, rememoration; retrospect, -ion; after-thought.

suggestion etc. (*information*) 527; prompting etc. *v.*; hint, reminder, token of remembrance, *memento*, *souvenir*, keepsake, relic, *memorandum*; remembrancer, flapper; memorial etc. (*record*) 551; commemoration etc. (*celebration*) 883.

things to be remembered, *memorabilia*.

art of –, artificial- memory; *memoria technica*; mnemo-nics, -technics; phrenotypics; Mnemosyne; memorandum-, note-, engagement-, prompt-book.

retentive –, tenacious –, green –, trustworthy –, capacious –, faithful –, correct –, exact –, ready –, prompt- memory.

V. remember, mind; retain the -memory, – remembrance- of; keep in view.

have –, hold –, bear –, carry –, keep –, retain- in *or* in the -thoughts, – mind, – memory, – remembrance; be in –, live in –, remain in –, dwell in –, haunt –, impress- one's -memory, – thoughts, – mind.

sink in the mind; run in the head; not be able to get it out of one's head; be deeply impressed with; rankle etc. (*revenge*) 919.

recur to the mind; flash -on the mind, – across the memory.

recognize, recollect, bethink oneself, recall, call up, conjure up, retrace; look –, trace- -back, – backwards; think –, look back- upon; review; call –, recall –, bring- to mind; remembrance; carry one's thoughts back; rake up the past.

suggest etc. (*inform*) 527; prompt; put –, keep- in mind; remind; fan the embers; call –, summon –, rip- up; renew; *infandum renovare dolorem*; task –, tax –, jog –, flap –, refresh –, rub up –, awaken- the memory; pull by the sleeve; bring back the memory, put in remembrance, memorialize.

get –, have –, learn –, know –, say –, repeat- by -heart, – rote; drive –, get- into -one's head; say one's lesson; repeat, – as a parrot; have at one's finger's ends.

commit to memory; memorize; con, – over; fix –, rivet –, imprint –, impress –, stamp –, grave –, engrave –, store –, treasure up –, bottle up –, embalm –, enshrine- in the memory; load –, store –, stuff –, burden- the memory with.

redeem from oblivion; keep the memory -alive, – green; *tangere ulcus*; keep up the memory of; commemorate etc. (*celebrate*) 883.

make a note of etc. (*record*) 551.

Adj. remember-ing, -ed etc. *v.*; mindful, reminiscential; retained in the memory etc. *v.*; pent up in one's memory; fresh; green, – in remembrance, still vivid; unforgotten, present to the mind; within one's -memory etc. *n.*; indelible; not to be forgotten, unforgettable, enduring; uppermost in one's thoughts; memorable etc. (*important*) 642.

Adv. by -heart, – rote; without book, *memoriter*.

in memory of; *in memoriam*; suggestive.

Phr. *manet altâ mente repostum*; *forsan et haec olim meminisse juvabit*.

506. Oblivion.—N. oblivion; forgetfulness etc. *adj.*; obliteration etc. 552, of –, insensibility etc. 823 to- the past.

short –, treacherous –, loose –, slippery –, failing- memory; decay –, failure –, lapse- of memory; memory like a sieve; waters of -Lethe, – oblivion, *amnesia*.

pardon, acquittal, amnesty, oblivion; absolution.

V. forget; be -forgetful etc. *adj.*; fall –, sink- into oblivion; have -a short memory etc. *n.* – no head.

forget one's own name, have on the tip of one's tongue, come in at one ear and go out at the other.

slip –, escape –, fade from –, die away from- the memory; lose, – sight of.

unlearn; efface etc. 552 –, discharge- from the memory; consign to -oblivion, – the tomb of the Capulets; think no more of etc. (*turn the attention from*) 458; cast behind one's back, wean one's thoughts from; let bygones be bygones etc. (*forgive*) 918.

Adj. forgotten etc. *v.*; unremembered, past recollection, bygone, out of mind; buried –, sunk- in oblivion; clean forgotten; gone out of one's -head, – recollection.

forgetful, oblivious, mindless, heedless, Lethean; insensible etc. 823- to the past.

Phr. *non mi ricordo*; the memory -failing, – deserting one, – being at (*or* in) fault.

507. Expectation.—N. expect-ation, -ance, -ancy; anticipation, reckoning, calculation; contingency; foresight etc. 510.

contemplation, prospection, look out; prospect, perspective, horizon, vista; destiny etc. 152.

suspense, waiting, abeyance; curiosity etc. 455; anxious –, ardent –, eager –, breathless –, sanguine- expectation; torment of Tantalus.

presumption, hope etc. 858; trust etc. (*belief*) 484; prognostication, auspices etc. (*prediction*) 511.

V. expect; look -for, – out for, – forward to; hope for, anticipate; have in -prospect, – contemplation; keep in view; contemplate, promise oneself; not -wonder etc. 870 -at, – if.

wait –, tarry –, lie in wait –, watch –, bargain- for; keep a -good, – sharp- look-out for; await; stand at 'attention,' abide, bide one's –, mark- time, watch.

foresee etc. 510; prepare for etc. 673; forestall etc. (*be early*) 132; count upon etc. (*believe in*) 484; think likely etc. (*probability*) 472; make one's mouth water.

lead one to expect etc. (*predict*) 511; have in store for etc. (*destiny*) 152.

prick up one's ears, hold one's breath.

Adj. expectant; expecting etc. *v.*; in -expectation etc. *n.*; on the watch etc. (*vigilant*) 459; open -eyed, -mouthed; agape, gaping, all agog; on -tenterhooks, – tiptoe, – the tiptoe of expectation; *aux aguets*; ready; curious etc. 455; looking forward to; prepared for; on the rack.

expected etc. *v.*; long expected, foreseen; in prospect etc. *n.*; prospective; in -one's eye, – view, – the horizon; impending etc. (*destiny*) 152.

Adv. expectantly; in the event of; on the watch etc. *adj.*; with -breathless expectation etc. *n.*; – bated breath, – eyes, – ears strained; *arrectis auribus*; on edge.

Phr. we shall see; *nous verrons*.

508. Inexpectation.—N. in-, non-expectation; false expectation etc. (*disappointment*) 509; miscalculation etc. 481; unforeseen contingency, the unforeseen, the unexpected.

surprise, sudden burst, thunderclap, blow, shock; bolt out of the blue; eye-opener; wonder etc. 870.

V. not -expect etc. 507; be taken by surprise; start; miscalculate etc. 481; not bargain for; come –, fall- upon.

be -unexpected etc. *adj.*; come -unawares etc. *adv.*; turn up, pop, drop from the clouds; come –, burst –, flash –, bounce –, steal –, creep- upon one; come –, burst- like a thunder-clap; -bolt; take –, catch- -by surprise, – unawares, – napping.

pounce –, spring a mine- upon.

surprise, startle, take aback, electrify, stun, stagger, take away one's breath, throw off one's guard; astonish etc. (*strike with wonder*) 870.

Adj. non-expectant; surprised etc. *v.*; unwarned, -aware; off one's guard; inattentive etc. 458.

un-expected, -anticipated, -prepared for, -looked for, -foreseen, -hoped for; dropped from the clouds; beyond –, contrary to –, against- expectation; out of one's reckoning; unheard of etc. (*exceptional*) 83; startling; sudden etc. (*instantaneous*) 113.

Adv. abruptly, unexpectedly, plump, pop, *à l'improviste*, unawares; without -notice, – warning, – saying 'by your leave;' like a -thief in the night, – thunderbolt; in an unguarded moment; suddenly etc. (*instantaneously*) 113.

Int. heyday! etc. (*wonder*) 870.

Phr. little did one -think, – expect; nobody would ever -suppose, – think, – expect; who would have thought?

509. Disappointment. [Failure of expectation.]—**N.** disappointment, disillusionment; blighted hope, balk; blow; slip 'twixt cup and lip; non-fulfilment of one's hopes; sad –, bitter- disappointment; trick of fortune; afterclap; false –, vain- expectation; miscalculation etc. 481; fool's paradise; much cry and little wool.

V. be disappointed; look -blank, – blue; look –, stand- aghast etc. (*wonder*) 870; find to one's cost; laugh on the wrong side of one's mouth; find one a false prophet.

disappoint; crush –, dash –, balk –, disappoint –, blight –, falsify –, defeat –, not realize- one's -hope, – expectation; balk, jilt, bilk; play one -false, – a trick; dash the cup from the lips; tantalize; dumb-found, -founder; disillusion, -ize; dissatisfy, disgruntle.

Adj. disappointed etc. *v.*; disconcerted, aghast; out of one's reckoning; disgruntled.

Phr. the mountain brought forth a mouse; *nascitur ridiculus mus*; *parturiunt montes*; *diis aliter visum*, the bubble burst; one's countenance falling.

510. Foresight.—N. foresight, prospicience, prevision, longsightedness; anticipation; providence etc. (*preparation*) 673.

fore-thought, -cast; pre-deliberation, -surmise; foregone conclusion etc. (*prejudgment*) 481; prudence etc. (*caution*) 864.

foreknowledge; *prognosis*; pre-cognition, -science, -notion, -sentiment; second sight; sagacity etc. (*intelligence*) 498.

prospect etc. (*expectation*) 507; foretaste; prospectus etc. (*plan*) 626.

V. foresee; look -forwards to, – ahead, – beyond; scent from afar; feel in one's bones; look –, pry –, peep into the future.

see one's way; see how the -land lies, – wind blows, – cat jumps.

anticipate; expect etc. 507; be beforehand etc. (*early*) 132; predict etc. 511; fore-know, -judge, -cast; surmise; have an eye to the -future, – main chance; *respicere finem*; keep a sharp look-out etc. (*vigilance*) 459; forewarn etc. 668.

Adj. foreseeing etc. *v.*; prescient; anticipatory; far-seeing, -sighted; sagacious etc. (*intelligent*) 498; weather-wise; provident etc. (*prepared*) 673; prospective etc. 507.

Adv. against the time when.

511. Prediction.—N. prediction, announcement; program, programme etc. (*plan*) 626; premonition etc. (*warning*) 668; *prognosis*, prophecy, vaticination, Mantology, prognostication, premonstration, augur-y, -ation; a-, ha-riolation; fore-, a-boding; bode-, abode-ment; omin-ation, -ousness; auspices, forecast; sign, presage, prognostic; omen etc. 512; horoscope, nativity; sooth, -saying; fortune-telling; divination; crystal gazing, necromancy etc. 992; prophet etc. 512.

[Divination by the stars] astrology, horoscopy, astromancy, judicial astrology.*

[Place of prediction] *adytum*.

prefigur-ation, -ement; prototype, type.

V. predict, prognosticate, prophesy, vaticinate, divine, foretell, soothsay, augurate, tell fortunes; cast a -horoscope, – nativity; advise; forewarn etc. 668.

presage, augur, bode; a-, fore-bode, -cast; fore-, be-token; pre-figure, -show; portend; fore show, -shadow, shadow forth, typify, ominate, signify, point to, precurse.

usher in, herald, premise, announce; lower.

hold out –, raise –, excite- -expectation, – hope; bid fair, promise, lead one to expect; be the -precursor etc. 64.

Adj. predicting etc. *v.*; predictive, prophetic, fatidical, vaticinal, oracular, Sibylline, haruspical, weatherwise.

ominous, presageful, portentous; augur-ous, -al, -ial, auspici-al, -ous; prescious, monitory, extispicious, premonitory, precusory, significant of, pregnant with, big with the fate of.

Phr. 'coming events cast their shadows before.'

*The following terms, expressive of different forms of divination, have been collected from various sources, and are here given as a curious illustration of bygone superstitions:

Divination *by oracles*, Theomancy; *by the Bible*, Bibliomancy; *by ghosts*, Psychomancy; *by spirits seen in a magic lens*, Cristallomantia; *by shadows or manes*, Sciomancy; *by appearances in the air*, Aeromancy, Chaomancy, *by the stars at birth*, Genethliacs; *by meteors*, Meteoromancy; *by winds*, Austromancy; *by sacrificial appearances*, Aruspicy (*or* Haruspicy), Hieromancy, Hieroscopy; *by the entrails of animals sacrificed*, Hieromancy; *by the entrails of a human sacrifice*, Anthropomancy; *by the entrails of fishes*, Ichthyomancy; *by sacrificial fire*, Pyromancy; *by red-hot iron*, Sideromancy; *by smoke from the alter*, Capnomancy; *by mice*, Myomancy; *by birds*, Orniscopy, Ornithomancy; *by a cock picking up grains*, Alectryomancy (*or* Alectoromancy); *by fishes*, Ophiomancy; *by herbs*, Botanomancy; *by water*, Hydromancy; *by fountains*, Pegomancy; *by a wand*, Rhabdomancy; *by dough of cakes*, Crithomancy; *by meal*, Aleuromancy, Alphitomancy; *by salt*, Halomancy; *by dice*, Cleromancy; *by arrows*, Belomancy; *by a balanced hatchet*, Axinomancy; *by a balanced sieve*, Coscinomancy; *by a suspended ring*, Dactyliomancy; *by dots made at random on paper*, Geomancy; *by precious stones*, Lithomancy; *by pebbles*, Pessomancy; *by pebbles drawn from a heap*, Psephomancy; *by mirrors*, Catoptromancy; *by writings in ashes*, Tephramancy; *by dreams*, Oneiromancy; *by the hand*, Palmistry, Chiromancy; *by nails reflecting the sun's rays*, Onychomancy; *by finger rings*, Dactylomancy; *by numbers*, Arithmancy; *by drawing lots*, Sortilege; *by passages in books*, Stichomancy; *by the letters forming the name of the person*, Onomancy, Nomancy; *by the features*, Anthroposcopy; *by the mode of laughing*, Geloscopy; *by ventriloquism*, Gastromancy; *by walking in a circle*, Gyromancy; *by dropping melted wax into water*, Ceromancy; *by currents*, Bletonism.

512. Omen.—N. omen, portent, presage, prognostic, augury, auspice; sigh etc. (*indication*) 550; herald, forerunner, harbinger etc. (*precursor*) 64.

bird of ill omen, signs of the times; gathering clouds; warning etc. 668.

prefigurement etc. 511.

513. Oracle.—N. oracle; prophet, -ess; seer, soothsayer, augur, fortune-teller, palmist, medium, clairvoyant, crystal gazer, witch, geomancer, *aruspex*; a-, ha-ruspice; Sibyl; Python, -ess; Pythia; Pythian –, Delphian- oracle; Monitor, Sphinx, Tiresias, Cassandra, Sibylline leaves; Zadkiel, Old Moore; sorcerer etc. 994; interpreter etc. 524.

514. Supposition.—N. supposition, assumption, postulation, condition, pre-supposition, hypothesis, postulate, *postulatum*, theory, *data*; pro-, position; *thesis*, theorem; proposal etc. (*plan*) 626.

bare –, vague –, loose- -supposition, – suggestion; conceit; conjecture; guess, – work; rough guess, shot; conjecturality; surmise, suspicion, inkling, suggestion, suggestiveness, association of ideas, hint; presumption etc. (*belief*) 484; divination, speculation.

theorist, speculator, doctrinarian, hypothesist.

V. suppose, conjecture, surmise, suspect, guess, divine; theorize; pre-sume, -surmise, -suppose; assume, fancy, wis, take it; give a guess, speculate, believe, dare say, take it into one's head, take for granted.

put forth; pro-pound, -pose; moot; hypothesize; start, put a case, submit, move, make a motion; hazard –, throw out –, put forward- a - suggestion, – conjecture.

allude to, suggest, hint, put it into one's head.

suggest itself etc. (*thought*) 451; run in the head etc. (*memory*) 505; marvel –, wonder- -if, – whether.

Adj. supposing etc. *v.*; given, mooted, postulatory; assumed etc. *v.*; supposit-ive, -itious; gratuitous, speculative, conjectural, hypothetical, suppositional, theoretical, academic, supposable, presumptive, putative.

suggestive, allusive, stimulating.

Adv. if, – so be; an; on the -supposition etc. *n.*; *ex hypothesi*; in -case, – the event of; *quasi*, as if, provided; perhaps etc. (*by possibility*) 470; for aught one knows.

515. Imagination.—N. imagination; originality; invention; fancy; inspiration; *verve*; empathy.

warm –, heated –, excited –, sanguine –, ardent –, fiery –, boiling –, wild –, bold –, daring –, playful –, lively –, fertile- - imagination, – fancy.

'mind's eye;' 'such stuff as dreams are made of.'

ideal-ity, -ism; romanticism, utopianism, castle-building; dreaming; frenzy; ecs-, ex-tasy; calenture etc. (*delirium*) 503; reverie, brown study, trance; somnambulism.

conception, *vorstellung*, ercogitation, 'a fine frenzy,' poetic frenzy, divine afflatus; cloud-, dream-land; flight –, fumes- of fancy; 'thick-coming fancies;' creation –, coinage- of the brain; imagery, word painting.

conceit, maggot, figment, myth, dream, vision, shadow, chimera; phan-tasm, -tasy; fantasy, fancy; whim, -sey; vagary, rhapsody, romance, *extravaganza*; air-drawn dagger, bugbear, nightmare; flying Dutchman, great sea-serpent, man in the moon, castle in the air, *château en Espagne*; Utopia, Atlantis, happy valley, millennium, fairy land; land of Prester John, kingdom of Micomicon; work of fiction etc. (*novel*) 594; poetry etc. 597; drama etc. 599; Arabian nights; *le pot au lait*; dream of Alnaschar etc. (*hope*) 858; day –, golden- dream

illusion etc. (*error*) 495; phantom etc. (*fallacy of vision*) 443; *Fata Morgana* etc. (*ignis fatuus*) 423; vapor etc. (*cloud*) 353; stretch of the imagination etc. (*exaggeration*) 549.

idealist, romanticist, visionary; mopus; romancer, dreamer; somnambulist; rhapsodist etc. (*fanatic*) 504.

V. imagine, fancy, conceive; ideal-, real-ize; dream, – of; 'give to airy nothing a local habitation and a name.'

create, originate, devise, invent, coin, fabricate; improvise, strike out something new.

set one's wits to work; strain –, crack- one's invention; rack –, ransack –, cudgel- one's brains; excogitate.

give -play, – the reins, – a loose- to the - imagination, – fancy; empathize; indulge in reverie.

conjure up a vision; fancy –, represent –, picture –, figure- to oneself; envisage.

float in the mind; suggest itself etc. (*thought*) 451.

Adj. imagined etc. *v.*; *ben trovato*; air-drawn, -built.

imagin-ing etc. *v.*, -ative; original, inventive, creative, fertile, productive; ingenious.

romantic, high-flown, flighty, extravagant, fanatic, enthusiastic, Utopian, Quixotic; preposterous, rhapsodical.

ideal, unreal; in the clouds, *in nubibus*; unsubstantial etc. 4; illusory etc. (*fallacious*) 495; fictitious, theoretical, hypothetical.

fabulous, legendary; myth-ic, -ological; chimerical; imagin-, vision-ary; notional; fan-cy, -ciful, -tastic, -tastical; whimsical; fairy, -like.

dreamy, entranced, vaporous.

516. Meaning. [Idea to be conveyed.] [Thing signified.]—**N.** meaning; signific-ation, -ance; sense, expression; im-, pur-port; drift, tenor, implication, connotation, essence, force, spirit bearing, coloring; scope.

matter; subject, -matter; argument, text, sum and substance; gist etc. 5.

general –, broad –, substantial – colloquial –, literal –, plain –, simple –, accepted –, natural –, unstrained –, true etc. (*exact*) 494 –, honest etc. 543 –, *primâ facie* etc. (*manifest*) 525- meaning.

literality; literal interpretation; after acceptation; allusion etc. (*latency*) 526; suggestion etc. (*information*) 527; synonym; figure of speech etc. 521; acceptation etc. (*interpretation*) 522.

V. mean, signify, express, connote, denote; im-, pur-port; convey, imply, breathe, indicate, bespeak, bear a sense; tell –, speak- of; touch on; point –, allude- to; drive at; involve etc. (*latency*) 526; delcare etc. (*affirm*) 535.

understand by etc. (*interpret*) 522.

Adj. meaning etc. *v.*; expressive, suggestive, meaningful, allusive; signific-ant, -ative, -atory; pithy; full of –, pregnant with- meaning.

declaratory etc. 535; intelligible etc. 518; literal, metaphrastic; synonymous; tantamount etc. (*equivalent*) 27; implied etc. (*latent*) 526; explicit etc. 525; literal etc. 562.

Adv. to that effect; that is to say etc. (*being interpreted*) 522.

literally; evidently, from the context.

517. Unmeaningness. [Absence of meaning.]—**N.** unmeaningness etc. *adj.*; scrabble, scribble, scrawl, daub, (*painting*), strumming (*music*).

empty sound, dead letter, *vox et praeterea nihil*; 'a tale told by an idiot, full of sound and fury, signifying nothing;' 'sounding brass and a tinkling cymbal.'

nonsense, jargon, gibberish, jabber, mere words, hocus-pocus, fustian, rant, bombast, balderdash, palaver, patter, flummery, *verbiage*, babble, *bavardage*, *baragouin*, platitude, *niaiserie*; inanity; rigmarole, rodomontade; truism; *nugae canorae*; twaddle, twattle, fudge, trash; stuff, – and nonsense; bosh, rubbish, rot, drivel, moonshine, wish-wash, fiddle-faddle, flapdoodle; absurdity etc. 497; vagueness etc. (*unintelligibility*) 519.

V. mean nothing; be unmeaning etc. *adj.*; twaddle, quibble, rant, gabble, scrabble etc. *n.*

Adj. unmeaning; meaning-, sense-less; nonsensical; void of -sense etc. 516.

in-, un-expressive; vacant, fatuous; not significant; insignificant,.

trashy, washy, inane, vague, trumpery, trivial, fiddle-faddle, twaddling, quibbling.

unmeant, not expressed; tacit etc. (*latent*) 526.

inexpressible, undefinable, incommunicable.

Int. rubbish! etc. 497.

518. Intelligibility.—N. intelligibility, clearness, clarity, explicitness etc. *adj.*; lucidity, perspicuity; legibility, plain speaking etc. (*manifestation*) 525; precision etc. 494; a word to the wise.

V. be -intelligible etc. *adj.*; speak -for itself, – volumes; tell its own tale, lie on the surface.

render -intelligible etc. *adj.*; popularize, simplify, clear up; elucidate etc. (*explain*) 522.

understand, comprehend; take, – in; catch, grasp, recognize, follow, collect, master, make out; see -with half an eye, – daylight, – one's way; enter into the ideas of; come to an understanding.

Adj. intelligible; clear, – as -day, – crystal, – noonday; lucid; per-, tran-spicuous; luminous, transparent; comprehensible.

easily understood, easy to understand, for the million, intelligible to the meanest capacity, popularized.

plain, distinct, explicit, clear-cut; positive; definite etc. (*precise*) 494.

graphic, vivid, telling; expressive etc. (*meaning*) 516; illustrative etc. (*explanatory*) 522.

un-ambiguous, -equivocal, -mistakable etc. (*manifest*) 525, -confused; legible, recognizable; obvious etc. 525.

Adv. in plain -terms, – words, – English.

Phr. he that runs may read etc. (*manifest*) 525.

519. Unintelligibility.—N. unintelligibility, incomprehensibility, imperspicuity; inconceivableness, vagueness etc. *adj.*; obscurity; ambiguity etc. 520; doubtful meaning; uncertainty etc. 475; perplexity etc. (*confusion*) 59; spinosity; *obscurum per obscurius*; mystification etc. (*concealment*) 528; latency etc. 526; transcendentalism.

paradox; enigma, riddle etc. (*secret*) 533; *dignus vindice nodus*; sealed book; steganography, freemasonry.

pons asinorum, asses' bridge; double –, high-Dutch, Greek, Hebrew; jargon etc. (*unmeaning*) 517.

obscurantist.

V. be -unintelligible etc. *adj.*; require -explanation etc. 522; have a doubtful meaning, pass comprehension.

render -unintelligible etc. *adj.*; conceal etc. 528; darken etc. 421; confuse etc. (*derange*) 61; perplex etc. (*bewilder*) 475.

not -understand etc. 518; lose, – the clue; miss; not know what to make of, be able to make nothing of, give it up; not be able to -account for, – make either head or tail of; be at sea etc. (*uncertain*) 475; wonder etc. 870; see through a glass darkly etc. (*ignorance*) 491.

not understand one another; play at cross purposes etc. (*misinterpret*) 523.

Adj. un-intelligible, -accountable, -decipherable, -discoverable, -knowable, -fathomable; incognizable, -explicable, -scrutable; inap-, incomprehensible; insol-vable, -uble; impenetrable.

illegible, indecipherable, as Greek to one, unexplained, paradoxical; enigmatic, -al; puzzling, baffling.

obscure, dark, muddy, clear as mud, seen through a mist, dim, nebulous, shrouded in mystery; undiscernible etc. (*invisible*) 447; misty etc. (*opaque*) 426; hidden etc. 528; latent etc. 526.

indefinite etc. (*indistinct*) 447; perplexed etc. (*confused*) 59; undetermined, vague, loose, ambiguous; mysterious; mystic, -al; transcendental; occult, recondite, esoteric, abstruse, crabbed.

incon-ceivable, -ceptible; searchless; above –, beyond –, past- comprehension; beyond one's depth; unconceived.

inexpressible, undefinable, incommunicable, unutterable, ineffable, unpronounceable.

520. Equivocalness. [Having a double sense.]—**N.** equivocalness etc. *adj.*; double -meaning etc. 516; ambiguity, *double entendre*, pun, paragram, *calembour*, quibble, *équivoque*, anagram; conundrum etc. (*riddle*) 533; word-play etc. (*wit*) 842; homonym, -y; amphibo-ly, -logy; ambiloquy.
Sphinx, Delphic oracle.
equivocation etc. (*duplicity*) 544; white lie, mental reservation etc. (*concealment*) 528.
V. be -equivocal etc. *adj.*; have two -meanings etc. 516; equivocate etc. (*palter*) 544.
Adj. equivocal, ambiguous, amphibolous, homonymous; double-tongued etc. (*lying*) 544.

521. Metaphor.—N. figure of speech; *facon de parler*, way of speaking, colloquialism.
phrase etc. 566; figure, trope, metaphor, tralatition, metonymy, enallage, *catachresis*, *synecdoche*, *autonomasia*; irony, satire, figurativeness etc. *adj.*; image, -ry; *metalepsis*, type, anagoge, simile, personification, *prosopopaeia*, allegory, apologue, parable, fable; allusion, adumbration; application; euphemism; euphuism.
V. employ -metaphor etc. *n.*; personify, allegorize, adumbrate, shadow forth, apply, allude –, refer- to.
Adj. metaphorical etc. *n.*; figurative, catachrestical, typical, tralatitious, parabolic, allegorical, allusive, anagogical; ironical; colloquial.
Adv. so to -speak, – say, – express oneself; as it were.
Phr. *mutato nomine de te fabula nattatur.*

522. Interpretation.—N. interpretation, definition; explan-, explic-ation; solution, answer; rationale; plain –, simple –, strict- interpretation; meaning etc. 516.
translation; rend-ering, -ition; reddition; literal –, free- translation; key, crib; secret; clew etc. (*indication*) 550; Rosetta stone.
exegesis; ex-pounding, -position; Hermeneutics; comment, -ary; inference etc. (*deduction*) 480; illustration, exemplification; gloss, annotation, *scholium*, note; e-, di-lucidation, enucleation; *éclaircissement*, *mot de l'énigme*.
symptomat-, semei-ology; metoposcopy, physiognomy; diagnosis, prognosis; paleography etc. (*philology*) 560.
accept-ion, -ation, -ance; light, reading, lection, construction, version.
equivalent, – meaning etc. 516; synonym; para-, meta-phrase; convertible terms, apposition; dictionary etc. 562; polyglot.
V. interpret, explain, define, construe, translate, render; do –, turn- into; transfuse the sense of.
find out etc. 480*a*- -the meaning etc. 516- of; read; spell –, figure –, make- out; decipher, decode, unravel, disentangle, puzzle out; find the key of, enucleate, resolve, solve; read between the lines.
account for; find –, tell- the cause etc. 153- of; throw –, shed- -light, – new light, – a fresh light- upon; clear up, elucidate.
illustrate, exemplify; unfold, expound, comment upon, annotate; popularize etc. (*render intelligible*) 518.
take –, understand –, receive –, accept- in a particular sense; understand by, put a construction on, be given to understand.
Adj. explanatory, expository; explica-tive, -tory; exegetical; hermeneutic, interpretive, illustrative, elucidative, annotative, scholiastic.
polyglot; literal; para-, meta-phrastic; cosignificative, synonymous; equivalent etc. 27.
Adv. in -explanation etc. *n.*; that is to say, *id est*, *videlicet*, to wit, namely, in other words.
literally, strictly speaking; in -plain, – plainer- -terms, – words, – English; more simply.

523. Misinterpretation.—N. misinterpretation, -apprehension, -understanding, -acceptation, -construction, -application; *catachresis*; cross -reading, – purposes; mistake etc. 495.
misrepresentation, perversion, exaggeration etc. 549; false -coloring, – construction; abuse of terms; parody, travesty; falsification etc. (*lying*) 544.
V. mis-interpret, -apprehend, -understand, -conceive, -judge, -doubt, -spell, -translate, -construe, -apply; mistake etc. 495.
misrepresent, pervert; garble etc. (*falsify*) 544; distort; detort; travesty, play upon words; stretch –, strain –, wrest- the -sense, – meaning; explain away; put a -bad, – false- construction on; give a false coloring, look through -rose colored –, – dark – spectacles.
be –, play- at cross purposes.
Adj. misinterpreted etc. *v.*; untranslat-ed, -able.
Adv. at cross purposes.

524. Interpreter.—N. interpreter, translator, ex-positor, -pounder, -ponent, -plainer; demonstrator.
scholiast, commentator, annotator; meta-, paraphrast.
spokesman, speaker, mouthpiece, prolocutor; diplomat etc. 758.
guide, courier, dragoman, *valet de place*, *cicerone*, showman; oneirocritic; Oedipus; oracle etc. 513.

525. Manifestation.—N. manifestation; unfolding; plainness etc. *adj.*; plain speaking; expression; showing etc. *v.*; exposition, demonstration, *séance*; exhibition, production; display, showing off etc. 882; premonstration. [Thing shown] exhibit, show.
indication etc. (*calling attention to*) 457; publicity etc. 531; disclosure etc. 529; openness etc. (*honesty*) 543, (*artlessness*) 703; *épachement*, prominence.
V. make –, render- -manifest etc. *adj.*; bring -forth, – forward, – to the front, – into view; give notice, express; represent, set forth, exhibit; show,

– up; expose; produce; hold up –, expose- to view; set –, place –, lay- before -one, – one's eyes; tell to one's face; trot out, put through one's paces, unfold, show off, show forth, unveil, bring to light, display, demonstrate, unroll; lay open; draw –, bring- out; bring out in strong relief; call –, bring- into notice; hold up the mirror; wear one's heart upon his sleeve; show one's -face, – colors; manifest oneself; speak out; make no -mystery, – secret- of; unfurl the flag; proclaim etc. (*publish*) 531.

indicate etc. (*direct attention to*) 457; disclose etc. 529; elicit etc. 480*a*; interpret etc. 522.

be -manifest etc. *adj.*; appear etc. (*be visible*) 446; transpire etc. (*be disclosed*) 529; speak for itself, stand to reason; stare one in the face; loom large, appear on the horizon, rear its head; give -token, – sign, – indication of; tell its own tale etc. (*intelligible*) 518; go without saying.

Adj. manifest, apparent; salient, striking, demonstrative, prominent, in the foreground, notable, pronounced.

flagrant; notorious etc. (*public*) 531; arrant; stark staring; unshaded, glaring.

defin-ed, -ite; distinct, conspicuous etc. (*visible*) 446; obvious, evident, incontestable, unmistakable, not to be mistaken, plain, clear, palpable, self-evident, autoptical; intelligible etc. 518; clear as -day, – daylight, – noonday; plain as -a pikestaff, – the sun at noonday, – the nose on one's face, – the way to the parish church.

ostensible, open, – as day; overt, patent, express, explicit; naked, bare, literal, downright, undisguised, exoteric.

unreserved; frank, plain spoken etc. (*artless*) 703; barefaced, brazen, bold, shameless, daring, flaunting, loud.

manifested etc. *v.*; disclosed etc. 529; expressible, capable of being shown, producible; in-, un-concealable.

Adv. manifestly, openly etc. *adj.*; before one's eyes, under one's nose, to one's face, face to face, above board, *cartes sur table*, on the stage, in plain sight, in open court, in the open, – streets; at the cross roads; in market overt; in the face of -day, – heaven; in -broad –, open- daylight; without reserve; at first blush, *primâ facie*, on the face of; in set terms.

Phr. *cela saute aux yeux*; he that runs may read; you can see it with half an eye; it needs no ghost to tell us; the meaning lies on the surface; *cela va sans dire*; *res ipsa loquitur*.

526. Latency.—N. latency, inexpression; hidden –, occult- meaning; occultness, occultism, mysticism, mystery, cabala, symbolism, anagoge; silence etc. (*taciturnity*) 585; concealment etc. 528; more than meets the -eye, – ear; Delphic oracle; *les dessous des cartes*, undercurrent.

allusion, insinuation, implication; innuendo etc. 527; adumbration; 'something rotten in the state of Denmark.'

snake in the grass etc. (*pitfall*) 667; secret etc. 533.

darkness, invisibility, impreceptibility.

latent influence, power behind the throne; friend at court, wire puller.

V. be -latent etc. *adj.*; lurk, smoulder, underlie, make no sign; escape -observation, – detection, – recognition; lie hid etc. 528.

laugh in one's sleeve; keep back etc. (*conceal*) 528.

involve, imply, implicate, connote, import, understand, allude to, infer, leave an inference; symbolize; whisper etc. (*conceal*) 528.

Adj. latent; lurking etc. *v.*; secret etc. 528; occult, symbolic, mystic; implied etc. *v.*; dormant.

un-apparent, -known, -seen etc. 441; in the background; invisible etc. 447; indiscoverable, dark; impenetrable etc. (*unintelligible*) 519; unspied, -suspected.

un-said, -written, -published, -breathed, -talked of, -told etc. 527, -sung, -exposed, -proclaimed, -disclosed etc. 529, -pronounced, -mentioned, -expressed; not expressed, tacit.

un-developed, -solved, -explained, -traced, -discovered etc. 480*a*, -tracked, -explored, -invented.

indirect, crooked, inferential; by -inference, – implication; implicit; constructive; allusive, covert, muffled; steganographic; under-stood, -hand, -ground; concealed etc. 528; delitescent.

Adv. by a side wind; *sub silentio*; in the background; behind -the scenes, – one's back, – the veil; below the surface; on the tip of one's tongue; secretly etc. 528; between the lines; by a mutual understanding.

Phr. 'thereby hangs a tale.' 'that is another story.'

527. Information.—N. information, enlightenment, acquaintance, knowledge etc. 490; publicity etc. 531.

communication, intimation; not-ice, -ification; e-, an-nunciation; announcement; representation, round robin, presentment.

case, estimate, specification, report, advice, monition; news etc. 532; return etc. (*record*) 551; account etc. (*description*) 594; statement etc. (*affirmation*) 535.

mention; acquainting etc. *v.*; instruction etc. (*teaching*) 537; outpouring; intercommunication, communicativeness.

informant, authority, teller, announcer, annunciator, harbinger, herald, intelligencer, commentator, columnist, reporter, exponent, mouthpiece; informer, keek, eavesdropper, delator, detective, sleuth; *mouchard*, spy, stool pigeon. newsmonger; messenger etc. 534; *amicus curiae*.

valet de place, *cicerone*, pilot, guide; guide-, hand-book; *vade mecum*; manual; map, plan, chart, gazetteer; itinerary etc. (*journey*) 266.

hint, suggestion, wrinkle, innuendo, inkling, whisper, passing word, word in the ear, subaudition, cue, by-play; gesture etc. (*indication*) 550; gentle – broad- hint; *verbum sapienti*; word to the wise; insinuation etc. (*latency*) 526.

V. tell; inform, – of; acquaint, – with; impart, – to; make acquainted with, bring to the ears of, apprise, advise, enlighten, awaken.

let fall, mention, express, intimate, represent, communicate, make known; publish etc 531; notify, signify, specify, convey the knowledge of.

let one –, have one to- know; serve notice, give one to understand; give notice; set –, lay –, put-before; point out, put into one's head; put one in possession of; instruct etc. (*teach*) 537; direct the attention to etc. 457.

an-nounce, -nunciate; report, – progress; bring –, send –, leave –, write- word; tele-graph, -phone; ring –, call- up; wire; retail, render an account; give an account etc. (*describe*) 594; state etc. (*affirm*) 535.

disclose etc. 529; show cause; explain etc. (*interpret*) 522.

hint; give an inkling of; give –, drop –, throw out- a hint; insinuate; allude –, make allusion- to; glance at; tip off, tip the wink etc. (*indicate*) 550; suggest, prompt, give the cue, breathe; whisper, – in the ear.

give a bit of one's mind; tell one plainly, – once for all; speak volumes.

un-deceive, -beguile; set right, correct, open the eyes of, disabuse.

be -informed of etc.; know etc. 490; learn etc. 539; get scent of, gather from; awaken –, open one's eyes- to; become -alive, – awake- to; keep posted; hear, overhear, understand.

come to one's -ears, – knowledge; reach one's ears.

Adj. informed etc. *v.*; *communiqué*; reported etc. *v.*; published etc. 531; advisory.

expressive etc. 516; explicit etc. (*open*) 525, (*clear*) 518; plain-spoken etc. (*artless*) 703.

declara-, nuncupa-, exposi-tory; declarative, enunciative, communicat-ive, -ory; oral.

Adv. from information received; according to -rumor, – report; in the air; from what one can gather.

Phr. a little bird told me.

528. Concealment.—N. concealment; hiding etc. *v.*; occultation, mystification.

seal of secrecy; screen etc. 530; disguise etc. 530; masquerade; masked battery; hiding place etc. 530; cipher, code, crypt-, stegan-ography; invisible –, sympathetic- ink; palimpsest; freemasonry.

stealth, -iness; obreption; slyness etc. (*cunning*) 702.

latit-ancy, -ation; seclusion etc. 893; privacy, secrecy, secretness; *incognita.*

reticence; reserve; mental –, reservation, aside; *arrière pensée*, suppression, evasion, white lie, misprision; silence etc. (*taciturnity*) 585; suppression of truth etc. 544; underhand dealing; close-, secretive-ness etc. *adj.*; mystery.

latency etc. 526; snake in the grass; secret etc. 533.

V. conceal, hide, secrete, stow away, put out of sight; lock –, seal –, bottle- up.

cover, screen, cloak, veil, shroud; screen from -sight, – observation; draw the veil; draw –, close- the curtain; curtain, shade, eclipse, throw a veil over; be-cloud, -fog, -mask; mask, disguise; ensconce, muffle, smother; whisper.

keep -from, – back, – to oneself; keep -snug, – close, – secret, – dark; bury; sink, suppress; keep -from, – out of- -view, – sight; keep in –, throw into- the -shade, – background; cover up one's tracks; stifle, hush up, withhold, reserve; fence with a question; ignore etc. 460.

code, codify, use a cipher.

keep -a secret, – one's own counsel; hold one's tongue etc. (*silence*) 585; make no sign, not let it go further; not breathe a -word, – syllable- about; not let the right hand know what the left is doing; hide one's light under a bushel, bury one's talent in a napkin.

keep –, leave- in -the dark, – ignorance; blind, – the eyes; blindfold, hoodwink, mystify; puzzle etc. (*render uncertain*) 475; bamboozle etc. (*deceive*) 545.

be -concealed etc. *v.*; suffer an eclipse; retire from sight, couch; hide oneself; lie -hid, – in ambush, – low, – *perdu*, – snug, – close; seclude oneself etc. 893; lurk, sneak, skulk, slink, pussyfoot, prowl; steal -into, – out of, – by, – along; play at -bopeep, – hind and seek; hide in holes and corners.

Adj. concealed etc. *v.*; hidden; veiled, secret, recondite, mystic, cabalistic, occult, dark; cryptic, -al, private, privy, *in petto*, auricular, clandestine, close, inviolate.

behind a -screen etc. 530; under -cover, – an eclipse; in -ambush, – hiding, – disguise; in a -cloud, – fog, – mist, – haze, – dark corner; in the -shade, – dark; clouded, wrapt in clouds; invisible etc. 447; buried, underground, *perdu*; incommunicado; secluded etc. 893.

un-disclosed etc. 529; -told etc. 527; covert etc. (*latent*) 526; mysterious etc. (*unintelligible*) 519.

irrevealable, inviolable; confidential; esoteric; not ot be spoken of.

obreptitious, furtive, stealthy, feline; skulking etc. *v.*; surreptitious, underhand, hole and corner; sly etc. (*cunning*) 702; secretive, evasive, noncommittal, reserved, reticent, uncommunicative, buttoned up; close, – as wax; taciturn etc. 585.

Adv. secretly etc. *adj.*; in -secret, – private, – one's sleeve, – holes and corners; in the dark etc. *adj.*

janius clausis, with closed doors, *à huis clos*; hugger-mugger, *à la dérobée*; under the -cloak of, – rose, – table; *sub rosâ*, *en tapinois*, in the background, aside, on the sly, with bated breath, *sotto voce*, in a whisper, without beat of drum, *à la sourdine*.

in –, strict- confidence; confidentially etc. *adj.*; between -ourselves, – you and me; *entre nous*, *inter nos*, under the seal of secrecy; in -code, – cipher.

underhand, by stealth, like a thief in the night; stealthily etc. *adj.*; behind -the scenes, – the curtain, – one's back, – a screen etc. 530; *incognito*; *in camerâ*.

Phr. it -must, – will- go no further; 'tell it not in Gath,' nobody the wiser.

529. Disclosure.—N. disclosure; retection; unveiling etc. *v.*; deterration, revealment, revelation; divulgence, expos-ition, -ure; *exposé*; whole truth; tell-tale etc. (*news*) 532.

acknowledgment, avowal; confession, -al; shrift.

bursting of a bubble; *dénouement*.

V. dis-close, -cover, -mask; draw –, draw aside –, lift –, raise –, lift up –, remove –, tear- the -veil, – curtain; un-mask, -veil, -fold, -cover, -seal, -kennel; take off –, break- the seal; lay -open, – bare; expose; open, – up; bare, bring to light; evidence; make -clear, – evident, – manifest; evince.

divulge, reveal, break; let into the secret; reveal the secrets of the prison-house; tell etc. (*inform*) 527; breathe, utter, blab, peach; let -out, – fall, – drop, – the cat out of the bag; betray; tell tales, – out of school; come out with; give -vent, – utterance- to; open the lips, blurt out, vent, whisper about; speak out etc. (*make manifest*) 525; make public etc. 531; unriddle etc. (*find out*) 480*a*; split; blow the gaff; break the news.

acknowledge, allow, concede, grant, admit, own, confess, avow, throw off all disguise, turn inside out, make a clean breast; show one's -hand, – cards; unburden –, disburden- one's -mind, – conscience, – heart; open –, lay bare –, tell a piece of- one's mind; unbosom oneself, own to the soft impeachment; say –, speak- the truth; turn -King's, – Queen's, – States's- evidence.

raise –, drop –, lift –, remove –, throw off- the mask; expose; debunk; lay open; un-deceive, -beguile, disabuse, set right, correct, open the eyes of; *désillusionner*.

be -disclosed etc.; transpire, come to light; come in sight etc. (*be visible*) 446; become known, escape the lips; come –, ooze –, creep –, leak –, peep –, crop- out; show its -face, – colors; discover etc. itself; break through the clouds, flash on the mind.

Adj disclosed etc. *v.*

Int. out with it!

Phr. the murder is out; a light breaks in upon one; the scales fall from one's eyes; the eyes are opened.

530. Ambush. [Means of concealment.]—**N.** hiding-place; secret -place, drawer; recess, hole, funk hole, holes and corners; closet, crypt, *adytum*, abditory, *oubliette*, safe, – deposit.

am-bush, -buscade; stalking horse; lurking-hole, -place; secret path, backstairs; retreat etc. (*refuge*) 666.

screen, cover, shade, blinder; veil, curtain, blind, *purdah*, cloak, cloud.

mask, vizor, visor, disguise, masquerade dress, domino; *camouflage*.

pitfall etc. (*source of danger*) 667; trap etc. (*snare*) 545.

V. ambush, ambuscade, lie in ambush etc. (*hide oneself*) 528; lie in wait for; set a trap for etc. (*deceive*) 545.

Adv. *aux aguets*.

531. Publication.—**N.** publication; public -announcement etc. 527; promulgation, propagation, proclamation, pronouncement, encylical, *pronunciamento*; circulation, indiction, edition, imprint, impression, printing; hue and cry.

publicity, notoriety, currency, flagrancy, cry, *bruit*; *vox populi*; report etc. (*news*) 532.

the Press, fourth estate, public press, newspaper, periodical, journal, gazette; house organ, trade publication, tabloid, daily, weekly, monthly, quarterly, annual, magazine, monograph, book; review; news sheet, special edition, supplement, feature, rotogravure, comic strips; leaflet, pamphlet; telegraphy; publisher etc. *v.*

circular, – letter; manifesto, advertisement, puff, placard, bill, *affiche*, broadside, poster; notice etc. 527; program.

V. publish; make -public, – known etc. (*information*) 527; speak –, talk- of; broach, utter; put forward; circulate, propagate, promulgate; spread –, abroad; rumor, diffuse, disseminate, evulgate; put –, give –, send- forth; emit, edit, get out; issue; cover, report; bring –, lay –, drag- before the public; give -out, – to the world; put –, bandy –, hawk –, buzz –, whisper –, bruit –, blaze- about; drag into the -open day, – limelight; voice.

proclaim, herald, blazon; blaze –, noise- abroad; sound a trumpet; trumpet –, thunder- forth; give tongue; announce with -beat of drum, – flourish of trumpets; proclaim -from the housetops, – at Charing Cross, at the cross roads; declare, declaim.

advertise, placard; post, – up; *afficher*, publish in the Gazette, send round the crier.

raise a -cry, – hue and cry, – report; set news afloat.

telegraph, cable, wireless, broadcast.

be -published etc; be –, become- public etc. *adj.*; come out; go –, fly –, buzz –, blow- about; get -about, – abroad, – afloat, – wind; find vent; see the light; go forth, take air, acquire currency, pass current, go -the rounds, – the round of the newspapers, – through the length and breadth of the land; *virum volitare per ora*, pass from mouth to mouth; spread; run –, spread- like wildfire.

Adj. published etc. *v.*; current etc. (*news*) 532; in circulation, public; notorious; flagrant, arrant; open etc. 525; trumpet-tongued; encyclical, promulgatory; exoteric.

Adv. publicly etc. *adj.*; in open court, with open doors; in the limelight.

Int. *Oyez!* O yes! notice!

Phr. notice is hereby given; this is –, these are- to give notice.

532. News.—**N.** news; information etc. 527; piece –, budget- of -news, – information; report, story, yarn, copy, filler, intelligence, tidings; stop press news.

word, advice, *aviso*, message; dis-, des-patch; telegram, cable, wireless telegram, radio-gram, marconi-gram, communication, errand, embassy; *bulletin*.

microphone; public address system, P.A.; walkie talkie, radio -telephone, -phone.

radio, wireless (Eng.), high fidelity, hi fi, radio set, transistor, receiver; speaker, loudspeaker, amplifier, tweeter, woofer; transmitter, broadcaster; AM –, FM –, short wave transmitter; radio station, studio, control room, network, hookup, circuit; frequency, kilocycles, megacycles; band, channel, modulation, amplification; broadcast, program, newscast, network show, commerical announcement, serial, sound effects; signature, station – identification, – break; radio listener, audiophile.

television, TV, video, color television; television –, live – broadcast, telecast, TV show; televising, telecasting, transmission, television channel, video, audio, beam, reception, image, test pattern; rain, snow, ghost; television –, TV – station, mobile unit, TVmobile, transmitter, televisor, boost, camera; set, monitor, tube, screen.

rumor, hearsay, *on dit*, flying rumor, news stirring, cry, buzz, *bruit*, fame; talk, *ouï-dire*, scandal, eavesdropping; town –, table- talk; tittle-tattle; *canard*, topic of the day, idea afloat.

fresh –, stirring –, old – stale- news; glad tidings; old –, stale- story.

narrator etc. (*describe*) 594; news-, scandal-monger; tale-bearer; tell-tale, gossip, tattler, busybody, chatterer; informer.

broad-, news-, sports-caster; commentator, announcer, master of ceremonies, M.C., programmer, sound man, radioman, ham, radioperator.

television technician, TV man, cameraman, soundman.

V. transpire etc. (*be disclosed*) 529; rumor etc. (*publish*) 531.

broadcast, radio, transmit, send, release, beam; sign – on, – off; go on –, go off – the air, monitor; listen –, tune – in.

tele-vise, -cast; color cast.

Adj. many-tongued; rumored; publicly –, currently- -rumored, – reported; rife, current, floating, afloat, going about, in circulation, in everyone's mouth, all over the town.

Adv. as the story -goes, – runs; as they say, it is said.

533. Secret.—N. secret; dead –, profound- secret; *arcanum*, mystery; latency etc. 526; Asian mystery; sealed book, secrets of the prison-house; *le dessous des cartes*.

enigma, riddle, puzzle, nut to crack, conundrum, charade, rebus, logogriph; mono-, ana-gram; acrostic, cross-word puzzle; Sphinx; *crux criticorum*.

maze, labyrinth, Hyrcynian wood.

problem etc. (*question*) 461; paradox etc. (*difficulty*) 704; unintelligibility etc. 519; *terra incognita* etc. (*ignorance*) 491.

Adj. secret etc. (*concealed*) 528.

534. Messenger.—N. messenger, envoy, emissary, legate; nuncio, internuncio; intermediary; ambassador etc. (*diplomatist*) 758.

marshal, flag-bearer, herald, crier, trumpeter, bellman, pursuivant, *parlementaire*, *apparitor*.

courier, runner, dawk, *estafette*; Hermes, Mercury, Iris, Ariel.

postman, letter carrier, telegraph boy, messenger boy, district messenger; despatch rider, commissionaire, erand-boy.

mail; post, -office; letter-bag; mail -boat, – train, – coach, – van, aerial mail; tele-graph, -phone; cable, wire; carrier-pigeon; wireless tele-graph, -phone; radiotele-graph, -phone.

journalist, newspaperman, reporter; gentleman –, representative- of the press; sob sister; penny-a-liner; special –, war –, own- correspondent; spy, scout; informer etc. 527.

535. Affirmation.—N. affirm-ance, -ation; statement, allegation, assertion, predication, declaration, word, averment.

asseveration, adjuration, swearing, oath, affidavit; deposition etc. (*record*) 551; avouchment, assurance; protest, -ation; profession; acknowledgment etc. (*assent*) 488; pledge.

vote, voice, suffrage, ballot.

remark, observation; position etc. (*proposition*) 514; saying, *dictum*, sentence, *ipse dixit*.

emphasis, positiveness, peremptoriness; dogmatism etc. (*certainty*) 474; dogmatist etc. 887.

V. assert; make -an assertion etc. *n.*; have one's say; say, affirm, predicate, declare, state, represent; protest, profess.

put -forth, – forward; advance, allege, propose, propound, enunciate, enounce, broach, set forth, hold out, maintain, contend, pronounce, pretend.

depose, depone, aver, avow, avouch, asseverate, swear; make –, take one's- oath; make –, swear –, put in- an affidavit; take one's Bible oath, kiss the book, vow, *vitam impendere vero*; swear till - one is black in the face, – all's blue; be sworn, call Heaven to witness; vouch, warrant, certify, assure, swear by bell, book and candle.

swear by etc. (*believe*) 484; insist –, take one's stand- upon; emphasize, lay stress on; assert - roundly, – positively; lay down, – the law; raise one's voice, dogmatize, have the last word; rap out; repeat; re-assert, -affirm.

announce etc. (*information*) 527; acknowledge etc. (*assent*) 488; attest etc. (*evidence*) 467; adjure etc. (*put to one's oath*) 768.

Adj. asserting etc. *v.*; declaratory, predicatory, pronunciative, affirmative, *soi-disant*; positive; certain etc. 474; express, explicit etc. (*patent*) 525; absolute, emphatic, flat, broad, round, pointed, marked, distinct, decided, confident, assertive, insistent, trenchant, dogmatic, definitive, formal, solemn, categorical, peremptory; unretracted; predicable, affirmable.

Adv. affirmatively etc. *adj.*; in the affirmative.

with emphasis, *ex cathedrâ*, without fear of contradiction.

I must say, indeed, i' faith, let me tell you, why, give me leave to say, marry, you may be sure, I'd have you to know; upon my -word, – honor; by my troth, egad, I assure you; by -jingo, – Jove, – George, – etc.; troth, seriously, sadly; in –, in sober- -sadness, – truth, – earnest; of a truth, truly, pardi, perdy; in all conscience, upon oath; be assured etc. (*belief*) 484; yes etc. (*assent*) 488; I'll - warrant, – warrant you, – engage, – answer for it, – be bound, – venture to say, – take my oath; in fact, as a matter of fact, forsooth, joking apart; so help me God; not to mince the matter.

Phr. quoth he; *dixi*.

536. Negation.—N. ne-, abne-gation; denial; dis-avowal, -claimer; abjuration; contra-diction, -vention; recusation, protest; rebuttal; recusancy etc. (*dissent*) 489; flat –, emphatic- -contradiction, – denial; *démenti*.

qualification etc. 469; repudiation etc. 610; retraction etc. 607; confutation etc. 479; refusal etc. 764; prohibition etc. 761.

V. deny; contra-dict, -vene; controvert, give denial to, gainsay, negative, shake the head.

dis-own, -affirm, -claim, -avow; recant etc. 607; revoke etc. (*abrogate*) 756.

dispute, impugn, traverse, rebut, join issue upon; bring –, call- in question etc. (*doubt*) 485.

deny -flatly, – peremptorily, – emphatically, – absolutely, – wholly, – entirely; give the lie to, belie.

repudiate etc. 610; set aside, ignore etc. 460; rebut etc. (*confute*) 479; qualify etc. 469; refuse etc. 764.

Adj. denying etc. *v.*; denied etc. *v.*; contradictory; negat-ive, -ory; revocatory; recusant etc. (*dissenting*) 489; at issue upon.

Adv. no, nay, not, nowise; not a -bit, – whit, – jot; not -at all, – in the least, – so; no such thing; nothing of the -kind, – sort; quite the contrary, *tout au contraire*, far from it; *tant s'en faut*; on no account, in no respect; by -no, – no manner of- means; negatively.

phr. there never was a greater mistake; I know better; *non haec in foedera.*

537. Teaching.—N. teaching etc. *v.*; instruction; edification; education; pedagogy; tuition; tutor-, tutel-age; direction, guidance.

qualification, preparation; train-, school-ing etc. *v.*; discipline; exer-cise, -citation; drill, practice.

persuasion, proselytism, propagandism, *propaganda*; in-doctrination, -culcation, oculation.

explanation etc. (*interpretation*) 522; lesson, lecture, sermon, homily; apologue, parable; discourse, prelection, preachment, disquisition.

exercise, task; *curriculum*; course, – of study; grammar, three R's, initiation, A.B.C. etc. (*beginning*) 66.

elementary –, primary –, secondary –, grammar school –, high school –, college –, university –, technical –, liberal –, classical –, religious –, denominational –, moral –, secular- education; technical –, vocational- training; university extension lectures; propaedeutics, moral tuition; evening classes, correspondence course.

physical education, gymnastics, calisthenics, eurythmics; *sloyd*.

V. teach, instruct, edify, school, tutor; cram, prime, coach; enlighten etc. (*inform*) 527.

in-culcate, -doctrinate, -oculate, -fuse, -stil, -fix, -graft, -filtrate; im-bue, -pregnate, -plant; graft, sow the seeds of, disseminate, propagandize.

give an idea of; put -up to, – in the way of; set right.

sharpen the wits, enlarge the mind; give new ideas, open the eyes, bring forward, 'teach the young idea how to shoot;' improve etc. 658.

expound etc. (*interpret*) 522; lecture; prelect; read –, give- a -lesson, – lecture, – sermon, – discourse; hold forth, preach; sermon-, moral-ize; point a moral.

train, discipline; bring up, – to; educate, form, ground, prepare, qualify, drill, exercise, practice, habituate, familiarize with, nurture, dry-nurse, breed, rear, take in hand; break, – in; tame; pre-instruct; initiate; inure etc. (*habituate*) 613.

put to nurse, send to school.

direct, guide; direct attention to etc. (*attention*) 457; impress upon the -mind, – memory; beat into, – the head; convince etc. (*belief*) 484.

Adj. teaching etc. *v.*; taught etc. *v.*; educational; scholastic, academic, doctrinal; disciplinal; instructive, didactic, hortative, pedagogic, tutorial.

Phr. the schoolmaster abroad.

538. Misteaching—N. mis-teaching, -information, -intelligence, -guidance, -direction, -persuasion, -instruction, -leading etc. *v.*; perversion, false teaching; sophistry etc. 477; college of Laputa; the blind leading the blind.

V. mis-inform, -teach, -direct, -guide, -instruct, -correct; pervert; put on a false –, throw off the- scent; deceive etc. 545; mislead etc. (*error*) 495; misrepresent; lie etc. 544; *ambiguas in vulgum spargere voces*, preach to the wise, teach one's grandmother to suck eggs.

render unintelligible etc. 519; bewilder etc. (*uncertainty*) 475; mystify etc. (*conceal*) 528; unteach.

Adj. misteaching etc. *v.*; unedifying.

Phr. *piscem natare doces.*

539. Learning.—N. learning; acquisition of -knowledge etc. 490, – skill etc. 698; acquirement, attainment; edification, scholarship, erudition; lore; information; self-instruction; study, reading, perusal; inquiry etc. 461.

ap-, prenticeship; pupil-age, -arity; tutelage, novitiate, matriculation.

docility etc. (*willingness*) 602; aptitude etc. 698.

V. learn; acquire –, gain –, receive –, take in –, drink in –, imbibe –, pick up –, gather –, get –, obtain –, collect –, glean- -knowledge, – information, – learning.

acquaint oneself with, master; make oneself -master of, – acquainted with; grind, cram; get –, coach- up; learn by -heart, – rote.

read, spell, peruse; con –, pore –, thumb- over; wade through; dip into; run the eye -over, – through; turn over the leaves.

study; be -studious etc. *adj.*; consume the midnight oil, mind one's book.

go to -school, – college, – the university; serve -an (*or* one's) apprenticeship, – one's time; learn one's trade; be -informed etc. 527; be -taught etc. 537.

Adj. studious; schol-astic, -arly; teachable; docile etc. (*willing*) 602; apt etc. 698; industrious etc. 682; learned erudite.

Adv. at one's books; *in statu pupillari* etc. (*learner*) 541.

540. Teacher.—N. teacher, trainer, instructor, institutor, master, tutor, don, director, Corypheus, dry nurse, coach, grinder, crammer; governor, bear-leader; governess, duenna; disciplinarian.

professor, lecturer, reader, prelector, prolocutor, preacher; Boanerges; pastor etc. (*clergy*) 996; schoolmaster, dominie, usher, pedagogue, abecedarian; schoolmistress, dame, monitor, proctor, pupil-teacher.

expositor etc. 524; preceptor, guide; mentor etc. (*adviser*) 695; pioneer, apostle, missionary, propagandist, moonshee; example etc. (*model for imitation*) 22.

professorship etc. (*school*) 542.

tutelage etc. (*teaching*) 537.

Adj. professorial, tutorial etc. 537.

541. Learner.—N. learner, scholar, student, *alumnus*, *élève*, pupil; ap-, prentice; articled clerk; school-boy, -girl, beginner, tyro, abecedarian, alphabetarian.

recruit, novice, neophyte, tenderfoot, inceptor, *débutant*, catechumen, probationer; undergraduate; freshman, frosh; sophomore, junior, senior; junior –, senior- soph; sophister, questionist, fellow-, commoner, pensioner, exhibitioner, sizar, scholar, fellow, advanced –, post graduate –, research- student.

class, form, grade, standard, remove; pupilage etc. (*learning*) 539.

disciple, follower, apostle, proselyte; fellow student, school-mate, -fellow, class mate, condisciple.

Adj. *in statu pupillari*, in leading strings, sophomoric.

542. School.—N. school, academy, university, *alma mater*, college, seminary, Lyceum; instit-ute, -ution, *conservatoire*; *palaestra*, *gymnasium*.

day –, boarding –, public –, preparatory –, elementary –, primary –, nursery –, dame's –, grammar –, Board –, County –, Council –, parochial –, denominational –, Sunday –, religious –, collegiate –, secondary –, continuation –, night –, correspondence –, secretarial –, military –, law –, medical –, business –, technical- school; technical –, training- college; Polytechnic; training ship; *Kindergarten*, nursery, *crèche*, reformatory.

pulpit, desk, reading desk, ambo, class-, lecture-room, theater, amphitheater, forum, stage, rostrum, platform, hustings, tribune.

school –, horn –, text-book; grammar, primer, abecedary, rudiments, manual, *vade mecum*, Lindley, Murray, Cocker.

professor-, lecture-, reader-ship; chair; schoolmaster etc. 540.

School Board, Council of Education; *propaganda*.

Adj. scholastic, academic, collegiate; educational.

Adv. *ex cathedrâ*.

543. Veracity.—N. veracity; truthfulness, frankness etc. *adj.*; truth, sooth, sincerity, candor, honesty, fidelity; plain dealing, *bona fides*; love of truth; probity etc. 939; ingenuousness etc. (*artlessness*) 703.

the truth the whole truth and nothing but the truth; honest –, sober- truth etc. (*fact*) 494; unvarnished tale; light of truth.

V. speak –, tell- the truth; speak by the card; paint in its –, show oneself in ones -true colors; make a clean breast etc. (*disclose*) 529; speak one's mind etc. (*be blunt*) 703; not -lie etc. 544, – deceive etc. 545.

Adj. truthful, true; ver-acious, -edical; scrupulous etc. (*honorable*) 939; sincere, candid, frank, open, straightforward, unreserved; open-, true-, simple- hearted; honest, trustworthy; undissembling etc. (dissemble etc. 544); guileless, pure; unperjured, ture blue, as good as one's word; unaffected, unfeigned, *bonâ fide*; outspoken, ingenuous etc. (*artless*) 703; undisguised etc. (*real*) 494.

Adv. truly etc. (*really*) 494; on oath; in plain words etc. 703; in –, with –, of a –, in good –, very- truth; as the -dial to the sun, – needle to the pole; honor bright; troth; in good -sooth, – earnest; unfeignedly, with no nonsense, in sooth, sooth to say, *bonâ fide*, *in foro conscientiae*; without equivocation; *cartes sur table*, from the bottom of one's heart; by my troth etc. (*affirmation*) 535.

544. Falsehood.—N. false-hood, -ness; fals-ity, -ification; misrepresentation; deception etc. 545; untruth etc. 546; guile; bad faith; lying etc. *v.*; misrepresentation; mendacity, perjury, false swearing; forgery, invention, fabrication; subreption; covin.

perversion –, suppression- of truth; *suppressio veri*; perversion, distortion, false coloring; exaggeration etc. 549; prevarication, equivocation, shuffling, fencing, evasion, fraud; *suggestio falsi* etc. (*lie*) 546; mystification etc. (*concealment*) 528; simulation etc. (*imitation*) 19; dis-simulation, -sembling; deceit.

sham; pretence, pretending, malingering.

lip-homage, – service; mouth honor; hollowness; mere -show, – outside, eye-wash, window dressing; duplicity, double dealing, insincerity, hypocrisy, cant, humbug, casuistry; jesuit-ism, -ry; pharisaism; Machiavelism, 'organized hypocrisy;' crocodile tears, mealy-mouthedness, quackery; charlatan-ism, -ry; gammon; bun-kum, -come; flam, ban, flim-flam, cajolery, flattery; Judas kiss; perfidy etc. (*bad faith*) 940; *il volto sciolto i pensieri stretti*.

unfairness etc. (*dishonesty*) 940; artfulness etc. (*cunning*) 702; misstatement etc. (*error*) 495.

V. be -false etc. *adj.*, – a liar etc. 548; speak -falsely etc. *adv.*; tell a -lie etc. 546; lie, fib; lie like a trooper; swear falsely, forswear, perjure oneself, bear false witness.

mis-state, -quote, -cite, -report, -represent; belie, falsify, pervert, distort; put a false construction upon etc. (*misinterpret*) 523.

prevaricate, equivocate. quibble; palter, – to the understanding; *répondre en Normand*; trim, shuffle, fence, mince the truth, beat about the bush, blow hot and cold, play fast and loose.

garble, gloss over, disguise, give a color to; give –, put- a -gloss, – false coloring- upon; color, varnish, cook, dress up, embroider; varnish right and puzzle wrong, exaggerate etc. 549.

invent, fabricate; trump –, get- up; forge, hatch, concoct; romance etc. (*imagine*) 515; cry 'wolf!'

dis-semble, -simulate; feign, assume, put on, pretend, make believe; play -false, – a double game; coquet; act –, play- a part; affect etc. 855; simulate, pass off for; counterfeit, fake, sham, make a show of; malinger; swing the lead; say the grapes are sour.

cant, play the hypocrite, sham Abraham, *faire pattes de velours*, put on the mask, clean the outside of the platter, lie like a conjuror; hang out –, hold out –, sail under- false colors; 'commend the poisoned chalice to the lips;' *ambiguas in vulgus spargere voces*; deceive etc. 545.

Adj. false, deceitful, mendacious, unveracious,

fraudulent, untruthful, dishonest; faith-, truth-, troth-less; un-fair, -candid; evasive; un-, dis-ingenuous; hollow, insincere, *Parthis mendacior*; forsworn.

canting; hypocrit-, jesuit-, pharisa-ical; tartuffish; Machiavelian; double-tongued, -faced, -handed, -minded, -hearted, -dealing; two-faced, bare-faced; Janus-faced; smooth-faced, -spoken, -tongued; plausible; mealy-mouthed; affected etc. 855.

collus-ive, -ory; artful etc. (*cunning*) 702; perfidious etc. 940, spurious etc. (*deceptive*) 545; untrue etc. 546; falsified etc. *v.*; covinous.

Adv. falsely etc. *adj.*; *à la Tartufe*, with a double tongue; out of whole cloth; slily etc. (*cunning*) 702.

545. Deception.—N. deception; falseness etc. 544; untruth etc. 546; impos-ition, -ture; fraud, deceit, guile; fraudulen-ce, -cy; covin; knavery etc. (*cunning*) 702; misrepresentation etc. (*falsehood*) 544.

delusion, gullery, bluff, spoof, *blague*; juggl-ing, -ery; sleight of hand, legerdemain; presti-giation, -digitation; magic etc. 992; conjur-ing, -ation; hocus pocus, jockeyship; trickery, coggery, hanky-panky, chicanery, pettifogging, sharp practice, *supercherie*, cozenage, circumvention, ingannation, collusion; treachery etc. 940; practical joke.

trick, cheat, wile, ruse, blind, feint, plant, bubble fetch, catch, chicane, juggle, reach, hocus, bite; thimble-rig, card-sharping, artful dodge, machination, swindle, hoax; tricks upon travellers; confidence trick; strategem etc. (*artifice*) 702; theft etc. 791.

snare, trap, pitfall, decoy, gin; sprin-ge, -gle; noose, hook; bait, decoy-duck, tub to the whale, baited trap, *guet-à-pens*; cobweb, net, meshes, toils, mouse-trap, bird-lime; ambush etc. 530; trap-door, sliding panel, false bottom; spring-net, -gun; mask, -ed battery; mine; booby trap.

Cornish hug; wolf in sheep's clothing etc. (*deceiver*) 548; disguise, -ment; false colors, masquerade, mummery, borrowed plumes; *pattes de velours*.

mockery etc. (*imitation*) 19; copy etc. 21; counterfeit, sham, brummagem, make-believe, forgery, fraud, fake; lie etc. 546; 'a mockery, a delusion, and a snare,' hollow mockery.

whited —, painted- sepulcher; tinsel, paste, false jewelry, scagliola, ormolu, German silver, Britannia metal, paint; jerry building; man of straw.

illusion etc. (*error*) 495; *ignis fatuus* etc. 423; *mirage* etc. 443.

V. deceive, take in; defraud, cheat, jockey, do, cozen, diddle, nab, gyp, chouse, double cross, play one false, bilk, cully, jilt, bite, pluck, swindle, victimize; abuse; mystify; blind one's eyes; blindfold, hoodwink, spoof, bluff; throw dust into the eyes, 'keep the word of promise to the ear and break it to the hope,' 'draw a herring across the trail.'

impose —, practice —, play —, put —, palm —, foist- upon; snatch a verdict.

circumvent, overreach; out-reach, -wit, maneuvre; steal a march upon, give the go-by to, leave in the lurch.

set —, lay- a -trap, — snare- for; bait the hook, forlay, spread the toils, lime; decoy, waylay, lure, beguile, delude, inveigle; tra-, tre-pan; kidnap; let-, hook-in; trick; en-, in-trap, -snare, entoil, benet; nick, springe; catch, — in a trap; sniggle, entangle, illaqueate, hocus, practice on one's credulity, dupe, gull, hoax, fool, befool, bamboozle; hum, -bug; gammon, stuff up, dope, sell; play a -trick, — practical joke- upon one; balk, trip up, throw a tub to a whale; fool to the top of one's bent, send on -a wild goose chase, — a fool's errand; make -game, — a fool, — an April fool, — an ass- of; trifle with, cajole, flatter; come over etc. (*influence*) 615; gild the pill, make things pleasant, divert, put a good face upon; dissemble etc. 544.

cog, — the dice, play with marked cards; live by one's wits, play at hide and seek; obtain money under false pretences etc. (*steal*) 791; conjure, juggle, practice chicanery; gerrymander.

play —, palm —, foist —, fob- off.

lie etc. 544; misinform etc. 538; mislead etc. (*error*) 495; betray etc. 940; be -deceived etc. 547.

Adj. deceived etc. *v.*; deceiving etc. *v.*; cunning etc. 702; prestigi-ous, -atory; decept-ive, -ious; deceitful, covinous; delus-ive, -ory; illus-ive, -ory; elusive, insidious, *ad captandum vulgus*.

untrue etc. 546; mock, sham, make-believe, counterfeit, faked, pseudo, spurious, so-called, pretended, feigned, trumped up, bogus, scamped, fraudulent, tricky, factitious, artificial, bastard; surreptitious, illegitimate, contraband, adulterated, sophisticated; unsound, rotten at the core; colorable; disguised; meretricious; tinsel, pinchbeck, plated; catch-penny; Brummagem; simulated etc. 544.

Adv. under -false colors, — the garb of, — cover of; over the left.

Phr. *fronti nulla fides.*

546. Untruth.—N. untruth, falsehood, lie, story, thing that is not, fib, bounce, crammer, taradiddle, whopper.

forgery, fabrication, invention; mis-statement, -representation; perversion, falsification, gloss, *suggestio falsi*; exaggeration etc. 549.

fiction, fable, nursery tale, romance etc. (*imagination*) 515; untrue —, false —, trumped up- -story, — statement; thing devised by the enemy; *canard*; shave, sell, hum, yarn, traveler's tale, Canterbury tale, cock and bull story, fairy tale, clap-trap.

myth, moonshine, bosh, all my eye, -and Betty Martin, mare's nest, farce.

irony; half truth, white lie, pious fraud; mental reservation etc. (*concealment*) 528.

pretence, pretext; false -plea etc. 617; subterfuge, evasion, shift, shuffle, make believe; sham etc. (*deception*) 545.

profession, empty words; Judas kiss etc. (*hypocrisy*) 544; disguise etc. (*mask*) 530.

V. have a false meaning; not ring true.

pretend, sham, feign, counterfeit, make believe.

Adj. untrue, false, trumped up; void of —, without- foundation; far from the truth, false as dicer's oaths; unfounded, *ben trovato*, invented, fabulous, fabricated, forged; fict-, fact-, supposit-, surrept-itious; e-, il-lusory; ironical; satirical; evasive; *soi-disant* etc. (*misnamed*) 565.

Phr. *se non e vero e ben trovato.*

547. Dupe.—N. dupe, gull, gudgeon, *gobemouche*, cull, cully, victim, sucker, pigeon, April fool; laughing stock etc. 857; Cyclops, simple Simon, flat, mug, greenhorn; fool etc. 501; puppet, cat's paw.

V. be -deceived etc. 545, – the dupe of; fall into a trap; swallow –, nibble at- the bait; bite; catch a Tartar.

Adj. credulous etc. 486; mistaken etc. (*error*) 495.

548. Deceiver.—N. deceiver etc. (deceive etc. 545); dissembler, hypocrite; sophist, Pharisee, Jesuit, Mawworm, Pecksniff, Joseph Surface, Tartufe, Janus; serpent, snake in the grass, cockatrice, Judas, wolf in sheep's clothing; Molly Maguire; jilt; shuffler.

liar etc. (lie etc. 544; story-teller, perjurer, false-witness, *mentuer à triple étage*, Scapin.

imposter, pretender, capper, decoy, fraud, *soi-disant*, humbug; adventurer; Cagliostro, Fernam Mendez Pinto; ass in lion's skin etc. (*bungler*) 701; actor etc. (*stage player*) 599.

quack, *charlatan*, mountebank, saltimbanco, *saltimbanque*, empiric, quacksalver, medicaster.

conjuror, juggler, magician, necromancer, trickster, prestidigitator, medium, jockey; crimp; decoy-duck, stool pigeon; rogue, knave, cheat; swindler etc. (*thief*) 792; jobber.

549. Exaggeration.—N. exaggeration; expansion etc. 194; hyperbole, stretch, strain, coloring; high coloring, caricature, *caricatura*; extravagance etc. (*nonsense*) 497; Baron Munchausen; men in buckram, yarn, fringe, embroidery, traveler's tale; Pelion upon Ossa.

storm in a teacup; much ado about nothing etc. (*over-estimation*) 482; puffery etc. (*boasting*) 884; rant etc. (*turgescence*) 577.

figure of speech, *façon de parler*; stretch of-fancy, – the imagination; flight of fancy etc. (*imagination*) 515.

false coloring etc. (*falsehood*) 544; aggravation etc. 835.

V. exaggerate, magnify, pile up, aggravate; amplify etc. (*expand*) 194; overestimate etc. 482; hyperbolize; over-charge, -state, -draw, -lay, -shoot the mark, -praise; make -much, – the most- of; strain, – a point; stretch, – a point; go great lengths; spin a long yarn; draw –, shoot with- a long-bow; deal in the marvelous.

out -Herod Herod, run riot, talk at random.

heighten, overcolor; color -highly, – too highly; embroider, *broder*; flourish; color etc. (*misrepresent*) 544; puff etc. (*boast*) 884.

Adj. exaggerated etc. *v.*; overwrought; bombastic etc. (*magniloquent*) 577; hyperbolical, on stilts; fabulous, extravagant, preposterous, egregious, *outré*, high-flying.

Adv. hyperbolically etc. *adj.*

550. Indication.—N. indication; symbol-ism, -ization; semeio-logy, -tics; sign of the times.

lineament, feature, *trait*, characteristic, trick, diagnostic; divining-rod; cloven hoof; footfall; means of recognition; earmark.

sign, symbol; ind-ex, -ice, -icator; point, -er; marker; exponent, note, token, symptom.

type, figure, emblem, cipher, device; representation etc. 554; epigraph, motto, posy.

gest-ure, -iculation; pantomime; wink, glance, leer; nod, shrug, beck; touch, nudge; grip; dactylology, -nomy; freemasonry, telegraphy, chirology, by-play, dumb-show; cue; hint etc. 527; clue, clew, key, scent, tract etc. 551.

signal, -post; rocket, blue light; watch-fire, -tower; telegraph, semaphore, flag-staff; cresset, fiery cross; calumet; heliograph, signal-, flash-lamp; radar, radar signal, pulse –, microwave –, radar; tracing, blips, pips.

mark, line, stroke, dash, score, stripe, streak, scratch, tick, dot, point, notch, nick, blaze; asterisk, red letter, Italics, heavy type, inverted commas, quotation marks, sublineation, underlining, jotting; print; impr-int, -ess, ession; note, annotation, mark of exclamation.

[For identification] badge, criterion; counter-check, -mark, -sign, -foil, duplicate, tally; label, tab, ticket, stub, billet, letter, counter, *tessera*, card, bill, check; witness, voucher; stamp; *cachet*; trade –, Hall- mark; broad arrow; signature; address –, visiting- card; *carte de visite*; credentials etc. (*evidence*) 467; passport, identity book; attestation; hand, – writing, sign-manual; cipher; monogram, – mark, seal, sigil, signet; autograph, -y, paraph, brand; superscription; in-, en-dorsement; title, heading, rubric, docket; *mot -de passe*, – *du guet*; *passe-parole*; shibboleth; watch-, catch-, pass-word; open *sesame*.

insignia, banner, -et, -ol; bandrol; flag, colors, streamer, standard, eagle, labarum, oriflamb, *oriflamme*; figure-head; ensign; pen-non, -nant, -dant; burgee, blue Peter, jack, ancient, gonfalon, union-jack; tricolor, stars and stripes; bunting.

hearldry, crest; coat of –, arms; armorial bearings, hatchment; e-, scutcheon; shield, supporters; livery, uniform; cockade, *epaulette*, brassard, chevron; garland, chaplet, love-knot, fillet, favor.

[Of locality] beacon, cairn, post, staff, flagstaff, hand, pointer, vane, cock, weathercock; guide-, hand-, finger-, directing-, sign-post; pillars of Hercules, pharos, signal fire; land-, sea-mark; lighthouse, balize; pole-, load-, lode-star; cynosure, guide; address, direction, name; sign, -board.

[Of the future] warning etc. 668; omen etc. 512; prefigurement etc. 511. [Of the past] trace record etc. 551. [Of danger] warning etc. 668; alarm etc. 669. [Of authority] scepter etc. 747. [Of triumph] trophy etc. 733. [Of quantity] gauge etc. 466. [Of distance] mile-stone, -post. [Of disgrace] brand, fool's cap, stigma, mark of Cain. [For detection] check, tell-tale; test etc. (*experiment*) 463.

notification etc. (*information*) 527; advertisement etc. (*publication*) 531.

word of command, call; bugle-, trumpet-call; reveille, taps; bell, alarum, cry; battle –, rallying-cry.

church, bell, angelus, sacring bell; muezzin.

exposition etc. (*explanation*) 522; proof etc. (*evidence*) 463; pattern etc. (*prototype*) 22.

V. indicate; be the -sign etc. *n.*- of; denote,

betoken; argue, testify etc. (*evidence*) 467; bear the -impress etc. *n.*- of; con-note, -notate.

represent, stand for; typify etc. (*prefigure*) 511; symbolize.

put -an indication, – a mark, – etc. *n.*; note, mark, tick, blaze, stamp, earmark; set one's seal upon; label, ticket, docket; dot, spot, score, dash, trace, chalk; print; im-print, -press, surprint; engrave, stereotype, electrotype.

signal, transmit, send, radiate, beam, deflect, echo, bounce back, return.

make a -sign etc. *n.*; signalize; give –, hang out- a signal; beck, -on; gesture; not; wink, glance, leer, nudge, shrug, tip the wink; gesticulate; raise –, hold up- the-finger, – hand; saw the air, suit the action to the word.

wave –, unfurl –, hoist –, hang out- a banner etc. *n.*; wave -the hand, – a kerchief; give the cue etc. (*inform*) 527; show one's colors; give –, sound- an alarm; beat the drum, sound the trumpets, raise a cry.

sign, seal, attest etc. (*evidence*) 467; underline etc. (*give importance to*) 642; call attention to etc. (*attention*) 457; give notice etc. (*inform*) 527.

Adj. indicat-ing etc. *v.*; -ive, -ory; de-, connotative; diacritical, representative, typical, symbolic, pantomimic, pathognomonic, symptomatic, ominous, characteristic, demonstrative, diagnostic, exponential, emblematic, armorial; individual etc. (*special*) 79.

known –, recognizable- by, indicated etc. *v.*; pointed, marked.

[Capable of being denoted] denotable; indelible.

Adv. in token of; symbolically etc. *adj.*; in dumb show.

Phr. *ecce signum*; *ex ungue leonem, ex pede Herculem.*

551. Record.—N. trace, vestige, relic, remains; scar, *cicatrix*; foot-step, -mark, -print; track, mark, wake, trail, spoor, scent, *piste.*

monument, hatchment, escutcheon, slab, tablet, trophy, achievement; obelisk, pillar, column, monolith, cromlech, dolmen; memorial; *memento* etc. (*memory*) 505; testimonial, medal, ribbon, order; commemoration etc. (*celebration*) 883.

record, note, minute; *dossier*; register, -try; census, roll etc. (*list*) 86; cartulary, diptych, Domesday book; entry, memorandum, indorsement, inscription, copy, duplicate, docket; notch etc. (*mark*) 550; muniment, deed etc. (*security*) 771; document; deposition, *procès-verbal*; affidavit; certificate etc. (*evidence*) 467.

note-, memorandum-, pocket-, commonplace-book; portfolio; scoring board, -sheet; bulletin board; card index, file; pigeon-holes, *excerpta*, *adversaria*, jottings, dottings.

gazette, -er; newspaper, magazine etc. 531; alman-ac, -ack; calendar, ephemeris, noctuary, diary, log, journal, account-, cash-, day-book, ledger.

archive, scroll, state-paper, Congressional Record, return, blue-book; statistics etc. 86; *compte rendu*; Acts –, Transactions –, Proceedings- of; Hansard's Debates; chronicle, annals; legend; history, biography etc. 594.

registration; en-, in-rolment; tabulation; entry, booking; signature etc. (*identification*) 550; recorder etc. 553; journalism.

drawing, photograph etc. 554; phonograph –, gramophone- record; music roll.

V. record; put –, place- upon record; go on record; chronicle, calendar, hand down to posterity; keep up the memory of etc. (*remember*) 505; commemorate etc. (*celebrate*) 883; report etc. (*inform*) 527; commit to –, reduce to- writing; put –, set down- -in writing, – in black and white; put –, jot –, take –, write –, note –, set-down; note, minute, put on paper; take –, make- a -note, – minute, – memorandum; make a return.

mark etc. (*indicate*) 550; sign etc. (*attest*) 467.

enter, book; post, – up; insert, make an entry of; mark –, tick- off; register, list, docket, enroll, inscroll; file etc. (*store*) 636.

Adv. on record.

552. Obliteration. [Suppression of sign.]—**N.** obliteration; erasure, rasure; effacement; interference; cancel, -lation; cassation; circumduction; deletion, blot; *tabula rasa.*

V. efface, obliterate, erase, rase, expunge, cancel; blot –, take –, rub –, scratch –, strike –, wipe –, wash –, sponge- out; wipe –, rub- off; wipe away; deface, render illegible; draw the pen through, apply the sponge.

interfere, jam, black-, block-out; clutter, screen.

be effaced etc.; leave no trace etc. 119; 'leave not a rack behind.'

Adj. obliterated etc. *v.*; out of print; printless; leaving no trace; intestate; un-recorded, -registered, -written.

Int. *dele*; out with it!

553. Recorder.—N. recorder, notary, clerk; regis-trar, -trary, -ter; prothonotary; amanuensis, secretary, scribe, stenographer, remembrancer, book-keeper, *custos rotulorum*, Master of the Rolls.

annalist; histori-an, -ographer; chronicler, journalist, reporter, columnist; biographer etc. (*narrator*) 594; antiquary etc. (*antiquity*) 122; memorialist.

draughtsman etc. 559; engraver 558; photographer, cinematographer, camera man.

Recording instrument, recorder, camera, phonograph, gramophone, dictaphone, telegraphone, telautograph, printing telegraph, tape recorder, ticker, time recorder, cash register, turnstile, speedometer, voting machine, seismograph, radar, oscilloscope, teletypewriter, pari-mutuel, photostat.

554. Representation.—N. represent-ation, -ment; imitation etc. 19; illustration, delineation, depictment, portrayal; imagery, portraiture, iconography; design, -ing; art, fine arts; painting etc. 556; sculpture etc. 557; engraving etc. 558; photography, radiography, skiagraphy.

person-ation, -ification; impersonation; drama etc. 599.

picture, drawing, sketch, draught, draft; tracing; copy etc. 21; photo-, helio-graph; daguerreo-, talbo-, calo-, helio-type; cabinet, *carte-de-visite*, snapshot; X-ray photograph; radio-gram, -graph, skia-graph, -gram.

image, likeness, icon, portrait; striking –, speaking- likeness; very image; effigy, fac-simile.

figure, – head; puppet, doll, *figurine*, aglet, manikin, lay-figure, model, *marionnette*, *fantoccini*, bust; waxwork, statue, -tte, automaton, Robot.

hieroglyphic, anaglyph; dia-, mono-gram, graph.

map, plan, chart; ground plan, projection, elevation; ichno-, carto-graphy; atlas; outline, scheme; view etc. (*painting*) 556.

artist, draughtsman etc. 559.

V. represent, delineate; depict, -ure; portray; picture; take –, catch- a likeness etc. *n.*; hit off, photograph, daguerreotype; figure; shadow -forth, – out; adumbrate; body forth; describe etc. 594; trace, copy; mold.

dress up; illustrate, symbolize.

paint etc. 556; carve etc. 557; engrave etc. 558.

person-ate, -ify; impersonate; assume a character; pose as; act; play etc. (*drama*) 599; mimic etc. (*imitate*) 19; hold the mirror up to nature.

Adj. represent-ing etc. *v.*, -ative; illustrative; represented etc. *v.*; imitative, figurative.

like etc. 17; graphic etc. (*descriptive*) 594.

555. Misrepresentation.—N. misrepresentation, distortion, exaggeration; daubing etc. *v.*; bad likeness, daub, sign-painting; scratch, caricature; *anamorphosis*.

V. misrepresent, distort, overdraw, travesty, parody, burlesque, exaggerate, caricature, daub.

Adj. misrepresented etc. *v.*

556. Painting.—N. painting; depicting; drawing etc. *v.*; design; perspective, skiagraphy; *chiaroscuro* etc. (*light*) 420; composition; treatment, values, atmosphere, tone, technique.

historical –, portrait –, miniature –, landscape –, marine –, flower –, scene- painting; scenography.

school, style; the grand style, high art, *genre*, portraiture; ornamental art etc. 847.

mono-, poly-chrome; *grisaille*.

pallet, palette; easel; brush, pencil, stump; blacklead, charcoal, crayons, chalk, pastel; paint etc. (*coloring matter*) 428; water-, body-, oil-color; oils, oil-paint; varnish etc. 356*a*; *gouache*, tempera, distemper, fresco, water-glass; enamel; encaustic painting; *graffito*, *gesso;* mosiac; tapestry.

picture, painting, piece, *tableau*, canvas; oil etc.-painting; fresco, cartoon; easel –, cabinet- picture; drawing, draught, draft; pencil etc. –, watercolor-drawing; sketch; outline; study.

portrait etc. (*representation*) 554; whole –, full –, half- length; kitcat, head; miniature; shade, *silhouette*; profile.

landscape, sea-piece, -scape; view, scene, prospect; interior; bird's- eye view; pan-, di-orama; still life.

picture –, art- gallery; *studio*, *atelier*.

V. paint, design, limn, draw, sketch, pencil, scratch, shade, stipple, hatch, dash off, chalk out, square up; color, dead-color, wash, varnish; draw in -pencil etc. *n.*; paint in -oils etc. *n.*; stencil; depict etc. (*represent*) 554.

Adj. painted etc. *v.*; pictorial, graphic, picturesque, decorative; classical, romantic, pre-Raphaelite, modern, cubist, futurist, vorticist.

pencil, oil etc. *n.*

Adv. in -pencil etc. *n.*

Phr. *fecit, delineavit.*

557. Sculpture.—N. sculpture, insculpture; carving etc. *v.*; statuary, ceramics, plastic arts.

high –, low –, bas- relief; relievo; *basso-*, *alto-*, *mezzo-relievo*; *intaglio*, anaglyph; medal, -lion; *cameo*.

marble, bronze, *terra cotta*; ceramic ware, pottery, porcelain, china, earthenware, faïence, enamel, *cloisonné*.

statue etc. (*image*) 554; cast etc. (*copy*) 21; glyptotheca.

V. sculpture, carve, cut, chisel, model, mold; cast.

Adj. sculptured etc. *v.*; in relief, anaglyptic, ceroplastic, ceramic; parian; marble etc. *n.*

558. Engraving.—N. engraving, chalcography; line –, mezzotint –, stipple –, chalk- engraving; dry-point, bur; etching, aquatinta; plate –, copper-plate –, steel –, wood-, process-, photo-engraving; xylo-, ligno-, glypto-, cero-, litho-, chromolitho-, photolitho-, zinco-, glypho- -graphy, -graph.

impression, print, engraving, plate; steel-, copper-plate; etching; mezzo-, aqua-, litho-tint; cut, woodcut, block; stereo-, grapho-, auto-, helio-type; half-tone; *photogravure*, *rotogravure*.

graver, *burin*, etching-point, style; plate, stone, wood-block, negative; die, punch, stamp.

printing; plate –, copper-plate –, intaglio –, anastatic –, lithographic –, color –, three color-printing; type-printing etc. 591.

illustr-, illumin-ation; *vignette*, initial letter, *cul de lampe*, tail-piece.

V. engrave, grave, stipple, scrape, etch; bite, – in; lithograph etc. *n.*; print.

Adj. insculptured; engraved etc. *v.*

Phr. *sculpsit, imprimit.*

559. Artist.—N. artist; painter, limner, drawer, sketcher, delineator; cartoon-, caricatur-ist, designer, engraver; draughtsman; copyist; enameller, -list.

historical –, landscape –, genre –, marine –, flower –, portrait –, miniature –, scene –, sign-painter; engraver; Apelles; sculptor, carver, chaser, modeller, lapidary, *figuriste*, statuary; Phidias, Praxiteles; Royal Academician.

photographer, retoucher.

560. Language.—N. language; phraseology etc. 569; speech etc. 582; tongue, lingo, vernacular, slang; mother –, vulgar –, native- tongue; household words; King's *or* Queen's English; idiom; dialect etc. 563.

volapuk, esperanto, ido, occidental, Ro.

confusion of tongues, Babel, *pasigraphie*; pantomime etc. (*signs*) 550; *onomatopaeia*.

phil-, gloss-, glott-ology; linguistics, chrestomathy; paleo-logy; -graphy; comparative grammar.

literature, letters, polite literature, *belles lettres*, muses, humanities, *literae humaniores*, republic of letters, dead languages, classics; genius of a language; scholarship etc. (*knowledge*) 490.

linguist etc. (*scholar*) 492.

V. speak, say, express by words etc. 566.

Adj. lingu-al, -istic; dialectic; vernacular, current, colloquial, slangy; bilingual, polyglot; literary.

561. Letter.—N. letter; character; hieroglyphic etc. (*writing*) 590; type etc. (*printing*) 591; capitals; majus-, minus-cule; alphabet, ABC, abecedary, christcross row, chrisscross row.

consonant, vowel, diphthong; mute, surd; sonant, liquid, labial, dental, palatal, gutteral.

syllable; mono-, dis-, poly-syllable; affix, prefix, suffix.

spelling, orthography, phon-ography, -etic spelling; ana-, meta-grammatism.

cipher, monogram, anagram; double – acrostic.

V. spell.

Adj. literal; alphabetical, abecedarian; syllabic; uncial etc. (*writing*) 590; phonetic, voiced, mute etc. *n*.

562. Word.—N. word, term, vocable; name etc. 564; phrase etc. 566; root, etymon; derivative; part of speech etc. (*grammar*) 567.

dictionary, vocabulary, word book, lexicon, index, glossary, thesaurus, *gradus, delectus*, concordance.

etymology, lexicology, derivation; phonology, orthoepy; gloss-, termin-, orism-ology; paleology etc. (*philology*) 560; comparative philology.

lexicograph-er, -y; glossographer etc. (*scholar*) 492; etymologist; logolept.

verbosity, verbiage, loquacity etc. 584.

Adj. verbal, literal; titular, nominal. [Similarly derived] conjugate, paraonymous; derivative.

Adv. verbally etc. *adj.*; *verbatim* etc. (*exactly*) 494.

563. Neology.—N. neolo-gy; -gism; newfangled expression; barbarism; caconym; archaism, black letter, monkish Latin; corruption; missaying, antiphrasis.

paronomasia, play upon words; wordplay etc. (*wit*) 842; *double-entente* etc. (*ambiguity*) 520; palindrome, paragram, clinch; abuse of -language, – terms.

dialect, brogue, *patois*, provincialism, broken English, *lingua franca*; Brit-, Gall-, Scott-, Hibernicism; American-ism; Gipsy lingo, Romany, pidgin English.

dog Latin, macaronics, gibberish, confusion of tongues, Babel; jargon.

colloquialism etc. (*figure of speech*) 521; byword; technicality, lingo, slang, cant, *argot*, St. Giles's Greek, thieves' Latin, peddler's French, flash tongue, Billingsgate, Wall Street slang.

pseudonym etc. (*misnomer*) 565; Mr. So-and-so; what d'ye call 'em, what's his name; thingum-my, -bob; *je ne sais quoi*.

neologist, coiner of words.

V. coin words.

Adj. neologic, -al; rare; archaic; obsolete etc. (*old*) 124; colloquial, dialectic, slang, cant.

564. Nomenclature.—N. nomenclature; naming etc. *v.*; nuncupation, nomination, baptism; orismology; *onomatopaeia*; antonomasia.

name; appella-tion, -tive; designation; title; head, -ing, caption; denomination; by-name, epithet.

style, proper name; prae-, ag-, cog-nomen; patronymic, surname; cognomination; com pellation, description; empty -title, – name; handle to one's name; namesake, eponym.

synonym, antonym.

term, expression, noun, by-word, convertible terms etc. 522; technical term; cant etc. 563.

V. name, call, term, denominate, designate, style, entitle, intitule, clepe, dub, christen, baptize, nickname, characterize, specify, define, distinguish by the name of; label etc. (*mark*) 550.

be -called etc. *v.*; take –, bear –, go (*or* be known) by –, go (*or* pass) under –, rejoice in- the name of.

Adj. named etc. *v.*; hight, yclept, known as; what one may -well, – fairly, – properly, – fitly- call.

nuncupa-tory, -tive; cognominal, titular, nominal; orismological.

565. Misnomer.—N. misnomer; *lucus a non lucendo*; Mrs. Malaprop; what d'ye call 'em etc. (*neologism*) 563.

nickname, *sobriquet*, by-name, handle, moniker; assumed -name, – title; *alias*; *nom de - guerre*, – *plume*, – *théâtre*; pseudonym, pen name, stage name.

V. mis-name, -call, - term; nickname; assume -a name, – an alias.

Adj. misnamed etc. *v.*; pseudonymous; *soi-disant*; self-called, -styled, -christened; so-called.

nameless, anonymous; without a –, having no-name; innominate, unnamed.

Adv. in no sense.

566. Phrase.—N. phrase, expression, set phrase; sentence, paragraph; figure of speech etc. 521; idi-om, -otism; turn of expression.

paraphrase etc. (*synonym*) 522; periphrase etc. (*circumlocution*) 573; motto etc. (*proverb*) 496.

phraseology etc. 569.

V. express, phrase; word, – it; give -words, – expression- to; voice; arrange in –, clothe in –, put into –, express by- words; couch in terms; find words to express; speak by the card.

Adj. expressed etc. *v.*; idiomatic.

Adv. in -round, – set, – good, set- terms; in set phrases.

567. Grammar.—N. grammar, accidence, syntax, *praxis*, analysis, paradigm, punctuation; parts of speech, inflexion, case, declension, conjugation; *jus et norma loquendi*; Lindley Murray etc. (*school-book*) 542; correct style; philology etc. (*language*) 560.

V. parse, analyze; decline, conjugate; punctuate.

Adj. grammatical; syntactic; inflexional.

568. Solecism.—N. solecism; bad –, false –, faulty- grammar; slip, error; slip of the -pen, – tongue; *lapsus calami*-, – *linguae*; *faux pas*; slipslop; bull.

V. use -bad, – faulty- grammar; solecize, commit a solecism; murder the -King's, – Queen's- English; break Priscian's head.

Adj. ungrammatical; in-correct, -accurate; faulty, improper, incongruous, abnormal.

569. Style.—N. style, diction, phraseology, wording; manner, strain; composition; mode of expression, choice of words, literary power, ready pen, pen of a ready writer; command of language etc. (*eloquence*) 582; authorship; *la morgue littéraire*.

V. express by words etc. 566; write.

570. Perspicuity.—N. perspicuity etc. (*intelligibility*) 518; plain speaking etc. (*manifestation*) 525; defin-iteness, -ition; exactness etc. 494; perspicuousness, logical acuteness.

Adj. lucid etc. (*intelligible*) 518; explicit etc. (*manifest*) 525; exact etc. 494.

571. Obscurity.—N. obscurity etc. (*unintelligibility*) 519; involution; hard words; ambiguity etc. 520; vagueness etc. 475, inexactness etc. 495; what d'ye call 'em etc. (*neologism*) 563; cloudiness, confusion.

Adj. obscure etc. *n.*; crabbed, involved, confused.

572. Conciseness.—N. conciseness etc. *adj.*; brevity, 'the soul of wit,' laconism; Tacitus; ellipsis; syncope; abridgment etc. (*shortening*) 201; compression etc. 195; epitome etc. 596; monostitch; portmanteau word, telescope word, protogram.

V. be -concise etc. *adj.*; condense etc. 195; abridge etc. 201; abstract etc. 596; come to the point.

Adj. concise, brief, short, terse, close; to the point, exact; neat, compact, condensed, pointed; laconic, curt, pithy, trenchant, summary; pregnant; compendious etc. (*compendium*) 596; succinct; elliptical, epigrammatic, crisp, sententious.

Adv. concisely etc. *adj.*; briefly, summarily; in -brief, – short, – a word, – few words, – a nutshell; for shortness sake; to -come to the point, – make a long story short, – cut the matter short, – be brief; it comes to this, the long and short of it is.

573. Diffuseness.—N. diffuseness etc. *adj.*; amplification etc. *v.*; dilating etc. *v.*; verbosity, *verbiage*, wordiness, cloud of words, *copia verborum*; flow of words etc. (*loquacity*) 584.

poly-, tauto-, batto-, perisso-logy; pleonasm, exuberance, redundance; thrice-told tale; prolixity; circumlocution, *ambages*; periphra-se, -sis; roundabout phrases; episode; expletive; penny-a-lining; padding, drivel, twaddle, rigmarole; richness etc. 577.

V. be -diffuse etc. *adj.*; run out on, descant, expatiate, enlarge, dilate, amplify, expand, inflate, pad; launch –, branch- out; rant.

maunder, prose; harp upon etc. (*repeat*) 104; dwell on, insist upon.

digress, ramble, *battre la campagne*, beat about the bush, perorate, spin a long yarn, protract; spin –, swell –, draw- out, drivel.

Adj. dif-, pro-fuse; wordy, verbose, largiloquent, copious, exuberant, effusive, pleonastic, lengthy; long, -some, -winded, -spun, -drawn out; diffusive, spun out, protracted, prolix, prosing, maundering; circumlocutory, periphrastic, ambagious, roundabout; digressive; dis-, ex-cursive; rambling, episodic; flatulent, frothy.

Adv. diffusely etc. *adj.*; at large, *in extenso*; about it and about it.

574. Vigor.—N. vigor, power, force; boldness, raciness etc. *adj.*; spirit, point, antithesis, piquancy; *verve*, glow, fire, warmth, ardor, enthusiasm; 'thoughts that breathe and words that burn;' strong language; punch; gravity, sententiousness; elevation, loftiness, sublimity.

eloquence; command of -words, – language.

Adj. vigorous, nervous, powerful, forcible, trenchant, mordant, biting, incisive, impressive; sensational.

spirited, lively, glowing, sparkling, racy, bold, slashing; pungent, *piquant*, full of point, pointed, pithy, antithetical; sententious.

lofty, elevated, sublime, grand, weighty, ponderous; eloquent; vehement, petulant, impassioned; poetic.

Adv. in -glowing, – good set, – no measured- terms.

575. Feebleness.—N. feebleness etc. *adj.*;

Adj. feeble, bald, tame, meager, insipid, nerve-les, jejune, vapid, trashy, cold, frigid, poor, dull, dry, languid; pros-ing, -y, -aic; unvaried, monotonous, weak, frail, washy, wishy-washy, sloppy; sketchy, slight; careless, slovenly, loose, lax; slip-shod, -slop; inexact; dis-jointed, -connected; puerile, childish; flatulent; rambling etc. (*diffuse*) 573.

576. Plainness.—**N.** plainness etc. *adj.*; simplicity, severity; plain -terms, – English; Saxon English; household words.

V. speak plainly; call a spade 'a spade;' plunge *in medias res*; come to the point.

Adj. plain, simple; un-ornamented, -adorned, -varnished; home-ly, -spun; neat; severe, chaste, pure, Saxon; commonplace, matter of fact, natural, prosaic, sober, unimaginative.

dry, unvaried, monotonous etc. 575.

Adv. in plain -terms, – words, – English, – common parlance; point blank.

577. Ornament.—**N.** ornament; floridness etc. *adj.*; turg-idity, -escence; altiloquence etc. *adj.*; orotundity; declamation, teratology; well-rounded periods; elegance etc. 578.

inversion, antithesis, alliteration, *paronomasia*; figurativeness etc. (*metaphor*) 521.

flourish; flowers of -speech, – rhetoric; euphuism, -emism.

big-, high-sounding words; macrology, *sesquipedalia verba*, sesquipedalianism; Alexandrine; inflation, pretension; rant, bombast, fustian, bunkum, balderdash, prose run mad; fine writing; Minerva press.

phrasemonger; euph-uist, -emist.

V. ornament, overlay with ornament, overcharge; smell of the lamp.

Adj. ornamented etc. *v.*; beautified etc. 847; ornate, florid, rich, flowery; euph-uistic, -emistic; sonorous; high-, big-sounding; inflated, swelling, tumid; turg-id, -escent; pedantic, pompous, stilted; high-flown, -flowing; sententious, rhetorical, declamatory; grandiose; grand-, magn-, altiloquent; sesquipedal, -ian; Johnsonian, mouthy; bombastic; fustian; frothy, flashy, flaming, flamboyant.

antithetical, alliterative; figurative etc. 521; artificial etc. (*inelegant*) 579.

Adv. *ore rotundo*; with rounded phrase.

578. Elegance.—**N.** elegance, purity, grace, ease, felicity, distinction, gracefulness, refinement, readiness etc. *adj.*; concinnity, euphony, numerosity, balance, rythym, symmetry, proportion; restraint; good taste, propriety.

well rounded –, well turned –, flowing-periods; the right word in the right place; antithesis etc. 577.

purist, stylist.

V. point an antithesis, round a period.

Adj. elegant, polished, classical, Attic, correct, Ciceronian, artistic; chaste, pure, Saxon, academical.

graceful, easy, readable, fluent, flowing, tripping; unaffected, natural, unlabored; mellifluous; euph-onious, -emistic; rhythmical, balanced, symmetrical.

felicitous, happy, neat; well –, neatly- -put, – expressed.

579. Inelegance.—**N.** inelegance; vulgarity, bad taste; stiffness etc. *adj.*; unlettered Muse; barbarism; slang etc. 563; solecism etc. 568; mannerism etc. (*affectation*) 855; euphuism; fustian etc. 577; cacophony; want of balance; words that -break the teeth, – dislocate the jaw.

V. be -inelegant etc. *adj.*

Adj. inelegant, graceless, ungraceful, unpolished; harsh, abrupt; dry, stiff, cramped, formal, *guindé*; forced, labored, awkward; artificial, mannered, ponderous; turgid etc. 577; affected, euphuistic; barbarous, uncouth, grotesque, rude, crude, halting; vulgar, offensive to ears polite.

580. Voice.—**N.** voice; vocality; organ, lungs, bellows; good –, fine –, powerful etc. (*loud*) 404 –, musical etc. 413- voice; intonation; tone etc. (*sound*) 402- of voice.

vocalization; cry etc. 411; strain, utterance, prolation, exclam-, ejacul-, vocifer-ation, enunci-, articul-ation; articulate sound; distinctness; clearness, – of articulation; stage whisper; delivery; attack.

accent, -uation; emphasis, stress; broad –, strong –, pure –, native –, foreign- accent; pronunciation.

[Word similarly pronounced] homonym.

orthoepy; euphony etc. (*melody*) 413.

gastri-, ventri-loquism; ventriloquist; polyphonism, -ist.

[Science of voice] phonology etc. (*sound*) 402.

V. sing, speak, utter, breathe, voice; give -utterance, – tongue; cry etc. (*shout*) 411; ejaculate, rap out; vocalize, prolate, articulate, enunciate, enounce, pronounce, accentuate, aspirate, deliver, mouth; emit, murmur, whisper, – in the ear, croon, yodel.

Adj. vocal, phonetic, oral; ejaculatory, articulate, distinct, stertorous; enunciative; accentuated, aspirated; euphonious etc. (*melodious*) 413.

581. Aphony—**N.** aphony, *aphonia*; dumbness etc. *adj.*; obmutescence; absence –, want- of voice; dysphony; silence etc. (*taciturnity*) 585; raucity; harsh etc. 410 –, unmusical etc. 414- voice; *falsetto*, 'childish treble;' mute, dummy, deaf mute.

V. keep silence etc. 585; speak -low, – softly; whisper etc. (*faintness*) 405.

silence; render -mute, – silent etc. 403; muzzle, muffle, suppress, smother, gag, strike dumb, dumbfound, -founder; drown the voice, put to silence, stop one's mouth, cut one short.

stick in the throat.

Adj. aphon-ous, -ic, dumb, mute; deaf-mute, –

and dumb; mum; tongue-tied; breath-, tongue-, voice-, speech-, word-less; mute as a -fish, – stock-fish, – mackerel; silent etc. (*taciturn*) 585; muzzled; in-articulate, -audible.

croaking, raucous, hoarse, husky, dry, hollow, sepulchral, hoarse as a raven.

Adv. with -bated breath, – the finger on the lips; *sotto voce*; in a -low tone, – cracked voice, – broken voice; in an aside.

Phr. *vox faucibus haesit.*

582. Speech.—N. speech, faculty of speech; locution, talk, parlance, verbal intercourse, prolation, oral communication, word of mouth, *parole*, palaver, prattle; effusion.

oration, recitation, delivery, say, address, speech, lecture, harangue, sermon, *tirade*, screed, formal speech, salutatory, peroration; prelection; speechifying; soliloquy etc. 589; allocution etc. 586; interlocution etc. 588.

oratory; elo-cution, -quence; rhetoric, declamation; grandi-, multi-loquence; burst of eloquence; facundity; talkativeness; flow –, command- of -words, – language; *copia verborum*; power of speech, gift of the gab; *usus loquendi.*

speaker etc. *v.*; spokesman, pro-, inter-locutor; mouthpiece, Hermes; ora-tor, -trix, -tress; Demosthenes, Cicero; rhetorician; stump –, platform- orator, tub-thumper; elocutionist; speech-maker, patterer, *improvisatore*.

V. speak, – of; say, utter, pronounce, deliver, give utterance to; utter –, pour- forth; breathe, let fall, come out with; rap –, blurt- out; have on one's lips; have at the -end, – tip- of one's tongue.

break silence; open one's -lips, – mouth; lift –, raise- one's voice; give –, wag the- tongue; talk, outspeak; put in a word or two.

hold forth; make –, deliver- -a speech etc. *n.*; speechify, harangue, declaim, stump, flourish, spout, rant, recite, lecture, preach, sermonize, discourse, be on one's legs; have –, say- one's say; expatiate etc. (*speak at length*) 573; speak one's mind.

soliloquize etc. 589; tell etc. (*inform*) 527; speak to etc. 586; talk together etc. 588.

be -eloquent etc. *adj.*; have -a tongue in one's head, – the gift of the gab etc. *n.*

pass –, escape- one's lips; fall from the -lips, – mouth.

Adj. speaking etc., spoken etc. *v.*; oral, lingual, phonetic, not written, unwritten, outspoken; eloquent, -cutionary; orat-, rhetorical; declamatory; grandiloquent etc. 577; talkative etc. 584.

Adv. orally etc. *adj.*; by word of mouth, *vivâ voce*, from the lips of.

Phr. quoth –, said- he etc.

583. Stammering. [Imperfect Speech.]—**N.** inarticulateness; stammering etc. *v.*; hesitation etc. *v.*; impediment in one's speech; aphasia, titubancy, traulism; whisper etc. (*faint sound*) 405; lisp, drawl, tardiloquence; nasal -tone, – accent; twang; *falsetto* etc. (*want of voice*) 581; broken -voice, – accents, – sentences.

brogue etc. 563; slip of the tongue, *lapsus linguae*.

V. stammer, stutter, hesitate, falter, hammer; balbu-tiate, -cinate; haw, hum and haw, be unable to put two words together.

mumble, mutter; maund, -er; whisper etc. 405; mince, lisp; jabber, gabble, gibber; sp-, spl-utter; muffle, mump; drawl, mouth; croak; speak -thick, – through the nose; snuffle, clip one's words; murder the -language, – King's (*or* Queen's) English; mis-pronounce, -say.

Adj. stammering etc. *v.*; inarticulate, guttural, nasal; tremulous.

Adv. *sotto voce* etc. (*faintly*) 405.

584. Loquacity.—N. loquac-ity, -iousness; talkativeness etc. *adj.*; garrulity; multiloquence, much speaking, effusion, wordiness.

jaw; gab, -ble; jabber, chatter; prate, prattle, cackle, clack; twaddle, trattle, rattle; *caquet*, *-terie*; blabber, *bavardage*, bibble-babble, gibble-gabble; small talk etc. (*converse*) 588.

fluency, flippancy, volubility, flowing tongue; flow, – of words; *flux de -bouche*, – *mots*, – *paroles*; *copia verborum, cacoëthes loquendi*; verbosity etc. (*diffuseness*) 573; gift of the gab etc. (*eloquence*) 582.

talker; chatter-er, -box; babbler etc. *v.*; rattle; ranter; sermonizer, proser, driveller; wind bag; gossip etc. (*converse*) 588; magpie, jay, parrot, poll, Babel; *moulin à paroles*.

V. be -loquacious etc. *adj.*; talk glibly, pour forth, patter; prate, palaver, prose, chatter, prattle, clack, jabber, jaw; rattle, – on; twaddle, twattle; babble, gabble; out-talk; talk oneself -out of breath, – hoarse; maunder, gush, blatter; talk a donkey's hind leg off; expatiate etc. (*speak at length*) 573; gossip etc. (*converse*) 588; din in the ears etc. (*repeat*) 104; talk -at random, – nonsense etc. 497; be hoarse with talking.

Adj. loquacious, talkative, conversational, garrulous, linguacious, multiloquous; chattering etc. *v.*; chatty etc. (*sociable*) 892; declamatory etc. 582; open-mouthed.

fluent, voluble, glib, flippant; long-tongued, -winded etc. (*diffuse*) 573.

Adv. trippingly on the tongue; glibly etc. *adj.*

Phr. the tongue running -fast, – loose, – on wheels.

585. Taciturnity.—N. silence, muteness, obmutescence; taciturnity, pauciloquy, costiveness, curtness; reserve, reticence etc. (*concealment*) 528; *aposiopesis.*

man of few words.

V. be -silent etc. *adj.*; keep silence; hold one's -tongue, – peace, – jaw; not speak etc. 582; say nothing; seal –, close –, put a padlock on- the -lips, – mouth; put a bridle on one's tongue; keep one's tongue between one's teeth; make no sign, not let a word escape one; keep a secret etc. 528; not have a word to say; lay –, place- the finger on the lips; render mute etc. 581.

stick in one's throat.

Adj. silent, mute, mum; silent as -a post, – a stone, – the grave etc. (*still*) 403; dumb etc. 581.

taciturn, sparing of words; close, – mouthed, –

tongued; laconic, costive, inconversable, curt; reserved; reticent etc. (*concealing*) 528.

Int. tush! silence! mum! hush! *chut!* hist! tut! etc. 403.

586. Allocution.—N. allocution, alloquy, address; speech etc. 582; apostrophe, interpellation, appeal, invocation, salutation; word in the ear.

[Feigned dialogue] dialogism.

platform etc. 542; audience etc. (*interview*) 588.

V. speak to, address, accost, make up to, apostrophize, appeal to, invoke; hail, salute; call to, halloo.

take -aside, – by the button, button-hole; talk to in private.

lecture etc. (*make a speech*) 582.

Int. soho! halloo! hey! hist! hi!

587. Response etc.; *see* Answer 462.

588. Interlocution.—N. interlocution; collocution, colloquy, converse, conversation, confabulation, talk, discourse, verbal intercourse; communion, oral communication, commerce; dia-, duo-, tria-logue.

causerie, chat, chit-chat; small –, table –, teatable –, town –, village –, idle- talk; tattle, gossip, tittle-tattle; babble, -ment; *tripotage*, cackle, prittle-prattle, *on dit*; talk of the -town, – village.

conference, parley, interview, audience, *pourparler*; *tête-à-tête*; reception, *conversazione*; congress etc. (*council*) 696; pow-wow.

hall of audience, *durbar*, coliseum, assembly hall, auditorium.

palaver, debate, logomachy, war of words, controversy.

talker, gossip, tattler; Paul Pry; tabby; chatterer etc. (*loquacity*) 584; interlocutor etc. (*spokesman*) 582; conversation-ist, -alist; dialogist.

'the feast of reason and the flow of soul;' *mollia tempora fandi*.

V. talk together, converse, confabulate; hold –, carry on –, join in –, engage in- a conversation; put in a word; shine in conversation; bandy words; parley; palaver; chat, gossip, tattle; prate etc. (*loquacity*) 584.

discourse –, confer –, commune –, commerce- with; hold -converse, – conference, – intercourse; talk it over; be closeted with; talk with one -in private, – *tête-à-tête*.

Adj. conversing etc. *v.*; interlocutory; conversational, -able; discursive, -coursive; chatty etc. (*sociable*) 892; colloquial, *tête-à-tête*, confabulatory.

589. Soliloquy.—N. soliloquy, monologue, apostrophe.

solilo-quist, -quizer, monologist.

V. soliloquize; say –, talk- to oneself; say aside, think aloud, apostrophize.

Adj. soliloquizing etc. *v.*

Adv. aside.

590. Writing.—N. writing etc. *v.*; chiro-, stelo-, cero-graphy, graphology; stylography; pen-craft, -script, -manship; quill-driving; typewriting.

writing, manuscript, MS., *literae scriptae*; these presents.

stroke –, dash- of the pen; *coup de plume*; line; pen and ink.

letter etc. 561; uncial writing, cuneiform character, arrow-head, Ogham, Runes, futhorc; hieroglyphic, hieratic, demotic; script; contraction.

short-hand; steno-, brachy-, tachy-graphy; secret writing, writing in cipher; crypt-, stegan-ography; phono-, pasi-, poly-, logo-graphy.

copy; tran-, re-script; draft, rough –, fair- copy; handwriting; signature, sign-manual; auto-, mono-, holo-graph; hand, fist; mark.

calligraphy; good –, running –, flowing –, cursive –, legible –, copperplate –, round –, bold-hand.

cacography, *griffonage*, *barbouillage*; bad –, cramped –, crabbed –, illegible- hand; scribble etc. *v.*; *pattes de mouche*; ill-formed letters; pot-hooks and hangers.

stationery; pen, quill, goose-quill, reed; stylographic-, fountain-pen; pencil, style, stylus; paper, foolscap, parchment, vellum, papyrus, pad, tablet, block, note book, slate, marble, pillar, table, black board.

ink-bottle, -pot, -stand, -well, -horn; typewriter.

transcription etc. (*copy*) 21; inscription etc. (*record*) 551; superscription etc. (*indication*) 550.

composition, authorship; *cacoethes scribendi*.

writer, scribe, amanuensis, scrivener, secretary, clerk, penman, copyist, transcriber, quill-driver; writer for the press etc. (*author*) 593.

shorthand writer, stenographer; typewriter, typist.

V. write, pen; copy, engross; write out, – fair; transcribe; scribble, scrawl, scrabble, scratch; interline; stain paper; write down etc. (*record*) 551; sign etc. (*attest*) 467; take down, – in shorthand; typewrite, type.

compose, indite, draw up, redact, draft, formulate; dictate; inscribe, throw on paper, dash off; concoct.

take -up the pen, – pen in hand; shed –, spill –, dip one's pen in- ink.

Adj. writing etc. *v.*; written etc. *v.*; in -writing, – black and white; under one's hand.

uncial, Runic, cuneiform, hieroglyphical etc. *n.*

Adv. *currente calamo*; pen in hand.

591. Printing.—N. printing; block –, type-printing, lino-, mono-type; plate printing etc. (*engraving*) 558; the press etc. (*publication*) 531; composition.

print, letterpress, text, matter, standing type; context, note, page, column; over-running; head-, foot-line, title.

typography; stereo-, electro-, apro-type; type,

black letter, heavy type, font, fount; pi, pie; capitals etc. (*letters*) 561; diamond, pearl, nonpareil, minion, brevier, bourgeois, long primer, small pica, pica, english, great primer.

folio etc. (*book*) 593; copy, impression, pull, proof, galley –, author's –, page- proof, revise.

printer, compositor, reader; printer's devil.

V. print; compose; put –, go- to press; pass –, see- through the press; publish etc. 531; bring out; appear in –, rush into- print.

Adj. printed etc. *v.*; in type; typographical etc. *n.*

592. Correspondence.—N. correspondence, letter, epistle, note, *billet*, post-, letter-card, missive, circular, form letter; favor, *billet-doux*; des-, dis-patch; *bulletin*, communication etc. 532; these presents; rescript, -ion; post etc. (*messenger*) 534; letter writer, correspondent.

V. correspond, – with; write –, send a letter- to; keep up a correspondence; drop a line to; despatch; communicate with; circularize.

Adj. epistolary.

593. Book.—N. book, -let; writing, work, volume, tome, opuscule; tract, -ate; *livret*; *brochure, libretto*, handbook, treatise, text-book, codex, manual, pamphlet, monograph, enchiridion, circular, publication; book of poems; novel; chap-book.

part, issue, number, *livraison*; album, portfolio; periodical, serial, magazine, *ephemeris*, annual, journal.

paper, bill, sheet, broadsheet, screed; leaf, -let; fly-leaf, page; quire, ream.

chapter, section, head, article, paragraph, passage, clause, supplement, appendix; *feuilleton.*

folio, quarto, octavo; duo-, sexto-, octo-decimo.

en-, cyclopedia, dictionary, lexicon, thesaurus, concordance, anthology, bibliography; compilation, compendium, catalogue etc. 86; library, bibliotheca; the press etc. (*publication*) 531.

writer, author, *littérateur*, essayist, journalist, publicist; scribe, penman, war –, special –, correspondent; pen, scribbler, the scribbling race; ghost, hack, literary hack, Grub-street writer; writer for –, gentlemen of –, representative of- the press; reporter, penny-a-liner; editor, sub-editor; playwright etc. 599; poet etc. 597.

bookseller, publisher; biblio-pole, -polist, -grapher; librarian; book -collector, – worm.

book -shop, – club, circulating –, lending –, public- library; publishing house.

knowledge of books, bibliography; book-learning etc. (*knowledge*) 490.

594. Description.—N. description, account, statement, report; *exposé* etc. (*disclosure*) 529; specification, particulars, scenario, plot; state –, summary- of facts; brief etc. (*abstract*) 596; return etc. (*record*) 551; *catalogue raisonné* etc. (*list*) 86; guide-book etc. (*information*) 527.

delineation etc. (*representation*) 554; sketch, vignette; monograph; minute –, detailed –, particular –, circumstantial –, graphic- account; narration, recital, rehearsal, relation.

histori-, chron-ography; historic Muse, Clio; history; bi-, autobi-ography; necrology, obituary.

narrative, history; memoir, memorials; annals etc. (*chronicle*) 551; tradition, legend, saga, epic, epos, story, tale, historiette; personal narrative, journal, letters, life, adventures, fortunes, experiences, confessions; anecdote, ana, *trait.*

work of fiction, short story, novelette, novel, romance, penny dreadful, shilling, shocker, Minerva press; fairy –, nursery- tale; fable, allegory, parable, apologue.

relator etc. *v.*; *raconteur*; historian etc. (*recorder*) 553; biographer, fabulist, novelist, story teller, romancer, teller of tales, spinner of yarns, anecdotist.

V. describe; set forth etc. (*state*) 535; draw a picture, picture; portray etc. (*represent*) 554; characterize, particularize; narrate, relate, recite, recount, sum up, run over, recapitulate, rehearse, fight one's battles over again.

unfold etc. (*disclose*) 529- a tale; tell; give –, render- an account of; report, make a report, draw up a statement.

detail; enter into –, descend to- -particulars, – details.

Adj. descriptive, graphic, narrative, epic, suggestive, well-drawn; historic; auto-, biographical, realistic, expository, tradition-al, -ary; legendary; fabulous, mythical; anecdotic, storied; described etc. *v.*

595. Dissertation.—N. dissertation, treatise, essay; *thesis*, theme; tract, -ate, -ation, excursus; discourse, memoir, disquisition, lecture, sermon, homily, pandect.

commentary, review, *critique*, criticism, article; lead-er, -ing article, editorial; argument, running commentary.

investigation etc. (*inquiry*) 461; study etc. (*consideration*) 451; discussion etc. (*reasoning*) 476; exposition etc. (*explanation*) 522.

commentator, critic, essayist, pamphleteer; publicist, reviewer, leader writer, editor, annotator.

V. dissert –, descant –, write –, touch- upon a subject; dissertate; treat of –, take up –, ventilate –, discuss –, deal with –, go into –, canvass –, handle –, do justice to- a subject; comment, criticize, interpret etc. 522.

Adj. dis-cursive, -coursive; disquisitional, disquisitionary; expository, critical.

596. Compendium.—N. compend, -ium; abstract, *précis*, epitome, *multum in parvo*, analysis, pandect, digest, sum and substance, brief, abridgment, summary, *aperçu*, draft, minute, note; synopsis, textbook, *conspectus*, outlines, syllabus, contents, heads, prospectus.

album; scrap –, note –, memorandum –, commonplace- book; extracts, *excerpta*, cuttings; fugitive -pieces, – writings; *spicilegium*, flowers, anthology, miscellany, *collectanea*, *analecta*; compilation.

recapitulation, *résumé*, review.

abbrevia-tion, -ture; contraction; shortening etc. 201; compression etc. 195.

V. abridge, abstract, epitomize, summarize; make –, prepare –, draw –, compile- an abstract etc. *n*.

recapitulate, review, skim, run over, sum up.

abbreviate etc. (*shorten*) 201; condense etc. (*compress*) 195; compile etc. (*collect*) 72; edit, blue pencil.

Adj. compendious, synoptic, analectic, analytical; abridged etc. *v*.

Adv. in -short, – epitome, – substance, – few words.

Phr. it lies in a nutshell.

597. Poetry.—N. poetry, poetics, poesy, Muse, Calliope, tuneful Nine, Parnassus, Helicon, Pierides, Pierian spring, afflatus, inspiration.

versification, rhyming, making verses; prosody, scansion, orthometry.

poem; epic, – poem; epopee, *epopaea*, ode, epode, idyl, lyric, eclogue, pastoral, bucolic, georgic, dithyramb, anacreontic, sonnet, roundelay, *rondel, rondoletto, rondeau, rondo*, triolet; madrigal, canzonet, *cento*, monody, elegy, palinode; rhapsody.

dramatic –, lyric- poetry; opera; posy, anthology.

song, ballad, lay, love –, drinking –, war –, folk –, sea- song; lullaby; music etc. 415; nursery rhymes.

[Bad poetry] doggerel, Hudibrastic verse, prose run mad; macaronics; macaronic –, leonine-verse; runes.

canto, stanza, distich, verse, line, couplet, triplet, quatrain, sestet; *strophe*, *antistrophe*, refrain, chorus, burden.

verse, rhyme, assonance, crambo, meter, measure, foot, numbers, strain, rhythm; accentuation etc. (*voice*) 580; iambus, dactyl, spondee, trochee, anapaest etc.; hex-, pent-ameter; Alexandrine; blank verse, alliteration.

elegiacs etc. *adj.*; elegiac etc. *adj.* -verse, – meter, – poetry.

poet, – laureate; laureate; minor poet, bard, lyrist, scald, troubadour, *trouvère*; mistrel; minne-, meister-singer; *improvisatore*; versifier, sonneteer; ballad monger; rhym-er, -ist, -ester; poetaster.

V. poetize, sing, versify, make verses, rhyme, scan.

Adj. poetic, -al; lyric, -al; tuneful; epic; dithyrambic etc. *n.*; metrical; a-, catalectic; elegiac, iambic, trochaic, spondaic, anapest; Ionic, Sapphic, Alcaic, Pindaric.

598. Prose.—N. prose, – writer, pros-aism, -aist, -er.

V. prose, write prose.

write -prose, – in prose.

Adj. pros-y, -aic; unpoetical.

rhymeless, unrhymed, in prose, not in verse.

599. Drama.—N. drama, the -drama, – stage, – theater, – play; theatricals, dramaturgy, histrionic art, buskin, sock, *cothurnus*, Melpomene and Thalia, Thespis.

play, stage-play, piece, five-act play, tragedy, comedy, opera, comic opera, *vaudeville, comedietta, lever de rideau*, curtain raiser, interlude, afterpiece, exode, farce, *divertissement, extravaganza*, burletta, harlequinade, pantomime, mimodrama, burlesque, *opéra bouffe*, musical comedy, review, revue, intimate revue, variety, cabaret entertainment, *ballet, spectacle*, masque, *drame, comédie drame*; melo-drama, -drame; *comédie larmoyante*, emotional drama, sensation drama, tragi-, farcical-comedy; mono-drame, -logue; duologue; trilogy; charade, *proverbe*; mystery, miracle –, morality play.

act, scene, *tableau*; in-, intro-duction; pro-, epilogue, curtain; *libretto*, book, script.

performance, representation, show, *mise en scène*, stagery, *jeu de théâtre*, stage-craft; acting; gesture etc. 550; impersonation etc. 554; stage business, gag, patter, buffoonery.

theater; play-, opera-house; house; music hall; *cabaret*; amphitheater, circus, hippodrome; puppet-show, *fantoccini*; *marionnettes*, Punch and Judy.

cinema, -tograph-, picture –, theater, the pictures, the movies, the talkies.

auditory, *auditorium*, front of the house, stalls, boxes, balcony, dress –, upper- circle, – boxes, amphitheater, pit, gallery; *foyer*; greenroom; dressing rooms, *coulisses*.

flat; drop, – scene; wing, screen, side-scene; transformation scene, curtain, act-drop, safety –, fire- curtain; *proscenium*, forestage.

stage, revolving stage, scene, the boards; star –, grave –, trap, mezzanine floor; flies; gridiron, floats, battens, footlights; lime –, spot –, flood –, bunch-lights; scenery, set, *décor*; orchestra.

theatrical -costume, – properties, props.

part, *rôle*, character, cast, *dramatis personae*; *répertoire*.

actor, player; stage –, strolling- player; old –, stager, performer; mime, -r; *artiste*; com-, tragedian, straight man; *tragédienne*, Thespian, Roscius, star.

pantomimist, clown, harlequin, *buffo*, buffoon, *farceur, grimacier*, pantaloon, columbine; *Pierrot, Pierrette*; punch, -inello; *pulcinell-o, -a*; mute, *figurante*, general utility; super, -numerary, extra.

mummer, guiser, guisard, gysart, masque.

mountebank, Jack Pudding; tumbler, posture-master, acrobat, equilibrist, juggler, contortionist; *danseuse*, *ballerina*, ballet -dancer, – girl, *coryphée*; *bayadère*, *geisha*; chorus -singer, – girl.

company; first tragedian, *prima donna*, lead, leading lady, protagonist; *jeune premier*; juvenile lead, *débutant, -e*; light –, genteel –, low- -comedy, – comedian; *soubrette*, walking gentleman, *amoroso*, heavy, heavy father, *ingénue, jeune veuve*, *commère*, *compère*.

property man, *costumier*, machinist, stage hand, electrician, prompter, call-boy; director, manager; stage –, acting –, business- manager; *entrepreneur*, *impresario*, producer, press agent.

dramatic -author, – writer; play-writer, -wright; dramatist, mimographer; dramatic critic.

V. act, play, perform; stage, produce, put on the stage; personate etc. 554; mimic etc. (*imitate*) 19; enact; play –, act –, go through –, perform- a part; rehearse, spout, gag, rant; 'strut and fret one's hour upon a stage;' tread the -stage, – boards; come out;, star.

Adj. dramatic; theatric, -al; scenic, histrionic, anctorial, comic, tragic, buskined, farcical, tragicomic, melodramatic, operatic; stagey spectacular; stagestruck.

Adv. on the -stage, – boards; before -the floats, – an audience; in the limelight, behind the footlights; behind the scenes.

600. Will.—N. will, volition, conation, velleity; will and pleasure, free-will; freedom etc. 748; discretion; choice, inclination, intent, purpose, option etc. (*choice*) 609; voluntariness; spontane-ity, -ousness; originality.

pleasure, wish, desire, mind; frame of mind etc. (*inclination*) 602; intention etc. 620; predetermination etc. 611; self-control etc. determination etc. (*resolution*) 604; will-power.

V.will, list; see –, think- -fit; determine etc. (*resolve*) 604; settle etc. (*choose*) 609; volunteer.

have a will of one's own; do what one chooses etc. (*freedom*) 748; have it all one's own way; have one's -will, – own way.

use –, exercise- one's discretion; take -upon oneself, – one's own course, – the law into one's own hands; do -of one's own accord, – upon one's own -responsibility, – authority; take the bit between one's teeth; take responsibility; originate etc. (*cause*) 153.

Adj. voluntary, volitive, volitional, wilful; free etc. 748; optional; discretion-al, -ary; volitient; dictatorial.

minded etc. (*willing*) 602; prepense etc. (*predetermined*) 611; intended etc. 620; autocratic; unbidden etc. (bid etc. 741); spontaneous; original etc. (*causal*) 153.

Adv. voluntarily etc. *adj.*; at -will, – pleasure; *à -volonté*, – *discrétion*; *al piacere*; *ad -libitum*, – *arbitrium*; as -one thinks proper, – it seems good to.

of one's own -accord, – free will; *proprio* –, *suo* –, *ex mero- motu*; out of one's own head; by choice etc. 609; purposely etc. (*intentionally*) 620; deliberately etc. 611.

Phr. *stet pro ratione voluntas*; *sic volo sic jubeo.*

601. Necessity.—N. involuntariness; instinct, blind –, natural- impulse; inborn –, innate- proclivity; the force of circumstances.

necessi-ty, -tation, necessarianism; obligation; compulsion etc. 744; subjection etc. 749; stern –, hard –, dire –, imperious –, inexorable –, iron –, adverse- -necessity, – fate; what must be.

desti-ny, -nation; fatality, fate, *kismet*, doom, foredoom, election, predestination; pre-, fore- ordination; lot, fortune; fatalism, determinism; inevitableness etc. *adj.*; spell etc. 993.

star, -s; planet, -s; astral influence; sky, Fates, Norns, *Parcae*, Sisters three, Clotho, Lachesis, Atropos; book of fate; God's will, will of Heaven; wheel of Fortune, Ides of March, Hobson's choice.

last -shift, – resort; *dernier ressort*; *pis aller* etc. (*substitute*) 147; necessaries etc. (*requirement*) 630.

necess-arian, -itarian; fatalist, determinist; automaton.

V. lie under a necessity; be -fated, – doomed, – destined etc., – in for, – under the necessity of; have no -choice, – alternative; be- obliged –, forced –, driven –, one's -fate etc. *n.*- to; be - pushed to the wall, – driven into a corner, – unable to help, – drawn irresistibly.

destine, doom, foredoom, devote; pre-destine, - ordain; cast a spell etc. 992; necessitate; compel etc. 744.

Adj. necessary; needful etc. (*requisite*) 630.

fated; destined etc. *v.*; fateful; elect; spell-bound.

compulsory etc. (*compel*) 744; uncontrollable, inevitable, unavoidable, irrestible, irrevocable, inexorable, binding; avoid-, resist-less; written in the book of fate.

involuntary, instinctive, automatic, blind, mechanical; un-conscious, -witting, -thinking; unintentional etc. (*undesigned*) 621; impulsive etc. 612.

Adv. necessarily etc. *adv.*; of -necessity, – course; *ex necessitate rei*; needs must; perforce etc. 744; *nolens volens*; will he nil he, willy nilly, *bon gré mal gré*, willing or unwilling, *coûte que coûte*, forcefully.

faute de mieux; by stress of; if need be.

Phr. it cannot be helped; there is no- help for, – helping- it; it -will, – must, – must needs- be, – be so, – have its way; the die is cast; *jacta est alea*; *che sarà sarà*; 'it is written;' one's- days are numbered, – fate is sealed; *Fata obstant*; *diis aliter visum.*

602. Willingness.—N. willingness, voluntariness etc. *adj.*; willing mind, heart.

disposition, inclination, leaning, *animus*; frame of mind, humor, mood, vein; bent etc. (*turn of mind*) 820; *penchant* etc. (*desire*) 865; aptitude etc. 698.

doc-ility, -ibleness, tractability; persuasi-bleness, -bility; pliability etc. (*softness*) 324.

geniality, cordiality; goodwill; alacrity, readiness, earnestness, forwardness, enthusiasm; zeal, eagerness etc. (*desire*) 865.

assent etc. 488; compliance etc. 762; pleasure etc. (*will*) 600.

labor of love, self-appointed task; volunteer, - ing, gratuitous service; unpaid worker, amateur.

V. be -willing etc. *adj.*; incline, lean to, mind, propend; had as lief; lend –, give –, turn- a willing ear; have -a, – half a, – a great- mind to; hold –, cling- to; desire etc. 865.

see –, think- -good, – fit, – proper; acquiescence etc. (*assent*) 488; comply with etc. 762.

swallow –, nibble at- the bait; gorge the hook; swallow hook, line and sinker; have –, make- no scruple of; make no bones of; jump –, catch- at; meet half way; volunteer, offer oneself etc. 763.

Adj. willing, minded, fain, disposed, inclined, favorable, favorably- minded, -inclined, -disposed; nothing loth; in the -vein, – mood, – humor, – mind.

ready, forward, enthusiastic, earnest, eager; bent upon etc. (*desirous*) 865; predisposed, propense.

docile; persua-dable, -sible; suasible, easily persuaded, facile, easy-going; amenable; tractable etc. (*pliant*) 324; genial, gracious, cordial, hearty; content etc. (*assenting*) 488.

voluntary, gratuitous, spontaneous; unasked etc. (ask etc. 765); unforced etc. (*free*) 748.

Adv. willing etc. *adj.*; fain, freely, as lief, heart and soul; with -pleasure, – all one's heart, – open arms; with -good, – right good- will; *de bonne volonté, ex animo*; *con amore*, heart in hand, nothing loth, without reluctance, of one's own accord, graciously, with a good grace, without demur.

à la bonne heure; by all -means, – manner of means; to one's heart's content; yes etc. (*assent*) 488.

Int. sure, -ly! of course!

603. Unwillingness.—N. unwillingness etc. *adj.*; indispos-ition, -edness; disinclination, aversation, aversion; nolleity, nolition; renitence; reluctance; indifference etc. 866; backwardness etc. *adj.*; slowness etc. 275; want of -alacrity, – readiness; indocility etc. (*obstinacy*) 606.

scrupul-ousness, -osity; qualms of conscience, delicacy, demur, scruple, qualm, shrinking, recoil; hesitation etc. (*irresolution*) 605; fastidiousness etc. 868.

averseness etc. (*dislike*) 867; dissent etc. 489; refusal etc. 764.

slacker, scrimshanker, *embusqué*, unwilling worker, forced labor.

V. be -unwilling etc. *adj.*; nill; dislike etc. 867; grudge, begrudge; not be able to find it in one's heart to, not have the stomach to.

demur, stick at, scruple, stickle; hang fire, run rusty, slack, shirk, scamp, give up, fight shy of, not pull fair; recoil, shrink, swerve; hesitate etc. 605; avoid etc. 623.

oppose etc. 708; dissent etc. 489; refuse etc. 764.

Adj. unwilling; not in the vein, loth, shy of, disinclined, indisposed, averse, reluctant, not content; adverse etc. (*opposed*) 708; laggard, backward, remiss, slack, slow to; renitent; indifferent etc. 866; scrupulous; squeamish etc. (*fastidious*) 868; repugnant etc. (*dislike*) 867; rest-iff, -ive; demurring etc. *v.*; unconsenting etc. (*refusing*) 764; involuntary etc. 601; grudging, irreconcilable.

Adv. unwilling etc. *adj.*; grudgingly, with a heavy heart; with -a bad, – an ill- grace; against –, sore against- -one's wishes, – one's will, – the grain; *invitâ Minervâ*; *à contre coeur*; *malgré soi*; in spite of -one's teeth, – oneself; *nolens volens* etc. (*necessity*) 601; perforce etc. 744; under protest; no etc. 536; not for the world, far be it from me; not if I can help it; if I must I must.

604. Resolution.—N. determination, will; iron –, unconquerable- will; will of one's own, decision, resolution, backbone, grit; strength of -mind, – will; resolve etc. (*intent*) 620; *intransigeance*; firmness etc. (*stability*) 150; energy, manliness, vigor; game, pluck; resoluteness etc. (*courage*) 861; zeal etc. 682; *aplomb*; desperation; devot-ion, -edness.

mastery over self; self-control, -command, -mastery, -possession, -reliance, -government, -restraint, -conquest, -denial; moral -courage, – strength, – fiber; perseverance etc. 604*a*; tenacity; obstinacy etc. 606; bull-dog; British lion.

V. have -determination etc. *n.*; know one's own mind; be -resolved etc. *adj.*; make up one's mind, will resolve, determine; decide etc. (*judgment*) 480; form –, come to- a -determination, – resolution, – resolve; conclude, fix, seal, determine once for all, bring to a crisis, drive matters to an extremity; take a decisive step etc. (*choice*) 609; take upon oneself etc. (*undertake*) 676.

devote oneself –, give oneself up- to; throw away the scabbard, kick down the ladder, nail one's colors to the mast, set one's back against the wall, set one's teeth, put one's foot down, burn one's bridges, take one's stand; stand firm etc. (*stability*) 150; steel oneself; stand no nonsense, not listen to the voice of the charmer.

buckle to; put –, lay –, set- one's shoulder to the wheel; put one's heart into; run the gantlet, make a dash at, take the bull by the horns; beard the lion in his den; rush –, plunge- *in medias res*; go in for; insist upon, make a point of; set one's heart, – mind- upon.

stick at nothing; make short work of etc. (*activity*) 682; not stick at trifles; go -all lengths, – the whole hog; persist etc. (*persevere*) 604*a*; go down with colors flying, die game; go through fire and water, ride in the whirlwind and direct the storm.

Adj. resolved etc. *v.*; determined; strong-willed, -minded; resolute etc. (*brave*) 861; self-possessed, plucky, tenacious; decided, definitive, peremptory, un-hesitating, -flinching, -shrinking; firm, cast iron, indomitable, game to the backbone; inexorable, relentless, not to be -shaken, – put down; *tenax propositi*; inflexible etc. (*hard*) 323; obstinate etc. 606; steady etc. (*persevering*) 604*a*; unbending, unyielding, irrevocable; firm as a rock; grim.

earnest, serious; set –, bent –, intent- upon.

steeled –, proof- against; *in utrumque paratus*.

Adv. resolutely etc. *adj.*; in –, in good- earnest; seriously, joking apart, earnestly, heart and soul; on one's metal; manfully, like a man, with a high hand; with a strong hand etc. (*exertion*) 686.

at any -rate, – risk, – hazard, – price, – cost, – sacrifice; at all -hazards, – risks, – events; cost what it may; *coûte que coûte*; *à tort et à travers*; once for all; neck or nothing; rain or shine; with colors nailed to the mast.

Phr. *spes sibi quisque*.

604a. Perseverance. —N. perseverance; continuance etc. (*inaction*) 143; permanence etc. (*absence of change*) 141; firmness etc. (*stability*) 150.

constancy, steadiness; singleness –, tenacity- of purpose; persistence, plodding, patience; sedulity etc. (*industry*) 682; pertina-cy, -city, -ciousness; iteration etc. 104.

bottom, game, pluck, stamina, backbone, grit; indefatiga-bility, -bleness; bulldog courage.

V. persevere, persist; hold -on, – out; die in the last ditch, be in at the death; stick –, cling –, adhere- to; stick to one's text, keep on; keep to –, maintain- one's -course, – ground; bear –, keep –, hold-up; plod; stick to work etc. (*work*) 686;

continue etc. 143; follow up; die -in harness, – at one's post.

Adj. persevering, constant; stead-y, -fast; undeviating, -wavering, -faltering, -swerving, -flinching, -sleeping, -flagging, -drooping; steady as time; uninter-, un-remitting; plodding; industrious etc. 682; strenuous etc. 686; pertinacious; persisting, -ent.

solid, sturdy, staunch, stanch, ture to oneself; unchangeable etc. 150; unconquerable etc. (*strong*) 159; indomitable, game to the last, indefatigable, untiring, unwearied, never tiring.

Adv. through -evil report and good report, – thick and thin, – fire and water; *per fas et nefas*; without fail, sink or swim, at any price, *vogue la galère*; in sickness and in health.

Phr. never say die; *vestigia nulla retrorsum*.

605. Irresolution.—N. irresolution, infirmity of purpose, indecision; in-, un-determination, loss of will power; unsettlement; uncertainty etc. 475; demur, suspense; hesi-tating etc. *v.*, -tation, -tancy; vacillation; ambivalence; changeableness etc. 149; fluctuation; alternation etc. (*oscillation*) 314; caprice etc. 608; lukewarmness.

fickleness, levity, *légèreté*; pliancy etc. (*softness*) 324; weakness; timidity etc. 860; cowardice etc. 862; half measures.

waverer, ass between two bundles of hay; shuttlecock, butterfly; timeserver, opportunist, turn coat.

V. be -irresolute etc. *adj.*; hang –, keep- in suspense; heave '*ad referendum*;' think twice about, pause; dawdle etc. (*inactivity*) 683; remain neuter; dilly dally. hesitate, boggle, hover, wobble, shilly-shally, hum and haw, demur, not know one's own mind; debate, balance; dally –, coquet- with; will and will not, *chasser-balancer*; go half-way, compromise, make a compormise; be thrown off one's balance, stagger like a drunken man; be afraid etc. 860; let 'I dare not' wait upon 'I would;' falter, waver.

vacillate etc. 149; change etc. 140; retract etc. 607; fluctuate; alternate etc. (*oscillate*) 314; keep off and on, play fast and loose; blow hot and cold etc. (*caprice*) 608.

shuffle, palter, blink; trim.

Adj. irresolute, infirm of purpose, double-minded, half-hearted; un-decided, -resolved, -determined; drifting; shilly-shally; fidgety, tremulous; wobbly; hesitating etc. *v.*; off one's balance; at a loss etc. (*uncertain*) 475.

vacillating etc. *v.*; unsteady etc. (*changeable*) 149; unsteadfast, fickle, unreliable, irresponsible, unstable, without ballast; capricious etc. 608; volatile, frothy; light, -some, -minded; giddy; fast and loose.

weak, feeble-minded, frail; timid etc. 860; cowardly etc. 862; facile; pliant etc. (*soft*) 324; unable to say 'no,' easy-going.

revocable, reversible.

Adv. irresolutely etc. *adj.*; irresolvedly; in faltering accents; off and on; from pillar to post; see-saw etc. 314.

Int. 'how happy could I be with either!'

606. Obstinacy.—N. obstinateness etc. *adj.*; obstinacy, tenacity; perseverance etc. 604*a*; immovability; old school; inflexibility etc. (*hardness*) 323; obdur-acy, -ation; dogged resolution; resolution etc. 604; ruling passion; blind side.

self-will, contumacy, perversity; pervica-cy, -city; indocility.

bigotry, intolerance, dogmatism; opinia-try, -tiveness; fixed idea etc.; intractibility, incorrigibility; (*prejudgment*) 481; fanaticism, zealotry, infatuation, monomania, opinionativeness.

mule; opin-ionist, -ionatist, -iator, -ator; stickler, dogmatist, die-hard, bitter-ender; bigot; zealot, enthusiast, fanatic.

V. be -obstinate etc. *adj.*; stickle, take no denial, fly in the face of facts; opinionate, be wedded to an opinion, hug a belief; have one's own way etc. (*will*) 600; persist etc. (*persevere*) 604*a*; have –, insist on having- the last word.

die -hard, – fighting, fight -against destiny, – to the last ditch; not yield an inch, stand out.

Adj. obstinate, tenacious, stubborn, obdurate, case-hardened; inflexible etc. (*hard*) 323; immovable, not to be moved; inert etc. 172; unchangeable etc. 150; inexorable etc. (*determined*) 604; mulish, obstinate as a mule, pig-headed.

dogged; sullen, sulky; un-moved, -influenced, -affected.

wilful, self-willed, perverse; res-ty, -tive, -tiff; pervicacious, wayward, refractory, unruly; head-y, -strong; *entete*; contumacious; cross-grained.

arbitrary, dogmatic, opinionated, positive, bigoted; prejudiced etc. 481; prepossessed, infatuated; stiff-backed, -necked, -hearted; hard-mouthed, hidebound; unyielding; im-pervious, -practicable, -persuasible; unpersuadable; in-, untractable; incorrigible, deaf to advice, impervious to reason; crotchety etc. 608.

Adv. obstinately etc. *adj.*

Phr. *non possumus*; no surrender.

607. Tergiversation.—N. change of -mind, – intention, – purpose; afterthought.

tergiversation, recantation; palinode, -ody; renunciation; abjur-ation, -ement; defection etc. (*relinquishment*) 624; going over etc. *v.*; apostasy; retract-ion, -ation; withdrawal, disavowal etc. (*negation*) 536; revo-cation, -kement; reversal; repentance etc. 950; *redintegratio amoris*.

coquetry, flirtation; vacillation etc. 605; backsliding, recidivation.

turn-coat, | -tippet; rat, apostate, renegade, mugwump; con-, per-vert; proselyte, deserter; backslider, recidivist; black leg.

time-server, -pleaser; timist, Vicar of Bray, trimmer, ambidexter; weathercock etc. (*changeable*) 149; Janus.

V. change one's -mind, – intention, – purpose, – note; abjure, renounce; withdraw from etc. (*relinquish*) 624; wheel –, turn –, veer- round; turn a *pirouette*; go over –, pass –, change –, skip- from one side to another; go to the right about; box the compass, shift one's ground, go upon another tack; back down, crawl, crawfish.

apostatize, change sides, go over, rat; recant, retract; revoke; rescind etc. (*abrogate*) 756; recall, forswear, abjure, unsay; come -over, – round- to an opinion.

draw in one's horns, eat one's words; eat –,

swallow- the leek; swerve, flinch, back out of, retrace one's steps, think better of it; come back –, return- to one's first love; turn over a new leaf etc. (*repent*) 950.

trim, shuffle, play fast and loose, blow hot and cold, coquet, flirt, hold with the hare but run with the hounds; straddle; *nager entre deux eaux*; wait to see how the -cat jumps, – wind blows.

Adj. changeful etc. 149; irresolute etc. 605; ductile, slippery as an eel, trimming, ambidextrous, timeserving; coquetting etc. *v.*

revocatory, reactionary.

Phr. 'a change came o'er the spirit of my dream.'

608. Caprice.—N. caprice, fancy, humor; whim, -sey, -wham; crotchet, *capriccio*, quirk, freak, maggot, fad, vagary, prank, fit, flim-flam, *escapade*, *boutade*, wild-goose chase; capriciousness etc. *adj.*; kink.

V. be -capricious etc. *adj.*; have a maggot in the brain; take it into one's head, strain at a gnat and swallow a camel; blow hot and cold; play -fast and loose, – fantastic tricks.

Adj. capricious; erratic, eccentric, fitful, hysterical; full of -whims etc. *n.*; maggoty; inconsistent, fanciful, fantastic, whimsical, crotchety, particular, humorsome, freakish, skittish, wanton, wayward; contrary; captious; arbitrary; unrestrained, undisciplined; not amenable to reason; uncomfortable etc. 83; penny wise and pound foolish; fickle etc. (*irresolute*) 605; frivolous, sleeveless, giddy, volatile.

Adv. by fits and starts, without rhyme or reason, at one's own sweet will.

Phr. *nil fuit unquam six impar sibi*; the deuce is in him.

609. Choice.—N. choice, option; discretion etc. (*volition*) 600; preoption; alternative; dilemma; *ambarras de choix*; adoption, cooptation; novation; decision etc. (*judgment*) 480.

election, poll, ballot, vote, voice, suffrage, plumper, cumulative vote; *plebiscitum*, *plébiscite*, *vox populi*; *referendum*, electioneering; voting etc. *v.*; franchise; ballot box; slate, ticket.

selection, excerption, gleaning, eclecticism; *excerpta*, gleanings, cuttings, scissors and paste; pick etc. (*best*) 650.

preference, prelation; predilection etc. (*desire*) 865.

V. offer for one's choice, set before; hold out –, present –, offer- the alternative; put to the vote.

use –, exercise –, one's- -discretion, – option; adopt, take up, embrace, espouse; choose, elect, coopt; take –, make- one's choice; make choice of, fix upon.

vote, poll, hold up one's hand; divide.

settle; decide etc. (*adjudge*) 480; list etc. (*will*) 600; make up one's mind etc. (*resolve*) 604.

select; pick, – and choose; pick –, single- out, excerpt; cull, glean, winnow; sift –, separate –, winnow- the chaff from the wheat; pick up, pitch upon; pick one's way; indulge one's fancy.

set apart, reserve, mark out for; mark etc. 550.

prefer; have -rather, – as lief; fancy etc. (*desire*) 865; be persuaded etc. 615.

take a -decided, – decisive- step; commit oneself to a course; pass –, cross- the Rubicon; cast in one's lot with; take for better or for worse.

Adj. optional; co-optative; discretional etc. (*voluntary*) 600; on approval.

ecletic; choosing etc. *v.*; preferential; chosen etc. *v.*; choice etc. (*good*) 648.

Adv. optionally etc. *adj.*; at pleasure etc. (*will*) 600; either, – the one or the other; or; at the option of; whether or not; once for all; for one's money.

by -choice, – preference; in preference; rather, before.

609a. Absence of Choice.—N. no –, Hobson's- choice; first come, first served; necessity etc. 601; not a pin to choose etc. (*equality*) 27; any, the first that comes.

neutrality, indifference; indecision etc. (*irresolution*) 605.

V. be -neutral etc. *adj.*; have no choice; waive, not vote; abstain –, refrain- from voting; leave undecided; make a virtue of necessity.

Adj. neu-tral, -ter; indifferent; undecided etc. (*irresolute*) 605.

Adv. either etc. (*choice*) 609.

610. Rejection.—N. rejection, repudiation, exclusion; declination; refusal etc. 764.

V. reject; set –, lay- aside; give up; decline etc. (*refuse*) 764; exclude, except, eliminate; pluck, spin; cast.

repudiate, scout, set at naught; fling –, cast –, thrown –, toss- -to the winds, – to the dogs, – overboard, – away; send to the right about; disclaim etc. (*deny*) 536; discard etc. (*eject*) 297, (*have done with*) 678.

Adj. rejected etc. *v.*; reject-aneous, -itious; not -chosen etc. 609, – to be thought of; out of the question.

Adv. neither, – the one nor the other; no etc. 536.

Phr. *non haec in foedera.*

611. Predetermination.—N. premeditation, -deliberation, -determination, -destination; foreordination; foregone conclusion; *parti pris*; resolve, propendency; intention etc. 620; project etc. 626.

V. pre-determine, -destine, -meditate, -resolve, -concert; foreordain; resolve beforehand.

Adj. pre-pense, -meditated etc. *v.*, -designed; advised, studied, designed, calculated; aforethought; intended etc. 620; foregone.

well-laid, -devised, -weighed; maturely considered; cut and dried; cunning.

Adv. advisedly etc. *adj.*; with premeditation, deliberately, all things considered, with eyes open, in cold blood; intentionally etc. 620.

612. Impulse.—N. impulse, sudden thought; *impromptu*, improvisation; inspiration, hunch, flash, spurt.

improvisatore, *improvisatrice*, improviser, extemporizer; creature of impulse.

V. flash on the mind.

say what comes uppermost; improvise, extemporize; rise to the occasion; spurt.

Adj. extemporaneous, impulsive, indeliberate; improvis-ed, -ate, -atory; un-, unpre-meditated; *improvisé*; unprompted, -guided; natural, unguarded; spontaneous etc. (*voluntary*) 600; instinctive etc. 601.

Adv. extem-pore, -poraneously; offhand, *impromptu*, *à l'improviste*; improviso; on the spur of the -moment, – occasion.

613. Habit.—N. habit, -ude; assuetude, -faction; wont; run, way.

common –, general –, natural –, ordinary –, habitual- -course, – run, – state- of things; matter of course; beaten -path, – track, – ground.

prescription, custom, use, usage, immemorial usage, practice; tradition; prevalence, observance; conventionalism, -ity; mode, fashion, vogue; *etiquette* etc. (*gentility*) 852; order of the day, cry; conformity etc. 82.

habitué, addict.

one's old way, old school, consuetude, *veteris vestigia flammae*; *laudator temporis acti*.

rule, standing order, precedent, routine; red-tape, -tapism; pipe-clay; rut, groove.

cacoëthes; bad –, confirmed –, inveterate –, intrinsic etc. 5- habit; addiction, trick.

training etc. (*education*) 537; seasoning, hardening, inurement; radication; second nature, acclimatization; knack etc. (*skill*) 698.

V. be -wont etc. *adj.*

fall into a custom etc. (*conform to*) 82; tread –, follow- the beaten -track, – path; *stare super antiquas vias*; move in a rut, run on in a groove, go round like a horse in a mill, go on in the old jobtrot way.

habituate, inure, harden, season, caseharden; accustom, familiarize; naturalize, acclimatize; keep one's hand in; train etc. (*educate*) 537.

get into the -way, – knack- of; learn etc. 539; cling –, adhere- to; repeat etc. 104; acquire –, contract –, fall into- a -habit, – trick; addict oneself –, take- to; accustom oneself to.

be -habitual etc. *adj.*; prevail; come into use, become a habit, take root; gain –, grow- upon one.

Adj. habitual; ac-, customary; prescriptive; accustomed etc. *v.*; traditional; of -daily, – everyday- occurrence; wonted, usual, general, ordinary, common, frequent, every-day, household, jog-trot; well-trodden, -known; familiar, vernacular, trite, commonplace, banal, bromidic, conventional, regular, set, stock, officinal, established, stereotyped; pre-vailing, -valent; current, received, acknowledged, recognized, accredited; of course, admitted, understood.

conformable etc. 82; according to -use, – custom, – routine; in -vogue, – fashion; fashionable etc. (*genteel*) 852.

wont; used – given – addicted –, attuned –, habituated etc. *v.*- to; in the habit of; *habitué*; at home in etc. (*skilful*) 698; seasoned; permeated –, imbued- with; devoted –, wedded- to; never free from.

hackneyed, fixed, rooted, deep-rooted, ingrafted, permanent, inveterate, besetting; naturalized; ingrained etc. (*intrinsic*) 5.

Adv. habitually etc. *adj.*; always etc. (*uniformly*) 16.

as -usual, – is one's wont, – things go, – the world goes, – the sparks fly upwards; *more -suo*, – *solito*.

as a rule, for the most part; generally etc. *adj.*; most often, – frequently.

Phr. *cela s'entend.*

614. Desuetude.—N. desuetude, disusage; disuse etc. 678; want of -habit, – practice; inusitation; newness to; new brooms.

infraction of usage etc. (*unconformity*) 83; non-prevalence; 'a custom more honored in the breach than the observance.'

V. be -unaccustomed etc. *adj.*; leave off –, cast off –, break off –, wean oneself of –, violate –, break through –, infringe- -a habit, – a custom, – a usage; break one's fetters; disuse etc. 678; wear off.

Adj. un-accustomed, -used, -wonted, -seasoned, -inured, -habituated, -trained; new; green etc. (*unskilled*) 699; fresh, original, unhackneyed.

unusual etc. (*unconformable*) 83; unconventional, non-observant; disused etc. 678.

Adv. just for once.

615. Motive.—N. motive, springs of action.

reason, ground, call, principle; mainspring, *primum mobile*, key-stone; the why and the wherefore; *pro* and *con*, reason why; secret –, ulterior- motive, *arrière-pensée*; intention etc. 620.

inducement, consideration; attraction etc. 288; loadstone; magnet, -ism, -ic force; allect-ation, -ive; temptation, enticement, *agacerie*, allurement, witchery; bewitch-ment, -ery; charm; spell etc. 993; fascination, blandishment, cajolery; seduc-tion, -ement; honeyed words, voice of the tempter, son of the Sirens; forbidden fruit, golden apple.

persuasi-bility, -bleness; attractability; impress-, suscept-ibility; softness; persuas-, attract-iveness; tantalization.

influence, prompting, dictate, instance; impuls-e, -ion; incit-ement, -ation; press, instigation; provocation etc. (*excitation of feeling*) 824; inspiration; per-, suasion; encouragement, advocacy; exhortation, advice etc. 695; solicitation etc. (*request*) 765; lobbying.

incentive, stimulus, spur, fillip, whip, goad, rowel, provocative, whet, dram.

bribe, lure; decoy, – duck; bait, trail of a red herring; bribery and corruption; sop, – for Cerberus.

prompter, tempter; seduc-er, -tor; suggester, coaxer, wheedler; instigator, firebrand, incendiary; Siren, Circe; *agent provocateur*; lobbyist.

V. induce, move; draw, – on; bring in its train, give an -impulse etc. *n.*- to; inspire; put up to, prompt, call up; attract, beckon.

stimulate etc. (*excite*) 824; spirit up, inspirit; a-, rouse; ecphorize; animate, incite, provoke, instigate, set on, actuate; act –, work –, operate-upon; encourage; pat –, clap- on the -back, – shoulder.

influence, weigh with, bias, sway, incline, dispose, predispose, turn the scale, inoculate; lead, – by the nose; have –, exercise- influence- -with, – over, – upon; go –, come- round one; turn the head, magnetize.

persuade; prevail -with, – upon; overcome, carry; bring -round, – to one's senses; draw –, win –, gain –, come –, talk- over; procure, enlist, engage; invite, court.

tempt, seduce, overpersuade, entice, allure, captivate, fascinate, intrigue, bewitch, carry away, charm, conciliate, wheedle, coax, lure, suggest; inveigle; tantalize; cajole etc. (*deceive*) 545.

tamper with, bribe, suborn, grease the palm, bait with a silver hook, gild the pill, make things pleasant, put a sop into the pan, throw a sop to, bait the hook.

enforce, force; impel etc. (*push*) 276; propel etc. 284; whip, lash, goad, spur, prick, urge; egg –, hound –, hurry- on; drag etc. 285; exhort; advise etc. 695; call upon etc.; press etc. (*request*) 765; advocate.

set -an example, – the fashion; keep in countenance; back up.

be -persuaded etc.; yield to temptation, come round; concede etc. (*consent*) 762; obey a call; follow -advice, – the bent, – the dictates of; act on principle.

Adj. impulsive, motive; suas-, persuas-, hortative, -ory; protreptical; inviting, tempting etc. *v.*; seductive, attractive, irresistible; fascinating etc. (*pleasing*) 829; provocative etc. (*exciting*) 824.

induced etc. *v.*; disposed; persuadable etc. (*docile*) 602; spellbound; instinct –, smitten- with; inspired etc. *v.*- by.

Adv. because, therefore etc. (*cause*) 155; from -this, – that- motive; for -this, – that- reason; for; by reason –, for the sake –, on the score –, on account- of; out of, from, as, forasmuch as.

for all the world; on principle.

615a. Absence of Motive.—N. absence of motive; caprice etc. 608; chance etc. (*absence of design*) 621.

V. have no motive; scruple etc. (*be unwilling*) 603.

Adj. without rhyme or reason; aimless etc. (*chance*) 621.

Adv. capriciously; out of mere caprice.

616. Dissuasion.—N. dissuasion, dehortation, expostulation, remonstrance; deprecation etc. 766.

discouragement, damper, wet blanket; warning.

cohibition etc. (*restraint*) 751; curb etc. (*means of restraint*) 752; check etc. (*hindrance*) 706.

reluctance etc. (*unwillingness*) 603; contraindication.

V. dissuade, dehort, cry out against, remonstrate, expostulate, warn, contraindicate.

disincline, indispose, shake, stagger; dispirit; discourage, -hearten, -enchant; deter; hold –, keep- back etc. (*restrain*) 751; render -averse etc. 603; repel; turn aside etc. (*deviation*) 279; wean from; act as a drag etc. (*hinder*) 706; throw cold water on, damp, cool, chill, blunt, calm, quiet, quench; deprecate etc. 766.

Adj. dissuading etc. *v.*; dissuasive; dehortatory, expostulatory; monit-ive, -ory.

dissuaded etc. *v.*; uninduced etc. (induce etc. 615); unpersuadable etc. (*obstinate*) 606; averse etc. (*unwilling*) 603; repugnant etc. (*dislike*) 867.

617. Plea. [Ostensible motive, ground, or reason assigned.]—**N.** plea, pretext; allegation, advocation; ostensible -motive, – ground, – reason; excuse etc. (*vindication*) 937; color; gloss, guise.

loop-, starting-hole; how to creep out of, salvo, come off.

handle, peg to hang on room, *locus standi*; stalking horse, *cheval de bataille*, cue.

pretence etc. (*untruth*) 546; put off, subterfuge, dust thrown in the eyes; blind; moonshine; mere –, shallow- pretext; lame -excuse, – apology, tub to a whale; flase plea, sour grapes; makeshift, shift, white lie; special pleading etc. (*sophistry*) 477; soft sawder etc. (*flattery*) 933.

V. plead, allege; shelter oneself under the plea of; excuse etc. (*vindicate*) 937; gloss over; lend a color to; furnish a -handle etc. *n.*, make a -pretext, – handle- of; use as a plea etc. *n.*; take one's stand upon, make capital out of; pretend etc. (*lie*) 544.

Adj. ostensible etc. (*manifest*) 525; excusing; alleged, apologetic; pretended etc. 545.

Adv. ostensibly; under -color, – the plea, – the pretence- of.

618. Good.—N. good, benefit, advantage; improvement etc. 658; interest, service, behoof, behalf; weal; main chance, *summum bonum*, common weal; 'consummation devoutly to be wished;' gain, boot; profit, harvest.

boon etc. (*gift*) 784; good turn; blessing, benison; world of good; piece of good -luck, – fortune; nuts, prize, windfall, godsend, waif, treasure trove.

good fortune etc. (*prosperity*) 734; happiness etc. 827.

[Source of good] goodness etc. 648; utility etc. 644; remedy etc. 662; pleasure-giving etc. 829.

Adj. commendable etc. 931; useful etc. 644; good etc., beneficial etc. 648.

V. benefit, profit, advantage, serve, help, avail; do good to, gain, prosper, flourish.

Adv. well, aright, satisfactorily, favorably, not amiss; all for the best; to one's -advantage etc. *n.*; in one's -favor, – interest etc. *n.*

Phr. so far so good.

619. Evil.—N. evil, ill, harm, hurt, mischief, nuisance; machinations of the devil, Pandora's box, ills that flesh is heir to.

blow, buffet, stroke, scratch, bruise, wound, gash, mutilation; mortal -blow, – wound; *im-*

medicabile vulnus; damage, loss etc. (*deterioration*) 659.

disadvantage, prejudice, drawback.

disaster, accident, casualty; mishap etc. (*misfortune*) 735; bad job, devil to pay; calamity, bale, woe, catastrophe, tragedy; ruin etc. (*destruction*) 162; adversity etc. 735.

mental suffering etc. 828. [Evil spirit] demon etc. 980. [Cause of evil] bane etc. 663. [Production of evil] badness etc. 649; painfulness etc. 830; evil doer etc. 913.

outrage, wrong, injury, foul play; bad –, ill-turn; disservice; spoliation etc. 791; grievance, crying evil.

V. be in trouble etc. (*adversity*) 735; harm, injure, hurt, do disservice to.

Adj. disastrous, bad etc. 649; awry, out of joint; disadvantageous, injurious, harmful.

Adv. amiss, wrong, ill, to one's cost.

620. Intention.—N. intent, -ion, -ionality; purpose; *quo animo*; project etc. 626; undertaking etc. 676; predetermination etc. 611; design, ambition.

contemplation, mind, *animus*, view, purview, proposal; study; look out.

final cause; *raison d'être*; *cui bono*; object, aim, end; 'the be all and the end all;' drift etc. (*meaning*) 516; tendency etc. 176; destination, mark, point, butt, goal, target, bull's-eye, quintain; prey, quarry, game.

decision, determination, resolve; set –, settled-purpose; *ultimatum*; resolution etc. 604; wish etc. 865; *arrière-pensée*; motive etc. 615.

[Study of final causes] teleology.

V. intend, purpose, design, mean; have to; propose to oneself; harbor a design; have in -view, – contemplation, – one's eye, – *petto*; have an eye to.

bid –, labor- for; be –, aspire –, endeavour-after; be –, aim –, drive –, point –, level- at; take aim; set before oneself; study to.

take upon oneself etc. (*undertake*) 676; take into one's head; meditate, contemplate; think –, dream –, talk- of; premeditate etc. 611; compass, calculate; dest-ine, -inate, propose.

project etc. (*plan*) 626; have a mind to etc. (*be willing*) 602; desire etc. 865; pursue etc. 622.

Adj. intended etc. *v.*; intentional, advised, express, determinate; prepense etc. 611; bound for; intending etc. *v.*; minded, disposed, inclined; bent upon etc. (*earnest*) 604; at stake, on the -anvil, – *tapis*; in -view; – prospect, – the breast of; *in petto*; teleological.

Adv. intentionally etc. *adj.*; advisedly, wittingly, knowingly, designedly, purposely, on purpose, by design, studiously, pointedly; with -intent etc. *n.*; deliberately etc. (*with premeditation*) 611; with one's eyes open, in cold blood.

for; with -a view, – an eye- to; in order -to, – that; to the end –, with the intent- that; for the purpose –, with the view –, in contemplation –, on account- of.

in pursuance of, pursuant to; *quo animo*; to all intents and purposes.

621. Chance.† [Absence of purpose in the succession of events.]—**N.** chance etc. 156; lot, fate etc. (*necessity*) 601; luck; good luck etc. (*good*) 618; bad luck etc. 735; wheel of fortune; mascot; swastika.

speculation, venture, stake, flutter, flier, gamble, game of chance; mere –, random- shot; blind bargain, leap in the dark; pig in a poke etc. (*uncertainty*) 475; fluke, pot-luck.

drawing lots; sorti-legy, -tion; *sortes*, – *Virgilianae*; *rouge et noir*, hazard, *roulette*, pitch and toss, chuck-farthing, cup-tossing, heads or tails, cross and pile, wager; bet, -ting; risk, stake, plunge; gambling; the turf.

stock exchange, bourse, board of trade, curb exchange.

gaming-, gambling-, betting-house; hell; betting ring, totalizator; dice, – box; dicer; gam-bler, -ester, plunger, stock operator, manipulator, punter; man of the turf; adventurer, speculator; bookmaker, layer, backer.

V. chance etc. (*hap*) 156; stand a chance etc. (*be possible*) 470.

toss up; cast –, draw- lots; leave –, trust- -to chance, – to the chapter of accidents; tempt fortune; chance it, take one's chance; run –, incur –, encounter- the -risk, – chance; stand the hazard of the die.

speculate, try one's luck, set on a cast, raffle, put into a lottery, buy a pig in a poke, shuffle the cards.

risk, venture, hazard, stake; lay, – a wager; make a bet, wager, bet, gamble, game, play for; play at chuck-farthing.

Adj. fortuitous etc. 156; unintentional, -ded; accidental; not meant; un-designed, -purposed; unpremeditated etc. 612; never thought of.

indiscriminate, promiscuous; undirected, random; aim-, drift-, design-, purpose-, cause-less; without purpose.

possible etc. 470.

Adv. casually etc. 156; unintentionally etc. *adj.*; unwittingly.

en passant, by the way, incidentally; as it may happen; at -random, – a venture, – haphazard; as luck would have it, by -chance, – good fortune; un-, -luckily.

† See note on 156.

622. Pursuit. [Purpose in action.]—**N.** pursuit; pursuing etc. *v.*; prosecution; pursuance; enterprise etc. (*undertaking*) 676; business etc. 625; adventure etc. (*essay*) 675; quest etc. (*search*) 461; scramble, hue and cry, game; hobby.

chase, hunt, *battue*, race, steeplechase, hunting, coursing; ven-ation, -ery; fox-chase; sport, -ing; shooting, angling, fishing, hawking.

pursuer; hunt-er, -sman; sportsman, Nimrod, the field; hound etc. 366.

V. pursue, prosecute, follow; run –, make –, be –, hunt – prowl- after; shadow; carry on etc. (*do*) 680; engage in etc. (*undertake*) 676; set about etc. (*begin*) 66; endeavor etc. 675; court etc. (*request*) 765; seek etc. (*search*) 461; aim at etc. (*intention*) 620; follow the trail etc. (*trace*) 461; fish for etc. (*experiment*) 463; press on etc. (*haste*) 684; run a race etc. (*velocity*) 274.

chase, give chase, course, dog, hunt, hound, stalk; tread –, follow- on the heels of etc. (*sequence*) 281.

rush upon; rush headlong etc. (*violence*) 173;

ride –, run- full tilt at; make a leap –, jump –, snatch- at; run down; start game.

tread a path; take –, hold- a course; shape –, direct –, bend- one's -steps, – course; play a game; fight –, elbow- one's way; follow up; take -to, – up; go in for; ride one's hobby.

Adj. pursuing etc. *v.*; in quest of etc. (*inquiry*) 461; in -pursuit, – full cry, – hot pursuit; on the scent.

Adv. in pursuance of etc. (*intention*) 620; after.

Int. tally-ho! yoicks! so-ho!

623. Avoidance. [Absence of pursuit.]—**N.** abst-ention, -inence; forbearance; refraining etc. *v.*; inaction etc. 681; neutrality.

avoidance, evasion, elusion; seclusion etc. 893.

avolation, flight; escape etc. 671; retreat etc. 287; recoil etc. 277; departure etc. 293; rejection etc. 610.

shirker etc. *v.*; slacker; truant; fugitive, refugee; runa-way, -gate; renegade; deserter.

V. abstain, refrain, spare, not attempt; not do etc. 681; maintain the even tenor of one's way.

eschew, keep from, let alone, have nothing to do with; keep –, stand –, hold- -aloof, – off; take no part in, have no hand in.

avoid, shun; steer –, keep- clear of; fight shy of; keep -one's, – at a respectful- distance; keep –, get- out of the way; evade, elude, turn away from; set one's face against etc. (*oppose*) 708; deny oneself.

shrink; hang –, hold –, draw- back; recoil etc. 277; retire etc. (*recede*) 287; flinch, blink, blench, shy, shirk, dodge, parry, make way for, give place to.

beat a retreat; turn -tail, – one's back; take to one's heels; run, -away, – for one's life; cut and run; be off, – like a shot; fly, flee; fly –, flee –, run away- from; take –, take to- flight; desert, elope; make –, scamper –, sneak –, shuffle –, sheer- off; break –, burst –, tear oneself –, slip –, slink –, steal- -away, – away from; slip cable, part company, turn on one's heel; sneak out of, play truant, give one the go by, give leg bail, take French leave, slope, decamp, flit, bolt, abscond, levant, skedaddle, absquatulate, cut one's stick, walk one's chalks, show a light pair of heels, make oneself scarce; escape etc. 671; go away etc. (*depart*) 293; abandon etc. 624; reject etc. 610.

lead one a -dance, – a merry chase, – pretty dance; throw off the scent, play at hide and seek.

Adj. unsought, unattempted; avoiding etc. *v.*; neutral; shy of etc. (*unwilling*) 603; elusive, evasive, distant; fugitive, runaway; shy, wild.

Adj. lest, in order to avoid.

Int. forebear! keep –, hands- off! *sauve qui peut!* devil take the hindmost.

624. Relinquishment.—**N.** relinquish-, abandon-ment; desertion, defection, secession, withdrawal; cave of Adullam; *nolle prosequi.*

discontinuance etc. (*cessation*) 142; renunciation etc. (*recantation*) 607; abrogation etc. 756; resignation etc. (*retirement*) 757; desuetude etc. 614; cession etc. (*of property*) 782.

V. relinquish, give up, abandon, desert, forsake, leave in the lurch; depart –, secede –, withdraw- from; back – out of, – down from, leave, go back on one's word, quit, take leave of, bid a long farewell; vacate etc. (*resign*) 757.

renounce etc. (*abjure*) 607; forego, have done with, drop; write off; disuse etc. 678; discard etc. 782; wash one's hands of; drop all idea of; *nolle-pros.*; lose interest in.

break –, leave- off; desist; stop etc. (*cease*) 142; hold –, stay- one's hand; quit one's hold; give over, shut up shop.

throw up the -game, – cards; give up the -point, – argument; pass to the order of the day, move the previous question, table the motion.

Adj. unpursued; relinquished etc. *v.*; relinquishing etc. *v.*

Int. avast etc.! (*stop*) 142.

625. Business.—**N.** business, occupation, employment; pursuit etc. 622; what one is doing-, – about; affair, concern, matter, case, undertaking.

matter in hand, irons in the fire; thing to do, *agendum*, task, work, job, chore, errand, transaction, commission, mission, charge, care; duty etc. 926.

part, *rôle*, cue; province, function, look-out, department, capacity, sphere, orb, field, line; walk, – of life; beat, round, routine; race, career.

office, place, post, incumbency, living situation, appointment, billet, berth, employ; service etc. (*servitude*) 749; engagement; undertaking etc. 676.

vocation, calling, profession, *métier*, cloth, faculty; industry, art; industrial arts; craft, mystery, handicraft; trade etc. (*commerce*) 794.

exercise; work etc. (*action*) 680; avocation; press of business etc. (*activity*) 682.

V. pass –, employ –, spend- one's time in; employ oneself -in, – upon; occupy –, concern- oneself with; make it one's -business etc. *n.*; undertake etc. 676; enter a profession; betake oneself to, turn one's hand to; have to do with etc. (*do*) 680.

drive a trade; carry on –, do –, transact- -business, – a trade etc. *n.*; keep a shop; ply one's task, – trade; labor in one's vocation; pursue the even tenor of one's way; attend to -business, – one's work.

officiate, serve, act; act –, play- one's part; do duty; serve –, discharge –, perform- the -office, – duties, – functions- of; hold –, fill- -an office, – a place, – a situation; hold a portfolio.

be -about, – doing, – engaged in, – employed in, – occupied with, – at work on; have one's hands in, have in hand; have on one's -hands, – shoulders; bear the burden; have one's hands full etc. (*activity*) 682.

be -in the hands of, – on the stocks, – on the anvil; pass through one's hands.

Adj. business-like; work-a-day; professional; official, functional; busy etc. (*actively employed*) 682; on –, in- -hand, – one's hands; afoot; on -foot, – the anvil; going on; acting.

Adv. in the course of business, all in a day's work; professionally etc. *adj*.

626. Plan.—**N.** plan, scheme, design, project; propos-al, -ition; suggestion; resolution, motion;

precaution etc. (*provision*) 673; deep-laid etc. (*premeditated*) 611- plan etc.; racket.

system etc. (*order*) 58; organization etc. (*arrangement*) 60; germ etc. (*cause*) 153; Five Year Plan.

sketch, skeleton, outline, draught, draft, *ébauche*, *brouillon*; rough-cast, – draft, – draught, – copy; proof, revise.

forecast, *programme*, prospectus, scenario; *carte du pays*; card; bill, protocol; order of the day, list of agenda, *memorandum*; bill of fare etc. (*food*) 298; base of operations; platform, plank.

rôle; policy etc. (*line of conduct*) 692.

contrivance, invention, expedient, receipt, nostrum, artifice, device, gadget; stratagem etc. (*cunning*) 702; trick etc. (*deception*) 545; alternative, loophole, shift etc. (*substitute*) 147; last shift etc. (*necessity*) 601.

measure, step; stroke, – of policy; master stroke; trump-, court-card; *chaval de bataille*, great gun; *coup*, – *d'état*; clever –, bold –, good- -move, – hit, – stroke; bright -thought, – idea, great idea.

intrigue, cabal, plot, frame-up, conspiracy, complot, machination; under-, counter-plot.

schem-ist, -atist; stragetist, machinator, schemer; projector, author, builder, artist, promoter, designer etc. *v.*; conspirator; *intrigant* etc. (*cunning*) 702.

V. plan, scheme, design, frame, contrive, project, forecast, sketch; conceive, devise, invent etc. (*imagine*) 515; set one's wits to work etc. 515; spring a project; fall –, hit- upon; strike –, chalk –, cut –, lay –, map-out; lay down a plan; shape –, mark- out a course; predetermine etc. 611; concert, preconcert, preestablish; prepare etc. 673; hatch, – a plot; concoct; take -steps, – measures.

cast, recast, systematize, organize; arrange etc. 60; digest, mature.

plot; counter-plot, -mine; dig a mine; lay a train; intrigue etc. (*cunning*) 702.

Adj. planned etc. *v.*; strategic, -al; planning etc. *v.*; in course of preparation etc. 673; under consideration; on the -*tapis*, – carpet, – table.

627. Method. [Path.]—**N.** method, way, manner, wise, gait, form, mole, fashion, tone, guise; *modus operandi*; procedure etc. (*line of conduct*) 692.

path, road, route, course; line of -way, – road; trajectory, orbit, track, beat, tack.

steps; stair, -case; flight of stairs, ladder, stile.

bridge, viaduct, gauntry, pontoon, stepping stone, plank, gangway, catwalk, drawbridge; pass, ford, ferry, tunnel, subway, elevated; pipe etc. 260.

door; gateway etc. (*opening*) 260; channel, passage, avenue, means of access, approach, perron, adit, entrance; artery, lane, alley, aisle, lobby, corridor, cloister; back- door, -stairs; secret passage; covert-way.

road-, path-, stair-way; thoroughfare; highway, pike, turnpike, trail, parkway, *boulevard*; turnpike –, royal –, coach- road; broad –, King's –, Queen's- highway; beaten -track, – path; horse –, bridle- road, – track, – path; pathway; walk, *trottoir*, foot-path, pavement, flags, side-walk; by –, cross- -road, – path, – way; cut; short -cut etc. (*mid-course*) 628; *carrefour*; private –, occupation- road; highways and byways; rail-, tram-road, -way; funicular, ropeway, causeway; defile, cutting; canal etc. (*conduit*) 350; street etc. (*abode*) 189.

Adv. how; in what -way, – manner; by what mode; so, in this way, after this fashion, on these lines.

one way or another, anyhow; somehow or other etc. (*instrumentality*) 631; by way of; *viâ*; *in transitu* etc. 270; on the high road to.

Phr. *hae tibi erunt artes.*

628. Mid-course.—N. middle-, mid-course; moderation, mean etc. 29; middle etc. 68; *juste milieu*, *mezzo termine*, golden mean, *aurea mediocritas*.

straight etc. (*direct*) 278 -course, – path; short –, cross- cut; short- circuit; great circle sailing.

neutrality; half –, half and half- measures; compromise.

V. keep in –, steer –, preserve- -a middle, – an even- course; go straight etc. (*direct*) 278.

go half way, compromise, make a compromise.

Adj. neutral, average, even, impartial, moderate, straight etc. (*direct*) 278.

629. Circuit.—N. circuit, round-about way, digression, divagation, *détour*, circum-ambience, -ambulation, bendibus, *ambages*, loop; winding etc. (*circuition*) 311; zigzag etc. (*deviation*) 279.

V. perform –, make- a circuit; go -round about, – out of one's way; make a *détour*; meander etc. (*deviate*) 27; circumambulate.

lead a pretty dance; beat about, – the bush; make two bites of a cherry.

adj. circuitous, indirect, round-about; zig-zag etc. (*deviating*) 279; circum-ambient, -ambulatory.

Adv. by -a side wind, – an indirect course; in a roundabout way; from pillar to post.

630. Requirement.—N. requirement, need, wants, necessities; necessaries, – of life; stress, exigency, pinch, *sine quâ non*, matter of necessity; case of -need, – life or death.

needfulness, essentiality, necessity, indispensability, urgency, prerequisite.

requisition etc. (*request*) 765, (*exaction*) 741; run upon; demand –, call- for.

desideratum etc. (*desire*) 865; want etc. (*deficiency*) 640.

charge, claim, command, injunction, requisition, mandate, order, *ultimatum*.

V. require, need, want, have occasion for, entail; not be able to -do without, – dispense with; prerequire.

render necessary, necessitate, create a necessity for, call for, put in requisition; make a requisition etc. (*ask for*) 765, (*demand*) 741.

stand in need of; lack etc. 640; desiderate; desire etc. 865; be -necessary etc. *adj.*

Adj. required etc. *v.*; requisite, needful,

necessary, imperative, essential, indispensable, prerequisite; called for; in -demand, – request.

urgent, exigent, pressing, instant, crying, absorbing.

in want of; destitute of etc. 640.

Adv. *ex necessitate rei* etc. (*necessarily*) 601; of –, out of stern- necessity; at a pinch.

Phr. there is no time to lose; it cannot be - spared, – dispensed with.

631. Instrumentality.—N. instrumentality; aid etc. 707; subservien-ce, -cy; mediation, intervention, -mediacy, medium, inter-medium, -mediary, vehicle, hand; agency etc. 170.

minister, handmaid, servant, slave, maid, valet; midwife, *accoucheur*, obstetrician; go-between; cat's paw; stepping-stone.

key; master –, pass –, latch- key; 'open seseme;' passport, *passe partout*, safe-conduct; influence.

instrument etc. 633; expedient etc. (*plan*) 626; means etc. 632.

V. subserve, minister, tend, mediate, intervene; come –, go- between, interpose; pull the strings; be -instrumental etc. *adj.*; pander to.

Adj. instrumental, useful etc. 644; ministerial, subservient, mediatorial; inter-mediate, -vening; conducive.

Adv. through, by, *per*; where-, there-, here by; by the -agency etc. 170- of; by dint of; by –, in- virtue of; through the -medium etc. *n.*- of; along with; on the shoulders of; by means of etc. 632; by –, with- -the aid etc. (*assistance*) 707- of.

per fas et nefas, by fair means or foul; somehow, – or other; by hook or by crook.

632. Means.—N. means, resources, revenue, wherewithal, ways and means, income; capital etc. (*money*) 800; stock in trade etc. 636; provision etc. 637; a shot in the locker; appliances etc. (*machinery*) 633; means and appliances; conveniences; cards to play; expendients etc. (*measures*) 626; two strings to one's bow; sheet anchor etc. (*safety*) 666; aid etc. 707; medium etc. 631.

V. find –, have –, possess- means etc. *n.*; provide the wherewithal.

Adj. instrumental etc. 631; mechanical etc. 633.

Adv. by means of, with; by -what, – all, – any, – some- means; where-, here-, there-with; wherewithal.

how etc. (*in what manner*) 627; through etc. (*by the instrumentality of*) 631; with –, by- the aid etc. (*assistance*) 707- of; by the -agency etc. 170- of.

633. Instrument.—N. machinery, mechanism, engineering.

instrument, organ, tool, implement, utensil, contrivance, machine, motor, engine, lathe, gin, mill, pump.

gear; tack-le, -ling, trice, rigging, gear, apparatus, appliances; plant, *matériel*; harness, trappings, fittings, accouterments; equip-ment, -age; appointments, furniture, upholstery; chattels; paraphernalia etc. (*belongings*) 780; *impedimenta.*

mechanical powers; lever, -age; mechanical advantage; crow, -bar; handspike, gavelock, jemmy, arm, limb, wing; oar, paddle; pulley, sheave; parbuckle; wheel and axle; wheel-, clock-work; wheels within wheels; piñion, gear wheel, spur –, bevel-gearing, chains, belting, crank, winch, capstan, windlass, crane, derrick, hoist, lift etc. 307; cam; pedal; wheel etc. (*rotation*) 312; inclined plane; wedge; screw; jack; spring, mainspring.

handle, hilt, haft, shaft, heft, shank, blade, trigger, tiller, helm, treadle, key; turnscrew, screwdriver, spanner, wrench.

hammer etc. (*impulse*) 276; edge tool etc. (*cut*) 253; borer etc. 262; vice, teeth etc. (*hold*) 781; nail, rope etc. (*join*) 45; peg etc. (*hang*) 214; support etc. 215; spoon etc. (*vehicle*) 272; arms etc. 727; oar etc. (*navigation*) 267.

Adj. instrumental etc. 631; mechanical, machinal, automatic, self-acting; brachial.

634. Substitute.—N. substitute etc. 147; deputy etc. 759; proxy, alternative, understudy.

635. Materials.—N. material, raw material, stuff, stock, staple; building materials, bricks and mortar; metal; stone; clay, brick; crockery etc. 384; compo, -sition; reinforced –, ferro-, concrete; cement; wood, ore, timber; gravel, cobbles, macadam, asphalt, tarmac.

materials; supplies, munition, fuel, grist, household stuff; *pabulum* etc. (*food*) 298; ammunition etc. (*arms*) 727; contingents; relay, reinforcement; baggage etc. (*personal property*) 780; means etc. 632.

Adj. raw etc. (*unprepared*) 674; wooden etc. *n.*

636. Store.—N. stock, fund, mine, vein, lode, quarry; spring; fount, -ain; well, -spring; milch-cow.

stock in trade, supply; heap etc. (*collection*) 72; treasure; reserve, *corps de réserve*, reserve fund, nest-egg, savings, *bonne bouche*.

crop, harvest, mow, vintage; yield, product, gleanings.

store, accumulation, hoard, rick, stack; lumber; relay etc. (*provision*) 637.

store-house, -room, -closet; depository, *dépôt*, *cache*, safe deposit, vault, pantechnicon, repository, -servatory, -pertory; *repertorium*; promptuary, warehouse, *entrepôt*, magazine, dump, buttery, larder, pantry, panary, lanary, still-room, spence; crib, garner, granary, silo, barn; bunker; thesaurus; bank etc. (*treasury*) 802; armoury; arsenal; dock; gallery, museum, library, conservatory, hot-house; manag-ery, -erie, aquarium, zoological gardens.

reservoir, cistern, tank, sump, pond, mill-pond; gasometer.

budget, quiver, bandolier, portfolio; coffer etc. (*receptacle*) 191.

conservation; storing etc. *v.*; storage.

dictionary etc. 562; list etc. 86.

V. store; put –, lay –, set- by; stow away; set –, lay- apart; store –, hoard –, treasure –, lay –, heap –, put –, garner –, save- up; *cache*; accumulate, amass, hoard, fund, garner, save, bank.

conserve, reserve; keep –, hold- back; husband, – one's resources.

deposit; stow, stack, load, dump; harvest; heap, collect etc. 72; lay -in, – down, – by, store etc. *adj.*; keep, file [papers] lay in etc. (*provide*) 637; preserve etc. 670; put by for a rainy day.

Adj. stored etc. *v.*; in -store, – reserve, – ordinary; spare, supernumerary.

637. Provision.—N. provision, supply; grist, – to the mill; subvention etc. (*aid*) 707; resources etc. (*means*) 632.

provising etc. *v.*; purveyance; reinforcement; commissary, commissariat.

rations; iron –, emergency- rations; provender etc. (*food*) 298; *viaticum*; ensilage.

caterer, purveyor, commissary, quartermaster, steward, housekeeper, manciple, feeder, batman, victualler, storekeeper, grocer, provision merchant, green-, grocer, *comprador*, *restaurateur*; sutler etc. (*merchant*) 797; innkeeper, publican, confectioner, baker, butcher, wine merchant, vintner.

V. provide; make -provision, – due provision for; lay in, – a stock, – a store.

sup-ply, -peditate; furnish; find, – one in; arm.

cater, victual, provision, purvey, forage; beat up for; stock, – with; make good, replenish; fill, – up; recruit, feed, ration.

have in -store, – reserve; keep, – by one, – on foot; have to fall back upon; store etc. 636; provide against a rainy day etc. (*economy*) 817.

638. Waste.—N. consumption, expenditure, exhaustion; dispersion etc. 73; ebb; leakage etc. (*exudation*) 295; loss etc. 776; wear and tear; waste; prodigality etc. 818; misuse etc. 679; wasting etc. *v.*; rubbish etc. (*useless*) 645.

mountain in labor.

v. spend, expend, use, consume, swallow up, exhaust, deplete; impoverish; spill, drain, empty; disperse etc. 73.

cast –, throw –, fling –, fritter- away; burn the candle at both ends, waste; squander etc. 818.

'waste its sweetness on the desert air;' cast -one's bread upon the waters, – pearls before swine; employ a steam engine to crack a nut, waste powder and shot, break a butterfly on a wheel; labor in vain etc. (*useless*) 645; cut a whetstone with a razor, pour water into a sieve; tilt at windmills.

leak etc. (*run out*) 295; run to waste; ebb; melt away, run dry, dry up.

Adj. wasted etc. *v.*; at a low ebb.

wasteful etc. (*prodigal*) 818; penny wise and pound foolish.

Phr. *magno conatu magnas nugas; le jeu n'en vaut pas la chandelle.*

639. Sufficiency.—N. sufficiency, adequacy, enough, withal, *quantum sufficit*, satisfaction, competence; no less.

mediocrity etc. (*average*) 29.

fill; fullness etc (*completeness*) 52; plen-itude, -ty; abundance; copiousness etc. *adj.*; amplitude, galore, lots, profusion; full measure; 'good measure pressed down, shaken together and running over.'

luxuriance etc. (*fertility*) 168; affluence etc. (*wealth*) 803; fat of the land; 'a land flowing with milk and honey;' cornucopia; horn of -plenty, – Amalthaea; mine etc. (*stock*) 636.

outpouring; flood etc. (*great quantity*) 31; tide etc. (*river*) 348; repletion etc. (*reduncance*) 641; satiety etc. 869; rich man etc. 803.

V. be -sufficient etc. *adj.*; suffice, do, just do, satisfy, pass muster; have -enough etc. *n.*; eat –, drink –, have- one's fill; roll –, swim- in; wallow in etc. (*superabundance*) 641.

abound, exuberate, teem, flow, stream, rain, shower down; pour, – in; swarm; bristle with.

render -sufficient etc. *adj.*; replenish etc. (*fill*) 52.

Adj. sufficient, enough, adequate, up to the mark, commensurate, competent, satisfactory, valid, tangible.

measured; moderate etc. (*temperate*) 953.

full etc. (*complete*) 52; ample; plen-ty, -tiful, -teous; plenty as blackberries; copious, abundant; abounding etc. *v.*; replete, enough and to spare, flush; choke-full; well-stocked, -provided; liberal; unstint-ed, -ing; stintless; without stint; un-sparing, -measured; lavish etc. 641; wholesale.

rich, luxuriant etc. (*fertile*) 168; affluent etc. (*wealthy*) 803; wantless; big with etc. (*pregnant*) 161.

un-exhausted, -wasted; exhaustless, inexhaustible.

Adv. sufficiently, amply etc. *adj.*; full; in -abundance etc. *n.*; with no sparing hand; to one's heart's content, *ad libitum*, without stint.

Phr. cut and come again.

640. Insufficiency.—N. insufficiency; inadequa-cy, -teness; incompetence etc. (*impotence*) 158; deficiency etc. (*incompleteness*) 53; imperfection etc. 651; shortcoming etc. 304; paucity; stint; scantiness etc. (*smallness*) 32; none to spare; bare subsistence.

scarcity, dearth; want, need, lack, poverty, exigency; inanition, starvation, famine, drought.

dole, pittance, mite; short -allowance, – commons; half-rations; banyan –, fast- day, Lent.

emptiness, poorness etc. *adj.*; depletion, vacancy, flaccidity; ebb-tide; low water; 'a beggarly account of empty boxes;' indigence etc. (*poverty*) 804; insolvency etc. (*non-payment*) 808; poor man etc. 804; bankrupt etc. 808.

V. be -insufficient etc. *adj.*; not -suffice etc. 639; come short of etc. 304; run dry.

want, lack, need, require; *caret*; be in want etc. (*poor*) 804; live from hand to mouth.

render- insufficient etc. *adj.*; drain of resources; impoverish etc. (*waste*) 638; stint etc. (*begrudge*) 819; put on short -commons, – allowance.

do -insufficiently etc. *adv.*; scotch the snake.

Adj. insufficient, inadequate; too -little etc. 32; not -enough etc. 639; unequal to; incompetent etc. (*impotent*) 158; 'weighed in the balance and found wanting;' perfunctory etc. (*neglect*) 460; deficient etc. (*incomplete*) 53; wanting etc. *v.*; imperfect etc. 651; ill-furnished, -provided, -stored, -off.

slack, at a low ebb; empty, vacant, bare; short –, out –, destitute –, devoid –, bereft etc. 789 –, denuded- of; dry, drained.

un -provided, -supplied, -furnished; unreplenished, -fed; un-stored, -treasured; empty-handed.

meager, poor, thin, scrimp, sparing, spare, stinted, stunted; skimpy; starv-ed, -eling; half-starved, emaciated, famine-stricken, famished, underfed, undernourished; jejune.

scant etc. (*small*) 32; scarce; not to be had, – for love or money, – at any price; scurvy; stingy etc. 819; at the end of one's tether; without - resources etc. 632; in want etc. (*poor*) 804; in debt etc. 806.

Adv. insufficiently etc. *adj.*; in default –, for want- of; failing.

641. Redundance.—N. redundance; too - much, – many; superabundance, -fluity, -fluence, -saturation; nimiety, transcendency, exuberance, profuseness; profusion etc. (*plenty*) 639; repletion, enough in all conscience, *satis superque*, lion's share; more than -enough etc. 639; plethora, engorgement, congestion, load, surfeit, sickener; turgescence etc. (*expansion*) 194; over-dose, -measure, supply, -flow, inundation etc. (*water*) 348; *avalanche*.

accumulation etc. (*store*) 636; heap etc. 72; drug, – in the market; glut; crowd; burden.

excess; sur-, over-plus, epact; margin; remainder etc. 40; duplicate; surplusage; expletive; work of –, supererogation; *bonus*, *bonanza*.

luxury; intemperance etc. 954; extravagance etc. (*prodigality*) 818; exorbitance, lavishment.

pleonasm etc. (*diffuseness*) 573; too many irons in the fire; embarassment of riches; money to burn.

V. super-, over-abound; know no bounds, swarm; meet one at every turn; creep –, bristle- with; overflow; run –, flow –, well –, brim-over; run riot; over-run, -stock, -lay, -charge, -dose, -feed, -burden, -load, -do, -whelm, -shoot the mark etc. (*go beyond*) 303; surcharge, supersaturate, gorge, glut, load, drench, whelm, inundate, deluge, flood; drug, – the market.

choke, cloy, accloy, suffocate; pile up, lay it on, – with a trowel, lay on thick; impregnate with; lavish etc. (*squander*) 818.

send –, carry- coals to Newcastle, – owls to Athens; teach one's grandmother to suck eggs; *pisces natare docere*; kill the slain, 'gild refined gold,' 'paint the lily;' butter one's bread on both sides, put butter upon bacon; employ a steam-engine to crack a nut etc. (*waste*) 638.

exaggerate etc. 549; wallow in; roll in etc. (*plenty*) 639; remain on one's hands, hang heavy on hand, go a begging.

Adj. redundant; too -much, – many; exuberant, inordinate, superabundant, excessive, overmuch, replete, profuse, lavish; prodigal etc. 818; exorbitant; overweening; extravagant; overcharged etc. *v.*; supersaturated, drenched, overflowing; running -over, – to waste, – down.

crammed –, filled- to overflowing; gorged, stuffed, ready to burst; dropsical, turgid, plethoric, full-blooded; obese etc. 194; voluminous.

superfluous, unnecessary, needless, supervacaneous, uncalled for, to spare, in excess; over and above etc. (*remainder*) 40; *de trop*; adscititious etc. (*additional*) 37; supernumerary etc. (*reserve*) 636; on one's hands, spare, duplicate, supererogatory, expletive; *un peu fort*.

Adj. over, too, over and above; over –, too-much; too far; without –, beyond – out of- measure; with ... to spare; over head and ears; up to one's eyes, – ears; *extra*; beyond the mark etc. (*transcursion*) 303; over one's head.

Phr. It never rains but it pours.

642. Importance.—N. importance, consequence, moment, prominence, consideration, mark, materialness.

import, significance, concern; emphasis, interest.

greatness etc. 31; superiority etc. 33; notability etc. (*repute*) 873; weight etc. (*influence*) 175; value etc. (*goodness*) 648; usefulness etc. 644.

gravity, seriousness, solemnity; no -joke, – laughing matter; pressure, urgency, stress; matter of life and death.

memorabilia, *notabilia*, great doings; red-letter day.

great -thing, – point; main chance, 'the be all and end all,' cardinal point, outstanding feature, substance, gist etc. (*essence*) 5; sum and substance, *gravamen*, head and front, important –, principal –, prominent –, essential- part; half the battle; *sine quâ non*; breath of one's nostrils etc. (*life*) 359; cream, salt, core, kernel, heart, nucleus; key, -note, -stone; corner stone; trumpcard etc. (*device*) 626; salient points.

top-sawyer, first fiddle, *prima donna*, chief, bigwig; triton among the minnows.

V. be -important etc. *adj.*, – somebody, – something; import, signify, matter, be an object; carry weight etc. (*influence*) 175; make a figure etc. (*repute*) 873; be in the ascendant, come to the front, lead the way, take the lead, play first fiddle, throw all else into the shade; lie at the root of; deserve –, merit –, be worthy- -of notice, – regard, – consideration.

attach –, ascribe –, give- importance etc. *n.*- to; value, care for; set store -upon, – by; mark etc. 550; mark with a white stone, underline; write –, put –, print- in -italics, – capitals, – large letters, – large type, – letters of gold; accentuate, emphasize, lay stress on.

make -a fuss, – a stir, – a piece of work, – much ado- about; make -of, – much of.

Adj. important; of -importance etc. *n.*; momentous, material; to the point; not to be -overlooked, – despised, – sneezed at; egregious; weighty etc. (*influential*) 175; of note etc. (*repute*) 873; notable, prominent, salient, signal; memorable, remarkable; worthy of -remark, – notice; never to be forgotten; stirring, eventful.

grave, serious, earnest, noble, grand, solemn, impressive, commanding, imposing.

urgent, pressing, critical, instant.

paramount, essential, vital, all-absorbing, radical, cardinal, chief, main, prime, primary, principal, leading, capital, foremost, overruling; of vital etc. importance.

in the front rank, first-rate, A1; superior etc. 33; considerable etc. (*great*) 31; marked etc. *v.*; rare etc. 137.

significant, telling, trenchant, emphatic, pregnant; *tanti*.

Adv. materially etc. *adj.*; in the main; above all, *par excellence*, to crown all.

643. Unimportance.—N. unimportance, insignificance, nothingness, immateriality.

triviality, trivia, fribble, levity, frivolity; paltriness etc. *adj.*; poverty; smallness etc. 32; vanity etc. (*uselessness*) 645; matter of -indifference etc. 866; no object; side issue.

nothing, – to signify, – worth speaking of, – particular, – to boast of, – to speak of; small –, no great –, trifling etc. *adj.*-matter; mere -joke, – nothing; hardly –, scarcely- anything; nonentity, cipher, figurehead; no great shakes, *peu de chose*; child's play; small beer.

toy, plaything, popgun, paper pellet, gimcrack, geegaw, bauble, trinket, *bagatelle*, kickshaw, knicknack, whim-wham, trifle, 'trifles light as air.'

trumpery, trash, rubbish, stuff, *fatras*, frippery; 'leather or prunello;' chaff, drug, froth, bubble, smoke, cobweb; weed; refuse etc. (*inutility*) 645; scum etc. (*dirt*) 653.

joke, jest, snap of the fingers; fudge etc. (*unmeaning*) 517; fiddlestick, – end; pack of nonsense, mere farce.

straw, pin, fig, continental, button, rush; bulrush, feather, halfpenny, farthing, brass farthing, doit, peppercorn, jot, rap, pinch of snuff, old song.

minutiae, details, minor details, small fry; dust in the balance, feather in the scale, drop in the ocean, flea-bite, molehill; fingle-fangle.

nine days' wonder, *ridiculus mus*; flash in the pan etc. (*impotence*) 158; much ado about nothing etc. (*overestimation*) 482; storm in a teacup.

V. be -unimportant etc. *adj.*; not -matter etc. 642; go for –, matter –, signify- -little, – nothing, – little or nothing; not matter a -straw etc. *n.*

make light of etc. (*underestimate*) 483; catch at straws etc. (*overestimate*) 482.

Adj. unimportant; of -little, – small, – no- -account, – importance etc. 642; immaterial; un-, non-essential; not vital; irrelevant, incidental, indifferent.

subordinate etc. (*inferior*) 34; *médiocre* etc. (*average*) 29; passable, fair, respectable, tolerable, commonplace; uneventful, mere, common; ordinary etc. (*habitual*) 613; inconsiderable, so-so, insignificant, inappreciable, nugatory.

trifling, trivial; slight, slender, light, flimsy, frothy, idle; puerile etc. (*foolish*) 499; airy, shallow; weak etc. 160; powerless etc. 158; frivolous, petty, niggling; pid-, ped-dling; fribble, inane, ridiculous, farcical; fini-cal, -kin; fiddle-faddle, namby-pamby, wishy-washy, milk and water.

poor, paltry, pitiful; contemptible etc. (*contempt*) 930; sorry, mean, meager, shabby, miserable, wretched, vile, scrubby, scrannel, weedy, niggardly, scurvy, putid, beggarly, worthless, twopenny-half penny, cheap, trashy, catchpenny, gimcrack, trumpery, one-horse; toy.

not worth -the pains, – while, – mentioning, – speaking of, – a thought, – a curse, – a straw, – rap etc. *n.*; beneath –, unworthy of- -notice, – regard, – consideration, – contempt; *de lanâ caprinâ*; vain etc. (*useless*) 645.

Adv. slightly etc. *adj.*; rather, somewhat, pretty well, fairly well, tolerably.

for aught one cares.

Int. no matter! pish! tush! tut! pshaw! pugh! pooh, -pooh! fudge! bosh! humbug! fiddle-stick, – end! fiddlededee! never mind! *n'importe!* what -signifies, – matter, – boots it, – of that, – 's the odds! a fig for! stuff ! nonsense! stuff and nonsense!

Phr. *magno conatu magnas nugas*; *le jeu n'en vaut pas la chandelle*; it -matters not, – does not signify; it is of no -consequence, – importance.

644. Utility.—N. utility; usefulness etc. *adj.*; efficacy, efficiency, adequacy; service, use, stead, avail; help etc. (*aid*) 707; applicability etc. *adj.*; subservience etc. (*instrumentality*) 631; function etc. (*business*) 625; value; worth etc. (*goodness*) 648; money's worth; productiveness etc. 168; *cui bono* etc. (*intention*) 620; utilization etc. (*use*) 677; step in the right direction.

common weal, public good; utilitarianism etc. (*philanthropy*) 910.

V. be -useful etc. *adj.*; avail, serve; subserve etc. (*be instrumental to*) 631; conduce etc. (*tend*) 176; answer –, serve- -one's turn, – a purpose.

act a part etc. (*action*) 680; perform –, discharge- -a function etc. 625; do –, render- -a service, – good service, – yeoman's service; bestead, stand one in good stead; be the making of; help etc. 707.

bear fruit etc. (*produce*) 161; bring grist to the mill; profit, remunerate; benefit etc. (*do good*) 648.

find one's -account, – advantage- in; reap the benefit of etc. (*be better for*) 658.

render useful etc. (*use*) 677.

Adj. useful; of -use etc. *n.*; serviceable, usable, proficuous, good for; subservient etc. (*instrumental*) 631; conducive etc. (*tending*) 176; subsidiary etc. (*helping*) 707.

advantageous etc. (*beneficial*) 648; profitable, gainful, remunerative, worth one's salt; in-, valuable; prolific etc. (*productive*) 168.

adequate; ef-ficient, -ficacious; effect-ive, -ual; practicable, expedient etc. 646.

applicable, available, ready, handy, at hand, tangible; commodious, adaptable; of all work.

Adv. usefully etc. *adj.*; *pro bono publico*.

645. Inutility.—N. inutility; uselessness etc. *adj.*; inefficacy, futility; inep-, inap-titude; unsubservience; inadequacy etc. (*insufficiency*) 640; inefficiency etc. (*incompetence*) 158; unskilfulness etc. 699; disservice; unfruitfulness etc. (*unproductiveness*) 169; labor -in vain, – lost, – of Sisyphus; lost -trouble, – labor; work of Penelope; sleeveless errand, wild goose chase, mere farce.

tautology etc. (*repetition*) 104; supererogation etc. (*redundance*) 641.

vanitas vanitatum, vanity, inanity, worthlessness, nugacity; triviality etc. (*unimportance*) 643.

caput mortuum, waste paper, dead letter; blunt tool.

litter, rubbish, lumber, odds and ends, cast-off clothes; button-top; shoddy; rags, orts, trash, refuse, sweepings, scourings, off-scourings, dross, slag, waste, rubble, dottle, drast, *débris*; stubble, leavings; broken meat; dregs etc. (*dirt*) 653; weeds, tares; rubbish heap, dust hole; *rudera*, deads.

fruges consumere natus etc. (*drone*) 683.

V. be -useless etc. *adj.*; go a begging etc. (*redundant*) 641; fail etc. 732.

seek –, strive- after impossibilities; use vain efforts, labor in vain, roll the stone of Sisyphus, beat the air, lash the waves; *battre l'eau avec un bâton*, *donner un coup d'épée dans l'eau*, fish in the air, milk the ram, drop a bucket into an empty well, sow the sand; bay the moon; preach –, speak- to the winds; whistle jigs to a milestone; kick against the pricks, *se battre contre des moulins*; lock the stable door when the steed is stolen etc. (*too late*) 135; hold a farthing candle to the sun; cast pearls before swine etc. (*waste*) 638; carry coals to Newcastle etc. (*redundance*) 641; wash a blackamoor white etc. (*impossible*) 471.

render -useless etc. *adj.*; dis-mantle, -mast, -mount, -qualify, -able; unrig; cripple, lame etc. (*injure*) 659; spike guns, clip the wings; put out of gear.

Adj. useless, inutile, inefficacious, futile, unavailing, bootless, inoperative etc. 158; inadequate etc. (*insufficient*) 640; in-, un- subservient: inept, inefficient etc. (*impotent*) 158; of no -avail etc. (*use*) 644; ineffectual etc. (*failure*) 732; incompetent etc. (*unskilful*) 699; 'stale, flat and unprofitable;' superfluous etc. (*redundant*) 641; dispensable; thrown away etc. (*wasted*) 638; abortive etc. (*immature*) 674.

worth-, value-less; unsaleable; not worth a straw etc. (*trifling*) 643; dear at any price.

vain, empty, inane; gain-, profit-, fruit-less; unserviceable, -profitable; ill-spent; unproductive etc. 169; *hors de combat*; barren, sterile, impotent, unproductive; effete, past work etc. (*impaired*) 659; obsolete etc. (*old*) 124; fit for the -dust-hole, – wastepaper basket; good for nothing; of no earthly use; not worth -having, – powder and shot; leading to no end, uncalled for; un-necessary, -needed, superfluous.

Adv. uselessly etc. *adj.*; to -little, – no, – little or no- purpose.

Int. *cui bono?* what's the good!

646. Expedience. [Specific subservience.]—**N.** expedien-ce, -cy; desirableness, -bility etc. *adj.*; fitness etc. (*agreement*) 23; utility etc. 644; propriety; advantage; opportunism, pragmatism.

high time etc. (*occasion*) 134.

V. be -expedient etc. *adj.*; suit etc. (*agree*) 23; befit; suit –, befit- the -time, – season, – occasion.

conform etc. 82.

Adj. expedient; desir-, advis-, accept-able; convenient; worth while, meet; fit, -ting; due, proper, eligible, seemly, becoming; befitting etc. *v.*; opportune etc. (*in season*) 134; *in loco*; suitable etc. (*accordant*) 23; applicable etc. (*useful*) 644; practical, effective, pragmatical; suitable, handy.

Adv. in the right place; conveniently etc. *adj.*; in the nick of time.

Phr. *operae pretium est.*

647. Inexpedience.—N. enexpedien-ce, -cy; undesira-bleness, -bility etc. *adj.*; discommodity, impropriety; unfitness etc. (*disagreement*) 24; inutility etc. 645; inconvenience, inadvisability; disadvantage.

V. be -inexpedient etc. *adj.*; come amiss etc. (*disagree*) 24; embarrass etc. (*hinder*) 706; put to inconvenience; pay too dear for one's whistle.

Adj. inexpedient, undesirable; un-, in-advisable; objectionable; troublesome, in-apt, -eligible, -admissable, -convenient; in-, dis-commodious; disadvantageous; inappropriate, unsuitable, unfit etc. (*inconsonant*) 24.

ill-contrived, -advised; unsatsifactory; unprofitable etc., unsubservient etc. (*useless*) 645; inopportune etc. (*unseasonable*) 135; out of –, in the wrong- place; improper, unseemly.

clumsy, awkward; cum-brous, -bersome; lumbering, unwieldy, hulky; unmanageable etc. (*impracticable*) 704; impedient (*in the way*) 706.

unnecessary etc. (*redundant*) 641.

Phr. it will never do.

648. Goodness. [Capability of producing good. Good qualities.]—**N.** goodness etc. *adj.*; excellence, merit; virtue etc. 944; value, worth, price.

super-excellence, -eminence; superiority etc. 33; perfection etc. 650; *coup de maître*; master-piece, *chef d'oeuvre*, prime, flower, cream, *élite*, pick, A1, none such, *nonpareil*, *crême de la crême*, flower of the flock, cock of the roost, salt of the earth; champion.

tid-bit; gem, – of the first water; *bijou*, precious stone, jewel, pearl, diamond, ruby, brilliant, treasure; good thing; *rara avis*, one in a thousand.

beneficence etc. 906; good man etc. 948.

V. be -beneficial etc. *adj.*; produce –, do- -good etc. 618; profit etc. (*be of use*) 644; benefit; confer a -benefit etc. 618.

be the making of, do a world of good, make a man of.

produce a good effect; do a good turn, confer an obligation; improve etc. 658.

do no harm, break no bones.

be -good etc. *adj.*; excel, transcend etc. (*be superior*) 33; bear away the bell.

stand the -proof, – test; pass -muster, – an examination.

challenge comparison, vie, emulate, rival.

Adj. harm-, hurt-less; unobnoxious; in-nocuous, -nocent, -offensive.

beneficial, valuable, of value; serviceable etc. (*useful*) 644; advantageous, profitable, edifying; salutary etc. (*healthful*) 656.

favorable, propitious etc. (*hopegiving*) 858; fair.

good, – as gold; excellent; better; superior etc. 33; above par; nice, fine; genuine etc. (*true*) 494.

best, choice, select, picked, elect, eximious, *recherché*, rare, priceless; unpara-goned, -lleled etc. (*supreme*) 33; superlatively etc. 33- good; super-fine, -excellent; bonzer; of the first water; first-rate, -class; high-wrought; exquisite, very best, crack, prime, tip-top, gilt-edged, capital, cardinal; standard etc. (*perfect*) 650: inimitable

admirable, estimable; praiseworthy etc. (*approve*) 931; pleasing etc. 829; *couleur de rose*, precious, of great price; costly etc. (*dear*) 814; worth -its weight in gold, – a king's ransom;

matchless, peerless, invaluable, inestimable, precious as the apple of the eye.

tolerable etc. (*not very good*) 651; up to the mark, un-exceptionable, -objectionable; satisfactory, tidy.

in -good, – fair- condition; fresh; unspoiled; sound etc. (*perfect*) 650.

Adv. beneficially etc. *adj.*; well etc. 618.

649. Badness. [Capability of producing evil. Bad qualities.]—**N.** hurtfulness etc. *adj.*; virulence.

evil doer etc. 913; bane etc. 663; plague-spot etc. (*insalubrity*) 657; evil star, ill wind; snake in the grass, skeleton in the closet; *amari aliquid*, thorn in the side; Jonah, jinx, hoodoo.

malignity; malevolence etc. 907; tender mercies [ironically].

ill-treatment, annoyance, molestation, abuse, oppression, persecution, outrage; misusage etc. 679; injury etc. (*damage*) 659.

badness etc. *adj.*; peccancy, abomination; painfulness etc. 830; pestilence etc. (*disease*) 655; guilt etc. 947; depravity etc. 945.

V. be -hurtful etc. *adj.*; cause –, produce –, inflict –, work –, do- evil etc. 619; damnify, endamage, hurt, harm, scathe; injure etc. (*damage*) 659; pain etc. 830.

wrong, aggrieve, oppress, persecute; trample –, tread –, bear hard –, put-upon; overburden; weigh -down, – heavy on; victimize; run down; molest etc. 830.

maltreat, abuse; ill-use, -treat; thwart, buffet, bruise, scratch, maul; smite etc. (*scourge*) 972; do -violence, – harm, – a mischief; stab, pierce, outrage.

do –, make- mischief; bring –, get- into trouble.

destroy etc. 162.

Adj. hurt-, harm-, scath-, bane-, bale-ful; injurious, deleterious, detrimental, noxious, pernicious, mischievous, full of mischief, mischief-making, malefie, malignant, nocuous, noisome; prejudicial; dis-serviceable, advantageous; wide-wasting.

unlucky, sinister; obnoxious, untoward, disastrous.

oppressive, burdensome, onerous; malign etc. (*malevolent*) 907.

corrupting etc. (corrupt etc. 659) virulent, venomous, envenomed, corrosive; poisonous etc. (*morbific*) 657; deadly etc. (*killing*) 361; destructive etc. (*destroying*) 162; inauspicious etc. 859.

bad, ill, arrant, as bad bad can be, dreadful; horrid, -rible; dire; rank, peccant, foul, fulsome; rotten, – at the core.

vile, base, villainous; mean etc. (*paltry*) 643; injured etc., deteriorated etc. 659; unsatisfactory, exception, -able, indifferent; below par etc. (*imperfect*) 651; ill-contrived, -conditioned; wretched, sad, grievous, deplorable, lamentable; piti-ful, -able, woeful etc. (*painful*) 830.

evil, wrong; depraved etc. 945; shocking; reprehensible etc. (*disapprove*) 932.

hateful, – as a toad; abominable, detestable, execrable, cursed, accursed, confounded; damn-ed, -able; infernal; diabolic etc. (*malevolent*) 907.

inadvisable etc. (*inexpedient*) 647; unprofitable etc. (*useless*) 645; incompetent etc. (*unskilful*) 699; irremediable etc. (*hopeless*) 859.

Adv. badly etc. *adj.*; wrong, ill; to one's cost; where the shoe pinches.

Phr. bad is the best; the worst come to the worst.

650. Perfection.—N. perfection; perfectness etc. *adj.*; indefectibility; inpecc-ancy, -ability.

pink, *beau idéal*, phoenix, paragon; pink –, acme- of perfection; *ne plus ultra*; summit etc. 210.

cygne noir; philosopher's stone; chrysolite, Koh-i-noor, black tulip.

model, standard, pattern, mirror, admirable Chrichton; trump; very prince of.

master-piece, -stroke, super-excellence etc. (*goodness*) 648; transcendence etc. (*superiority*) 33.

V. be -perfect etc. *adj.*; transcend etc. (*be supreme*) 33.

bring to perfection, perfect, ripen, mature; consummate, complete etc. 729; put in trim etc. (*prepare*) 673; put the finishing touch to.

Adj. perfect, faultless, ideal; indefective, -ficient, -fectible; immaculate, spotless, impeccable; free from -imperfection etc. 651; un-blemished, -injured etc. 659; sound, – as a roach; in perfect condition; scathless, intact, harmless; seaworthy etc. (*safe*) 644; right as a trivet; *in seipso totus teres atque rotundus*; consummate etc. (*complete*) 52; finished etc. 729; complete in itself.

best etc. (*good*) 648; model, standard; inimitable, unparagoned, unparalleled etc. (*supreme*) 33; superhuman, divine; beyond all praise etc. (*approbation*) 931; *sans peur et sans reproche*.

Adj. to perfection, to the limit; perfectly etc. *adj.*; *ad unguem*; clean, – as a whistle.

651. Imperfection.—N. imperfection; imperfectness etc. *adj.*; deficiency; inadequacy etc. (*insufficiency*) 640; peccancy etc. (*badness*) 649; immaturity etc. 674.

fault, defect, weak point; screw loose; rift within the lute; fly in the ointment; flaw etc. (*break*) 70; gap etc. 198; twist etc. 243; taint, attainder; bar sinister, hole in one's coat; blemish etc. 848; weakness etc. 160; half-blood, touch of the tar brush; shortcoming etc. 304; drawback; seamy side.

mediocrity; no great -shakes, – catch; not much to boast of.

V. be -imperfect etc. *adj.*; have a -defect etc. *n.*; lie under a disadvantage; spring a leak.

not –, barely- pass muster; fall short etc. 304.

Adj. imperfect; not -perfect etc. 650; de-ficient, -fective; faulty, unsound, mutilated, tainted; out of -order, – tune; cracked, leaky; sprung; warped etc. (*distort*) 243; lame; injured etc. (*deteriorated*) 659; peccant etc. (*bad*) 649; frail etc. (*weak*) 160; inadequate etc. (*insufficient*) 640; crude etc. (*unprepared*) 674; incomplete etc. 53; found wanting; below par; shorthanded; below –, under- its full -strength, – complement.

indifferent, middling, ordinary, mediocre; average etc. 29; so-so; *così-così*, milk and water; tolerable, fair, passable; pretty -well, – good; rather –, moderately- good; good –, well-enough; decent; not -bad, – amiss; inobjectionable, admissable, bearable, only better than nothing.

secondary, inferior; second-rate, -best, one-horse.

Adv. almost etc.; to a limited extent, rather etc. 32; pretty, moderately; only; considering, all things considered, enough.

Phr. *surgit amari aliquid.*

652. Cleanness.—N. cleanness etc. *adj.*; purity; cleaning etc. *v.*; purification, defecation etc. *v.*; purgation, lustration; de-, abs-tersion; epuration, mundation, ablution, lavation, colature; disinfection etc. *v.*; drain-, sewerage.

lavatory, bath, -room; swimming pool, natatorium; public baths; hot –, cold –, Turkish –, Swedish –, Russian – vapor- bath; *hammam*, laundry, washhouse; washerwoman, laundress, laundryman; scavenger, cleaner, sweeper, goodie; crossing sweeper, white wings, dustman, sweep.

brush; broom, besom, carpet-sweeper, vacuum-cleaner, mop, squilgee, rake, shovel, sieve, riddle, screen, filter; scraper, strigil.

napkin, *serviette*, cloth, table-, carving-cloth, table-linen, napery, maukin, handkerchief, towel, sudary; doyley, doily, duster, sponge, mop, swab.

cover, drugget, mat, doormat.

soap, wash, lotion, detergent, cathartic, purgative; purifier etc. *v.*; dentifrice, tooth-powder, -paste; mouth wash; disinfectant.

V. be –, render- clean etc. *adj.*

clean, -se; mundify, rinse, wring, flush, full, wipe, mop, sponge, scour, swab, scrub, holystone, brush up.

wash, shampoo, lave, launder, buck; abs-, deterge; clear, purify; de-purate, -spumate, -fecate; purge, expurgate; Bowdlerize; elutriate, lixiviate, edulcorate, clarify, refine, rack; fil-ter, -trate; drain, strain.

disinfect, sterilize, pasteurize, fumigate, ventilate, deodorize; whitewash.

sift, winnow, screen, riddle, pick, weed, comb, rake, brush, sweep.

rout –, clear –, sweep etc.- out; make a clean sweep of.

Adj. clean, -ly; pure; immaculate; spot-, stain-, taint-less; without a stain, un-stained, -spotted, -soiled, -sullied, -tainted, -infected, -adulterated; aseptic; sweet, – as a nut.

neat, spruce, tidy, trim, gimp, clean as a new penny, like a cat in pattens; cleaned etc. *v.*; kempt.

Adv. neatly etc. *adj.*; clean as a whistle.

653. Uncleanness.—N. uncleanness etc. *adj.*; impurity; immundi-ty, -city; impurity etc. [of mind] 961.

defilement, contamination etc. *v.*; defedation; soil-ure, -iness; abomination; leaven; taint, -ure; fetor etc. 401.

decay; putre-scence, -faction; corruption; mold, must, mildew, dry-rot, *mucor*, rubigo, caries.

slovenry; slovenliness etc. *adj.*; squalor.

dowdy, drab, slut, malkin, slattern, sloven, slammerkin, scrub, draggletail, mudlark, dustman, sweep; beast.

dirt, filth, soil, slop; dust, cobweb, flue; smoke, soot, smudge, smut, grime, raff.

sordes, dregs, grounds, lees; sedi-, settle-ment; heel-tap; dross, -iness; mother, precipitate, *scoria*, ashes, cinders, recrement, slag; scum, froth.

hog-wash, swill, ditch-, dish-, bilge-water; rinsings, cheese-parings; sweepings etc. (*useless refuse*) 645; off-, out-scourings; off-scum; *caput mortuum*, *residuum*, sprue, feculence, clinker, draff; scurf, -iness; *exuviae*, morphew; fur, -fur; dandruff; tartar.

riffraff; vermin, louse, cootie, flea, bug.

mud, mire, quagmire, *alluvium*, silt, sludge, slime, slush, slosh.

spawn, offal, garbage, carrion; *excreta* etc. 299; slough, peccant humor, pus, matter, suppuration, *llenteria*; *feces*, excrement, ordure, dung; sew-, sewer-age; muck, coprolite; guano, manure, compost.

dunghill, *coluvies*, mixen, midden, bog, laystall, sink, w.c., water-, earth-closet, latrine, privy, iakes, John's, cess, -pool; sump, sough, *cloaca*, drain, sewer, common sewer; Cloacina; dust-hole.

sty, pig-sty, lair, den, Augean stable, sink of corruption; slum, rookery.

V. be –, become- unclean etc. *adj.*; rot, putrefy, fester, rankle, reek; stink etc. 401; mold, -er; go - bad etc. *adj.*

render -unclean etc. *adj.*; dirt, -y; soil, smoke, tarnish, slaver, spot, smear, daub, blot, blur, smudge, smutch, smirch; d-, dr-abble, -aggle; spatter, slubber; be-smear etc.; -mire, -slime, -grime, -foul; splash, stain, distain, maculate, sully, pollute, defile, debase, contaminate, taint, leaven; corrupt etc. (*injure*) 659; cover with -dust etc. *n.*; drabble in the mud.

wallow in the mire; slob-, slab-ber.

Adj. unclean, dirty, filthy, grimy; soiled etc. *v.*; not to be handled with kid gloves; dusty, snuffy, smutty, sooty, smoky; thick, turbid, dreggy; slimy.

uncleanly, slovenly, untidy, sluttish, dowdy, slatternly, draggletailed; un-combed, -kempt, -scoured, -swept, -wiped, -washed, -strained, -purified; squalid.

nasty, coarse, foul, impure, offensive, abominable, beastly, reeky, reechy; fetid etc. 401.

moldy, lentiginous, musty, mildewed, rusty, moth-eaten, mucid, rancid, bad, gone bad, touched, fusty, reasty, rotten, corrupt, tainted, high, fly-blown, maggoty; putr-id, -escent, -efied; purulent, carious, peccant, fec-al, -ulent; stercoraceous, excrementitious; scurfy, impetiginous; gory, bloody; rotting etc. *v.*; rotten as -a pear, – cheese.

crapulous etc. (*intemperate*) 954; gross etc. (*impure in mind*) 961.

654. Health.—N. health, sanity; soundness etc. *adj.*; vigor; good –, perfect –, excellent –, rude –, robust- health; bloom, *mens sana in corpore sano*; Hygeia; incorrupti-on, -bility; good state –, clean bill- of health, eupepsia.

V. be in health etc. *adj.*; bloom, flourish.

keep -body and soul together, – on one's legs; enjoy -good, – a good state of - health; have a clean bill of health.

return to health; recover etc. 660; get better etc. (*improve*) 658; take a -new, – fresh- lease of life; convalesce, be convalescent, recruit; restore to health; cure etc. (*restore*) 660.

Adj. health-y, -ful; in -health etc. *n.*; well, sound, strong, fit, hearty, hale, fresh, blooming, green, whole; florid, flush, hardy, stanch, staunch, brave, robust, vigorous, weather-proof; convalescent.

un-scathed, -injured, -maimed, -marred, -tainted; sound of wind and limb, safe and sound; without a scratch.

on one's legs; sound as a -roach, – bell; fresh as -a daisy, – a rose, – April; picture of health; bursting with health; fit as a fiddle; hearty as a buck; in -fine, – high- feather; in -good case, – full bloom; in fine fettle; pretty bobbish, tolerably well, as well as can be expected.

sanitary etc. (*health-giving*) 656; sanatory etc. (*remedial*) 662.

655. Disease.*—N. disease, illness, sickness etc. *adj.*; ailing etc. *v.*; 'the ills that flesh is heir to;' morb-idity, -osity; infirmity, ailment, indisposition; complaint, disorder, malady; distemper, -ature.

visitation, attack, seizure, stroke, fit, epilepsy, apoplexy, shock, shell-shock.

delicacy, loss of health, valetudinarianism, invalidism, cachexy; *cachexia*, atrophy, *marasmus*; indigestion, *dyspepsia*; decay etc. (*deterioration*) 659; malnutrition, decline, consumption, palsy, paralysis, prostration; occupational diseases.

taint, pollution, infection, contagion, septicity, septicaemia, blood poisoning, pyaemia, epi-, endemic; murrain, plague, pestilence, virus, pox.

sore, ulcer, abscess, fester, boil; pimple etc. (*swelling*) 250; carbuncle, gathering, whitlow, imposthume, peccant humor, issue; rot, canker, cancer, *carcinoma*, *caries*, mortification, corruption, gangrene, *sphacelus*, leprosy, eruption, rash, breaking out, venereal disease.

fever, calenture; inflammation.

fatal etc. (*hopeless*) 859- -disease etc.; dangerous illness, galloping consumption, churchyard cough; general breaking up, break up of the system.

[Disease of the mind] neurasthenia; idiocy etc. 499; insanity etc. 503.

martyr to disease; cripple; 'the halt, the lame and the blind;' valetudinar-y, -ian; invalid, patient, case; sick-room, -chamber, hospital etc. 662.

[Science of disease] path-, eti-, nos-ology, therapeutics, diagnosis, prognosis.

V. be -ill etc. *adj.*; ail, suffer, labor under, be affected with, complain of; droop, flag, languish, halt; sicken, peak, pine, waste away, fail, lose strength; gasp.

keep one's bed; feign sickness etc. (*falsehood*) 544; malinger.

lay -by, – up; take –, catch- -a disease etc. *n.*, – an infection; be stricken by; break out.

Adj. diseased; ailing etc. *v.*; ill, – of; taken ill, seized with; indisposed, unwell, sick, squeamish, poorly, seedy; affected –, afflicted- with illness; laid up, confined, bed-ridden, invalided, in hospital, on the sick list; out of -health, – sorts; valetudinary.

un-sound, -healthy; sickly, morbose, healthless, infirm, chlorotic, unbraced, drooping, flagging, lame, halt, crippled, halting.

morbid, tainted, vitiated, peccant, contaminated, poisoned, septic, tabid, mangy, leprous, cankered; rotten, – to, – at- the core; withered, palsied, paralytic, tuberculous; dyspeptic.

touched in the wind, broken-winded, spavined, gasping; *hors de combat* etc. (*useless*) 645.

weak-ly, -ened etc. (*weak*) 160; decrepit; decayed etc. (*deteriorated*) 659; incurable etc. (*hopeless*) 859; in declining health; cranky; in a bad way, in danger, prostrate; moribund etc. (*death*) 360.

morbific, epidemic etc. 657.

*Extended lists of different diseases are beyond the scope of this work.

656. Salubrity.—N. salubrity, salubriousness; healthiness etc. *adj.*

fine -air, – climate; eudiometer.

[Preservation of health] *hygiène*; valetudinarian, -ism, preventorium, sanitarian; *sanitarium*, *sanitorium*, immunity.

V. be -salubrious etc. *adj.*; agree with, be good for; assimilate etc. 23.

Adj. salu-brious, -tary, -tiferous, wholesome; health-y, -ful; sanitary, prophylactic, benign, bracing, tonic, invigorating, good for, nutritious, hyg-eian, -ienic.

in-noxious, -nocuous, -nocent; harmless, uninjurious, uninfectious; immune.

sanative etc. (*remedial*) 662; restorative etc. (*reinstate*) 660; useful etc. 644.

657. Insalubrity.—N. insalubrity, unhealthiness etc. *adj.*; non-naturals; plague spot; malaria etc. (*poison*) 663; death in the pot, contagion.

Adj. insalubrious; un-healthy, -wholesome; noxious, noisome, foul; morbi-fic, -ferous; mephitic, septic, azotic, deleterious; pesti-lent, -ferous, -lential; virulent, venomous, envenomed, poisonous, toxic, narcotic.

contagious, infectious, catching, taking, communicable, epidemic, zymotic, sporadic, endemic, pandemic, epizoötic.

innutritious, indigestible, ungenial; uncongenial etc. (*disagreeing*) 24.

deadly etc. (*killing*) 361.

658. Improvement.—N. improvement; a-, melioration; betterment; mend, amendment, emendation; mending etc. *v.*; advancement; advance etc. (*progress*) 282; ascent etc. 305; promotion, preferment; elevation etc. 307; increase etc. 35.

cultiv-, civiliz-ation; menticulture, culture, march of intellect; eugenics, euthenics, meliorism, telesis.

reform, -ation; revision, radical reform; second thoughts, correction, *limae labor*, refinement, elaboration; purification etc. 652; repair etc. (*restoration*) 660; recovery etc. 660.

revise; revised –, new- edition.

reformer, radical, progressive.

V. improve; be –, become –, get- better; mend, amend.

advance etc. (*progress*) 282; ascend etc. 305; increase etc. 35; fructify, ripen, mature; pick up, come about, rally, take a favorable turn; turn -over a new leaf, – the corner; raise one's head, sow one's wild oats; recover etc. 660.

be -better etc. *adj.*, – improved by; turn to -right, – good, – best- account; profit by, reap the benefit of; make -good use of, – capital out of; place to good account; take advantage of.

render better, improve, emend, make over, better; a-, meliorate; correct.

improve –, refine- upon; rectify; enrich, mellow, elaborate, fatten.

promote, cultivate, advance, forward, enhance; bring -forward, – on; foster etc. 707; invigorate etc. (*strengthen*) 159.

touch –, rub –, brush –, furbish –, bolster –, vamp –, brighten –, warm- up; polish, cook, make the most of, set off to advantage; prune; repair etc. (*restore*) 660; put in order etc. (*arrange*) 60.

review, revise, edit, redact; make -corrections, – improvements etc. *n.*; doctor etc. (*remedy*) 662; purify etc. 652.

relieve, refresh, revive, infuse new blood into, recruit, re-invigorate, renew, revivify, freshen, build -afresh, – anew; uplift, inspire.

re-form, -model, -organize; new model, civilize.

view in a new light, think better of, appeal from Philip drunk to Philip sober.

palliate, mitigate; lessen etc. 36- an evil.

Adj. improving etc. *v.*; progressive, improved etc. *v.*; better, – off, – for; all the better for; better advised.

reform-, emend-atory; reparatory etc. (*restorative*) 660; remedial etc. 662.

corrigible, improvable, curable, accultural.

Adv. on -consideration, – reconsideration, – second thoughts, – better advice; *ad melius inquirendum*; on the -mend, – up grade.

659. Deterioration.—N. deterioration, debasement; want, ebb; recession etc. 287; retrogradation etc. 283; decrease etc. 36.

degenera-cy, -tion, -teness; degradation; depravation, -ement; depravity etc. 945; demoralization, retrogression.

impairment, inquination, injury, damage, loss, detriment, delaceration, outrage, havoc, inroad, ravage, scath; perversion, prostitution, vitiation, discoloration, oxidation, pollution, defedation, poisoning, venenation, leaven, contamination, canker, corruption, adulteration, alloy.

decl-ine, -ension, -ination; decadence, -cy; falling off etc. *v.*; caducity, decreptitude, senility.

decay, dilapidation, ravages of time, wear and tear; cor-, e-rosion; mouldi-, rotten-ness; moth and rust, dry-rot, blight, marasmus, atrophy, collapse; disorganization; *délabrement* etc. (*destruction*) 162.

wreck, mere wreck, honeycomb, *magni nominis umbra.*

V. be –, become- -worse, – deteriorated etc. *adj.*; have seen better days, deteriorate, degenerate, fall off; wane etc. (*decrease*) 36; ebb; retrograde etc. 283; decline, droop; go down etc. (*sink*) 306; go -downhill, – on from bad to worse, – farther and fare worse; jump out of the frying pan into the fire.

run to -seed, – waste; swale, sweal; lapse, be the worse for; break, – down; spring a leak, crack, start; shrivel etc. (*contract*) 195; fade, go off, wither, molder, rot, rankle, decay, go bad; go to – fall into- decay; 'fall into the sear and yellow leaf,' rust, crumble, shake; totter, – to its fall; perish etc. 162; die etc. 360.

[Render less good] deteriorate; weaken etc. 160; put back; taint, infect, contaminate, poison, empoison, envenom, canker, corrupt, exulcerate, pollute, vitiate, inquinate; de-, em-base; denaturalize, leaven; de-flower, -bauch, -file, -prave, -grade; stain etc. (*dirt*) 653; discolor; alloy, adulterate, sophisticate, tamper with, prejudice.

pervert, prostitute, demoralize, brutalize; render vicious etc. 945; compromise.

embitter, ex-, acerbate, aggravate.

injure, impair, labefy, damage, harm, hurt, shend, scathe, spoil, mar, despoil, dilapidate, waste; overrun; ravage; pillage etc. 791.

wound, stab, pierce, maim, lame, surbate, cripple, hough, hamstring, hit between the wind and water, scotch, mangle, mutilate, disfigure, blemish, deface, warp.

blight, rot; cor-, e-rode, eat away; wear away, – out; gnaw, – at the root of; sap, mine, undermine, shake, sap the foundations of, break up; dis-organize, -mantle, -mast; destroy etc. 162.

damnify etc. (*aggrieve*) 649; do one's worst, knock down; deal a blow to; play -havoc, – sad havoc, – the mischief, – the deuce, – the very devil- -with, – among; decimate.

Adj. unimproved etc. (improve etc. 658); deteriorated etc. *v.*; altered, – for the worse; injured etc. *v.*; sprung; withering, spoiling, etc. *v.*; on the -wane, – decline; tabid; degenerate; worse; the –, all the- worse for; out of -repair, – tune; imperfect etc. 651; the worse for wear; battered; weather-ed, -beaten; stale, *passé*, shaken, dilapidated, frayed, faded, wilted, shabby, second-hand, second-rate, threadbare; worn, – to- -a thread, – a shadow, – the stump, rags; reduced, – to a skeleton, skeletonized; far gone.

decayed etc. *v.*; moth-, worn-eaten; mildewed, rusty, moldy, spotted, seedy, time-worn, moss-grown; discolored; effete, wasted, crumbling, moldering, rotten, cankered, blighted, tainted; depraved etc. (*vicious*) 945; decrep-id, -it; broken down; done, – for, – up; worn out, used up; fit for the -dust-hole, – wastepaper basket; past work etc. (*useless*) 645.

at a low ebb, in a bad way, on one's last legs, washed -up; – out; undermined, deciduous; nodding to its fall etc. (*destruction*) 162; tottering etc. (*dangerous*) 665; past cure etc. (*hopeless*) 859; fatigued etc. 688; backward, retrograde etc. (*retrogressive*) 283; deleterious etc. 649; behind the times.

Adv. on the down grade; beyond hope.

Phr. out of the frying pan into the fire; *aegrescit medendo.*

660. Restoration.—N. restor-ation, -al; reinstatement, -placement, -habilitation, -

establishment, -construction; reporduction etc. 163; re-novation, -newal; reviv-al, -escence; refreshment etc. 689; re-suscitation, -animation, -vivification, -viction; Phoenix; reorganization.

renaissance, renascence, rebirth, second youth, rejuvenation, rejuvenescence, new birth; regeneration, -cy, -teness; palingenesis, reconversion, resurgence, resurrection.

redress, retrieval, reclamation, recovery; convalescence; resumption, *résumption*.

recurrence etc. (*repetition*) 104; *réchauffé, rifacimento*.

cure, recure, sanation; healing etc. *v.*; redintegration; rectification, instauration.

repair, reparation, mending; recruiting etc. *v.*; cicatrization; disinfection; tinkering.

reaction; redemption etc. (*deliverance*) 672; restitution etc. 790; relief etc. 834.

mender, repairer, renewer; tinker, cobbler; doctor etc. 662; *vis medicatrix* etc. (*remedy*) 662.

curableness.

V. return to the original state; recover, rally, revive; come -to, – round, – to oneself; pull through, weather the storm, be oneself again; get -well, – round, – the better of, – over, – about; rise from -one's ashes, – the grave; resurge, resurrect; survive etc. (*outlive*) 110; resume, reappear; come to, – life again; live –, rise- again; relive.

heal, skin over, cicatrize; right itself.

restore, put back, place *in statu quo*; re-instate, -place, -seat, -habilitate, -establish, -estate, -install.

re-construct, -build, -organize, -constitute; reconvert; re-new, -novate; recondition; regenerate; rejuvenate.

re-deem, -claim, -cover, -trieve; rescue etc. (*deliver*) 672.

redress, recure; cure, heal, remedy, doctor, physic, medicate; break of; bring round, set on one's legs.

re-suscitate, -vive, -animate, -vivify, -call to life; reproduce etc. 163; warm up; reinvigorate, refresh etc. 689.

redintegrate, make whole; recoup etc. 790; make -good, – all square; rectify; put –, set- -right, – to rights, – straight; set up, correct; put in order etc. (*arrange*) 60; refit, recruit; fill up, – the ranks; reinforce.

repair, mend; put in -repair, – thorough repair, – complete repair; retouch, botch, vamp, tinker, doctor, cobble; do –, patch –, plaster –, vamp-up; darn, fine-draw, heel-piece; stop a gap, stanch, staunch, caulk, calk, careen, splice, bind up wounds.

Adj. restored etc. *v.*; *redivivus*, convalescent; in a fair way; none the worse; rejuvenated, renascent.

restoring etc. *v.*; restorative, recuperative; sana-, repara-tive, -tory; curative, remedial.

restor-, recover-, san-, remedi-, retriev-, cur-able.

Adv. *in statu qho*; as you were.

Phr. *revenons a nos moutons.*

661. Relapse.—N. relapse, lapse; falling back etc. *v.*; retrogradation etc. (*retrogression*) 283; deterioration etc. 659.

[Return to, or recurrence of a bad state] backsliding, recidivation, recrudescence.

V. relapse, lapse; fall –, slide –, sink- back; have a relapse; return; retrograde etc. 283; recidivate; fall off etc. 659- again.

662. Remedy.—N. remedy, help, redress; antidote, anti-toxin, -biotic; anti-, counter-poison, prophylactic, antiseptic, germicide, bactericide, corrective, restorative, stimulant, pick-me-up, tonic; sedative etc. 174; palliative; febrifuge; alterant, -ative; specific; emetic, carminative; narcotic etc. *adj.*; Nepenthe, Mithridate.

cure; radical –, perfect –, certain- cure; sovereign remedy.

physic, medicine, patent medicine, Galenicals, simples, drug, wonder –, miracle – drugs; potion, draught, dose, pill, bolus, lozenge, tablet, tabloid, capsule; electuary; linct-us, -ure; medicament.

nostrum, receipt, recipe, prescription; catholicon, panacea, elixir, *elixir vitae*, philosopher's stone; balm, balsam, cordial, theriac, ptisan.

salve, ointment, cerate, oil, lenitive, lotion, cosmetic; plaster; epithem, embrocation, liniment, cataplasm, sinapism, arquebusade, traumatic, vulnerary, pepastic, poultice, collyrium, depilatory.

compress, pledget; bandage etc. (*support*) 215.

treatment, medical treatment, regimen; diet-ary, -etics; *vis medicatrix*, – *naturae*; *médicine expectante*; seton, blood-letting, bleeding, venesection, phlebotomy, cupping, leeches; operation, surgical operation; tonsillectomy, appendectomy; injection, electrolysis, massage.

pharma-cy, -cology, -ceutics; acology; materia medica, pharmacopoeia, therapeutics, therapy, posology, pathology etc. 655; home-, hetero-, all-, hydr-opathy; cold water –, open air- cure; dietetics; sur-, chirur-gery, osteopathy; healing art, leechcraft, practice of medicine; ortho-paedy, -praxy; dentistry, midwifery, obstetrics, gynecology.

faith -cure, – healing, Christian science; psychotherapy, -analysis, psychiatry.

hospital, infirmary, clinic; pest-, lazar-house; lazaretto, lazaret; lock hospital; *maison de santé*; *ambulance*; dispensary; *sanatorium*, *sanitarium*, spa, baths, pump-room, well; *hospice*; Red Cross; nursing home; asylum.

doctor, physician, surgeon; medical –, general-practitioner, consultant, specialist; medical attendant; medical student, medico; chemist, apothecary, pharmacopolist, druggist; leech; Aesculapius, Hippocrates, Galen; *accoucheur*, gynecologist, midwife, oculist, aurist, dentist; operator; osteopath, bonesetter; nurse, monthly nurse, sister; dresser; *masseur*, *masseuse*.

V. apply a -remedy etc. *n.*; doctor, dose, physic, nurse, minister to, attend, dress the wounds, plaster, bandage, poultice; heal, cure, work a cure, kill or cure, remedy, stay (disease), snatch from the jaws of death; prevent etc. 706; relieve etc. 834; palliate etc. 658; restore etc. 660; drench with physic; consult, operate, extract, deliver; bleed, cup, let blood, transfuse; electrolyse; psychoanalyse.

Adj. remedial; restorative etc. 660; corrective, palliative, healing; sana-tory, -tive; prophylactic; salutiferous etc. (*salutary*) 656; medic-al, -inal; therapeutic, surgical, chirurgical, orthopedic, epulotic, paregoric, tonic, corroborant, analeptic, balsamic, anodyne, hypnotic, neurotic, narcotic, sedative, lenitive, demulcent, emollient; depuratory; deter-sive, -gent; abstersive, disinfectant, febrifugal, alternative; traumatic, vulnerary.

dietetic, alimentary; nutrit-ious, -ive; peptic; alexi-pharmic, -teric; remedi-, cur-able.

663. Bane. —**N.** bane, curse, thorn in the -side, -flesh, bugbear, *bête noire*; evil etc. 619; hurtfulness etc. (*badness*) 649; painfulness etc. (*cause of pain*) 830; scourge etc. (*punishment*) 975; *damnosa hereditas*; white elephant.

sting, fang, thorn, tang, bramble, briar, nettle.

poison, leaven, virus, venom; intoxicant; arsenic, Prussic acid, antimony, tartar emetic, strychnine, nicotine, cyanide of potassium, corrosive sublimate; curare; hyoscine etc.; poison-, mustard-, tear-gas; carbon di-, mon-oxide; ptomaine poisoning, botulism; miasm, mephitis, malaria, azote, sewer gas; pest, stench etc. 401.

rust, worm, moth, moth and rust, fungus, mildew; dry-rot; canker, -worm; cancer; torpedo; viper etc. (*evil-doer*) 913; demon etc. 980.

hemlock, hellebore, nightshade, *belladonna*, henbane, aconite; Upas tree.

drugs, dope, opium, morphia, morphine, cocaine, heroin, hashish, bhang.

[*Science of poisons*] Toxicology.

Adj. baneful etc. (*bad*) 649; poisonous etc. (*unwholesome*) 657.

664. Safety.—N. safety, security, impregnability; invulnera-bility, -bleness etc. *adj.*; danger -past, – over; storm blown over; coast clear; escape etc. 671; means of escape, safety-valve; safeguard, palladium, sheet anchor, rock, tower of strength.

guardian-, ward-, warden-ship; tutelage, custody, safe keeping; preservation etc. 670; protection, auspices.

safe-conduct, escort, convoy; guard, sheild etc. (*defense*) 717; guardian angel, tutelary -god, – deity, – saint; *genius loci.*

protector, guardian; ward-en, -er; preserver, custodian, *duenna chaperon*, third person.

watch-, ban-dog; Cerberus; watch-, patrol-, police-man, constable, peeler, bobby, copper, cop, bull, flat-foot, detective, armed guard; sentinel, sentry, scout etc. (*warning*) 668; garrison; guard-ship.

[Means of safety] refuge etc., anchor etc. 666; precaution etc. (*preparation*) 673; quarantine, *cordon sanitaire*. [Sense of security] confidence etc. 858.

V. be -safe etc. *adj.*; keep one's head above water, tide over, save one's bacon; ride out –, weather- the storm; light upon one's feet; bear a charmed life; escape etc. 671; possess nine lives.

make –, render- -safe etc. *adj.*; protect, watch over; take care of etc. (*care*) 459; preserve etc. 670; cover, screen, shelter, shroud, flank, ward; guard etc. (*defend*) 717; secure etc. (*restrain*) 751; intrench, fence round etc. (*circumscribe*) 229; house, nestle, ensconce; take charge of.

escort, convoy; garrison; watch, mount guard, patrol, scout, spy.

make assurance double sure etc. (*caution*) 864; take up a loose thread; take precautions etc. (*prepare for*) 673; take in a reef; double reef topsails.

seek safety; take –, find- shelter etc. 666; run into port.

Adj. safe, secure, sure; in -safety, – security; have an anchor to windward; on the safe side; under the -shield of, – shade of, – wing of, – shadow of one's wing; under -cover, – lock and key; out of -danger, – the meshes, – harm's way; in -harbor, – port; on sure ground, at anchor, high and dry, above water, on *terra firma*; unthreatened, -molested; protected etc. *v.*; cavendo tutus; panoplied etc. (*defended*) 717.

snug, sea-, air-worthy; weather-, water-, fire-, bomb-proof.

defensible, tenable, proof against, invulnerable; un-assailable, -attackable; im-pregnable, -perdible; founded on a rock; inexpugnable.

safe and sound etc. (*preserved*) 670; harmless; scathless etc. (*perfect*) 650; unhazarded; not -dangerous etc. 665.

protecting etc. *v.*; guardian, tutelary; perservative etc. 670; trustworthy etc. 939.

Adv. *ex abundanti cautelâ*; with impunity.

Phr. all's well; all clear; *salva res est*; *suave mari magno*; safety first.

665. Danger.—N. danger, peril, insecurity, jeopardy, risk, hazard, venture, precariousness, slipperiness; instability etc. 149; defenselessness etc. *adj.*

exposure etc. (*liability*) 177; vulnerability; vulnerable point, heel of Achilles; forlorn hope etc. (*hopelessness*) 859.

[Dangerous course] leap in the dark etc. (*rashness*) 863; road to ruin, *facilis descensus Averni*, hair-breadth escape.

cause for alarm; source of danger etc. 667. [Approach of danger] rock –, breakers- ahead; storm brewing, clouds -in the horizon, – gathering; warning etc. 668; alarm etc. 669. [Sense of danger] apprehension etc. 860.

V. be -in danger etc. *adj.*; be exposed to –, run into –, incur –, encounter- -danger etc. *n.*; run a risk; lay oneself open to etc. (*liability*) 177; lean on –, trust to- a broken reed; feel the ground sliding from under one, have to run for it; have the -chances, – odds- against one.

hang by a thread, totter; tremble on the -verge, – brink; sleep – stand -on a volcano; sit on a barrel of gunpowder, live in a glass house.

bring –, place –, put in -danger etc. *n.*; endanger, expose to danger, imperil; jeopard, -ize, compromise; sail too near the wind etc. (*rash*) 863; put one's head in the lion's mouth.

adventure, risk, hazard, venture, stake, set at hazard; run the gauntlet etc. (*dare*) 861; engage in a forlorn hope.

threaten etc. 909- danger; run one hard; lay a trap for etc. (*deceive*) 545.

Adj. in -danger etc. *n.*; endangered etc. *v.*; fraught with danger; danger-, hazard-, peril-, parl-, pericul-ous; unsafe, unprotected etc. (safe, protect etc. 664); insecure, untrustworthy, unreliable; built upon sand, on a sandy basis.

defence-, fence-, guard-, harbor-less; unshielded; vulnerable, expugnable, unsheltered, exposed; open to etc. (*liable*) 177.

aux abois, at bay; on -the wrong side of the wall, – a lee shore, – the rocks.

at stake, in question; precarious, aleatory, critical, ticklish; slip-pery, -py; hanging by a thread etc. *v.*; with a halter round one's neck; between - the hammer and the anvil, – Scylla and Charybdis, – two fires; on the -edge, – brink, – verge of a- -precipice, – volcano; in the lion's den, on slippery ground, under fire; not out of the wood.

un-warned, -admonished, -advised; unprepared etc. 674; off one's guard etc. (*inexpectant*) 508.

tottering; un-stable, -steady; shaky, top-heavy, tumble-down, ramshackle, crumbling, waterlogged; help-, guide-less; in a bad way; reduced to –, at- the last extremity; trembling in the balance; nodding to its fall etc. (*destruction*) 162.

threatening etc. 909; ominous, ill-omened; alarming etc. (*fear*) 860; explosive; poisonous etc. 657.

adventurous etc. (*rash*) 863, (*bold*) 861.

Int. stop! look out! beware! take care!

Phr. ***incidit in Scyllam qui vult vitare Charybdim; nam tua res agitur paries dum proximus ardet.***

666. Refuge. [Means of safety.]—**N.** refuge, sanctuary, retreat, fastness; stronghold, keep, last resort; ward; prison etc. 752; asylum, ark, home, almshouse, refuge for the destitute; hiding-place etc. (*ambush*) 530; *sanctum sanctorum* etc. (*privacy*) 893.

roadstead, anchorage; breakwater, mole, port, haven; harbor, – of refuge; sea-port; pier, jetty, embankment, quay.

covert, shelter, abri, screen, lee-wall, wing, shield, umbrella; splash-, dash-board, mudguard.

wall etc. (*inclosure*) 232; fort etc. (*defence*) 717.

anchor, kedge; grap-nel, -pling iron; sheet-, mushroom-anchor, main-stay; support etc. 215; check etc. 706; ballast.

jury-mast; vent-peg; safety -valve, – lamp; lightning conductor.

means of escape etc. (*escape*) 671; life-boat, swimming belt, cork jacket; life preserver, breeches buoy; parachute, plank, stepping-stone.

safeguard etc. (*protection*) 664.

V. seek –, take –, find- refuge etc. *n.*; seek –, find- safety etc. 664; throw oneself into the arms of; claim sanctuary; take to the -hills, – woods; make port, reach shelter, bar –, bolt –, lock -the door, – gete; let the portcullis down; raise the drawbridge.

667. Pitfall. [Source of danger.]—**N.** rocks, reefs, coral reef, sunken rocks, snags; sands, quicksands, Goodwin sands, sandy foundation; slippery ground; breakers, shoals, shallows, bank, shelf, flat, lee shore, iron-bound coast; rock –, breakers- ahead; derelict.

precipice; abyss, chasm, pit, crevasse; maelstrom, whirlpool, eddy, vortex, rapids, current, bore, tidal wave; storm, squall, hurricane, whirlwind; volcano; ambush etc. 530; pitfall, trap-door; trap etc. (*snare*) 545.

sword of Damocles; wolf at the door, snake in the grass, viper in one's bosom, death in the pot; latency etc. 526.

ugly customer, dangerous person, *le chat qui dort*; firebrand, hornet's nest.

Phr. *latet anguis in herbâ*; *proximus ardet Ucalegon.*

668. Warning.—N. warning, caution, *caveat*; notice etc. (*information*) 527; premoni-tion, -shment; prediction etc. 511; contraindication; symptom; lesson, dehortation; admonition, monition; alarm etc. 669.

handwriting on the wall, *tekel upharsin*, yellow flag; fog-signal, -horn; siren; monitor, warning voice, Cassandra, signs of the times, Mother Carey's chickens, stormy petrel, bird of ill omen, gathering clouds, clouds in the horizon, cloud no bigger than a man's hand, death-watch.

watch-tower, beacon, signal-post; light-house etc. (*indication of locality*) 550.

sent-inel, -ry; watch, -man; watch and ward; watch-, ban-, house-dog; patrol, vedette, picket, bivouac, scout, spy, spial; advanced –, rear-guard, lookout, flagman.

cautiousness etc. 864.

V. warn, caution; fore-, pre-warn; ad-, premonish; give -notice, – warning; menace etc. (*threaten*) 909; put on one's guard; sound the alarm etc. 669; croak.

beware, ware; take -warning, – heed at one's peril; watch out for; keep watch and ward etc. (*care*) 459.

Adj. warning etc. *v.*; premonitory, monitory, cautionary; admonitory, -tive; ominous, threatening, lowering, minatory, symptomatic.

warned etc. *v.*; on one's guard etc. (*careful*) 459; (*cautious*) 864.

Adv. *in terrorem* etc. (*threat*) 909.

Int. beware! ware! take care! mind –, take care- what you are about; mind! look out!

Phr. *ne reveillez pas le chat qui dort*; *foenum habet in cornu.*

669. Alarm. [Indication of danger.]—**N.** alarm; alarum, larum, alarm bell, tocsin, *alerte*, beat of drum, sound of trumpet, note of alarm, hue and cry, signal of distress, S.O.S.; blue-lights; war-cry, -whoop; warning etc. 668; fog-signal, -horn; siren; yellow flag; danger signal; red -light, – flag; fire -bell, – alarm; burglar alarm, police whistle, watchman's rattle.

false alarm, cry of wolf; bug-bear, -aboo.

V. give –, raise –, sound –, beat- the *or* an - alarm etc. *n.*; alarm; warn etc. 668; ring the tocsin; *battre la générale*; cry wolf.

Adj. alarming etc. *v.*

Int. *sauve qui peut! qui vive?* who goes there?

670. Preservation.—N. preservation; safe keeping; conservation etc. (*storage*) 636; maintenance, upkeep, support, sustentation, conservatism; *vis conservatrix*; salvation etc. (*deliverance*) 672; drying etc. *v.*

[Means of preservation] prophylaxis; preserv-er, -ative; canned goods; cold pack; hygi-astics, -antics; cover, durgget; *cordon sanitaire.*

[Superstitious remedies] charm etc. 993.

V. preserve, maintain, keep, sustain, support; keep -up, – alive; not willingly let die; shore –, bank- up; nurse; save, rescue; be –, make- safe etc. 664; take care of etc. (*care*) 459; guard etc. (*defend*) 717.

stare super antiquas vias; hold one's own; hold –, stand- -one's ground etc. (*resist*) 719.

embalm, dry, cure, smoke, salt, pickle, season, kyanize, bottle, pot, tin, can; husband etc. (*store*) 636.

Adj. preserving etc. *v.*; conservative; prophylatic; preserva-tory, -tive; hygienic.

preserved etc. *v.*; un-impaired, -broken, -injured, -hurt, -singed, -marred; safe, – and sound; intact, with a whole skin, without a scratch.

Phr. *nolumus leges Angliae mutari.*

671. Escape.—N. escape, scape; avolation, elopment, flight, get-away; evasion etc. (*avoidance*) 623; retreat; narrow –, hairbreadth- escape; close –, near- shave; come off, impunity.

[Means of escape] loophole etc. (*opening*) 260, path etc. 627; secret -door, – passage; refuge etc. 666; vent, – peg; safety-valve; drawbridge, fire-escape.

reprieve etc. (*deliverance*) 672; liberation etc. 750.

refugee etc. (*fugitive*) 623.

V. escape, scape; make –, effect –, make good- one's escape, make a get-away; get -off, – clear off, – well out of; *échapper belle*, save one's bacon; weather the storm etc. (*safe*) 664; escape scot-free.

elude etc., make off etc. (*avoid*) 623; march off etc. (*go away*) 293; give one the slip; slip through the -hands, – fingers; slip the collar, wriggle out of; break -loose, – from prison; break –, slip –, get- away; find -vent, – a hole to creep out of.

Adj. escap-ing, -ed etc. *v.*; stolen away, fled.

Phr. the bird has flown.

672. Deliverance.—N. deliverance, extrication, rescue; repriev-e, -al; respite; ransom; liberation etc. 750; truce, armistice; redemption, salvation; riddance; gaol delivery; exemption, day of grace; redeemableness.

V. deliver, extricate, rescue, save, redeem, ransom, free, liberate, release, set free, redeem, emancipate; bring -off, – through; *tirer d'affaire*, get the wheel out of the rut; snatch from the jaws of death, come to the rescue; rid; retrieve etc. (*restore*) 660; be –, get- rid of.

Adj. saved etc. *v.*; extric-, redeem-, rescu-able.

Phr. to the rescue!

673. Preparation.—N. preparation; providing etc. *v.*; provi-sion, -dence; anticipation etc. (*foresight*) 510; precaution, -concertation, disposition; forecast etc. (*plan*) 626; rehearsal, not of preparation.

[Putting in order] arrangement etc. 60; clearance; adjustment etc. 23; tuning; equipment, outfit, accoutrement, armament, array.

ripening etc. *v.*; maturation, evolution; elaboration, concoction, digestion; gestation, hatching, incubation, sitting.

groundwork, datum, first stone, cradle, stepping-stone; foundation, scaffold etc. (*support*) 215; scaffolding, *échafaudage*.

[Preparation -of men] training etc. (*education*) 537; inurement etc. (*habit*) 613; novitiate; [– of food] cook-ing, -ery; brewing, culinary art; [– of the soil] till-, plough-, sow-ing; semination, cultivation.

[State of being prepared] prepared-, readi-, ripe-, mellow-ness; maturity; *un impromptu fait à loisir.*

[Preparer] preparer, teacher, coach, trainer, pioneer; *avant-courrier*, *-coureur*; sappers and miners, paver, navvy; packer, stevedore; warmingpan; precursor etc. 64.

V. prepare; get –, make- ready; make preparations, settle preliminaries, get up, sound the note of preparation; address oneself to.

set –, put- in order etc. (*arrange*) 60; forecast etc. (*plan*) 626; prepare –, plough –, dress- the ground; till –, cultivate- the soil; predispose, sow the seed, lay a train, dig a mine; lay –, fix- the -foundations, – basis, -groundwork; dig the foundations, erect the scaffolding; lay the first stone etc. (*begin*) 66.

rough-hew; cut out work; block –, hammer-out; lick into shape etc. (*form*) 240.

elaborate, mature, ripen, mellow, season, bring to maturity; nurture etc.

(*aid*) 707; hatch, cook, brew; temper; anneal, smelt; dry, cure etc. 670.

equip, arm, man; fit-out, -up; furnish, rig, dress, garnish, betrim, accouter, array, fettle, fledge; dress –, furbish –, brush –, vamp- up; refurbish; sharpen one's tools, trim one's foils, set, prime, attune; whet the -knife, – sword; wind –, screw- up; adjust etc. (*fit*) 27; put in- trim, – train, – gear, – working order, – tune, – a groove for, – harness; pack, stow away, store.

train etc. (*teach*) 537; inure etc. (*habituate*) 613; breed; prepare etc.- for; rehearse; make provision for; take -steps, – measures, – precautions; provide, – against; beat up for recruits; open the door to etc. (*facilitate*) 705.

set one's house in order, make all snug; clear -decks, – for action; close one's ranks; shuffle the cards.

prepare oneself; serve an apprenticeship etc. (*learn*) 539; lay oneself out for, get into harness, gird up one's loins, buckle on one's armor, *reculer pour mieux sauter*, prime and load, shoulder arms, get the steam up, put the horses to.

guard –, make sure- against; forearm, make sure, prepare for the evil day, have a rod in pickle, provide against a rainy day, feather one's nest; lay in provisions etc. 637; make investments; keep on foot.

be -prepared, – ready etc. *adj.*; hold oneself in readiness, watch and pray, keep one's powder dry; lie in wait for etc. (*expect*) 507; anticipate etc. (*foresee*) 510; *principiis obstare*; *veniente occurrere morbo.*

Adj. preparing etc. *v.*; in -preparation, – course

of preparation, – agitation, – embryo, – hand, – train; afoot, afloat; on -foot, – the stocks, – the anvil; under consideration etc. (*plan*) 626; brewing, hatching, forthcoming, brooding; in -store for, – reserve.

precautionary, provident; prepara-tive, -tory; provisional, inchoate, under revision; preliminary etc. (*precedent*) 62.

prepared etc. *v.*; in readiness; ready, – to one's hand, – made, cut and dried; ready for use, reach me down; made to one's hand, handy, on the table, made to order; in gear; in working -order, – gear; snug; in practice.

ripe, mature, mellow; practiced etc. (*skillet*) 698; labored, elaborate, highly-wrought, smelling of the lamp, worked up.

in -full feather, – best bib and tucker; in –, at- harness; in – the saddle, – arms, – battle array, – war paint; up in arms; armed -at all points, – to the teeth, – *cap-à-pie*; sword in hand; booted and spurred.

in utrumque –, *semper- paratus*; on the alert etc. (*vigilant*) 459; at one's post.

Adv. in -preparation, – anticipation of; afoot, astir, abroad; abroach.

674. Non-preparation.—N. non-, absence of –, want of- preparation; unpreparedness; in-culture, inconcoction, improvidence.

immaturity, crudity; rawness etc. *adj.*; abortion; disqualification.

[Absence of art] nature, state of nature; virgin soil, unweeded garden; rough diamond, neglect etc. 460.

rough copy etc. (*plan*) 626; germ etc. 153; raw material etc. 635.

improvisation etc. (*impulse*) 612.

V. be -unprepared etc. *adj.*; want –, lack- preparation; lie fallow; *s'embarquer sans biscuits*; live from hand to mouth.

[Render unprepared] dismantle etc. (*render useless*) 645; undress etc. 226.

extemporize, improvise.

surprise, pay a surprise visit, take by surprise, drop in upon, take unawares; take pot-luck.

Adv. un-prepared etc. prepare etc. 673] without -preparation etc. 673; incomplete etc. 53; rudimental, embryonic, abortive; immature, unripe, raw, green, crude; coarse; rough, -cast, -hewn; in the rough; un-hewn, -formed, -fashioned, -wrought, -labored, -blown, -cooked, -boiled, -concocted, -cút, -polished.

callow, un-hatched, -fledged, -nurtured, -licked, -taught, -educated, -cultivated, -trained, -tutored, -drilled, -exercised; precocious, premature; un-, in-digested; un-mellowed, -seasoned, -leavened.

fallow; un-sown, -tilled; natural, in a state of nature; undressed; in dishabille, *en déshabille, en négligé*.

un-, dis-qualified; unfitted; ill-digested; unbegun, -ready, -arranged, -organized, -furnished, -provided, -equipped, -trimmed; out of -gear, – order; dismantled etc. *v.*

shiftless, improvident, unthrifty, thoughtless, unguarded; happy-go-lucky; caught napping etc. (*inexpectant*) 508; unpremeditated etc. 612.

Adv. extempore etc. 612.

675. Essay.—N. essay, trial, endeavor, aim, attempt; venture, adventure, speculation, *coup d'essai, début*; probation etc. (*experiment*) 463.

V. try, essay; experiment etc. 463; endeavor, strive; tempt, tackle, take on, attempt, make an attempt; venture, adventure, speculate, take one's chance, tempt fortune; try one's -fortune, – luck, – hand; use one's endeavor; feel –, grope –, pick- one's way.

try hard, push, make a bold push, use one's best endeavor; do one's best etc. (*exertion*) 686.

Adj. essaying etc. *v.*; experimental etc. 463; tentative, empirical, probationary

Adv. experimentally etc. *adj.*; on trial, at a venture; by rule of thumb.

if one may be so bold.

676. Undertaking.—N. undertaking, compact etc. 769; engagement etc. (*promise*) 768; enter-, em-prise; venture etc. 675; pilgrimage; matter in hand etc. (*business*) 625; move; first move etc. (*beginning*) 66.

V. undertake; engage –, embark- in; launch –, plunge- into; volunteer; apprentice oneself to; engage etc. (*promise*) 768; contract etc. 769; take upon -oneself, – one's shoulders; devote oneself to etc. (*determination*) 604.

take -up, – in hand; tackle; set –, go- about; set –, fall- -to, – to work; launch forth; set up shop; put in -hand, – execution; set forward; break the neck of a business, be in for; put one's hand to; betake oneself to, turn one's hand to, go to do; begin etc. 66; broach, institute, etc. (*originate*) 153; put –, lay- one's -hand to the plough, – shoulder to the wheel.

have in hand etc. (*business*) 625; have many irons in the fire etc. (*activity*) 682.

Adj. undertaking etc. *v.*; on the anvil etc. 625; adventurous, venturesome.

Int. here goes!

677. Use.—N. use; employ, -ment; exer-cise, -citation; appli-cation, -ance; adhibition, disposal; consumption; agency etc. (*physical*) 170; usufruct; usefulness etc. 644; recourse, resort, avail, pragmatism.

[Conversion to use] utilization, service, wear.

[Way of using] usage.

V. use, make use of, employ, put to use; apply, put in -action, – operation, – practice; set -in motion, – to work.

ply, work, wield, handle, manipulate; play, – off; exert, exercise, practice, avail oneself of, profit by; resort –, have recourse –, recur –, take –, betake oneself- to; take -up with, – advantage of; lay one's hands on, try.

render useful etc. 644; mold; turn to -account, – use; convert to use, utilize, administer; work up; call –, bring- into play; put into requisition; call –, draw- forth; press –, enlist- into the service; bring to bear upon, devote, dedicate, consecrate, apply, adhibit, dispose of; make a -handle, – cat's paw- of.

fall beak upon, make a shift with; make the -most, – best- of.

use –, swallow- up; consume, absorb, expend; tax, task, wear, put to task.

Adj. in use; used etc. *v.*; well-worn, -trodden. useful etc. 644; subservient etc. (*instrumental*) 631; utilitarian; pragmatical.

678. Disuse.—N. forbearance, abstinence; disuse; relinquishment etc. 782; desuetude etc. (*want of habit*) 614.

V. not use; do without, dispense with, let alone, not touch, forbear, abstain, spare, waive, neglect; keep back, reserve.

lay -up, – by, – on the shelf, – up in a napkin; shelve; set –, put –, lay- aside; disuse, leave off, have done with; supersede; discard etc. (*eject*) 297; dismiss, give warning.

throw aside etc. (*relinquish*) 782; make away with etc. (*destroy*) 162; cast –, heave –, throw- overboard; cast to the -dogs, – winds; dismantle etc. (*render useless*) 645.

lie –, remain- unemployed etc. *adj.*

Adj. not used etc. *v.*; un-employed, -applied, -disposed of, -spent, -exercised, -touched, -trodden, -essayed, -gathered, -culled; uncalled for, not required.

disused etc. *v.*; done with; run down, used up, cast off.

679. Misuse.—N. mis-use, -usage, employment, -application, -appropriation.

abuse, profanation, prostitution, desecration, waste etc. 638.

V. mis-use, -employ, -apply, -appropriate.

desecrate, abuse, profane, prostitute; waste etc. 638; over-task, -tax, -work; squander etc. 818.

cut a whetstone with a razor, employ a steam-engine to crack a nut; catch at a straw.

Adj. misused etc. *v.*

680. Action.—N. action, performance; doing etc. *v.*; perpetration; exercise, citation; movement, operation, evolution, work; labor etc. (*exertion*) 686; *praxis*, execution; procedure etc. (*conduct*) 692; handicraft; business etc. 625; agency etc. (*power at work*) 170.

deed, act, overt act, stitch, touch, gest; transaction, job, doings, dealings, proceeding, measure, step, maneuver, bout, passage, move, stroke, blow; *coup*, – *de main*, – *d'état*; *tour de force* etc. (*display*) 882; feat, exploit, stunt; achievement etc. (*completion*) 729; handiwork, workmanship, craftsmanship; manufacture; stroke of policy etc. (*plan*) 626.

actor etc. (*doer*) 690.

V. do, perform, execute; achieve etc. (*complete*) 729; transact, enact; commit, perpetrate, inflict; exercise, prosecute, carry on, work, practice, play.

employ oneself, ply one's task; officiate, have in hand etc. (*business*) 625; labor etc. 686; be at work; pursue a course; shape one's course etc. (*conduct*) 692.

act, operate; take -action, – steps; strike a blow, lift a finger, stretch forth one's hand; take in hand etc. (*undertake*) 676; put oneself in motion; put in practice; carry into execution etc. (*complete*) 729; act upon.

be -an actor etc. 690; take –, act –, play –, perform- a part in; participate in; have a -hand in, – finger in the pie; have to do with; be a -party to, – participator in; bear –, lend- a hand; pull an oar, run in a race; mix oneself up with etc. (*meddle*) 682.

be in action; come into operation etc. (*power at work*) 170.

Adj. doing etc. *v.*; acting; in action; in harness; on duty; at work; in operation etc. 170; up to one's ears in work, in the midst of things.

Adv. in the -act, – midst of, – thick of; red-handed, *in flagrante delicto*; while one's hand is in.

681. Inaction.—N. inaction, passiveness, abstinence from action; non-interference; Fabian –, conservative- policy; neglect etc. 460; stagnation, vegetation; loafing.

inactivity etc. 683; rest etc. (*repose*) 687; quiescence etc. 265; want of –, in- occupation; unemployment; idle hours, time hanging on one's hands, *dolce far niente*; sinecure.

V. not -do, – act, – attempt; be -inactive etc. 683; abstain from doing, do nothing, hold, spare; not -stir, – move, – lift- a -finger, – foot, – peg; fold one's arms, – hands; leave –, let alone; let -be, – pass, – things take their course, – it have its way, – well alone; *quieta non movere*; *stare super antiquas vias*; rest and be thankful, live and let live; lie –, rest- upon one's oars, *laisser aller*, – *faire*; stand aloof; refrain etc. (*avoid*) 623; keep oneself from doing; remit –, relax- one's efforts; desist etc. (*relinquish*) 624; stop etc. (*cease*) 142; pause etc. (*be quiet*) 265.

wait, lie in wait, bide one's time, take time, tide it over.

cool –, kick- one's heels; loaf, while away the -time, – tedious hours; pass –, fill –, beguile- the time; talk against time; waste time etc. (*inactive*) 683.

lie -by, – on the shelf, – in ordinary, – idle, – to, – fallow; keep quiet, slug; have nothing to do, whistle for want of thought; twiddle one's thumbs.

undo, do away with; take -down, – to pieces; destroy etc. 162.

Adj. not doing etc. *v.*; not done etc. *v.*; undone; passive; un-occupied, -employed; out of -employ, – work, – a job; fallow; *désoeuvré*.

Adv. *re infectâ*, at a stand, *les bras croisés*, with folded arms; with the hands -in the pockets, – behind one's back; *pour passer le temps*.

Int. so let it be! stop! etc. 142; hands off!

Phr. nothing doing; *cunctando restituit rem*.

682. Activity.—N. activity; briskness, liveliness etc. *adj.*; animation, life, vivacity, spirit, verve, dash, energy, go.

nimbleness, agility; smartness, quickness etc. *adj.*; velocity etc. 274; alacrity, promptitude; des-, dis-patch; expedition; haste etc. 684; punctuality etc. (*early*) 132.

eagerness, zeal, ardor, *perfervidum ingenium*, *empressement*, earnestness, intentness; *abandon*; vigor etc. (*physical energy*) 171; devotion etc. (*resolution*) 604; exertion etc. 686.

industry, assiduity; assiduousness etc. *adj.*; sedulity; laboriousness; drudgery etc. (*labor*) 686; painstaking, diligence; perseverance etc. 604*a*; indefatigation; habits of business.

vigilance etc. 459; wakefulness; sleep-, restlessness; *pervigilium, insomnia*; racketing.

movement, bustle, hustle, stir, fuss, ado, bother, pottering; fidget, -iness; flurry etc. (*haste*) 684.

officiousness; dabbling, meddling; inter-ference, -position, -meddling, butting in, intrusiveness; tampering with, intrigue.

press of business, no sinecure, plenty to do, many irons in the fire, great doings, busy hum of men, battle of life, thick of -things, – the action; the madding corwd.

housewife, busy bee; new brooms; sharp fellow, blade; hustler, devotee, enthusiast, fan, zealot, fanatic; meddler, intermeddler, intriguer, busybody, kibitzer, pickthank.

V. be -active etc. *adj.*; busy oneself in; stir, -about, – one's stumps; bestir –, rouse- oneself; speed, hasten, peg away, lay about one, bustle, fuss; raise –, kick up- a dust; push; make a -push, – fuss, – stir; go ahead, push forward; flight –, elbow- one's way; make progress etc. 282; toil etc. (*labor*) 686; drudge, plod, persist etc. (*persevere*) 604*a*; keep -up the ball, – the pot boiling.

look sharp; have all one's eyes about one etc. (*vigilance*) 459; rise, arouse oneself, get up early, hustle, push; be about, keep moving, steal a march, kill two birds with one stone; seize the opportunity etc. 134; lose no time, not lose a moment, make the most of one's time, not suffer the grass to grow under one's feet, improve the shining hour, make short work of; dash off; make haste etc. 684; do one's best, take pains etc. (*exert oneself*) 686; do –, work- wonders.

have -many irons in the fire, – one's hands full, – much on one's hands; have other -things to do, – fish to fry; be busy; not have a moment -to spare, – that one can call one's own.

have one's fling, run the round of; go all lengths, stick at nothing, run riot.

outdo; over-do, -act, -lay, -shoot the mark; make a toil of a pleasure.

have a hand in etc. (*act in*) 680; take an active part, put in one's oar, have a finger in the pie, mix oneself up with, trouble one's head about, intrigue; agitate.

tamper with, meddle, moil; inter-meddle, -fere, -pose; obtrude; poke –, thrust- one's nose in, butt in.

Adj. active; brisk, – as a lark, – as a bee; lively, animated, vivacious; alive, – and kicking; frisky, spirited, stirring.

nimble, – as a squirrel; agile; light-, nimble-footed; featly, tripping.

quick, prompt, yare, instant, ready, alert, spry, sharp, smart, slick, go-ahead; fast etc. (*swift*) 274; quick as a lamplighter, expeditious; awake, broad awake; wide awake etc. (*intelligent*) 498.

forward, eager, ardent, strenuous, zealous, enterprising, pushing, in earnest; resolute etc. 604.

industrious, assiduous, diligent, sedulous, notable, painstaking; intent etc. (*attention*) 457; indefatigable etc. (*persevering*) 604*a*; unwearied; unsleeping, sleepless, never tired; plodding, hard-working etc. 686; business-like, workaday.

bustling; restless, – as a hyena; fussy, fidgety, pottering; busy, – as a hen with one chicken.

working, laboring, at work, on duty, in harness; up in arms; on one's legs, at call; up and -doing, – stirring.

busy, occupied; hard at -work, – it; up to one's ears in, full of business, busy as a bee.

meddling etc. *v.*; meddlesome, pushing, officious, overofficious, *intrigant*.

astir, stirring; a-going, -foot; on foot; in full swing; eventful; on the alert etc. (*vigilant*) 459.

Adv. actively etc. *adj.*; with -life and spirit, – might and main etc. 686, – haste etc. 684, – wings; full tilt, *in mediis rebus*.

Int. be –, look- -alive, – sharp! move –, push- on! keep moving! go ahead! stir your stumps! *age quod agis!*

Phr. *carpe diem* etc. (*opportunity*) 134; *nulla dies sine lineâ*; *nec mora nec requies*; no sooner said than done etc. (*early*) 132; catch a weasel asleep.

683. Inactivity.—N. inactivity; inaction etc. 681; inertness etc. 172; obstinacy etc. 606.

lull etc. (*cessation*) 142; quiescence etc. 265; rust, -iness.

idle-, remiss-ness etc. *adj.*; sloth, indolence, indiligence; otiosity, dawdling etc. *v.*

dullness etc. *adj.*; languor; segni-ty, -tude; lentor; sluggishness etc. (*slowness*) 275; procrastination etc. (*delay*) 133; torp-or, -idity, -escence; stupor etc. (*insensibility*) 823; somnolence; drowsiness etc. *adj.*; nodding etc. *v.*; oscitation, -ancy; pandiculation, hypnotism, lethargy; heaviness, heavy eye-lids, sand in the eyes.

sleep, slumber; sound –, heavy –, balmy- sleep; Morpheus, dreamland; coma, trance, catalepsy, hypnosis, *ecstasis*, dream, hibernation, nap, doze, snooze, *siesta*, wink of sleep, forty winks, snore; Hypnology.

dull work; pottering; relaxation etc. (*loosening*) 47; Castle of Indolence.

[Cause of inactivity] lullaby, *berceuse*; anesthetic, sedative etc. 174; torpedo.

idler, drone, droil, dawdle, mopus; do-little, *fainéant*, dummy, sleeping partner; afternoon farmer; truant etc. (*runaway*) 623; lounger, *lazzarone*, floater, loafer, tramp, beggar, cadger; lubber, -bard; slow-coach etc. (*slow*) 275; opium –, lotus- eater; slug; lag-, slug-gard, lie-abed; slumberer, dormouse, marmot; waiter on Providence, *fruges consumere natus*.

V. be -inactive etc. *adj.*; do nothing etc. 681; move slowly etc. 275; let the grass grow under one's feet; take one's time, dawdle, poke, drawl, droil, lag, hang back, slouch; loll, -op; lounge, loaf, loiter; go to sleep over; sleep at one's post; *ne battre que d'une aile*.

take -it easy, – things as they come; lead an easy life, vegetate, swim with the stream, eat the bread of idleness; loll in the lap of -luxury, – indolence; waste –, consume –, kill –, lose time; burn daylight, waste the precious hours.

idle –, trifle –, fritter –, fool- away time; spend –, take- time in; ped-, pid-dle; potter, putter, dabble, faddle, fribble, fiddle-faddle; dally, dilly-dally.

sleep, slumber, be asleep; hibernate; oversleep; sleep like a -top, – log, – dormouse; sleep -soundly, – heavily; doze, drowze, snooze, nap; take a -nap etc. *n.*; dream; snore; settle –, go –, go off- to sleep; drop off; fall –, drop- asleep; close –, seal up- -the -eyes, – eyelids; weigh down the eyelids; get sleepy, nod, yawn; go to bed, turn in.

languish, expend itself, flag, hang fire; relax.

render -idle etc. *adj.*; sluggardize; mitigate etc. 174.

Adj. inactive; motionless etc. 265; unoccupied etc. (*doing nothing*) 681.

indolent, lazy, slothful, idle, otiose, lusk, remiss, slack, inert, torpid, sluggish, languid, supine, heavy, dull, leaden, lumpish; exanimate, soulless; listless; dron-y, -ish; lazy as Ludlam's dog.

dilatory, laggard; lagging etc. *v.*; slow etc. 275; rusty, flagging; lackadaisical, maudlin, fiddle-faddle; pottering etc. *v.*; shilly-shally etc. (*irresolute*) 605.

sleeping etc. *v.*; alseep; fast –, dead –, sound-alseep; in a sound sleep; sound as a top, dormant, comatose; in the -arms, – lap- of Morpheus.

sleep-y, -ful; dozy, drowsy, somnolent, torpescent; lethargic, -al; heavy, – with sleep; napping; somni-fic, -ferous; sopor-ous, -ific, -iferous; hypnotic; balmy, dreamy; un-, una-wakened.

sedative etc. 174.

Adv. inactively etc. *adj.*; at leisure etc. 685.

Phr. the eyes begin to draw straws.

684. Haste.—**N.** haste, urgency; des-, dis-patch; acceleration, spurt, spirt, forced march, rush, dash; velocity etc. 274; precipit-ancy, -ation, -ousness etc. *adj.*; impetuosity; *brusquerie*; hurry, scurry, scuttle, drive, scramble, push, hustle, bustle, fuss, fidget, flurry, flutter, splutter.

V. haste, hasten; make -haste, – a dash etc. *n.*; hurry –, dash –, whip –, push –, press- -on, – forward; hurry, skurry, scuttle along, bundle on, dart to and fro, bustle, flutter, scramble; plunge, – headlong; run, race, speed; dash off; rush etc. (*violence*) 173.

bestir oneself etc. (*be active*) 682; lose -no time, – not a moment, – not an instant; make short work of; make the best of one's -time, – way.

be -precipitate etc. *adj.*; jump at; be in -haste, – a hurry etc. *n.*; have -no time, – not a moment- -to lose, – to spare; work -under pressure, – against time.

quicken etc. 274; accelerate, expedite, put on, precipitate, urge, whip, spur, flog, goad.

Adj. hasty, hurried, *brusque*; scrambling, cursory, precipitate, headlong, furious, boisterous, impetuous, hot-headed; feverish, fussy; pushing.

in -haste, – a hurry etc. *n.*; in -hot, – all- haste; breathless, pressed for time, hard pressed, urgent.

Adv. with -haste, – all haste, – breathless speed; in haste etc. *adj.*; apace etc. (*swiftly*) 274; amain; all at once etc. (*instantaneously*) 113; at short notice etc., immediately etc. (*early*) 132; posthaste; by -express, – telegraph, – wire, – wireless, – air mail.

hastily, precipitately etc. *adj.*; helter-skelter, hurry-skurry, holusbolus; slap-dash, -bang; full-tilt, -drive; heels over head, head and shoulders, headlong, *à corps perdu.*

by -fits and starts, – spurts; hop, skip and jump.

Phr. *sauve qui peut*, devil take the hindmost, no time to be lost; no sooner said than done etc. (*early*) 132; a word and a blow.

Int. hurry up! look alive! get a move on! buck up! double march! rush! urgent!

685. Leisure.—**N.** leisure; spare -time, – hours, – moments; vacant hour; time, – to spare, – on one's hands; holiday etc. (*rest*) 687; *otium cum dignitate*, ease.

V. have -leisure etc. *n.*; take one's -time, – leisure, – ease; repose etc. 687; move slowly etc. 275; while away the time etc. (*inaction*) 681; be -master of one's time, – an idle man; *desipere in loco.*

Adj. leisurely; slow etc. 275; deliberate, quiet, calm, undisturbed; at -leisure, – one's ease, – a loose end.

Phr. time hanging heavy on one's hands.

686. Exertion.—**N.** exertion, effort, strain, tug, pull, stress, force, pressure, throw, stretch, struggle, spell, spurt, spirt; stroke –, stitch- of work.

'a stong pull, a long pull and a pull all together;' dead lift; heft; gymnastics, sports; exer-cise, -citation; wear and tear; ado; toil and trouble; uphill –, hard –, warm- work; harvest time.

labor, work, toil, travail, manual labor, sweat of one's brow, swink, operoseness, drudgery, slavery, fagging, hammering; *limae labor.*

trouble, pains, duty; resolution etc. 604; energy etc. (*physical*) 171.

V. exert oneself; exert –, tax- one's energies; use exertion.

labor, work, toil, moil, sweat, fag, drudge, slave, drag a lengthened chain, wade through, strive, strain; make –, stretch- a long arm; pull, tug, ply; ply –, tug at- the oar; do the work; take the laboring oar.

bestir oneself (*be active*) 682; take trouble, trouble oneself.

work hard; rough it; put forth -one's strength, – a strong arm; fall to work, bend the bow; buckle to, set one's shoulder to the wheel etc. (*resolution*) 604; work like a -Briton, – horse, – carthorse, – galley-slave, – coalheaver; labor –, work-day and night; redouble one's efforts; do double duty; work double -hours, – tides; sit up, burn the -midnight oil, – candle at both ends; stick to etc. (*persevere*) 604*a*; work –, fight- one's way; lay about one, hammer at.

take pains; do one's -best, – level best, – utmost; do -the best one can, – all one can, – all in one's power, – as much as in one lies, – what lies in one's power; use one's -best, – utmost- endeavor, try one's -best, – utmost; play one's best card; put one's -best, – right- leg foremost; have one's whole soul in one's work, put all one's strength into, strain every nerve; spare no -efforts, – pains; go all lengths; go through fire and water etc. (*resolution*) 604; move heaven and earth, leave no stone unturned.

Adj. laboring etc. *v.*

laborious, operose, elaborate; strained; toil-, trouble-, burden-, weari-some; uphill; herculean, gymnastic, athletic, palestric.

hardworking, painstaking, strenuous, energetic. hard at work, on the stretch.

Adv. laboriously etc. *adj.*; lustily; with -might and main, – all one's might, – a strong hand, – sledge-hammer, – much ado; to the best of one's abilities, *totis viribus*, *vi et armis*, *manibus pedibusque*, tooth and nail, *unguibus et rostro*,

hammer and tongs, heart and soul; through thick and thin etc. (*perseverance*) 604*a*.
by the sweat of one's brow, *suo Marte*.

687. Repose.—N. repose, rest, silken repose; sleep etc. 683.
relaxation, breathing time; halt, pause etc. (*cessation*) 142; respite.
day of rest, *dies non*, Sabbath, Lord's day, holiday, red-letter day, vacation, recess.
V. repose; rest, – and be thankful; take -rest, – one's ease.
relax, unbend, slacken; take breath etc. (*refresh*) 689; rest upon one's oars; pause etc. (*cease*) 142; stay one's hand.
lie down; recline, – on a bed of down, – on an easy chair; go to -rest, – bed, – sleep etc. 683.
take a holiday, shut up shop; lie fallow etc. (*inaction*) 681.
Adj. reposing etc. *v.*; unstrained.
Adv. at rest.

688. Fatigue.—N. fatigue; weariness etc. 841; yawning, drowsiness etc. 683; lassitude, tiredness, fatigation, exhaustion; sweat.
anhelation, shortness of breath, panting; faintness; collapse, prostration, swoon, fainting, *deliquium*, syncope, lipothymy.
V. be -fatigued etc. *adj.*; yawn etc. (*get sleepy*) 683; droop, sink, flag; lose -breath, – wind; gasp, pant, puff, blow, drop, swoon, faint, succumb.
fatigue, tire, weary, bore, irk, fag, jade, harass, exhaust, knock up, wear out, prostrate.
tax, task, strain; over-task, -work, -burden, -tax, -strain.
Adj. fatigued etc. *v.*; weary etc. 841; drowsy etc. 683; drooping etc. *v.*; haggard; toil-, way-worn; footsore, surbated, weatherbeaten; faint; done –, used –, knock- up; exhausted, prostrate, spent; over-tired, -spent, -fatigued; forspent; unre-freshed, -stored.
worn, – out; battered, shattered, pulled down, seedy, altered.
breath-, wind-less; short of –, out of -breath, – wind; blown, puffing and blowing; short-breathed; anhelous; broken-, short-winded.
ready to drop, more dead than alive, dog -tired, – weary, walked off one's legs, tired to death, on one's last legs, played out, *hors de combat*.
fatiguing etc. *v.*; tire-, irk-, weari-some; weary; trying.

689. Refreshment.—N. bracing etc. *v.*; recovery of -strength etc. 159; restoration, revival etc. 660; repair, refection, refocillation, refreshment, regalement, bait; relief etc. 834.
V. brace etc. (*strengthen*) 159; reinvigorate; air, freshen up, refresh, recruit; repair etc. (*restore*) 660; fan, revocillate.
breathe, respire; draw –, take –, gather –, take a long –, regain –, recover- breath; get better, raise one's head; recover –, regain –, renew- one's strength etc. 159; perk up.
come to oneself etc. (*revive*) 660; feel like a giant refreshed.
Adj. refreshing etc. *v.*; recuperative etc. 660.
refreshed etc. *v.*; un-tired, -wearied.

690. Agent.—N. doer, actor, agent, performer, perpetrator, operator; execu-tor, -trix; practitioner, worker, stager.
bee, ant, working bee, laboring oar, shaft horse, servant –, maid- of all work, general servant, factotum.
workman, artisan; crafts-, handicrafts-man; mechanic, operative; working –, laboring- man; hewers of wood and drawers of water, laborer, navvy; hand, man, day laborer, journeyman, hack; mere -tool etc. 633; porter, docker, stevedore, beast of burden, drudge, fag.
maker, artificer, artist, wright, manufacturer, architect, contractor, builder, mason, bricklayer, smith, forger, Vulcan; black-, tin-smith; carpenter; ganger, platelayer.
machinist, mechanician, engineer, electrician, plumber, gasfitter etc.
semp-, sem-, seam-stress; needle-, char-, work-woman; tailor, cordwainer.
minister etc. (*instrument*) 631; servant etc. 746; representative etc. (*commissioner*) 758; (*deputy*) 759.
co-worker, fellow-worker, party to, participator in, co-operator, colleague, associate, collaborator, *particeps criminis, dramatis personae*; *personnel*.
Phrs. *'quorum pars magna fui.'*

691. Workshop.—N. work-shop, -house; laboratory; manufactory, mill, factory, armory, arsenal, mint, forge, loom; cabinet, *studio*, *bureau*, *atelier*; hive, – of industry; nursery; hot-house, -bed; kitchen, kitchenette; dock, -yard; slip, yard, wharf; found-ry, -ery; furnace; vineyard, orchard, farm, kitchen garden.
melting pot, crucible, alembic, caldron, mortar, *matrix*.

692. Conduct.—N. dealing, transaction etc. (*action*) 680; business etc. 625.
tactics, game, policy, polity; general-, statesman-seaman-ship; strate-gy, -gics; plan etc. 626.
husbandry; house-keeping, -wifery; stewardship; *ménage*; regimen, *régime*; econom-y, -ics; political economy; management; government etc. (*direction*) 693.
execution, manipulation, treatment, campaign, career, life, course, walk, race.
conduct; behavior; de-, com-portment; carriage, *maintien*, demeanor, guise, bearing, manner, mien, air, observance.
course –, line- of -conduct, – action, – proceeding; *rôle*; process, ways, practice, procedure, *modus operandi*; method etc., path etc. 627.
V. transact, execute; des-, dis-patch; proceed with, discharge; carry -on, – through, – out, – into effect; work out; go –, get- through; enact; put into practice; officiate etc. 625.

behave –, comport –, demean –, carry –, bear –, conduct –, acquit- oneself.

run a race, lead a life, play a game; take –, adopt- a course; steer –, shape- one's course; play one's- part, – cards; shift for oneself; paddle one's own canoe.

conduct; manage etc. (*direct*) 693.

deal –, have to do- with; treat, handle a case; take -steps, – measures.

Adj. conducting etc. *v.*; strategical, business-like, practical, economic, executive.

693. Direction.—N. direction; manage-ment, -ry; government, gubernation, conduct, legislation, regulation, guidance; steer-, pilot-age; reins, – of government; helm, rudder, controls, joy stick, needle, compass, binnacle; guiding –, load –, lode –, pole- star; cynosure.

super-vision, -intendence; *surveillance*, oversight; eye of the master; control, charge, auspices; board of control etc. (*council*) 696; command etc. (*authority*) 737.

premier-, senator-ship; director etc. 694; chair, seat, portfolio.

statesmanship; state-, king-craft.

minis-try, -tration; administration; steward-, proctor-ship; agency.

V. direct, manage, govern, conduct; order, prescribe, cut out work for; head, lead; lead –, show- the way; take the lead, lead on; regulate, guide, steer, pilot; take –, be at- the helm; have –, handle –, hold –, take- the reins, handle the ribbons; drive, tool; tackle.

super-intend, -vise; overlook, control, keep in order, look after, see to, oversee, legislate for; administer, ministrate; patronize; have the -care, – charge- of; have –, take- the direction; pull the -strings, – wires; rule etc. (*command*) 737; have –, hold- -office, – the portfolio; preside, – at the board; take –, occupy –, be in- the chair; pull the stroke oar.

Adj. directing etc. *v.*; executive, supervisory, hegemonic.

Adv. at the -helm, – head of, in charge of; under the auspices of.

694. Director.—N. director, manager, governor, rector, comptroller; super-intendent, -visor; intendant; over-seer, -looker; foreman, boss, straw boss; supercargo, husband, inspector, visitor, ranger, surveyor, aedile, moderator, monitor, task-master; master etc. 745; leader, ringleader, demagogue, corypheus, conductor, fugleman, precentor, bellwether, agitator.

guiding star etc. (*guidance*) 693; adviser etc. 695; guide etc. (*information*) 527; pilot; helmsman; steers-man, -mate; man at the wheel; wire-puller.

driver, whip, Jehu, charioteer; coach-, car-, cab-man, jarvey; postilion, *vetturino*, muleteer, teamster; whipper in; engineer, engine driver, motorman, *chauffeur*.

head, – man; principal, president, speaker; chair, -man; captain etc. (*master*) 745; superior; dean; mayor etc. (*civil authority*) 745; vice-president, prime minister, premier, vizier, grand vizier; dictator.

officer, functionary, minister, official, red-tapist, bureaucrat; man –, Jack- in office; office-bearer; person in authority etc. 745.

statesman, strategist, legislator, lawgiver, politician, administrator, statist, statemonger; Minos, Draco; arbiter etc. (*judge*) 967; king maker, power behind the throne.

board etc. (*council*) 696.

secretary, – of state; Reis Effendi; vicar etc. (*deputy*) 759; steward, factor; agent etc. 758; bailiff, middleman; ganger, clerk of works; land-reeve; factotum, major-domo, seneschal, house-keeper, shepherd, *croupier*; proctor, procurator, curator, librarian.

Adv. *ex officio*.

695. Advice.—N. advice, counsel, adhortation; word to the wise; suggestion, submonition, recommendation, advocacy, consultation.

exhortation etc. (*persuasion*) 615; expostulation etc. (*dissuasion*) 616; admonition etc. (*warning*) 668; guidance etc. (*direction*) 693.

instruction, charge, injunction.

adviser, prompter; counsel, -lor; monitor, mentor, Nestor, *magnus Apollo*, senator; teacher etc. 540.

guide, manual, chart etc. (*information*) 527.

physician, leech, archiater; arbiter etc. (*judge*) 967.

refer-ence, -ment; consultation, conference, parley, *pourparler* etc. 696.

V. advise, counsel; give -advice, – counsel, – a piece of advice; suggest, prompt, submonish, recommend, prescribe, advocate; exhort etc. (*persuade*) 615.

enjoin, enforce, charge, instruct, call; call upon etc. (*request*) 765; dictate.

expostulate etc. (*dissuade*) 616; admonish etc. (*warn*) 668.

advise with; lay heads –, consult- together; compare notes; hold a council, deliberate, be closeted with.

confer, consult, refer to, call in; take –, follow- advice; follow implicitly; be advised by, have at one's elbow, take one's cue from.

Adj. recommendatory; hortative etc. (*persuasive*) 615; dehortatory etc. (*dissuasive*) 616; admonitory etc. (*warning*) 668; consultative.

Int. go to!

696. Council.—N. council, committee, sub-committee, *comitia*, court, chamber, cabinet, board, bench, staff; consultation.

senate, *senatus*, parliament, house, – of Lords, – Peers, – Commons, legislature, legislative assembly, federal council, chamber of deputies, directory, *reichsrath*, *rigsdag*, *cortes*, storthing, witenagemote, *junta*, divan, *musnud*, *sanhedrim*, Amphictyonic council; *duma*, *zemstvo*, *soviet*, *cheka*, *ogpu*; *Dail Eireann*; caput, consistory, chapter, syndicate; court of appeal etc. (*tribunal*) 966; board of -control, – works; vestry; county –, borough –, district –, parish –, town- council, local board.

cabinet –, privy- council, royal commission; cockpit, convocation, synod, congress, congregation, convention, diet, states-general, aulic council.

League of Nations, assembly, *caucus*, conclave, *clique*, conventicle; meeting, sitting, *séance*, conference, session, hearing, palaver, *pourparler*, *durbar*, pow-wow, house; *quorum*.

senator; member, – of parliament; councilor, M.P., representative of the people.

Adj. senatorial, curule, parliamentary.

697. Precept.—N. precept, direction, instruction, charge; prescript, -ion; *recipe*, receipt; golden rule; maxim etc. 496.

commandment, rule, ruling, canon, law, code, *corpus juris*, *lex scripta*, common –, unwritten –, canon- law; the Ten Commandments; act, statute, convention, rubric, stage direction, regulation; form, -ula, -ulary; technicality; nice point.

order etc. (*command*) 741.

698. Skill.—N. skill, skilfulness, address; dexter-ity, -ousness; adroitness, expertness etc. *adj.*; proficiency, competence, craft, callidity, facility, knack, trick, sleight; master-y, -ship; excellence, panurgy; ambidext-erity, -rousness; sleight of hand etc. (*deception*) 545.

sea-, air-, marks-, horse-manship; tight-, rope-dancing.

accomplish-, acquire-, attain-ment; art, science; techn-icality, -ology, -ique; practical –, technical-knowledge; technocracy; finish, technic.

knowledge of the world, world wisdom, *savoir-faire*; tact; mother wit etc. (*sagacity*) 498; discretion etc. (*caution*) 864; *finesse*; craftiness etc. (*cunning*) 702; management etc. (*conduct*) 692; *ars celare artem*; self-help.

cleverness, talent, ability, ingenuity, capacity, parts, talents, faculty, endowment, *forte*, turn, gift, genius, flair, feeling; intelligence etc. 498; sharpness, readiness etc. (*activity*) 682; invention etc. 515; apt-ness, -itude; turn –, capacity –, genius-for; felicity, capability, *curiosa felicitas*, qualification, habilitation.

proficient etc. 700.

masterpiece, *coup de maître*, *chef- d'oeuvre*, *tour de force*; good stroke etc. (*plan*) 626.

V. be -skilful etc. *adj.*; excel in, be master of; have -a turn for etc. *n.*

know -what's what, – a hawk from a handsaw, – what one is about, – on which side one's bread is buttered, – what's o'clock, – a thing or two; have cut one's -eye, – wisdom- teeth.

see -one's way, – where the wind lies, – which way the wind blows; have -all one's wits about one, – one's hand in; *savoir vivre*; *scire quid valeant humeri quid ferre recusent*

look after the main chance; cut one's coat according to one's cloth; live by one's wits; exercise one's discretion, feather the oar, sail near the wind; stoop to conquer etc. (*cunning*) 702; play one's -cards well, – best card; hit the right nail on the head, put the saddle on the right horse.

take advantage of, make the most of; profit by etc. (*use*) 677; make a hit etc. (*succeed*) 731; make a virtue of necessity; make hay while the sun shines etc. (*occasion*) 134.

Adj. skilful, dexterous, adroit, expert, apt, slick, handy, quick, deft, ready, resourceful, gain; smart etc. (*active*) 682; proficient, good at, up to, at home in, master of, a good hand at, *au fait*, thoroughbred, masterly, crack, accomplished; conversant etc. (*knowing*) 490.

experienced, practiced, skilled; up –, well up-in; in -practice, – proper cue; competent, efficient, qualified, capable, fitted, fit for, up to the mark, trained, initiated, prepared, primed, finished.

clever, able, ingenious, felicitous, gifted, talented, endowed, cute, inventive etc. 515; shrewd, sharp etc. (*intelligent*) 498; cunning etc. 702; alive to, up to snuff, not to be caught with chaff; discreet.

neat-handed, fine-fingered, ambidextrous, sure-footed; cut out –, fitted- for.

technical, artistic, scientific, daedalian, ship-shape; workman-, business-, statesman-like.

Adv. skilfully etc. *adj.*; well etc. 618; artistically; with -skill, – consummate skill; *secundum artem*, *suo Marte*; to the best of one's abilities etc. (*exertion*) 686; like a machine.

699. Unskillfulness.—N. unskillfulness etc. *adj.*; want of -skill etc. 698; incompeten-ce, -cy; in-ability, -felicity, -dexterity, -experience; clumsiness; disqualification, unproficiency; quackery.

folly, stupidity etc. 499; indiscretion etc. (*rashness*) 863; thoughtlessness etc. (*inattention*) 458, (*neglect*) 460.

mis-management, -conduct; impolicy; maladministration; mis-rule, -government, -application, -direction, -feasance.

absence of rule, rule of thumb; bungling etc. *v.*; failure etc. 732; screw loose; too many cooks.

blunder etc. (*mistake*) 495; *étourderie*, *gaucherie*, act of folly, *balourdise*; botch, -ery; bad job, sad work.

sprat sent out to catch a whale, much ado about nothing, wildgoose chase.

bungler etc. 701; fool etc. 501.

layman, amateur.

V. be -unskillful etc. *adj.*; not see an inch beyond one's nose; blunder, bungle, boggle, fumble, muff, botch, bitch, flounder, loppet, stumble, trip; hobble etc. 275; put one's foot in it; make a -mess, – hash, – sad work- of; overshoot the mark.

play -tricks with, – Puck; mismanage, -conduct, -direct, -apply, -send.

stultify –, make a fool of –, commit- oneself; act foolishly; play the fool; put oneself out of court; lose one's -head, – cunning.

begin at the wrong end; do things by halves etc. (*not complete*) 730; make two bites of a cherry; play at cross purposes; strain at a gnat and swallow a camel etc. (*caprice*) 608; put the cart before the horse; lock the stable door when the horse is stolen etc. (*too late*) 135.

not know -what one is about, – one's own interest, – on which side one's bread is buttered; stand in one's own light, quarrel with one's bread and butter, throw a stone in one's own garden, kill the goose which lays the golden eggs, pay dear for one's whistle, cut one's own throat, burn one's fingers; knock –, run- one's head against a stone wall; fall into a trap, catch a Tartar, bring the house about one's ears; have too many -eggs in one basket (*imprudent*) 863, – irons in the fire.

mistake etc. 495; take the shadow for the substance etc. (*credulity*) 486; be in the wrong box, aim at a pigeon and kill a crow; take –, get- the wrong sow by the ear, – the dirty end of the stick; put -the saddle on the wrong horse, – a square peg into a round hole, – new wine into old bottles.

cut a whetstone with a razor; hold a farthing candle to the sun etc. (*useless*) 645; fight with –, grasp at- a shadow; catch at straws, lean on a broken reed, reckon without one's host, pursue a wildgoose chase; go on a fool's –, sleeveless-errand; go further and fare worse; loose –, miss-one's way; fail etc. 732.

Adj. un-skillful etc. 698; unskilled, inexpert; bungling etc. *v.*; awkward, clumsy, unhandy, lubberly, *gauche*, *maladroit*; left-, heavy-handed; slovenly, slatternly; gawky.

adrift, at fault.

in-, un-apt; inhabile; un-tractable, -teachable; giddy etc. (*inattentive*) 458; inconsiderate etc. (*neglectful*) 460; stupid etc. 499; inactive etc. 683; incompetent; un-, dis-, ill-qualified; unfit; quackish; raw, green, inexperienced, rusty, out of practice.

un-accustomed, -used, -trained etc. 537; -initiated, -conversant etc. (*ignorant*) 491; shiftless; unbusinesslike, unpractical; unstatesmanlike.

un-, ill-, mis-advised; ill-devised, -imagined, -judged, -contrived, -conducted; un-, mis-guided; misconducted, foolish, wild; infelicitous; penny wise and pound foolish etc. (*inconsistent*) 608.

Phr. one's fingers being all thumbs; the right hand forgets its cunning.

il se noyerait dans une goutte d'eau.

incidit in Scyllam qui vult vitare Charybdim; *out of the frying pan into the fire.*

700. Proficient.—N. proficient, expert, adept, dab; *connoisseur* etc. (*scholar*) 492; master, -hand; top-sawyer, *prima donna*, first fiddle, *chef de cuisine*; protagonist; past master; profess-or, -ional, specialist.

picked man; medalist, prizeman.

veteran; old -stager, – campaigner, – soldier, – file, – hand; man of -business, – the world.

nice –, good –, clean- hand; practised –, experienced- -eye, – hand; marksman; good –, dead –, crack- shot; rope-dancer, funambulist, acrobat, contortionist; cunning man; conjuror etc. (*deceiver*) 548; wizard etc. 994.

genius; master-mind, – head, – spirit.

cunning –, sharp -blade, – fellow; jobber; cracksman etc. (*thief*) 792; politician, tactician, diplomat, -ist, strategist.

pantologist, admirable Crichton, Jack of all trades; prodigy of learning; walking encyclopedia; mine of information.

701. Bungler.—N. bungler; blunderer, -head; marplot, fumbler, lubber, lout, oaf, duffer, stick, clown; bad –, poor- -hand, – shot; butter-fingers.

no conjuror, flat, muff, slow coach, looby, lubber, swab; clod, yokel, hick, awkward squad, novice, greenhorn, jaywalker, *blanc-bec*.

land lubber; fresh water –, fair weather- sailor; horse-marine; fish out of water, ass in lion's skin, jackdaw in peacock's feathers; quack etc. (*deceiver*) 548; Lord of Misrule.

sloven, slattern, trapes.

Phr. *il n'a pas inventé la poudre*; he will never set the Thames on fire.

702. Cunning.—N. cunning, craft; cunningness, craftiness etc. *adj.*; subtlety, artificiality; maneuvring etc. *v.*; temporization; circumvention.

chicane, -ry; sharp practice, knavery, jugglery; concealment etc. 528; nigger in the woodpile; guile, duplicity etc. (*falsehood*) 544; foul play.

diplomacy, politics; Machiavellism; jobbery, back-stairs influence, gerrymandering.

art, -ifice; device, machination; plot etc. (*plan*) 626; maneuver, stratagem, dodge, artful dodge, wile; trick, -ery etc. (*deception*) 545; *ruse, – de guerre; finesse*, side-blow, thin end of the wedge, shift, go by, subterfuge, evasion; white lie etc. (*untruth*) 546; juggle, *tour de force*; tricks of the trade, – upon travelers; imposture, deception; *espièglerie*, net, trap etc. 545.

Ulysses, Machiavel, sly boots, fox, reynard; Scotch-, Yorkshire-man; Jew, Yankee; intriguer, *intrigant*, schemer, trickster.

V. be -cunning etc. *adj.*; have cut one's eyeteeth; contrive etc. (*plan*) 626; live by one's wits; maneuver; intrigue, gerrymander, *finesse*, double, temporize, stoop to conquer, *reculer pour mieux sauter*, circumvent, steal a march upon; overreach etc. 545; throw off one's guard; surprise etc. 508; outdo, get the better of, snatch from under one's nose; snatch a verdict; waylay, undermine, introduce the thin end of the wedge; play -a deep game, – tricks with; have an axe to grind; *ambiguas in vulgum spargere voces*; flatter, make things pleasant.

Adj. cunning, crafty, artful; skilful etc. 698; subtle, feline, vulpine; cunning as a -fox, – serpent; deep, – laid; profound; designing, contriving; intriguing etc. *v.*; strategic, diplomatic, politic, Machiavellian, time-serving; artificial; trick-y, -sy; wily, sly, slim, insidious, stealthy, foxy; underhand etc. (*hidden*) 528; subdolous; deceitful etc. 545; double-tongued, -faced; shifty; crooked; arch, pawky, shrewd, acute; sharp, – as a needle; canny, astute, leery, knowing, up to snuff, too clever by half, not to be caught with chaff.

Adv. cunningly etc. *adj.*; slily, on the sly, by a side wind.

Phr. diamond cut diamond.

703. Artlessness.—N. artlessness etc. *adj.*; nature, simplicity; innocence etc. 946; *bonhomie, naiveté, abandon*, candor, sincerity; singleness of -purpose, – heart; honesty etc. 939; plain speaking; *épanchement*.

rough diamond, matter of fact man; *le palais de vérité*; *enfant terrible*.

V. be -artless etc. *adj.*; look one in the face; wear one's heart upon his sleeves for daws to peck at; think aloud; speak -out, – one's mind; be free with one, call a spade a spade.

Adj. artless, natural, pure, native, simple, plain, inartificial, untutored, unsophisticated, *ingénu,* unaffected, *naïve*; sincere, frank; open, – as day; candid, ingenuous, guileless, unsuspicious, childlike; honest etc. 939; innocent etc. 946; Arcadian; undesigning, straightforward; unreserved, unvarnished, above-board; simple-, single-minded; frank-, open-, single-, simple-hearted; open and above-board.

free-, plain-, out-spoken; blunt, downright, direct, matter of fact, unpoetical; unflattering.

Adv. in plain -words, – English; without mincing the matter; not to mince the matter etc. (*affirmation*) 535.

Phr. *Davus sum non Oedipus*; *liberavi animam meam.*

704. Difficulty.—N. difficulty; hardness etc. *adj.*; impracticability etc. (*impossibility*) 471; tough –, hard –, uphill- work; hard –, Herculean –, Augean- task; task of Sisyphus, Sisyphean labor, tough job, teaser, rasper, dead lift.

dilemma, embarrassment; perplexity etc. (*uncertainty*) 475; involvement; intricacy; entanglement etc. 59; cross fire; awkwardness, delicacy, ticklish card to play, deadlock, knot, Gordian knot, *dignus vindice nodus,* net, meshes, maze; coil etc. (*convolution*) 248; crooked path.

nice –, delicate –, subtle –, knotty-point; vexed question, *vexata quaestio,* poser; puzzle etc. (*riddle*) 533; paradox; hard –, nut to crack; bone to pick, *crux, pons asinorum,* where the shoe pinches.

nonplus, quandary, strait, pass, pinch, pretty pass, stress, brunt; critical situation, crisis; trial, rub, emergency, exigency, scramble.

scrape, hobble, slough, quagmire, hot water, hornet's nest; sea –, peck- of troubles; pretty kettle of fish; pickle, stew, *imbroglio,* mess, muddle, botch, fuss, bustle, ado; false position; set fast, stand; dead -lock, – set; fix, horns of a dilemma, *cul de sac*; hitch; stumbling block etc. (*hindrance*) 706.

V. be -difficult etc. *adj.*; run one hard, go against the grain, try one's patience, put one out; put to one's -shifts, – wit's end; go hard with –, try- one; pose, perplex etc. (*uncertain*) 475; bother, nonplus, gravel, bring to a dead lock; be -impossible etc. 471; be in the way of etc. (*hinder*) 706.

meet with –, labor under –, get into –, plunge into –, struggle with –, contend with –, grapple with- difficulties; labor under a disadvantage; be -in difficulty etc. *adj.*

fish in troubled waters, buffet the waves, swim against the stream, scud under bare poles.

have -much ado with, – a hard time of it; come to the -push, – pinch; bear the brunt.

grope in the dark, lose one's way, weave a tangled web, walk among eggs.

get into a -scrape etc. *n.*; bring a hornet's nest about one's ears; be put to one's shifts; flounder, boggle, struggle; not know which way to turn etc. (*uncertain*) 475; get -tangled up, – wound up; *perdre son latin*; stick - at, – in the mud, – fast; come to a -stand, – dead lock; hold the wolf by the ears.

render -difficult etc. *adj.*; encumber, embarrass, ravel, entangle; put a spoke in the wheel etc. (*hinder*) 706; lead a pretty dance.

Adj. difficult, not easy, hard, tough; trouble-, toil-, irk-some; operose, laborious, onerous, arduous, Herculean, formidable; sooner –, more easily- said than done; difficult –, hard- to deal with; ill-conditioned, crabbed; not -to be handled with kid gloves, – made with rosewater.

awkward, unwieldy, unmanageable; intractable, stubborn etc. (*obstinate*) 606; perverse, refractory, plaguy, trying, thorny, rugged; knot-ted, -ty; invious; path-, track-less; labyrinthine etc. (*convoluted*) 248; intricate, complicated etc. (*tangled*) 59; impracticable etc. (*impossible*) 471; not -feasible etc. 470; desperate etc. (*hopeless*) 859.

embarrassing, perplexing etc. (*uncertain*) 475; delicate, ticklish, critical; beset with –, full of –, surrounded by –, entangled by –, encompassed with- difficulties.

under a difficulty; in -difficulty, – hot water, – the suds, – a cleft stick, – a fix, – the wrong box, – a scrape etc. *n.*; – deep water, – a fine pickle; *in extremis*; between -two stools, – Scylla and Charybdis; surronded by -shoals, – breakers, – quicksands; at cross purposes; not out of the wood.

reduced to straits; hard –, sorely- pressed; run hard; pinched, put to it, straitened; hard -up, – put to it, – set; put to one's shifts; puzzled, at a loss etc. (*uncertain*) 475; at -the end of one's tether, – one's wit's end, – a nonplus, – a standstill; graveled, nonplussed, stranded, aground; stuck –, set- fast; up a tree, at bay, *aux abois*, driven -into a corner, – from post to pillar, – to extremity, – to one's wit's end, – to the wall; *au bout de son latin*; out of one's -depth, – reckoning; put –, thrown -out.

accomplished with difficulty; hard-fought, -earned.

Adv. with -difficulty, – much ado; hardly etc. *adj.*; uphill; against the -stream, – grain; *à rebours*; *invitâ Minervâ*; in the teeth of; at –, upon- a pinch; at long odds.

Phr. ay there's the rub; *hic labor hoc opus*; things are come to a pretty pass.

705. Facility.—N. facility, ease; easiness etc. *adj.*; capability; feasibility etc. (*practicability*) 470; flexibility, pliancy etc. 324; smoothness etc. 255; convenience.

plain –, smooth –, straight- sailing; mere child's play, holiday task.

smooth water, fair wind; smooth – royal- road; clear -coast, – stage; *tabula rasa*; *full play* etc. (*freedom*) 748.

disen-cumbrance, -tanglement; deoppilation; permission etc. 760.

V. be -easy etc. *adj.*; go on –, run- smoothly; have -full play etc. *n.*; go –, run- on all fours; obey the helm, work well.

flow –, swim –, drift –, go- with the- -stream, – tide; see one's way; have -it all one's own way, – the game in one's own hands; walk over the course, win -at a canter, – hands down; make -light of, – nothing of; be at home in etc. (*skilful*) 698.

render -easy etc. *adj.*; facilitate, smooth, ease; popularize; lighten, – the labor; free, clear; disencumber, -embarrass, -entangle, -engage; deobstruct, unclog, extricate, unravel; untie –, cut- the knot; disburden, unload, exonerate, emancipate, free from, deoppilate; humor etc. (*aid*) 707; lubricate etc. 332; relieve etc. 834.

leave -a hole to creep out of, – a loophole, – the matter open; give -the reins to, – full play, – full swing; make way for; open the -door to, – way; prepare –, smooth –, clear- the -ground, – way, – path, – road; pave the way, bridge over; permit etc. 760.

Adj. easy, facile; feasible etc. (*practicable*) 470; easily -managed, – accomplished; within reach, accessible, easy of access, for the million, open to.

manageable, wieldy; towardly, tractable; submissive; yielding, ductile; pliant etc. (*soft*) 324; glib, slippery; smooth etc. 255; on -friction wheels, – velvet; convenient.

un-, dis-burdened, -encumbered, -embarrassed; exonerated; un-loaded, -obstructed, -trammeled, -impeded, -restrained etc. (*free*) 748; at ease, light.

at –, quite at- home; in -one's element, – smooth water.

Adv. easily etc. *adj.*; readily, smoothly, swimmingly, *ad lib.*, on easy terms, single-handed.

Phr. touch and go

Int. all clear!

706. Hindrance.—N. prevention, preclusion, obstruction, stoppage; prohibition; inter-ruption, -ception, -clusion; hindrance, impedition; retardment, -ation; constriction; embarrassment, oppilation; coarctation, stricture, restriction; anchor etc. 666; restraint etc. 751 & 752; inhibition etc. 761; blockade etc. (*closure*) 261; picketing.

inter-ference, -position; obtrusion; discouragement, -countenance, -approval, -approbation; opposition etc. 708.

impediment, let, obstacle, obstruction, knot, knag; check, hitch, *contretemps, impasse,* screw loose, grit in the oil.

bar, stile, barrier; turn-stile, -pike; gate, portcullis; bulwark, parapet, barricade etc. (*defence*) 717; wall, dead wall, breakwater, groyne; bulkhead, block, buffer; stopper etc. 263; boom, dam, weir, burrock.

drawback, objection; stumbling-block, -stone; lion in the path; snag; snags and sawyers.

en-, in-cumbrance; clog, skid, shoe, spoke; brake, drag, – chain, – weight; stay, stop; preventive, prophylactic; contraception; load, burden, fardel, *onus,* millstone round one's neck, *impedimenta*; dead weight; lumber, pack; nightmare, Ephialtes, incubus, old man of the sea; remora.

difficulty etc. 704; insuperable etc. 471- obstacle; estoppel; ill wind; head wind etc. (*opposition*) 708; trammel, tether etc. (*means of restraint*) 752; hold back, counterpoise; damper, wet blanket, hinderer, marplot, kill-joy, dog in the manger, interloper; trail of a red herring; opponent etc. 710.

V. hinder, impede, impedite, embarrass.

keep –, stave –, ward- off; picket; obviate; a-, ante-vert; turn aside, draw off, prevent, forefend, nip in the bud; retard, slacken, check, let; counteract, -check; preclude, debar, foreclose, estop; inhibit etc. 761; shackle etc. (*restrain*) 751; restrict, restrain, cohibit.

obstruct, filibuster, stop, stay, bar, bolt, lock; block, – up; belay, barricade; block –, stop- the way; dam up etc. (*close*) 261; put on the -brake etc. *n.*; scotch –, lock –, put a spoke in- the wheel; put a stop to etc. 142; traverse, contravene; inter-rupt, -cept; oppose etc. 708; hedge -in, – round; cut off; interclude.

inter-pose, -fere, -meddle etc. 682.

cramp, hamper; clog, – the wheels; cumber; en-, in-cumber; handicap; choke; saddle –, load- with; overload, lay; lumber, trammel, tie one's hands, put to inconvenience; in-, discommode; discompose; hustle, drive into a corner; choke off.

run –, fall- foul of; cross the path of, break in upon.

thwart, frustrate, disconcert, balk, foil, baffle, snub, override, circumvent; defeat etc. 731; spike guns etc. (*render useless*) 645; spoil, mar, clip the wings of; cripple etc. (*injure*) 659; put an extinguisher on; damp; dishearten etc. (*dissuade*) 616; discountenance, throw cold water on, spoil sport; lay –, throw- a wet blanket on; cut the ground from under one, take the wind out of one's sails, undermine; be –, stand- in the way of; act as a drag; hang like a millstone round one's neck.

Adj. hindering etc. *v.*; obstr-uctive, -uent; impedi-tive, -ent; intercipient; prophylactic etc. (*remedial*) 662.

in the way of, unfavorable; onerous, burdensome; cumb-rous, -ersome; obtrusive.

hindered etc. *v.*; wind-bound, water-logged, heavy laden; hard pressed.

unassisted etc. (*see* assist etc. 707); single-handed, alone; deserted etc. 624.

707. Aid.—N. aid, -ance; assistance, help, opitulation, succor; support, lift, advance, furtherance, promotion; coadjuvancy etc. (*co-operation*) 709.

patronage, championship, countenance, favor, interest, advocacy, auspices.

sustentation, subvention, subsidy, bounty, alimentation, nutrition, nourishment, maintenance; manna in the wilderness; food etc. 298; means etc. 632.

ministr-y, -ation; subministration; accomodation.

relief, rescue; help at a dead lift; supernatural aid; *deus ex machinâ*.

supplies, reinforcements, succors, contingents, recruits; support etc. (*physical*) 215; adjunct, ally etc. (*helper*) 711.

V. aid, assist, help, succor, lend one's aid; come to the aid etc. *n*- of; contribute, subscribe to; bring –, give –, furnish –, afford –, supply- -aid etc. *n.*; render assistance; give –, stretch –, lend –, bear –, hold out- a -hand, – helping hand; give one a -lift, – cast, – turn; take -by the hand, – in tow; help a lame dog over a stile, lend wings to.

relieve, rescue; set -up, – agoing, – on one's legs; bear –, pull- through; give new life to, be the making of; reinforce, recruit; set –, put –, push- forward; give -a lift, – a shove, – an impulse- to; promote, further, forward, advance; speed, expedite, quicken, hasten.

support, sustain, uphold, prop, hold up, bolster.

cradle, nourish; nurture, nurse, dry nurse, suckle, put out to nurse; manure, cultivate, force; foster; cherish, foment; feed –, fan- the flame.

serve; do service to, tender to, pander to; ad-, sub-, minister to; tend, attend, wait on; take care of etc. 459; entertain; smooth the bed of death.

oblige, accomodate, consult the wishes of; humor, cheer, encourage.

second, stand by; back, – up; pay the piper, abet; work –, make interest –, stick up –, take up the cudgels- for; take up –, espouse –, adopt- the cause of; advocate, beat up for recruits, press into the service; squire, give moral support to, keep in countenance, countenance, patronize; lend - oneself, – one's countenance- to; smile –, shine- upon; favor, befriend, take up, take in hand, enlist under the banners of; side with etc. (*co-operate*) 709.

be of use to; subserve etc. (*instrument*) 631; benefit etc. 648; render a service etc. (*utility*) 644; conduce etc. (*tend*) 176.

Adj. aiding etc. *v.*; auxiliary, adjuvant, helpful; coadjuvant etc. 709; subservient, ministrant, ancillary, accessory, subsidiary.

at one's beck; friendly, amicable, favorable, propitious, well-disposed; neighborly; obliging etc. (*benevolent*) 906.

Adv. with –, by- -the aid etc. *n.*- of; on –, in- behalf of; in -aid, – the service, – the name, – favor, – furtherance- of; on account of; for the sake of, on the part of; *non obstante*.

Int. help! save us! to the rescue! S.O.S.!

708. Opposition.—N. opposition, antagonism, oppug-nancy, -nation; impugnation; contravention; counteraction etc. 179; counterplot.

cross-fire, under-current, head-wind.

clashing, collision, conflict, lack of harmony, contest.

competition, two of a trade, rivalry, emulation, race; war to the knife.

absence of -aid etc. 707; resistance etc. 719; restraint etc. 751; hindrance etc. 706.

V. oppose, conteract, run counter to; withstand etc. (*resist*) 719; control etc. (*restrain*) 751; hinder etc. 706; antagonize, oppugn, fly in the face of, go dead against, kick against, fall foul of; set –, pit- against; face, confront, cope with; make a -stand, – dead set- against; set -oneself, one's face- against; protest –, vote –, raise one's voice- against; disfavor, turn one's back upon; set at naught, slap in the face, slam the door in one's face.

be –, play- at cross purposes; counter-work, - mine; thwart, overthwart.

stem, breast, encounter; stem –, breast- the - tide, – current, – flood; buffet the waves; beat up –, make head- against; grapple with; kick against the pricks etc. (*resist*) 719; contend etc. 720 –, do battle etc. (*warfare*) 722- -with, – against.

contra-dict, -vene; belie; go –, run –, beat –, militate- against; come in conflict with.

emulate etc. (*compete*) 720; rival, spoil one's trade.

Adj. oppos-ing, -ed etc. *v.*; adverse, antagonistic; ambivalent; contrary etc. 14; at variance etc. 24; at issue, at war with; in opposition; 'agin the Government.'

un-favorable, -friendly; hostile, inimical, cross, unpropitious.

in hostile array, front to front, with crossed bayonets, at daggers drawn; up in arms; resistant etc. 791.

competitive, emulous.

Adv. against, *versus*, counter to, in conflict with, at cross purposes.

against the -grain, – current, – stream, – wind, – tide; with a headwind; with the wind - ahead, – in one's teeth.

in spite, in despite, in defiance; in the -way, – teeth, – face- of; across; a-, over-thwart; where the shoe pinches.

though etc. 30; even; *quand même*; *per contra*.

Phr. *nitor in adversum*.

709. Co-operation.—N. co-operation; coadjuvancy, -tancy; coagency, coefficiency; concert, concurrence, complicity, participation; union etc. 43; amalgamation, combination etc. 48; collusion.

association, alliance, colleagueship, jointstock, copartnership, trust, cartel, pool, ring, combine, interlocking directorate; confederation etc. (*party*) 712; federation, coalition, fusion; a long pull, a strong pull and a pull all together; log-rolling, freemasonry.

unanimity etc. (*assent*) 488; *esprit de corps*, party spirit; clan-, partisan-ship; reciprocity, concord etc. 714.

V. co-operate, co-adjute, concur; conduce etc. 178; combine, cartelize, unite one's efforts; keep –, draw –, pull –, club –, hang –, hold –, league –, band –, be banded- together; stand –, put- shoulder to shoulder; act in concert, join forces, fraternize, cling to one another, conspire, concert, lay one's heads together; confederate, be in league with; collude, understand one another, play into the hands of, hunt in couples.

side –, take side –, go along –, go hand in hand –, join hands –, make common cause –, strike in –, unite –, join –, mix oneself up –, take part –, play along –, cast in one's lot- with; join –, enter into- partnership with; rally round, follow the lead of; come to, pass over to, come into the views of; be –, row –, sail- in the same boat; sail on the same tack.

be a party to, lend oneself to; participate; have a -hand in, – finger in the pie; take –, bear- part in; second etc. (*aid*) 707; take the part of, play the game of; espouse a -cause, – quarrel.

Adj. co-operating etc. *v.*; in -co-operation etc. *n.*, – league etc. (*party*) 712; coadju-vant, -tant; hand and glove with.

favorable etc. 707- to; un-opposed etc. 708.

Adj. as one man etc. (*unanimously*) 488; shoulder to shoulder; in co-operation with.

710. Opponent.—N. opponent, antagonist, adversary; adverse party, opposition; enemy etc. 891; assailant.

oppositionist, obstructive; obscurantist; brawler, wrangler, brangler, disputant, extremist, irreconcilable, diehard, bitter-ender.

malcontent; Jacobin, Fenian etc. 742; demagogue, reactionist.
passive resister, conscientious objector.
rival, competitor, contestant.

711. Auxiliary.—N. auxiliary; recruit; assistant; adju-vant, -tant; adjunct; help, er, -mate, -ing hand; midwife; colleague, partner, mate, *confrère*, co-operator; coadju-tor, -trix; collaborator.
ally; friend etc. 890; confidant, *fidus Achates*, pal, chum, buddy, *alter ego*.
confederate; ac-, complice; accessory, – after the fact; *particeps criminis*.
aide-de-camp, secretary, clerk, associate, marshal; right-hand; candle-, bottle-holder; hand-maid; servant etc. 746; puppet, cat's-paw; stooge, dependent, creature, jackal; tool, *âme damnée*; satellite, adherent, parasite.
votary, disciple, secta-rian, -ry; seconder, backer, upholder, supporter, abettor, advocate, partisan, champion, patron, friend at court, mediator.
friend in need, Jack at a pinch, *deus ex machinâ*, guardian angel, fairy godmother; special providence, tutelary genius.

712. Party.—N. party, faction, side, denomination, class, communion, set, crowd, crew, band, horde, posse, phalanx; regiment etc. 726; family, clan etc. 166.
Tories, Conservatives, Unionists, Whigs, Liberals, Radicals, Labour party, Socialists, Communists etc.; Republicans, Democrats, Farmer-Labor; *Fascisti*, Revolutionaries etc. 742.
community, body, fellowship, sodality, solidarity; con-, fraternity; sorority; brother-, sisterhood.
Freemasons, Knights Templars, Odd Fellows, Ku Klux Klan etx.
knot, gang, *clique*, ring, circle; *coterie*, club, *casino*.
corporation, corporate body, guild; establishment, company, copartnership, firm, house, joint concern, joint-stock company, trust, investment trust, combine etc. 709.
society, association; instit-ute, -ution; union; trade-union; league, syndicate, alliance, *Verein*, *Bund*, *Zollverein*, combination; league –, alliance- offensive and defensive; coalition; federation; confedera -tion, -cy; junto, cabal, *camarilla*, *camorra*, *brigue*; freemasonry; party spirit etc. (*co-operation*) 709.
staff; cast, *dramatis personae*.
V. unite, join; club together etc. (*co-operate*) 709; cement –, form- a party etc. *n.*; associate etc. (*assemble*) 72.
Adj. in -league, – partnership, – alliance etc. *n.*
bonded –, banded –, linked etc. (*joined*) 43- together; embattled; confederated, federative, joint, corporate, leagued, fraternal, masonic, cliquish.
Adv. hand in hand, side by side, shoulder to shoulder, *en masse*, in the same boat.

713. Discord.—N. disagreement etc. 24; discord, -accord, -sidence, -sonance; jar, clash, shock; jarring, jostling etc. *v.*; screw loose.
variance, difference, dissension, misunderstanding, cross purposes, odds, *brouillerie*; division, split, rupture, disruption, division in the camp, house divided against itself, rift within the lute; disunion, breach; schism etc. (*dissent*) 489; feud, faction.
quarrel, dispute, rippet, spat, tiff, *tracasserie*, squabble, altercation, words, high words; wrangling etc. *v.*; jangle, brabble cross questions and crooked answers, snip-snap; family jars.
polemics; litigation; strife etc. (*contention*) 720; warfare etc. 722; outbreak, open rupture; breaking off of negotiations, recall of ambassadors; declaration of war.
broil, brawl, row, racket, hubbub, rixation; embroilment, embranglement, *imbroglio*, *fracas*, breach of the peace, piece of work, scrimmage, rumpus; breeze, squall; riot, disturbance etc. (*disorder*) 59; commotion etc. (*agitation*) 315; bear garden, Donnybrook Fair.
subject of dispute, ground of quarrel, battle ground, disputed point; bone -of contention, – to pick; apple of discord, *casus belli*; question at issue etc. (*subject of inquiry*) 461; vexed question, *vexata quaestio*, brand of discord.
troublous times; cat-and-dog life; contentiousness etc. *adj.*; enmity etc. 889; hate etc. 898; Kilkenny cats; disputant etc. 710; strange bedfellows.
V. be discordant etc. *adj.*; disagree, come amiss etc. 24; clash, jar, jostle, pull different ways, conflict, have no measures with, misunderstand one another; live like cat and dog; differ; dissent etc. 489; have a -bone to pick, – crow to pluck- with.
fall out, quarrel, dispute; litigate; controvert etc. (*deny*) 536; squabble, wrangle, jangle, brangle, bicker, nag; spar etc. (*contend*) 720; have -words etc. *n.* with; fall foul of.
split; break –, break squares –, part company- with; declare war, try conclusions; join –, put in- issue; pick a quarrel, fasten a quarrel on; sow –, stir up- -dissension etc. *n.*; embroil, estrange, entangle, disunite, widen the breach; set -at odds, – together by the ears; set –, pit- against; rub up the wrong way.
get into hot water, fish in troubled waters, brawl; kick up a -row, – dust; turn the house out of window.
Adj. discordant; disagreeing etc. *v.*; out of tune, dissonant, inharmonious, harsh, grating, jangling, ajar, on bad terms; dissentient etc. 489; inconsistent, contradictory, incongruous, discrepant; un- reconciled, -pacified.
quarrelsome, unpacific; gladiatorial, controversial, polemic, disputatious; factious; liti-gious, -gant; pettifogging.
at odds, at loggerheads, at daggers drawn, at variance, at issue, at cross purposes, at sixes and sevens, at feud, at high words; up in arms, together by the ears, in hot water, embroiled.
torn, disunited.
Phr. *quot homines tot sententiae*; no love lost between them, *non nostrum tantas componere lites*.

714. Concord.—N. concord, accord, harmony, symphony, homology; aggreement etc. 23; sympathy etc. (*love*) 897; response; union, unison, unity; bonds of harmony; peace etc. 721; unanimity etc. (*assent*) 488; league etc. 712; happy family.

rapprochement; *réunion*; amity etc. (*friendship*) 888; reciprocity; alliance, ***entente cordiale***, good understanding, conciliation, arbitration, peacemaker etc. 724.

V. agree etc. 23; accord, harmonize with; fraternize; be -concordant etc. *adj.*; go hand in hand; blend –, tone in- with; run parallel etc. (*concur*) 178; understand one another; pull together etc. (*co-operate*) 709; put up one's horses together, sing in chorus.

side –, sympathize –, go –, chime in –, fall in- with; come round; be pacified etc. 723; assent etc. 488; enter into the -ideas, – feelings- of; reciprocate.

hurler avec les loups; go –, swim- with the stream.

pour oil on troubled waters, keep in good humor, render accordant, put in tune; come to an understanding, meet half-way; keep the –, remain at- peace.

Adj. concordant, congenial; agreeing etc. *v.*; in-accord etc. *n.*; harmonious, united, cemented; banded together etc. 712; allied; friendly etc. 888; fraternal; conciliatory; at one with; of one mind etc. (*assent*) 488.

at peace, in still water; tranquil etc. (*pacific*) 721.

Adv. with one voice etc. (*assent*) 488; in concert with, hand in hand; on one's side, unanimously.

715. Defiance.—N. defiance; daring etc. *v.*; dare, challenge, *cartel*; threat etc. 909; war-cry, -whoop.

V. defy, dare, beard; brave etc. (*courage*) 861; bid defiance to; set at -defiance, – naught; hurl defiance at; dance the war dance; snap the fingers at, laugh to scorn; disobey etc. 742.

show -fight, – one's teeth, – a bold front; bluster, look big, stand akimbo; double –, shake- the fist; threaten etc 909.

challenge, call out; throw –, fling- down the -gauntlet, – gage, – glove.

Adj. defiant; defying etc. *v.*; with arms akimbo; rebellious, insolent; reckless, greatly daring.

Adv. in -defiance, – the teeth- of; under one's very nose.

Int. do your worst! come if you dare! come on! marry come up! hoity toity!

Phr. *noli me tangere*; *nemo me impune lacessit*.

716. Attack.—N. attack; assault, – and battery; onset, onslaught, charge.

aggression, drive, offence; incursion, inroad; invasion; irruption; outbreak; *estrapade*, *ruade*; *coup de main*, sally, *sortie*, *camisade*, raid, foray; run -at, – against; dead set at.

storm, -ing; boarding, *escalade*; siege, investment, obsession, bombardment, cannonade; air raid.

fire, volley; platoon –, file –, rapid-fire; *fusillade*; sharp-shooting, sniping; broadside; raking –, cross –, machine gun- fire; – volley of grapeshot, *feu d'enfer*; salvo.

cut, thrust, lunge, pass, *passado*, *carte* and *tierce*, home thrust, *coup de pied*; kick, punch, etc. (*impulse*) 276.

battue, *razzia*, *Jacquerie*, *dragonnade*; devastation etc. 162.

assailant, aggressor, invader.

base of operations, point of attack.

V. attack, assault, assail; set –, fall- upon; charge, impugn, break a lance with, enter the lists.

assume –, take- the offensive; be –, become- the aggressor; strike the first blow, fire the first shot, throw the first stone at; lift a hand –, draw the sword- against; take up the cudgels; advance –, march- against; march upon, invade, harry; come on, show fight.

strike at, poke at, thrust at; aim –, deal- a blow at; give –, fetch- one a -blow, – kick; have a -cut, – shot, – fling, – shy- at; be down –, pounce- upon; fall foul of, pitch into, launch out against; bait, slap on the face; make a -thrust, – pass, – set, – dead set- at; dunt; bear down upon.

close with, come to close quarters, bring to bay.

ride full tilt against; let fly at, dash at, run a tilt at, rush at, tilt at, run at, fly at, hawk at, have at, let out at; make a -dash, – rush at; attack tooth and nail; strike home; drive –, press- one hard; be hard upon, run down, strike at the root of.

lay about one, run amuck.

fire -upon, – at, – a shot at; shoot at, pop at, level at, let off a gun at; open fire, pepper, bombard, shell, pour a broadside into; fire -a volley, – red-hot shot; spring a mine.

throw -a stone, – stones- at; stone, lapidate, pelt; hurl -at, – against, – at the head of.

beset, besiege, beleaguer; lay siege to, invest, open the trenches, plant a battery, sap, mine; storm, board, scale the walls.

cut and thrust, bayonet, butt; kick, strike etc. (*impulse*) 276; whip etc. (*punish*) 972.

Adj. attacking etc. *v.*; aggressive, offensive, obsidional.

up in arms; on the warpath; over the top.

Adv. on the offensive.

Int. 'up and at them!'

717. Defense.—N. defense, protection, guard, ward; shielding etc. *v.*; propugnation; preservation etc. 670; guardianship.

self-defense, -preservation; resistance etc. 719.

safeguard etc. (*safety*) 664; screen etc. (*shelter*) 666, (*concealment*) 530; barrage; fortification; muni-tion, -ment; bulwark, fosse, moat, ditch, intrenchment, trench, dugout, gas mask; dike, dyke; parapet, parados, sunk fence, embankment, mound, mole, bank; earth- field-work, gabions; fence, wall, dead wall, contravallation; paling etc. (*inclosure*) 232; palisade, haha, stockade, *stoccado, laager, sangar*; barri-er, -cade; boom; portcullis, *chevaux de frise*; aba-, abat-, abba-tis; *vallum*, circumvallation, battlement, rampart, scarp; e-, counter-scarp; glacis, casemate.

mine, countermine.

buttress, abutment; shore etc. (*support*) 215.

breastwork, *banquette*, curtain, mantlet, bastion, demilune, redan, ravelin; advanced –, horn –, out- work, lunette; barb-acan, -ican; redoubt; fortelage, -alice; lines; coast defense.

loop-hole, machicolation; sally-port, postern gate.

hold, stronghold, fastness; asylum etc. (*refuge*) 666; keep, donjon, fortress, citadel; capitol, castle; tower, – of strength; fort, barracoon, pah, sconce, martello tower, peel-house, block-house, rath; wooden walls; turret, barbette.

buffer, corner-stone, fender, apron, mask, gauntlet, thimble, carapace, armor, shield, buckler; target, targe, aegis, breastplate, cuirass, plastron, habergeon, mail, coat of mail, brigandine, hauberk, lorication, helmet, helm, basinet, sallet, salade, heaume, morion, murrion, armet, cabaset, vizor, casquetel, siege-cap, head-piece, casque, steel helmet, tin hat; *pickelhaube,* csako; shako etc. (*dress*) 225; bearskin; panoply; truncheon etc. (*weapon*) 727.

garrison, picket, piquet; defender, protector; guardian etc. (*safety*) 664; trabant, body guard, champion; knight-errant, Paladin; propugner.

V. defend, forfend, fend; shield, screen, shroud; fence round etc. (*circumscribe*) 229; fence, intrench; guard etc. (*keep safe*) 664; guard against; take care of etc. (*vigilance*) 459; bear harmless; keep –, ward –, beat- off; hinder etc. 706.

parry, repel, propugn, put to flight; give a warm reception to [*ironical*]; hold –, keep- at bay, – arm's length.

stand –, act- on the defensive; show fight; maintain –, stand- one's ground; stand by; hold one's own; bear –, stand- the brunt; fall back upon, hold, stand in the gap.

Adj. defending etc. *v.*; defensive; mural; armed, – at all points, – *cap-à-pie,* – to the teeth; panoplied; accoutred, harnessed; iron plated, -clad; loop-holed, castellated, machicolated; casemated; defended etc. *v.*; proof against, bomb-, bullet-proof; protective.

Adv. defensively; on the -defense, – defensive; in defense; at bay, *pro aris et focis.*

Int. no surrender! *il ne passeront pas!*

Phr. defense not defiance.

718. Retaliation.—N. retaliation, reprisal, retort; counter-stroke, -blast, -plot, -project; retribution, *lex talionis*; reciprocation etc. (*reciprocity*) 12.

requital, desert, tit for tat, give and take, blow for blow, *quid pro quo,* a Roland for an Oliver, measure for measure, an eye for an eye, diamond cut diamond, the biter bit, a game at which two can play; boomerang.

recrimination etc. (*accusation*) 938; revenge etc. 919; compensation etc. 30; reaction etc. (*recoil*) 277.

V. retaliate, retort, turn upon; pay -off, – back; pay in -one's own, – the same- coin; cap; reciprocate etc. 148; turn the tables upon, return the compliment; give -a *quid pro quo* etc. *n.*, – as much as one takes; give and take, exchange -blows, – fisticuffs; be -quits, – even- with; pay off old scores.

serve one right, be hoist on one's own petard, throw a stone in one's own garden, cathch a Tartar.

Adj. retaliating etc. *v.*; retalia-tory, -tive; retributive, recriminatory, reciprocal.

Adv.. in retaliation; *en revanche.*

Phr. *mutato nomine de te fabula narratur; par pari refero; tu quoque*; you're another; *suo sibi gladio hunc jugulo.*

719. Resistance.—N. resistance, stand, front, oppugnation; opposition etc. 708; renitence, reluctation, recalcitration, recalcitrance; repugnance; kicking etc. *v.*

repulse, rebuff.

insurrection etc. (*disobedience*) 742; strike; turn –, lock –, barring- out; *levée en masse, Jacquerie*; riot etc. (*disorder*) 59.

V. resist; not -submit etc. 725; repugn, reluctate, withstand; stand up –, strive –, bear up –, be proof –, make head- against; stand, – firm, – one's ground, – the brunt of, – out; hold -one's ground, – one's own, – out.

breast the -wave, – current; stem the -tide, – torrent; face, confront, grapple with; show a bold front etc. (*courage*) 861; present a front; make a –, take one's- stand.

kick, – against; recalcitrate, kick against the pricks; oppose etc. 708; fly in the face of; lift the hand against etc. (*attack*) 716; rise up in arms etc. (*war*) 722; strike, turn out; draw up a round robin etc. (*remonstrate*) 932; revolt etc. (*disobey*) 742; make a riot.

prendre le mors aux dents; take the bit between the teeth; sell one's life dearly, die hard, keep at bay; repel, repulse.

Adj. resisting etc. *v.*; resist-ive, -ant; refractory etc. (*disobedient*) 742; recalcitrant, re-nitent, -pulsive, -pellant; up in arms.

proof against; unconquerable etc. (*strong*) 159; stubborn, unconquered; indomitable etc. (*persevering*) 604*a*; unyielding etc. (*obstinate*) 606.

Int. hands off! keep off!

720. Contention.—N. contention, strife; contest, -ation; struggle; belligerency; opposition etc. 708.

controversy, polemics; debate etc. (*discussion*) 476; war of words, logomachy, litigation; paper war, ink slinging; high words etc. (*quarrel*) 713; sparring etc. *v.*

competition, rivalry; corrival-ry, -ship; agonism, *concours,* match, race, horse-racing, heat, steeple chase, point-to-point race, handicap; boat race, regatta; field-day; sham fight, Derby day; turf, sporting, bull-fight, tauromachy, *gymkhana,* rodeo, Olympiad.

wrestling, *ju-jitsu,* pugilism, boxing, fisticuffs, spar, mill, set-to, scrap, round, bout, event; prize-fighting; quarter-staff, single stick; gladiatorship, gymnastics; athletic-s, – sports; games of skill etc. 840.

shindy; *fracas* etc. (*discord*) 713; clash of arms; tussle, scuffle, broil, fray; affray, -ment; velitation; col , luctation; brabble, *brique,* scramble, *mêlée,* scrimmage, stramash, bush-fighting.

free –, stand up –, hand to hand –, running-fight.

conflict, skirmish; ren-, en-counter; *rencontre,* collision, affair, brush, fight; battle, – royal; combat, action, engagement, joust, tournament; tilt, -ing; tourney, list; pitched battle, guerilla warfare.

death-struggle, struggle for life or death, Armageddon; hard knocks, sharp contest, tug of war.

naval -engagement, – battle; *naumachia,* sea-fight.

duel, -lo; single combat, monomachy, satisfaction, *passage d'armes,* passage of arms, affair of honor; triangular duel; hostile meeting, digladiation; appeal to arms etc. (*warfare*) 722.

deeds –, feats- of arms; pugnacity; combativeness etc. *adj.*; bone of contention etc. 713.

V. contend; contest, strive, struggle, scramble, wrestle; spar, square; exchange -blows, – fisticuffs; scrap, mix with, fib, justle, tussle, tilt, box, stave, fence; skirmish; fight etc. (*war*) 722; wrangle etc. (*quarrel*) 713.

contend etc. –, grapple –, engage –, close –, buckle –, bandy –, try conclusions –, have a brush etc. *n.* –, tilt- with; encounter, fall foul of, pitch into, clapperclaw, run a tilt at; oppose etc. 708; reluct.

join issue, come to blows, be at loggerheads, set-to, come to the scratch, exchange shots, measure swords, meet hand to hand; take up the -cudgels, – glove, – gauntlet; enter the lists; couch one's lance; give satisfaction; appeal to arms etc. (*warfare*) 722.

lay about one; break the peace.

compete –, cope –, vie –, race- with; outvie, emulate, rival; run a race; contend etc. –, stipulate –, stickle- for; insist upon, make a point of.

Adj. contending etc. *v.*; together by the ears, at loggerheads, at war, at issue.

competitive, rival; belligerent; contentious, combative, bellicose, unpeaceful; warlike etc. 722; quarrelsome etc. 901; pugnacious; pugilistic, gladiatorial; palestric, -al.

Phr. *a verbis ad verbera*; a word and a blow.

721. Peace.—N. peace; amity etc. (*friendship*) 888; harmony etc. (*concord*) 714; tranquility etc. (*quiescence*) 265; truce etc. (*pacification*) 723; pacificism; pipe –, calumet- of peace.

piping time of peace, quiet life; neutrality.

V. be at peace; keep the peace etc. (*concord*) 714; make peace etc. 723.

Adj. pacific; peace-able, -ful; calm, tranquil, untroubled, halcyon; bloodless; neutral.

Phr. the storm blown over; the lion lies down with the lamb.

722. Warfare.—N. warfare; fighting etc. *v.*; hostilities; war, arms, the sword; Mars, Bellona, grim visaged war, *horrida bella*, Armageddon.

appeal to -arms, – the sword; ordeal –, wager- of battle; *ultima ratio regum*, arbitrament of the sword.

battle array, campaign, crusade, expedition; mobilization; state of siege; battle-field etc. (*arena*) 728; warpath.

art of war, tactics, strategy, castrametation; general-, soldier-ship; aerial –, submarine –, naval –, chemical-, atomic-, guerilla- warfare; military evolutions, ballistics, gunnery; chivalry; poison gas; gun-powder, shot, – and shell.

battle, tug of war etc. (*contention*) 720; service, campaigning, active service, tented field; fiery cross, trumpet, clarion, bugle, pibroch, slogan; war-cry, -whoop; battle cry, beat of drum, rappel, tom-tom; word of command; pass-, watch-word.

war to the -death, – knife; *guerre à -mort*, – *outrance*; open –, internecine –, civil- war.

V. arm; raise –, mobilize- troops; raise up in arms; take up the cudgels etc. 720; take up –, fly to –, appeal to- -arms, – the sword; draw –, unsheathe- the sword; dig up the hatchet; go to –, declare –, wage –, let slip the dogs of- war; cry havoc; kindle –, light- the torch of war; raise one's banner, send round the fiery cross; hoist the black flag; throw –, fling- away the scabbard; enrol, enlist, join up; take the field; take the law into one's own hands; do –, give –, join –, engage in –, go to- battle; flesh one's sword; set to, fall to, engage, measure swords with, draw the trigger, cross swords; come to -blows, – close quarters; fight; combat; contend etc. 720; battle –, break a lance- with.

serve; see –, be on- -service, – active service; campaign; wield the sword, shoulder a musket, smell powder, be under the fire; spill –, imbrue the hands in- blood; be on the warpath.

carry on -war, – hostilities; keep the field; fight the good fight; go over the top; cut one's way through; fight -it out, – like devils, – one's way, – hand to hand; sell one's life dearly.

Adj. conten-ding, -tious etc. 720; armed, – to the teeth, – cap-à-pie; sword in hand; in –, under –, up in- arms; at war with; bristling with arms; in -battle array, – open arms, – the field; embattled.

unpacific, unpeaceful; belligerent, combative, armigerous, bellicose, martial, warlike; mili-tary, -tant; soldier-like, -ly; chivalrous; strategical, internecine.

Adv. *flagrante bello*, in the -thick of the fray, – cannon's mouth; at the -swords's point, – point of the bayonet.

Int. *vae victis!* to arms! to your tents O Israel!

Phr. the battle rages.

723. Pacification.—N. pacification, conciliation; reconcil-iation, -ement; shaking of hands, accomodation, arrangement, adjustment; terms, compromise; amnesty, deed of release.

peace-offering; olive-branch; overtures; pipe –, calumet –, preliminaries- of peace.

truce, armistice; suspension of -arms, – hostilities; breathing-time; convention; *modus vivendi*; flag of truce, white flag, *parlementaire*, *cartel*.

hollow truce, *pax in bello*; drawn battle.

V. pacify, tranquilize, compose; allay etc. (*moderate*) 174; reconcile, propitiate, placate, conciliate, meet half-way, hold out the olive-branch, heal the breach, make peace, restore harmony, bring to terms.

settle –, arrange –, accommodate- -matters, – differences; set straight; make up a quarrel, *tantas componere lites*; come to -an understanding, – terms; bridge over, hush up; make -it, – matters- up; shake hands.

raise a siege; put up –, sheathe- the sword; bury the hatchet, lay down one's arms, turn swords into ploughshares; smoke the calumet of peace, close the temple of Janus; keep the peace etc. (*concord*) 714; be -pacified etc.; come round.

Adj. conciliatory, pacificatory; composing etc *v.*; pacified etc. *v.*

Phr. *requiescat in pace.*

724. Mediation.—N. media-tion, -torship, -tization; inter-vention, -position, -ference, -meddling, -cession; parley, negotiation, arbitration; flag of truce etc. 723; good offices, peace -offering; diploma-tics, -cy; compromise etc. 774.

mediator, intercessor, peacemaker, make-peace, negotiator, go-between; diplomatist etc. (*consignee*) 758; moderator, propitiator, umpire, arbitrator.

V. media-te, -tize; inter-cede, -pose, -fere, -vene; step in, negotiate; meet half-way; arbitrate; *magnas componere lites*.

Adj. mediatory, propitiatory, diplomatic.

725. Submission.—N. submission, yielding, acquiescence, compliance; non-resistance; obedience etc. 743; submissiveness, deference.

surrender, cession, capitulation, resignation.

obeisance, homage, kneeling, genuflexion, courtesy, curtsy, *salaam*, *kowtow*, prostration.

V. succumb, submit, yield, bend, resign, defer to, accede.

lay down –, deliver up- one's arms; hand over one's sword; lower –, haul down –, strike- one's flag, – colors; deliver the keys of the city.

surrender, – at discretion; cede, capitulate, come to terms, retreat, beat a retreat; draw in one's horns etc. (*humility*) 879; give -way, – ground, – in, – up, cave in, suffer judgment by default, bend, – to one's yoke, – before the storm; reel back; bend –, knuckle- -down, – to, – under; knock under.

humble oneself; eat -dirt, – the leek, – humble pie; bite –, lick- the dust; be –, fall- at one's feet; craven; crouch before, throw oneself at the feet of; swallow the -leek, – pill; kiss the rod; turn the other cheek; *avaler des couleuvres*, gulp down.

obey etc. 743; kneel to, bow to, pay homage to, cringe to, truckle to; bend the -neck, – knee; kneel, fall on one's knees, bow submission, courtesy, curtsy, *kowtow*; make obeisance.

pocket the affront; make -the best of, – a virtue of necessity; grin and abide, shrug the shoulders, resign oneself; submit with a good grace etc. (*bear with*) 826.

Adj. surrendering etc. *v.*; submissive, resigned, crouching; down-trodden; down on one's marrow bones; on one's bended knee; weak-kneed, un-, non-resisting; pliant etc. (*soft*) 324; undefended.

untenable, indefensible; humble etc. 879.

Phr. have it your own way; it can't be helped; amen etc. (*assent*) 488.

726. Combatant.—N. combatant; disputant, controversialist, polemic, litigant, belligerent; competitor, rival, corrival; fighter, assailant, aggressor; champion, Paladin; moss-trooper, swashbuckler, fire-eater, duellist, bully, bludgeon-man, rough, fighter, fighting-man, prize-fighter, pugilist, pug, boxer, bruiser, the fancy, gladiator, athlete, wrestler; fighting-, game-cock; swordsman, *sabreur*.

warrior, soldier, Amazon, man-at-arms, armigerent; campaigner, veteran; red-coat, military man, *rajpoot*, brave.

armed force, troops, soldiery, military, forces, sabaoth, the army, standing army, regulars, the line, troops of the line, militia, territorials, yeomanry, volunteers, trainband, fencible; auxiliary –, reserve- forces; reserves, *posse comitatus*, national guard, *gendarme*, beefeater; guards, -man; yeoman of the guard, life guards, household troops.

janissary; myrmidon; Mama-, Mame-luke; spahee, *spahi*, Cossack, Croat, Pandour; irregular, free lance, *franc-tireur, bashi-bazouk, guerilla, condottiere*; mercenary.

levy, draught, commando; *Land-wehr, -sturm*; conscript, recruit, rookie, cadet, raw levies.

private, – soldier; Tommy Atkins, rank and file, peon, trooper, doughboy, sepoy, *askari, legionnaire*, legionary, food for powder, cannon fodder; officer etc. (*commander*) 745; subaltern, ensign, shave-tail, standard bearer, non-com; spear-

pike-man; halberdier, lancer; musketeer, carabineer, rifleman, sharpshooter, yager, skirmisher; grenadier, fusileer; archer, bowman.

horse and foot; horse –, foot- soldier; cavalry, horse, artillery, horse –, field –, heavy –, mountain- artillery, infantry, light horse, *voltigeur, Uhlan*, mounted rifles, dragoon, hussar, trooper; light –, heavy- dragoon; heavy; *cuirassier*; gunner, cannoneer, bombardier, artillery-man, matross; sapper, – and miner; engineer; light infantry, rifles, *chasseur, zouave*; military train, supply and transport, coolie.

army, – corps, *corps d'armée*, host, division, column, wing, detachment, *escadrille*, garrison, flying column, brigade, regiment, *corps*, battalion, squadron, company, platoon, battery, subdivision, section, squad; piquet, picket, guard, rank, file; legion, phalanx, cohort; cloud of skirmishers; impi.

war-horse, charger, *destrier*.

armored -train, – car; tank.

marine, man of war's man etc. (*sailor*) 269; navy, first line of defense, wooden walls; naval forces, fleet, flotilla, armada, squadron.

man-of-war, warship; H.M.S., U.S.S.; capital ship; line-of-battle ship, battle ship; super-, dreadnought, battle –, armored –, protected – light- cruiser; scout, flotilla leader; destroyer, torpedo boat; submarine, submersible, U-boat; submarine chaser, eagle boat, mystery ship, Q-boat; mine- layer, -sweeper; ship of the line, iron-clad, turret- ship, ram, Monitor, floating battery; first-rate, frigate, sloop of war, corvette, gunboat, bomb- vessel, fire-boat; flag ship, guard ship, cruiser; airplane carrier; privateer; tender; depôt –, parent- ship; store –, troop- ship; transport, catamaran.

aircraft etc. 273; air force, scout, fighter, bomber, troop carrier, aerial patrol, seaplane, flying boat, torpedo plane; airship, Zeppelin; rigid –, semi-rigid –, non-rigid- airship; dirigible –, free –, captive –, kite –, observation- balloon.

anti-aircraft guns, searchlights, sound locators; catapult.

727. Arms.—N. arm, -s; weapon, deadly weapon; arma-ment, -ture; panoply, stand of arms; armor etc. (*defense*) 717; armory etc. (*store*) 636.

ammunition; powder, – and shot; explosive; propellant; gun-powder, -cotton; dynam-, melin-, cord-, lydd-ite; trinitrotoluene, T.N.T., ammonal; cartridge; ball cartridge, *cartouche*, fire-ball; dud, black Marie; 'villainous saltpeter;' poison –, mustard –, lachrymatory –, tear- gas.

sword, saber, broadsword, cutlass, falchion, scimitar, cimeter, brand, whinyard, bilbo, glaive, glave, rapier, skean, Toledo, Ferrara, tuck, claymore, creese, kris, *kukri*, dagger, dirk, hanger, poniard, stiletto, stylet, dudgeon, bayonet; sword-bayonet, -stick; side arms, foil, blade, steel; axe, bill; pole-, battle-axe; gisarm, halberd, partisan, tomahawk, bowie-knife; at-, att-, yat-aghan; yatachan; good –, trusty –, naked- sword; cold –, naked-steel.

club, mace, truncheon, staff, bludgeon, cudgel, life-preserver, shillelagh, sprig; hand-, quarter-staff; bat, cane, stick, knuckle-duster, sand bag.

gun, piece; fire-arms; artillery, ordnance; siege –, battering-train; park, battery; cannon, gun of position, heavy –, siege –, field –, mountain –, anti-aircraft –, breech loading –, quick firing-gun; field piece, mortar, trench mortar; mine –, flame- -thrower, napalm; howitzer, carronade, culverin, basilisk; falconet jingal, swivel, *pederero, bouche à feu*; smooth bore, rifled cannon; Armstrong –, Lancaster –, Paixhan –, Whitworth –, Parrott –, Krupp –, Gatling –, Maxim –, Vickers –, Hotchkiss –, Lewis –, machine- gun; tommy gun, Thompson's submachine gun; *mitrailleu-r, -se*; pompom; blow pipe.

small arms; musket, -ry, firelock, flintlock, fowling-piece, shot gun, rifle, *fusil*, caliver, carbine, blunderbuss, musketoon, Brown Bess, matchlock, harquebuss, *arquebuse*, haguebut; petronel; smallbore; breech-, muzzle-loader; Minié –, Enfield –, Westly Richards –, Snider –, Springfield –, Martini-Henry –, Lee-Metford –, Lee-Enfield –, Mauser –, Männlicher –, magazine –, repeating- rifle; needle-gun, *chassepot*; pis-tol, -et; revolver, automatic pistol, automatic; wind-, air-gun; flame –, gas- projector.

bow, cross-bow, arbalest, balister, catapult, sling; battering-ram etc. (*impulse*) 276; gunnery; ballistics etc. (*propulsion*) 284.

missile, bolt, projectile, shot, pellet, ball; grape; grape –, canister –, bar –, cannon –, langrel –, langrage –, round –, chain- shot; explosive; incendiary –, expanding –, soft-nosed –, dum-dum- bullet; slug, stone, brickbat; hand –, rifle-grenade; high explosive –, incendiary –, stink-, A-, H-, atomic –, hydrogen – bomb; petard, torpedo, carcass, rocket; congreve, – rocket; shrapnel, *mitraille*; thunderbolt; mine, land mine, infernal machine.

pike, lance, spear, spontoon, javelin, assagai, throwing stick, dart, djerrid, arrow, reed, shaft, bolt, boomerang, harpoon, gaff.

728. Arena.—N. arena, field, platform; scene of action, theater; walk, course; hustings; stage, boards etc. (*playhouse*) 599; amphitheater; Coli-, Colos-seum; Flavian amphitheater, hippodrome, circus, race-course, track, *stadium*, *corso*, turf, cockpit, bear-garden, play-ground, playing fields, *gymnasium, palaestra*, ring, lists; tilt-yard, -ing ground; *Campus Martius, Champ de Mars*; aerodrome, airport, air base, flying field.

theater –, seat- of war; battle-field, -ground; field of -battle, – slaughter; no man's land; Aceldama, camp; the enemy's camp; trysting- place etc. (*place of meeting*) 74.

729. Completion.—N. completion; accomplish-, achieve-, fulfil-ment; performance, execution; des-, dis-patch; consummation, culmination, climax; finish, conclusion, effectuation; close etc. (*end*) 67; terminus etc. (*arrival*) 292; winding up; *finale, dénouement*, catastrophe, issue, upshot, result; final –, last –, crowning –, finishing- -touch, – stroke; last finish, *coup de grâce*; crowning of the edifice; coping-, keystone; missing link etc. 53; superstructure, *ne plus ultra*, work done, *fait accompli*.

elaboration; finality; completeness etc. 52.

V. effect, -uate; accomplish, achieve, compass, consummate, hammer out; bring to -maturity, – perfection; perfect, complete; elaborate.

do, execute, make; go –, get- through; work out, enact, bring -about, – to bear, – to pass, – through, – to a head.

des-, dis-patch; knock –, finish –, polish- off; make short work of; dispose of, set at rest; perform, discharge, fulfil, realize; put in -practice, – force; carry -out, – into effect, – into execution; make good; be as good as one's word.

do thoroughly, not do by halves, go the whole hog; drive home; be in at the death etc. (*persevere*) 604*a*; carry through, play out, exhaust, deliver the goods, fill the bill.

finish, bring to a close etc. (*end*) 67; wind up, stamp, clinch, seal, set the seal on, put the seal to; give the -final touch etc. *n.* to; put the -last, – finishing- hand to; crown, – all; cap.

ripen, culminate; come to a -head, – crisis; come to its end; die -a natural death, – of old age; run -its course, – one's race; touch –, reach –, attain- the goal; reach etc. (*arrive*) 292; get in the harvest.

Adj. completing, final; conclu-ding, -sive; crowning etc. *v.*; exhaustive, complete, mature, perfect, consummate.

done, completed etc. *v.*; done for, sped, wrought out; highly wrought etc. (*preparation*) 673; thorough etc. 52; ripe etc. (*ready*) 673.

Adv. completely etc. (*thoroughly*) 52; to crown all, out of hand.

Phr. the race is run; *actum est*; *finis coronat opus*; *consummatum est*; *c'en est fait*; it is all over; the game is played out, the bubble has burst.

730. Non-Completion.—N. non-completion, -fulfilment; shortcoming etc. 304; incompleteness etc. 53; drawn -battle, – game; work of Penelope, task of Sisyphus.

non-performance, inexecution; neglect etc. 460.

V. not -complete etc. 729; leave -unfinished etc. *adj.*, – undone; neglect etc. 460; let -alone, – slip; lose sight of.

fall short of etc. 304; do things by halves; scotch the snake, not kill it; hang fire; be slow to; collapse etc. 304.

Adj. not completed etc. *v.*; incomplete etc. 53; uncompleted, unfinished; unaccomplished; unperformed, unexecuted; sketchy, addle.

in progress, in hand; going on, proceeding; on one's hands; on the fire; on the stocks; in preparation; lacking the finishing touch.

Adv. *re infectâ*.

731. Success.—N. success, -fulness; speed; advance etc. (*progress*) 282.

trump card; hit, stroke; lucky –, fortunate –, good- -hit, – stroke; bold –, master- stroke; *coup de maître*, checkmate; half the battle, prize; profit etc. (*acquisition*) 775; best seller.

continued success; good fortune etc. (*prosperity*) 734; time well spent.

advantage over; edge; upper-, whiphand; ascendancy, mastery; expugnation, conquest, victory, subdual; subjugation etc. (*subjection*) 749.

triumph etc. (*exultation*) 884; proficiency etc. (*skill*) 698; conqueror, victor, winner, champion; master of the -situation, – position.

V. succeed; be -successful etc. *adj.*; gain one's -end, – ends; crown with success.

gain –, attain –, carry –, secure –, win- -a point, – an object; put over; make a go of; manage to, contrive to; accomplish etc. (*effect, complete*) 729; do –, work- wonders.

come off -well, – successfully, – with flying colors; make short work of; take –, carry- by storm; bear away the bell; win -one's spurs, – the battle; win –, carry –, gain- the -day, – prize, – palm; climb on the bandwagon; have -the best of it, – it all one's own way, – the game in one's own hands, – the ball at one's feet, – one on the hip; walk over the course; carry all before one, remain in possession of the field; score a success, win hands down.

speed; make progress etc. (*advance*) 282; win –, make –, work –, find- one's way; strive to some purpose; prosper etc. 734; drive a roaring trade; make profit etc. (*acquire*) 775; reap –, gather- the -fruits, – benefit of, – harvest; make one's fortune, get in the harvest, turn to good account; turn to account etc. (*use*) 677.

triumph, be triumphant; gain –, obtain- -a victory, – an advantage; chain victory to one's car.

surmount –, overcome –, get over- -a difficulty, – an obstacle etc. 706; *se tirer d'affaire*; make head against; stem the -torrent, – tide, – current; weather -the storm, – a point; turn a corner, keep one's head above water, tide over; master; get –, have –, gain- the -better of, – best of, – upper hand, – ascendancy, – whip hand, – start of; distance; surpass etc. (*superiority*) 33.

defeat, conquer, vanquish, discomfit; over-come, throw, -power, -master, -match, -set, -ride, -reach; out-wit, -do, -flank, -maneuver, -general, -vote; take the wind out of one's adversary's sails; beat, – hollow; rout, lick, drub, floor, worst; put -down, – to flight, – to the rout, – *hors de combat*; – out of court.

silence, quell, nonsuit, checkmate, upset, confound, nonplus, trump; baffle etc. (*hinder*) 706; circumvent, elude; trip up – the heels of; drive -into a corner, – to the wall; run hard, put one's nose out of joint.*

settle, do for; break the -neck of, – back of; capsize, sink, shipwreck, drown, swamp; subdue; subjugate etc. (*subject*) 749; reduce; make the enemy bite the dust; victimize, roll in the dust, trample under foot, put an extinguisher upon.

answer, – the purpose; avail, prevail, take effect, do, turn out well, work well, take, tell, bear fruit; hit -it, – the mark, – the right nail on the head; nick it; turn up trumps, make a hit; find one's account in.

Adj. succeeding etc. *v.*; successful; prosperous etc. 734; triumphant; flushed –, crowned- with success; victorious; set up; in the ascendant; unbeaten etc. (*see* beat etc. *v.*); well-spent; felicitous, effective, in full swing.

Adv. successfully etc. *adj.*; with flying colors, in triumph, swimmingly; *à merveille*, beyond all hope; to some –, good- purpose; to one's heart's content.

Phr. *veni vidi vici*, the day being one's own, one's star in the ascendant; *omne tulit punctum*.

732. Failure.—N. failure; non-success, -fulfilment; dead failure, successlessness; abortion, miscarriage; *brutum fulmen* etc. 158; labor in vain etc. (*inutility*) 645; no go; inefficacy; inefficaciousness etc. *adj.*; vain –, ineffectual –, abortive- -attempt, – efforts; flash in the pan, 'lame and impotent conclusion;' frustration; slip 'twixt cup and lip etc. (*disappointment*) 509.

blunder etc. (*mistake*) 495; fault, omission, miss, oversight, slip, trip, stumble, claudication, footfall; false –, wrong- step; *faux pas*, titubation, *bévue*, *faute*, lurch; botchery etc. (*want of skill*) 699; scrape, jam, mess, muddle, foozle, *fiasco*, breakdown.

mishap etc. (*misfortune*) 735; split, collapse, smash, blow, explosion.

repulse, rebuff, defeat, rout, overthrow, discomfiture; beating, drubbing, *quietus*, nonsuit, subjugation; check-, fool's-mate.

fall, downfall, ruin, perdition; wreck etc. (*destruction*) 162; death-blow; bankruptcy etc. (*non-payment*) 808.

losing game, *affaire flambée*.

victim, prey; bankrupt.

V. fail; be -unsuccessful etc. *adj.*; not -succeed etc. 731; make -vain efforts etc. *n.*; do –, labor –, toil- in vain; lose one's labor, take nothing by one's motion; bring to naught, make nothing of; wash a blackamoor white etc. (*impossible*) 471; roll the stone of Sisyphus etc. (*useless*) 645; do by halves etc. (*not complete*) 730; lose ground etc. (*recede*) 283; flunk; fall short of etc. 304.

miss, – one's aim, – the mark, – one's footing, – stays; slip, trip, stumble; make a -slip etc. *n.*, – blunder etc. 495, – mess of, – botch of; bitch it, miscarry, abort, go up like a rocket and come down like the stick, reckon without one's host; get the wrong sow by the ear etc. (*blunder, mismanage*) 699.

limp, halt, hobble, titubate; fall, tumble; lose one's balance; fall -to the ground, – between two stools; flounder, falter, stick in the mud, run aground, split upon a rock; run –, knock –, dash- one's head against a stone wall; break one's back; break down, sink, drown, founder, have the ground cut from under one; get into -trouble, – a mess, – a scrape; come to grief etc. (*adversity*) 735; go to -the wall, – the dogs, – pot; lick –, bite- the dust; be -defeated etc. 731; have the worst of it, lose the day, come off second best, lose; fall a prey to; succumb etc. (*submit*) 725; not have a leg to stand on.

come to nothing, end in smoke; fall -to the ground, – through, – dead, – still-born, – flat; slip through one's fingers; hang –, miss- fire; flash in the pan, collapse; topple down etc. (*descent*) 305; go to wrack and ruin etc. (*destruction*) 162.

go amiss, go wrong, go cross, go hard with, go on a wrong tack; go on –, come off –, turn out

—, work- ill; take -a wrong, — an ugly- turn; gang agley.

be all -over with, — up with; explode; dash one's hopes etc. (*disappoint*) 509; defeat the purpose; upset the apple cart; sow the wind and reap the whirlwind, jump out of the frying pan into the fire.

Adj. unsuccessful, successless; failing, tripping etc. *v.*; at fault; unfortunate etc. 735.

abortive, addle, still-born; fruitless, sterile, bootless; ineffect-ual, -ive; inefficient etc. (*impotent*) 158; inefficacious; lame, hobbling, *décousu*; insufficient etc. 640; unavailing etc. (*useless*) 645; of no effect.

aground, grounded, swamped, stranded, cast away, wrecked, foundered, capsized, shipwrecked, non-suited; foiled; defeated etc. 731; struck —, borne —, broken- down; down-trodden; over-borne, -whelmed; all up with; beaten to a frazzle.

lost, undone, ruined, broken; bankrupt etc. (*not paying*) 808; played out; done -up, — for; dead beat, ruined root and branch, *flambé*, knocked on the head; destroyed etc. 162.

frustrated, thwarted, crossed, unhinged, disconcerted, dashed; thrown -off one's balance, — on one's back, — on one's beam ends; unhorsed, in a sorry plight; hard hit.

stultified, befooled, dished, hoist on one's own petard, victimized, sacrificed.

wide of the mark etc. (*error*) 495; out of one's reckoning etc. (*inexpectation*) 508; left in the lurch; thrown away etc. (*wasted*) 638; unattained; uncompleted etc. 730.

Adv. unsuccessfully etc. *adj.*; to little or no purpose, in vain, *re infectâ.*

Phr. the bubble has burst, the game is up, all is lost; the devil to pay; *parturiunt montes* etc. (*disappointment*) 509.

733. Trophy.—N. trophy; medal, prize, palm; ribbon, blue ribbon, *cordon bleu*; citation; cup, laurel, -s; bays, crown, chaplet, wreath, civic crown; Victoria Cross, V.C., *Croix de Guerre,* Iron Cross; Distinguished Service Cross, Medal of Honor, Congressional Medal; insignia etc. 550; feather in one's cap etc. (*honor*) 873; decoration etc. 877; garland, triumphal arch.

triumph etc. (*celebration*) 883; flying colors etc. (*show*) 882.

monumentum aere perennius.

734. Prosperity.—N. prosperity, welfare, well-being; affluence etc. (*wealth*) 803; success etc. 731; thrift, roaring trade; chicken in every pot, the full dinner paid; good —, smiles of- fortune; blessings, godsend.

luck; good —, run of- luck; sunshine; fair -weather, — wind; palmy —, bright —, halcyon- days; piping times, tide, flood, high tide.

Saturnia regna, Saturnian age; golden -time, — age; bed of roses; fat of the land, milk and honey, loaves and fishes, fleshpots of Egypt.

made man, lucky dog, *enfant gâté,* spoiled child of fortune.

upstart, *parvenu, nouveau riche,* profiteer, skip-jack, mushroom.

V. prosper, thrive, flourish; be -prosperous etc. *adj.*; drive a roaring trade; go on -well, — smoothly, — swimmingly; sail before the wind, swim with the tide; run -smooth, — smoothly, — on all fours.

rise —, get on- in the world; work —, make- one's way; look up; lift —, raise- one's head, make one's -fortune, — pile, feather one's nest.

flower, blow, blossom, bloom, fructify, bear fruit, fatten, batten.

keep oneself afloat; keep —, hold- one's head above water; light —, fall- on one's -legs, — feet; drop into a good thing; bear a charmed life; bask in the sunshine; have a -good, — fine- time of it; have a run, — of luck; have the -good fortune etc. *n.* to; take a favorable turn; live -on the fat of the land, — in clover.

Adj. prosperous; thriving etc. *v.*; in a fair way, buoyant; well -off, — to do, — to do in the world; set up, at one's ease; rich etc. 803; in good case; in -full, — high- feather; fortunate, lucky, in luck; born -with a silver spoon in one's mouth, — under a lucky star; on the sunny side of the hedge.

auspicious, propitious, providential.

palmy, halcyon; agreeable etc. 829; *couleur de rose.*

Adv. prosperously etc. *adj.*; swimmingly; as good luck would have it; beyond all -expectation, — hope, — one's wildest dreams.

Phr. one's star in the ascendant, all for the best, one's course runs smooth.

735. Adversity.—N. adversity, evil etc. 619; failure etc. 732; bad —, ill —, evil —, adverse —, hard- -fortune, — hap, — luck, — lot; frowns of fortune; evil -dispensation, — star, — genius; ups and downs of life, broken fortunes; hard -case, — lines, — life; sea —, peck- of troubles; hell upon earth; slough of despond; jinx.

trouble, humiliation, hardship, curse, blight, blast, load, pressure.

pressure of the times, iron age, evil day, time out of joint; hard —, bad —, sad- times; rainy day, cloud, dark cloud, gathering clouds, ill wind; visitation, infliction; affliction etc. (*painfulness*) 830; bitter -pill, — cup; care, trial; the sport of fortune.

mis-hap, -chance, -adventure, -fortune; disaster, calamity, catastrophe; accident, casualty, cross, reverse, check, *contretemps,* rub, pinch, setback.

losing game; falling etc. *v.*; fall, down-fall, come-down; ruin-ation, -ousness; undoing; extremity; ruin etc. (*destruction*) 162.

V. be -ill off etc. *adj.*; go hard with; fall on evil, — days; go on ill; not -prosper etc. 734.

go -downhill, — to rack and ruin etc. (*destruction*) 162, — to the dogs; fall, — from one's high estate; decay, sink, decline, go down in the world; have seen better days; bring down one's grey hairs with sorrow to the grave; come to grief; be all -over, — up- with; bring a -wasp's, — hornet's- nest about one's ears.

Adj. unfortunate, unblest, unhappy, unlucky; im-, un-prosperous; luck-, hap-less; out of luck; in trouble, in a bad way, in an evil plight; under a cloud; clouded; ill —, badly- off; in adverse circumstances; poor etc. 804; behindhand, down in the world, decayed, undone; on the road to ruin, on its last legs, on the wane; in one's utmost need.

planet-struck, devoted; born -under an evil star, – with a wooden ladle in one's mouth; ill-fated, -starred, -omened; inconspicuous, ominous, doomed, unpropitious.

adverse, untoward; disastrous, calamitous, ruinous, dire, deplorable.

Adv. if the worst come to the worst, as ill luck would have it, from bad to worse, out of the frying pan into the fire.

Phr. one's star is on the wane; one's luck -turns, – fails; the game is up, one's doom is sealed, the ground crumbles under one's feet, *sic transit gloria mundi, tant va la cruche à l'eau qu'à la fin elle se casse.*

736. Mediocrity.—N. moderate –, average- circumstances; respectability; middle classes, *bourgeoisie*; mediocrity; golden mean etc. (*mid-course*) 628, (*moderation*) 174.

V. jog on; go –, get on- -fairly, – quietly, – peaceably, – tolerably, – respectably; steer a middle course etc. 628.

Adj. middling, so-so, fair, medium, moderate, mediocre, second-, third- etc. -rate.

737. Authority.—N. authority; influence, patronage, power, preponderance, credit, *prestige*, prerogative, jurisdiction; right etc. (*title*) 924.

divine right, dynastic rights, authoritativeness; absolut-eness, -ism; despotism, tyranny; *jus nocendi.*

command, empire, sway, rule; domin-ion, -ation; sovereignty, supremacy, suzerainty; lord-, head-ship; chiefdom; seignior-y, -ity, hegemony, patriarchate, patriarchy; master-y, -ship, -dom; government etc. (*direction*) 693; dictation, control.

hold, grasp; grip, -e; reach; iron sway etc. (*severity*) 739; fangs, clutches, talons; rod of empire etc. (*scepter*) 747.

reign, regnancy, *régime,* dynasty; director-, dictator-ship; protector-ate, -ship; caliphate, pashalic, electorate; presiden-cy, -tship; administration; pro-, consulship; prefecture; seneschalship; magistra-ture, -cy; raj.

empire; monarchy; king-hood, -ship; royalty, regality, autocracy, monocracy, arist-archy, -ocracy; oligarchy, democracy, demogogy; republic, -anism, federalism; socialism, collectivism; communism, bolshevism, syndicalism; mob law, mobocracy, ochlocracy, ergatocracy; *vox populi, imperium in imperio*; bureaucracy; beadle-, humble-dom; stratocracy; martial law, military -power, – government; feodality, feudal system, feudalism.

Thearchy, diarchy; du-, tri-, heter-archy; du-, triumvirate; auto-cracy, -nomy; limited monarchy; constitutional -government, – monarchy; home rule, autonomy; self-government, -determination; representative government; Soviet government.

gyn-archy, -ocracy, -aeocracy; petticoat government, matriarchate, matriarchy.

[Vicarious authority] commission etc. 755; deputy etc. 759; permission etc. 760.

country, state, realm, commonwealth, canton, constituency, toparchy, municipality, polity, body politic, *posse comitatus.*

person in authority etc. (*master*) 745; judicature etc. 965; cabinet etc. (*council*) 696; usurper; seat of -government, – authority; head-quarters.

[Acquisition of authority] accession; installation etc. 755; usurpation.

V. authorize etc. (*permit*) 760; warrant etc. (*right*) 924; dictate etc. (*order*) 741; have –, hold –, possess –, exercise –, exert –, wield- -authority etc. *n.*

be -at the head of etc. *adj.*; hold –, be in –, fill an- office; hold –, occupy- a post; be -master etc. 745.

rule, sway, command, control, administer; govern etc. (*direct*) 693; lead, preside over, reign; possess –, be seated on –, occupy- the throne; sway –, wield- the scepter; wear the crown.

have –, get- the -upper, – whip- hand; gain a hold upon, preponderate, dominate, boss, rule the roost; over-ride, -rule, -awe; lord it over, hold in hand, keep under, make a puppet of, lead by the nose, hold in the hollow of one's hand, turn round one's little finger, bend to one's will, hold one's own, wear the breeches; have -the ball at one's feet, – it all one's own way, – the game in one's own hand, – on the hip, – under one's thumb; be master of the situation; take the lead, play first fiddle, set the fashion; give the law to; carry with a high hand, lay down the law; 'ride in the whirlwind and direct the storm;' rule with a rod of iron etc. (*severity*) 739.

ascend –, mount- the throne, take the reins, – into one's hand; assume -authority etc. *n.*, – the reins of government; take –, assume the- command.

be -governed by, – in the power of; be under -the rule of, – the domination of.

Adj. ruling etc. *v.*; regnant, at the head, dominant, paramount, supreme, predominant, preponderant, in the ascendant, influential; gubernatorial; imperious; authoritative, executive, administrative, clothed with authority, official, *ex officio,* ministerial, bureaucratic, departmental, imperative, peremptory, overruling, absolute; hegemonic, -al; arbitrary; compulsory etc. 744; stringent.

regal, sovereign; royal, -ist; monarchical, kingly; imperial, -istic; princely; feudal; aristo-, auto-cratic; oligarchic etc. *n.*; democratic, republican, dynastic.

at one's command; in one's -power, – grasp; under control; authorized etc. (*due*) 924.

Adv. in the name of, by the authority of, *de par le Roi,* in virtue of; under the auspices of, in the hands of.

at one's pleasure; by a -dash, – stroke- of the pen; *ex mero motu*; *ex cathedrâ.*

Phr. the grey mare the better horse; 'every inch a king.'

738. Laxity. [Absence of authority.]—**N.** laxity; lax-, loose-, slack-ness; toleration etc. (*lenity*) 740; freedom etc. 748.

anarchy, interregnum; relaxation; loosening etc. *v.*; remission; dead letter, *brutum fulmen*, misrule; license, licentiousness; insubordination etc. (*disobedience*) 742; lynch law etc. (*illegality*) 964; nihilism.

[Deprivation of power.] dethronement, deposition, usurpation, abdication.

V. be -lax etc. *adj.*; *laisser -faire*, – *aller*; hold a loose rein; give -the reins to, – rope enough, – a loose to; tolerate; relax; misrule.

go beyond the length of one's tether; have one's -swing, – fling; act without -instructions, – authority; act on one's own responsibility, usurp authority.

dethrone, depose; abdicate.

Adj. lax, loose; slack; remiss etc. (*careless*) 460; weak.

relaxed; licensed; reinless, unbridled; anarchical; unauthorized etc. (*unwarranted*) 925.

739. Severity.—N. severity; strictness, formalism, harshness etc. *adj.*; rigor, stringency, austerity; inclemency etc. (*pitilessness*) 914*a*; arrogance etc. 885.

arbitrary power; absolut-, despot-ism; dictatorship, autocracy, tyranny, domineering, oppression; assumption, usurpation; inquisition, reign of terror, martial law; iron -heel, – rule, – hand, – sway; tight grasp; brute -force, – strength; coercion etc. 744; strong –, tight- hand.

hard -lines, – measure; tender mercies [ironical.]; sharp practice; bureaucracy, red tape; pipe-clay, officialism.

tyrant, disciplinarian, martinet, stickler, formalist, bashaw, despot, hard master, Draco, oppressor, inquisitor, extortioner, harpy, vulture, bird of prey.

V. be -severe etc. *adj.*

assume, usurp, arrogate, take liberties; domineer, bully etc. 885; tyrannize, inflict, wreak, stretch a point, put on the screw; be hard upon; bear –, lay- a heavy hand on; be –, come- down upon; ill-treat; deal-hardly with, – hard measure to; rule with a rod of iron, chastise with scorpions; dye with blood; oppress, override; trample –, tread- -down, – upon, – under foot; crush under an iron heel, ride roughshod over; rivet the yoke; hold –, keep- a tight hand; force down the throat; coerce etc. 744; give no quarter etc. (*pitiless*) 914*a*.

Adj. severe; strict, hard, harsh, dour, rigid, stiff, stern, rigorous, uncompromising, exacting, exigent, *exigeant*, inexorable, inflexible, obdurate, austere, relentless, Spartan, Draconian, stringent, strait-laced, puritanical, prudish, searching, unsparing, ironhanded, hard-headed, peremptory, absolute, positive, arbitrary, imperative; coercive etc. 744; tyrannical, despotic, masterful, extortionate, grinding, withering, oppressive, inquisitorial; inclement etc. (*ruthless*) 914*a*; cruel etc. (*malevolent*) 907; haughty, arrogant etc. 885.

Adv. severely etc. *adj.*; with a -high, – strong, – tight, – heavy-hand.

at the point of the -sword, – bayonet.

Phr. *Delirant reges plectuntur Achivi.*

740. Leniency.—N. leni-ency, -ence, -ty; moderation etc. 174; toler-ance, -ation; mildness, gentleness; favor; indulgen-ce, -cy; clemency, mercy, forbearance, quarter; compassion etc. 914.

V. be -lenient etc. *adj.*; tolerate, bear with; *parcere subjectis*, give quarter.

indulge, allow one to have his own way, spoil.

Adj. lenient; mild, – as milk; gentle, soft; tolerant, indulgent, easy-going; clement etc. (*compassionate*) 914; forbearing; complaisant, long-suffering.

741. Command.—N. command, order, ordinance, act, *fiat*, bidding, *dictum*, hest, behest, call, beck, nod.

des-, dis-patch; message, direction, injunction, charge, instructions; appointment, fixture.

demand, exaction, imposition, requisition, claim, reclamation, revendication; *ultimatum* etc. (*terms*) 770; request etc. 765; requirement.

dictation; dict-, mand-ate; *caveat*, decree, decree -nisi, – absolute, *senatus consultum*; precept; pre-, re-script; writ, ordination, bull, edict, decretal, dispensation, prescription, brevet, placet, ukase, *firman*, hatti-sheriff, warrant, passport, *mittimus, mandamus*, summons, subpoena, *nisi prius*, interpellation, citation; word, – of command; *mot d'ordre*; bugle –, trumpet- call; beat of drum, tattoo; order of the day; enactment etc. (*law*) 963; *plébiscite* etc. (*choice*) 609.

V. command, order, decree, enact, ordain, dictate, direct, give orders.

prescribe, set, appoint, mark out; set –, prescribe –, impose- a task; set to work, put in requisition etc. 926.

bid, enjoin, charge, call upon, instruct; require, – at the hands of; exact, impose, tax, task; demand; insist on etc. (*compel*) 744.

claim, lay claim to, revendicate, reclaim.

cite, summon; call –, send- for; subpoena; beckon.

issue a command; make –, issue –, promulgate- -a requisition, – a decree, – an order etc. *n.*; give the -word of command, – word, – signal; call to order; give –, lay down- the law; assume the command etc. (*authority*) 737; remand.

be -ordered etc.; receive an order etc. *n.*

Adj. commanding etc. *v.*; authoritative etc. 737; decret-ory, -ive, -al; imperative, jussive, decisive, final.

Adv. in a commanding tone; by a -stroke, – dash- of the pen; by order, at beat of drum, on the first summons; at the word of command.

Phr. the decree is gone forth; *sic volo sic jubeo*; *le Roi le veut.*

742. Disobedience.—N. disobedience, insubordination, contumacy; infraction, -fringement; violation, non-compliance; non-observance etc. 773.

revolt, rebellion, mutiny, outbreak, rising, uprising, putsch, insurrection, *émeute*; riot, tumult etc. (*disorder*) 59; strike etc. (*resistance*) 719; barring out; defiance etc. 715.

mutinousness etc. *adj.*; mutineering; sedition, treason; high –, petty –, misprison of- treason; *premunire*; *lèse- majesté*; violation of law etc. 964; defection, secession, revolution, *sabotage*, bolshevism, *Sinn Fein.*

insurgent, mutineer, rebel, revolter, rioter, traitor, *carbonaro*, *sansculottes*, red republican, communist, Fenian, chartist, *frondeur*; seceder, runagate, brawler, anarchist, demagogue; suffragette; Spartacus, Masaniello, Wat Tyler, Jack Cade; bolshevist, bolshevik, maximalist, ringleader.

V. disobey, violate, infringe; shirk; set at defiance etc. (*defy*) 715; set authority at naught, run riot, fly in the face of, bolt, take the law into one's own hands; kick over the traces.

turn –, run- restive; champ the bit; strike etc. (*resist*) 719; rise, – in arms; secede; mutiny, rebel.

Adj. disobedient; uncompl-ying, -iant; unsubmissive; unruly, ungovernable; insubordinate, impatient of control; rest-iff, -ive; refractory, contumacious; recusant etc. (refuse) 764; recalcitrant; resisting etc. 719; lawless, mutinous, seditious, insurgent, riotous, revolutionary.

disobeyed, unobeyed; unbidden.

743. Obedience.—N. obedience; observance etc. 772; compliance; submission etc. 725; subjection etc. 749; non-resistance; passiveness, passivity, resignation.

allegiance, loyalty, fealty, homage, deference, devotion, fidelity, constancy.

submiss-ness, -iveness; ductility etc. (*softness*) 324; obsequiousness etc. (*servility*) 886.

V. be -obedient etc. *adj.*; obey, bear obedience to; submit etc. 725; comply, answer the helm, come at one's call; do -one's bidding, – what one is told, – suit and service; attend to orders, serve -devotedly, –, loyally, – faithfully.

follow, – the lead of, – to the world's end; serve etc. 746; play second fiddle.

Adj. obedient; compl-ying, -iant; law-abiding, loyal, faithful, leal, devoted; at one's -call, – command, – orders, – beck and call; under -beck and call, – control.

restrainable; resigned, passive; submissive etc. 725; henpecked; pliant etc. (*soft*) 324.

unresist-ed, -ing.

Adv. obediently etc. *adj.*; in compliance with, in obedience to.

Phr. to hear is to obey; as –, if- you please; at your service.

744. Compulsion.—N. compulsion, coercion, coaction, constraint, eminent domain, duress, enforcement, press, conscription.

force; brute –, main –, physical- force; the sword, *ultima ratio*; club –, mob –, lynch- law; *argumentum baculinum, le droit du plus fort*, martial law.

restraint etc. 751; necessity etc. 601; *force majeure*; Hobson's choice; the spur of necessity.

V. compel, force, make, drive, coerce, constrain, enforce, necessitate, oblige.

force upon, press; cram –, thrust –, force- down the throat; say it must be done, make a point of, insist upon, take no denial; put down, dragoon.

extort, wring from; put –, turn- on the screw; drag into; bind, – over; pin –, tie- down; require, tax, put in force; commandeer; restrain etc. 751.

Adj. compelling etc. *v.*; coercive, coactive; inexorable etc. 739; compuls-ory, -atory; obligatory, stringent, peremptory, binding.

forcible, not to be trifled with; irresistible etc. 601; compelled etc. *v.*; fain to.

Adv. by -force etc. *n.*, – force of arms; on compulsion, perforce; *vi et armis*, under the lash; at the point of the -sword, – bayonet; forcibly; by a strong arm.

under protest, in spite of one's teeth; against one's will etc. 603; *nolens volens* etc. (*of necessity*) 601; by stress of -circumstances, – weather; under press of; *de rigueur*.

745. Master.—N. master, *padrone*; lord, – paramount; command-er, -ant; captain; chief, -tain; *sahib*, sirdar, sachem, sheik, head, senior, governor, *duce*, ruler, dictator; leader etc. (*director*) 694.

lord of the ascendant, cock of the -walk, – roost; grey mare; mistress.

potentate; liege, – lord; suzerain, sovereign, monarch, autocrat, despot, tyrant, oligarch, overlord.

crowned head, emperor, king, anointed king, majesty, *imperator*, protector, president, stadtholder, judge.

caesar, kaiser, czar, sultan, grand Turk, caliph, imaum, shah, padishah, sophi, mogul, great mogul, khan, cham; lama, tycoon, mikado, inca, cazique; domn; vaivode; wai-, way-wode; landamman; seyyid, cacique.

prince, duke etc. (*nobility*) 875; arch-duke, doge, elector; seignior; mar-, land-grave; rajah, emir, nizam, nawab, negus.

empress, queen, sultana, czarina, princess, infanta, duchess, margravine, begum, maharani.

regent, viceroy, exarch, palatine, khedive, hospodar, beglerbeg, three-tailed bashaw, pasha, pashaw, bashaw, bey, beg, dey, sherif, tetrarch, satrap, mandarin, subhadar, nabob, maharajah; burgrave; laird etc. (*proprietor*) 779; High Commissioner.

the -authorities, – powers that be, – government; staff, *état major*, aga, official, man in office, person in authority.

[Naval authorities] admiral, -ty, – of the fleet; rear-, vice-, port-admiral; senior-, naval officer, S.N.O., commodore, captain, commander, lieutenant-commander, lieutenant, sub-lieutenant, midshipman, warrant –, petty- officer, leading seaman; skipper, mate, master.

[Military authorities] marshal, field-marshal, *maréchal*; general, -issimo; commander-in-chief, *seraskier, hetman*; lieutenant-, major-general; commandant; colonel, lieutenant-colonel, major, captain, centurion, skipper, lieutenant, second-lieutenant, officer, staff-officer, *aide de camp*, brigadier, brigade-major, adjutant, *jemidar*, ensign, cornet, cadet, subaltern, warrant officer, quartermaster, noncommissioned officer, N.C.O.; sergeant, -major; top-sergeant, color sergeant; corporal, -major; lance-, acting-corporal; drum major; shavetail.

[Air authorities] air -marshal, – commodore; group captain, squadron leader, wing commander, flight lieutenant, flying –, pilot- officer.

[Civil authorities] judge etc. 967; mayor, -alty; prefect, chancellor, archon, provost, magistrate, syndic; alcalde, alcaid; burgomaster, *corregidor*, seneschal, alderman, warden, constable, portreeve; lord mayor, sheriff; officer etc. (*executive*) 965.

746. Servant.—N. subject, liegeman; servant, retainer, follower, henchman, servitor, domestic, menial, help, lady help, *employé, attaché*; official.

retinue, suite, *cortège*, staff, court.

attendant, squire, usher, page, buttons, donzel, footboy; dog robber; train-, cup-bearer; waiter, busboy, tapster, butler, livery servant, lackey, footman, flunkey, valet, *valet de chambre*; boots; scout, gyp; equerry, groom; jockey, hostler, ostler, tiger, orderly, messenger, cad, gillie, caddie; *wallah*; journeyman, herdsman, swineherd.

bailiff, castellan, seneschal, chamberlain, *major-domo*, groom of the chambers.

secretary; under –, assistant- secretary; clerk; clerical staff, stenographer, subsidiary; agent etc. 758; subaltern; under-ling, -strapper; man.

maid, -servant, waitress; handmaid; *confidente*, lady's maid, abigail, *soubrette*; nurse, *bonne, ayah*; nurse-, nursery-, house-, parlor-, waiting-, chamber-, kitchen-, scullery-, between –, laundry –, dairy-maid; *femme –, fille- de chambre*; *camarista*; *chef de cuisine, cordon bleu*, cook, scullion, Cinderella; maid –, servant- of all work, tweeny, general servant, girl, slavey; laundress, bed-maker, goodie, char-woman etc. (*worker*) 690.

serf, vassal, slave, negro, helot; bondsman, -woman; bondslave; *âme damnée, odalisque*, ryot, *adscriptus glebae*; vill-ain, -ein; bead-, bede-sman; sizar; pension-er, -ary; client; dependant, -ent; hanger on, stooge, satellite; parasite etc. (*servility*) 886; led captain; *protégé*, ward, hireling, mercenary, puppet, creature.

badge of slavery; bonds etc. 752.

V. serve; minister to, wait –, attend –, dance attendance –, pin oneself- upon; squire, tend, hang on the sleeve of, char, do for; fag; valet.

Adj. in the train of; in one's -pay, – employ; at one's call etc. (*obedient*) 743; in bonds.

747. Scepter. [Insignia of authority.]—**N.** scepter, regalia, rod of empire, sword of state, mace, *fasces*, wand; staff, – of office; *bâton*, truncheon; flag etc. (*insignia*) 550; ensign –, emblem –, badge –, insignia- of authority, rank marks, brassard, badge, sash; cocked –, brass- hat.

epaulette, aiguilette, crown, star, eagle, bar, double bar, pip, stripe, chevron, curl, ring, anchor, shoulder-strap, tab.

throne, chair, musnud, divan, dais, woolsack.

toga, pall, mantle, robes of state, ermine, purple.

crown, coronet, diadem, tiara, triple crown, miter, crozier, cardinal's hat etc.; cap of maintenance; decoration; title etc. 877; portfolio.

key, signet, seals, talisman; helm; reins etc. (*means of restraint*) 752.

748. Freedom.—N. freedom, liberty, independence; license etc. (*permission*) 760; facility etc. 705.

scope, range, latitude, play; free –, full- -play, – scope; free stage and no favor; swing, full swing, elbow-room, margin, rope, wide berth; Liberty Hall.

franchise, denization; free –, freed-, liveryman; denizen.

autonomy, self-government, homerule, self-determination, liberalism, free trade; non-interference etc. 706.

immunity, exemption; emancipation etc. (*liberation*) 750; en-, af-franchisement; rights, privileges.

free land, freehold; allodium; frankalmoigne, mortmain.

independent, free-lance, -thinker, -trader.

V. be -free etc. *adj.*; have -scope etc. *n.*, – the run of, – one's own way, – a will of one's own, – one's fling; do what one -likes, – wishes, – pleases, – chooses; go at large, feel at home, paddle one's own canoe; stand on one's -legs, – rights; shift for oneself.

take a liberty; make -free with, – oneself quite at home; use a freedom; take -leave, – French leave.

set free etc. (*liberate*) 750; give the reins to etc. (*permit*) 760; allow –, give- scope etc. *n.* to; give a horse his head.

make free of; give the -freedom of, – franchise; en-, af-franchise.

laisser -faire, – aller; live and let live; leave to oneself; leave –, let- alone; mind one's own business.

Adj. free, – as air; out of harness, independent, at large, loose, scot free; left -alone, – to oneself.

in full swing; uncaught, unconstrained, unbuttoned, unconfined, unrestrained, unchecked, unprevented, unhindered, unobstructed, unbound, uncontrolled, untrammeled.

unsubject, ungoverned, unenslaved, unenthralled, unchained, unshackled, unfettered, unreined, unbridled, uncurbed, unmuzzled, unimpeded.

unrestricted, unlimited, unconditional; absolute; discretionary etc. (*optional*) 600.

unassailed, unforced, uncompelled.

unbiassed, unprejudiced, uninfluenced, spontaneous.

free and easy; at –, at one's- ease; *dégagé*, quite at home; wanton, rampant, irrepressible, unvanquished.

exempt; freed etc. 750; freeborn; autonomous, freehold, allodial; *gratis* etc. 815.

unclaimed, going a begging.

Adv. freely etc. *adj.*; *ad libitum* etc. (*at will*) 600.

749. Subjection.—N. subjection; depend-ence, -ance, -ency; subordination; thrall, thraldom, enthralment, subjugation, bondage, serfdom; feudal- -ism, -ity; vassalage, villenage; slavery, enslavement, involuntary servitude.

service; servi-tude, -torship; tendence, employ, tutelage, clientship; liability etc. 177; constraint etc. 751; oppression etc. (*severity*) 739; yoke etc. (*means of restraint*) submission etc. 725; obedience etc. 743.

V. be -subject etc. *adj.*; be –, lie- at the mercy of; depend –, lean –, hang- upon; fall -a prey to, – under; play second fiddle.

be a -mere machine, – puppet, – football; not dare to say one's soul is his own; drag a chain.

serve etc. 746; obey etc. 743; submit etc. 725.

break in, tame; subject, subjugate; master etc. 731; tread -down, – under foot; weigh down; drag at one's chariot wheels; reduce to -subjection, –

slavery; en-, in-, be-thral; enslave, lead captive; take into custody etc. (*restrain*) 751; rule etc. 737; drive into a corner, hold at the sword's point; keep under; hold in -bondage, – leading strings, – swaddling clothes.

Adj. subject, dependent, subordinate; feud-al, -atory; in subjection to, under control; in -leading strings, – harness; subjected, enslaved etc. *v.*; constrained etc. 751; subservient, servile, fawning, slavish, obsequious, cringing; down-trodden; overborne, -whelmed; under the lash, on the hip, led by the nose, henpecked; the -puppet, – sport, – plaything- of; under one's -orders, – command, – thumb; like dirt under one's feet; a slave to; at the mercy of; in the -power, – hands, – clutches- of; at the feet of; at one's beck and call etc. (*obedient*) 743; liable etc. 177; parasitical; stipendiary.

Adv. under.

750. Liberation.—N. liberation, disengagement, release, disenthrallment, enlargement, emancipation; af-, en-franchisement; manumission; discharge, dismissal.

deliverance etc. 672; redemption, extrication, acquittance, absolution; acquittal etc. 970; escape etc. 671.

V. liberate, free; set -free, – clear, – at liberty; render free, emancipate, release; en-, af-franchise; manumit; enlarge; dis-band, -charge, -miss, -enthral; let go, loose, out, slip; cast, turn- adrift; deliver etc. 672; absolve etc. (*acquit*) 970; reprieve.

unfetter etc. 751; untie etc. 44; loose etc. (*disjoin*) 44; loosen, relax; un-bolt, -bar, -close, -cork, -clog, -hand, -bind, -latch, -chain, -harness; dis-engage, -entangle; clear, extricate, unloose.

gain –, obtain –, acquire- one's -liberty etc. 748; get -rid, – clear- of; deliver oneself from; shake off the yoke, slip the collar; break -loose, – prison; tear asunder one's bonds, cast off trammels; escape etc. 671.

Adj. at -liberty, – large, free, liberated etc. *v.*; out of harness etc. 748; adrift.

Int. unhand me! let me go!

751. Restraint.—N. restraint; hindrance etc. 706; coercion etc. (*compulsion*) 744; cohibition, constraint, repression; discipline, control, self-restraint etc. 604.

confinement; durance, duress; im-, prisonment; incarceration, coarctation, entombment, mancipation, durance vile, thrall, -dom, limbo, captivity; blockade; quarantine; detention.

arrest, -ation; custody, keep, care, charge, ward, restringency.

curb etc. (*means of restraint*) 752; *lettres de cachet.*

limitation, restriction, protection, monopoly; prohibition etc. 761; economic pressure.

prisoner etc. 754.

V. restrain, check; put –, lay- under restraint; en-, in-, be-thral; restrict; debar etc. (*hinder*) 706; constrain; coerce etc. (*compel*) 744; curb, control; hold –, keep- -back, – from, – in, – in check, – within bounds; hold in -leash, – leading strings; withhold.

keep under; repress, suppress; smother; pull in, rein in; hold, – fast; keep a tight hand on; prohibit etc. 761; in-, co-hibit.

enchain; fasten etc. (*join*) 43; fetter, shackle; en-, trammel; bridle, muzzle, gag, pinion, manacle, handcuff, tie one's hands, hobble, bind hand and foot; swathe, swaddle; pin –, peg- down; tether, picket; tie, – up, – down; secure; forge fetters.

confine; shut –, clap –, lock –, box –, mew –, bottle –, cork –, seal –, button- up; shut –, hem –, bolt –, wall –, rail- in; impound, pen, coop; enclose etc. (*circumscribe*) 229; cage; in-, en-cage; close the door upon, cloister; imprison, immure; incarcerate, entomb; clap –, lay- under hatches; put in -irons, – a strait waistcoat; throw –, cast- into prison; put into bilboes.

arrest; take -up, – charge of, – into custody; take –, make- -prisoner, – captive; captivate; lead -captive, – into captivity; send –, commit- to prison; commit; give in -charge, – custody; subjugate etc. 749.

Adj. re-, con-strained; imprisoned etc. *v.*; pent up; jammed in, wedged in; under restraint, – lock and key, – hatches; serving –, doing- time; in swaddling clothes; on *parole*; in custody etc. (*prisoner*) 754; cohibitive, coactive etc. (*compulsory*) 744.

stiff, restringent, straitlaced, hide-bound.

ice-, wind-, weather-bound; 'cabined, cribbed, confined;' in Lob's pound, laid by the heels.

Adv. in captivity, under arrest, behind the bars in -prison, – jail, – durance vile.

752. Prison. [Means of restraint.]—**N.** prison, -house; jail, gaol, cage, coop, den, death house, condemned –, cell; stronghold, fortress, keep, donjon, dungeon, *Bastille, oubliette*, bridewell, house of correction, hulks, tool-booth, panopticon, penitentiary, guard-room, clink, can, stir, tronk, jug, lock-up, hold; round –, watch –, station –, sponging-house; station; house of detention, black hole, pen, fold, pound; enclosure etc. 232; penal settlement; chain gang; debtors' prison; reformatory; federal penitentiary, state prison; criminal lunatic asylum; bilboes, stocks, limbo, quod.

Dartmoor, Newgate, Fleet, Marshalsea; King's (*or* Queen's) Bench; Sing Sing, Dannemora.

bond; strap, bandage, splint, tourniquet; irons, pinion, gyve, fetter, shackle, trammel, manacle, handcuff, bracelets, darbies, strait waistcoat, strait-jacket.

yoke, collar, halter, harness; muzzle, gag, bit, brake, curb, snaffle, bridle; rein, -s; ribbons, lines, bearing-rein; martingale, leading string; tether, picket, band, guy, chain; cord etc. (*fastening*) 45.

bolt, bar, lock, padlock, rail, wall; paling, palisade; fence; barrier, barricade.

brake, drag etc. (*hindrance*) 706.

753. Keeper.—N. keeper, custodian, *custos*, ranger, warder, jailer, gaoler, turnkey, castellan, guard; watch, -dog, -man; Charley; sen-try, -tinel; watch and ward; *concierge*, coast-guard, *guarda costa*, gamekeeper.

escort, body guard, convoy.

protector, governor, duenna; guardian; governess etc. (*teacher*) 540; nurse, *bonne*, *ayah*, *amah*.

754. Prisoner.—N. prisoner, captive, *détenu*, close prisoner.

jail-bird, ticket-of-leave man.

V. stand committed; be -imprisoned etc. 751.

Adj. imprisoned etc. 751; in -prison, – quod, – durance vile, – limbo, – custody, – charge, – chains; under -lock and key, – hatches; on *parole*; detained at his Majesty's pleasure.

755. Commission. [Vicarious authority.]—**N.** commission, delegation; con-, as-signment; procuration; deputation, legation, mission, embassy; agency, agentship; power of attorney, proxy; clerkship.

errand, charge, *brevet*, diploma, *exequatur*, permit etc. (*permission*) 760.

appointment, nomination, return; charter; ordination; installation, inauguration, investiture; accession, coronation, enthronement.

vicegerency; regency, regentship.

viceroy etc. 745; consignee etc. 758; deputy etc. 759.

V. commission, delegate, depute; consign, assign; charge; in-, en-trust; turn over to; commit, – to the hands of; authorize etc. (*permit*) 760.

put in commission, accredit, engage, hire, bespeak, appoint, name, nominate, return, ordain; install, induct, inaugurate, invest, crown; en-roll, -list.

employ, empower; give power of attorney to; set –, place- over; send out.

be commissioned, be accredited; represent, stand for; stand in the -stead, – place, – shoes- of.

Adj. commissioned etc. *v.*

Adv. *per procuratione.*

756. Abrogation.—N. abrogation, annulment, nullification; cancelling etc. *v.*; cancel; revo-cation, -kement; repeal, rescission, defeasance.

dismissal, *congé*, demission; depos-al, -ition; sack, dethronement; disestablish-, disendow-ment; deconsecration.

aboli-tion, -shment; dissolution.

counter-order, -mand; repudiation, retractation; recantation etc. (*tergiversation*) 607.

V. abrogate, annul, cancel; destroy etc. 162; abolish; revoke, repeal, rescind, reverse, retract, recall; over-rule, -ride; set aside; disannul, dissolve, quash, nullify, declare null and void; dis-establish, -endow; deconsecrate.

disclaim etc. (*deny*) 536; ignore, repudiate; recant etc. 607; divest oneself, break off.

counter-mand, -order; do away with; sweep –, brush- away; throw -overboard, – to the dogs; scatter to the winds, cast behind.

dismiss, discard; cast –, turn- -off, – out, – adrift, – out of doors, – aside, – away; send -off, – away, – about one's business; discharge, get rid of, fire out, fire etc. (*eject*) 297; jilt.

cashier; break; oust; set down, unseat, -saddle; un-, de-, disen-throne; depose, uncrown; unfrock, strike off the roll; dis-bar, -bench.

be -abrogated etc.; receive its quietus.

Adj. abrogated etc. *v.*; *functus officio*.

Int. get along with you! begone! go about your business! away with!

757. Resignation.—N. resignation, retirement, abdication, renunciation, abjuration, disclaimer, abandonment, relinquishment.

V. resign; give –, throw- up; lay down, throw up the cards, wash one's hands of, abjure, renounce, forego, disclaim, abandon, relinquish, retract, demit; deny etc. 536.

abrogate etc. 756; desert etc. (*relinquish*) 624; get rid of etc. 782.

abdicate; vacate, – one's seat; accept the stewardship of the Chiltern Hundreds; retire; tender –, send in –, hand in- one's resignation.

Adj. abdicant, renunciatory etc. *v.*

Phr. 'Othello's occupation's gone.'

758. Consignee.—N. consignee, trustee, nominee, committee.

delegate; commiss-ary, -ioner; emissary, envoy, commissionaire; messenger etc. 534.

diplomatist, diplomat, *corps diplomatique*, embassy; am-, em-bassador; representative, resident, consul, legate, nuncio, internuncio, *chargé d' affaires*, *attaché*.

vicegerent etc. (*deputy*) 759; plenipotentiary.

functionary, placeman, curator; treasurer etc. 801; agent, factor, bailiff, steward, clerk, secretary, attorney, solicitor, proctor, broker, underwriter, commission agent, auctioneer, one's man of business; factotum etc. (*director*) 694; caretaker.

negotiator, go between; middleman; under agent, *employé*; servant etc. 746.

salesman; commercial, – traveler; bagman, *commis-voyageur*, touter.

newspaper –, own –, war –, special- correspondent; reporter.

759. Deputy.—N. deputy, substitute, vice, proxy, *locum tenens*, delegate, representative, next friend, surrogate, secondary.

regent, vicegerent, vizier, minister, vicar; premier etc. (*director*) 694; chancellor, prefect, provost, warden, lieutenant, archon, consul, proconsul; viceroy etc. (*governor*) 745; commissioner etc. 758; plenipotentiary, *alter ego*.

team, eight, eleven; champion.

V. be -deputy etc. *n.*; stand –, appear –, hold a brief –, answer- for; represent; stand –, walk- in the shoes of; stand in the stead of.

substitute, ablegate, accredit; commission, empower, delegate etc. 755.

Adj. acting; vice, -regal; accredited to.

Adv. in behalf of, by proxy.

760. Permission.—N. permission, leave; allow-, suffer-ance; toler-ance, -ation; liberty, law, license, concession, grace; indulgence etc. (*lenity*) 740; favor, dispensation, exemption, release; connivance; vouchsafement.

authorization, warranty, accordance, admission.

permit, warrant, *brevet*, precept, sanction, authority, *firman*; pass, -port; furlough, license, *carte blanche*, ticket of leave; grant, charter, patent.

V. permit; give -permission etc. *n.*, – power;

let, allow, admit; suffer, bear with, tolerate, recognize; concede etc. 762; accord, vouchsafe, favor, humor, gratify, indulge, stretch a point; wink at, connive at; shut one's eyes to.

grant, empower, charter, enfranchise, privilege, confer a privilege, license, authorize, warrant; sanction; entrust etc. (*commission*) 755.

give -*carte blanche*, – the reins to, – scope to etc. (*freedom*) 748; leave -alone, – it to one, – the door open; open the -door to, – floodgates; give a loose to.

let off; absolve etc. (*acquit*) 970; release, exonerate, dispense with.

ask –, beg –, request- -leave, – permission.

Adj. permitting etc. *v.*, permissive, indulgent; permitted etc. *v.*; patent, chartered, permissible, allowable, lawful, legitimate, legal; legalized etc. (*law*) 963; licit; unforbid, -den; unconditional.

Adv. permissibly; by –, with –, on- -leave etc. *n.*; *speciali gratiâ*; under favor of; *pace*; *ad libitum* etc. (*freely*) 748, (*at will*) 600; by all means etc. (*willingly*) 602; yes etc. (*assent*) 488.

761. Prohibition.—N. pro-, in-hibition; *veto*, disallowance; interdict, -ion; injunction; embargo, ban, *verboten*, taboo, proscription; *index expurgatorius*; restriction etc. (*restraint*) 751; hindrance etc. 706; forbidden fruit.

V. pro-, in-hibit; forbid, put one's *veto* upon, disallow; bar; debar etc. (*hinder*) 706; forefend.

keep -in, – within bounds; restrain etc. 751; cohibit, withhold, limit, circumscribe, clip the wings of, restrict, narrow; interdict, taboo; put –, place- under -an interdiction, – the ban; proscribe, censor; exclude, shut out; shut –, bolt –, show- the door; warn off; dash the cup from one's lips; forbid the banns.

Adj. prohibit-ive, -ory; interdictive; proscriptive; restrictive, exclusive; forbidding etc. *v.*

prohibited etc. *v.*; not -permitted etc. 760; unlicensed, contraband, under the ban of; illegal etc. 964; unauthorized, not to be thought of.

Adv. on no account etc. (*no*) 536.

Int. forbid it heaven! etc. (*deprecation*) 766. hands –, keep- off! hold! stop! avast!

Phr. that will never do.

762. Consent.—N. consent; assent etc. 488; acquiescence; approval etc. 931; compliance, agreement, concession; yield-ance, -ingness; accession, acknowledgment, acceptance, agnition.

settlement, ratification, confirmation, adjustment.

permit etc. (*permission*) 760; promise etc. 768.

V. consent; assent etc. 488; yield assent, admit, allow, concede, grant, yield; come -over, – round; give in to, acknowledge, agnize, give consent, comply with, acquiesce, agree to, fall in with, accede, accept, embrace an offer, close with, take at one's word, have no objection.

satisfy, meet one's wishes, settle, come to terms etc. 488; not -refuse etc. 764; turn a willing ear etc. (*willingness*) 602; jump at; deign, vouchsafe; promise etc. 768.

Adj. consenting etc. *v.*; agreeable, compliant; agreed etc. (*assent*) 488; unconditional.

Adv. yes etc. (*assent*) 488; by all means etc. (*willingly*) 602; if –, as- you please; be it so, so be it, well and good, of course.

763. Offer.—N. offer, proffer, presentation, tender, bid, overture; propos-al, -ition; motion, invitation; candidature; offering etc. (*gift*) 784.

V. offer, proffer, present, tender; bid; propose, move; make -a motion, – advances; start; invite, hold out, place- at one's disposal, – in one's way, put forward.

hawk about; offer for sale etc. 796; press etc. (*request*) 765; lay at one's feet.

offer –, present- oneself; volunteer, come forward, be a candidate; stand –, bid- for; seek; be at one's service; go a begging; bribe etc. (*give*) 784.

Adj. offer-ing, -ed etc. *v.*; in the market, for sale, to let, disengaged, on hire.

764. Refusal.—N. refusal, rejection; non-, incompliance; denial; declining etc. *v.*; declension; peremptory –, flat –, point blank- refusal; repulse, rebuff; discountenance.

recusancy, renunciation, abnegation, negation, protest, disclaimer; dissent etc. 489; revocation etc. 756.

V. refuse, reject, deny, decline; nill, negative; refuse –, withhold- one's assent; shake the head; close the -hand, – purse, grudge, begrudge, be slow to, hang fire.

be deaf to; turn -a deaf ear to, – one's back upon; set one's face against, discountenance, not hear of, have nothing to do with, wash one's hands of, stand aloof, forswear, set aside, cast behind one; not yield an inch etc. (*obstinacy*) 606.

resist, cross; not -grant etc. 762; repel, repulse; shut –, slam- the door in one's face; rebuff; send -back, – to the right about, – away with a flea in the ear; deny oneself, not be at home to; discard etc. (*repudiate*) 610; rescind etc. (*revoke*) 756; disclaim, protest; dissent etc. 489.

Adj. refusing etc. *v.*; rest-ive, -iff; recusant; uncomplying, noncompliant, unconsenting, uncomplaisant, protestant; not willing to hear of, deaf to.

refused etc. *v.*; ungranted, out of the question, not to be thought of, impossible.

Adv. no etc. 536; on no account, not for the world; no thank you.

Phr. *non possumus*; [ironically] your humble servant; *bien obligé*.

765. Request.—N. requ-est, -isition; claim etc. (*demand*) 741; petition, suit, prayer; begging letter, round-robin.

motion, overture, application, canvass, address, appeal, apostrophe; imprecation; rogation; proposal, proposition.

orison etc. (*worship*) 990; incantation etc. (*spell*) 993.

mendicancy; asking, panhandling, begging etc. *v.*; postulation, solicitation, invitation, entreaty, importunity, supplication, instance, impetration, imploration, obsecration, obtestation, invocation, interpellation.

V. request, ask; beg, crave, sue, pray, petition, solicit, invite, pop the question, make bold to ask; beg -leave, – a boon; apply to, call to, put to; call -upon, – for; make –, address –, prefer –, put up- a -request, – prayer, – petition; make -application, – a requisition; ask –, trouble- one for; claim etc. (*demand*) 741; offer up prayers etc. (*worship*) 990; whistle for.

beg hard, entreat, beseech, plead, supplicate, implore, apostrophize; conjure, adjure; obtest; cry to, kneel to, appeal to; invoke, evoke; impetrate, imprecate, ply, press, urge, beset, importune, dun, tax, clamor for; cry -aloud, – for help; fall on one's knees; throw oneself at the feet of; come down on one's marrow-bones.

beg from door to door, send the hat round, go a begging; mendicate, mump, cadge, panhandle, beg one's bread.

dance attendance on, besiege, knock at the door.

bespeak, canvass, tout, make interest, court; seek, bid for etc. (*offer*) 763; publish the banns.

Adj. requesting etc. *v.*; precatory; suppli-ant, -cant, -catory; invoc-, imprec-, rog-atory; postulant, mendicant.

importunate, clamorous, urgent; solicitous; cap in hand; on one's -knees, – bended knees, – marrow-bones.

Adv. prithee, do, please, pray; be so good as, be good enough; have the goodness, vouchsafe, will you, I pray thee, if you please.

Int. for -God's, – heaven's, – goodness', – mercy's- sake.

766. Deprecation. [Negative request.]—**N.** deprecation, expostulation; remonstrance; intercession, mediation.

V. deprecate, protest, expostulate, enter a protest, intercede for.

Adj. deprecatory, expostulatory, intercessory, mediatorial.

deprecated, protested.

un-, unbe-sought; unasked etc. (*see* ask etc. 765).

Int. cry you mercy! God forbid! forbid it Heaven! Heaven -forefend, – forbid! far be it from! hands off! etc. (*prohibition*) 761.

767. Petitioner.—N. petitioner, solicitor, applicant; suppli-ant, -cant; suitor, candidate, claimant, postulant, aspirant, competitor, bidder; place –, pot- hunter; prizer.

beggar, mendicant, mumper, sturdy beggar, cadger, panhandler.

canvasser, barker, touter etc. 768.

sycophant, parasite etc. 886.

768. Promise.—N. promise, undertaking, word, troth, plight, pledge, *parole*, word of honor, vow; oath etc. (*affirmation*) 535; profession, assurance, warranty, guarantee, insurance, obligation; contract etc. 769.

engagement, pre-engagement; affiance; betroth, -al, -ment; marriage -compact, – vow.

V. promise; give a -promise etc. *n.*; undertake, engage; make –, form- an engagement; enter -into, – on- an engagement; bind –, tie –, pledge –, commit –, take upon- oneself; vow; swear etc. (*affirm*) 535; give –, pass –, pledge –, plight- one's -word, – honor, – credit, – troth; betroth, plight faith; take the vows.

assure, warrant, guarantee, vouch for, avouch, covenant etc. 769; attest etc. (*bear witness*) 467.

hold out an expectation; contract an obligation; become -bound to, – sponsor for; answer –, be answerable- for; secure; give security etc. 771; underwrite.

adjure, administer an oath, put to one's oath, swear a witness.

Adj. promising etc. *v.*; promissory; votive; under hand and seal; upon -oath, – affirmation.

promised etc. *v.*; affianced, pledged, bound; committed, compromised; in for it.

Adv. as one's head shall answer for; upon my honor.

Phr. in for a penny, in for a pound.

768a. Release from engagement.—**N.** release etc. (*liberation*) 750.

Adj. absolute; unconditional etc. (*free*) 748.

769. Compact.—N. compact, contract, agreement, bargain, deal, transaction; affidation; pact, -ion; bond, covenant, indenture.

stipulation, settlement, convention; compromise, *cartel*.

protocol, treaty, *concordat, Zollverein, Sonderbund*, charter, *Magna Charta*, Pragmatic Sanction.

negotiation etc. (*bargaining*) 794; diplomacy etc. (*mediation*) 724; negotiator etc. (*agent*) 758.

ratification, completion, signature, seal, sigil, signet.

V. contract, covenant, agree for, engage etc. (*promise*) 768.

treat, negotiate, stipulate, make terms; bargain etc. (*barter*) 794.

make –, strike- a bargain; come to -terms, – an understanding; compromise etc. 774; set at rest; close, – with; conclude, complete, settle; confirm, ratify, clench, subscribe, underwrite; en-, in-dorse; put the seal to; sign, seal etc. (*attest*) 467; indent.

take one at one's word, bargain by inch of candle.

Adj. contractual, agreed etc. *v.*; conventional; under hand and seal; signed, sealed and delivered.

Phr. *caveat emptor.*

770. Conditions.—N. conditions, terms; articles, – of agreement.

clauses, provisions; proviso etc. (*qualification*) 469; covenant, stipulation, obligation, *ultimatum, sine quâ non*; *casus foederis*.

V. make –, come to- -terms etc. (*contract*) 769; make it a condition, stipulate, insist upon, make a point of; bind, tie up.

Adj. conditional, provisional, guarded, fenced, hedged in.

Adv. conditionally etc. (*with qualification*) 469; provisionally, *pro re natâ*; on condition; with a reservation.

771. Security.—N. security; guaran-ty, -tee; gage, waranty, bond, tie, pledge, plight, mortgage, debenture, hypothecation, bill of sale, lien, pignus, pawn, pignoration; real security; bottomry; collateral, vadium.

stake, deposit, earnest, handsel, caution.

promissory note; bill, – of exchange; I.O.U.: personal security, covenant, specialty; *parole* etc. (*promise*) 768.

acceptance, indorsement, signature, execution, stamp, seal.

spon-sor, -sion, -sorship; surety, bail; mainpernor, hostage.

recognizance; deed –, covenant- of indemnity.

authentication, verfication, warrant, certificate, voucher, docket, doquet; record etc. 551; probate, attested copy.

receipt; ac-, quittance; discharge, release.

muniment, title-deed, instrument; deed, – poll; assurance, insurance, indenture; charter etc. (*compact*) 769; charter-poll; paper, parchment, settlement, will, testament, last will and testament, codicil.

V. give -security, – bail, – substantial bail; go bail; pawn, impawn, hock, spout, mortgage, hypothecate, impignorate.

guarantee, warrant, assure; accept, indorse, underwrite, insure.

execute, stamp; sign, seal etc. (*evidence*) 467.

let, set; grant –, take –, hold- a lease; hold in pledge; lend on security etc. 787.

Adj. secure, -ed; pledged etc. *v.*; in pawn, on deposit.

772. Observance.—N. observance, performance, compliance; obedience, etc. 743; fulfilment, satisfaction, discharge; acquit-tance, -tal.

adhesion, acknowledgment; fidelity etc. (*probity*) 939; exact etc. 494- observance.

V. observe, comply with, respect, acknowledge, abide by; cling to, adhere to, be faithful to, act up to; meet, fulfil; carry -out, – into execution; execute, perform, keep, satisfy, discharge; do one's office.

perform –, fulfill –, discharge –, acquit oneself of- an obligation; make good; make good –, keep- one's -word, – promise; redeem one's pledge; keep faith with, stand to one's engagement.

Adj. observant, faithful, true, loyal; honorable etc. 939; true as the -dial to the sun, – needle to the pole; punct-ual, -ilious; meticulous; literal etc. (*exact*) 494; as good as one's word.

Adv. faithfully etc. *adj.*

773. Non-observance.—N. non-observance etc. 772; evasion, inobservance, failure, omission, neglect, laches, laxity, informality.

infringement, infraction; violation, transgression. retractation, repudiation, nullification; protest; forfeiture.

lawlessness; disobedience etc. 742; bad faith etc. 940.

V. fail, neglect, omit, elude, evade, give the go by to, cut, set aside, ignore; shut –, close- one's eyes to, avoid.

infringe, transgress, pirate, violate, break, trample under foot, do violence to, drive a coach and six through.

discard, protest, repudiate, fling to the winds, set at naught, nullify, declare null and void; cancel etc. (*wipe off*) 552.

retract, go back from, be off, forfeit, go from one's word, palter; stretch –, strain- a point.

Adj. violating etc. *v.*; lawless, transgressive; elusive, evasive; lax, casual; non-observant.

unfulfilled etc. (*see* fulfil etc. 772).

774. Compromise.—N. com-promise, -mutation, -position; middle term, *mezzo termine*; compensation etc. 30; adjustment, mutual concession.

V. com-promise, -mute, -pound; take the mean; split the difference, meet one half way, give and take; come to terms etc. (*contract*) 769; submit to –, abide by- arbitration; patch up, bridge over, fix up, arrange; adjust, – differences; agree; make -the best of, – a virtue of necessity; take the will for the deed.

775. Acquisition.—N. acquisition; gaining etc. *v.*; obtainment; procur-ation, -ement; purchase, descent, inheritance; gift etc. 784.

recovery, retrieval, revendication, replevin; redemption, salvage, trover; find, *trouvaille*, foundling.

gain, thrift; money-making, -grubbing; lucre, filthy lucre, loaves and fishes, the main chance, pelf; emolument etc. 973; wealth etc. 803.

profit, earnings, winnings, innings, clean-up, pickings, perquisite, net profit; income etc. (*receipt*) 810; pro-ceeds, -duce, -duct; out-come, -put; return, fruit, crop, harvest, tilth; second crop, aftermath; benefit etc. (*good*) 618.

sweepstakes, trick, prize, pool.

[Fraudulent acquisition] subreption; theft, stealing etc. 791.

V. acquire, get, gain, win, earn, obtain, procure, gather, annex; collect etc. 72; pick, – up; glean, take etc. 789.

find; come –, pitch –, light- upon; scrape -up, – together; get in, reap and carry, net, bag, sack, bring home, secure, come across, derive, draw, get in the harvest.

profit; make –, draw- profit; turn to -profit, – account; make -capital out of, – money by; obtain a return, reap the fruits of; reap –, gain- an advantage; turn -a penny, – an honest penny; make the pot boil, bring grist to the mill; make –, coin –, raise- money; raise -funds, – the wind; fill one's pocket etc. (*wealth*) 803.

treasure up etc. (*store*) 636; realize, clear; produce etc. 161; take etc. 789.

get back, recover, regain, retrieve, revendicate, replevy, redeem, come by one's own.

come -by, – in for; receive etc. 785; inherit; step into, – a fortune, – the shoes of; succeed to.
get -hold of, – between one's finger and thumb, – into one's hand, – at; take –, come into –, enter into- possession.
be -profitable etc. *adj.*; pay, answer.
accrue etc. (*be received*) 785.
Adj. acquir-ing, -ed etc. *v.*; acquisitive; productive, profitable, advantageous, gainful, remunerative, paying, lucrative.

776. Loss.—N. loss; de-, perdition; forfeiture, lapse.
privation, bereavement; deprivation etc. (*dispossession*) 789; riddance.
V. lose; incur –, experience –, meet with- a loss; miss; mislay, let slip, allow to slip through the fingers, squander; be without etc. (*exempt*) 777*a*; forfeit.
get rid of etc. 782; waste etc. 638.
be lost, lapse.
Adj. losing etc. *v.*; not having etc. 777*a*.
shorn of, deprived of; denuded, bereaved, bereft, *minus*, cut off; dispossessed etc. 789; rid of, quit of; out of pocket.
lost etc. *v.*; long lost; irretrievable etc. (*hopeless*) 859; irredentist; off one's hands.
Int. farewell to! adieu to! good riddance!

777. Possession.—N. possession, seisin; ownership etc. 780; occupancy; hold, -ing; tenure, tenancy, feodality, dependency; villenage; socage, chivalry, knight service.
exclusive possession, impropriation, monopoly, corner; retention etc. 781; pre-possession, -occupancy; nine points of the law.
future possession, heritage, inheritance, heirship, reversion, fee, seigniority, feud, fief.
bird in hand, *uti possidetis*, *chose* in possession.
V. possess, have, hold, occupy, enjoy; be -possessed of etc. *adj.*; have -in hand etc. *adj.*; own etc. 780; command.
inherit; come -to, – in for.
engross, monopolize, forestall, regrate, impropriate, have all to oneself, corner; have a firm hold of etc. (*retain*) 781; get into one's hand etc. (*acquire*) 775.
belong to, appertain to, pertain to; be -in one's possession etc. *adj.*; vest in.
Adj. possessing etc. *v.*; worth; possessed of, seized of, master of, in possession of; endowed –, blest –, instinct –, fraught –, laden –, charged –, instilled –, with.
possessed etc. *v.*; on hand, by one; in hand, in store, in stock; in one's -hands, – grasp, – possession; at one's -command, – disposal; one's own etc. (*property*) 780.
unsold, unshared.

777a. Exemption.—N. exemption; exception, immunity, privilege, release etc. 927*a*; absence etc. 187.
V. not -have etc. 777; be -without etc. *adj.*
Adj. exempt from, devoid of, without, unpossessed of, unblest with, immune from.
not -having etc. 777; unpossessed; untenanted etc. (*vacant*) 187; without an owner.
unobtained, unacquired.

778. Participation. [Joint possession.]—**N.** participation; co-, joint-tenancy; possession –, tenancy- in common; joint –, common- stock; co-, partnership; communion; community of -possessions, – goods; communalism, communism, socialism, collectivism; co-operation etc. 709; profit sharing.
snacks, co-portion, picnic, hotchpotch; co-heirship, -parceny, -parcenary; gavelkind.
participator, sharer; co-, partner; shareholder; co-, joint-tenant; tenants in common; co-heir, -parcener.
communist, socialist.
V. par-ticipate, -take; share, – in; come in for a share; go -shares, – snacks, – halves; share and share alike.
have –, possess –, be seized- -in common, – as joint tenants etc. *n.*
join in; have a hand in etc. (*co-operate*) 709.
Adj. partaking etc. *v.*; communistic, socialistic, co-operative, profit sharing.
Adv. share and share alike.

779. Possessor.—N. possessor, holder; occupant, -ier; tenant; person –, man- -in possession etc. 777; renter, lodger, lessee, under-lessee; zemindar, ryot; tenant -on sufferance, – at will, – from year to year, – for years, – for life.
owner; propriet-or, -ress, -ary; impropriator, master, mistress, lord.
land-holder, -owner, -lord, -lady; lord -of the manor, – paramount; heritor, laird, vavasor, landed gentry, mesne lord.
cestui-que-trust, beneficiary, mortgagor.
grantee, feoffee, relessee, devisee; legat-ee, -ary.
trustee; holder etc.- of the legal estate; mortgagee.
right –, rightful- owner.
[Future possessor] heir, – apparent; – presumptive; heiress; inherit-or, -ress, -rix; reversioner, remainder-man.

780. Property.—N. property, possession, *suum cuique, meum et tuum*.
owner-, proprietor, lord-ship; seignority; empire etc. (*dominion*) 737.
interest, stake, estate, right, title, claim, demand, holding; tenure etc. (*possession*) 777; vested –, contingent –, beneficial –, equitable- interest; use, trust, benefit; legal –, equitable- estate; seisin.
absolute interest, paramount estate, freehold; fee, – simple, – tail; estate -in fee, – in tail, – tail; estate in tail -male, – female, – general.
limitation, term, lease, settlement, strict settlement, particular estate; estate -for life, – for years, – *pur autre vie*; remainder, reversion, expectancy, possibility.

dower, dowry, *dot*, jointure, marriage portion, appanage, inheritance, heritage, patrimony, alimony; legacy etc. (*gift*) 784.

assets, belongings, means, resources, circumstances; wealth etc. 803; money etc. 800; what one -is worth, – will cut up for; estate and effects.

landed –, real- -estate, – property; realty; land, -s; subdivision; plot, site; tenements; hereditaments; corporeal –, incorporeal- hereditaments; acres; ground etc. (*earth*) 342; acquest; messuage.

territory, state, kingdom, principality, realm, empire, protectorate, margravate, dependancy, colony, sphere of influence, mandate.

manor, honor, domain, demesne; farm, ranch, plantation, *hacienda*; allodium etc. (*free*) 748; fieff, feoff, feud, zemindary, dependency.

free-, copy-, lease-holds; chattels real; fixtures, plant, heirloom easement; folkland; right of -common, – user.

personal -property, – estate, – effects; personalty, chattels, goods, effects, movables; stock, – in trade; things, traps, rattle-traps, paraphernalia; equipage etc. 633.

parcels, appurtenances.

impedimenta; lug-, bag-gage; bag and baggage; pelf; cargo, lading.

rent-roll; income etc. (*receipts*) 810.

patent, copyright; *chose* in action; credit etc. 805; debt etc. 806.

V. possess etc. 777; be the possessor etc. 779-of own; have for one's own, – very own; come in for, inherit, enfeoff

savor of the realty.

be one's own -property etc. *n.*; belong to; ap-, pertain to.

Adj. one's own; landed, predial, manorial, allodial, seignorial; free-, copy-, lease-hold; feu-, feo-dal; hereditary, entailed, personal.

Adv. to one's -credit, – account; to the good.

to one and -his heirs for ever, – the heirs of his body, – his heirs and assigns, – his executors, administrators and assigns.

781. Retention.—N. retention; retaining etc. *v.*; keep, detention, custody; tenacity, firm hold, grasp, gripe, grip, iron grip.

fangs, teeth, claws, talons, nail, hook, tentacle, *tenaculum*; bond etc. (*vinculum*) 45.

clutches, tongs, forceps, pincers, nippers, pliers, tweezers, vise.

paw, hand, finger, wrist, fist, neaf, neif.

bird in hand; captive etc. 754.

V. retain, keep; hold, – fast, – tight, – one's own, – one's ground; clinch, clench, clutch, grasp, gripe, hug, have a firm hold of.

secure, withold, detain; hold –, keepback; keep close; husband etc. (*store*) 636; reserve; have –, keep- in stock etc. (*possess*) 777; enfail, tie up, settle.

Adj. retaining etc. *v.*; retentive, tenacious.

unforfeited, undeprived, undisposed, uncommunicated.

incommunicable, inalienable; in mortmain; in strict settlement.

Phr. *uti possidetis.*

782. Relinquishment.—N. relinquishment, abandonment etc. (*of a course*) 624; renunciation, expropriation, dereliction; cession, surrender, dispensation; resignation etc. 757; riddance.

derelict etc. *adj.*; jetsam; waif, foundling, orphan.

v. relinquish, give up, surrender, yield, cede; let -go, – slip; spare, drop, resign, forego, renounce, abjure, abandon, expropriate, give away, dispose of, part with; lay -aside, – apart, – down, – on the shelf etc. (*disuse*) 678; set –, put- aside; make away with, cast behind; discard, cast off, dismiss; maroon.

give -notice to quit, – warning; supersede; be –, get- -rid of, – quit of; eject etc. 297.

rid –, disburden –, divest –, dispossess- oneself of; wash one's hands of; divorce, desert; disinherit, cut off.

cast –, throw –, pitch –, fling- -away, – aside, – overboard, – to the dogs; cast –, throw –, sweep- to the winds; put –, turn –, sweep- away; jettison.

quit one's hold.

Adj. relinquished etc. *v.*; cast off, derelict; unowned, unappropriated, unculled; left etc. (*residuary*) 40; divorced; disinherited.

Int. away with!

783. Transfer.—N. transfer, conveyance, assignment, alienation, aballenation; demise, limitation; conveyancing; transmission etc. (*transference*) 270; enfeoffment, bargain and sale, lease and release; exchange etc. (*interchange*) 148; barter etc. 794; substitution etc. 147.

succession, reversion; shifting -use, – trust; devolution.

V. transfer, convey; alien, -ate; assign; grant etc. (*confer*) 784; consign; make –, hand- over; pass, hand, transmit, negotiate; hand down; exchange etc. (*interchange*) 148.

change -hands, – from one to another; devolve, succeed; come into possession etc. (*acquire*) 775; take over.

abalienate; disinherit; dispossess etc. 789; substitute etc. 147.

Adj. alienable, negotiable, transferable, reversional.

Phr. estate coming into possession.

784. Giving.—N. giving etc. *v.*; bestowal, donation; present-ation, -ment; accordance; con-, cession; delivery, consignment, dispensation, communication, endowment; invest-ment, -iture; award.

almsgiving, charity, liberality, generosity; philanthropy etc. 910.

[Thing given] gift, donation, present, *cadeau*; fairing; free gift, boon, favor, benefaction, grant, offering, oblation, sacrifice, immolation.

grace, act of grace, *bonus, bonanza.*

allowance, contribution, subscription, subsidy, tribute, subvention.

bequest, legacy, devise, will, dotation, appanage; dowry; voluntary -settlement, – conveyance etc. 783; amortization.

alms, largess, bounty, dole, sportule, donative, help, oblation, offertory, Peter's pence, *honorarium*, gratuity, Maundy money, Christmas box, Easter offering, vail, tip, *douceur*, drink money, *pourboire, trinkgeld, backsheesh*; fee etc. (*recompense*) 973; consideration.

bribe, bait, ground-bait; peace-offering, handsel.

giver, grantor etc. *v.*; donor, feoffer, settlor; almoner; testator; investor, subscriber, contributor; fairy godmother; Santa Claus, benefactor etc. 816.

V. deliver, hand, pass, put into the hands of; hand –, make –, deliver –, pass –, turn- over.

present, give away, dispense, dispose of; give –, deal –, dole –, mete –, fork –, shell –, squeeze- out.

pay etc. 807; render, impart, communicate.

concede, cede, yield, part with, shed cast; spend etc. 809.

give, bestow, confer, grant, accord, award, assign.

entrust, consign, vest in.

make a present; allow, contribute, subscribe, donate, furnish its quota.

invest, endow, settle upon; bequesth, leave, devise.

furnish, supply, help; ad-, minister to; afford, spare; accommodate –, indulge –, favor- with; shower down upon; lavish, pour on, thrust upon; tip, bribe; tickle –, grease- the palm; offer etc. 763; sacrifice, immolate.

Adj. giving etc. *v.*; given etc. *v.*; allow-ed, -able; concessional; communicable; charitable, eleemosynary, sportulary, tributary; *gratis* etc. 815.

785. Receiving.—N. receiving etc. *v.*; acquisition etc. 775; reception etc. (*introduction*) 296; suscipiency, acceptance, admission.

re-, ac-cipient; assignee, devisee; lega-tee, -tary; grantee, feoffee, donee, relessee, lessee.

sportulary, stipendiary; beneficiary; pension-er, -ary; almsman.

income etc. (*receipt*) 810.

v. receive; take etc. 789; acquire etc. 775; admit.

take in, catch, touch; pocket; put into one's -pocket, – purse; accept; take off one's hands.

be received; come -in, – to hand; pass –, fall- into one's hand; go into one's pocket; fall to one's -lot, – share; come –, fall- to one; accrue; have -given etc. 784 to one.

Adj. receiving etc. *v.*; re-, suscipient.

received etc. *v.*; given etc. 784; second-hand.

not given, unbestowed etc. (*see* give, bestow etc. 784).

786. Apportionment.—N. apportion-, allot-, consign-, assign-, appoint-ment; appropriation; dispensation, -tribution; allocation, division, deal; repartition; administration.

dividend, portion, contingent, share, allotment, lot, cut, split, measure, dose; dole, meed, pittance; *quantum*, ration; ratio, proportion, quota, *modicum*, mess, allowance.

V. apportion, divide; cut, split, divvy; distribute, administer, dispense; billet, allot, detail, cast, share, mete; portion –, parcel –, dole- out; deal, carve.

partition, assign, appropriate, appoint.

come in for one's share etc. (*participate*) 778.

Adj. apportioning etc. *v.*; respective.

Adv. respectively, each to each.

787. Lending.—N. lending etc. *v.*; loan, advance, accommodation, feneration; mortgage etc. (*security*) 771; investment.

mont de piété, pawnshop, hock shop, spout, my uncle's.

lender, pawnbroker, money lender, usurer, Jew, Shylock.

V. lend, advance, loan, accommodate with; lend on security; pawn etc. (*security*) 771.

intrust, invest; place –, put- out to interest; sink, risk.

let, demise, lease, set, under-, sub-let.

Adj. lending etc. *v.*; lent etc. *v.*; unborrowed etc. (*see* borrowed etc. 788).

Adv. in advance; on -loan, – security.

788. Borrowing.—N. borrowing, pledging, pawning.

borrowed plumes; plagiarism etc. (*thieving*) 791.

replevin.

V. borrow, desume; pawn.

hire, rent, farm; take a -lease, – demise; take –, hire- by the -hour, – mile, – year etc.

raise –, take up- money; float bonds; raise the wind; fly a kite, borrow of Peter to pay Paul; run into debt etc. (*debt*) 806.

make use of, plagiarize, pirate.

replevy.

789. Taking.—N. taking etc. *v.*; reception etc. (*taking in*) 296; deglutition etc. (*taking food*) 298; appropriation, prehension, prensation; capture, caption; ap-, de-prehension; abreption, seizure; abduction, -lation; subtraction etc. (*subduction*) 38; abstraction, ademption.

dispossession; depriv-ation, -ement; bereavement; divestment; disherison; distraint, distress; sequestration, confiscation, attachment, execution; eviction etc. 297.

rapacity, extortion, vampirism, predacity, blood-sucking; theft etc. 791.

resumption; repris-e, -al; recovery etc. 775.

clutch, swoop, wrench; grip etc. (*retention*) 781; haul, take, catch; scramble.

taker, captor, capturer; vampire; extortioner.

V. take, catch, hook, nab, bag, sack, pocket, put into one's pocket, scrounge; receive; accept.

reap, crop, cull, pluck; gather etc. (*get*) 775; draw.

ap-, im-propriate; assume, possess oneself of; take possession of; commandeer; lay –, clap- one's hands on; help oneself to; make free with, dip one's hands into, lay under contribution; intercept; scramble for; deprive of.

take –, carry –, bear- -away, – off; abstract; hurry off –, run away- with; abduct; steal etc. 791; ravish; seize; pounce –, spring- upon; swoop -to, – down upon; take by -storm, – assault; snatch, reave.

snap up, nip up, whip up, catch up; kidnap, crimp, capture, lay violent hands on.

get –, lay –, take –, catch –, lay fast –, take firm- hold of; lay by the heels, take prisoner; fasten upon, grip, grapple, embrace, gripe, clasp, grab, clutch, collar, throttle, take by the throat, claw, clinch, clench, make sure of.

catch at, jump at, make a grab at, snap at, snatch at; reach, make a long arm, stretch forth one's hand.

take -from, – away from; deduct etc. 38; retrench etc. (*curtail*) 201; dispossess, ease one of, snatch from one's grasp; tear –, tear away –, wrench –, wrest –, wring- from; extort; deprive of, bereave; disinherit, cut off with a shilling.

oust etc. (*eject*) 297; divest; levy, distrain, confiscate; sequest-er, -rate, accroach; usurp; despoil, strip, fleece, shear, displume, impoverish, eat out of house and home; drain, – to the dregs; gut, dry, exhaust, swallow up; absorb etc. (*suck in*) 296; draw off; suck, – like a leech, – the blood of.

retake, resume; recover etc. 775.

Adj. taking etc. *v.*, privative, prehensile; predaceous, -al, -atory, -atorial; rap-acious, -torial; ravenous; parasitic; all-devouring, -engulfing.

bereft etc. 776.

Adv. at one fell swoop.

Phr. give an inch and take an ell.

790. Restitution.—N. restitution, return; ren-, red-dition; reinstatement, restoration; reinvestment, recuperation; repatriation; rehabilitation etc. (*reconstruction*) 660; reparation, atonement, indemnity, compensation, recompense.

release, replevin, redemption; recovery etc. (*getting back*) 775; remitter, reversion.

V. return, restore; recondition; give –, carry –, bring- back; render, – up; give up; let go, unclutch; dis-, re-gorge; regurgitate; recoup, reimburse, repay, indemnify, reinvest, remit, rehabilitate; repair etc. (*make good*) 660.

redeem, recover etc. (*get back*) 775; take back again; revest, revert.

Adj. restoring etc. *v.*; recuperative etc. 660; in full restitution, to compensate for.

Phr. *suum cuique.*

791. Stealing.—N. stealing etc. *v.*; theft, thievery, robbery, latrociny, direption; abstraction, appropriation; plagiar-y, -ism; rape, kidnapping, depredation; raid, hold up.

spoliation, plunder, pillage; sack, -age; rapine, *brigandage*, highway robbery, foray, *razzia*; blackmail; piracy, privateering, buccaneering; filibustering, -ism; burglary; house-breaking; cattle-stealing, -rustling, -lifting.

peculation, embezzlement; fraud etc. 545; larceny, petty larceny, pilfering, shop-lifting.

thievishness, rapacity, kleptomania, Alsatia; den of -Cacus, – thieves.

license to plunder, letters of marque.

V. steal, thieve, rob, purloin, pilfer, filch, lift, prig, bag, nim, crib, cabbage, palm; abstract; appropriate, plagiarize.

convey away, carry off, abduct, kidnap, shanghai, impress, crimp; make –, walk –, run-off with; run away with; spirit away; seize etc. (*lay violent hands on*) 789.

plunder, pillage, rifle, sack, loot, ransack, spoil, spoliate, despoil, strip, sweep, gut, forage, levy black-mail, pirate, pickeer, maraud, lift cattle, rustle, poach, smuggle, run.

stick –, hold- up.

swindle, peculate, embezzle; sponge, mulct, rook, bilk, pluck, pigeon, skin, fleece, diddle; defraud etc. 545; obtain under false pretences; live by one's wits

rob –, borrow of- Peter to Paul; set a thief to catch a thief.

disregard the distinction between *meum* and *tuum*.

Adj. thieving etc. *v.*; thievish, light-fingered; furacious, -tive; piratical; pred-aceous, -al, -atory, -atorial; raptorial etc. (*rapacious*) 789.

stolen etc. *v.*

Phr. *sic vos non vobis.*

792. Thief.—N. thief, robber, *homo trium literarum*, pilferer, rifler, filcher, plagiarist.

spoiler, depredator, pillager, marauder; harpy, shark, land-shark, falcon, moss-trooper, bushranger, Bedouin, brigand, freebooter, bandit, thug, dacoit, pirate, corsair, viking, Paul Jones; buccan-eer, -ier; piqu-, pick-eerer; rover, ranger, privateer, filibuster; rapparee, wrecker, picaroon; smuggler, poacher, plunderer; racketeer.

highwayman, Dick Turpin, Claude Duval, Macheath, knight of the road, footpad, sturdy beggar; abductor, kidnapper.

cut-, pick-purse; pick-pocket, light-fingered gentry; sharper; card-, skittle-sharper; crook; thimble-rigger; rook, Greek, blackleg, leg, welsher, defaulter; Autolycus, Cacus, Barabbas, Jeremy Diddler, Robert Macaire, artful dodger, trickster; swell mob, *chevalier d'industrie*; shop-lifter.

swindler, peculator; forger, coiner, counterfeiter, shoful; fence, receiver of stolen goods, duffer; smasher.

burglar, housebreaker; cracks-, mags-man; Bill Sikes, Jack Sheppard, Jonathan Wild, Raffles, cat burglar.

793. Booty.—N. booty, spoil, plunder, price, loot, graft, swag, pickings, boodle; *spolia opima*, prey; blackmail; stolen goods.

Adj. looting etc. *n.*; manubial, spoliative.

794. Barter.—N. barter, exchange, scorse, truck system; interchange etc. 148.

a Roland for an Oliver; *quid pro quo*; commutation, -position.

trade, commerce, mercature, buying and selling, bargain and sale; traffic, business, nundination, custom, shopping; commercial enterprise, speculation, jobbing, stock-jobbing, *agiotage*, brokery, arbitrage.

dealing, transaction, negotiation, bargain.

free trade.

V. barter, exchange, truck, scorse, swop; interchange etc. 148; commutate etc. (*substitute*) 147; compound for.

trade, traffic, buy and sell, give and take, nundinate; carry on –, ply –, drive- a trade; be in -

business, – the city; keep a shop, deal in, employ one's capital in.

trade –, deal –, have dealings- with; transact –, do- business with; open –, keep- an account with.

bargain; drive –, make- a bargain; negotiate, bid for; dicker, haggle, higgle; chaffer, huckster, cheapen, beat down; stickle, – for; out-, under-bid; ask, charge; strike a bargain etc. (*contract*) 769.

speculate, give a sprat to catch a herring; buy in the cheapest and sell in the dearest market; rig the market.

Adj. commercial, mercantile, trading; interchangeable, marketable, staple, in the market, for sale.

wholesale, retail.

Adv. across the counter; on 'change.

795. Purchase.—N. purchase, emption; buying, purchasing, shopping; pre-emption, refusal.

coemption, bribery; slave trade.

buyer, purchaser, *emptor*, vendee; patron, employer, client, customer, *clientèle*.

V. buy, purchase, invest in, procure; rent etc. (*hire*) 788; repurchase, buy in.

keep in one's pay, bribe, suborn; pay etc. 807; spend etc. 809.

make –, complete- a purchase; buy over the counter; pay cash for.

shop, market, go a shopping.

Adj. purchased etc. *v.*

Phr. *caveat emptor.*

796. Sale.—N. sale, vent, disposal; auction, roup, Dutch auction; custom etc. (*traffic*) 794.

vendi-bility, -bleness.

seller, salesman; peddler, smous; vender, vendor, consignor; merchant etc. 797; auctioneer.

V. sell, vend, dispose of, effect a sale; sell -over the counter, – by auction etc. *n.*; dispense, retail; deal in etc. 794; sell -off, – out; turn into money; realize; bring -to, – under- the hammer; put up to auction; auction, offer –, put up- for sale; hawk, peddle, bring to market; offer etc. 763; undersell; dump, unload.

let; mortgage etc. (*security*) 771.

Adj. under the hammer, in the market, for sale.

saleable, marketable, vendible, in demand, having a ready sale; unsaleable etc., unpurchased, unbought; on one's hands.

797. Merchant.—N. merchant, trader, dealer, monger, chandler, salesman; changer; regrater; shop-keeper, -man; trades-man, -people, -folk.

retailer; chapman, hawker, huckster, higgler; peddler, smous, pedlar, *colporteur*, cadger, Autolycus; sutler, *vivandière*; coster-man, -monger; market woman; cheap jack; caterer etc. 637; tallyman.

money-broker, -changer, -lender; stock-broker, -jobber; cambist, usurer, moneyer, banker.

jobber; broker etc. (*agent*) 758; buyer etc. 795; seller etc. 796.

concern; firm etc. (*partnership*) 712.

798. Merchandise.—N. merchandise, ware, commodity, effects, goods, article, stock, produce, staple commodity; stock in trade etc. (*store*) 636; cargo etc. (*contents*) 190.

799. Mart.—N. mart; market, -place, *forum*; fair, bazaar, staple; stock –, exchange; 'change, *bourse*, Wall Street, Rialto, hall, guildhall; toll-booth, custom-house; Tattersalls.

shop, stall, booth; wharf; office, chambers, counting-house, *bureau*; coun-, comp-ter.

ware-house, -room; *dépôt*, interposit, *entrepôt*, *emporium*, establishment; store etc. 636.

open market, market-overt.

800. Money.—N. money -matters, – market; finance; accounts etc. 811; funds, treasure; capital, stock; assets etc. (*property*) 780; wealth etc. 803; supplies, ways and means, wherewithal, sinews of war, almighty dollar, needful, cash.

sum, amount; balance, -sheet; sum total; proceeds etc. (*receipts*) 810.

currency, circulating medium, specie; coin, – of the realm; piece, hard cash, dollar, sterling coin; pounds, shillings and pence; L s. d., guineas; pocket, breeches pocket, purse; money in hand; the best, ready, – money; filthy lucre, shekels, roll, jack, rhino, blunt, dust, bawbees, brass, dibs, dough, mopus, tin, salt, chink, oof, spondulics, pile, wads.

precious metals, gold, silver, copper, nickel; bullion, bar, ingot, nugget.

petty cash; pocket-, pin-money; small –, change; small coin, loose cash; doit, stiver, rap, mite, farthing, *sou*, penny, shilling, bob, tanner, tester, groat, guinea, ducat; *rouleau*; *wampum*; good –, round –, lump- sum; power –, mint –, tons- of money; plum, lac of rupees, millions, money-bags, miser's hoard, stocking, mine of wealth etc. 803.

[Science of coins] numismatics, chrysology.

paper-money; money –, postal –, Post Office-order; note, – of hand; bank –, treasury- note; Bradbury; promissory note; I.O.U., bond; bill, – of exchange; draft, check, order, warrant, *coupon*, debenture, exchequer bill, *assignat*, greenback, gold –, silver- certificate.

copper, nickel, dime, quarter, two bits, half a dollar, dollar, buck, simoleon, fiver, tenner, a twenty, a sawbuck, a century, a grand; eagle, double eagle.

gold standard, bimetallism, fiat money; rate of –, exchange; in-, de-flation.

remittance etc. (*payment*) 807; credit etc. 805; liability etc. 806; solvency etc. 803.

draw-er, -ee; oblig-or, -ee; moneyer, coiner, counterfeiter, forger.

false –, bad- money; base –, counterfeit- coin, flash note, slip, kite; Bank of Elegance.

argumentum ad crumenam.

V. amount to, come to, mount up to; touch the pocket; draw, – upon; endorse etc. (*security*) 771; issue, utter, circulate; discount etc. 813.

forge, counterfeit, coin, circulate –, pass- bad money.

Adj. monetary, pecuniary, crumenal, fiscal, financial, sumptuary, numismatical; sterling; solvent etc. 803.

801. Treasurer.—N. treasurer; bursar, -y; purser, purse-bearer; cash-keeper, banker; depositary; questor, receiver, steward, trustee, chartered –, accountant; Accountant-General, almoner, liquidator, paymaster, cashier, teller; cambist; money-changer etc. (*merchant*) 797.

financier, Chancellor of the Exchequer, minister of finance; Secretary of the Treasury, Director of the Budget, Controller of Currency.

802. Treasury.—N. treasury, bank, exchequer, almonry, fisc, hanaper, bursary; safe; strong-box, -hold, -room; coffer; chest etc. (*receptacle*) 191; depository etc. 636; till, -er; cash-box, -register, purse, pocketbook, wallet; money-bag, -belt, -box, *porte-monnaie*.

purse-strings; pocket, breeches pocket.

sinking fund; stocks; government –, public –, parliamentary- -stocks, – funds, – securities, bonds; gild-edged securities; Consols, Liberty bonds, government bonds, *crédit mobilier*.

803. Wealth.—N. wealth, riches, fortune, handsome fortune, opulence, affluence; good –, easy- circumstances; independence; competence etc. (*sufficiency*) 639; solvency, soundness, solidity.

provision, livelihood, maintenance; alimony, dowry; means, resources, substance; property etc. 780; command of money.

income etc. 810; capital, money; round sum etc. (*treasure*) 800; mint of money, mine of wealth, *El Dorado*, Pactolus, Golconda, Potosi, *bonanza*; philosopher's stone.

long –, full –, well lined –, heavy- purse; purse of Fortunatus.

pelf, Mammon, lucre, filthy lucre; loaves and fishes; fleshpots of Egypt.

rich –, moneyed –, warm- man; man of substance; capitalist, millionaire, Nabob, Croesus, Midas, Plutus, Dives, Timon of Athens; Timo-, Pluto-cracy; Danaë.

V. be -rich etc. *adj.*; roll –, wallow- in -wealth, – riches; have money to burn.

afford, well afford; command -money, – a sum; make both ends meet, hold one's head above water.

become -rich etc. *adj.*; fill one's -pocket etc. (*treasury*) 802; feather one's nest, clean up –, make- a fortune; make money etc. (*acquire*) 775.

enrich, imburse.

worship -Mammon, – the golden calf.

Adj. wealthy, rich, affluent, opulent, moneyed, monied, worth -a great deal, – much; well -to do, – off; warm; well –, provided for.

made of money; rich as Croesus; rolling in -riches, – wealth.

flush, – of -cash, – money, – tin; in -funds, – cash, – full feather; solvent, solid, sound, pecunious, out of debt, all straight; able to pay 20s in the L.

Phr. one's ship coming in.

804. Poverty.—N. poverty, indigence, penury, pauperism, destitution, want; need, -iness; lack, necessity, privation, distress, difficulties, wolf at the door.

bad –, poor –, needy –, embarrassed –, reduced –, straitened- circumstances; slender –, narrow- means; straits; hand to mouth existence, *res angusta domi*, low water, impecuniosity.

beggary; mendi-cancy, -city; broken –, loss of-fortune; insolvency etc. (*non-payment*) 808.

empty -purse, – pocket; light purse; beggarly account of empty boxes.

poor man, pauper, mendicant, mumper, beggar, starveling; *pauvre diable*.

V. be -poor etc. *adj.*; want, lack, starve, live from hand to mouth, have seen better days, go down in the world, be on one's uppers, come upon the parish; go to -the dogs, – wrack and ruin; not have a -penny etc. (*money*) 800, – shot in one's locker; beg one's bread; *tirer le diable par la queue*; run into debt etc. (*debt*) 806.

render -poor etc. *adj.*; impoverish; reduce, – to poverty; pauperize, fleece, ruin, bring to the parish.

Adj. poor, indigent; poverty-striken; badly –, poorly –, ill- off; poor as -a rat, – a church mouse, – Job's turkey, – Job; fortune-, dower-, money-, penni-less; unportioned, unmoneyed; impecunious; broke, flat; out –, short- of -money, – cash; without –, not worth a rap etc. (*money*) 800; *qui n'a pas le sou*, out of pocket, hard up; out at -elbows, – heels; seedy, bare-footed; beggar-ly, -ed; destitute; fleeced, strapped, stripped; bereft, bereaved; reduced.

in want etc. *n.*; needy, necessitous, distressed, pinched, straitened; put to one's -shifts, – last shifts; unable to -keep the wolf from the door, – make both ends meet; embarrassed, under hatches; involved etc. (*in debt*) 806; insolvent etc. (*not paying*) 808.

Adv. *in formâ pauperis*.

Phr. *zonam perdidit*.

805. Credit.—N. credit, trust, tick, score, tally, account.

letter of credit, circular note; duplicate; mortgage, lien, debenture, paper credit, floating capital; draft; securities.

creditor, lender, lessor, mortgagee; dun; usurer.

V. keep –, run up- an account with; entrust, credit, accredit.

place to one's -credit, – account; give –, take-credit; fly a kite.

Adj. credit-ing, -ed; accredited.

Adv. on -credit etc. *n.*; to the -account, – credit- of.

806. Debt.—N. debt, obligation, liability, indebtment, debit, score.

arrears, deferred payment, deficit, default; insolvency etc. (*non-payment*) 808; bad debt.

interest; usance, usury; premium; floating -debt, – capital.

debtor, debitor; mortgagor; defaulter etc. 808; borrower.

V. be -in debt etc. *adj.*; owe; incur –, contract-a debt etc. *n.*; run up -a bill, – a score, – an account; go on tick, put on the cuff; borrow etc. 788; run –, get- into debt; outrun the constable.

answer –, go bail- for; back one's note.

Adj. indebted; liable, chargeable, answerable for.

in -debt, – embarrassed circumstances, – difficulties; incumbered, involved; involved –, plunged –, deep –, over head and ears- in debt; deeply involved; fast tied up; insolvent etc. (*not paying*) 808; *minus*, out of pocket.

unpaid; unrequieted, unrewarded; owing, due, in arrear, outstanding.

807. Payment.—N. pay-, defray-ment; discharge; ac-, quittance; settlement, clearance, liquidation, satisfaction, reckoning, arrangement.

acknowledgment, release; receipt, – in full, – in full of all demands; voucher.

repayment, reimbursement, retribution; pay etc. (*reward*) 973; money paid etc. (*expenditure*) 809.

ready money etc. (*cash*) 800; stake, remittance, instalment.

payer, liquidator etc. 801.

V. pay, defray, make payment; pay -down, – on the nail, – ready money, – at sight, – in advance; cash, honor a bill, acknowledge; redeem; pay in kind.

pay one's -way, – shot, – footing; pay -the piper, – sauce for all, – costs; do the needful; come across; shell –, fork- out; come down with, – the dust; tickle –, grease- the palm; expend etc. 809; put –, lay- down.

discharge, settle, quit, acquit oneself of; account –, reckon –, settle –, be even –, be quits- with; strike a balance; settle –, balance –, square- accounts with; quit scores; foot the bill; wipe –, clear- off old scores; satisfy; pay in full; satisfy –, pay in full of- all demands; clear, liquidate; pay -up, – old debts.

disgorge, make repayment; repay, refund, reimburse, retribute; make compensation etc. 30.

Adj. paying etc., paid etc. *v.*; owing nothing, out of debt, all straight, clear of -debt, – encumbrance; unowed, never indebted.

Adv. to the tune of; on the nail; money –, cash-down; cash on delivery.

808. Non-payment.—N. non-payment; default, defalcation; protest, repudiation; application of the sponge; whitewashing.

insolvency, bankruptcy, failure; overdraft, overdrawn account; insufficiency etc. 640; run upon a bank.

waste paper bonds; dishonored –, protested-bills; bogus cheque.

bankrupt, insolvent debtor, lame duck, man of straw, welsher, stag, defaulter, absconder, levanter.

V. non -pay etc. 807; fail, break, stop payment; become -insolvent, – bankrupt; be gazetted.

protest, dishonor, repudiate, nullify.

pay under protest; button up one's pockets, draw the purse strings; apply the sponge; pay over the left shoulder, get whitewashed; swindle etc. 791; run up bills, fly kites.

Adj. not paying; in debt etc. 806; behindhand, in arrear; beggared etc. (*poor*) 804; unable to make both ends meet; *minus*; worse than nothing.

insolvent, bankrupt, in the gazette, gazetted, ruined.

unpaid etc. (*outstanding*) 806; *gratis* etc. 815; unremunerated.

809. Expenditure.—N. expenditure, money going out; out-goings, -lay; expenses, disbursement; prime cost etc. (*price*) 812; circulation; run upon a bank.

[Money paid] payment etc. 807; pay etc. (*remuneration*) 973; bribe etc. 973; fee, footing, garnish; subsidy; tribute, Peter's pence; contingent, quota; donation etc. 784.

pay in advance, earnest, handsel, deposit, instalment.

investment; purchase etc. 795.

V. expend, spend; run –, get- through; pay, disburse; open –, loose –, untie- the purse strings; lay –, shell –, fork- out; bleed; make up a sum, invest, sink money.

fee etc. (*reward*) 973; pay one's way etc. (*pay*) 807; subscribe etc. (*give*) 784; subsidize, bribe.

Adj. expend-ing, -ed etc. *v.*; sumptuary, liberal etc. 816; openhanded, lavish etc. 818; extensive etc. 814.

810. Receipt—N. receipt, accountable –, conditional –, binding –, return- receipt; value received, money coming in; income, incomings, innings, revenue, return, proceeds; gross receipts, net profit; earnings etc. (*gain*) 775.

rent, – roll; rent-al, -age; rack-rent.

premium, *bonus*; sweepstakes, tontine, prize, drawing.

pension, annuity; jointure etc. (*property*) 780; alimony, pittance; emolument etc. (*remuneration*) 973.

V. receive etc. 785; take money; draw –, derive- from; get, be in receipt of, acquire etc. 775; take etc. 789.

bring in, yield, afford, pay, return; accrue etc. (*be received from*) 785.

Adj. receiv-ing, -ed etc. *v.*; profitable etc. (*gainful*) 775.

811. Accounts.—N. accounts, accompts; commercial –, monetary- arithmetic; statistics etc. (*numeration*) 85; money matters, finance, budget, bill, score, reckoning, account.

books, account book, ledger; day –, cash –, pass- book; journal; debtor and creditor –, cash –, petty cash –, running- account; account-current; balance, – sheet; *compte rendu*, account settled.

book-keeping, audit; double –, single- entry; reckoning etc. 85.

chartered –, certified public –, accountant; auditor, actuary, bookkeeper; financier etc. 801; accounting party.

V. keep accounts, enter, post, book, credit, debit, carry over; take stock; balance –, make up –, square –, settle –, wind up –, cast up –, add up –, tot up- accounts; make accounts square.

bring to book, audit, tax, surcharge and falsify.

falsify –, garble –, cook –, doctor- an account.

Adj. monetary etc. 800; account-able, -ing; statistical.

812. Price.—N. price, amount, cost, expense, prime cost, charge, figure, demand, damage, fare, hire; wages etc. (*remuneration*) 973.

dues, duty, toll, tax, impost, cess, sess, tallage, levy, capitation-, poll-, income-, sur-, sales-, supertax; gabel, *gabelle*; gavel, *octroi*, custom, tariff, excise, assessment, taxation, benevolence, tithe, tenths, exactment, ransom, salvage; broker-, wharf-, lighter-, ton-, freight-age.

worth, rate, value, valuation, appraisement, money's worth, par value; penny etc. -worth; price current, market price, quotation; what it will -fetch etc. *v.*

bill etc. (*account*) 811; shot.

V. bear –, set –, fix- a price; appraise, assess, price, charge, demand, ask, require, exact, run up; distrain; run up a bill etc. (*debt*) 806; have one's price; liquidate.

amount to, come to, mount up to; stand one in. fetch, sell for, cost, bring in, yield, afford.

Adj. priced etc. *v.*; to the tune of, *ad valorem*; mercenary, venal.

Phr. no penny, no paternoster; *point d'argent, point de Suisse*, no longer pipe, no longer dance, no song, no supper.

one may have it for.

813. Discount.—N. discount, abatement, concession, reduction, depreciation, allowance, qualification, set off, drawback, poundage, *agio*, percentage; rebate, -ment; backwardation, contango, salvage, tare and tret.

V. discount, bate; a-, re-bate; deduct, reduce, mark down, take off, allow, give, make allowance; tax, depreciate.

Adj. discounting etc. *v.*

Adv. at a discount, below par.

814. Dearness.—N. dearness etc. *adj.*; high –, famine –, fancy- price; overcharge; extravagance; exorbitance, extortion; heavy pull upon the purse; Pyrrhic victory.

V. be -dear etc. *adj.*; cost -much, – a pretty penny; rise in price, look up.

overcharge, bleed, fleece, skin, extort.

pay -too much, – through the nose, –, too dear for one's whistle.

Adj. dear; high, -priced; of great price, expensive, costly, precious, dear bought; unreasonable extravagant, exorbitant, extortionate.

at a premium; not to be had, – for love or money; beyond –, above- price; priceless, of priceless value.

Adv. dear, -ly; at great –, heavy- cost; *à grands frais*.

Phr. prices looking up; *le jeu ne vaut pas la chandelle.*

815. Cheapness.—N. cheapness, low price; depreciation; bargain; good penny etc.- worth, *bon marché.*

[Absence of charge] gratuity; free -quarters, – seats, – admission, – warren; pass, Annie Oakley; run of one's teeth; nominal price, peppercorn rent; labor of love.

drug in the market.

V. be -cheap etc. *adj.*; cost little; come down –, fall- in price.

buy for -a mere nothing, – an old song; have one's money's worth; cheapen, beat down.

Adj. cheap; low, – priced; moderate, reasonable; in-, un-expensive; well –, worth the money; *magnifique et pas cher*; good –, cheap- at the price; dirt –, dog- cheap; cheap, -as dirt, – and nasty; catchpenny.

reduced, marked down, half-price, depreciated, unsaleable.

gratuitous, *gratis*, free, for love, – nothing; cost-, expense-less; without charge, not charged, untaxed; scot –, shot –, rent- free; free of -cost, – expense; honorary, unbought, unpaid, complimentary.

Adv. for a mere song; at -cost price, – prime cost, – a reduction, – a bargain; on the cheap.

816. Liberality.—N. liberality, generosity, munificence; bount-y, -eousness, -ifulness; hospitality; charity etc. (*beneficence*) 906.

benefactor, free giver, Lady Bountiful.

V. be -liberal etc. *adj.*; spend –, bleed- freely; shower down upon; open one's purse strings etc. (*disburse*) 809; spare no expense, give -with both hands, – *carte blanche.*

Adj. -liberal, free, generous; charitable etc. (*beneficent*) 906; hospitable; bount-iful, -eous; handsome; unsparing, ungrudging; open-, free-, full handed; open, large, free hearted; munificent, princely, unstinting.

overpaid.

Adv. liberally, ungrudgingly, with open hand.

817. Economy.—N. economy, frugality; thrift, -iness; prudence, care, husbandry, good housewifery, savingness, retrenchment.

savings; prevention of waste, save-all; cheese parings and candle ends; parsimony etc. 819.

V. be -economical etc. *adj.*; economize, save; retrench; cut- down expenses, – one's coat according to one's cloth, make both ends meet, keep within compass, meet one's expenses, pay one's way; keep one's head above water; husband etc. (*lay by*) 636; save –, invest- money; put out to interest; provide –, save- -for, – against- a rainy day; feather one's nest; look after the main chance.

Adj. economical, frugal, careful, thrifty, saving, chary, spare, sparing; parsimonious etc. 819.

underpaid.

Adv. sparingly etc. *adj.*; *ne quid nimis.*

818. Prodigality.—N. prodi-gality, -gence; unthriftiness, waste, -fulness; profus-ion, -eness; extravagance; squandering etc. *v.*; lavishness; malversation.

prodigal; spend-, waste-thrift; losel, play-boy, spender, squanderer, locust.

V. be -prodigal etc. *adj.*; squander, lavish, sow broadcast; pour forth like water; pay through the nose etc. (*dear*) 814; spill, waste, dissipate, exhaust, drain, eat out of house and home, overdraw, outrun the constable; run -out, – through; misspend; throw -good money after bad, – the helve after the hatchet; burn the candle at both ends; make ducks and drakes of one's money;

squander one's substance, spend money like water; fool –, potter –, muddle –, fritter –, throw-away one's money; pour water into a sieve, kill the goose that lays the golden eggs; *manger son blé en herbe*.

Adj. prodigal, profuse, thriftless, unthrifty, improvident, wasteful, losel, extravagant, lavish, dissipated, over liberal; full-handed etc. (*liberal*) 816.

penny wise and pound foolish.

Adv. with an unsparing hand; money burning one's pocket; recklessly profuse.

Int. hang the expense!

819. Parsimony.—N. parsimony, parcity; parsimoniousness, stinginess etc. *adj.*; stint; illiberality, avarice, tenacity, avidity, rapacity, extortion, venality, cupidity; selfishness etc. 943; *auri sacra fames*.

miser, niggard, churl, screw, tightwad, skinflint, crib, codger, muckworm, money-grubber, pinch-fist, scrimp, lickpenny, hunks, curmudgeon, *Harpagon*, Silas Marner, harpy, extortioner, usurer.

V. be -parsimonious etc. *adj.*; grudge, begrudge, stint, skimp, pinch, gripe, screw, dole out, hold back, withhold, starve, famish, live upon nothing, skin a flint.

drive a -bargain, – hard bargain; cheapen, beat down; stop one hole in a sieve; have an itching palm, grasp, grab.

Adj. parsimonious, penurious, stingy, miserly, mean, shabby, peddling, scrubby, pennywise, near, niggardly, frugai to excess; close; fast-, close-, strait-handed; close-, hard-, tight-fisted; tight, sparing; chary; grudging, griping etc. *v.*; illiberal, ungenerous, churlish, hidebound, sordid, mercenary, venal, covetous, usurious, avaricious, greedy, extortionate, rapacious.

Adv. with a sparing hand.

820. Affections.—N. affections, character, qualities, disposition, nature, spirit, tone; temper, -ament; *diathesis*, idiosyncrasy; cast –, habit –, frame- of -mind, – soul; predilection, turn; natural –, turn of mind; bent, bias, predisposition, proneness, proclivity; propen-sity, -sedness, -sion, -dency; vein, humor, mood, grain, mettle; sympathy etc. (*love*) 897.

soul, heart, breast, bosom, inner man; heart's -core, – strings, – blood; heart of hearts, *penetralia mentis*; secret and inmost recesses of the –, cockles of one's- heart; inmost -heart, – soul; back-bone.

passion, pervading spirit; ruling –, master-passion; *furore*; fulness of the heart, heyday of the blood, flesh and blood, flow of soul, force of character.

V. have –, possess- -affections etc. *n.*; be of a -character etc. *n.*; be -affected etc. *adj.*; breathe.

Adj. affected, characterized, formed, molded, cast; at-, tempered; framed; pre-, disposed; prone, inclined; having a -bias etc. *n.*; tinctured –, imbued –, penetrated –, eaten up- with.

inborn, inbred, ingrained, in the grain, congenital, inherent, bred in the bone; deep-rooted, ineffaceable, inveterate; pathoscopic.

Adv. in one's -heart etc. *n.*; at heart; heart and soul etc. 821; in the -vein, – mood.

821. Feeling.—N. feeling; suffering etc. *v.*; endurance, tolerance, sufferance, supportance, experience, response; sympathy etc. (*love*) 897; impression, inspiration, affection, sensation, emotion, pathos, deep sense.

fire, warmth, glow, unction, *gusto*, vehemence; ferv-or, -ency; heartiness, cordiality; earnestness, eagerness; *empressment*, ardor, zeal, passion, enthusiasm, *verve, furore*, fanaticism; excitation of feeling etc. 824; fulness of the heart etc. (*disposition*) 820; passion etc. (*state of excitability*) 825; ecstasy etc. (*pleasure*) 827.

blush, suffusion, flush; hectic; tingling, thrill, kick, turn, shock; agitation etc. (*irregular motion*) 315; quiver, heaving, flutter, flurry, fluster, twitter, tremor; throb, -bing; pulsation, palpitation, painting; trepid-, perturb-ation; ruffle, hurry of spirits, pother, stew, ferment.

V. feel; receive an -impression etc. *n.*; be -impressed with etc. *adj.*; entertain –, harbor –, cherish- -feeling etc. *n.*

respond; catch the -flame, – infection; enter the spirit of.

bear, suffer, support, sustain, endure, brook, thole, aby; abide etc. (*be composed*) 826; experience etc. (*meet with*) 151; taste, prove; labor –, smart- under; bear the brunt of, brave, stand.

swell, glow, warm, flush, blush, change color, mantle; turn -color, – pale, – red, – black in the face; blench, crimson, whiten, pale, tingle, thrill, heave, pant, throb, palpitate, go pit-a-pat, tremble, quiver, flutter, twitter; stagger, reel; shake etc. 315; be -agitated, – excited etc. 824; look -blue, – black; wince, draw a deep breath.

impress etc. (*excite the feelings*) 824.

Adj. feeling etc. *v.*; sentient; sensuous; sensorial, -y; emo-tive, -tional; of –, with- feeling etc. *n.*

warm, quick, lively, smart, strong, sharp, acute, cutting, piercing, incisive; keen, – as a razor; trenchant, pungent, racy, *piquant*, poignant, caustic.

impressive, deep, profound, indelible; deep-, home-, heart-felt; swelling, soul-stirring, deep-mouthed, heart-expanding, electric, thrilling, rapturous, ecstatic.

earnest, wistful, eager, breathless; fer-vent, -vid; gushing, passionate, warmhearted, hearty, cordial, sincere, zealous, enthusiastic, glowing, ardent, burning, red-hot, fiery, flaming; boiling, – over.

pervading, penetrating, absorbing; rabid, raving feverish, fanatical, hysterical; impetuous etc. (*excitable*) 825; overmastering.

impressed –, moved –, touched –, affected –, penetrated –, seized –, imbued etc. 820- with; devoured by; wrought up etc. (*excited*) 824; struck all of a heap; rapt; in a -quiver etc. *n.*; enraptured etc. 829.

Adv. heart and soul, from the bottom of one's heart, *ab imo pectore*, *de profundis*, at heart, *con amore*, heartily, devoutly, over head and ears.

Phr. the heart -big, – full, – swelling, – beating, – pulsating, – throbbing, – thumping, – beating high, – melting, – overflowing, – bursting, – breaking.

822. Sensibility.—N. sensi-bility, -bleness, -tiveness; moral sensibility; impress-, affect-ibility; suscepti-bleness, -bility, -vity; mobility; viva-city, -ciousness; tender-, soft-ness; sentimental-ity, -ism.

excitability etc. 825; fastidiousness etc. 868; physical sensibility etc. 375.

sore -point, – place; where the shoe pinches.
V. be -sensible etc. *adj.*; have a -tender, – warm, – sensitive- heart.

take to –, treasure up in the- heart; shrink. 'die of a rose in aromatic pain;' touch to the quick.

Adj. sensi-ble, -tive; impressi-ble, -onable; suscepti-ve, -ble; alive to, impassion-able, -ed; gushing; warm-, tender-, soft-hearted; tender –, as a chicken; soft, sentimental, romantic; enthusiastic, highflying, spirited, mettlesome, vivacious, lively, expressive, mobile, tremblingly alive; excitable etc. 825; over-sensitive, without skin, thin-skinned; fastidious etc. 868.

Adv. sensibly etc. *adj.*; to the -quick, – inmost core.

823. Insensibility.—N. insensi-bility, -bleness; moral insensibility; inertness, *inertia, vis inertiae*; impassi-bility, -bleness; inappetency, apathy, phlegm, dulness, hebetude, supineness, lukewarmness, insusceptibility, unimpressibility.

cold -fit, – blood, – heart; cold-, cool-ness; frigidity, *sang-froid*; stoicism, imperturbation etc. (*inexcitability*) 826; *nonchalance*, unconcern, dry eyes; *insouciance* etc. (*indifference*) 866; recklessness etc. 863; callousness; heart of stone, stock and stone, marble, deadness.

torp-or, -idity; obstupefaction, lethargy, coma, trance, sleep etc. 683, suspended animation, stupor, -efaction; paralysis, palsy; numbness etc. (*physical insensibility*) 376.

neutrality; quietism, vegetation.

V. be -insensible etc. *adj.*; have a rhinoceros hide; show -insensibility etc. *n.*; not -mind, – care, – be affected by; have no desire for etc. 866; have –, feel –, take- no interest in; *nil admirari*; not care a -straw etc. (*unimportance*) 643 for; disregard etc. (*neglect*) 460; set at naught etc. (*make light of*) 483; turn a deaf ear to etc. (*inattention*) 458; vegetate.

render -insensible, – callous; blunt, obtund, numb, benumb, paralyze, chloroform, deaden, hebetate, stun, stupefy; brut-ify, -alize.

inure; harden, – the heart; steel, case-harden, sear.

Adj. insensible, unconscious; impassi-ve, -ble; blind to, deaf to, dead to; un-, in-susceptible; unimpress-ionable, -ible; passion-, spirit-, heart-, soulless; unfeeling, unmoral.

apathetic; leuco-, phlegmatic; dull, frigid; cold, -blooded, -hearted; unemotional; cold as charity; flat, obtuse, inert, supine, sluggish, torpid; sleepy etc. (*inactive*) 683; languid, half-hearted, tame; numb, -ed; comatose; anesthetic etc. 376; stupefied, chloroformed, palsy-stricken.

indifferent, lukewarm; Laodicean; careless, mindless, regardless; inattentive etc. 458; neglectful etc. 460; disregarding.

unconcerned, *nonchalant, pococurante, insouciant, sans souci*; unambitious etc. 866.

un-affected, -ruffled, -impressed, -inspired, -excited, -moved, -stirred, -touched, -shocked, -struck; unblushing etc. (*shameless*) 885; unanimated; vegetative.

callous, thick-skinned, pachydermatous, impervious; hard, -ened; inured, case-hardened; steeled –, proof- against; imperturbable etc. (*inexcitable*) 826; unfelt.

Adv. insensibly etc. *adj.*; *aequo animo*; without being -moved, – touched, – impressed; in cold blood; with -dry eyes, – withers unwrung.

Phr. never mind; it is of no consequence etc. (*unimportant*) 643; it cannot be helped; nothing coming amiss; it is all -the same, – one- to.

824. Excitation.—N. excitation of feeling; mental –, excitement; suscitation, galvanism, stimulation, piquancy, provocation inspiration, calling forth, infection; interest, animation, agitation, perturbation; subjugation, fascination, intoxication; en-, ravishment; entrancement, high pressure.

unction, impressiveness etc. *adj.*; emotional appeal; melodrama; psychological moment, crisis; sensationalism.

trail of temper, *casus belli*; irritation etc. (*anger*) 900; passion etc. (*state of excitability*) 825; thrill etc. (*feeling*) 821; repression of feeling etc. 826.

V. excite, affect, touch, move, impress, strike, interest, intrigue, animate, inspire, impassion, smite, infect; stir –, fire –, warm- the blood; set astir; a-, wake; a-, waken; call forth; e-, pro-voke; raise up, summon up, call up, wake up, blow up, get up, light up; raise; get up steam, rouse, arouse, stir, fire, kindle, enkindle, apply the torch, set on fire, inflame, illuminate.

stimulate; ex-, suscitate; inspirit; spirit up, stir up, work up, infuse life into, give new life to, bring –, introduce- new blood; quicken; sharpen, whet; work upon etc. (*incite*) 615; hurry on, give a fillip, put on one's mettle.

fan the -fire, – flame; blow the coals, stir the embers; fan, – into a flame; foster, heat, warm, foment, raise to a fever heat; keep -up, – the pot boiling; revive, rekindle; rake up, rip up.

stir –, play on –, come home to- the feelings; touch -a string, – a chord, – the soul, – the heart; go to one's heart, penetrate, pierce, go through one, touch to the quick, open the wound; possess –, pervade –, penetrate –, imbrue –, absorb –, affect –, disturb- the soul.

absorb, rivet the attention; sink into the -mind, – heart; prey on the mind; intoxicate; over-whelm, -power; *bouleverser*, upset, turn one's head.

fascinate; enrapture etc. (*give pleasure*) 829.

agitate, perturb, ruffle, fluster, flutter, shake, disturb, faze, startle, shock, stagger; give one a -shock, – turn; strike -dumb, – all of a heap; stun, astound, electrify, galvanize, petrify.

irritate, sting; cut, – to the -heart, – quick; try one's temper; fool to the top of one's bent, pique; infuriate, madden, make one's blood boil; lash into fury etc. (*wrath*) 900.

be -excited etc. *adj.*; flash up, flare up; catch the infection; thrill etc. (*feel*) 821; mantle; work oneself up; seethe, boil, simmer, foam, fume, flame, rage, rave; run mad etc. (*passion*) 825.

Adj. excited etc. *v.*; wrought up, on the *qui vive*, astir, sparkling; in a -quiver etc. 821, – fever, – ferment, – blaze, – state of excitement; in hysterics; black in the face, over-wrought; hot, red-hot, flushed, feverish; all -of a twitter, – of a flutter, – of a dither, – in a pucker; with -quivering lips, – tears in one's eyes.

flaming; boiling, – over; ebullient, seething; foaming, – at the mouth; fuming, raging, carried away by passion, wild, raving, frantic, mad, distracted, distraught, beside oneself, out of one's wits, amuck, ready to burst, *bouleversé*, demoniacal.

lost, *eperdu*, tempest-tossed; haggard; ready to sink.

stung to the quick, up, on one's high ropes.

exciting etc. *v.*; impressive, warm, glowing, fervid, swelling, imposing, spirit-stirring, thrilling; high-wrought; soul-stirring, -subduing; heart-swelling, -thrilling; agonizing etc. (*painful*) 830; telling, sensational, melodramatic, hysterical; overpowering, -whelming; more than flesh and blood can bear.

piquant etc. (*pungent*) 392; spicy, appetizing, provocative, *provaquant*, tantalizing.

Adv. till one is black in the face.

Phr. the heart -beating high, – going pit-a-pat, – leaping into one's mouth; the blood -being up, – boiling in one's veins; the eye -glistening, – 'in a fine frenzy rolling;' the head turned.

825. Excitability. [Excess of sensitiveness.]—**N.** excitability, impetuosity, vehemence; boisterousness etc. *adj.*; turbulence; impatience, intolerance, non-endurance; irritability etc. (*irascibility*) 901; itching etc. (*desire*) 865; wincing; disquiet, -ude; restlessness; fidge-ts, -tiness; agitation etc. (*irregular motion*) 315.

trepidation, perturbation, ruffle, hurry, -skurry, fuss, flurry; fluster, flutter; pother, stew, ferment; whirl; thrill etc. (*feeling*) 821; state –, fever- of excitement; transport.

passion, excitement, flush, heat; fever, -heat; fire, flame, fume, blood boiling; tumult; effervescence, ebullition; boiling, – over; whiff, gust, storm, tempest; scene, breaking out, burst, fit, paroxysm, explosion; out-break, -burst; agony.

violence etc. 173; fierceness etc. *adj.*; rage, fury, *furor*, *furore*, desperation, madness, distraction, raving, delirium, brain storm; frenzy, hysterics; intoxication; tearing –, raging- passion, towering rage; anger etc. 900.

fascination, infatuation, fanaticism; Quixot-ism, -ry; *tête montée*.

V. be -impatient etc. *adj.*; not be able to -bear etc. 826; bear ill, wince, chafe, champ the bit; be in a -stew etc. *n.*; be out of all patience, fidget, fuss, not have a wink of sleep; toss, – on one's pillow.

lose one's temper etc. 900; break –, burst –, fly- out; go –, fly- -off, – off the handle, – off at a tangent; explode; flare up, flame up, fire up, burst into a flame, take fire, fire, burn; boil, – over; foam, fume, rage, rave, rant, tear; go –, run- -wild, – mad; go into hysterics; run -riot, – amuck; *battre la campagne, faire le diable à quatre*, play the deuce; raise -Cain, – the devil.

Adj. excitable, easily excited, in an excitable state; high strung; irritable etc. (*irascible*) 901; impatient, intolerant.

feverish, febrile, hysterical; delirious, mad, moody, maggoty-headed.

unquiet, mercurial, electric, galvanic, hasty, hurried, restless, fidgety, fussy; chafing etc. *v.*

startlish, mettlesome, high mettled, skittish.

vehement, demonstrative, violent, wild, furious, fierce, fiery, hot-headed, mad-cap.

over-zealous, enthusiastic, impassioned, fanatical; rabid etc. (*eager*) 865.

rampant, clamorous, uproarious, turbulent, tempestuous, tumultuary, boisterous.

impulsive, impetuous, passionate; uncontroll-ed, -able; ungovernable, irrepressible, stanchless, inextinguishable, burning, simmering, volcanic, ready to burst forth.

excit-ed, -ing etc. 824.

Int. pish! pshaw!

Phr. *noli me tangere*.

826. Inexcitability. [Absence of excitability, or of excitement.]—**N.** inexcit-, imperturb-, inirritability; even temper, tranquil mind, dispassion; tolerance, toleration, patience.

passiveness etc. (*physical inertness*) 172; hebetude, -ation; impassibility etc. (*insensibility*) 823; stupefaction.

coolness, calmness etc. *adj.*; composure, placidity, indisturbance, imperturbation, *sang-froid*, tranquility, serenity; quiet, -ude; peace of mind, mental calmness.

staidness etc. *adj.*; gravity, sobriety, Quakerism; philosophy, equanimity, stoicism, command of temper; self-possession, -control, -command, -restraint; presence of mind.

submission etc. 725; resignation; suffer-, support-, endur-, long-suffer-, forbear-ance; longanimity; fortitude; patience -of Job, – 'on a monument,' – 'sovereign o'er transmuted ill;' moderation; repression –, subjugation- of feeling; restraint etc. 751.

tranquilization etc. (*moderation*) 174.

V. be -composed etc. *adj.*

laisser -faire, – *aller*; take things -easily, – as they come; take it easy, run on, live and let live; take -easily, – cooly, – in good part; *aequam serva e mentem*.

bear, – well, – the brunt; go through, support, endure, brave, disregard.

tolerate, suffer, stand, bide; abide, aby; bear –, put up –, abide- with; acquiesce; submit etc. (*yield*) 725; submit with a good grace; resign –, reconcile- oneself to; brook, digest, eat, swallow, pocket, stomach; make -light of, – the best of, – a virtue of necessity; put a good face on, keep one's countenance; carry -on, – through; check etc. 751- oneself.

compose, appease etc. (*moderate*) 174; propitiate; repress etc. (*restrain*) 751; render insensible etc. 823; overcome –, allay –, repress- one's -excitability etc. 825; master one's feelings.

make -oneself, – one's mind- easy; set one's mind at -ease, – rest.

calm –, cool- down; thaw, grow cool.

be -borne, – endured; go down.

Adj. in-, un-excitable; imperturbable; unsusceptible etc. (*insensible*) 823; un-, dispassionate; cold-blooded, inirritable; enduring etc. *v.*; stoical, Platonic, philosophic, staid, stayed; sober, – minded; grave; sober –, grave- as a judge; sedate, demure, cool-, level-headed; steady.

easy-going, peaceful, placid, calm; quiet, – as a mouse; tranquil, serene; cool, – as -a cucumber, – custard; undemonstrative.

temperate etc. (*moderate*) 174; composed, collected; un-excited, -stirred, -ruffled, -disturbed, -perturbed, -impassioned; unoffended; unresisting.

meek, tolerant; patient, – as Job; submissive etc. 725; tame; content, resigned, chastened, subdued, lamblike; gentle, – as a lamb; *suaviter in modo*; mild, – as mother's milk; soft as peppermint; armed with patience, bearing with, clement, forbearant, long-suffering.

Adv. 'like patience on a monument smiling at grief;' *aequo animo*, in cold blood etc. 823; more in sorrow than in anger.

Int. patience! and shuffle the cards.

827. Pleasure.—N. pleasure, gratification, enjoyment, fruition; ob-, de-lectation; relish, zest; *gusto* etc. (*physical pleasure*) 377; satisfaction etc. (*content*) 831; complacency.

well-being; good etc. 618; snugness, comfort, ease; cushion etc. 215; *sans souci*, mind at ease.

joy, gladness, delight, glee, cheer, sunshine; cheerfulness etc. 836.

treat, refreshment; frolic, fun, lark, gambol, merry-making; amusement etc. 840; luxury etc. 377; hedonism.

mens sana in corpore sano.

happiness, felicity, bliss; beati-tude, -fication; enchantment, transport, rapture, ravishment, ecstasy; *summum bonum*; paradise, elysium etc. (*heaven*) 981; third –, seventh- heaven; unalloyed - happiness etc.

honeymoon; palmy –, halcyon- days; golden - age, – time; *Saturnia regna*, Eden, Arcadia, happy valley, Agapemone; Cockaigne.

V. be pleased etc. 829; feel –, experience- pleasure etc. *n.*; joy; enjoy –, hug- oneself; be in - clover etc. 377, – elysium etc. 981; tread on enchanted ground; fall –, go- into raptures.

feel at home, breathe freely, bask in the sunshine.

be -pleased etc. 829- with; receive –, derive- pleasure etc. *n.*- from; take -pleasure etc. *n.*- in; delight in, rejoice in, indulge in, luxuriate in; gloat over etc. (*physical pleasure*) 377; enjoy, relish, like; love etc. 897; take -to, – a fancy to; have a liking for; enter into the spirit of.

take in good part.

treat oneself to, solace oneself with.

Adj. pleased etc. 829; not sorry; glad, -some; pleased as Punch.

happy, blest, blessed, blissful, beatified; happy as -a king, – the day is long; thrice happy, *ter quaterque beatus*; enjoying etc. *v.*; joyful etc. (*in spirits*) 836; hedonic.

in -a blissful state, – paradise etc. 981; – raptures, – ecstasies, – a transport of delight.

comfortable etc. (*physical pleasure*) 377; at ease; content etc. 831; *sans souci*, in clover.

overjoyed, entranced, enchanted; enraptured; en-, ravished; transported; fascinated, captivated.

with -a joyful face, – sparkling eyes.

pleasing etc. 829; ecstatic, beat-ic, -ific; painless, unalloyed, without alloy, cloudless.

Adv. happily etc. *adj.*; with pleasure etc. (*willingly*) 60; with -glee etc. *n.*

phr. one's heart leaping with joy.

828. Pain.—N. mental suffering, pain, dolor; suffer-ing, -ance; ache, smart etc. (*physical pain*) 378; passion.

displeasure, dissatisfaction, discomfort, discomposure, disquiet; *malaise*; inquietude, uneasiness, vexation of spirit; taking; discontent etc. 832.

dejection etc. 837; weariness etc. 841.

annoyance, irritation, worry, infliction, visitation; plague, bore; bother, -ation; stew, vexation, mortification, chagrin, *esclandre*; *mauvais quart d'heure.*

care, anxiety, solicitude, trouble, trial, ordeal, fiery ordeal, shock, blow, cark, dole, fret, burden, load.

concern, grief, sorrow, distress, affliction, woe, bitterness, gloom, heartache; heavy –, aching –, bleeding –, broken- heart; heavy affliction, gnawing grief; unhappiness, infelicity, misery, tribulation, wretchedness, desolation; despair etc. 859; extremity, prostration, depth of misery.

nightmare, *ephialtes*, incubus.

anguish, agony; throe, tor-ture, -ment; crucifixion, martyrdom; pang, twinge, stab; the rack, the stake; purgatory etc. (*hell*) 982.

hell upon earth; iron age, reign of terror; slough of despond etc. (*adversity*) 735; peck –, sea- of troubles; ills that flesh is heir to etc. (*evil*) 619; miseries of human life; unkindest cut of all.

sufferer, victim, prey, martyr, object of compassion, wretch, shorn lamb.

V. feel –, suffer –, experience –, undergo –, bear –, endure- pain etc. *n.*; smart, ache etc. (*physical pain*) 378; suffer, bleed, ail; be the victim of; bear – take up- the cross.

labor under afflictions; quaff the bitter cup, have a bad time of it; fall on evil days etc. (*adversity*) 735; go hard with, come to grief, fall a sacrifice to, drain the cup of misery to the dregs, sup full of horrors.

sit on thorns, be on pins and needles, wince, fret, chafe, worry oneself, be in a taking, fret and fume, take -on, – to heart.

grieve; mourn etc. (*lament*) 839; yearn, repine, pine, droop, languish, sink; give way; despair etc. 859; break one's heart; weigh upon the heart etc. (*inflict pain*) 830.

Adj. in –, in a state of –, full of- pain etc. *n.*; suffering etc. *v.*; pained, afflicted, worried, displeased etc. 830; aching, griped, sore etc. (*physical pain*) 378; on the rack; in limbo; between hawk and buzzard.

un-comfortable, -easy; ill at ease; in a -taking, – way; disturbed; discontented etc. 832; out of humor etc. 901*a*; weary etc. 841.

heavy laden, stricken, crushed, a prey to, victimized, ill-used.

unfortunate etc. (*hapless*) 735; to be pitied, doomed, devoted, accursed, undone, lost, stranded.

unhappy, infelicitous, poor, wretched, miserable, woe-begone; cheerless etc. (*dejected*) 837; careworn.

concerned, sorry; sorrow-ing, -ful; cut up, chagrined, horrified, horror-stricken; in –, plunged in –, a prey to- grief etc. *n.*; in tears etc. (*lamenting*) 839; steeped to the lips in misery; heart-stricken, -broken, -scalded; broken-hearted; in despair etc. 859.

Phr. 'the iron entered into our soul;' *haeret lateri lethalis arundo*;' one's heart bleeding.

829. Pleasurableness. [Capability of giving pleasure; cause or source of pleasure.]—**N.** pleasurable-, pleasant-, agreeable-ness etc. *adj.*; pleasure giving, jocundity, delectability; amusement etc. 840.

attraction etc. (*motive*) 615; attractiveness, -

ability; invitingness etc. *adj.*; charm, fascination, captivation, enchantment, witchery, seduction, winsomeness, winning ways, amenity, amiability, sweetness.

loveliness etc. (*beauty*) 845; sunny –, bright-side; sweets etc. (*sugar*) 396; goodness etc. 648; manna in the wilderness, land flowing with milk and honey.

treat; regale etc. (*physical pleasure*) 377; dainty; tit-, tid-bit; nuts, *sauce piquante*.

V. cause –, produce –, create –, give –, afford –, procure –, offer –, present –, yield- pleasure etc. 827.

please, charm, delight; gladden etc. (*make cheerful*) 836; take, captivate, fascinate; enchant, entrance, enrapture, transport, bewitch; en-, ravish.

bless, beatify; satisfy; gratify –, desire etc. 865; slake, satiate, quench; indulge, humor, flatter, tickle; tickle the palate etc. (*savory*) 394; regale, refresh; enliven; treat; amuse etc. 840; take –, tickle –, hit- one's fancy; meet one's wishes; win –, gladden –, rejoice –, warm the cockles of- the heart; do one's heart good.

attract, allure etc. (*move*) 615; stimulate etc. (*excite*) 824; interest, intrigue.

make things pleasant, popularize, gild the pill, sweeten.

Adj. causing pleasure etc. *v.*; pleasure-giving; pleas-ing, -ant, -urable; agreeable, cushy; grat-eful, -ifying; leef, lief, acceptable; welcome, – as the roses in May; welcomed; favorite; to one's -taste, – mind, – liking, – heart's content; satisfactory etc. (*good*) 648.

refreshing; comfortable; cordial; genial; glad, -some; sweet, delectable, nice, dainty; delic-ate, -ious; dulcet; luscious etc. 396; palatable etc. 394; luxurious, voluptuous; sensual etc. 377.

attractive etc. 615; inviting, prepossessing, engaging; win-ning, -some; taking, fascinating, captivating, killing; seduc-ing, -tive; alluring, enticing; appetizing etc. (*exciting*) 824; cheering etc. 836; bewitching; interesting, absorbing, enchanting, entrancing, enravishing.

charming; delightful, felicitous, exquisite; lovely etc. (*beautiful*) 845; ravishing, rapturous; heartfelt, thrilling, ecstatic; beat-ic, -ific; seraphic; empyrean; elysian etc. (*heavenly*) 981.

palmy, halcyon, Saturnian.

Phr. *decies repetita placebit*.

830. Painfulness. [Capability of giving pain; cause or source of pain.]—**N.** painfulness etc. *adj.*; trouble, care etc. (*pain*) 828; trial; af-, in-fliction; cross, blow, stroke, burden, load, curse; bitter -pill, – draught, – cup; waters of bitterness.

annoyance, grievance, nuisance, vexation, mortification, sickener; bore, bother, pother, hot water, sea of troubles, hornet's nest, plague, pest.

cancer, ulcer, sting, thorn; canker etc. (*bane*) 663; scorpion etc. (*evil-doer*) 913; dagger etc. (*arms*) 727; scourge etc. (*instrument of punishment*) 975; carking –, canker worm of- care.

mishap, misfortune etc. (*adversity*) 735; *désagrément, esclandre*, rub.

source of -irritation, – annoyance; wound, sore subject, skeleton in the closet; thorn in -the flesh, – one's side; where the shoe pinches, gall and wormwood.

sorry sight, heavy news, provocation; affront etc. 929; head and front of one's offending.

infestation, molestation; malignity etc. (*malevolence*) 907.

V. cause –, occasion –, give –, bring –, induce –, produce –, create –, inflict- pain etc. 828; pain, hurt, wound.

pinch, prick, gripe etc. (*physical pain*) 378; pierce, lancinate, cut.

hurt –, wound –, grate upon –, jar upon- the feelings; wring –, pierce –, lacerate –, break –, rend- the heart; make the heart bleed; tear –, rend- the heart-strings; draw tears from the eyes.

sadden; make -unhappy etc. 828; plunge into sorrow, grieve, fash, afflict, distress; cut -up, – to the heart.

displease, annoy, incommode, discommode, discompose, trouble, disquiet, disturb, thwart, cross, perplex, molest, tease, rag, tire, irk, vex, mortify, wherret, worry, plague, bother, pester, bore, pother, harass, harry, badger, heckle, bait, beset, infest, persecute, importune, be troublesome.

wring, harrow, torment, torture; put to the -rack, – question; break on the wheel, rack, scarify; cruci-ate, -fy; convulse, agonize; barb the dart; plant a -dagger in the breast, – thron in one's side.

irritate, provoke, sting, nettle, try the patience, pique, fret, rile, tweak the nose, chafe, gall; sting –, wound –, cut- to the quick; aggrieve, affront, enchafe, enrage, ruffle, sour the temper; give offence etc. (*resentment*) 900.

maltreat, bite, snap at, assail, bully; smite etc. (*punish*) 972.

sicken, disgust, revolt, nauseate, disenchant, repel, offend, shock, stink in the nostrils; go against –, turn- the stomach; make one sick, set the teeth on edge, go against the grain, grate on the ear; stick in one's -throat, – gizzard; rankle, gnaw, corrode, horrify, appal, freeze the blood; chill the spine; make the -flesh creep, – hair stand on end; make the blood -curdle, – run cold; make one shudder.

haunt, – the memory; weigh –, prey- on the -heart, – mind, – spirits; bring one's grey hairs with sorrow to the grave; add a nail to one's coffin.

Adj. causing pain, hurting etc. *v.*; hurtful etc. (*bad*) 649; painful; dolor-ific, -ous; unpleasant; un-, dis-pleasing; disagreeable, unpalatable, bitter, distasteful; uninviting; unwelcome; undesir-able, -ed; obnoxious; unacceptable, unpopular, thankless.

unsatisfactory, untoward, unlucky, uncomfortable.

distressing; afflict-ing, -ive; joy-, cheer-, comfortless; dismal, disheartening; depress-ing, -ive; dreary, melancholy, grievous, piteous; woeful, rueful, mournful, deplorable, pitiable, lamentable; sad, affecting, touching, pathetic.

irritating, provoking, stinging, annoying, aggravating, mortifying, galling; unaccommodating, invidious, vexatious; trouble-, tire-, irk-, weari-some; plagu-ing, -y; awkward.

importunate; teas-, pester-, bother-, harass-, worry-, torment-, cark-ing.

in-toler-, -suffer-, -support-able; un-bear-, -endur-able; past bearing; not to be -borne, – endured; more than flesh and blood can bear; enough to -drive one mad, – provoke a saint, – make a parson swear, – try the patience of Job.

shocking, terrific, grim, appalling, crushing; dreadful, fearful, frightful; thrilling, tremendous, dire; heart-breaking, -rending, -wounding, corroding, -sickening; harrowing, rending.

odious, hateful, execrable, repulsive, repellent, abhorrent; horri-d, -ble, -fic, -fying; offensive; nause-ous, -ating; disgust-, sicken-, revolt-ing; nasty; loath-some, -ful; fulsome; vile etc. (*bad*) 649; hideous etc. 846.

sharp, acute, sore, severe, grave, hard, harsh, cruel, biting, acrimonious, caustic; cutting, corroding, consuming, racking, excruciating, searching, searing, grinding, grating, agonizing; envenomed.

ruinous, disastrous, calamitous, tragical; desolating, withering; burdensome, onerous, oppressive; cumb-rous, -ersome.

Adv. painfully etc. *adj.*; with -pain etc. 828; deuced.

Int. *hinc illae lachrymae!* woe is me!

Phr. *surgit amari aliquid*; the place being too hot to hold one; the iron entering the soul.

831. Content.—N. content, -ment, -edness; complacency, satisfaction, entire satisfaction, ease, heart's ease, peace of mind; serenity etc. 826; cheerfulness etc. 836; ray of comfort; comfort etc. (*well-being*) 827.

re-, conciliation; resignation etc. (*patience*) 826.

waiter on Providence.

V. be -content etc. *adj.*; rest satisfied, – and be thankful; take the good the gods provide, let well alone, feel oneself at home, hug oneself, lay the flattering unction to one's soul.

take -up with, – in good part; assent etc. 488; be reconciled to, make one's peace with; get over it; take -heart, – comfort; put up with etc. (*bear*) 826.

render -content etc. *adj.*; set at ease, comfort; set one's -heart, – mind- at -ease, – rest; speak peace; conciliate, reconcile, win over, propitiate, disarm, beguile; content, satisfy; gratify etc. 829.

be -tolerated etc. 826; go down, – with; do.

Adj. content, -ed; satisfied etc. *v.*; at -ease, – one's ease, – home; with the mind at ease, *sans souci, sine curâ*, easy-going, not particular; conciliatory; unrepining, of good comfort; resigned etc. (*patient*) 826; cheerful etc. 836.

un-afflicted, -vexed, -molested, -plagued; serene etc. 826; at rest; snug, comfortable; in one's element.

satisfactory, satisfying, ample, sufficient, adequate, tolerable.

Adv. to one's heart's content; *à la bonne heure*; all for the best.

Int amen etc. (*assent*) 488; very well, so much the better, well and good; it –, that- will do; it cannot be helped.

Phr. nothing comes amiss.

832. Discontent.—N. discontent, -ment; dissatisfaction; dissent etc. 489; labor unrest.

disappointment, mortification; cold comfort; regret etc. 833; repining, taking on etc. *v.*; inquietude, vexation of spirit, soreness; heart-burning, -grief; querulousness etc. (*lamentation*) 839; hypercriticism.

malcontent, grumbler, growler, croaker, *laudator temporis acti*; censurer, complainer, faultfinder, murmurer, Adullamite, Diehard, Bitterender.

the Opposition, cave of Adullam, indignation meeting, 'winter of our discontent.'

V. be -discontented etc. *adj.*; quarrel with one's bread and butter; repine; regret etc. 833; wish one at the bottom of the Red Sea; take -on, – to heart; shrug the shoulders; make a wry –, pull a long- face; knit one's brows; look -blue, – black, – black as thunder, – blank, – glum.

take -in bad part, – ill; fret, chafe, make a piece of work; grumble, croak, grouse; lament etc. 839.

cause -discontent etc. *n.*; dissatisfy, disappoint, mortify, put out, disconcert; cut up; dishearten.

Adj. discontented; dissatisfied etc. *v.*; unsatisfied, ungratified; dissident; dissentient etc. 489; malcontent, exigent, exacting, hypercritical.

repining etc. *v.*; regretful etc. 833; down in the mouth etc. (*dejected*) 837.

in high dudgeon, – a fume, – the sulks, – the dumps, – bad humor; glum, sulky; sour, – as a crab; soured, sore; out of -humor, – temper.

disappointing etc. *v.*; unsatisfactory.

Int. so much the worse!

Phr. that –, it- will never do.

833. Regret.—N. regret, repining; home sickness, nostalgia; *mal –, maladie- du pays*; lamentation etc. 839; contrition, compunction, penitence etc. 950.

bitterness, heart-burning.

laudator temporis acti etc. (*discontent*) 832.

V. regret, deplore; bewail etc. (*lament*) 839; repine, cast a longing lingering look behind; rue, – the day; repent etc. 950; *infandum renovare dolorem.*

prey –, weigh –, have a weight- on the mind; leave an aching void.

Adj. regretting etc. *v.*; regretful; home-sick.

regretted etc. *v.*; much to be regretted, regrettable; lamentable etc. (*bad*) 649.

Int. what a pity! hang it!

Phr. 'tis -pity, – too true.

834. Relief.—N. relief; deliverance; refreshment etc. 689; easement, softening, alleviation, mitigation, palliation etc. 174; soothing, lullaby; cradle song, *berceuse*

solace, consolation, comfort, encouragement.

lenitive, restorative etc. (*remedy*) 662; poultice etc. *v.*; cushion etc. 215; crumb of comfort, balm in Gilead; aspirin.

V. relieve, ease, alleviate, mitigate, palliate, soothe, addulce; salve; soften, – down; foment, stupe, poultice; assuage, allay.

cheer, comfort, console; encourage, bear up, pat on the back, give comfort, set at ease; enliven, gladden –, cheer- the heart.

remedy; cure etc. (*restore*) 660; refresh; pour -balm into, – oil on.

smoothe the ruffled brow of care, temper the wind to the shorn lamb, lay the flattering unction to one's soul.

disburden etc. (*free*) 705; take off a load of care.

be relieved; breathe more freely, draw a long breath; take comfort; dry –, wipe- the -tears, – eyes.

Adj. relieving etc. *v.*; consolatory, soothing; assua-ging, -sive; bal-my, -samic; lenitive, palliative; anodyne etc. (*remedial*) 662; curative etc. 660.

835. Aggravation.—N. aggravation, heightening; exacerbation; exasperation; overestimation etc. 482; exaggeration etc. 549.

V. aggravate, render worse, heighten, embitter, sour; ex-, acerbate; exasperate, envenom; tease, provoke, enrage.

add fuel to the -fire, – flame; fan the flame etc. (*excite*) 824; go from bad to worse etc. (*deteriorate*) 659.

Adj. aggravated etc. *v.*; worse, unrelieved; aggravable; aggravating etc. *v.*

Adv. out of the frying pan into the fire, from bad to worse, worse and worse.

Int. so much the worse!

836. Cheerfulness.—N. cheerfulness etc. *adj.*; geniality, gaiety, *l'allegro*, cheer, good humor, spirits; high –, animal –, flow of- spirits; glee, high glee, light heart; sunshine of the -mind, – breast; *gaieté de coeur*, *bon naturel*.

liveliness etc. *adj.*; life, alacrity, vivacity, animation, *allégresse*; jocundity, joviality, jollity; levity; jocularity etc. (*wit*) 842.

mirth, merriment, hilarity, exhilaration; laughter etc. 838; merry-making etc. (*amusement*) 840; heyday, rejoicing etc. 838; marriage bells.

nepenthe, Euphrosyne.

optimism etc. (*hopefulness*) 858; self-complacency.

V. be -cheerful etc. *adj.*; have the mind at ease, smile, put a good face upon, keep up one's spirits; view -the bright side of the picture, – things *en couleur de rose*; *ridentem dicere verum*, cheer up, brighten up, light up, bear up; chirp, take heart, cast away care, drive dull care away, perk up.

rejoice etc. 838; carol, chirrup, lilt; frisk, rollick, give a loose to mirth.

cheer, enliven, elate, exhilarate, gladden, inspirit, animate, raise the spirits, inspire; put in good humor; cheer –, rejoice- the heart; delight etc. (*give pleasure*) 829.

Adj. cheerful; happy etc. 827; cheer-y, -ly; of good cheer, smiling; blithe; in –, in good- spirits; in high -spirits, – feather; happy as -the day is long, – a king; gay, – as a lark; *allegro*; light, -some, -hearted; buoyant, *débonnaire*, bright, free and easy, airy; janty, jaunty, canty; spright-ly, -ful; spry; spirit-ed, -ful; lively; animated, breezy, vivacious; brisk, – as a bee; sparkling; sportive; full of -play, – spirit; all alive.

sunny, palmy; hopeful etc. 858.

merry, – as a -cricket, – grig, – marriage bell; joyful, joyous, jocund, jovial; jolly, – as a thrush, – as a sandboy; blithesome; glee-ful, -some; hilarious, rattling.

winsome, bonny, hearty, buxom.

play-ful, -some; *folâtre*, playful as a kitten, tricksy, frisky, frolicsome; gamesome; jocose, jocular, waggish; mirth-, laughter-loving; mirthful, rollicking.

elate, -d; exulting, jubilant, flushed; rejoicing etc. 838; cock-a-hoop.

cheering, inspiriting, exhilarating; cardiac, -al; pleasing etc. 829; flourishing, halcyon.

Adv. cheerfully etc. *adj.*

Int. never say die! come! cheer up! hurrah! etc. 838; 'hence loathed melancholy!' begone dull care! away with melancholy!

837. Dejection.—N. dejection; dejectedness etc. *adj.*; depression, prosternation; lowness –, depression- of spirits; weight –, oppression –, damp- on the spirits; low –, bad –, drooping –, depressed- spirits; heart sinking; heaviness –, failure- of heart.

heaviness etc. *adj.*; infestivity, gloom; weariness etc. 841; *taedium vitae*, disgust of life; *mal du pays* etc. (*regret*) 833.

melancholy; sadness etc. *adj.*; *il penseroso*, *melancholia*, dismals, mumps, mopes, lachrymals, dumps, blues, blue devils, doldrums, vapors, megrims, spleen, horrors, hypochondriasis, pessimism; despondency, slough of Despond; disconsolateness etc. *adj.*; hope deferred, blank despondency.

prostration, – of soul; broken heart; despair etc. 859; cave of -despair, – Trophonius.

demureness etc. *adj.*; gravity, solemnity; long –, grave- face.

hypochondriac, seek-sorrow, self-tormentor, *heautontimorumenos*, *malade imaginaire*, *médecin tant pis*; croaker, pessimist; mope, mopus.

[Cause of dejection] affliction etc. 830; sorry sight; *memento mori*; damper, wet blanket, Job's comforter; death's head, skeleton at the feast.

V. be -dejected etc. *adj.*; grieve; mourn etc. (*lament*) 839; take on, give way, lose heart, despond, droop, sink.

lower, look downcast, frown, pout; hang down the head; pull –, make- a long face; laugh on the wrong side of the mouth; grin a ghastly smile; look -blue, – like a drowned man; lay –, take- to heart.

mope, brood over; fret; sulk; pine, – away; yearn; repine etc. (*regret*) 833; despair etc. 859.

refrain from laughter, keep one's countenance; be –, look- grave etc. *adj.*; repress a smile, keep a straight face.

depress; dis-courage, -hearten; dis-pirit; damp, dull, deject, lower, sink, dash, knock down, unman, prostrate, break one's heart; frown upon; cast a -gloom, – shade- on; sadden; damp –, dash –, wither- one's hopes; weigh –, lie heavy –, prey- on the -mind, – spirits; damp –, depress- the spirits.

Adj. cheer-, joy-, spirit-less; uncheer-ful, -y; unlively; unhappy etc. 828; melancholy, dismal, somber, dark, gloomy, adust, *triste*, clouded, murky, lowering, frowning, lugubrious, Acherontic, funereal, mournful, lamentable, dreadful.

dreary, flat; dull, – as -a beetle, – ditchwater; depressing etc. *v.*

'melancholy as a gib cat;' oppressed with –; a prey to- melancholy; down-cast, -hearted; down -in the mouth, – on one's luck; heavy-hearted; in the -dumps, – suds, – sulks, – doldrums; in doleful dumps, in bad humor; sullen; mumpish, dumpish; mopish, moping; moody, glum; sulky etc. (*discontented*) 832; out of -sorts, – humor, – heart, – spirits; ill at ease, low-spirited, in low spirits, a cup too low; weary etc. 841; dis-couraged, -heartened; desponding; chop-, jaw-, crest-fallen.

sad, pensive, *penseroso*, tristful; dole-some, -ful; woebegone, lachrymose, in tears, melancholic, hypped, hypochondriacal, bilious, jaundiced, atrabilious, saturnine, splenetic; lackadaisical.

serious, sedate, staid, stayed; grave, – as -a judge, – an undertaker, – a mustard pot; sober, solemn, demure; grim; grim-faced, -visaged; rueful, wan, long-faced.

disconsolate; un-, in-consolable; forlorn, comfortless, desolate, *désolé*, sick at heart; soul-, heart-sick; *au désepoir*; in despair etc. 859; lost.

overcome; broken-, borne-, bowed-down; heart-stricken etc. (*mental suffering*) 828; cut up, dashed, sunk; unnerved, unmanned; down-fallen, -trodden; broken hearted; care-worn.

Adv. with -a long face, – tears in one's eyes; sadly etc. *adj*.

Phr. the countenance falling; the heart -failing, – sinking within- one.

838. Rejoicing. [Expression of pleasure.]—**N.** rejoicing, exultation, triumph, jubilation, heyday, flush, revelling; merry-making etc. (*amusement*) 840; jubilee etc. (*celebration*) 883; *paean, Te Deum* etc. (*thanksgiving*) 990, congratulation etc. 896, applause etc. 971.

smile, simper, smirk, grin; broad –, sardonic-grin.

laughter, giggle, titter, crow, cheer, chuckle, snicker, snigger, shout; Homeric laughter, horse –, hearty- laugh; guffaw; burst –, fit –, shout –, roar –, peal- of laughter; cachinnation.

risibility; derision etc. 856.

Momus; Democritus the Abderite; rollicker; Laughter holding both his sides.

V. rejoice; thank –, bless- one's stars; congratulate –, hug- oneself; rub –, clap- one's hands; smack the lips, fling up one's cap; dance, skip, caleer; sing, carol, chirrup, chirp; hurrah; cry for –, leap with- joy; exult etc. (*boast*) 884; triumph; hold jubilee etc. (*celebrate*) 883; make merry etc. (*sport*) 840; sing a paean of joy.

smile, simper, smirk; grin, – like a Cheshire cat; mock, laugh in one's sleeve; laugh, – outright; giggle, titter, snigger, crow, smicker, chuckle, snicker, cackle; burst -out, – into a fit of laughter; shout, split, roar.

shake –, split –, hold both- one's sides; roar –, die- with laughter.

raise laughter etc. (*amuse*) 840.

Adj. rejoicing etc. *v.*; jubilant, exultant, triumphant; flushed, elated; laughing etc. *v.*; risible; ready to -burst, – split, – die with laughter; convulsed with laughter.

laughable etc. (*ludicrous*) 853.

Int. hip, hip, -hurrah! huzza! aha! hail! tolderolloll! tra-la la! Heaven be praised! *io triumphe! tant mieux!* so much the better.

Phr. the heart leaping with joy.

839. Lamentation. [Expression of pain.]—**N.** lament, -ation; wail, complaint, plaint, murmur, mutter, grumble, groan, moan, whine, whimper, sob, sigh, suspiration, heaving, deep sigh.

cry etc. (*vociferation*) 411; scream, howl; outcry, wail of woe, frown, scowl.

tear; weeping etc. *v.*; flood of tears, fit of crying, lachrymation, melting mood, weeping and gnashing of teeth.

plaintiveness etc. *adj.*; languishment; condolence etc. 915.

mourning, weeds, willow, cypress, crêpe, crape, deep mourning; sackcloth and ashes; knell etc. 363; dump, deathsong, dirge, coronach, keen, *nenia*, requiem, elegy, *epicedium*; threne; mon-, thren-ody; jeremiad; ululation.

mourner, professional mourner, keener; grumbler etc. (*discontent*) 832; Niobe; Heraclitus.

V. lament, mourn, deplore, grieve, weep over; be-wail, -moan; keen; condole with etc. 915; fret etc. (*suffer*) 828; wear –, go into –, put on- mourning; wear -the willow, – sackcloth and ashes; *infandum renovare dolorem* etc. (*regret*) 833; give sorrow words.

sigh; give –, heave –, fetch- a sigh; 'waft a sigh from Indus to the pole;' sigh 'like furnace;' wail.

cry, weep, sob, greet, blubber, pipe, snivel, bibber, whimper, pule; pipe one's eye; drop –, shed- -tears, – a tear; melt –, burst- into tears; *fondre en larmes*; cry -oneself blind, – one's eyes out.

scream etc. (*cry out*) 411; mew etc. (*animal sounds*) 412; groan, moan, whine, yammer; roar; roar –, bellow- like a bull; cry out lustily, rend the air, yell.

frown, scowl, make a wry face, grimace, gnash one's teeth, wring one's hands, tear one's hair, beat one's breast, roll on the ground, burst with grief.

complain, murmur, mutter, grumble, growl, clamor, make a fuss about, croak, grunt, maunder; deprecate etc. (*disapprove*) 932.

cry out before one is hurt, complain without cause.

Adj. lamenting etc. *v.*; in mourning, in sackcloth and ashes; crying, sorrowing, -ful etc. (*unhappy*) 828; mourn-, tear-ful; lachrymose; plaint-ive, -ful, quer-ulous, -imonious; in the melting mood.

in tears, with tears in one's eyes; with -moistened, – watery- eyes; bathed –, dissolved- in tears; 'like Niobe all tears.'

elagiac, epicedial, threnetic.

Adv. *de profundis; les larmes aux yeux.*

Int. heigh-ho! alas! alack! O dear! ah –, woe is- me! lackadaisy! well –, lack –, alack- a day! well-a-way! alas the day! *O tempora! O mores!* what a pity! *miserabile dictu!* O lud lud! too true!

Phr. tears -standing in, – starting from- the eyes; -eyes -suffused, – swimming, – brimming –, over- flowing- with tears.

840. Amusement.—N. amuse-, entertain-ment; diver-sion, -tissement; reaction, relaxation, solace; pastime, *passetemps*, sport; labor of love; pleasure etc. 827.

fun, frolic, merriment, whoopee, jollity; jovial-ity, -ness; heyday; laughter etc. 838; jocos-ity, -eness; droll-, buffoon-, tomfool-ery; mummery, masquing, pleasantry; wit etc. 842; quip, quirk.

play; game, – at romps; gambol, romp, prank, antic, rig, lark, spree, skylarking, vagary, trick, monkey trick, *gambade, fredaine, escapade, échappée*, bout, *espièglerie*; practical joke etc. (*ridicule*) 856.

dance; round –, square –, solo –, step –, tap –, clog –, skirt –, sand –, folk –, morris-dance, *pas seul*, step, turn, *chassé*, cut, shuffle, double shuffle; hop, reel, rigadoon, saraband, hornpipe, bolero, fandango, pavan, tarantella, minuet, waltz, polka; galop, -ade; Schottische, *pas de quatre*, Boston, one-, two-step, rumba, tango, maxixe, fox-, turkey-trot, shimmy, ragtime, cakewalk, jazz, blues, Charleston; jig, breakdown, fling, strathspey; *allemande*; gavot, -te; mazurka, morisco; quadrille, lancers, country dance, *cotillon*, polonaise, Sir Roger de Coverley, Swedish dance; *ballet* etc. (*drama*) 599; ball; *bal*, – *masqué*, – *costumé*; masquerade, fancy dress ball; *thé dansant*; Terpsichore, choreography, Russian ballet, classical dancing; eurythmics; nautch dance, *danse du ventre*, cancan.

festivity, merry-making; party etc. (*social gathering*) 892; *fête*, festival, gala, *ridotto*; revel-s, -ry, -ling; carnival, brawl, saturnalia, high jinks; feast, banquet etc. (*food*) 298; regale, *symposium*, wassail; carous-e, -al; jollification, junket, wake, pic-nic, *fête champêtre*, garden party, gymkhana, regatta, track meet, field day, jamboree, treat.

round of pleasures, dissipation, a short life and a merry one, racketing, holiday making, high jinks.

rejoicing etc. 838; jubilee etc. (*celebration*) 883.

bonfire, fireworks, *feu-de-joie*, rocket, catherine wheel, roman candle etc.

holiday; gala –, red letter –, play- day; high days and holidays; high –, Bank- holiday; May –, Derby- day; Saint –, Easter –, Whit- Monday; King's birthday, Empire Day; *mi-carême*; *Bairam*; wayzgoose, bean feast, beano.

place of amusement, theater etc. 599; concert-, ball-, assembly-room; music-hall, cinema, movies, talkies, vaudeville; hippodrome, circus, rodeo; *casino*, *kursaal*; winter garden; park, pleasance, arbor; garden etc. 371; pleasure-, play-, cricket-, football-, polo-, croquet-, archery-, hunting-ground; golf links, race course, stadium, gridiron, bowl, speedway, racing track, ring; gymnasium, swimming pool; shooting gallery; tennis-, racket-court; bowling-green, -alley; croquet-lawn, rink, skating rink; roller-coaster, roundabout, carousel, merry-go-round; swing; *montagne russe*; switchback, scenic railway etc.

game, – of -chance, – skill; athletic sports, gymnastics; fencing; archery, rifle-shooting; tournament, pugilism etc. (*contention*) 720; sporting etc. 622; horse-racing, the turf; aquatics etc. 267; skating, roller skating; ski-running, -joring, -jumping, bobsleighing, luging, tobogganing, winter sports; sliding; cricket, tennis, lawn –, table –, deck-tennis, rackets, fives, squash, ping pong, trap bat and ball, battledore and shuttlecock, badminton, *la grâce*; pall mall, tip-cat, croquet, golf, curling, hockey, basketball, soccer, football, Rugby, Association, *pallone*, polo; tent-pegging, tilting at the ring, quintain, greasy pole; quoits, *discus*; throwing the hammer, putting the -weight, – shot, tossing the caber; knurr and spell; leap-frog; hop, skip and jump; French and English, tug of war; blind man's buff, hunt the slipper, hide-and-seek, kiss in the ring; snapdragon; cross questions and crooked answers; jig-saw puzzle; rounders, base-ball, *la crosse* etc.; angling; swimming, diving, water-polo.

billiards, pool, pyramids, snooker, bagatelle; bowls, skittles, ninepins, kail, American bowls.

cards; bridge, auction, contract, whist, rubber; round game, coon-can, loo, cribbage, *bésique*, pinocle, euchre, drole, *écarté*, skat, picquet, all-fours, quadrille, ombre, reverse, Pope Joan, commit; bo-, boa-ston; *vingt-et-un*; *quinze*, thirty-one, put-and-take, speculation, connections, brag, cassino, lottery, commerce, snip-snap-snorem, lift smoke, blind hookey, Polish bank, poker, banker; faro; Earl of Coventry, Napoleon, nap, patience, pairs; old maid, fright, beggar-my-neighbor; *baccarat*, *chemin de fer*, *monté*, *roulette*.

chess, draughts, backgammon, dominoes, checkers, mah jong, merelles, nine men's morris, go-bang, solitaire; game of –, fox and-goose; lotto; etc.

morra; gambling etc. (*chance*) 621.

toy, plaything, bauble; doll etc. (*puppet*) 554; teetotum; knick-knack etc. (*trifle*) 643; magic lantern etc. (*show*) 448; peep-, puppet-, raree-, gallanty-show; marionettes, Punch and Judy; toy-shop; 'quips and cranks and wanton wiles, nods and becks and wreathed smiles.'

sportsman, gamester, gambler etc. 621; reveler, master of the -ceremonies, – revels; *arbiter elegantiarum*.

V. amuse, entertain, divert, eliven; tickle, – the fancy; titillate, raise a smile, put in good humor; cause –, create –, occasion –, raise –, excite –, produce –, convulse with- laughter; set the table in a roar, be the death of one.

recreate, solace, cheer, rejoice; please etc. 829; interest; treat, regale.

amuse oneself; game; play, – a game, – pranks, – tricks; sport, disport, toy, wanton, revel, junket, feast, carouse, banquet, make merry; drown care; drive dull care away; frolic, gambol, frisk, romp; caper; dance etc. (*leap*) 309; keep up the ball; run a rig, sow one's wild oats, have one's fling, paint the town red, take one's pleasure; see life; *desipere in loco*, play the fool.

make –, keep- holiday; go a Maying.

while away –, beguile- the time; kill time, dally.

Adj. amusing, entertaining, diverting etc. *v.*; recreative, lusory; pleasant etc. (*pleasing*) 829; laughable etc. (*ludicrous*) 853; witty etc. 842; festive, -al; jovial, jolly, jocund, roguish, rompish; sporting; playful – as a kitten; sportive, ludibrious.

amused etc. *v.*; 'pleased with a feather, tickled with a straw.'

Adv. 'on the light fantastic toe,' at play, in sport.

Int. *vive la bagatelle! vogue la galère!*

Phr. *Deus nobis haec otia fecit*; *dum vivimus vivamus*.

841. Weariness.—N. weariness, defatigation, boredom, *ennui*; lassitude etc. (*fatigue*) 688; drowsiness etc. 683.

disgust, nausea, loathing, sickness; satiety etc. 869; *taedium vitae* etc. (*dejection*) 837.

wearisome-, tedious-ness etc. *adj.*; dull work, tedium, monotony, twice told tale.

bore, button-hole, proser, wet blanket; heavy hours, 'the enemy' [time].

V. weary; tire etc. (*fatigue*) 688; bore; bore –, weary –, tire- -to death, – out of one's life, – out of all patience; set –, send- to sleep.

pall, sicken, nauseate, disgust.

harp on the same string; drag its -slow, – weary- length along.

never hear the last of; be -tired etc. *adj.* -of, – with; yawn; died with *ennui.*

Adj. wearying etc. *v.*; wearing; weari-, tire-, irksome; uninteresting, stupid, bald, devoid of interest, dry, monotonous, dull, arid, tedious, humdrum, mortal, flat; pros-y, -ing; slow; soporific, somniferous, dormitive.

disgusting etc. *v.*; unenjoyed.

weary; tired etc. *v.*; drowsy etc. (*sleepy*) 683; uninterested, flagging, used up, worn out, *blasé*, life-weary, weary of life; sick of.

Adv. wearily etc. *adj.*; *usque ad nauseam.*

Phr. time hanging heavily on one's hands; *toujours perdrix*; *crambe repetita.*

842. Wit.—N. wit, -tiness; attic -wit, – salt; atticism; salt, *esprit*, point, fancy, whim, humor, drollery, pleasantry.

farce, buffoonery, fooling, tomfoolery; harlequinade etc. 599; broad -farce, – humor; fun, *espièglerie*; *vis comica.*

jocularity; jocos-ity, -eness; facetiousness; waggery, -ishness; whimsicality; comicality etc. 853.

smartness, ready wit, banter, *badinage, persiflage*, retort, repartee, *quid pro quo*, ridicule etc. 856.

facetiae, quips and cranks; jest, joke, capital joke; standing -jest, – joke; conceit, quip, quirk, crank, quiddity, *concetto, plaisanterie*, brilliant idea; merry –, bright –, happy- thought; sally; flash, – of wit, – of merriment; scintillation; *mot*, – pour rire; witticism, smart saying, *bon mot, jeu d'esprit*, epigram; jest book; dry joke, *quodlibet*, cream of the jest.

word-play, *jeu de mots*; play -of, – uponwords; pun, -ning; *double entente* etc. (*ambiguity*) 520; quibble, verbal quibble, conundrum etc. (*riddle*) 533; anagram, acrostic, double acrostic, *nugae canorae*, trifling, idle conceit, *turlupinade.*

old joke, Joe Miller, chestnut, hoary-headed jest.

V. joke, jest, cut jokes; crack a joke; perpetrate a -joke, – pun; make -fun of, – merry with; set the table in a roar etc. (*amuse*) 840; scintillate.

retort, flash back; banter etc. (*ridicule*) 856; *ridentem dicere verum*; joke at one's expense.

Adj. witty, attic, salty; quick-, nimble-witted; keen, clever, smart, brilliant, pungent, jocular, jocose, funny, waggish, facetious, whimsical, humorous, gilbertian; playful etc. 840; merry and wise; pleasant, sprightly, *spirituel*, sparkling, epigrammatic, full of point, *ben trovato*; comic etc. 853.

Adv. in joke, in jest, in sport, in play.

843. Dullness.—N. dullness, heaviness, flatness; infestivity etc. 837; stupidity etc. 499; want of originality, dearth of ideas.

prose, matter of fact; heavy book, *conte à dormir debout*; platitude.

V. be -dull etc. *adj.*; prose, platitudinize, take *au sérieux*, be caught napping.

render -dull etc. *adj.*; damp, depress, throw cold water on, lay a wet blanket on; fall flat upon the ear; hang fire.

Adj. dull, – as ditch water; dry, insipid, jejune; unentertaining, uninteresting, unlively, unimaginative; heavisome, heavy-gaited; insulse; dry as dust; pros-y, -ing, -aic; matter of fact, commonplace, banal, pointless; 'weary, flat, stale and unprofitable.'

stupid, slow, flat, sluggish, ponderous, humdrum, monotonous; melancholic etc. 837; stolid etc. 499; plodding.

Phr. *Davus sum non Oedipus.*

844. Humorist.—N. humorist, wag, wit, reparteeist, epigrammatist, gag man, punster; *bel esprit*, life of the party; wit-snapper, -cracker, -worm; joker, jester, jokesmith, Joe Miller, *drôle de corps, gaillard*, spark, *persiffleur*, banterer.

buffoon, *farceur*, merry-andrew, mime, tumbler, acrobat, mountebank, charlatan, posturemaster, harlequin, punch, *pulcinella*, scaramouch, clown; wearer of the -cap and bells, – motley; motley fool; pantaloon, gipsy; jack -pudding, – in the green, – a dandy; zany; mad-cap, pickle-herring, witling, caricaturist, *grimacier.*

845. Beauty.—N. beauty, the beautiful, *le beau ideal*, loveliness.

[Science of the perception of beauty] Callaesthetics.

form, elegance, grace, beauty unadorned; symmetry etc. 242; comeliness, fairness etc. *adj.*; pulchritude, polish, gloss; good -effect, – looks; *belle tournure*; bloom, brilliancy, radiance, splendor, gorgeousness, magnificence; sublimi-ty, -fication.

concinnity, delicacy, refinement; charm, *je ne sais quoi*, style, *chic*, swank.

Venus, – of Milo; Aphrodite, Hebe, the Graces, Peri, Houri, Cupid, Apollo, Hyperion, Adonis, Antinous, Narcissus; Helen of Troy.

peacock, butterfly; flower, flow'ret gay, rose, lily, asphodel; garden; flower of, pink of; *bijou*; jewel etc. (*ornament*) 847; work of art.

pleasurableness etc. 829.

beautifying; landscape gardening; decoration etc. 847; calisthenics.

V. be -beautiful etc. *adj.*; shine, beam, bloom; become one etc. (*accord*) 23; set off, grace, flatter one.

render -beautiful etc. *adj.*; beautify; polish, burnish; gild etc. (*decorate*) 847; set out.

'snatch a grace beyond the reach of art.'

Adj. beaut-iful, -eous; handsome; pretty; lovely, graceful, elegant; delicate, dainty, refined, exquisite; fair, personable, comely, seemly; bonny; good-looking; well-favored, -made, -formed, -proportioned; proper, shapely; symmetrical etc. (*regular*) 242; harmonious etc. (*color*) 428; sightly.

fit to be seen, passable, not amiss.

goodly, dapper, tight, jimp; gimp; janty, jaunty; natty, quaint, trim, tidy, neat, spruce, smart, tricksy.

bright, -eyed; rosy-, cherry-cheeked; rosy, ruddy; blooming, in full bloom.

brilliant, shining; beam-y, -ing; sparkling, swanky, splendid, resplendent, dazzling, glowing; glossy, sleek.

showy, specious; rich, gorgeous, superb, magnificent, grand, fine, sublime, imposing; majestic 873.

artistic, -al; aesthetic; pict-uresque, -orial; *fait à piendre*, paintable; well-composed, -grouped, -varied; curious.

enchanting etc. (*pleasure-giving*) 829; attractive etc. (*inviting*) 615; becoming etc. (*accordant*) 23; ornamental etc. 847.

undeformed, undefaced, unspotted; spotless etc. (*perfect*) 650.

846. Ugliness.—N. ugliness etc. *adj.*; deformity, inelegance; disfigurement etc. (*blemsih*) 848; want of symmetry, inconcinnity; distortion etc. 243; squalor etc. (*uncleanness*) 653.

forbidding countenance, vinegar aspect, hanging look, wry face, *'spretae injuria formae.'*

eyesore, object, figure, sight, fright, specter, scarecrow, hag, harridan, satyr, witch, toad, baboon, monster, Caliban, Aesop, *'monstrum horrendum informe ingens cui lumen ademptum.'*

V. be -ugly etc. *adj.*; look ill, grin horribly a ghastly smile, make faces.

render -ugly etc. *adj.*; deface; dis-, de-figure; deform, spoil, distort etc. 243; blemish etc. (*injure*) 659; soil etc. (*render unclean*) 653.

Adj. ugly, – as -sin, – a toad, – a scarecrow, – a dead monkey; plain, bald etc. 226; homely etc. (*unadorned*) 849; ordinary, unornamental, inartistic; unsightly, unseemly, uncomely, unshapely, unlovely; sightless, seemless; not fit to be seen; unbeaut-eous, -iful; beautiless; shapeless etc. (*amorphous*) 241; course; garish, over-decorated etc. 882.

mis-shapen, -proportioned; monstrous; gaunt etc. (*thin*) 203; dumpy etc. (*short*) 201; curtailed of its fair proportions; ill-made, -shaped, -proportioned; crooked etc. (*distorted*) 243; hard-featured, -visaged; ill-, hard-, evil-favored; ill-looking; unprepossessing.

graceless, inelegant; ungraceful, ungainly, uncouth; stiff; rugged, rough, gross, rude, awkward, clumsy, slouching, rickety; gawky; lump-ing, -ish; lumbering; hulk-y, -ing; unwieldy.

squalid, haggard; grim, -faced, -visaged; grisly, ghastly; ghost-, death-like; cadaverous, gruesome.

frightful, hideous, odious, uncanny, forbidding, repellant, repulsive; horri-d, -ble; shocking etc. (*painful*) 830.

foul etc. (*dirty*) 653; dingy etc. (*colorless*) 429; gaudy etc. (*color*) 428; disfigured etc. *v.*; discolored (*blemished*) etc. 848.

847. Ornament.—N. ornament, -ation, -al art; ornat-ture, -eness; adorn-ment, decoration, embellishment; architecture.

garnish, polish, varnish, French polish, gilding, japanning, lacquer, ormolu, enamel.

cosmetics, rouge, powder, lipstick, lip salve, mascara; manicure, nail polish; permanent –, Marcel –, finger-wave.

pattern, diaper, powdering, panelling, graining, pargeting, inlay, detail; texture etc. 329; richness; tracery, molding, beading, reeding, fillet, listel, strapwork, *coquillage*, flourish, *fleur-de-lis*, arabesque, fret, *anthemion*; egg and -tongue, – dart; *astragal*, zigzag, *acanthus, cartouche*; pilaster etc. (*projection*) 250; cyma, ogee.

em-, broidery, needlework; knitting, crochet, tatting, brocade, *brocatelle*, beads, bugles; galloon, lace, gimp, *guipure*, fringe, trapping, border, edging, insertion, *motif*, trimming; *passementerie*; drapery, hanging, tapestry, arras; millinery, ermine.

wreath, festoon, garland, lei, chaplet, flower, nosegay, *bouquet*, posy, 'daisies pied and violets blue.'

tassle, knot; shoulder-knot, *épaulette*, epaulet, aigulet, *aiguilette*, frog; star, rosette, bow; feather, plume, *panache, aigrette*.

jewel, -ry, -lery; bijoutry; *bijou, -terie*; diadem, tiara; pendant, trinket, locket, necklace, armilla, bracelet, bangle, armlet, anklet, ear-, nose- ring, carcanet, chain, *châtelaine*, albert, brooch, torque.

gem, precious stone; diamond, brilliant, beryl, aquamarine, alexandrite, cat's eye, emerald, calcedony, chrysoprase, cornelian, jasper, bloodstone, agate, heliotrope; girasol, -e; onyx, plasma; sard, -onyx; garnet, lapis-lazuli, opal, peridot, chrysolite, sapphire, ruby; spinel, -le; balais; oriental –, topaz; turquois, -e; zircon, jacinth, hyacinth, carbuncle, amethyst; moonstone; pearl, coral.

finery, frippery, gewgaw, gimcrack, knick-knack, tinsel, spangle, sequin, *clinquant*, pinch-beck, paste; excess of ornament etc. (*vulgarity*) 851; gaud, pride, ostentation; frills and furbelows.

illustration, illumination, *vignette*; *fleuron*; head-, tail-piece; *cul-de-lampe*; flowers of rhetoric etc. 577; work of art, article of vertu, *bric-à-brac*, curio, *bibelot*.

V. ornament, embellish, enrich, decorate, adorn, beautify, adonize.

smarten, furbish, polish, gild, varnish, whitewash, enamel, japan, lacquer, paint, grain.

garnish, trim, dizen, bedizen, prink, prank; trick –, fig- out; deck, bedeck, dight, bedight, array; dress, – up, preen, spruce up, titivate; spangle, bespangle, powder; embroider, work; chase, tool, emboss, fret; emblazon, blazon, illuminate; illustrate.

become etc. (*accord with*) 23.

Adj. ornamented, beautified etc. *v.*; ornate, rich, gilt, begilt, tesselated, enamelled, inlaid; festooned; topiary.

smart, gay, tricksy, flowery, glittering; new-gilt, -spangled; fine, – as -a Mayday queen, – fivepence, – a carrot fresh scraped; pranked out, bedight, well-groomed.

in full dress etc. (*fashion*) 852; *en grande -tenue*, – *toilette*; in best bib and tucker, in Sunday best, *endimanché*; dressed to advantage.

showy, flashy; gaudy etc. (*vulgar*) 851; garish; gorgeous.

ornamental, decorative; becoming etc. (*accordant*) 23.

848. Blemish.—N. blemish, disfigurement, deformity; defect etc. (*imperfection*) 651; flaw; injury etc. (*deterioration*) 659; spots on the sun; eyesore.

stain, blot, slur; spot, -tiness; speck, -le; blur, freckle, mole, *macula*, patch, blotch, birthmark, blain, maculation, tarnish, smudge, smear; dirt etc. 653; bruise, black eye, scar, wem; pustule; excrescence, pimple etc. (*protuberance*) 250.

V. disfigure etc. (*injure*) 659; speckle; render ugly etc. 846.

Adj. pitted, freckled, discolored, bloodshot, bruised, disfigured; stained etc. *n.*; imperfect etc. 651; injured etc. (*deteriorated*) 659.

849. Simplicity.—N. simplicity; plain-, homeli-ness; undress, nudity, nakedness, beauty unadorned, chastity, chasteness.

V. be -simple etc. *adj.*

render -simple etc. *adj.*; simplify, chasten, strip of ornament.

Adj. simple, plain; home-ly, -spun; ordinary, household.

natural, unaffected; free from -affectation, – ornament; *simplex munditiis*; *sans façon, en déshabillé*, nude, naked.

chaste, inornate, severe.

un-adorned, -ornamented, -decked, -garnished, -arranged, -trimmed, -varnished.

bald, flat, dull, blank.

850. Taste. [Good taste.]—**N.** taste; good –, refined –, cultivated- taste; delicacy, refinement, fine feeling, gust, *gusto*, tact, *finesse*; nicety etc. (*discrimination*) 465; polish, elegance, grace.

virtu; dilettanteism, virtuosity; fine art; cul-ture, -ivation.

[Science of taste] esthetics.

man of -taste etc.; *connoisseur*, judge, critic, *conoscente, virtuoso, amateur, dilettante*, Aristarchus, Corinthian, *arbiter elegantarum*, stagirite, euphemist.

'caviar to the general.'

V. appreciate, judge, criticize, discriminate etc. 465.

Adj. in good taste; tasteful, tasty; unaffected, pure, chaste, classical, attic; cultivated, refined; dainty; esthetic, artistic; elegant etc. 578; euphemistic.

to one's -taste, – mind; after one's fancy; *comme il faut*; *tiré à quatre épingles*.

Adv. elegantly etc. *adj.*

Phr. *nihil tetigit quod non ornavit.*

851. Vulgarity. [Bad taste.]—**N.** vulgar-ity, -ism; barbar-, Vandal-, Gothic-ism; *mauvais goût*, bad taste; Babbittry; *gaucherie*, awkwardness, want of tact; ill-breeding etc. (*discourtesy*) 895; ungentlemanly behavior.

coarseness etc. *adj.*; indecorum, misbehavior.

low-, homeli-ness; low life, *mauvais ton*, rusticity; boorishness etc. *adj.*; brutality; rowdy-, ruffian-, blackguard-ism; ribaldry; slang etc. (*neology*) 563.

bad joke, *mauvaise plaisanterie*.

[Excell of ornament] gaudi-, tawdri-ness; false ornament; finery, frippery, trickery, tinsel, gewgaw, *clinquant*.

rough diamond, tomboy, hoyden, cub, unlicked cub; clown etc. (*commonalty*) 876; Hun, Goth, Vandal, Boeotian; vulgarian; snob, cad, bounder, gent; *parvenu* etc. 876; frump, dowdy; slattern etc. 653.

V. be -vulgar etc. *adj.*; misbehave; talk –, smell of the- shop.

Adj. in bad taste, vulgar, unrefined, gutter.

coarse, indecorus, ribald, gross; unseemly, unbeseeming, unpresentable; *contra bonos mores*; ungraceful etc. (*ugly*) 846.

dowdy, slovenly etc. (*dirty*) 653; ungenteel, shabby genteel; low etc. (*plebeian*) 876;uncourtly; uncivil etc. (*discourteous*) 895; ill-bred, -mannered; underbred; ungentleman-ly, -like; unladylike, unfeminine; wild, – as an unbacked colt.

unkempt, uncombed, untamed, unlicked, unpolished, uncouth, plebeian; incondite; heavy, rude, awkward; home-ly, -spun, -bred; provincial, hick, countrified, rustic, uncultivated, freshwater; boorish, clownish; savage, brutish, blackguard, rowdy, snobbish; barbar-ous, -ic; Gothic, unclassical, doggerel, heathenish, tramontane, outlandish; Bohemian.

obsolete etc. (*antiquated*) 124; unfashionable, old-fashioned, out of date; new-fangled etc. (*unfamiliar*) 83; fantastic, odd etc. (*ridiculous*) 853.

particular; affected etc. 855; meretricious; extravagant, monstrous, horrid; shocking etc. (*painful*) 830.

gaudy, tawdry, bedizened, tricked out, gingerbread; obtrusive, flaunting, loud, flashy, garish, showy.

852. Fashion.—N. fashion, style, *ton*, *bon ton*, society; good –, polite society; drawing room, civilized life, civilization, town, *beau monde*, high life, court; world; fashionable –, gay- world; Vanity Fair; show etc. (*ostentation*) 822.

manners, breeding etc. (*politeness*) 894; air, demeanor etc. (*appearance*) 448; *savoir faire*; gentlemanliness, gentility, decorum, propriety, *bienséance*; conventions –, dictates- of society; Mrs. Grundy; convention, -ality; punctilio; form, -ality; etiquette, point of etiquette; custom etc. 613; mode, vogue, style, go; rage etc. (*desire*) 865; prevailing taste, *dernier cri*, dress etc. 225.

man –, woman- of -fashion, – the world; height –, pink –, star –, glass –, leader- of fashion; *arbiter elegantiarum* etc. (*taste*) 850; upper ten thousand etc. (*nobility*) 875; *élite* etc. (*distinction*) 873.

V. be -fashionable etc. *adj.*, – the rage etc. *n.*; have a run, pass current.

follow –, conform to –, fall in with- the fashion etc. *n.*; go with the stream etc. (*conform*) 82; *savoir -vivre*, – *faire*; keep up appearances, behave oneself.

set the –, bring into- fashion; give a tone to –, cut a figure in- society, rub shoulders with nobility, keep one's carriage.

Adj. fashionable; in -fashion etc. *n.*; *à la mode, comme il faut*; admitted –, admissible- in -society etc. *n.*; presentable, decorous, punctilious, conventional etc. (*customary*) 613; genteel; well-bred, -mannered, -behaved, -spoken; gentleman-like, -ly; ladylike; civil, polite etc. (*courteous*) 894.

polished, refined, thoroughbred, courtly; *distingué*, aristocratic, unembarrassed, poised, *dégagé*; ja-, jau-nty; dashing, fast, showy, high toned, toney.

modish, stylish, in the latest style, *recherché*; new-fangled etc. (*unfamiliar*) 83.

in -court, – full, – evening- dress; *en grande tenue* etc. (*ornament*) 847.

Adv. fashionably etc. *adj.*; for fashion's sake.

853. Ridiculousness.—N. ridiculousness etc. *adj.*; comical-, odd-ity etc. *adj.*; extravagance, drollery.

farce, comedy; burlesque etc. (*ridicule*) 856; buffoonery etc. (*fun*) 840; frippery; doggerel verses; Irish bull, Hibernianism, Hibernicism; Spoonerism; absurdity etc. 497; bombast etc. (*unmeaning*) 517; anticlimax, bathos; monstrosity etc. (*unconformity*) 83; laughing stock etc. 857.

V. be -ridiculous etc. *adj.*; pass from the sublime to the ridiculous; make one laugh; play the fool, make a fool of oneself, commit an absurdity.

play a joke on, make a -fool of, – sucker of, – monkey of.

Adj. ridiculous, ludicrous; comic, -al; droll, funny, laughable, *pour rire*, grotesque, farcical, odd; whimsical, – as a dancing bear; fanciful, fantastic, queer, rum, quizzical, waggish, quaint, *bizarre*; eccentric etc. (*unconformable*) 83; strange, outlandish, out of the way, *baroque*, *rocaille*, rococo; awkward etc. (*ugly*) 846.

absurd, extravagant, *outré*, monstrous, preposterous, bombastic, inflated, stilted, burlesque, mock heroic.

drollish; serio-, tragic-comic; gimcrack, contemptible etc. (*unimportant*) 643; doggerel; ironical etc. (*derisive*) 856; risible.

Phr. *'risum teneatis amici?' rideret Heraclitus.*

854. Fop.—N. fop, fine gentleman; swell; dand-y, -iprat; exquisite, coxcomb, toff, beau, macaroni, blade, blood, buck, man about town, fast man; fribble, jemmy, spark, popinjay, puppy, prig, *petit maître*; jacka-napes, -dandy; man milliner; Jemmy Jessamy, carpet-knight, masher, Dundreary, Johnnie, dude.

belle, fine lady, *coquette*, flirt.

855. Affectation.—N. affectation; affectedness etc. *adj.*; acting a part etc. *v.*; pretence etc. (*falsehood*) 544; (*ostentation*) 882; boasting etc. 884.

charlatanism, quakery, shallow profundity, humbug, pretension, airs, pedantry, purism, precisianism, euphuism, prunes and prisms; teratology etc. (*altiloquence*) 577.

mannerism, *simagrée*, grimace.

conceit, foppery, dandyism, man millinery, coxcombry, puppyism.

stiffness, formality, buckram; prudery, demureness, coquetry, mock modesty, *minauderie*, sentimentalism; *mauvaise honte*, false shame.

affector, performer, actor; pedant, pedagogue, *doctrinaire*, purist, euphuist, mannerist; shoneen; *grimacier*; lump of affectation, *précieuse ridicule*, *bas bleu*, blue stocking, poetaster; prig, hypocrite; charlatan etc. (*deceiver*) 548; *petit maître* etc. (*fop*) 854; flatterer etc. 935; *coquette*, prude, puritan; precisian, formalist.

V. affect, act a part, put on; give oneself airs etc. (*arrogance*) 885; boast etc. 884; coquet; simper, mince, attitudinize, strike a pose, pose; flirt a fan; over-act, -play, -do.

Adj. affected, full of affectation, pretentious, pedantic, stilted, stagey, theatrical, big-sounding, *ad captandum*, canting, insincere.

not natural, unnatural; self-conscious; *maniéré*; artificial; over-wrought, -done, -acted; euphuistic etc. 577.

stiff, starch, formal, prim, smug, demure, *tiré à quatre épingles*, quakerish, puritanical, prudish, pragmatical, priggish, conceited, coxcomical, foppish, dandified; fini-cal, -kin, -cky, mincing, simpering, namby-pamby, sentimental, languishing.

856. Ridicule.—N. ridicule, derision; sardonic -smile, – grin; irrision; snigger; scoffing etc. (*disrespect*) 929; mockery, quiz, banter, irony, *persiflage*, raillery, chaff, *badinage*; quizzing etc. *v.*

squib, satire, skit, quip, quib, grin.

parody, burlesque, travesty; farce etc. (*drama*) 599; caricature, take-off.

buffoonery etc. (*fun*) 840; practical joke, horse-play.

V. ridicule, deride; laugh at, grin at, smile at; snigger; laugh in one's sleeve; banter, rally, chaff, joke, twit, quiz, poke fun at, jolly, roast, rag; fleer; play –, play tricks- upon; fool, – to the top of one's bent; show up.

satirize, parody, caricature, burlesque, travesty.

turn into ridicule; make merry with; make -fun, – game, – a fool, – an April fool- of; rally; scoff etc. (*disrespect*) 929.

raise a laugh etc. (*amuse*) 840; play the fool, make a fool of oneself.

be ridiculous etc. 853.

Adj. deris-ory, -ive; mock; sarcastic, ironical, quizzical, burlesque, Hudibrastic; scurrilous etc. (*disrespectful*) 929.

Adv. in -ridicule etc. *n.*

857. Laughing-stock. [Object and cause of ridicule.]**—N.** laughing-, jesting-, gazing-stock; butt, game, fair game; April fool etc. (*dupe*) 547.

original, oddity; queer –, odd- fish; quiz, square toes; old –, fogey *or* fogy.

monkey; buffoon etc. (*jester*) 844; pantomimist etc. (*actor*) 599.

jest etc. (*wit*) 842.

858. Hope.—N. hope, -s; desire etc. 865; fervent hope, sanguine expectation, trust, confidence, reliance; faith etc. (*belief*) 484; affiance, assurance; secur-eness, -ity; reassurance.

good -omen, – auspices; promise; well-grounded hopes; good –, bright- prospect; clear sky.

as-, pre-sumption; anticipation etc. (*expectation*) 507.

hopefulness, buoyancy, optimism, enthusiasm, heart of grace, aspiration; optimist, utop-ian, -ist; Pollyanna.

castles in the air, *châteaux en Espagne*, hope chest, *le pot au lait*, Utopia, millennium; day –, golden- dream; dream of Alnaschar; airy hopes, fool's paradise; *mirage* etc. (*fallacies of vision*) 443; fond hope.

beam –, ray –, gleam –, glimmer –, dawn –, flash –, star- of hope; cheer; bit of blue sky, silver lining of the cloud, bottom of Pandora's box, balm in Gilead.

anchor, sheet-anchor, main-stay; staff etc. (*support*) 215; heaven etc. 981.

V. hope, trust, confide, rely on, put one's trust in, lean upon; pin one's -hope, – faith- upon etc. (*believe*) 484.

feel –, entertain –, harbor –, indulge –, cherish –, feed –, foster –, nourish –, encourage –, cling to –, live in- hope etc. *n.*; see land; feel –, rest- -assured, – confident etc. *adj.*

presume; promise oneself; expect etc. (*look forward to*) 507.

hope for etc. (*desire*) 865; anticipate.

be -hopeful etc. *adj.*; look on the bright side of, view on the sunny side, make the best of it, hope for the best; put -a good, – a bold, – the best- face upon; keep one's spirits up; take heart, – of grace; be of good -heart, – cheer; flatter oneself, lay the flattering unction to one's soul.

catch at a straw, hope against hope, count one's chickens before they are hatched.

give –, inspire –, raise –, hold out- hope etc. *n.*; raise expectations; encourage, hearten, cheer, assure, reassure, buoy up, embolden; promise, bid fair, augur well, be in a fair way, look up, flatter, tell a flattering tale.

Adj. hoping etc. *v.*; in -hopes etc. *n.*; hopeful, confident; secure etc. (*certain*) 484; sanguine, in good heart, buoyed up, buoyant, elated, flushed, exultant, enthusiastic; utopian.

unsus-pecting, -picious; fearless, free –, exempt from- -fear, – suspicion, – distrust, – despair; undespairing, self-reliant.

probable, on the high road to; within sight of -shore, – land; promising, propitious; of –, full of- promise; of good omen; auspicious, *de bon augure*; reassuring; encouraging, cheering, inspiriting, looking up, bright, roseate, *couleur de rose*, rose-colored.

Adv. hopefully etc. *adj.*

Phr. *nil desperandum*; never say die, *dum spiro spero, latet scintillula forsan*, all is for the best, *spero meliora*; the wish being father to the thought; 'hope told a flattering tale;' *rusticus expectat dum defluat amnis*.

859. Hopelessness. [Absence, want, or loss of hope.]—**N.** hopelessness etc. *adj.*; despair, desperation; despondency etc. (*dejection*) 837; pessimism.

hope deferred, dashed hopes; vain expectation etc. (*disappointment*) 509.

airy hopes etc. 858; forlorn hope; bad -job, – business; *enfant perdu*; gloomy –, black spots in the- horizon; slough of Despond, cave of Despair.

Job's comforter; bird of -bad, – ill-omen.

V. despair; lose –, give up –, abandon –, relinquish- -all hope, – the hope of; give -up, – over; yield to despair; falter; despond etc. (*be dejected*) 837; *jeter le manche après la cognée*.

inspire –, drive to- despair etc. *n.*; disconcert; dash –, crush –, shatter –, destroy- one's hopes; hope against hope.

Adj. hopeless, desperate, despairing, in despair, *au désespoir*, forlorn; inconsolable etc. (*dejected*) 837; broken-hearted.

out of the question, not to be thought of; impracticable etc. 471; past -hope, – cure, – mending, – recall; at one's last gasp etc. (*death*) 360; given -up, – over.

incurable, cureless, immedicable, remediless, beyond remedy; incorrigible; irre-parable, -mediable, -coverable, -versible, -trievable, -claimable, -deemable, -vocable; ruined, undone; immitigable.

unpromising, unpropitious; inauspicious, ill-omened, threatening, clouded over, lowering, ominous.

Phr. *'lasciate ogni speranza voi ch' entrate;'* its days are numbered; the worst come to the worst.

860. Fear.—**N.** fear, timidity, diffidence, want of confidence; apprehensive-, fearful-ness etc. *adj.*; solicitude, anxiety, care, apprehension, misgiving; mistrust etc. (*doubt*) 485; suspicion, qualm; hesitation etc. (*irresolution*) 605.

nervous-, restless-ness etc. *adj.*; in-, dis-quietude; flutter, trepidation, fear and trembling, perturbation, tremor, quivering, shaking, trembling, throbbing heart, palpitation, ague fit, cold sweat; abject fear etc. (*cowardice*) 862; mortal funk, heart-sinking, despondency; despair etc. 859.

fright; affright, -ment; alarm, pavor, dread, awe, terror, horror, dismay, consternation, panic, scare, stampede [of horses].

intimidation, terrorism, reign of terror.

[Object of fear] bug-bear, -aboo; scarecrow; hobgoblin etc. (*demon*) 980; daymare, nightmare, Gorgon, Medusa, mormo, ogre, Hurlothrumbo, raw head and bloody bones, fee faw fum, *bête noire*, *enfant terrible*.

alarmist etc. (*coward*) 862.

V. fear, stand in awe of; be -afraid etc. *adj.*; have -qualms etc. *n.*; apprehend, sit upon thorns, eye askance; distrust etc. (*disbelieve*) 485.

hesitate etc. (*be irresolute*) 605; falter, funk, cower, crouch; skulk etc. (*cowardice*) 862; let 'I dare not' wait upon 'I would;' take -fright, – alarm; start, wince, flinch, shy, shrink; fly etc. (*avoid*) 623.

tremble, shake; shiver, – in one's shoes; shudder, flutter; shake –, tremble- -like an aspen leaf, – all over; quake, quaver, quiver, quail; get the wind up.

grow –, turn- pale; blench, stand aghast; not dare to say one's soul is one's own.

inspire –, excite- -fear, – awe; raise apprehensions; give –, raise –, sound- an alarm; alarm, startle, scare, cry 'wolf,' disquiet, dismay; fright, -en; affright, terrify; astound; frighten from one's propriety; frighten out of one's -wits, – senses, – seven senses; awe; strike -all of a heap, – an awe into, – terror; harrow up the soul, appal, unman, petrify, horrify.

make one's -flesh creep, – hair stand on end, – blood run cold, – teeth chatter; chill one's spine; take away –, stop- one's breath; make one -tremble etc.

haunt, obsess, beset; prey –, weigh- on the mind.

put in -fear, – bodily fear; terrorize, intimidate, cow, daunt, over-awe, abash, deter, discourage; browbeat, bully; threaten etc. 909.

Adj. fearing etc. *v.*; frightened etc. *v.*; in -fear, – a fright etc. *n.*; haunted with the -fear etc. *n.*- of.

afraid, fearful; tim-id, -orous; nervous, diffident, coy, faint-hearted, tremulous, shaky, afraid of one's shadow, apprehensive, restless, fidgety; more frightened than hurt.

aghast; awe-, horror-, terror-, panic- -struck, -stricken; frightened to death, white as a sheet; pale, – as -death, – ashes, – a ghost; breathless, in hysterics.

inspiring fear etc. *v.*; alarming; formidable, redoubtable; perilous etc. (*danger*) 665; portentous; fear-ful, -some; dread, -ful; fell; dire, -ful; shocking; terri-ble, -fic; tremendous; horri-d, -ble, -fic; ghastly; awful, awe-inspiring, eerie, weird; revolting etc. (*painful*) 830.

Adv. *in terrorem.*

Int. 'angels and ministers of grace defend us!'

Phr. *ante tubam trepidat*; *horresco referens*, one's heart failing one, *obstupui steteruntque comae et vox faucibus haesit.*

861. Courage. [Absence of fear.]—**N.** courage, bravery, valor; resolute-, bold-ness etc. *adj.*; spirit, daring, gallantry, intrepidity; contempt –, defiance- of danger; derring-do; audacity; rashness etc. 863; dash; defiance etc. 715; confidence, self-reliance.

man-liness, -hood; nerve, pluck, mettle, game; heart, – of grace; spunk, gameness, grit, face, virtue, hardihood, fortitude; firmness etc. (*stability*) 150; heart of oak; bottom, backbone etc. (*perseverance*) 604*a*.

resolution etc. (*determination*) 604; tenacity, bull-dog courage.

prowess, heroism, chivalry.

exploit, feat, achievement; heroic -deed, – act; bold stroke.

man, – of mettle; hero, demigod, paladin, heroine, Amazon, Hector, Joan of Arc; lion, tiger, panther, bulldog; game-, fighting-cock; bully, fire-eater etc. 863; dare-devil.

V. be -courageous etc. *adj.*; dare, venture, make bold; face –, front –, affront –, confront –, brave –, defy –, despise –, mock- danger; look in the face; look -full, – boldly, – danger- in the face; face; meet, – in front; brave, beard; defy etc. 715.

take –, muster –, summon up –, pluck up- courage; nerve oneself, take heart; take –, pluck up- heart of grace; hold up one's head, screw one's courage to the sticking place; come -to, – up to- the scratch; stand, – to one's guns, – fire, – against; bear up – against; hold out etc. (*persevere*) 604*a*.

put a bold face upon; show –, present- a bold front, face the music; envisage; show fight.

bell the cat, take the bull by the horns, beard the lion in his den, march up to the cannon's mouth, go through fire and water, run the gauntlet, go over the top.

give –, infuse –, inspire- courage; reassure, encourage, embolden, inspirit, cheer, hearten, nerve, put upon one's mettle, rally, raise a rallying cry; pat on the back, make a man of, keep in countenance.

Adj. courageous, brave; val-iant, -orous; gallant, intrepid; spirit-ed, -ful; high-spirited, -mettled; mettlesome, game, plucky; man-ly, -ful; resolute; stout, -hearted; iron-, lion-hearted; heart of oak; Penthesilean.

bold, – spirited; daring, audacious; fear-, daunt-, dread-, awe-less; un-daunted, -appalled, -dismayed, -awed, -blenched, -abashed, -alarmed, -flinching, -shrinking, -blenching; apprehensive; confident, self-reliant; bold as -a lion, – brass.

enterprising, adventurous; ventur-ous, -esome; dashing, chivalrous; soldierly etc. (*warlike*) 722; heroic.

fierce, savage; pugnacious etc. (*bellicose*) 720.

strong-minded, hardy, doughty; firm etc. (*stable*) 150; determined etc. (*resolved*) 604; dogged, indomitable etc. (*persevering*) 604*a*.

up to, – the scratch; upon one's mettle; reassured etc. *v.*; unfeared, undreaded.

Phr. one's blood being up.

862. Cowardice. [Excess of fear.]—**N.** cowardice, pusillanimity; cowardliness etc. *adj.*; timidity, effeminacy.

poltroonery, baseness; dastard-ness, -y; abject fear, funk; Dutch courage; fear etc. 860; white feather, faint heart.

coward, poltroon, dastard, sneak, recreant; shy –, dunghill- cock; coistril, milksop, white-liver, nidget, cur, craven, one that cannot say 'Boo' to a goose; Bob Acres, Jerry Sneak.

alarm-, terror-, pessim-ist; runagate etc. (*fugitive*) 623; shirker.

V. quail etc. (*fear*) 860; be -cowardly etc. *adj.*, – a coward etc. *n.*; funk; cower, skulk, sneak; flinch, shy, fight shy, slink, turn tail; run away etc. (*avoid*) 623; show the white feather, have cold feet, show a yellow streak.

Adj. coward, -ly; fearful, shy; tim-id, -orous; skittish; poor-spirited, spirit-less, soft, effeminate.

weak-minded; infirm of purpose etc. 605; weak-, faint-, chicken-, lily-, pigeon-hearted; yellow; white-, lily-, milk-livered; milksop, smock-faced; unable to say 'Boo' to a goose.

dastard, -ly; base, craven, sneaking, dunghill, recreant; unwar-, unsoldier-like.

'in face a lion but in heart a deer.'

unmanned; frightened etc. 860.

Int. *sauve qui peut!* devil take the hindmost!

Adv. in fear and trembling, in fear of one's life, in a blue funk.

Phr. *ante tubam trepidat*, one's courage oozing out.

863. Rashness.—**N.** rashness etc. *adj.*; temerity, want of caution, imprudence, indiscretion; over-confidence, presumption, audacity.

precipit-ancy, -ation; impetuosity; levity; foolhardi-hood, -ness; heed-, thought-lessness etc. (*inattention*) 458; carelessness etc. (*neglect*) 460; desperation; Quixotism, knight-errantry; fire-eating.

gam-ing, -bling; blind bargain, leap in the dark, fool's paradise; too many eggs in one basket.

desperado, rashling, mad-cap, dare-devil, Hotspur, fire-eater, bully, *bravo*, Hector, scapegrace, *enfant perdu*; Don Quixote, knight-errant, Icarus; adventurer; gam-bler, -ester; dynamitard.

V. be -rash etc. *adj.*; stick at nothing, play a desperate game; run into danger etc. 665; play with -fire, – edge tools.

carry too much sail, sail too near the wind, ride at single anchor, go out of one's depth.

take a leap in the dark, buy a pig in a poke.

donner tête baissée; knock one's head against a wall etc. (*be unskilful*) 699; rush on destruction; kick against the pricks, tempt Providence, go on a forlorn hope.

count one's chickens before they are hatched; reckon without one's host; catch at straws; trust to –, lean on- a broken reed.

Adj. rash, incautious, indiscreet, injudicious; imprudent, improvident, temerarious; uncalculating; heedless; careless etc. (*neglectful*) 460; without ballast, heels over head; giddy etc. (*inattentive*) 458; wanton, reckless, wild, madcap; desperate, devil-may-care.

hot-blooded, -headed, -brained; head-long, -strong; break-neck; fool-hardy, harebrained; precipitate, impulsive.

over-confident, -weening; ventur-esome, -ous; adventurous, Quixotic; fire-eating, cavalier; free-and-easy.

off one's guard etc. (*inexpectant*) 508.

Adv. post haste, *à corps perdu*, hand over head, *tête baissée*, head- foremost; happen what may.

Phr. neck or nothing, the devil being in one.

864. Caution.—N. caution; cautiousness etc. *adj.*; discretion, prudence, cautel, heed, circumspection, calculation, deliberation; safety first.

foresight etc. 510; vigilance etc. 459; warning etc. 668.

coolness etc. *adj.*; self-possession, -command; presence of mind, *sang froid*; well-regulated mind; worldly wisdom, Fabian policy.

V. be -cautious etc. *adj.*; take -care, – heed, – good care; have a care; mind, – what one is about; be on one's guard etc. (*keep watch*) 459; make assurance double sure; ca' canny.

bespeak etc. (*be early*) 132.

think twice, look before one leaps, keep one's weather eye open, count the cost, look to the main chance, cut one's coat according to one's cloth; feel one's -ground, – way; see how the land lies etc. (*foresight*) 510; wait to see how the cat jumps; bridle one's tongue; *reculer pour mieux sauter* etc. (*prepare*) 673; let well alone, let sleeping dogs lie, *ne pas réveiller le chat qui dort*.

keep out of -harm's way, – troubled waters; keep at a respectful distance, stand aloof; keep –, be- on the safe side.

husband one's resources etc. 636.

caution etc. (*warn*) 668.

Adj. cautious, wary, guarded; on one's guard etc. (*watchful*) 459; *cavendo tutus*; *in medio tutissimus*.

care-, heed-ful; cautelous, stealthy, chary, shy of, circumspect, prudent, canny, safe, non-committal, discreet, politic; sure-footed etc. (*skilful*) 698.

unenterprising, unadventurous, cool, steady, self-possessed; over-cautious.

suspicious, leery, vigilant.

Adv. cautiously, gingerly etc. *adj.*

Int. have a care! look out! *cave canem!*

Phr. *timeo Danaos*; *festina lente*.

865. Desire.—N. desire, wish, fancy, fantasy; want, need, exigency.

mind, inclination, leaning, bent, *animus*, partiality, *penchant*, predilection; propensity etc. 820; willingness etc. 602; liking, love, fondness, relish.

longing, hankering; solicitude, anxiety; yearning, coveting; aspiration, ambition, vaulting ambition; eagerness, zeal, ardor, *empressement*, breathless impatience, over-anxiety; solicitude, impetuosity etc. 825.

appet-ite, -ition, -ence, -ency; sharp appetite, keenness, hunger, stomach, twist; thirst, -iness; drouth, mouth-watering; itch, -ing; prurience, *cacoëthes*, cupidity, lust, concupiscence.

edge of -appetite, – hunger; torment of Tantalus; sweet –, lickerish- tooth; itching palm; longing –, wistful –, sheep's-eye.

avidity; greed, -iness; covetous-, ravenous-ness etc. *adj.*; grasping, craving, canine appetite, rapacity, voracity etc. (*gluttony*) 957.

passion, rage, *furore*, mania, *manie*; inextinguishable desire; dips-, klept-, mon-omania.

[Person desiring] desirer, lover, *amateur*, votary, devotee, aspirant, solicitant, candidate; cormorant etc. 957; sycophant.

[Object of desire] *desideratum*; want etc. (*requirement*) 630; 'consummation devoutly to be wished;' attraction, magnet, allurement, fancy, temptation, seduction, lure, fascination, *prestige*, height of one's ambition, idol; whim, -sey; maggot; hobby, -horse.

Fortunatus's cap, wishing cap, love potion.

V. desire; wish, – for; be -desirous etc. *adj.*; have a -longing etc. *n.*; hope etc. 858.

care for, affect, like, list; take to, cling to, take a fancy to; fancy; prefer etc. (*choose*) 609.

have -an eye, – a mind- to; find it in one's heart etc. (*be willing*) 602; have a fancy for, set one's eyes upon; cast a sheep's eye –, look sweet- upon; take into one's head, have a heart, be bent upon; set one's -cap at, – heart upon, – mind upon, covet.

want, miss, need, lack, desiderate, feel the want of; would fain -have, – do; would be glad of.

be -hungry etc. *adj.*; have a good appetite, play a good knife and fork; hunger –, thirst –, crave –, lust –, itch –, hanker –, run mad- after; raven –, die- for; burn to.

desiderate; sigh –, cry –, gape –, gasp –, pine –, pant –, languish –, yearn –, long –, be on thorns –, hope- for; aspire after; catch at, grasp at, jump at.

woo, court, solicit; fish –, spell –, whistle –, put up- for; ogle.

cause –, create –, raise –, excite –, provoke- desire; whet the appetite; appetize, titillate, allure, attract, take one's fancy, tempt; hold out -temptation, – allurement; tantalize, make one's mouth water, *faire venir l'eau à la bouche*.

gratify desire etc. (*give pleasure*) 829.

Adj. desirous; desiring etc. *v.*; orectic, appetitive; inclined etc. (*willing*) 602; partial to; fain, wishful, optative; anxious, wistful, curious; at a loss for, sedulous, solicitous.

craving, hungry, sharp-set, peckish, ravening, with an empty stomach, esurient, lickerish, thirsty, athirst, parched with thirst, pinched with hunger, famished, dry, drouthy; hungry as a -hunter, – hawk, – horse, – church mouse.

greedy, – as a hog; over-eager, voracious; ravenous, – as a wolf; open-mouthed, covetous, rapacious, grasping, extortionate, exacting, sordid, *alieni appetens*; insati-able, -ate; unquenchable, quenchless; omnivorous.

unsatisfied, unsated, unslaked.

eager, avid, keen; burning, fervent, ardent; agog; all agog; breathless; impatient etc. (*impetuous*) 825; bent –, intent –, set- -on, – upon; mad after, *enragé*, rabid, dying for, devoured by desire.

aspiring, ambitious, vaulting, sky-aspiring.

desirable; popular; desired etc. *v.*; in demand; pleasing etc. (*giving pleasure*) 829; appeti-zing, -ble; tantalizing.

Adv. wistfully etc. *adj.*; fain.

Int. would -that, – it were! O for! *esto perpetua!* if only!

Phr. the wish being the father to the thought; *sua cuique voluptas*; *hoc erat in votis*, the mouth watering, the fingers itching; *aut Caesar aut nullus*.

866. Indifference.—N. indifference, neutrality; coldness etc. *adj.*; unconcern, *insouciance, nonchalance*; want of -interest, – earnestness; anorexy, inappetency; apathy etc. (*insensibility*) 823; supineness etc. (*inactivity*) 683; disdain etc. 930; recklessness etc. 863; inattention etc. 458.

V. be -indifferent etc. *adj.*; stand neuter; take no interest in etc. (*insensibility*) 823; have no -desire etc. 865. – taste, – relish- for; not care for; care nothing -for, – about; not care a -straw etc. (*unimportance*) 643 -about, – for; not mind.

set at naught etc. (*make light of*) 483; spurn etc. (*disdain*) 930.

Adj. indifferent, cold, frigid, lukewarm; cool, – as a cucumber; unconcerned, *insouciant*, phlegmatic, *pococurante*, easy-going, devil-may-care, careless, listless, lackadaisical, feckless; half-hearted; un-ambitious, -aspiring, -desirous, -solicitous, -attracted.

un-attractive, -alluring, -desired, -desirable, -cared for, -wished, -valued, all one to.

insipid etc. 391; vain.

Adv. for aught one cares.

Int. never mind.

867. Dislike.—N. dis-like, -taste, -relish, -inclination, -placency.

reluctance; backwardness etc. (*unwillingness*) 603.

repugnance, disgust, queasiness, turn, nausea, loathing; avers-eness, -ation, -ion; abomination, antipathy, abhorrence, horror; mortal –, rooted- antipathy, – horror; hatred, detestation; hate etc. 898; animosity etc. 900; hydrophobia.

sickener; gall and wormwood etc. (*unsavory*) 395; shuddering, cold sweat.

V. dis-, mis-like, -relish; mind, object to; have rather not, not care for; have –, conceive –, entertain –, take- -a dislike, – an aversion- to; have no -taste, – stomach- for.

shun, avoid etc. 623; eschew; withdraw –, shrink –, recoil- from; not be able to -bear, – abide, – endure; shrug the shoulders at, shudder at, turn up the nose at, look askance at; make a -mouth, – wry face, – grimace; make faces.

loathe, nauseate, abominate, detest, abhor; hate etc. 898; take amiss etc. 900; have enough of etc. (*be satiated*) 869.

cause –, excite- dislike; disincline, repel, sicken; make –, render- sick; turn one's stomach, nauseate, wamble, disgust, shock, stink in the nostrils; go against the -grain, – stomach; stick in the throat; make one's blood run cold etc. (*give pain*) 830; pall.

Adj. disliking etc. *v.*; averse to, loth, adverse; shy of, sick of, out of conceit with; disinclined; heart-, dog-sick; queasy.

disliked etc. *v.*; uncared for, unpopular; out of favor; repulsive, repugnant, repellent; abhorrent, insufferable, fulsome, nauseous; loath-some, -ful; offensive; disgusting etc. *v.*; disagreeable etc. (*painful*) 830; unsavory etc. 395.

Adv. *usque ad nauseam*.

Int. faugh! foh! ugh!

868. Fastidiousness.—N. fastidiousness etc. *adj.*; nicety, meticulosity, hypercriticism, difficulty in being pleased, *friandise*, epicurism, *omnia suspendens naso*.

discrimination, discernment, good taste, perspicacity.

epicure, gourmet.

[Excess of delicacy] prudery, prudishness, primness.

V. be -fastidious etc. *adj.*; split hairs, discriminate, have a sweet tooth.

mince the matter; turn up one's nose at etc. (*disdain*) 930; look a gift horse in the mouth, see spots on the sun.

Adj. fastidious, meticulous, exacting, nice, delicate, *délicat*, finical, finicky, difficult, dainty, lickerish, squeamish, thin-skinned; s-, queasy; hard –, difficult- to please; querulous, particular, over-particular, straitlaced, prudish, prim, scrupulous; censorious etc. 932; hypercritical, discriminating, discerning, perspicacious.

Phr. *noli me tangere*.

869. Satiety.—N. satiety, satisfaction, saturation, repletion, glut, surfeit; weariness etc. 841.

spoiled child; *enfant gâté*; too much of a good thing, *toujours perdrix*; *crambe repetita*.

V. sate, satiate, satisfy, saturate; cloy, quench, slake, pall, glut, gorge, surfeit; bore etc. (*weary*) 841; tire etc. (*fatigue*) 688; spoil.

have -enough of, – quite enough of, – one's fill, – too much of; be -satiated etc. *adj.*

Adj. satiated etc. *v.*; overgorged; *blasé*, used up, sick of, heart-sick.

Int. enough! hold! *eheu jam satis!*

870. Wonder.—N. wonder, marvel; astonish-, amaze-, wonder-, bewilder-ment; amazedness etc. *adj.*; admiration, awe; stup-or, -efaction; stound, fascination; sensation; surprise etc. (*inexpectation*) 508; cynosure.

note of admiration; thaumaturgy etc. (*sorcery*) 992.

V. wonder, marvel, admire; be -surprised etc. *adj.*; start; stare; open –, rub –, turn up- one's eyes; gloar; gape, open one's mouth, hold one's breath; look –, stand- -aghast, – agog; look blank etc. (*disappointment*) 509; *tomber des nues*; not believe one's -eyes, – ears, – senses.

not be able to account for etc. (*unintelligible*) 519; not know whether one stands on one's head or one's heels.

surprise, astonish, amaze, astound; dumbfound, -er; startle, dazzle; strike, – with -wonder, – awe; electrify; stun, stupefy, petrify, confound, bewilder, flabbergast; stagger, throw on one's beam ends, fascinate, turn the head, take away one's breath, strike dumb; make one's -hair stand on end, – tongue cleave to the roof of one's mouth; make one stare.

take by surprise etc. (*be unexpected*) 508.

be -wonderful etc. *adj.*; beggar –, baffle-description; stagger belief.

Adj. surprised etc. *v.*; aghast, all agog, breathless, agape; open-mouthed; awe-, thunder-, moon-, planet-struck; spell-bound; lost in -amazement, – wonder, – astonishment; struck all of a heap, unable to believe one's senses, like a duck in thunder.

wonderful, wondrous; surprising etc. *v.*; unexpected etc. 508; unheard of; mysterious etc. (*inexplicable*) 519; miraculous; *foudroyant*.

in-describable, -expressible, -effable; un-utterable, -speakable.

monstrous, prodigious, stupendous, marvelous; in-conceivable, -credible; in-, un-imaginable; strange etc. (*uncommon*) 83; passing strange.

striking etc. *v.*; over-whelming; wonder-working.

Adv. wonderfully etc. *adj.*; fearfully; for a –, in the name of- wonder; strange to say; *mirabile -dictu*, – visu; to one's great surprise.

with -wonder etc. *n.*, – gaping mouth, – open eyes, – upturned eyes; eyes starting out of one's head.

Int. lo, – and behold! O! hey-day! halloo! what! indeed! really! surely! humph! hem! good -lack, – heavens, – gracious! – lord! by jove! gad so! well a day! dear me! only think! lack-a-daisy! my -stars, – goodness! gracious goodness! goodness gracious! mercy on us! heavens and earth! God bless me! bless -us, – my heart! odzookens! *O gemini!* ad-zooks! hoity-toity! strong! Heaven save –, bless-the mark! can such things be! zounds! 'sdeath! what -on earth, – in the world! who would have thought it! etc. (*inexpectation*) 508; fancy! did you ever? you don't say so! what do you say to that! how now! where am I? well I'm blowed! etc.

Phr. *vox faucibus haesit*; one's hair standing on end.

871. Expectance. [Absence of wonder.]—**N.** expectan-ce, -cy etc. (*expectation*) 507; calmness, composure, tranquillity, serenity, coolness, imperturbability etc. 826.

nine days' wonder.

V. expect etc. 507; not -be surprised, – wonder etc. 870; *nil admirari*, make nothing of.

Adj. expecting etc. *v.*; unamazed, astonished at nothing; *blasé* etc. (*weary*) 841; unimaginative, calm, serene, imperturbable etc. 826; expected etc. *v.*; foreseen.

common, ordinary etc. (*habitual*) 613.

Int. no wonder; of course; why not?

872. Prodigy.—N. prodigy, phenomenon; wonder, -ment; genius, marvel, miracle; freak, monster etc. (*unconformity*) 83; curiosity, lion, infant prodigy, sight, spectacle; *jeu –*, *coup- de théâtre*; gazing-stock; sign; portent etc. 512.

bursting of a -shell, – bomb; volcanic eruption, peal of thunder; thunder-clap, -bolt.

what no words can paint; wonders of the world; *annus mirabilis*; *dignus vindice nodus*.

873. Repute.—N. distinction, mark, name, figure; repute, reputation, character; good –, high-repute; note, notability, notoriety, *éclat*, 'the bubble reputation,' vogue, celebrity; fame, famousness; renown; populairty, *aura popularis*; esteem, approval, approbation etc. 931; credit, *succès d'estime*, *prestige*, talk of the town; name to conjure with.

glory, honor; luster etc. (*light*) 420; illustriouness etc. *adj.*

account, regard, respect; reputableness etc. *adj.*; respectability etc. (*probity*) 939; good -name, – report; fair name.

dignity; stateliness etc. *adj.*; solemnity, grandeur, splendor, nobility, majesty, sublimity.

rank, standing, brevet rank, precedence, *pas*, station, place, *status*; position, – in society; order, degree, *locus standi*, caste, condition.

greatness etc. *adj.*; eminence; height etc. 206; importance etc. 642, pre-, super-eminence; high mightiness, primacy; top of the -ladder, – tree.

elevation; ascent etc. 305; super-, ex-altation; dignification, aggrandizement.

dedication, consecration, enthronement, canonization, apotheosis, deification, celebration, enshrinement, glorification.

hero, man of mark, great card, celebrity, worthy, lion, *rara avis*, notability, somebody; man of rank etc. (*nobleman*) 875; pillar of the -state, – society, – church.

chief etc. (*master*) 745; first fiddle etc. (*proficient*) 700; scholar etc. 492; cynosure, mirror; flower, pink, pearl; paragon etc. (*perfection*) 650; choice and master spirits of the age; *élite*; star, sun, constellation, galaxy.

ornament, honor, feather in one's cap, halo, aureole, nimbus; halo –, blaze- of glory; blushing honors; laurels etc. (*trophy*) 733.

memory, posthumous fame, niche in the temple of fame; immor-tality, -tal name; *magni nominis umbra*.

V. be conscious of glory; be proud of etc. (*pride*) 878; exult etc. (*boast*) 884; be vain of etc. (*vanity*) 880.

be -distinguished etc. *adj.*; shine etc. (*light*) 420; shine forth, figure; make –, cut- a -figure, – dash, – splash.

rival, surpass; out-shine, -rival, -vie, -jump; emulate, vie with, eclipse; throw –, cast- into the shade; overshadow.

live, flourish, glitter, scintillate, flaunt; gain –, acquire- honor etc. *n.*; play first fiddle etc. (*be of importance*) 642; bear the -palm, – bell; lead the way; take -precedence, – the wall of; gain –, win- -laurels, – spurs, – golden opinions etc. (*approbation*) 931; graduate, take one's degree, pass one's examination, win a -scholarship, – fellowship.

make -a, – some- -noise, – noise in the world; leave one's mark, exalt one's horn, star, have a run, be run after; enjoy popularity, come -into vogue, – to the front; raise one's head.

enthrone, signalize, immortalize, deify, exalt to the skies; hand one's name down to posterity.

consecrate; dedicate to, devote to; enshrine, inscribe, blazon, lionize, blow the trumpet, crown with laurel.

confer –, reflect- honor etc. *n.* on; shed a luster on; redound to one's honor, ennoble.

give –, do –, pay –, render- honor to; honor, accredit, pay regard to, dignify, glorify; sing praises to etc. (*approve*) 931; look up to; exalt, aggrandize, elevate, nobilitate.

Adj. distinguished, *distingué*, noted; of -note etc. *n.*; honored etc. *v.*; popular; fashionable etc. 852.

in good odor; in –, in high- favor; reput-, respect-, credit-able.

remarkable etc. (*important*) 642; notable, notorious; celebrated, renowned, in every one's mouth, talked of; fam-ous, -ed; far-famed; conspicuous, to the front; foremost; in the -front rank, – ascendant.

imperishable, deathless, immortal, never fading, *aere perennius*; time-honored.

illustrious, glorious, splendid, brilliant, radiant; bright etc. 420; full-blown; honorific.

eminent, prominent; high etc. 206; in the zenith; at the -head of, – top of the tree; peerless, of the first water; superior etc. 33; super-, pre-eminent.

great, dignified, proud, noble, honorable, worshipful, lordly, grand, stately, august, princely, imposing, solemn, transcendent, majestic, sacred, sublime, heaven-born, heroic, *sans peur et sans reproche*; sacrosanct.

Int. hail! all hail! *ave! viva! vive!* long life to! glory –, honor- be to!

Phr. one's name -being in every mouth, – living for ever; *sic itur ad astra, fama volat, aut Caesar aut nullus*; not to know him argues oneself unknown; none but himself could be his parallel, *palmam qui meruit ferat.*

874. Disrepute.—N. disrepute, discredit; ill-, bad- -repute, -name, -odor, -favor; disapprobation etc. 932; in-gloriousness, derogation; a-, debasement; abjectness etc. *adj.*; degradation, dedecoration; 'a long farewell to all one's greatness;' odium, obloquy, opprobrium, ignominy.

dishonor, disgrace; shame, humiliation; scandal, baseness, vileness; perfidy, turpitude etc. (*improbity*) 940; infamy.

tarnish, taint, defilement, pollution.

stain, blot, spot, blur, stigma, brand, reproach, imputation, slur.

crying –, burning- shame; *scandalum magnatum*, badge of infamy, blot in one's escutcheon; bend –, bar- sinister; champain, point champain; by- word of reproach; Ichabod.

argumentum ad verecundiam; sense of shame etc. 879.

V. be -inglorious etc. *adj.*; incur -disgrace etc. *n.*; have –, earn- a bad name; put –, wear- a halter round one's neck; disgrace –, expose- oneself.

play second fiddle; lose caste; pale one's ineffectual fire; recede into the shade; fall from one's high estate; keep in the background etc. (*modesty*) 881; be conscious of disgrace etc. (*humility*) 879; look -blue, – foolish, – like a fool; cut a -poor, – sorry- figure; laugh on the wrong side of the mouth; make a sorry face, go away with a flea in one's ear, slink away.

cause -shame etc. *n.*; shame, disgrace, put to shame, dishonor; throw –, cast –, fling –, reflect- dishonor etc. *n.* upon; be a -reproach etc. *n.* to; derogate from.

tarnish, stain, blot, sully, taint; discredit, degrade, debase, defile; beggar; expel etc. (*punish*) 972.

impute shame to, brand, post, stigmatize, vilify, defame, slur, cast a slur upon, hold up to shame, send to Coventry; tread –, trample- under foot; show up, drag through the mire, heap dirt upon; reprehend etc. 932.

bring low, put down, snub; take down a peg, – lower, – or two.

obscure, eclipse, outshine, take the shine out of; throw –, cast- into the shade; overshadow; leave –, put- in the background; push into a corner, put one's nose out of joint; put out, – of countenance.

upset, throw off one's center; discompose, disconcert; put to the blush etc. (*humble*) 879.

Adj. disgraced etc. *v.*; blown upon; shorn of -its beams, – one' glory; overcome, down-trodden; loaded with -shame etc. *n.*; in -bad repute etc. *n.*; out of -repute, – favor, – fashion, – countenance; at a discount; under -a cloud, – an eclipse; unable to show one's face; in the -shade, – background; out at elbows, down in the world, down and out.

inglorious; nameless, renownless, obscure, unknown to fame; un-noticed, -noted, -honored, -glorified.

shameful; dis-graceful, -creditable, -reputable; despicable; questionable; unbecoming, unworthy; derogatory; degrading, humiliating, *infra dignitatem*, dedecorous; scandalous, infamous, too bad, unmentionable; ribald, opprobrious; arrant, shocking, outrageous, notorious, shady.

ignominious, scrubby, dirty, abject, vile, beggarly, pitiful, low, mean, shabby; base etc. (*dishonorable*) 940.

Adv. to one's shame be it spoken.

Int. fie! shame! for shame! *proh pudor! O tempora! O mores!* ough! *sic transit gloria mundi!*

875. Nobility.—N. nobility, rank, condition, distinction, optimacy, blood, *pur sang*, birth, high descent, order; quality, gentility; blue blood of Castile; *ancien régime*.

high life, *haut monde*; upper -classes, – ten thousand; *élite*, aristocracy, great folks; fashionable world etc. (*fashion*) 852; salariat.

peer, -age; house of -lords, – peers; lords, – temporal and spiritual; *noblesse*; baronage, knightage; noble, -man; lord, -ling; grandee, *magnifico, hidalgo*; don, -ship; aristocrat, swell, three-tailed bashaw; gentleman, squire, squireen, patrician, laureate.

gentry, gentlefolk; squirarchy, better sort, *magnates, primates, optimates.*

king etc. (*master*) 745; prince, crown prince, *Dauphin*; duke; marquis, -ate; earl, viscount, baron, thane, banneret; baronet, -cy; knight, -hood; count, armiger, laird; sig-, seig-nior; esquire, boyar, margrave, vavasor, sheik, emir, ameer, scherif, *pasha*, effendi, sahib.

queen etc. 745; princess, begum, duchess, marchioness; countess etc.; lady, dame.

personage –, man- of -distinction, – mark, – rank; nota-bles, -bilities; celebrity, big-wig, magnate, great man, star; *magni nominis umbra*; 'every inch a king;' grand Panjandrum

V. be -noble etc. *adj.*

Adj. noble, exalted; of -rank etc. *n.*; princely, titled, patrician, aristocratic; high-, well-born; of gentle blood; genteel, *comme il faut*, gentlemanlike, courtly etc. (*fashionable*) 852; highly respectable.

Adv. in high quarters.

876. Commonalty.—N. commonalty, democracy; obscruity; low -condition, – life, – society, – company; *bourgeoisie*; mass of -the people, – society; Brown, Jones, and Robinson; Tom, Dick, and Harry; lower –, humbler- - classes, – orders; vulgar –, common- herd; rank and file, *hoc genus omne*; the -many, – general, – crowd, – people, – populace, – multitude, – million, – masses, – mobility, – peasantry; king Mob; proletariat, *fruges consumere nati*, great unwashed; man in the street

mob; rabble, – rout; chaff, rout, horde, *canaille*, scum –, *residuum* –, dregs- of -the people, – society; swinish multitude, *faex populi*; *profanum* –, *ignobile- vulgus*; vermin, riff-raff, tag-rag and bobtail; small fry.

commoner, one of the people, democrat, plebeian, republican, proletary, *prolétaire, roturier*, Mr. Snooks, *bourgeois, épicier*, Philistine, cockney; *grisette, demi-monde*.

peasant, countryman, boor, carle, churl; vill-ain, -ein; serf, kern, tyke, tike, chuff, ryot, fellah; longshoreman; swain, clown, hind; clod, -hopper; hobnail, yokel, hick, rube, cider squeezer, bog-trotter, bumpkin; ploughman, -boy; rustic, chawbacon, tiller of the soil; hewers of wood and drawers of water, groundling; gaffer, loon, put, cub, Tony Lumpkin, looby, lout, under-ling; *gamin*, guttersnipe, street arab, mudlark; rough, rowdy, ruffian, roughneck; pot-wallopper, slubberdegullion; vulgar –, low- fellow; cad, curmudgeon.

upstart, *parvenu, nouveau-riche*, skipjack; nobody, – one knows; *hesterni quirites, pessoribus orti*; *bourgeois gentilhomme*, *novus homo*, snob, gent, mushroom, no one knows who, adventurer; man of straw.

beggar, panhandler, gaberlunzie, muckworm, mudlark, *sans-culotte*, raff, tatterdemalion, caitiff, ragamuffin, Pariah, outcast of society, tramp, weary Willie, bum, vagabond, *chiffonaier*, rag-picker, Cinderella, cinderwench, scrub, jade; boots, gossoon.

Goth, Vandal, Hottentot, savage, barbarian, Yahoo; unlicked cub, rough diamond.

barbar-ousness, -ism; Boeotia.

V. be -ignoble etc. *adj.*, – nobody etc. *n.*

Adj. ignoble, common, mean, low, base, vile, sorry, scrubby, beggarly, below par; no great shakes etc. (*unimportant*) 643; home-ly, -spun; vulgar, low-minded; snobbish, *parvenu*.

plebeian, proletarian; of -low, – mean- - parentage, – origin, extraction; low-, base-, earthborn, low bred; mushroom, dunghill, risen from the ranks; unknown to fame, obscure, untitled.

rustic, uncivilized; lout-, boor-, clown-, churl-, brut-, raff-ish; rude, unlicked, unpolished.

barbar-ous, -ian, -ic, -esque; cockney, born within sound of Bow bells.

underling, menial, servile, subaltern.

Adv. below the salt.

877. Title.—N. title, honor; knighthood etc. (*nobility*) 875.

royal –, serene- highness, excellency, grace; lordship, worship, Rt. Hon., rever-ence, -end; esquire, sir; madam, *madame*; master, mistress, Mr., Mrs., *signor, señor, Mein Herr, mynheer*; your –, his- honor; handle to one's name.

decoration, laurel, palm, wreath, garland, bays, medal, ribbon, riband, blue ribbon, *cordon*, cross, crown, coronet, star, garter; feather, – in one's cap; chevron, epaulet, *épaulette*, colors, cockade; livery; order, arms, armorial bearings, shield, scutcheon, crest, reward etc. 973.

878. Pride.—N. dignity, self-respect, *mens sibi conscia recti*.

pride; haughtiness etc. *adj.*; high notions, *hauteur*; vainglory, crest; arrogance etc. (*assumption*) 885; pomposity etc. 882.

proud man, highflier; fine -gentleman, – lady; *grande dame*.

V. be -proud etc. *adj.*; put a good face on; look one in the face; stalk abroad, perk oneself up; presume, swagger, strut; rear –, lift up –, hold up- one's head; hold one's head high, look big, take the wall, 'bear like the Turk no rival near the throne,' carry with a high hand; ride the –, mount on one's- high horse; set one's back up, bridle, toss the head; give oneself airs etc. (*assume*) 885; boast etc. 884.

pride oneself on; glory in, take pride in; pique –, plume –, hug- oneself; stand upon, be proud of; put a good face on; not -hide one's light under a bushel, – put one's talent in a napkin; not think small beer of oneself etc. (*vanity*) 880.

Adj. dignified; stately; proud, -crested; lordly, baronial; lofty-minded; high-souled, -minded, - mettled, -handed, -plumed, -flown, -toned.

haughty, paughty, insolent, lofty, high, mighty, swollen, puffed up, flushed, blown; vain-glorious; purse-proud, fine; proud as -a peacock, Lucifer; bloated with pride.

supercilious, disdainful, bumptious, magisterial, imperious; high-handed, – and mighty; overweening, consequential; arrogant etc. 885; unblushing etc. 880.

stiff, -necked; starch; perked –, stuck- up; in buckram, straitlaced; prim etc. (*affected*) 855.

on one's -high horses, – tight ropes, – high ropes; on stilts; *en grand seigneur*.

Adv. with head erect, with one's nose in the air.

Phr. *odi profanum vulgus et arceo*.

879. Humility.—N. hum-ility, -bleness; meek-, low-ness; lowli-ness, -hood; abasement, self-abasement, -effacement; submission etc. 725; resignation.

condescension; affability etc. (*courtesy*) 894.
modesty etc. 881; verecundity, blush, suffusion, confusion; sense of -shame, – disgrace; humiliation, mortification; let –, set- down.
V. be -humble etc. *adj.*; deign, vouchsafe, condescend; humble –, demean- oneself; stoop, – to conquer; carry coals; submit etc. 725; submit with a good grace etc. (*brook*) 826; yield the palm.
lower one's -tone, – note; sing small, draw in one's horns, sober down; hide one's -face, – diminished head; not dare to show one's face, take shame to oneself, not have a word to say for oneself; feel –, be conscious of- -shame, – disgrace; drink the cup of humiliation to the dregs; eat -humble pie, – one's words, – dirt; be humiliated, receive a snub.
blush -for, – up to the eyes; redden, change color; color up; hang one's head, look foolish, feel small.
render humble; humble, humiliate; let –, set –, take –, tread –, frown- down; snub, abash, abase, make one sing small, strike dumb; teach one -his distance, – his place; take down a peg, – lower; throw –, cast- into the shade etc. 874; stare –, put- out of countenance; put to the blush; confuse, ashame, mortify, disgrace, crush; send away with a flea in one's ear.
get a set down.
Adj. humble, lowly, meek; modest etc. 881; humble-, sober-minded; unoffended; submissive etc. 725; servile etc. 886.
condescending; affable etc. (*courteous*) 894.
humbled etc. *v.*; bowed down, resigned; abashed, ashamed, dashed; out of countenance; down in the mouth; down on one's -knees, – marrow-bones; humbled in the dust, brow-beaten; chap-, crest-fallen; dumbfoundered, flabbergasted, struck all of a heap.
shorn of one's glory etc. (*disrepute*) 874.
Adv. with -downcast eyes, – bated breath, – bended knee; on all fours, on one's feet.
under correction, with due deference.
Phr. I am your -obedient, – very humble- servant; my service to you.

880. Vanity.—N. vanity; conceit, -edness; self-conceit, -complacency, -confidence, -sufficiency, -esteem, -love, -approbation, -praise, -glorification, -laudation, -gratulation, -applause, -admiration; *amour-propre*; selfishness etc. 943.
airs, pretensions, mannerism; egotism; prigg-ism, -ishness; coxcombery, gaudery, vainglory, elation; pride etc. 878; ostentation etc. 882; assurance etc. 885.
vox et praeterea nihil; *cheval de bataille*.
ego-ist, -tist; peacock, coxcomb etc. 854; Sir Oracle etc. 887.
V. be -vain etc. *adj.*, – vain of; pique oneself etc. (*pride*) 878; lay the flattering unction to one's soul.
have -too high, – an overweening- opinion of -oneself, – one's talents; blind oneself as to one's own merit; not think -small beer, – *vin ordinaire*- of oneself; put oneself forward; fish for compliments; give oneself airs etc. (*assume*) 885; boast etc. 884.
render -vain etc. *adj.*; inspire with -vanity etc. *n.*; inflate, puff up, turn up, turn one's head.

Adj. vain, – as a peacock; conceited, assured, overweening, pert, forward, perky; vain-glorious, high-flown; ostentatious etc. 882; puffed up, inflated, flushed.
self-satisfied, -confident, -sufficient, -flattering, -admiring, -applauding, -glorious, -opinionated; *entêté* etc. (*wrong-headed*) 481; wise in one's own conceit, pragmatical, overwise, pretentious, priggish; egotistic, -al; *soi-disant* etc. (*boastful*) 884; arrogant etc. 885.
un-abashed, -blushing; un-constrained, -ceremonious; free and easy.
Adv. vainly etc. *adj*.
Phr. how we apples swim!

881. Modesty.—N. modesty; humility etc. 879; diffidence, timidity; retiring disposition, unobtrusiveness, bashfulness etc. *adj.*; *mauvaise honte*; blush, -ing; verecundity; self-knowledge.
reserve, constraint; demureness etc. *adj.*; blushing honors.
V. be -modest etc. *adj.*; retire, reserve oneself; give way to; draw in one's horns etc. 879; hide one's face.
keep -private, – in the background, – one's distance; pursue the noiseless tenor of one's way, 'do good by stealth and blush to find it fame,' hide one's light under a bushel, cast a sheep's eye.
Adj. modest, diffident; humble etc. 879; timid, timorous, bashful; shy, nervous, skittish, coy, sheepish, shamefaced, blushing, over-modest.
unpreten-ding, -tious; un-obtrusive, -assuming, -ostentatious, -boastful, -aspiring; poor in spirit.
out of countenance etc. (*humbled*) 879.
reserved, constrained, demure.
Adv. humbly etc. *adj.*; quietly, privately; without -ceremony, – beat of the drum; *sans facon*.

882. Ostentation.—N. ostentation, display, show, flourish, parade, *étalage*, pomp, array, state, solemnity; dash, splash, glitter, strut, swank, side, swagger, pomposity; preten-se, -sions; showing off; fuss.
magnificence, splendor; *coup d'oeil*; grand doings.
coup de théâter; stage -effect, – trick; clap-trap; *mise en scène*; *tour de force*; *chic*.
demonstration, flying colors; tomfoolery; flourish of trumpets etc. (*celebration*) 883; pageant, -ry; spectacle, exhibition, procession; turn –, set- out; grand function; *fête*, gala, field-day, review, march past, promenade, insubstantial pageant.
dress; court –, full –, evening –, ball –, fancy- dress; tailoring, millinery, man-millinery, frippery; foppery, equipage.
ceremon-y, -ial; ritual; form, -ality; etiquette; punct-o, -ilio, -ilious-ness; starched-, stateli-ness.
mummery, solemn mockery, mouth honor.
attitudinarian; fop etc. 854.
V. be -ostentatious etc. *adj.*; come –, put oneself- forward; attract attention, star it.
make –, cut- a -figure, – dash, – splash; strut, blow one's own trumpet; figure, – away; make a show, – display; glitter.
show -off, – one's paces; parade, march past;

display, exhibit, put forward, hold up; trot –, hang- out; sport, brandish, blazon forth; dangle, – before the eyes.

cry up etc. (*praise*) 931; *prôner*, flaunt, emblazon, prink, set off, mount, have framed and glazed.

put a good, – smiling- face upon; clean the outside of the platter etc. (*disguise*) 544.

Adj. ostentatious, showy, dashing, pretentious, ja-, jau-nty; grand, pompous, palatial; high-sounding; turgid etc. (*big-sounding*) 577; garish, gorgeous; gaudy, – as a -peacock, – butterfly, – tulip; flaunting, flashing, flaming, glittering; gay etc. (*ornate*) 847; colorful.

splendid, magnificent, sumptuous.

theatrical, dramatic, spectacular, scenic, ceremonial, ritual, -istic.

solemn, stately, majestic, formal, stiff, ceremonious, punctilious, starch-ed, -y.

en grande tenue, in best bib and tucker, in Sunday best, *endimanché*.

Adv. with -flourish of trumpet, – beat of drum, – flying colors, – a brass band.

ad captandum vulgus.

883. Celebration.—N. celebration solemnization, jubilee, diamond jubilee, commemoration, ovation, paean, triumph, jubilation.

triumphal arch, bonfire, salute; salvo, – of artillery; *feu de joie*, flourish of trumpets, *fanfare*, colors flying, illuminations, fireworks.

inauguration, installation, presentation; *début*, coming out, birthday anniversary, bi-, ter-, centenary; silver –, golden –, diamond- wedding, -day; coronation; Lord Mayor's show; harvest home, red letter day, festival; trophy etc. 733; *Te Deum* etc. (*thanksgiving*) 990; fête etc. 882; holiday etc. 840.

V. celebrate, keep, signalize, do honor to, commemorate, solemnize, hallow, mark with a red letter, hold high festival, maffick.

pledge, drink to, toast, hob and nob.

inaugurate, install, instate, induct, chair.

rejoice etc. 838; kill the fatted calf, hold jubilee, roast an ox, fire a salute.

Adj. celebrating etc. *v.*; commemorative, celebrated, immortal.

Adv. in -honor, – commemoration, – celebration of.

Int. hail! all hail! *io -paean, – triumphe!* 'see the conquering hero comes!'

884. Boasting.—N. boasting etc. *v.*; boast, vaunt, crake; preten-ce, -sions; puff, -ery; flourish, *fanfaronnade*; gasconade; bluff, swank, brag, -gardism; bravado, bunkum, Buncombe; highfalutin; jact-itation, -ancy; bounce, rant, bluster; venditation, vaporing, rodomontade, bombast, fine talking, tall talk, magniloquence, teratology, heroics; jingoism, Chauvinism; exaggeration etc. 549; gas, hot air.

vanity etc. 880; *vox et praeterea nihil*; much cry and little wool, *brutum fulmen*.

exultation; glorification; flourish of trumpets; triumph etc. 883.

boaster; bragg-art, -adocio; hot air merchant; Gascon, *fanfaron*, pretender, fourflusher, *soi-disant*; windbag, blowhard, bluffer; chauvinist; blusterer etc. 887; charlatan, jack-pudding, trumpeter; puppy etc. (*fop*) 854.

V. boast, make a boast of, brag, vaunt, puff, show off, flourish, crake, crack, trumpet, strut, swagger, vapor, bluff; draw the long bow.

exult, crow over, neigh, chuckle, triumph; glory, gloat, jubilate; throw up one's cap; talk big, *se faire valoir*, *faire claquer son fouet*, take merit to oneself, make a merit of, sing *Io triumphe*, holloa before one is out of the wood.

Adj. boasting etc. *v.*; magniloquent, flaming, Thrasonic, stilted, gasconading, braggart, boastful, pretentious, *soi-disant*; vain-glorious etc. (*conceited*) 880.

elate, -d; jubilant, triumphant, exultant; in high feather; flushed, – with victory; cock-a-hoop; on stilts.

vaunted etc. *v.*

Adv. vauntingly etc. *adj.*; with a brass band.

Phr. 'let the galled jade wince.'

885. Insolence. [Undue assumption of superiority.]—**N.** insolence; haughtiness etc. *adj.*; arrogance, airs; overbearance, brashness, bumptiousness, contumely, disdain; domineering etc. *v.*; tyranny etc. 739.

impertinence; cheek, nerve, sauce; sauciness etc. *adj.*; flippancy, dicacity, petulance, procacity, bluster; swagger, -ing etc. *v.*; bounce; terrorism; jingoism, chauvinism.

as-, pre-sumption; beggar on horseback; usurpation.

impudence, assurance, audacity, self-assertion, hardihood, front, face, brass; shamelessness etc. *adj.*; effrontery, hardened front, face of brass.

assumption of infallibility.

malapert, saucebox etc. (*blusterer*) 887.

V. be -insolent etc. *adj.*; bluster, vapor, swagger, swell, give oneself airs; snap one's fingers, kick up a dust; swear etc. (*affirm*) 535; rap out oaths; roister.

arrogate; as-, pre-sume; make -bold, – free; take a liberty, give an inch and take an ell.

domineer, bully, dictate, hector; lord it over, bulldoze; *traiter de haut*, *regarder de haut en bas*; exact; snub, huff, beard, fly in the face of; put to the blush; bear –, beat- down; browbeat, intimidate; trample –, tread- -down, – under foot; dragoon, ride roughshod over, terrorize.

out-face, -look, -stare, -brazen, -brave; stare out of countenance; brazen out; lay down the law; teach one's grandmother to suck eggs; assume a lofty bearing; talk –, look- big; put on big looks, act the *grand seigneur*; mount –, ride- the high horse; toss the head, carry with a high hand.

tempt Providence, want snuffing.

Adj. insolent, haughty, arrogant, imperious, magisterial, dictatorial, arbitrary; high-handed, high and mighty; contumelious, supercilious, overbearing, intolerant, domineering; overweening, high-flown.

flippant, pert, cavalier, saucy, forward, impertinent, fresh, malapert.

precocious, assuming, would-be, bumptious.

bluff; brazen-, browed-faced, shameless, aweless, unblushing, unabashed; bold-, bare-faced; dead –, lost- to shame.

impudent, audacious, presumptuous, free and easy, devil-may-care, rollicking; janty, jaunty; roistering, blustering, hectoring, swaggering, vaporing; thrasonic, fire-eating, 'full of sound and fury.'

Adv. insolently, with a high hand; *ex cathedrâ*.

Phr. one's bark being worse than his bite.

886. Servility.—N. servility; slavery etc. (*subjection*) 749; obsequiousness etc. *adj.*; subserviency; abasement; pros-tration, -ternation; genuflexion etc. (*worship*) 990; fawning etc. *v.*; tuft-hunting, time-serving, flunkeyism; sycophancy etc. (*flattery*) 933; humility etc. 879.

sycophant, parasite, yes-man; toad, -y, -eater; tuft-hunter; snob, flunkey, lap-dog, spaniel, lickspittle, smell-feast, *Graeculus esuriens*, hanger on, stooge, *cavaliere servente*, led captain, carpet knight; time-server, fortune-hunter, Vicar of Bray, Sir Pertinax Mac Sycophant, pick-thank; flatterer etc. 935; doer of dirty work; *âme damnée*, tool; reptile; slave etc. (*servant*) 746; courtier; sponge, jackal; truckler.

V. cringe, bow, stoop, kneel, bend the knee; fall on one's knees, prostrate oneself; worship etc. 990.

sneak, crawl, crouch, cower, truckle to, grovel, fawn, toady, lick the feet of, kiss the hem of one's garment.

pay court to; feed –, fatten –, batten- on; dance attendance on, pin oneself upon, hang on the sleeve of, *avaler des couleuvres*, keep time to, fetch and carry, do the dirty work of.

go with the stream, follow the crowd, worship the rising sun, hold with the hare and run with the hounds.

Adj. servile, obsequious; supple, – as a glove; soapy, oily, pliant, cringing, fawning, slavish, groveling, sniveling, mealy-mouthed; beggarly, sycophantic, parasitical; abject, prostrate, down on one's marrow-bones; base, mean, sneaking; crouching etc. *v.*

Adv. hat –, cap- in hand.

887. Blusterer.—N. bluster-, swagger-, vapor-, roister-, brawl-er; brazen-face; *fanfaron*; braggart etc. (*boaster*) 884; bully, terrorist, rough, roughneck; hooligan, hoodlum, larrikin, ruffian; Mohock, -hawk; drawcansir, swashbuckler, Captain Boabdil, Sir Lucius O'Trigger, Thraso, Pistol, Parolles, Bombastes Furioso, Hector, Chrononhotonthologos; jingo; desperado, dare-devil, fire-eater; fury etc. (*violent person*) 173; rowdy.

puppy etc. (*fop*) 854; prig; Sir Oracle, dogmatist, *doctrinaire*, stump orator, jack-in-office; saucebox, malapert, jackanapes, minx; bantam-cock.

888. Friendship.—N. friendship, amity; friendliness etc. *adj.*; brotherhood, fraternity, sodality, confraternity, sorosis, sisterhood; harmony etc. (*concord*) 714; peace etc. 721.

firm –, staunch –, intimate –, familiar –, bosom –, cordial –, tried –, devoted –, lasting –, fast –, sincere –, warm –, ardent- friendship.

cordiality, fraternization, *entente cordiale*, good understanding, *rapprochement*, sympathy, fellow-feeling, response, welcomeness; *camaraderie*.

affection etc. (*love*) 897; favoritism; goodwill etc. (*benovolence*) 906; partiality.

acquaintance, familiarity, intimacy, intercourse, fellowship, knowledge of; introduction.

V. be -friendly etc. *adj.*, – friends etc. 890; – acquainted with etc. *adj.*; know; have the ear of; keep- company with etc. (*sociality*) 892; hold communication –, have dealings –, sympathize- with; have a leaning to; bear good will etc. (*benevolence*) 906; love etc. 897; make much of; befriend etc. (*aid*) 707; introduce to.

set one's horses together; hold out –, extend the right hand of -friendship, – fellowship; become -friendly etc. *adj.*; make -friends etc. 890 with; break the ice, be introduced to; make –, pick –, scrape- acquaintance with; get into favor, gain the friendship of.

shake hands with, fraternize, embrace; receive with open arms, throw oneself into the arms of; meet half way, take in good part.

Adj. friendly, amic-able, -al; well affected, unhostile, neighborly, brotherly, fraternal, sisterly, sympathetic, harmonious, hearty, cordial, warm-hearted, devoted.

friends –, well –, at home –, hand in hand- with; on -good, – friendly, – amicable, – cordial, – familiar, – intimate- -terms, – footing; on -speaking, – visiting- terms; in one's good -graces, – books.

acquainted, familiar, intimate, thick, hand and glove, hail fellow well met, free and easy; welcome.

Adv. amicably etc. *adj.*; with open arms; *sans cérémonie*; arm in arm.

889. Enmity.—N. enmity, hostility; unfriendliness etc. *adj.*; discord etc. 713.

alienation, estrangement; dislike etc. 867; hate etc. 898; antagonism.

heartburning; animosity etc. 900; malevolence etc. 907.

V. be -inimical etc. *adj.*; keep –, hold- at arm's length; be at loggerheads; bear malice etc. 907; fall out; take umbrage etc. 900; harden the heart, alienate, estrange.

Adj. inimical, unfriendly, hostile; at -enmity, – variance, – swords points, – daggers drawn, – open war with; up in arms against; in bad odor with.

on bad –, not on speaking- terms; cool; cold, -hearted; estranged, alienated, disaffected, irreconcilable.

890. Friend.—N. friend, – of one's bosom, intimate acquaintance, neighbor, well-wisher; *alter ego*; best –, bosom –, fast- friend; *amicus usque ad aras*; *fidus Achates*; *persona grata*.

favorer, *fautor*, patron, backer, Maecenas; tutelary saint, good genius, advocate, partisan, sympathizer; ally; friend in need etc. (*auxiliary*) 711.

associate, compeer, comrade, mate, companion, *confrère, camarade*, *confidante*, colleague; old –, crony; side-kick; chum, buddy, bunkie, roommate, pal; play-fellow, -mate; classmate, schoolfellow; bed-fellow, -mate; maid of honor.

compatriot; fellow –, countryman, – townsman.

shop-, ship-, mess-mate; fellow –, boon –, pot-companion; co-partner.

Arcades ambo, Pylades and Orestes, Castor and Pollux, Nisus and Euryalus, Damon and Pythias, *par nobile fratrum*.

host, Amphitryon, Boniface; guest, visitor, frequenter, *habitué*; *protégé*.

891. Enemy.—N. enemy; antagonist, foeman; open –, bitter- enemy; opponent etc. 710; back friend.

public enemy, enemy to society, traitor, anarchist etc. 743.

Phr. every hand being against one.

892. Sociality.—N. soci-ality, -ability, -ableness etc. *adj.*; social intercourse; consociation; intercourse, -community; consort-, companion-, fellow-, comrade-ship; clubbism; *esprit de corps*.

conviviality; good -fellowship, – company, *camaraderie*; joviality, jollity, *savoir -vivre*, festivity, festive board, merry-making; loving cup; hospitality, heartiness; cheer.

welcome, -ness; greeting; hearty –, warm –, welcome- reception; urbanity etc. (*courtesy*) 894; intimacy, familiarity.

good –, jolly- fellow, good mixer, Rotarian; *bon enfant*.

social –, family- circle; circle of acquaintance, *coterie*, society, company.

social -gathering, – *réunion*; assembly etc. (*assemblage*) 72; party, entertainment, reception, *levée*, at home, *conversazione*, *soirée*, *matinée*, evening –, morning –, afternoon –, garden –, dinner –, tea –, cocktail- party; symposium, singsong; kettle-, drum; *partie carrée*, dish of tea, *ridotto*, rout, housewarming; ball, prom, hop, dance, *thé dansant*; festival etc. (*amusement*) 840; wedding breakfast; 'the feast of reason and the flow of soul.'

visit, -ing; round of visits; call, morning call; interview etc. (*interlocution*) 588; assignation; tryst, -ing place; appointment.

club etc. (*association*) 712.

V. be -sociable etc. *adj.*; know; be -acquainted etc. *adj.*; associate –, sort –, keep company –, walk hand in hand -with; eat off the same trencher, club together, consort, bear one company, join; make acquaintance with etc. (*friendship*) 888; make advances, fraternize, embrace; intercommunicate.

be –, feel –, make oneself- at home with; make free with; crack a bottle with; take pot luck with, receive hospitality, live at free quarters.

visit, pay a visit; interchange -visits, – cards; call -at, – upon; leave a card; drop in, look in; look one up, beat up one's quarters.

entertain; give a -party etc. *n.*; be at home, see one's friends, hang out, keep open house, do the honors; receive, – with open arms; welcome; give a warm reception etc. *n.* to; kill the fatted calf.

Adj. sociable, companionable, clubbable, clubby, conversable, cosy, cosey, chatty, conversational; homiletical.

convivial; fest-ive, -al; jovial, jolly, hospitable.

welcome, – as the roses in May; *fêté*, entertained.

free and easy, hail fellow well met, familiar, on visiting terms, acquainted.

social, neighborly; international, cosmopolitan, gregarious.

Adv. *en famille*, in the family circle; *sans -façon*, – *cérémonie*, arm in arm.

893. Seclusion. Exclusion.—N. seclusion, privacy; retirement; concealment; reclusion, recess; snugness etc. *adj.*; delitescence; rustication, *rus in urbe*; solitude; solitariness etc. (*singleness*) 87; isolation; loneliness etc. *adj.*; estrangement from the world, anchoritism, voluntary exile; aloofness.

cell, hermitage; convent etc. 1000; *sanctum sanctorum*; study, library, den; hide-out.

depopulation, desertion, desolation; wilderness etc. (*unproductive*) 169; howling wilderness; rotten borough, Old Sarum.

exclusion, excommunication, banishment, exile, ostracism, proscription; cut, – direct; dead cut.

inhospit-ality, -ableness etc. *adj.*; un-, dissociability; domesticity, Darby and Joan.

recluse, hermit, eremite, cenobite; anchor-et, -ite; Simon Stylites; Troglodyte, Timon of Athens, Santon, *solitaire*, ruralist, disciple of Zimmermann, closet cynic, Diogenes; outcast, Pariah, castaway, outsider, pilgarlic; wastrel, foundling, orphan.

V. be –, live- secluded etc. *adj.*; keep –, stand –, hold oneself aloof, – in the background; keep snug; shut oneself up; deny –, seclude- oneself; creep into a corner, rusticate, *aller planter ses choux*; retire, – from the world; hermetize, take the veil; abandon etc. 624.

cut, – dead; refuse to -associate with, – acknowledge; look cool –, turn one's back –, shut the door- upon; repel, blackball, excommunicate, exclude, exile, expatriate; banish, outlaw, maroon, ostracize, proscribe, cut off from, send to Coventry, keep at arm's length, draw a cordon round; boycott, blockade, lay an embargo on, isolate.

depopulate; dis-, un-people.

Adj. secluded, sequestered, retired, delitescent, private, bye; out of the -world, -way; in a backwater; 'the world forgetting by the world forgot.'

snug, domestic, stay-at-home.

unsociable; un-, dis-social; inhospitable, cynical, inconversable, unclubbable, *sauvage*, eremetic.

solitary; lone-ly, -some; isolated, single.

excluded, estranged; unfrequented; uninhabitable, -ed; tenantless; un-tenanted, -occupied; abandoned; deserted, – in one's utmost need; unfriended; kith-, friend-, home-less; lorn, forlorn, desolate.

un-visited, -introduced, -invited, -welcome; under a cloud, left to shift for oneself, derelict, outcast, outside the gates.

banished etc. *v.*; under an embargo.

Phr. *noli me tangere*.

894. Courtesy.—N. courtesy; respect etc. 928; good -manners, – behavior, – breeding; manners; politeness etc. *adj.*; *bienséance*, urbanity, comity, gentility; gentle –, breeding; polish, presence, cultivation, culture; civili-ty, -zation; amenity, suavity; good -temper, – humor; amiability, easy temper, complacency, soft tongue, mansuetude; condescension etc. (*humility*) 879; affability, complaisance, *prévenance*, amiability, gallantry, chivalry; pink of -politeness, – courtesy.

compliment; fair –, soft –, sweet- words; honeyed phrases, flattering remarks, ceremonial; salutation, reception, presentation, introduction, *accueil*, greeting, recognition; welcome, *abord*, respects, *devoir*, regards, remembrances; kind -regards, – remembrances; love, best love, duty; deference.

obeisance etc. (*reverence*) 928; bow, courtesy, curtsy, scrape, *salaam*, *kow-tow*, bowing and scraping; kneeling; genuflexion etc. (*worship*) 990; obsequiousness etc. 886; capping, shaking hands etc. *v.*; grip of the hand, embrace, hug, squeeze, *accolade*, loving cup, *vin d'honneur*, pledge; love token etc. (*endearment*) 902; kiss, buss, salute.

mark of recognition, not; 'nods and becks and wreathed smiles;' valediction etc. 293; condolence etc. 915.

V. be -courteous etc. *adj.*; show -courtesy etc. *n.*

mind one's P's and Q's, behave oneself, be all things to all men, conciliate, speak one fair, take in good part; make –, do- the amiable; look as if butter would not melt in one's mouth; mend one's manners.

receive, do the honors, usher, greet, hail, bid welcome; welcome, – with open arms; shake hands; hold out –, press –, squeeze- the hand; bid God speed; speed the parting guest; cheer, serenade.

salute; embrace etc. (*endearment*) 902; kiss, – hands; drink to, pledge, hob and nob; move to, nod to; smile upon.

uncover, cap; touch –, take off- the hat; doff the cap; pull the forelock; present arms; make way for; bow; make one's bow; scrape, curtsy, courtesy; bob a -curtsy, – courtesy; kneel; bow –, bend- the knee; salaam, *kowtow*.

visit, wait upon, present oneself, pay one's respects, pay a visit etc. (*sociability*) 892; dance attendance on etc. (*servility*) 886; pay attentions to; do homage to etc. (*respect*) 928.

prostrate oneself etc. (*worship*) 990.

give –, send- one's duty etc. *n.* to.

render -polite etc. *adj.*; polish, civilize, humanize.

Adj. courteous, polite, civil, mannerly, urbane; well-behaved, -mannered, -bred, -brought up, gently bred, of gentle -breeding, – manners, good-mannered, polished, civilized, cultivated; refined etc. (*taste*) 850; gentlemanlike etc. (*fashion*) 852; gallant, chivalrous, on one's good behavior.

fine –, fair –, soft- spoken; honey-mouthed, -tongued; oily, unctuous, bland, suave; obliging, conciliatory, complaisant, complacent; obsequious etc. 886.

ingratiating, winning; gentle, mild; good-humored, cordial, gracious, amiable, tactful, addressful, affable, genial, friendly, familiar; neighborly.

Adv. courteously etc. *adj.*; with a good grace; with -open, – outstretched- arms; *à bras ouverts*; *suaviter in modo*, in good humor.

Int. hail! welcome! well met! *ave!* all hail! good -day, – morning etc., – morrow! God speed! *pax vobiscum!* may your shadow never be less! *chin-chin!*

895. Discourtesy.—N. discourtesy; ill-breeding; ill –, bad –, ungainly- manners; insuavity; grouchiness; un-courteousness etc. *adj.*, tactlessness; rusticity, inurbanity; illiberality, incivility, displacency.

disrespect etc. 929; procacity, impudence; barbar-ism, -ity; misbehavior, brutality, blackguard-ism, conduct unbecoming a gentleman, *grossièreté*, *brusquerie*; vulgarity etc. 851.

churlishness etc. *adj.*; spinosity, perversity; moroseness etc. (*sullenness*) 901*a*.

bad-, ill-temper; sternness etc. *adj.*; austerity; moodishness, captiousness etc. 901; cynicism; tartness etc. *adj.*; acrimony, acerbity, virulence, asperity.

scowl, black looks, frown; short answer, rebuff; hard words, contumely; unparliamentary language, personality.

bear, bruin, brute, grouch, blackguard, beast; unlicked cub; frump, cross-patch; saucebox etc. 887.

V. be -rude etc. *adj.*; insult etc. 929; treat with discourtesy; take a name in vain; make -bold, – free- with; take a liberty; stare out of countenance, ogle, point at, put to the blush.

cut; turn -one's back upon, – on one's heel; give the cold shoulder; keep at -a distance, – arm's length; look -cool, – coldly, – black- upon; show the door to, send away with a flea in the ear.

lose one's temper etc. (*resentment*) 900; sulk etc. 901*a*; frown, scowl, glower, pout; snap, snarl, growl.

render -rude etc. *adj.*; brut-alize, -ify.

Adj. dis-, un-courteous; uncourtly; ill-bred, -mannered, -behaved, -conditioned; unbred; unmanner-ly, -ed; im-, un-polite; un-polished, -civilized, -genteel; ungentleman-like, -ly; unladylike; blackguard; vulgar etc. 851; dedecorous; foul-mouthed, -spoken; abusive.

un-civil, -gracious, -ceremonious; cool; pert, forward, obtrusive, impudent, rude, saucy, precocious; insolent etc. 885.

repulsive; un-complaisant, -accommodating, -neighborly, -gallant; inaffable; un-gentle, -gainly; rough, rugged, bluff, blunt, gruff; churl-, boor-, bear-ish; brutal, *brusque*; stern, harsh, austere; cavalier.

tart, sour, crabbed, sharp, short, trenchant, sarcastic, crusty, biting, caustic, virulent, bitter, acrimonious, venomous, contumelious; snarling etc., *v.*; surly, – as a bear; perverse; grim, sullen etc. 901*a*; peevish etc. (*irascible*) 901.

Adv. discourteously etc. *adj.*; with -discourtesy etc. *n.*, – a bad grace.

896. Congratulations.—N. con-, gratulation; felicitation; salute etc. 894; condolence etc. 915; compliments of the season; good –, best- wishes.

V. con-, gratulate; felicitate, compliment; give –, wish one- joy; tender –, offer- one's congratulations; wish -many happy returns of the day, – a merry Christmas and a happy new year.

congratulate oneself etc. (*rejoice*) 838.

Adj. con-, gratulatory.

897. Love.—N. love; fondness etc. *adj.*; liking; inclination etc. (*desire*) 865; regard, dilection, admiration, fancy.

affection, sympathy, fellow-felling; tenderness etc. *adj.*; heart, brotherly love; benevolence etc. 906; attachment.

yearning, tender passion, *affaire de coeur*, *amour*, gallantry, passion, flame, devotion, fervor, enthusiasm, transport of love, rapture, enchantment, infatuation, adoration, idolatry.

narcissism, Oedipus complex, Electra complex.

Cupid, Venus, Eros; myrtle; true lover's knot; love -token, – suit, – affair, – tale, – story; the old story, plighted love; courtship etc. 902; *amourette*.

maternal love.

attractiveness, charm; popularity; favorite etc. 899.

lover, suitor, follower, admirer, adorer, wooer, amoret, beau, sweetheart, inamorato, swain, young man, flame, love, truelove; leman, Lothario, gallant, paramor, *amoroso*, *cavaliere servente*, captive, *cicisbeo*; *caro sposo*, Don Juan, sheik, ladies' man, squire of dames, Knave of Hearts.

inamorata, lady-love, idol, darling, duck, Dulcinea, angel, goddess, *cara sposa*; mistress.

betrothed, affianced, *fiancée*.

flirt, *coquette*; amorette; pair of turtle doves; abode of love, *agapemone*.

V. love, like, affect, fancy, care for, take an interest in, be partial to, sympathize with; be -in love etc. *adj.* with; have –, entertain –, harbor –, cherish- a -love etc. *n.* for; regard, revere; take to, bear love to, be wedded to; set one's affections on; make much of, feast one's eyes on; hold dear, prize, treasure; hug, cling to, cherish, pet, caress etc. 902.

burn; adore, idolize, love to distraction, *aimer eperdument*; dote -on, – upon.

take a fancy to, fall for, be stuck on, look sweet upon; become -enamored etc. *adj.*; fall in love with, lose one's heart; desire etc. 865.

excite love; win –, gain –, secure –, engage- the -love, – affections, – heart; take the fancy of; have a place in –, wind round- the heart; attract, attach, endear, charm, fascinate, captivate, bewitch, seduce, enamor, enrapture, turn the head.

get into favor; ingratiate –, insinuate –, worm- oneself; propitiate, curry favor with, pay one's court to, make a date with, *faire l'aimable*, set one's cap at, flirt, coquet.

Adv. loving etc. *v.*; fond of; taken –, struck- with; smitten, bitten; attached to, wedded to; enamored; charmed etc. *v.*; in love; lovesick; over head and ears in love.

affectionate, tender, sweet upon, sympathetic, loving, fond, amorous, amatory; erotic, uxurious, ardent, passionate, rapturous, devoted, motherly.

loved etc. *v.*; beloved; well –, dearly- beloved; dear, precious, darling, pet, little; favorite, popular.

congenial; to –, after- one's -mind, – taste, – fancy, – own heart.

in one's good -graces etc. (*friendly*) 888; dear as the apple of one's eye, nearest to one's heart.

lovable, adorable; lovely, sweet; attractive, seductive, winning; charming, engaging, interesting, enchanting, captivating, fascinating, intriguing, bewitching; amiable, like an angel, angelic, seraphic.

898. Hate.—N. hate, hatred, vials of hate; Hymn of Hate.

dis-affection, -favor; alienation, estrangement, coolness; enmity etc. 889; animosity etc. 900.

umbrage, pique, grudge; dudgeon, spleen; bitterness, – of feeling; ill –, bad- blood; acrimony; malice etc. 907; implacability etc. (*revenge*) 919.

repugnance etc. (*dislike*) 867; odium, unpopularity; loathing, detestation, antipathy; object of -hatred, – execration; abomination, aversion, *bête noire*; enemy etc. 891; bitter pill; source of annoyance etc. 830.

V. hate, detest, abominate, abhor, loathe; recoil –, shudder- at; shrink from, view with horror, hold in abomination, revolt against, execrate; scowl etc. 895; disrelish etc. (*dislike*) 867.

owe a grudge; bear -spleen, – a grudge, – malice etc. (*malevolence*) 907; conceive an aversion to.

excite –, provoke- hatred etc. *n.*; be -hateful etc. *adj.*; stink in the nostrils; estrange, alienate, repel, set against, sow dissension, set by the ears, envenom, incense, irritate, rile, ruffle, vex; horrify etc. 830.

Adj. hating etc. *v.*; abhorrent; averse from etc. (*disliking*) 867; set against.

bitter etc. (*acrimonious*) 895; implacable etc. (*revengeful*) 919.

un-loved, -beloved, -lamented, -deplored, -mourned, -cared for, endured, -valued; disliked etc. 867.

crossed in love, forsaken, rejected, love-lorn, jilted.

obnoxious, hateful, odious, abominable, repulsive, offensive, shocking; disgusting etc. (*disagreeable*) 830.

invidious, spiteful; malicious etc. 907.

insulting, irritating, provoking.

[Mutual hate] at -daggers drawn, – swords points; not on speaking terms etc. (*enmity*) 889.

Phr. no love lost between.

899. Favorite.—N. favorite, pet, cosset, minion, idol, jewel, spoiled child, *enfant gâté*; led captain; crony; fondling; apple of one's eye, man after one's own heart; *persona grata*.

love, dear, darling, duck, honey, jewel; mopsey, moppet; sweetheart etc. (*love*) 897.

general –, universal- favorite; idol of the people; matinée idol, movie –, radio- star.

900. Resentment.—N. resentment, displeasure, animosity, anger, wrath, indignation; vexation, exasperation, bitter resentment, wrathful indignation.

pique, umbrage, huff, miff, soreness, dudgeon, acerbity, virulence, bitterness, acrimony, asperity, spleen, gall; heart-burning, -swelling; rankling.

ill –, bad- -humor, – temper; irascibility etc. 901; ill blood etc. (*hate*) 898; revenge etc. 919.

excitement, irritation; warmth, bile, choler, ire, fume, pucker, dander, ferment, ebullition; towering -passion, – rage, *acharnement*, angry mood, taking, pet, tiff, passion, fit, tantrums.

burst, explosion, paroxysm, storm, rage, fury, desperation; violence etc. 173; fire and fury; vials of wrath; gnashing of teeth, hot blood, high words.

scowl etc. 895; sulks etc. 901*a*.

[Cause of umbrage] affront, provocation, offence; indignity etc. (*insult*) 929; grudge, crow to pluck, sore subject; red rag to a bull; *casus belli.*

Furies, Erinys, Eumenides, Alecto, Megaera, Tisiphone.

buffet, slap in the face, box on the ear, rap on the knuckles.

V. resent; take -amiss, – ill, – to heart, – offence, – umbrage, – huff, – exception; take in -ill part, – bad part, – dudgeon; *ne pas entendre raillerie*; breathe revenge, cut up rough.

fly –, fall –, get- into a -rage, – passion; bridle –, bristle –, froth –, fire –, flare- up; open –, pour out- the vials of one's wrath.

pout, knit the brow, frown, scowl, lower, snarl, growl, gnarl, gnash, snap; redden, color; look -black, – black as thunder, – daggers; bite one's thumb; show –, grind- one's teeth; champ the bit.

chafe, mantle, fume, kindle, fly out, take fire; boil, – over; boil with -indignation, – rage; rage, storm, foam; vent one's -rage, – spleen; lose one's temper, stand on one's hind legs, stamp the foot, kick up a row, fly off the handle, cut up rough; stamp –, quiver –, swell –, foam- with rage; burst with anger; raise Cain, breathe fire and fury.

have a fling at; bear malice etc. (*revenge*) 919.

cause –, raise- anger; affront, offend; give -offence, – umbrage; anger; hurt the feelings; insult, discompose, fret, ruffle, nettle, heckle, huff, pique; excite etc. 824; irritate, stir the blood, stir up bile; sting, – to the quick; rile, provoke, chafe, wound, incense, inflame, enrage, aggravate, add fuel to the flame, fan into a flame, widen the breach, envenom, embitter, exasperate, infuriate, kindle wrath; stick in one's gizzard; rankle etc. 919.

put out of humor; put one's -monkey, – back-up; set –, get- one's back up; raise one's -gorge, – dander, – choler; work up into a passion; make -one's blood boil, – the ears tingle; throw into a ferment, madden, drive one mad; lash into -fury, – madness; fool to the top of one's bent; set by the ears.

bring a hornet's nest about one's ears.

Adj. angry, wrath, irate; ire-, wrath-ful; cross etc. (*irascible*) 901; sulky etc. 901*a*; bitter, virulent; acrimonious etc. (*discourteous*) etc. 895; violent etc. 173.

warm, burning; boiling, – over; fuming, raging; foaming, – at the mouth; convulsed with rage.

offended etc. *v.*; waxy, *acharné*; wrought, worked up; indignant, hurt, sore, peeved; set against.

fierce, wild, rageful, furious, mad with rage, fiery, infuriate, rabid, savage; relentless etc. 919.

flushed with -anger, – rage; in a -huff, – stew, – fume, – pucker, – passion, – rage, – fury; on one's high ropes, up in arms; in high dudgeon.

Adv. angrily etc. *adj.*; in the height of passion; in the heat of -passion, – the moment.

Phr. one's -blood, – back, – monkey- being up; *fervens difficili bile jecur*; the gorge rising, eyes flashing fire; the blood -rising, – boiling; *haeret lateri lethalis arundo*.

901. Irascibility.—N. irascibility, temper; crossness etc. *adj.*; susceptibility, procacity, petulance, irritability, tartness, acerbity, protervity; pugnacity etc. (*contentiousness*) 720.

excitability etc. 825; bad –, fiery –, crooked –, irritable etc. *adj.*- temper; *genus irritabile*, hot blood.

ill humor etc. (*sullenness*) 901*a*; asperity etc., churlishness etc. (*discourtesy*) 895.

huff etc. (resentment) 900; a word and a blow.

Sir Fretful Plagiary; brabbler, Tartar; shrew, vixen, virago, termagant, dragon, scold, Xanthippe; porcupine; spit-fire; fire-eater etc. (*blusterer*) 887; fury etc. (*violent person*) 173.

V. be -irascible etc. *adj.*; have a -temper etc. *n.*, – devil in one; fire up etc. (*be angry*) 900.

Adj. irascible; bad-, ill-tempered; irritable, susceptible; excitable etc. 825; thin-skinned etc. (*sensitive*) 822; fretful, fidgety; on the fret.

hasty, over-hasty, quick, warm, hot, testy, touchy, techy, tetchy; like -touchwood, – tinder; huffy; pet-tish, -ulant; waspish, snapp-y, -ish, peppery, fiery, passionate, choleric, shrewish, 'sudden and quick in quarrel.'

querulous, captious, mood-y, -ish; quarrelsome, contentious, disputatious; pugnacious etc. (*bellicose*) 720; cantankerous, exceptious; restive etc. (*perverse*) 901*a*; churlish etc. (*discourteous*) 895.

cross, – as -crabs, – two sticks, – a cat, – a dog, – the tongs; like a bear with a sore head; fractious, peevish, *acariâtre*.

in a bad temper; sulky etc. 901*a*; angry etc. 900.

resent-ful, -ive; vindictive etc. 919.

Int. pish!

901a. Sullenness.—N. sullenness etc. *adj.*; morosity, spleen; churlishness etc. (*discourtesy*) 895; irascibility etc. 901.

moodiness etc. *adj.*; perversity; obstinacy etc. 606; torvity, spinosity; crabbedness etc. *adj.*

ill –, bad- -temper, – humor; sulks, dudgeon, mumps, doleful dumps, doldrums, fit of the sulks, *bouderie*, black looks, scowl; huff etc. (*resentment*) 900.

V. be -sullen etc. *adj.*; sulk; frown, scowl, lower, glower, grouse, grouch, crab, gloam, pout, have a hang-dog look, glout.

Adj. sullen, sulky; ill-tempered, -humored, -affected, -disposed; in -an ill, – a bad, – a shocking- -temper, – humor; out of -temper, – humor; knaggy, torvous, crusty, crabbed; sore as a boil; surly etc. (*discourteous*) 895.

moody; spleen-ish, -ly; splenetic, cankered.

cross, -grained; perverse, wayward, humorsome; restive; cantankerous, refractory, intractable, exceptious, sinistrous, deaf to reason, unaccommodating, rusty, crust, froward.

dogged etc. (*stubborn*) 606.

grumpy, glum, grim, grum, morose, frumpish; in the -sulks etc. *n.*; out of sorts; scowl-, glower-, growl-ing.

peevish etc. (*irascible*) 901.

902. Endearment. [Expression of affection or love.]—**N.** endearment, caress; blandish-, blandi-ment; *épanchement*, fondling, billing and cooing, dalliance.

embrace, salute, kiss, buss, smack, osculation,

deosculation; amorous glances; ogle, side glance, sheep's eyes.

courtship, wooing, suit, addresses, the soft impeachment; love-making; an affair; serenading; caterwauling.

flirting etc. *v.*; flirtation, gallantry; coquetry, spooning.

ture lover's knot, plighted love, engagement, bethrothal; love -tale, – token, – letter; *billet-doux*, valentine.

honeymoon; Strephon and Chloe, 'Arry and 'Arriet.

V. caress, fondle, pet, dandle, nurse; pat, – on the -head, – cheek; chuck under the chin, smile upon, coax, wheedle, cosset, coddle, cocker; make -of, – much of, pamper; cherish, foster, kill with kindness.

clasp, hug, cuddle; fold –, strain- in one's arms; nestle, nuzzle, neck, embrace, kiss, buss, smack, blow a kiss; salute etc. (*courtesy*) 894.

bill and coo, spoon, toy, dally, flirt, coquet; galli-, gala-vant; philander; make love; pay one's -court, – addresses, – attentions- to; serenade; court, woo; set one's cap at; be –, look- sweet upon; ogle, cast sheep's eyes upon; *faire les yeux doux*.

fall in love with, win the affections etc. (*love*) 897; die for.

propose; make –, have an offer; pop the question; plight one's -troth, – faith; become -engaged, – betrothed.

Adj. caressing etc. *v.*; 'sighing like furnace;' love-sick, spoony.

carressed etc. *v.*

903. Marriage.—N. marriage, matrimony, wedlock, union, intermarriage, *vinculum matrimonii*, nuptial tie, knot.

married state, coverture, bed, cohabitation.

match; betrothment etc. (*promise*) 768; wedding, nuptials, Hymen, bridal; e-, spousals; leading to the altar etc. *v.*; nuptial benediction, *epithalamium*,

torch –, temple- of Hymen; hymeneal altar; honeymoon.

bride, bridegroom; brides-maid; -man.

best –, grooms-man, page, usher.

married -man, – woman, – couple; neogamist, Benedick, partner, spouse, mate, yokemate; husband, man, consort, baron; old –, good- man; wife of one's bosom; help-meet, -mate, rib, better half, grey mare, old woman, good wife; feme, – coverte; squaw, lady; matron, -age, -hood; man and wife; wedded pair, Darby and Joan.

affinity, soul-mate.

mono-, bi-, di-, deutero-, tri-, poly-gamy; mormonism; poly-andry; Turk, Bluebeard.

unlawful –, left-handed –, companionate –, morganatic –, ill-assorted- marriage; *mésalliance*; *mariage de convenance*; an affair.

match-maker, marriage broker, matrimonial agent.

V. marry, wive, take to oneself a wife; be -married, – spliced; go –, pair- off; wed, espouse, lead to the hymeneal altar, take 'for better, for worse,' give one's hand to, bestow one's hand upon; remarry; intermarry.

marry, join, handfast; couple etc. (*unite*) 43; tie the nuptial knot; give -away, – in marriage; affy, affiance; betroth etc. (*promise*) 768; publish –, bid- the banns; be asked in church.

Adj. married etc. *v.*; one, – bone and one flesh.

marriageable, nubile.

engaged, betrothed, affianced.

matrimonial, marital, conjugal, connubial, wedded; nuptial, hymeneal, spousal, bridal.

Phr. the gray mare the better horse.

904. Celibacy.—N. celibacy, singleness, single blessedness; bachelor-hood, -ship; miso-gamy, -gyny.

virginity, *pueelage*; maiden-hood, -head.

unmarried man, bachelor, agamist, old bachelor; miso-gamist, -gynist; celibate.

unmarried woman, spinster; maid, -en; virgin, *feme sole*, old maid; bachelor girl; nun etc.

V. live single; keep bachelor hall.

Adj. un-married, -wedded; wife-, spouse-less; single, virgin, celibate.

905. Divorce.—N. divorce, -ment; separation; judicial separation, separate maintenance; *separatio a -mensâ et thoro*, – *vinculo matrimonii*.

widowhood, viduage, viduity, weeds.

widow, -er; relict; dowager; *divorcée*; cuckold.

V. live -separately, – apart; separate, divorce, dissspouse, put away; wear the horns.

906. Benevolence.—N. benevolence, Christian charity; God's -love, – grace; good-will; philanthropy etc. 910; unselfishness etc. 942.

good -nature, – feeling, – wishes; kind-, kindliness etc. *adj.*; lovingkindness, benignity, brotherly love, charity, humanity, fellow-feeling, sympathy; goodness –, warmth- of heart; *bon-homie*; kind-heartedness; amiability, milk of human kindness, tenderness; love etc. 897; friendship etc. 888.

toleration, consideration, generosity; mercy etc. (*pity*) 914.

charitableness etc. *adj.*; bounty, alms-giving; good works, beneficence, the luxury of doing good.

acts of kindness, a good turn; good –, kind- -offices, – treatment.

good Samaritan, sympathizer, well-wisher, philanthropist, *bon enfant*; altruist.

V. be -benevolent etc. *adj.*; have one's heart in the right place, bear good will; wish -well, – God speed; view –, regard- with an eye of favor; take in good part; take –, feel- an interest in; be –, feel- interested- in; sympathize with, feel for; fraternize etc. (*be friendly*) 888.

enter into the feelings of others, do as you would be done by, meet halfway.

treat well; give comfort, smooth the bed of death; do -good, – a good turn; benefit etc. (*goodness*) 648; render a service, be of use; aid etc. 707.

Adj. benevolent; kind, -ly; wellmeaning; amiable; obliging, accommodating, indulgent, considerate, gracious, complacent, good-humored.

warm-, soft-, kind-, tender-, large-, broad-hearted; merciful etc. 914; philanthropic etc. 910; charitable, beneficent, humane, benign, benignant; bount-eous, -iful etc. 816.

good-, well-natured; spleenless; sympath-izing, -etic; complaisant etc. (*courteous*) 894; kindly, well-meant, -intentioned.

fatherly, motherly, brotherly, sisterly; pat-, mat-, frat-ernal; friendly etc. 888.

Adv. with -a good intention, – the best intentions.

Int. God speed! much good may it do!

907. Malevolence.—N. malevolence; bad intent, -ion; un-, dis-kindness; ill -nature, – will, – blood; bad blood; enmity etc. 889; hate etc. 898; malignity; malice, – aforethought, – prepense; maliciousness etc. *adj.*; spite, despite; resentment etc. 900.

uncharitableness etc. *adj.*; incompassionateness etc. 914*a*; gall, venom, rancor, rankling, virulence, mordacity, acerbity; churlishness etc. (*discourtesy*) 895.

hardness of heart, heart of stone, obduracy; cruelty; cruelness etc. *adj.*; brutality, savagery; ferity, -ocity; barbarity, inhumanity, immanity, truculence, ruffianism; evil eye, cloven -foot, – hoof; Inquisition; torture.

ill –, bad- turn; affront etc. (*disrespect*) 929; outrage, atrocity; ill usage; intolerance, bigotry, persecution; tender mercies [ironical]; 'unkindest cut of all.'

V. be -malevolent etc. *adj.*; bear –, harbor- -spleen, – a grudge, – malice; betray –, show- the cloven foot.

hurt etc. (*physical pain*) 378; annoy etc. 830; injure, harm, wrong; do -harm, – an ill office- to; outrage; disoblige, malign, plant a thorn in the breast.

molest, worry, harass, haunt, harry, bait, tease, throw stones at; play the devil with; hunt down, dragoon, hound; persecute, oppress, grind; maltreat; ill-treat, -use.

wreak one's malice on, do one's worst, break a butterfly on the wheel; dip –, imbrue- one's hands in blood; have no mercy etc. 914*a*.

Adj. male-, unbene-volent; unbenign; ill-disposed, -intentioned, -natured, -conditioned, -contrived; evil-minded, -disposed.

malicious; malign, -ant; rancorous; de-, spiteful; mordacious, caustic, bitter, envenomed, acrimonious, virulent; un-amiable, -charitable; maleficent, venomous, grinding, galling.

harsh, disobliging; un-kind, -friendly, -gracious; treacherous; inofficious; invidious; uncandid; churlish etc. (*uncourteous*) 895; surly, sullen etc. 901*a*.

cold, -blooded, -hearted; hard-, flint-, marble-, stony-hearted; hard of heart, unnatural; ruthless etc. (*unmerciful*) 914*a*; relentless etc. (*revengeful*) 919.

cruel; brut-al, -ish; savage, – as a -bear, – tiger; ferine, feral, ferocious; inhuman; barbarous, fell, untamed, tameless, truculent, incendiary; bloodthirsty etc. (*murderous*) 361; atrocious.

fiend-ish, -like; demoniacal; diabolic, -al; devilish, infernal, hellish, Satanic.

Adv. malevolently etc. *adj.*; with -bad intent etc. *n.*

908. Malediction.—N. malediction, malison, curse, imprecation, denunciation, execration, anathema, ban, proscription, excommunication, commination, thunders of the Vatican, fulmination, *maranatha*, aspersion, vilification, vituperation, scurrility.

abuse; foul –, bad –, strong –, unparliamentary- language, Limehouse; Billingsgate, sauce, evil speaking; cursing etc. *v.*; profane swearing, oath.

threat etc. 909; more bark than bite; invective etc. (*disapprobation*) 932.

V. curse, accurse, imprecate, damn, swear at; slang; curse with bell, book and candle; invoke –, call down- curses on the head of; devote to destruction.

execrate, beshrew, scold; anathematize etc. (*censure*) 932; hold up to execration, denounce, proscribe, excommunicate, fulminate, thunder against; threaten etc. 909; curse up hill and down dale.

curse and swear; swear, – like a trooper; fall a cursing, rap out an oath, damn, cuss.

Adj. curs-ing, -ed etc. *v.*; maledictory.

Int. woe to! beshrew! *ruat coelum!* ill –, woe-betide! confusion seize! damn! confound! blast! curse! devil take! hang! out with! a plague –, out-upon! aroynt! *honi soit!*

Phr. *delenda est Carthago.*

909. Threat.—N. threat, menace; defiance etc. 715; abuse, minacity, intimidation; fulmination; commination etc. (*curse*) 908; gathering clouds etc. (*warning*) 668.

V. threat, -en; menace; snarl, growl, gnarl, mutter, bark, bully.

defy etc. 715; intimidate etc. 860; keep –, hold up –, hold out- *in terrorem*; shake –, double –, clinch- the fist at; thunder, talk big, fulminate, use big words, bluster, look daggers.

Adj. threatening, menacing; mina-tory, -cious; comminatory, abusive; *in terrorem*; ominous etc. (*predicting*) 511; defiant etc. 715; under the ban.

Int. *vae victis!* at your peril! do your worst!

910. Philanthropy.—N. philanthropy; altruism, humanit-y, -arianism; universal benevolence; *deliciae humani generis;* cosmopolitanism, utilitarianism, the greatest happiness of the greatest number, social science, sociology.

common weal, public welfare, socialism, communism.

patriotism, civism, nationality, love of country, *amor patriae*, public spirit.

chivalry, knight errantry; generosity etc. 942.

philanthropist, altruist etc. 906; utilitarian, Benthamite, socialist, communist, cosmopolite, citizen of the world, *amicus humani generis*; knight errant; patriot.

Adj. philanthropic, altruistic, humanitarian, utilitarian, cosmopolitan; public-spirited, patriotic; humane, large-hearted etc. (*benevolent*) 906; chival-ric, -rous, generous etc. 942.

Adv. *pro -bono publico*, – *aris et focis.*

Phr. '*humani nihil a me alienum puto.*'

911. Misanthropy.—N. misanthropy, incivism; egotism etc. (*selfishness*) 943; moroseness etc. 901*a*; cynicism; defeatism.

misanthrope, misanthropist, egotist, cynic, man-hater, Timon, Diogenes.
woman-hater, misogynist.
Adj. misanthropic, antisocial, unpatriotic; egotistical etc. (*selfish*) 943; morose etc. 901*a*.

912. Benefactor.—N. benefactor, savior, good genius, tutelary saint, patron, guardian angel, fairy godmother, good Samaritan; *pater patriae*; salt of the earth etc. (*good man*) 948; auxiliary etc. 711.

913. Evil-doer. [*Maleficent being.*]**—N.** evil--doer, – worker; wrong doer etc. 949; mischief maker, marplot; oppressor, tyrant; firebrand, incendiary, pyromaniac, anarchist, destroyer, Hun, *Boche*, Vandal, iconoclast; communist; terrorist, *apache*, gunman, gangster, racketeer.
savage, brute, ruffian, barbarian, semi-barbarian, caitiff, desperado; Mo-hock, -hawk; bludgeon man, bully, rough, hooligan, larrikin, dangerous classes, ugly customer; thief etc. 792.
cockatrice, scorpion, hornet; viper, adder; snake, – in the grass; serpent, cobra, asp, rattlesnake, anaconda; canker-, wire-worm; locust, Colorado beetle; torpedo; bane etc. 663.
cannibal; Anthropophag-us, -ist; bloodsucker, vampire, ogre, ghoul, gorilla; vulture; gyr-, ger-falcon.
wild beast, tiger, hyaena, butcher, hangman; cut-throat etc. (*killer*) 361; blood-, sleuth-, hell-hound.
hag, hellhag, beldam, Jezebel.
monster; fiend etc. (*demon*) 980; homicidal maniac, devil incarnate, demon in human shape; Frankenstein's monster.
harpy, siren, vampire; Furies, Eumenides etc. 900.
Attila, scourge of the human race.
Phr. *foenum habet in cornu.*

914. Pity.—N. pity, compassion, commiseration; bowels, – of compassion; condolence etc. 915; sympathy, fellow-feeling, tenderness, yearning, forbearance, humanity, mercy, clemency, exorability; leniency etc. (*lenity*) 740; charity, ruth, long-suffering.
melting mood; *argumentum ad misericordiam*; quarter, grace, *locus poenitentiae*.
sympathizer, champion, partisan.
V. pity; have –, show –, take- pity etc. *n.*; commiserate, compassionate; condole etc. 915; sympathize; feel –, be sorry –, yearn- for; weep, melt, thaw, enter into the feelings of.
forbear, relent, relax, give quarter, wipe the tears, *parcere subjectis*, give a *coup de grâce*, put out of one's misery; be cruel to be kind.
raise –, excite- pity etc. *n.*; touch, soften; melt, – the heart; appeal to one's better feelings; propitiate, disarm.
ask for -mercy etc. *n.*; supplicate etc. (*request*) 765; cry for quarter, beg one's life, kneel; deprecate.
Adj. pitying etc. *v.*; pitiful, compassionate, sympathetic, touched.
merciful, clement, ruthful; humane; humanitarian etc. (*philanthropic*) 910; tender, – hearted, – as a chicken; soft, – hearted; unhardened; lenient etc. 740; exorable, forbearing; melting etc. *v.*; weak.
Int. for pity's sake! mercy! have –, cry you-mercy! God help you! poor -thing, – dear, – fellow! woe betide! *quis talia fando temperet a lachrymis!*
Phr. one's heart bleeding for; *haud ignara mali miseris succurrere disco.*

914a. Pitilessness.—N. pitilessness etc. *adj.*; inclemency; inexorability, hardness of heart; inflexibility; severity etc. 739; malevolence etc. 907.
V. have no –, shut the gates of- mercy etc. 914; give no quarter.
Adj. piti-, merci-, ruth-, bowel-less; unpitying, unmerciful, inclement; in-, un-compassionate; inexorable, inflexible; harsh etc. 739; cruel etc. 907; unrelenting etc. 919.

915. Condolence.—N. condolence; lamentation etc. 839; sympathy, consolation.
V. condole with, console, sympathize etc. 914; share one's misery; feel for; express –, testify- pity; afford –, supply- consolation; lament etc. 839- with; send one's condolences.

916. Gratitude.—N. gratitude, thankfulness, gratefulness, feeling of obligation.
acknowledgement, recognition, thanksgiving, giving thanks.
thanks, praise, benediction; paean; *Te Deum* etc. (*worship*) 990; grace, – before, – after-meat; thank-offering.
requital.
V. be -grateful etc. *adj.*; thank; give –, render –, return –, offer –, tender- thanks etc. *n.*; acknowledge, requite.
feel –, be –, lie- under an obligation; *savoir gré*; not look a gift horse in the mouth; never forget, overflow with gratitude; thank –, bless- one's stars; fall on one's knees.
Adj. grateful, thankful, obliged, beholden, indebted to, under obligation.
Int. thanks! many thanks! gramercy! much obliged! thank you! thank Heaven! Heaven be praised!

917. Ingratitude.—N. ingratitude, thanklessness, oblivion of benefits; unthankfulness.
'benefits forgot;' thankless -task, – office.
V. be -ungrateful etc. *adj.*; forget benefits; look a gift horse in the mouth.
Adj. un-grateful, -mindful, -thankful; thankless, ingrate, wanting in gratitude, insensible of benefits.
forgotten; un-acknowledged, -thanked, -requited, -rewarded; ill-requited.
Int. thank you for nothing! *'et tu Brute!'*

918. Forgiveness.—N. forgiveness, pardon, condonation, grace, remission, absolution, amnesty, oblivion; indulgence; reprieve.

conciliation; reconciliation etc. (*pacification*) 723; propitiation.

excuse, exoneration, quittance, release, indemnity; bill –, act –, covenant –, deed- of indemnity; exculpation etc. (*acquittal*) 970.

longanimity, placability, forbearance; *amantium irae*; *locus poenitentiae*.

V. forgive, – and forget; pardon, condone, think no more of, let bygones be bygones, shake hands; forget an injury, bury the hatchet; clean the slate.

excuse, pass over, overlook; wink at etc. (*neglect*) 460; bear with; allow –, make allowances- for; let one down easily, not be too hard upon, pocket the affront; blot out one's transgression.

let off, remit, absolve, give absolution, reprieve; acquit etc. 970.

beg –, ask –, implore- pardon etc. *n.*; conciliate, propitiate, placate; make up a quarrel etc. (*pacify*) 723; let the wound heal.

Adj. forgiving, placable, conciliatory.

forgiven etc. *v.*; un-resented, -avenged, revenged.

Adv. cry you mercy.

Phr. *veniam petimusque damusque vicissim*; more in sorrow than in anger.

919. Revenge.—N. revenge, -ment; vengeance; avenge-ment, -ance; sweet revenge, *vendetta*, death-feud, eye for an eye, blood for blood, a Roland for an Oliver; retaliation etc. 718; day of reckoning.

rancor, vindictiveness, implacability; malevolence etc. 907; ruthlessness etc. 914*a*.

avenger, vindicator, Nemesis, Eumenides.

V. re-, a-venge; take –, have one's- revenge; breathe -revenge, – vengeance; wreak one's -vengeance, – anger; give no quarter.

have -accounts to settle, – a crow to pluck, – a rod in pickle; pay off old scores.

keep the wound green; harbor -revenge, – vindictive feeling; bear malice; rankle, – in the breast; have at one's mercy.

Adj. revenge-, venge-ful; vindictive, rancorous; pitiless etc. 914*a*; ruthless, rigorous, avenging, retaliative.

unforgiving, unrelenting; inexorable, stony-hearted, implacable; relent-, remorse-less.

aeternum servans sub pectore vulnus; rankling, immitigable.

Phr. *manet -cicatrix,– altâ mente repostum*. revenge is sweet.

920. Jealousy.—N. jealous-y, -ness; jaundiced eye, heartburning; green-eyed monster; yellows; Juno.

V. be -jealous etc. *adj.*; view with -jealousy, – a jealous eye.

Adj. jealous, – as a Barbary pigeon; jaundiced, yellow-eyed, horn-mad.

921. Envy.—N. envy; enviousness etc. *adj.*; rivalry; *jalousie de métier*.

V. envy, covet, lust after, crave, burst with envy, regard with envious eyes.

Adj. envious, invidious, covetous; *alieni appetens*.

922. Right.—N. right; what -ought to, – should- be; fitness etc. *adj.*; *summum jus*.

justice, equity; equitableness etc. *adj.*; propriety; fair play, impartiality, measure for measure, give and take, *lex talionis*, square deal.

Astraea, Nemesis, Themis.

scales of justice, even-handed justice, retributive justice, *suum cuique*; clear stage –, fair field- and no favor; Queensberry rules.

morals etc. (*duty*) 926; law etc. 963; honor etc. (*probity*) 939; virtue etc. 944.

V. be -right etc. *adj.*; stand to reason.

see -justice done, – one righted, – fair play; do justice to; recompense etc. (*reward*) 973; hold the scales even, give and take; serve one right, put the saddle on the right horse; give -every one, – the devil- his due; *audire alteram partem*.

deserve etc. (*be entitled to*) 924.

Adj. right, good; just, reasonable; fit etc. 924; equ-al, -able, -itable; evenhanded, fair, – and square.

legitimate, justifiable, rightful; as it -should, – ought to- be; lawful etc. (*permitted*) 760, (*legal*) 963.

deserved etc. 924.

Adv. rightly etc. *adj.*; in -justice, – equity, – reason.

without -distinction of, – regard to, – respect to- persons; upon even terms.

Int. all right!

923. Wrong.—N. wrong; what -ought not to, – should not- be; *malum in se*; unreasonableness, grievance; shame.

injustice; unfairness etc. *adj.*; iniquity, foul play, partiality, leaning; favor, -itism; nepotism, party spirit, partisanship; undueness etc. 925; unlawfulness etc. 964.

robbing Peter to pay Paul etc. *v.*; the wolf and the lamb; vice etc. 945.

a custom more honored in the breach than the observance.

V. be -wrong etc. *adj.*; cry to heaven for vengeance.

do -wrong etc. *n.*; be -inequitable etc. *adj.*; favor, lean towards; encroach; impose upon; reap where one has not sown; give an inch and take an ell; rob Peter to pay Paul.

Adj. wrong, -ful; bad, too bad; unjust, -fair; in-, un-equitable; unequal, partial, one-sided.

objectionable; un-reasonable, -allowable, -warrantable, -justifiable; not cricket, not playing the game; improper, unfit; unjustified etc. 925; illegal etc. 964; iniquitous, criminal; immoral etc. 945; injurious etc. 649.

in the wrong, – box.

Adv. wrongly etc. *adj.*

Phr. it will not do; this is too bad.

924. Dueness.—N. due, -ness; right, privilege, prerogative, prescription, title, claim, pretension, demand, birthright.

immunity, license, liberty, franchise; vested -interest, – right; licitness.

sanction, authority, warranty, charter; warrant etc. (*permission*) 760; constitution etc. (*law*) 963; tenure; bond etc. (*security*) 771.

deserts, merits, dues.

claimant, appellant; plaintiff etc. 938.

V. be -due etc. *adj.*to, – the due etc. *n.*of; have -right, – title, – claim- to; be entitled to; have a claim upon; belong to etc. (*property*) 780.

deserve, merit, be worthy of, richly deserve.

demand, claim; call upon –, come upon –, appeal to- for; re-vendicate, -claim; exact; insist -on, – upon; challenge; take one's stand, make a point of, require, lay claim to, assert, assume, arrogate, make good; substantiate; vindicate a -claim, – right; make out a case.

give –, confer- a right; sanction, entitle; authorize etc. 760; sanctify, legalize, ordain, prescribe, allot.

give every one his due etc. 922; pay one's dues; have one's -due, – rights; stand upon one's rights.

use a right, assert, enforce, put in force, lay under contribution.

Adj. having a right to etc. *v.*; entitled to; claiming; deserving, meriting, worthy of.

privileged, allowed, sanctioned, warranted, authorized; ordained, prescribed, constitutional, chartered, enfranchised.

prescriptive, presumptive; absolute, indefeasible; un-, in-alienable.

imprescriptible, inviolable, unimpeachable, unchallenged; sacrosanct.

due to, merited, deserved, condign, richly deserved, *emeritus*.

allowable etc. (*permitted*) 760; lawful, licit, legitimate, legal; legalized etc. (*law*) 963.

square, unexceptionable, right; equitable etc. 922; due, *en règle*; fit, -ting; correct, proper, meet, befitting, becoming, seemly; decorous; creditable, up to the mark, right as a trivet; just –, quite- the thing; *selon les règles*.

Adv. duly, *ex officio*, *de jure*; by -right, – divine right; as is -fitting, – proper, – fitting and proper; *jure divino*, *Dei gratiâ*, in the name of.

Phr. *civis Romanus sum*.

925. Undueness. [Absence of right.]—**N.** undueness etc. *adj.*; *malum prohibitum*; impropriety; illegality etc. 964.

falseness etc. *adj.*; emptiness –, invalidity- of title; illegitimacy.

loss of right, disfranchisement, forfeiture.

usurpation, assumption, tort, violation, breach, encroachment, presumption, seizure, stretch, exaction, imposition, lion's share.

usurper, pretender, Carlist; imposter.

V. be -undue etc. *adj.*; not be -due etc. 924.

infringe, encroach, trench on, exact; arrogate, – to oneself; give an inch and take an ell; stretch –, strain- a point; usurp, violate, do violence to; sail under false colors.

dis-franchise, -entitle, -qualify; invalidate.

relax etc. (*be lax*) 738; misbehave etc. (*vice*) 945; misbecome.

Adj. undue; unlawful etc. (*illegal*) 964; unconstitutional, *ultra vires*; illicit; un-authorized, -warranted, -allowed, -sanctioned, -justified; un-, dis-entitled, -qualified; un-privileged, -chartered.

illegitimate, bastard, spurious, false; usurped, tortious.

un-deserved, -merited, -earned; unfulfilled.

forfeited, disfranchised.

improper; un-meet, -fit, -befitting, -seemly; un-, mis-becoming; seemless; *contra bonos mores*; not the thing, out of the question, not to be thought of; preposterous, pretentious, would- be.

926. Duty.—N. duty, what ought to be done, moral obligation, accountableness, liability, *onus*, responsibility; bounden –, imperative- duty; call, – of duty.

allegiance, fealty, tie; engagement etc. (*promise*) 768; part; function, calling etc. (*business*) 625.

morality, morals, decalogue; case of conscience; conscientiousness etc. (*probity*) 939; conscience, inward monitor, still small voice within, sense of duty, tender conscience.

dueness etc. 924; propriety, fitness, seemliness, amenableness, decorum; the -thing, – proper thing; the -right, – proper- thing to do.

[Science of morals] eth-ics, -ology; deon-, aretology; moral –, ethical-philosophy; casuistry, polity.

observance, fulfilment, discharge, performance, acquittal, satisfaction, redemption; good behavior.

V. be -the duty of, – incumbent etc. *adj.*on, – responsible etc. *adj.*; behoove, become, befit, beseem; belong –, pertain- to; fall to one's lot; devolve on; lie -upon, – on one's head, – at one's door; rest -with, – on the shoulders of.

take upon oneself etc. (*promise*) 768.

be –, become- -bound to, – sponsor for; be responsible for; incur a -responsibility etc. *n.*; be –, stand –, lie- under an obligation; have to answer for, owe it to oneself.

impose a -duty etc. *n.*; enjoin, require, exact; bind, – over; saddle with, prescribe, assign, call upon, look to, oblige.

enter upon –, perform –, observe –, fulfil –, discharge –, adhere to –, acquit oneself of –, satisfy- -a duty, – an obligation; act one's part, redeem one's pledge, do justice to, be at one's post; do duty; do one's duty etc. (*be virtuous*) 944.

be on one's good behavior, mind one's P's and Q's.

Adj. obligatory, binding; imperative, peremptory; stringent etc. (*severe*) 739; behooving etc. *v.*; incumbent –, chargeable- on; under obligation; obliged –, bound –, tied- by; saddled with.

due –, beholden –, bound –, indebted- to; tied down; compromised etc. (*promised*) 768; in duty bound.

amenable, liable, accountable, responsible, answerable.

right, meet etc. (*due*) 924; moral, ethical, casuistical, conscientious, ethological.

Adv. with a safe conscience, as in duty bound, on one's own responsibility, at one's own risk, *suo periculo*; *in foro conscientiae*; *quamdiu se bene gesserit*; at one's post, on duty.

Phr. *dura lex sed lex*.

927. Dereliction of Duty.—N. dere; liction of duty; fault etc. (*guilt*) 947- sin etc. (*vice*) 945; non-observance, -performance, -co-operation; neglect, carelessness, laziness, incompetence, eye-service, relaxation, infraction, violation, transgression, failure, evasion, indolence; dead letter.

slacker, loafer, striker, non-co-operator.

V. violate; break, – through; infringe; set - aside, – at naught; trample -on, – under foot; slight, neglect, evade, renounce, forswear, repudiate; wash one's hands of; escape, transgress, fail.

call to account etc. (*disapprobation*) 932.

927a. Exemption.—N. exemption, freedom, irresponsibility, immunity, liberty, license, release, exoneration, excuse, dispensation, absolution, franchise, renunciation, discharge; exculpation etc. 970; *aegrotat*.

V. be -exempt etc. *adj.*

exempt, release, acquit, discharge, quit-claim, remise, remit; free, set at liberty, let off, pass over, spare, excuse, dispense with, give dispensation, license; stretch a point; absolve etc. (*forgive*) 918; exonerate etc. (*exculpate*) 970; save the necessity.

Adj. exempt, free, immune, at liberty, scot free; released etc. *v.*; unbound, unencumbered; irresponsible, unaccountable, not answerable; excusable.

928. Respect.—N. respect, regard, consideration; courtesy etc. 894; attention, deference, reverence, honor, esteem, estimation, veneration, admiration; approbation etc. 931.

homage, fealty, obeisance, genuflexion, kneeling, prostration; obsequiousness etc. 886; salaam, *kowtow*, bow, presenting arms, salute.

respects, regards, duty, *devoirs*, *égards*.

devotion etc. (*piety*) 987.

V. respect, regard; revere, -nce; hold in reverence, honor, venerate, hallow; esteem etc. (*approve of*) 931; think much of; entertain –, bear- respect for; have a high opinion of; look up to, defer to; pay -attention, – respect etc. *n.*- to; do –, render- honor to; do the honors, hail; show courtesy etc. 894; salute, present arms; do –, pay- homage to; pay tribute to; kneel to, bow to, bend the knee to; fall down before, prostrate oneself, kiss the hem of one's garment; worship etc. 990.

keep one's distance, make room, observe due decorum, stand upon ceremony.

command –, inspire- respect; awe, impose, overawe, dazzle.

Adj. respecting etc. *v.*; respectful, deferential, decorous, reverential, obsequious, ceremonious, bare-headed, cap in hand, on one's knees; prostrate etc. (*servile*) 886.

respected etc. *v.*; in high -esteem, – estimation; time-honored, venerable, *emeritus*.

Adv. in deference to; with -all, – due, – the highest- respect; with submission.

saving your -grace, – presence; *salva sit reverentia*; *pace tanti nominis*.

Int. hail! all hail! *esto perpetua!* may your shadow never be less!

929. Disrespect.—N. dis-respect, -esteem, -estimation, -favor, -repute; low estimation; disparagement etc. (*dispraise*) 932; (*detraction*) 934.

irreverence; slight, neglect; *spretae injuria formae*; superciliousness etc. (*contempt*) 930.

vilipendency, contumely, affront, dishonor, insult, indignity, outrage, discourtesy etc. 895; practical joking; scurrility, scoffing, sibilation; ir-, derision; mockery; irony etc. (*ridicule*) 856; sarcasm.

hiss, hoot, gibe, flout, jeer, scoff, gleek, taunt, sneer, quip, fling, wipe, slap in the face.

V. hold in disrespect etc. (*despise*) 930; misprize, disregard, slight, undervalue, depreciate, trifle with, set at naught, pass by, push aside, overlook, turn one's back – on, laugh in one's sleeve; be -disrespectful etc. *adj.*, – discourteous etc. 895; treat with -disrespect etc. *n.*; set down, browbeat.

dishonor, desecrate; insult, affront, outrage.

speak slightingly of; disparage etc. (*dispraise*) 932; vilipend, call names; throw –, fling- dirt; drag through the mud, point at, indulge in personalities; make -mouths, – faces; bite the thumb; take –, pluck- by the beard; toss in a blanket, tar and feather.

have –, hold- in derision; deride, scoff, sneer, laugh at, snigger, ridicule, gibe, mock, jeer, taunt, twit, niggle, gleek, gird, flout, fleer; roast, turn into ridicule; guy, burlesque etc. 856; laugh to scorn etc. (*contempt*) 930; smoke; fool; make -game, – a fool, – an April fool- of; play a practical joke; rag; lead one a dance, run the rig upon, have a fling at, scout, hiss, hoot, mob.

Adj. disrespectful; aweless, irreverent; disparaging etc. 934; insulting etc. *v.*; supercilious etc. (*scornful*) 930; rude, derisive, contemptuous, sarcastic; scurri-le, -lous; contumelious.

un-respected, -worshipped, -envied, -saluted; undis-regarded.

Adv. disrespectfully etc. *adj.*

930. Contempt.—N. contempt, disdain, scorn, sovereign contempt; despi-sal, -ciency; vilipendency, contumely; slight, sneer, spurn, by-word.

contemptuousness etc. *adj.*; scornful eye; smile of contempt; derision etc. (*disrespect*) 929.

[State of being despised] despisedness.

V. despise, contemn, scorn, disdain, feel contempt for, view with a scornful eye, disregard, slight, not mind; pass by etc. (*neglect*) 460.

look down upon; hold -cheap, – in contempt, – in disrespect; think -nothing, – small beer- of; make light of; underestimate etc. 483; esteem - slightly, – of small or no account; take no account of, care nothing for; set no store by; not care a - straw etc. (*unimportance*) 643; set at naught, laugh in one's sleeve, snap one's fingers at, shrug one's shoulders, turn up one's nose at, pooh-pooh, damn with faint praise; sneeze –, whistle –, sneer- at; curl up one's lip, toss the head, *traiter de haut*; laugh at etc. (*be disrespectful*) 929.

point the finger of –, hold up to –, laugh to- scorn; scout, hoot, flout, hiss, scoff at.

turn -one's back, – a cold shoulder- upon; tread –, trample- -upon, – under foot; spurn, kick; fling to the winds etc. (*repudiate*) 610; send away with a flea in the ear.

Adj. contemptuous; disdain-, scorn-ful; withering, contumelious, supercilious, cynical, haughty, bumptious, cavalier; derisive.

contemptible, despicable; pitiable; pitiful etc. (*unimportant*) 643; despised etc. *v.*; downtrodden; unenvied.

Adv. contemptuously etc. *adj.*

Int. a fig for etc. (*unimportant*) 643; bah! never mind! away with! hang it! fiddle-de-dee!

931. Approbation.—N. approbation; approval, -ement; sanction, advocacy; nod of approbation; esteem, estimation, good opinion, golden opinions, admiration; love etc. 897; appreciation, regard, account, popularity, *kudos*, credit; repute etc. 873.

commendation, praise; laud, -ation; good word; meed –, tribute- of praise; encomium; eulog-y, -ium; *éloge*, panegyric; homage, hero worship; benediction, blessing, benison.

applause, plaudit, clap; clapping, – of hands; accl-aim, -amation; cheer; paean, hosannah; shout –, peal –, chorus –, thunders- of -applause etc. Kentish fire; Prytaneum; blurb.

V. approve; think -good, – much of, – well of, – highly of; esteem, value, prize; set great store -by, – on.

do justice to, appreciate; honor, hold in esteem, look up to, admire; like etc. 897; be in favor of, wish God speed; hail, – with satisfaction.

stand –, stick- up for; uphold, hold up, countenance, sanction; clap –, pat- on the back; keep in countenance, endorse, give credit, recommend; mark with a white -mark, – stone.

commend, praise; be-, laud; compliment, pay a tribute, bepraise; clap, – the hands; applaud, cheer, acclaim, acclamate, encore; panegyrize, eulogize, cry up, *prôner*, puff; extol, – to the skies; magnify, glorify, exalt, boost, swell, make much of; flatter etc. 933; bless, give a blessing to; have –, say- a good word for; speak -well, – highly, – in high terms- of; sing –, sound –, chaunt –, resound- the praises of; sing praises to; cheer –, applaud- to the -echo, – very echo.

redound to the -honor, – praise, – credit- of; do credit to; deserve -praise etc. *n.*; recommend itself; pass muster.

be -praised etc.; receive honorable mention; be in -favor, – high favor- with; ring with the praises of, win golden opinions, gain credit, find favor with, stand well in the opinion of; *laudari a laudato viro*.

Adj. approving etc. *v.*; in favor of; lost in admiration.

commendatory, complimentary, benedictory, laudatory, panegyrical, eulogistic, encomiastic, acclamatory, lavish of praise, uncritical.

approved, praised etc. *v.*; un-censured, -impeached; popular, in good odor; in high esteem etc. (*respected*) 928; in –, in high- favor.

deserving –, worthy of- praise etc. *n.*; praiseworthy, commendable, of estimation; good etc. 648; meritorious, estimable, creditable, plausible, unimpeachable; beyond all praise.

Adv. commendably, with credit, to admiration; well etc. 681; with three times three.

Int. hear, hear! well done! *brav-o! -a! -i! bravissimo! euge! macte virtute!* so far so good, that's right, quite right; *optime!* one cheer more; may your shadow never be less! *esto perpetua!* long life to! *viva! enviva!* God speed! *valete et plaudite! encore! bis!*

Phr. *probatum est.*

932. Disapprobation.—N. disappro-bation, -val; improbation; dis-esteem, -valuation, -placency; odium; dislike etc. 867; dissent etc. 489.

dis-praise, -commendation; blame, censure, obloquy; detraction etc. 934; disparagement, depreciation; denunciation; condemnation etc. 971; ostracism; boycott; black-list, -ball; *index -expurgatorius, – librorum prohibitorum*.

animadversion, reflection, stricture, objection, exception, criticism; sardonic -grin, – laugh; sarcasm, insinuation, innuendo; bad –, poor –, left-handed- compliment.

satire; sneer etc. (*contempt*) 930; taunt etc. (*disrespect*) 929; cavil, carping, censoriousness; hypercriticism etc. (*fastidiousness*) 868.

reprehension, remonstrance, expostulation, reproof, reprobation, admonition, increpation, reproach; rebuke, reprimand, castigation, jobation, lecture, curtain lecture, blow up, wigging, dressing, – down; rating, scolding, trimming; correction, set down, rap on the knuckles, *coup de bec*, rebuff; slap, – on the face; home thrust; hit; frown, scowl, black look.

diatribe; jeremiad; *tirade*, philippic.

clamor, outcry, hue and cry; hiss, -ing; sibilation, cat-call; execration etc. 908.

chiding, upbraiding etc. *v.*; exprobration, abuse, vituperation, invective, objurgation, contumely, personal remarks; hard –, cutting –, bitter- words.

evil-speaking; bad language etc. 908; personality.

V. disapprove; dislike etc. 867; lament etc. 839; object to, take exception to; be scandalized at, think ill of; view with -disfavor, – dark eyes, – jaundiced eyes; *nil admirari*, disvalue, improbate.

frown upon, look grave; bend –, knit- the brows; shake the head at, shrug the shoulders; turn up the nose etc. (*contempt*) 930; look -askance, – black upon; look with an evil eye; make a wry -face, – mouth- at; set one's face against.

dis-praise, -commend, -parage; deprecate, speak ill of, not speak well of, slate, condemn etc. (*find guilty*) 971.

blame; lay –, cast- blame upon; censure, *fronder*, reproach, pass censure on, reprobate, impugn.

remonstrate, expostulate, recriminate.

reprehend, chide, admonish; bring –, call- -to account, – over the coals, – to order; take to task, reprove, lecture, bring to book; read a -lesson, – lecture- to; rebuke, correct.

reprimand, chastise, castigate, lash, blow up, trounce, trim, *laver la tête*, overhaul; give it one, – finely; gibbet.

accuse etc. 938; impeach, denounce; hold up to -reprobation, – execration; expose, brand, gibbet, stigmatize; show –, pull –, take- up; cry 'shame' upon; be outspoken; raise a hue and cry against.

execrate etc. 908; exprobrate, speak daggers, vituperate; abuse, –, like a pickpocket; scold, rate, objurage, upbraid, fall foul of; jaw; rail, – at, – in good set terms; bark at; anathematize, call names; call by -hard, – ugly- names; a-, re-vile; vili-fy, -pend; bespatter; backbite; clapperclaw; rave –, thunder –, fulminate- against; load with reproaches; lash with the tongue.

exclaim –, protest –, inveigh –, declaim –, cry out –, raise one's voice- against.

decry; cry –, run –, frown- down; clamor, hiss,

hoot, mob, ostracize; draw up –, sing- a round robin; black-ball, -list.

animadvert –, reflect- upon; glance at; cast -reflection, – reproach, – a slur- upon; insinuate, damn with faint praise; 'hint a fault and hesitate dislike;' not to be able to say much for.

scoff at, point at; twit, taunt etc. (*disrespect*) 929; sneer at etc. (*despise*) 230; satirize, lampoon; defame etc. (*detract*) 934; depreciate, find fault with, criticize, cut up; pull –, pick- to pieces; take exception; cavil; peck –, nibble –, carp- at; be -censorious etc. *adj.*; pick -holes, – a hole, – a hole in one's coat; make a fuss about.

take –, set- down; snub, snap one up, give a rap on the knuckles; throw a stone -at, – in one's garden; have a -fling, – snap- at; have words with, pluck a crow with; give one a -wipe, – lick with the rough side of the tongue.

incur blame, excite disapprobation, scandalize, shock, revolt; get a bad name, forfeit one's good opinion, be under a cloud, come under the ferule, bring a hornet's nest about one's ears.

take blame, stand corrected; have to answer for.

Adj. disapproving etc. *v.*; scandalized.

disparaging, condemnatory, damnatory, denunciatory, reproachful, abusive, objurgatory, clamorous, vituperative; defamatory etc. 934.

satirical, sarcastic, sardonic, cynical, dry, sharp, cutting, biting, severe, virulent, withering, trenchant, hard upon; censorious, critical, captious, carping, hypercritical; fastidious etc. 868; sparing of –, grudging- praise.

disapproved, chid etc. *v.*; in bad odor, blown upon, unapproved; unblest; at a discount, exploded; weighed in the balance and found wanting.

blameworthy, reprehensible etc. (*guilt*) 947; to –, worthy of- blame, answerable, uncommendable, exceptionable, not to be thought of, bad etc. 649; vicious etc. 945.

un-lamented, -bewailed, -pitied.

Adv. with a wry face; reproachfully etc. *adj.*

Int. it is too bad! it -won't, – will never- do! marry come up! Oh! come! 'sdeath!

forbid it Heaven! God –, Heaven- forbid! out –, fie- upon it! away with! tut! *O tempora! O mores!* shame! fie, – for shame! out on you!

tell it not in Gath!

933. Flattery.—N. flattery, adulation, gloze; bland-ishment, -iloquence; cajolery; fawning, wheedling etc. *v.*; captation, coquetry, sycophancy, obsequiousness, flunkeyism, toad-eating, tuft-hunting; snobbishness.

incense, honeyed words, flummery; bun-kum, -combe; blarney, *placebo*, butter; soft -soap, – sawder; rose water.

voice of the charmer, mouth honor; lip-homage; euphemism; unctuousness etc. *adj.*

V. flatter, praise to the skies, puff; wheedle, cajole, glaver, coax; fawn, –, upon; humor, gloze, soothe, pet, coquet, slaver, butter; be-spatter, -slubber, -plaster, -slaver; lay it on thick, overpraise; earwig, cog, collogue; truckle –, pander *or* pandar –, pay court- to; court; creep into the good graces of; curry favor with, hang on the sleeve of; fool to the top of one's bent; lick the dust.

lay the flattering unction to one's soul, gild the pill, make things pleasant.

overestimate etc. 482; exaggerate etc. 549.

Adj. flattering etc. *v.*; adulatory; mealy-, honey-mouthed; honeyed; smooth, – tongued; soapy, oily, unctuous, blandiloquent, specious; fine-, fair-spoken; plausible, servile, sycophantic, fulsome; courtier-ly, -like.

Adv. *ad captandum.*

934. Detraction.—N. detraction, disparagement, depreciation, vilification, obloquy, scurrility, scandal, defamation, aspersion, traducement, slander, calumny, obtrectation, evil-speaking, backbiting, *scandalum magnatum*.

personality, libel, squib, lampoon, skit, pasquinade; *chronique scandaleuse*.

sarcasm, cynicism; criticism (*disapprobation*) 932; invective etc. 932; envenomed tongue; *spretae injuria formae*.

detractor etc. 936.

V. detract, derogate, decry, depreciate, disparage; run –, cry- down; minimize, make light of; belittle, sneer at etc. (*contemn*) 930; criticize, pull to pieces, pick a hole in one's coat, asperse, cast aspersions, blow upon, bespatter, blacken; vilify, -pend; avile; give a dog a bad name, brand, malign, backbite, libel, lampoon, traduce, slander, defame, calumniate, bear false witness against; speak ill of behind one's back.

'damn with faint praise, assent with civil leer; and without sneering, others teach to sneer.'

fling dirt etc. (*disrespect*) 929; anathematize etc. 932; dip the pen in gall, view in a bad light.

Adj. detracting etc. *v.*; defamatory, detractory, derogatory; disparaging, libellous; scurril-e, -ous; abusive; foul-spoken, -tongued, -mouthed; slanderous; calumni-ous, -atory; sar-castic, -donic; satirical, cynical.

935. Flatterer.—N. flatterer, adulator; eulogist, -phemist; optimist, encomiast, *laudator*, whitewasher, booster.

toad-y, -eater; sycophant, courtier, pickthank, Sir Pertinax MacSycophant; *flâneur*, *prôneur*; puffer, touter, *claqueur*; claw-back, ear-wig, doer of dirty work; parasite, hanger on etc. (*servility*) 886.

936. Detractor.—N. detractor, reprover; censor, -urer; cynic, critic, caviller, carper, word-catcher.

defamer, backbiter, slanderer, knocker, Sir Benjamin Backbite, lampooner, satirist, traducer, libeller, calumniator, dearest foe, dawplucker, Thersites; Zoilus; good-natured –, candid- friend [satirically]; reviler, vituperator, castigator; shrew etc. 901.

disapprover, *laudator temporis acti*.

937. Vindication.—N. vindication, justification, warrant; exoneration, exculpation; acquittal etc. 970; whitewashing.

extenuation; pallia-tion, -tive; softening, mitigation.

reply, defense; recrimination etc. 938.

apology, gloss, varnish; plea etc. 617; salvo; excuse, extenuating circumstances; allowance, – to be made; *locus poenitentiae*.

apologist, vindicator, justifier; defendant etc. 938.

justifiable charge, true bill.

V. justify, warrant; be an -excuse etc. *n.*- for; lend a color, furnish a handle; vindicate; ex-, disculpate; acquit etc. 970; clear, set right, exonerate, whitewash.

extenuate, palliate, excuse, soften, apologize, varnish, slur, gloze; put a -gloss, – good face- upon; mince; gloss over, bolster up, help a lame dog over a stile.

advocate, defend, plead one's cause; stand –, stick –, speak- up for; contend –, speak- for; bear out, keep in countenance, support; plead etc. 617; say in defense; plead ignorance; confess and avoid, propugn, put in a good word for.

take the will for the deed, make allowance for, do justice to; give -one, – the Devil- his due.

make good; prove -the truth of, – one's case; be justified by the event.

Adj. vindicat-ed, -ing etc. *v.*; vindicat-ive, -ory; palliative; exculpatory; apologetic.

excusable, defensible, pardonable; veni-al, -able; specious, plausible, justifiable.

Phr. *'honi soit qui mal y pense.'*

938. Accusation.—**N.** accusation, charge, imputation, slur, inculpation, exprobration, delation; crimination; in-, ne-, re-crimination; *tu quoque* argument; invective etc. 932.

de-nunciation, -nouncement; libel, challenge, citation, arraignment; im-, ap-peachment; indictment, bill of indictment, true bill; lawsuit etc. 969; condemnation etc. 971.

gravamen of a charge, head and front of one's offending, *argumentum ad hominem*; scandal etc. (*detraction*) 934; *scandalum magnatum*.

accuser, prosecutor, plaintiff, complainant, petitioner; relator, informer; appellant.

accused, defendant, prisoner, panel, co-, respondent; litigant.

V. accuse, charge, tax, impute, twit, taunt with, reproach.

brand with reproach; stigmatize, slur; cast a -stone at, – slur on; incriminate; inculpate, implicate; call to account etc. (*censure*) 932; take to- blame, – task; put in the black book.

inform against, indict, denounce, arraign; im-, ap-peach; have up, show up, pull up, challenge, cite, lodge a complaint; prosecute, bring an action against etc. 969.

charge –, saddle- with; lay to one's -door, – charge; lay the blame on, bring home to; cast –, throw- in one's teeth; cast the first stone at.

have –, keep- a rod in pickle for; have a crow to pluck with.

trump up a charge.

Adj. accusing etc. *v.*; accusat-ory, -ive; imputative, denunciatory; re-, criminatory.

accused etc. *v.*; suspected; under -suspicion, – a cloud, – *surveillance*; in -custody, – detention; in the -lock up, – watch house, – house of detention.

accusable, imputable; in-defensible, -excusable; un-pardonable, -justifiable; vicious etc. 945.

Int. look at home; *tu quoque* etc. (*retaliation*) 718.

939. Probity.—**N.** probity, integrity, rectitude; uprightness etc. *adj.*; honesty, faith; honor; good faith, *bona fides*; purity, clean hands.

fairness etc. *adj.*; fair play, justice, equity, impartiality, principle; grace.

constancy; faithfulness etc. *adj.*; fidelity, loyalty; incorrupt-ion, -ibility.

trustworthiness etc. *adj.*; truth, candor, singleness of heart; veracity etc. 543; tender conscience etc. (*sense of duty*) 926.

punctil-iousness, -io; delicacy, nicety; scrupulosity, -ousness etc. *adj.*; scruple; point, – of honor; punctuality.

dignity etc. (*repute*) 873; respectability, -bleness etc. *adj.*; gentleman; man of -honor, – his word; *fidus Achates*, *preux chevalier*; *galantuomo*; truepenny, trump, brick; true Briton, white man, sportsman.

court of honor, a fair field and no favor; *argumentum ad verecundiam*.

V. be -honorable etc. *adj.*; deal -honorably, – squarely, – impartially, – fairly; speak the truth etc. (*veracity*) 543; tell the truth and shame the devil, *vitam impendere vero*; show a proper spirit, make a point of; do one's duty etc. 944; play the game.

redeem one's pledge etc. 926; keep –, be as good as- one's -promise, – word; keep faith with, not fail.

give and take, *audire alteram partem*, give the devil his due, put the saddle on the right horse.

redound to one's honor.

Adj. upright; honest, – as daylight; veracious etc. 543; virtuous etc. 944; honorable; fair, right, just, equitable, impartial, even-handed, square; fair –, open- and aboveboard.

constant, – as the northern star; faithful, loyal, staunch; true, – blue, – to one's colors, – to the core, – as the needle to the pole; true-hearted, trust-y, -worthy; as good as one's word, to be depended on, incorruptible.

manly, straightforward etc. (*ingenuous*) 703; frank, candid, open-hearted.

conscientious, tender-conscienced, right-minded; high-principled, -minded; scrupulous, religious, strict; nice, punctilious, correct, punctual; respect-, reput-able; gentlemanlike.

inviol-able, -ate; un-violated, -broken, -betrayed; un-bought, -bribed.

innocent etc. 946; pure; stainless; un-stained, -tarnished, -sullied, -tainted, -perjured; uncorrupt, -ed; unde-filed, -praved, -bauched; *integer vitae scelerisque purus*; *justus et tenax propositi*.

chivalrous, jealous of honor, *sans peur et sans reproche*; high-spirited.

supra-mundane, unworldly, overscrupulous.

Adv. honorably etc. *adj.*; *bona fide*; on the square, in good faith, honor bright, *foro conscientiae*, with clean hands; by fair means.

940. Improbity.—**N.** improbity; dishon-esty, -our; deviation from rectitude; disgrace etc. (*disrepute*) 874; fraud etc. (*deception*) 545; lying etc. 544; bad –, Punic- faith; *mala –*, *Punica*, *fides*; infidelity; faithlessness etc. *adj.*; Judas kiss, betrayal; scrap of paper.

breach of -promise, – trust, – faith; prodition, disloyalty, divided allegiance, treason, high treason; apostacy etc. (*tergiversation*) 607; non-observance etc. 773.

shabbiness etc. *adj.*; villainy; baseness etc. *adj.*; abjection, debasement, turpitude, moral turpitude, laxity, trimming, shuffling.

perfidy; perfidiousness etc. *adj.*; treachery, double-dealing; unfairness etc. *adj.*; knavery, roguery, rascality, foul-play; jobb-ing, -ery; Tammany, graft; venality, nepotism; corruption, job, shuffle, fishy transaction, barratry; sharp practice, heads I win, tails you lose; mouth-honor etc. (*flattery*) 933.

V. be -dishonest etc. *adj.*; play false; break one's -word, – faith, – promise; jilt, betray, forswear; shuffle etc. (*lie*) 544; live by one's wits, sail near the wind; play with marked cards.

disgrace –, dishonor –, demean –, degrade- oneself; derogate, stoop, grovel, sneak, lose caste; sell oneself, go over to the enemy; seal one's infamy.

Adj. dishon-est, -orable; un-conscientious, -scrupulous; fraudulent etc. 545; knavish; disgraceful etc. (*disreputable*) 874; wicked etc. 945.

false-hearted, disingenuous; unfair, one-sided; double, -tongued, -faced; time-serving, crooked, tortuous, insidious, Machiavellian, dark, slippery; questionable; fishy; perfidious, treacherous, perjured.

infamous, arrant, foul, base, vile, low, ignominious, blackguard.

contemptible, abject, mean, shabby, little, paltry, dirty, scurvy, scabby, sneaking, groveling, scrubby, rascally, pettifogging; beneath one; not cricket.

low-minded, -thoughted; base-minded.

undignified, indign; unbe-coming, -seeming, fitting; de-rogatory, -grading; *infra dignitatem*; ungentleman-ly, -like; un-knightly, -chivalric, -manly, -handsome; recreant, inglorious.

corrupt, venal; debased, mongrel.

faithless, of bad faith, false, unfaithful, disloyal; untrustworthy; trust-, troth-less; lost to shame, dead to honor.

Adv. dishonestly etc. *adj.*; *malâ fide*, like a thief in the night, by crooked paths; by foul means.

Int. *O tempora! O mores!*

941. Knave.—N. knave, rogue, villain; Seapin, rascal; Lazarillo de Tormes; bad man etc. 949; blackguard etc. 949.

traitor, betrayer, arch-traitor, conspirator, stool pigeon, Judas, Catiline; reptile, serpent, snake in the grass, wolf in sheep's clothing, sneak, Jerry Sneak, tell-tale, squealer, mischief-maker, trimmer; renegade etc. (*tergiversation*) 607; truant, recreant; sycophant etc. (*servility*) 886.

942. Disinterestedness.—N. disinterestedness etc. *adj.*; generosity; liberal-ity, -ism; altruism; benevolence etc. 906; elevation, loftiness of purpose, exaltation, magnanimity; chival-ry, -rous spirit; heroism, sublimity.

self-denial, -abnegation, -effacement, -sacrifice, -immolation, -control etc. (*resolution*) 604; stoicism, devotion, martyrdom, *suttee*.

labor of love.

V. be -disinterested etc. *adj.*; make a sacrifice, lay one's head on the block; put oneself in the place of others, do as one would be done by, do unto others as we would men should do unto us.

Adj. disinterested; unselfish; self-denying, -sacrificing, -devoted; generous.

handsome, liberal, noble; noble-, high-minded; princely, great, high, elevated, lofty, exalted, spirited, stoical, magnanimous; great-, large-hearted, chivalrous, heroic, sublime.

un-bought, -bribed; uncorrupted etc. (*upright*) 939.

943. Selfishness.—N. selfishness etc. *adj.*; self-love, -indulgence, -worship, -interest; ego-tism, -ism; egocentrism, narcissism; *amour propre* etc. (*vanity*) 880; nepotism.

worldliness etc. *adj.*; world wisdom.

illiberality; meanness etc. *adj.*

time-server; tuft-, fortune-hunter; self-seeker; jobber, worldling; egotist, egoist, monopolist, nepotist, profiteer; temporizer, trimmer; dog in the manger, charity that begins at home.

V. be -selfish etc. *adj.*; please –, indulge –, coddle- oneself; consult one's own -wishes, – pleasure; look after one's own interest; feather one's nest; take care of number one, have an eye to the main chance, know on which side one's bread is buttered; give an inch and take an ell; wangle.

Adj. selfish; self-seeking, -indulgent, -interested; wrapt up –, centered- in self; egotistic, -al; egoistical; egocentric.

illiberal, mean, ungenerous, narrowminded; mercenary, venal; covetous etc. 819.

unspiritual; earthly, -minded; mundane; worldly, -minded, -wise; time-serving.

interested; *alieni appetens sui profusus*.

Adv. ungenerously etc. *adj.*; to gain some private ends; from selfish –, interested- motives.

Phr. *après nous le déluge*.

944. Virtue.—N. virtue; virtuousness etc. *adj.*; morality; moral rectitude; integrity etc. (*probity*) 939; nobleness etc. 873.

morals; ethics etc. (*duty*) 926; cardinal virtues.

merit, worth, desert, excellence, credit; self-control etc. (*resolution*) 604; self-denial etc. (*temperance*) 953.

well-doing; good -actions, – behavior; discharge –, fulfilment –, performance- of duty; well spent life; innocence etc. 946.

V. be -virtuous etc. *adj.*; practice -virtue etc. *n.*; do –, fulfil –, perform –, discharge- one's duty; redeem one's pledge etc. 926; act well, – one's part; fight the good fight; acquit oneself well; command –, master- one's passions; keep -straight, – in the right path.

set -an, – a good- example; be on one's -good, – best- behavior.

Adj. virtuous, good; innocent etc. 946; meritorious, deserving, worthy, desertful, correct; dut-iful, -eous; moral; right, -eous, -minded; well-intentioned, creditable, laudable, commendable, praiseworthy; above –, beyond- all praise; excellent, admirable; sterling, pure, noble.

exemplary; match-, peer-less; saint-ly, -like; heaven-born, angelic, seraphic, godlike.

Adv. virtuously etc. *adj.*; *e merito*.

945. Vice.—N. vice; evil-doing, – courses; wrong doing; wickedness, viciousness etc. *adj.*; iniquity, peccability, demerit; sin, Adam; old – offending- Adam.

immorality, impropriety, indecorum, scandal, laxity, looseness of morals; want of -principle, – ballast; obliquity, backsliding, infamy, demoralization, pravity, depravity, pollution; hardness of heart; brutality etc. (*malevolence*) 907; corruption etc. (*debasement*) 659; knavery etc. (*improbity*) 940; profligacy; lust etc. 961; flagrancy, atrocity; cannibalism.

infirmity; weakness etc. *adj.*; weakness of the flesh, frailty, imperfection; error; weak side; foible; fail-ing, -ure; crying –, besetting- sin; defect, deficiency, shortcoming; cloven foot.

lowest dregs of vice, sink of iniquity, Alsatian den; *gusto picaresco*.

fault, crime; criminality etc. (*guilt*) 947.

sinner etc. 949.

V. be -vicious etc. *adj.*; sin, commit sin, do amiss, err, transgress; misdemean –, forget –, misconduct- oneself; mis-do, -behave; fall, lapse, slip, trip, offend, trespass; deviate from the -line of duty, – path of virtue etc. 944; take a wrong course, go astray; hug a -sin, – fault; sow one's wild oats.

render -vicious etc. *adj.*, demoralize, brutalize, corrupt etc. (*degrade*) 659.

Adj.* vicious; sinful; sinning etc. *v.*, wicked, iniquitous, bad, immoral, unrighteous, wrong, criminal; naughty, incorrect; undut-eous, -iful.

unprincipled, lawless, disorderly, *contra bonos mores*, indecorous, unseemly, improper; dissolute, profligate, scampish; unworthy; worth-, desert-less; disgraceful, recreant; reprehensible, blameworthy, uncommendable; dis-creditable, -reputable.

base, sinister, scurvy, foul, gross, vile, black, grave, facinorous, felonious, nefarious, shameful, scandalous, infamous, villainous, of a deep dye, heinous; flag-rant, -itious; atrocious, incarnate, accursed.

Mephistophelian, satanic, diabolic, hellish, infernal, stygian, fiend-ish, -like, hell-born, demoniacal, devilish.

mis-created, -begotten; demoralized, corrupt, depraved.

evil-minded, -disposed; ill-conditioned; malevolent etc. 907; heart-, grace-, shame-, virtueless; abandoned, lost to virtue; unconscionable; sunk –, lost –, deep –, steeped- in iniquity.

incorrigible, irreclaimable, obdurate, reprobate, past praying for; culpable, reprehensible etc. (*guilty*) 947.

unjustifiable; in-defensible, -excusable; inexpiable, unpardonable, irremissible.

weak, frail, lax, infirm, imperfect, indiscreet; demoralizing, degrading.

Adv. wrong; sinfully etc. *adj.*; without excuse.

Int. *O tempora! O mores!*

*Most of these adjectives are applicable both to the act and to the agent.

946. Innocence.—N. innocence; guiltlessness etc. *adj.*; incorruption, impeccability.

clean hands, clear conscience, *mens sibi conscia recti*.

innocent, new born babe, lamb, dove.

V. be -innocent etc. *adj.*; *nil conscire sibi nullâ pallescere culpâ*.

acquit etc. 970; exculpate etc. (*vindicate*) 937.

Adj. innocent, not guilty, unguilty; guilt-, fault-, sin-, stain-, blood-, spot-less; clear, immaculate; *rectus in curiâ*; un-spotted, -blemished, -erring; undefiled etc. 939; unhardened, Saturnian; Arcadian etc. (*artless*) 703.

in-, un-culpable; unblam-ed, -able; blameless, inerrable, above suspicion; irrepr-oachable, -ovable, -ehensible; un-exceptionable, -objectionable, -impeachable; salvable; venial etc. 937.

harmless; in-offensive, -noxious, -nocuous; dove-, lamb-like; pure, harmless as doves; innocent as -a lamb, – the babe unborn; more sinned against than sinning.

virtuous etc. 944; un-reproved, -impeached, -reproached.

Adv. innocently etc. *adj.*; with clean hands; with a -clear, – safe- conscience.

947. Guilt.—N. guilt, -iness; culpability; crimin-ality, -ousness; deviation from rectitude etc. (*improbity*) 940; sinfulness etc. (*vice*) 945; peccability.

mis-conduct, -behavior, -doing, -deed; malpractice, fault, sin, error, transgression; dereliction, delinquency; indiscretion, lapse, slip, trip, *faux pas*, *peccadillo*; flaw, blot, omission; fail-ing, -ure.

offence, trespass; mis-demeanor, feasance, -prision, tort; mal-efaction, -feasance, -versation; crime, felony.

enormity, atrocity, outrage; deadly –, mortal –, unpardonable- sin; died without a name.

corpus delicti.

Adj. guilty, to blame, culpable, peccable, in fault, censurable, reprehensible, blameworthy, uncommendable, illaudable; weighed in the balance and found wanting; exceptionable, objectionable.

Adv. *in flagrante delicto*; red-handed, in the very act.

948. Good Man.—N. good man, worthy.

good woman, goddess, *madonna*, virgin.

model, paragon etc. (*perfection*) 650; good example; hero, demigod, seraph, angel; innocent etc. 946; saint etc. (*piety*) 987; benefactor etc. 912; philanthropist etc. 910; Aristides.

brick, trump, rough diamond, ugly duckling.

salt of the earth; one in ten thousand; one of the best.

Phr. *si sic omnes!*

949. Bad Man.—N. bad man, wrongdoer, worker of iniquity; evil-doer etc. 913; sinner; the -wicked etc. 945; bad example.

rascal, scoundrel, villain, miscreant, caitiff; wretch, reptile, viper, serpent, cockatrice, basilisk, urchin; tiger, monster; devil etc. (*demon*) 980; devil incarnate; demon in human shape, Nana Sahib; hell-hound, -cat; rake-hell.

bad woman, jade, Jezebel, adultress, etc. 962.

scamp, scapegrace, rip, runagate, ne'er-do-well, reprobate, *roué*, rake; limb; one who has sold himself to the devil, fallen angel, *âme damnée*, *vaurien*, *mauvais sujet*, loose fish, sad, dog; lost –, black-sheep; castaway, recreant, defaulter; prodigal etc. 818; libertine etc. 962.

rough, rowdy, ugly customer, ruffian, hoodlum, bully; Jonathan Wild; hangman; incendiary; thief etc. 792; murderer etc. 361.

culprit, delinquent, criminal, melefactor, misdemeanant; felon; convict, jail-bird, ticket-of-leave man; outlaw.

blackguard, *polisson*, loafer, sneak; raps-, rascallion; cullion, mean wretch, varlet, kern, *âme-de-boue*, *drôle*; cur, dog, hound, whelp, mongrel; lown, loon, runnion, outcast, vagabond; rogue etc. (*knave*) 941; scum of the earth, riff-raff; *Arcades ambo*.

Int. sirrah!

950. Penitence.—N. penitence, contrition, compunction, repentance, remorse; regret etc. 833.

self-reproach, -reproof, -accusation, -condemnation, -humiliation; stings –, pangs –, qualms –, prickings –, twinge –, twitch –, touch –, voice- of conscience; compunctious visitings of nature.

acknowledgment, confession etc. (*disclosure*) 529; apology etc. 952; recantation etc. 607; penance etc. 952; resipiscence.

awakened conscience, deathbed repentance, *locus poenitentiae*, stool of repentance, cutty stool.

penitent, Magdalen, prodigal son, returned prodigal, a sadder and wiser man.

V. repent, be sorry for; be -penitent etc. *adj.*; rue; regret etc. 833; think better of; recant etc. 607; knock under etc. (*submit*) 725; plead guilty; sing -*miserere*, – *de profundis*; cry *peccavi*; own oneself in the wrong; acknowledge, confess etc. (*disclose*) 529; humble oneself; beg pardon etc. (*apologize*) 952; turn over a new leaf, put on the new man, turn from sin; reclaim; repent in sackcloth and ashes etc. (*do penance*) 952; learn by experience.

Adj. penitent; repenting etc. *v.*; repentant, contrite; conscience-smitten, -stricken; self-accusing, -convicted.

penitenti-al, -ary; chastened, reclaimed; not hardened; un-hardened.

Adv. *meâ culpâ*.

Phr. *peccavi*; *erubuit*; *salva res est*; *vous l'avez voulu, Georges Dandin*.

951. Impenitence.—N. impenitence, irrepentance, recusance.

hardness of heart, seared conscience, induration, obduracy.

V. be -impenitent etc. *adj.*; steel –, harden- the heart; die -game, – and make no sign.

Adj. impenitent uncontrite, obdurate; hard, -ened; seared, recusant; unrepentant; relent-, remorse-, grace-, shrift-less.

lost, incorrigible, irreclaimable.

unre-claimed, -formed; unrepented, unatoned.

952. Atonement.—N. atonement, reparation; compromise, composition; compensation etc. 30; quittance, quits; indemni-ty, -fication; expiation, redemption, reclamation, conciliation, propitiation.

amends, apology, *amende honorable*, satisfaction; peace –, sin –, burnt- offering; scapegoat, sacrifice.

penance, fasting, maceration, sackcloth and ashes, white sheet, shrift, flagellation, lustration; purga-tion, -tory.

V. atone, – for; expiate; propitiate; make -amends, – good; reclaim, redeem, repair, ransom, absolve, purge, shrive, do penance, stand in a white sheet, repent in sackcloth and ashes.

set one's house in order, wipe off old scores, make matters up; pay the -forfeit, – penalty.

apologize, beg pardon, express regret, *faire amende honorable*, give satisfaction; come –, fall-down on one's -knees, – marrow bones.

Adj. propitiatory, expiatory; sacrific, -ial, -atory; piacul-ar, -ous.

953. Temperance.—N. temperance, moderation, sobriety, soberness.

forbearance, abnegation; self-denial, -restraint, -control etc. (*resolution*) 604.

frugality; vegetarianism, teetotalism, total abstinence, prohibition; abst-inence, -emiousness, asceticism etc. 955; system of -Pythagoras, – Cornaro; Pythagorism, Stoicism.

vegetarian; Pythagorean, gymnosophist; teetotaler etc. 958; abstainer.

V. be -temperate etc. *adj.*; abstain, forbear, refrain, deny oneself, spare; know when one has had enough; take the pledge; look not upon the wine when it is red.

Adj. temperate, moderate, sober, frugal, sparing; abst-emious, -inent; within compass; measured etc. (*sufficient*) 639.

Pythagorean; vegetarian; teetotal, pussy-foot.

954. Intemperance.—N. intemperance; sensuality, animalism, carnality; pleasure; effeminacy, silkiness; luxur-y, -iousness; lap of -pleasure, – luxury.

indulgence; high-, free- living, in-abstinence, self-indulgence; voluptuousness etc. *adj.*; epicurism, -eanism; sybaritism.

dissipation; licentiousness etc. *adj.*; debauchery; crapulence.

revel-s, -ry; debauch, carousal, jollification, drinking bout, wassail, Saturnalia, orgies; excess, too much; intoxication etc. 959.

Circean cup; drug habit etc. 663.

V. be -intemperate etc. *adj.*; indulge, exceed; live -well, – high, – on the fat of the land; give a loose to -indulgence etc. *n.*; dine not wisely but too well; wallow in -voluptuousness etc. *n.*; plunge into dissipation.

revel, rake, live hard, run riot, sow one's wild oats; slake one's -appetite, – thirst; swill; pamper.

Adj. intemperate, inabstinent, intoxicated etc. 958; sensual, self-indulgent; voluptuous, luxurious, licentious, wild, dissolute, rakish, fast, debauched.

brutish, crapulous, swinish, piggish, hoggish, bestial.

Paphian, Epicurean, Sybaritical; bred –, nursed- in the lap of luxury; indulged, pampered, full-fed.

954a. Sensualist.—N. Sybarite, voluptuary, Sardanapalus, man of pleasure, carpet knight; epicure, -an; *gourm-et, -and;* gormandizer, gutling, glutton, pig, hog; votary –, swine- of Epicurus; sensualist; Heliogabalus; free –, hard- liver; libertine etc. 962; hedonist.

955. Asceticism.—N. asceticism, puritanism, sabbatarianism; cynicism, austerity; total abstinence.

mortification, maceration, sackcloth and ashes, flagellation; penance etc. 952; fasting etc. 956; martyrdom.

ascetic; anchor-et, -ite; martyr; *Heautontimorumenos*; hermit etc. (*recluse*) 893; puritan, sabbatarian, cynic.

Adj. ascetic, austere, puritanical; cynical; over-religious.

956. Fasting.—N. fasting; exrophagy; famishment, starvation; banting.

fast, *jour maigre*; fast –, banyan-day; Lent, quadragesima; Rama-dan, -zan; spare –, meager-diet; lenten -diet, – entertainment; *soupe maigre*, short -rations, – commons; Barmecide feast; hunger strike.

V. fast, starve, clem, famish, perish with hunger; dine with Duke Humphrey, make two bites of a cherry.

Adj. lenten, quadragesimal; unfed; starved etc. *v.*; half-starved; fasting etc. *v.*; hungry etc. 865.

957. Gluttony.—N. gluttony; greed; greediness etc. *adj.*; voracity.

epicurism; good –, high- living; edacity, gulosity, crapulence; gutt-, guzz-ling; over-indulgence.

good cheer, blow out; feast etc. (*food*) 298; gastronomy.

epicure, *bon vivant*, *gourmand*; glutton, cormorant, hog, belly-god, Apicius, gastronome, gormandizer.

V. gormandize, gorge; over-gorge, -eat- oneself; engorge, eat one's fill, cram, stuff, stodge, glut, satiate; gutt-le, guzz-le; bolt, devour, gobble up; gulp etc. (*swallow food*) 298; raven, eat out of house and home.

have the stomach of an ostrich; play a good knife and fork etc. (*appetite*) 865.

Adj. gluttonous, greedy; gormandizing etc. *v.*; edacious, omnivorous, crapulent, swinish, voracious, devouring.

pampered; over-fed, -gorged.

958. Sobriety.—N. sobriety; teetotalism, temperance etc. 953.

water-drinker; teetotal-er, -ist; abstainer, Good Templar, Rechabite, band of hope; prohibitionist, pussyfoot.

V. take the pledge.

Adj. sober, – as a judge; dry, on the water wagon.

959. Drunkenness.—N. drunkenness etc. *adj.*; intemperance; drinking etc. *v.*; inebri-ety, -ation; ebri-ety, -osity; befuddlement; insobriety; intoxication; temulency, bibacity, wine-bibbing; com-, potation; deep potations, bacchanals, *bacchanalia*, libations.

oino-, dipso-mania; *delirium tremens*, d.t., alcohol, -ism.

drink; alcoholic drinks, alcohol, booze; gin, blue ruin, grog, brandy, port wine; punch, -bowl; cup, rosy wine, flowing bowl; drop, – too much; dram; beer, wine, spirits etc. (*beverage*) 298; cocktail, nip, peg; stirrup cup.

drunkard, sot, toper, tippler, bibber, wine-bibber; hard –, gin –, dram- drinker; soak, soaker, sponge, tun; love-, toss-pot; thirsty soul, reveller, carouser; Bacchanal, -ian; Bacch-al, -ante; devotee to Bacchus, dipsomaniac.

V. get –, be- drunk etc. *adj.*; see double; take a -drop, – glass- too much; drink, tipple, tope, booze, bouse, guzzle, swill, soak, sot, lush, bib, swig, carouse; sacrifice at the shrine of Bacchus; take to drinking; drink -hard, – deep, – like a fish; have one's swill, drain the cup, splice the main brace, take a hair of the dog that bit you.

liquor, – up; wet one's whistle, take a whet; lift one's elbow; crack a –, pass the- bottle; toss of etc. (*drink up*) 298, go to the -ale, – public house.

make one-drunk etc. *adj.*; inebriate, fuddle, fuzzle, get into one's head.

Adj. drunk, tipsy; intoxicated; inebri-ous, -ate, -ated; in one's cups; in a state of -intoxication etc. *n.*; temulent, -ive, fuddled, mellow, cut, boosy, fou, fresh, merry, elevated, squiffy; plastered, befuddled, sozzled; flush, -ed; flustered, disguised, groggy, beery; topheavy; potvaliant, glorious; potulent; over-come, -taken; whittled, screwed, tight, primed, oiled, corned, raddled, sewed up, lushy, nappy, muddled, muzzy, bosky, obfuscated, maudlin; crapulous, dead –, blind- drunk.

inter pocula; in –, the worse for- liquor, having had a drop too much, half seas over, three sheets in the wind; under the table, blind to the world, one over the eight.

drunk as -a piper, – a fiddler, – a lord, – Chloe, – an owl, – David's sow, – a wheelbarrow.

drunken, bibacious, bibulous, sottish; given –, addicted- to -drink, – the bottle; toping etc. *v.*; wet.

Phr. *nunc est bibendum.*

960. Purity.—N. purity; decency, decorum, delicacy; continence, chastity, honesty, virtue, modesty, shame; pudicity, *pucelage*, virginity.

vestal, virgin, Joseph, Hippolytus; Lucretia, Diana; prude.

Adj. pure, undefiled, modest, delicate, decent, decorous; *virginibus puerisque*; chaste, continent, virtuous, honest, Platonic.

961. Impurity.—N. impurity; uncleanness etc. (*filth*) 653; immodesty; grossness etc. *adj.*; indelicacy, indecency; impudicity; obscenity, ribaldry, smut, bawdry, *double entendre*, *équivoque*; Aretinism; pornography.

concupiscence, lust, carnality, flesh, salacity; pruriency, lechery, lasciviency, lubricity, lewdness.

incontinence, intrigue, *faux pas*; *amour*, *-ette*; gallantry; dabauchery, libertinism, *libertinage*, fornication; *liaison*; wenching, venery, dissipation.

seduction; defloration, defilement, abuse, violation, rape; incest.

social evil, harlotry, stupration, whoredom, concubinage, cuckoldom, adultery, advoutry, *crim. con.*; free love.

seraglio, harem, zenana; brothel, bagnio, stew, bawdy-house, *lupanar*, house of ill fame, *bordel*, kip.

V. be -impure etc. *adj.*; intrigue; debauch, defile, assault, attack, seduce; prostitute; abuse, violate, deflower; commit -adultery etc. *n.*

Adj. impure; unclean etc. (*dirty*) 653; not to be mentioned to ears polite; immodest, shameless; indecorous, -delicate, -decent; loose, suggestive, *risqué*, coarse, gross, broad, free, equivocal, smutty, fulsome, ribald, obscene, bawdy, pornographic.

concupiscent, prurient, lickerish, rampant, lustful; carnal, -minded; lewd, lascivious, lecherous, libidinous, erotic, ruttish, salacious; Paphian; voluptuous; incestuous.

unchaste, light, wanton, licentious, adulterous, debauched, dissolute; of -loose character, – easy virtue; frail, gay, riggish, incontinent, meretricious, rakish, gallant, dissipated; no better than she should be; on the -town, – streets, – *pavé*, – loose.

adulterous, incestuous, bestial.

962. Libertine.—N. libertine; voluptuary etc. 954*a*; rake, debauchee, loose fish, rip, rake-hell, fast man; *intrigant*, gallant, seducer, fornicator, lecher, satyr, goat, whoremonger, *paillard*, adulterer, gay deceiver, Lothario, Don Juan, Bluebeard.

adulteress, advoutress, courtesan, prostitute, strumpet, tart, hustler, chippy, broad, harlot, whore, punk, *fille de joie*; woman, – of the town; street-walker, Cyprian, miss, piece; frail sisterhood, fallen woman; demirep, wench, trollop, trull, baggage, hussy, drab, bitch, jade, skit, rig, quean, mopsy, slut, minx, harridan; woman -of easy virtue etc. (*unchaste*) 961; wanton, fornicatress; Jezebel, Messalina, Delilah, Thaïs, Phryne, Aspasia, Lais, *lorette*, *cocotte*, *petite dame*, *grisette*; *demimonde*; white slave.

concubine, mistress, fancy woman, kept woman, doxy, *chère amie*, *bona roba*.

pimp; pand-er, -ar; bawd, *conciliatrix*, procuress, mackerel; wittol.

963. Legality.—N. legality; legitima-cy, -teness, legitimization.

legislature; law, code, *corpus juris*, constitution, pandect, charter, act, enactment, statute, rule; canon etc. (*precept*) 697; ordinance, institution, regulation; by-, bye-law, rescript; decree etc. (*order*) 741; *ordonnance*; standing order; *plébiscite* etc. (*choice*) 609.

legal process; form, -ula, -ality; rite; arm of the law; *habeas corpus*.

[Science of law] jurisprudence, nomology; legislation, codification.

equity, common law; *lex* –, *lex nonscripta*, unwritten law; law of nations, international law, *jus gentium*; *jus civile*; civil –, criminal –, canon –, statute –, ecclesiastical- law; *lex mercatoria*.

constitutional-ism, -ity; justice etc. 922.

V. legalize, legitimize; enact, ordain; decree etc. (*order*) 741; pass a law; legislate; codify, formulate; authorize.

Adj. legal, legitimate; according to law; vested, constitutional, chartered, legalized; lawful etc. (*permitted*) 760; statut-able, -ory; legislat-orial, -ive.

Adv. legally etc. *adj.*; in the eye of the law; *de jure*.

964. Illegality. [Absence or violation of law.]—**N.** lawlessness; breach –, violation- of law; disobedience etc. 742; unconformity etc. 83.

arbitrariness etc. *adj.*; antinomy, violence, brute force, despotism, outlawry.

mob –, lynch –, club –, Lydford –, martial –, drumhead- law; *coup d'état*; *le droit du plus fort*; *argumentum baculinum*.

illegality, informality, unlawfulness, illegitimacy, bar sinister.

trover and conversion; smuggling, boot-legging, rum-running, poaching; simony.

speakeasy, speakie, blind pig.

V. offend against –, violate- the law; set the law at defiance, ride rough-shod over, drive a coach and six through a statute; make the law a dead letter, take the law into one's own hands.

smuggle, run, poach.

Adj. illegal; prohibited etc. 761; not allowed, unlawful, illegitimate, illicit, contraband, actionable.

unchartered, unconstitutional; unwarrant-ed, -able; unauthorized; informal, unofficial; in-, extrajudicial.

lawless, arbitrary; despotic, -al; summary, irresponsible; un-answerable, -accountable.

null and void; a dead letter.

Adv. illegally etc. *adj.*; with a high hand, in violation of law.

965. Jurisdiction. [Executive.]—**N.** jurisdiction, judicature, administration of justice, soc; executive, commission of the peace; magistracy etc. (*authority*) 737.

judge etc. 967; tribunal etc. 966; municipality, corporation, bailiwick, shrievalty; lord lieutenant; lord –, mayor, city manager, alderman etc. 745; sheriff, bailie, shrieve, chief –, constable; police, – force; constabulary, bumbledom.

officer; proctor, high –, commissioner; bailiff, tipstaff, bum-bailiff, catchpoll, beadle; police-man, -constable, -sergeant; *sbirro*, *alguazil*, *gendarme*, kavass, *lictor*, macebearer, *huissier*, bedel.

press-gang; exciseman, gauger, custom-house officer, *douanier*.

coroner, edile, aedile, portreeve, paritor; *posse comitatus*.

V. judge, sit in judgment.

Adj. executive, administrative, municipal;

inquisitorial, causidical; judic-atory, -iary, -ial; juridical.

Adv. *coram judice.*

966. Tribunal.—N. tribunal, court, board, bench, judicatory, curia; court of -justice, – law, – arbitration; inquisition; guild.

justice –, judgment –, mercy- seat; woolsack; bar, – of justice; dock; forum, hustings, *bureau*, drum-head; jury-, witness-box.

senate-house, town-hall, theater; House of -Lords, – Commons.

assize, eyre; ward-, burgh-mote; superior courts of Westminister; court of -record, – oyer and terminer, – assize, – appeal – error; High court of -Judicature, – Appeal; Judicial Committee of the Privy Council; Star-Chamber; Court of -Chancery, – King's *or* Queen's Bench, – Exchequer, – Common Pleas, – Probate, – Arches, – Admiralty, – Criminal Appeal; Lords Justices' –, Rolls –, Vice Chancellor's –, Stannary –, Divorce –, Palatine –, ecclesiastical –, county –, police- court; sessions; quarter –, petty-sessions; court -leet, – baron, – of pie poudre, – of common council; board of green cloth.

court-martial; drum-head court-martial; *durbar*, divan; Areopagus; *rota*.

Adj. judicial etc. 965; appellate; curial.

967. Judge.—N. judge; justi-ce, -ciar, -ciary; chancellor; justice –, judge- of assize; recorder, common serjeant; puisne –, assistant –, county court- judge; conservator –, justice- of the peace, J.P.; court etc. (*tribunal*) 966; grand –, petty –, coroner's- jury; panel, juror, juryman; twelve men in a box; magistrate, police magistrate, stipendiary, the great unpaid, beak; his -worship, – honor, – lordship; deemster, moderator.

Lord -Chancellor, – Justice; Master of the Rolls, Vice-Chancellor; Lord Chief -Justice, – Baron; Mr. Justice; Baron, – of the Exchequer.

jurat, assessor; arbi-ter, -trator; umpire; refer-ee, -endary; revising barrister; domesman; censor etc. (*critic*) 480; official –, receiver.

archon, tribune, praetor, *ephor*, syndic, *podestà*, mullah, ulema, mufti, cadi, kadi; Rhadamanthus.

litigant etc. (*accusation*) 938.

V. adjudge etc. (*determine*) 480; try a -case, – prisoner.

Adj. judicial etc. 965.

Phr. 'a Daniel come to judgment.'

968. Lawyer.—N. lawyer, jurist, legist, civilian, pundit, publicist, jurisconsult, legal adviser, advocate; barrister, – at law; counsel, -lor; King's *or* Queen's counsel; K.C.; Q.C.; silk gown, leader; junior, – counsel; stuff gown, serjeant-at-law; bencher, tubman; judge etc. 967.

bar, legal profession, gentleman of the long robe; junior –, outer –, inner- bar; Inns of Court; equity draftsman, conveyancer, pleader, special pleader.

solicitor, attorney, proctor; notary, – public; scrivener, cursitor; writer, – to the signet; S.S.C.; limb of the law; pettifogger.

V. practice -at, – within- the bar; plead; call –, to called- -to, – within- the bar; take silk.

Adj. learned in the law; at the bar; forensic.

969. Lawsuit.—N. lawsuit, suit, action, cause, petition; litigation; dispute etc. 713.

citation, arraignment, prosecution, impeachment; accusation etc. 938; presentment, true bill, indictment.

apprehension, arrest; committal; imprisonment etc. (*restraint*) 751.

writ, summons, subpoena, *latitat*, *nisi prius*; *habeas corpus*.

pleadings; declaration, bill, claim; *procès-verbal*, bill of right, information, *corpus delicti*; affidavit, state of facts; answer, replication, plea, demurrer, rebutter, rejoinder; surre-butter, -joinder.

suitor, party to a suit; litigant etc. 938; libellant.

hearing, trial; verdict etc. (*judgment*) 480; appeal, – motion; writ of error; *certiorari*.

case, decision, precedent, ruling; decided case, reports.

V. go to –, appeal to the- law; bring to -justice, – trial, – the bar; put on trial, pull up; accuse etc. 938; prefer –, file- a claim etc. *n.*; take the law of, inform against.

serve with a writ, cite, apprehend, arraign, sue, prosecute, bring an action against, indict, impeach, attach, distrain, commit; arrest; summon, -s; give in charge etc. (*restrain*) 751.

empanel a jury, implead, join issue; close the pleadings; set down for hearing.

try, hear a cause; sit in judgment; adjudicate etc. 480.

Adj. litigious etc. (*quarrelsome*) 713; *qui tam*; *coram* –, *sub- judice*.

Adv. *pendente lite*.

Phr. *adhuc sub judice lis est.*

970. Acquittal.—N. acquit-tal, -ment; clearance, exculpation, exoneration; discharge etc. (*release*) 750; *quietus*, absolution, compurgation, reprieve, respite; pardon etc. (*forgiveness*) 918.

[Exemption from punishment] impunity, immunity.

V. acquit, exculpate, exonerate, clear; absolve, whitewash, assoil, discharge, release; liberate etc. 750.

reprieve, respite; pardon etc. (*forgive*) 918; let off, – scot free.

Adj. acquitted etc. *v.*; un-condemned, -punished, -chastised; recommended to mercy.

971. Condemnation.—N. condemnation, conviction, proscription, damnation; death warrant; penalty etc. 974.

attain-der, -ture, -tment.

V. condemn, convict, cast, bring home to, find guilty, damn, doom, sign the death warrant, sentence, pass sentence on, attaint, confiscate, proscribe, sequestrate; non-suit.

disapprove etc. 932; accuse etc. 938.

stand condemned.

Adj. condem-, dam-natory; condemned etc. *v.*; non-suited etc. (*failure*) 732; self-convicted.

Phr. *mutato nomine de te fabula narratur.*

972. Punishment.—N. punishment, punition; chast-isement, -ening; correction, castigation.

discipline, infliction, trial; judgment; penalty etc. 974; retribution; thunderbolt, Nemesis; requital etc. (*reward*) 973; penology; retributive justice.

lash, scaffold etc. (*instrument of punishment*) 975; imprisonment etc. (*restraint*) 751; chain gang; transportation, banishment, expulsion, deportation, exile, involuntary exile, ostracism; penal servitude, hard labor; galleys etc. 975; beating etc. *v.*; flagellation, fustigation, gantlet, *strappado*, *estrapade*, *bastinado*, *argumentum baculinum*, stick law, rap on the knuckles, box on the ear; blow etc. (*impulse*) 276; stripe, cuff, kick, buffet, pummel; slap, – in the face; wipe, douse; *coup de grâce*; torture, rack; picket, -ing; *dragonnade*; capital punishment, extreme penalty; execution; hanging etc. *v.*; de-capitation, -collation; *garrot-te*, *-to*; electrocution, lethal chamber; crucifixion, impalement; martyrdom, *auto-da-fé*; *noyade*; *hara-kiri*, happy despatch.

V. punish; chast-ise, -en; castigate, correct, inflict punishment, administer correction, deal retributive justice.

visit upon, pay; pay –, serve- out; settle with, get even with, get one's own back; do for; make short work of, give a lesson to, strafe, serve one right, make an example of; have a rod in pickle for; give it one.

strike etc. 276; deal a blow to, administer the lash, smite; slap, – the face; smack, cuff, box the ears, spank, thwack, thump, beat, lay on, swinge, buffet; thresh, thrash, pummel, drub, leather, trounce, baste, belabor; lace, – one's jacket; dress, give a -dressing, – down; trim, warm, wipe, tund, cob, bang, strap, comb, lash, lick, larrup, whallop, whop, flog, scourge, whip, birch, cane, give the stick, switch, flagellate, horsewhip, *bastinado*, towel, rub down with an oaken towel, rib roast, dust one's jacket, fustigate, pitch into, lay about one, beat black and blue; beat to a -mummy, – jelly; give a black eye; hit on the head; sandbag.

tar and feather; pelt, stone, lapidate; mast-head, keelhaul.

execute; bring to the -block, – gallows; behead; de-capitate, -collate; guillotine; hang, turn off, gibbet, bowstring, hang, draw and quarter; shoot; decimate; burn; electrocute; break on the wheel, crucify; em-, im-pale; flay; lynch; put to death.

torture; put -on, – to- the rack; picket.

banish, exile; trans-, de-port; expel, ostracize; rusticate; drum out; dismiss, -bar, -bench; strike off the roll, unfrock; post.

suffer, – for, – punishment; be -flogged, – hanged etc.; come to the gallows, dance upon nothing, die in one's shoes; be rightly served.

Adj. punishing etc. *v.*; penal; puni-tory, -tive; inflictive, castigatory; punished etc. *v.*

Int. *à la lanterne!*

973. Reward.—N. reward, recompense, remuneration, prize, meed, guerdon, reguerdon; indemni-ty, -fication, price; quittance; compensation; reparation, *ersatz*, assythment, redress; retribution, reckoning, acknowledgment, requital, amends, sop; atonement; consideration, return, *quid pro quo*; salvage, perquisite; vail etc. (*donation*) 784; *douceur*, bribe, bait, baksheesh, tip; hush-, smart-money; black-mail; carcelage; *solatium*.

allowance, salary, stipend, wages; pay, -ment; emolument; tribute; batta, shot, scot; premium, fee, *honorarium*; hire.

crown etc. (*decoration of honor*) 877.

V. re-ward, -compense, -pay, -quite; re-, munerate; compensate; fee, tip, bribe; pay one's footing etc. (*pay*) 807; make amends, indemnify, atone; satisfy, acknowledge.

get for one's pains, reap the fruits of.

Adj. remunerat-ive, -ory; munerary, compensatory, retributive, reparatory.

974. Penalty.—N. penalty; retribution etc. (*punishment*) 972; pain, pains and penalties; *peine forte et dure*; penance etc. (*atonement*) 952; the devil to pay.

fine, mulct, amercement; forfeit, -ure; escheat, damages, deodand, sequestration, confiscation, *premunire*.

V. penalize, fine, mulct, amerce, sconce, confiscate; sequest-rate, -er; escheat; estreat, forfeit.

975. Scourge. [Instrument of punishment.]—**N.** scourge, rod, cane, stick; ra-, rat-tan; birch, – rod; rod in pickle; switch, ferule, cudgel, truncheon; rubber hose.

whip, lash, strap, thong, cowhide, knout; cat, – o'-nine-tails, *sjambok*, quirt; rope's end.

pillory, stocks, whipping-post; cuck-, duck-ing stool; brank; triangle, wooden horse, maiden, thumbscrew, boot, rack, wheel, iron heel; treadmill, crank, galleys.

scaffold; block, axe, *guillotine*; stake; cross; gallows, gibbet, Tyburn tree; drop, noose, rope, halter, bowstring; electric chair, lethal chamber.

house of correction etc. (*prison*) 752.

gaol-, jail-er; executioner; hang-, heads-man; Jack Ketch; lyncher.

976. Deity.—N. Deity, Divinity; God-head, -ship; Omnipotence, Providence.

[Quality of being divine] divin-eness, -ity.

God, Lord, Jehovah, *Deus*; The -Almighty, – Supreme Being, – First Cause; *Ens Entium*; Author –, Creator- of all things; Author of our being; The -Infinite, – Eternal; The All-powerfull, -wise, -merciful, -holy; The Omni-potent, -scient.

[Attributes and perfections] infinite -power, – wisdom, – goodness, – justice, – truth, – love, – mercy; omni-potence, -science, -presence; unity, immutability, holiness, glory, majesty, sovereignty, infinity, eternity.

The -Trinity, – Holy Trinity, – Trinity in Unity, – Triune God; Three in One and One in Three.

God the Father; The -Maker, – Creator, – Preserver.

[Functions] creation, preservation, divine government; The-ocracy, -archy; providence; ways –, dealings –, dispensations –, visitations- of Providence.

God the Son, Jesus, Christ; The -Messiah, – Anointed, – Savior, – Redeemer, – Mediator,

– Intercessor, – Advocate, – Judge; The Son of - God, – Man, – David; The Only Begotten; The Lamb of God, The Word; Em-, Im-manuel; The - King of Kings and Lord of Lords, – King of Glory, – Prince of Peace, – Good Shepherd, – Way, – Truth, – Life, – Bread of Life, – Light of the World; The -Lord our, – Sun of- Righteousness.

The -Incarnation, – Hypostatic Union, – Word made Flesh.

[Functions] salvation, redemption, atonement, propitiation, mediation, intercession, judgment.

God the Holy Ghost, The Holy Spirit, Paraclete; The -Comforter, – Consoler, – Spirit of Truth, – Dove.

[Functions] inspiration, unction, regeneration, sanctification, consolation.

eon, aeon, special providence, *Deus ex machinâ*; *Avatar*.

V. create, uphold, preserve, govern etc.

atone, redeem, save, propitiate, mediate etc.

predestinate, elect, call, ordain, bless, justify, sanctify, glorify etc.

Adj. almighty, holy, hallowed, sacred, divine, heavenly, celestial; messianic; sacrosanct; all-powerful, -wise, -seeing, -knowing; omnipotent, omniscient; supreme.

super-human, -natural; ghostly, spiritual, hyper-physical, unearthly; the-istic, -ocratic, deistic; anointed.

Adv. *jure divino*, by divine right; *Deo volente*, D.V.

977. Angel. [Beneficent spirits.]—**N.** angel, archangel; heavenly host, choir invisible, host of heaven, sons of God; Michael, Gabriel etc.; seraph, -im; cherub, -im; ministering spirit, morning star; saint, *Madonna*; Our Lady, the Blessed Virgin, the Virgin Mary.

Adj. angelic, seraphic, cherubic.

978. Satan. [Maleficent spirits.]—**N.** Satan, the Devil, Lucifer, Ahrimanes, Belial; Sammael, Zamiel, Beelzebub, the Prince of the Devils; Mephistopheles, his satanic majesty.

the tempter; the evil -one, – spirit; the -author of evil, – wicked one, – old Serpent; the Prince of -darkness, – this world, – the power of the air; the -foul, – arch- fiend; the devil incarnate; the - common enemy, – angel of the bottomless pit; Abaddon, Apollyon, Mammon.

fallen agnels, unclean spirits, devils; the -rulers, – powers- of darkness; inhabitants of Pandemonium; demon etc. 980.

diabolism; devil-ism, -ship, -dom, -ry, -worship; *diablerie*; satanism, manicheism; the cloven foot; black magic etc. 992.

Adj. satanic, diabolic, devilish, infernal, hell-born.

979. Jupiter.—**N.** god, -dess; heathen gods and goddesses; Pantheon; Jupiter, Jove, Zeus, Apollo, Mars, Mercury, Neptune, Vulcan, Bacchus, Pluto, Saturn, Cupid, Eros, Pan; Juno, Ceres, Proserpina, Dina, Minerva, Pallas, Athenae, Venus, Aphrodite, Vesta; The Fates etc. 601.

Allah, Brahma, Vishnu, Siva, Shiva, Krishna, Juggernaut, Buddha; Ra, Isis, Osiris; Belus, Bel, Baal, Asteroth etc.; Thor, Odin; Mumbo Jumbo; good –, tutelary- genius; demiurge, familiar, – spirit; Sibyl; fairy, fay; sylph, -id; Ariel, peri, nymph, nereid, dryad, oread, sea-maid, Banshee, Benshie, Ormuzd; Oberon, Titania, Mab, hamadryad, naiad, mermaid, kelpie, Ondine, nix, nixie, sprite; denizens of the air; pixy etc. (*bad spirit*) 980.

mythology; heathen –, fairy- mythology; Lemprière, folklore.

Adj. fairy-, sylph-like; sylphic.

980. Demon.—**N.** demon, -ry, -ism, -ology; evil genius, fiend, familiar, – spirit, devil; bad –, unclean- spirit; cacodemon, incubus, Frankenstein's monster, succubus and succuba, Titan, Shedim, Mephistopheles, Asmodeus, Moloch, Belial, Ahriman, fury, The Furies etc. 900; harpy; Friar Rush.

vampire, ghoul; af-, ef-freet; afrite; ogre, -ss; gnome, gin, djinn, imp, deev, *lamia*; bo-gie, -gle; nis, kobold, flibbertigibbet, fairy, brownie, pixy, elf, dwarf, urchin, Puck, Robin Goodfellow; lepre-cluri-chaune; troll, dwerger, sprite, oaf, changeling, bad fairy, nixe, pigwidgeon, Will-o'-the-wisp; Erl King.

[Supernatural appearance] ghost, specter, apparition, genie, spirit, shade, shadow, vision, phantom etc. 443; materialization (*spiritualism*) 992; hob-, goblin; wraith, spook, werwolf, boggart, banshee, *loup-garou*, *lemures*; evil eye.

nisse, necks; mer-man, -maid, -folk; siren, Lorelei; satyr, faun.

Adj. supernatural, weird, uncanny, unearthly, spectral; ghost-ly, -like; elf-in, -like; fiend-ish, -like; impish, demoniacal; haunted.

981. Heaven.—**N.** heaven; kingdom of - heaven, – God; heavenly kingdom; throne –, presence- of God; inheritance of the saints in light.

Paradise, Eden, abode of the blessed; Holy City, New Jerusalem; celestial bliss, glory.

[Mythological -heaven] Olympus; [– paradise] Elysium, Elysian fields, Arcadia, bowers of bliss, garden of the Hesperides, Islands of the Blessed; happy hunting-ground; third –, seventh-heaven; Valhalla (Scandinavian); Nirvana (Buddhist).

future state, eternity, eternal life, life after death, eternal home, resurrection, translation; resuscitation etc. 660; apotheosis, deification.

Adj. heavenly, celestial, supernal, unearthly, from on high, paradisiacal, beatific, elysian, Olympian, Arcadian.

982. Hell.—**N.** hell, bottomless pit, place of torment; habitation of fallen angels; Pandemonium, Abaddon, Domdaniel.

hell fire; everlasting -fire, – torment; lake of fire and brimstone; fire that is never quenched, worm that never dies.

purgatory, limbo, gehenna, abyss.

[Mythological hell] Tartarus, Hades, Avernus, Styx, Stygian creek, pit of Acheron, Cocytus,

Phlegethon, Lethe; infernal regions, *inferno*, shades below, realms of Pluto.

Pluto, Rhadamanthus, Erebus, Charon, Cerberus; Tophet.

Adj. hellish, infernal, stygian.

983. Theology. [Religious Knowledge.]—**N.** Theology (natural and revealed); Theo-gony, -sophy; Divinity; Hagio-logy, -graphy; Caucasian mystery; monotheism; religion; religious -persuasion, – sect, – denomination; cult; creed etc. (*belief*) 484; articles –, declaration –, profession –, confession- of faith.

theolog-ue, -ian; divine, schoolman, canonist, monotheist.

Adj. theological, religious; canonical; denominational; sectarian etc. 984.

983a. Orthodoxy.—N. orthodoxy; strictness, soundness, religious truth, true faith; truth etc. 494.

Christian-ity, -ism; Catholic-ism, -ity; 'the faith once delivered to the saints;' hyperorthodoxy etc. 984; iconoclasm.

the Holy –, the Orthodox- Church; Catholic –, Universal –, Apostolic –, Established- Church; temple of the Holy Ghost; Church –, body –, members –, disciples –, followers- of Christ; Christian, – community; true believer; canonist etc. (*theologian*) 983; Christendom, collective body of Christians, the Church Militant.

canons etc. (*belief*) 484; thirty-nine articles; Apostles' –, Nicene –, Athanasian- Creed; Church Catechism; textuary.

Adj. orthodox, sound, literal, strict, faithful, catholic, schismless, Christian, evangelical, scriptural, divine, monotheistic; true etc. 494.

984. Heterodoxy. [Sectarianism.]—**N.** heterodoxy; error etc. 495; false doctrine, heresy, schism; schismantic-ism, -alness; recusancy, backsliding, apostasy; atheism etc. (*irreligion*) 989.

bigotry etc. (*obstinacy*) 606; fanaticism, iconoclasm; hyperorthodoxy, precisianism, bibliolatry, hagiolatry, sabbatarianism, puritanism; idolatry etc. 991; superstition etc. (*credulity*) 486; dissent etc. 489.

sectar-ism, -ianism; nonconformity; secularism; syncretism, religious sects; the clash of creeds.

protestant-, advent-, Arian-, Erastian-, Calvin-, quaker-, method-, anabapt-, Pusey-, tractarian-, ritual-, Origen-, Sabellian-, Socinian-, De-, The-, mon-, material-, positiv-, latitudinairan-ism etc.

High –, Low –, Broad –, Free- Church; ultramontanism; monasticism; pap-ism, -istry; papacy; Anglican-, Catholic-, Roman-ism; popery, Scarlet Lady, Church of Rome, Greek Church; Christian Science, The Church of Christ Scientist.

pagan-, heathen-, ethic-ism; mythology; animism; poly-, di-, tri-, pan-theism; dualism; heathendom.

Juda-, Gentil-, Mahometan-, Islam-, Turc-, Brahmin-, Hindoo-, Buddh-, Lama-, Confucian-, Shinto-, Sabian-, Gnostic-. Soofee-, Hylothe-, Mormon-ism.

Theosophy; Spiritualism, Occultism.

heretic, antichrist; pagan, heathen; pai-, pay-nim; *giaour*; gentile; pan-, poly-theist; idolator; misbeliever, apostate, backslider.

bigot etc. (*obstinacy*) 606; fanatic, dervish, abdal, iconoclast.

latitudinarian, limitarian, Deist, Theist, Unitarian; positivist, materialist; agnostic, sceptic etc. 989.

schismatic; sectar-y, -ian, -ist; seceder, separatist, recusant, dissenter; non-conformist, -juror; Huguenot, Protestant; orthodox dissenter, Congregationalist, Independent; Episcopalian, Presbyterian; Lutheran, Calvinist, Quaker, Methodist, Weslayan; Ana-, Baptist; Dunker; Mormon, Latter-day Saint, Irvingite, Sandemanian, Glassite, Erastian; Sub-, Supra-lapsarian; Gentoo, Antinomian, Swedenborgian, Adventist, Plymouth Brother; Theosophist etc.

Catholic, Roman Catholic, Romanist, papist, ultramontane; Old Catholic, tractarian, Anglican, Puseyite, ritualist; Puritan.

Jew, Hebrew, Rabbist; Mahometan, Mohammedan, Mussulman, Moslem, Islamite, Osmanli; Brahm-in, -an; Parsee, Sofi, Soofee; Buddhist; Zoroastrian, Magi, Gymnosophist, fire-worshipper, Sabian, Gnostic, Sadducee, Rosicrucian etc.

Adj. heterodox, heretical; un-orthodox, -scriptural, -canonical; antiscriptural, apocryphal; un-, anti-christian; schismatic, recusant, iconoclastic; sectarian; dis-senting, -sident; secular etc. (*lay*) 997.

pagan; heathen, -ish; ethnic, -al; gentile, painim; pan-, poly-theistic; agnostic, sceptic.

Judaical, Mohammedan, Moslem, Brahminical, Buddhist etc. *n.*; Romish, Protestant etc. *n.*

bigoted etc. (*prejudiced*) 481; (*obstinate*) 606; superstitious etc. (*credulous*) 486; fanatical; idolatrous etc. 991; visionary etc. (*imaginative*) 515.

985. Revelation.—N. revelation, inspiration, *afflatus*.

Word, – of God; Scripture; the -Scriptures, – Bible, – Book of Books; Holy -Writ, – Scriptures; inspired writings, Gospel.

Old Testament, Septuagint, Vulgate, Pentateuch; Octateuch; the -Law, – Jewish Law, – Prophets; major –, minor- Prophets; Hagio-grapha, -logy; Hierographa; Apocrypha.

New Testament; Gospels, Evangelists, Acts, Epistles, Apocalypse, Revelations.

Talmud; Mishna, Masorah.

prophet etc. (*seer*) 513; evangelist, apostle, disciple, saint; the –, the Apostolical- fathers; Holy Men of old, inspired -writers, – penmen.

Adj. scriptural, biblical, sacred, prophetic; evangel-ical, -istic; apostolic, -al; inspired, theopneustic, apocalyptic, ecclesiastical, canonical, textuary.

986. Pseudo-Revelation.—N. the -Koran, – Alcoran; Ly-king, Shaster, Vedas, Zendavesta, Vedidad, Purana, Edda; Go-, Gau-tama; Book of Mormon.

[False prophets and religious founders] Buddha, Zoroaster, Zerdhusht, Confucius, Mahomet.

[Idols] golden calf etc. 991; Baal, Moloch, Dagon.

987. Piety.—N. piety, religion, theism, faith; religiousness, holiness etc. *adj.*; saintship; religionism; sanctimony etc. (*assumed piety*) 988; reverence etc. (*respect*) 928; humility, veneration, devotion; prostration etc. (*worship*) 990; grace, unction, edification; sancti-ty, -tude; consecration.

spiritual existence, odor of sanctity, beauty of holiness.

theopathy, beatification, adoption, regeneration, conversion, justification, sanctification, salvation, inspiration, bread of life; Body and Blood of Christ.

believer, convert, theist, Christian, devotee, pietist; the -good, – righteous, – just, – believing, – elect; Saint, *Madonna*.

the children of -God, – the kingdom, – light.

V. be -pious etc. *adj.*; have -faith etc. *n.*; believe, receive Christ; revere etc. 928; worship etc. 950; be -converted etc.

convert, edify, sanctify, hallow, keep holy, beatify, regenerate, inspire, consecrate, enshrine.

Adj. pious, religious, devout, devoted, reverent, godly, heavenly minded, humble; pure, – in heart; holy, spiritual, pietistic; saint-ly, -like; seraphic, sacred, solemn.

believing, faithful, Christian, Catholic.

elected, adopted, justified, sanctified, regenerated, inspired, consecrated, converted, unearthly, not of the earth.

988. Impiety.—N. impiety; sin etc. 945; irreverence; profan-eness etc. *adj.*, -ity, -ation; blasphemy, desecration, sacrilege; scoffing etc. *v.*

[Assumed piety] hypocrisy etc. (*falsehood*) 544; pietism, cant, pious fraud; lip-devotion, -service, -reverence; mis-devotion, formalism, austerity; sanctimon-y, -iousness etc. *adj.*; pharisaism, precisianism; sabbat-ism, -arianism; *odium theologicum*, sacerdotalism; bigotry etc. (*obstinacy*) 606, (*prejudice*) 481.

hardening, backsliding, declension, perversion, reprobation apostacy, recusancy.

sinner etc. 949; scoffer, blasphemer; sacrilegist; worldling; hypocrite etc. (*dissembler*) 548; Scribes and Pharisees; Tartufe, Maw-worm.

bigot; saint [ironically] ; Pharisee, sabbatarian, formalist, methodist, puritan, pietist, precisian, religionist, devotee, ranter, fanatic, wowser.

the -wicked, – evil, – unjust, – reprobate; son of -men, – Belial, – the wicked one; children of darkness.

V. be -impious etc. *adj.*; profane, desecrate, blaspheme, revile, scoff; swear etc. (*malediction*) 908; commit sacrilege.

snuffle; turn up the whites of the eyes; idolize.

Adj. impious; irreligious etc. 989; desecrating etc. *v.*; profane, irreverent, sacrilegious, blasphemous.

un-hallowed, -sanctified, -regenerate; hardened, perverted, reprobate.

hypocritical etc. (*false*) 544; canting, pietistical, sanctimonious, unctuous, pharisaical, over-righteous, righteous over much.

bigoted, fanatical etc. 481 and 606; priest-ridden.

Adv. under the -mask, – cloak, – pretence, – form, – guise- of religion.

989. Irreligion.—N. irreligion, indevotion; ungodliness etc. *adj.*; laxity, quietism, apathy, indifference, passivity.

scepticism, doubt; un-, dis-belief; incredul-ity, -ousness etc. *adj.*; want of -faith, – belief; pyrrhonism; doubt etc. 485; agnosticism.

atheism, deism; hylotheism; materialism; positivism; nihilism.

infidelity, freethinking, antichristianity, rationalism.

atheist, anti-christian, sceptic, unbeliever, deist, infidel, pyrrhonist; *giaour*, heathen, alien, gentile, Nazarene; *esprit fort*, freethinker, latitudinarian, rationalist; materialist, positivist, nihilist, agnostic.

V. be -irreligious etc. *adj.*; disbelieve, lack faith; doubt, question etc. 485.

dechristianize; serve Mammon, love darkness better than light.

Adj. irreligious; in-, un-devout; devout-, god-, grace-less; un-godly, -holy, -sanctified, -hallowed; atheistic, without God.

sceptical, free-thinking; un-believing, -converted; incredulous, faithless, lacking faith; deistical; un-, anti-christian.

worldly, mundane, earthly, carnal, unspiritual; worldly etc.- minded.

Adv. irreligiously etc. *adj.*

990. Worship.—N. worship, adoration, devotion, aspiration, latria, homage, service, humiliation; kneeling, genuflexion, prostration.

prayer, invocation, supplication, rogation, intercession, orison, holy breathing; petition etc. (*request*) 765; collect, litany, Lord's prayer, paternoster, *Ave Maria*, rosary; bead-roll; latria, dulia, hyperdulia, vigils; revival; cult.

thanksgiving; giving –, returning- thanks; grace, praise, glorification, benediction, doxology, hosanna; h-, allelujah; *Te Deum*, *non nobis Domine*, *nunc dimittis*; paean.

psalm, -ody; hymn, plainsong, chant, chaunt, response, anthem, motet; antiphon, -y.

oblation, sacrifice, incense, libation; burnt –, votive –, thank-offering; offertory, collection.

discipline; self-discipline, -examination, -denial; fasting.

divine service, office, duty; morning prayer; mass, matins, evensong, vespers, compline; holy day etc. (*rites*) 998.

worshipper, congregation, communicant, celebrant.

V. worship, lift up the heart, aspire; revere etc. 928; adore, do service, pay homage; humble oneself, kneel; bow –, bend- the knee; fall -down, – on one's knees; prostrate oneself, bow down and worship, recite the rosary.

pray, invoke, supplicate; put –, offer- up -prayers, – petitions; beseech etc. (*ask*) 765; say one's prayers, tell one's beads.

return –, give- thanks; say grace, bless, praise, laud, glorify, magnify, sing praises; give benediction, lead the choir, intone, chant, sing.

propitiate, offer sacrifice, fast, deny oneself; vow, offer vows, give alms.

work out one's salvation; go to church; attend -service, – mass; communicate etc. (*rite*) 998.

Adj. worshipping etc. *v.*; devout, devotional, reverent, pure, solemn; fervid etc. (*heartfelt*) 821.

Int. h-, allelujah! hosanna! glory be to God! O Lord! pray God that! God -grant, – bless, – save, – forbid! *sursum corda.*

991. Idolatry.—N. idol-atry, -ism; demon-ism, -olatry; idol –, demon –, devil –, fire- worship; zoolatry, fetishism, Mari-, Bibli-, ecclesi-, heli-olatry.

deification, apotheosis, canonization; hero worship.

sacrifices, hecatomb, holocaust; human sacrifices, immolation, mactation, infanticide, self-immolation, *suttee.*

idol, golden calf, graven image, fetish, *avatar*, Juggernaut, joss, *lares et penates*; Baal etc. 986.

idolator etc. *n.*

V. worship -idols, – pictures, – relics; put on a pedestal, bow down to, prostrate oneself before, make sacrifice to; deify, canonize, idolize.

Adj. idolatrous.

992. Sorcery.—N. sorcery; superstition; occult -art, – sciences; black –, magic; the black art, necromancy, theurgy, thaumaturgy; demon-ology, -omy, -ship; *diablerie*, bedevilment; witch-craft, -ery; glamor; fetis-hism, -ism; ghost dance; hoodoo, voodoo; Shamanism [Esquimaux], vampirism; conjuration; bewitchery, exorcism, enchantment, incantation, obsession, possession, mysticism, second sight, mesmerism, animal magnetism; od –, odylic- force; electro-biology, *clairvoyance*; spiritualism, spirit-rapping, table-turning; thought reading, telepathy, thought transference, automatic writing, *planchette*, ouija board; crystal gazing; spirit manifestation, materialization, astral body, ectoplasm etc.

divination etc. (*prediction*) 511; sortilege, ordeal, *sortes Virgiliance*; hocus-pocus etc. (*deception*) 545; oracle etc. 513.

V. practice -sorcery etc. *n.*; cast a -horoscope, – nativity; conjure, exorcise, charm, enchant; bewitch, -devil; overlook, look on with the evil eye; entrance, mesmerize, magnetize; fascinate etc. (*influence*) 615; taboo; wave a wand; rub the -ring, – lamp; cast a spell; call up spirits, – from the vasty deep; raise spirits from the dead; raise –, lay-ghosts; command genii.

Adj. magic, -al; mystic, weird, cabalistic, talismanic, phylacteric, incantatory; charmed etc. *v.*

993. Spell.—N. spell, charm, incantation, exorcism, weird, cabala, exsufflation, cantrap, runes, abracadabra, hocus-pocus, open *sesame*, countercharm, Ephesian letters, bell, book and candle, Mumbo-jumbo, evil-eye, fee-faw-fum.

talisman, amulet, periapt, telesm, phylactery, philter, wish-bone, merry-thought, mascot, scarab, swastika; fetish; *agnus Dei.*

wand, caduceus, rod, divining rod, lamp of Aladdin, magic carpet, seven-league boots; magic ring; wishing –, Fortunatus's- cap.

994. Sorcerer.—N. sorcerer, magician; thaumat-, the-urgist; conjuror, necromancer, seer, wizard, witch; fairy etc. 980; *lamia*, hag, warlock, charmer, exorcist, voodoo, mage, diviner, dowser; cunning –, medicine- man, witch doctor; Shaman, figure-flinger, ecstatica, medium, *clairvoyant*, mesmerist, hypnotist; *deus ex machinâ*; astrologer; soothsayer etc. 513.

Katerfelto, Cagliostro, Merlin, Comus, Mesmer, Rosicrucian; Hecate, Circe, Lilith, siren, weird sisters; witch of Endor.

995. Churchdom.—N. church, -dom; ministry, apostleship, priesthood, prelacy, hierarchy, church government, christendom, pale of the church.

clerical-, sacerdotal-, episcopalian-, ultramontan-ism; Theocracy; ecclesiolog-y, -ist; priestcraft, *odium theologicum.*

monach-ism, -y; monasticism, monkhood.

[Ecclesiastical offices and dignities] pontificate, primacy, archbishopric, archiepiscopacy; prelacy; bishop-ric, -dom; episcop-ate, -acy; see, diocese; deanery, stall; canon-ry, -icate; prebend, -aryship; benefice, incumbency, glebe, advowson, living, cure, – of souls; rectorship; vicar-iate, -ship; pastor-ate, -ship; deacon-ry, -ship; -curacy; chaplain, -cy, -ship; cardinal-ate, -ship; abbacy, presbytery.

holy orders, ordination, institution, consecration, induction, reading in, preferment, translation, presentation.

popedom, papacy; the -Vatican, – apostolic see, – see of Rome; religious sects etc. 984.

council etc. 696; conclave, college of cardinals, convocation, synod, consistory, chapter, vestry, presbytery; sanhedrim, *congé d'élire*; ecclesiastical courts, consistorial court, court of Arches.

V. call, ordain, induct, prefer, translate, consecrate, present, elect, bestow.

take -orders, – the veil, – vows.

Adj. ecclesi-astical, -ological; clerical, sacerdotal, priestly, prelatical, pastoral, ministerial, capitular, theocratic; hierarchical, archiepiscopal; episcopal, -ian; canonical; mon-astic, -achal; monkish; abbati-al, -cal; pontifical, papal, apostolic; untramontane, priest-ridden.

996. Clergy.—N. clergy, clericals, ministry, priesthood, presbytery, the cloth, the pulpit.

clergyman, divine, ecclesiastic, churchman, priest, presbyter, hierophant, pastor, shepherd, minister, clerk in holy orders; father, – in Christ; *padre*, *abbé*, *curé*; patriarch; reverend; black coat; confessor; sky pilot.

dignitaries of the church; ecclesi-, hier-arch; eminence, reverence, elder, primate, metropolitan, archimandrite, archbishop, bishop, prelate, diocesan, suffragan, dean, subdean, archdeacon, prebendary, canon, rural dean, rector, parson, vicar, perpetual curate, residentiary, beneficiary, incumbent, chaplain, curate, – in charge; deacon, -ess; preacher; lay reader, lecturer; capitular; missionary, propagandist, Jesuit, revivalist, field preacher.

churchwarden, sidesman; clerk, precentor, choir; almoner, *suisse*, verger, beadle, sexton, sacristan; acol-yth, -othyst, -yte; thurifer; chorister, choir boy.

[Roman Catholic priesthood] Pope, *Papa*, Holy

Father, pontiff, high priest, cardinal; ancient –, flamen; confessor, penitentiary; spiritual director.

cenobite, conventual, abbot, prior, monk, friar, lay brother, beadsman, mendicant, pilgrim, palmer; canon-regular, -secular; Jesuit, Franciscan, Friars minor, Minorites; Observant, Capuchin, Dominican, Carmelite; Augustinian; Gilbertine; Austin-, Black-, White-, Grey-, Crossed-, Crutched- Friars; Bonhomme, Carthusian, Benedictine, Cistercian, Trappist, Cluniac, Premonstratensian, Maturine; Templar, Hospitaller.

abb-, prior-, canon-ess; mother superior; *religieuse*, nun, sister, *beguine*, novice, postulant.

[Under the Jewish dispensation] prophet, priest, high priest, Levite; Rabbi, -n; scribe.

[Mohammedan etc.] mullah, ulema, imauam, sheik; so-fi, -phi; mufti, hadji, muezzin, dervish; fakir, -quir; brahmin, gooroo, druid, bonze, santon, abdal, Lama, talapoin, caloyer etc.

V. take orders etc. 995.

Adj. the –, the very –, the Right- Reverend; ordained, in orders, called to the ministry.

997. Laity.—N. laity, flock, fold, congregation, assembly, brethren, people.

temporality, secularization.

layman, civilian; parishioner, catechumen; secularist.

V. secularize.

Adj. secular, lay, laical, civil, temporal, profane.

998. Rite.—N. rite; ceremon-y, -ial; ordinance, observance, function, duty; form, -ulary; solemnity, sacrament; incantation etc. (*spell*) 993; service, psalmody etc. (*worship*) 990; liturgies.

ministration; preach-ing, -ment; predication, sermon, homily, exhortation, lecture, discourse, pastoral.

baptism, christening, chrism; immersion; baptismal regeneration; font; circumcision.

confirmation; imposition –, laying on- of hands; churching, purification, ordination etc. (*churchdom*) 995; excommunication.

Eucharist, Lord's supper, communion; the –, the holy- sacrament; celebration, high celebration; *missa cantata*; offertory; introit; consecration; con-, tran-substantiation; real presence; elements, bread and wine; mass; high –, low –, dry- mass.

matrimony etc. 903; burial etc. 363; visitation of the sick.

seven sacraments, impanation, extreme unction, last rites, *viaticum*, invocation of saints, canonization, transfiguration, auricular confession; fasting; maceration, flagellation, sackcloth and ashes; penance etc. (*atonement*) 952; absolution; telling of beads, reciting the rosary, processional; thurification, incense, holy water, aspersion.

relics, rosary, beads, reliquary, host, cross, rood, crucifix, pax, pix, pyx, *agnus Dei*, censer, thurible, patera, urceole; chalice, patten, Holy Grail, sangrail; seven-branch candle stick, monstrance, sacring bell.

ritual, rubric, canon, ordinal; liturgy, prayer-book, book of common prayer, pietas, euchology, litany, lectionary; missal, breviary, mass-book, bead-roll.

psalter; psalm –, hymn- book; hymn-al, -ology; psalmody.

ritual-, ceremonial-ism; sabbat-ism, -arianism; ritualist, sabbatarian.

holyday, feast, fast; Sabbath, Passover, Pentecost; Advent, Christmas, Noel, Epiphany, Lent, Shrove Tuesday, Ash Wednesday, Maundy Thursday; Passion –, Holy- week; Good Friday, Easter, Ascension Day, Whitsuntide; Trinity Sunday, Corpus Christi; All-Saints' –, – Souls'- Day; Candle-, Lam-, Martin-, Michael-mas; hogmanay; Ramadan, -zan; Bairam etc. etc.

V. perform service, do duty, minister, officiate, baptize, dip, sprinkle; confirm, lay hands on; give –, administer –, take –, receive –, attend –, partake of- the -sacrament, – communion; communicate; celebrate mass; administer –, receive- extreme unction; anele, shrive, absolve, confess; do penance; genuflect; cross oneself, make the sign of the cross.

excommunicate, ban with bell, book and candle.

preach, sermonize, predicate, lecture.

Adj. ritual, -istic; ceremonial, liturgic; baptismal, eucharistical; paschal.

999. Canonicals. N. canonicals, vestments, robe, gown, Geneva gown, frock, pallium, surplice, cassock, dalmatic, scapulary, cope, scarf, tunicle, chasuble, alb, *alba*, stole; fan-on, -nel; tonsure, cowl, hood; calo-te, -tte; bands; capouch, amice, orarium, ephod; apron, lawn sleeves, pontificals, pall; miter, tiara, triple crown; shovel –, cardinal's- hat; biretta; crosier; pastoral staff; costume etc. 225.

1000. Temple.—N. place of worship; house of -God, – prayer.

temple, cathedral, minister, church, kirk, chapel, meeting-house, bethel, tabernacle, conventicle, *basilica*, fane, holy place, chantry, oratory.

synagogue; mosque; marabout; pantheon; pagoda; joss-house; dagobah, tope; kiosk.

parsonage, rectory, vicarage, manse, deanery, glebe, church house; Vatican; bishop's palace; Lambeth.

altar, shrine, sanctuary, Holy of Holies, *sanctum sanctorum*, sacrarium, -isty; communion –, holy –, Lord's- table; table of the Lord; pyx; baptistery, font; piscina, stoup; aumbry; sedile; reredos; rood-loft, – screen; jube.

chancel, quire, choir, nave, aisle, transept, lady chapel, vestry, crypt, cloisters, porch; triforum, clerestory, churchyard, *golgotha*, calvary, Easter sepulcher; stall, pew, sitting; pulpit, ambo, lectern, reading-desk, confessional, prothesis, credence, baldachin, *baldacchino*; jesse, apse, belfry; chapter-house; presbytery.

monastery, priory, abbey, friary, convent, nunnery, cloister.

Adj. claustral, cloistered; monast-ic, -erial; conventual.

INDEX

The numbers refer to the headings under which the words or phrases occur. When the same word or phrase may be used in various senses, the several headings under which it, or its synonyms, will be found, according to those meanings, are indicated by the words printed in Italics. These words in Italics are not intended to explain the meaning of the word or phrase to which they are annexed, but only to assist in the required reference.

When the word given in the Index is itself the title or heading of a category, the number of reference is printed in blacker type, thus: **abode 189.**

A

A 1 642, 648
a – fortiori 33
 – se 10
à – fond 52
 – outrance, – plomb 212
 – propos *relative* 9
 apt 23
 occasion 134
 – propos de bottes 10
A.B. 269
ab – extra 220
 – initio 66
 – intra 221
 – ovo 66
 – ovo usque ad mala 52
 – uno disce omnes 16
abacist 85
aback 235
 take – 508
abacus 85
Abaddon 978, 982
abaft 235
abalienate 783
abandon
 depart from 293
 – *a purpose* 624
 – *property* 782
 – *hope* 859
 – *society* 893
abandon
 lively 682
 artless 703
 relinquish 757
abandoned
 neglected 460
 forsaken 893
 vicious 945
abase 308, 879
abased 886
abasement 874, 886
abash *daunt* 860
 humiliate 879
abat jour 260
abate *lessen* 36
 – *a price* 813
abattis 717
abattoir 361
abba 166
abbacy 995
abbatial 995
abbatis 717
abbess 996
abbey 1000
abbot 996
abbreviation 201, 596
A B C *beginning* 66
 teaching 537
 letters 561
abdal *fanatic* 984
 clergy 996
abdicate
 – *a throne* 738
 resign 757
abditory 530
abdomen 191, 221
abducent 289
abduct *take* 789
 steal 791
 repel 289
abeam 236
abecedarian 540, 541
abecedary
 school 542
 letter 561
aberrant
 exceptional 83
 deviating 279
 divergent 291
 erroneous 495
aberration [*see* aberrant]
 variation 20a
 mental – 503
abet 707
abettor 711
abeyance
 extinction 2
 suspense 142
 expectation 507
 in – 172
abhor 867, 898
abhorrent 830
abide *endure* 106
 remain 110
 continue 141, 143
 dwell 186
 quiet 265
 expect 507
 not – 867
 – by 488, 772
 – with 826
abigail 746
abilities, to the best of one's – 686
ability 157, 698
abiogenesis 161
abject
 vile 874, 940
 servile 886
 – fear 862
abjure 607, 757, 780
ablation 38, 789
ablaze 382, 420
able 157, 689
 – seaman 269
able-bodied 159
ablegate 185, 759
ablepsy 442
ablude 15
ablution 652
abnegation
 denial 536
 refusal 764
 forbearance 953
 self – 942
abnormal 83, 568
 – mind 503
abnormis sapiens 498
aboard *present* 186
 ship 273
 go – 293
abode 189
 presage 511
 take up one's – 150, 184
abodement 511
abois, aux –
 dying 360
 danger 665
 difficulty 704
abolish 162, 756
abominable
 bad 649
 foul 653
 hateful 898
abominate 867, 898
abord 894
aboriginal 66, 153
aborigines 188
aborticide 361
abortion 674, 732
abound 639
about *relative to* 9
 nearly 32
 near 197
 around 227
 be – *busy with* 625
 active 682
 beat – 629
 come – 658
 get – *public* 531
 recover 660
 go – *turn* 311
 going – *news* 532
 not know what one is – 699
 put –
 turn round 283
 round – 311
 send – one's business 756
 set – 676
 turn – *invert* 218
 what it is – 454
 what one is – 625
 – it and about it 573
 – to 121
 – to be 152
above 206
 – all 33, 642
 – board
 manifest 525
 artless 703
 fair 939
 – comprehension 519
 – ground 359
 – the mark 33
 – par 31, 648
 – praise 944
 – price 814
 – stairs 206
 – suspicion 946
 – water *safe* 664
above-mentioned
 preceding 62
 repeated 104
 prior 116
abracadabra 993
Abraham,
 sham – 544
abrasion
 paring 38
 filing 330, 331
abreast 216, 236
abreption 789
abri 666
 – tente d' – 233
abridge *lessen* 36
 shorten 201
 – *in writing* 572, 596
abridgment
 compendium 596
abroach 673
abroad
 extraneous 57
 distant 196
 uncertain 475
 get – *public* 531
abrogation 756
abrupt *sudden* 113
 violent 173
 steep 217
 unexpected 508
 style 579
abruption 44
abscess 655
abscissa 466
abscission
 retrenchment 38
 division 44
abscond
 escape 623
 not pay 808
absence 187
 – of choice 609a
 – of influence 175a
 – of intellect 450a
 – of mind 458
 – of motive 615a
absentee 187
absinthe 298
absolute
 not relative 1
 great 31
 complete 52
 certain 474
 affirmative 535
 authoritative 737
 severe 739
 free 748
 unalienable 924
 make – 467, 480
 – interest 980
absolution 978
absolutism 506, 739
absolve
 liberate 750
 forgive 918
 exempt 927a
 shrive 952
 acquit 970
absonant 414, 477
absorb *combine* 48
 take in 296
 consume 677
 – the mind 457, 458
 – the soul 824
 – ed in thought 451
absorbing 630, 821, 829
absquatulate 623
abstain 623
 disuse 678
 temperance 953
 – from action 681
 – from voting 609a
abstainer 958, 958
abstemious 953
absterge 652
abstersive 662
abstinence [*see* abstain]
 total – 953, 955
abstract
 separate 44
 abridge 596
 take 789
 steal 791
 in the – *apart* 44
 alone 87
 – idea 453
 – oneself inattention 458
 – thought 451
 attention 457
abstracted
 inattentive 458
abstruse 519
absurdity
 impossible 471
 nonsense **497**
 ridiculous 853
abundant *great* 31, 63
 enough 639

abundanti cautelâ, ex – 664
abuse *deceive* 545
ill-treat 649
misuse 679
malediction 908
threat 909
upbraid 932
violate 961
– of language 563
– of terms 523
abusive 895, 934
abut *near* 197 *touch* 199, 215
abutment 717
aby *remain* 141
endure 821, 826
abysmal *deep* 208
abyss *space* 180
depth 208
interval 198
danger 667
hell 982
A.C. 106
academic
teaching 537, 542
theory 514
academical
style 578
academicals
225 *robes*
academician 492
Royal – 559
academy 542
acanthus 847
a capite ad calcem 52
acariâtre 901
acarpous 169
acatalectic 597
acaudal 38
accede 488, 725, 762
accelerate
early 132
stimulate 173
velocity 274
hasten 684
accension 384
accent *sound* 402
tone of voice 580
rhythm 597
accentuate 642
accentuated 580
accept *assent* 488
consent 762
receive 785
take 789
acceptable 646, 829
acceptance 771
acceptation 522
acception 522
access 286
easy of – 705
means of – 627
accessible 470, 705
accession
adjunct 39
increase 35
addition 37
- to office 737, 755
consent 762
accessory
extrinsic 6
additive 37
adjunct 39
accompanying 88
aid 707
auxiliary 711
acciaccatura 413
accidence 567
accident *event* 151
chance 156
disaster 619
misfortune 735
fatal – 361
accidental
extrinsic 6
fortuitous 156
undesigned 621
accidents,
trust to the chapter of – 621
accipient 785
acclamation
assent 488
approbation 931
acclimatize 370, 613
acclivity 217
accloy 641
accolade 894
accommodate
suit 23
adjust 27
aid 707
reconcile 723
give 784
lend 787
– oneself to 82
accommodation
space 180
accommodating
kind 906
accompaniment
adjunct 39
coexistence **88**
musical 415
accompany
add 37
coexist 88
concur 120
music 416
accompli, fait – 729
accomplice 711
accomplish
execute 161
complete 729
succeed 731
accomplishment
490, 698
accompts 811
accord
uniform 16
agree 23
music 413
assent 488
concord 714
grant 760
give 784
of one's own – 602
according
– as *qualification* 469
– to *evidence* 467
– to circumstances 8
– to law 963
– to rule
conformably 82
– rumor 527
accordingly
logically 476
accordion 417
accost 586
accoucheur 631, 662
accouchment 161
account *list* 86
adjudge 480
description 594
credit 805
money - 811
fame 873
approbation 931
call to – 932
find one's – in
useful 644
success 731
make no – of 483, 930
not – for 519
on – of *motive* 615
behalf 707
on no – 536
send to one's – 361
take into – 457, 469
small – 643
to one's – 780
turn to –
improve 658
use 677
success 731
gain 775
– as *deem* 484
– book 551
– for 155, 522
– with 794, 807
accountable
liable 177
debit 811
duty 926
accountant 301, 811
certified public – 811
accounts **811**
accouple 43
accoutered
armed 717
accouterment
dress 225
appliance 633
equipment 673
accoy 174
accredit
commission 755, 759
money 805
honor 873
accredited 484, 613
– to 755, 759
accretion 35, 46
accrimination 938
accroach 789
accrue *add* 37
result 154
acquire 775
be received 785, 810
accubation 213
accueil 894
accultural 35
accumbent 213
accumulate
collect 72
store 636
redundance 641
accurate 494
– knowledge 490
accurse 908
accursed
disastrous 649
undone 828
vicious 945
accusation **938**
accuse
disapprove 932
charge 938
lawsuit 969
accustom 613
ace *small* 32
unit 87
within an – 197
aceldama *kill* 361
arena 728
acephalous 59
acerbate 659, 835
acerbity
acrimony 395
sourness 397
rudeness 895
spleen 900, 901
malevolence 907
acervate 72
acetous 397
acetylene 388
acharné 900
Achates, fidus – 890, 939
ache *physical* 378
mental 828
Acheron
pit of – 982
Acherontic
moribund 360
gloomy 837
achievable 470
achieve *end* 67
produce 161
do 680
accomplish 729
achievement 551, 861
Achilles, heel of –
vulnerable 665
achromatism **429**
acicular 253
acid 397
acid test 463
acknowledge
answer 462
assent 488
disclose 529
avow 535
consent 762
observe 772
pay 807
thank 916
repent 950
reward 973
acknowledged
custom 613
acme 210
– of perfection 650
Acology 662
acolyte 996
acomous 226
aconite 663
acoustic 418
– organs 418
acoustics 402
acquaint
– oneself with 539
– with 527
acquaintance
knowledge 490
information 527
friend 890
make – with 888
acquiesce
assent 488
willing 488
consent 762
tolerate 826
acquire
develop 161
get 775
receive 785
– a habit 613
– learning 539
acquirement
knowledge 490
learning 539
talent 698
receipt 810
acquisition
knowledge 490
gain 775
acquit
liberate 750
exempt 927a
vindicate 937
innocent 946
absolve 970
acquit oneself
behave 692
– of a debt 807
– of a duty 926
– of an obligation 772
acquittal **506, 970**
acquittance 771
acres *space* 180
land 342
property 780
Acres, Bob 862
acrid 392, 395
acridity 171
acrimony
physical 171
caustic 830
discourtesy 895
hatred 898
anger 900
malevolence 907
acroamatism 490
acrobat
strength 159
actor 599
proficient 700
mountebank 844
Acropolis 210
across 219, 708
acrostic 533, 561, 842
act *imitate* 19
physical 170
- of a play 599
personate 599
voluntary 680
statute 697
in the – 680, 947
– **a part** *feign* 544
– one's part 625, 926
– upon
physical 170
mental 615
take steps 680
– up to 772
– well one's part 944
– without authority 738
acting *deputy* 759
actinic 420
actinometer 445
action *physical* 170
voluntary **680**
battle 720
law 969
line of – 692

aedile 965
aegis 717
aegrescit medendo 659
aegrotat 927a
aeolian 349
— harp 417
aequam servare mentem 826
aequo animo 823 826
aerate 334, 353
aere perennius 873
aerial 273
elevated 206
flying 267
gas 334
air 338
– navigation 267
– navigator 269
– mail 534
– patrol 726
– perspective 428
– warfare 722
aerie 189
aerify 334
aerodonetics 267
aerodrome 728
aerodynamics 267, 334, 349
aerolite 318
aerology 338
aeromancy 511
aeromechanics 267
aerometer 338
aeronaut 269
aeronautical 273
aeronautics 267, 338
aeroplane 273
aerostat *balloon* 273
aerostatics 267, 334
aerostation 338
aery 317
Aesculapius 662
Aesop 846
aesthetic
sensibility **375**
beauty 845
taste 850
aestival 125
aeternum servans sub pectore vulnus 919
afar 196
affable 879, 894
affair *event* 151
topic 454
business 625
battle 720
love 902, 903
– of honour 720
affaires, charge d' – 758
affaire de coeur 897
affect *relate to* 9
tend to 176
qualify 469
feign 544
touch 824
desire 865
love 897
affectation **855**
affected with
feeling 821
disease 655
affectibility 822
affecting 830
affection 821, 897
affections **820**
affettuoso 415
affiance 768, 858
affianced 897, 903
affiche 531
affidation 769
affidavit
affirmation 535
record 551
lawsuit 969
affiliation
relation 9
kindred 11
attribution 155
affine 11
affinitive 9
affinity 9, 17
mate 905
affirmation **535**, 488
affix *add* 37
sequel 39
fasten 43
letter 561
afflation 349
afflatus 349, 597, 985
afflict 830
– with illness 655
affliction *pain* 828
infliction 830
adversity 735
affluence
sufficiency 639
prosperity 734
wealth 803
affluent *river* 348
afflux 286
afford *supply* 784
wealth 803
yield 810
sell for 812
– aid &c. 707
afforestation 371
affranchise
make free of 748
liberate 750
affray 720
affreet 980
affriction 331
affright 860
affront *molest* 830
provocation 900
insult 929
– danger 861
affuse 337
afield 186
afire 382
afloat *extant* 1
unstable 149
going on 151
ship 273
navigation 267
ocean 341
news 532
preparing 673
keep oneself – 734
set – *publish* 531
afoot *on hand* 625
preparing 673
astir 682
afore 116
aforementioned 116
aforesaid
preceding 62
repeated 104
prior 116
aforethought 611
aforetime 116
afraid 860
be – *irresolute* 605
– to say *uncertain* 475
afresh 104, 123
Afric heat 382
Afrikander 57
afrite 980
aft 235
after *in order* 63
in time 117
too late 135
rear 235
pursuit 622
be – *intention* 620
pursuit 622
go – *follow* 281
– all *for all that* 30
qualification 469
on the whole 476
– time 133
after acceptation 516
after-age 124
after-clap 509
after-crop 65, 168
after-dinner 117
after-glow 40, 65, 420
after-growth 65
after-life 152
aftermath
sequel 65
fertile 168
profit 775
aftermost 235
afternoon 126
– farmer 683
after-part 65, 235
after-piece 599
after-taste 65, 390
after-thought
thought 451
memory 505
change of mind 607
after-time 121
afterwards 117
age 745
agacerie 615
again 90, 104
– and again 136
come – *periodic* 138
fall off – 661
live – 660
against
counteraction 179
anteposition 237
provision 673
voluntary opposition 708
chances – 473
declaim – 932
false witness – 934
go – 708
set – *actively* 898
set one's face 764, 932
stand up – *resist* 719
raise &c. one's voice – 489
– one's will 744
– one's expectation 508
– the grain *difficult* 704
painful 830
dislike 867
– the stream 704
– the time when 510
– one's will 744
– one's wishes 603
agamist 904
agape *open* 260
curious 455
expectant 507
wonder 870
Agapemone 827, 897
agate 847
age *time* 106
period 108
long time 110
era 114
present time 118
oldness 124
advanced life **128**
of – 131
from age to – 112
age quod agis! 682
agency
physical **170**
instrumentality 631
means 632
employment 677
voluntary action 680
direction 693
commission 755
agenda 625, 626
agent *physical* 153
intermediary 228
voluntary **690**
consignee 759
– provocateur 615
agentship 755
ages: for – 110
– ago 122
agglomerate 46, 72
agglutinate 46
aggrandize
in degree 35
in bulk 194
honor 873
aggravate
increase 35
vehemence 173
exaggerate 549
render worse 659
distress 835
exasperate 900
aggravating 830
aggravation **835**
aggregate 50, 72, 84
aggregation 46
aggression 716
aggressor 726
aggrieve 649, 830
aggroup 72
aghast
disappointed 509
fear 860
wonder 870
agile 274, 682
agio 813
agiotage 794
agitate *move* 315
inquire 461
activity 682
excite the feelings 824
– a question 476
agitation [*see* agitate]
changeableness 149
energy 171
motion **315**
in – *preparing* 673
agitator *leader* 694
aglet 554
agley, gang – 732
aglow 382, 420
agnate 11
agnition 762
agnomen 564
agnostic 487
agnosticism 984, 989
agnus Dei 993, 998
ago 122
not long – 123
agog *expectant* 507
desire 865
wonder 870
agoing 682
set – 707
agonism 720
agonizing 824, 830
agony 378, 828
– of death 360
– of excitement 825
agrarian 371
agree *accord* 23
concur 178
assent 488
concord 714
consent 762
compact 769
compromise 774
– in opinion 488
– with *salubrity* 656
agreeable
comfortable 82
physically 377
mentally 829
agreeably to 82
agreement **23** [*see* agree]
compact 769
agrestic 371
agriculture **371**
agronomy 371
aground *fixed* 150
in difficulty 704
failure 732
ague-fit 860
aguets, aux – *expectation* 507
ambush 530
aguish *cold* 383
ah me! 839
aha! *rejoicing* 838
ahead 234, 280
go – *progression* 282
shoot – *transcursion* 303
activity 682
rock – 665, 667
Ahrimanes 987, 980
aid **707**, 906
by the – of 631, 632
aide-de-camp 711, 745

aidless 160
aigrette 847
aiguille 253
aiguillette 747, 847
aigulet 847
ail 655, 828
aileron 267, 273
ailment 655
aim 278, 620, 675
– a blow at 716
aimable 894
faire l' – 897
aimer éperdument 897
aimless *without motive* 615a
chance 621
air *unsubstantial* 4
broach 66
lightness 320
gas 334
atmospheric 338
wind 349
tune 415
appearance 448
refresh 689
demeanor 692
fashionable 852
beat the – 645
fill the – 404
fine – *salubrity* 656
fish in the – 645
fowls of the – 366
in the – 527
rend the – 404
take – 531
air-balloon 273
air base 728
air-commodore 745
aircraft 273, 726
air-drawn 515
airdrome 273
air-force 726
air-gun 727
airing 266
air-mail 273
airman 269
airmanship 698
air-marshal 745
air-passage 351
air-pipe 351
airport 273, 292, 728
air-pump 349
air-raid 716
airs *affectation* 855
pride 878
vanity 880
arrogance 885
air-shaft 351
air service 267
airship 273, 726
air-tight 261
airways 267
airworthy 273, 664
airy [*see* air]
windy 349
unimportant 643
gay 836
– hopes 858, 859
give to – nothing a local habitation &c. 515
aisle *passage* 260
way 627
in a church 1000
ait 346
ajar *open* 260
discordant 713
ajee 217
ajutage 260, 350
akimbo *angular* 244
stand – 715
akin *related* 9
consanguineous 11
similar 17
al fresco 220
alabaster *white* 430
alack! 839
alacrity *willing* 602
active 682
cheerful 836
Aladdin's lamp 993
alar 267
alarm *warning* 668
notice of danger 669
fear 860
cause for – 665
give an – *indicate* 550
alarmist 862
alarum 114, 550, 669
alas! 839
alate 267
alb 999
albeit 30
albert
chain 847
albification 430
albinescence 430
albinism 430
albino 443
album 593, 596
albumen
semi-liquid 352
protein 357
Alcaic 597
alcaid 745
alcalde 745
alcazar 189
alchemy 144
alcohol 995
Alcoran 986
alcove 191, 252
Aldebaran 423
alderman 745
ale 298
alea, jacta est – 601
aleatory 665
Alecto 173
alectromancy 511
alehouse 189
go to the – 959
alembic
conversion 144
vessel 191
furnace 386
laboratory 691
alentours 197
alert *watchful* 457, 459
active 682
alerte 669
aleuromancy 511
Alexandrine
ornate style 577
verse 597
alexandrite 848
alexipharmic 662
alexiteric 662
algebra 85
algid 383
algology 369
algorithm 85
alguazil 965
alias
otherwise 18
pseudonym 565
alibi 187
alien *irrelevant* 10
foreign 57
transfer 783
gentile 989
alienable 783
alienate
transfer 783
estrange 44, 889
set against 898
alienation
mental – 503
alieni appetens
grasping 865
envious 921
selfish 943
alienism 54
align 278
alight *stop* 265
arrive 292
descend 306
on fire 382
alike 17
share and share – 778
aliment *food* 298
alimentary 662
– canal 350
alimentation
aid 707
alimony
property 780
provision 803
income 810
aliquot 51, 84
aliter visum, diis – 601
alive
living 359
intelligent 498
active 682
cheerful 836
be – with 102
keep – *continue* 143
keep the memory – 505
look – 684
– to *attention* 457
cognizant 490
informed 527
able 698
sensible 822
alkahest 335
all *whole* 50
complete 52
generality 78
– absorbing 642
in – ages 112
– aboard 495
– agog 865
– in all 50
– along 106
– along of 154
– but 32
– colors 440
– considered 451, 480
– day long 110
– devouring 190
in – directions 278
– engrossing 190
at – events *compensation* 30
qualification 469
true 494
resolve 604
– fours *easy* 705
cards 840
– in good time 152
– hail! *welcome* 292
honor to 873
celebration 883
courtesy 894
– hands *everybody* 78
on – hands 488
– of a dither 824
– of a heap 72
– knowing 976
– manner of *difference* 15
multiform 81
with – one's might 686
– at once 113
– one 27, 866
– out 52
– over *end* 67
universal 78
destruction 162
space 180
at – points 52
– in one's power 686
– powerful
mighty 159
God 976
in – quarters 180
with – respect 928
in – respects 52, 494
– right! 922
– Saints' day 998
– searching 461
– seeing 976
on – sides 227
– sorts *diverse* 16a
mixed 41
multiform 81
– talk 4
– things to all men 894
– the time 106
at – times 136
– together 50
– ways 243, 279
– wise 976
– the world and his wife 78
of – work
useful 644
maid 746
Allah 979
allay
moderate 174
pacify 723
relieve 834
– excitability 826
allective 615
allege *evidence* 467
assert 535
plea 617
allegiance 743, 926
allegory 464, 521, 594
allegro *music* 415
cheerful 836
allelujah 990
allemande 840
all-embracing 76
alleviate 174, 834
alley *court* 189
passage 26
way 627
alliance *relation* 9
kindred 11
physical co-operation 178
voluntary co-operation 709
party 712
union 714
allied to *like* 17
alligation 43
allign 278
alliteration
similarity 17
style in writing 577
poetry 597
allocation 60, 786
allocution 586
allodium *free* 748
property 780
allopathy 662
alloquy 586
allot *arrange* 60
distribute 786
due 924
allow *assent* 488
admit 529
permit 760
consent 762
give 784
– to have one's own way 740
allowable 760, 924
allowance
qualification 469
gift 784
allotment 786
discount 813
salary 973
with grains of – 485
make – for *forgive* 918
vindicate 937
alloy *mixture* 41
combination 48
debase 659
allude *hint* 514
mean 516
refer to 521
latent 526
inform 527
allure *move* 615
create desire 865
alluring 829
allusive
relative 9
alluvial *level* 213
land 342
plain 344
alluvium
deposit 40
land 342
soil 653
ally *combine* 48
auxiliary 711
friend 891
alma mater 542
almanac
list 86
chronometry 114
record 551
almighty 157
Almighty, the – 976
almoner
treasurer 801

giver 784
church officer 996
almonry 802
almost *nearly* 32
not quite 651
– all 50
– immediately 132
alms *gift* 784
benevolence 906
worship 990
almshouse 189, 666
almsman 785
Alnaschar's dream 515, 858
aloes 395
aloft 206
alogy 497
alone *single* 87
unaided 706
let – *not use* 678
not restrain 748
along 200
get – *progress* 282
go – *depart* 293
go – with *concur* 178
assent 488
co-operate 709
– of *caused by* 154
– with *added* 37
together 88
by means of 631
alongside *near* 197
parallel 216
laterally 236
aloof *distant* 196
high 206
secluded 893
stand – *inaction* 681
refuse 764
cautious 864
alopecia 226
aloud 404
think – 589
naïveté 703
Alp 206
alpenstock 215
Alpha 66
– and Omega 50
alphabet
beginning 66
letters 561
alphabetarian 541
alphabeticize 60
alphitomancy 511
alpine *high* 206
Alpine Club 268, 305
already
antecedently 116
even now 118
past time 122
Alsatia 791, 945
also 37
altar 903, 1000
alter 140
– the case 468
– one's course 279
alter ego *similar* 17
auxiliary 711
deputy 759
friend 890
alterable 149
alteram partem, audire – 468, 922
alterative
substitute 634
remedy 662
altercation 713
altered *worn* 688
– for the worse 659
alternate
reciprocal 12
sequence 63
discontinuous 70
periodic 138
changeable 149
oscillate 314
alternative
substitute 147
choice 609
plan 626
although
compensation 30
counteraction 179
unless 469
altiloquence 577
altimetry
height 206
angle 244
measurement 466
altitude *height* 206
– and azimuth 466
alto 410, 416
– part 415
alto-rilievo 250, 557
altogether 50, 51
nude 226
altruism 910, 942
altruist 906
alum 397
alumnus 541
alveolus 252
always
uniformly 16
generally 78
during 106
perpetually 112
habitually 613
a.m. 114, 125
amability 829, 894
amah 753
amain 173, 684
amalgam, -ate 41, 48
amalgamation 709
Amalthea's horn 639
amantium iræ 918
amanuensis 553, 590
amaranthine 112
amari aliquid
bad 649
imperfect 651
painful 830
amaritude 395
amass *whole* 50
collect 72
store 636
amateur *volunteer* 602
layman 699
taste 850
votary 865
amatory 897
amaurosis 442
amaze 870
amazingly 31
Amazon
woman 374
warrior 726
courage 861
ambages
convolutions 248
circumlocution 573
circuit 629
ambagious 573
ambassador
messenger 534
representative 758
recall of –s 713
amber 356*a*
– color 436
ambidexter
right and left 238
fickle 607
clever 698
ambient 227
ambigu 41
ambiguas spargere voces
uncertain 475
misteach 538
false 544
cunning 702
ambiguous
uncertain 475
unintelligible 519
equivocal 520
obscure 571
ambiloquy 520
ambit 230
ambition 620, 865
ambivalence 605, 708
amble 266
ambo *school* 542
pulpit 1000
ambo, Arcades –
alike 17
friends 890
bad men 949
ambrosia 298
ambrosial 394, 490
ambulance
vehicle 272
hospital 662
ambulation 266
ambuscade 530
ambush 530, 667
lie in – 528
âme – de boue 949
– damnée
catspaw 711
servant 746
servile 886
bad man 949
– qui vive 101, 187
ameer 875
ameliorate 658
amen *assent* 488
submission 725
content 831
amenable 177, 602, 926
not – to reason 608
amend 658
amendatory 20
amende honorable 952
amends
compensation 50
atonement 952
reward 973
amenity 829, 894
amentia 503
amerce 974
American organ 417
Americanism 563
amethyst
purple 437
jewel 847
amiable
courteous 894
loving 897
kind 906
amicable 707, 888
amice 999
amicus – curiæ 527
– humani generis 910
– usque ad aras 890
amidships 68
amidst 41, 228
amiss 619
come – *disagree* 24
mistime 135
inexpedient 647
do – 945
nothing comes – 823
take – 867, 900
amity *concord* 714
peace 721
friendship 888
ammunition 635, 727
amnesia 506
amnesty 506, 723, 918
amnis, rusticus expectat dum defluat – *hope* 858
amœbæan 63
amok 503
among 41, 228
amor patriæ 910
amore, con – 602, 821
amoroso 599
amorous 897
– glances 902
amorphous 83, 241
amorphism 241
amortization 784
amotion 270
amount
quantity 25
degree 26
sum of money 800
price 812
gross – 50
– to 27, 85
amour 897, 961
– propre 880
ampere 466
amphibian 366
amphibious 83
amphibology 520
Amphictyonic council 696
amphigouri 497
amphitheatre
prospect 441
school 542
theater 599
arena 728
Amphitryon 890
amphora 191
ample *much* 31
spacious 180
large 192
broad 202
copious 639
amplify
expand 194
exaggerate 549
diffuse style 573
amplitude
quantity 25
degree 26
size 192
breadth 202
enough 639
ampoulé 191
ampulla 191
amputate 38
amuck 824
run – 503
amulet 247, 993
amusare la bocca, per – 394
amuse 829, 840
amusement 840
place of – 840
amussim, ad – 494
amylaceous 352
an *if* 514
ana 594
Anabaptist 984
anabasis 35
anachronism
false time 115
inopportune 135
error 495
anacoluthon 70
anaconda 913
anacreontic 597
anaglyph 554, 557
anagoge 521, 526
anagram
double sense 520
secret 533
letter 561
wit 842
analecta 596
analeptic 662
analgesia 376
analogy 9, 17
analogous 12
analysis
decomposition 49
arrangement 60
algebra 85
inquiry 461
experiment 463
reasoning 476
grammar 567
compendium 596
analyst 461, 463
anamorphosis
distortion 243
optical 443
misrepresentation 555
anapest 597
anaphylaxis 375
anarchist
destroyer 165
disobedient 742
evil-doer 913
anarchy 59, 738
anastatic printing 558
anastomosis 43, 219
anastrophe 218
anathema 908
anathematize 908
censure 932
detract 934
anatomize *dissect* 44
investigate 461
anatomy
dissection 44
leanness 203
texture 329
anatomy

science 357
comparative – 368
anatriptic 331
ancestral
bygone 122
old 124
aged 128
ancestry 166
anchor
connection 45
stop 265
safeguard 666
badge 747
hope 858
at – *fixed* 150
stationed 184
safe 664
cast – *settle* 184
arrive 292
have an – to windward 664
sheet – *means* 632
anchorage
location 184
roadstead 189
refuge 866
anchored 150
anchorite 893, 955
ancien régime 875
ancient *old* 124
flag 550
– times 122
ancientness 122
ancillary 707
and 37, 88
andante 415
andiron 386
androgynous 83
anecdote 594
anele 998
anemia 160
anemography 349
ἀνεμώλια βάζειν 497
anemometer
wind 349
measure 466
anent 9
aneroid 338
anesthesia 376, 381, 683
anew *again* 104
newly 123
anfractuosity 248
angel
object of love 897
good person 948
supernatural being **977**
fallen –
bad man 949
devil 978
guardian –
safety 664
auxiliary 711
benefactor 912
– of Death 362
– 's visits 137
angelic 944
angels and ministers of grace defend us! 860
angelus 550
anger 900
more in sorrow than in – 826, 918
angiology 329
angle 244
try 463
at an – 217
Anglicanism 984
angling 622, 840
anguille au genou, rompre l' – 158, 471
anguilliform 205, 248
anguis in herbâ 667
anguish
physical 378
moral 828
angular 244
– velocity 264
angularity 244
angusta domi, res – 804
angustation 203
anhelation 688
anhydrate 340
anhydrous 340
aniline dyes 437
anility 128, 499
animadvert
consider 451
attend to 457
reprehend 932
animal **366**
female – 374
– cries 412
– economy 350
– gratification 377
– life 364
– physiology 368
– spirits 836
– and vegetable kingdom 357
animalcule 193, 366
animalism
sensuality 954
animality **364**
animate
induce 615
excite 824
enliven 836
animation
life 359
animality 364
activity 682
vivacity 836
suspended – 823
animism 984
animo, ex – 602
quo – 620
animosity
dislike 867
enmity 889
hatred 898
anger 900
animus
willingness 602
intention 620
desire 865
ankle 244
– deep 208, 209
anklet 847
ankylosis 150
annalist 114, 553
annals
chronology 114
record 551
account 594
anneal 673
annex
addition 37
adjunct 39
junction 43
acquire 775
Annie Oakley 815
annihilate 2, 162
anniversary 138
anno 106
Anno Domini
era 106
old age 124
annotation 522, 550
annotator 524
scholar 492
interpreter 524
editor 595
annotto 434
announce
predict 511
inform 527
publish 531
assert 535
announcer 527
annoy
molest 649, 907
disquiet 830
annoyance 828
source of – 830
annual *periodic* 138
plant 367
book 593
annuity 810
annul 162, 750
annular 247
annunciate 527
annus magnus 108
anodyne
lenitive 174
remedial 662
relief 834
anoint *coat* 223
lubricate 332
oil 355
anointed
deity 976
king 745
anomaly 59, 83
disorder 59
irregularity 83
anon 132
anonymous 565
anopsia 442
anorexy 866
another
different 15
repetition 104
– story 468, 526
go upon – tack 607
– time 119
answer
to an inquiry **462**
confute 479
solution 522
succeed 731
pecuniary profit 775
pleadings 969
require an – 461
– for *deputy* 759
promise 768
go bail 806
I'll – for it 535
– the helm 745
– the purpose 731
– to *correspond* 9
– one's turn 644
answerable
agreement 23
liable 177
bail 806
duty 926
censurable 932
ant 690
Antaeus 159, 192
antagonism
difference 14
physical 179
voluntary 708
enmity 889
antagonist 710, 891
antagonistic 24
antarctic 237
antecedence 62, 116
antecedent 64
antechamber 191
ante Christum 106
antedate 115
antediluvian 124
antelope 274
antemundane 124
antenna 379
anteposition 62
anterior
in order 62
in time 116
in place 234
– to reason 477
anteroom 191
antevert 706
anthem 990
anthemion 847
anthology
book 533
collection 596
poem 597
anthracite 388
anthropoid 372
anthropology
zoology 368
mankind 372
anthropomancy 511
anthropophagi 913
anthroposcopy 511
anthroposophy 372
antic 840
anti-aircraft gun 564, 727
antichambre, faire – 133
antichristian 984, 989
antichronism 115
anticipate
anachronism 115
priority 116
future 121
early 132
expect 507
foresee 510
prepare 673
hope 858
in – 116
anticlimax
decrease 36
bathos 497, 853
anticlinal 217
anticyclone 265
antidote 662
antigropelos 225
antilogarithm 84
antilogy 477
antimony 663
Antinomian 984
antinomy 964
Antinous 845
antiparallel 217
antipathy 867, 898
antiphon *music* 415
answer 462
worship 990
antiphrasis 563
antipodes
difference 14
distance 196
contraposition 237
antipoison 660
antiquary
past times 122
scholar 492
historian 553
antiquas vias, stare super – 613, 670
antiquated 128
antique 124
antiquity 122
antiscriptural 984
antiseptic 652, 662
antisocial 911
antistrophe 597
antithesis
contrast 14
difference 15
opposite 237
style 574, 577
antitoxin 662
antitype 22
antler 253
antonomasia
metaphor 521
nomenclature 564
antonym 14
antrum 252
anvil *support* 215
on the –
intended 620
in hand 625
preparing 673
anxiety *pain* 828
fear 860
desire 865
anxious expectation 507
any *some* 25
part 51
no choice 609*a*
at – price 604*a*
at – rate
certain 474
true 494
at all hazards 604
anybody 78
anyhow 460, 627
anything one knows, for – 491
aorist 109, 119
aorta 350
apace *early* 132
swift 274
apache 913
apart 44, 87
set – 636
wide – 196
apartment 191
–s 189
–s to let
imbecile 499
apathetic 275
apathy
indifference 465
insensibility 823
irreligion 989
ape *imitate* 19
Apelles 559
aperçu 596
aperture 260

apex 210
aphasia 583
aphelion 196
aphonic 403
aphony 581
aphorism 496
aphrodite 845, 979
apiary 370
apiculture 370
Apicius 957
apiece 79
apish 19, 499
aplanatic 429
aplomb
stability 150
self-possession 498
resolution 604
Apocalypse 985
Apocrypha 985
apocryphal
uncertain 475
erroneous 495
heterodox 984
apodictic 478
apodosis 67
apogee 210
apograph 21
Apollo *sun* 318
music 416
luminary 423
beauty 845
god 979
magnus – 500, 695
Apollyon 978
apologue
metaphor 521
teaching 537
description 594
apology *excuse* 617
vindication 937
penitence 950
atonement 952
apophthegm 496
apophysis 250
apoplexy 158, 655
aporetic 487
aposiopesis 585
apostasy
recantation 607
dishonor 940
heterodoxy 984
apostate
convert 144
turncoat 607
impiety 988
apostle *teacher* 540
disciple 541
inspired 985
–'s creed 983a
apostolic 985
– church 983a
– see 995
apostrophe
address 586
soliloquy 589
appeal 765
apothecary 662
–'s weight 319
apothegm 496
apotheosis
resuscitation 163
canonization 873
heaven 981
hero worship 991
apozem 335, 384
appal 830, 860
appanage
property 780
gift 784
apparatus 633
apparel 225
apparent
visible 446
appearing 448
probable 472
manifest 525
heir – 779
apparition
fallacy of vision 443
spirit 980
apparitor 534
appeach 938
appeal 586, 765
court of – 966
– to arms 722
– motion 969
– from Philip drunk to Philip sober 658
– to *call to witness* 467
– to for (*claim*) 924
appear 446, 525
– for 759
– in print 591
appearance 448
make one's – 292
to all – 448
probable 472
appearances
keep up – 852
appease 174
appellant 924, 938
appellate 966
appellation 564
append *add* 37
sequence 63
hang 214
appendage 39
appendectomy 662
appendix
adjunct 39
sequel 65
end 67
book 593
appertain
related to 9
component 56
belong 777
property 780
appetite 865
tickle the –
savory 394
appetizing 865
exciting 824
applaud 931
apple – of discord 713
golden –
allurement 615
– of one's eye *good* 648
love 897
favorite 899
– off another tree 15
how we –s swim! 880
apple-green 435
apple-pie order 58
appliance *use* 677
–s *means* 632
machinery 633
applicable *relevant* 23
useful 644
expedient 646
applicability 9
applicant 767
application *study* 457
metaphor 521
use 677
request 765
apply, *use* 677
– a match 384
– the match to a train 66
– the mind 457
– a remedy 662
appoggiatura 413
appointment
employment 625
order 741
charge 755
assignment 786
interview 892
appointments
gear 633
apportion *arrange* 60
disperse 73
allot 786
apportionment 786
appositeness 9
apposition
relation 9
relevancy 23
closeness 199
paraphrase 522
appraise 466, 812
appreciate
realize 450, 451
measure 466
judge 480
know 490
taste 850
approve 931
apprehend
believe 484
know 490
fear 860
seize 789
apprehension
idea 453
taking 789
apprentice 541
– oneself 676
apprenticeship 539, 673
apprise 527
apprised of 490
approach
of time 121
impend 152
nearness 197
move 286
path 627
approaching 9
approbation 931
appropinquation 286
appropriate *fit* 23
peculiar 79
expedient 646
assign 786
take 789
steal 791
approval 488, 931
on – 609
approximate
related to 9
resemble 17
in mathematics 85
nearness 197
approach 286
appulse *meeting* 199
collision 276
approach 286
convergence 290
appurtenance
part 51
component 56
belongings 780
accompaniment 88
appurtenant 9
après nous le déluge 943
apricot *color* 439
April
– fool 547, 857
make an – fool of 545
– showers 149
apron *extension* 39
clothing 225
defence 717
canonicals 999
àpropos [*see* à]
aprotype 591
apse 1000
apt *consonant* 23
tendency 176, 177
docile 539
willing 602
clever 698
aqua-fortis 335
aquamarine 435
aquarium 370
Aquarius 348, 636
aquatic *water* 337
aquatics 267
aquatinta 558
aqueduct 350
aqueous 337
aquiline 244
A.R. 106
Arab *wanderer* 268
horse 271
street – 876
araba 272
arabesque 847
Arabian
– perfumes 400
– nights 515
arable 371
arbalest 727
arbiter *critic* 480
director 694
adviser 695
judge 967
– elegantiarum
revels 840
taste 850
fashion 852
arbitrage 794
arbitrament 480
judgment 480
– of the sword 722
arbitrary
without relation 10
irregular 83
wilful 606
capricious 608
authoritative 737
severe 739
insolent 885
lawless 964
– power 739
arbitrate
adjudicate 480
mediate 724
arbitration
court of – 966
submit to – 774
arbitrium, ad – 600
arbor 215, 312
arbor *abode* 189
summer-house 191
plaisance 840
arborescent
ramifying 242
rough 256
trees 367
arboriculture 371
arc 245
heat 382
arcade *street* 189
curve 245
gateway 260
Arcades ambo
alike 17
friends 890
bad men 949
Arcadia 827, 981
Arcadian 703, 946
arcanum 533
arch *great* 31
support 215
curve 245
convex 250
concave 252
clever 498
cunning 702
triumphal – 733, 883
archaic *old* 124
archaism 122, 563
archangel 977
archbishop 996
archbishopric 995
archdeacon 996
archduchy 181
archduke 745
archegenesis 161
archeologist
pastimes 122
scholar 492
archeology 122
archer 726
archery 840
Arches, court of – 966, 995
archetype 22
archetypal 20
Archeus 359
archfiend 978
archiater 695
archiepiscopal 995
archimandrite 996
archipelago 346
architect 164, 690
architectonic 161
architecture
arrangement 60
construction 161
fabric 329
ornament 847
architrave 210
archive 551
archlute 417
archon *ruler* 745
deputy 759
judge 967
archtraitor 941

arctic *northern* 237
cold 383
arctics 225
arcuation 245
ardent *fiery* 382
eager 682
feeling 821
loving 897
– expectation 507
– imagination 515
ardet, proximus – 665, 667
ardor *vigor* 574
activity 821
feeling 821
desire 865
arduous 704
area 181, 182
arefaction 340
arena *space* 180
region 181
field of view 441
field of battle **728**
arenaceous 330
areola 247
areolar 219
areometer 321
Areopagus 966
arête 253
aretinism 961
aretology 926
Argand lamp 423
argent 430
argillaceous 324
argosy 273
argot 563
argonaut 269
argue *evidence* 467
reason 476
indicate 550
dissectation 595
argument *disagreement* 24
topic 454
discussion 476
meaning 516
have the best of an – 478
argumentum
– baculinum
compel 744
lawless 964
punish 972
– ad crumenam 800
– ad hominem
reasoning 476
accuse 938
– ad verecundiam 939
Argus-eyed 441, 459
argute 498
aria 415
arianism 984
arid 340
unproductive 169
uninteresting 841
Ariel *courier* 268
swift 274
messenger 534
spirit 979
arietation 276
arietta 415
aright *well* 618
Ariman [*see* Ahrimanes]
ariolation 511
arioso 415
aris et focis, pro –
defence 717
philanthropy 910
arise *exist* 1
begin 66
happen 151
mount 305
appear 446
– from 154
Aristarchus 850
Aristides
good man 948
aristocracy
power 737
fashion 852
nobility 875
ἄριστον μέτρον 628
Arithmancy 511
arithmetic 85
ark *abode* 189
asylum 666
arm *part* 51
power 157
instrument 633
provide 637
prepare 673
war 722
weapon 727
make a long – 200
– chair 215
– in arm
together 88
friends 888
sociable 892
– of the law 963
– of the sea 343
armada 726
Armageddon 720, 722
armament 673, 727
armed 717
– at all points 673
– force 726
– guard 664
armet 717
armful 25
armiger 875
armigerent 726
armigerous 722
armilla 247, 847
armillary sphere 466
armipotent 157
armistice
cessation 142
respite 672
pacification 723
armless 158
armlet *ring* 247
gulf 343
ornament 847
armor *cover* 223
defence 717
arms 727
buckle on one's – 673
– plated 223
armored
– car 726
– cruiser 726
– train 726
armorial bearings 550, 877
armory *store* 636
workshop 691
arm's length
at – 196
keep at –
repel 289
defence 717
enmity 889
seclusion 893
discourtesy 895
arms **727** [*see* arm]
heraldry 550
war 722
honors 877
clash of – 720
deeds of – 720
with folded – 681
in – *infant* 129
throw oneself into the – of 666, 880
under – 722
up in – *active* 682
discord 713
resistance 719
resentment 900
enmity 889
Armstrong gun 727
army *collection* 72
multitude 102
troops 726
aroma 400
around 227
lie – 220
arouse *move* 615
excite 824
– oneself 682
aroynt *begone* 297
malediction 908
arquebusade 662
arquebuse 727
arraign 938, 969
arrange
set in order 60
plan 626
compromise 774
– with creditors 807
– itself 58
arrange – matters
pacify 723
– music 413, 416
– in a series 69
– under 76
arrangement 23, **60**
[*see* arrange]
order 58
temporary – 111
arrant *identical* 31
manifest 525
notorious 531
bad 649
disreputable 874
base 940
arras 847
array *order* 58, 60
series 69
assemblage 72
multitude 102
dress 225
prepare 673
adorn 847
ostentation 882
battle – 722
arrear, in – 53, 808
arrears *debt* 806
arrectis auribus
hear 418
expect 507
arrest *stop* 142
restrain 751
in law 969
– the attention 457
arrière-pensée
after-thought 65
mental reservation 528
motive 615
set purpose 620
arrival **292**
arrive *happen* 151
reach 292
complete 729
– at a conclusion 480
– at the truth 480*a*
arrogant *severe* 739
proud 878
insolent 885
arrogate 885, 924
– to oneself
undue 925
arrondissement 181
arrosion 331
arrow *swift* 274
missile 284
arms 727
broad – 550
arrow-head
form 253
writing 590
'Arry and 'Arriet 902
ars celare artem 698
arsenal *store* 636
workshop 661
arsenic 663
arson 384
art *representation* 554
business 625
skill 698
cunning 702
fine – 850
work of – 845, 847
– gallery 556
artery 350, 627
artes, hae tibi erunt – 627
artesian well 343
artful 544, 702
– dodge 545, 702
article *thing* 3
part 51
matter 316
chapter 593
review 595
goods 798
articled clerk 541
articles
thirty-nine – 983*a*
– of agreement 770
– of faith 484, 983
articulate 366
articulation
junction 43
speech 580
articulo, in –
transient 111
dying 360
artifice 626, 702
artificer 690
artificial
fictitious 545
cunning 702
affected 855
– language 579
artillery
explosion 404
arms 727
artilleryman 726
artisan 690
artist *painter* &c. **559**
contriver 626
agent 690
artiste *music* 416
drama 599
artistic *skilful* 698
beautiful 845
taste 850
– language 578
artlessness **703**
aruspex 513
aruspicy 511
arundo, haeret lateri lethalis – 828
as *motive* 615
– broad as long 27
– can be 52
– good as 27
– if *similar* 17
suppose 514
– little as may be 32
– it may be
circumstance 8
event 151
chance 156
– much again 90
– soon as 120
– they say 496, 532
– things are 7
– things go 151, 613
– to 9
– usual 82
– it were 17, 521
– you were 141, 283
– well as 37
– the world wags 151
ascend *be great* 31
increase 35
rise 305
improve 658
ascendancy
power 157
influence 175
success 731
ascendant
lord of the – 745
in the –
influence 175
important 642
success 731
authority 737
repute 873
one's star in the –
prosperity 734
ascension
[*see* ascend]
calefaction 384
– Day 998
ascent
[*see* ascend]
gradient 217
rise **305**
glory 873
ascertain *fix* 150
determine 480
ascertained 474, 490
ascertainment 480*a*
asceticism **955**
ascititious

intrinsic 6
additional 37
supplementary 52
ascribe 155
aseptic 652
ash 384
– colored 432
– blond 430
ashen 429
Ash Wednesday 998
ashamed 879
ashes *corpse* 362
dirt 653
lay in – 162
pale as – 429, 860
rise from one's – 660
ashore 342
go – *arrive* 292
ashy 429
Asian mystery 533
aside *laterally* 236
whisper 405
private 528
say – 589
set &c. – *displace* 185
neglect 460
negative 536
reject 610
disuse 678
abrogate 756
discard 782
step – 279
asinine *ass* 271
fool 499
ask *inquire* 461
request 765
for sale 794
price 812
– leave 760
askance 217
eye – *fear* 860
look – *vision* 441, 443
dissent 489
dislike 867
disapproval 932
askari 726
asked in church 903
askew 217, 243
aslant 217
asleep 683
aslope 217
Asmodeus 980
asomatous 317
asp *animal* 366
evil-doer 913
Aspasia 962
aspect *feature* 5
state 7
situation 183
appearance 448
aspen leaf
shake like an – 315, 860
asperity
roughness 256
discourtesy 895
anger 900
irascibility 901
asperse 934
aspersion
malediction 908
rite 998
asphalt
smooth 255
resin 356a
material 635
asphodel 845
aspic 352
asphyxia 360
asphyxiate 361
aspirant 767, 865
aspirate 580
aspirator 349
aspire *rise* 305
hope 858
desire 865
worship 990
aspirin 834
asportation 270
asquint 217
ass *beast of burden* 271
fool 501
make an – of
delude 545
– between two bundles of hay 605
–'s bridge 519
– in lion's skin
cheat 548
bungler 701
assafetida 401
assagai 727
assail 716, 830
assailant 710, 726
assassin, -ate 361
assault 716, 961
take by – 789
assay 463
asseguay 727
assemblage 72
assembly
council 696
society 892
religious 997
assembly hall 588
assembly room 189
assent *belief* 484
agree 488
willing 602
consent 762
content 831
assert 535, 924
assess *measure* 466
determine 480
tax 812
assessor
judge 967
assets 780, 800
asseverate 535
assiduity 110
assiduous 682
assign
commission 755
transfer 270, 783
give 784
allot 786
– as cause 155
– a duty 926
– places 60
assignat 800
assignation 892
place of – 74
assignee *donee* 785
assimilate
uniform 16
resemble 17
imitate 19
agree 23
transmute 144
assist 707
– at 186
assistant 711
assister *be present* 186
assize *measure* 466
tribunal 966
justice of – 967
associate *mix* 41
unite 43
collect 72
accompany 88
colleague 690
auxiliary 711
friend 890
– with 892
association
[see associate]
relation 9
combination 48
co-operation 709
partnership 712
– of ideas
intellect 450
thought 451
intuition 477
hint 514
– football 840
assoil *acquit* 970
assonance
music 413
poetry 597
assort *arrange* 60
assortment 72, 75
assuage 174, 834
assuetude 613
assume *believe* 484
suppose 514
falsehood 544
take 789
insolent 885
right 924
– authority 737
– a character 554
– command 741
– a form 144
– the offensive 716
assumed name 565
assumption
[see assume]
severity 739
hope 858
usurpation 925
assurance
speculation 156
certainty 474
belief 484
assertion 535
promise 768
security 771
hope 858
vanity 880
insolence 885
make – double sure *safe* 664
caution 864
assuredly
assent 488
assythment 973
astatic 320
asterisk 550
astern 235
put the engines – 275
fall – 283
asteroid 318
Asteroth 979
asthenia 160
astigmatism 443
astir 682
set – 824
astonish 870
astonished
– at nothing 871
astonishing
great 31
astound *excite* 824
fear 860
surprise 870
astra, sic itur ad – 360, 873
astraddle 215
Astraea 922
astragal 847
astral 318
– body 717, 992
– influence 601
– plane 317
astray 475, 495
go – *deviate* 279
sin 945
astriction 43
astride 215
astringent 195
astrolabe 466
astrologer 994
astrology 511
astromancy 511
astronomy 318
astute 498, 702
asunder 44, 196
as poles – 237
asylum *hospital* 663
retreat 666
defence 717
asymptote 290
at, be – 620
up and – them! 716
ataghan 727
atavism 144, 163
ataxia 158
atelier 556, 691
athanasia 112
Athanasian creed 983a
athanor 386
atheism 989
atheist 487
Athenae 979
Athens, owls to – 641
athirst 865
athlete *strong* 159
gladiator 726
athletic *strong* 159
strenuous 686
– sports
contest 720
games 840
athwart
oblique 217
crossing 219
opposing 708
Atkins, Tommy 726
Atlantis 515
Atlas *arrangement* 60
list 86
strength 159
support 215
maps 554
atmosphere
circumambience 227
air 338
painting 556
atmospheric blue 438
atoll 346
atom *small* 32, 193
atomic energy 157
atomics 316
atomizer 336
atoms
crush to – 162
atomy 193
atonement
restitution 790
expiation 952
amends 973
religious 976
atony 160
atrabilious 837
atramentous 431
atrium 191
atrocity
malevolence 907
vice 945
guilt 947
atrophy
shrinking 195
disease 655
decay 659
atropos 601
attach *join* 43
love 897
legal 969
– importance to 642
attaché
employé 746
diplomatic 758
– case 191
attack *singing* 580
disease 655
assault 716
debauch 961
attaghan 727
attain *arrive* 292
succeed 731
– majority 131
attainable 470
attainder
taint 651
at law 971
attainment
knowledge 490
learning 539
skill 698
attar 400
attempter 41, 174
attempered 820
attempt 675
vain – 732
– impossibilities 471
attend
accompany 88
be present 186
follow 281
apply the mind 457
medically 662
aid 707
serve 746
– to business 625
– to orders 743
attendance on
dance – 886
attendant
[see attend]
attention 457
care 459
respect 928

attract – 882
call to – 457
call – to 550
give – 418
pay –s to 894
pay one's –s to 902
attenuate
decrease 36
weaken 158
reduce 195
rarefy 322
attenuated 203
attest
bear testimony 467
affirm 535
adjure 768
attested copy 771
attic *simple* 42
garret 191
summit 210
style 578
wit 842
taste 850
Attila 913
attire 225
attitude
circumstance 8
situation 183
posture 240
attitudinarian 882
attitudinize 855
attollent 307
attorney
consignee 758
at law 968
power of – 755
attract
bring towards 288
induce 615
allure 865
excite love 897
– the attention 457
visible 446
attraction
[*see* attract]
natural power 157
bring towards 288
attractive
[*see* attract]
pleasing 829
beautiful 845
attrahent 288
attribute
speciality 79
accompaniment 88
power 157
–s of the Deity 976
– to 155
attribution 155
attrite 330
attrition 330, 331
attroupement 72
attune *music* 415
prepare 673
attuned to
habit 613
attunement 23
auburn 433
A.U.C. 106
auction 796, 840
auctioneer 758, 796
auctorial 599
audacity
courage 861
rashness 863
insolence 885
audible 402
become – 418
scarcely – 405
audience
hearing 418
conversation 588
before an – 599
audire alteram partem
counter-evidence 468
right 922
justice 939
audit
numeration 85
examination 461
accounts 811
auditive 418
auditor
hearer 418
accountant 811
auditorium 189, 588
auditory
sound 402
hearing 418
theater 599
– apparatus 418
au fait 698
au fond 5
auf wiedersehen 293
Augean
– stable 653
– task 704
auger 262
aught 51
for – one cares
unimportant 643
indifferent 866
for – one knows
ignorance 491
conjecture 514
augment
increase 35
thing added 39
expand 194
augur 513
– well 858
augurate 511
augury 512
august 873
Augustinian 996
auk 366
auld lang syne 122
aulic council 696
aumbry 1000
aunt 11
aura *wind* 349
sensation 380
aurea mediocritas 628
aureate 436
aureola 420
aureole 420, 873
aureolin 436
auribus, arrectis – 418
auricular *hearing* 418
clandestine 528
– confession 998
auri sacra fames 819
aurist 662
aurora
dawn 125
light 420, 423
twilight 422
– australes 423
– borealis 423
Auroral 236
ausculation 418
auspice *omen* 512
auspices
influence 175
prediction 511
protection 664
direction 693
aid 707
under the – of 693, 737
auspicious
opportune 134
prosperous 734
hopeful 858
austerity
harsh taste 395
severe 739
discourteous 895
ascetic 955
pietism 988
austral 237
austromancy 511
authentic 467
certain 474
true 494
authentication
evidence 467
security 771
author 164, 593
projector 626
dramatic – 599
– of our being 976
– of evil 978
– 's proof 591
authoritative 474, 741
authority
testimony 467
sage 500
informant 527
power 737
permission 760
right 924
ensign of – 747
person in – 745
do upon one's own – 600
authorized *due* 924
legalized 963
authorship
production 161
style 569
writing 590
autobiography 594
autocar 272
autochthonous 188
autocracy 737, 739
autocrat 745
autocratic 600, 737
auto-da-fe 384, 972
autograph 550, 590
Autolycus *thief* 792
pedlar 797
automaniac 504
automatic 601, 633
- pistol 727
- writing 992
automaton 554, 601
automobile 272
automobilist 268
automotive 266
autonomasia 521
autonomy 737, 748
autopsy
post-mortem 363
vision 441
autoptical 446, 535
autotype 558
autumn 126
auxiliary 711
additional 34
helpful 707
– forces 726
avail *benefit* 618
useful 644
succeed 731
of no – 645
– oneself of 677
avalanche *fall* 306
snow 383
redundance 641
avaler les couleuvres 725, 886
avant-courier 64, 673
avant-propos 64
avarice 819
avast! *stop* 142, 265
desist 624
forbid 761
avatar *change* 140
deity 976
idol 991
avaunt! 297, 440
ave! *honor* 873
courtesy 894
Ave maria 990
avenge 919
avenue
plantation 371
way 627
aver 535
average *mean* 29, 628
médiocre 651
– circumstances 736
take an – 466
Averni, facilis descensus – 217, 665
Avernus 982
averruncate 297, 301
aversion *unwillingness* 603
dislike 867
hate 898
avert 706
– the eyes 442
aviary 370
aviation 267
aviator 269
avidity *avarice* 819
desire 865
airette 273
avile 932, 934
avion 273
aviso 532
avocation 625
avoidance 623
avoidless 474, 601
avoirdupois 319
avolation 623, 671
avouch 535, 768
avow *assent* 488
disclose 529
assert 535
avulsion 44, 301
avuncular 11
await *future* 121
be kept waiting 133
impend 152
expect 507
awake *attentive* 457
careful 459
intelligent 498
active 682
– to life immortal 360
awaken *inform* 527
excite 824
– the attention 457
– the memory 505
award *adjudge* 480
give 784
aware 490
away 187, 196
break – 623
fly – 293
move – 287
take – from 789
get &c. – 671
throw &c. –
eject 297
reject 610
waste 638
relinquish 782
– from *unrelated* 10
– with! 930, 932
do – with *undo* 681
abrogate 756
awe *fear* 860
wonder 870
respect 928
aweless *fearless* 861
insolent 885
disrespectful 329
awful 31, 860
– silence 403
awhile 111
awkward
inelegant 579
inexpedient 647
unskilful 699
difficult 704
painful 830
ugly 846
vulgar 851
ridiculous 853
– squad 701
awl 262
awn 253
awning 223, 424
awry *oblique* 217
distorted 243
evil 619
axe *edge tool* 253
impulse 276
weapon 727
for beheading 975
have an – to grind 702
Axinomancy 511
axiom 496
axiomatic 474
axis *support* 215
center 222
rotation 312
axle 312
wheel and – 633
axle load 466
axletree 215
ay 488
ayah 746, 753
aye *ever* 112
yes 488
azimuth

horizontal 213
direction 278
measurement 466
– circle 212
azoic 358
azote 663
azotic 657
azure 438
azygous *single* 87

B

Baal 979, 986
Babbittry 851
babble *rivulet* 348
faint sound 405
unmeaning 517
talk 584, 588
babbler 501
babbling
foolish 499
babe 129
innocent as the – unborn 946
Babel *confusion* 59
discord 414
tongues 560
jargon 563
loquacity 584
baboon 846
baby *infant* 129
fool 501
– linen 225
babyhood 127
babyish 499
baccarat 840
bacchanals 959
Bacchus 979
drink 959
bachelor 904
– of arts 492
– girl 374
bacillus 193
back *rear* 235
shoulder 250
aid 707
behind one's –
latent 526
hidden 528
come – 292
give – 790
fall – *relapse* 661
go – 283
go – from *retract* 773
have at one's – 215
hold – *avoid* 623
keep – *reserve* 636
look – 505
on one's – *impotent* 158
horizontal 213
failure 732
pat on the –
incite 615
encourage 861
approve 931
pay – *retaliate* 718
put – *deteriorate* 659
restore 660
send – 764
take – again 790
carry one's thoughts – 505
some time – 122
spring – 277
trace – 505
turn – 283
turn one's – 283
turn one's – upon
repel 289
inattention 458
avoid 623
oppose 508
seclusion 893
discourtesy 895
disrespect 929
contempt 930
set one's – against the wall 604
– to back 235
– down 283
– one's note 806
– out *retire* 283
change sides 607
relinquish 624
– pedal 273
– up *support* 215
influence 615
aid 707
put one's – up
anger 900
set one's – up
pride 878
backbite 932, 934
backbiter 936
backbone
intrinsic 5
energy 171
frame 215
center 222
resolution 604
persevere 604*a*
soul 820
game to the – 604
back door 627
back down 607
backer 711
back-fire 406
back friend 891
backgammon 840
background
distance 196
rear 235
in the –
latent 526
ignoble 874
keep in the –
hide 528
modest 881
seclusion 893
put one in the – 874
throw into the – 460
backsheesh 784, 973
backside 235
backslider 607
backsliding
regression 283
tergiversation 607
relapse 661
vice 945
heterodox 984
impiety 988
backstairs
ambush 530
way 627
– influence 702
backward
tardy 133
regression 283
unwilling 603
deteriorate 659
backwardation 813
backwards 283
bend – 325
– and forwards
interchange 148
oscillation 314
backwater 275, 283
in a – 893
backwoodsman
inhabitant 188
agriculture 371
bacon
butter upon – 641
save one's – 664, 671
Baconian method 461
bacteria 193
bactericide 660
baculinum, argumentum –
compel 744
lawless 964
punish 972
bad 649
unclean 653
wrong 923
– blood 898, 907
go – 653, 659
– business 859
– case 477
– chance 473
put a – construction on 523
– debt 806
– fairy 980
– faith 940
– grace 895
– habit 613
– hand 701
– humor
discontent 832
dejection 837
anger 900
sullen 901*a*
not a – idea 498
– intent 907
– job *evil* 619
botch 699
hopeless 859
– joke 851
– language 908
view in a – light 934
– luck &c. 735
– man **949**
– money 800
– name 932, 934
in – odor 889
take in – part 832, 900
– repute 874
– smell 401
– spirit 980
– spirits 837
– taste 579, 851
– temper 900, 901, 901*a*
on – terms 713, 889
– time of it 828
– turn 619, 907
in a – way
disease 655
worse 659
danger 665
adversity 735
– woman 949
from – to worse
aggravation 835
badaud 501
badge 550
– of authority 747
– of infamy 874
– of slavery 746
badger 830
– dog 366
badinage 842, 856
badly off
adversity 735
poor 804
badminton 840
badness **649**
Baedeker 266
baffle *hinder* 706
defeat 731
– description
unconformable 83
wonder 870
baffling
puzzling 519
bag *put up* 184
receptacle 191
protrude 250
acquire 775
take 789
steal 791
– and baggage 780
bagatelle
trivial 643
pastime 840
baggage 270
minx 129
materials 635
property 780
hussy 962
baggy 47
bagman 758
bagnio 961
bagpipes 417
bah! 930
bail 771
go – 806
leg – 623
bailie 965
bailiff
director 694
servant 746
factor 758
officer 965
bailiwick
region 181
jurisdiction 965
Bairam
holiday 840
rite 998
bairn 129
bait *attraction* 288
food 298
trap 545
lure 615
refresh 689
attack 716
bribe 784
harass 830
swallow the – 547
bake 384
bakehouse 386
baker 637
baker's dozen 98
baking heat 382
bal 840
balais 847
balaclava helmet 225
balance *equal* 27
mean 29
compensate 30
remainder 40
numeration 85
weigh 319
compare 464
style 578
hesitate 605
money 800
accounts 811
in the – 475
the mind losing its – 503
off one's –
irresolute 605
fail 732
want of – 579
– accounts with
pay 807
balanced 150, 242
balbucinate 583
balbutiate 583
balcony 250
theater 599
bald *bare* 226
style 575
uninteresting 841
ugly 846
plain 849
baldachin 223, 1000
balderdash 517, 577
baldric 230, 247
bale *bundle* 72
load 190
ladle 270
evil 619
– out 297
baleful 649
balister 727
balize 550
balk *disappoint* 509
deceive 545
hinder 706
Balkanize 713
ball *globe* 249
missile 284
shot 727
dance 840
party 892
– at one's feet 731, 737
keep up the – 143, 682
ballad 415, 597
– monger 597
ballast
compensation 30
weight 319
wisdom 498
safety 666
without – *rash* 863
vicious 945
ballerina 599
ballet 599, 840
ballet-dancer 599
ballistics
projectiles 284
war 722
arms 727
ballon d'essai 463
balloon 273, 726
balloonist 269
balloonry 267
ballot 535, 609
ball-room 840
balm *moderate* 174
fragrance 400
remedy 662

ask 765
– one's bread 765
poor 804
– leave 760
– one's life 914
– pardon 952
– the question 477
beget 161
begetter 164, 166
beggar *idler* 683
petitioner 767
poor 804
degrade 874
low person 876
sturdy – 792
– description 83, 870
– my neighbor 840
– on horseback 885
beggared
bankrupt 808
beggarly *mean* 643
vile 874
vulgar 876
servile 886
– account of empty boxes 640, 804
begging
go a –
too much 641
useless 645
offered 763
free 748
letter 765
begilt 847
begin 66
– again 104
beginner 541
beginning 66
begird 227, 229
beglerbeg 745
begone
depart 293
ejection 297
abrogate 756
– dull care 836
Begotten, the only – 976
begrime 653
begrudge
unwilling 603
refuse 764
stingy 819
beguile *mislead* 495
deceive 545
reconcile 831
– the time
inaction 681
amusement 840
beguine 996
begum 745, 875
behalf 618, 707
in – of 759
behave oneself
conduct 692
fashion 852
courtesy 894
behavior 692
on one's good – 894, 944
behead 361, 972
behemoth 192
behest 741
behind
in order 63
in space 235
sequence 281
– the age 124, 491
– one's back 187
speak ill of – one's back 934
– the bars 751
– the scenes
cause 153
unseen 447
cognizant 490
latent 526
hidden 528
playhouse 599
– time 133
behindhand
late 133
shortcoming 304
adversity 735
insolvent 808
behold 441, 457
beholden 916, 926
beholder 444
behoof 618
behoove 926
being 1, 3
created – 366
human – 372
time – 106
Bel 979
belabor 276, 972
belated *late* 133
ignorant 491
belaud 931
belay *join* 43
restrain 706
belch 297
beldam 130, 913
beldame 173
beleaguer 716
bel esprit 844
belfry 206, 1000
Belial 978, 980
sons of – 988
belie *deny* 536
falsify 544
contradict 708
belief **484,** 983
easy of – 472
hug a – 606
believe
[*see* belief]
suppose 514
reason to – 472
– who may 485
not – one's senses 870
believer
religious 987
true – 983*a*
belike 472
belittle
decrease 36
underestimate 482
disparage 934
bell 417, 550
alarm – 669
bear away the –
goodness 648
success 731
repute 873
church – 350
cracked – 408*a*
passing – 363
– book and candle
swear 535
curse 908
spell 993
rite 998
– the cat 861
– shape 249, 252
belladonna 663
belle 374, 854
a la – étoile 220, 845
belles-lettres 560
belli, casus – 824
bellicose 720, 722
bellied 250
belligerent
contentious 720
warlike 722
combatant 726
belling 412
bellman 354
bello, flagrante – 722
Bellona 722
bellow *loud* 404
cry 411
animal cry 412
wail 839
bellows 349, 580
bells, peal of – 407
bellwether 64, 694
belly *receptacle* 191
inside 221
convex 250
–ful 52, 639
– god 957
– timber 298
belomancy 511
belong to *related* 9
component 56
included 76
attribute 157
property 777, 780
duty 926
beloved 897
below 207
here – 318
– the mark 32
– par 34, 207
bad 649
indifferent 651
discount 813
ignoble 876
– its full strength 651
– stairs 207
belt *outline* 230
ring 247
strait 343
swimming – 666
belting 633
Belus 979
belvedere 441
bemask 528
bemingle 41
bemire 653
bemoan 839
bemused 458
bench *support* 215
council 696
tribunal 966
Bench, King's – 752
bencher 968
bend *oblique* 217
angle 244
curve 245
incline 278
deviate 279
depression 308
circuit 311
give 324
submit 725
– backwards 235
– the bow 686
– the brows 932
– one's course 27
– the knee
bow down 308
submit 725
humble 879
servile 886
courtesy 894
respect 928
worship 990
– one's looks upon 441
– the mind 457
– over 250
– to rules &c. 82
– sinister 874
– one's steps 622
– to *tend* 176
– towards 278
– to one's will 737
beneath 207
one 940
– notice 643
Benedick 903
Benedictine 996
benediction
gratitude 916
approval 931
worship 990
nuptial – 903
benefaction 784
benefactor 816, 912
benefice 995
beneficent 906
beneficial 648
– interest 780
beneficiary
possessor 779
receive 785
clergy 996
benefit *good* 618
use 644
do good 648
aid 707
acquisition 775
property 780
benevolence 906
reap the – of 131
benefits forgot 917
bene gesserit, quamdiu se – 926
benet 545
benevolence
tax 812
love 897
kindness **906**
universal – 910
Bengal heat 382
benighted
dark 421
ignorant 491
benign 656, 906
benignant 906
benison 618, 931
Benjamin's mess 33, 50
Benshie 979
bent *tendency* 176
angle 244
turn of mind 820
desire 865
fool to the top of one's – 856
– on *willing* 602
resolved 604
intention 620
desirous 865
Benthamite 910
ben trovato
likely 472
imagination 515
untruth 546
wit 842
benumb
insensible 376
cold 385
deaden affections 823
beplaster 933
bepraise 931
bequest 270
gift 784
bereavement
death 360
loss 776
take away 789
bereft *poor* 804
– of life 360
– of reason 503
béret 225
berg, ice – 383
bergamot 400
berlin 272
berth *lodging* 189
bed 215
office 625
beryl *green* 435
jewel 847
beseech 765, 990
beseem 926
berserk 173, 503
beset *surround* 227
follow 281
attack 716
entreat 765
annoy 830
haunt 860
– with difficulties 704
besetting 78, 613
– sin 945
beshrew 908
beside *except* 83
near 197
alongside 236
– the mark 10, 495
– oneself 503, 824
besides 37
besiege
surround 227
attack 716
solicit 765
bésique 840
besmear 233, 653
besom 652
besotted 481
bespangle 847
bespatter *dirt* 653
disapprove 932
flatter 933
detract 934
bespeak *early* 132
evidence 467
indicate 516
engage 755
ask for 765
bespeckle 440
bespot 440
besprinkle 41, 440
best 648, 650

– setter 662
bonehouse 363
boner 495
bones [see bone]
corpse 362
music 417
break no – 648
make no – 602, 705
boneyard 363
bonfire 382
festivity 840
celebration 883
make a – of 384
bonhomie 703, 906
bonhomme 996
Boniface 890
bonne 746, 753
– bouche *end* 67
pleasant 377
savory 394
saving 636
à la – heure 602, 831
de – volonté 602
bonnet 225
bonny 836, 845
bono: cui –
intention 620
utility 644
inutility 645
pro – publico 644, 910
bonus *extra* 641
gift 784
money 810
bony 323
bonze 996
bonzer 648
booby 501
– trap 545
boodle 793
book *register* 86
publication 531
record 551
volume 593
script 599
enter accounts 811
at one's –s 539
bring to –
evidence 467
account 811
reprove 932
mind one's – 539
school – 542
without –
by heart 505
– of Books 985
– club 593
– of fate 601
– learning 490
– shop 593
book-case 191
booked *dying* 360
bookish 490
bookkeeper 553
bookkeeping 811
bookless
unlearned 493
bookmaking 156
bookseller 593
bookworm 492, 593
boom
support 215
sail 267
rush 274
impulse 276
sound 404
obstacle 706
defence 717
boomerang
recoil 277
retribution 718
weapon 727
boon 784
beg a – 765
– companion 890
boor *clown* 876
boorish 851, 895
boost 276, 482, 931
booster 935
boot *box* 191
dress 225
advantage 618
punishment 975
to – *added* 37
– legging 964
booted and spurred 673
booth 189, 799
bootless 645, 732
boots *dress* 225
servant 746
low person 876
what – it? 643
booty 793
booze 959
bo-peep 441, 528
bordel 961
border *edge* 231
limit 233
flower bed 371
ornament 847
– upon 197, 199
bore *diameter* 202
hole 260
tide 348, 667
fatigue 688
trouble 828
plague 830
weary 841
bored 456
boreal
Northern 237
cold 383
Boreas 349
boredom 841
borer 262
born 359
– so 5
– under an evil star 735
– under a lucky star 734
borne 826
– down *failure* 732
defection 837
borné 499
borough 181, 189
rotten – 893
– council 696
borrow 19, 788
– of Peter &c. 147
borrowed plumes
deception 545
borrower 806
borrowing 788
bosh *absurdity* 497
unmeaning 517
untrue 546
trifling 643
bosky 959
bosom *breast* 221
mind 450
affections 820
in the – of 229
– of one's family 221
– friend 890
boss 250, 694, 737
straw – 694
boston 840
botanic garden 369, 371
Botanomancy 511
Botany 367, **369**
botch *bungle* 59
mend 660
unskilful 699
difficulty 704
fail 732
both 89
listen with – ears 418
burn the candle at – ends 641
butter one's bread on – sides 641
bother
uncertainty 475
bustle 682
difficulty 704
trouble 828
harass 830
bothy 189
bottle
receptacle 191
preserve 670
bee in a – 407
crack a – 298
pass the – 959
smelling – 400
– green 435
– holder
auxiliary 177
mediator 724
– up *remember* 505
hide 528
restrain 751
bottom
lowest part 211
support 215
posterior 235
combe 252
ship 273
pluck 604a
courage 861
at – 5
at the – of
cause 153
go to the – 310
probe to the – 461
from the – of one's heart *veracity* 543
feeling 821
– upwards 218
– land 180, 207
bottomless 208
– pit 982
angel of the – pit 978
bottomry 771
botulism 663
bouche:
bonne – *end* 67
savory 394
saving 636
pleasant 829
– à feu 727
bouderie 901a
boudoir 191
bouffe, opera 599
bouge 250
bough *part* 51
curve 245
tree 367
bought *flexure* 245
bougie 423
boulder 249
boulevards 227
bouleversement
revolution 146
destruction 162
excite 824
bouillabaise 298
bouillon 298
bounce *violence* 173
jump 309
lie 546
boast 884
insolence 885
– upon 202, 508
bouncing *large* 192
bound
circumscribe 229
swift 274
leap 309
certain 474
I'll be – 535
– back *recoil* 277
– by 926
– for *direction* 278
destination 620
– to *promise* 768
responsible 926
boundary 233
bounden duty 926
bounder 851
boundless 105, 180
bounds 230, 233
keep within –
moderation 174
shortcoming 304
restrain 751
prohibit 761
– of possibility 470
bountiful 816, 906
Lady – 816
bounty *gift* 784
bouquet
fragrant 400
beauty 847
bourgeois
middle class 29
type 591
commoner 876
bourdon 215
bourgeon 194
bourn 233
bourse 621, 799
bouse 959
bout *turn* 138
job 680
fight 720
prank 840
drinking – 954
bout
au – du compte 476
au – de son latin
sophistry 477
ignorance 491
difficulty 704
boutade 497, 608
boutonnière 400
bovine 366, 499
bow *be inferior* 34
fore part 234
curve 245
projection 250
stoop 308
fiddlestick 417
weapon 727
ornament 847
servility 886
reverence 894
respect 928
bend the – 686
draw the long – 884
– down *worship* 990, 991
– out 297
– submission 725
– window 260
Bow bells
born within sound of – 876
Bowdlerize 652
bowed down 837, 879
bowelless 914a
bowels *inside* 221
– of compassion 914
– of the earth 208
bower 189, 191
–s of bliss 981
bowery 424
bowie knife 727
bowl *vessel* 191
rotate 312
stadium 840
flowing – 959
– along *walk* 266
swift 271
bowlder 249
bowline 45
bowler *hat* 225
bow-legged 243
bowling-green 213, 840
bowls 840
bowman 726
bowshot 197
bowsprit 234
bowstring *execution* 972, 975
box *house* 189
chest 191
seat 215
theater 599
fight 720
horse – 272
musical – 417
wrong – *error* 495
unskilful 699
dilemma 704
– the compass
direction 278
rotation 312
change of mind 607
– the ear 900, 972
– up 751
boxer 726
boy 129
– scout 534
boyar 875
boyhood 127
boycott 55, 297, 893
brabble 713, 720
brabbler 901
brace *tie* 43
fasten 45
two 89
strengthen 159
support 214
music 413

refresh 689
bracelet *circle* 247
handcuff 752
ornament 847
bracer 392
braces 45
brachial 633
Brachygraphy 590
bracing 656
bracken 367
bracket *tie* 43, 45
couple 89
support 215
brackish 392
brad 45
bradawl 262
Bradbury 800
Bradshaw 266
brae 206
brag *cards* 840
boast 884
braggart 884
Braggadocio 884
Brahma 979
Brahmin 984, 996
braid *tie* 43
ligature 45
net 219
variegate 440
brain *kill* 361
intellect 450
skill 498
blow one's –s out 361
coinage of the – 515
suck one's –s 461
rack one's –s 451, 515
brainless 499
brainpan 450
brainsick 458
brain-storm 503, 825
brainwork 451
brainy 498
brake *carriage* 272
copse 367
hindrance 706
curb 752
apply the – 275
brakeman 268
bramble *thorn* 253
bane 663
bran 330
brancard 272
branch *member* 51
class 75
posterity 167
fork 244
tree 367
– off 91, 291
– out *ramify* 91
diffuse style 573
branching
symmetry 242
brand *burn* 384
fuel 388
torch 423
mark 550
sword 727
disrepute 874
censure 932
stigmatize 934
– of discord 713
– new 123
– with reproach 938
brandish
oscillate 314
flourish 315
display 882
brandy 959
brangle 713
brangler 710
brank 975
bras
les – croisés 681
à – ouverts 894
brashness 885
brass *alloy* 41
money 800
insolence 885
bold as – 861
– band 417, 882
with a – 884
– colored 439
– hat 745
– farthing 643
brassard 550, 747
brat 129
brattice 224, 228
bravado 884
brave *confront* 234
healthy 654
defy 715
warrior 726
bear 821, 826
courage 861
– a thousand years 110
bravo
assassin 361
desperado 863
applause 931
bravura 415
brawl *cry* 411
discord 713
revel 840
brawler
disputant 710
rioter 742
blusterer 887
brawny 159, 192
bray *grind* 330
cry 412
Bray, Vicar of – 607, 886
braze 43
brazen 525, 885
– browed 885
– faced 885
brazier 386
breach *crack* 44
gap 198
quarrel 713
violation 925
custom honored in the – 614
– of faith 940
– of law 83, 964
– of the peace 713
bread 298
beg – 765
selfish 943
quarrel with – and butter 699
– of idleness 683
– of life *Christ* 976
piety 987
– upon the waters 638
– and wine 998
breadbasket 191
breadth 202
chiaroscuro 420
break
fracture 44
discontinuity 70
change 140
gap 198
carriage 272
crumble 328
disclose 529
cashier 756
violate 773, 927
bankrupt 808
– away 623
– bread 298
– bulk 297
– camp 293
– of day *morning* 125
twilight 422
– down *destroy* 162
fall short 304
decay 659
fail 732
dance 840
– one's fetters 614
– forth 295
– ground 66
– a habit 614
– the heart *pain* 828, 830
dejection 837
– the ice 888
– in *ingress* 294
domesticate 370
teach 537
tame 749
– in upon *derange* 61
inopportune 135
hinder 706
– a lance 716, 722
– a law 83
– loose 671, 750
– one's neck
powerless 158
die 360
– the neck of
task 676
success 731
– the news 529
– no bones 648
– of 660
– off *cease* 142
relinquish 624
abrogate 756
– out *begin* 66
violent 173
disease 655
excited 825
– the peace 173, 720
– Priscian's head 568
– prison 750
– the ranks 61
– short 328
– silence 582
– the teeth 579
– the thread 70
– through the clouds *visible* 446
disclose 529
– through a custom 614
– up *disjoin* 44
decompose 49
end 67
revolution 146
destroy 162
– up of the system, 360, 665
– on the wheel
physical pain 378
mental pain 830
punishment 972
– with 713
– with the past 146
– word *deceive* 525
improbity 940
breaker
of horses 268
reef 346
wave 348
breakers 348, 667
surrounded by – 704
– ahead 665
breakfast 298
breakneck
precipice 217
rash 863
breakwater
refuge 666
obstruction 706
breast *interior* 221
confront 234
convex 250
mind 450
oppose 708
soul 820
at the – 129
in the – of 620
– the current 719
– high 206
breastplate 717
breastwork 717
breath *instant* 113
breeze 349
life 359
animality 364
faint sound 405
with bated – 581
hold – *quiet* 265
expect 507
wonder 870
not a – of air 265, 382
out of – 688
in the same – 120
shortness of – 688
take – 265, 689
take away one's – *unexpected* 508
fear 860
wonder 870
breathe *exist* 1
blow 349
live 359
faint sound 405
evince 467
mean 516
inform 527
disclose 529
utter 580
speak 582
refresh 689
– freely 827, 834
– one's last 360
not – a word 528
breathing time 687, 723
breathless
voiceless 581
out of breath 688
feeling 821
fear 860
eager 865
wonder 870
– attention 457
– expectation 507
– impatience 865
– speed 684
bred in the bone 820
breech 235
– loader 727
breeches 225
wear the – 737
– buoy 666
– maker 225
– pocket
money 800, 802
breed *kind* 75
multiply 161
progeny 167
animals 370
rear 537
breeding 161, 852, 894
breeze *wind* 349
discord 713
breezy 836
brethren 997
breve 413
brevet
warrant 741
commission 755
permit 760
– rank 873
breviary 998
brevier 591
brevity 201, 572
brew 41, 673
brewing
impending 152
storm – 665
bribe *equivalent* 30
tempt 615
offer 763
gift 784
buy 795
expenditure 809
reward 973
bric-à-brac 847
brick *hard* 323
pottery 384
material 635
trump 939, 948
make -s without straw 471
– color 434
brickbat 727
bricklayer 690
bride 903
bridewell 752
bridge 45, 627
– over *join* 43
facilitate 705
make peace 723
compromise 774
cards 840
bridle *restrain* 751
rein 752
– road 627
– one's tongue 585, 864
– up 900
brief *time* 111
space 201
concise 572
compendium 596

hold a – for 759
– case 191
briefly *anon* 132
brier
sharp 253
pipe 390
bane 663
brig 273
brigade 726
brigadier 745
brigand 792
brigandage 791
brigandine 717
brigantine 273
bright *shine* 420
color 428
intelligent 498
cheery 836
beauty 845
glory 873
– days 734
– eyed 845
– prospect 858
– side 829
look at the – side 836, 858
– thought
sharp 498
good stroke 626
wit 842
brighten up
furbish 658
brigue 712, 720
brilliant
shining 420
good 648
wit 842
beautiful 845
gem 847
glorious 873
– idea 842
brilliantine 356
brim 231
– over 641
brimful 52
brimstone 388
brindled 440
brine 341, 392
bring 270
– about 153, 729
– back 790
– back to the memory 505
– to bear upon
relation 9
– *action* 170
– into being 161
– to a crisis 604
– forth 161
– forward
evidence 467
manifest 525
teach 537
improve 658
– grey hairs to the grave 735, 830
– grist to the mill 644
– home 775
– home to 155
– in *receive* 296
income 810
price 812
– to life 359
– to light 480*a*
– low 874
– to maturity 673, 729
– to mind 505
– under one's notice 457
– off 672
– out
discover 480*a*
manifest 525
publish 591
– over
persuade 484
– to perfection 677
– into play 677
– to a point 74
– in question 461
– up the rear 235
– round
persuade 615
restore 660
– to terms 723
– to *convert* 144
halt 265
– together 72
– in its train 88
– to trial 969
– up *develop* 161
vomit 297
educate 537
– in a verdict 480
– word 527
brink 231
on the –
almost 32
coming 121
near 197
– of the grave 360
briny 392
– ocean 341
brio *music* 415
active 682
brisk *prompt* 111
energetic 171
active 682
cheery 836
bristle 253
– up *stick up* 250
angry 900
– with 639, 641
– with arms 722
bristly 256
Britannia metal 545
Briticism 563
British 188
– lion 604
Briton, true – 939
work like a – 686
brittleness 328
britzska 272
broach *begin* 66
found 153
reamer 262
tap 297
publish 531
assert 535
broad *general* 78
space 202
lake 343
emphatic 535
indelicate 961, 962
– accent 580
– awake 459, 682
– daylight 420, 525
– farce 842
– grin 838
– highway 627
– hint 527
– meaning 516
– minded 498
broadcast
disperse 73
spread 78
publish 531
sow – 818
broadcloth 219
broadhearted 906
broadsheet 593
broad-shouldered 159
broadside 236
publication 531
cannonade 716
broadsword 727
Brobdingnagian 192
brocade 847
brochure 593
Brocken, specter of the 443
broder 549
brogue *boot* 225
dialect 563
broidery 847
broil *heat* 382
fry 384
fray 713, 720
broke *poor* 804
broken
discontinuous 70
weak 160
– color 428
– down
decrepit 659
failing 732
dejected 837
– English 563
– fortune 735, 804
– heart 828, 837
hopeless 859
– reed 160, 665
– meat 645
– voice 581, 583
– winded
disease 655
fatigue 688
broker 758, 797
brokerage *pay* 812
brokery 794
bromidic 613
bronchia 351
bronze *alloy* 41
brown 433
sculpture 557
brooch 847
brood 102, 167
– over 451, 847
brooding
preparing 673
brook *stream* 348
bear 821, 826
broom 652
broth 298
brothel 961
brother *kin* 11
similar 17
equal 27
brotherhood 712
brotherly
friendship 888
love 897
benevolence 906
brougham 272
brought to bed 161
brouillerie 713
brouillon 626
brow *top* 210
edge 231
front 234
browbeat
intimidate 860
swagger 885
disrespect 929
–en *humbled* 879
brown 433
– Bess 727
– study 451, 458
Brown, Jones and Robinson 876
brownie 980
browse 298
bruin 895
bruise *powder* 330
hurt 619
injure 649
blemish 848
bruiser 726
bruit
report 531, 532
brumal 126, 383
brumous 353
Brummagem 545
brunette 433
brunt *beginning* 66
impulse 276
bear the –
difficulty 704
defence 717
endure 821, 826
brush *rough* 256
rapid motion 274
graze 379
clean 652
fight 720
paint – 556
– away *reject* 297
abrogate 756
– up *clean* 652
furbish 658
prepare 673
brushwood 367
brusque *violent* 173
haste 684
discourtesy 895
brutal *vulgar* 851
rude 895
savage 907
brutalize
[*see* brutal]
corrupt 659
deaden 823
vice 945
brute *animal* 366
rude 895
maleficent 913
– force
strength 159
violence 173
animal 450*a*
severe 739
compulsion 744
lawless 964
– matter 316, 358
Brute, et tu 917
brutish [*see* brute]
vulgar 851
ignoble 876
intemperate 954
brutum fulmen
impotent 158
failure 732
lax 738
boast 884
bubble
unsubstantial 4
transient 111
little 193
convexity 250
light 320
water 348
air 353
error 495
deceit 545
trifle 643
– burst
fall short 304
disappoint 509
fail 732
– reputation 873
– and squeak 298
– up *agitation* 315
buccaneer 791, 792
bucentaur 273
Bucephalus 271
buck *stag* 366
male 373
wash 652
money 800
fop 854
– basket 191
– jump 309
– up 684
bucket 191
kick the – 360
drop – in empty well 645
like –s in well 314
buckle *tie* 43
fastening 45
distort 243
curl 248
– on one's armor 673
– to 604, 686
– with *grapple* 720
buckler 717
buckram 855, 878
men in – 549
bucolic
pastoral 370
poem 597
bud 367
beginning 66
germ 153
expand 194
graft 300
– from 154
Buddha 979, 986
Buddhism 984
budding *young* 127
buddy 711, 890
budge 264
budget *heap* 72
bag 191
store 636
finance 811
– of news 532
buff 436
blind man's – 840
native – 226
buffer
hindrance 706
defence 717
buffet 191
strike 276
agitate 315
evil 619
bad 649
affront 900
smite 972
– the waves 704,

708
bar 189
buffo 599
buffoon *actor* 599
humorist 844
butt 857
buffoonery 840, 842
bug 653
bugaboo 669, 860
bugbear
imaginary 155
bane 663
alarm 669
fear 860
buggy 272
bugle
instrument 417
war-cry 722
ornament 847
– call 550, 741
build *construct* 161
form 240
– anew 658
– upon a rock 150
– up *compose* 54
– upon *belief* 484
builder 626, 690
building material 635
buildings 189
built on *basis* 211
bulb 249, 250
bulge 250
bulk 50, 192
– large 31
bulkhead 228, 706
bull *animal* 366
male 373
error 495
absurdity 497
solecism 568
police 664
ordinance 741
– in a china shop 59
like a – at a gate 173
take the – by the horns 604, 861
Bull, John – 188
bullcalf 501
bulldog *animal* 366
pluck 604, 604*a*
courage 861
bulldoze 885
bullet *ball* 249
arms 727
missile 284
bulletin 532, 592
– board 551
bullfight 720
bullhead 501
bullion 800
bullseye *centre* 222
lantern 423
aim 620
bully *fighter* 726
maltreat 830
frighten 860
courage 861
rashness 863
bluster 885
blusterer 887
threaten 909
evil doer 913
bad man 949
bulrush
worthless 643
bulwark 706, 717
bum 876
bumbailiff 965
bumbledom 737, 965
bumboat 273
bump 250, 276
– off 361
bumper 52
bumpkin 876
bumptious
proud 878
insolent 885
contemptuous 930
bun 298
bunch *collection* 72
protuberance 250
– light 599
bunchbacked 243
Buncombe
[*see* bunkum]
Bund 712
bundle *packet* 72
go 266
– on 275, 684
– out 297
bung 263
– up 261
bungalow 189
bungle 59, 699
bungler **701**
bunion 259
bunk 186, 215
bunker 181
bunkie 890
bunkum *lie* 544
style 577
boast 884
flattery 933
bunting 550
buoy *raise* 307
float 320
hope 858
buoyant
floating 305
light 320
elastic 325
prosperous 734
cheerful 836
hopeful 858
bur *clinging* 46
sharp 253
rough 256
in engraving 558
burden *lading* 190
weight 319
melody 413
poetry 597
too much 641
clog 706
oppress 828
care 830
– the memory 505
– of a song
repetition 104
burdensome
[*see* burden]
hurtful 649
laboring 686
bureau *chest* 191
office 691
shop 799
tribunal 960
bureaucracy 737
bureaucrat 694
burgee 550
burgeon
[*see* bourgeon]
burgess 188
burgh 189
burgher 188
burghmote 966
burglar 792
– alarm 669
burglary 791
burgomaster 745
burgrave 745
burial 363
buried *deep* 208
imbedded 229
hidden 528
– in a napkin 460
– in oblivion 506
burin 558
burke 361
burlesque
imitation 19
travesty 21
absurdity 497
misrepresent 555
drama 599
comic 853
ridicule 856
burletta 599
burly 192
burn *near* 197
rivulet 348
hot 382
consume 384
near the truth 480*a*
excited 825
love 897
punish 972
– the candle at both ends
waste 638
exertion 686
prodigal 818
– daylight 683
– one's bridges 604
– one's fingers 699
– in 384
– out 385
– to 865
burner 423
burning [*see* burn]
passion 821
angry 900
– glass 445
– with curiosity 455
– pain 378
– shame 874
burnish *polish* 255
shine 420
beautify 845
burnous 225
burnt [*see* burn]
red 434
– offering 952, 990
burr 410
burrock 706
burrow *lodge* 184
excavate 252
bursar 801
bursary 802
burst *disjoin* 44
instantaneous 113
explosion 173
brittle 328
sound 406
paroxysm 825
bubble –
disclosure 529
all over 729
ready to –
replete 641
excited 824
– of anger 900
– away 623
– of eloquence 582
– of envy 921
– into a flame 825
– forth *begin* 66
expand 194
be seen 446
–ing with health 654
– with grief 839
– in 294
– of laughter 838
– out 295
– upon *arrive* 292
unexpected 508
– into tears 839
burthen
[*see* burden]
bury *enclose* 229
inter 363
conceal 528
– the hatchet 918
– one's talent 528
busboy 746
busby 225
bush *branch* 51
jungle 344
shrub 367
beat about the – 629
bushel *much* 31
multitude 102
receptacle 191
size 192
hid under a – 460
not hide light under a – 878
bush-fighting 720
bushing 224
bushranger 792
bushy 256
business *event* 151
topic 454
occupation **625**
commerce 794
full of – 682
man of –
proficient 700
consignee 758
mind one's –
incurious 456
attentive 457
careful 459
let alone 748
send about one's – 297
stage – 599
business-like
orderly 58
business 625
active 682
practical 692
skilful 698
buskin *dress* 225
drama 599
buss *boat* 273
courtesy 894
endearment 902
bust 554
bustle *energy* 171
dress 225
agitation 315
activity 682
haste 684
difficulty 704
bustling
[*see* bustle]
eventful 151
busy 682
busybody 532, 682
but
on the other hand 30
except 83
limit 233
qualifying 469
– now 118
butcher *kill* 361
provisions 637
evil-doer 913
butler 746
butt *cask* 191
push 276
aim 620
attack 716
laughing-stock 857
– in 294, 682
– end 67
butte 206
butter 357
flattery 933
– bread on both sides 641
– not melt in mouth 894
buttered *side*
know – *skill* 698
selfish 943
not know – 699
butter-fingers 701
butterfly
variegated 440
fickle 605
beauty 845
gaudy 882
break – on wheel
waste 638
spite 907
butter-scotch 396
buttery 636
buttock 235
button *fasten* 43
fastening 45
little 193
hanging 214
knob 250
trifle 643
take by the – 586
– hole 586
– up *close* 261
restrain 751
– up one's pockets 808
buttoned-up
reserved 528
buttonholder 841
buttons *page* 746
button-top
useless 645
buttress
strengthen 159
support 215
defence 717
butyraceous 355
buxom 836
buy 795
– a pig in a poke 621
– and sell 794
buzz *hiss* 409
insect cry 412

bane 663
painful 830
candelabrum 423
candent 382
candid *white* 430
sincere 543
ingenuous 703
honorable 939
candidate 767, 865
candidature 763
candle 423
bargain by inch of – 769
burn – at both ends 686
not fit to hold a – to 34
– ends 40, 817
– holder 711
– light 126, 422
– power 466
– stick 423, 998
hold – to sun 645
Candlemas 998
candor
veracity 543
artlessness 705
honor 939
candy *dense* 321
sweet 396
cane *weapon* 727
punish 972
scourge 975
canescent 430
Canicula 423
canicular 382
caniculated 259
canine 366
– appetite 865
canister 191
canker *disease* 655
deterioration 659
bane 663
pain 830
canned goods 670
cannel coal 388
cankered
sullen 901*a*
cankerworm 663
evil-doer 913
care 830
cannibal 913
cannibalism 945
cannon
collision 276
loud 404
arms 727
– fodder 726
–'s mouth *war* 722
courage 861
cannonade 716
cannonball 249, 274
cannoneer 726
cannot 271
cannular 260
canny 498, 702
ca' – 864
canoe 273
paddle one's own – 748
canon *rule* 80
ravine 198
music 415
belief 484
precept 697
priest 996
rite 998
– law 697
canonical
regular 82
inspired 985
ecclesiastical 995
canonicals 999
canonist 983
canonization
repute 873
deification 991
rite 998
canonry 995
canopy 223
– of heaven 318
canorous 413
cant *oblique* 217
jerk 276
hypocrisy 544
neology 563
impiety 988
cantabile 415
cantankerous 901, 901*a*
cantata 415
missa – 998
cantatrice 416
canteen 189, 191
canter 266, 274
win at a – 705
canterbury
receptacle 191
Canterbury tale 546
cantharides 171
canticle 415
cantilever 215
canting 855
cantle 51
cantlet 32, 51
canto 597
canton 181, 737
cantonment 184, 189
cantrap 993
canty 836
canvas *sail* 267
picture 556
under press of – 274
canvass
investigate 461
discuss 476
dissert 595
solicit 765
canvasser 767
canyon 350
canzonet 415, 597
caoutchouc 325
cap *be superior* 33
height 206
summit 210
cover 223
hat 225
retaliate 718
complete 929
salute 894
fling up one's – 838
Fortunatus's – 993
set one's – at 897, 902
– and bells 844
– fits 23
– in hand
request 765
servile 886
respect 928
– of maintenance 747
capability
endowment 5
power 157
skill 698
facility 705
capacious *space* 180
– memory 505
capacity
endowment 5
power 157
space 180
size 192
intellect 450
wisdom 498
office 625
talent 698
cap-à-pie
complete 52
armed –
prepared 673
defence 717
war 722
caparison 225
cape *height* 206
cloak 225
projection 250
capella, alla – 415
caper *leap* 309
dance 840
capful *quantity* 25
small 32
– of wind 349
capillament 205
capillary
hairlike 205
thin 203
capital *city* 189
top 201
letter 561
important 642
excellent 648
money 800
wealth 803
make – out of
pretext 617
acquire 775
print in –s 642
– messuage 189
– punishment 972
ship 726
capitalist 803
capitation 85
– tax 812
capitol 189, 717
capitular 995, 996
capitulate 725
capnomancy 511
capon 373
caponize 38, 158
capote 225
capouch 999
capper 548
capriccio *music* 415
whim 608
caprice **608**
out of – 615*a*
capricious
irregular 139
changeable 149
irresolute 605
whimsical 608
capriole 309
capsize 218, 731
capsized 732
capstan 307, 633
capstone 210
capsular 252
capsule *vessel* 190
tunicle 223
medicine 662
captain 269, 745
captandum, ad –
sophistry 477
deception 545
affectation 855
ostentation 882
flattery 933
captation 933
captious
capricious 608
irascible 901
censorious 932
caption
taking 789
beginning 66
heading 564
captivate
induce 615
restrain 751
please 829
captivated 827
captivating 829, 897
captive
prisoner 754
adorer 897
lead – 749
make – 751
– balloon 273
captivity 751
capture 789
Capuchin 996
caput 696
– mortuum 645, 653
caquet 584
car 272
carabineer 726
carack 273
caracole 309
caracoler 266
carafe 191
caramel 396
carambole 276
carapace 717
cara sposa 897
carat 309
caravan 266, 272
caravansary 189
caravel 273
carbine 727
carbohydrates 298
carbon 388
– dioxide 663
– monoxide 663
carbonaro 742
carbonization 384
carboy 191
carbuncle *red* 434
abscess 655
jewel 847
carcanet 847
carcass
structure 329
corpse 362
bomb 727
carcelage 973
carcinoma 655
card *unravel* 60
ticket 550
plan 626
address – 550
by the – 82
great – 873
house of –s 328
leave a – 892
on the –s 152, 177, 470
play one's – 692
play one's best – 686
play one's –s well 698
playing –s 840
shuffle the –s
begin again 66
change 140
chance 621
prepare 673
speak by the –
care 459
veracity 543
phrase 566
throw up the –s 757
ticklish – 704
trump – 626
– index 60, 86, 551
–s to play 632
cardcase 191
cardiac 836
cardigan 225
cardinal *intrinsic* 5
dress 225
red 434
important 642
excellent 648
priest 995, 996
–'s hat 747
– points 278
– virtues 944
cardioid 245
card-sharper 792
card-sharping 545
care *attention* **459**
business 625
adversity 735
custody 751
economy 817
pain 828
fear 860
for aught one –s 643, 866
begone dull – 836
drive – away 840
have the – of 693
take – 665, 864
take – of 459
– for *important* 642
desire 865
love 897
careen *slope* 217
repair 660
career 625, 692
careless
inattentive 458
neglectful 460, 927
feeble 575
insensible 823
indifferent 866
caress 897, 902
caret *incomplete* 53
want 640
careworn 828, 837
cargo 270
large quantity 31
contents 190
property 780
goods 798
– boat 273
caricature
likeness 19
copy 21

exaggerate 549
misrepresent 555
ridicule 856
caricaturist 844
caries 49, 653, 655
carillon 417
cariole 272
carious 563
carking 828
– care 830
carle 876
Carlist 925
car-load 31
carman 694
Carmelite 996
carminative 662
carmine 434
carnage 361
carnal 364
intemperate 954
impure 961
irreligious 989
carnation 434
carnival 840
carnivorous 298
carol
music 415, 416
cheerful 836
rejoice 838
caro sposo 897
carouse *feast* 298
festivity 840
intemperance 954
drinking 959
carousel 840
carp at 932
carpe diem 134
carpenter 690
carper 936
carpet 211
on the –
topic 454
project 626
– bag 191
– knight *fop* 854
servile 886
sybarite 954a
– sweeper 652
carrefour 627
carriage *gait* 264
transference 270
vehicle 272
aspect 448
conduct 692
keep one's – 852
carried
– by acclamation &c. 488
– away by passion 824
carrier 271
– pigeon 534
carrion 362, 653
carronade 727
carroty 434
carry
conduce to 176
support 215
transfer 270
induce 615
reap and – 775
– all before one 731
– coals 879
– conviction 484
– into execution 729, 772
– with a high hand
authority 737
pride 878
insolence 885
– in the mind 505
– off *take* 789
steal 791
– on [*see below*]
– oneself 692
– out *conduct* 692
complete 729
– over
transfer 270
accounts 811
– a point 731
– by storm 731
– through 692, 729
– weight
influence 175
evidence 467
importance 642
carry on
continue 143
pursue 622
do 680
conduct 692
undertake 326
– an argument 476
– business 625
– an enquiry 461
– a trade 794
– war 722
cart 272
– away 185
– before the horse
disorder 59
inversion 218
bungling 699
– horse 271
work like a – horse 686
– load 31, 190
cartage 270
carte *list* 86
à la – 298
– blanche 760, 816
– du pays 626
– and tierce 716
– de visite 550
photograph 554
cartel
combination 709
defiance 715
truce 723
compact 769
cartelize 709
carter 268
cartes sur table 525, 543
Carthago, delenda est – 908
Carthusian 996
cartilage
dense 321
hard 323
tough 327
cartography 466, 554
cartoon 21, 556
cartoonist 559
cartouche
ammunition 727
ornament 847
cartridge 727
cartulary 86, 551
caruncle 250
carve *cut* 44
make 161
form 240
sculpture 557
apportion 786
– one's way 282
carvel 273
carver 559
caryatides 215
Cary's chickens, Mother – 668
cascade 348
case *state* 7
box 191
sheath 223
topic 454
argument 476
specification 527
grammar 567
affair 625
patient 655
law-suit 969
be the – 1, 494
in good – 654, 734
in –
circumstance 8
event 151
supposition 514
make out a – 467, 924
– in point 23, 82
caseation 321
caseharden
strengthen 159
habituate 613
case hardened
callous 376, 823
obstinate 606
casemate 189, 717
casement 260
casern 189
cash *money* 800
pay 807
in – 803
pay – for 795
– account 811
– book 551
– box 802
– down 807
– register 85, 553, 802
cashier *dismiss* 756
treasurer 801
casing 223
casino 712; 840
cask 191
casket 191
casque 717
Cassandra 513, 668
cassation 552
casserole 191
Cassiopeia's chair 318
cassock 999
cast *mold* 21
small quantity 32
spread 73
tendency 176
form 240
throw 284
tinge 428
aspect 448
drama 599
reject 610
plan 626
company 712
give 784
allot 786
condemn 971
give one a – 707
set on a – 621
– about for 463
– accounts 811
– adrift *disperse* 73
eject 297
liberate 750
dismiss 756
– anchor 265, 292
– aside 460
– aspersions 934
– away 610, 638
lost 732
– behind one
forget 506
refuse 764
relinquish 782
– away care 836
– off clothes 645
– of countenance 448
– of the dice 156
– in a different mold 18
– dishonor &c. upon 874
– to the dogs 162
– down 308, 837
– in the eye 443
– the eyes back 122
– eyes on 441
– the eyes over 457
– a gloom 837
– off a habit 614
– iron 323
resolute 604
– in one's lot with 609
– lots 621
– luster upon 420
– of mind 820
– a nativity 511, 992
– one's net 463
– off *divest* 226
disused 678
dismiss 756
relinquish 782
– over-board 678
– the parts 60
– reflection upon 932
– in the same mold 17
– a shade 421
– the skin 226
– a slur 874
accuse 938
– a spell 992
– off trammels 750
– up *add* 85
happen 151
eject 297
castanet 417
castaway *exile* 893
reprobate 949
caste 75, 873
lose – 940
castellan 746, 753
castellated 717
caster *cruet* 191
wheel 312
castigate 932, 972
castigator 936
casting 21
casting – vote 480
– weight 28, 30
castle *at chess* 148
abode 189
defence 717
– in the air
impossible 471
imagination 515
hope 858
Castle of Indolence 683
castor *hat* 225
Castor and Pollux 89, 890
castrametation 189, 722
castrate *subduct* 38
impotent 158
casual *extrinsic* 6
chance 156
uncertain 475
lax 773
casualty *event* 151
killed 361
evil 619
misfortune 735
casuist 476
casuistry
sophistry 477
falsehood 544
duty 926
casus belli
quarrel 713
irritation 824, 900
casus foederis 770
cat *nine lives* 359
animal 366
keen sight 441
fall on one's feet 734
cross 901
gib –, tom – *male* 373
rain –s and dogs 348
let – out of bag 529
– boat 273
– burglar 792
– call *whistle* 417
disapproval 932
–'s cradle 219
– and dog life 713
as the – jumps
event 151
see how the – jumps 510
fickleness 607
caution 864
– o' nine tails 975
– in pattens 652
–'s paw *dupe* 547
instrumental 631
use 677
auxiliary 711
catabasis 36
catachresis 521, 523
cataclysm
convulsion 146
destruction 162
deluge 348
catacomb 363
catacoustics 402
catadupe 348
catafalque 363
catalectic 597
catalepsy 265, 376, 683

catalogue 60, 86
catalysis 49, 140
catamaran 273, 726
catemenial 138, 299
cataphonics 402
cataplasm 662
catapult 284, 726, 727
cataract
waterfall 348
blindness 442, 443
catarrh 299
catastrophe
disaster 619
finish 729
misfortune 735
end 67
catch *imitate* 19
fastening 45
song 415
detect 480a
joke 497
gather the meaning 518
cheat 545
receive 785
take 789
by –es 70
no great – 651
– at *willing* 602
desire 865
– the attention 457
– one's death 360
– a disease 655
– the ear 418
– the eye 446
– fire 384
– a glimpse of 441
– an idea 498
– the infection
excitation 824
– a likeness 554
– a sound 418
– at straws
overrate 482
credulous 486
unskilful 699
rash 863
– by surprise 508
– a Tartar *dupe* 547
retaliate 718
– in a trap 545
– tripping 480a
– up 789
catching
infectious 657
catchpenny
deceiving 545
trumpery 643
cheap 815
catchpoll 965
catchword 550
catechism 461, 484
church – 983a
catechize 461
catechumen 541, 997
categorical
positive 474
demonstrative 478
affirmative 535
categorically true 494
category 7, 75
in the same – 9
catena 69
catenary 245
catenation 69
cater 298, 637
caterpillar tractor 271
caterwaul
cat-cry 412
discord 414
courting 902
cates 298
catgut 417
– scraper 416
cathartic 652
cathedrâ, ex –
affirm 535
school 542
authority 737
audacity 885
cathedral 1000
Catherine wheel 840
catholic
universal 78
religious 987
– church 983a
Roman – 984
catholicon 662
Catiline 941
catopsis 441
catoptrics 420
catoptromancy 511
cattle 271, 366
– truck 272
catwalk 273, 627
Caucasian mystery 983
caucus 696
caudal 67, 235
caudate 214
caudex 215
Caudine forks 162
cauf 370
caught tripping 491
caulk 660
cause *source* **153**
law-suit 969
final – 620
take up the – of 707
tell the – of 522
–d by 154
causeless
casual 156
aimless 621
causerie 588
causeway 627
causidical 965
caustic
energetic 171
feeling 821
painful 830
gruff 895
malevolent 907
– curve 245
cautel 864
cautelâ, ex abundanti – 664
cautery 384
caution *warn* 668
prudence 864
security 771
want of – 863
cavalcade 69, 266
cavalier
horseman 268
rash 863
insolent 885
discourteous 895
contemptuous 930
cavaliere servente
servile 886
lover 897
cavalry 726
cavatina 415
cave *dwelling* 189
cell 191
cavity 252
– canem 864
– of Adullam 624, 832
– in *hollow* 252
submit 725
caveat
warning 668
command 741
– emptor 769
cavendo tutus 664, 864
cavern [*see* cave]
cavernous 252
caviar 392, 393
– to the general 850
cavil *sophistry* 477
dissent 489
censure 932
caviler 936
cavity 252
caw 412
cayak 273
cayenne 392, 393
cazique 745
cease 142
– to breathe 360
– to exist 2
ceaseless 112
cecal 261
cecity 442
cecum 261
cede *submit* 725
relinquish 782
give 784
ceiling 206, 210, 223
celare artem, ars – 698
cela va sans dire
conformity 82
consequence 154
celebrant 990
celebration **883**, 998
celebrity 873, 875
celerity 274
celeste 417
celestial
physical 318
religious 976
heaven 981
celibacy **904**
cell *abode* 189
receptacle 191
cavity 221, 252
prison 752
hermitage 893
cellar 191
cellaret 191
cello 417
cellophane 223
cellular 191, 252
cement
medium 45
unite 43, 46, 48
covering 223
hard 323
material 635
– a party 712
cemented
concord 714
cemetery 363
cenobite 893, 996
cenotaph 363
censer 998
censor
moderate 174
critic 480
ban 761
detractor 936
censorious 480, 932
censurable 947
censure 932
censurer 936
census 85, 86
record 551
centaur 83, 366
centenarian 130
centenary
hundred 98
period 138
celebration 883
center 68, 222
– round 72, 290
centesimal 99
cento 597
centrality 222
centralize
combine 48
centrifugal 291
centripetal 290
centroidal 222
centuple 98
centurion 745
century
hundred 98
period 108
long time 110
money 800
ceramic
bake 384
– ware 557
cerate 662
Cerberus
janitor 263
custodian 664
hades 932
sop for – 615
cereal 298
cerebration 451
cerebrum 450
cere-cloth 363
cerement
covering 223
wax 356
burial 363
ceremonious 928
ceremony
parade 882
courtesy 894
rite 998
Ceres 979
cerise 434
cerography 558, 590
Ceromancy 511
ceroplastic 557
certain *special* 79
indefinite number 100
sure 474
belief 484
true 494
make – of 480a
of a – age 128
to a – degree 32
certainly *yes* 488
certainness 474
certainty **474**
certes 474, 488
certificate
evidence 467
record 551
security 771
certify 467, 535
certiorari 969
certitude 474
cerulean 438
cess *tax* 812
sewer 653
cessation **142**
cession
surrender 725
of property 782
gift 784
cesspool 653
cestui-que trust 779
cestus 45, 247
chafe
physical pain 378
warm 384
irritate 825
mental pain 828, 830
discontent 832
incense 900
chaff *trash* 643
ridicule 856
vulgar 876
not to be caught with – 698, 702
winnow – from wheat 609
chaffer 794
chafing-dish 386
chagrin 828
chain *fasten* 43
vinculum 45
series 69
measure 200
interlinking 219
measure 466
gearing 633
imprison 752
ornament 847
drag a – 749
drag a lengthened – 686
in –s 754
chain gang 752, 972
chain-shot 727
chair *support* 215
vehicle 272
professorship 542
throne 747
celebration 883
president 694
in the – 693
chairman 694
chaise 272
chalcography 558
chalet 189
chalice 191, 998
chalk *earth* 342
white 430
mark 550
drawing 556
– from cheese 14, 491
– out *plan* 626
challenge
question 461
doubt 485
claim 924
defy 715

chess 840
chessboard 440
chest 191, 802
chestnut-color 433
cheval-de-bataille
plea 617
plan 626
vanity 880
cheval-glass 445
chevalier 875
– d'industrie 792
chevaux de frise
253, 717
chevron
angle 217
indication 550
badge 747
decoration 877
chew 298
– the cud 451
– tobacco 392
chiaroscuro
light 420
grey 432
painting 556
chiasma 43
chic 845, 882
chicane
sophistry 477
deceit 545
cunning 702
chicken 129, 366
– in every pot 733
count –s before hatched 858, 863
tender as a – *soft* 324
sensitive 822
compassionate 914
chickenhearted 862
chide 932
chief *principal* 642
master 745
evidence in – 467
– constable 765
– part 31
Chief Justice 967
chiefdom 737
chieftain 745
chiffonnier 876
chiffonnière 191
chignon 225
chilblain 383
child
infant 129
offspring 167
fool 501
– of God 987
–'s play 643, 705
with – 161
childbirth 161
childhood 127
childish
credulous 486
foolish 499
feeble 575
– treble 581
childlike 703
chiliad 98
chill *cold* 383
render cold 385
indispose 616
– the spine 830, 860
chillies 393
Chiltern Hundreds 757
chime
repetition 104
roll 407
resonance 408
melody 413
– in with *agree* 23
conform 82
assent 488
concord 714
chimera 83, 515
chimney 260, 351
– corner 189
– pot 249
china 384, 557
China to Peru 180
chine 235
chinese white 430
chink *gap* 198
sound 408
money 800
chip *small* 32
detach 44
bit 51
reduce 195
– of the old block
similar 17
copy 21
offspring 167
chippy 962
Chirography 590
Chirology 550
Chiromancy 511
chirp
bird-note 412
sing 416
cheerful 836
rejoice 838
chirrup [*see* chirp]
chirurgery 662
chisel
fabricate 161
form 240
sharp 253
sculpture 557
chit 129, 193
chit-chat 588
chitterlings 221
chivalry *war* 722
tenure 777
courage 861
courtesy 894
philanthropy 910
honor 939
generosity 942
chlamys 225
chloroform 376, 823
chlorophyl 435
chlorotic 655
chock full 52
chocolate
food 298
color 433
choice *will* 600
election 609
excellent 648
absence of – **609a**
by – 600
– spirits 873
– of words 569
choir *sing* 416
church music 996
church 1000
– boy 996
– invisible 360, 977
choke *close* 261
stifle 361
redundant 641
hinder 706
–full *complete* 52
replete 639
–off 706
choler 900
choleric 901
choose 609
do what one –s 748
chop *disjoin* 44
change 140
– logic 476
– up 201
chopfallen 837
chopper 330
chopping
large 192
– sea 348
chops *mouth* 66
jaws 231
food 298
choral 415
chord 413
chore 625
choreography 840
chorister 416, 996
chorography 183
chorus
shout 411
song 415
singers 416
unanimity 488
poetry 597
opera 599
concord 714
– girl 599
chose
– in action 780
– in possession 777
chouse 545
choux gras, faire ses – 377
chrestomathy 560
chrism 998
Christ 976
Church of – 893*a*
receive – 987
Christ-cross-row 561
christen 564, 998
Christendom 983*a*, 995
Christian 983*a*, 987
– charity 906
– science 662, 984
Christmas 138, 998
Christmas-box 784
chromatic
color 428
– scale *music* 413
chromato-pseudoblepsis 443
chromatrope 445
chrome 436
chromolithograph 558
chromosphere 318
chronic 110
chronicle
measure time 114
annals 551
chronicler 553
chronography
measure time 114
description 594
chronology 114
chronometry 114
Chrononhotonthologos 887
chrysalis 129
chrysoprase 847
chrysolite 847
perfection 650
chrysology 800
chubby 192
chuck *throw* 284
animal cry 412
– it 142
– under chin 902
chuck-farthing 621
chuckle
animal cry 412
laugh 838
exult 884
chuff 876
chum 711, 890
chunk 51
Church
infallible 474
orthodox 983*a*
Christendom 995
temple 1000
dignitaries of – 996
go to – 990
High –, Low – &c. 984
– of Christ 983*a*
– bell 550
– house 1000
churchdom 995
churching 998
churchman 996
churchwarden 996
pipe 392
churchyard 363, 1000
– cough 655
churl *boor* 876
churlish
niggard 819
rude 895
sulky 901*a*
malevolent 907
churn 315, 352
chut! *silent* 403
taciturn 585
chute 348
chutney 393
chypre 400
cibarious 298
cicatrix 551
manet – 919
cicatrize 660
Cicero 582
cicerone 524, 527
ciceronian 578
cicisbeo 897
cicuration 370
cider 298
cider squeezer 876
ci-devant 122
cigar 392
ci-git 363
cilia 205, 256
cimeter 727
Cimmerian 421
cinch 45
cincture 247
cinder
combustion 384
dirt 653
Cinderella
servant 746
commonalty 876
cinema 448, 599, 840
cinematograph 448
cinematographer 553
cinerary 363
cineration 384
cinereous 432
cingle 230
cinnabar 434
cinnamon 393, 433
cinque 98
cipher
unsubstantial 4
number 84
compute 85
zero 101
concealment 528
mark 550
letter 561
unimportant 643
writing in – 590
Circe 615, 994
–an cup 377, 954
circination 312
circle *region* 181
embrace 227
form 247
party 712
describe a – 311
great – sailing 628
– of acquaintance 892
– of the sciences 490
circlet 247
circling 248
circuit *region* 181
outline 230
winding 248
tour 266
indirect path 311
indirect course **629**
circuition 311
circuitous 279, 311
– method 629
circular *round* 247
publication 531
letter 592
pamphlet 593
– note 805
circularity 247
circularize 592
circulate
circuit 311
rotate 312
publish 531
circulating medium 800
circulation
[*see* circulate]
in – *news* 532
– of money 809
circumambient 227, 229, 311, 629
circumambulate
travel 266
go round 311, 629
circumaviate 311
circumbendibus 248, 629
circumcision 44, 998
circumduction 552
circumference 230
circumferential 227
circumflex 311

circumfluent
lie round 227
move round 311
circumforaneous
traveling 266
circuition 311
circumfuse 73
circumgyration 312
circumjacence 227
circumlocution 573
circumnavigate
navigation 267
circuition 311
circumrotation 312
circumscribe
surround 229
limit 233, 761
circumscription 229
circumspection
attention 457
care 459
caution 459
circumstance
phase 8
event 151
circumstances
property 780
bad – 804
depend on – 475
good – 803
under the – 8
circumstantial 8
– account 594
– evidence 467
probability 472
circumstantiality 459
circumstantiate 467
circumvallation
enclosure 229, 232
defence 717
line of – 233
circumvent
environ 227
move round 311
cheat 545
cunning 702
hinder 706
defeat 731
circumvest 225
circumvolution
winding 248
rotation 312
circus
buildings 189
drama 599
arena 728
amusement 840
cirrus 353
cistern
receptacle 191
store 636
Cistercian 996
cit 188
citadel 717
citation 467, 733
cite
quote as example 82
as evidence 467
summon 741
accuse 938
arraign 969
cithern 417
citizen 188
– of the world 910
citriculture 371
citrine 436
city 189
in the – 794
city manager 965
civet 400
civic 372
civil *courteous* 894
laity 997
– authorities 745
– crown 733
– law 963
– war 722
civilian *lawyer* 968
layman 997
civilization
improvement 658
fashion 852
courtesy 894
civilized life 852
civism 910
clack *clatter* 407
animal cry 412
talkative 584
clad 225
claim *requisition* 630
demand 741
property 780
right 924
lawsuit 969
– the attention 457
claimant
petitioner 767
right 924
clair-obscur 420
clairvoyance 992
clairvoyant 513, 994
clamant 411
clamber 305
clammy 352
clamor *cry* 411
wail 839
– against 932
– for 765
clamorous
[*see* clamor]
loud 404
excitable 825
clamp *fasten* 43
fastening 45
clan *race* 11
class 75
family 166
party 712
clandestine 528
clangor 404
clank 410
clannishness 481
clanship 709
clap *explosion* 406
applaud 931
thunder –
prodigy 872
– the hands
rejoice 838
– on 31
– on the shoulder 615
– together 43
– up *imprison* 751
clapperclaw
contention 720
censure 932
claptrap
pretence 546
display 882
claquer 935
faire – son fouet 884
clarence 272
claret color 434
clarify 652
clarinet 417
clarion *music* 417
war 722
clarity 518
clash *disagree* 24
cross 179
concussion 276
sound 406
oppose 708
discord 713
– of arms 720
clasp *fasten* 43
fastening 45
stick 46
come close 197
belt 230
embrace 902
class *arrange* 60
category 75
learners 541
party 712
– prejudice 481
– room 542
classic *old* 124
symmetry 242
classical
elegant writing 578
taste 850
– art 556
– dancing 840
– education 537
– music 415
classicist 492
classics 560
classify 60
classmate 890
clatter 404, 407
claudication
slowness 275
failure 732
clause *part* 51
passage 593
condition 770
clausis, janius – 528
claustral 110
clavate 250
clavichord 417
clavier 417
claw *hook* 781
grasp 789
– back 935
clay *soft* 324
earth 342
corpse 362
material 635
– pipe 392
clay-cold 383
claymore 727
clean
entirely 52
perfect 650
unstained 652
– bill of health 654
– breast
disclose 529
– forgotten 506
– hand
proficient 700
with – hands
honesty 939
innocence 946
– out *empty* 297
– shaven 226
– sweep
revolution 146
destruction 162
clean-up 775
clear *simple* 42
sound 413
light 420
transparent 425
visible 446
certain 474
intelligible 518
manifest 525
easy 705
liberate 750
profit 775
vindicate 937
innocent 946
acquit 975
all – 664, 705
coast – 664
get – off 671
keep – of 623
make – 529
– for action
prepare 673
– articulation 580
– conscience 946
– the course 302
cut 510
– the ground
facilitate 705
– of *distant* 196
– off *pay* 807
– out *empty* 297
clean 652
– sighted
vision 441
shrewd 498
– sky *hope* 858
– stage
occasion 134
easy 705
right 922
– thinking 498
– the throat 297
– up *light* 420
intelligible 518
interpret 522
clearheaded 498
clear-obscure 420
cleat 45
cleavage
cutting 44
structure 329
cleave *sunder* 44
adhere 46
bisect 91
cleaver 253
cledge 342
clef 413
cleft *divided* 44
bisected 91
chink 198
in a – stick
difficulty 704
clem 956
clement
lenient 740
long-suffering 826
compassionate 914
clench *compact* 769
retain 781
take 789
clepe 564
clepsydra 114
clerestory 191, 1000
clergy 996
clerical 995, 996
– error 495
– staff 746
clerk *scholar* 492
recorder 553
writer 590
helper 711
servant 746
agent 758
clergy 996
articled – 541
– in holy orders 995
– of works 694
clerkship
commission 755
cleromancy 511
clever
intelligent 498
skilful 698
smart 842
too – by half 702
clew *ball* 249
interpretation 522
indication 550
seek a – 461
click 406
client
dependant 746
customer 795
clientship
subjection 749
cliff *height* 206
vertical 212
steep 217
land 342
climacteric 128
climate *region* 181
weather 338
fine – 656
climatology 338
climax
supremacy 33
summit 210
culmination 729
climb 305
– on the band-wagon 731
clime 181
clinal 217
clinch *fasten* 43
close 261
certify 474
pun 563
complete 729
clutch 781
snatch 789
– an argument 47
– the fist at 909
clincher 479
cling *adhere* 46
– to *near* 197
willing 602
persevere 604a
habit 613
observe 772
desire 865
love 897
– to hope 858
– to one another 709
clinic 662
clink
resonance 408
stridor 410

prison 752
clinker *brick* 384
dirt 653
clinometer
oblique 217
angle 244
clinquant
ornament 847
vulgar 851
Clio 594
clip *shorten* 201
– the wings
powerless 158
speed 264
slow 275
useless 645
hinder 706
prohibit 761
– one's words 583
clipper 273
clipping
small piece 51
clique *conclave* 696
party 712
cloaca *conduit* 350
foul 653
Cloacina 653
cloak *dress* 225
conceal 528
disguise 530
cloaked 223
cloche 371
clock 114
clockwork 633
by – *uniform* 16
order 58
regular 80
clod *lump* 192
earth 342
fool 501
bungler 701
clodhopper 876
clodpated
stupid 499
clog *shoe* 225
hinder 706
– dance 840
cloison 228
cloisonné 557
cloister *arcade* 189
way 627
restraint 751
convent 1000
close *similar* 17
tight 43
end 67
field 181
court 189
near 197
narrow 203
shut 261
dense 321
warm 382
hidden 528
concise 572
taciturn 585
complete 729
stingy 819
examine –ly 457
keep – *hide* 528
retain 781
tread – upon 281
– the door upon
restrain 751
– the ears 419
– the eyes
die 360
not see 442
– one's eyes to
not attend 458
set at naught 773
– at hand
to-morrow 121
imminent 152
near 197
– the hand
refuse 764
– in upon 290
– inquiry 461
–ly packed 72
– prisoner 754
– quarters 197
approach 286
attack 716
battle 722
– one's ranks 673
– study
thought 451
attention 457
– up 197, 290
– with *cohere* 46
assent 488
attack 716
contend 720
consent 762
compact 769
close-mouthed 585
closet
receptacle 191
ambush 530
closeted with
conference 588
advice 695
close-up 197
closure 142, **261**
clot *solidify* 321
earth 342
cloth *vocation* 625
napkin 652
clergy 996
clothes 225
grave – 363
– basket 191
clothier 225
Clotho 601
clotpoll 501
clotted 352
cloud
assemblage 72
multitude 102
mist 353
shade 424
screen 520
break through the –s 446
drop from the –s 508
in a – 475, 528
in the –s
lofty 206
inattentive 458
dreaming 515
under a –
insane 503
adversity 735
disrepute 874
secluded 893
censured 932
accused 938
– burst 348
–capt 206
– of dust 330, 353
–s gathering
dark 421
danger 665
warning 668
– no bigger than a man's hand 668
– of skirmishers 726
– of smoke 353
– of words 573
clouded
variegated 440
dejected 837
hopeless 859
– perception 499
cloudiness 571
cloudland 515
cloudless
light 420
happy 827
cloudy *dim* 422, 426
clough 206
clout 276
cloven 91
cloven foot
mark 550
malevolence 907
vice 945
Satan 978
see the – 480*a*
show the – 907
clover
luxury 377
prosperity 734
comfort 827
clown
pantomime 599
bungler 702
buffoon 844
vulgar 851
rustic 876
cloy 641, 869
club
place of meeting 74
house 189
association 712
weapon 727
sociality 892
– law
compulsion 744
lawless 964
– together
co-operate 709
clubby 892
club car 272
clubfooted 243
cluck 412
clue 550
seek a – 461
clump
assemblage 72
projecting mass 250
– of trees 367
clumsy
unfit 647
awkward 699
ugly 846
Cluniac 996
clurichaune 980
cluster 72
clutch *retain* 781
seize 789
clutches 737
in the – of 749
clutter 407
coacervation 72
coach
carriage 272
teach 537
tutor 540, 673
– painter 540
– road 627
drive a – and six through 964
– up 539
coachhouse 191
coachman 268, 694
coaction 744
coadjutant 709
coadjutor 711
coadjuvancy 709
coagency 178, 709
coagmentation 72
coagulate
cohere 46
density 321
semi-liquid 352
coal 388
call over the –s 932
carry –s 879
– black 431
carry –s to Newcastle 641
coalesce
identity 13
combine 48
coalheaver
work like a – 686
coalition 43, 709, 712
coaming 232
coaptation 23
coarctation
decrease 36
contraction 195
narrow 203
impede 706
restraint 751
coarse *harsh* 410
dirty 653
unpolished 674
garish 846
vulgar 851
impure 961
– grain 329
coast *border* 231
slide 266
navigate 267
land 342
– defence 717
– line 230
coaster 273
coastguard 753
coat *layer* 204
paint 223
habit 225
cut – according to cloth 698
– of arms 550
– of mail 717
coating, inner – 224
coax *persuade* 615
endearment 902
flatter 933
cob *horse* 271
punish 972
cobalt 438
cobble *mend* 660
cobbler 225
cobbles 635
coble 273
cobra 913
cobweb *light* 320
fiction 545
flimsy 643
dirt 653
–s of antiquity 124
–s of sophistry 477
cocaine 376, 381, 663
cochineal 434
cock *bird* 366
male 373
game – 861
– boat 273
– and bull story 546
– the eye 441
– of the roost
best 648
master 745
– up *vertical* 212
convex 250
cockade *badge* 550
title 877
cock-a-hoop
gay 836
exulting 884
Cockaigne 827
cockatrice
monster 83
piercing eye 548
evil-doer 913
miscreant 949
cockcrow 125
cocked hat 225, 745
cocker *fold* 258
caress 902
Cocker
school book 542
according to – 82
cockle *fold* 258
– of one's heart 820
cockleshell 273
cockloft 191
cockney
Londoner 188
plebeian 876
cockpit *hold* 191
council 696
arena 728
cockshut
morning 125
evening 126
dusk 422
cock-sparrow 193
cocksure 484
cockswain 269
cocktail 298, 959
– party 892
cocoa 298
cocotte 962
coction 384
Cocytus 982
cod *shell* 223
coddle 902
– oneself 943
code *conceal* 528
precept 697
law 963
codex 593
codger 819
codicil *sequel* 65
testament 771
codify 60, 963
codlin 129
coefficient
factor 84
accompany 88

co-operate 709
Coelebs 904
coemption 795
coequal 27
coerce *compel* 744
restrain 751
coetaneous 120
coeternal
perpetual 112
synchronous 120
coeur, à contre – 603
coeval 120
– with birth 5
coexist *exist* 1
accompany 88
synchronism 120
contiguity 199
coextension
equality 27
parallelism 216
symmetry 242
coffee 298
coffee-house 189
coffee-pot 191
coffer *chest* 191
store 636
money chest 802
cofferdam 55
coffin 363
add a nail to one's – 830
cog *tooth* 253
boat 273
deceive 545
flatter 933
cogent
powerful 157
– reasoning 476
cogitate 451
cogitative faculties 450
cognate
consanguineous 11
related 9
similar 16
cognition 490
cognitive faculties 450
cognizance 490
take – of
intellect 490
attention 457
cognomen 564
cognoscence 490
cog-wheel 312
cohabitation
location 184
marriage 903
coheir 778
coherence *unite* **46**
dense 321
cohesive 46
cohibit
restrict 706
restrain 751
prohibit 761
cohobation 336
cohort 726
cohue 72
coif 225
coiffure 225
coign of vantage 33
coil *disorder* 59
curve 245
convolution 248
circuition 311
shuffle off this mortal – 360
coin *fabricate* 161
imagine 515
money 800
– money 775
– words 563
coincidence
identity 13
in time 120
chance 156
concurrence 178
in place 199
in opinion 488
coiner *thief* 792
coistril 862
coition 42
coke 388
colander 260
colature 652
cold *frigid* **383**
color 429, 438
style 575
insensible 823
indifferent 866
in – blood
premeditated 611
purposely 620
unfeeling 823
dispassionate 826
– comfort 832
– shoulder
discourtesy 895
contempt 930
– stool 727
– storage 387
– sweat *fear* 860
dislike 867
– water cure 662
throw – water on
dissuade 616
hinder 706
dull 843
cold feet 862
coldhearted
unfeeling 823
hostile 889
malevolent 907
cold pack 670
Coliseum 189, 588, 728
collaboration 178
collaborator 690, 711
collapse
prostration 158
contract 195
shortcoming 304
deteriorate 659
fatigue 688
failure 732
collar *dress* 225
circlet 247
shackle 752
seize 789
slip the – 750
collate 464
collateral
relation 9, 11
parallel 216
lateral 236
security 771
– evidence 467
collation
repast 298
comparison 464
colleague
accompany 88
co-worker 696
co-operation 709
auxiliary 711
friend 890
collect
assemble 72
opine 480
understand 518
acquire 775
prayer 990
– evidence 467
– knowledge 539
– one's thoughts 451
collectanea
assemblage 72
compendium 596
collected *calm* 826
collection
assemblage 72
offertory 998
collectively
whole 50
generality 78
together 88
collectivism 737, 778
college 542
go to – 539
– of cardinals 996
– education 537
colleen 129
colley 366
collide 276
collier 273
colligate 72
collimation 216, 278
colliquate 335
collision *disagreement* 24
clash 179
percussion 276
opposition 708
encounter 720
collocate
arrange 60
assemble 72
place 184
collocution 588
collogue 933
colloid 352
collop 51, 298
colloquial
figure of speech 521
neology 563
conversation 588
– meaning 516
colluctation 720
collusion *deceit* 545
conspiring 709
collusive 544
colluvies 653
collyrium 662
Cologne
eau de – 398
colon 142
colonel 745
colonist 188
colonize 184, 294, 295
colonnade
series 69
houses 189
colony 184, 188, 780
colophon 65
colophony 356*a*
Colorado beetle 913
color *hue* **428**
tone 431
appearance 448
probability 472
disguise 544
paint 556
plea 617
be angry 900
all –s 440
change –
shame 879
give a – to
change 140
qualify 469
probable 472
falsehood 472
lend a – to
plea 617
vindicate 937
man of – 431
show in true –s 543
– blindness 443
– printing 558
– sergeant 745
–ed spectacles 424
– too highly 549
– up *redden* 434
blush 879
colorable
ostensible 472
deceptive 545
coloration 428
coloratura 415, 416
colorful 882
coloring
[*see* color]
meaning 516
false – 523
– matter 428
colorless
weak 160
pale 429
colors
ensign 550
decoration 877
with – flying
resolution 604
false – 544, 545
flying –
display 882
celebration 883
lower one's – 735
nail one's – to the mast 604
show one's –
manifest 525
disclose 529
true to one's – 939
Colosseum 728
colossus 192, 206
colporteur 797
colstaff 215
colt *young* 129
horse 271
fool 501
columbine 599
columella 215
column *series* 69
height 206
support 215
cylinder 249
caravan 266
monument 551
printing 591
troop 726
columnist 527, 553
colures 318
coma *inactive* 683
insensible 376, 823
comb *teeth* 253
clean 652
punish 972
combat 720, 722
combat, hors de –
useless 645
tired 688
combatant **726**
combe 252
comber 348
combination **48**
arithmetical 84
party 712
combine *unite* 48
co-operate 709
combustible 388
combustion 384
come *happen* 151
approach 286
arrive 292
cheer up! 836
out upon! 932
to – *future* 121
destiny 152
– about 658
– across
discover 480*a*
acquire 775
pay up 807
– after
sequence 63
posterior 117
– between 631
cut and – again 639
– of age 131
– amiss
disagreeable 24
ill-timed 135
– back 283
– before 116
– by 775
– at one's call 743
– to a determination 604
– down with 807
– into existence
be 1
begin 66
– first *superior* 33
precede 62
– forth
egress 295
appear 446
– forward 763
– from 154
– to the front 303
– and go 314
– to hand 785
– to a head
climax 33
complete 52
– in *ingress* 294
receipt 785
– in for
property 778, 780
– to one's knowledge 527
– to life 359
– what may 474
– near 286
– to nothing
unproductive 169
fail 732

– of 154
– off *event* 151
disjoin 44
loop-hole 617
escape 671
– on *future* 121
destiny 152
I defy you 715
attack 716
– to oneself 660
– into operation 170
– out
disclosure 529
publication 531
on the stage 599
– out of *effect* 154
egress 295
– out with
disclose 529
speak 582
– over
influence 615
consent 762
– to pass *state* 7
event 151
– to pieces 44
– to the point
speciality 79
attention 457
concise 572
– to the rescue 672
– round
period 138
conversion 144
belief 484
assent 488
change of mind 607
influence 615
restoration 660
be pacified 723
consent 762
– to the same thing 27
– short of
inferior 34
fall short 304
– to one's senses 502
– to a stand 142
– to terms
assent 488
contract 769
it –s to this
concisely 572
– to *equal* 27
whole 50
arithmetic 85
become 144
effect 154
inherit 777
money 800
price 812
– together
assemble 72
converge 290
– under 76
– upon
unexpected 508
acquire 775
claim 924
– into use 613
– into view 446
– into the views of
co-operate 709
– off well 731
– into the world 359
come-down 306, 735
comedy
drama 599
comic 853
comely 845
comestible 298
comet
wanderer 268
star 318
cometary 111
comfit 396
comfort
pleasure **377**
delight 827
content 831
relief 834
give – 906
comfortable
pleasing 829
comforter
covering 223
Comforter 976
comfortless
painful 830
dejected 837
comic *wit* 842
ridiculous 853
– opera 599
– strips 531
coming [*see* come]
impending 152
– events
prediction 511
– out 883
– time 121
comitia 696
comity 894
comma 142
inverted –s 550
command *high* 206
requisition 630
authority 737
order **741**
possess **777**
at one's –
obedient 743
– belief 484
– of language
writing 574
speaking 582
– of money 803
– one's passions 944
– respect 928
– one's temper 826
– a view of 441
commandant 745
commander 269
commandeer 744, 789
commanding
[*see* command]
important 642
commando 726
commandment 697
comme deux gouttes d'eau 17
comme il faut
taste 850
fashion 852
genteel 875
commemorate 883
commence 66
commencement de la fin *end* 67
destruction 162
commend 931
– the poisoned chalice 544
commendable 944
commensurate
accordant 23
numeral 85
adequate 639
comment
reason 476
judgment 480
interpretation 522
criticize 595
commentary 595
commentator 492, 524, 527
commerce
conversation 588
barter 794
cards 840
commercial 811
– arithmetic 811
– traveler 758
commère 599
commination 908, 909
commingle 41
comminute 330
commiserate 914
commissariat 637
commissary
provisions 637
consignee 758
commission
task 625
delegate **755**, 759
Royal – 696
– of the peace 965
commissioner 758
commissionaire
doorkeeper 263
messenger 534
consignee 758
commissure 43
commis-voyageur 758
commit *do* 680
delegate 755
cards 840
arrest 969
– an absurdity 853
– oneself to a course 609
– to the flames 384
– to memory 505
– oneself
clumsy 699
promise 768
– to prison 751
– sin 945
– to writing 551
committee
council 696
consignee 758
(*director* 694)
commix 41
commode 191
commodious 644
commodity 798
commodore 745
common
general 78
ordinary 82
plain 344
habitual 613
trifling 643
base 876
in – *related* 9
participate 778
right of – 780
short –s 640
tenant in – 778
make – cause 709
– consent 488
– council 966
– course 613
– herd 876
– law *old* 124
law 697, 963
– measure 84
– origin 153
– parlance 576
– place 82
– place book
record 551
compendium 596
– saying 496
– sense 498
– sewer 653
– stock 778
– weal
mankind 372
good 681
utility 644
philanthropy 910
Common Pleas Court of – 966
commonalty **876**
commoner 876
commonplace
usual 82
known 490
plain 576
habit 613
unimportant 643
dull 843
commons 298
commonwealth
territory 181
community 372
authority 737
commorant 188
commotion 315
communalism 778
commune
township 181
commune with 588
– oneself 451
communibus annis 29
communicant 990
communicate
join 43
tell 527
correspond 592
give 784
sacrament 998
communication
news 532
of disease 657
oral – 582, 588
communion
discourse 588
society 712
participation 778
sacrament 998
hold – with 888
– table 1000
communiqué 527
communism 737
communist
party 712
rebel 742
participation 778
philanthropy 910
evil doer 913
community
party 712
– at large 372
– of goods 778
commutation
compensation 30
substitution 147
interchange 148
compromise 774
barter 794
commutual 12
compact
joined 43
united 87
receptacle 191
small 193
compressed 195
compendious 201
dense 321
bargain **769**
compages
whole 50
structure 329
compagination 43
companion *match* 17
accompaniment 88
ladder 305
friend 890
companionable 892
companionship 892
companionway 305
company
assembly 72
actors 599
party, partnership 712
troop 726
sociality 892
bear – 88
in – with 88
comparable 9
comparative 464
degree 26
– anatomy 368
comparatively 32
compare 464
– notes 695
comparison **464**
compartition 44
compartment
part 51
region 181
place 182
cell 191
carriage 272
compass
degree 26
space 180
surround 227
measure 466
intend 620
guidance 693
achieve 729
box the –
azimuth 278
rotation 312
keep within –
moderation 174
fall short 304
economy 817
points of the – 236
in a small – 193
– about 229

– of thought 498
compassion 914
object of – 828
compatible
consentaneous 23
possible 470
compatriot
inhabitant 188
friend 890
compeer *equal* 27
friend 890
compel 744
compellation 564
compendency 43
compendious 201
compendium **596**
book 593
compensate
make up for 30
requite 973
compensation **30**
compère 599
competence
power 157
sufficiency 639
skill 698
wealth 803
competition
opposition 708
contention 720
competitor
opponent 710
combatant 726
candidate 767
compilation
collect 72
book 593
compendium 596
compile 54
complacent
pleased 827
content 831
courteous 894
kind 906
complain 839
complainant 938
complaint
illness 655
murmur 839
lodge a – 938
– without cause 839
complaisant
lenient 740
courteous 894
kind 906
complement
adjunct 39
remainder 40
part 52
arithmetic 84
complementary
correlation 12
colour 428
complete
entire 52
accomplish 729
compact 769
– answer 479
– circle 311
in a – degree 31
completeness **52**
completion **729**
complex 59
complexion
state 7
color 428
appearance 448
compliance
conformity 82
obedience 743
consent 762
observance 772
complicate
derange 61
complicated
disorder 59
convolution 248
complice 711
complicity 709
compliment
courtesy 894, 896
praise 931
poor – 932
–s of season 896
complimentary
free 815
complot 626
comply [*see* compliance]
compo *coating* 223
material 635
component **56**
componere lites 723, 724
comport
– oneself 692
– with 23
compos mentis 502
compose
make up 54, 56
produce 161
moderate 174
music 416
write 590
printing 591
pacify 723
assuage 826
composed
self-possessed 826
composer
music 413
composite 41
composition **54**
[*see* compose]
combination 48
piece of music 415
picture 556
style 569
writing 590
building material 635
compromise 774
barter 794
atonement 952
compositor
printer 591
compost 653
composure 826, 871
compotation 959
compote 298
compound
mix 41
combination 48
limited space 182
enclosure 232
compromise 774
– arithmetic 466
– for *substitute* 147
barter 794
comprador 637
comprehend
compose 54
include 76
know 490
understand 518
comprehension [*see* comprehend]
intelligence 498
comprehensive 76
complete 50
general 78
wide 192
– argument 476
compress
contract 195
curtail 201
condense 321
remedy 662
compressible 322
comprise 76
comprobation
evidence 467
demonstration 478
compromise
dally with 605
mid-course 628
taint 659
danger 665
pacify 723
compact 769
compound **774**
atone 952
compromised
promised 768
compter 799
compte rendu
record 551
accounts **811**
comptroller 694
compulsion **744**
compunction 833, 950
compurgation
evidence 467
acquittal 970
compute 85
comrade 890
comradeship 892
con *think* 451
get by heart 505
learn 539
conation 600
conatu magnas nugas, magno –
waste 638
unimportance 643
conatus 176
concamerate 245
concatenation
junction 43
continuity 69
concavity **252**
conceal
invisible **447**
hide 528
cunning 702
concealment **528**, 893
concede
assent 488
admit 529
permit 760
consent 762
give 784
conceit *idea* 453
folly 499
supposition 514
imagination 515
wit 842
affectation 855
vanity 880
conceited
dogmatic 481
conceivable 470
conceive *begin* 66
beget 161
teem 168
believe 484
understand 490
imagine 515
plan 626
concent 413
concentrate
assemble 72
centrality 222
converge 290
concentric 216, 222
conception
[*see* conceive]
intellect 450
idea 453
concern
relation 9
event 151
business 625
importance 642
firm 797
grief 828
– oneself with 625
concert
agreement 23
synchronism 120
music 415
act in – 709
in – *musical* 413
concord 714
– measures 626
concertina 417
concerto 415
concert-room 840
concession
permission 760
consent 762
compromise 774
giving 784
discount 813
concesso, ex –
reasoning 476
assent 488
concetto 842
conchoid 245
conchology 223
concierge 163, 753
conciliate
talk over 615
pacify 723
satisfy 831
courtesy 894
atonement 952
conciliatory [*see* conciliate]
concord 714
forgiving 918
conciliatrix 962
concinnity
agreement 23
style 578
beauty 845
conciseness **572**
concision 201
conclave
assembly 72
council 696
church 995
conclude
end 67
infer 480
resolve 604
complete 729
compact 769
conclusion
[*see* conclude]
sequel 65
germination 161
judgment 480
try –s 476
forgone – 611
hasty – 481
conclusive
[*see* conclude]
answer 462
evidence 467
certain 474
proof 478
– reasoning 476
concoct *lie* 544
write 590
plan 626
prepare 673
concomitant
accompany 88
same time 120
concurrent 178
concord *agree* 23
music **413**
assent 488
harmony **714**
concordance 562
book 593
concordant **173**
concordat 769
concordia discors 24, 59
concours **720**
concourse
assemblage 72
convergence 290
concremation 384
concrete *existent* 3
mass 16
definite 79
density 321
hardness 323
materials 635
concubinage 961
concubine 926
concupiscence 865, 961
concur
co-exist 120
causation 178
converge 290
assent 488
concert 709
concurrence **178**, 216
concussion 276
condemnation 932, **971**
condemned cell 752
condense
compress 195
dense 321
condensed
concise 572
condescend 879
condign 924
condiment **393**
condisciple 541
condition *state* 7
modification 469
supposition 514
term 770
repute 873
rank 875
in – *plump* 192
in good – 648
on – 770
in perfect – 650

physical – 316
conditional 8
conditions **770**
condolence 914, **915**
condone 918
condottiere
traveller 268
fighter 726
conduce
contribute 153
tend 176
concur 178
avail 644
conducive 631
conduct
transfer 270
music 416
procedure **692**
lead 693
safe –
passport 631
safety 664
– a funeral 363
– an inquiry 461
– to 278
conduction 264
conductor 269
conveyer 271
director 694
lightning – 666
conduit **350**
conduplicate 89
condyle 250
cone *round* 249
pointed 253
confabulation 588
confection 396
confectionary 396
confectioner 637
confederacy
co-operation 709
party 712
confederate 711
confer *advise* 695
give 784
– benefit 648
– power 157
– privilege 760
– right 924
– with 588
conference [*see* confer]
council 696
confess *assent* 488
avow 529
penitence 950, 998
– and avoid 937
confession [*see* confess]
auricular – 998
– of faith 983
confessional 1000
confessions
biography 594
confessor 996
confidant 711
confidante
servant 746
friend 890
confidence
trust 484
hope 858
courage 861
in – 528
– trick 545
confident 535
configuration 240
confine
region 182
circumscribe 229
limit 231, 233
imprison 751
confined
narrow judgment 481
ill 655
confinement
childbed 161
confines of
on the – 197
confirm
corroborate 467
assent 488
consent 762
compact 769
rite 998
confirmed 150
– habit 613
confiscate *take* 789
condemn 971
penalty 974
confiture 396
conflagration 382, 384
conflexure 245
conflict
opposition 708
discord 713
contention 720
conflicting
contrary 14
counteracting 179
– evidence 468
confluence
junction 43
convergence 290
river 348
conflux
assemblage 72
convergence 290
conform *assent* 488
– to rule 494
conformable 23, 178
conformation 54, 240
conformity **82**, 178
confound
disorder 61
destroy 162
not discriminate 465a
perplex 475
defeat 731
astonish 870
curse 908
confounded
great 31
bad 649
confraternity
party 712
friendship 888
confrère
colleague 711
friend 890
confrication 331
confront *face* 234
compare 464
oppose 708
resist 719
– danger 861
– witnesses 467
confucianism 984
Confucius 986
confuse *derange* 61
perplex 458
obscure 519
not discriminate 465a
abash 879
confused *disorder* 59
invisible 447
uncertain 475
style 571
confusion
[*see* confuse]
– seize 908
– of tongues 560, 563
– of vision 443
– worse-confounded 59
confutation **479**
congé 293, 756
– d'élire 995
congeal *dense* 321
cold 385
congeneric
similar 17
included 76
congenial
related 9
agreeing 23
concord 714
love 897
congenital 5, 820
congeries 72
congestion 641
conglaciation 385
conglobation 72
conglomerate
cohere 46
assemblage 72
council 696
dense 321
conglutinate 46
congratulate 896
– oneself 838
congratulation **896**
congregation
assemblage 72
worshippers 990
laity 997
Congregationalist 984
congress
assembly 72
convergence 290
conference 588
council 698
Congressional Medal 733
Congressional Record 551
congreve *fuel* 388
– rocket 727
congruous
agreeing 23
(*expedient* 646)
conical *round* 249
pointed 253
conjecture 475, 514
conjoin 43
conjoint 48
conjointly 37
conjugal 903
conjugate
words 562
grammar 567
– in all its tenses &c. 104
conjugation
junction 43
pair 89
phase 144
grammar 567
conjunction 43
in – with 37
conjuncture
contingency **8**
occasion 134
conjure *deceive* 545
entreat 765
sorcery 992
name to – with 873
– up *recall* 505
– up a vision 505
conjuror
deceiver 548
sorcerer 994
connaître les dessous des cartes 490
connate
intrinsic 5
kindred 11
cause 153
connatural
uniform 16
similar 17
connect *relate* 9
link 43
connection
[*see* connect]
kin 11
in – with 9
connections
cards 840
connective 45
conned, well – 490
connive
overlook 460
co-operate 709
allow 760
connoisseur
critic 480
scholar 492
taste 850
connotate 550
connote 516, 550
imply 526
connubial 903
connuted 9
conoscente 850
conquer 731
conquered
(*failure* 732)
conquering hero comes 883
conqueror 731
consanguinity **11**
consciarecti, mens–
pride 878
innocence 946
conscience
knowledge 490
moral sense 926
in all – *great* 31
affirmation 535
awakened – 950
qualms of – 603
clear – 946
stricken – 950
tender – 926
honor 939
conscientious 926
scrupulous 939
– objector 489
conscious
intuitive 450
knowledge 490
– of disgrace 874
– of glory 873
conscript 726
conscription 744
consecrate *use* 677
dedicate 873
sanctify 987
holy orders 995
consecration
rite 998
consectory 478
– reasoning 476
consecution 63
consecutive
following 63
continuous 69
– fifth 414
consecutively
slowly 275
consensus 488
– of opinion 23
consent *assent* 488
compliance **762**
with one – 178
consentaneous
agreeing 23
(*expedient* 646)
consequence
event 151
effect 154
importance 642
in – 478
of no – 643
take the –s 154
consequent 63
consequential
deducible 478
arrogant 878
consequently
reasoning 476
effect 154
conservation
permanence 141
storage 636
preservation 670
conservatism 141, 670
conservative 141, 712
– policy 681
conservatoire 542
conservator
of the peace 967
conservatory
receptacle 191
floriculture 371
furnace 386
store 636
conserve 396, 636
consider *think* 451
attend to 457
examine 461
adjudge 480
believe 484
considerable
in degree 31
in size 192
important 642
considerate
careful 459
judicious 498
benevolent 906
consideration
purchase money 147
thought 451

idea 453
attention 457
qualification 469
inducement 615
importance 642
gift 784
benevolence 906
respect 928
requital 973
deserve – 642
in – of
compensation 30
reasoning 476
on – 658
take into –
thought 451
attention 457
under –
topic 454
inquiry 461
plan 626
considered, all things –
collectively 50
judgment 480
premeditation 611
imperfection 651
consign
transfer 270
commission 755
property 783
give 784
– to the flames 384
– to oblivion 506
– to the tomb 363
consignee 758
consignor 796
consignment
commission 755
gift 784
apportionment 786
consilience 178
consist
– in 1
– of 54
consistence
density 321
consistency
uniformity 16
agreement 23
consistently with 82
consistory
council 696
church 995
consolation
relief 834
condole 915
religious 976
console
table 215
Consoler
the – 976
consolidate
unite 46, 48
condense 321
consols 802
consommé 298
consonant
agreeing 23
musical 413
letter 561
consort
accompany 88
associate 892
spouse 903
– with 23
consortium 23
consortship 892
conspection 441
conspectus 596
conspicuous
visible 446
famous 873
conspiracy 626
conspirator 626
traitor 941
conspire
concur 178
co-operate 709
constable
policeman 664
governor 745
officer 965
constant
fixed 5
uniform 16
continuous 69
regular 80
continual 112
frequent 136
regular 138
immutable 150
exact 494
persevering 604a
obey 743
faithful 939
– flow 69
constellation
stars 318
luminary 423
glory 873
consternation 860
constipation
closure 261
density 321
constituency 181, 737
constituent 51, 56
constitute
compose 54, 56
produce 161
constitution
nature 5
state 7
composition 54
structure 329
charter 924
law 963
constitutional
walk 226
– government 737
constrain
compel 744
restrain 751
abash 881
constraint 195
constrict 195, 706
constringe 195
construct 161
construction 161
form 240
structure 329
meaning 522
put a false – upon 523
constructive
latent 526
– evidence 467
constructor 164
construe 522
consubstantiation 998
consuetude 618
consul 758, 759
consulship 737
consult 695
– one's pillow 133
– one's own wishes 943
– the wishes of 707
consultant 662
consultation 695, 696
consume
destroy 162
waste 638
use 677
– away 36
– time
time 106
inactivity 683
consumere natus, fruges – 683
consuming 830
consummate
great 31
complete 52
completed 729
– skill 698
consummation
end 67
completion 729
– devoutly to be wished
good 618
desire 865
consumption [*see* consume]
decrease 36
shrinking 195
disease 655
contact 199
come in –
arrive 292
contagion
transfer 270
disease 655
unhealthy 657
contain
be composed of 54
include 76
container 191
contaminate
soil 653
spoil 659
contaminated
diseased 655
contango 133, 813
contemn 930
contemper 174
contemplate
view 441
think 451
expect 507
purpose 620
contemporary 120
contemporation 171
contempt 930
– of danger 861
contemptible
unimportant 643
dishonorable 940
contend
reason 476
assert 535
fight 720
– with difficulties 704
– for
vindicate 937
content
assenting 488
willing 602
calm 826
satisfied **831**
to one's heart's –
sufficient 639
success 731
contention 720
contentious 901
contents
ingredients 56
list 86
components **190**
synopsis 596
conterminate
end 67
limit 233
conterminous 199
contesseration 72
contest 709, 720
contestant 710
context 591
from the – 516
contexture 329
contiguity 199
continence 960
continent
land 342
continental 643
contingency
event 151
uncertainty 475
expectation 507
contingent
conditional 8
casual 156
liable 177
possible 470
uncertain 475
supply 635
aid 707
allotted 786
donation 809
unforeseen 508
– duration **108a**
– interest 780
continual
perpetual 112
frequent 136
continuance 143
continuation
adjunct 39
sequence 63
sequel 65
– school 542
continue
endure 106, 110
persist 143
continued 69
– success 731
continuity 69
uniformity 16
contortion
distortion 243
convolution 248
contortionist 599, 700
contour
outline 230
appearance 448
contra 14
per – 708
– bonos mores
vulgar 851
improper 925
vice 945
contraband
deceitful 545
prohibited 761
illicit 964
contrabasso 417
contraception 706
contract
shrink 195
narrow 203
promise 768
bargain 769
bridge 840
– a debt 806
– a habit 613
– an obligation 768
contractility 195
contraction 195
short-hand 590
compendium 596
contractor 690
contradict
contrary 14
answer 462
dissent 489
deny 536
oppose 708
contradictory
disagreement 24
evidence 468
discord 713
contradistinction 15
contraindicate
dissuade 616
warning 668
contraire, tout au – 536
contralto 408, 416
contraposition
inversion 218
reversion **237**
contrapuntist 413
contrariety 14
contrary
opposite 14
antagonistic 179
captious 608
opposing 708
quite the – 536
– to expectation
improbable 473
unexpected 508
– to reason 471
contrast
contrariety 14
difference 15
comparison 464
contravallation 717
contravene
contrary 14
counterevidence 468
deny 536
hinder 706
oppose 708
contre coeur, à – 603
contre-coup 277
contretemps
ill-timed 135
hindrance 706
misfortune 735
contribute
cause 153
tend 176
concus 178
aid 707
give 784
contribution 784
lay under – 789, 924

contrition
abrasion 331
regret 833
penitence 950
contrivance 633
contrive
produce 161
plan 626
– to *succeed in* 731
contriving
cunning 702
control
power 157
influence 175
regulate 693
authority 737
restrain 751
board of – 696
under –
obedience 743
subjection 749
controller of currency 801
controls 273, 693
controversial
discussion 476
discordant 713
controversialist 476, 726
controversy
disagreement 24
discussion 476
debate 588
contention 720
controvert
deny 536
controvertible
uncertain 475
debatable 476
untrue 495
contumacy
obstinacy 606
disobedience 742
contumely
arrogance 885
rudeness 895
disrespect 929
scorn 930
reproach 932
contund 330
contuse 330
conundrum *pun* 520
riddle 533
wit 842
convalescence 654, 660
convection 270
convenance
mariage de – 903
convene 72
conveniences 632
convenient 646, 705
convent 1000
conventicle
assembly 72
council 696
chapel 1000
convention
agreement 23
assembly 72
rule 80
council 696
precept 697
treaty of peace 723
compact 769
–s of society 852
conventional 82, 613
conventual 996, 1000
convergence **290**
convergent 286
conversable
talk 588
sociable 892
conversant
know 490
skilful 698
conversation 588
conversational
loquacious 584
interlocution 588
sociable 892
conversazione 588, 892
converse
reverse 14
talk 588
conversely 468
conversion **144**
trover and – 964
convert
change to 140, 144
opinion 484
tergiversation 607
religion 987
– to use 677
convertible 13, 27
– terms 522
convexity **250**
convey
transfer 270
mean 516
assign 783
– away 791
– the knowledge of 527
conveyance
[*see* convey]
vehicle 272
conveyancer 968
conveyancing 783
convict
convince 484
condemned 949
condemn 971
convicted, self – 950
conviction
confutation 479
belief 484
prove guilty 971
convince
belief 484
confute 479
teach 537
convivial 892
convocate 72
convocation
council 696
church 995
convoke 72
convolution
coil **248**
rotation 312
convoy
accompany 88
transfer 270
guard 664
escort 753
convulse
derange 61
violent 173
agitate 315
bodily pain 378
mental pain 830
convulsed with
– laughter 838
– rage 900
convulsion
[*see* convulse]
disorder 59
revolution 146
in –s 325
coo 412
cook *heat* 384
falsify 544
improve 658
prepare 673
servant 746
too many –s 699
– accounts 811
cool *moderate* 174
cold 383
refrigerate 385
grey 432
dissuade 616
cautious 864
indifferent 866
unamazed 871
unfriendly 889
discourteous 895
look – upon
unsocial 893
take –ly 826
– down 826
– one's heels
kept waiting 133
inaction 681
cooler 387
coolheaded
judicious 498
unexcitable 826
coolie
bearer 271
military 726
coolness
insensibility 823
estrangement 898
coon-can 840
coop *abode* 189
restrain 751
prison 752
co-operation
physical 178
voluntary **709**
participation 778
co-operator 690, 711
co-optation 609
co-ordinate
equal 27
arrange 60
measure 466
cootie 653
cop 664
copal 356*a*
coparcener 778
copartner
accompanying 88
participator 778
associate 890
copartnership
co-operation 709
party 712
cope *equal* 27
oppose 708
contend 720
canonicals 999
copia verborum
diffuse 573
loquacious 584
coping stone
top 210
completion 729
copious
diffuse style 573
abundant 639
coportion 778
copper *money* 800
policeman 664
copper-colored 433, 439
copper-plate –
engraving 558
writing 590
coppice 367
coprolite 653
copse 367
copula 45
copulation 43
copy
imitate 19
facsimile **21**
prototype 22
news 532
record 551
represent 554
write 590
for the press 591
plan 626
– book 22
copyhold 780
copyist
imitator 19
artist 559
writer 590
copyright 780
coquet *lie* 544
change the mind 607
affected 855
endearment 902
flattery 933
– with
irresolute 605
coquette
affected 854, 855
flirt 897
coquillage 847
coracle 273
coral 847
– reef 667
coram judice
jurisdiction 965
lawsuit 969
cor Anglais 417
corbeille 191
corbel 215
cord *tie* 45
filament 205
cordage 45
cordated 245
cordial
pleasure 377
dram 392
willing 602
remedy 662
feeling 821
grateful 829
friendly 888
courteous 894
cordiform 245
cordite 727
cordon
inclosure 232
circularity 247
decoration 877
– bleu 733, 746
– sanitaire
safety 664
preservation 670
corduroy 259
cordwainer
shoemaker 225
artificer 690
core *gist* 5
source 153
center 222
gist 642
true to the – 939
coriaceous 327
Corinthian 850
co-rival
[*see* corrival]
cork *plug* 263
lightness 320
– jacket 666
– up *close* 261
restrain 751
corking pin 45
corkscrew
spiral 248
perforator 262
circuition 311
cormorant
desire 865
gluttony 957
corn
projection 250
Cornaro 953
cornea 441
corned 959
cornelian 847
corneous 323
corner *place* 182
receptacle 191
angle 244
monopoly 777
– creep into a – 893
in a dark – 528
drive into a – 706
push into a – 874
rub off –s 82
– turn a – 311
turn the – 658
– stone
support 215
importance 642
defence 717
cornet *music* 417
officer 745
cornice 210
corniculate 253
cornification 323
Cornish hug 545
corno 417
cornopean 417
cornucopia 639
cornute
projecting 250
sharp 253
corollary
adjunct 39
deduction 480
corona 247
coronach 839
coronation
enthronement 755
celebration 883
coroner 363, 965
–'s jury 967
coronet *hoop* 247

insignia 747
title 877
corporal
corporeal 316
officer 745
corporate 43
– body 712
corporation
bulk 192
convex 250
association 712
jurisdiction 965
corporeal 3, 316, 364
– hereditaments 780
corporeity 316
corps *assemblage* 72
troops 726
à – perdu
haste 684
rash 863
– de reserve 636
corpse 362
corpulence 192
corpus 316
– Christi 998
– delicti
guilt 947
lawsuit 969
– juris
precept 697
law 963
corpuscle
small 32
little 193
corradiation
focus 74
convergence 290
corral 232, 370
correct
orderly 58
true 494
inform 527
disclose 529
improve 658
repair 660
due 924
censure 932
honorable 939
virtuous 944
punish 972
– ear 416, 418
– memory 505
– reasoning 476
– style
grammatical 567
elegant 578
correction
[*see* correct]
house of – 752
under – 879
corrective 662
corregidor 745
correlation
relation 9
reciprocity **12**
correspondence
correlation 12
similarity 17
agreement 23
writing **592**
– course 537
correspondent
messenger 534
journalist 593
consignee 758
corresponding
similar 17
agreeing 23
corridor *region* 181
place 191
passage 627
– train 272
corrigendum 495
corrigible 658
corrival 726
corrivalry 720
corrivation 348
corroborant 662
corroboration
evidence 467
assent 488
corrode *burn* 384
erode 659
afflict 830
corrosive
[*see* corrode]
acrid 171
destructive 649
– sublimate 663
corrugate
derange 61
constrict 195
roughen 256
rumple 258
furrow 259
corruption
decomposition 49
neology 563
foulness 653
disease 655
deterioration 659
improbity 940
vice 945
corrupting
noxious 649
corsage 225
corsair 273, 792
corse 362
corselet 225
corset 225
corso 728
cortège
adjunct 39
continuity 69
accompaniment 88
journey 266
suite 746
cortes 696
cortex
cortical 223
coruscate 420
corvette 273, 726
corybantic 503
coryphée 599
Corypheus
teacher 540
director 694
coscinomancy 511
cosey 892
cosignificative 522
cosine 217
cosmetic
remedy 662
ornament 847
cosmic 318
cosmogony &c. 318
cosmopolitan
abode 189
mankind 372
philanthropic 910
sociality 892
cosmorama 448
cosmos 60, 318
Cossack 726
cosset
darling 899
caress 902
cost 812
pay –s 807
to one's –
evil 619
badness 649
– what it may 604
– price 815
costermonger 797
costless 815
costly 814
costive
taciturn 585
costume 225
theatrical – 599
costumé 225
bal – 840
costumier 225
theatrical 599
cosy *snug* 377
sociable 892
cot *abode* 189
bed 215
cote 189
cotenancy 778
coterie *class* 75
junto 712
society 892
coterminous 120
cothurnus 599
cotillon 840
cottage 189
– piano 417
cottager 188
cotter 188
cotton 205
– seed oil 356
couch *lie* 213
bed 215
stoop 308
lurk 528
– one's lance 720
– in terms 566
couchant 213
couci-couci 651
cough 349
churchyard – 655
couleur de rose
good 648
prosperity 734
view en – 836
coulisses 599
coulter 253
council
senate **696**
church 995
hold a – 695
– of education 542
– school 542
councillor 696
counsel
advice 695
lawyer 968
keep one's own – 528
take – *think* 451
inquire 461
be advised 695
count *clause* 51
item 79
compute 85
estimate 480
lord 875
– one's chickens before they are hatched 858, 863
– the cost 864
– upon
believe 484
expect 507
to be –ed on one's fingers 103
countenance
face 234
appearance 448
favor 707
approve 931
keep in –
conform 82
induce 615
encourage 861
vindicate 937
keep one's –
brook 826
not laugh 837
out of –
abashed 879
put out of – 874
stare out of – 885
– falling
disappointment 509
dejection 837
counter *contrary* 14
number 84
table 215
stern 235
token 550
shop-board 799
over the –
barter 794
buy 795
sell 796
run – 179
– to 708
counteract
compensate 30
physically 179
hinder 706
voluntarily 708
counteraction 14, **179**
counterbalance 30
counterblast
counteract 179
retaliate 718
countercharge 462
counterchange
correlation 12
interchange 148
countercharm 993
countercheck
mark 550
hindrance 706
counterclaim 30
counter-evidence **468**
counterfeit
imitate 19
copy 21
simulate 544
sham 545
coinage 792
counterfoil 550
countermand 756
countermarch 266, 283
countermark 550
countermine
plan 626
oppose 708
countermotion 283
counterorder 756
counterpane 223
counterpart
match 17
copy 21
reverse 237
counterplot
plan 626
oppose 708
retaliate 718
counterpoint 415
counterpoise
compensate 30
weight 319
hinder 706
counter-poison 662
counterpole 14
counter-project 718
counter-protest 468
counter-revolution 146
counterscarp 717
countersign
evidence 467
assent 488
mark 550
counterstroke 718
countervail
outweigh 28
compensate 30
evidence 468
counterwork 708
countess 875
counting-house 799
countless 105
countrified 189
vulgar 851
country
region 181
abode 189
rural 371
authority 737
love of – 910
country-dance 840
countryman
commonalty 876
friend 890
county 181
– seat 189
– town 189
– school 542
– council 696
– court 966
coup
instantaneous 113
action 680
– de bec
attack 716
censure 932
– d'épée dans l'eau 645
– d'essai 675
– d'état
revolution 146
plan 626
action 680
lawless 964
– de grâce
end 67
death-blow 361
completion 729
punishment 972
– de main
violence 173
action 680
attack 716
– de maître
excellent 648

skilful 698
success 731
– d'oeil
sight 441
appearance 448
display 882
– de plume 590
– de soleil
hot 384
mad 503
à – sûr 474
– de théâtre
appearance 448
display 882
coupé 272
couple
unite 43
two 89
–d with
added 37
accompanied 88
coupler 45
couplet 89, 597
coupling 45
coupon 800
courage **861**
moral – 604
– oozing out 862
courant, au – 490
coureur, avant – 673
courier
traveler 268
guide 524
messenger 534
course *order* 58
continuity 69
time 106, **109**
layer 204
motion 264
locomotion 266, 267
direction 278
dinner 298
river 348
pursuit 622
way 627
conduct 692
arena 728
bend one's – 266
in due – 134
hold a – 278
in the – of
during 106
keep one's –
progress 282
persevere 604*a*
let things take their –
continue 143
inaction 681
follow as of – 478
mark out a – 626
of –
conformity 82
effect 154
certain 474
assent 488
necessity 601
willingly 602
custom 613
consent 762
expect 871
race – 840
run its –
end 67
complete 729
take a – 622
take its – 151
– of action 692
– of business 625
– of events 151
– of inquiry 461
– of preparation 673
– runs smooth 734
– of study 537
– of things 151
– of time 121
courser
horse 271
swift 274
coursing
kill 361
pursue 622
court *close* 181, 182
house 189
hall 191
flatness 213
invite 615
pursue 622
council 696
retinue 746
solicit 765
gentility 852
wish 865
woo 902
flatter 933
tribunal 966
bring into – 467
friend at – 526, 711
pay – to
servile 886
love 897, 902
flatter 933
put out of – 731
– card 626
– of honor 939
courteous 894
courtesan 962
courtesy
stoop 308, 314
submit 725
politeness **894**
show –
respect 928
courtier
servile 886
flatterer 935
–like 933
courtly 852
courtship 902
courtyard 182
cousin 11
coûte-que-coûte
certainly 474
necessary 601
resolution 604
cove *cell* 191
hollow 252
bay 343
covenant
compact 769
condition 770
security 771
covenanter 488
Coventry
Earl of –
cards 840
send to –
eject 297
disrepute 874
seclusion 893
cover
compensate 30
include 76
superpose, lid 223
dress 225
stopper 263
meal 298
conceal 528
retreat 530
report 531
keep clean 652
keep safe 664
preserve 670
under –
hidden 528
pretence 545
safe 664
with dust 653
covercle 223
covering **223**
coverlet 223
Coverley, Sir Roger de – 840
covert *abode* 189
invisible 447
latent 526
refuge 666
feme –e 903
– way 627
coverture 903
covet *desire* 865
envy 921
covetous
miserly 819
covey
assemblage 72
multitude 102
cow
animal 366
female 374
intimidate 860
coward 862
cowardice **862**
cowboy 370
cower *stoop* 308
fear 860
cowardice 862
servile 886
cowherd 370
cowhide 223, 975
cowhouse 189
cowkeeper 370
cowl *sacerdotal* 999
dress 225
cowled 223
cowl-staff 215
co-worker 690
coxcomb 854
coxcombry
affectation 855
vanity 880
coxswain 269
coy *timid* 860
modest 881
cozen 545
crab *sourness* 397
–like motion
deviation 279
regression 283
grouch 901*a*
crabbed *sour* 397
unintelligible 519
obscure style 571
difficult 704
uncivil 895
sulky 901*a*
crack *split* 44
discontinuity 70
instantaneous 113
fissure 198
furrow 259
brittle 328
sound 406
excellent 648
injure 659
skilful 698
boast 884
– a bottle
food 298
social 892
drunken 959
– of doom
end 67
future 121
destruction 162
– one's invention 515
– a joke 842
– shot 700
crackbrained 503
cracked
unmusical 410
fanatical 481
mad 503
faulty 651
– bell 408*a*
– voice 581
cracker 406
crackle 406
cracksman 792
crack-up 162
cradle
beginning 66
infancy 127
origin 153
placing 184
bed 215
training 673
aid 707
in the – 129
– song 415
craft *shipping* 273
business 625
skill 698
cunning 702
craftiness 498
craftsman 690
craftsmanship 680
crag *pointed* 253
hard 323
land 342
craggy
rough 256
craig *height* 206
crake 884
cram *crowd* 72
stuff 194
choke 261
teach 537
learn 539
gorge 957
– down the throat
induce belief 484
compel 744
crambe repetita
weariness 841
satiety 869
crambo 597
crammed 52
– to overflowing 641
crammer *lie* 546
teacher 537
cramp
fastening 45
paralyze 158
weaken 160
little 193
compress 195
spasm 378
hinder 706
cramped *style* 579
cran 191
cranch
[*see* craunch]
crane *angle* 244
elevate 307
instrument 633
– neck 245
craniology &c. 450
cranium 450
crank
fanatic 504
instrument 633
wit 842
treadmill 975
crankle *fold* 258
crankling
rough 256
cranky *weak* 160
ill health 655
cranny 198
crape
crinkle 248
mourning 839
crapulence
intemperance 954
gluttony 957
drunken 959
crash
destruction 162
collision 276
gain entrance 294
sound 406
crasis *nature* 5
coherence 48
composition 54
crass 31
– ignorance 491
crassitude
breadth 202
thickness 352
crate
receptacle 191
vehicle 272
crater *deep* 208
hollow 252
craunch
shatter 44
chew 298
pulverize 330
cravat 225
crave *ask* 765
desire 865
envy 921
craven *submit* 725
cowardly 862
craw 191
crawfish 607
crawl *time* 109
creep 275
back down 283, 606
servile 886
– with 102
crawling 102
crayons 556
craze 481
crazy *weak* 160
mad 503
creachy 160
creak 410
cream
emulsion 352
oil 356
important part

physical pain 378
mental pain 830
crucible
dish 191
conversion 144
furnace 386
experiment 463
laboratory 691
put into the – 163
crucifix 219, 998
crucifixion 828
cruciform 219
crucify
physical torture 378
mental agony 830
execution 972
crucis, experimentum – 463
crude *color* 428
- *style* 579
unprepared 674
cruel
painful 830
inhuman 907
– to be kind 914
cruelly *much* 31
cruet 191
cruise
vessel 191
navigation 267
cruiser 726
cruising 267
crumb *small* 32
powder 330
– of comfort 834
crumble
decrease 36
weak 160
destruction 162
brittle 328
pulverize 330
spoil 659
– into dust
decompose 49
– under one's feet 735
crumbling
[*see* crumble]
dangerous 665
crumenal 800
crump
distorted 243
curved 245
crumple
ruffle 256
fold 258
– up *destroy* 162
crush 195
crunch
shatter 44
chew 298
pulverize 330
crupper 235
crusade 722
crush *crowd* 72
destroy 162
compress 195
pulverize 330
humble 879
– under an iron heel 739
– one's hopes
disappoint 509
hopeless 859
crushed 828
crushing 830
crust 223
crustacean 366
crusty 895, 901*a*
crutch
support 215
angle 244
-ed Friars 996
crux 219, 704
– criticorum 533
cry *human* **411**
animal 412
publish 531, 532
call 550
voice 580
vogue 613
weep 839
far – to 196
full – *loud* 404
raise a – 550
– aloud
implore 765
– out against
dissuade 616
censure 932
– down 932, 934
– for 865
– before hurt 839
– for joy 838
– you mercy
deprecate 766
pity 914
forgive 918
– shame 932
– to *beseech* 765
– up 931
– for vengeance 923
– wolf *false* 544
alarm 669
– and little wool
overrate 482
boast 884
disappoint 509
crying [*see* cry]
urgent 630
weary 841
– evil 619
– shame 874
– sin 945
crypt *cell* 191
grave 363
ambush 530
altar 1000
cryptic 475, 528
cryptography
hidden 528
writing 590
crystal *hard* 323
transparent 425
snow – 383
– gazer 513
– gazing 511, 992
– oil 356
clear as – 519
crystalline
dense 321
hard 323
transparent 425
crystallization 321, 323
csako 225, 717
cub *young* 129
vulgar 851
clown 876
unlicked – 241
cubby-hole 191
cube
three dimensions 92, 93
form 244
cubicle 191
cubist 556
cubit 200
cucking stool 975
cuckold 905
cuckoldom 961
cuckoo
imitation 19
repetition 104
sound 407
cry 412
cuddle 196, 902
cudgel *beat* 276
weapon 727
punish 975
take up the –s
aid 707
attack 716
contention 720
– one's brains
think 451
imagine 515
cue *hint* 527
watchword 550
plea 617
rôle 625
take one's – from 695
in proper – 698
cuff *sleeve* 225
blow 276
punishment 972
cui bono 644, 645
cuique voluptas sui – 865
cuirass 717
cuirassier 726
cuisine 298
batterie de – 957
culbute
inversion 218
fall 306
cul-de-lampe
engraving 558
ornament 847
cul-de-sac
concave 252
closed 261
difficulty 704
culinary 298
– art 673
cull *dupe* 547
choose 609
take 789
cullender 260
cullibility 486
cullion 949
cully *deceive* 545, 547
culm 388
culminate
maximum 33
height 206
top 210
complete 729
culpability *vice* 945
guilt 947
culprit 949
cult 983
cultivate *till* 365, 371
sharpen 375
improve 658
prepare 673
aid 707
cultivated
courteous 894
– taste 850
cultivator 371
culture
knowledge 490
improvement 658
taste 850
politeness 894
culverin 727
culvert 350
cum multis aliis 37, 102
cumber *load* 319
obstruct 706
cumbersome
incommodious 647
disagreeable 830
cummerbund 225
cumulative 72
increasing 35
assembled 72
– evidence 467
– vote 609
cumulus 353
cunctando restituit rem 681
cunctation 133
cuneiform 244
– character 590
cunning
prepense 611
sagacious 698
artful **702**
– fellow 700
– man 994
cup *vessel* 191
hollow 252
beverage 298
remedy 662
trophy 733
tipple 959
between – and lip 111
in one's –s 959
– that cheers &c. 298
– of humiliation 879
dash the – from one's lips 509
– too low 837
cupbearer 746
cupboard 191
cupellation 384
Cupid *beauty* 845
love 897
gods 979
cupidity
avarice 819
desire 865
cupola *height* 206
roof 223
dome 250
cup-tossing 621
cur *dog* 366
coward 862
sneak 949
curable 658, 660, 662
curacy 995
curare 663
curate 996
curative 660
curator 694, 758
curb *moderate* 174
slacken 275
dissuade 616
restrain 751
shackle 752
curb exchange 621
curbstone 233
curd *density* 321
pulp 354
(*cohere* 46)
curdle *condense* 321
(*cohere* 46)
make the blood – 830
curdled 352
cure *reinstate* 660
remedy 662
preserve 670
benefice 995
curé 996
cureless 859
curfew 126
curia 966
curio 847
curiosa felicitas 698
curiosity
unconformity 83
inquiring **455**
phenomenon 872
curious
exceptional 83
inquisitive 455
true 494
beautiful 845
desirous 865
curiously *very* 31
curl *bend* 245
convolution 248
hair 256
cockle up 258
badge 747
– up one's lip 930
curling *game* 840
curmudgeon
miser 819
plebeian 876
currency
publicity 531
money 800
current *existing* 1
usual 78
present 118
happening 151
flow 264
of water 348
of air 349
rife 531, 532
language 560
habit 613
danger 667
account – 811
against the – 708
go with the – 82
pass –
believed 484
fashion 852
stem the – 708
– belief 488
– of events 151
– of ideas 451
– of time 109
currente calamo 590
curricle 272
curriculum 537
curry *food* 298
rub 331
condiment 392, 393
– favour with
love 897
flatter 933

– with faint
praise 932, 934
damnable 649
damnatory
disapprove 932
condemn 971
damnify
damage 649
spoil 659
damnosa hereditas
663
Damocles
sword of – 667
Damon and Pythias 890
damozel 129
damp
moderate 174
moist 339
cold 385
sound 405
dissuade 616
hinder 706
depress 837
dull 843
– the sound 408*a*
damper 387
damsel
youth 129
female 374
Dan to Beersheba
52, 180
Danaë 803
Danaos, timeo –
doubt 485
caution 864
dance
jump 309
oscillate 314
agitate 315
rejoice 838
sport 840
sociality 892
lead the – 175
lead one a –
run away 623
circuit 629
difficult 704
practical joke 929
St. Vitus' – 315
– attendance
waiting 133
follow 281
servant 746
petition 765
servility 886
– the back step
283
– upon nothing
972
– the war dance
715
dance-band 417
dance-music 415
dander 900
Dandie Dinmont
366
dandiprat 193
dandle 902
dandruff 653
dandy
ship 273
fop 854
dandyism 855
danger 665
in – *liable* 177
source of – 667
– past 664
– signal 669
dangerous
[*see* danger]
– classes 913
– illness 655
– person 667
dangle *hang* 214
swing 314
display 882
dangler 281
Daniel *sage* 500
judge 967
dank 339
Dannemora 752
danseuse 599
dapper
little 193
elegant 845
dapple 433
dappled 440
darbies
handcuffs 752
Darby and Joan
secluded 893
married 903
dare *defy* 715
face danger 861
– not 860
– say *probable* 472
believe 484
suppose 514
dare-devil
courage 861
rash 863
bluster 887
daring 861
unreserved 525
– imagination 515
dark
obscure 421
dim 422
black 431
blind 442
invisible 447
unintelligible 519
latent 526
joyless 837
insidious 940
in the –
ignorant 491
leap in the –
experiment 463
chance 621
rash 863
keep – *hide* 528
– ages 491
– , loud 735
view with – eyes
932
– lantern 423
darkly
see through a
glass – 443
darkness [*see* dark]
421
children of – 988
love – better than
light 989
powers of – 978
darky 431
darling *beloved* 897
favorite 899
darn 660
dart *swift* 274
propel 284
missile 727
– to and fro 684
Dartmoor 752
Darwinism 357
dash
small quantity 32
mix 41
swift 276
fling 284
mark 550
courage 861
cut a – *repute* 873
display 882
– at *resolution* 604
attack 716
– board 666
– cup from lips 761
– down 308
– hopes
disappoint 509
fail 732
dejected 837
despair 859
– on 274
– off *paint* 556
write 590
active 682
haste 684
– of the pen 590
dashed [*see* dash]
humbled 879
dashing
fashionable 852
brave 861
ostentatious 882
dastard 862
data *evidence* 467
reasoning 476
supposition 514
date *time* 106
chronology 114
datum 673
daub *cover* 223
paint 428
misrepresent 555
dirt 653
daughter 167
daunt 860
dauntless 861
Dauphin 875
davenport 191, 215
davit 214
Davus sum non Oedipus
unintelligent 499
artless 703
dull 843
Davy Jones' locker
310
dawdle *tardy* 133
slow 275
inactive 683
dawk 534
dawn
precursor 64
begin 66
priority 116
morning 125
light 420
dim 422
glimpse 490
dawplucker 936
day
period 108
present time 118
light 410
all – 110
clear as –
certain 474
intelligible 518
manifest 525
close of – 126
decline of – 126
denizens of the –
366
good old –'s 122
have had its – 124
one fine – 119
open as – 703
order of the – 613
red letter – 642
see the light of –
446
– after day
diuturnal 110
frequent 136
– by day
repeatedly 104
time 106
periodic 138
– after the fair
135
–s gone by 122
– of judgment 121
happy as the – is
long 827, 836
– and night
frequent 136
labor – and night
686
–s numbered
transient 111
death 360
– one's own 731
– of rest 686
– star 423
– after to-morrow
121
– before yesterday
122
–s of week 138
all in –'s work 625
daybed 215
daybook *record* 551
accounts 811
daybreak
morning 125
dim 422
day-dream
fancy 515
hope 858
day-laborer 690
daylight 125, 420
see – *intelligible*
518
– saving 114
daymare 859
daze 420
dazed 376
dazzle
light 420
blind 422, 443
put out 458
astonish 870
awe 928
dazzling
[*see* dazzle]
beautiful 845
de: – die in diem
time 106
periodic 138
– facto 1
– fond en comble
52
– novo 104
– omnibus rebus
81
– profundis 821
deacon 996
deaconry 995
dead *complete* 52
inert 172
colorless 429
lifeless 360
insensible 376
– against
contrary 14
oppose 708
more – than alive
688
– asleep 683
– beat
powerless 158
– certainty 474
– color 556
– cut 893
– drunk 959
– failure 732
– flat 213
– heat 27
– languages 560
– letter
impotent 158
unmeaning 517
useless 645
laxity 738
exempt 927
illegal 964
– level 16
– lift *exertion* 686
difficulty 704, 706
– lock *cease* 142
stoppage 265
– march 363, 415
– of night
midnight 126
dark 421
– reckoning
numeration 85
measurement 466
– secret 533
– set against 708
– set at
attack 716
– shot 700
– silence 403
– sound 408*a*
– stop 142
– to 823
– wall
hindrance 706
defence 717
– weight 706
– water 343
deaden
weaken 158
moderate 174
sound 405
mute 408*a*
benumb 823
dead-house 363
deadlock 142, 704
deadly *killing* 361
pernicious 649
unhealthy 657
– sin 947
– weapon 727
deads 645
deaf 419
inattentive 458
– to advice 606
– and dumb 581
turn – ear to
neglect 460
unbelief 487
refuse 764
– to reason 901*a*

censure 932
detract 934
defamer 936
defatigation 841
default
incomplete 53
shortcoming 304
neglect 460
insufficiency 640
debt 806
non-payment 808
in – of 187
judgment by – 725
defaulter *thief* 792
non-payer 808
rogue 949
defeasance 756
defeat
confute 479
succeed 731
failure 732
– one's hope 509
defeatism 911
defecate 652
defecation 299
defect
decrement 40*a*
incomplete 53
imperfect 651
failing 945
defection
relinquishment 624
disobedience 742
defective
incomplete 53
insufficient 640
imperfect 651
defence
plea 462
resist **717**
vindication 937
first line of – 726
defenceless
impotent 158
weak 160
exposed 665
defendant 938
defensible *safe* 664
excusable 937
defensive alliance 712
defer 133
– to *assent* 488
submit 725
respect 928
deference
obedience 743
humility 879
courtesy 894
respect 928
defiance **715**, 909
threat 909
in – *opposition* 708
set at – *disobey* 742
– of danger 861
deficiency
[*see* deficient]
vice 945
deficient
inferior 34
incomplete 53
shortcoming 304
insufficient 640
imperfect 651
deficit
incompleteness 53
debt 806
defigure 846
defile
interval 198
march 266
dirt 653
spoil 659
shame 874
impure 961
define
specify 79
limit 233
explain 522
name 564
definite
[*see* define]
visible 446
certain 474
exact 494
intelligible 518
manifest 525
perspicuous 570
definition
interpretation 521
definitive *final* 67
affirmative 535
decided 604
deflagration 384
deflate 195
deflation
currency 800
deflect
curve 245
deviate 279
deflower
spoil 659
violate 961
defluxion
egress 295
flowing 348
defœdation 653, 659
deform 241
deformity
distortion 243
ugliness 846
blemish 848
defraud *cheat* 545
swindle 791
defray 807
deft *suitable* 23
clever 698
defunct 360, 362
defy 715
disobey 742
threaten 909
– danger 861
dégagé *free* 748
fashion 852
degenerate 659
deglutition 298
degradation
deterioration 659
shame 874
dishonor 940
degree **26**
term 71
honor 873
by –s 26
by slow –s 275
degustation 390
dehiscence 260
dehort
dissuade 616
advise 695
dehydrate 340
Dei gratiâ 924
deification 873, 981
deify
hono
idolatry 991
deign
condescend 762
consent 879
Deism
heterodoxy 984
irreligion 989
Deity **976**
tutelary – 664
dejection
excretion 299
melancholy **837**
déjeûner 298
délabrement 162
delaceration 659
delation 938
delator 527
delay 133
dele 552
delectable
savory 394
agreeable 829
delectation 827
delectus 562
delegate
transfer 270
commission 755
consignee 758
deputy 759
delenda est Carthago
destroy 162
curse 908
delete 162
deleterious
pernicious 649
unwholesome 657
deletion 552
deletory
destructive 162
deliberate
slow 275
think 451
attentive 457
leisure 685
advise 695
cautious 864
deliberately
[*see* deliberate]
late 133
with premeditation 611
delicacy *weak* 160
slender 203
dainty 298
brittleness 328
texture 329
savory 394
color 428
exact 494
scruple 603
ill health 655
difficult 704
pleasing 829
beauty 845
taste 850
fastidious 868
honor 939
pure 960
delicate ear 418
délice 377
delicious *taste* 394
pleasing 829
delicti, corpus –
guilt 947
lawsuit 969
delicto, in flagrante – 947
delight
pleasure 827
pleasing 829
Delilah 962
delimit 233
delineate
outline 230
represent 554
describe 594
delineator 559
delineavit 556
delinquency 304, 947
delinquent 949
deliquation 335
deliquesce 36
deliquescence 335
deliquium
paralysis 158
fatigue 688
delirant reges plectuntur Achivi 739
delirium
raving 503
passion 825
– tremens 503, 959
delitescence
invisible 447
latency 526
seclusion 893
deliver
transfer 270
utter 580, 582
birth 662
rescue 672
liberate 750
give 784
relieve 834
– as one's act and deed 467
– the goods 729
– judgment 480
– a speech 582
deliverance **672**
delivery
[*see* deliver]
bring forth 161
cash on – 807
dell 252
Delphic oracle
prophetic 513
equivocal 520
latent 526
delta 342
delude *error* 495
deceive 545
deluge *crowd* 72
water 337
flood 348
redundance 641
delusion
[*see* delude]
insane 503
self – *credulous* 486
delve *dig* 252
till 371
– into *inquire* 461
demagogue
director 694
malcontent 710
rebel 742
demagogy 737
demand
inquire 461
order 741
ask 765
price 812
claim 924
in – *require* 630
desire 865
saleable 796
demarcation 233
dematerialize 317
demean oneself
conduct 692
humble 879
dishonor 940
demeanor
aid 448
conduct 692
fashion 852
demency 503
dementia 503
demerit 945
demesne
abode 189
property 780
demi- 91
demigod *hero* 861
angel 948
demigration 266
demijohn 191
demi-jour 422
demi-lune 717
demi-monde
plebeian 876
licentious 962
démenti 536
demirep 962
demise *death* 360
transfer 783
lease 787
demisemiquaver 413
demission 756
demit 757
demiurge
deity 979
demivolt 309
demobilize 73
democracy *rule* 737
commonalty 876
Democrats
party 712
Democritus 838
demoiselle 129
demolish 479
demon *violent* 173
bane 663
devil **980**
– in human shape 913, 949
– worship 991
demoniacal
malevolent 907
furious 824
wicked 945
demonology
demons 980
sorcery 992
demonstration
number 85
proof **478**
manifest 525
ostentation 882
ocular – 441, 446
demonstrative
manifest 525
indicative 550
vehement 825
demonstrator 524
demoralize

unnerve 158
spoil 659
vicious 945
Demosthenes 582
demotic 590
demulcent
mild 174
soothing 662
demur
disbelieve 485
dissent 489
unwilling 603
hesitate 605
without – 602
demure
grave 826
sad 837
affected 855
modest 881
demurrage 132
demurrer 969
den *abode* 189
study 191, 893
sty 653
prison 752
– of thieves 791
denary 98
denaturalize
corrupt 659
denaturalized
abnormal 83
dendriform 242, 367
dendrology 369
denial
negation 536
refusal 764
self– 953
denigrate 431
denization 748
denizen
inhabitant 188
freeman 748
–s of the air 979
–s of the day 366
Denmark, rotten in the state of – 526
denomination
class 75
name 564
sect 712
religious – 983
denominational
dissent 489
theological 983
– education 537
denominator 84
denote
specify **79**
mean 516
indicate 550
dénouement
end 67
result 154
disclosure 529
completion 729
denounce
curse 908
disapprove 932
accuse 938
dense
crowded 72
ignorant 493
density **321**
dent 252, 257
dental 561
denticulated 253, 257
dentifrice 652
dentistry 662
denude 226
denuded *loss* 776
– of
insufficient 640
denunciation
[*see* denounce]
deny *dissent* 489
negative 556
refuse 764
– oneself
avoid 623
seclude 893
temperate 953
ascetic 990
Deo volente 470, 976
deobstruct 705
deodand 974
deodorize 399
clean 652
deontology 926
deoppilation 705
deorganization 61
deosculation 902
depart 293
– from
deviate 15, 279
relinquish 624
– this life 360
departed
non-existent 2
department
class 75
region 181
business 625
departure 293
new – 66
point of – 293
depend *hang* 214
contingent 475
– upon
be the effect of 154
evidence 467
trust 484
– on circumstances 475
depended on, to be –
certain 474
reliable 484
honorable 939
dependency 777, 780
dependent
effect 154
liable 177
hanging 214
puppet 711
servant 746
subject 749
deperdition 776
dephlegmation 340
depict 554, 556
describe 594
depilation 226
depilatory 662
depletion 638, 640
deplorable *bad* 649
disastrous 735
painful 830
deplore *regret* 833
complain 839
remorse 950
deploy 194
depone 535
deponent 467
depopulate
eject 297
desert 893
deportation
removal 270
emigration 297
expulsion 972
deportment 692
depose
evidence 467
declare 535
dethrone 738, 756
deposit *place* 184
precipitate 321
store 636
security 771
payment 809
depositary 801
deposition
[*see* depose, deposit]
record 551
depository 636
depôt *terminal* 292
store 636
shop 799
– ship 726
deprave *spoil* 659
depraved *bad* 649
vicious 945
deprecation **766**
pity 914
disapprove 932
depreciation
decrease 36
underestimate 483
discount 813
cheap 815
disrespect 929
censure 932
detraction 934
accusation 938
depredation 791
depredator 792
deprehension 789
depression
lowness 207
depth 208
concavity 252
lowering **308**
dejection 837
dulness 843
depressing
painful 830
deprive *subduct* 38
take 798
– of life 361
– of power 158
– of property 789
– of strength 160
deprived of 776
depth *physical* **208**
mental 498
out of one's – 304 310
– bomb 727
– of misery 828
– of thought 451
– of winter 383
depurate *clean* 652
improve 658
depuratory 662
deputation 755
depute 755
deputies, chamber of – 696
deputy **759**
dequantitate 36
derangement **61**
mental – 503
Derby-day 720
derelict *land* 342
danger 667
relinquish 782
outcast 893
dereliction
relinquishment 624, 782
guilt 947
– of duty **927**
deride
ridicule 856
disrespect 929
contempt 930
derivation
origin 153, 154, 155
verbal 562
derive
attribute 155
deduce 480
acquire 775
income 810
dermal 223
dermatology 223
dernier
– cri 850
– ressort 601
dérobée, à la – 528
derogate
underrate 483
disparage 934
dishonor 940
– from 874
derogatory
shame 874
dishonor 940
derrick 307, 633
derring-do 861
dervish 996
désagrément 830
descant *music* 415
diffuseness 573
loquacity 584
dissert 595
descend *slope* 217
go down 306
– to particulars
special 79
describe 594
descendant 167
descensus Averni, facilis – 665
descent *lineage* 166
fall **306**
inheritance 775
description
kind 75
name 564
narration **594**
descriptive music 415
descry 441
desecrate
misuse 679
disrespect 929
profane 988
desert
unproductive 169
empty 187
plain 344
run away 623
relinquish 624, 782
merit 944
waste sweetness
on – air 638
deserted
outcast 893
deserter 144, 607, 623
desertless 945
deserts 924
deserve
be entitled to 924
merit 944
– notice 642
– belief 484
désespoir, au –
dejected 837
hopeless 859
déshabillé, en –
not dressed 226
unprepared 674
homely 849
desiccate 340
desiccator 340
desiderate *need* 630
desire 865
desideratum
inquiry 461
requirement 630
desire 865
design
prototype 22
form 240
delineation 554
painting 556
intention 620
plan 626
designate
specify 79
call 564
designation 75
designed
aforethought 611
designer 164, 559
designing
cunning 702
designless 621
désillusioner 529
desinence *end* 67
discontinuance 142
desipience 499
desipere in loco 840
desirable 646
desire **865**
will 600
have no – for 866
desist
discontinue 142
relinquish 624
inaction 681
desk *box* 191
support 215
school 542
pulpit 1000
désobligeant 272
désoeuvré 681
desolate *alone* 87
ravage 162
afflicted 828
dejected 837
secluded 893
desolating
painful 830
désorienté 475
despair *grief* 828, 859
despatch *eject* 297
kill 361
news 532
epistle 592

nature 5
state 7
temperament 820
diatonic 413
diatribe 932
dibble
perforator 262
till 371
dibs *money* 800
dicacity 885
dice 156, 621
on the – 470
dicer 621
false as –'s oaths 546
dichotomy
bisect 91
angle 244
dichroism 440
dichromatic 443
dickens 978
dicker 794
dicky 215, 225
dictaphone 553
dictate
write 590
enjoin 615
advise 695
authority 737
command 741
dictator 694, 745
–'s of society 852
dictatorial
dogmatic 481
wilful 600
insolent 885
dictatorship 737, 739
diction 569
dictionary
list 86
words 562
book 593
dictum
judgment 480
maxim 496
affirmation 535
command 741
didactic 537
didder 383
diddle 545, 791
Diddler, Jeremy – 792
diduction 44
die *mould* 22
expire 360
engraving 558
hazard of the – 621
never say – 604*a*
not willingly let – 670
– away
vanish 4
decrease 36
cease 142
the – is cast 601
– with ennui 841
– for *desire* 865
endearment 902
– game 951
– hard
obstinate 606
resist 719
– in harness 143, 604*a*
– in the last ditch 604*a*
– with laughter 838
– from the memory 536
– and make no sign 951
– out 2, 4
– of a rose in aromatic pain 822
– in one's shoes 972
– a violent death 361
– hard 710, 832
dies non *never* 107
rest 687
diet *food* 298
council 696
spare – 956
dietetics 662
differ 15
discord 713
agree to – 489
beg to – 439
– in opinion 489
– toto coelo
contrary 14
dissimilar 18
dissent 489
difference 15
[see differ]
numerical 84
perception of – 465
split the – 774
– engine 85
different 15
multiform 81
– time **119**
differentia 15
differential 15, 84
– calculus 85
differentiate 79, 465
differentiation
calculation 85
discrimination 465
difficult 704
– to please 868
difficulties
poverty 804
in – 806
difficulty **704**
question 461
diffide 485
diffident 860, 881
diffluent 348
diffraction 470
– grating 445
diffuse *mix* 41
disperse 73
publish 531
style 573
diffuseness 104, **573**
dig *deepen* 208
excavate 252
till 371
– out 461
– the foundations 673
– up 455, 480*a*
digamy 903
digest *arrange* 60
boil 384
think 451
compendium 596
plan 626
prepare 673
brook 826
diggings 189
dight *dress* 225
ornament 847
digit 84
digitate 44
digitated 253
digladiation 720
dignify 873
dignitary
clergy 996
dignity
glory 873
pride 878
honour 939
dignus vindice nodus
unintelligible 519
difficulty 704
prodigy 872
digress
deviate 279
style 573
digression
circuit 629
dihedral 89
– angle 244
diis alitur visum
disappointment 509
necessity 601
dijudication 480
dike *gap* 108
fence 232
furrow 259
gulf 343
conduit 350
defence 717
dilaceration 44
dilapidation 659
dilate
increase 35
swell 194
widen 202
rarefy 322
expatiate 573
dilatory
slow 275
inactive 683
dilection 89
dilemma
uncertain 475
logic 476
choice 609
difficulty 704
dilettante 492, 850
dilettantism
knowledge 490
diligence
coach 272
diligent
active 682
– thought 457
dilly-dally
irresolution 605
inactivity 683
dilucidation 522
diluent 335
dilute *weaken* 160
water 337
diluvian 124
dim *dark* 421
faint 422
invisible 447
unintelligible 519
dime 800
dimension 192
dimidiate 91
diminish
lessen 36
contract 195
– the number 103
diminutive 32, 193
diminuendo
decreasingly 36
music 415
dimness **422**
dimple 252, 257
dimsightedness **443**
unwise 499
din 404
– in the ear
repeat 104
drum 407
loquacity 584
dine 298
– with Duke Humphrey 87
ding 408
ding-dong
repeat 104
chime 407
dining-car 272
dining-room 191
dingle 252
dingy *boat* 273
dark 421, 422
colorless 429
black 431
gray 432
dinner 298
– jacket 225
party 892
dint *power* 157
concavity 252
blow 276
by – of
instrumentality 631
dio, sub – 220, 338
diocesan 996
diocese 181, 995
Diogenes
recluse 893
cynic 911
lantern of –
inquiry 461
dioptrics 420
diorama *view* 448
painting 556
diorism 465
dip *slope* 217
concavity 252
ladle 270
direction 278
insert 300
descent 306
plunge 310
water 337
candle 423
baptize 998
– one's hands into
take 789
– into
glance at 457
inquire 461
learn 539
diphthong 561
diploma
evidence 467
commission 755
diplomacy
artfulness 702
mediation 724
negotiation 769
diplomatist
messenger 534
expert 700
consignee 758
dipper 191
dipsomania
insanity 503
desire 865
drunkenness 959
dipsomaniac 504
diptych 86, 551
dire *hateful* 649
disastrous 735
grievous 830
fearful 860
direct
straight 246
teach 537
artless 703
command 741
– attention to **457**
– one's course
motion 278
pursuit 622
– the eyes to **441**
direction
[see direct]
tendency **278**
indication 550
management **693**
precept 697
directly *soon* **132**
director
teacher 540
theater 599
manager **694**
master 745
– of the budget 801
directorship 737
directory *list* 86
council 696
diremption 44
direption 791
dirge
funeral 363
song 415
lament 839
dirigible balloon 273, 726
dirk 727
dirt 653
throw –
defame 874
disrespect 929
– cheap 815
like – under one's feet 749
dirty *dim* 222
opaque 426
unclean 653
disreputable 874
dishonorable 940
– end of stick 699
– sky 353
– weather 349
do – work
servile 886
flatterer 935
diruption 162
disability
impotence 158
disable 158
weaken 160
disabuse 527, 529
disaccord 713
disadvantage
evil 619
inexpedience 647

at a – 34
lie under a – 651
disadvantageous 647, 649
disaffection
dissent 489
enmity 889
hate 898
disaffirm 536
disagreeable 830, 867
disagreement
difference 15
incongruity **24**
dissent 489
discord 713
disallow 761
disannul 756
disappearance **449**
disappointment
balk **509**
fail 732
discontent 832
disapprobation 706, **932**
disapprover 936
disarm *disable* 158
weaken 160
reconcile 831
propitiate 914
disarrange 61
disarray
disorder 59
undress 226
disaster *evil* 619
failure 732
adversity 735
calamity 830
disastrous *bad* 649
disavow 536
disband
separate 44
disperse 73
liberate 750
disbar
abrogate 756
punish 972
disbarment 55
disbelief 485, 487
religious 989
disbench 756, 972
disbowel 297
disbranch 44
disburden
facilitate 705
– one's mind 529
– oneself of 782
disburse 809
disc 220, 234
discard *eject* 297
relinquish 624
disuse 678
abrogate 756
refuse 764
repudiate 773
surrender 782
– from one's thoughts 458
discarded 495
disceptation 476
discern *see* 441
know 490
discernible 446
discernment 498, 868
discerption 44
discharge
violence 173
propel 284
emit 297
excrete 299
sound 406
acquit oneself 692
complete 729
liberate 750
abrogate 756
pay 807
exempt 927*a*
acquit 970
– a duty 926, 944
– a function
business 625
utility 644
– itself *egress* 295
river 348
– from the memory 506
– from the mind 458
– an obligation 772
discind 44
disciple *pupil* 541
votary 711
Christian 985
disciplinarian
master 540
martinet 739
discipline
order 58
teaching 537
training 673
restraint 751
punishment 972
religious 990
disclaim *deny* 536
repudiate 756
abjure 757
refuse 764
disclosure 480*a*, **529**
discoid *layer* 204
frontal 220
flat 251
discoloration 429
discolored
shabby 659
ugly 846
blemish 848
discomfit 731
discomfiture 732
discomfort
physical 378
mental 828
discommend 932
discommode
hinder 706
annoy 830
discommodious 645, 647
discompose
derange 61
put out 458
hinder 706
pain 830
disconcert 874
anger 900
discomposure 828
disconcert
derange 61
distract 458
disappoint 509
hinder 706
discontent 832
confuse 879
disconcerted
hopeless 859
disconformity 83
discongruity 24
disconnected
style 575
disconnection
irrelation 19
disjunction 44
discontinuity 70
disconsolate 837
discontent **832**
discontinuance
cessation 142
relinquishment 624
discontinuity **70**
discord
difference 15
disagreement 24
of sound **414**
of color 428
dissension **713**
discount
decrease 36
decrement 40*a*
money **813**
at a –
disrepute 874
disapproved 932
discountenance
disfavor 706
refuse 764
discourage
dissuade 616
sadden 837
frighten 860
discourse
teach 537
speech 582
talk 588
dissert 595
sermon 998
discourtesy **895**
discous 202
discover
perceive 441
solve 462
find 480*a*
disclose 529
– itself
be seen 446
discovery 480*a*
discredit
disbelief 485
dishonor 874
discreditable
vicious 945
discreet *careful* 459
cautious 864
discrepancy 15
discrepant 24, 713
discrete
separate 44, 70
single 87
discretion *will* 600
choice 609
skill 698
caution 864
surrender at – 725
use – 609
years of – 131
discrétion à – 600
discrimination
difference 15
nice perception **465**
wisdom 498
taste 850
fastidiousness 868
disculpate 937
discumbency 213
discursion 266
discursive
moving 264
migratory 266
wandering 279
argumentative 476
diffuse style 573
conversable 588
disserting 595
discus 840
discuss *eat* 298
reflect 451
inquire 461
reason 476
dissert 595
discussion
[*see* discuss]
open to – 475
under – 461
disdain
indifference 866
fastidious 868
arrogance 885
pride 878
contempt 930
disease **655**
occupational – 655
–d mind 503
disembark 292
disembarrass 705
disembody
decompose 49
disperse 73
spiritualize 317
disembogue
emit 295
eject 297
flow out 348
disembowel 297, 301
disembroil 60
disenable 158
disenchant
discover 480*a*
dissuade 616
displease 830
disencumber 705
disendow 756
disengage
detach 44
facilitate 705
liberate 750
disengaged
to let 763
disentangle
separate 44
arrange 60
unroll 313
decipher 522
facilitate 705
liberate 750
disenthral 750
disenthrone 756
disentitle 925
disespouse 905
disestablish
displace 185
abrogate 756
disesteem 929, 932
disfavor
oppose 708
hate 898
disrespect 929
view with – 932
disfigure
deface 241
injure 659
deform 846
blemish 848
disfranchise 925
disgorge *emit* 297
flow out 348
restore 790
pay 807
disgrace
shame 874
dishonor 940
sense of – 879
disgraceful
vice 945
disgruntle 509
disguise
unlikeness 18
conceal 528
mask 530
falsify 544
untruth 546
disguised in drink 959
disgust *taste* 395
offensive 830
weary 841
dislike 867
hatred 898
– of life 837
dish *destroy* 162
plate 191
food 298
– of tea 892
dishabille
undress 225
unprepared 674
dishearten
dissuade 616
pain 830
discontent 832
deject 837
dished 252, 732
disherison 789
dishevel
loose 47
untidy 59
disorder 61
disperse 73
intermix 219
dishonest *false* 544
base 940
dishonour
disrepute 874
disrespect 929
baseness 940
– bills 808
dish-water 653
disillusion 509
disincline
dissuade 616
dislike 867
disinclined 603
disinfect
purify 652
restore 660
disinfectant 662
disingenuous
false 544
dishonorable 940
disinherit
relinquish 782
transfer 783
deprive 789
disintegrate
separate 44
decompose 49
pulverize 330
disinter *exhume* 363

discover 480a
disinterested **942**
disjecta membra
separate 44
disorder 59
dispersed 73
– poetae 597
disjoin 44
disjointed
disorder 59
powerless 158
style 575
disjunction **44**
disjunctive 70
diskindness 907
dislike **867**
reluctance 603
hate 898
dislocate
separate 44
put out of joint 61
dislocated
disorder 59
dislodge
displace 185
eject 297
disloyal 940
dismal
depressing 830
dejected 837
dismantle
destroy 162
divest 226
render useless 645
injure 659
disuse 678
dismask 529
dismast
render useless 645
injure 659
disuse 678
dismay 860
dismember
separate 44
disperse 73
dismiss
send away 289
discharge 297
discard 678
liberate 750
abrogate 756
relinquish 782
punish 972
– from the mind 452, 458
dismount
arrive 292
descend 306
render useless 645
disnest 185
disobedience **742**
non-observance 773
disoblige 907
disorder
confusion **59**
derange 61
turbulent 173
disease 655
–ed intellect 503
disorderly
unprincipled 945
disorganize
derange 61
destroy 162
spoil 659
disorganized 59
disown 536
dispair 44
disparage
underrate 483
disrespect 929
dispraise 932
detract 934
disparity
different 15
dissimilar 18
disagreeing 24
unequal 28
isolated 44
dispart 44
dispassionate 826
– opinion 484
dispatch
[*see* despatch]
dispel *scatter* 73
destroy 162
displace 185
repel 289
dispensable
useless 645
dispensary 662
dispensation
[*see* dispense]
command 741
licence 760
relinquishment 782
exemption 927a
–s of Providence 976
dispense
disperse 73
give 784
apportion 786
retail 796
– with
disuse 678
permit 760
exempt 927a
cannot be –d with 630
dispeople
eject 297
expatriate 893
disperse
separate 44
scatter 73
diverge 291
waste 638
dispersion **73**
– of light 420
chromatic – 428
dispirit
discourage 616
sadden 837
displacement
derange 61
remove **185**
transfer 270
displacency
dislike 867
incivility 895
disapprobation 932
displant 185
display *appear* 448
show 525
parade 882
displease 830
displeasure 828
anger 900
displosion 173
displume 789
disport 840
disposal
[*see* dispose]
at one's – 763, 777
dispose
arrange 60
tend 176
induce 615
– *of use* 677
complete 729
relinquish 782
give 784
sell 796
disposed 620
disposition
nature 5
order 58
arrangement 60
inclination 602
mind 820
dispossess
transfer 783
take away 789
– oneself of 782
dispraise 932
dispread 73
disprize 483
disproof
counter-evidence 468
confutation 479
disproportion
irrelation 10
disagreement 24
disprove 479
disputable **475**, 485
disputant 710, 726
disputatious 901
dispute
discuss 476
doubt 485
deny 536
discord 713
in – 461
disqualification
incapacitate 158
useless 645
unprepared 674
unskilful 699
disentitle 925
disquiet
changeable 149
agitation 315
excitement 825
uneasiness 828
give pain 830
disquietude
apprehension 860
disquisition 539, 595
disregard
overlook 458
neglect 460
make light of 483
insensible to 823, 826
disrespect **929**
contempt 930
– of time 115
disrelish 867, 898
disreputable 874
vicious 945
disrepute **874**, 929
disrespect **929**
despise 930
disrobe 226
disruption
disjunction 44
destruction 162
discord 713
dissatisfaction
disappointment 509
sorrow 828
discontent 832
dissect
anatomize 44, 49
investigate 461
dissemblance 18
dissemble 544
dissembler 548
disseminate
scatter 73
pervade 186
publish 531
teach 537
dissension 713
sow – 898
dissent
disagree **489**
refuse 764
heterodoxy **984**
dissentient 15
dissentious 24
dissertation **595**
disservice
disadvantage 619
useless 645
disserviceable 649
dissever 44
dissidence
disagreement 24
dissent 489
discord 713
discontent 832
heterodoxy 984
dissilience 173
dissimilarity **18**
dissimulate 544
dissipate *scatter* 73
destroy 162
pleasure 377
prodigality 818
amusement 840
intemperance 954
dissolute 961
dissocial 893
dissociate 44
dissociation
irrelation 10
separation 44
dissolute 961
profligate 945
intemperate 954
dissolution
[*see* dissolve]
decomposition 49
destruction 162
death 360
dissolve *vanish* 2, 4
liquefy 335
disappear 449
abrogate 756
dissolving views 448, 449
dissonance
disagreement 24
unmusical 414
discord 713
dissuasion **616**
dissyllable 561
distaff
– side 374
distain *dirty* 653
ugly 846
distal 196
distance **196**
overtake 282
go beyond 303
defeat 731
angular – 244
keep at a –
discourtesy 895
keep one's –
avoid 623
modest 881
respect 928
teach one his – 879
– of time
long time 110
past 122
distaste 867
distasteful 830
distemper 299, 428
color 428
painting 556
disease 655
distend 194
distended 192
distich 89, 597
distil *come out* 295
extract 301
evaporate 336
drop 348
distinct
disjoined 44
audible 402
visible 446
intelligible 518
manifest 525
express 535
articulate 580
distinction
difference 15
discrimination 465
style 578
fame 873
rank 875
– without a difference 27
distinctive 15
– feature 79
distinctness 15
distingué 852, 873
distinguish
perceive 441
discriminate 465
by the name of 564
distinguishable 15
distinguished
superior 33
repute 873
Distinguished Service Cross 733
distortion
obliquity 217
twist **243**
of vision 443
misinterpret 523
falsehood 544
misrepresent 555
ugly 846
distract 458
distracted
confused 475
insane 503
excited 824
distraction
passion 825
love to – 897
distrain *take* 789
appraise 812
attach 969

distrait 458
distraught 824
distress
distraint 789
poverty 804
affliction 828
cause pain 830
signal of – 669
distressingly
excessively 31
distribute
arrange 60
disperse 44, 73
allot 786
district 181
– council 696
distrust
disbelief 485
fear 860
distrustful 487
disturb
derange 61
change 140
agitate 315
excite 824
distress 828, 830
disturbance 59
disunion
discord 24
separation 44
disorder 59
discord 713
disuse
desuetude 614
relinquish 624
unemploy **678**
disused
old 124
disvalue 932
ditch
inclosure 232
trench 259
water 343
conduit 350
defence 717
to the last – 606
ditch-water 653
ditheism 984
dither 315
dithyramb
music 415
poetry 597
dithyrambic 503
ditto 13, 104
say – to 488
ditty 415
– box 191
diurnal 138
diuturnity **110**
diva 416
divagate 279, 629
divan *sofa* 215
council 696
throne 747
tribunal 966
divaricate *differ* 15
bifurcate 91
diverge 291
dive *swim* 267
fly 267
plunge 306, 310
– into *inquire* 461
divellicate 44
diver 208
divergence
difference 15
variation 20a
disagreement 24
deviation 279
separation **291**
divers *different* 15
multiform 81
many 102
– coloured 440
diverse 15
diversify
very 20a
change 140
diversion
change 140
deviation 279
pleasure 377
amusement 840
diversity
difference 15
irregular 16a
dissimilar 18
multiform 81
– of opinion 489
divert *turn* 279
deceive 545
amuse 840
– the mind 452, 458
divertissement
diversion 377
drama 599
amusement 840
Dives 803
divest *denude* 226
take 789
– oneself of
abrogate 756
relinquish 782
divestment **226**
divide *differ* 15
separate 44
part 51
arrange 60
arithmetic 85
bisect 91
vote 609
apportion 786
dividend *part* 51
number 84
portion 786
divina particula aurae 450
divination
prediction 511
sorcery 992
divine *predict* 511
guess 514
perfect 650
of God 976, 983, 983a
clergyman 996
divine afflatus 515
– right
authority 737
due 924
– service 990
diving 840
diving-bell 208
divining-rod 550, 993
Divinity *God* 976
theology 983
divisible
number 84
division
[see divide]
part 51
class 75
arithmetic 85
discord 713
military 726
divisor 84
divorce
separation 44
relinquish 782
matrimonial **905**
Divorce Court 966
divulge 529
divulsion 44
divvy 786
dixi 535
dizen 847
dizzard 501
dizzy
dimsighted 443
confused 458
vertigo 503
– height 206
– round 312
djerrid 727
djinn 980
do *fare* 7
suit 23
produce 161
cheat 545
act 680
complete 729
succeed 731
I beg 765
all one can – 686
plenty to – 682
thing to – 625
– away with
destroy 162
eject 297
abrogate 756
– battle 722
– one's bidding 743
– business 625
– to death 361
– as done by 906, 942
– for *destroy* 162
kill 361
conquer 731
serve 746
punish 972
– good 906
– harm 907
– honor 873
– into
translate 522
– justice to 595
– like 19
– little 683
– no harm 648
– nothing 681
– nothing but 136
– one's office 772
– as others do 82
– over 223
– as one pleases 748
– a service
useful 644
aid 707
– up 660
have to – with 680, 692
– without 678
– the work 686
– wrong 923
docere, pisces natare – 641
docile *domesticated* 370
learning 539
willing 602
docimastic 463
dock *diminish* 36
cut off 38
port 189
shorten 201
edge 231
store 636
tribunal 966
docked
incomplete 53
docker 690
docket
list 86
evidence 467
note 550
record 551
security 771
dockyard 691
doctor
learned man 492
restore 660
remedy 662
after death the – 135
– accounts 811
when –s disagree 475
doctrinaire
positive 474
pedant 492
affectation 855
blusterer 887
doctrinal 537
doctrinarian 514
doctrine *tenet* 484
knowledge 490
document 551
documentary evidence 467
dodder 315
doddering 128
dodecahedron 244
dodge *change* 140
shift 264
deviate 279
oscillate 314
pursue 461
avoid 623
stratagem 702
dodger, artful – 792
dodo 366
extinct as the – 122
doe *swift* 274
deer 366
female 374
doer
originator 164
agent 690
doff 226
– the cap 894
dog *follow* 281
animal 366
male 373
pursue 622
wretch 949
cast to the –s
destroy 162
reject 610
disuse 678
abrogate 756
relinquish 782
fire – 386
go to the –s
destruction 162
fail 732
adversity 735
poverty 804
sea – 269
watch –
safety 664
warning 668
keeper 753
hair of – that bit you 959
let sleeping –s lie 141
– in manger 706, 943
–tired 686
–s of war 722
dog-cart 272
dog-cheap 815
dog-days 382
doge 745
dogged
obstinate 606
valour 861
sullen 901a
dogger 273
doggerel
verse 597
ridiculous 851, 853
dog-hole 189
dog-Latin 563
dogma *tenet* 484
theology 983
dogmatic
certain 474
positive 481
assertion 535
obstinate 606
dogmatist 887
dog's ear 258
dog robber 746
dog-sick 867
dog-star 423
dog-trot 275
dog-weary 688
doily 852
doing
up and – 682
what one is – 625
doings
events 151
actions 680
conduct 692
doit *trifle* 643
coin 800
dolce far niente 681
doldrums
dejection 837
sulks 901a
dole
small quantity 32
scant 640
give 784
allot 786
parsimony 819
grief 828
doleful 837
– dumps 901a
doll *small* 193
image 554
dollar 800
dolman 225
dolmen 363, 551
dolor
physical 378
moral 828
dolorem, infandum renovare – 833
dolorous 830
dolphin 341

– the cup of misery 828
– into 348
– pipe 249
– of resources 640
drake *male* 373
fire – 423
dram *drink* 298
pungent 392
stimulus 615
– drinking 959
drama 599
dramatic 599
ostentation 882
– author 599
– critic 599
– poetry 597
dramatis personæ
mankind 372
play 599
agents 690
party 712
drapery 225, 847
drast 645
drastic 171
draught
[*see also* draft]
depth 208
traction 285
drink 298
stream of air 349
delineation 554, 556
plan 626
physic 662
troops 726
– off 73
draughts
game 840
draughtsman
artist 559
draw *equality* 27
compose 54
pull 285
delineate 554, 556
– aside 279
– off the attention 458
– back
deduction 40*a*
regret 283
avoid 623
– breath
refresh 689
feeling 821
relief 834
– a cheque 800
– a curtain 424
– down 153
– forth 677
– from 810
– on futurity 132
– in one's horns
tergiversation 607
humility 879
– in 195
– an inference 480
– the line 465
– lots 621
– near *time* 121
approach 286
– off *eject* 297
hinder 706
take 789
– on *time* 121
event 151
induce 615
– out
protract 110
late 133
prolong 200
extract 301
discover 480*a*
exhibit 525
diffuse style 573
– over *induce* 615
– a parallel 9
– the pen through 552
– a picture 594
– profit 775
– and quarter 972
– the sword
attack 716
war 722
– the teeth of 158
– together
assemble 72
co-operate 709
– towards 288
– up *order* 58
stop 265
write 590
– up a statement 594
– upon *money* 800
– the veil 528
drawback *evil* 619
imperfection 651
hindrance 706
discount 813
drawbar 45
drawbridge
way 627
escape 671
raise the – 666
drawcansir 887
drawee 800
drawer
receptacle 191
artist 559
– of water 690
drawers
dress 225
drawhead 45
drawing
delineation 554, 556
prize 810
drawing-room
assembly 72
room 191
fashion 852
drawl *prolong* 200
creep 275
in speech 583
sluggish 683
drawn *equated* 27
– battle
– irresistibly 601
pacification 723
incomplete 730
dray 272
– horse 271
drayman 268
dread 860
dreadful *great* 31
bad 649
dire 830
depressing 837
fearful 860
dreadless 861
dreadnought
warship 726
dream
unsubstantial 4
error 495
fancy 515
sleep 683
golden – 858
– of *think* 451
intend 620
– on other things 458
dreamer
madman 504
imaginative 515
dreamy
unsubstantial 4
inattentive 458
sleepy 683
dreary
monotonous 16
solitary 87
melancholy 830, 837
dredge *collect* 72
extract 301
raise 307
dregs
remainder 40
refuse 645
dirt 653
– of the people 876
– of vice 945
drench *drink* 298
water 337
redundance 641
– with physic 662
drencher 248
drenching rain 348
dress
uniformity 16
agree 23
equalize 27
clothes 225
prepare 673
ornament 847
ostentation 882
full – 852
– circle 599
– the ground 371
– up *falsehood* 544
represent 554
– wounds 662
– to advantage 847
dress-coat 225
dresser
sideboard 215
surgeon 662
dressing 932, 972
– room 191, 599
dressing-gown 225
dressmaker 225
dribble 295, 348
driblet 25, 32
drift
accumulate 72
distance 196
motion 264
flying 267
float 267
transfer 270
direction 278
deviation 279
approach 286
wind 349
meaning 516
intention 620
snow – 383
drifter 273
drifting 605
driftless 621
drill *fabric* 219
bore 260
auger 262
teach 537
prepare 673
– hall 191
drink
swallow 296
liquor 298
tipple 959
– one's fill
enough 639
– in *imbibe* 296, 298
– in learning 539
– to *celebrate* 883
courtesy 894
drinking-bout 954
drink-money 784
drip 295, 348
dripping *wet* 330
fat 356
drive *airing* 266
impel 276
propel 284
break in 370
urge 615
haste 684
direct 693
attack 716
compel 744
– at *mean* 516
intend 620
– a bargain
barter 794
parsimony 819
– care away 836
– a coach and six through 83
– into a corner
difficult 704
hinder 706
defeat 731
subjection 749
– to despair 859
– matters to an extremity 604
– from *repel* 289
– one hard 716
– home 729
– in 300
– to the last 133
– out 297
– trade
business 625
barter 794
drivel *slobber* 297
imbecile 499
mad 503
rubbish 517
driveler 501, 584
driver 268
director 694
driving rain 348
drizzle 348
droil 683
droit du plus fort 744
drôle *cards* 840
drole 949
– de corps 844
drollery
amusement 840
wit 842
ridiculous 853
dromedary 271
drone *slow* 275
sound 407, 412, 413
inactive 683
drool 297
droop
weak 160
hang 214
sink 306
disease 655
decline 659
flag 688
sorrow 828
dejection 837
drop *small quantity* 32
discontinue 142
powerless 158
bring forth 161
spherule 249
emerge 295
fall 306
trickle 348
relinquish 624
discard 782
gallows 975
let – 308
ready to –
fatigue 688
– asleep 683
– astern 283
– from the couds 508
– dead 360
– by drop
by degrees 26
in parts 51
– in the bucket 32
– in upon 674
– into a good thing 734
– into the grave 360
– a hint 527
– all idea of 624
– in *arrive* 292
immerse 300
sociality 892
– the mask 529
– off *decrease* 36
die 360
sleep 683
– in the ocean
trifling 643
– the subject 458
– too much 959
dropping fire 70
drop-scene 599
dropsical 194, 641
droshki 272
dross
remainder 40
slag 384
trash 643, 645
dirt 653
drought
dryness 340
insufficiency 640
drouth *desire* 865
drove
assemblage 72
multitude 102
drover 370
drown
affusion 337
kill 361
ruin 731, 732
– care 840
– the voice 581
drowsy *slow* 275

sleepy 683
weary 841
drub
defeat 731, 732
punish 972
drudge *labour* 686
worker 682, 690
drug
render insensible 376
superfluity 641
trash 643
remedy 662
bane 663
– in the market 815
drugget
cover 223
clean 652
preserve 670
druggist 662
druid 996
drum
repeat 104
cylinder 249
sound 407
music 417
party 892
beat of –
signal 550
alarm 669
war 722
command 741
parade 882
ear – 418
muffled –
funeral 363
non-resonance 408*a*
– and fife band 417
– fire 407
– out 972
drum-head 964, 966
drum-major 745
drummer 416
drunken 959
reel like a – man 315
drunkenness **959**
dry *arid* 340
style 575, 576, 579
hoarse 581
scanty 640
preserve 670
exhaust 789
tedious 841
dull 842
thirsty 865
cynical 932
teetotal 958
run – 640
with – eyes 823
– dock 189
– joke 842
– land 342
– the tears 834
– up 340, 638
dryad 979
dry-as-dust
antiquarian 122
dull 843
dryness **340**
dry-nurse
teach 537
teacher 540
aid 707
dry-point 558
dry-rot
dirt 653
decay 659
bane 663
dualism 984
duality **89**
duarchy 737
dub 564
dubious 475
ducat 800
duce 745
duchess 745, 875
duchy 181
duck *stoop* 308
plunge 310
water 337
darling 897, 899
play –s and drakes
recoil 277
prodigality 818
–'s egg
zero 101
– in thunder 870
ducking-stool 975
duckling 127
duck-pond 370
duct 350
ductile
elastic 323
flexible 324
trimming 607
easy 705
docile 749
dud 158, 727
dude 854
duds 225
dudgeon
dagger 727
discontent 832
churlishness 895
hate 898
anger 900
sullenness 901*a*
due
expedient 646
owing 806
proper 924, 926
give his – to
right 922
vindication 937
fair 939
in – course 109
occasion 134
– respect 928
– sense of 498
– time
soon 132
– to
cause and effect 154, 155
give – weight **465**
duel 720
duelist 726
dueness **924**
duenna
teacher 540
guardian 664
keeper 753
dues 812
duet 415
duff 298
duffer
bungler 701
smuggler 792
dug 250
dug-out
old man 130
boat 273
defence 717
duke *ruler* 745
noble 875
dulce domum 189
dulcet
sweet 396
sound 405
melodious 413
agreeable 829
dulcify 174, 396
dulcimer 417
Dulcinea 897
dulcorate 396
dulia 990
dull *weak* 160
inert 172
moderate 174
blunt 254
insensible 376, 381
sound 405
dim 422
colorless 429
ignorant 493
stolid 499
style 575
inactive 683
unapt 699
callous 823
dejected 837
weary 841
prosing 843
simple 849
– of hearing 419
– sight 443
dullard 501
dullness **843**
duly 924
duma 696
dumb 581
– animal 366
– show 550
– waiter 307
strike –
ignorant 493
astonish 870
humble 879
dumbfounder
disappoint 509
silence 581
astonish 870
humble 879
dummy
substitute 147
impotent 158
speechless 581
inactive 683
dump *music* 415
store 636
lament 839
undersell 796
dumpling 298
dumps
discontent 832
dejection 837
sulk 901*a*
dumpy *little* 193
short 201
thick 202
dun *dim* 422
colorless 429
grey 432
importune 765
creditor 805
dunce
ignoramus 493
fool 501
dunderhead 501
dune 206
dung 653
dungeon 752
dunghill
dirt 653
cowardly 862
baseborn 876
– cock 366
Dunker 984
dunt 716
duo 415
duodecimal 99
duodecimo
little 193
book 593
duodenary 98
duologue
interlocution 588
drama 599
dupe
credulous 486
deceive 545
deceived **547**
duplex 90, 189
duplicate
imitate 19
copy 21
double 90
tally 550
record 551
redundant 641
pawn 805
duplication
imitation 19
doubling **90**
repetition 104
duplicature
fold 258
duplicity
duality 89
falsehood 544
dura lex sed lex 926
durable
long time 110
stable 150
durance 141, 751
in – 754
duration 106
contingent – **108a**
infinite – 112
durbar
conference 588
council 696
tribunal 966
duress
compulsion 744
restraint 751
during 106
– pleasure &c. 108*a*
durity 323
dusk
evening 126
half-light 422
dusky
dark 421
black 431
dust *levity* 320
powder 330
corpse 362
trash 643
dirt 653
money 800
come to –
die 360
come down with the – 807
humbled in the – 879
kick up a – 885
level with the – 162
lick the –
submit **725**
fail 732
make to bite the – 731
turn to –
deorganized 358
die 360
– in the balance 643
throw – in the eyes
blind 442
deceive 545
plead 617
– one's jacket 972
duster 652
dust-bin, dust-hole 191, 645
fit for the –
useless 645
dirty 653
spoilt 659
dustman
cleaner 652
dust-storm 330
dusty
powder 330
dirt 653
Dutch
double – 519
high – 519
– auction 796
– courage 862
Dutchman, flying 515
dutiful 944
duty
business 625
work 686
tax 812
courtesy 894
obligation **926**
respect 928
worship 990
rite 998
do one's –
virtue 944
on – 680, 682
duumvirate 737
Duval, Claude – 792
D.V. 470, 976
dwarf
lessen 36
small 193
elf 980
dwell
reside 186
abide 265
– upon
descant 573
dweller 188
dwelling 184, 189
dwindle *lessen* 36
shrink 195
dyad 89
dye 428
dying 360
dyke [*see* dike]
dynamic energy 157
dynamics 276

dynamitard 863
dynamite 727
dynamo 153
dynasty 737
dysentery 299
dyspepsia 655
dysphony 581

E

each 79
– to each 786
– other 12
– in his turn 148
eager
willing 602
active 682
ardent 821
desirous 865
– expectation 507
eagle
standard 550
money 800
– boat 726
– eye *sight* 441
intelligence 498
– winged *swift* 274
insignia 747
eagre 348
ean 161
ear 418
corn 154
come to one's –s 527
din in the –
loud 404
drum 407
all – 418
have the – of
belief 484
friendship 888
lend an –
hear 418
attend 457
meet the – 418
nice – 418
no – 419
offend the – 410
pick up the –s
attention 457
expectation 507
put about one's –s 308
quick – 418
reach one's –s 527
ring in the – 408
set by the –s
discord 713
hate 898
resentment 900
split the –s 404
together by the –s
discord 713
contention 720
up to one's –s
redundance 641
active 680, 682
willing – 602
word in the – 586
– for music 416, 418
in at one – out at the other
inattention 458
forget 506
not for –s polite 961
make the –s tingle
anger 900
– ache 378
ear-drum 418
earl 875
earless 419
earliness **132**
early 132
get up – 682
earmark 550
earn 775
earnest *willing* 602
determined 604
emphatic 642
pledge 771
pay in advance 809
eager 821
in –
affirmation 535
veracious 543
strenuous 682
ear-piercing 410
ear-ring 847
ear-shot 197
out of – 405
ear-splitting 404
earth *ground* 211
world 318
land 342
corpse 362
what on –
inquiry 461
wonder 870
– closet 653
earthenware
baked 384
sculpture 557
earthling 372
earthly 318
end of one's – career 360
of no – use 645
earthly-minded 943, 989
earthquake 146, 173
earthwork 717
earwig *flatter* 933, 935
ear-witness 467
ease *bodily* 377
style 578
leisure 685
facility 705
mental 827
content 831
at one's –
prosperous 734
mind at –
cheerful 836
set at – *relief* 834
take one's – 687
– off *deviate* 297
– one of *take* 789
easel *support* 215
painting 556
– picture 556
easement
property 780
relief 834
easily
[*see* easy]
let one down – 918
– accomplished 705
– deceived 486
– persuaded 602
East 236, 278
Easter *period* 138
rite 998
– Monday
holiday 840
– offering
gift 784
– sepulcher 1000
easy *gentle* 275
style 578
facile 705
make oneself – about 484
take it –
inactive 683
inexcitable 826
– ascent 217
– of belief 472
– chair
support 215
repose 687
– circumstances 803
– going
willing 602
irresolute 605
lenient 740
inexcitable 826
contented 831
indifferent 866
– sail
moderate 174
slow 275
– temper 894
– terms 705
– to understand 518
– virtue 961
eat *food* 298
tolerate 826
– dirt 725, 879
– one's fill
enough 639
gorge 957
– heartily 298
– one's words 879
– out of house and home *take* 789
prodigal 818
gluttony 957
– of the same trencher 892
– one's words 607
eatables 298
eaten up with 820
eau, battre l' – 645
faire venir l' – à la bouche 865
mettre de l' – dans son vin 174
eaves 250
eavesdropper 455, 527
eavesdropping 418, 532
ébauche 626
ebb *decrease* 36
contract 195
regress 283
recede 287
waste 638
spoil 659
low – 36
low 207
depression 308
insufficient 640
– and flow 314
– of life 360
ebb-tide *low* 207
dry 340
ebony 431
ebriety 959
ebullient
violent 173
hot 382
excited 824
ebullition
energy 171
violence 173
agitation 315
heating 384
excitation 825
anger 900
écarté 840
ecce
– iterum Crispinus 104
– signum 550
eccentric 220
irregular 83
foolish 499
crazed 503, 504
capricious 608
ecchymosis 299
ecclesiastic
church 995
clergy 996
ecclesiastical
canonical 985
– court 966
– law 963
ecclesiolatry 991
écervelé 458
échafaudage 673
échappée 840
échapper belle 671
échelon 279
echo *imitate* 19
copy 21
repeat 104
reflection 277
resonance 408
answer 462
assent 488
applaud to the – 931
awake –es 404
éclaircissement 522
éclat 873
eclectic 609
eclipse *surpass* 33
disappearance 449
hide 528
outshine 873, 874
partial – *dim* 422
total – *dark* 421
under an –
invisible 447
out of repute 874
ecliptic 318
eclogue 597
economic pressure 751
economy
order 58
conduct 692
frugality **817**
animal – 359
écorcher les oreilles 410
ecphorize 615
écru 433
ecstasis 683
ecstasy
frenzy 515
transport 821
rapture 827
ecstatic 829
ecstatica 994
ectoplasm 992
ectype 21
ecumenical 78
edacity 957
Edda 986
eddy
whirlpool 348
current 312
danger 667
edematous 194, 324
Eden 827
edge *energy* 171
height 206
brink **231**
sidle 279
advantage 731
cutting – 253
on – 256, 507
take the – off 174
– of hunger 865
– in 228
– one's way 282
edge-tools 253
play with – 863
edgewise 217
edging
obliquity 217
border 231
ornament 847
edible 298
edict 741
edification
building 161
teaching 537
learning 539
piety 987
edifice 161
edifying *good* 648
edile 965
edit
publication 531
condense 596
revise 658
edition, new – 658
editor 593
educate 537
educated 490
self – 490
education
teaching 537
knowledge 490
man of – 492
higher – 490
educational 537, 542
educe *extract* 301
discover 480*a*
educt 40
eduction 40*a*
edulcorate 396, 652
eel 248
wriggle like an – 315
eerie 860
efface
delete 162
disappear 449
obliterate 552
– from the memory 506
effect
consequence **154**
product 161
impression 375

complete 729
carry into – 692
with crushing – 162
in – 5
take – 731
to that – 516
effective
capable 157
useful 644
effectuation 729
expedient 646
effects 780, 798
effectual 731
effectually 52
effectuate 729
effeminate
weak 160
womenlike 374
timorous 862
sensual 954
effeminize 158
effendi 875
effervesce
energy 171
violence 173
agitate 315
bubble 353
excited 825
effervescent 338
effete *old* 128
weak 160
useless 645
spoiled 659
efficacious
[see efficient]
efficient
power 157
agency 170
utility 644
skill 698
effigy 21, 554
effleurer *skim* 267, 460
efflorescence 330
effluxion of time 109
effluence *egress* 295
flow 348
effluvium 334, 398
efflux 295
efformation 240
effort 686
effreet 980
effrontery 885
effulgence 420
effuse
pour out 295, 297
excrete 299
speech 582
loquacity 584
effusion of blood 361
effusive 573
eft 366
eftsoons 117
egad 535
égards 928
egesta 299
egestion 297
egg *beginning* 66
cause 153
food 298
walk among –s 704
too many –s in one basket
unskilful 699
(*imprudent* 863)
– and dart
ornament 847
– on 615
egg-shaped 247, 249
ego *intrinsic* 5
speciality 79
immaterial 317
non – 6
egocentrism 943
egotism
vanity 880
cynicism 911
selfishness 943
egregious
exceptional 83
absurd 497
exaggerated 549
important 642
egregiously 31, 33
egress 295
Egyptian darkness 421
eheu! fugaces labuntur anni 111
eiderdown 223
eidouranion 318
Eiffel tower 206
eight *number* 98
boat 273
representative 759
eisteddfod 72, 416
eighty 98
either *choice* 609
happy with – 605
ejaculate
propel 284
utter 580
ejection 185, 297
ejecta 299
ejector 349
eke *also* 37
– out *complete* 52
spin out 110
ekka 272
El Dorado 803
elaborate
improve 658
prepare 673
laborious 686
work out 729
elaine 356
élan 276
elapse 109, 122
elastic fluid 334
elasticity
power 157
strength 159
energy 171
spring 325
elate *cheer* 836
rejoice 838
hope 858
vain 880
boast 884
elbow *angle* 244
projection 250
push 276
at one's –
near 197
advice 695
lift one's –
drink 959
out at –s
undress 226
poor 804
disrepute 874
– one's way
progress 282
pursuit 622
active 682
elbow-chair 215
elbow-grease 331
elbow-room 180, 748
elder *older* 124
aged 128
veteran 130
clergy 996
elect *choose* 609
good 648
predestinate 976
pious 987
clergy 996
election
numerical 84
necessity 601
electioneering 609
elector 745
electorate 737
Electra complex 897
electric
swift 274
sensation 821
excitable 825
car 272
– blue 438
– chair 974
– light 423
– piano 417
electrician 599, 690
electricity 157, 388
electrify
unexpected 508
excite 824
astonish 870
electro-biology 992
electrocution 972
electrolier 214, 423
electrolyze 49
electro-magnetism 157
electromobile 272
electron 32
electronics 157
electroplate 223
electrotype 21, 591
electuary 662
eleemosynary 784
elegance
in style 578
beauty 845
taste 859
Bank of – 800
elegy *interment* 363
poetry 597
lament 839
element
component 50
beginning 66
cause 153
matter 316
in one's –
facility 705
content 831
devouring – 382
out of its – 195
elementary 42
– education 537
– school 542
elements
Eucharist 998
elench 477
elephant
large 192
carrier 271
white – *bane* 663
elevated
tipsy 959
elevation
height 206
vertical 212
raising **307**
plan 554
– of style 574
improvement 658
glory 873
– of mind 942
angular – 244
élève 541
eleven 98
representative 759
eleventh hour
evening 126
late 133
opportune 134
elf *infant* 129
little 193
imp 980
elicit *cause* 153
draw out 301
discover 480a
manifest 525
eligible 646
Elijah's mantle 63
eliminant 299
eliminate
subduct 38
simplify 42
exclude 55
weed 103
extract 301
reject 610
elision 44, 201
élite *best* 648
distinguished 873
aristocratic 875
elixation 384
elixir 662
– of life 471
elk 223
ell 200
take an –
take 789
insolence 885
wrong 923
undue 925
selfish 943
ellipse 247
ellipsis *shorten* 201
style 572
ellipsoid 247, 249
elocation 185, 270
elocution 582
éloge 931
elongation 196, 200
elopement 623, 671
eloquence 572, 582
else 37
elsewhere 187
elucidate 522
elude
sophistry 477
avoid 623
escape 671
succeed 731
palter 773
elusive 545
elusory 546
elutriate 652
elysian 829, 981
Elysium 827, 981
elytron 223
Elzevir edition 193
emaciation 195, 203, 640
emanate 151
go out of 295
excrete 299
– from 544
emanation 398
emancipate
facilitate 705
free 748, 750
emasculate
impotent 158
embalm
interment 363
perfume 400
preserve 670
– in the memory 505
embankment
esplanade 189
refuge 666
fence 717
embar 229
embargo
stoppage 265
prohibition 761
exclusion 893
embark
transfer 270
depart 293
– in *begin* 66
engage in 676
embarquer sans biscuits, s' 674
embarras de – choix 609
embarrass 641, 704, 706
embarrassed 804, 806
embarrassing 475
embase 659
embassy
errand 532
commission 755
consignee 758
embattled
arranged 60
leagued 712
war array 722
embed
locate 184
base 215
enclose 221
insert 300
embellish 847
embers 384
embezzle 791
embitter
deteriorate 659
aggravate 835
acerbate 900
emblazon
color 428
ornament 847
display 882
emblem 550, 747
embody
join 43
combine 48
form a whole 50
compose 54
embolden
hope 858
encourage 861

embolism 228, 261, 300
embonpoint 192
embosomed
lodged 184
interjacent 228
circumscribed 229
emboss *convex* 250
ornament 847
embouchure 260
embowel 297
embrace
cohere 46
compose 54
include 76
enclose 227
choose 609
take 789
friendship 888
sociality 892
courtesy 894
endearment 902
– an offer 760
embrangle 61
embranglement 713
embrasure 257, 260
embrocation 662
embroider
variegate 440
lie 544
ornament 847
embroidery
adjunct 39
exaggeration 549
embroil *derange* 61
discord 713
embroilment 59
embrown 433
embryo
beginning 66
cause 153
in – *destined* 152
preparing 673
embryology 357
embryonic 193, 674
embus 293
embusqué 603
emendation 658
emerald *green* 435
jewel 847
emerge 295, 446
emergency
circumstance 8
event 151
difficulty 704
emeritus 500, 928
emersion 295, 446
emery
sharpener 253
– paper
smooth 255
emetic *remedy* 662
émeute 742
emication 420
emigrant 57, 268
emigrate 266, 295
emigré 268, 295
eminence
height 206
fame 873
church dignitary 996
eminent domain 744
eminently 33
emir 745, 875
emissary
messenger 534
consignee 758
emission 297
emit *eject* 297
publish 531
voice 580
– vapour 336
Emmanuel 976
emmet 193
emollient 662
emolument
acquisition 775
receipt 810
remuneration 973
emotion 821
–al appeal 824
–al drama 599
empale 260, 972
empanel 86, 969
empathy 515
emperor 745
emphasis 580
emphatic 535, 642
emphatically 31
empierce
perforate 260
insert 300
empire 737, 789
– day 840
empiric 548
empirical 463, 675
empiricism 463
emplane 293
employ
business 625
use 677
servitude 749
commission 755
in one's – 746
– one's capital in 794
– oneself 680
– one's time in 625
employé
servant 746
agent 758
employer 795
empoison 659
emporium 799
empower
power 157
commission 755
accredit 759
permit 760
empress 745
empressement
activity 682
emotion 821
desire 865
emprise 676
emption 795
emptor 795
caveat – 769
empty *clear* 185
vacant 187
deflate 195
drain 297
ignorant 491
waste 638
deficient 640
useless 645
beggarly account of – boxes
poverty 804
– one's glass 298
– purse 804
– sound 517
– stomach 865
– title *name* 564
undue 925
– words 546
empty-handed 640
empty-headed 4, 491
empurple 437
empyrean *sky* 318
blissful 829
empyreuma 41
empyrosis 384
emulate *imitate* 19
goodness 648
rival 708
compete 720
glory 873
emulsion 352
emunctory 350
en – bloc 50
– masse 50
– passant
parenthetical 10
transient 111
à propos 134
– rapport 9
– règle *order* 58
conformity 82
– route
journey 266
progress 282
enable 157
enact *drama* 599
action 680
conduct 692
complete 729
order 741
law 963
enallage 521
enamel *coating* 223
painting 556
ornament 847
enameller 559
enamor 897
encage 751
encamp 184, 189
encampment 184
encaustic 556
enceinte
with child 161
region 181
inclosure 232
enchafe 830
enchain 751
enchant *please* 829
enchanted 827
enchanting 845, 897
enchantment
sorcery 992
enchase 43, 259
enchiridion 593
enchorial 188
encincture 229
encircle 76, 227, 311
enclave *close* 181
boundary 233
enclose 227, 229
enclosure
region 181
envelope 232
fence 752
encomiast 935
encomium 931
encompass 227, 233
–ed with difficulties 704
encore 104, 931
encounter
undergo 151
clash 276
meet 292
withstand 708
contest 720
– danger 665
– risk 621
encourage
animate 615
aid 707
comfort 834
hope 858
embolden 861
encroach
transcursion 303
do wrong 923
infringe 925
encumber 704, 706
encumbrance
clear of – 807
encyclical 531
encyclopedia 490, 593
walking – 700
encyclopedical
general 78
– knowledge 490
encysted 229
end
termination **67**
effect 154
object 620
at an – 142
come to its – 729
one's journey's – 292
on – 212
put an – to
destroy 162
kill 361
begin at the wrong – 699
– one's days 360
–s of the earth 196
– to end *space* 180
touching 199
length 200
– of life 360
– in smoke 732
– of one's tether
sophistry 477
ignorant 491
insufficient 640
difficult 704
endamage 649
endanger 665
endear 897
endearment **902**
endeavor
pursue 622
attempt 675
use one's best – 686
– after 620
endemic
special 79
interior 221
disease 657
endimanché 847, 882
endless
multitudinous 102
infinite 105
perpetual 112
endlessly 16
endlong 200
endocrine 221
endogenous 367
endorse
evidence 467
assent 488
compact 769
- *a bill* 800
approve 931
endorsement 550
endosmose 302
endow
confer power 157
endowed with
possessed of 777
endowment
intrinsic 5
power 157
talent 698
gift 784
endrogynous 83
endue 157
endure *time* 106
last 110
persist 143
continue 141
undergo 151
feel 821
submit to 826
unable to – 867
– for ever 112
– pain 828
enduring
indelible 505
endwise 212
enemy *time* 841
foe 891
the common – 978
thing devised by the – 546
– to society 891
energumen 504
energy *power* 157
strength 159
physical **171**
resolution 604
activity 682
enervate 158, 160
enfant, bon – 906
– gâté
prosperity 734
satiety 869
favorite 899
– perdu
hopeless 859
reckless 863
– terrible
curiosity 455
artless 703
object of fear 860
enfeeble 160
enfeoff 780, 783
Enfield rifle 727
enfilade
lengthwise 200
pierce 260
pass through 302
enfold 229
enforce *urge* 615
advise 695
compel 744
require 924
enfranchise
free 748
liberate 750
permit 760
enfranchised 924
engage
bespeak 132

epicurean 954
Epicurus, system of – 954
epicy-cle, -cloid 247
epidemic
general 78
disease 655
insalubrity 657
epidermis 223
epigenesis 161
epigram 496, 842
epigrammatic 572
epigrammatist 844
epigraph 550
epilepsy 315, 655
epilogue
sequel 65
end 67
drama 599
èpingles, tiré à quatre – 855
Epiphany 998
episcopal 995
Episcopalian 984
episcopate 995
episode
adjunct 39
discontinuity 70
interjacence 228
episodic
irrelative 10
style 573
epistle 592
Epistles 985
epistrophe 104
epistyle 210
epitaph 363
epithalamium 903
epithem 662
epithet 564
epitome
miniature 193
short 201
concise 572
epizoötic 657
epoch *time* 106
instant 113
date 114
present time 118
epode 597
eponym 564
epopoea 597
epos 594
epulation 298
epulotic 662
epuration 652
equable 16, 922
equal *even* 27
equitable 922
– chance 156
– times 120
– to *power* 157
equality 13, **27**
equalize 213
equanimity 826
equate 27, 30
equations 85
equator 68, 318
equatorial 68, 236
equerry 746
equestrian 268
equibalanced 27
equidistant 68
equilibration 27
equilibrist 599
equilibrium 27
equine *carrier* 271
horse 366
equinox 125, 126
equip 225, 673
equipage
vehicle 272
instruments 633
display 882
equiparent 27
equipment 633
equipoise &c. 27, 30
equiponderate 30
equitable *wise* 498
just 922
due 924
honorable 939
– interest 780
equitation 266
equity *right* 922
honor 939
law 963
in – 922
– draftsman 968
equivalent
identical 13
equal 27
compensation 30
substitute 147
translation 522
equivocalness
dubious 475
double meaning **520**
impure 961
equivocate
sophistry 477
palter 520
lie 544
equivocation
[*see* equivocate]
without – 543
équivoque
double meaning 520
impure 961
era *time* 106, 108
date 114
eradicate
destroy 162
extract 301
erase *destroy* 162
obliterate 331, 552
Erastian 984
erasure 552
Erato 416
ere 116
– long 132
– now 116
past 122
Erebus *dark* 421
hell 982
erect *build* 161
vertical 212
raise 307
with head – 878
– the scaffolding 673
erewhile 116, 122
ergatocracy 737
ergo 476
ergotism 480
ergotize 485
eriometer 445
Erinys 900
Erl King 980
ermine
badge of authority 747
ornament 847
erode 36, 659
Eros 897, 979
erosion 36
erotic 897, 961
err – *in opinion* 495
– *morally* 945
errand
message 532
business 625
commission 755
errand-boy 534
errant 279
erratic
irregular 139
changeable 149
wandering 279
capricious 608
erratum 495
erroneous 495
error *fallacy* **495**
vice 945
guilt 947
court of – 966
writ of – 969
ersatz 973
erst 122
erubescence 434
erubuit salva res est 95
eruct 297
eructate 297
erudition 490, 539
eruption
upheaval 146
violence 173
egress 295, 297
disease 655
volcanic – 872
escadrille 726
escalade
mounting 305
attack 716
escalator 307
escalop 248
escapade
absurdity 497
freak 608
prank 840
escape
flight **671**
liberate 750
evade 927
means of – 664, 666
– the lips
disclosure 529
speech 582
– the memory 506
– notice &c.
invisible 447
inattention 458
latent 526
escarp 717
escarpment
stratum 204
height 206
oblique 217
escharotic
caustic 171
pungent 392
eschatology 67
escheat 144, 974
eschew
avoid 623
dislike 867
esclandre 828, 830
escort
accompany 88
safeguard 664
keeper 753
escritoire 191
esculent 298
escutcheon 550
esophagus 260
esoteric
private 79
concealed 528
Espagne, château en – *fancy* 515
hope 858
espalier 232
especial 79
especially 33
espial 441
espiéglerie
cunning 702
fun 840
wit 842
espionnage 441, 461
esplanade
houses 189
flat 213
espouse
choose 609
marriage 903
– a cause *aid* 707
co-operate 709
esprit
shrewdness 498
wit 842
bel – 844
– de corps
bias 481
co-operation 709
sociality 892
(*party* 712)
– fort
thinker 500
irreligious 989
espy 441
esquire 875, 877
essay
experiment 463
dissertation 595
endeavor **675**
essayist 593, 595
esse 1
essence
nature 5
scent 398
essential
intrinsic 5
great 31
required 630
important 642
essentially
intrinsically 5
substantially 3
essential stuff 5
establish
settle 150
create 161
place 184
evidence 467
demonstrate 478
– equilibrium 27
established
permanent 141
habit 613
– church 983*a*
establishment
party 712
shop 799
estafette 534
estaminet 189
estate *condition* 7
property 780
come to man's – 131
esteem
believe 484
repute 873
approve 931
in high – 928
estimable 648
estimate
measure 466
adjudge 480
information 527
– too highly 482
estimation
[*see* esteem, estimate]
estime
succès d' – 873
estival 382
esto perpetua!
perpetuity 112
permanence 141
desire 865
estop 706
estrade 213
estrange
alienate 44, 889
discord 713
hate 898
estranged
secluded 893
estrapade
attack 716
punishment 972
estreat 974
estuary 343
estuation 384
esurient 865
et – cetera
add 37
include 76
plural 100
– hoc genus omne
similar 17
include 76
multiform 81
étalage 882
état major 745
etch *furrow* 259
engraving 558
eternal 112
– home 981
Eternal, the – 976
eterne 112
eternify 112
eternity 112
an – 110
launch into – 360, 361
ether
lightness 320
rarity 322
vapor 334
anesthetic 376
ethereal 4
ethicism 984
ethics 926
Ethiopian 431
–'s skin 150
Ethiopian's skin
unchangeable 150
ethnology 372
ethnic 984
ethology 926
ethos 5
etiolate 429, 430

etiology *causes* 155, 359
knowledge 490
disease 655
etiquette
custom 613
fashion 832
ceremony 882
étoile, à la belle –
out of doors 220
in the air 338
Eton jacket 225
étourderie
inattention 458
unskilfulness 699
etymological 560
etymology 562
etymon *origin* 153
verbal 562
Eucharist 998
euchology 998
euchre 840
eudiometer
air 338
salubrity 656
euge! 931
eugenics 658
eulogist 935
eulogize 482
eulogy 931
Eumenides *fury* 900
evil-doers 913
revenge 919
eunuch 158
eupepsia 651
euphemism
metaphor 521
style 577, 578
flattery 933
euphemist
man of taste 850
flatterer 935
euphony 413, 578
Euphrosyne 836
euphuism
metaphor 521
elegant style 577
affected style 579
affectation 855
Eurasian 41
eureka! 462, 480*a*
Euripus 343
Eurus 349
eurythmics 537, 840
eurythmy 242
Euterpe 416
euthanasia 360
euthenics 658
evacuate
quit 293
excrete 295
emit 297
evacuation 299
evade *sophistry* 477
avoid 623
not observe 773
exempt 927
evagation 279
evanescent
small 32
transient 111
little 193
disappearing 449
evangelical 983*a*, 985
Evangelists 985
evanid 160
evaporable 334
evaporate
unsubstantial 4
transient 111
vaporize 336
evaporation 340
evasion
sophistry 477
concealment 528
falsehood 544
untruth 546
avoidance 623
escape 671
cunning 702
non-observance 773
dereliction 927
eve 126
on the – of
transient 111
prior 116
future 121
evection 61
even
uniform 16
equal 27
still more 33
regular 138
level 213
straight 246
flat 251
smooth 255
although 409
in spite of 708
– course 628
– now 118
– so
for all that 30
yes 488
– temper 826
– terms 922
– tenor
uniform 16
order 58
continuity 58
pursue the – tenor
continue 143
avoid 623
business 625
be – with
retaliate 718
pay 807
get – with 972
even-handed 922, 939
evening **126**
shades of – 422
– classes 537
– star 423
evenness 16
evensong 126, 990
event 151
bout 720
in the – of
circumstance 8
expectation 507
supposition 514
justified by the – 937
eventful 151
remarkable 642
stirring 682
eventide 126
eventual 121
eventuality **151**
eventually
effect 154
ever 16, 112
did you – ? 870
– and anon 136
– changing 149
– recurring 104
ever so 31
– little 32
– long 110
– many 102
evergreen
continuous 69
lasting 110
always 112
fresh 123
everlasting 112
– life 152
– fire 982
evermore 112
eversion 218
evert 140
every 78
– hand against one 891
– day
conformity 82
frequent 136
habit 613
– description 81
– inch 50
in – mouth
assent 488
news 532
repute 873
– other 138
in – quarter 180
in – respect 494
on – side 227
at – turn 186
– whit 52
everybody 78
everyone 78
– his due 922
– in his turn 148
everywhere 180, 186
evict 297
evidence **467**
disclose 529
ocular – 446
évidence, en – 446
evident
concrete 3
visible 446
certain 474
manifest 525
evidently 516
evil *harm* **619**
badness 649
impious 988
– day
prepare for – 673
adversity 735
– eye *vision* 441
malevolence 907
disapprobation 932
demon 980
sorcery 992
spell 993
– favored 846
– fortune 735
– genius 980
– hour 135
– one 978
– plight 735
through – report &c. 604*a*
– star 649
evil-doer **913**
evil-doing 945
evil-minded 907, 945
evil-speaking
malediction 908
censure 932
detraction 934
evince *show* 467
prove 478
disclose 529
eviscerate 297, 301
eviscerated 4
evoke *cause* 153
call upon 765
excite 824
evolution
numerical 85
production 161
motion 264
extraction 301
circuition 311
turning out **313**
organization 357
training 673
action 680
military –s 722
evolve
discover 480*a*
evolved from 154
[*and see* evolution]
evulgate 531
evulsion 301
evviva! 931
ewe 366, 374
– lamb 366
ewer 191
ex
– animo 602
– cathedra 542
– officio 494, 924
– parte 467
– pede Herculem 82
– post facto 122, 133
– tempore
instant 113
occasion 134
exacerbate
increase 35
exasperate 173
aggravate 659, 835
exact *similar* 17
special 79
true 494
style 572
require 741
tax 812
insolence 885
claim 924, 926
– meaning 516
– memory 505
– observance 772
– truth 494
exacting
severe 739
discontented 832
grasping 865
fastidious 868
exaction
[*see* exact]
undue 925
exactly
just so 488
exaggeration
increase 35
expand 194
overestimate 482
magnify **549**
misrepresent 555
exalt
increase 35
elevate 307
extol 931
– one's horn 873
exalté 504
tête –e 503
exalted *high* 206
repute 873
noble 875
magnanimous 942
examination
[*see* examine]
evidence 467
undergo – 461
examine 457, 461
example
pattern 22
instance 82
bad – 949
good – 948
make an – of 974
set a good – 944
exanimate
dead 360
supine 360
exarch 745
exasperate
exacerbate 173
aggravate 835
enrage 900
excavate 252
excecation 442
exceed *surpass* 33
remain 40
transgress 303
intemperance 954
excel *surpass* 33
– in *skilful* 698
excellence 648, 944
excellence, par – 642
excellency 877
excelsior 305
except *subduct* 38
exclude 55
reject 610
exception
unconformity 83
qualification 469
exemption 777*a*
disapproval 932
take –
qualify 469
resent 900
exceptionable
bad 649
guilty 947
exceptional
original 20
extraneous 57
unconformable 83
in an – degree 31
exceptious 901, 901*a*
exceptis excipiendis 469
excern 297
excerpt 609
excerpta *parts* 51
compendium 596

selections 609
excerption 609
excess
remainder 40
redundance 641
intemperance 954
excessive 31
exchange
reciprocity 12
interchange 148
transfer 783
barter 794
mart 799
bill of – 771
rate of – 800
– blows &c.
retaliation 718
battle 720
Exchequer 802
Baron of – 967
Court of – 966
– bill 800
excise 812
exciseman 965
excision 38
excitability **825**, 901
excitation **824**
excite *energy* 171
violence 173
- *morally* 824
– attention 457
– desire 865
– hope 811
– an impression 375
– love 897
excited fancy 515
excitement 824, 825
anger 900
exclaim 411
– against 932
exclamation 580
mark of – 550
exclude
leave out 42, **55**
reject 610
prohibit 761
banish 893
exclusion **55, 57**
exclusive
simple 42
omitting 55
special 79
irregular 83
forbidding 761
– of 38
– possession 777
– thought 457
excogitate 451, 515
excommunicate
banish 893
curse 908
rite 998
excoriate 226
excrement
excretion 299
dirt 653
excrescence
projection 250
blemish 848
excreta
excretion 299
dirt 653
excretion 297, **299**
excruciating 378, 830
exculpate
forgive 918
vindicate 937
acquit 970
excursion 266, 311
excursionist 268
excursive
deviating 279
- *style* 573
excursus 595
excuse *plea* 617
forgive 918
exempt 927*a*
vindicate 793
execrable 649, 830
execrate 898, 908
execution
music 416
action 680
conduct 692
signing 771
observance 772
punishment 972
carry into –
complete 729
put in –
undertaking 676
executioner 975
executive
conduct 692
direction 693
authority 737
judicature 965
executor 690
to one and his –s &c., *property* 780
exegetical 522
exemplar 22
exemplary 944
exemplify
quote 82
illustrate 522
exempt *free* 748
dispensation 927*a*
– from *absent* 187
unpossessed 777*a*
exemption
exception 83
qualification 469
deliverance 692
permission 760
non-possession **777***a*
non-liability **927***a*
exenterate 297
exequatur 755
exequies 363
exercise
operation 170
teach 537
task 625
use 677
act 680
exert 686
– authority 737
– discretion 600
– the intellect 451
– power 157
exergue 231
exert *use* 677
– authority 737
– oneself 686
exertion 171, **686**
exfoliate 226
exhalation
ejection 297
excretion 299
vapor 336
breath 349
odor 398
exhaust
paralyze 158
empty 195
waste 638
fatigue 688
complete 729
drain 789
squander 818
exhausted
inexistent 2
exhauster 349
exhaustive
complete 52
– inquiry 461
exhaustless
infinite 105
enough 639
exhibit *evidence* 467
show 525
display 882
exhilarate 836
exhort
persuade 615
advise 695
exhortation 998
exhume
past times 122
disinter 363
exigeant 739
exigency *crisis* 8
requirement 630
dearth 640
difficulty 704
need 865
exigent
exacting 739
discontented 832
exiguous 103, 193
exile
transport 185
banish 893
punish 972
voluntary – 893
exility 203
eximious 648
existence *being* **1**
thing 3
- *in time* 118
- *in space* 186
come into – 151
exit
departure 293
egress 295
disappear 449
give – to 297
ἐξοχήν, κατ' –
supreme 33
important 642
exode 599
exodus 293
exogenous 367
exonerate
disburden 705
release 760
forgive 918
exempt 927*a*
vindicate 937
acquit 970
exorable 914
exorbitant
enormous 31
redundant 641
dear 814
exorcise 297
exorcism 992, 993
exorcist 994
exordium 64, 66
exosmose 302
exostosis 250
exoteric 525, 531
exotic *alien* 10
exceptional 83
plant 367
expand *increase* 35
swell 194
- *in breadth* 202
rarefy 322
- *in writing* 573
expanse 180, 192
expansion **194**
expatiate
range 266
- *in writing* &c. 573
- *in discourse* 584
expatriate 295, 893
expect
look forward to 507
hope 858
not wonder 871
future 121
reason to – 472
expectance **871**
expectancy 780
expectante, médecine –
wait 133
remedy 662
expectation **507**
beyond – 508
hold out an – 768
expected
as well as can be – 654
expectorate 297
expedience **646**
expedient
plan 626
means 632
useful 646
temporary – 147
expedite *early* 132
quickening 274
hasten 684
aid 707
expedition
[*see* expedite]
march 266
activity 682
war 722
expel *push* 284
eject 297
punish 972
expend *waste* 638
use 677
pay 809
– itself 683
expenditure **809**
expense *price* 812
joke at one's – 842
spare no – 816
expenseless 815
expenses 809
expensive 814
experience
meet with 151
knowledge 490
undergo 821
learn by – 950
experienced 698
– eye &c. 700
experiences
narrative 594
experiment **463**, 675
Experimental Philosophy 316
experimentum crucis *test* 463
proof 478
expert 698, 700
expiate 952
expire *end* 67
run its course 109
die 360
expired *past* 122
explain 462, 522
– away 523
explainer 524
expletive 573, 641
explication 522
explicit *clear* 518
potent 525
explode. *burst* 173
confute 479
failure 732
passion 825
exploded *past* 122
antiquated 124
error 495
blown upon 932
exploit 680, 861
exploitation 461
explore 461, 463
explorer 268
explosion
[*see* explode]
revolution 146
violence 173
sound 406
anger 900
explosive
dangerous 665
ammunition 727
exponent
numerical 84
interpreter 524
informant 527
index 550
export 295
expose *denude* 226
confute 479
disclose 529
censure 932
– to danger 665
– oneself
disreputable 874
– to view
visible 446
manifest 525
exposé
disclosure 529
description 594
exposed to
liable 177
exposition [*see* expose]
explanation 522
expositor 524, 540
expository
explaining 522
informing 527
describing 594
disserting 595
expostulate
dissuade 616
advise 695
deprecate 766
reprehend 932
exposure [*see*

fame *greatness* 31
news 532
renown 873
familiar
known 490
habitual 613
sociable 892
affable 894
– *spirit* 979, 980
on – terms 888
familiarize
teach 537
habit 613
famille, en – 892
family
kin 11
class 75
ancestors 166
posterity 167
party 712
in the bosom of one's – 221
happy – 714
– circle 892
– jars 713
– likeness 17
– tie 11
in the – way 161
famine 640
– price 814
famine-stricken 640
famish
stingy 810
fasting 956
famished
insufficient 640
hungry 865
famous 873
famously 31
fan *blow* 349
cool 385
refresh 689
stimulate 824
flirt a – 855
– the embers 505
– the flame
violence 173
heat 384
aid 707
excite 824
– into a flame
anger 900
–shaped 194
fanatic
madman 504
imaginative 515
zealot 682
religious – 988
fanatical
misjudging 481
insane 503
emotional 821
excitable 825
heterodox 984
over-righteous 988
fanaticism 606
fanciful
imaginative 515
capricious 608
ridiculous 853
fancy *think* 451
idea 453
believe 484
suppose 514
imagine 515
caprice 608
choice 609
pugilism 726
wit 842
desire 865
wonder 870
love 897
after one's – 850
indulge one's – 609
take a – to
delight in 827
desire 865
take one's –
please 829
– dog 366
– dress 840
– price 814
– woman 962
fandango 840
fandi, mollia tempora – 588
fane 1000
fanfare *loudness* 404
celebration 883
fanfaron 887
fanfaronnade 884
fangs *venom* 663
rule 737
retention 781
fan-light 260
fan-like 202
fannel 999
fanon 999
fantasia 415
fantastic *odd* 83
absurd 497
imaginative 515
capricious 608
unfashionable 851
ridiculous 853
fantasy
imagination 515
desire 865
fantoccini 554, 599
faquir 996
far – away 196
– be it from
unwilling 603
deprecation 766
– between
disjunction 44
few 103
interval 198
– from it
unlike 18
shortcoming 304
no 536
– from the truth 546
– and near 180
– off 196
– and wide 31, 180, 196
farce
absurdity 497
untruth 546
drama 599
wit 842
ridiculous 853
mere –
unimportant 643
useless 645
farceur
actor 599
humorist 844
fardel
bundle 72
hindrance 706
fare *state* 7
food 298
price 812
bill of –
list 86
farewell
departure 293
relinquishment 624
loss 776
– to greatness 874
far-famed 873
far-fetched 10
far-flung 73
far-gone
much 31
insane 503
spoiled 654
farinaceous 330
farm *till* 371
property 780
rent 788
farmer 188, 342, 371
afternoon – 683
farm-house 189
Farmer-Labor 712
faro 840
farrago 59
farrier 370
farrow
produce 161
litter 167
multitude 102
far-sighted 442, 510
farther 196
[*and see* further]
farthing
quarter 97
worthless 643
coin 800
– candle 422
farthingale 225
fasces 747
fascia 205, 247
fascicule 51
fasciculated 72
fascinate
influence 615
excite 824
please 829
astonish 870
love 897
conjure 992
fascinated
pleased 827
fascination [*see* fascinate]
infatuation 825
desire 870
fascine 72
Fascisti 712
fas et nefas, per – 604*a*, 631
fash 830
fashion
state 7
form 240
custom 613
method 627
ton **852**
after a –
middling 32
after this – 617
follow the – 82
be in the – 488
man of – 852
set the –
influence 175
authority 737
for –'s sake 852
fast *joined* 43
steadfast 150
rapid 274
fashionable 852
intemperate 954
not eat 956
worship 990
rite 998
stick – 704
– asleep 683
– by 197
– day 956
– friend 890
– and loose
sophistry 477
falsehood 544
irresolute 605
tergiversation 607
caprice 608
– man *fop* 854
libertine 962
fasten *join* 43
hang 214
restrain 751
– on the mind 451
– a quarrel upon 713
– upon 789
fastening 45
fast-handed 819
fastidious
censorious 932
fastidiousness **868**
fasting
insufficiency 640
worship 990
penance 952
abstinence **956**
fastness
asylum 666
defence 717
fat *corpulent* 192
expansion 194
unctuous 355
oleaginous 356
kill the –ted calf
celebration 883
sociality 892
– in the fire
disorder 59
violence 173
– of the land
pleasure 377
enough 639
prosperity 734
intemperance 95
fata – Morgana
occasion 134
ignis fatuus 423
– obstant 601
fatal 361
– disease 655
fatalism 601
fatality 601
fate *end* 67
necessity 601
chance 621
be one's – 156
sure as – 474
Fates 601, 979
fat-head 501
father *eldest* 128
paternity 166
priest 996
Apostolical –s 985
gathered to one's –s 360
heavy – 599
– upon 155
Father, God the – 976
fatherland 189
fatherless 158
fatherly 906
fathom
length 200
investigate 461
solve 462
measure 466
discover 480*a*
knowledge 490
fathomless 208
fatidical 511
fatigation 688
fatigue **688**
fatras 643
fatten
expand 194
improve 658
prosperous 734
– on *parasite* 886
– upon
feed 298
fatuity 4, 499
fatuous 517
fat witted 499
faubourg 227
fauces 231
faucet 252
faugh! 867
fault
break 70
error 495
imperfection 651
failure 732
vice 945
guilt 947
at –
uncertain 475
ignorant 491
unskilful 699
find – with 932
faultless 650, 946
faulty 495, 651
faun 980
fauna 366
faut: comme il –
taste 850
fashion 852
il s'en – bien 489
tant s'en – 536
faute 732
– de mieux
substitution 147
necessity 601
fauteuil 215
fautor 890
faux pas
error 568
failure 732
misconduct 947
intrigue 961
favor
resemble 16
badge 550
letter 592
aid 707
indulgence 740

unimportant 643
contempt 930
fiddlefaddle
unmeaning 517
trifle 643
dawdle 683
fiddler 416
fiddlestick 417
– end 643
fidelity
veracity 543
obedience 743
observance 772
honor 939
fidget *changes* 149
activity 682
hurry 684
excitability 825
fidgety
irresolute 605
fearful 860
irascible 901
fiducial 156
fiduciary 484
fidus Achates
auxiliary 711
associate 743
friend 890
fie *disreputable* 874
– upon it
censure 932
fief 777
field *opportunity* 134
scope 180
region 181
plain 344
agriculture 371
business 625
arena 728
property 780
the – *hunting* 622
beasts of the – 300
playing –s 728
the potter's – 361
take the – 722
– artillery 726
the – of blood 361
– of inquiry
topic 454
inquiry 461
– of view
vista 441
idea 453
field-day
contention 720
amusement 840
display 882
field-glass 445
field-marshal 745
field-piece 727
field-preacher 996
field-work 717
fiend 913, 980
fiend-like
malevolent 907
wicked 945
fiend 980
fierce *violent* 173
passion 825
daring 861
angry 900
fiery *violent* 173
hot 382
strong feeling 821
excitable 825
angry 900
irascible 901
– cross 550, 722
– furnace 386
– imagination 515
– ordeal 828
fife 417
fifer 416
fifth 98, 99
fifty 98
fig
unimportance 643
in the name of the prophet –s! 497
– out 847
fight
contention 720
warfare 722
show –
defence 717
courage 861
– one's battles again 594
– against destiny 606
– the good fight 944
– it out 722
– shy *avoid* 603, 623
coward 862
– one's way
pursue 622
active 682
exertion 686
fighter 726
fighting-cock 726, 861
fighting-man 726
figment 515
figurante 599
figurate number 84
figuration 240
figurative
metaphorical 521
representing 554
– *style* 577
figure
number 84
form 240
appearance 448
metaphor 521
indicate 550
represent 554
price 812
ugly 846
cut a –
repute 873
display 882
poor – 874
– to oneself 515
– of speech 521
– out 522
exaggeration 549
figure-flinger 994
figure-head 4, 550, 554, 643
figurine 554
figuriste 559
filaceous 205
filament 205
filamentous 256
filch 791
filcher 762
file *subduct* 38
arrange 60
row 69
assemblage 72
list 86
reduce 195
smooth 255
pulverize 330
record 551
store 636
soldiers 726
– a claim &c. 969
– off *march* 266
diverge 291
file-fire 716
filial 167
filiation
consanguinity 11
attribution 155
posterity 167
filibuster 133, 706, 792
filibustering 791
filiform 205
filigree 219
filings 330
fill *complete* 52
occupy 186
contents 190
stuff 224
provision 637
eat one's – 957
have one's –
enough 639
satiety 869
– the bill 229
– an office
business 625
government 737
– out
expand 194
–ed to overflowing 641
– one's pocket 803
– time 106
– up *compensate* 30
compose 54
close 261
restore 660
– up the time
inaction 681
fille
– de chambre 746
– de joie 962
filled
– to overflowing 641
filler 532
fillet *band* 45
filament 205
circle 247
insignia 550
ornament 847
fillibeg 225
filling 224
fillip
impulse 276
propulsion 284
stimulus 615
excite 824
filly 271
film *layer* 204
opaque 426
semitransparent 427
– over the eyes
dim sight 443
cinema 448
ignorant 491
filmy *texture* 329
filter *percolate* 295
clean 652
filth 653
–y lucre 800
filtrate 652
fimbriated 256
fin 267
final *ending* 67
conclusive 474
completing 729
court of – appeal 474
– cause 620
– stroke 729
– touch 729
finale *end* 67
completion 729
finality 67, 729
finally
for good 141
on the whole 476
finance 800, 811
minister of – 801
financier 801
finch 366
find
eventuality 151
adjudge 480
discover 480a
acquire 775
– one's account in 644
– the cause of 522
– a clue to 480a
– to one's cost 509
credence 484
– it in one's heart 602
– in *provide* 637
– the key of 522
– the meaning 522
– means 632
– oneself *be* 1
present 186
– out 480a
– vent 671
– one's way 731
– one's way into 294
finding
judgment 480
fine *small* 32
large 192
thin 203
rare 322
not raining 340
exact 494
good 648
beautiful 845
adorned 847
proud 878
mulct 974
in – *end* 67
after all 476
– air 656
arts 554
– feather 159, 654
– feeling 850
– frenzy 515
– gentleman
fop 854
proud 878
– grain 329
– lady 854, 878
one – morning 106
some – morning 119
– powder 330
– talking
overrate 482
boast 884
– writing 577
– time of it 734
– voice 580
fine-draw 660
fine-fingered 698
fine-spoken 894, 933
fine-spun *thin* 203
sophistry 477
fine-toned 413
finem, respicere – 510
finery 847, 851
finesse *tact* 698
artifice 702
taste 850
finger *touch* 379
hold 781
lay the – on
point out 457
discover 480a
lift a – 680
not lift a – 681
point the – at 457
turn round one's little – 737
–'s breadth 203
at one's s' end
near 197
know 490
remember 505
– on the lips
aphony 581
taciturnity 585
– in the pie
cause 153
interfere 228
act 680
active 682
co-operate 709
fingerling 193
finger-post 550
finger-print 467
finger-stall 223
fingle-fangle 643
finical
trifling 643
affected 855
fastidious 868
finicky 855, 868
finikin 643
finis 67
– coronat opus 729
finish *end* 67
symmetry 242
complete 729
skill 698
finished
absolute 31
perfect 650
skilled 698
finishing
– stroke 361
– touch 729
finite 32
fiord 343
fire *energy* 171
heat 382
make hot 384
stoke 388
vigor 574
discharge 756
enthusiasm 821
excite 824, 825
catch – 384

hell – 982
on – 382
open – *begin* 66
play with – 863
signal – 550
take –
excitable 825
angry 900
between two –s 665
under – 665, 722
– at 716
– the blood 824
– and fury 900
– the first shot 716
– of genius 498
– off 284
– a salute 883
– and sword 162
– up *excite* 825
anger 900
– a volley 716
go through – and water
resolution 604
perseverance 604*a*
courage 861
fire-alarm 669
fire-annihilator 385
fire-arms 727
fire-ball *fuel* 388
arms 727
fire-balloon 273
fire-barrel 388
fire-bell 669
fire-boat 726
fire-brand
fuel 388
instigator 615
dangerous man 667
incendiary 913
fire-brigade 385
fire-curtain 599
fire-drake 423
fire-eater
fighter 726
blusterer 887
fire-eating
rashness 863
insolence 885
fire-engine 348
fire-escape 671
fire-extinguisher 385
fire-fly 423
fireless cooker 386
fire-light 422
firelock 727
fireman *stoker* 268
extinguisher 385
fire-place 386
fire-proof 385, 644
fireside 189
firewood 388
firework
fire 382
luminary 423
celebration 883
amusement 840
fire-worship 991
fire-worshipper 984
firing *fuel* 388
explosion 406
firkin 191
firm
junction 43
stable 150
hard 323
resolute 604
partnership 712
merchant 797
brave 861
stand – 719
– as a rock 604
– belief 484
– hold 781
firmament 318
firman 741, 760
first 66
– blush
morning 125
leading 280
vision 441
appearance 448
manifest 525
– blow 716
– cause 976
– that comes 609*a*
– fiddle
importance 642
proficient 700
authority 737
– come first served 609*a*
– and foremost 66
– impression 66
– and last 87
– line 234
come back to –
love 607
– move 66
– opportunity 132
at – sight 448
– stage 66
– stone
preparation 673
attack 716
on the – summons 741
of the – water
best 648
repute 873
first-born 124, 128
first-fruits 154
first-hand 20, 467
firstlings 128, 154
first-rate
important 642
excellent 648
man-of-war 726
firth 343
fisc 802
fiscal 800
fish *food* 298
sport 361, 622
animal 366
food for –es 362
other – to fry
ill-timed 135
busy 682
queer – 857
– in the air 645
– for compliments 880
– for *seek* 4
experiment 463
desire 865
– hatchery 370
– out *inquire* 461
discover 480*a*
– in troubled waters
difficult 704
discord 713
– up *raise* 307
find 480*a*
– out of water
disagree 24
unconformable 83
displaced 185
bungler 701
fisherman 361
fishery 370
fishing *kill* 361
pursue 622
fishing-boat 273
fishpond 343, 370
fish-trail 267
fishy transaction 940
fisk 266, 274
fissile 328
fission 44
fissure 44
chink 198
fist
handwriting 590
grip 781
shake the –
defy 515
threat 909
fisticuffs 720
fistula 260
fit *state* 7
agreeing 23
equal 27
paroxysm 173
agitation 315
caprice 608
expedient 646
healthy 654
disease 655
excitement 825
anger 900
right 922
due 924
duty 926
in –s 315
think – 600
– of abstraction 458
– of crying 839
– for 698
– out *dress* 225
prepare 673
– to be seen 845
by –s and starts
irregular 59
discontinuous 70
agitated 315
capricious 608
haste 684
fitful
irregular 139
changeable 149
capricious 608
fittings 633
five 98
division by – 99
– act play 599
– and twenty 98
Five Year Plan 626
fiver 800
fives *game* 840
fix *join* 43
arrange 60
establish 150
place 184
immovable 265
solidify 321
resolve 604
difficulty 704
– the eyes upon 441
– the foundations 673
– the memory 505
– the time 114
– the thoughts 457
– up 774
– upon *discover* 480*a*
choose 609
fixed *intrinsic* 5
permanent 141
stable 150
quiescent 265
habitual 613
– idea 481
– opinion 484
– periods 138
fixity 141
fixity of purpose 141
fixture
appointment 741
property 780
fizgig 423
fizz 409
fizzle 353
– out 304
flabelliform 194
flabbergast 870, 879
flabby 324
flabbiness 324
flaccid *weak* 160
soft 324
empty 640
flag *weak* 160
flat stone 204
floor 211
smoothness 255
slow 275
leaf 367
sign 550
path 627
infirm 655
inactive 683
tired 688
weary 841
lower one's – 725
red – *alarm* 669
yellow –
warning 668
alarm 669
– man 668
– ship 726
– of truce 723
flag-bearer 534
flagellation
penance 952
asceticism 955
flogging 972
rite 998
flagelliform 205
flageolet 417
flagitious 945
flagon 191
flagrant
great 31
manifest 525
notorious 531
atrocious 945
flagrante
– bello 722
– delicto
sure enough 474
act 680
guilt 947
flagration 384
flagstaff *tall* 206
signal 550
flail 276
flair 450, 698
flake 204
snow – 383
– white 430
flam 544
flambé 732
flambeau 423
flamboyant 577
flame *fire* 382
light 420
luminary 423
passion 824, 825
love 897
catch the –
emotion 821
consign to the –s 384
add fuel to the – 173
in –s 382
– up 825
–colored
red 434
orange 439
flame-projector 527
flamen 996
flaming *violent* 173
feeling 821
excited 824
ostentatious 882
boasting 884
flâneur 935
flange *support* 215
rim 231
projection 250
flank *side* 236
protect 664
flannel 384
flap *adjunct* 39
hanging 214
move to and fro 315
– the memory 505
flapdoodle 517
flapper *girl* 129
flapping *loose* 47
flare *violent* 173
glare 420
light 423
– up
excited 824, 825
angry 900
flaring *color* 428
flash *instant* 113
violent 173
fire 382
light 420
eyes – fire 900
– lamp 550
– light 423
– across the memory 505
– on the mind
thought 451
disclose 529
impulse 612
– note 800
– in the pan
unsubstantial 4
transientness 111

impotent 158
unproductive 169
failure 732
– tongue 563
– up *excited* 824
– upon
unexpected 508
– of wit 842
flashing
ostentatious 882
flashy
gaudy color 428
style 577
ornament 847
vulgar 851
flask 191
flat *inert* 172
abode 189
story 191
low 207
horizontal 213
vapid 391
low tone 408
musical note 413
positive 535
dupe 547
back-scene 599
shoal 667
bungler 701
poor 804
insensible 823
dejected 837
weary 841
dull 843
simple 849
fall – 732
– contradiction 536
– iron 255
– refusal 764
flatfoot 664
flatness **251**
flatter *deceive* 545
cunning 702
please 829
grace 845
encourage 858
approbation 931
adulation 933
– oneself
probable 472
hope 858
– the palate 394
flatterer **935**
flattering
– remarks 894
– tale
hope 858
– unction to one's soul
content 831
vain 880
flattery 933
flattery 544, **933**
flatulent
gaseous 334
air 338
wind 349
- *style* 573, 575
flatus 334, 349
flaunt 873, 882
flaunting *vulgar* 85
gaudy 428
unreserved 525
flautist 416
Flavian amphitheater 728
flavor 390
flavoring 393
flavous 436
flaw *break* 70
crack 198
error 495
imperfection 651
blemish 848
fault 947
– in an argument 477
flaxen 436
flay *divest* 226
punish 972
flea *jumper* 309
dirt 653
– in one's ear
repel 289
eject 297
refuse 764
disrepute 874
abashed 879
discourteous 895
contempt 930
flea-bite 643
flea-bitten 440
fleck 32
flecked 440
flection 279
fled *escaped* 671
fledge 673
fledgling 123
flee *avoid* 623
fleece *tegument* 223
strip 789
rob 791
impoverish 804
surcharge 814
fleer *ridicule* 856
insult 929
fleet *ships* 273
swift 274
navy 726
Fleet *prison* 752
fleeting 4, 111
flesh *bulk* 192
animal 364
mankind 372
carnal 961
gain – 194
ills that – is heir to *evil* 619
disease 655
in the – 359
one – 903
way of all – 360
weakness of the – 945
– and blood
substance 3
materiality 316
animality 364
affections 820
make the – creep
pain 830
fear 860
flesh-color 434
flesh-pots 298
– of Egypt 734, 803
fleshly 316
fleur-de-lis 847
fleuron 847
flexible 324, 705
flexion
curvature 245
fold 258
deviation 279
flexuous 248
flexure 245, 258
flibbertigibbet 980
flicker
changing 149
waver 314
flutter 315
light 420
dim 422
flickering 139
flier 621
flies *theatre* 599
flight *flock* 102
volitation 267
swiftness 274
departure 293
avoidance 623
escape 671
– lieutenant 745
put to –
propel 284
repel 717
vanquish 731
– of fancy 515
– of stairs 305, 627
– of time 109
flighty *inattentive* 458
mad 503
fanciful 515
flim-flam 544, 608
flimsy *unsubstantial* 4
weak 160
rarity 322
soft 324
sophistical 477
trifling 643
flinch *swerve* 607
avoid 623
fear 860
cowardice 862
fling *propel* 284
jig 840
jeer 929
have one's –
active 682
laxity 738
freedom 748
amusement 840
– aside 782
have a – at
attack 716
resent 900
disrespect 929
censure 932
– away *reject* 610
waste 638
relinquish 782
– down 308
– to the winds
destroy 162
not observe 773
flint *hard* 323
flint-hearted 907
flintlock 727
flip *beverage* 298
flippant *fluent* 584
pert 885
flipper *paddle* 267
flirt *propel* 284
coquet 607, 854
love 897
endearment 902
– a fan 855
flit *elapse* 109
changeable 149
move 264
travel 266
swift 274
depart 293
run away 623
flitter
small part 32
changeable 149
flutter 315
flitting 111
float *establish* 150
navigate 267
boat 273
buoy up 305
lightness 320
before the –s
on the stage 599
– on the air 405
– before the eyes 446
– bonds 788
– in the mind
thought 451
imagination 515
floater 683
floating
[*see* float]
rumoured 532
– battery 726
– capital 805
debt 806
– dock 189
flocculent
woolly 256
soft 324
pulverulent 330
flock
assemblage 72
multitude 102
laity 997
–s and herds 366
– together 72
floe *ice* 383
flog 972
hasten 684
flood *much* 31
crowd 72
river 348
abundance 639
redundance 641
prosperity 734
stem the – 708
– of light 420
– of tears 839
flood-gate
limit 233
egress 295
conduit 350
open the –s
eject 297
permit 760
flood-light 423, 599
flood-mark 466
flood-tide
increase 35
complete 52
height 206
advance 282
water 337
floor *level* 204
base 211
horizontal 213
support 215
overthrow 731
ground – 191
flop 315
Flora 369
floral 367
florescence 154
floriculture 371
florid *color* 428
red 434
– *style* 577
health 654
florist 371
floss 256
flotilla 273, 726
flotsam and jetsam 73
flounce
trimming 231
jump 309
agitation 315
flounder
change 149
toss 315
uncertain 475
bungle 699
difficulty 704
fail 732
flour 330
flourish
brandish 314, 315
exaggerate 549
language 577
speech 582
prosper 618
healthy 654
prosperous 704
ornament 847
repute 873
display 882
boast 884
– of trumpets
loud 404
cheerfulness 836
publish 531
ostentation 882
celebrate 883
boast 884
flout 929, 936
flow *course* 109
hang 214
motion 264
stream 348
murmur 405
abundance 639
– from
result 154
– of ideas 451
– in 294
– into *river* 348
– out 295
– over 641
– of soul
conversation 588
affections 820
cheerful 836
social 892
– with the tide 705
– of time 109
– of words 582, 584
flower *essence* 5
produce 161
vegetable 367
prosper 734
beauty 845
ornament 847
repute 873

foozle 732
fop **854**
foppery 882
foppish 855
for *cause* 155
tendency 176
reason 476
motive 615
intention 620
preparation 673
have –
price **812**
– all that
notwithstanding 30
qualification 469
– all the world like 17
– aught one knows 156
– better for worse 78
– ever 112
– example 82
– form's sake 82
– good
complete 52
diuturnity 110
permanence 141
– the most part
great 31
general 78
special 79
– the nonce 118
– nothing 815
– a season 106
– a time 111
– the time being 106
forage
food 298
provision 637
steal 791
forage-cap 225
foramen 260
foraminous 260
forasmuch as
relating to 9
cause 155
reason 476
motive 615
foray *attack* 716
robbery 791
forbear
avoid 623
spare 678
lenity 740
sufferance 826
pity 914
abstain 953
forbearance 918
forbid 761
God –
dissent 489
deprecation 766
censure 932
prayer 990
forbidden fruit
seduction 615
prohibition 761
forbidding
ugly 846
force *corps* 72
power 157
strength 159
agency 170
energy 171
violence 173
cultivate 371, 707
cascade 348
- *of style* 574
urge 615
exertion 686
compulsion **744**
armed – 726
brute – 964
put in – 924
– of argument **476**
– of arms 744
– of character 820
– down the throat
severe 739
compel 744
– majeure **744**
– open 173
– one's way
progression 282
passage 302
forced *irrelative* 10
- *style* 579
be – to 601
– labor 603
– march 744
forcefully 601
forceps
extraction 301
grip 781
forces 726
forcible [*see* force]
ford 302, 627
fore 234
fore and aft
complete 52
lengthwise 200
– schooner 273
fore part 234
forearm 673
forebears 166
forebode 511
forecast
foresight 510
prediction 511
plan 626
foreclose 706
foredoom 152, 601
forefathers 166
forefend
prohibit 761
forefinger 379
forego
relinquish 624
renounce 757
surrender 782
foregoing 62, 116
foregone
past 122
– conclusion
prejudged 481
predetermined 611
foreground 234
in the –
manifest 525
forehead 234
foreign
alien 10
extraneous 57
– accent 580
– parts 196
foreigner 57
forejudge
prejudge 481
foresight 510
foreknow 510
foreland 206, 254
forelay 545
fore ock
pull the – 894
take time by the –
early 132
occasion 134
foreman 694
foremost
superior 33
beginning 66
front 234
in advance 280
important 642
reputed 873
forenoon 125
forensic 968
foreordain 152
foreordination 601, 611
forerun 62, 116, 280
forerunner 64, 512
foresee 507, 510
foreseen 871
foreshadow 152, 511
foreshorten 201
foreshow 511
foresight 116, **510**
caution 864
forest 367
forestage 599
forestry 371
forestall
prior 116
early 132
possession 777
foretaste 510
foretell 511
forethought 459, 510
foretoken 511
forewarn 511, 668
foreword 64
forfeit *fail* 773
lose 776
penalty 974
– one's good opinion 932
forfeiture
disfranchisement 925
forfend 706, 717
forgather 72
forge *imitate* 19
produce 161
furnace 386
trump up 544
workshop 691
– fetters 751
forged
false 546
forger
maker 690
thief 792
forgery
deception 545
forget 506
hand – cunning 699
– benefits 917
– injury 918
– oneself 945
forgive **918**
forgo
relinquish 624
renounce 757
surrender 782
forgotten
past 122
ingratitude 917
not to be – 505
– by the world 893
fork *bifid* 91
pointed 244
– lightning 423
– out
give 784
pay 807
expenditure 809
forlorn
dejected 837
hopeless 859
deserted 893
– hope
danger 665
rashness 863
form *state* 7
likeness 21
make up 54
order 58
arrange 60
convert 144
produce 161
bench 215
shape **240**
educate 537
pupils 541
manner 627
beauty 845
fashion 852
etiquette 882
law 963
rite 998
– letter 592
– part of 56
– a party 712
– a resolution 604
formal [*see* form]
regular 82
definitive 535
- *style* 579
affected 855
stately 882
– speech 582
formalism 739, 988
formalist 82
formality [*see* formal]
ceremony 852
affectation 855
law 963
formation
composition 54
production 161
shape 240
formative 153
formed [*see* form]
attempered 820
former
in order 62
prior in time 116
past 122
formication 380
formidable 704, 860
formless 241
formula *rule* 80
arithmetic 84
maxim 496
precept 697
law 963
formulary 998
formulate 590
fornication 961
fornicator 962
foro conscientiæ
veracity 543
duty 926
probity 939
forsake 624
forsaken 898
forsooth 535
forspent 688
forswear *lie* 544
tergiversation 607
refuse 764
transgress 927
improbity 940
fort 666, 717
fort
le droit du plus –
compulsion 744
illegality 964
un peu – 641
fortalice 717
forte 415, 698
fortelage 717
forth 282
come –
egress 295
visible 446
go – *depart* 293
the decree has gone – 741
forthcoming 152, 673
forthwith 132
fortification 717
fortify 159
fortiori, a – 467, 476
fortissimo 404
fortiter in re 171
fortitude 826, 861
fortnightly 138
fortress 717, 752
fortuitous
extrinsic 6
chance 156
undersigned 621
– concourse of atoms 59
fortunate
opportune 134
successful 731
prosperous 734
Fortunatus's – cap
wish 865
spell 993
– purse 803
fortune *chance* 156
fate 601
wealth 803
be one's – 151
clean up a – 803
evil – 621, 735
good – 734
make one's –
succeed 731
wealth 803
tempt –
hazard 621
essay 675
trick of – 509
try one's – 675
wheel of – 601, 621
fortune-hunter 886, 943
fortuneless 804
fortune-teller 513
fortune-telling 511

fortunes of
narrative 594
forty 98
– winks 683
forum 799
school 542
tribunal 966
forward *early* 132
transmit 270
advance 282
willing 602
improve 658
active 682
help 707
vain 880
insolent 885
uncourteous 895
bend – 234
come –
in sight 446
offer 763
display 882
look – to 507
move – 282
press – *haste* 684
put – *aid* 507
offer 763
put oneself – 880
set – 676
– in *knowledge* 490
foss 348
fosse
inclosure 232
ditch 259
defence 717
fossil
ancient 124
hard 323
organic 357
dry bones 362
foster *aid* 707
excite 824
caress 902
– a belief 484
fou 959
foudroyant 870
foul
collide 276
bad 649
dirty 653
unhealthy 657
ugly 846
base 940
vicious 945
fall – of
oppose 708
quarrel 713
attack 716
fight 720
censure 932
run – of
impede 706
– fiend 978
– means 940
– language
malediction 908
– odor 401
– play *evil* 619
cunning 702
wrong 923
improbity 940
foul-mouthed 895
foul-spoken 934
found 153, 215
foundation
beginning 66
stability 150
base 211
support 215
lay the –s 673
sandy – 667
shake to its –s 315
founded
well – 472
– on *base* 211
evidence 467
founder
originator 164
sink 310
fail 732
religious –s 986
foundery 691
founding 22
foundling
trover 775
derelict 782
outcast 893
fount *type* 591
fountain
source 153
river 348
store 636
– head 210
– pen 590
four 95
on all –s 13, 23
horizontal 213
easy 705
prosperous 734
humble 879
– in hand 272
– score &c. 98
– square 244
– times 96
from the – winds 278
fourflusher 884
fourfold 96
four-oar 273
four-poster 215
fourth 96, 97
musical 413
– estate 531
four-wheeler 272
fowl 366
fowling-piece 727
fox *animal* 366
cunning 702
– chase 622
fox-trot 840
foxy *color* 433, 434
cunning 720
foyer 191, 599
fracas
disorder 59
noise 404
discord 713
contention 720
fraction *part* 51
numerical 84
less than one **100a**
fractious 901
fracture
disjunction 44
discontinuity 70
fissure 198
fragile 160, 328
fragment
small 32, 193
part 51, 100*a*
fragrance **400**
fragrant weed 392
frail *weak* 160
brittle 328
feeble 575
irresolute 605
imperfect 651
failing 945
impure 961
– sisterhood 962
frais, à grands – 481
frame
condition 7
make 161
support 215
border 231
form 240
substance 316
structure 329
contrive 626
cucumber – 371
have –d and glazed 822
– of mind
inclination 602
disposition 820
frame-up 626
framework
support 215
structure 329
franchise
voting 609
freedom 748
right 924
exemption 927*a*
Franciscan 996
franc-tireur 726
frangible 160, 328
frank *open* 525
sincere 543
artless 703
honorable 939
frankalmoigne 748
Frankenstein 913, 980
frankincense 400
frantic
violent 173
delirious 503
excited 824
fraternal
brother 11
concord 714
friendly 888
fraternity
[*see* fraternal]
party 712
fraternize
co-operate 48, 709
agree 714
sympathize 888
associate 892
fratricide 361
Frau 374
fraud
falsehood 544
deception 545
pretender 548
dishonor 940
pious – 988
fraught *full* 52
pregnant 161
possessing 777
– with danger 665
fray *rub* 331
battle 720
in the thick of the – 722
frayed 659
frazzle
beaten to a – 732
freak 608, 872
– of Nature 83
freckle 848
freckled 440
fredaine 840
free
detached 44, 47
unconditional 52
liberate 672
unobstructed 705
at liberty 748, 750
gratis 815
liberal 816
insolent 885
exempt 927*a*
impure 961
– balloon 273
– and easy
cheerful 836
adventurous 863
vain 880
insolent 885
friendly 888
sociable 892
– fight 720
– from
simple 42
never – from 613
– gift 784
– from imperfection 650
– lance 726
– land 748
– liver 954*a*
– love 961
make – of 748
– play 170, 748
– quarters
cheap 815
hospitality 892
– space 180
– stage 748
– trade
commerce 794
– translation 522
– will 600
make – with
frank 703
take 789
sociable 892
uncourteous 895
freebooter 792
freeborn 748
freedman 748
freedom **748**
free-handed 816
freehold 780
freely
willingly 602
freeman 748
freemasonry
unintelligible 519
secret 528
sign 550
co-operation 709
party 712
free-spoken 703
freethinker 989
freeze
benumb 381
cold 385
– the blood 830
freezing 385
– mixture 387
freight *lade* 184
cargo 190
transfer 270
freightage 812
freighter 273
freight train 272
French
peddler's – 563
– and English 840
– horn 417
– leave *avoid* 623
freedom 748
– polish 847
frenetic 503
frenzy
madness 503
imagination 515
excitement 825
frequency **136**
frequent
in number 104
in time 136
in space 186
habitual 613
visit 892
fresco *cold* 383
painting 556
al –
out of doors 220
in the air 338
fresh *additional* 37
new 123
flood 348
cold 383
color 428
remembered 505
unaccustomed 614
good 648
healthy 654
impertinent 885
tipsy 959
– breeze 349
– color 434
– news 532
freshen 658, 689
freshet 348
freshman 541
freshwater 851
freshwater sailor 701
fret *suffer* 378
grieve 828
gall 830
discontent 832
sad 837
ornament 847
irritate 900
– and fume 828
fretful 901
fret-work 219
friable 328, 330
friandise 868
friar 996
–'s lantern 423
– Rush 980
Black –s 996
friary 1000
fribble
slur over 460
trifle 643
dawdle 683
fop 854
fricassee 298
frication 331
friction *force* 157
obstacle 179
rubbing **331**
on – wheels 705
friend 711, **890**

candid – 936
next – 759
friendless 893
friendly 714, 894
friends, be – 888
see one's – 892
friendship 9, **888**
frieze 210
frigate 726
fright
cards 840
alarm 860
frightful 31, 830, 846
frightfully 31
frightfulness 860
frigid
cold 383
- *style* 575
callous 823
indifferent 866
frigidarium 387
frigorific 385
frill 231, 248
frills and furbelows 847
fringe
border 231
lace 256
exaggeration 549
ornament 847
frippery
trifle 643
ornament 847
finery 851
ridiculous 853
ostentation 882
frisk *prance* 266
leap 309
search 461
gay 836
amusement 840
frisky 682, 836
frith *chasm* 198
strait 343
forest 367
fritinancy 412
fritter *small* 32
– away *lessen* 36
waste 638
– away time 683
fritters 298
frivolous
unreasonable 477
foolish 499
capricious 608
trivial 643
frizz *curve* 245, 248
fold 258
frock *dress* 225
canonicals 999
– coat 225
frog *fastening* 45
leaper 309
ornament 847
frolic 827, 840
frolicsome 836
from *motive* 615
– this cause 155
– day to day 106, 138
– end to end 52
– that time 117
– time immemorial 122
– time to time 136
frond 367
fronder
censure 932
frondeur
disobey 742
front *foremost* 66
wig 225
fore part **234**
resist 719
insolence 885
bring to the –
manifest 525
come to the –
surpass 303
important 642
repute 873
in – 280
present a – 719
– danger 861
– to front 708
– of the house 599
– rank 234
in the – rank
important 642
repute 873
frontage 234
frontal 220
fronti nulla fides
doubt 485
deception 545
frontier 199, 233
fronting 237
frontispiece 64
frosh 541
frost 283
frosted 430
– glass 427
frostbite 383
froth
bubble 353
trifle 643
dirt 653
– up *angry* 900
frothy 320, 353
- *style* 573, 577
irresolute 605
frounce 258
frouzy 401
froward 901*a*
frown *lower* 837
scowl 839
discourteous 895
angry 900
sulky 901*a*
disapprove 932
– down
abash 879
–s of fortune 735
frozen 383, 385
fructify
produce 161
be productive 168
improve 658
prosper 734
frugal 817, 953
– to excess 819
fruges consumere natus *drone* 683
peasant 876
frugivorus 298
fruit *result* 154
produce 161
food 298
profit 775
forbidden – 615
reap the –s
succeed 731
reward 973
– tree 367
fruitful 168
fruition 161, 827
fruitless
unproductive 169
useless 645
failure 732
frump 851, 895
frumpish 901*a*
frustrate 179, 706
frustrated 732
frustum 51
fry *shoal* 102
child 129
heat 384
small –
unimportant 643
commonalty 876
frying-pan 386
out of – into fire
worse 659
clumsy 699
failure 732
misfortune 735
aggravation 835
fuddled 959
fudge 517, 643
fuel **388**, 638
add – to the flame 835
– oil 388
increase 35
heat 384
aggravate 835
anger 900
fugaces labuntur anni 111
fugacious 111
fugitive
transient 111
emigrant 268
avoiding 623
– writings 596
fugleman
pattern 22
director 694
fugue 415
fulciment 215
fulcrum 215
fulfil
complete 729
– a duty 926
– an obligation 772
fulgent 420
fuliginous
dim 422
opaque 426
black 431
full *much* 31
complete 52
large 192
loud 404
abundant 639
cleanse 652
hands –
active 682
receipt in – 807
– blooded 641
– bloom 131
health 654
beauty 845
– blown 131
expanded 194
glorious 873
– of business 682
– colored 428
– cry *loud* 404
bark 412
pursuit 622
– dinner pail 734
dress 225
ornament 847
fashion 852
show 882
– drive 274
– feather
prepared 673
– force 159
– gallop 274
– heart 820
– of incident 151
– many 102
– of meaning 516
– measure 639
– of people 186
– play
facility 705
freedom 748
– of point 842
– scope 748
– score 415
– size 912
– of sound and fury &c.
unmeaning 517
– speech 274
– stop
cease 142
rest 265
– swing
strong 159
active 682
successful 731
free 748
– as a tick 52
– tide 348
– tilt *active* 682
haste 684
– view 446
– of whims 608
full-fashioned 240
full-fed 954
full-flavored 392
full-grown 131, 192
full-handed 816, 818
full-length 556
full-mouthed 412
full-toned 413
fully 31
fulminate
violent 173
propel 284
loud 404
malediction 908
threat 909
– against
accuse 932
fulness
[*see* full]
in the – of time 109
fulsome
nauseous 395
fetid 401
bad 649
abhorrent 867
adulatory 933
impure 961
fulvid 436
fulvous 436
fumble
derange 61
handle 379
grope 463
awkward 699
fumbler 701
fume
violent 173
exhalation 334, 336
froth 353
heat 382
odor 398
excitement 824, 825
anger 900
in a –
discontented 832
–s of fancy 515
fumid 426
fumigate
vaporize 336
cleanse 652
fumigator 388
fumo, dare pondus – 481
fun 827, 840, 842
make – of 856
funambulist 700
function
algebra 84
office 170
business 625
utility 644
pomp 882
rite 998
duty 926
functionary
director 694
consignee 758
functus officio 756
fund *store* 636
sinking – 802
fundamental
intrinsic 5
base 211
support 215
– bass 413
– note 413
fundamentally 31
funds 800
in – 803
public – 802
funebrial 363
funeral 363
– pace 275
– march 415
funereal
interment 363
dismal 837
fungiform 249
fungology 369
fungosity 250
fungus
projection 250
vegetable 367
foetor 401
bane 663
funicle 205
funicular 627
funk 860, 862
– hole 530
funnel *opening* 260
conduit 350
air-pipe 351
funnel-shaped 252
funny *odd* 83
boat 273
humorous 842

comic 853
fur *covering* 223
hair 256
warm 384
dirt 653
furacious 791
furbelow 231
furbish
improve 658
prepare 673
adorn 847
furcated 244
furcation 91
furcular 244
furfur 653
furfuraceous 330
Furies *anger* 900
evil-doers 913
demons 980
furious *violent* 173
haste 684
passion 825
anger 900
furiously 31
furl 312
furlong 200
furlough 760
furnace 386
workshop 691
like a – *hot* 382
sighing like –
lament 839
in love 902
furnish
provide 637
prepare 673
give 784
– aid 707
– a handle 617
– its quota 784
furniture 633
– van 272
furor
insanity 503
passion 825
furore
emotion 820, 821
passion 825
desire 865
furrow 259
further
added 37
distant 196
aid 707
go – and fare worse
worse 659
bungle 699
not let it go – 528
furthermore 37
furtive
clandestine 528
stealing 791
furuncle 250
fury *violence* 173
excitation 825
anger 900
demon 980
furze 367
fuscous 433
fuse *join* 43
combine 48
heat 382, 384
torch 388
fuselage 215
fusel oil 356
fusiform 244, 253
fusil 727
fusileer 726
fusillade 361, 716
fusion *union* 48
heat 384
co-operation 709
fuss *agitation* 315
activity 682
haste 684
difficulty 704
excitement 825
ostentation 882
kick up a – 173
make a – about
importance 642
lament 839
disapprove 932
fussy *crotchety* 481
bustling 682
excitable 825
fustian
absurd 497
unmeaning 517
- *style* 577, 579
fustigate 972
fusty 124, 401, 653
futhorc 590
futile 497, 645
future 121
eye to the – 510
– possession 777
– state
destiny 152
heaven 981
futurity 121
fuzzle 959
fuzzy 447

G

gab 284
gift of the – 582
gabardine 225
gabble 517, 583
gabelle 812
gaberlunzie 876
gabion 717
gable *side* 236
– end 67
Gabriel 977
Gaby 501
gad
about 266, 268
gadget 626
gad-so 870
gaff 727
gaffer *old* 130
man 373
clown 876
gag
closure 261
render mute 403, 581
dramatic 599
muzzle 751
imprison 752
gage *measure* 466
security 771
throw down the – 715
gaggle 412
gag-man 844
gaieté de cœur 836
gaiety
[*see* gay] 836
gaillard 844
gain
increase 35
advantage 618
skilful 698
acquisition 775
– the confidence of 484
– credit 931
– one's ends 731
– ground
progress 282
improve 658
– head 175
– laurels 873
– learning 539
– over 615
– a point 731
– private ends 943
– the start
priority 116
early 132
– strength 35
– time
protract 110
early 132
late 133
– upon
approach 286
pass 303
become a habit 613
– a victory 731
gainful *useful* 644
gainless 646
gainsay 536
gait 264, 627
gaiter 225
gala 840, 882
galactic circle 318
galantuomo 939
galavant 902
galaxy
assemblage 72
multitude 102
stars 318
luminary 423
glory 873
gale 349
Galen 662
galenicals 662
galimatias 497
galipot 191
galopade 840
galore 639
gall *hurt* 378
bitter 395
annoy 830
anger 900
malevolence 907
dip the pen in – 934
gallant *brave* 861
courteous 894
love 897
licentious 961, 962
gallantry
dalliance 902
gallanty-show 448, 840
galled jade wince, let the – 884
galleon 273
gallery *room* 191
passage 260
auditory 599
museum 636
picture – 556
galley *ship* 273
punishment 972, 975
work like a – slave 686
– proof 591
galliass 273
Gallicism 563
galligaskin 225
gallimaufry 41
galliot 273
gallipot 191
gallivant 902
galloon 847
gallop
pass away 111
ride 266
scamper 274
galloping consumption 655
galloway 271
gallows 361, 975
come to the – 972
galoche 225
galore 102
galvanic
excitable 825
galvanism 157
galvanize 824
gamache 225
Gamaliel
brought up at the feet of – 492
gambade *leap* 309
prank 840
gamble 156
gambado
gaiter 225
leap 309
gambit 66
gambling
chance 621
rashness 863
gambling-house 621
gamboge 436
gambol 309, 827, 840
game *lame* 160
food 298
animal 366
savory 394
resolute 604
persevering 604a
aim 620
gamble 612
pursuit 622
tactics 692
amusement 840
laughing-stock 857
brave 861
make – of
deceive 545
ridicule 856
disrespect 929
play the – 709, 939
– in one's hands
easy 705
succeed 731
command 737
– to the last 604a
– at which two can play 718
– up 732
game-cock 726, 861
game-keeper 370, 753
gameness 861
gamesome 836
gamester
chance 621
play 840
rash 863
gamin 876
gaming-house 621
gammer *old* 130
woman 374
gammon 544, 545
gamey 392
gamut 413
gander 373
gang
assemblage 72
go 264
party 712
– agley 732
ganger 690
gangrene 655
gangster 361, 913
gangway 260, 627
gantlet 972
run the –
resolution 604
dare 861
gaol 752
– delivery 672
gaoler 753, 975
gap 70, 198, 252
stand in the – 717
gape *open* 260
curiosity 455
wonder 870
– for *desire* 865
gaping [*see* gape]
expectant 507
gar 161
garage 191
garb 225
under the – of 545
garbage 653
garble
take from 38
exclude 55
erroneous 495
misinterpret 523
falsify 544
– accounts 811
garbled
incomplete 53
garden *grounds* 189
horticulture 371
beautiful 845
botanic – 371
zoological – 370
– party 840
gardener 371
gardens *street* 189
Gargantua 192
gargle 337
gargoyle 350
garish
light 420
color 428
ugly 846
ornament 847
vulgar 851
display 882
garland
circle 247
sign 550
trophy 733
ornament 847

– ready 673
– rid of 672
– a sight of 441, 490
– through
end 67
transact 692
complete 729
expend 809
– to
extend to 196
arrive 292
– together 72
– into trouble 732
– the wind up 860
– up *produce* 161
ascend 305
raise 307
learn 539
fabricate 544
prepare 673
rise early 682
foment 824
– into the way of 613
get-away 671
gewgaw
trifle 643
ornament 847
vulgar 851
geyser 382, 386
ghastly
pale 429
hideous 846
frightful 860
ghaut 203
ghetto 189
ghost *shade* 362
fallacy of vision 443
soul 450
writer 593
apparition 980
give up the – 360
needs no – to tell us 525
pale as a –
colorless 429
fear 860
– dance 992
ghost-like
ugly 846
ghostly
intellectual 450
supernatural 976, 980
Ghost, Holy – 976
ghoul 913, 980
ghyll 348
giant
large 192
tall 206
– refreshed
strong 159
refreshed 689
–'s strides
distance 196
swift 294
giaour 984, 989
gibber 583
gibberish 517, 563
gibbet
brand 932
execute 972
gallows 975
gibble-gabble 584
gibbous 249, 250
gib-cat *male* 373
gibe 929
giblets 298
gibus 225
giddy
inattentive 458
vertiginous 503
irresolute 605
capricious 608
bungling 699
giddy-head 501
giddy-paced 315
gift *power* 157
talent 698
given 784
– of the gab 582
look a – horse in the mouth
fastidious 868
ungrateful 917
gifted 698
gig 272, 273
gigantic
strong 159
large 192
tall 206
giggle 838
giglamps 445
Gilbertian 842
Gilbertine 996
gild *coat* 223
color 439
ornament 847
– refined gold 641
– the pill
deceive 545
tempt 615
please 829
flatter 933
Gilead, balm in – 834, 858
Giles's Greek, St. – 563
gill 348
gillie 746
gilt 436, 847
– edged 648
gimbals 312
gimcrack
weak 160
brittle 328
trifling 643
ornament 847
ridiculous 853
gimlet 262
gimp
clean 652
pretty 845
decoration 847
gin *trap* 545
instrument 633
intoxicating 959
demon 980
gin mill 189
gin palace 189
gingerbread
weak 160
vulgar 851
gingerly 174, 459, 864
gingle 408
gipsy
wanderer 268
wag 844
– lingo 563
giraffe 206
girandole 423
girasol 847
gird *bind* 43
strengthen 159
surround 227
jeer 929
– up one's loins
brace 159
prepare 673
girder 45, 215
girdle *bond* 45
encircle 227
circumference 230
circle 247
put a – round the earth 311
girl 129, 374
girlhood 127
girt 45
girth
bond 45
circumference 230
gisarm 727
gist *essence* 5
meaning 516
important 642
gît, ci – 363
gittern 417
give *yield* 324
melt 382
bestow 784
discount 813
– away 782, 784
in marriage 903
– back 790
– birth to 161
– with both hands 816
– in charge
restrain 751
– chase 622
– consent 762
– one credit for 484
– in custody 751
– expression to 566
– forth 531
– the go by 623
– a horse his head 748
– in *submit* 725
– into *consent* 762
– light 420
– the mind to 457
– notice
inform 527
warn 668
– it one
censure 932
punish 972
– out *emit* 297
publish 531
bestow 784
– over *cease* 142
relinquish 624
lose hope 859
– place to
substitute 147
avoid 623
– play to the imagination 515
– points to 27
– quarter 740
– rise to 153
– one the slip 671
– security 771
– and take
reciprocate 12
compensation 30
interchange 148
retaliation 718
compromise 774
barter 794
equity 922
honour 939
– tongue 531
– a turn to 140
– one to understand 527
– up
not understand 519
unwilling 603
reject 610
relinquish 624
submit 725
resign 757
surrender 782
restore 790
hopeless 859
– up the ghost 360
– way *weak* 160
brittle 328
submit 725
pine 828
despond 837
modest 881
given [*see* give]
circumstances 8
supposition 514
received 785
– over *dying* 360
– time 134
– to 613
giving **784**
gizzard 191
stick in one's – 900
glabrous 225
glacial 383
glaciate 385
glacier 383
glacis 217, 717
glad 827, 829
give the – eye 441
would be – of 865
– tidings 532
gladden 834, 836
glade *hollow* 252
opening 260
shade 424
gladiator 726
gladiatorial 361, 713, 720
gladsome 827, 829
Gladstone bag 191
glair 352
glaive 727
glamor 992
glance *look* 441
sign 550
see at a – 498
– at
take notice of 457
allude to 527
censure 932
– off *deviate* 279
diverge 291
gland 221
glare *light* 420
stare 441
imperfect vision 443
visible 446
glaring
[*see* glare]
great 31
color 428
visible 446
manifest 525
glass *vessel* 191
smooth 255
brittle 328
transparent 425
lens 445
musical –es 47
see through a – darkly 491
– of fashion 852
live in a – house
brittle 328
visible 446
danger 665
– too much 959
glass-coach 272
glasshouse 191, 371
Glassite 984
glassy [*see* glass]
shining 420
colorless 429
glaucous 435
glave 727
glaver 933
glaze 255
gleam *small* 32
light 420
glean 609, 775
gleanings 636
glebe *land* 342
ecclesiastical 995
church 1000
glee *music* 415
satisfaction 827
merriment 836
gleek 929
glen 252
glengarry 225
glib *voluble* 584
facile 705
glide *lapse* 109
move 264
travel 266
fly 267
– into
conversion 144
glider 273
glimmer
light 420
dim 422
visible 446
slight knowledge 490, 491
glimpse 441, 490
glint 420
glissade 306
glisten 420
glitter
shine 420
appear 446
illustrious 882
glittering
ornament 847
display 882
gloam 901*a*
gloaming 126, 422
gloar *look* 441
wonder 970
gloat 884
– on *look* 441
– over 441
pleasure 377

delight 827
globated 249
globe
sphere 249
world 318
on the face of the – 318
– trotter 268
globule 32, 249
glomeration 72
gloom 421, 827, 837
gloomy horizon 859
glorification 884
glorify
honor 873
approve 931
worship 990
glorious
illustrious 873
tipsy 959
glory
light 420
honor 873
heaven 981
King of – 976
– in 878, 884
– be to God 990
gloss *smooth* 255
sheen 420
interpretation 522
falsehood 546
plea 617
beauty 845
– of novelty 123
– over
neglect 460
sophistry 477
falsehood 544
vindicate 937
glossary 86, 562
glossographer 492
glossologist 492
glossology 560, 562
glossy [*see* gloss]
glottology 560
glout 901*a*
glove 225
take up the – 720
throw down the – 715
glow *warm* 382
shine 420
appear 446
color 428
style 574
passion 821
glower
glare 443
discourteous 895
sullen 901*a*
glowing
[*see* glow]
orange 439
excited 824
beautiful 845
– terms 574
glow-worm 423
gloze 933, 937
glucose 396
glue *cement* 45
cementing 46
semiliquid 352
glum
discontented 832
dejected 837
sulky 901*a*
glut
redundance 641
satiety 869
gluttony 957
glutinous 352
glutton 954*a*, 957
gluttony 957
glycerine 332, 356
glyphography 558
glyptography 558
glyptotheca 557
gnarl *protuberance* 250
anger 900
threat 909
gnarled 256, 321
gnash one's teeth 839, 900
gnat *little* 193
strain at a – &c.
caprice 608
gnaw *eat* 298
rub 331
injure 659
gnawing
– grief 828, 830
– pain 378
gnome 496, 980
gnomic 496
gnomon 114
Gnostic 984
go
cease to exist 2
energy 171, 682
move 264
recede 287
depart 293
fade 429
disappear 449
fashion 852
come and – 314
as things – 613
– about
turn round 311
published 531
undertake 676
– across 302
– after
in time 117
in motion 281
– ahead
energetic 171
precede 280
advance 282
active 682
– against 708
– astray 495
– away 293
– back 283, 624
– bad 659
– bail 771
– before 280
– between
interjacent 228
instrumental 631
mediate 631, 724
– beyond 303
– by the board 158
– about your business
ejection 297
dismissal 756
– by
conform to 82
elapse 109
past 122
outrun 303
subterfuge 702
give the – by to
neglect 460
deceive 545
avoid 623
not observe 773
– by the name of 564
– deep into 461
– down *sink* 306
decline 659
– down with
believed 484
tolerated 826
content 831
– farther and fare worse 659
– forth *depart* 293
publish 531
– halves 91
– hand in hand
accompany 88
same time 120
– hard 704
– on ill 735
– in 294
– in for
resolution 604
pursuit 622
– into
ingress 294
inquire 461
dissert 595
– all lengths
complete 52
resolve 604
exertion 686
– mad 503
– near 286
– no further
keep secret 528
– for nothing
sophistry 477
unimportant 643
– off *explode* 173
depart 293
die 360
wither 659
marry 903
– on *time* 106
continue 143
advance 282
– on for ever 112
– one better 303
– out
cease 142
egress 295
extinct 385
– out of one's head 506
– over
passage 302
explore 461
apostate 607
faithless 940
– to pieces 162
– on record 551
– round 311
– shares 778
– to sleep 683
– through
meet with 151
pass 302
explore 461
perform 599
conduct 692
complete 729
endure 826
– to *extend* 196
travel 266
direction 278
remonstrance 695
– up 305
– to war 722
– with
assent 488
concord 714
– with the stream
conform 82
servile 886
– from one's word 773
goad 615
hasten 684
goal *end* 67
reach 292
object 620
reach the –
complete 729
goat *substitute* 147
jumper 309
lecher 962
he – *male* 373
play the – 499
gob 269
gobang 840
gobbet
small piece 32
food 298
gobble *cry* 412
gormandize 957
eat 298
gobemouche 501, 547
go-between 758
goblet 191
goblin 980
go-cart 272
GOD 976
house of – 1000
kingdom of – 981
sons of – 977
–'s acre 363
– bless me! 870
– bless you
farewell 293
– forbid 766
–'s grace 906
– grant 990
– knows 491
–'s love 906
for –'s sake 765
–'s will 601
– willing 470
god 979
household –s 189
tutelary – 664
goddess *love* 897
good woman 948
heathen 979
Godhead 976
godlike 987
godly 944
godsend *good* 618
prosperity 734
Godspeed
farewell 293
hope 858
courtesy 894
benevolence 906
approbation 931
goer *horse* 271
goes [*see* go]
as one – 270
here – 676
Gog and Magog 192
goggle 441
– eyes 443
goggles 445
going [*see* go]
general 78
rumor 532
– to happen 152
– on
incomplete 53, 730
current 151
transacting 625
goiter 250
Golconda 803
gold *yellow* 436
orange 439
money 800
write in letters of – 642
worth its weight in – 648
gold certificate 800
golden [*see* gold]
– age
prosperity 734
pleasure 827
– apple 615
– calf
wealth 803
idol 985
idolatry 991
– dream
imagination 515
hope 858
– mean
moderation 174
mid-course 628
– opinions 931
– opportunity 134
– rule
precept 697
– season of life 127
– wedding 883
golf 840
Golgotha 363, 1000
Goliath 159, 192
goloshes 225
gondola 273
gondolier 269
gone [*see* go]
past 122
absent 187
dead 360
– bad 653
– by
antiquated 124
– out of one's recollection 506
gonfalon 550
gong 417
goniometer 244, 466
good
complete 52
palatable 394
assent 488
benefit **618**
beneficial 648
right 922
virtuous 944
pious 987
as – as 197
be so – as 765
do – 906

for –
diuturnal 110
permanent 141
make –
evidence 467
provide 637
restore 660
complete 729
substantiate 924
vindicate 937
atone for 952
so far so – 931
think – 931
to the – 780
turn to – account 731
what's the – 645
– actions 944
– at 698
– auspices 858
– behavior
contingent 108*a*
duty 926
virtue 944
in one's – books 888
– bye 293
in – case 192
– chance 472
– cheer *food* 298
cheerful 826
– circumstances 803
– condition 192
– day
arrival 292
departure 293
courtesy 894
– effect
goodness 648
beauty 845
– enough
not perfect 651
be – enough 765
put a – face upon
cheerful 836
proud 878
– fellow 892
– fight *war* 722
virtue 944
– for
useful 644
salubrious 656
– fortune 734
– Friday 998
– genius
friend 890
benefactor 912
god 979
in one's – graces 888
– hand 700
– humor
concord 714
cheerfulness 836
amuse 840
courtesy 894
kindly 906
– intention 906
– judgment 498
– lack! 870
– living
food 298
gluttony 957
– look-out 459
– looks 845
– luck 734
– man *man* 373
husband 903
worthy **948**
– manners 894
much – may it do 906
– morrow 292
– name 873
– nature 906
– night 293
– for nothing
impotence 158
useless 645
in – odor
repute 873
approbation 931
– offices
mediation 724
kind 906
– old time 122
– omen 858
– opinion 931
take in – part
pleased 827
courteous 894
kind 906
– pennyworth 815
– at the price 815
to – purpose 731
– repute 873
– sense 498
– society 852
– taste 578, 850
– temper 894
– thing 648
– time *early* 132
opportune 134
prosperous 734
– turn
kindness 906
– understanding 714
– wife
woman 374
spouse 903
– will
willingness 602
benevolence 906
– word
approval 931
vindication 937
– as one's word
veracity 543
observance 772
probity 939
– works 906
goodie 652, 746
goodly
great 31
large 192
handsome 845
good mixer 892
goodness
[*see* good] **648**
virtue 944
have the –
request 765
– gracious! 870
– of heart 906
goods *effects* 270, 780
merchandise 798
good taste 868
Goodwin sands 667
goody 374
gooroo 996
goose *hiss* 409
game of – 840
giddy as a – 458
tailor's – 255
kill the – with golden eggs 699, 818
a wild – chase 545
gooseberry
old – 978
play – 459
– eyes 411, 443
goosecap 501
goose egg 101
gooseflesh 383
goosequill 590
goose-skin 383
Gordian knot 59, 704
gore *stab* 260
blood 361
gorge *ravine* 198
conduit 350
fill 641
satiety 869
gluttony 957
raise one's – 900
– the hook 602
gorge de pigeon 440
gorgeous
colour 428
beauty 845
ornament 847
ostentation 882
Gorgon 860
gorilla 913
gormandize 298, 954*a*, 957
gorse 367
gory *red* 434
murderous 361
unclean 653
gospel
certainty 474
truth 494
take for – 484
Gospels 985
gossamer
filament 205
light 320
texture 329
gossip *news* 532
babbler 584
conversation 588
gossoon 876
Gotama 986
Goth 851, 876
Gotham, wise men of – 501
gothic
amorphous 241
gouache 556
gouge *concave* 252
perforator 262
goulash 298
gourd 191
gourmand 954*a*, 957
gourmet 868, 954*a*
gout 378
goût, haut – 392
goutte d'eau, il se noyerait dans une – 699
govern 693, 737
governess 540
[*see* govern]
ruling power 745
divine – 976
petticoat – 699
governor
tutor 540
director 694
ruler 745
keeper 753
gowk 501
gown *dress* 225
canonicals 999
gownsman 492
grab *take* 789
miser 819
grabble 379
grace *style* 578
permission 760
concession 784
elegance 845
polish 850
title 877
pity 914
forgiveness 918
honor 939
piety 987
worship 990
act of – 784
God's – 906
with a bad – 603
with a good –
willing 602
courteous 894
in one's good –s 888
heart of – 861
say – 990
submit with a good – 826
– before meat 916
grâce: coup de – 914
la – 840
graceless
inelegant 579
ugly 846
vicious 945
impenitent 951
irreligious 989
Graces 845
gracile 203
gracious
willing 602
courteous 894
kind 906
good – 870
grade *degree* 26
arrange 60
term 71
ascent 217
on the down – 658
on the up – 659
gradatim
gradually 26
in order 58
continuous 69
slow 275
gradation
degree 26
order 58
continuity 69
gradient 217
gradual *degree* 26
continuous 69
slow 275
graduate
adjust 23
calibrate 26
arrange 60
series 69
measure 466
scholar 492, 873
graduated scale 466
gradus 86, 562
Graeculus esuriens 886
graft *join* 43
locate 184
insert 300
trees 371
teach 537
booty 794
corruption 940
Grail
holy – 998
grain *essence* 5
small 32
tendency 176
little 193
rough 256
weight 319
texture 329
powder 330
paint 428
temper 820
ornament 847
against the –
rough 256
unwilling 603
opposing 708
in the – 820
–s of allowance
qualification 469
doubt 485
like –s of sand
incoherent 47
gram 319
gramercy 916
graminivorous 298
grammar
beginning 66
teaching 537
school 542
language **567**
bad – 568
comparative – 560
grammarian 492
gramophone 417, 418, 553
granary 636
grand
great 31
style 574
important 642
money 800
handsome 845
glorious 873
ostentatious 882
– climacteric 128
– doings 882
– duchy 181
– jury 967
en – seigneur
proud 878
insolent 885
en –e tenue
ornament 847
show 882
– piano 417
– style 556
– tour 266
– Turk 745
– vizier 694
grandam 130
grandchildren 167
grandee 875
grande dame 878
grandeur 873

grandfather 130, 166
grandiloquent 577
grandiose 577
grandmother 166
simple 501
teach – 538
grandsire 130, 166
grange 189
granite 323
granivorous 298
grano salis, cum 469, 485
grant *admit* 529
permit 760
consent 762
confer 784
God – 990
– a lease 771
granted 488
take for –
believe 484
suppose 514
grantee
possessor 779
receiver 785
granular 330
granulate 330
granule 32
grapes, sour –
unattainable 471
falsehood 544
excuse 617
grape-shot
attack 716
arms 727
graph 554
graphic
intelligible 518
painting 556
descriptive 594
graphite 332
graphito 556
graphology 590
graphometer 244
graphotype 558
grapnel 666
grapple
fasten 43
clutch 789
– with
- *a question* 461
- *difficulties* 704
oppose 708
resist 719
contention 720
grappling-iron
fastening 45
safety 666
grasp
comprehend 518
power 737
retain 781
seize 789
in one's – 737
possess 777
tight – *severe* 739
– at 865
– of intellect 498
grasping
miserly 819
covetous 865
grass 344, 367
let the – grow under one's feet
neglect 460
inactive 683
not let the – &c.
active 682
grasshopper 309
grass-plat 371
grate *rub* 330
physical pain 378
stove 386
– on the ear
harsh sound 410
– on the feelings 830
grated
barred 219
grateful
physically pleasant 377
agreeable 829
thankful 916
grater 260, 330
gratification
animal – 377
moral – 827
gratify 829
permit 760
please 829
grating [*see* grate]
lattice 219
harsh 713
gratis 815
gratitude 916
gratuitous
inconsequent 477
supposititious 514
voluntary 602
payless 815
gratuity
gift 784
gratis 815
gratulate 896
gravaman 642
– of a charge 938
grave *great* 31
engrave 259, 558
tomb 363
important 642
composed 826
distressing 830
sad 837
heinous 945
beyond the – 360
look –
disapprove 932
rise from the – 660
silent as the – 403
sink into the – 360
on this side of the – 359
– in the memory 505
– note 408
– trap 599
gravel
earth 342
material 635
puzzle 704
graveolent 398
graven image 991
graver 558
graving dock 189
gravitate
descend 306
weigh 319
– towards 176
gravity *force* 157
weight **319**
vigor 574
importance 642
sedateness 826
seriousness 827
center of – 222
specific –
weight 319
density 321
gravy 333
– boat 191
gray 432 [and *see* grey]
graze *touch* 199
browse 298
rub 331
brush 379
grazier 370
gré, savoir – 916
grease
lubricate 332
oil 356
– the palm
tempt 615
give 784
pay 807
greasy 355
great *much* 31
big 192
glorious 873
magnanimous 942
(*important* 642)
– bear 318
– circle sailing 628
– coat 225
– doings
importance 642
bustle 682
– folks 875
– gun 626
– hearted 942
– Mogul 745
– number 102
– primer 591
– quantity 31
greater 33
– number 102
– part 31
nearly all 50
greatest 33
greatness 31
greave 225
greed
desire 865
gluttony 957
greedy
avaricious 819
green
new 123
young 127
lawn 344
grass 367
unripe 397
color 435
credulous 486
novice 491
unused 614
healthy 654
immature 674
unskilled 699
board of – cloth 966
– memory 505
– old age 128
greenback 800
green-eyed monster 920
greenhorn
novice 493
dupe 547
bungler 701
greenhouse
receptacle 191
horticulture 371
greenness 435
green-room 599
greensward 344
Greenwich time 114
greenwood 367
Greek
unintelligible 519
sharper 792
St. Giles's – 563
– Church 984
– Kalends 107
greet *weep* 839
hail 894
greeting
sociality 802
–'s! 292
gregarious 892
grenade 727
grenadier
tall 206
soldier 726
grey 432
– beard 130
– friar 996
– hairs 128
bring – hairs to the grave
adversity 735
harass 830
– mare
ruler 737
master 745
wife 903
– matter
brain 498
–hound
swift 274
animal 366
ocean –hound 273
gridelin 437
gridiron
flatness 213
crossing 219
stove 386
stage 599
stadium 840
grief 828
come to – 735
grievance
evil 619
painful 830
wrong 923
grieve *mourn* 828
pain 830
dejected 837
complain 839
grievous 649, 830
grievously 31
griffin 83, 366, 493
griffo 41
griffonage 590
grig *merry* 836
grill 382, 384, 461
– room 189
grille 219
grim
resolved 604
painful 830
doleful 837
ugly 846
discourteous 895
sullen 901a
–visaged war 722
grimace 243, 839, 855
grimacier
actor 599
humorist 844
affected 855
grimalkin 366
grimy 652
grin *laugh* 838
ridicule 856
– and abide 725
– a ghastly smile
dejected 837
ugly 846
grind
reduce 195
sharpen 253
pulverize 330
pain 378
learn 539
oppress 907
– the organ 416
– one's teeth 900
grinder
teacher 330
noise 404
grinding 739, 830
grindstone 253, 330
grip
indication 550
power 737
retention 781
clutch 789
– of the hand 894
gripe [*see* grip]
pain 378
parsimony 819
grisaille
grey 432
painting 556
grisette
woman 374
commonalty 876
libertine 962
grisly 846
grist
materials 635
provision 637
– to the mill
useful 644
acquire 775
gristle 321, 327
grit
strength 159
powder 330
stamina 604a
courage 861
– in the oil
hindrance 706
gritty 323
grizzled
grey 432
variegated 440
groan 411, 839
groat 800
grocer 637
grocery 396
grog 298, 959
groin 244
groom 370, 746
– well
– of the chambers 746
–'s man 903

training 537
exercise 686
contention 720
sport 840
gymnosophist
abstainer 953
sectarian 984
gynander 83
gynarchy 727
gynecaeum 374
gynecology 662
gyniatrics 374
gynics 374
gyp 545, 746
gyre 311
gyrate 312
gyrfalcon 913
gyromancy 511
gyrostat 312
gysart 599
gyve 752

H

habeas corpus 963, 969
haberdasher 225
habergeon 717
habiliment 225
habilitation 698
habit
essence 5
coat 225
custom 613
want of – 614
–s of business 682
– of mind 820
habitant 188
habitat 189
habitation 189
habit-maker 225
habitual
unvariable 16
orderly 58
ordinary 82
customary 613
habituate 537, 613
habitude
state 7
habit 613
habitué 613
hacienda 189, 780
hack *cut* 44
shorten 201
horse 271
writer 594
worker 690
literary – 593
hackle 44
hackney-coach 272
hackneyed
known 490
trite 496
habitual 613
Hades 982
Hadji
traveler 268
priest 996
hae tibi erunt artes 627
haeret lateri lethalis arundo
displeasure 828
anger 900
haft 633
hag *age* 128
ugly 846
wretch 913
witch 994
haggard
insane 503
tired 688
wild 824
ugly 846
haggis 298
haggle *cut* 44
chaffer 794
Hagiographa 985
Hagiolatry 984
Hagiology 983, 985
haguebut 727
ha-ha *trench* 198, 719
haik 225
hail *welcome* 292
ice 383
call 586
rejoicing 838
honor to 873
celebration 883
courtesy 894
salute 928
approve 931
–fellow well met
friendship 888
sociality 892
hailstone 383
hair *small* 32
filament 205
roughness 256
to a – 494
–'s breadth
near 197
narrow 203
–breadth escape
danger 665
escape 671
–s on the head
multitude 102
make one's – stand on end
distressing 830
fear 860
wonder 870
hairless 226
hairy *rough* 256
halberd 727
halberdier 726
halcyon *calm* 174
peace 721
prosperous 734
joyful 827, 829
hale 654
half 91
– the battle
important 642
success 731
– distance 68
– a dozen *six* 98
several 102
see with – an eye
intelligent 498
intelligible 518
manifest 525
– a gale 349
– and half
equal 27
mixed 41
incomplete 53
– a hundred 98
– light 422
– measures
incomplete 53
vacillating 605
mid-course 628
– moon 245
– price 815
– rations 640
– scholar 493
– seas over 959
– sight 443
– speed
moderate 174
slow 275
– truth 546
half-blind 443
half-blood
mixture 41
unconformity 83
imperfect 651
half-frozen 352
half-hearted
irresolute 605
insensible 823
indifferent 866
half-learned 491
half-melted 352
halfpenny
trifle 643
half-starved
insufficient 640
fasting 956
half-way
small 32
middle 68
between 228
go – *irresolute* 605
mid-course 628
meet –
willing 602
compromise 774
half-witted 499, 501
hall *chamber* 189
receptacle 191
mart 799
music – 599
– of audience 588
– mark 550
hallelujah 990
halliard 45
halloo *cry* 411
look here! 457
call 586
wonder 870
hallow
celebrate 883
respect 928
hallowed 976
hallucination
error 495
insanity 503
halo *light* 420
glory 873
Halomancy 511
halser 45
halt *cease* 142
weak 160
rest 265
go slowly 275
lame 655
fail 732
at the – 265
halter *rope* 45
restraint 752
punishment 975
wear a – 874
with a – round one's neck 665
halting
style 579
– place 292
halve [*see* half]
halves
do by –
neglect 460
not complete 730
not do by – 729
go – 778
ham *house* 189
hamadryad 979
hammam 386, 652
hamlet 189
hammer
repeat 104
knock 276
stammer 583
under the –
auction 796
between the – and the anvil 665
– at *think* 451
work 686
– out *form* 240
prepare 673
complete 729
hammock 215
hamper *basket* 191
obstruct 706
hamstring 158, 659
hanaper 802
hand
measure of length 200
side 236
transfer 270
man 372
organ of touch 379
indicator 550
writing 590
medium 631
agent 690
grasp 781
transfer 783
at – *future* 121
destined 152
near 197
useful 644
bad – 590
bird in – 781
come to – 292, 785
fold one's –s 681
give one's – to
marry 903
good –
writing 590
skill 698
proficiency 700
helping – 707, 711
hold in – 737
hold out the – 894
hold up the –
vote 609
in –
incomplete 53
business 625
preparing 673
not finished 730
possessed 777
money 800
in the –s of
authority 737
subjection 749
lay –s on
discover 480a
use 677
take 789
rite 998
much on one's –s 682
on one's –s
business 625
redundant 641
not finished 730
for sale 796
on the other – 468
no – in 623
poor – 701
put into one's –s 784
put one's – to 676
ready to one's – 673
shake –s 918
stretch forth one's – 680
take by the – 707
take in –
teach 537
undertake 676
time hanging on one's –s
inaction 681
leisure 685
weary 841
try one's – 675
turn one's – 675
turn one's – to 625
under one's –
in writing 590
promise 768
compact 769
– back 683
– cart 272
– of death 360
– down
record 551
transfer 783
have one's –s full 682
– gallop 274
– glass 445
– and glove 709, 888
– in hand
joined 43
accompanying 88
same time 120
concur 178
co-operate 709
party 712
concord 714
friend 888
social 892
– to hand
touching 199
transfer 270
fight 720, 722
– over head
inattention 458
neglect 460
reckless 863
have a – in
cause 153
act 680
co-operate 709
have one's – in
skill 698
keep one's – in 613
live from – to mouth
insufficient 640

unprepared 674
poor 804
–s off! *avoid* 623
leave alone 681
prohibition 761
– over
transfer 783
give 784
win –s down 731
with the –s in the pockets 681
hand-bag 191
hand-barrow 272
handbook
travel 266
information 527
book 593
handcuff 751, 752
handfast 903
handful
quantity 25
small 32
few 103
handicap
equalize 27
inferiority 34
encumber 706
race 720
handicraft 625, 680
handicraftsman 690
effect 154
doing 680
handkerchief
clothes 225
cleaner 652
handle
feel, touch 379
name 565
dissert 595
plea 617
instrument 633
use 677
manage 693
furnish a – 937
make a – of 677
– a case 693
– to one's name
name 564
honor 877
handmaid
instrumentality 631
auxiliary 711
servant 746
handpost 550
handsel
begin 66
security 771
gift 784
pay 809
handsome
liberal 816
beautiful 845
disinterested 942
– fortune 803
handspike 633
handstaff 727
handwriting
signature 550
autograph 590
– on the wall
warning 668
handy
near 197
useful 644, 646
ready 673
dexterous 698
hang
pendency 214
kill 361
curse 908
execute 972
– about 133, 197
– back 133, 623
– in the balance 133
– in doubt 485
– fire *late* 133
cease 142
unproductive 169
inert 172
slow 275
reluctance 603
inactive 683
not finish 730
fail 732
refuse 764
dullness 843
– on hand 641
– down the head 837
– over the head 152
– it! *regret* 833
contempt 930
– out a light 420
– upon the lips of 418
– on
accompany 88
– out
display 882
entertain 892
– over
destiny 152
height 206
project 250
– out a signal 550
– on the sleeve of
servant 746
servility 886
flattery 933
– in suspense 605
– by a thread 665
– together
joined 43
cohere 46
concur 178
co-operate 709
– upon
effect 154
dependency 749
hangar 191, 273
hang-dog look 901*a*
hanged if, I'll be – 489
hanger
weapon 727
suspender 45, 214
pothooks and –s 590
– on
accompaniment 88
servant 746
servile 886
hanging [*see* hang]
elevated 307
ornament 847
– look 846
hangman
evil-doer 913
bad man 949
executioner 975
hank *tie* 45
hanker 865
hanky-panky 545
Hansard 551
hansom 272
hap 156
haphazard
chance 156, 621
hapless
unfortunate 735
(*miserable* 828)
(*hopeless* 859)
haply
possibly 470
(*by chance* 156)
happen 151
– as it may
chance 621
– what may
certain 474
reckless 863
happening 151
happiness
[*see* happy]
the greatest – of the greatest number 910
happy *fit* 23
opportune 134
style 578
glad 827
cheerful 836
– despatch 972
– go lucky 674
– hunting grounds 981
– returns of the day 896
– thought 842
– valley
imagination 515
delight 827
harangue 582
hara-kiri 972
harass
fatigue 688
vex 830
worry 907
harbinger
precursor 64
omen 512
informant 527
harbor
abode 189
haven 292
refuge 666
cherish 821
natural – 343
– a design 620
in – 664
– an idea 451
– revenge 919
harborless 665
hard *strong* 159
dense 323
physically insensible 376
sour 397
difficult 704
severe 739
morally insensible 823
grievous 830
impenitent 951
blow – 349
go –
difficult 704
failure 732
adversity 735
pain 828
hit – 276
look – at 441
not be too – upon 918
strike –
energy 171
impulse 276
try – 675
work – 686
– at it 682
– bargain 819
– of belief 487
– to believe 485
– by 197
– case 735
– cash 800
– earned 704
– and fast rule 80
– fought 704
– frost 383
– of hearing 419
– heart
malevolent 907
vicious 945
impenitent 951
– hit 732
– knocks 720
– life 735
– lines
adversity 735
severity 739
– liver 954*a*
– lot 735
– master 739
– measure 739
– names 932
– necessity 601
– nut to crack 704
– to please 868
– pressed
haste 684
difficulty 704
hindrance 706
– put to it 704
– set 704
– tack 298
– task 703
– time 704
– up 704, 804
– upon
attack 715
severe 739
censure 932
– winter 383
– words
obscure 571
rude 895
censure 932
– work 686
– at work 682
harden [*see* hard]
strengthen 159
accustom 613
– the heart
insensible 823
enmity 889
impenitence 951
hardened
impious 988
– front
insolent 885
hardening
habit 613
hard-featured 846
hard-fisted 819
hard-headed 498, 739
hardihood 861, 885
hardly
scarcely 32
deal – with 739
– any *few* 103
– anything
small 32
unimportant 643
– ever 137
hard-mouthed 606
hardness 323
– of heart 914*a*
hardship 735
hardy
strong 159
healthy 654
brave 861
hare 274
hold with the – and run with the hounds
fickle 607
servile 886
hare-brained 458, 863
harem 961
hariolation 511
hark 418, 457
– back 283
harl 205
harlequin
changeable 149
nimble 274
motley 440
pantomimic 599
humorist 844
harlequinade 599
harlot 962
harlotry 961
harm
evil 619
badness 649
malevolence 907
harmattan 349
harmless
impotent 158
good 648
perfect 650
salubrious 656
safe 664
innocent 946
bear – 717
harmonica 417
harmonics 413
harmonist 413
harmonize 178, 416
harmonium 417
harmony
agreement 23
order 58
music 413
color 428
concord 714
peace 721
friendship 888
harness
fasten 43
fastening 45
accouterment 225
yoke 370
instrument 633
restraint 752
in –
prepared 673

in action 680
active 682
subjection 749
– up 293
harp
repeat 104
musical instrument 417
weary 841
Harpagon 819
harper 416
harpist 416
harpoon 727
harpsichord 417
harpy
relentless 739
thief 792
miser 819
evil-doer 913
demon 980
harquebuss 727
harridan 846, 962
harrier 366
harrow
agriculture 371
– up the soul 860
harrowing 830
harry *pain* 830
attack 716
persecute 907
Harry, old – 978
harsh
acrid 171
sound 410
style 579
discordant 713
severe 739
disagreeable 830
morose 895
malevolent 907
– voice 581
hart 366, 373
hartal 142, 489
harum-scarum 59, 458
haruspice 513
Haruspicy 511
harvest
effect 154
profit 618
store 636
acquisition 775
get in the –
complete 729
succeed 731
– home
celebration 883
– time
autumn 126
exertion 686
has been 122
hash *mix* 41
cut 44
confusion 59
food 298
make a – 699
hashish 863
hasp 43, 45
hassock 215
hastate 253
haste
velocity 274
activity 682
hurry **684**
hasten
promote 707
hasty
transient 113
hurried 684
impatient 825
irritable 901
– pudding 298
hat 225
cardinal's – 999
send round the – 765
shovel – 999
– in hand 886
hatch
produce 161
gate 232
opening 260
chickens 370
fabricate 544
shading 556
plan 626
prepare 673
– a plot 626
hatches, under –
restraint 751
prisoner 754
poor 804
hatchet
cutting 253
bury the – 918
dig up the – 722
throw the helve after the – 818
hatchet-faced 203
hatchment
funeral 363
arms 550
record 551
hatchway 260
hate 867, **898**
hateful 649, 830
hath been, the time – 122
hatrack 215
hatter 225
mad as a – 503
hatti-sheriff 741
hatred [*see* hate]
object of – 898
hauberk 717
haud passibus æquis 28, 275
haugh 344
haughty
proud 878
insolent 885
contemptuous 930
haul *drag* 285
catch of fish &c. 789
– down one's flag 725
– in 10
haunch 236
haunt *focus* 74
presence 186
abode 189
alarm 860
persecute 907
– the memory
remember 505
trouble 830
haunted 980
haut
traiter de –
insolence 885
contempt 930
hautboy 417
haut-goût 392
haut-monde 875
hauteur 878
have *confute* 479
ken 49
possess 777
– the advantage 28, 33
– at 716
– no choice 609*a*
– done! 142
– to do with 9
– no end 112
– other fish to fry 135
– it
discover 480*a*
believe 484
– one to know 527
– some knowledge of 490
– nothing to do with 10
– for one's own 780
– rather 609
– one's rights 924
– the start 116
– in store 152, 637
– to 620
– up 638
– it your own way
submission 725
haven 292, 666
haversack 191
havoc
destruction 162
cry – *war* 722
play – *spoil* 659
haw 583
hawk *spit* 297
stammer 583
eye of a – 498
– about
publish 531
offer 763
sell 796
– at 716
between – and buzzard 315, 828
know a – from a handsaw 465, 698
hawker 796
hawk-eyed 441
hawking *chase* 622
hawser 45
hay while the sun shines, make – 134
haycock 72
hazard
chance 156, 621
danger 665
at all –s 604
– a conjecture 514
– a proposition 477
haze *mist* 353
uncertainty 475
in a –
hidden 528
hazel 433
hazy *opaque* 426
he 373
head *precedence* 62
beginning 66
class 75
summit 210
coiffure 225
lead 280
froth 353
person 372
intellect 450
topic 454
wisdom 498
picture 556
nomenclature 564
chapter 593
direct 693
director 694
master 745
at the – of
direction 693
authority 737
repute 873
bow the – 308
bring to a – 729
come into one's – 451
come to a – 729
drive into one's – 505
gain – 175
get into one's –
thought 451
learn 505
belief 484
intoxicate 959
give a horse his – 748
hang one's – 879
have in one's – 490
from – to heels 52, 200
hit on the – 912
knock on the – 361
knock one's – against
impulse 276
unskilful 699
fail 732
lie on one's – 926
lift up one's – 878
make – against
oppose 708
resistance 719
success 731
never entered into one's – 458
have no – 506
on one's – 218
off one's – 503
can't get out of one's – 505
over – and ears
deep 641
debt 806
love 897
put into one's –
supposition 514
information 527
put out of one's – 458
run in the – 505
not know whether one stands on – or heels
uncertain 475
wonder 870
take into one's –
thought 451
caprice 608
intention 620
turn the – 824
trouble one's – about 457
as one's – shall answer for 768
with – erect 878
from – to foot 200
– and front
important 642
– and front of one's offending
provocation 830
charge 938
– over heels
inversion 218
rotation 312
– light 423
– line 591
– and shoulders
irrelevant 10
complete 52
haste 684
make neither – nor tail of 519
hold one's – up 307
– above water
safe 664
prosperous 743
wealth 803
with a – on 353
headache 378
head-dress 225
header 310
head-foremost
violent 173
rash 863
head-gear 225
heading *prefix* 64
beginning 66
indication 550
title 564
headland
height 206
projection 250
headlong
hurry 684
rush 863
rush –
violence 173
headman 694
headmost
front 234
precession 280
head-piece
summit 210
intellect 450
helmet 717
ornament 847
head-quarters
focus 74
abode 189
authority 737
head-race 350
head-stone 363
heads
compendium 596
– or tails 156, 621
lay – together
advice 695
co-operate 709
– I win tails you lose
unfair 940
headship 737
headsman 975

headstrong
violent 173
obstinate 606
rash 863
headway *space* 180
navigation 267
progression 282
headwind 708
headwork 451
heady 606
heal *restore* 660
remedy 662
let the wound –
forgive 918
– the breach
pacify 723
healing art 662
health **654**
picture of – 654
healthiness 655
health resort 189
healthy 656
heap *quantity* 31
collection 72
store 636
too many 641
heaps 102
rubbish – 645
hear
audition 418
be informed 527
not – of (refuse) 764
– a cause
adjudge 480
lawsuit 969
– hear! 931
– and obey 743
– out 457
hearer 418
hearing **418**, 696
[*see* hear]
gain a – 175
give a – 418
hard of – 419
out of – 196
within – 197
hearken 457
hearsay 532
– evidence 467
hearse 363
heart
intrinsicality 5
interior 221
centre 222
mind 450
willingness 602
essential 642
affections 820
courage 861
love 897
man after one's own – 899
with all one's – 438, 602
at – 820, 821
from bottom of – 543
beating – 821, 824
break the – 830
by –
memory 505
go to one's – 824
in good – 858
with a heavy – 603
know by – 490
lay to – 837
learn by – 539
lift up the – 990
lose – 837
lose one's – 897
nearest to one's – 897
not find it in one's – 603
have a place in the – 897
put one's – into 604
set one's – upon 604
take –
content 831
hope 858
courage 861
take to –
sensibility 822
discontent 832
dejection 837
anger 900
warm – 822
wind round the – 897
– bleeding for 914
to one's –'s content
willing 602
enough 639
success 731
pleasure 829
–'s core
mind 450
affections 820
– expanding 821
– failing one 837, 860
do one's – good 829
– of grace 858
– in hand 602
– leaping with joy 827, 838
– leaping into one's mouth 824
– of oak
strong 159
hard 323
– in right place 906
– sinking *fear* 860
– and soul
completely 52
willing 602
resolute 604
exertion 686
feeling 821
– of stone 823, 907
– swelling 824
heartache 828
heart-breaking 821, 830
heart-broken 828
heartburning
discontent 832
regret 833
enmity 889
anger 900
jealousy 920
hearten 858, 861
heartfelt 821, 829
hearth
home 189
fireplace 386
heartless 823, 945
heart-rending 830
heartsease 831
heart-shaped 245
heart-sick
dejection 837
dislike 867
satiety 869
heart-stricken 828
heart-strings, tear the – 830
hearty
willing 602
healthy 654
feeling 821
cheerful 836
friendly 888
social 892
– laugh 838
– meal 298
– reception 892
heat *warmth* **382**
make hot 384
contest 720
excitement 824, 825
dead – 27
– of passion 900
– wave 382
heated imagination 515
heater 386
heath *moor* 344
plant 367
heathen 984, 989
– mythology 979
heathenish 851
heather *moor* 344
plant 367
heaume 717
heautontimorumenos 837, 955
heave *raise* 307
emotion 821
– the lead 208, 466
– a sigh 839
– in sight 446
– to 265
heaven 827, **981**
call – to witness 535
in the face of – 525
light of – 420
move – and earth 686
will of – 601
– forfend! 766
– knows 475, 491
– be praised 838, 916
for –'s sake 765
heaven-born
wise 498
repute 873
virtue 944
heaven-directed 498
heaven-kissing 206
heavenly
celestial 318
rapturous 829
divine 976
of heaven 981
– bodies 318
– host 977
– kingdom 981
heavenly-minded 987
heavens 318
– and earth! 870
Heaviside layer 338
heavisome 843
heavy *great* 31
inert 172
weighty 319
stupid 499
actor 599
sleepy 683
dull 843
brutish 851
– affliction 828
– artillery 726
– cost 814
– dragoon 726
– father 599
– gaited 843
– gun 727
– hand
clumsy 699
severe 739
– on hand 641
– heart *loth* 603
pain 828
dejection 837
– hours 841
– on the mind 837
– news 830
– sea
agitation 515
waves 348
– sleep 683
– type 591
– wet 298
heavy-laden 706, 828
hebdomadal 138
Hebe 845
hebetate 823, 826
hebetude
imbecile 499
insensible 823
inexcitable 826
Hebrew
unintelligible 519
Jew 984
Hecate 994
hecatomb
number 98
sacrifice 991
heckle 830, 900
hectic 382, 821
Hector *brave* 861
rash 863
bully 885, 887
hedge
compensate 30
inclosure 232
– in
circumscribe 229
hinder 706
conditions 770
hedgehog 253
hedonism 377, 827
hedonist 954*a*
heed *attend* 457
care 459
beware 668
caution 864
heedful 457
heedless
inattentive 458
neglectful 460
oblivious 506
rash 863
heel *support* 215
lean 217
deviate 279
go round 311
iron – 975
lay by the –s 162
turn on one's –
go back 283
go round 311
avoid 623
– of Achilles 665
heel-piece
sequel 65
back 235
repair 660
heel-tap
remainder 40
dress 653
heels *lowness* 207
at the – of
near 197
behind 235
cool one's – 681
follow on the – of 281
laid by the – 751
lay by the – 789
show a light pair of – 623
take to one's – 623
tread on the – of
near 197
follow 281
approach 286
– over head
inverted 218
hasty 684
rash 863
heft *handle* 633
exertion 686
hegemony
influence 175
direction 693
authority 737
heifer 366
heigho! 839
height *degree* 26
altitude **206**
summit 210
at its –
great 31
supreme 33
draw oneself up to his full – 307
– finder 206
heighten
increase 35
elevate 307
exaggerate 549
aggravate 835
hegira [*see* hejira]
heinous 945
heir *futurity* 121
posterity 167
inheritor 779
heirloom 780
heirship 777
hejira 293
Helen of Troy 845
heliacal 318
helical 248
Helicon 597
helicon-horn 417

helicopter 273
Heliogabalus 954*a*
heliograph
signal 550
picture 556
heliography 550
light 420
painting 556
Helios 423
heliotrope 847
heliotype 558
helix 248
hell *abyss* 208
gaming-house 62
gehenna **982**
– upon earth
misfortune 735
pain 828
– broke loose 59
hell-born 945, 978
hellebore 663
hell-hound 913, 949
hellish
malevolent 907
vicious 945
hell 982
helluo librorum 492
helm *handle* 633
scepter 747
(*authority* 737)
answer the – 713
at the – 693
obey the – 705
take the – 693
helmet 225, 717
helminthology 368
helmsman 269, 694
helot 746
help *benefit* 618
utility 644
remedy 662
aid 707
servant 746
give 784
it can't be –ed
submission 725
never mind 823
content 831
God – you 914
so – me God 535
– oneself to 789
helper 711
helpless 158, 665
helpmate
auxiliary 711
wife 903
helter-skelter 59, 684
helve
throw the – after the hatchet 818
hem *edge* 231
fold 258
indeed! 870
kiss the – of one's garment 886
– in *enclose* 220
restrain 751
hemi- 91
hemisphere 181
hemispheric 250
hemlock 663
hemorrhage 299
hemp 205
hen 366, 374
female 374
– with one chicken
busy 682
henbane 663
hence
arising from 155
departure 293
deduction 476
– loathed melancholy 836
henceforth 121
henchman 746
hencoop 370
hendiadis 91
henna 433
henpecked 743, 749
heptagon 244
heptarchy 98
Heraclitus 839
rideret – 853
herald
precursor 64
precession 280
predict 511
forerunner 512
proclaim 531
messenger 534
heraldry 550
herb 367
herbage 365
herbal 369
herbivorous 298
herborize 369
herculean
strong 159
exertion 686
difficult 704
Herculem, ex pede – 550
Hercules 159, 215
pillars of – 233, 550
herd 72, 102
herdsman 746
here
situation 183
presence 186
arrival 292
come –! 286
– below 318
– goes 676
– and there
dispersed 73
few 103
place 182, 183
– there and everywhere
diversity 16*a*
space 180
omnipresence 186
– to-day and gone to-morrow 111
hereabouts 183, 197
hereafter 121, 152
hereby 631
hereditament 780
hereditary
intrinsic 5
derivative 154, 167
heredity 167
herein 221
heresy 495, 984
heretic 984
heretofore 122
hereupon 106
herewith 88, 632
heritage
futurity 121
possession 777
property 780
heritor 779
hermaphrodite 83
– brig 273
hermeneutics 522
Hermes 534, 582
hermetically 261
hermit 893, 955
hermitage
house 189
cell 191
seclusion 893
hero *brave* 861
glory 873
good man 948
– worship 931, 991
Herod, out-Herod – 549
heroic [*see* hero]
magnanimous 942
mock – 853
heroics 884
heroin 663
heroine 861
herpetology 368
Herr 373
herring
pungent 392
– pond 341
draw a – across the trail 545
trail of a red 615, 706
herring-gutted 203
hesitate
uncertain 475
sceptical 485
stammer 583
reluctant 603
irresolute 605
fearful 860
Hesperian 236
Hesperides, garden of the – 981
Hesperus 423
Hessian boot 225
hest 741
hesterni quirites 876
heterarchy 737
heteroclite 83
heterodoxy 489, **984**
heterogeneous
unrelated 10
different 15
mixed 41
multiform 81
exceptional 83
heterogeneity 15, 16*a*
heteromorphism 16*a*
hetman 745
hew *cut* 44
shorten 201
fashion 240
– down 308
hewers of wood
workers 690
commonalty 876
hexagon 98, 244
hexahedron 244
hexameter 98, 597
hey! 586
heyday
exultation 838
festivity 840
wonder 870
– of the blood 820
– of youth 127
hiation 260
hiatus 198
hibernal 383
hibernate 683
Hibernicism 497, 563
hic:
– jacet 363
– labor hoc opus 704
hick 701, 851, 876
hiccup 349
hid under a bushel 460
hidalgo 875
hidden 528
– meaning 526
hide *skin* 223
conceal 528
– diminished head
inferior 34
decrease 36
humility 879
– one's face
modesty 881
– and seek
deception 545
avoid 623
game 840
hide-bound 751, 819
hideous 846
hide-out 893
hiding-place
abode 189
ambush 530
refuge 666
hie 264, 274
– to 266
hiemal 126
hierarch 996
hierarchy 995
hieratic 590
hieroglyphic
representation 554
letter 561
writing 590
hierographa 985
hieromancy 511
hierophant 996
hieroscopy 511
higgle 794
higgledy piggledy 59
higgler 797
high *much* 31
lofty 206
fetid 401
treble 410
foul 653
noted 873
proud 878
from on – 981
on – 206
think –ly of 931
– art 556
– celebration 998
– color
color 428
red 434
exaggerate 549
– commissioner 745
– days and holidays 840
in a – degree 31
– descent 875
– and dry
stable 150
safe 664
in – esteem 928
in – feather
strong 159
health 654
cheerful 836
boasting 884
– glee 836
– hand
violent 173
resolved 604
authority 737
severe 739
pride 878
insolence 885
lawless 964
– jinks 840
ride the – horse 878
– hat 225
– life *fashion* 852
rank 875
– living
intemperance 954
gluttony 957
– mass 998
– mightiness 873
– and mighty
pride 878
insolence 885
– note 410
– notions 878
– places 210
– pressure
energy 171
excitation of feeling 824
– price 814
– priest 996
in – quarters 875
– relief 448
– repute 873
–ly respectable 875
on the – road to
way 627
hope 858
on one's – ropes
excitation 824
pride 878
anger 900
– seas 341
in – spirits 836
– tide *wave* 348
prosperity 734
– time *late* 133
occasion 134
– in tone
white 430
– treason
disobedience 742
dishonor 940
– words
quarrel 713
anger 900
high-ball 298
high-born 875

riding 266
skill 698
horseplay 856
horse power 466
horse-shoe 245
horse-whip 972
hortation 615, 695
hortative 537
horticulture 371
hortus siccus 369
hosanna 931, 990
hose
stockings 225
pipe 348, 350
extinguisher 385
hosier 225
hospice 189, 662
hospitable 816, 892
hospital 189, 662
in – 655
hospitality
[*see* hospitable]
hospodar 745
host *collection* 72
multitude 102
army 726
friend 890
rite 998
reckon without one's –
error 495
unskilful 699
rash 863
– of heaven 977
– in himself 175
hostage 771
hostel 189
hostelry 189
hostile
disagreeing 24
opposed 708
enmity 889
in – array 708
– meeting 720
hostilities 722
hostility 889
hostler 746
hot *violent* 173
warm 382
pungent 392
red 434
orange 439
excited 824
irascible 901
make – 384
– air 482, 884
– bath 386
– blood *rash* 863
angry 900
irascible 901
blow – and cold
inconsistent 477
falsehood 544
tergiversation 607
caprice 608
in – haste 684
in – pursuit 622
– water
difficulty 704
quarrel 713
painful 830
– water bottle 386
hot air merchant 884
hot-bed *cause* 153
centre 222
workshop 691
Hotchkiss gun 727
hotchpotch
mixture 41
confusion 59
participation 778
hotel 189
hot-headed 684, 825
hothouse
conservatory 371, 636
furnace 386
workshop 691
hot-press 255
Hotspur 863
Hottentot 876
hough 659
hound *animal* 366
hunt 622
persecute 907
wretch 949
hold with the hare but run with the –s 607
– on 615
houppelande 225
hour *period* 108
point of time 113
present time 118
improve the shining – 682
one's – is come
occasion 134
death 360
– after hour 110
hour-glass
chronometer 114
contraction 195
narrow 203
Houri 845
hourly *time* 106
frequent 136
periodical 138
house *family* 166
locate 184
abode 189
theater 599
make safe 664
council 696
firm 712
before the – 454
keep – 184
eat out of – and home
prodigal 818
gluttony 957
turn out of – and home 297
– of cards 160
– of correction
prison 752
punishment 975
– of death 363
– of detention 752
– divided against itself 713
bring the – about one's ears 699
– of Commons 696, 966
– of God 1000
– of Lords 696, 875, 966
set one's – in order 952
– of peers 696, 875
– of prayer 1000
– built on sand 160
turn – out of window 713
housebreaker 792
housebreaking 791
house-dog 366
household
inhabitants 188
abode 189
– gods 189
– stuff 635
– troops 726
– words
known 490
language 560
plain 576, 849
householder 188
housekeeper 637, 694
housekeeping 692
houseless 185
housemaid 746
house-organ 531
Houses of Parliament 191, 696
house-top 210
proclaim from – 531
house-room 180
house-warming 892
housewife 682
housewifery 692, 817
housing
lodging 189
covering 223
horse-cloth 225
hovel 189
hoveller 269
hover *high* 206
rove 266
soar 267
ascend 305
irresolute 605
– about
move 264
– over
near 197
how *way* 627
means 632
– comes it?
attribution 155
inquiry 461
– now 870
howbeit 30
however
degree 26
notwithstanding 30
except 83
howitzer 727
howker 273
howl
wind 349
human cry 411
animal cry 412
lamentation 839
howler 495
howling wilderness 169, 893
hoy 273
hoyden *girl* 129
rude 851
hub 222
hubble-bubble 392
hubbub *stir* 315
noise 404
discord 713
huckster 794, 797
huddle
disorder 59
derange 61
collect 72
hug 197
– on 225
Hudibrastic 856
– verse 597
hue 428
– and cry *cry* 411
proclaim 531
pursuit 622
alarm 669
raise a – and cry 932
hueless 429
huff 885, 900
huffy 901
hug *cohere* 46
border on 197
retain 781
courtesy 894
love 897
endearment 902
– a belief 606
– oneself
pleasure 827
content 831
rejoicing 838
pride 878
– the shore
navigation 267
approach 286
– a sin 945
huge 31, 192
hugger-mugger 528
Huguenot 984
huis clos, à – 528
huissier 965
huke 225
hulk *body* 50
ship 273
hulks 752
hulky *big* 192
unwieldy 647
ugly 846
hull 50
hullabaloo 404, 411
hullo! 292
hum
faint sound 405
continued sound 407
animal sound 412
sing 416
deceive 545, 546
– and haw
stammer 583
irresolute 605
busy – of men 682
human 372
– race 372
– sacrifices 991
humane
benevolent 906
philanthropic 910
merciful 914
humanitarian 372, 910
humanities 560
humanize 894
humano capiti cervicem jungere equinam 24
humation 363
humble *meek* 879
modest 881
pious 987
–r classes 876
– oneself
submit 725
meek 879
penitent 950
worship 990
eat – pie 725, 879
your – servant
dissent 489
refusal 764
humbug
falsehood 544
deception 545
deceiver 548
trifle 643
affectation 855
humdrum 841, 843
humectate 337, 339
humid 339
humiliate 308
humiliation
adversity 735
disrepute 874
sense of shame 879
worship 990
self – 950
humility **879, 987**
humming-top 417
hummock 206, 250
humorist **844**
humor *essence* 5
tendency 176
liquid 333
disposition 602
caprice 608
aid 707
indulge 760
affections 820
please 829
wit 842
flatter 933
(*fun* 840)
in the – 602
out of – 901*a*
peccant –
unclean 853
disease 655
humorous 842
humorsome
capricious 608
sulky 901*a*
hump 250
hump-backed 243
humph! 870
Humphrey, dine with Duke – 956
Humpty-dumpty 193
Hun 165, 851, 913
hunch 250, 612
hunch-backed 243
hundred
number 98
many 102
region 181
the same a – years hence 460
hundredth 99
hundredweight 319
hunger 865
hunger-strike 956
hunks 819

hunt *inquiry* 461
pursuit 622
– after 622
– in couples 709
– down 907
– out *inquiry* 461
discover 480a
– slipper 840
hunter *horse* 271
killer 361
pursuer 622
place &c. – 767
hunting 361, 622
hunting-ground 840
happy – 981
hurdle 272
hurdy-gurdy 417
hurl 284
– against 716
– defiance 715
hurler avec les loups 82, 714
Hurlothrumbo 860
hurly-burly 315
hurrah 411, 836, 838
hurricane 349, 667
– deck 210
hurry *haste* 684
excite 825
– forward 684
– off with 789
– on 615
– of spirits 821
– up 684
hurst 367
hurt
physical pain 378
evil 619
maltreat 649
injure 659
more frightened than – 860
– the feelings
pain 830
anger 900
hurtful 649
hurtle 276
hurtless 648
husband
store 636
director 694
spouse 903
husbandman 371
husbandry
agriculture 371
conduct 692
economy 817
hush *moderate* 174
stop 265
silence 403
taciturn 585
– up
conceal 528
pacify 723
hush-money 30, 973
husk 223, 226
husky *strong* 159
dry 340
faint sound 405
hoarse 581
hussar 726
hussy 962
hustings
school 542
arena 728
tribunal 966
hustle
perturb 61
push 276
agitate 315
activity 682
hinder 706
hustler 682, 962
hut 189
hutch 189
huzza 838
hyacinth
jewel 847
hyaline 425
hybrid
mixture 41
exception 83
hydra
monster 83, 366
productive 168
– headed 163
hydrant 348, 385
hydraulics 333, 348
hydro-aeroplane 273
hydrodynamics 333, 348
hydrography 341
hydrology 333
hydrolysis 49
hydromancy 511
hydromel 396
hydropathy 662
hydrophobia 867
hydroplane 273
hydrostatics 333
hyemal 383
hyena 913
hyetology 348
hygeian 656
hygiantics 670
hygienic 656, 670
hygre 348
hygrometry 339
hyle 316
hylism 316
hylotheism 984, 989
Hymen 903
hymeneal 903
hymn *song* 415
worship 990
– of hate 898
hymn-book 998
hyoscine 663
hypallage 218
hyperbation 218
hyperbola 245
hyperbole 549
hyperborean
far 196
cold 383
hypercriticism
misjudgment 481
discontent 832
fastidiousness 868
censure 932
hyperdulia 990
Hyperion 423, 845
– to a satyr 14
hyperorthodoxy 984
hyperphysical 976
hypertrophy 194
hyphen 45
hypnology 683
hypnotic
remedy 662
sleep 683
hypnotize 376
hypocaust 386
hypochondriac
madman 504
low spirits 837
hypochondriasis 837
hypocrisy
falsehood 544
religious – 988
hypocrite 548, 855
play the – 544
hypostasis 1, 3
Hypostatic union 976
hypothecate 771
hypothenuse 217
hypothesis 514
hypothesize 514
hypothetical 475, 514
hypped *insane* 503
dejected 837
hypsometer 206
Hyrcynian wood 533
hysteria
insanity 503
hysteric *violent* 173
hysterical
spasmodic 608
emotional 821
excitable 825
hysterics 173
in – *excited* 824
frightened 860
hysteron proteron 218

I

I 79
iambic 597
ibidem 13
Icarus
navigator 269
rash 863
fate of – 306
ice *cold* 383
refrigerate 385
iceberg 383
ice-bound 383
restraint 751
ice-chest 385
ice-house 387
ice-yacht 273
Ichabod 874
ichnography 554
ichor 333
ichthyology 368
ichthyomancy 511
ichthyophagous 298
icicle 383
icon 554
iconoclasm 983a, 984
iconoclast 165, 913
iconography 554
icosahedron 244
id est 522
idea
small quantity 32
notion 453
give an – of 537
ideal *unreal* 2
completeness 52
erroneous 495
imaginary 515
perfect 650
ideality 450, 515
idée fixe 481
identification
identity 13
comparison 464
discovery 480a
identity 13
– book 206
Ideology 450
Ides of March 601
idiocrasy
essence 5
tendency 176
idiocy 499
idiom 560, 566
idiomatic 79
idiosyncrasy
essence 5
speciality 79
unconformity 83
tendency 176
temperament 820
idiot 501
tale told by an – 517
idiotic
foolish 499
idiotism
folly 499
phrase 566
idle *foolish* 499
trivial 643
slothful 683
lie – *inaction* 681
– conceit 842
– hours 681
be an – man
leisure 685
– talk 588
– time away 683
idler 683
Ido 560
idol *desire* 865
favorite 899
fetich 991
– of the people 899
idolater 984
idolatry 897, 991
idolize *love* 897
impiety 988
idoneous 23
idyl 597
if *circumstance* 8
qualification 469
supposition 514
– you please 765
– possible 470
igloo 189
igneous 382
ignis fatuus
luminary 423
phantom 443
ignite 384
ignoble 876
ignominy 874, 940
ignoramus 493
ignorance 491
keep in – 528
plead – 937
ignoratio elenchi 477
ignore
neglect 460
incredulity 487
not known 491
repudiate 756, 773
ignotum per ignotius 477
ilk 13
ill *evil* 619
badness 649
sick 655
go on – *fail* 732
adversity 735
look – 846
take –
discontent 832
anger 900
– betide 908
– blood *hate* 898
malevolence 907
– at ease *pain* 828
dejection 837
house of – fame 961
–s that flesh is heir to *evil* 619
disease 655
– humor
anger 900
sullenness 901a
– luck 735
as – luck would have it 135
– off
insufficient 640
adversity 735
poor 804
do an – office to 907
bird of – omen 668
– repute 874
– turn *evil* 619
spiteful 907
– usage 907
– will 907
wind *bad* 649
hindrance 706
adversity 735
ill-adapted 24
ill-advised
foolish 499
inexpedient 647
unskilful 699
ill-affected 901a
illapse
conversion 144
ingress 294
illaqueate 545
ill-assorted 24
illation 480
illaudable 947
ill-balanced 28
ill-bred 851, 895
ill-conditioned
bad 649
difficult 704
discourteous 895
malevolent 907
vicious 945
ill-conducted 699
ill-contrived
inexpedient 647
bad 649
unskilful 699
malevolent 907

465a
indispensable 630
indispose
dissuade 616
indisposed
unwilling 603
sick 655
indisputable 474
indissoluble, indissolvable
joined 43
whole 50
stable 150
dense 321
indistinct 447
indistinction 465*a*
indistinguishable
identical 13
invisible 447
indisturbance 265, 826
indite 590
individual
whole 50
special 79
unity 87
person 372
indivisible *whole* 50
dense 321
indocility 158, 606
indoctrinate 537
indolence 683, 927
indomitable
strong 159
determined 601
persevering 604*a*
resisting 719
courage 861
indoor 221
indorse 769, 771
indorsement 550, 551
indraught 343, 348
indubitable 474
induce *cause* 153
power 157
produce 161
motive 615
induct 883
induction
inquiry 461
reasoning 476
drama 599
appointment 755
- *of a priest* 995
indulge *lenity* 740
allow 760
please 829
intemperance 954
gluttony 959
– one's fancy 609
– in 827
– oneself 943
– in reverie
inattention 458
fancy 515
– with *give* 784
indulgence
[*see* indulge]
absolution 918
indulgent *kind* 906
induration
hardening 323
impenitence 951
Indus to the pole, from – 180
industry 625, 682
hive of – 691
indweller 188
indwelling 5
inebriety 959
inedible 395
ineffable *great* 31
inexpressible 521
wonderful 870
ineffaceable 820
ineffectual
incapable 158
useless 645
failing 732
– attempt 732
pale its – fire 422
inefficacious
incapable 158
useless 645
failing 732
inefficient 158
inelastic *soft* 324
– fluid 333
inelasticity **326**
inelegance **579,** 846
ineluctable 474
inept 24, 158, 645
inequality **28**
inequitable 923
ineradicable
intrinsic 5
stable 150
inerrable 946
inertia 172
inertness
physical **172**
inactive 683
moral 823
inestimable 648
inevitable 474, 601
inexact
erroneous 495
feeble 575
inexcitability **826**
inexcusable
accusable 938
vicious 45
inexecution 730
inexhaustible 105, 639
inexistence **2**
inexorable
unavoidable 601
resolved 604
stern 739
compelling 744
pitiless 914*a*
revengeful 919
inexpectation **508**
inexpedience **647**
inexpensive 815
inexperience 491, 699
inexpert 699
inexpiable 945
inexplicable 519
inexpressible
great 31
unmeaning 517
unintelligible 519
wonderful 870
inexpressibles 225
inexpression
latency 526
inexpensive 517
inexpugnable 664
inextension **180a**
littleness 193
immateriality 317
inextinguishable
stable 150
strong 159
excitable 825
– desire 865
inextricable
coherent 46
disorder 59
impossible 471
infallibility 474
assumption of – 885
infamy *shame* 874
dishonor 940
vice 945
infancy 66, 127
infandum renovare dolorem 505, 833
infant **129**
fool 501
– prodigy 872
Infanta 745
infanticide 361, 991
infantine 129
foolish 499
infantry 726
infarction 261
infatuation
misjudgment 481
credulity 486
folly 499
insanity 503
obstinacy 606
passion 825
love 897
infeasible 471
infect *mix with* 41
contaminate 659
excite 824
infectâ, re –
shortcoming 304
non-completion 730
failure 732
infection
transference 270
disease 655
infectious 270, 657
infecund 169
infelicity
inexpertness 699
misery 828
infelicitous 24
infer 472
inference 476, 480
by – 467
inferential
demonstrative 478
latent 526
inferiority
in degree **34**
in size 195
imperfection 651
personal – 34
infernal *bad* 649
malevolent 907
wicked 945
satanic 978
– machine 727
– regions 982
infertility 169
infest 830
infestivity 837, 843
infibulation 43
infidel 487, 989
infidelity
dishonor 940
irreligion 989
infiltrate *mix* 41
intervene 228
interpenetrate 294
moisten 337, 339
teach 537
infiltration
passage 302
Infinite, the – 976
infinite 105
– goodness 976
infinitely *great* 31
infinitesimal
small 32
little 193
– calculus 85
infinity **105**
infirm *weak* 160
disease 655
vicious 945
– of purpose 605
infirmary 662
infirmity
[*see* infirm]
infix 537
inflame
render violent 173
burn 384
excite 824
anger 900
inflamed 382
inflammable 384, 388
inflammation
heating 384
disease 655
inflate *increase* 35
expand 194
blow 349
inflated
overestimation 482
style 573, 577
ridiculous 853
vain 880
inflation
[*see* inflate]
rarefaction 322
currency 800
inflect 245
inflexible *hard* 323
resolved 604
obstinate 606
stern 739
inexorable 914*a*
inflexion
change 140
curvature 245
grammar 567
inflict *act upon* 680
severity 739
– evil 649
– pain
bodily pain 378
mental pain 830
– punishment 972
infliction
adversity 735
mental pain 828, 830
punishment 972
influence 153
change 140
physical – **175**
inducement 615
instrumentality 631
authority 737
absence of – **175a**
sphere of – 780
make one's – felt 631
influx 294
infold 232
inform 527
– against
accuse 938
go to law 969
informal 83, 964
informality 773
informant 527
information
knowledge 490
communication **527**
learning 539
lawsuit 969
pick up – 539
informer 532
informity 241
infra dignitatem 874, 940
infraction
trespass 303
disobedience 742
non-observance 773
exemption 927
– of usage &c.
unconformity 83
desuetude 614
infrangible
combined 46
dense 321
infra-red rays 420
infrequency **137**
infrigidation 385
infringe
transgress 303
disobey 742
not observe 773
undueness 925
dereliction 927
– a law &c. 83
infundibular 252, 269
infuriate
violent 173
excite 824
anger 900
infuscate 431
infuse *mix* 41
insert 300
teach 537
– courage 861
– life into 824
– new blood 658
infusible 321
infusion [*see* infuse]
liquefaction 335
infusoria 193
ingannation 545
ingathering 72
ingemination 90
ingenerate 5
ingenious 515, 698
ingenite 5
ingenium, perfervidum – 682
ingénu *artless* 703
ingénue *actress* 599
ingenuity 698

ingenuous 703
ingesta 298
ingestion 296
ingle 388
inglorious 874, 940
ingluvies 191
ingot 800
ingraft *add* 37
join 43
insert 300
teach 537
ingrafted
extrinsic 6
habit 613
ingrain
insinuate 228
color 428
ingrained
intrinsic 5
combined 48
habit 613
character 820
ingrate 917
ingratiate 897
ingratiating 894
ingratitude **917**
ingredient 51, 56
ingress **294**
forcible – 300
ingurgitate 296
ingustible 391
inhabile 699
inhabit 186
inhabitant **188**
inhale *receive* 296
breathe 349
smell 398
inharmonious
discord 713
– color 428
– sound 414
inhere 1
inherent 5, 820
inherit 775, 777
inheritance 780
– of the saints 981
inherited
intrinsic 5
inheritor 779
inhesion 5
inhibit *hinder* 706
restrain 751
prohibit 761
inhospitable 893
inhuman 907
inhume 363
inimaginable
impossible 471
improbable 473
wonderful 870
inimical 708, 889
inimitable
non-imitation 20
supreme 33
very good 648
perfect 650
iniquity 923, 945
worker of – 949
inirritability 826
initial 66
– letter 558
initiate *begin* 66
admit 296
teach 537
initiated *skilful* 698
initiative 66
inject 300, 337
injection 662
injudicial 964
injudicious 499, 863
injunction
acquirement 630
advice 695
command 741
prohibition 761
injure *evil* 619
damage 659
spite 907
injuria formae, spretae – 846, 930
injury *evil* 619
badness 649
damage 659
injustice 923
ink 431
pen and – 590
before the – is dry 132
– slinging 720
inkle 45
inkling
knowledge 490
supposition 514
information 527
inkstand 590
inland 221
inlay 440, 847
inlet *beginning* 66
interval 198
opening 260
ingress 294
- *of the sea* 343
inly 221
inmate 188
inmost 221
to the – core 822
– soul 820
– thoughts 451
inn 189
– s of Court 968
innate 5, 601
innavigable 471
inner 221
– coating 224
– man *intellect* 450
affections 820
innermost recesses 221
innings *land* 342
acquisition 775
receipt 810
innkeeper 601
innocence **946**
innocent *fool* 501
good 648
healthy 656
artless 703
guiltless 946
innocuous *good* 648
healthy 656
innocent 946
innominate 565
innovation
variation 20a
new 123
change 140
innoxious
salubrious 656
innocent 946
innuendo *hint* 527
censure 932
innumerable 105
innutritious 657
inobservance 773
inoccupation 681
inoculate
insert 300
teach 537
influence 615
inodorous **399**
inoffensive 648, 946
inofficious 907
inoperative
powerless 158
unproductive 169
useless 645
inopportune
untimely 135
inexpedient 647
inordinate 31, 641
inorganization **358**
inornate 849
inosculate *join* 43
intersect 219
convoluted 248
inquest 461
inquietude
changeable 149
uneasy 828
discontent 832
apprehension 860
inquinate 659
inquire 461
– into 595
inquirer 461
inquiring mind 455
inquiry **461**
inquisition
inquiry 461
severity 739
torture 907
tribunal 966
inquisitive 455
inquisitorial
prying 455
inquiry 461
severe 739
jurisdiction 965
inroad *ingress* 294
devastation 659
invasion 716
inrolment 551
insalubrity **657**
insanity **503**
insatiable 865
inscribe 590, 873
inscription 551
inscroll 551
inscrutable 519
insculpture 557
insculptured 558
insecable 43, 87
insect *minute* 193
animal 366
– cry 412
insecure
uncertain 475
danger 665
insensate
foolish 499
insane 503
insensibility
slow 275
physical **376**
moral **823**
– of benefits 917
– to the past 506
inseparable 43, 46
insert *locate* 184
interpose 228
enter 294
put in 300
record 551
– itself 300
insertion **300**
adjunct 39
ornament 847
inservient 645
inseverable 43, 87
inside 221
– out 218
turn – out 529
insidious
deceitful 545
cunning 702
dishonourable 940
insight 465, 490
insignia 550
– of authority **747**
insignificant
unmeaning 517
unimportant 643
insincere 544, 855
insinuate
intervene 228
ingress 294
insert 300
latency 526
hint 527
ingratiate 897
blame 932
insipid
style 575
dull 840
insipidity
tasteless **391**
indifferent 866
insist *argue* 476
command 741
– upon *affirm* 535
dwell on 573
be determined 604
contend 720
compel 744
conditions 770
due 924
insnare 545
insobriety 959
insolation 382, 384
insolence 878, 885
insoluble *dense* 321
unintelligible 519
insolvable 519
insolvent
poverty 804
debt 806
non-payment 808
insomnia 682
insouciance
thoughtlessness 458
supineness 823
indifference 866
inspan 293
inspect 441, 457
inspector 444
inquisitor 461
judge 480
director 694
inspiration
wisdom 498
imagination 515
poetry 577
impulse 612
motive 615
feeling 821
Deity 976
revelation 985
religious - 987
inspire *improve* 658
prompt 615
animate 824
cheer 836
– courage 861
– hope 858
– respect 928
inspirit *incite* 615
animate 824
encourage 861
inspiriting
hopeful 858
inspissate 321, 352
instability 149
install *locate* 184
commission 755
celebrate 883
instalment
portion 51
payment 807, 809
instance
example 82
motive 615
solicitation 765
instant *moment* 113
present 118
destiny 152
required 630
importance 642
active 682
lose not an – 684
on the – 132
instantaneity **113**
instanter 113, 132
instar omnium 17, 82
instate 883
instauration 660
instead 147
instep 245
instigate 615
instil *extrinsic* 6
mix 41
insert 300
teach 537
instinct
intellect 450
intuition 477
impulse 601
– with *motive* 615
possession 777
brute – 450*a*
instinctive
inborn 5
institute *begin* 66
cause 153
produce 161
academy 542
society 712
– an inquiry 461
institution
academy 542
society 712
political - 963
church 995
institutor 540
instruct *teach* 537
advise 695
precept 697
order 741
instructed 490
instructor 540
instrument
implement **633**

stable 150
necessary 601
resolute 604
hopeless 859
irrigate 337
irriguous 339
irrision 856, 929
irritabile, genus – 901
irritable 825, 901
irritate *violent* 173
excite 824
pain 830
provoke 898
incense 900
irritation
[*see* irritate]
pain 828
source of – 830
irritating
[*see* irritate]
stringent 171
irruption 294, 716
Irvingite 984
Ishmael 83
is: that – 118
– to be 152
Isis 979
Islamism 984
island 181, 346
–s of the blessed 981
islander 188
isle 346
isobar 338
isocheimal 383
isochronal 114
isochronous 27, 120
isolate 44, 893
isolated 10, 87
isomorphism 240
isoperimetrical 27
isothermal 382
– layer 338
isotonic 413
issue *distribute* 73
focus 74
event 151
effect 154
posterity 167
depart 293
egress 295
stream 348, 349
inquiry 461
publication 531
book 593
ulcer 655
dénouement 729
money 800
at – *discussion* 476
dissent 489
negation 536
opposition 708
discord 713
contention 720
in – 461
join – *lawsuit* 969
– a command 741
issueless 169
isthmus
connection 45
narrow 203
land 342
italics *mark* 550
put in –
importance 642
itch *titillation* 380
desire 865
itching palm 819
item
addition 37, 39
part 51
speciality 79
unit 87
iteration 104
itinerant 266, 268
itinerary 266, 527
itur ad astra, sic – 360
ivory 430
Ixion 312

J

jab 276
jabber
unmeaning 517
stammer 583
chatter 584
jacent 213
jacet, hic – 363
jacinth 847
jack
rotation 312
ensign 550
instrument 633
money 800
Jack – Cade 742
– Ketch 975
– o' lantern 423
– in office
director 694
bully 887
– at a pinch 711
– Pudding
actor 599
humorist 844
boaster 884
before one can say '– Robinson' 132
– tar 269
– of all trades 700
jack-a-dandy 844, 854
jackal
auxiliary 711
servility 886
jackanapes 854, 887
Jackass 271
jack-boot 225
jackdaw in peacock's feathers 701
jacket 225
cork – 666
Jacobin 710
Jacquerie 716, 719
jacta est alea 601
jactitation
tossing 315
boasting 884
jaculation 284
jade *horse* 271
fatigue 688
low woman 876
scamp 949
drab 962
jag 257
jagged 244
jail 752
– bird
prisoner 754
bad man 949
jailer 753, 975
jakes 653
jalousie de métier 921
jam *squeeze* 43
crowd 72
food 298
pulp 354
sweet 396
scrape 732
– in *interpose* 228
jamb 215
jamboree 840
jammed in 751
jangle
harsh sound 410
quarrel 713
janissary 726
janitor 263
janty *gay* 836
pretty 845
stylish 852
showy 882
insolent 885
January 138
januis clausis 528
Janus *deceiver* 607
tergiversation 607
close the temple of – 723
Janus-faced 544
japan *coat* 223
resin 356a
ornament 847
jar *clash* 24
vessel 191
agitation 315
stridor 410
discord 713
– upon the feelings 830
jardinière 191
jargon
absurdity 497
no meaning 517
unintelligible 519
neology 563
jarvey 694
jasper 847
jaundiced
yellow 436
prejudiced 481
dejected 837
jealous 920
view with – eyes
disapprove 932
jaunt 266
jaunting car 272
jaunty [*see* janty]
javelin 727
jaw *chatter* 584
scold 932
jaw-fallen 837
jaws *mouth* 231
eating 298
– of death 360
jay 584
jaywalker 701
jazz 415, 840
– band 417
jealous of honor 939
jealousy 920
suspicion 485
jecur, difficili bile – 900
jeer 929
Jehovah 976
Jehu 268, 694
jejune *insipid* 391
style 575
scanty 640
dull 843
jell 352
jelly 298, 352
beat to a – 972
jemidar 745
jemmy *lever* 633
dandy 854
je ne sais quoi
exceptional 83
what d'ye call 'em 563
beauty 845
jennet 271
jeopardy 665
jerboa 309
jeremiad
lament 839
invective 932
Jericho, send to – 297
jerk *start* 146
throw 284
pull 285
agitate 315
jerkin 225
jerks, by – 70
Jerry Sneak 862, 941
jersey 225
Jerusalem
the new – 981
Jessamy, Jemmy – 854
jesse 1000
jest *trifle* 643
wit 842
jest-book 842
jester 844
jesting-stock 857
Jesuit *deceiver* 548
priest 996
jesuitical 477, 544
Jesus 976
jet *ship* 273
stream 348
— black 431
— propulsion 267
jetsam 73, 782
jettison 782
jetty *protection* 250
harbor 666
jeu
le – n'en vaut pas la chandelle
waste 638
unimportant 643
dear 814
– d'esprit 842
– de mots 842
– de théâtre 599
jeune
– premier 599
– veuve 599
jewel *gem* 648
ornament 847
favorite 899
jewelery; false – 545
Jezebel *wicked* 913
wretch 949
courtesan 962
jib *front* 234
regression 283
cut of one's –
form 240
appearance 448
jibe 140
jiffy 113
jig 840
jig-saw puzzle 840
jilt *disappoint* 509
deceive 545
deceiver 548
cast off 756
dishonor 940
jilted 898
jimp 845
jingal 727
jingle 408
jingo 887
jingoism 884
jinks, high – 840
jinriksha 272
jinx 649, 735
Joan of Arc 861
job *business* 625
action 680
unfair 940
tough – 704
Job:
patience of – 826, 830
poor as – 804
–'s comforter
dejection 837
hopeless 859
jobation 932
jobber
deceiver 548
tactician 700
merchant 797
trickster 943
jobbernowl 501
jobbery 702, 940
jobbing *barter* 794
jockey *rider* 268
deceive 545
deceiver 548
servant 746
jocose 836, 842
jocoseness *fun* 840
jocular 836, 842
jocund 836, 840
jocundity 829
Joe Miller 842, 844
jog *push* 276
shake 315
– the memory 505
– on *continue* 143
trudge 266
slow 275
advance 282
mediocrity 736
joggle 315
jog-trot
trudge 266
slow 275
habit 613

landscape
prospect 448
– gardening
agriculture 71
beauty 845
– painting 556
– painter 559
land-shark 792
land-slip 306
landsman 342
Landsturm 726
land-surveying 466
Landwehr 726
lane 189, 260, 627
langrel 727
lang-syne 122
language 560
command of – 582
strong –
vigor 574
malediction 908
languid *weak* 160
inert 172
slow 275
- *style* 575
inactive 683
torpid 823
languish
decrease 36
ill 655
inactive 683
repine 828
– for 865
languishing
weak 160
affected 855
languishment
lament 839
languor
[*see* languid]
lank 200
lanky 203, 206
lantern
window 260
lamp 423
magic – 448
– of Diogenes 461
– jaws 203
lanterne, à la – 972
lanuginous 256
lanyard 45
Laodicean 822
lap *abode* 189
support 215
interior 221
wrap 225
encompass 227, 229
drink 298
– of luxury
pleasure 377
inactivity 683
voluptuousness 954
lap-dog *animal* 366
servile 886
lapel 39
lapidary 559
lapidate *kill* 361
attack 716
punish 972
lapidescence 323
lapis lazuli
blue 438
jewel 847
lappet 39, 214
lapse *course* 109
past 122
conversion 144
fall 306
degeneracy 659
relapse 661
loss 776
vice 945
guilt 947
– of memory 506
– of time 109
lapsus calami 495
lapsus linguae
mistake 495
solecism 568
stammering 583
Laputa, college of 538
larboard 239
larceny 791
lard 356
lardaceous 355
larder 636
contents of the – 298
lares et penates
home 189
idols 991
large
quantity 31
size 192
at – *diffuse* 573
free 748
become – 194
– number 102
– type 642
large-hearted
liberal 816
benevolent 906
disinterested 942
larger 194
largest 784
largest portion 192
larghetto 275, 415
largiloquent 573
largo 275, 415
lariat 45, 247
lark *ascent* 305
pleasure 827
spree 840
with the – 125
larmes:
fondre en – 839
– aux yeux 839
larmoyante, comédie – 599
larrikin 887, 913
larrup 972
larum 404, 669
larva 129
larynx 351
lascar 269
lasciate ogni speranza 859
lascivious 961
lash *tie together* 43
violence 173
incite 615
censure 932
punish 972
scourge 975
under the – *compelled* 744
subject 749
– into fury 909
– with the tongue 931
– the waves 645
lass *girl* 129
lassitude 680, 841
lasso 45, 247
last *model* 22
- *in order* 67
endure 106
durable 110
- in time 122
continue 141
at – 133
breathe one's – 360
game to the – 604*a*
never hear the – of 104
– but one &c. 67
die in the – ditch 604*a*
– for ever 112
at the – extremity 665
– finish 729
– gasp 360
go to one's – home 360
on – legs *weak* 160
dying 360
spoiled 659
adversity 735
– resort 666
– rites 998
– shift 601
– sleep 360
– stage 67
– straw 153
– stroke 729
– touch 729
– word
affirmation 535
obstinacy 606
– year &c. 122
latch 43, 45
latchet 45
latch-key 631
late *past* 122
new 123
tardy 133
dead 360
too – 135
lately 122, 123
latency 526
lateness 133
latent 172, 526
– organism 153
later 117
laterality 236
lateritious 434
latest 118
latet anguis in herbâ 66
lath 205
thin as a – 203
lathe
region 181
machine 633
lather 332, 353
Latin
au bout de son – 704
perdre son – 704
thieves' – 563
latitancy 528
latitat 969
latitude *extent* 180
region 181
breadth 202
measurement 466
freedom 748
– and longitude
situation 183
latitudinarian 984, 989
latration 412
latria 990
latrines 653
latrociny 791
latter *sequent* 63
past 122
Latter-day Saint 984
latterly 123
lattice *crossing* 219
opening 260
laud 931, 990
laudable 944
laudanum 174
laudari a laudato viro 931
laudator 935
– temporis acti
past 122
habit 613
discontent 832
detractor 936
laudatory 931
laugh 838
make one – 853
raise a – 840
– at *ridicule* 856
sneer 929
(*undervalue* 483)
– to scorn *defy* 715
despise 930
– in one's sleeve
latent 526
ridicule 856
disrespect 929
contempt 930
– on the wrong side of one's mouth
disappointed 509
dejected 837
in disrepute 874
laughable 853
laughing:
no – matter 642
– gas 376
laughing-stock 857
laughter-loving 836
launch *begin* 66
boat 273
propel 284
– forth 676
– into 676
– into eternity 360, 361
– out 573
– out against 716
laundress 652, 746
laundry *room* 191
heat 386
clean 652
– maid 746
– man 652
laureate 875
poet – 597
laurel *trophy* 733
glory 873
decoration 877
repose on one's –s 265
lava *excretion* 299
semiliquid 352
lavatory 652
lave *water* 337
clean 652
lavender *colour* 437
laver la tête 932
lavish *profuse* 641
give 784
squander 818
– of praise 931
law *regularity* 80
statue 697
permission 760
legality 963
court of – 966
give the – 737
go to – 969
Jewish – 985
lay down the –
certainty 474
affirm 535
command 741
learned in the – 968
set the – at defiance 964
take the – into one's own hands 722, 712
– of the Medes and Persians 80, 148
take the – of 969
law-abiding 743
lawful
permitted 760
due 924
legal 963
lawgiver 694
lawless 59
irregular 83
mutinous 742
non-observant 773
vicious 945
arbitrary 964
lawn *plain* 344
grass 367
agriculture 371
– sleeves 999
– tennis 840
lawsuit 969
lawyer 968
lax *incoherent* 47
soft 324
error 495
- *style* 575
remiss 738
non-observance 773
dishonorable 940
licentious 945
irreligious 989
laxity 738
lay *moderate* 174
place 184
ley 344
music 415
poetry 597
bet 621
secular 997
– about one
active 682
exertion 686
attack 716
contend 720
punish 972
– one's account for

484
– apart
exclude 55
relinquish 782
– aside
neglect 460
reject 610
disuse 678
give up 782
– on the table 133
– the axe at the root of tree 162
– bare 529
– before 527
– brother 996
– by *store* 636
sickness 655
disuse 678
– to one's charge 938
– claim to 924
– in the dust 162
– eggs 161
– at the door of 155
– down [*see* below]
– at one's feet 763
– figure *nonentity* 4
model 22
representation 554
– one's finger upon 480*a*
– the first stone 66
– the flattering unction to one's soul 831, 834
– the foundations 153, 673
– ghosts 992
– hands on
use 677
take 789
rite 998
– under hatches 751
– one's head on the block 942
– heads together 695, 709
– in *eat* 298
store 636
provide 637
– on 972
open *divest* 226
opening 260
show 525
disclose 529
– oneself open to 177
– out
horizontal 213
corpse 363
plan 626
expend 809
– oneself out for 673
– over 133
– reader 996
– under restraint 751
– in ruins 162
– siege to 716
– stress on 642
– to *attribute* 155
rest 265
– it on thick
cover 223
too much 641
flatter 933
– together 43
– train 626
– up *store* 636
sickness 655
disuse 678
– waste 162
lay down *locate* 184
horizontal 213
assert 535
renounce 757
relinquish 782
pay 807
– one's arms
pacification 723
submission 725
– the law
certain 474
assert 535
command 741
insolence 885
– one's life 360
– a plan 626
layer **204**
layette 225
layman 699, 997
laystall 653
lazaret 662
lazar-house 662
lazy 683, 927
lazzarone 683
lb. 319
lea *land* 342
plain 344
leach 335
lead *superiority* 33
in order 62
pioneer 64
influence 175
tend 176
soundings 208
- *in motion* 280
heavy 319
rôle 599
induce 615
direct 693
authority 737
heave the – 466
red – 434
take the –
influence 175
importance 642
authority 737
white – 420
– to the altar 903
– astray 495
– captive
subject 749
restraint 751
– a merry chase 623
– the choir 990
– a dance
run away 623
circuit 629
difficulty 704
disrespect 929
– the dance 280
– one to expect 511
– a life 692
– on 693
– to no end 645
– by the nose 737
– off 62
– the way
precedence 62
begin 66
precession 280
importance 642
direction 693
repute 873
leaden *dim* 422
colorless 429
grey 432
inactive 683
leader
precursor 64
dissertation 595
director 694
counsel 968
– writer 593
leading
beginning 66
important 642
– article 595
– lady 599
– note *music* 413
– part 175
– question 461
– seaman 745
– strings
childhood 127
child 129
pupil 541
subject 749
restraint 751, 752
leads 223
leaf *part* 51
layer 204
plant 367
- *of a book* 593
turn over a new – 658
– green 435
leafless 226
leaflet 531
leafy 256
league *length* 200
co-operation 709
party 712
– of Nations 696
leak *crack* 198
dribble 295
waste 638
spring a –
injury 659
– out
disclosure 529
leaky *imperfect* 651
leal 743
lean *thin* 203
oblique 217
– on 215
– to *shed* 191
willing 602
– towards 923
– upon *belief* 484
subjection 749
hope 858
leaning
tendency 176
willingness 602
desire 865
friendship 888
favoritism 923
leap
sudden change 146
ascent 305
jump **309**
–s and bounds 274
make a – at 622
– in the dark
experiment 463
uncertain 475
chance 621
rash 863
– with joy 838
– year 138
leap-frog 840
learn 490, 539
– by experience 950
– by heart 505
learned 490
learner **541**
learning 490, **539**
lease *property* 780
lending 787
grant a – 771
take a new – of life 654
– and release 783
leasehold 780
leash *tie* 43
three 92
hold in – 751
least
– *in quantity* 34
– *in size* 193
at the – 32
leather *skin* 223
tough 327
beat 972
nothing like – 481
– bottle 191
– or prunello 643
leave *remainder* 40
part company 44
relinquish 624
permission 760
bequeathe 784
French – 623
take – *depart* 293
freedom 748
– alone
inaction 681
freedom 748
permit 760
– the beaten track 83
– to chance 621
– an inference 526
– a loophole 705
– in the lurch
pass 303
decisive 545
– no trace
be no more 2
disappear 449
obliterate 552
– it to one 76
– to oneself 748
– off *cease* 142
desuetude 614
relinquish 624
disuse 678
– out 55
– out of one's calculation 460
– a place 293
– ad referendum 605
give me – to say 535
– undecided 609*a*
– undone 730
– a void *regret* 833
– word 527
leaven
component 56
cause 153
lighten 320
qualify 469
unclean 653
deterioration 659
bane 663
leavings
remainder 40
useless 645
lecher 962
lechery 961
lectern 1000
lection *special* 79
interpretation 522
lectionary 998
lecture *teach* 537
speak 582
dissertation 595
censure 932
sermon 998
– room 542
lecturer
teacher 540
preacher 996
lectureship 542
led – captain
follower 746
servile 886
favorite 899
– by the nose 749
ledge *height* 206
horizontal 213
shelf 215
projection 250
ledger *list* 86
record 551
accounts 811
lee 236
leech 662, 695
leef 829
leek eat the –
recant 607
submit 725
Lee-Metford
rifle 727
leer *stare* 441
dumb-show 550
leery 702, 864
lees 653
lee-shore 665, 667
leet, court – 966
lee-wall 666
leeward 236
lee-way *space* 180
tardy 133
navigation 267
deviation 279
progression 282
shortcoming 304
left *residuary* 40
sinistral 239
over the – 545
– alone 748
– in the lurch 732
– to shift for oneself 893
pay over the – shoulder 808
left-handed
clumsy 699
– compliment 932
– marriage 903
leg *support* 215
walker 266

thief 792
best – foremost 686
fast as –s will carry 274
have a – to stand on 470
keep on one's –s 654
last –s *spoiled* 659
fatigue 688
light on one's –s 734
make a – 894
not a – to stand on
illogical 477
confuted 479
failure 732
off one's –s
propulsion 284
on one's –s
upright 212
elevation 307
speaking 582
in health 654
active 682
free 748
set on one's –s 660
– bail 623
legacy 270, 780, 784
legal *permitted* 760
legitimate 924
relating to law 963
adviser 968
– estate 780
legality **963**
legate 534
legatee 779, 785
legation 755
legato 415
legend 551, 594
legendary
imaginary 515
legerdemain 146, 545
légèreté 605
leggings 225
leghorn hat 225
legible 518
– hand 590
legion
multitude 102
army 726
legionary 726
legislation 693, 963
legislative assembly 696
legislator 694
legislature 693, 696
legist 968
legitimate *true* 494
permitted 760
right 922
due 924
legal 963
legume 367
lei 847
leisure **685**
at one's – *late* 133
leisurely 275
leman 897
lemma 476
lemon *color* 436
Lemprière 979
lemures 980
lend 787
– aid 707
– countenance 707
– a hand 680
– oneself to
assent 488
co-operate 709
– on security 789
– wings to 707
lender *creditor* 805
lending **787**
length **200**
go all –s
resolution 604
activity 682
exertion 686
at – *in time* 133
full – *portrait* 556
go great –s 549
– and breadth of 50
– and breadth of the land
space 180
publication 531
– of time 110
lengthen 35, 200
– out
diuturnity 110
late 133
lengthwise 200
lengthy *long* **200**
diffuse 573
lenient
moderate 174
mild 740
compassionate 914
lenify 174
lenitive
moderating 174
remedy 662
relieving 834
lenity **740**
lens 445
Lent 956, 998
lenten 956
lenticular 245, 250
lentor *slowness* 275
spissitude 352
inactivity 683
lentous 352
leonem, ex ungue – 550
leonine verses 597
leopard
variegated 440
–'s spots
unchanging 150
leprechaune 980
leprosy 655
lerret 273
lèse-majesté 742
less *inferior* 34
subduction 38
– than no time 113
lessee
possessor 779
receiver 785
lessen
– in quantity or degree 36
– in size 195
– an evil 658
lesson *teaching* 537
warning 668
give a – to
punish 972
read a – to
censure 932
say one's –
memory 505
lessor 805
lest 623
let *hindrance* 706
permit 760
lease 771
lend 787
sell 796
apartments to –
fool 499
to – 763
– alone *besides* 37
permanence 141
quiescence 265
avoid 623
disuse 678
inaction 681
not complete 730
free 748
– be
permanence 141
continuance 143
inaction 681
– blood 297
– 'I dare not' wait upon 'I would' 605
– down
depress 308
humble 879
– down easily
forgive 918
– fall *drop* 308
inform 527
speak 582
– fly *violence* 173
propel 284
– fly at 716
– go *neglect* 460
liberate 750
relinquish 782
restitution 790
– in *interpose* 228
admit 296
trick 545
– into *inform* 490
disclose 529
– one know 527
– off *violent* 173
propel 284
permit 760
forgive 918
exempt 927a
acquit 970
– out *disperse* 73
lengthen 200
eject 297
disclose 529
liberate 750
– out at 716
– pass 460
– slip
miss an opportunity 135
neglect 460
not complete 730
lose 776
relinquish 782
– the matter stand over 133
– things take their course 143
– well alone
content 831
caution 864
lethal 361
– chamber 975
lethalis arundo, haeret lateri – 900
lethargy 683, 823
Lethe 982
waters of – 506
lethiferous 361
letter *mark* 550
character **561**
epistle 592
to the – 494
– card 524
– of credit 805
– of the law 494
– writer 592
letter-bag 534
letter-carrier 534
lettered 490
letterpress 591
letters
knowledge 490
language 560
description 594
in large – 642
man of – 492
– of marque 791
lettres de cachet 751
leucophlegmatic 823
leucorrhea 299
Levant *east* 236
levant *abscond* 623
levanter *wind* 349
defaulter 808
levée *assemblage* 72
sociality 892
– en masse 719
level *uniform* 16
equal 27
destroy 162
horizontal 213
instrument 213, 217
flat 251
smooth 255
lower 308
– at *direct* 278
intend 620
attack 716
– best 686
– headed 826
– off 27
– with the ground 207
lever *cause* 153
instrument 633
– de rideau 599
leverage 175
leviathan 192
levigate 255, 330
levitate 320
Levite 996
levity *lightness* **320**
irresolution 605
trifle 643
jocularity 836
rashness 863
levy *muster* 72
military 726
distrain 789
demand 812
lewd 961
Lewis gun 727
lex – mercatoria 963
– scripta 697
– scripta et non-scripta 963
– talionis
retaliation 718
right 922
lexicography 562
lexicology 562
lexicon 86, 562
ley 344
liability **177**
debt 806
duty 926
liaison 961
liar 548
libation
potation 298
drunkenness 959
worship 990
libel 934, 938
libelant 989
libeller 936
liberal *ample* 639
– party 712
generous 816
disinterested 942
over – 818
– education
knowledge 490
teaching 537
liberalism
freedom 748
liberality
giving 784
generosity **816**
liberate 672
liberation **750**
liberavi animam meam 703
libertinage 961
libertine **962**
libertinism 961
liberty *freedom* 748
permission 760
right 924
exemption 927a
gain one's – 750
set at – *free* 750
exempt 927a
take a –
arrogate 739
make free 748
insolence 885
discourtesy 895
libidinous 961
libitum, ad –
at will 600
enough 639
freely 748
librarian 593, 694
library *room* 191, 593
books 593
storehouse 636
librate 314
libretto 593, 599
licence *laxity* 738
permission 760
right 924
exemption 927a
– to plunder 791
licentiate 492
licentious *lax* 738
dissolute 954

lion
courage 861
prodigy 872
repute 873
come in like a – 183
as dewdrops from the –'s mane 483
in the –'s den 665
– lies down with the lamb 721
put one's head in the –'s mouth 665
– in the path 706
–'s share *more* 33
chief part 50
too much 641
undue 925
lioness 374
lion-hearted 861
lionize 455, 873
lip *beginning* 66
edge 231
side 236
prominence 250
between cup and – 111
finger on the –s
silent 581
speechless 585
hang on the –s of 418
open one's –s
speak 582
seal the –s 585
smack the –
taste 390
savory 394
– homage
flattery 933
– service
falsehood 544
hypocrisy 988
– wisdom 499
lip salve 847
lipstick 847
lipothymy 688
lippitude 443
liquefaction 335, 384
liquescence 335
liqueur 298, 396
liquid
fluid 333
sound 405
letter 561
liquidate 807, 812
liquidator 801
liquor *potable* 298
fluid 333
in – 959
– up 959
liquorice 396
liquorish [*see* lickerish]
lisp 583
lissom 324
list *catalogue* **86**
strip 205
leaning 217
fringe 231
hear 418
record 551
will 600
choose 609
arena 728
desire 865
enter the –s
attack 716
contend 720
listed 440
listel 847
listen 418
– in 455
– to 457
be –ed to 175
– to reason 498
listless
inattentive 458
inactive 683
indifferent 866
litany 990, 998
lite, pendente – 969
literae scriptae 590
literal
imitated 19
exact 494
manifest 525
letter 561
word 562
orthodox 983a
– meaning 516
– translation 522
literarum
homo multarum – 492
homo trium – 792
literary 560
– hack 593
– man 492
– power 569
literati 492
literatim [*see* literal]
literature 490, 560
lithe 324
lithic 323
lithograph 558
lithology 358
lithomancy 511
lithotint 558
litigant
litigious 713
combatant 726
accusation 938
litigation
quarrel 713
contention 730
lawsuit 969
litigious 713
litter *disorder* 59
derange 61
multitude 102
brood 167
support 215
vehicle 272
useless 645
littéraire, la morgue – 569
littérateur 492, 593
little
- *in degree* 32
- *in size* 193
darling 897
mean 940
cost – 815
do – 683
make – of 483
signify – 643
think – of 458
- did one think 508
– by little
degree 26
slowly 275
– Mary 191
– one 129
to – purpose
useless 645
failure 732
littleness **193**
littoral 342
liturgy 978
live *exist* 1
continue 141
energetic 171
dwell 186
life 359
repute 873
– apart 905
– to fight again 110
– from hand to mouth 674
– hard 954
– in hope 858
– and let live
inaction 681
freedom 748
inexcitability 826
– in the memory 505
– upon nothing 819
– on 298
– separately 905
by one's wits 545
livelihood 803
livelong 110
lively *keen* 375
- *style* 574
active 682
acute 821
sensitive 822
sprightly 836
– imagination 515
– pace 274
liver 83; hard – 954a
white – 862
liver-colored 433
livery *suit* 225
color 428
badge 550
decoration 877
– servant 746
liveryman 748
live wire 171
livid *dark* 431
grey 432
purple 437
living *life* 359
business 625
benefice 995
good – 957
– beings 357
–room 191
– soul 372
– thing 366
livraison 593
livret 593
lixiviate 335, 652
lixivium 335
llama 271
lo! 457, 870
load *quantity* 31
fill 52
lade 184
cargo 190
weight 319
store 636
redundance 641
hindrance 706
adversity 735
anxiety 828
oppress 830
prime and – 673
take off a – of care 834
– the memory 505
– with 706
– with reproaches 932
loads 102
loadstar [*see* lodestar]
loaf *mass* 192
do nothing 681
dawdle 683
loafer
stroller 268
inactive 683
neglect 927
bad man 949
loam 342
loan 787
loathe 867, 898
loathing
[*see* loathe]
weariness 841
hate 898
loathsome
unsavory 395
painful 830
dislike 867
loaves and fishes
prosperity 734
acquisition 775
wealth 803
Lob's pound, in – 751
lobby 191, 615, 627
lobbying 615
lobe 51
local
– habitation 184, 189
– board 966
locale 183
locality 182, 183
localize 184
location **184**
loch 343
loci, genius – 664
lock *fasten* 43
fastening 45
tuft 256
canal 350
hindrance 706
prison 752
dead – 265
in the –up 938
under – and key
safe 664
restraint 751
prisoner 754
– hospital 662
–out 55, 719
– the stable door
too late 135
useless 645
unskilful 699
–, stock and barrel 50
– up *hide* 528
imprison 751
locker 191
locket 847
lock-up *prison* 752
loco, in –
agreeing 23
situation 183
expedience 646
locofoco 388
locomotion 264
– by air 267
– by land 266
– by water 267
locomotive 266, 271
locular 191
locum tenens
substitute 147
inhabitant 188
deputy 759
locus:
– poenitentiae 937
– standi
support 215
plea 617
social rank 873
locust *prodigal* 818
evil-doer 913
swarm like –s 102
locution 582
lode 636
lodestar
attraction 288
indication 550
direction 693
lodestone 288, 615
lodge *place* 184
presence 186
dwelling 189
– a complaint 938
lodgement 184
lodger
inhabitant 188
possessor 779
lodging 189
loft 191, 210
lofty *high* 206
- *style* 574
proud 878
insolent 885
magnanimous 942
log *velocity* 274
fuel 388
record 551
heave the – 466
sleep like a – 683
logarithm 84
loggerhead 501
at –s *discord* 713
contention 720
enmity 889
loggia 191
logic 476
– of facts 467
logician 476
logical acuteness 570
logography 590
logogryph 533
logolept 562
logomachy
discussion 476
words 588
dispute 720
logometer 85
logometric 84
log-rolling 709

love *desire* 865
courtesy 894
affection **897**
favorite 899
abode of – 897
labor of –
willing 602
inexpensive 815
amusement 840
disinterested 942
God's – 906
make – 902
no – lost 713
– affair 897
– of country 910
– lock 256
not for – or money 640, 814
love-knot *token* 550
love-lorn 898
lovely 845, 897
love-making 902
love-pot 959
love-potion 865
lover [*see* love]
love-sick 897, 902
love-story 897, 902
love-token 897, 902
loving-cup 892, 894
loving-kindness 906
low *small* 32
not high 207
– *sound* 405
moo 412
vulgar 851
disreputable 874
common 876
base 940
bring – 308
– condition 876
– comedy 599
at a – ebb
small 32
inferior 34
depressed 308
waste 638
deteriorated 659
– fellow 876
– life 851
– note 408
– origin 876
– price 815
– spirits 837
– tide 207
– tone *black* 431
mutter 581
– water *low* 207
dry 340
insufficient 640
poor 804
low-born 876
low-brow 491
low-lands 207
low-minded 876, 940
lower *inferior* 34
decrease 36
overhang 214
depress 308
dark 421
dim 422
predict 511
sad 837
irate 900
sulky 901a
– one's flag 725
– one's note 879
– orders 876
lowering 668, 859
lowly 879
lown 501, 949
lowness [*see* low] **207**
humility 879
loy 272
loyal *obedient* 743
observant 772
honourable 939
lozenge 244, 662
L. s. d. 800
lubbard [*see* lubber]
lubber 683, 701
lubberly 192, 699
lubricant 332
lubrication 255, **332**
lubricity
slippery 255
unctuous 355
impure 961
lucent 420
lucid
luminous 420
transparent 425
intelligible 518
– *style* 570
– interval 502
lucidus ordo 58
lucifer 388
Lucifer 423, 978
lucimeter 445
luck *chance* 156, 621
prosperity 701
good – 858
luckless 735
lucky 134, 731
lucrative 775
lucre 775, 803
Lucretia 960
luctation 720
lucubration 451
luculent 420
lucus a non lucendo 18, 565
lud! O – 839
ludibrious 840
ludicrous 853
luff 267
lug *pull* 285
ear 418
luge 272
luggage 270, 780
– van 272
lugger 273
lugubrious 837
lukewarm
temperate 382
irresolute 605
torpid 823
indifferent 866
lull *cessation* 142
mitigate 174
silence 403
– to sleep 265
lullaby
moderate 174
song 415
verses 597
inactivity 683
relief 834
lumbago 378
lumbar 235
lumbar *disorder* 59
slow 275
store 636
useless 645
hindrance 706
lumbering 647, 846
lumber-room 191
lumbriciform 249
luminary *star* 318
light **423**
sage 500
luminescence 420
luminous *light* 420
intelligible 518
– paint 423
lump *whole* 50
chief part 51
amass 72
mass 192
projection 250
weight 319
density 321
in the – 50
– of affectation 855
– sum 800
– together *join* 43
combine 48
assemble 72
lumpish [*see* lump]
inactive 683
ugly 846
Luna 318
lunacy 503
lunar 318
– caustic 384
lunatic 503, 504
luncheon 298
lune avec les dents, prendre la – 158, 471
lunette 717
lunge 276, 716
lungs *wind* 349
loudness 404
shout 411
voice 580
luniform &c. 245
lupanar 961
lurch *incline* 217
sink 306
oscillation 314
failure 732
leave in the –
outstrip 303
deceive 545
relinquish 624
left in the –
defeated 732
lure *attraction* 288, 865
deceive 545
entice 615
lurid *dark* 421
dim 422
red 434
lurk *unseen* 447
latent 526
hidden 528
lurking-place 530
luscious 394, 829
lush *vegetation* 365
drunkenness 959
lushy 959
lusk 683
lusory 840
lust 865, 961
– after 921
luster
brightness 420
chandelier 423
glory 873
lustily 404, 686
cry out – 839
lustless 158
lustration 652, 952
lustrum 108
lusty 159, 192
lusus naturæ 80
lute *cement* 45, 46
guitar 417
luteous 436
Lutheran 984
luxation 44
luxuriant 168, 639
luxuriate in 377, 827
luxurious
pleasant 377
delightful 829
intemperate 954
luxury
physical - 377
redundance 641
enjoyment 827
sensuality 954
lycanthropy 503
Lyceum 542
Lydford law 964
Lydian measure 415
lyddite 727
lying
decumbent 213
deceptive 544
faithless 986
Ly-king 986
lymph *fluid* 333
water 337
transparent 425
lymphatic 337
lynch 972
– law 964
lyncher 975
lynching 361
lynx-eyed 441, 498
lyre 417
lyric 415
– poetry 597
lyrist 597

M

Mab 979
macadamize 255, 635
Macaire, Robert – 792
macaroni 854
macaronic
absurdity 497
neology 563
verses 597
Macchiavel [*see* Machiavelism]
mace
weapon 727
scepter 747
mace-bearer 965
maceration
saturation 337
atonement 952
asceticism 955
rite 998
Macheath 792
Machiavelism
falsehood 544
cunning 702
dishonesty 940
machicolation 257, 717
machination
trick 545
plan 626
cunning 702
–s of the devil 619
machinator 626
machine 633
like a – 698
– gun 407, 727
be a mere – 749
machinist
theatrical - 599
workman 690
macilent 203
mackerel
mottled 440
procuress 962
– sky 349, 353
mackintosh 225
macrobiotic 110
macrocosm 318
macrography 441
macrology 577
mac Sycophant, Sir Pertinax – 886, 935
mactation 991
macte virtute 931
macula 848
maculate
unclean 653
maculation 440, 848
mad *insane* 503
excited 824
drive one – 900
go – 825
– after 865
– with rage 900
madam 374
mad-brained 503
madcap
violent 173
lunatic 504
excitable 825
buffoon 844
rash 863
madder *color* 434
made
– to one's hand 673
– man 734
– to order 673
madefaction 339
madman **504**
Madonna
good 948
angel 977
pious 987
madrigal *music* 415
verses 597
Maecenas 492, 890
Maelstrom
whirl 312
water 348
pitfall 667
maestro 415
maffick 883
magazine
periodical 53
record 551

Marshalsea 752
marsupial 191, 366
mart 799
Marte, suo –
exertion 686
skill 698
martello tower 717
martial 722
court– 966
– law 737, 739
compulsory 744
illegal 964
– music 415
martinet 739
martingale 752
Martinmas 998
martyr
bodily pain 378
mental pain 828
ascetic 955
– to disease 655
martyrdom
killing 361
agony 378, 828
unselfish 942
punishment 972
marvel 870, 872
– whether 514
marvelous 31, 870
deal in the – 549
Masaniello 742
mascara 847
mascot 993
masculine 159, 373
mash *mix* 41
disorder 59
soft 324
semiliquid 253
pulpify 354
masher 854
mask *dress* 225
shade 424
concealment 528
ambush 530
deceit 545
shield 717
put on the – 544
mason 690
Masorah 985
masque 599
masqué, bal – 840
masquerade
dress 225
concealment 528
disguise 530
frolic 840
mass *quantity* 25
much 31
whole 50
heap 72
size 192
gravity 319
density 321
worship 990
rite 998
attend – 990
in the – 50
– book 998
– of society 876
massacre 361
massage 33, 379, 662
masse, en – 712
masses, the – 876
massive *large* 31
huge 192
heavy 319
dense 321
mast 206
master
boy 129
influence 175
man 373
know 490
understand 518
learn 539
teacher 540
director 694
proficient 698, 700
succeed, conquer 731
ruler **745**
possession 777
possessor 779
title 877
eye of the – 693
hard – 739
past – 700
– of Arts 492
– one's feelings 826
– hand 700
– key *open* 260
instrument 631
– mariner 269
– mind *sage* 500
proficient 700
– passion 820
– one's passions 944
– of the position 731
– of the revels 840
– of the Rolls 553, 967
– of self 604
– of the situation 731, 737
– spirit of the age 500, 873
– of one's time 685
masterdom 737
masterpiece
good 648
perfect 650
skill 698
master-stroke 626, 731
mastery 731, 737
get the – over 175
masthead
punish 972
mastic *viscid* 352
resin 356a
masticate 298
mastiff 366
mat *support* 215
woven 219
misty 427
cover 652
matador 361
match *coincide* 13
similar 17
copy 19
equal 27
fuel 388
contest 720
marriage 903
matchless
supreme 33
excellent 648
virtuous 944
matchlock 727
mate *similar* 17
equal 27
duplicate 89
mariner 269
auxiliary 711
master 745
friend 890
wife 903
check– 732
maté 298
mater alma – 542
–familias 166
materia medica 662
material
substance 316
stuff 635
important 642
– for thought 454
– point 32
materialism
matter 316
heterodoxy 984
irreligion 989
materiality **316**
materialize 446
materials **635**
matériel 633
maternal
parental 166
benevolent 906
– love 897
maternity 166
mathematical
precise 494
– point 193
mathematics 25
mathesis 25
matin 125
matinée 892
matins 990
matrass 191
matriarch 11, 166
matriarchate 737
matriculate 86
matriculation 539
matrilinear 11, 166
matrimony
mixture 41
wedlock 903
matrix *mold* 22
workshop 691
matron 374, 903
matronly 128, 131
matross 726
matter *substance* 3
material world 316
topic 454
meaning 516
type 591
business 625
importance 642
pus 653
no – 460
what – 643
what's the – 455, 461
– of course
conformity 82
certain 474
habitual 613
– in dispute 461
– of fact *event* 151
certainty 474
truth 494
language 576
artless 703
dull 843
– in hand 454, 625
– of indifference 866
– nothing 643
mattock 253
mattress 215
mature *old* 124
adolescent 131
conversion 144
scheme 626
perfect 650
improve 658
prepare 673
complete 729
– thought 451
maturely considered 611
maturine 996
maturity [*see* mature]
bring to – 729
matutinal 125
matzoon 298
maudlin
inactive 683
drunk 959
mauger 30
maukin 562
maul *hammer* 276
hurt 649
maulstick 215
maund *basket* 191
mumble 583
maunder
diffuse style 573
mumble 583
talk 584
lament 839
maundy
– money 784
– Thursday 988
Mauser rifle 727
mausoleum 363
mauvais
– goût 851
– quart d'heure 828
– sujet 949
– ton 851
mauvaise:
– honte
affectation 855
modesty 881
– plaisanterie 851
mauve 437
maw 191
mawkish 391
Mawworm
deceiver 548
sham piety 988
maxim 80, **496**
Maxim gun 727
maximal 33
maximalist 742
maximum 33, 210
maxixe 840
may be 470
as it – 156
May-day 138, 840
May-fly 111
mayhap 470
mayor 745, 965
maypole 206
mayonnaise 298
May-queen 847
mazard 298
maze
disorder 59
convolution 248
enigma 533
difficulty 704
in a –
uncertain 475
mazed 503
mazurka 840
me 317
me judice 484
meâ culpâ 950
mead *plain* 344
sweet 396
meadow *plain* 344
grass 367
– land 371
meager *small* 32
incomplete 53
thin 203
- *style* 575
scanty 640
poor 643
– diet 956
meal *repast* 298
powder 330
mealy-mouthed
falsehood 544
servile 886
flattering 933
mean *average* **29**
small 32
middle 68, 228
signify 516
intend 620
contemptible 643
stingy 819
shabby 874
ignoble 876
sneaking 886
base 940
selfish 943
golden – 174
take the – 774
– nothing 517
– parentage 876
– time 114
– wretch 949
meander
convolution 248
deviate 279
circuition 311
river 348
– around Robin Hood's barn 279
meandering
diffuse 573
meanest capacity 499
intelligible to the – 518
meaning **516**
meaningless 517
means
appliances **632**
property 780
wealth 803
by all – 602
by any – 632
by no – 536
– of access 627
meantime 106
meanwhile 106
measurable 466
within – distance 470
measure *extent* 25

degree 26
moderation 174
music 413
compute 466
verse 597
proceeding 626
action 680
apportion 786
angular – 244
full – 629
out of – 641
without – 641
– of inclination 217
measured
moderate 174
sufficient 639
temperate 953
measureless 105
measurement 25, **466**
measures
have no – with 713
take – *plan* 626
prepare 673
conduct 692
– of length 200
meat 298
broken – 645
one man's – is another man's poison 15
mechanic 690
mechanical 601, 633
– warfare 722
– powers 633
mechanician 690
mechanism 633
medal
record 551
sculpture 557
palm 733
decoration 877
– of Honor 733
medalist 700
medallion 557
meddle 682
médecin tant pis 837
médecine expectante 133, 662
Medes and Persians, law of the – 80, 141
mediaeval 124
mediaevalism 122
medial 29, 68
median 228
mediant 413
medias res, in – 68
plunge – 300, 576
mediation—*instrumentality* 631
intercession **724**
deprecation 766
Christ 976
mediator 711
Mediator
Saviour 976
medical 662
medicament 662
medicaster 548
medicate
compound 41
heal 660
medicine 662
– man 994
medico 662
mediety 68
mediis rebus, in – 682
medio tutissimus, in – 864
mediocritas, aurea – 628
mediocrity
average 29
smallness 32
imperfect 651
– *of fortune* **736**
meditate *think* 451
purpose 620
mediterranean 68, 228
medium *mean* 29
middle 68
atmosphere 227
intermediary 228
color 428
oracle 513
impostor 548
instrument 631
seer 994
transparent – 425
medley 41, 59
music 415
chance – 156
medullary 994
Medusa 860
meed
apportion 786
reward 973
– of praise 931
meek 826, 879
meerschaum 392
meet *agreement* 23
assemble 72
touch 199
converge 290
arrive 292
expedient 646
fulfil 772
proper 924
make both ends –
wealth 803
economy 817
unable to make both ends –
poverty 804
not pay 808
– with attention 457
– one's death 360
– the ear 418
– one at every turn
present 186
redundant 641
– one's expenses 817
– the eye 446
– in front 861
– half way
willing 602
concord 714
pacification 723
mediation 724
compromise 774
friendship 888
benevolence 906
– hand to hand 720
– one's wishes
consent 762
pleasurable 829
– with *event* 151
find 480*a*
meeting [*see* meet]
junction 43
hostile – 720
place of – 74
meeting-house
hall 189
chapel 1000
megacosm 318
Megaera 173, 900
megalomania 482, 504
megaphone 404, 418
megascope 445
megatherium 124
megrims *fits* 315
melancholy 837
mehari 271
Mein Herr 877
meister-singer 597
melancholia
insanity 503
dejection 837
melancholy 830, 837
away with – 836
mélange 41
mêlée *disorder* 59
contention 720
melinite 727
meliora, spero – 858
meliorate 658
meliorism 658
melius inquirendum, ad – 658
melliferous
sweet 396
mellifluous
music 413
– *language* 578
mellow
old 128
grow into 144
soft 324
sound 413
color 428
improve 658
prepare 673
tipsy 959
melodeon 417
melodious 413
melodist 416
melodrama 599, 824
melody **413**
Melpomene 599
melt *convert* 144
liquefy 335
fuse 384
pity 914
– in the air 405
– away
cease to exist 2
unsubstantial 4
decrease 36
disappear 111, 449
waste 638
– the heart 914
– into one 48
– into tears 839
melting-pot 691
member *part* 51
component 56
councillor 696
membrane 204
même, quand – 708
memento 505
– mori 363, 837
meminisse juvabit 505
memoir 594, 595
memorabilia
reminiscences 505
important 642
memorable 642
memorandum
memory 505
record 551
plan 626
– book 505, 551
compendium 596
memorial
record 551
memorialist 553
memorialize 505
memorials 594
memoriam, in – 363, 505
memory **505**
fame 873
failing – 506
short – 506
in the – of man 122
– runneth not to the contrary 124
mem-sahib 374
menace 909
ménage 692
menagerie
collection 72
animals 370
store 636
mend 658, 660
– one's manners 894
mendacity 544
mendicancy 765, 804
mendicant
beggar 767
poor 804
monk 996
menhir 363
menial 746, 876
meniscus 245, 445
mens sana 502
– in corpore sano 827
mens sibi conscia recti 878
mensâ et thoro, separatio a – 905
menses 299
menstrual 138
menstruum 335
mensuration 466
mental 450
– calm 826
– excitement 824
– pabulum 454
– philosophy 450
– reservation 528
– suffering 828
menteur à triple étage 548
menticulture 658
mention 527
above –ed 104
not worth –ing 643
mentis gratissimus error 481
mentor *sage* 500
teacher 540
adviser 695
menu 86, 298
Mephistopheles 980
Mephistophelian 945
mephitic 401, 657
mephitis 663
meracious 392
mercantile 794
mercatoria, lex – 963
mercature 794
mercenary
soldier 726
servant 746
price 812
parsimonious 819
selfish 943
mercer 225
merchandise **798**
merchant **797**
merchantman 273
merciful 914
merciless 914*a*
mercurial
changeable 149
mobile 264
quick 274
excitable 825
Mercury 979
traveler 268
quick 274
messenger 534
mercy *lenity* 740
pity 914
at the – of
liable 177
subject 749
cry you – 766
have at one's – 919
have no – 914*a*
– on us! 870
for –'s sake 765
– seat 966
mere *simple* 32
lake 343
trifling 643
– nothing
small 32
trifle 643
buy for a – nothing 815
– pretext 617
– words 477
– wreck 659
merelles 840
meretricious
false 495
vulgar 851
licentious 961
merfolk 980
merge *combine* 48
include 76
insert 300
plunge 337
– in 56
– into *become* 144

merged 228
meridian
region 181
room 125
summit 210
light 420
– of life 131
merit
goodness 648
due 924
virtue 944
make a – of 884
– notice 642
merito, e – 944
meritorious 931
Merlin 994
mermaid 341
monster 83
mythology 979, 980
merman 341
mero motu, ex – 600
merriment
cheerful 836
amusement 840
merry *cheerful* 836
drunk 959
make – *sport* 840
make – with *wit* 842
ridicule 856
wish a – Christmas &c. 896
– and wise 842
merry-andrew 844
merry-go-round 312, 840
merry-making 827, 840, 892
merry-thought 842
mersion 337
meruit ferat, palmam qui – 873
merveille, à – 731
mesa 344
mésalliance 24, 903
meseems 484
mesh 198, 219
meshes *trap* 545
difficulty 704
– of sophistry 477
meshwork 219
mesial
middle 68
mesmerism 992
mesmerist 994
mesne lord 779
mess *mixture* 41
disorder 59
barracks 191
meal 298
difficulty 704
portion 786
make a –
unskilful 699
fail 732
message
intelligence 532
command 741
Messalina 962
messenger 271
envoy **534**
servant 746
– balloon 463
Messiah 976
messianic 976
messmate 890
messuage 189
messy 59
metabolism 140
metacenter 222
metachronism 115
metage 466
metagenesis 140
metagrammatism 561
metal 635
Brittania – 545
metallic *sound* 410
metalepsis 521
metallurgy 358
metamorphosis 140
metaphor
comparison 464
figure **521**
(*analogy* 17)
metaphrase 522
metaphrast 524
metaphrastic 516
metaphysics 450
metastasis, metathesis
change 140
inversion 218
displacement 270
mete *measure* 466
distribute 786
– out *give* 784
metempsychosis 140
meteor 318, 423
meteoric 173, 420
meteorology 338
meteoromancy 466
meter 466
meter
length 200
poetry 597
metheglin 396
methylated spirit 388
methinks 484
method *order* 58
way **627**
want of – 59
methodical 60
Methodist 984
methodist
journalist 988
methodize 60
Methuselah 130
old as – 12
since the days of – 124
meticulous 772
métier 625
métis 83
metonymy 521
metoposcopy
front 234
appearance 44
interpret 522
metrical
measured 466
verse 597
metrology 466
moderation 174
mid-course 628
metropolis 189
metropolitan
archbishop 996
mettle *spirit* 820
courage 861
man of – 861
on one's –
resolved 604
put on one's –
excite 824
encourage 861
mettlesome
energetic 171
sensitive 822
excitable 825
brave 861
mettre de l'eau dans son vin 160
meum et tuum 780
disregard distinction between – 791
mew *moult* 226
cry 412
– up 751
mewed up 229
mewl 412
mews 189
mezzanine floor 191, 599
mezzo rilievo
convex 250
sculpture 557
mezzo termine
middle 68
mid-course 628
compromise 774
Mezzofanti 492
mezzosoprano 416
mezzotint 420, 558
miasm 663
mica 425
micacious 204
mi-carême 840
Micawber 460
Michael 977
Michaelmas 998
Micomicon 515
microbe 163, 193
microcosm 193
micrography 193, 441
micrometer 193
micro-organism 193
microphone 418
microscope 193, 445
microscopic 32, 193
mid 68
Midas 803
mid-course **628**
mid-day 125
midden 653
middle - *in degree* 29
- *in order* **68**
- *in space* 222, 228
– classes 736
– constriction 203
– course 29, 628
– man *director* 694
agent 758
– point 29
– term 68
compromise 774
middlemost 222
middling 29, 32, 68, 651
middy 225, 269
midge 193
midget 193
midland 342
midnight *night* 126
dark 421
– oil 539, 689
mid-progress 282
midriff 68, 228
midshipman 269, 745
midships 68
midst - *in order* 68
central 222
interjacent 228
in the – of
mixed with 41
doing 680
midsummer **125**
– day 138
midway 68
midwife
instrument 631
remedy 662
auxiliary 711
midwifery 161, 662
mien 448, 692
miff 900
might *power* 157
violence 173
energy 686
mightily 31
mighty *much* 31
strong 159
large 192
haughty 878
migraine 378
migrate 266, 295
mikado 745
milch cow
productive 168
animal 366
store 636
mild *moderate* 174
warm 382
insipid 391
lenient 740
calm 826
courteous 894
mildew 653, 663
mildewed
spoiled 659
mile 200
milestone 550
whistle jigs to a – 645
milieu, juste – 174, 628
militant 722
church – 983*a*
military
warfare 722
soldiers 726
– authorities 745
– band 417
– power 737
– time 132
– train 726
militate against 708
militia 726
milk *moderate* 174
semiliquid 352
cows &c. 370
white 430
mild 740
– a he-goat into a sieve 471
flow with – and honey *plenty* 639
prosperity 734
pleasant 829
– of human kindness 906
– the ram 645
– and water
weak 160
insipid 391
unimportant 643
imperfect 651
milk-livered 862
milksop
incapable 158
fool 501
coward 862
milky [*see* milk]
semitransparent 427
whiteness 430
– way 318
mill 330
notch 257
machine 633
workshop 691
fight 720
like a horse in a – 312
millennium
number 98
period 108
futurity 121
utopia 515
hope 858
millesimal 99
millet seed 193
milliard 98
milliner 225
man – 854
millinery *dress* 225
ornament 847
display 882
man – 855
million 98
multitude 102
people 372
populace 876
for the –
intelligible 518
easy 705
-s *money* 800
millionaire 803
mill-pond *level* 213
pond 343
store 636
mime 19, 599, 844
mimeograph 19
mimeotype 19
mimic 19
mimodrama 599
minacity 909
minaret 206
minatory 668
minauderie 855
mince *cut up* 44
slow 275
food 298
stammer 583
affected 855
extenuate 937
– the matter 868
not – the matter
affirm 525
artless 703
– the truth 544
mincemeat of
make – 162
mincing 855

greater – 536
misteaching 538
mister 373
misterm 565
misthink 481
mistime 135
mistral 349
mistranslate 523
mistress *lady* 374
master 745
possessor 779
title 877
love 897
concubine 962
mistrust 485
misty [*see* mist]
semi-transparent 427
misunderstand
misinterpret 523
misunderstanding 495, 713
misuse 679
mite *bit* 32
small 193
insufficiency 649
money 800
little – 129
miter *junction* 43
angle 244
crown 747, 999
Mithridate 662
mitigate *abate* 174
improve 658
relieve 834
mitigation
[*see* mitigate]
extenuation 937
mitraille 727
mitrailleur 727
mitten 225
mittimus 741
mix 41
– oneself up with
meddle 682
co-operate 709
– with 720
mixen 653
mixture 41
mere – 59
mix-up 59
mizzen 235
mizzle 348
mnemonics 505
Mnemosyne 505
moa 366
moan 405
cry 411
lament 839
moat *enclosure* 232
ditch 259
canal 350
defence 717
mob *crowd* 72
multitude 102
vulgar 876
hustle 929
scold 932
king – 876
– cap 225
– law
authority 737
illegality 964
mobile
inconstant 149
movable 264
sensitive 822
mobility, the – 876
mobilize
assemblage 72
render movable 264
– troops 722
mobocracy 737
mobster 361
moccasin 225
mock *imitate* 17, 19
repeat 104
erroneous 495
deceptive 545
chuckle 838
ridicule 856
disrespect 929
– danger 861
– modesty 855
– sun 423
mockery
[*see* mock]
unsubstantial 4
solemn – 882
– delusion and snare
sophistry 477
deception 545
mocking-bird 19
modal 6, 7, 8
mode *state* 7
music 413
habit 613
method 627
fashion 852
– of expression 569
mode, à la – 852
model *copy* 21
prototype 22
rule 80
form 240
representation 554
sculpture 557
perfection 650
good man 948
new – 658
– after 19
– condition 80
modeller 559
moderate
average 29
small 32
allay **174**
slow 275
sufficient 639
cheap 815
temperate 953
– circumstances
mediocrity 736
moderately
imperfect 651
moderation [*see* moderate] **174**
mid-course 628
inexcitability 826
moderato *music* 415
moderator 174
lamp 423
director 694
mediator 724
judge 967
modern 123
music 415
art 556
modest *small* 32
modesty
humility **881**
purity 960
mock – 855
modicum *little* 32
allotment 786
modification
difference 15
variation 20*a*
change 140
qualification 469
modish 852
modulation
variation 20*a*
change 140
music 413
module 22
modulus 84
modus: – operandi
method 627
conduct 692
– in rebus 174
– vivendi 723
mogul 745
Mohammedan 984
Mohawk
swaggerer 887
evil-doer 913
moiety 51, 91
moil *active* 682, 686
exertion 686
moisture *wet* 337
humid **339**
mokes 219
molar 330
molasses 396
mole *mound* 206
mold *condition* 7
matrix 22
convert 144
form 240
structure 329
earth 342
vegetation 367
model 554
carve 557
decay 653
turn to account 677
molded 820
– on 19
molder 653, 659
molding 847
moldy 653, 659
prominence 250
color 432
refuge 666
defence 717
spot 848
molecular 32
molecule 193
molehill *little* 193
low 207
trifling 643
molest *trouble* 830
molestation
damage 649
malevolence 907
mollia tempora 134
– fandi 588
mollify *allay* 174
soften 324
mollusk 366
mollycoddle 158
Molly Maguire 548
Moloch
slaughter 361
demon 980
heathen deity 986
molten 384
moment
- *of time* 113
importance 642
for the – 111
lose not a – 684
not have a – 682
on the spur of the – 612
momentous 152
momentum 276
Momus 838
monachism 995
monad 193
monarch 745
monarchy 737
monastery 1000
monastic 995
monasticism 984
monetary 800
– arithmetic 11
money 800
wealth 803
bad – 800
command of – 803
for one's – 609
made of – 803
make – 775
raise – 788
save – 817
throw away one's – 818
– to burn 641, 803
– burning one's pocket 818
– coming in 810
– down 807
– going out 809
– market 800
– matters 811
– paid 809
–'s worth
useful 644
price 812
cheap 815
money-bag 800, 802
money-belt 800
money-broker 797
money-changer 797, 801
moneyed 803
moneyer 797
money-grubbing 775
moneyless 804
monger 797
mongrel
mixture 41
anomalous 83
dog 366
base 949
moniker 565
moniliform 249
monism 984
monition 527, 668
information 527
warning 668
monitor *hear* 418
oracle 513
pupil-teacher 540
director 694
adviser 695
war-ship 726
inward – 926
monitory
prediction 511
dissuasion 616
warning 668
monk 996
monkey
imitative 19
support 215
catapult 276
ridiculous 857
play the – 499
–jacket 225
– trick
absurdity 497
sport 840
– up 900
monkhood 995
monkish Latin 563
monochord 417
monochrome 429, 556
monocracy 737
monoculous 443
monode 445
monodrame 599
monody 597, 839
monogamist 904
monogamy 903
monogram
sign 550
cipher 533
diagram 554
letter 561
monograph
publication 531
writing 590
book 593
description 594
monolith 551
monolithic 983*a*
monologue
soliloquy 589
drama 599
monomachy 720
monomania 503
obstinacy 606
fanaticism 825
monomaniac 504
monomark 550
monoplane 273
monopolist 943
monopoly
restraint 751
possession 777
monostich 572
monosyllable 561
monotheism 983
monotonous
uniform 16
equal 27
repetition 104
permanent 141
- *style* 575
weary 841
dull 843
monotype 591
monsoon 349
monsieur 370
monster
exception 83
large 192
ugly 846
prodigy 872
evil-doer 913
ruffian 949
monstrance 998
monstrosity
[*see* monster]

mutable 149
mutation 140
mutatis mutandis
correlation 12
change 140
interchange 148
mutato nomine de te &c.
parable 521
retaliation 718
mute *funeral* 363
silent 403
sordine 405, 408*a*, 417
letter 561
speechless 581
taciturn 585
dramatis persona 599
deaf – 419
render – 581
mutilate
retrench 38
deform 241
injure 659
mutilated 53
mutilation 619
mutineer 742
mutiny 742
mutt 366
mutter
faint sound 405
mumble 583
grumble 839
threaten 909
mutton-chop
whiskers 256
mutual 12, 148
mutualize 12
mutual understanding 23
muzzle
powerless 158
edge 231
opening 260
silence 403
render speechless 581
restrain 751
gag 752
muzzle-loader 727
muzzy 458
in liquor 959
my: all – eye 546
– stars! 870
mycology 369
mynheer 877
myology 329
myomancy 511
myopia 443
myriad 98, 102
myrmidon 726
myrrh 400
myrtle 897
myself *I* 79
immateriality 317
mysterious
invisible 447
uncertain 475
obscure 519
concealed 528
mystery
[*see* mysterious]
latency 526
secret 533
play 599
craft 625
– ship 726
mystic
uncertain 475
obscure 519
latent 526
concealed 528
sorcery 992
puzzle 475
mystify *falsify* 477
hide 528
misteach 538
deceive 545
myth 515, 546
mythology 979, 984

N

nab *deceive* 545
seize 789
Nabob 745, 803
nacelle 273
nacre 440
nadir 211
nag *horse* 271
quarrel 713
nager entre deux eaux 607
Naiad 341, 979
nail *fasten* 43
fastening 45
measure of length 200
peg 214
sharp 253
hard 323
retain 781
on the –
present 118
pay 807
hit the right – on the head
discover 480*a*
skill 698
– polish 847
naïveté 703
naked *denuded* 226
manifest 525
simplicity 849
– eye 441
– fact 151
– steel 727
– sword 727
– truth 494
namby-pamby 643, 855
name
indication 550
appellation 564
appoint 755
celebrity 873
assume a – 565
call –s
disrespect 929
disapprobation 932
fair – 873
good – 873
in the – of
aid 707
authority 737
due 924
– to conjure with 873
nameless 565, 874
namely 79, 522
namesake 564
Nana Sahib 949
Nanny-goat 374
nap *down* 256
texture 329
sleep 683
cards 840
nape *back* 235
napery 652
Napier's bones 85
napkin 652
buried in a – 460
lay up in a – 678
napless 226
Napoleon *food* 298
cards 840
napping
inattentive 458
inexpectant 508
dull 843
nappy *frothy* 353
tipsy 959
narcissism 897, 943
Narcissus 845
narcosis 376
narcotic 657, 662
nard 356
narration 594
narrow
contract 195
thin 203
intolerant 481
restrict 761
– down 42
– end of the wedge 66
– escape 671
– house 363
– means 804
– search 461
narrow-minded 481, 943
narrowness **203**
narrows 343
nasal accent 583
nascent 66
nascitur: – ridiculus mus 509
– a sociis 82
naso, omnia suspendens – 868
nasty
unsavory 395
foul 653
offensive 830
cheap and – 815
natâ, pro re – 770
natal *birth* 66
indigenous 188
natation 267
natatorium 652
nathless 30
nation 372
national 188, 372
– guard 726
nationality 372, 910
nations, law of 963
native
inhabitant 188
artless 703
– accent 580
– land 189
– soil 189
– tongue 560
nativity *birth* 66
cast a –
predict 511
sorcery 992
natty 845
natura il fece e poi roppe la stampa 87
naturae, vis medicatrix – 662
natural *intrinsic* 5
musical note 413
true 494
fool 501
- *style* 576, 578
spontaneous 621
not prepared 674
artless 703
simple 849
– course of things 613
– death *death* 360
completion 729
– impulse 601
– meaning 516
– order of things 82
– state 90
– turn 820
Natural – History 357
– Philosophy 316
– Theology 983
naturalist 357
naturalization
conformity 82
conversion 144
location 184
naturalize
habit 613
naturalized
inhabitant 188
naturally 154
nature *essence* 5
rule 80
tendency 176
world 318
reality 494
artlessness 703
affections 820
animated – 357
organized – 357
second – 613
state of –
naked 226
raw 674
in –'s garb 226
naught *nothing* 4
zero 101
bring to – 732
set at –
make light of 483
opposition 708
disobey 742
not observe 773
disrespect 929
contempt 930
naughty 945
naumachia 720
nausea 841, 867
nauseate 395, 830
nauseous
unsavory 395
unpleasant 830
disgusting 867
nautch dancer 840
nautical 267
naval 267
– authorities 745
– engagement 720
– forces 726
nave *middle* 68
centre 222
church 1000
navel 68, 222
navigation **267**
navigator 269
navvy 673, 690
navy 273, 726
– blue 438
nay 536
– rather 14
Nazarene 989
naze 250
N.C.O. 745
ne plus ultra
supreme 33
complete 52
distance 196
summit 210
limit 233
perfection 650
completion 729
neaf 781
neap 195, 207
– tide 36, 340
near *like* 17
- *in space* 197
- *in time* 121
soon 132
impending 152
approach 286
stingy 819
bring – 17
draw – 197
come – 286
– one's end 360
– at hand 132
– the mark 32
– run 32
– side 239
– sight 443
– the truth 480*a*
– upon 3
sail – the wind
skilful 698
rash 863
nearly 32
nearness **197**
neat *simple* 42
order 58
in writing 572, 576, 578
clean 652
spruce 845
–'s foot oil 356
– as a pin 58
neat-handed 698
neatherd 370
neb 250
nebula *stars* 318
mist 353
nebular *dim* 422
nebulous *misty* 353
obscure 519
necessarian 601
necessaries 630
necessarily 154
necessitate 630
necessity *fate* **601**
requirement 630
compulsion 744
indigence 804
make a virtue of – 698
neck
contraction 195
narrow 203

nihil – ad rem 10
– tetigit quod non ornavit 850
nihilism 989
nihilist 165
nihility 2, 4
nil 2, 4
– admirari
insensible 823
no wonder 871
disapproval 932
– conscire sibi nullâ pallescere culpâ 946
– desperandum 858
nill *unwilling* 604
refuse 764
nim 791
nimble 274, 682
nimble-witted 498, 842
nimbus
cloud 353
halo 420
glory 873
nimiety 641
nimis, ne quid – 817
nimium ne crede colori 485
n'importe 643
Nimrod 361, 622
nincompoop 501
nine 98
tuneful –
music 416
poetry 597
– days' wonder
transient 111
unimportant 643
no wonder 871
– lives 359
– men's morris 840
– points of the law 777
ninefold 98
ninepins 840
ninety 98
ninny 501
Niobe 839
nip *cut* 44
destroy 162
shorten 201
dram 298
freeze 385
pungent 392
drink 959
– in the bud
check 201
kill 361
hinder 706
– up 789
nipperkin 191
nippers 781
nipple 250
Nirwana 981
nis 980
nisi prius 741, 969
Nisus and Euryalus 890
nisus formativus 161
nitency 420
niter 392
nitor in adversum 708
nitrous oxide 376
nit-wit 499, 501
niveous *cold* 383
white 430
nixe *demon* 980
nixie *fairy* 979
nizam 745
nizy 501
N or M 78
no *zero* 101
dissent 489
negation 536
refusal 764
unable to say – 605
on – account 761
have – business there 83
– chicken 128, 131
– choice 601, 609*a*
– conjuror 501, 701
– consequence 643
in – degree 32
at – great distance 197
– doubt 474, 488
have – end 112
– end of *great* 31
multitude 102
length 200
– fear 473
– go 304, 732
at – hand 32
matter of – import 4
with – interval 199
– one knows who 876
– less 639
– longer 122
– love lost between them 898
– man's land 187, 778
– matter
neglect 460
unimportant 643
and – mistake 474
– more
inexistent 2
past 122
dead 360
– more than 32
have – notion of 489
– object 643
– one 4, 187
– other 13, 87
to – purpose
shortcoming 304
useless 645
failure 732
give – quarter 361
– scholar 493
make – scruple of 602
– great shakes
small 32
trifling 643
imperfect 651
– sooner said than done 113, 132
– stranger to 490
– such thing
non-existent 2
unsubstantial 4
contrary 14
dissimilar 18
– surrender 606, 717
– thank you 764
at – time 107
– wonder 871
Noah's ark 41, 72
nob 210
nobilitate 873
nobility 875
noble *great* 31
important 642
rank 873
peer 875
disinterested 942
virtuous 944
noblesse 875
nobody
unsubstantial 4
zero 101
absence 187
low-born 876
– knows
ignorance 491
– knows where
distance 196
– present 187
– would think 508
noctambulation 266
noctivagant
travel 266
dark 421
noctograph 421
noctuary 421, 551
nocturnal
night 126
dark 421
black 431
nocturne 415
nocuous 649
nod *wag* 314
assent 488
signal 550
sleep 683
command 741
bow 894
– of approbation 931
– of assent 488
nodding to its fall 162, 306
noddle 210, 450
noddy 501
node 250
nodosity 250, 256
nods and becks and wreathed smiles 894
nodule 250
nodular 256
nodus, dignus vindice – 704
Noel 998
noggin 191
noise 402, 404
– abroad 531
make a – in the world 873
noiseless 403
noisome
fetid 401
bad 649
unhealthy 657
nolens volens 601
noli me tangere
defiance 715
excitable 825
fastidious 868
nolition 603
nolle prosequi 624
nolumus leges Angliae mutari
permanence 141
continuance 143
preservation 670
nom de: – guerre 565
– plume 565
nomad 268
nomadic 266
Nomancy 511
nomenclature 564
nominal
unsubstantial 4
word 562
name 564
– price 815
nomination 564, 755
nominee 758
nominis umbra 4
Nomology 963
non:
– compos mentis 503
– constat 477
– deficit alter 100
– est inventus 187
– haec in foedera 536, 610
– nobis Domine 990
– obstante 707
– placet 489
– possumus
impossible 471
obstinate 606
refusal 764
– nostrum tantas componere lites 471, 713
lex – scripta 963
– semper erit aestas 111
– sequitur 477
– sum qualis eram 140, 160
non-addition 38
non-admission 55
nonage 127
nonagenarian 98
non-appearance 447
non-assemblage 73
non-attendance 187
nonce 118
for the – 118, 134
nonchalance
neglect 460
insensibility 823
indifference 866
non-coincidence 14
non-cohesive 47
non-com. 726
non-commissioned officer 745
non-committal 528, 864
non-completion 730
non-compliance 742, 764
nonconformity
difference 15
exception 83
dissent 489
sectarianism 984
non-content 489
non-cooperation 489, 927
nondescript 83
none 101
– else 87
– to spare 640
– such
superior 33
exceptional 83
very good 648
– in the world 4
– the worse 660
non-endurance 825
nonentity
inexistence 2
unsubstantial 4
unimportant 643
non esse 2
non-essential 6, 643
non-existence 2
non-expectance 508
non-extension 180*a*
non-fulfilment 730, 732
– of one's hopes 509
non-imitation 20
non-interference
inaction 681
freedom 748
nonius 466
non-juror 489, 984
non-naturals 657
nonny 501
non-observance
inattention 458
desuetude 614
infraction 773
dereliction 927
nonpareil 648
type 591
non-payment 808
non-performance
non-completion 730
dereliction 927
non-plus
uncertain 475
difficulty 704
conquer 731
non-preparation 674
non-prevalence 614
non-residence 187
non-resistance 725, 743
non-resonance 408a
nonsense
absurdity 497
unmeaning 517
trash 643
talk – *folly* 499
non-subsistence 2
non-success 732
nonsuch [*see* none]
nonsuit *defeat* 731
fail 732
condemn 971
nonum prematur in annum 133

numeral 84, 85
numeration **85**
numerator 84
numerical 85
numerose
many 102
numerous 102
numismatics 800
numps 501
numskull 501
nun 996
nunc dimittis 990
nuncio 534, 758
nuncupation
naming 564
nuncupatory
informing 527
nunindation 794
nunnery 1000
nuptials 903
nurse *remedy* 662
preserve 670
help 707
servant 746
custodian 753
fondle 902
put to – 537
nurseling 129
nursery *infancy* 127
nest 153
room 191
garden 371
school 542
workshop 691
– rhymes 597
– tale 546, 594
nursing home 493
nurture *feed* 298
educate 537
prepare 673
aid 707
– a belief 484
– an idea 451
nut
– to crack
fanatic 504
riddle 533
difficulty 704
– oil 365
nut-brown 433
nutmeg 393
nutmeg-grater 330
nuts 618, 829
nutshell *small* 32
lie in a – 572
little 193
compendium 596
nutation 314
nutriment 298
nutrition 707
nutritious *food* 298
healthy 656
remedy 662
nutty 499
nuzzle 902
nyctalopy 443
nymph *girl* 129
woman 374
mythology 979
sea – 341
nystagmus 443

O

O! *wonder* 870
discontent 932
– for *desire* 865
oaf *fool* 501
bungler 701
changeling 980
oak *strong* 159
heart of –
hard 323
brave 861
oakum 205
oar *paddle* 267
oarsman 269
instrument 633
laboring – 686
lie upon one's –s 681
ply the –
navigate 267
exert 686
pull an – 680
put in an – 228, 682
rest on one's
cease 142
quiescence 265
repose 687
stroke – 693
oarsman 269
oasis *separate* 44
exceptional 83
land 342
oast-house 386
oath
assertion 535
bad language 908
on – 543
rap out –s 885
upon – 768
oatmeal 298
obbligato 88, 415
obduction 223
obdurate
obstinate 606
severe 739
malevolent 907
graceless 945
impenitent 951
obedience **743**
obeisance *bow* 308
submission 725
courtesy 894
reverence 928
obelisk 206, 551
Oberon 979
obese 194
obesity 192
obey 743
be subject to 749
– a call 615
– the helm 705
– rules 82
obfuscate 421, 426
obfuscated
drunk 959
obit 360, 363
post – 360, 363
obiter dictum
irrelevant 10
occasion 134
interjacent 228
obituary 360, 594
object *thing* 3
matter 316
take exception 469
intention 620
ugly 846
disapprove 932
be an –
important 642
– to *dislike* 867
– lesson 82
objection 706, 932
no – 762
objectionable
inexpedient 647
wrong 923, 947
objective
extrinsic 6
material 316
objector
conscientious – 710
objurgate 932
oblate 201
– spheroid 249
oblation *gift* 784
religious 990
oblectation 827
obligation
necessity 601
promise 768
conditions 770
debt 806
confer an – 648
feeling of – 916
under an – 916, 926
oblige *benefit* 707
compel 744
duty 926
oblige, bien –
refusal 764
obliged
necessity 601
grateful 916
duty 926
obligee 800
obliging
helping 707
courteous 894
kind 906
obliquation 279
obliquity
slope **217**
vice 945
– of judgment 481
– of vision 443
obliteration **552**
– of the past 506
oblivion **506**
nothingness 2
pardon 506
forgiveness 918
redeem from – 505
– of benefits 917
– of time 115
oblivious 506
oblong 200
– spheroid 249
obloquy
disrepute 874
disapprobation 932
detraction 934
obmutescence 581, 585
obnoxious
pernicious 649
unpleasing 830
hateful 898
– to *liable* 177
obnubilated 422
oboe 417
obreption 528
obscene 653, 961
obscurantist 421, 519, 710
obscure *dark* 421
dim 422
unseen 447
uncertain 475
unintelligible 519
eclipse 874
ignoble 876
obscurity *style* **571**
obscurum per obscurius 519
obsecration 765
obsequies 363
obsequious
subject 749
servile 886
courteous 894
respectful 928
flattery 932
observance *rule* 82
attention 457
habit 613
practice 692
fulfilment **772**
duty 926
rite 998
observant
friar 996
observation
intellect 450
idea 453
attention 457
assertion 535
– car 272
observatory 318
observe [*see* observance, observation]
remark 535
– a duty 926
– rules 82
observer 444
obsess 860, 992
obsession 716
obsidional 716
obsolete *old* 124
words 563
effete 645
obstacle 179, 706
obstant, Fata – 601
obstetrician 631
obstetrics 161, 662
obstinacy **606**
prejudice 481
obstipation 261
obstreperous 173, 404
obstruct *close* 261
hinder 706
– the passage of light 426
– the view 424
obstructive
opponent 710
obstruent 706
obstupefaction 823
obstupui steteruntque comæ 860
obtain *exist* 1
prevail 78
get 775
– under false pretences 791
obtainable 470
obtenebration 421
obtestation 765
obtrectation 934
obtrude
interfere 228
insert 300
meddle 682
obtruncate 201
obtrusion 228, 706
obtrusive
interfering 228
vulgar 851
rude 895
obtund *mitigate* 174
blunt 254
deaden 376
paralyze 823
obturate 261
obturator 263
obtuse *blunt* 253
insensible 376
imbecile 499
dull 823
– angle 244
obtuseness 456*a*
obumbrate 421
obverse 234
obviate 706
obvious *visible* 446
evident 474
clear 518
manifest 525
ocarina 417
occasion
juncture 8
opportunity **134**
cause 153
befit the – 646
have – for 630
on the present – 118
on the spur of – 612
occasional 475
occasionally 136
occidental 236, 560
occiput 235
occision 361
occlusion 261
unintelligible 919
latent 526
hidden 528
– art 992
occultism 984
occultation 449, 528
occupancy 186, 777
occupant 188, 779
occupation
business 625
in the – of 188
– road 627
occupied 682
– by 188
– with 457, 625
occupier 188, 779
occupy 186, 777
– the chair 693
– oneself with 457, 625
– the mind 451, 457
– a post 737
– time 106
occur 1, 151
– to the mind 451
– in a place 186
occurrence 151
of daily – 613
occursion 276

ocean 341
plough the – 267
oceanography 341
ocher 433, 439
yellow – 436
ochlocracy 737
o'clock 114
know what's – 698
octagon 244
octahedron 244
Octateuch 895
octave
eight 98
music 413
period 108
octavo 593
octet 98
octifid 99
octodecimo 593
octogenarian 98, 130
octoroon 41
octroi 812
octuple 98
ocular 441
– demonstration
see 441
visible 446
– inspection 441
oculis subjecta fidelibus 446
oculist 662
od force 992
odalisque 746
odd *remaining* 40
exception 83
single 87
insane 503
vulgar 851
ridiculous 853
– fellows 712
– fish 857
oddity 857
oddments 51
odds *inequality* 28
superiority 33
chance 156
discord 713
at – 24, 713
long – 704
what's the – 643
– against one 665
the – are 472
– and ends
remainder 40
mixture 41
part 51
useless 645
ode 597
odi profanum vulgus 878
Odin 979
odious
disagreeable 830
ugly 846
hateful 898
odium *disgrace* 874
hatred 898
blame 932
odium theologicum 481, 988
church 995
odograph 200
odometer 200
odontoid 250, 253
odor 398
in bad – 932
– of sanctity 897
odylic force 992
odzookens 870
Oedipus 462, 524
– complex 897
Davus sum non – 703
oeil de maitre 459
o'er [*see* over]
oeuvre 161
of: – all things 33
– course 82, 154
– late 123
– one mind 23
– no effect 169
– old 122
– a piece
uniform 16
similar 17
agreeing 23
off 196
be – 623
keep – 623
make – with 791
move – 287
sheer – 287
stand – 287
start – 293
– one's balance 605
throw – one's center 874
– one's guard 260, 508
– one's hands 776
take – one's hands 785
– one's head 503
– one's legs 284, 309
– one's mind 452
– and on
periodical 138
changeable 149
irresolute 605
throw – the scent
uncertain 475
avoid 623
– side 238
– with you 297
offal 653
offence *attack* 716
anger 900
guilt 947
offend 830, 945
– against the law 964
offensive
unsavory 395
fetid 401
foul 653
aggressive 716
displeasing 830
distasteful 867
obnoxious 898
– and defensive alliance 712
– to ears polite 579
offer *proposal* **763**
– the alternative 609
– a choice 609
– of marriage 902
– oneself 763
– up prayers 990
– sacrifice 990
– for sale 796
offering *gift* 784
burnt – 990
sin – 952
offertory *gift* 784
worship 990
rite 998
off-hand *soon* 132
inattentive 458
careless 460
spontaneous 612
office *doing* 170
room 191
business 625
mart 799
worship 900
do one's – 772
good –s 724, 906
hold – 693
kind –s 906
do an ill – 907
man in – 694
officer *director* 694
commander 745
constable 965
offices
kitchen &c. 191
official *certain* 474
true 494
business 625
man in office 694
authoritative 737
master 745
servant 746
officialism 739
officiate
business 625
act 680
conduct 692
religious 998
officio ex –
officer 694
authority 737
duly 924
officinal 613
officious 682
offing 196, 341
offscourings 645, 653
offset
compensation 30
offspring 167
offshoot *adjunct* 39
part 51
effect 154
offspring 167
offspring *effect* 154
posterity 167
offuscate 121, 426
often *repeated* 104
frequent 136
most – 613
– to be met with 136
ogee 847
Ogham 590
ogive 215
ogle *look* 441
desire 865
rude 895
endearment 902
ogpu 696
ogre *bugbear* 860
evil-doer 913
demon 980
oil *lubricate* 332
grease 355, **356**
pour – on
relieve 834
– on the troubled waters 174, 714
– lamp 423
– stove 386
oiled *drunk* 959
oilcloth 223
oilskin 386
oil-painting 556
oily *smooth* 255
greasy 355
servile 886
courteous 894
flattery 933
oinomania 959
ointment
grease 356
remedy 662
O.K. 58
old 124
of – 122
– age 128
die of – age 729
– bachelor 904
– clothes 225
– fashioned 851
– fogey 501, 857
– joke 842
– maid *cards* 840
spinster 904
– man *veteran* 130
husband 903
– man of the sea 706
– Nick 978
– school 124
obstinate 606
habit 613
pay off – scores 718
– song
repetition 104
trifle 643
cheap 815
– stager
veteran 130
actor 599
proficient 700
– story
repetition 104
stale news 532
love 897
– times 122
one's – way 613
– woman *fool* 501
wife 903
Oldbuck 122
olden 124
older 128
oldest inhabitant
not in memory of – 137
old-fashioned 124, 851
oldness 124
oleagine 356
oleaginous 355
oleomargarine 356
oleum addere camino 35, 173
olfactory 398
olid 401
oligarch 745
oligarchy 737
olio 41
olive-branch
infant 129
offspring 167
pacification 723
olive-green 435
olla podrida 41
Olympiad 720
Olympus 981
omber 840
ombres chinoises 448
omega *end* 67
omelet 298
omen 512
ominate 511
ominous
predicting 511
indicating 550
danger 665
hopeless 859
omission
incomplete 53
exclusion 55
neglect 460
failure 732
non-observance 773
guilt 947
omitted 2, 187
omne tulit punctum 731
omnibus 272
omnifarious 81
omnific 168
omniform 81
omnigenous 81
omnipotence 157, 976
omnipresence 186, 976
omniscience 490, 976
omnium gatherum
mixture 41
confusion 59
assemblage 72
omnivorous
eating 298
desire 865
gluttony 957
omphalos 68
on *forwards* 282
– account of 155
– all accounts 52
– that account 155
– approval 463
– an average 29
– the brink of 32
– the cards 152
– foot *duration* 106
event 151
doing 170
– the fire 730
– all fours 13, 23
– the other hand 30
– one's head 218
– the increase 35
– a large scale 31
– these lines 627
– the move 264
– the nail 118
– no account 32
– no occasion 107
– a par 27
– the part of 9
– the point of 111
– the present oc-

rejection 610
refusal 764
hopeless 859
undue 925
– reach 196, 471
– one's reckoning
uncertain 475
error 495
inexpectation 508
disappointment 509
– repair 659
– repute 874
– season 135
– shape 243
put – sight
invisible 447
neglect 460
conceal 528
– sorts *disorder* 59
dejection 837
– the sphere of 196
– spirits 837
– one's teens 131
– time
unmusical 414
imperfect 651
spoiled 659
discord 713
– the way
irrelevant 10
exceptional 83
absent 187
distant 196
ridiculous 853
secluded 893
get – the way 623
go – one's way 629
– one's wits 824
– work 681
– the world
dead 360
secluded 893
outbalance 30, 33
outbid 794
outbrave 885
out-brazen 885
outbreak
beginning 66
violence 173
egress 295
discord 713
attack 716
revolt 742
passion 825
outburst
violence 173
egress 295
revolt 825
outcast
unconformable 83
pariah 876
secluded 893
bad man 949
outcome *effect* 154
egress 295
produce 775
outcry *noise* 411
complaint 839
censure 932
outdo *superior* 33
transcursion 303
activity 682
cunning 702
conquer 731
outdoor 220
outer 220
outermost 220
outface 885
outfit 225, 673
outflank *flank* 236
defeat 731
outgate 295
outgeneral 731
outgo 303
outgoing 295
outgoings 809
outgrow 194
outgrowth 154
out-Herod 33, 174
outhouse 191
outing 266
outjump
transcursion 303
repute 873
outlander 57
outlandish
foreign 10
extraneous 57
irregular 83
barbarous 851
ridiculous 853
outlast 110
outlaw *irregular* 83
secluded 893
reprobate 949
outlawry 964
outlay 809
outleap 303
outlet *opening* 260
egress 295
outline *contour* 230
form 240
features 448
sketch 554
painting 556
plan 626
outlines
rudiments 66
principles 596
outlive 110, 141
outlook *view* 448
outstare 885
outlying
remaining 40
exterior 220
outmaneuver
trick 545
defeat 731
outnumber 102
outpost
distant 196
circumjacent 227
front 234
outpouring
egress 295
information 527
abundance 639
output *egress* 295
produce 775
outrage
violence 173
evil 619
badness 649
injury to 659
malevolence 907
disrespect 929
guilt 947
outrageous
excessive 31
violent 173
scandalous 874
outrance: à –
great 31
complete 52
violent 173
guerre – 722
outrank 33, 62
outré
exceptional 83
exaggerate 549
ridiculous 853
outre mer 196
outreach 545
outreckon 482
outride 303
outrider 64
outrigger
support 215
boat 273
outright 52
outrival
superior 33
surpass 303
fame 873
outrun 303
– the constable
debt 806
prodigal 818
outscourings 653
outset 66, 873
outshine 873, 874
outside
extraneous 57
exterior 220
appearance 448
– the gates 893
more – 544
– car 272
clean the – of the platter
ostentation 882
outsider 57, 893
outskirts 196, 227
outspan 292
outspeak 582
outspoken *say* 582
artless 703
be – *censure* 932
outspread 202
outstanding
remaining 40
outside 220
– debt 806
– feature 642
outstare 885
outstep 303
outstretched 202
with – arms 894
outstrip 303
outtalk 584
outvie 720, 873
outvote 731
outward 220
– bound 293
outweigh 33, 175
outwit 545, 731
outwork
defence 717
outworn 124
oval 247
ovate 247
ovation 883
oven 386
like an – *hot* 382
over *more* 33
remainder 40
end 67
past 122
high 206
too much 641
all – *completed* 729
all – with
destroyed 162
dead 360
failure 732
adversity 735
danger – 664
get – 660
fight one's battles – again 594
hand – 783
make – 784
set – 755
turn – 218
– and above
superior 33
added 37
remainder 40
redundance 641
– again 104
– against 237
– the border 196
– head and ears
complete 52
height 206
feeling 821
– the hills and far away 196
– the mark 33
– one's head 208, 641
– the way 237
overabound 641
overact *bustle* 682
affect 855
overall 225
over-anxiety 865
overarch 223
overawe *sway* 737
intimidate 860
respect 928
overbalance
unequal 28
compensation 30
superior 33
overbear 175
overbearing 885
overboard, throw –
eject 297
reject 610
disuse 678
abrogate 756
relinquish 782
overborne 732, 749
overburden
redundant 641
bad 649
fatigue 688
overcast *cloudy* 353
dark 421
dim 422
over-cautious 864
overcharge
exaggerate 549
style 577
redundance 641
dearness 814
overcoat 225
overcolor 549
overcome
prevail 175
induce 615
conquer 731
sad 837
disgraced 874
tipsy 959
– an obstacle 731
over-confident 486, 863
over-credulous 486
over-curious 455
overdate 115
overdecorated 846
over-distension 194
overdo
redundance 641
bustle 682
affectation 855
overdose 641
overdraft 808
overdraw
exaggerate 549
misrepresent 555
prodigal 818
over-due 115, 133
over-eager 865
overeat oneself 957
over-estimation **482**
overfatigued 688
overfed 957
overfeed 641
overflow *stream* 348
redundance 641
– with gratitude 916
overgo 303
overgorged 869, 957
overgrown *much* 31
large 192
expanded 194
overhang *high* 206
overhanging
destiny 152
over-hasty 901
overhaul *count* 85
attend to 457
inquire 461
censure 932
overhead 206
overhear *hear* 418
be informed 527
overindulgence 957
overjoyed 827
overjump 303
overlap 225, 303
overlay *cover* 223
exaggerate 549
excess 641
overdo 682
hinder 706
– with ornament
writing 577
overleap 303
over-liberal 818
overlie 223
overload
redundance 641
hinder 706
overlook *slight* 458
neglect 460
superintend 693
forgive 918
disparage 929
bewitch 992
overlooked 642
not to be – 642
overlooker 694
overlord 745
overlying 206
overmaster 731
overmastery 821

P

speech 582
– spelling 561
phonics 402
phonograph 417, 418
phonography
sound 402
letter 361
writing 590
phonology 562
Phosphor 423
phosphorescence 420, 423
phosphorus 423
photo-engraving 558
photograph *like* 17
photographer 559
photography 445
light 420
representation 554
photogravure 558
photolysis 49
photometer 445
photosphere 318
photostat 553
phrase *part* 51
music 413
language **566**
phrasemonger 577
phraseology 569
phrenetic 503
phrenitis 503
phrenology 450
phrenotypics 505
Phryne 962
phthisozoics 361
phylacteric
sorcery 992
phylactery
maxim 496
spell 993
physic
cure 660
remedy 662
physical 316
– education
material 316
teaching 537
– force
strength 159
compulsion 744
– nature 3
– pleasure **377**
– pain **378**
– science 316
physician
remedy 662
advice 695
Physics 316
physiognomy
face 234
appearance 448
interpret 522
Physiology
organization 357
life 359
Vegetable – 369
physique
strength 159
animality 364
phytivorous 298
Phytology 369
pi 591
piacere, al – 600
piacular 952
pianino 417
pianissimo 415
pianist 416
piano *gentle* 174
music 415
– organ 417
– player 417
pianoforte 417
pianola 417
piazza 189, 191
pibroch *music* 415
war 722
pica 591
picaresco, gusto – 945
picaroon 792
piccolo 410, 417
pick *axe* 253
eat 298
select 609
best 648
clean 652
gain 775
– a-back 215
– the brains of 461
– holes
censure 932, 934
– the lock 480*a*
– me up 662
– out *extract* 301
select 609
– to pieces
separate 44
destroy 162
find fault 932
– a quarrel 713
– one's steps 459
– up *learn* 539
get better 658
gain 775
– one's way 675
pickaninny 129
pickaxe 253
picked 648
– men 700
pickeer 791
pickeerer 792
pickelhaube
armor 717
picket *join* 43
locate 184
fence 229
guard 668
defence 717
soldiers 726
restrain 751
imprison 752
torture 972
– boat 273
pickings 775, 793
pickle *condition* 7
macerate 337
pungent 392
condiment 393
preserve 670
difficulty 704
have a rod in – 673
pickle-herring 844
pickpocket 792
abuse like a – 932
pickthank *busy* 682
servile 886
flatterer 937
picnic *food* 298
participation 778
amusement 840
picquet 840
pictorial
painting 556
beauty 845
picture
appearance 448
representation 554
painting 556
description 594
– to oneself 515
picture-gallery 556
picture-theater 599
picturesque
painting 556
beauty 845
piddle *dawdle* 683
piddling *trivial* 643
pidgin English 563
pie *food* 298
sweet 396
printing 591
piebald 440
piece *adjunct* 59
bit 31
painting 556
drama 599
cannon 727
coin 800
courtesan 962
fall to –s 162
go to –s 162
in –s 330
of a – 42
pull to –s 162
give a – of advice 695
– of good fortune 618
– of music 415
– of news 532
– out 52
– together 43
– of work 713
make a – of work about 642
pièce
– justificative 467
– de résistance 298
piecemeal 51
pied *variegated* 440
pied de la lettre, au – 494
pie-poudre, court of – 966
pier 189, 666
pierce
perforate 260
bodily pain 378
chill 385
hurt 649
wound 659
affect 824
mental pain 830
– the head 410
– the heart 830
piercer 262
piercing *cold* 383
loud 404
shrill 410
intelligent 498
feeling 821
– eye 441
– pain 378
pier-glass 445
Pierian spring 597
pierre fendre, à – 383
Pierrot 599
pietas 998
piété, mont de – 787
pietism 988
pietist 987, 988
piety **987**
pig *animal* 366
sensual 954*a*
– in a poke
uncertain 475
chance 621
rash 863
– together 72
pigeon
dupe 547
steal 791
gorge de – 440
pigeon-hearted 862
pigeon-hole 191, 260
piggin 191
piggish 954
pig-headed 499, 606
pigment 428
pigmy 193
pignoration 771
pignus 771
pig-sticking 361
pigsty 653
pigtail 214
pigwidgeon 193, 980
pike *hill* 206
sharp 253
highway 627
weapon 727
pikeman 726
pikestaff *tall* 206
plain 525
pilaster
support 215
projection 250
ornament 847
pile *stake* 45
heap 72
edifice 161
post 215
velvet 256
money 800
funeral – 363
– up 549, 641
pile-driver 276
pilfer *steal* 791
pilferer 792
pilgarlic
outcast 893
pilgrim 268, 996
pilgrimage 266, 676
pill *sphere* 249
medicine 662
bitter – 735
pillage 659, 791
pillager 792
pillar *stable* 150
lofty 206
support 215
monument 551
tablet 590
–s of Hercules 550
– of the state &c. 873
from – to post
transfer 270
agitation 315
irresolute 505
circuit 629
pillion 215
pillory 975
pillow
support 215
soft 324
consult one's –
temporize 133
reflect 451
pilot *mariner* 269
inform 527
guide 693
director 694
pilot-balloon 463
pilot-boat 273
pilot-officer 745
pilot-jacket 225
pilous 256
pimp 962
pimple 250, 848
pin *fasten* 43
fastening 45
locate 184
sharp 253
axis 312
trifle 643
might hear a – drop 403
point of a – 193
not a – to choose 27, 609*a*
– down 744, 751
– one's faith upon 484
– oneself upon 746, 886
pinafore 225
pince-nez 445
pincers 781
pinch *emergency* 8
contract 195
pain 378
chill 385
need 630
difficulty 704
adversity 735
grudge 819
hurt morally 830
at a – 630, 704
jack at a – 711
where the shoe –s 830
– of snuff 643
pinchbeck 545, 847
pinched [*see* pinch]
thin 203
poor 804
– with hunger 865
pinching 383, 819
Pindaric 597
ping-pong 840
pine *disease* 655
dejection 837
suffer in mind 828
– away 837
– for 865
pinery 371
pinguid 355
pin-hole 260
pinion *fasten* 43
wing 267
instrument 633
restrain 751
fetter 752
pink *notch* 257
pierce 260
thrust 276

color 434
perfection 650
glory 873
pink of *beauty* 845
– fashion 852
– perfection 650
– politeness 894
pinnace 273
pinnacle 210
pinocle 840
pin-prick 180*a*
pins *legs* 266
– and needles
bodily pain 378
numb 381
mental pain 828
pinscher 366
Pinto, Fernam Mendez – 548
pioneer
precursor 64
leader 234
teacher 540
prepare 673
pious 987
– fraud 546, 988
pip 747
pipe *tube* 260
conduit 350
vent 351
tobacco 392
sound 410
cry 411
music 416, 417
weep 839
no – no dance 812
– one's eye 839
– of peace 721, 723
pipeclay *habit* 613
strictness 739
piper 416
pay the – 707, 807
piping – hot 382
– time 721, 734
pipkin 191
piquant
pungent 392
– *style* 574
impressive 821
piquante, sauce – 393, 829
pique *fly* 267
excite 824
pain 830
hate 898
anger 900
– oneself
pride 878
piqueerer 792
piquet 717, 726
pirate 773, 791, 792
piroque 273
pirouette 218, 312
turn a – 607
Pisa, tower of – 217
pis-aller 147
piscatorial 366
pisces natare docere 538, 641
pisciculture 370
piscina 350, 1000
pish! *absurd* 497
trifling 643
excitable 825
irascible 901
piste 551
Pistol 887
pistol 727
pistol-shot 197
piston 263
pit *deep* 208
hole 252
opening 260
extract 301
grave 363
theater 599
danger 667
bottomless – 982
– of Acheron 982
– against 708, 713
– against one another 464
pit-a-pat
agitation 315
rattle 407
feeling 821
excitation 824
pitch *degree* 26
term 71
location 184
height 206
summit 210
erect 212
throw 284
descent 306
depression 308
reel 311
resin 356*a*
musical – 413
black 431
absolute – 416
– of one's breath 411
– dark 421
– into *attack* 716
contend 720
punish 972
– overboard 782
– one's tent 292
– and toss 621
– upon *reach* 292
discover 480*a*
choose 609
get 775
pitched battle 720
pitcher 191
pitchfork 273, 284
rain –s 348
pitch-pipe 417
piteous 830
piteously *much* 31
pitfall 545, **667**
pith *gist* 5
strength 159
interior 221
center 222
meaning 516
important part 642
pithless 158
pithy *meaning* 516
concise 572
vigorous 574
pitiable *bad* 649
painful 830
contemptible 930
pitied, to be – 828
pitiful
unimportant 643
bad 649
disrepute 874
pity 914
pitiless 914*a*
revengeful 919
pittance
quantity 25
dole 640
allotment 786
income 810
pitted 848
pituitous 352
pity **914**
express – 915
what a –
regret 833
lament 839
for –'s sake 914
pivot *junction* 43
cause 153
support 215
axis 222, 312
pix *box* 191, 998
assay 463
pixy 980
pizzicato 415
placable 918
placard 531
placate 723, 918
place
circumstances 8
order 58
arrange 60
term 71
situation **100**, 100
locate 184
abode 189
office 625
rank 873
give – to 623
have – 1
in – 183
in – of 147
make a – for 184
out of – 185
take – 151
– to one's credit 805
– itself 58
– in order 60
– upon record 551
– under
include 76
placebit, decies repetita – 829
placebo 933
place-hunter 767
placeman 758
placet 488, 741
placid 826
placket 260
plagiarism
imitation 19
borrowing 788
theft 791
plagiarist 792
Plagiary, Sir Fretful – 901
plagiedral 217
plague *disease* 655
pain 828
worry 830
plague-spot 657
plaguy 704, 830
plaid *shawl* 225
variegation 440
plaidoyer 476
plain
horizontal 213
country **344**
obvious 446
meaning 518
manifest 525
style 576
artless 703
ugly 846
simple 849
speak –ly 576
tell one –ly 527
– English 576
– dealing 543
– interpretation 522
– question 461
– sailing 705
– sense 498
– speaking 525, 703
– terms
intelligible 518
interpreted 522
language 576
– truth 494
– words 703
plainness **576**
plainsong 990
plain-spoken 525, 703
plaint 411, 839
plaintiff 938
plaintive 839
plaisance
[*see* pleasance]
plaisanteric 842
plaister 223
plait 219, 258
plan *itinerary* 266
information 527
representation 554
scheme **626**
according to – 82
planchette 992
plane *horizontal* 213
flat 251
smooth 255
fly 267
aeroplane 273
soar 305
inclined – 633
planet *world* 318
luminary 423
fate 601
planet-struck
adversity 735
wonder 870
planimeter 466
planish 255
plank *board* 204
program 626
path 627
safety 666
plant *place* 184
insert 300
vegetable 367
agriculture 371
trick 545
tools 633
property 780
– a battery 716
– a dagger in the breast 830
– oneself 184
– a thorn in the side 830
plantation
location 184
agriculture 371
estate 780
planter 188
planter ses choux, aller – 893
plaque 204
plash *lake* 343
stream 348
sound 405, 408
plashy 345
plasm 22
plasma 847
plasmic 240
plaster *cement* 45
covering 223
remedy 662
– up *repair* 660
plastered 959
plastic *alterable* 149
form 240
soft 324
– arts 557
plastron 717
plat *weave* 219
ground 344
plate *dish* 191
layer 204
covering 223
flat 251
food 298
engraving 558
– layer 690
– printing 558, 501
plateau 213, 344
plated 545
platform
horizontal 213
support 215
stage 542
scheme 626
arena 728
– orator 582
platinum-blond 430
platitude 517, 843
Platonic
contemplative 451
inexcitable 826
chaste 960
– bodies 244
Platonism 451
platoon 726
– fire 716
platter 191
layer 204
flat 251
clean the outside of the – 544
plaudit 931
plausible
probable 472
sophistical 477
false 544
approbation 931
flattery 933
vindication 937
play *operation* 170
influence 175
scope 180
oscillation 314
music 416
drama 599
use 677
action 680
freedom 748
amusement 840
at – 840
bring into – 677

punctilio 939
at the – of 197
come to the –
special 79
attention 457
reasoning 476
plain language 576
culminating – 210
disputed – 713
from all –s 180
full of – 574
give –s to 27
go straight to the – 278
in – *relative* 9
agreeing 23
conformable 82
knotty – 704
make a – of
resolution 604
contention 720
compulsion 744
conditions 770
due 924
honor 939
nice – 697
on the – of 111, 121
to the – 572, 642
– an antithesis 578
– at *direction* 278
direct attention 457
intend 620
discourtesy 895
disrespect 929
censure 932
– of attack 716
at the – of the bayonet 173
– of the compass 278
– of convergence 74
– of death 360
– in dispute 461
– of etiquette 852
in – of fact 1
– the finger of scorn 930
– of honor 939
– of land 250
– a moral 537
– out 155, 457, 527
– to – race 720
at the – of the sword
violence 173
severity 739
compulsion 744
– to *attribute* 155
direction 278
probable 472
predict 511
mean 516
– of view 441, 448
point d'appui 215
point-blank
direct 278
plain language 576
refusal 764
point-champain 874
pointed
great 31
sharp 253
affirmation 535
marked 550
concise 572
language 574
pointedly
intention 620
pointer *dog* 366
indicator 550
pointless 843
poise 27, 319, 852
mental – 498
poison 659, 666
– gas 722, 727
poisoned 655
commend the – chalice 544
poisonous 657, 665
poke
pocket 191
pig in a –
uncertain 475
chance 621
dawdle 683
rash 863
– at 276, 716
– the fire 384
– fun at 856
– one's nose in 682
– out *project* 250
poker 386
cards 840
polacca 273
polacre 273
polar 210
cold 383
– co-ordinates 466
polarization 420
polariscope 445
polarity
duality 89
counteraction 179
contraposition 237
pole *measure of length* 200
tall 206
summit 210
axis 222
punt 267
rotation 312
greasy – 840
opposite –s 237
from – to pole 180
pole-axe 727
polecat 401
pole-star 550, 693
polemic
discussion 476
discord 713
contention 720
combatant 726
polemoscope 445
police 965
– court 966
– magistrate 967
policeman 664, 965
policy 626, 692
polish *smooth* 255
rub 331
furbish 658
beauty 845
ornament 847
taste 850
politeness 894
– off *finish* 729
Polish bank 840
polished
- *language* 578
fashionable 852
polite 894
polisson 949
polite 894
offensive to ears – 579
– literature 560
– society 852
politic *wise* 498
cunning 702
cautious 864
body –
mankind 372
government 737
political economy 692
politician
director 694
proficient 700
politics 702
polity *conduct* 692
authority 737
duty 926
polka 840
poll 85, 609
– tax 812
pollard 193, 201
tree 367
Poll-parrot 584
pollute *soil* 653
corrupt 659
disgrace 874
pollution
disease 655
vice 945
Pollyanna 858
polo 840
polonaise 840
poltroon 862
polyandry 903
polychord 417
polychromatic 428, 440
polychrome 440, 556
polygamy 903
polygastric 191
polyglot 522, 560
polygon
buildings 189
figure 244
polygraphy 590
polylogy 573
polymorphic 81
polyphonism 580
polypus 250
polyscope 445
polysyllable 561
polytheism 984
pomade 356
pomatum 356
pommel
support 215
round 249
beat 972
Pomona 369
pomp 882
pom-pom 727
pomposity 882
pompous
language 577
poncho 225
pond 343, 636
fish – 370
ponder 451
ponderable 316, 319
ponderation 319, 480
ponderous 319
- *style* 574, 579
dull 843
pondus fumo, dare – 481
poniard 727
pons asinorum 519, 704
pontifical 995
pontificals 999
pontificate 995
pontiff 996
pontoon
vehicle 272
boat 273
way 627
pony 271
poodle 366
pooh, pooh!
unimportance 643
contempt 930
pool *lake* 343
combination 709
prize 775
billiards 840
poop 235
poor *weak* 160
- *reasoning* 477
- *style* 575
insufficient 640
trifling 643
indigent 804
unhappy 828
cut a – figure 874
– hand 701
– head 499
– house 189
– man 804
– in spirit 881
– stick 501
– thing 914
poorly 160, 655
– off 804
poor-spirited 862
pop *noise* 406
unexpected 508
– at 716
– in *ingress* 294
insertion 300
– off *die* 360
– a question 461
– the question
request 765
endearment 902
– upon *arrive* 292
discover 480a
Pope
infallibility 474
priest 996
Popedom 995
Pope Joan 840
Popery 984
pop-gun *trifle* 643
popinjay 854
poplar *tall* 206
poppy *sedative* 174
populace 876
popular
in demand 865
celebrated 873
favorite 897
approved 931
– opinion 488
popularis, aura – 873
popularize
render intelligible 518
facilitate 705
make pleasant 829
populate 184
population 188, 372
populi, vox –
publication 531
election 609
authority 737
populous
crowded 72
multitude 102
presence 186
porcelain
baked 384
sculpture 557
porch *entrance* 66
lobby 191
mouth 231
opening 260
church 1000
porcupine 253, 901
pore *opening* 260
egress 295
conduit 350
– over *look* 441
apply the mind 457
learn 539
porism 461, 480
pornographic 961
porous 260
porpoise 192
porridge 298
porringer 191
port *abode* 189
sinistral 239
gait 264
arrival 292
carriage 448
harbor 666
in – 664
make – 666
– admiral 745
– fire 388
– wine 959
portable *small* 193
transferable 270
light 320
portage 270
portal *entrance* 66
mouth 231
opening 260
portative 193, 270
portcullis 706, 717
let down the – 666
porte-monnaie 802
portend 511
portent 512
portentous
prophetic 511
fearful 860
porter *janitor* 263
carrier 271, 690
porterage 270
portfolio *case* 191
book 593
magazine 636
direction 693
insignia 747
porthole 260

vegetation 367
praise *thanks* 916
commendation 931
worship 990
praiseworthy 931, 944
prame 273
prance 266, 315
prandial 298
prank *caprice* 608
amusement 840
adorn 847
prate 584
prattle 582, 584
pravity 945
praxis
grammar 567
action 680
Praxiteles 559
pray 765, 990
prayer 765, 990
house of – 1000
prayer-book 998
preach *teach* 537
speak 582
predication 998
– to the winds 645
– to the wise 538
preacher
teacher 540
priest 996
preachment 998
preadamite 124, 130
preamble 61
preapprehension 481
prebend 995
prebendary 996
precarious
transient 111
uncertain 475
dangerous 665
precatory 765
precaution
care 459
expedient 626
safety 664
preparation 673
precede
superior 33
- *in order* 62
- *in time* 116
- *in motion* 280
precedence 873
precedent
[*see* precede]
prototype 22
precursor 64
habit 613
legal decision 969
follow –s 82
precentor 694, 996
precept *adage* 496
maxim 697
order 641
permit 760
preceptor 540
precession 62, 280
précieuse ridicule 855
precinct *region* 181
place 182
environs 227
boundary 233
precious *great* 31
excellent 648
valuable 814
beloved 897
– metals 800
– stone 648, 847
precipice
vertical 212
slope 217
dangerous 667
on the verge of a – 665
precipitancy 684, 863
precipitate
early 132
sink 308
consolidate 321
refuse 653
haste 684
rash 863
– oneself 306
precipitous 217
précis 596
precise *exact* 494
preciosity 578
precisely
literally 19
assent 488
precisianism
affectation 855
heterodoxy 984
over-religious 988
preclude 55, 706
precocious
early 132
immature 674
pert 885
rude 895
precognition
forethought 490
knowledge 510
preconceived idea 481
preconception 481
preconcert 611, 626
preconcertation 673
precursor
- *in order* 62, 64
- *in time* 116
predict 511
predatory 789, 791
predecessor 64
predeliberation 510, 611
predella 215
predesigned 611
predestination
fate 152
necessity 601
predetermination 611
Deity 976
predetermination 611
predial
land 342
agriculture 371
manorial 780
predicament 8, 75
predicate
affirm 535
preach 998
prediction 511
predilection
bias 481
affection 820
desire 865
predispose 615, 673
predisposed
willing 602
predisposition 176, 820
predominant 175, 737
predominate 33
pre-eminent 33, 873
pre-emption 795
preen 847
pre-engage 132
pre-engagement 768
pre-establish 626
pre-examine 461
pre-exist 1, 116
preface 62, 64
prefect 745, 759
prefecture 737
prefer *choose* 609
– a claim 969
– a petition 765
preference 62
preferment
improvement 658
ecclesiastical - 995
prefigure 511
prefix 62, 64
letter 561
pre-glacial 124
pregnable 158
pregnant
producing 161
productive 168
predicting 511
- *style* 572
important 642
– with meaning 516
prehensile 789
prehension 789
pre-historic 124
pre-instruct 537
prejudge 481
prejudicate 481
prejudice
misjudge 481
evil 619
detriment 659
prejudicial 481, 649
prelacy 995
prelate 996
prelation 609
prelection 537, 582
prelector 540
preliminaries:
settle – 673
– of peace 723
preliminary 62, 64
prelude 62, 64
beginning 66
music 415
premature 132, 674
premeditate 611, 620
prémices 154
premier 694, 759
– pas 66
premiership 693
premise *prefix* 62
precede 116
announce 511
premises
precursor 64
prior 116
ground 182
evidence 467
logic 476
premium
debt 805
receipt 810
reward 783
at a – 814
premonish 668
premonitory 511, 668
Premonstratensian 996
premonstration
appearance 448
prediction 511
manifestation 525
premunire 742, 974
prendre la balle au bond 134
prenotion
misjudgment 481
foresight 510
prensation 789
prentice 541
prenticeship 539
preoccupancy
possession 777
preoccupation
inattention 458
preoption 609
preordain 152, 601
preparation 673
music 413
instruction 537
in – 730
in course of – 626
preparatory
preceding 62
prepare the way
facilitate 705
prepared *expectant* 507
ready 698
preparing
destined 152
prepense
spontaneous 600
predetermined 611
intended 620
malice – 907
prepollence 157
πρέπον, τό – 850, 926
preponderance
superiority 33
influence 175
dominance 737
prepossessed
obstinate 606
prepossessing 829
prepossession
prejudice 481
possession 777
preposterous
great 31
absurd 497
exaggerated 549
ridiculous 853
undue 925
prepotency 157
pre-Raphaelite 122, 124, 556
pre-require 630
pre-resolve 611
prerogative 737, 924
presage 511, 512
presbyopia 443
presbyter 996
Presbyterian 984
presbytery 995, 996, 1000
prescience 510
prescious 511
prescribe *direct* 693
advice 695
order 741
entitle 924
enjoin 926
prescript 697, 741
prescription
remedy 662
prescriptive *old* 124
unchanged 141
habitual 613
due 924
presence
in space 186
appearance 448
breeding 894
in the – of
near 197
real – 998
saving one's – 928
– of God 981
– of mind 826, 864
presence-chamber 191
present
- *in time* 118
- *in space* 186
offer 763
give 784
church preferment 995
at – 118
these –s 590, 592
– arms 894, 928
– a bold front 861
– a front 719
– itself *event* 151
visible 446
thought 451
– oneself
presence 186
offer 763
courtesy 894
– to the mind 457, 505
– time 118
instant 113
– to the view 448
presentable 852
presentation 883, 894
presentiment
instinct 477
prejudgment 481
foresight 510
presently 132
presentment
information 527
law proceeding 969
preservation
continuance 141
conservation 670
Divine attributes 976
preserve *sweets* 396
preserver 664
preshow 511

privity 490
privy *hidden* 528
latrines 653
– to 490
Privy Council 966
prize *good* 618
palm 733
gain 775
booty 793
receipt 810
love 897
approve 931
reward 973
win the – 731
– open 173
prizer 767
prize-fighter 726
prize-fighting 720
prizeman 700
pro: – and con 476, 615
– formâ 82
– hâc vice
special 79
present time 118
occasion 134
seldom 137
– rata 23
– re natâ
circumstances 8
relation 9
special 79
occasion 134
conditions 770
– tanto 26, 32
tempore 111
proa 273
probability 156, **472**
probable 858
probate 771
Probate Court 966
probation
trial 463
demonstration 478
probationary 463, 675
probationer 541
probative 478
probatum est 478, 931
probe *depth* 208
perforator 262
investigate 461
measure 466
probity **939**
problem *topic* 454
question 461
enigma 533
problematical 475
proboscis 250
procacity
insolence 885
rudeness 895
irascibility 901
procedure
method 627
action 680
conduct 692
proceed *time* 109
advance 282
– from 154
– with 692
proceeding
incomplete 53
event 151
action 680
not finished 730
course of – 692
proceedings 551
proceeds *gain* 775
money 800
receipts 810
procerity 206
procès-verbal
record 551
law proceeding 969
process
projection 250
conduct 692
legal – 963
– engraving 558
– of time 109
in – of time 117
procession
continuity 69
march 266
ceremony 882
processional
rite 998
prochronism 115
proclaim 531
proclivity 176, 820
proconsul 759
proconsulship 737
procrastination 133, 460, 683
procreant 168
procreate 161, 168
procreator 166
procrustean 82
– law 80
Procrustes:
stretch on the bed of – 27
proctor *teacher* 540
officer 694, 965
consignee 758
lawyer 968
proctorship 693
procumbent 213
procurator 694
procuration 170, 755
procure *cause* 153
induce 615
get 775
buy 795
procuress 962
procurement 170
prod 276
prodigal 641, 816
prodigality **818**
prodigious 31, 870
prodigy 83, **872**
– of learning 700
prodition 940
prodrome 64
produce
increase **35**
cause 153
effect 154
create 161
prolong 200
show 525
stage 599
fruit 775
merchandise 798
– itself 446
producer **164**
product
multiple 85
effect 154
harvest 636
gain 775
finished – 154
production 54, **161**
[*and see* produce]
productive
cause 153
power 157
inventive 515
profitable 775
productiveness **168**
proem 64
proemial
preceding in order 62
beginning 66
profane
desecrate 679
impious 988
laical 997
– swearing 908
profanum vulgus 876
profession
assertion 535
pretence 546
business 625
promise 768
enter a – 625
– of faith 484, 983
professional 700
– mourner 363, 830
professor 492, 540, 700
professorship 542
proffer 763
proficient
knowledge 490
skill 698
adept **700**
proficuous **644**
profile
outline 230
side 236
appearance 448
portraiture 556
profit
increase 35
advantage 618
utility 644
acquisition 775
– by *use* 677
– sharing 778
profitable
useful 644
good 648
gainful 775
profitless 646
profligacy 945
profluent
progressive 282
stream 348
profound
great 31
deep 208
learned 490
wise 498
sagacious 702
feeling 821
– attention 457
– knowledge 490
– secret 533
profundis, de – 839, 950
profuse
diffuse style 573
redundant 641
prodigal 818
profusion 102, 639
prog 298
progenerate 161
progenitive 163
progenitor 166
progeny 167
prognosis 510, 511, 522, 655
prognostic 511, 512
prognosticate 511
prognostication 507
program
catalogue 86
publication 531
plan 626
progress
growth 144
motion 264
advance 282
in – *incomplete* 53, 730
make – 282
in mid – 270
– of science 490
– of time 109
progression
gradation 58
series 69
numerical – 84
motion **282**
progressive
continuous 60
course 109
advancing 282
improving 658
prohibition **761**
exclusion 55
stoppage 706
teetotalism 953, 958
project *bulge* 250
impel 284
intend 620
plan 626
projectile 727
projection *map* 554
projector
lantern 423
film 445
designer 626
prolation 580, 582
prole, sine – 169
prolegomena 64
prolepsis 64, 115
proletarian 876
prolific 168
prolix 573
prolocutor
interpreter 524
teacher 540
speaker 582
prologue
precursor 64
drama 599
prolong
protract 110
late 133
continue 143
lengthen 200
prolongation 63, 143
prolusion 64
prom 892
promenade 266
display 882
on pier 189
Promethean 359
prominent
convex 250
manifest 525
important 642
eminent 873
prominently 31, 33
promiscuous
mixed 41
irregular 59
indiscriminate 465*a*
casual 621
promise
predict 511
engage **768**
hope 858
keep one's – 939
keep – to ear and break to hope 545
– oneself 507, 858
promissory 768
– note 771, 800
promontory
height 206
projection 250
land 342
promote 153, 658, 707
promoter 626
promotion 658
prompt *early* 132
remind 505
tell 527
induce 615
active 682
advise 695
– memory 505
prompter
drama 599
motive 615
adviser 695
promptuary 636
promulgate 531
– a decree 741
pronation and supination 218
prone
horizontal 213
proneness
tendency 176
disposition 820
prôner 882, 931
prôneur 935
prong 91
pronounce
judge 480
assert 535
voice 580
speak 582
pronounced 525
pronouncement 531
pronunciamento 531
pronunciation 580
pronunciative 535
proof *hard* 323
insensible 376
test 463
demonstration 478
printing 591
draft 626
ocular – 446

– an inquiry 461
– the tenor of one's way 625, 881
pursuer 622
pursuit 622
pursuivant 534
pursy 194
purulent 653
purvey 637
purview 620
pus 653
Puseyite 984
push *exigency* 8
impel 276
progress 282
propel 284
essay 675
activity 682
haste 684
come to the – 704
– aside 460, 929
– forward 682, 707
– from 289
– to the last 133
– on *haste* 684
– out *eject* 297
pushing 282, 284, 682
pusillanimity 862
puss 366
play – in the corner 148
pussy-foot 528, 958
pustule 250, 848
put *place* 184
fool 501
cards 840
clown 876
neatly – 576
– across 484
– about
turn back 283
go round 311
publish 531
– aside
exclude 55
inattention 458
neglect 460
disuse 678
– away
- *thought* 452
relinquish 782
divorce 905
– back
turn back 283
deteriorate 659
restore 660
– before 527
– by 636
– a case 82, 514
– in commission 755
– a construction on 522
– on the cuff 806
– down
destroy 162
record 551
conquer 731
compel 744
pay 807
humiliate 874
– an end to
end 67
stop 142
destroy 162
- *oneself* 361
– in force
complete 729
compel 744
– forth
expand 194
suggest 514
publish 531
assert 535
- *a question* 461
- *strength* 686
– forward
suggest 514
publish 531
ostentation 882
– one's hand to 676
– the horses to 673
– in [*see below*]
– to inconvenience 647
– a mark upon 457
– one's nose out of joint 33
– off *late* 133
divest 226
depart 293
plea 617
– on *clothe* 225
deceive 544
hasten 684
affect 855
– out [*see below*]
– on paper 551
– over 484, 731
– a question 461
– right 660
– the saddle on the right horse 155
– the seal to 729, 769
– to [*see below*]
– together *join* 43
combine 48
assemble 161
– one's trust in 484
– up [*see below*]
– upon 545, 649
put in *arrive* 292
insert 300
– an affidavit 535
– hand 676
– one's head 514
– mind 505
– motion 264
– order 60
– the place of 147
– one's pocket 785
– practice 692
– remembrance 505
– shape 60
– trim 60, 673
– the way of 470
– a word 582, 588
put out
destroy 162
outside 220
extinguish 385
darken 421
distract the attention 458
uncertain 475
difficult 704
discontent 832
– of countenance 874
oneself – of court
sophistry 477
bungling 699
– of gear 158
– of one's head 458
– of joint 61
– of one's misery 914
– to nurse 707
– of order 59
put to *attribute* 155
request 765
– the blush 879
– death 361
– the door 261
– it 704
– one's oath 768
– press 591
– the proof 463
– the question 830
– the rack 830
– rights 60
– sea 293
– shame 874
– silence 581
– the sword 361
– task 677
– use 677
– the vote 609
put up *assemble* 72
locate 184
store 636
– to auction 796
– for 865
– a petition 765
– a prayer 990
– for sale 796
– a shutter 424
– the sword 723
– to 615
– with 147, 826
putative
attributed 155
believed 484
supposed 514
putid 643
putrefy 653
putrescence 49
putrid 653
putsch 742
puttee 225
putter 683
putting the weight 840
putty 45
puzzle *uncertain* 475
conceal 528
enigma 533
– out 522
puzzled 475, 533
puzzle-headed 499
puzzling 519
pyemia 655
pyjamas 225
Pylades and Orestes 890
pylon 206
pyramid *heap* 72
height 206
point 253
pyramids
billiards 840
pyre 363
pyriform 249
pyrology 282
pyromaniac 384, 504, 913
pyromancy 511
pyrometer 389
pyrotechnics 423
pyrotechny 382
Pyrrhic victory 814
pyrrhonism 487, 989
Pythagorean 953
Pythia *oracle* 513
Python, -ess 513
pyx *vessel* 191, 998
temple 1000

Q

Q-boat 726
Q.C. 968
Q.E.D. 478
quack *cry* 412
imposter 548
quackery
falsehood 544
want of skill 699
affectation 855
quacksalver 548
quad 189
quadragesima 956
quadrangle
four-sided 95
precinct 182
house 189
angular 244
quadrant 244, 247
quadrate with 23
quadratic 95
quadrature
four 95
angle 244
quadrennial 95
quadrible 96
quadrifid 97
quadriga 95, 272
quadrilateral
sides 236
angles 244
quadrille 840
quadripartition 97
quadrisection 97
quadrivalent 95
quadroon 41
quadruped 366
quadruplet 96
quadruplex 96
quadruplication 96
quaere 461
quaff 298
– the bitter cup 828
quaggy 345
quagmire
marsh 345
dirty 653
difficult 704
quail 860, 862
quaint *odd* 83
pretty 845
ridiculous 853
quake *oscillate* 314
shake 315
cold 383
fear 860
quakerish 826, 855
Quakerism 984
qualification
[*see* qualify]
power 157
modification **469**
skill 698
discount 813
qualify *change* 140
modify 469
deny 536
teach 537
qualis ab incepto 141
qualities
character 820
quality *nature* 5
power 157
tendency 176
nobility 875
qualm *disbelieve* 485
unwilling 603
fear 860
qualms of conscience 950
quamdiu se bene gesserit 108*a*
quand même
compensating 30
opposed 708
quandary 475, 704
quantity 25, 31, 102
quantum *amount* 25
allotment 786
– mutatus 140
– sufficit 639
quaquaversum 278
quarantine 664, 751
quarrel 24, 713
– with one's bread and butter
bungling 699
discontent 832
quarrelsome 901
quarry *object* 620
mine 636
quart 97
quarter *cut up* 44
fourth 95
quadrisection 97
period 108
region 181
locate 184
abode 189
side 236
direction 278
forbearance 740
money 800
mercy 914
give – 914
give no –
kill 361
severe 739
pitiless 914*a*
revenge 919
– of a hundred 98
– upon 184
quarter-day 138
quarter-deck 210
quarterly
periodical 531
quartermaster 637
quartern 95
quarteron 41
quarters *abode* 189
take up one's – 184

R

rational
– *quantity* 84
intellectual 450
judicious 498
sane 502
rationale *cause* 153
attribution 155
answer 462
interpretation 322
rationalism 476, 989
rationalization 60
rats in the upper story 503
rattan 975
ratten 158
rattle *noise* 407
music 417
prattle 584
death – 360
watchman's – 669
on 584
rattle-snake 913
rattle-traps 780
rattling 836
– pace 274
raucity 405, 410
raucous *hoarse* 581
ravage 162, 659
ravages of time 659
rave *madness* 503
excitement 824, 825
– against 932
ravel *untwist* 60
derange 61
entangle 219
difficulty 704
ravelin 717
ravelled 59
raven *black* 431
hoarse 581
gorge 957
– for 865
ravening 173, 865
ravenous 789, 865
raver 504
ravine *interval* 198
narrow 203
dike 259
channel 350
raving *mad* 503
feeling 821
excitement 824, 825
ravish *seize* 789
please 829
ravished
pleased 827
ravishment 824
raw *immature* 123
sensitive 378
cold 383
color 428
unprepared 674
unskilled 699
– head and bloody bones 860
– levies 726
– material 635
raw-boned 203
ray 420
– of comfort 831
rayah 745
rayless 421
raze 162
– to the ground 308
razor 253
cut a whetstone with a – 638
misuse 679
unskilful 699
keen as a – 821
razzia
destruction 162
attack 716
plunder 791
re, in – 9
reabsorb 296
reach *degree* 26
equal 27
distance 196
fetch 270
arrive at 292
river 348
deceive 545
grasp 737
take 789
within – *near* 197
possible 470
– the ear
hearing 418
information 527
– of thought 498
– to *distance* 196
length 200
reach-me-down 673
reaction
compensation 30
reversion 145
counteraction 179
recoil 277
restoration 660
reactionary 145, 607
reactionist 710
read 522, 539
well – 490
– a lecture 537
readable 578
reader *teacher* 540
printer 591
clergyman 996
readership 542
readily 705
reading
speciality 79
knowledge 490
interpretation 522
learning 539
– glass 445
– in 995
reading-desk 1000
readjust 23, 27
readmit 296
ready
expecting 507
willing 602
useful 644
prepare 673
active 682
skilful 698
cash 800
get – 673
make – 673
– to burst forth 825
– made 673
– memory 505
– money 800
– pen 569
– to sink 824
– wit 842
reaffirm 535
reagent 463
real *existing* 1
substantial 3
– *number* 84
true 494
– estate 780
– property 780
– security 771
realism 494
realistic 17
realize
speciality 79
intellect 450
think 451
discover 480a
believe 484
conceive 490
imagine 515
accomplish 729
acquire 775
sell 796
really *wonder* 870
realm *region* 181
people 372
government 737
property 780
realness 1
realty 780
ream 593
reamer 262
reanimate
reproduce 163
life 359
resuscitate 660
reap *shorten* 201
agriculture 371
take 789
– the benefit of
be better for 658
– and carry 775
– the fruits
succeed 731
acquire 775
reward 973
– where one has not sown 923
– the whirlwind
product 154
failure 732
reappear
repetition 104
reproduce 163
visible 446
restore 660
rear *sequel* 65
end 67
bring up 161
erect 212
back **235**
elevate 307
teach 537
in the – 281
– its head
manifest 525
– one's head
pride 878
rear-admiral 745
reason *cause* 153
intellect 450
thought 451
argue 476
wisdom 498
motive 615
by – of 615
feast of – 588
in – *moderate* 174
right 922
listen to – 498
stand to –
certain 474
proof 478
manifest 525
what's the – ? 461
without rhyme or – 615a
– in a circle 477
– why 153, 615
reasonable
moderate 174
probable 472
judicious 498
sane 502
cheap 815
right 922
– prospect 472
reasoner 476
reasoning 476
reasonless 499
reasons 476
reassemble 72
reassert 535
reassure 858, 861
reasty 401, 653
reave 789
rebate
subtract 38
decrement 40a
moderate 174
discount 813
rebeck 417
rebel 742
rebellion 715
rebellow 412
rebirth 660
reboation 412
rebound 277, 283
rebours, à –
reversion 145
regression 283
difficult 704
rebuff *recoil* 277
resist 719
repulse 732
refuse 764
discourtesy 895
censure 932
rebuild 660
rebuke 932
rebus 533
rebut *answer* 462
counter evidence 468
confute 479
deny 536
rebutter 462, 969
recalcitrant 719, 742
recalcitrate 277, 719
recalescence 382
recall
recollect 505
recant 607
cancel 756
– to life 660
recant *deny* 536
retract 607
resign 756
recapitulate
enumerate 85
repeat 104
describe 594
summarize 596
recast
revolution 146
scheme 626
recede 283, 287
– into the shade 874
receipt
scheme 626
prescription 662
precept 697
security 771
payment 807
– *of money* **810**
– in full 807
receive *include* 76
admit 296
belief 484
assent 488
acquire **775**
take in 785
take 789
– *money* 810
welcome 892, 894
– Christ 987
received *known* 490
habitual 613
– maxim 496
receiver
vessel 191
treasurer 801
official – 967
– of stolen goods 792
receiving 785
recension 85
recent 122, 123
receptacle 191
reception
comprehension 54
inclusion 76
arrival 292
ingestion **296**
interview 588
receiving 785
welcome 892, 894
warm – 892
reception-room 191
recess
receptacle 191
corner 244
regression 283
ambush 530
vacation 687
retirement 893
recesses
interior 221
secret – of one's heart 820
recession
motion from **287**
Rechabite 958
réchauffé *copy* 21
repetition 104
food 298
made hot 384
restored 660
recherché 648, 852
recidivation
regression 283
relapse 607, 661
recipe *remedy* 662
precept 697
recipient 191, 785
reciprocal 12, 84
reciprocate
correlation 12

refluence *recoil* 277
regress 283
reflux *decrease* 36
recoil 277
regress 283
current 348
refocillate
strengthen 159
refresh 689
reform *convert* 144
improve 658
reformatory 542, 752
reformer 658
refound 144
refraction
deviation 279
light 420
fallacy of vision 443
refractory
obstinate 606
difficult 704
mutinous 742
ill-tempered 901a
refrain *poetry* 597
avoid 623
do nothing 681
temperate 953
– from laughter 837
– from voting 609a
refrain 104
refresh
strengthen 159
cool 385
refit 658
restore 660
recruit 689
relieve 834
– the memory 505
refreshing 377, 829
refreshment
food 298
recruiting **689**
delight 827
refrigeration
anesthetic 376
making cold **385**
refrigerator **387**
reft 44
refuge **666**
refugee 268, 623
refulgence 420
refund 807
refurbish 673
refusal **764**
pre-emption 795
refuse *remains* 40
useless 645
not consent 764
– assent 489
– to associate with 893
– to believe 487
– to hear 460
refute 479
refuted 495
regain 775
breath 680
regal 737
regale *feast* 298
physical pleasure 377
refresh 689
pleasing 829
amusement 840
regalia 747
regality 737
regard
relation 9
view 441
attention **457**
judge 480
credit 873
love 897
respect 928
approbation 931
have – to 457
merit – 642
pay – to
believe 484
honor 873
– as 484
regardful 457, 459
regardless 458, 823
regards 894, 928
regatta 720, 840
regency 755
regenerate
reproduce 163
restore 660
piety 987
regeneration
divine function 976
baptismal – 998
regent 745, 759
regicide 361
régime
circumstances **8**
conduct 692
authority 737
ancien – 875
regimen *diet* 298
remedy 662
conduct 692
regiment 72, 726
regimentals 225
region **181**
register
arrange 60
list 86
chronicle 114
record 551, 553
registrar 553
registration 551
registry 114
règle: en – 924
regnant 175, 737
regni, anno – 106
regorge 790
regrade 283
regrate 777
regrater 797
regression **283**
regret **833**, 950
express – 952
regretted, to be – 833
reguerdon 973
regular
uniform 16
complete 52
order 58
arrangement 60
rule 80
conformity 82
periodic 138
symmetric 242
habitual 613
by – intervals 58
– return 138
regulars 726
regulate
adjust 23
arrange 60
direct 693
regulated by
conformity 82
regulation 697, 963
regurgitate
return 283
flow 348
restore 790
rehabilitate 660, 790
rehearse
repeat 104
try 463
describe 594
drama 599
prepare 673
Reichsrath 696
reign 175, 737
– of terror 739, 860
reimburse 790, 807
rein 752
– in 275, 751
reincarnation 163
reindeer 271
re infectâ 304, 681
reinforce
strengthen 159
restore 660
aid 707
reinforced concrete 635
reinforcement
addition 37
adjunct 39
materials 635
provision 637
aid 707
reinless 738
reins [*see* rein]
direction 693
give the – to
facilitate 705
lax 738
permit 760
hold the – 693
take the – 737
give – to the imagination 515
reinstall 660
reinstate 660, 790
reinvest 790
reinvigorate 658, 689
Reis Effendi 694
reiterate 104
reject
exclude 55
eject 297
refuse 764
rejected
hateful 898
rejection **610**
rejoice *exult* 838
amuse 840
– the heart
gratify 829
cheer 836
– in 827
– in the name of 564
rejoicing **838**
rejoin *assemble* 72
arrive 292
rejoinder
answer 462
law pleadings 969
rejuvenescence 660
rekindle
ignite 384
excite 824
relapse
turn back 145, 283
fall back **661**
relate *narrate* 594
– to *refer* 9
related *kin* 11
relation **9**
kin 11
narrative 594
relationship 9
relative 11, 464
– position
relativity 9
relator
accuser 938
relax *loose* 47
weaken 160
moderate 174
slacken speed 275
soften 324
inactive 683
repose 687
misrule 738
liberate 750
relent 914
– one's efforts 681
– the mind 452
relaxation
[*see* relax]
amusement 840
dereliction 927
relaxed *weak* 160
relay 635, 637
release *death* 360
deliverance 672
liberate 750
exempt 760
from engagement **768a**
security 771
restore 790
repay 807
forgive 918
exempt 927a
discharge 970
deed of – 923
relegate *banish* 55
transfer 270
remove 297
relent *moderate* 174
soften 324
pity 914
relentless
resolute 604
severe 739
wrathful 900
malevolent 907
revenge 919
impenitent 951
relessee
possessor 779
receiver 785
relevancy 9, 23
relevé 298
reliable 474
reliance
confidence 484
hope 858
relic *remainder* 40
reminiscence 505
token 551
relics *corpse* 362
sacred 998
relict 40, 905
relief
prominence 250
aid 707
comfort **834**
bas – 250, 557
in strong – 446, 525
relieve *improve* 658
aid 707
comfort 834
relievo 250, 557
religieuse 996
religion 983, 987
under the mask of – 988
religionist 988
religious
honorable 939
theological 983
pious 987
over– 955
– education 537
– persuasion 983
– sects 984
religiously exact 494
relinquish 757
– hope 859
– life 360
property 782
– a purpose 624
recant 607
relinquishment **624, 782**
reliquary 191, 998
reliquiæ 362
relish *pleasure* 377
savor 390
condiment 393
savory 394
delight 827
desire 865
relive 660
relucent 420
reluct 720
reluctance
dissuasion 616
unwilling 603
dislike 867
reluctation 719
relume 384, 420
rely 484, 858
rem acu tetigisti 23
remain *be left* 40
endure 106
long time 110
continue 141
be present 186
stand 265
– firm 150
– on one's hands 641
– in one's mind 505
– neuter 605
– in possession of the field 731
remainder **40**
estate 780
in – *posterior* 117
remainder-man 779
remains

remainder 40
corpse 362
vestige 551
organic – 357
remand *defer* 133
order 741
remanet 40
remark *observe* 457
affirmation 535
worthy of – 642
remarkable
great 31
exceptional 83
important 642
remarry 903
Rembrandtesque 160
remediable, remedial 660, 662
remediless 859
remedy 660, **662**
remembrance 505
remembrances 894
rememoration 505
remigration
regression 283
arrival 292
egress 295
remind 505
that –s me 134
reminiscence 505
remise 927*a*
remiss
neglectful 460
reluctant 603
idle 683
lax 738
remission
cessation 142
moderation 174
laxity 738
forgiveness 918
exemption 927*a*
remit
[*see* remission]
– one's efforts 681
remittance 807
remittent
periodic 138
remitter 790
remnant 40
remodel
convert 144
revolutionize 146
improve 658
remonstrance 615, 766, 932
remora *cohere* 46
hindrance 706
remorse 950
remorseless 919
remote 10, 196
– age 122
– cause 153
– future 121
remotest idea, not have – 491
remotion 270
remount 147
remove *subduct* 38
term 71
displace 185
transfer 270
recede 287
depart 293
dinner 298
extract 301
school 541
– the mask 529
removedness
distance 196
remugient 412
remunerate 973
remunerative 644, 775
renaissance 660
renascence 660
renascent 163
rencounter
contact 199
meeting 292
fight 720
rend 44
– the air 404, 411, 839
– the heart-strings 830
render *convert* 144
interpret 522
give 784
restore 790
– an account
inform 527
describe 594
– *hors de combat* 645
– a service 644
rendering
covering 223
rendezvous 72, 74
rendition
interpretation 522
restore 790
renegade
convert 144
turncoat 607
fugitive 623
apostate 941
renew *twice* 90
repeat 104
reproduce 163
recollect 505
improve 658
restore 660
– one's strength 689
reniform 245
renitence
counteraction 179
hardness 323
elasticity 325
unwillingness 603
resistance 719
renitency
light 420
renounce
recant 607
relinquish 624
resign 757
abnegate 764
- *property* 782
repudiate 927
renovare dolorem, infandum – 833
renovate 160, 660
renovated *new* 123
renown 873
renownless 874
rent *tear* 44
fissure 198
hire 788
purchase 795
rental 810
renter 188, 779
rent-free 815
rent-roll 780, 810
rents *houses* 189
renunciation
[*see* renounce]
exemption 927*a*
reorganize
order 60
convert 144
improve 658
restore 660
repair
mend 658
make good 660
refresh 689
out of – 659
– to 266
reparation
[*see* repair]
compensation 30
restitution 790
atonement 952
reward 973
repartee 462, 842
reparteeist 844
repartition 786
repass, pass and – 314
repast 298
repatriation 790
repay 790, 807, 973
repeal 756
repeat *imitate* 19
duplication 90
iterate 104
reproduce 163
affirm 535
– by rote 505
repeated 104, 136
repeater
watch 114
fire-arm 727
repel *repulse* 289
deter 616
defend 717
resist 719
refuse 764
give pain 830
disincline 867
banish 893
excite hate 898
repent 950
repercussion 277
répertoire 399
repertory 636
repetend
arithmetical 84
iteration 104
repetition 19, **104**
repine
pain 828
discontent 832
regret 833
sad 837
replace
substitute 147
locate 184
restore 660
replenish 52, 637
repletion
filling 639
redundance 641
satiety 869
replevin
recovery 775
borrow 788
restore 790
replica 21
replication
answer 462
law pleadings 969
reply 462, 937
répondre en Normand 544
report *noise* 406
judgment 480
inform 527
publish 531
news 532
rumor 532
record 551
statement 594
good – 873
through evil report and good 604*a*
– progress 527
reporter
informant 527
messenger 534
recorder 553
journalist 593, 758
reports *law* 969
repose
quiescence 265
leisure 685
rest **687**
– confidence in 484
– on *support* 215
evidence 467
– on one's laurels 142
reposit 184
repository 636
repostum, manet alta mente – 919
repoussé 250
reprehend 932
reprehensible 945, 947
represent *similar* 17
imitate 19
exhibit 525
intimate 527
declare 535
denote 550
delineate 554
commission 755
deputy 759
– to oneself 515
representation
[*see* represent]
copy 21
portrait **554**
drama 599
representative
typical 79
commissioner 758
deputy 759
– government 737
– of the people 696
– of the press
messenger 534
writer 593
repress 751
– one's feelings 826
– a smile 837
reprieve
respite 133, 970
deliverance 672
release 750
pardon 918
reprimand 932
reprint
copy 21
repetition 104
reproduce 183
reprisal
retaliation 718
resumption 789
reprise 40*a*
reproach
disgrace 874
blame 932
accusation 938
reprobate
disapproved 932
vicious 945
bad man 949
sinner 988
reprobation 932, 988
reproduce
imitate 19
repeat 104
renovate 163
reproduction [*see* reproduce] 21, **163**
reproductive 163
reproof 932
reprover 936
reptile
animal 366
servile 886
knave 941
miscreant 949
republic
country 181
people 372
government 737
– of letters 560
republican
party 712
government 737
commonalty 876
republicanism 737
repudiate
exclude 55
deny 489
reject 610
abrogate 756
violate 773
not pay 808
evade 927
repugn 719
repugnance
incongruity 24
resistance 719
dislike 867
hate 898
repulse *recoil* 277
repel 289
resist 719
failure 732
refusal 764
repulsion 157, **289**
repulsive
[*see* repulse]
unsavory 395
painful 830
ugly 846
disliked 867
discourteous 895
hateful 898
repurchase 795
reputable 873, 939
reputation 873
repute **873**

beat a – 623
retreating
concave 252
retrench *subduct* 38
shorten 201
lose 789
economize 817
retribution
retaliation 718
payment 807
punishment 972
reward 973
retrieve *restore* 660
acquire 775
retriever *dog* 366
retroaction
counteraction 179
recoil 277
regression 283
retroactive
past 122
retrocession
regression 283
recession 287
retrograde
moving back 283
deteriorated 659
relapsing 661
retrogression
regression 283
deterioration 659
relapse 661
retrospection
past 122
thought 451
memory 505
retroussé 245
retroversion 218
retrude 289
return *list* 86
repeat 104
periodic 138
reverse 145
recoil 277
regression 283
arrival 292
answer 462
report 551
relapse 661
appoint 755
profit 775
restore 790
proceeds 810
reward 973
in –
compensation 30
– the compliment
interchange 148
retaliate 718
– to the original state 660
–ed prodigal 950
– thanks 916, 990
return game 104
return match 104
reunion *junction* 43
réunion
assemblage 72
concord 714
lieu de – 74
point de – 74
social – 892
revamp 140
revanche, en – 718
reveal 529
– itself 446
reveille 550
réveiller le chat qui dort, ne pas – 668, 864
revel 840, 954
– in *enjoy* 377
revelation
disclosure 480*a*, 529
theological 985
Revelations 985
reveller 840
drunkard 959
revelling 59, 838
revendicate
claim 741
acquisition 775
due 924
revenge **919**
breathe – 900
revenons à nos moutons 283, 660
revenue 632, 810
reverberate 277, 408
reverberatory 386
revere *love* 897
respect 928
piety 987
reverence *title* 877
respect 928
piety 987
clergy 996
reverenced 500
reverend 877, 996
reverent 987, 990
reverential 928
reverie
train of thought 451
inattention 458
imagination 515
reversal 218, 607
reverse *contrary* 14
inversion 218
- of a medal 235
anteposition 237
adversity 735
abrogate 756
cards 840
– of the shield 468
reverseless 150
reversible 605
reversion
[*see* reverse]
posterity 117
return **145**
possession **777**
property 780
succession 783
remitter 790
reversioner 779
revert *repeat* 104
return 145
turn back 283
revest 790
– to 457
revest 790
revet 223
reviction 660
review *consider* 457
inquiry 461
judge 480
recall 505
periodical 531
dissertation 595
compendium 596
entertainment 599
revise 658
parade 882
reviewer 480, 595
revile 932, 988
reviler 936
revise *copy* 21
consider 457
printing 591
plan 626
improve 658
revising barrister 967
revision, under – 673
revisit 186
revival
reproduction 163
restoration 660
worship 990
revivalist 996
revive
reproduce 163
improve 658
resuscitate 660
excite 824
revivify
reproduce 163
life 359
improve 658
resuscitate 660
revocable 605
revoir, au – 293
revoke 607, 756
revolt *resist* 719
disobey 742
shock 830
disapproval 932
– against *hate* 898
– at the idea
dissent 489
revolting
painful 830
revolution
periodicity 138
change **146**
rotation 312
disobedience 742
revolutionize 140, 146
revolve
[*see* revolution]
– in the mind 451
revolver 727
revue 599
intimate – 599
revulsion
reversion 145
revolution 146
inversion 218
recoil 277
reward **973**
reword 104
Reynard
animal 366
cunning 702
rez-de-chaussée 191, 207
rhabdology 85
rhabdomancy 511
Rhadamanthus 967, 982
rhapsodical
irregular 139
imaginary 515
rhapsodist
fanatic 504
rhapsody
discontinuity 70
music 415
nonsense 497
fancy 515
poetry 597
rhetoric *speech* 582
flowers of – 577
rheum
excretion 299
fluidity 333
water 337
rhino 800
rhinoceros hide 376, 823
rhomb 244
rhumb 278
rhyme
similarity 17
verse 597
without – or reason
absurd 497
caprice 608
motiveless 615*a*
rhymeless 598
rhymester 597
rhythm
periodicity 138
melody 413
elegance 578
verse 597
rhythmical
- *style* 578
rialto 799
rib *support* 215
ridge 250
wife 903
ribald *vulgar* 851
disreputable 874
impure 961
riband
[*see* ribbon]
ribbed 259
ribbon *tie* 45
filament 205
record 550
decoration 877
–s *reins* 152
handle the – 693
ribroast 972
rich *savory* 394
color 428
language 577
abundant 639
wealthy 803
beautiful 845
ornament 847
– man 803
riches 803
richesses, embarras de – 641, 803
richly *much* 31
– deserve 924
rick 72, 846
rickety *weak* 160
ugly 846
imperfect 651
rickshaw 272
ricochet 277
ricordo, non mi – 506
rid *deliver* 672
get – of *eject* 297
liberation 750
loose 776
relinquish 782
riddance 672, 776, 782
good – 776
riddle *arrange* 60
sieve 260
secret 533
clean 652
ride *get above* 206
move 266
break in 370
– at anchor 265
– full tilt at 622, 716
– hard 274
– one's hobby 622
– rough shod
violence 173
severity 739
insolence 885
illegality 964
– out the storm 664
– and tie
periodicity 138
journey 266
– the whirlwind 604, 737
rideau, lever de – 599
ridentem dicere verum 836, 842
rider *appendix* 39
equestrian 268
rideret Heraclitus 853
ridge *narrow* 203
height 206
prominence 250
ridicule **856**, 929
ridiculous
absurd 497
foolish 499
trifling 643
grotesque 853
ridiculousness **853**
riding *district* 181
journey 266
ridotto 840, 892
rifacimento 104, 660
rife *existence* 1
general 78
influence 175
riff-raff *dirt* 653
commonalty 876
bad folk 949
rifle *musket* 727
plunder 791
– shot 406
rifled cannon 727
rifleman 726
rifler 792
rifles 726
rifle-shooting 840
rift 44, 198
– within the lute 651, 713
rig *dress* 225
prepare 673
frolic 840
strumpet 962
– the market 794
run the – upon 929
rigadoon 840
rigging *ropes* 45
gear 225
instrument 633

rutilant 420
ruttish 961
ryot *servant* 746
possessor 779
commonalty 876

S

sabaoth 726
sabbatarian
ascetic 955
sectarian 984
false piety 988
ritualistic 998
Sabbath *rest* 687
rite 998
sabbatism 988
Sabellianism 984
saber 361, 727
Sabianism 984
sable 223, 431
sabot 225
sabotage 162, 742
sabreur *slayer* 361
soldier 726
sabulous 330
sac 191
– de nuit 225
sacatra 83
saccharine 396
saccular 191
sacerdotal 995
sacerdotalism 988
sachel 191
sachem 745
sachet 400
sack *bag* 191
discharge 297, 756
gain 775
take 789
plunder 791
give the – to 297
sackbut 297
sackcloth and ashes
lament 839
atonement 952
ascetic 955
rite 998
sacrament 998
sacrarium 1000
sacred
dignified 873
holy 976
revelation 985
piety 987
sacrifice
destroy 162
gift 784
atonement 952
worship 990
idolatry 991
at any – 604
fall a – 828
make a – 942
make the supreme – 361
self – 942
sacrificed 732
sacrilege 988
sacring bell 550, 998
sacristan 996
sacristy 1000
sacrosanct
honorable 873
inviolable 924
holy 976
sad *great* 31
grey 432
bad 649
painful 830
dejected 837
– disappointment 509
– dog 949
– times 735
– work 699
sadden 830, 837
sadder and wiser man 950
saddle 215
in the – 673
– on 37, 43
– on the right horse
discovery 480a
skill 698
right 922
fair 939
– with *add* 37
attribute 155
quarter on 184
clog 706
impose a duty 926
accuse 938
– on the wrong horse 495, 699
– up 293
saddle-bags 191
Sadducee 984
sadness, in – 535
safe *cupboard* 191
hiding place 530
secure 664
treasury 802
cautious 864
– conduct 631
– conscience 926, 946
– deposit 636
– keeping 670
– and sound 654
on the – side 864
safety 664
– bicycle 272
– curtain 599
– first 665, 864
– match 388
– valve 666
saffron *color* 436
sag 214, 217, 245
saga 594
sagacious 498, 510
sage 498, **500**
– maxim 496
saggar 386
sagittal 253
sagittary 83
sagum 225
Sahara 169
sahib 373, 745, 875
saick 273
said *preceding* 62
repeated 104
prior 116
it is – 532
thou hast – 488
more easily – than done 704
sail *navigate* 267
ship 273
set out 293
easy – 174
full – 274
press of – 274
shorten – 275
take in – 174
take the wind out of one's –s 706
too much – 863
under – 267
– before the wind 734
– near the wind 698
– too near the wind 863
sailing: plain – 705
– vessel 273
sailor 269
fair weather – 701
saint *angel* 977
revelation 985
piety 987
false piety 988
tutelary – 664
Saint Monday 840
saintly 944, 987
sais quoi, je ne – 563
sake:
for the – of 615, 707
for goodness – 765
salaam
bow 308
submit 725
courtesy 894
respect 928
salacity 961
salad 41
– oil 356
salade 717
salamander 386
salariat 875
salary 973
sale **796**
bill of – 771
for – *offer* 763
barter 794
saleable 796
salebrosity 256
salesman 797
salient
projecting 250
sharp 253
manifest 525
important 642
– angle 244
– points 642
saline 392
saliva 299, 332
salivate 297
salle-à-manger 191
sallet 717
sallow
colorless 429
yellow 436
sally *issue* 293
attack 716
wit 842
sally-port 295, 717
salmagundi 41
salmi 298
salmon-colored 434
saloon 189, 191
salt *sailor* 269
pungent 392
condiment 393
importance 642
preserve 670
money 800
wit 842
below the – 876
worth one's – 644
– of the earth 648, 948
– water 341
saltation 309
saltatory 315
saltinbanco 548
saltpeter 392, 727
saltum, per – 315
salubrity **656**
salutary 656
salutatory 582
salute
allocution 586
celebration 883
courtesy 894
kiss 902
respect 928
salutiferous
[*see* salutary]
salva:
– res est 664
– sit reverentia 928
salvable 946
salvage
acquisition 775
tax 812
discount 813
reward 973
salvation
preservation 670
deliverance 672
religious 976
piety 987
work out one's – 990
salve *unguent* 356
remedy 662
relieve 834
salver 191
salvo *exception* 83
explosion 406
qualification 469
plea 617
attack 716
excuse 937
– of artillery
celebration 883
Samaritan, good – 906, 912
same 13
all the – to 823
in the – boat 709
in the – breath 113, 120
go over the – ground 104
of the – mind 488
on the – tack 709
adds up to the – thing 27
at the – time 30, 120
sameness 16
samiel 349
samisen 417
Sammael 978
samovar 191
sampan 273
sample 82, 463
Samson 159
sana, mens – 502
– in corpore sano 827
sanation 660
sanative 662
sanatorium 662
sanctification 976
sanctify 926, 987
sanctimony 988
sanction
permission 760
dueness 924
approbation 931
sanctitude 987
sanctity 987
sanctuary 666, 1000
sanctum 191
– sanctorum
abode 189
privacy 893
temple 1000
sand *powder* 330
–bag 727
built upon – 665
–dance 840
sow the – 645
sandal 225
sand-blind 442
Sandemanian 984
sand-paper 255
sands *danger* 667
– on the seashore
multitude 102
sand-storm 330
sandwich-wise 228
sandy *yellow* 436
sane 502
sangar 717
sang-froid
insensibility 823
inexcitability 826
presence of mind 864
sangrail 998
sanguinary 361
sanguine *red* 434
hopeful 858
– expectation 507, 858
– imagination 515
sanhedrim 696, 995
sanies 333
sanitaire, cordon – 670
sanitarian 656
sanitarium 656, 662
sanitary 656
sanity *mental* **502**
bodily - 654
sans 187
– cérémonie 888, 892
– façon
simple 849
modest 881
social 892
– pareil 33
– peur et sans reproche
perfect 650
heroic 873
honorable 939
– souci
insensible 823

impose 741
lease 771, 787
make a dead – at 716
– about 66, 676
– abroach 73
– one's affections on 897
– afloat 153, 531
– against
oppose 708
quarrel 713
hate 898
angry 900
– against one another 464
– agoing
impulse 276
propulsion 284
aid 717
– apart
separate 44
exclude 55
select 609
– aside
displace 185
disregard 458
neglect 460
negative 536
reject 610
disuse 678
annul 756
refuse 764
not observe 773
relinquish 782
dereliction 927
– one's back up 878
– before
inform 527
choice 609
– before oneself 620
– by 636
– one's cap at 897, 902
– on a cast 621
– down [*see below*]
– by the ears 898
– at ease 831
– an example
model 22
motive 615
– the eyes on 441
– one's face against
oppose 708
refuse 764
disapprove 932
– the fashion
influence 175
authority 737
fashion 852
– fast 704
– on fire
ignite 384
excite 824
– on foot 66
– foot on 294
– forth *show* 525
assert 535
describe 594
– forward 293
– free 750
– going [*see* – agoing]
– one's hand to 467
– one's heart upon 604, 865
– at hazard 665
– in *begin* 66
rain 348
– on its legs 150
– on one's legs 159, 669
– in motion 264, 677
– to music 416
– at naught
make light of 483
reject 610
oppose 708
defy 715
disobey 742
not observe 773
dereliction 927
– no store by 483, 930
– off
compensation 30
depart 293
improve 658
discount 813
adorn 845
display 882
– on 615
– in order 60
– out *arrange* 60
begin 66
depart 293
decorate 845
display 882
– over 755
– phrase 566
– a price 85, 812
– purpose 620
– at rest *end* 67
answer 462
adjudge 480
complete 729
compact 769
– right
inform 527
disclose 529
teach 537
reinstate 660
vindicate 937
– to rights 60
– sail 293
– the seal on 729
– one's seal to 467
– store by 642
– straight 246, 723
– the table in a roar 840
– one's teeth 604
– terms
manifest 525
phrase 566
style 574
– a trap for 545
– to 720, 722
– in towards 286
– up
printing 54
originate 153
strengthen 159
produce 161
upright 212
raise 307
successful 731
prosperous 734
– up shop 676
– upon
resolved 604
attack 716
desirous 865
– too high a value upon 482
– watch 459
– one's wits to work *think* 451
imagine 515
plan 626
– to work
undertake 676
impose 741
set-back 735
set down
record 551
unseat 756
humiliate 879
slight 929
censure 932
give one a –
confute 479
– as 484
– for 484
– a cause for hearing 969
– to 155
– in writing 551
setaceous 256
seton 662
setose 256
settee 215
setter 366
settle *regulate* 60
establish 150
be located 184
bench 215
come to rest 265
subside 306
kill 361
decide 480
choose 609
vanquish 731
consent 762
compact 769
pay 807
– accounts 807, 811
– down 133
stability 150
moderate 174
locate oneself 184
– into 144
– matters 723
– preliminaries 673
– property 781
– the question 478
– to sleep 683
– upon *give* 784
– with 807, 992
settled [*see* settle]
characteristic 5
ended 67
account – 811
– opinion 484
– purpose 620
settlement [*see* settle]
location 184
colony 188
dregs 653
compact 769
deed 771
property 780
strict – 781
settler 188
settlor 784
seven 98
–league boots 274, 992
wake the – sleepers 404
seventy 98
sever 38, 44
several *special* 79
plural 100
many 102
– times 104
severalize 465
severally 44, 79
severalty 44
severance 38
severe
energetic 171
symmetry 242
exact 494
- *style* 576
harsh 739
painful 830
simple 849
critical 932
severely *very* 31
severity 739
sew 43
sewage 299, 653
sewed up
drunk 959
sewer 350, 653
sewerage 652, 653
sewer-gas 663
sewing-silk 205
sex *kind* 75
women 374
fair – 374
sexagenarian 98, 130
sexagenary 99
sextant 217, 244, 247
sextet 98
sextodecimo 593
sexton 363, 996
sextuple 98
seyyid 745
sforzando 415
shabbiness 34
shabby *trifling* 643
deteriorated 659
stingy 819
mean 874
disgraceful 940
shabby-genteel 851
shack 189
shackle
fastening 45
hinder 706
restrain 751
fetter 752
shade *degree* 26
small quantity 32
manes 362
darkness 421
shadow 424
color 428
conceal 528
screen 530
paint 556
ghost 980
eye – 443
in the – 528, 874
shadow of a – 32, 422
throw into the –
surpass 303
conceal 528
glory 873
throw all else into the – 642
thrown into the – 34, 874
under the – of 664
without a – of doubt 474
shades:
– below 982
– of death 360
– of difference 15
– of evening 422
shading 421
– off 26
shadow
unsubstantial 4
copy 21
small 32
accompaniment 88
thin 203
be behind 235
sequence 281
dark 421
shade 424
pursue 461, 622
dream 515
demon 980
fight with a – 699
follow as a – 281
partial – 422
without a – of turning 141
worn to a –
thin 203
worse for wear 659
– of coming events 511
– forth *dim* 422
predict 511
metaphor 521
represent 554
may your – never be less
courtesy 894
respect 928
approbation 931
take the – for the substance
credulous 486
mistake 495
unskilful 699
under the – of one's wing 664
shadowy 4, 447
shady 874
shaft *deep* 208
frame 215
pit 260
missile 284
axis 312
air-pipe 351
handle 633
weapon 727
shaggy 256
shagreen 223
shah 745
shake *totter* 149
weak 160
vibrate 314
agitation 315
shiver 383

not believe 487
permit 760
not observe 773
– the gates of mercy 914*a*
– in 751
– oneself up 893
– out 55, 761
– up shop *end* 67
cease 142
silence 403
relinquish 624
repose 687
– up *close* 261
confute 479
imprison 751
shutter 424
shuttle 314
shuttlecock 605
shy *deviate* 279
draw back 283
propel 284
avoid 623
fearful 860
cowardly 862
modest 881
fight – of 623
have a – at 716
– of belief 487
– cock 862
– of *doubtful* 485
unwilling 603
cautious 864
dislike 867
Shylock 787
Siamese twins 89
sib 11
Siberia 383
sibi gladio hunc jugulo, suo – 718
sibilation *hiss* **409**
disrespect 929
disapprobation 932
Sibyl *oracle* 513
ugly 846
Sibylline 511
– leaves 513
sic *imitation* 19
exact 494
si – omnes! 948
– transit gloria mundi 111
– volo sic jubeo 600
– vos non vobis 791
siccity 340
sick *ill* 655
make one – 830, 867
visitation of the – 998
– at heart 837
– of *weary* 841
dislike 867
satiated 869
in –ness and in health 604
sick-chamber 655
sicken *nauseate* 395
disease 655
pain 830
weary 841
disgust 867
sickener
too much 641
sickle 244, 253
sickly *weak* 160
sick-room 655
side
consanguinity 11
edge 231
laterality 236
party 712
ostentation 882
at one's – 197
on every – 227
on one – 243
on one's – 714
look only at one – of the shield 481
pass from one – to another 607
take up a – 476
wrong – up 218
– by side
accompaniment 88
near 197
laterality 236
party 712
from – to side 314
– with *aid* 707
co-operate 709
concord 714
side-arms 727
side-blow 702
sideboard 191
side-car 272
side-dish 298
side-drum 417
side-kick 890
side issue 643
sideling 279
sidelong 236
sideration 158
sidereal 318
– time 114
siderite 288
Sideromancy 511
side-saddle 215
side-scene 599
sideslip 267
sidesman 996
side-track 287
sidewalk 627
sideways 217, 236
side-wind
oblique 217
circuit 629
cunning 702
sidle *oblique* 217
lateral 236
deviate 279
siege 716
lay – to 716
state of – 722
siege-train 727
siesta 683
sieve *sort* 60
perforate 260
clean 652
memory like a – 506
pour water into a – 638, 818
stop one hole in a – 819
sift *simplify* 42
sort 60
inquire 461
discriminate 465
clean 652
– the chaff from the wheat 609
sigh 405, 839
– for 865
sighing like furnace 902
sight *much* 31
multitude 102
vision 441
appearance 448
ugly 846
prodigy 872
at – 132, 441
dim – 443
in – 446
in – of 197, 441
in plain – 525
keep in – 457
within – of shore 858
sightless
blind 442
invisible 447
ugly 846
sightly 845
sights, see – 455
sightseeing 441
sightseer 444, 455
sigil *seal* 550
evidence 769
sigmoidal 248
sign *attest* 467
omen 512
indication 550
record 551
write 590
compact 769
prodigy 872
give – of 525
make no – 585
– of the cross 998
–s of the times
indication 550
omen 512
warning 668
–s of the zodiac 318
signal *great* 31
sign 550
important 642
give the – 741
– of distress 669
signalize
indicate 550
glory 873
celebrate 883
signally 31
signal oil 356
signal-post 668
signature
mark, identification 550
writing 590
compact 769
security 771
sign-board 550
signet
mark, identification 550
sign of authority 747
compact 769
writer to the – 968
significant 642
[*see* signify]
evidence 467
important 642
signifies, what – 643
signify
forebode 511
mean 516
inform 527
signior 875
sign-manual 550, 590
signor 373, 877
signora 374
sign-painter 559
sign-painting 555
sign-post 550
signum, ecce – 550
sike 348
silence *disable* 158
no sound **403**
confute 479
latency 526
concealment 528
aphony 581
taciturn 585
check 731
silencer 405, 408
silentio, sub –
silent 403
inattention 458
latent 526
silhouette
outline 230, 448
shadow 421
portrait 556
siliquose 191
silk 255, 324
– gown
barrister 968
– hat 225
make a – purse out of a sow's ear 471
silken repose 686
silkiness 954
sill 215
silly
credulous 486
imbecile 499
insane 503
silo 636
silt *deposit* 321
dirt 653
silvan 367
silver *bright* 420
white 430
grey 432
money 800
bait with a – hook 615
german – 545
– lining of the cloud 858
– wedding 883
silver certificate 800
silver-toned 413
silviculture 371
simagrée 855
similarity 17
– of form 240
simile
similarity 17
comparison 464
metaphor 521
similitude 17, 21
simmer
agitation 315
boil 382, 384
excitement 824
simmering 825
simoleon 800
Simon Pure
the real – 494
Simon, Simple – 501, 547
Simon Stylites 893
simony 964
simoon 249, 382
simper *smile* 838
affectation 855
simple *mere* 32
unmixed 42
credulous 486
ignorant 493
silly 499
- *language* 576
herb 662
artless 703
unadorned 849
– meaning 516
simple-hearted 543
simpleness **42**
Simple Simon 501, 547
simpleton 501
simplex munditiis 849
simplicity
[*see* simple] **849**
ignorance 491
simplify
[*see* simple]
elucidate 518
simply 32, 87
more – 522
simulacrum 19
simulate
resemble 17
imitate 19
cheat 544
simultaneous 120
sin 945, 947
sinapism 662
since *under the circumstances* 8
after 117
cause 155
reason 476
sincere
veracious 543
ingenuous 703
feeling 821
sine 217
sine: – curâ 831
– die 107, 133
– ictu 158
– quâ non
required 630
important 642
condition 770
sinecure 681
no – 682
sinew 159
sinewless 158
sinews of war 800
sinful 945
sing *bird* 412
resonance 408
music 416
voice 580
poetry 597
rejoice 838
– Io triumphe 884
– out 411
– praises

smooth *uniform* 16
calm 174
flattery 213, 251
not rough 255
easy 705
– the bed of death 707, 906
– down 174
– over 174
– the ruffled brow of care 834
– sailing 705
– water *easy* 705
– the way 705
smooth-bore 727
smoothly, go on – *prosperous* 734
smoothness 255
smooth-tongued 544, 933
smother
repress 174
kill 361
stifle sound 581
restrain 751
smoulder *inert* 172
burn 382
latent 526
smous 796, 797
smudge 431, 653, 848
smug *affected* 855
smuggle
introduce 228
steal 791
illegal 904
smuggler 792
smut
dirt 653
impurity 961
smutch 431
snack
small quantity 32
food 298
snacks, go – 778
snaffle 752
snag *projection* 250
sharp 253
danger 667
hindrance 706
snail *slow* 275
snake *undulation* 248
serpent 366
hissing 406
miscreant 913
scotch the – 640
– in the grass
hidden 528
deceiver 548
bad 649
source of danger 667
evil-doer 913
knave 941
snake-like
convoluted 248
snap *break* 44
eat 298
brittle 328
noise **406**
rude 895
– at *seize* 789
bite 830
censure 932
– of the fingers
trifle 643
– one's fingers at
defy 715
insolence 885
despise 930
– the thread 70
– up *seize* 789
– one up
censure 932
-shot 554
snap-dragon 840
snappish 901
snare *deception* 545
snarl *growl* 412
rude 895
angry 900
threaten 909
snatch
small quantity 32
seize 789
– at *pursue* 622
seize 789
– a grace beyond the reach of art 845
– from one's grasp 789
– from the jaws of death 662, 672
– from under one's nose 702
– a verdict 545, 702
snatches, by – 70
sneak *hide* 528
coward 862
servile 886
base 940
knave 941
bad man 949
– off, – out of 623
sneer *disparage* 929
contempt 930
blame 932
sneeze *blow* 349
snuffle 409
– at *despise* 930
sneezed at, not to be – 642
snick 32, 51
snicker 838
sniff *blow* 349
odor 398
discovery 480a
sniffle 349
snigger *laugh* 838
ridicule 856
disrespect 929
sniggle 545
snip
small quantity 32
cut 44
short 201
tailor 225
sniping 716
snippet 32
snip-snap 713
snip-snap-snorem 840
snivel *weep* 839
sniveling
servile 886
snob *vulgar* 851
plebeian 876
servile 886
snobbishness
flattery 933
snood
headdress 225
circle 247
snooker 840
Snooks, Mr. – 876
snooze 683
snozzle 250
snore 411, 683
snort 411, 412
snout 250
snow *ship* 273
ice 383
white 430
snow-ball 72
snow-blindness 443
snow-drift 72
snow-shoe 272
snow-storm 383
snub *short* 201
hinder 706
cast a slur 874
humiliate 879
bluster 885
censure 932
snub-nosed 243
snuff *blow* 349
pungent 392
odor 398
up to – 698, 702
go out like the – of a candle 360
– out 162, 421
– up 296, 398
snuff-color 433
snuffing, want – *pert* 885
snuffle *blow* 349
hiss 409
stammer 583
hypocrisy 988
snuffy 653
snug *closed* 261
comfortable 377
safe 664
prepared 673
content 831
secluded 893
keep – 528, 893
make all – 673
snuggery 189
snugness 827
so *similar* 17
very 31
therefore 476
method 627
– be it 488, 762
– far so good 618
– let it be 681
– much the better 831, 838
– much the worse 832, 835
– to speak 17, 521
soak *immerse* 300
water 337
moist 339
drunkenness 959
– up 340
So-and-so, Mr. – *neology* 563
soap *lubricate* 332
oil 356
cleanser 652
soapy *unctuous* 355
servile 886
flattery 933
soar *great* 31
height 206
fly 267
rise 305
sob 839
sober *moderate* 174
wise 498
sane 502
style 576
grave 837
temperate 953
abstinent 958
– down 174, 502
humility 879
in – sadness
affirmation 535
– senses 502
– truth *fact* 494
sober-minded 502
calm 826
humble 879
sobriety 958
sobriquet 565
sob sister 534
so-called 545, 565
soc *jurisdiction* 965
socage 777
soccer 840
sociable
carriage 272
sociality 892
social *mankind* 372
sociable 892
– circle 892
– evil 961
– gathering 892
– science 910
socialism
government 737
participation 778
philanthropy 910
socialist 712
sociality 892
society
mankind 372
party 712
fashion 852
sociality 892
position in – 873
Socinianism 984
sociology 712
sock *hosiery* 225
drama 599
socket 191, 252
socle 215
Socratic method 461
sod 344
beneath the – 363
sodality 712, 888
sodden 339, 384
sofa 215
Sofi 984, 996
soft *stop!* 142
weak 160
moderate 174
smooth 255
not hard 324
moist 339
marsh 345
silence! 403
- *sound* 405
dulcet 413
credulous 486
silly 499
lenient 740
tender 822
timid 862
own to the – impeachment 529
– music 415
– pedal 405
– sawder 617, 933
– soap 356, 933
– tongue, – words 894
soften [*see* soft]
moderate 174
relieve 834
pity 914
palliate 937
softening of the brain 158
softer sex 374
soft-hearted 914
softling 160
softness 324
persuasibility 615
soft-spoken 894
soggy 339
soho
attention 457
parley 586
hunting 622
soi-disant
asserting 535
pretender 548
misnomer 565
vain 880
boastful 884
soil *region* 18
land 342
dirt 653
deface 846
till the – 371, 673
soirée 892
sojourn 186, 189
sojourner 188
soke 181
solace *relief* 834
recreation 840
– oneself with
pleasure 827
solar 318
– system 318
– time 114
solatium 973
sold to the devil 949
soldan [*see* sultan]
solder *join* 43
cement 45
cohere 46
soldier 726
soldier-like 722, 861
sole *alone* 87
base 211
support 215
feme – 904
solecism 568
soleil, coup de –
hot 384
mad 503
solemn
affirmation 535
important 642
grave 837
glorious 873
ostentatious 882
religious 987
worship 990
– mockery 882
– silence 403
solemnity *rite* 998
solemnization 883
sol-fa 416

solfeggio 415
solicit *induce* 615
request 765
desire 865
– the attention 457
solicitor *agent* 758
petitioner 767
lawyer 968
solicitous 865
solicitude *care* 459
pain 828
anxiety 860
desire 865
solid *complete* 52
dense 321
certain 474
learned 490
exact 494
wise 498
persevering 604*a*
solvent 803
– angle 244
solidarity
party 712
solidify 321
soliloquy **589**
solitaire *game* 840
hermit 893
solitary, **solitude** *alone* 87
secluded 893
solmization 416
solo 87, 415
– dance 840
Solomon, **Solon** *wise* 498
sage 500
solstice 125, 126
soluble *fluid* 333
liquefy 335
solus 87
solution
liquefaction 335
answer 462
explanation 522
– of continuity 70
solve *liquefy* 335
discover 480*a*
unriddle 522
solvent
liquefier 335
monied 803
somatics 316
somber *dark* 421
black 431
grey 432
sad 837
sombrero 225
some *indefinite quantity* 25
small quantity 32
more than one 100
–body *person* 372
important or distinguished 642
in – degree
degree 26
small 32
at – other time 119
in – place 182
– ten or a dozen 102
– time ago 122
– time or other 119
somehow or other
cause 155
instrument 631
somersault 218
something *thing* 3
small degree 32
matter 316
– else 15
– like 17
– or other 475
sometimes 136
somewhat
a little 32
a trifle 643
somewhere 182
– about 32
somnambulism
walking 266
trance 515
somnambulist
walker 268
dreamer 515
somniferous
sleepy 683
weary 841
somnolence 683
son 167
Son, God the – **976**
sonant 402
letter 561
sonata 415
Sonderbund **769**
song *music* 415
poem 597
death – 360, 839
love– 597
for a mere – 815
no – no supper 812
old – 643
songster 416
soniferous 402
sonnet 597
sonneteer 597
sonorous *sound* 402
loud 404
language 577
sons of:
– Belial 988
– God 977
Soofeeism 984
soon *transient* 111
future 121
early 132
too – for 135
sooner: – or later
another time 119
future 121
– said than done 704
soot 431, 653
sooth 511
in good – 543
soothe
allay 174
relieve 834
flatter 933
soothing
faint sound 405
– syrup 174
soothsay 511
soothsayer 513, 994
soothsaying 511
sop
small quantity 32
food 298
fool 501
inducement 615
reward 973
– to Cerberus 458
– in the pan 615
soph 492, 541
Sophi 745, 996
sophism 477, 497
sophist *scholar* 492
dissembler 548
sophister 492
student 541
sophistical 477
sophisticate *mix* 41
debase 659
sophisticated
spurious 545
sophistry **477**
sophomore 541
soporific 683, 841
soporous 683
soprano 410, 416
sorbet 298
sorcerer **994**
sorcery **992**
sordes 653
sordet 417
sordid *stingy* 819
covetous 865
sordine 417
sore
bodily pain 378
disease 655
mental suffering 828, 830
discontent 832
anger 900
– as a boil 901*a*
– place 822
– subject 830, 900
sorely *very* 31
s'orienter 278
sorites 476
sorority 712
sorrel 433, 434
sorrow 828
give – words 839
sorry *trifling* 643
grieved 828
mean 876
make a – face 874
cut a – figure 874
be – for 750, 914
in a – plight 732
– sight 830, 837
sort *degree* 26
arrange 60
kind 75
– with
sociality 892
sortable, **sortance**
agreement 23
sortes
chance 156, 621
– Virgilianae
sorcery 992
sortie 716
sortilege
prediction 511
sorcery 992
sortilegy 621
sortition 621
sorts, out of –
ill-health 655
sulky 901*a*
S.O.S. 669, 707
so-so *small* 32
trifling 643
imperfect 651
sostenuto 415
sot *fool* 501
drunkard 959
sot à triple étage 501
sotto voce
faint sound 405
conceal 528
voiceless 581
sou *money* 800
qui n'a pas le – 804
soubrette 599, 746
sough *conduit* 350
noise 405
cloaca 653
soul *essence* 5
person 372
intellect 450
genius 498
affections 820
cure of –s 995
flow of – 588
not a – 187
not dare to say one's – is his own *subjection* 749
fear 860
– of wit 572
have one's whole – in his work 686
soulless 683, 823
soul-mate 905
soul-sick 837
soul-stirring 821, 824
sound *great* 31
conformable 82
stable 150
strong 159
fathom 208
bay 343
noise **402**
investigate 461
measure 466
true 494
wise 498
sane 502
good 648
perfect 650
healthy 654
solvent 803
orthodox 983*a*
catch a – 418
safe and – 654, 670
– the alarm
indication 550
warning 668
alarm 669
fear 860
– asleep 683
full of – and fury
unmeaning 517
insolent 885
– the horn 416
– of limb 654
– locator 726
– mind 502
– the praises of 931
– the note of preparation 673
– reasoning 476
– a retreat 283
– sleep 683
– a trumpet
publish 531
alarm 669
– of wind 654
sounding: big – 577
– brass 517
sounding-board 417
soundings 208
soundless
unfathomable 208
silent 403
soup 298, 352
soupçon 32, 41
souplé 298
sour *acid* 397
discontented 832
embitter 835
uncivil 895
sulky 901
– grapes
impossible 471
excuse 617
– the temper 830
source *beginning* 66
cause 153
sourdet 417
sourdine 417
à la – *noiseless* 405
concealed 528
sourdough 463
soured 832
sourness **397**
sous tous les rapports 52
souse 310, 337
South *direction* 278
North and –
opposite 237
Southern
antipodes 237
– Cross 318
souvenir 505
sovereign
superior 33
all-powerful 159
authorities 737
ruler 745
– contempt 930
– remedy 662
Soviet 696, 737
sow *scatter* 73
pig 366
agriculture 371
female 374
get the wrong – by the ear
misjudgment 481
error 495
mismanage 699
fail 732
– broadcast 818
– dissension 713, 898
– the sand 645
– the seed
prepare 673
– the seeds of
cause 153
teach 537
– one's wild oats
improve 658
amusement 840
vice 945
intemperance 954

sozzled 959
spa *town* 189
sanatorium 662
space *distribute* 60
time 106
extension **180**
musical 413
ship 273
celestial –s 318
wide open –'s 180
spaddle 272
spade 272
call a – a spade
plain language 576
straightforward 703
spade-husbandry 371
spahi 726
span *join* 43
link 45
duality 89
time 106
transient 111
distance 196
near 196
length 200
short 201
measure 466
new 191
spangle *spark* 420
ornament 847
spaniel *dog* 366
servile 886
spanish fly 171
spank *swift* 274
flog 972
spanking *large* 192
– pace 274
spanner 633
spar *beam* 214
quarrel 713
contend 720
spare *extra* 37
small 193
meagre 203
refrain 623
store 636
scanty 640
redundant 641
disuse 678
inaction 681
relinquish 782
give 784
economy 817
exempt 927a
temperate 953
enough and to – 639
not a moment to – 682
to – 641
– diet 956
– no expense 816
– no pains 686
– room 180
– time 685
spared: be –
live 359
it cannot be – 630
sparge 337
spargefaction
scatter 73
wet 337
sparing [*see* spare]
small 32
economy 817
parsimony 819
temperate 953
with a – hand 819
with no – hand 639
– of praise 932
– of words 585
spark *small* 32
heat 382
light 420
luminary 423
wag 844
fop 854
as the –s fly upwards *habit* 613
sparkle
bubble 353
glisten 420
sparkling
vigorous 574
excitement 824
cheerful 836
wit 842
beauty 845
with – eyes 827
sparse 73
sparsity 103
Spartacus 742
spartan 739
spasm
sudden change 146
violence 173
agitation 315
pain 378
spasmodic
discontinuous 70
irregular 139
changeable 149
violent 173
spat 225, 713
spate 348
spathic 204
spatter *dirt* 653
spatterdash 225
spatula 191, 272
spavined 655
spawn *produce* 161
offspring 167
dirt 653
spay 38, 158
speak 560, 580, 582
– one fair 894
– for 937
– ill of 932, 934
– for itself 518, 528
– low 581
– of *meaning* 516
publish 531
speak 582
– out *make manifest* 525
artless 703
– softly 581
– to 586
– up 411
– up for 937
– volumes 467
– well of 931
speakeasy 189, 964
speaker
interpreter 524
chairman 694
speakie 964
speaking: much – 584
way of – 521
– likeness 554
on – terms 888
speaking-trumpet 418
spear 260, 727
– shaped 253
spearman 726
special 79
– correspondent 593
special pleader 968
special pleading
sophistry 477
speciali gratiâ 760
specialist 662, 700
speciality **79**
specialty
security 771
specie 800
species *kind* 75
appearance 448
human – 372
specific *special* 79
remedy 662
– gravity 321
specification 594
specify
particularize 79
tell 527
name 564
specimen 82
specious
probable 472
sophistical 477
beauty 845
flattering 933
pardonable 937
speck 32
speckle 440, 848
spectacle
appearance 448
prodigy 872
show 882
drama 599
spectacles 445
look through rose colored – 523
spectacular 882
spectator **444**
spectral 4, 980
spectre
fallacy of vision 443
ugly 846
ghost 980
spectroscope
light 420
color 428
optical instrument 445
spectrum
color 428
variegation 440
optical illusion 443
speculate
view 441
think 451
suppose 514
chance 621
essay 675
traffic 794
speculation
experiment 463
cards 840
speculative 463, 514
speculum 445
veluti in – 446
sped *completed* 729
speech **582**
figure of – 521
parts of – 567
speechify 582
speechless 403, 581
speechmaker 582
speed
velocity 274
activity 682
haste 684
help 707
succeed 731
with breathless – 684
God – 731, 906
speedily *soon* 132
speedometer 200, 274, 553
speedway 840
speer 455, 461
spell *period* 106
influence 175
read 539
letter 561
necessity 601
motive 615
exertion 686
charm **993**
cast a – 992
wonder 870
knurr and – 840
– for 865
– out *interpret* 522
spell-bound 601, 615
spence 636
spencer 225
spend *effuse* 297
waste 638
give 784
purchase 795
expend 809
– freely 816
– time 106
– time in 683
– one's time in 625
spender 818
spendthrift 818
spent 160, 688
spermaceti 356
spermatic 168
spermatize 168
spero, dum spiro – 858
spes sibi quisque 604
spew 297
sphacelus 655
sphere *rank* 26
domain 74
space 180
region 181
ball 249
world 318
business 625
– of influence 181, 780
spheroid 249
spherule 249
sphery 318
sphinx *monster* 83
oracle 513
ambiguous 520
riddle 533
spial 668
spice
small quantity 32
mixture 41
pungent 392
condiment 393
spiced 390
spicilegium 72, 596
spick and span 123
spiculate 253
spiculum 253
spicy 400, 824
spigot 263
spike *sharp* 253
pierce 260
plug 263
– guns 158, 645
spikebit 262
spikenard 356
spill *filament* 205
stopper 263
shed 297
splash 348
match 388
waste 638
lavish 818
– blood 722
– and pelt 59
spin *flying* 267
rotate 312
pluck 610
– out *protract* 110
late 133
prolong 200
diffuse style 573
– the wheel 140
– a long yarn 549
spindle 312
spindling 203
spindle-shanks 203
spindle-shaped 253
spindrift 353
spine 222, 253
spinel 847
spinet *copse* 367
harpsichord 417
spinney 367
spinner of yarns 594
spinosity
unintelligible 519
discourtesy 895
sullenness 901a
spinous *prickly* 253
spinster 374, 904
spiracle 351
spiral 248
spire *height* 206
convolution 248
peak 253
soar 305
spirit *essence* 5
immateriality 317
fuel 388
intellect 450
meaning 516
vigorous language 574
activity 682
affections 820
courage 861
ghost 980
bad – 980
keep one's – up
hope 858
with life and – 682

unclean – 978
– away 791
– up 615, 824
Spirit, the Holy – 976
spirited
language 574
active 682
sensitive 822
cheerful 836
brave 861
generous 942
spiritless
insensible 823
sad 837
cowardly 862
spirit-level 213
spiritoso *music* 415
spirit-rapping 992
spirits *drink* 298, 959
cheer 836
spirit-stirring 824
spiritual
immaterial 317
psychical 450
heterodoxy 984
divine 976
pious 987
– director 996
– existence 987
spiritualism
immateriality 317
intellect 450
sorcery 992
spiritualize 317
reasoning 476
spirituel 842
spirt *eject* 297
stream 348
haste 684
exertion 686
spirtle *disperse* 73
splash 348
spissitude 321, 352
spit *pointed* 253
perforate 260
eject 297
rotate 312
rain 348
– fire *irascible* 901
spite 907
in – of
disagreement 24
notwithstanding 30
counteraction 179
opposition 708
in – of one's teeth
unwilling 603
compulsion 744
spiteful 898, 907
hating 898
spittle 299
spittoon 191
splanchnology 329
splash *affuse* 337
stream 348
spatter 653
parade 882
make a –
fame 873
display 882
–board 666
splay 291
–footed 243
spleen
melancholy 837
hatred 898
anger 900
sullen 901*a*
harbor – 907
spleenless 906
splendor
bright 420
beautiful 845
glorious 873
display 882
splenetic 837, 901*a*
splice *join* 43
cross 219
interjacent 228
repair 660
– the main brace
tipsy 959
spliced, be –
marriage 903
splint 215
splinter
small piece 32
divide 44
filament 205
brittle 328
split *divide* 44
discontinuity 70
bisect 91
brittle 328
divulge 529
quarrel 713
fail 732
portion 786
laugh 838
– the difference 29, 774
– the ears } 404
– the head } 410
– hairs
discriminate 465
sophistry 477
fastidiousness 868
– upon a rock 732
– one's sides 838
splutter *energy* 171
spit 297
stammer 583
haste 684
spoil *vitiate* 659
hinder 706
lenity 740
plunder 791
booty 793
deface 846
satiate 869
– sport 706
– trade 708
spoiled child 869, 899
– of fortune 734
spoiler 792
spoke *radius* 200
tooth 253
obstruct 706
put a – in one's wheel *render*
powerless 158
hinder 706
spokesman 524, 582
spolia opima 793
spoliate 791
spoliative 793
spondee 597
spondulics 800
sponge *moisten* 339
dry 340
pulp 354
clean 652
despoil 791
hanger on 886
drunkard 959
apply the –
obliterate 552
non-payment 808
– out 552
sponging-house 752
spongy *porous* 252
soft 324
marshy 345
sponsion 771
sponsor
witness 467
security 771
be – for
promise 768
obligation 926
sponsorship 771
spontaneous
voluntary 600
willing 602
impulsive 612
spontoon 727
spoof 545
spook 980
spool 312
spoon
receptacle 191
ladle 272
bill and coo 902
born with a silver – in one's mouth 734
Spoonerism 218, 853
spoonful 25, 32
spoon-like 252
spoon-meat 298
spoony *foolish* 499
lovesick 902
spoor 551
sporadic 73, 137, 657
spore 330
sport *killing* 361
chase 622
amusement 840
show off 882
in – *pastime* 840
humor 842
the – of 749
– of fortune 735
sporting *killing* 361
contention 720
amusement 840
– dog 366
sportive 836, 840
sports 686
sportsman 361, 622, 840
sportulary 784, 785
sportule 784
sporule 330
spot *place* 182
discover 480*a*
mark 550
dirt 653
blemish 848
blot 874
on the –
instantly 113
present time 118
soon 132
in one's presence 186
spotless *perfect* 650
clean 652
innocent 946
spot light 423, 599
spots in the sun, see – *fastidious* 868
spotted
variegated 440
damaged 659
spousal 903
spouse 88, 903
spouseless 904
spout *egress* 295
flow out 348
conduit 350
speak 582
act 599
pawn 771, 787, 788
sprag 215
sprain 158, 160
sprat to catch a:
– herring 794
– whale 699
sprawl *length* 200
horizontal 213
descend 306
spray *sprig* 51
vaporizer 336
foam 353
spread *enlarge* 35
disperse 73
broadcast 78
expanse 180
expand 194
diverge 291
feast 298
publish 531
– abroad 531
– canvas 267
– out 194
– sail 267
– a shade 421
– to 196
– the toils 545
spree 840
spretae injuria formae *ugly* 846
disrespect 929
detraction 934
sprig *branch* 51
child 129
shillelagh 727
sprightly 836, 842
spring *early* 125
source 153
strength 159
velocity 274
recoil 277
fly 293
leap 309
elasticity 325
rivulet 348
instrument 633
store 636
–s of action 615
– back 277
– to one's feet 307
– from 154
– a leak 651, 659
– a mine
destroy 162
unexpected 508
attack 716
– a project 626
– up *begin* 66
event 151
grow 194
ascend 305
visible 446
hot – 382
– upon 789
spring balance 319
springe 545
spring-gun 545
spring tide
greatness 31
increase 35
completeness 52
youth 127
high 206
low 207
wave 348
water 337
springy 325
sprinkle *add* 37
mix 41
scatter 73
wet 337
rain 348
variegate 440
baptize 998
sprinkler 348, 385
sprinkling
small quantity 32
sprint 274
sprit *sprout* 167
support 215
sprite 979, 980
sprout *grow* 35
germinate 161
offspring 167
expand 194
– from *result* 154
spruce 652, 845
– up 847
sprue 653
sprung 651, 659
spry 682, 836
spud 272
spume 353
spun out 110, 573
spunk 861
spur
pointed 250
sharp 253
incite 615
hasten 684
win –s *succeed* 731
glory 873
on the – of the moment
instantly 113
now 118
soon 132
opportune 134
impulse 612
– gearing 633
the – of necessity 745
spurious
erroneous 495
false 544
deceptive 545
illegitimate 925
spurlos versenkt 2, 449
spurn *reject* 55
disdain 930
spurred 253
spurt

retract one's – 283
take – *plan* 626
prepare 673
conduct 692
tread in the – of 281
stercoraceous 653
stereography 591
stereometry 466
stereopticon 445
stereoscope 445
stereoscopic 446
stereotype *copy* 21
mark 550
engraving 558
printing 591
stereotyped
uniform 16
stable 150
habit 613
sterile 169, 645, 732
sterilize 652
sterling *true* 494, 944
– coin 800
stern *rear* 235
severe 739
discourteous 895
– necessity 601, 603
– truth 494
sternmost 235
sternutation
sneeze 349
sound 409
sternway 267
stertorous 402, 580
stet 150
– pro ratione voluntas 600
stethoscope 418
stevedore 271, 613, 690
stew *food* 298
heat 382
cook 384
difficulty 704
emotion 821
excitement 825
annoyance 828
bagnio 961
in a – *angry* 900
steward 637
director 694
agent 758
treasurer 801
stewardship 692, 693
stewpan 386
stichomancy 511
stick *adhere* 46
cease 142
staff 215
stab 260
remain quiet 265
fool 501
bungler 701
weapon 727
scourge 975
dirty end of the – 699
give the – to 972
– at *doubt* 485
averse 603
– fast *firm* 150
difficulty 704
– in one's gizzard 830, 900
– in 300
– law 972
– in the mud 304, 732
– at nothing
resolve 604
active 682
rash 863
– out 250
– to 143, 604*a*
– in the throat
hoarse 581
not say 585
dislike 867
– up 212, 307, 791
– up for *aid* 707
applaud 931
vindicate 937
stickle 603, 616
– for 720, 794
stickler 606
severity 739
sticky
cohering 46
viscid 352
stiff *rigid* 323
style 579
severe 739
coactive 751
ugly 846
affected 855
haughty 878
pompous 882
breeze 349
stiffen 323
stiff-necked 606
stiffness
stability 150
stifle *kill* 361
silence 403
conceal 528
stifled
faint sound 405
stifling *hot* 382
stigmatize 874
censure 932
accuse 938
stile *way* 627
hindrance 706
help a lame dog over a – 707
stiletto 262, 727
still
on the other hand 30
moderate 174
not moving 265
vaporization 336
furnace 386
silent 403
– less 467
– life *matter* 316
painting 556
– more
superior 33
evidence 467
– small voice 405
in – water 714
still-born 360, 732
stillroom 636
stillicidium 348
stilted
elevated 307
- *style* 577
ridiculous 853
affected 855
boasting 884
stilts *support* 215
on – *high* 206
elevated 307
hyperbolical 549
proud 878
boasting 884
stimulant 662
stimulate
energy 171
violence 173
incite 615
excite 824
stimulating
suggestive 514
stimulus 615
sting *pain* 378
tingle 380
poison 663
excite 824
mental suffering 830
anger 900
stinging
pungent 392
stingo 298
stingy 819
stink 401
– in the nostrils
unpleasant 830
dislike 867
hate 898
stink-bomb 727
stink-pot 401
stint *degree* 26
limit 233
scanty 640
begrudge 819
stintless 639
stipend *salary* 973
stipendiary
subject 749
receiving 785
magistrate 967
stipple
variegate 440
painting 556
engraving 558
stipulate 769, 770
– for 720
stipule 51
stir *energy* 171
move 264
agitation 315
excite 375
activity 682
jail 752
emotion 824
make a – 642, 682
– about 682
– the blood 824, 900
– up dissension 713
– the embers 163, 824
– the feelings 824
– the fire 384
– a question 461, 476
– one's stumps 266, 682
– up *mix* 41
violent 173
excite 824
stirps *kin* 11
source 153
paternity 166
stirring *events* 151
important 642
active 682
– news 532
stirrup
support 215
with a foot in the – 293
stirrup-cup 293, 959
stitch *junction* 43
pain 378
work 680
– in time 132
– of work 686
stive 384
stiver 800
stoat 401
stoccado 717
stock *kinship* 11
quantity 25
origin 153
paternity 166
collar 225
soup 298
fool 501
habitual 613
materials 635
store 636
property 780
merchandise 798
money 800
in – 777
laughing – 857
lay in a – 637
take – *inspect* 457
accounts 811
– exchange 799
– still 265
– in trade
means 632
store 636
property 780
merchandise 798
– with 637
stockade 717
stocked, well – 639
stock exchange 621
stock-farm 370
stocking 225
hoard 800
stock-jobbing 794
stock operator 621
stocks *prison* 752
funds 802
punishment 975
on the –
business 625
preparation 673
incomplete 730
– and stones 316, 823
stocky 201
stodge 957
stoicism
insensibility 823
inexcitability 826
disinterested 942
temperance 953
stoke 388
stoker 268
stole 999
stolen: – away 671
– goods 793
stolid 499, 843
stomach *pouch* 191
taste 390
brook 826
desire 865
not have the – to 603
turn the – 830
– of an ostrich 957
stomacher 225
stone *heavy* 319
dense 321
hard 323
kill 361
lithography 558
material 635
attack 716
weapon 727
punish 972
corner – 642
go down like a – 310
cast the first – at 938
heart of – 823, 907
key– 642
musical –s 417
no – unturned 461, 686
philosopher's 662
precious – 648
stepping – 627
throw a – at
attack 716
censure 932
accuse 938
throw –s at 907
tomb– 363
mark with a white – 642
throw a – in one's own garden 699
– dead 360
– of Sisyphus 645
stone-blind 442
stone-colored 432
stone-deaf 419
stone's throw 197
stoneware 384
stony 323
stony-hearted 907, 919
stooge 711, 746, 886
stook 72
stool 215
between two –s 704
– of repentance 950
– pigeon 527, 548
stoop *slope* 217
lower 308
humble 879
servile 886
dishonorable 940
– to conquer 702
stop *end* 67
cease 142
close 261
rest 265
silent 403
danger 665
inaction 681
hinder 706
prohibit 761
put a – to 142
– the breath 361
– the ears 419
– a flow 348

– the first blow 716
– one's flag 725
– hard 171
– all of a heap 824, 860
– home 171
– in with
imitate 19
assent 488
cooperate 709
– the iron while it is hot 134
– a light 384, 420
– the lyre 416
– the mind 457
– out something new 146, 515
– off *exclude* 55
– one 451
– out *exclude* 55
destroy 102
invent 515
obliterate 552
scheme 626
– off the roll 756, 972
– at the root of 162
– root 150
– sail 275
– tents 293
– terror 860
– up 416
– with wonder 870
striker 927
striking 525
– likeness 554
strikingly
greatly 31
string *tie* 43
ligature 45
continuity 69
filament 205
musical note 413
– together 60, 69
stringed instruments 417
stringent
energetic 171
authoritative 737
strict 739
compulsory 744
strings: *music* 417
leading – 541
pull the – 175, 693
two – to one's bow 632
stringy 205, 327
strip *adjunct* 39
narrow 203
filament 205
divest 226
take 780
rob 791
stripe *length* 200
variegation 440
mark 550
badge 747
blow 972
stripling 129
stripped *poor* 804
strive *endeavour* 675
exert 686
contend 720
– against 720
stroke *impulse* 276
touch 379
mark 550
evil 619
expedient 626
disease 655
action 680
success 731
painful 830
at a – 113
good – 626
– of death 360
– of the pen
writing 590
command 741
– of policy 626
– of time 113
– of word 686
– the wrong way 256
stroll 266
strolling player 599
strong *great* 31
powerful 159
energetic 171
tough 327
taste 390
pungent 392
fetid 401
healthy 654
feeling 821
wonderful! 870
smell – of 398
– accent 580
– argument 476
by a – arm 744
– box 802
with a – hand
resolution 604
exertion 686
severity 739
– language 574
– pull 686
– point 476
strong-headed 498
stronghold
refuge 666
defence 717
prison 752
strong-minded 498, 861
strong-scented 398
strong-willed 604
strop 253
strophe 597
strow 73
struck [*see* stricken, strike]
awe– 860
– down 732
– all of a heap
emotion 821
wonder 870
humbled 879
– with *love* 897
structural *state* 7
structure
production 161
form 240
texture 329
organization 357
struggle *exert* 686
difficulty 704
contend 720
strum 416, 517
strumpet 962
strung
highly – 825
strut *walk* 266
pride 878
parade 882
boast 884
– and fret one's hour upon a stage 359, 599
strychnine 663
stub 40, 550
stubbed 201
stubble *remains* 40
useless 645
stubborn
strong 159
hard 323
obstinate 606
resistance 719
stubby 201
stucco 45, 223
stuck [*see* stick]
– fast 150, 704
be – on 897
stuck-up 878
stud *hanging-peg* 214
knob 250
horses 271
studded *many* 102
spiked 253
variegated 440
student 541
stud-farm 370
studied
predetermined 611
studio *room* 191
painting 556
workshop 691
studious
thoughtful 451
docile 539
intending 620
study *copy* 21
room 191
thought 451
attention 457
research 461
learning 539
painting 556
intention 620
retreat 893
brown – 515
stuff *substance* 3
contents 190
expand 194
line 224
matter 316
texture 329
absurdity 497
unmeaning 517
material 635
trifle 643
overeat 957
such – as dreams are made of 515
– gown 968
– in 300
– the memory with 505
– and nonsense
unsubstantial 4
absurdity 497
unmeaning 517
– up *close* 261
hoax 545
stuffed
redundancy 641
stuffing *contents* 190
lining 224
stopper 263
stuffy 321, 382
stultified 732
stultify oneself 699
stultiloquy 497
stumble *fall* 306
flounder 315
error 495
unskilful 699
failure 732
– on *chance* 156
discover 480a
stumbling-block
difficulty 704
hindrance 706
stump
remainder 40
trunk 51
walk 266
drawing 556
speak 582
stir your –s
active 682
worn to the – 659
– along *slow* 275
stump orator 582, 887
stumpy *short* 201
stun *physically*
insensible 376
loud 404
deafen 419
unexpected 508
morally insensible 823
affect 824
astonish 870
stung [*see* sting]
– to the quick 824
stunt *shorten* 201
performance 680
stunted 193, 195
insufficient 640
stupe 834
stupefaction 826
stupefy
- *physically* 376
- *morally* 823
astonish 870
stupendous
great 31
large 192
wonderful 870
stupid
unsubstantial 4
misjudging 481
credulous 486
unintelligent 499
tiresome 841
dull 843
stupor
insensibility 823
wonder 870
stupration 961
sturdy *strong* 159
persevering 604a
– beggar 767, 792
stutter 583
sty *house* 189
enclosure 232
dirt 653
Stygian *dark* 421
diabolic 945
infernal 982
cross the – ferry
die 360
– shore
death 360
style *state* 7
time 114
painting 556
graver 558
name 564
diction 569
writing 590
beauty 845
fashion 852
stylet
awl 262
dagger 727
stylist 578
Stylites, Simon – 893
stylographic pen 590
stylography 590
stylus 590
styptic 397
Styx 982
suasible 602
suasion 615
suave mari magno 664
suaviter in modo 826, 894
suavity 894
sub 34
spe rati 475
subacid 397
subaction 330
subahdar 745
subalpine 206
subaltern
inferior 34
soldier 726
officer 745
servant 746
plebeian 876
subaqueous 208
subastral 318
subaudition 527
subcommittee 696
subconscious 317
subcontrary 237
subcutaneous 221
subdean 996
subdichotomy 91
subdititious 147
subdivide 44
subdivision
part 51
class 75
military 726
realty 780
subdolous 702
subdominant 413
subdual 731
subduction 38
subdue *calm* 174
succeed 731
subdued
morally 826
sub-editor 593
subitaneous 113
subito 113
subjacent 207
subject *dominate* 175
liable 177
topic 454
meaning 516

servant 746
enthral 749
– of dispute 713
– to examination 461
– of inquiry 461
– of thought 454
– to 469, 475
subjection **749**
subjective
intrinsic 5
immaterial 317
intellectual 450
subjoin 37
subjugate 731, 749
subjugation 732, 824
subjunctive 37
sublapsarian 984
sublation 38
sublevation 307
sub-lieutenant 745
sublimate
elevate 307
lighten 320
vaporize 336
sublime *high* 206
language 574
beauty 845
glory 873
magnanimous 942
from the – to the ridiculous 853
subliminal 317
sublineation 550
sublunary 318
submarine
deep 208
ship 272
warship 726
– chaser 726
– warfare 722
submediant 413
submerge
destroy 162
immerse 300
plunge 310
steep 337
submersible 273, 726
submersion 208
subministration 707
submission **725**
obedience 743
submissive
tractable 705
enduring 826
humble 879
submit to arbitration 774
submonish 695
submultiple 84
subordinate
inferior 34
unimportant 643
subject 749
subordination 58
suborn 615, 795
subpoena 741, 969
subreption
falsehood 544
acquisition 775
subrogation 147
subscribe
assent 488
aid 707
agree to 769
give 784
subscript 39, 65
subscription
gift 784
subsequent
- *in order* 63
- *in time* 117
subserviency
servility 886
subservient
instrumental 631
aid 707
subject 749
subside 36, 306
subsidiary *aid* 707
servant 746
subsidy
assistance 707
gift 784
pay 809
subsist *exist* 1
continue 141
live 359
subsistence 298
subsoil 221, 342
substance
existence 1
thing 3
quantity 25
inside 221
matter 316
texture 329
important part 642
wealth 803
in – 596
man of – 803
substantial
existing 1
hypostatic 3
material 316
dense 321
true 494
– meaning 516
substantiality **3**
substantially
intrinsically 5
– true 494
substantiate 467, 924
substantive 1, 3
substitute
inferior 34
change 147
means **634**
deputy 759
substitution **147**
substratum
substance 3
layer 204
base 211
support 215
interior 221
materiality 316
substructure 211
subsultory 315
subsume 54
subtend 237
subterfuge 617
sophistry 477
lie 546
cunning 702
subterranean 208
subtile *light* 320
rare 322
- *texture* 329
subtilize *rarefy* 322
sophistry 477
subtle *slight* 32
light 320
cunning 702
– point 704
– reasoning 476
subtlety 477, 498
subtraction
subduction 38
arithmetic 85
taking 789
subtrahend 38, 84
suburb *town* 189
near 197
environs 227
subvention
support 215
aid 707
gift 784
subversion 146
subvert *destroy* 162
invert 218
depress 308
subway 627
– train 272
succedaneum 147
succeed *follow* 63
posterior 117
success 731
transfer 783
– to *acquire* 775
succès d'estime 873
success **731**
succession
sequence 63
continuity 69
repetition 104
posteriority 117
transfer 783
in quick – 136
in regular – 138
– of ideas 451
– of time 109
successless 732
successor 65, 117
succinct 572
succor 707
succubus 980
succulent
nutritive 298
juicy 333
semiliquid 352
succumb
fatigue 688
yield 725
fail 732
succussion 315
such: – as 17
– being the case 8
– like 17
– a one 372
suchwise 8
suck
draw off 297
drink 298
take 789
– in 296
– the blood of 789
sucker 260, 547
suckle 707
suckling *infant* 129
suction *force* 157
reception 296
sudary 652
sudation 299
sudatory 386
sudden
transient 111
instantaneous 113
soon 132
unexpected 508
– burst 508
– death 360
– and quick in quarrel 901
– thought 612
sudorific 382
suds *froth* 353
in the – 704, 837
sue *demand* 765
go to law 969
suet 356
suffer *physical pain* 378
disease 655
allow 760
feel 821
endure 826
moral pain 828
– for 972
– punishment 972
sufferance, tenant on – 779
suffice 639
sufficiency **639**
suffix *adjunct* 39
sequence 63
sequel 65
letter 561
sufflation 349
suffocate *kill* 361
excess 641
suffocating 382, 401
suffocation 361
suffragan 996
suffrage 609
suffragette 742
suffusion
mixture 41
feeling 821
blush 879
sugar 396
sugar-loaf 253
suggest *suppose* 514
inform 527
influence 615
advise 695
– itself 451, 515
– a question 461
suggestio falsi 546
suggestion 626, 695
suggestive
reminder 505
significant 516
descriptive 594
bawdy 961
sui generis 83
suicidal 162
suicide *killing* 361
suisse *beadle* 996
Suisse, point d'argent point de – 812
suit *accord* 23
series 69
class 75
clothes 225
expedient 646
petition 765
courtship 902
follow – 19
law– 969
love– 897
– the action to the word 550
– the occasion 646
do – and service 743
suit case 191
suitable 23, 646
– season 134
suite *sequel* 65
series 69
escort 88
retinue 746
– of rooms 189, 191
suitor
petitioner 767
lover 897
lawsuit 969
sulcated 259
sulky *carriage* 272
obstinate 606
discontented 832
dejected 837
sullen 901*a*
sullen
obstinate 606
gloomy 837
discourteous 895
sulky 901*a*
sullenness **901a**
sully 653, 874
sulphur 388
– colored 436
sultan 745
sultry 382
sum *number* 84
money 800
– and substance
meaning 516
synopsis 596
important part 642
– total 800
– up *reckon* 85
description 594
compendium 596
sumless 105
summation 37, 85
summary
transient 111
early 132
short 201
concise 572
compendious 596
illegal 964
– of facts 594
summer *season* 125
support 215
heat 382
Indian – 125
St. Luke's – 125
St. Martin's – 125
– lightning 423
– time 114
summer-house 191
summerset 218
summit *top* **210**
summon 741, 969
– up 505, 824
– up courage 861
summum:
– bonum 618, 827
– jus 922
sump *base* 211
pool 343
slough 345
store 636

cess 653
sumpter-horse 271
sumptuary 800, 809
sumptuous 882
sum-total 50
sun 318
luminary 423
glory 873
bask in the – 377
going down of the – 126
farthing candle to the – 645
under the – 180, 318
as the – at noon-day *bright* 420
certain 474
plain 525
– oneself 384
Sun:
– of Righteousness 976
sunbeam 420
–s from cucumbers 471
sunburn *heat* 384
sunburnt *brown* 433
Sunday:
– Monday &c. 138
–'s best 847, 882
– school 542
sunder 44
sundial 114
sundown 126
sundry 102
sunk [*see* sink]
deep 208
– fence 717
– in iniquity 945
– in oblivion 508
sunken rocks 667
sunless 421
sunlight 420
sunny *warm* 382
luminous 420
cheerful 836
sunny side 829
view the – 858
– of the hedge 734
sun-painting 556
sunrise 125
sunset 126
at – 133
sunshade 223, 424
sunshine *light* 420
prosperity 734
happy 827
cheerful 836
sunstroke 384, 503
sun-up 125
suo: – periculo 926
– sibi gladio hunc jugulo
absurdity 479
retaliation 718
sup *small quantity* 32
feed 298
– full of horrors 828
super *theatrical* 599
superable 470
superabound 641
superadd 37
superannuated 128
superb 845
supercargo 694
supercherie 545
supercilious
proud 878
insolent 885
disrespectful 929
scornful 930
superdreadnought 726
supereminence 648, 873
supererogation 641, 645
superexaltation 873
superexcellence 648
superfetation 37, 168
superficial
shallow 209
outside 220
misjudging 481
ignorant 491
– extent 180
superficies 220
superfine 648
superfluitant 305
superfluity 40, 641
superfluous 645
superhuman 650, 976
superimpose 233
superimposed 206
superincumbent 206, 319
superinduce
change 140
cause 153
produce 161
superintend 693
superintendent 694
superior *greater* 33
– *in size* 194
important 642
good 648
director 694
superiority 33
superjunction 37
superlative 33
superlatively good 648
superman 33
supernal 206, 210, 981
supernatant 206, 305
supernatural 976, 980
– aid 707
supernumerary
adjunct 39
theatrical 599
reserve 636
redundant 641
superpose 37, 223
supersaturate 641
superscription 550, 590
supersede
substitute 147
disuse 678
relinquish 782
supersensible 317
superstition
credulity 486
error 495
religion 984
superstratum 220
superstructure 729
supertax 812
supertonic 413
supervacaneous 641
supervene
extrinsic 6
be added 37
succeed 117
happen 151
supervise 693
supervisor 694
supination 213
supine
horizontal 213
inverted 218
sluggish 683
mentally torpid 823
suppeditate 637
supper 298
supplant 147
supple *soft* 324
servile 886
supplement
addition 37
adjunct 39
completion 52
publication 531
book 593
suppletory 37
suppliant 765, 767
supplicate *beg* 765
pity 914
worship 990
supplies
materials 635
aid 707
money 800
supply *store* 636
provide 637
give 784
– aid 707
– deficiencies 52
– the place of 147
– and transport 726
support *perform* 170
sustain 215
evidence 467
preserve 670
aid 707
feel 821
endure 826
vindicate 937
– life 359
supporter 711
–s *heraldic* 550
suppose 514
supposing 469
supposition 514
supposititious 546
suppress
destroy 162
conceal 528
silent 581
restrain 751
suppression of truth 544
suppuration 653
suppute 85
supralapsarian 984
supramundane 939
supremacy 33, 737
supreme 33
summit 210
authority 737
in a – degree 31
Supreme Being 976
surbate 659
surbated 688
surcease 142
surcharge 641
– and falsify 811
surcingle 45
surcoat 225
surd *number* 84
deaf 419
silent letter 561
sure *certain* 474
belief 484
safe 664
make – against 673
make – of
inquire 461
take 789
you may be – 535
to be – *assent* 488
on – ground 664
security 771
sure-footed
careful 459
skilful 698
cautious 864
surely 489, 602, 870
sureness 474
surety 474, 664
surf 348, 353
surface *outside* 220
texture 329
below the – 526
lie on the – 518, 525
skim the – 460
Surface, Joseph – 548
surfeit 641, 869
surge *swarm* 72
swell 305
rotation 312
wave 348
surgeon 662
surgery 662
surgit amari aliquid 651
surly *gruff* 895
sullen 901a
unkind 907
surmise 514
surmount *be superior* 33
tower 206
transcursion 303
ascent 305
– a difficulty
overcome 731
surmountable 470
surname 564
surpass
be superior 33
grow 194
go beyond 303
outshine 873
surplice 999
surplus 40, 641
surplusage 641
surprint 550
surprise
non-expectation 508
unprepared 674
wonder 870
surprisingly 31
surrebutter &c.
answer 462
pleadings 969
surrender 725, 782
– one's life 360
surreptitious
furtive 528
deceptive 545
untrue 546
surrogate 759
surround 227, 229
surroundings
amidst such and such – 183
sursum corda 990
surtax 812
surtout *coat* 225
surveillance
care 459
direction 693
under – 938
survene 151
survey 441, 466
surveyor 85, 694
survive *remain* 40
long time 110
permanent 141
susceptibility
power 157
tendency 176
liability 177
sensibility 375
motive 615
impressibility 822
irascibility 901
suscipient 785
suscitate *cause* 153
produce 161
stir up 173
excite 824
suspect *doubt* 485
suppose 514
suspected 938
suspectless 484
suspend *defer* 133
discontinue 142
hang 214
suspended animation 823
suspender 45, 214
suspense
cessation 142
uncertainty 475
expectation 507
irresolution 605
in – *inert* 172
suspension
cessation 142
hanging 214
music 413
– of arms 723
suspicion *doubt* 485
incredulity 487
knowledge 490
supposition 514
fear 860
under – 938
suspiration 839
sustain
continue 143
strength 159
perform 170
support 215
preserve 670
aid 707
endure 821

T

T, to a – 494
tab 39, 550, 747
tabard 225
tabby *mottled* 440
gossip 588
tabefaction 195
tabernacle 189, 1000
house 189
temple 1000
tabid *shrunk* 195
thin 203
disease 655
deteriorated 659
table
arrangement 60
list 86
defer 133
layer 204
support 215
flat 251
repast 298
writing 590
on the – 626, 673
turn the –s 218, 468
under the –
hidden 528
drunk 959
– of the Lord 1000
the motion 624
tableau *list* 86
appearance 448
painting 556
theatrical 599
table-cloth 652
table d'hôte 298
table-land 213, 344
tabescent 195
tablet *layer* 204
flat 251
record 551
writing 590
remedy 662
table-talk 532, 588
tablets of the memory 505
table-turning 992
tabloid 531, 662
taboo 762, 992
tabor 417
tabouret 215
tabret 417
tabula rasa
inexistence 2
absence 187
ignorance 491
obliterated 552
facility 705
tabulate 60, 69
tabulation 551
tachometer 274
tachygraphy 590
tachy case 191
tacit 526
taciturnity **585**
Tacitus
concise style 572
tack *join* 43
nails 45
change course 140
sharp 253
direction 278
turn 279
food 289
way 627
go upon another – 607
wrong – 732
– to *add* 37
tackle
fastening 45
gear 633
try 675
undertake 676
manage 693
tacky 352
tact *touch* 379
discrimination 465
wisdom 498
skill 698
taste 850
want of – 851
tactful 894
tactician 700
tactics 602, 722
tactless 895
tactile &c. 379
tadpole 129
taedium vitae 837, 841
tag *small* 32
addition 37
adjunct 39
fastening 45
sequel 65
end 67
point 253
sheep 366
– after 281
tagrag and bobtail 876
tail *sequel* 65
end 67
pendent 214
back 235
aircraft 273
estate – 780
turn – 623
– off *decrease* 36
tail-coat 225
tailor 225, 690
tailoring 225, 882
tail-piece *sequel* 65
rear 235
engraving 558
ornament 847
tail-race 350
taint
imperfection 651
dirt 653
decay 659
disgrace 874
tainted 401, 655
taintless 652
taj 225
take *eat* 298
believe 484
know 490
understand 518
succeed 731
receive 785
appropriate 789
captivate 829
give and – 718
– a back 508, 870
– an account of 85
– action 680
– advice 695
– after 17
– aside 586
– away
annihilate 2
subtract 38
remove 185
seize 789
– back again 790
– a back seat 34
– by [*see below*]
– the cake 33
– care 668, 864
– care of 459, 664
– no care of 460
– off 293
– one's chance 621, 675
– one's choice 609
– things as they come 683, 826
– comfort 831, 834
– the consequences 154
– coolly 826
– a course 692
– its course 143, 151
– no denial 606, 744
– a disease 655
– down
swallow 298
depress 308
record 551
write 590
dismantle 681
humiliate 874
censure 932
– easily 826
– effect 151, 170
– an ell 885
– exception 932
– one's fancy 829, 865
– fire 384
– flight 623
– from 38, 789
– for [*see below*]
– the good the gods provide 831
– heart 831, 836
– to heart 828, 832
– heed 864
– a hint 498
– hold of 46, 789
– hold of the mind 484
– ill 832
– in [*see below*]
– an infection 655
– no interest in 823
– into [*see below*]
– it 484, 514
– the lead 62
– a leaf out of another's book 19
– a lease 788
– leave of 624
– a liberty 748
– away life 361
– a likeness 554
– measures 626
– money 810
– no note of 460
– no note of time 115
– notice 457
– one's oath 535
– off [*see below*]
– oneself off 293
– on [*see below*]
– one with another 29
– out 301, 552
– over 783
– part with 709
– pattern by 19
– a peep 441
– pen in hand 590
– to pieces 44, 681
– place 151
– the place of 147
– possession of 589
– precedence 33, 62
– its rise 66, 154
– root 150, 184
– the shine out of 33
– ship 267
– steps 673, 680
– stock 85
– time
duration 106
late 133
leisure 685
– time by the forelock 132
– to *habit* 613
pursuit 622
use 677
like 827
desire 865
love 897
– on trust 484
– a turn 140
– up [*see below*]
– upon oneself 676, 768
– warning 668
– wing 293
– one at one's word 769
take by
– the button 586
– the hand 707
– surprise 508, 674
take for 484
– better or for worse 609
– gospel 486
– granted 484
take in *include* 54
shorten 201
admit 296
understand 518
deceive 545
receive money 785
– good part
be calm 826
be pleased 827
content 831
– hand *teach* 537
undertake 676
aid 707
– an idea 498
– sail 275
take into
– account
include 76
discriminate 465
qualify 469
– consideration 451
– custody 751
– one's head 514, 608
take off *mimic* 19
destroy 162
remove 185
divest 226
depart 293
discount 813
ridicule 856
– one's hands 785
– the hat 894
take on
attempt 675
discontent 832
melancholy 837
– credit 484
– trust 484
take up
elevate 307
inquire 461
dissent 595
choose 609
undertake 676
befriend 707
arrest 751
borrow 788
censure 932
– arms 722
– a case 476
– one's abode 184
– the cudgels 710, 720
– an inquiry 461
– money 788
– one's pen 590
– with
attention 457
use 677
content 831
taken, be –
die 360
– ill 655
– with 897
taker 789
taking **789**
infectious 657
in a – *pained* 828
angry 900
talapoin 996
talbotype 556
tale
counting 85
narrative 594
thereby hangs a – 526
twice-told –
diffuse style 573
weary 841
tale-bearer 532
talent 698
bury one's – in a napkin 528
not put one's – in a napkin 878
talionis, lex – 718, 922
taliped 243
talisman 747, 993
talismanic 992
talk
unsubstantial 4
rumor 532
speak 582
conversation 588
small – 588
– big *boast* 884

insolent 885
threat 909
- glibly 584
- nonsense 497
- of *signify* 516
publish 531
intend 620
- to oneself 589
- oneself out of breath 584
- over
confer 588
persuade 615
- to in private 586
- at random
illogical 477
loquacity 584
- together 588
- against time
time 106
protract 110
inaction 681
- of the town
gossip 588
fame 873
talkative 582, 584
talked of 873
talkies 599, 840
talking, fine –
over-estimation 482
tall 206
- hat 225
- talk 884
tallage 812
tallies 85
tallow 356
- candle 423
tallow-faced 429
tally *agree* 23
list 85, 86
sign 550
credit 805
- with *conform* 82
tally-ho 622
tally-man 797
talma 225
Talmud 985
talons
authority 737
claws 781
talus 217
tam-o'-shanter 225
tambourine 417
tame *inert* 172
moderate 174
domesticate 370
teach 537
feeble 575
subjugate 749
insensible 823
calm 826
tameless
violent 173
malevolent 907
Tammany 940
tamp 261, 276
tamper with
alter 140
seduce 615
injure 659
meddle 682
tan *color* 433
tandem
at length 200
vehicle 272
tang *taste* 390
bane 663
tangent 199
angle 217
fly off at a –
deviate 279
diverge 291
excitable 825
tangere ulcus 505
tangible
material 316
touch 379
exact 494
sufficient 639
useful 644
tangle 61, 219
tangled 59, 704
weave a – web 704
tango 840
tank *pool* 343
reservoir 636
armored vehicle 726
tankard 191
tanker 273
tant: – mieux 838
- s'en faut 489
- soit peu 32
tantaene animis coelestibus irae 900
tantalize *balk* 509
induce 615
desire 865
tantalizing
exciting 824
Tantalus: torment of – 507, 865
tantamount 27, 516
tantara 407
tantas componere lites 723
tanti 642
tantivy *speed* 274
tantrums 900
tap *open* 260
plug 263
hit 276
let out 295, 297
sound 406
turn on the – 297
tap-dance 840
tape *string* 205
measure 466
- machine 553
taper *contract* 195
narrow 203
candle 423
- to a point 253
tapestry 556, 847
tapinois, en – 528
tapis: on the –
event 151
topic 454
intention 620
plan 626
tap-root 153
taps 550
tapster 746
tar *cover* 223
sailor 269
pitch 356a
- and feather 929, 972
taradiddle 546
tarantass 272
tarantella 840
tarboosh 225
tardiloquence 583
tardy 133, 275
tare 40*a*
- and tret 813
tares 645
targe 717
target 620
shield 717
tariff 812
tarmac 635
tarn 343
tarnish
discoloration 429
soil 653
deface 848
disgrace 874
tarpaulin 223
tarry *remain* 110, 265
later 133
continue 141
- for *expect* 507
tart *pastry* 298, 396
acid 397
rude 895
irascible 901
harlot 962
tartan 440
tartane 273
Tartar *choleric* 901
catch a – *dupe* 547
unskilful 699
retaliation 718
tartar *dirt* 653
- emetic 663
Tartarus 982
Tartufe
hypocrisy 544
deceiver 548
impiety 988
task *lesson* 537
business 625
put to use 677
fatigue 688
command 741
hard – 704
set a – 741
take to – 932
- the memory 505
taskmaster 694
tass 191
tassel 847
taste *sapidity* **390**
experience 821
good taste **850**
man of – 850
to one's – *savory* 394
pleasant 829
love 897
tasteful 850
tasteless *insipid* 391
tasty 394, 850
tâtonner 463
tatter
small quantity 32
tatterdemalion 876
Tattersalls 799
tatters *garments* 225
tear to – 162
tatting 847
tattle 588
tattler 532, 588
tattoo
drumming 407
mottled 440
summons 741
taught [*see* teach]
fastened 43
taunt 929, 938
tauromachy 720
taut 43
tautology 104, 573
tavern 189
tawdry 851
tawny 433, 436
tax *inquire* 461
employ 677
fatigue 688
command 741
compel 744
request 765
accounts 811
impost 812
discount 813
accuse 938
- one's energies 686
- the memory 505
taxi 266
taxi-cab 272
taxi-driver 268
taxidermy 368
taxis 60
taxonomy 60
tazza 191
Te Deum 990
te fabula narratur, de – *retaliate* 718
condemn 971
tea 298
teach 537
- one's grand-mother 641, 885
- one his place 879
teachable 539
teacher **540**, 673
teaching **537**
false – 538
teacup, storm in a –
overrate 482, 549
exaggerate 549
teagown 225
team *assemblage* 69, 72
teamster 694
tea-party 892
tea-pot 191
tear *separate* 44
violence 173
move rapidly 274
excite 825
weeping 839
- away from 789
- oneself away 623
- asunder one's bonds 750
- one's hair 839
- out 301
- to pieces
separate 44
destroy 162
- up *destroy* 162
tear-gas 663, 727
tearful 839
tearing passion 839
tears: draw – 830
shed – 839
- in one's eyes
excited 824
sad 837
tease *annoy* 830
spite 907
teaser *difficult* 704
teasing 830
teat 250
tea-table talk 588
technic 698
technica, memoria – 505
technical
conformable 82
workmanlike 698
- college 542
- education 537
- knowledge 698
- school 542
- term 564
technicality
special 79
cant term 563
formulary 697
technique 556, 698
technocracy 698
technology 698
techy 901
tedious 841
while away the – hours 681
tedium 841
teem
produce 161
productive 168
abound 639
- with *multitude* 102
teemful 168
teeming *crowd* 72
teemless 169
'teens 98
in one's – 127, 129
teeter 314
teeth 330, 781
armed to the – 673, 717, 722
between the – 405
cast in one's – 938
chattering of – 383
have cut one's eye – 698
in the – of 704, 708
grind one's – 900
the run of one's – 815
set one's – 604
show one's – 900
in spite of one's – 708, 744
make one's – chatter 385, 860
set the – on edge
scrape 331
saw 397
stridor 410
pain the feelings 830
tee 66
teetotalism 953, 958
teetotum 312, 840
teg 366
tegument 223
teind 99
teinoscope 445
tekel upharsin 668
telautograph 553
telegram 532
telegraph

solecism 568
stammering 583
on the tip of one's –
near 197
forget 506
latent 526
speech 582
wag the – 582
– cleave to the roof of one's mouth 870
have a – in one's head 582
– of land 342
– running loose 584
keep one's – between one's teeth 585
tongueless 581
tongue-tied 581
tonic
musical note 413
healthy 656
medicine 662
– sol fa 415
tonicity 159
tonnage 192
tonsillectomy 662
tonsils 351
tonsure 999
tonsured 226
tontine 810
tony 501
Tony Lumpkin 876
too
also 37
excess 641
– bad
disreputable 874
wrong 923
censure 932
– clever by half 702
in a – great degree 31
– far 641
– hot to hold one 830
– late 133
– late for 135
– little 640
– many 641
– much [*see below*]
– soon 132
– soon for 135
– true 833 839
too much
redundance 641
intemperance 954
have – of 869
make – of 482
– for 471
– of a good thing 869
tool *instrument* 633
steer 693
catspaw 711
ornament 847
servile 886
edge – 253
mere – 690
toot 406
tooth *fastening* 45
projection 250
sharp 253
roughness 256
notch 257
texture 329
taste 390
sweet –
desire 865
fastidious 868
– and nail
violence 173
exertion 686
attack 716
– paste &c. 652
toothache 378
toothed 253
toothsome 394
top *supreme* 33
summit 210
roof 223
spin 312
sleep like a – 683
fool to the – of one's bent 545
go over the – 861
– to bottom 52
– coat 225
– hat 225
at the – of the heap 210
– of the ladder 873
at the – of one's speed 274
from – to toe 200
at the – of the tree 210, 873
at the – of one's voice 404, 411
toparchy 737
topaz 436, 847
top-boot 225
tope *tomb* 363
trees 367
drink 959
temple 1000
topee 225
toper 959
top-full 52
top-gallant mast, 206, 210
top-heavy
unbalanced 28
inverted 218
dangerous 665
tipsy 959
Tophet 982
topiary 847
topic 454
– of the day 532
topical 183
top-mast 206
topmost 210
topography 183
topographer 466
topple
unbalanced 28
perish 162
decay 659
– down *fall* 306
– over 28, 306
topsail schooner 273
topsawyer 642, 700
top sergeant 745
topsy-turvy 14, 218
toque 225
tor 206
torch 388, 423
apply the – 824
light the – of war 722
– of Hymen 903
Tories 712
torment
physical 378
moral 828, 830
place of – 982
Tormes, Lazarillo de – 941
torn [*see* tear]
discord 713
tornado 312, 349
torpedo *bane* 663
sluggish 683
weapon 727
evil-doer 913
– boat 726
– boat destroyer 726
– plane 276
torpid, torpor
inert 172
inactive 683
insensible 823
torque 847
torrefy 384
torrent
violence 173
rapid 274
flow 348
rain in –s 348
torrid 382
torsion 248
torso 50
tort 925, 947
tort et à travers, à –
disagreement 24
absurdity 497
resolution 604
tortious 925
tortile 248
tortive 248
tortoise 275
tortoise-shell 440
tortuous
twisted 248
dishonorable 940
torture
physical 378
moral 828, 830
cruelty 907
punishment 972
– a question 476
torvity 901*a*
toss *derange* 61
throw 284
oscillate 314
agitate 315
– in a blanket 929
– the caber 840
– the head
pride 878
insolence 885
contempt 930
– off *drink* 298
– overboard 610
– on one's pillow 825
– up 156, 621
tosspot 959
tot *child* 129
tot homines, tot sententiæ 15
total 50, 84
sum – 800
– abstinence 953, 955
– eclipse 421
totality 52
totalizator 621
totally 52
totidem verbis 19, 494
totient 84
toties quoties 136
totis viribus 686
totitive 84
toto: in – 52
– cœlo 52
totter
changeable 149
weak 160
limp 275
oscillate 314
agitate 315
decay 659
danger 665
– to its fall 162
touch *relate to* 9
small quantity 32
mixture 41
conduct 199
sensation **379, 380**
music 416
test 463
indication 550
act 680
receive 785
excite 824
pity 914
– and go
instant 113
soon 132
changeable 149
easy 705
– the guitar 416
– the hat 894
– the heart 824
– on 516
– to the quick 822
– up 658
– upon 595
in – with 9
touched *crazy* 503
tainted 653
compassion 914
– in the wind 655
– with *feeling* 821
touching 830
touchstone 463
touchwood
fuel 388
irascible 901
touchy 901
tough *coherent* 46
tenacious 327
difficult 704
toujours perdrix
repetition 104
weary 841
satiety 869
toupee 256
tour 266
tour de force
skill 698
stratagem 702
display 882
touring car 272
tourist 268
tournament 720
tourniquet 263
tournure 230, 448
belle – 845
tous les rapports, sous – 494
tousle 61
tout *solicit* 765
tout: – au contraire 14
– court 265
– ensemble 50
– le monde 78
touter *agent* 758
solicitor 767
eulogist 935
tow 285
take in – *aid* 707
towage 812
towardly 705
towards 278
draw – 288
move – 286
towel *clean* 652
flog 972
tower
stability 150
edifice 161
abode 189
height 206
soar 305
defence 717
– of strength
strong 159
influential 175
safety 664
towering *great* 31
furious 173
large 192
high 206
– passion 900
– rage 900
town *city* 189
fashion 852
man about – 854
on the – 961
all over the – 532
talk of the – 873
– council 696
town-hall 189, 966
township 181
townsman 188
fellow – 892
town-talk 532, 588
toxic 657
toxicology 663
toxophilite 284
toy *trifle* 643
amusement 840
fondle 902
toy-dog 366
toy-shop 840
trabant 717
tracasserie 713
trace *inquire* 461
discover 480*a*
mark 550
record 551
delineate 554
– back 122
– out 480*a*
– to 155
– up 461
tracery
lattice 219
curve 245
ornament 847
traces *harness* 45
trachea 351
tracing 21

trousers 225
trousseau 225
trouvaille 775
trouvère 597
trover 775, 964
trow *think* 451
believe 484
know 490
trowel 191
troy-weight 319
truant *absent* 187
runaway 623
idle 682
apostate 941
truce *cessation* 142
deliverance 672
peace 721
pacification 723
flag of – 724
trucidation 361
truck *summit* 210
vehicle 272
barter 794
truck driver 268
truck farm 371
truckle to
submit 725
servile 886
flatter 933
truckle-bed 215
truck-load 31
truckman 268
truculent 907
trudge 266, 275
truditur dies die 109
true *real* 1
straight 246
assent 488
accurate 494
veracious 543
faithful 772
honorable 939
orthodox 983*a*
– bill
vindicate 937
accuse 938
lawsuit 969
see in its – colors 480*a*
– meaning 516
– to nature 17
– to oneself 604*a*
– saying 496
– to scale 494
true-hearted 543, 939
true-love 897
true-lover's knot 897, 902
true-penny 939
truism *axiom* 496
unmeaning 517
trull 962
truly *very* 31
assent 488
really 494
indeed 535
trump *perfect* 650
honorable 939
good man 948
turn up –s 731
– card *device* 626
success 731
– up *falsehood* 544
accuse 938
trumped up 468, 545, 546
trumpery 517, 643
trumpet *music* 417
war cry 722
boast 884
flourish of –s
ostentation 882
celebration 883
boasting 884
ear– 418
penny –
skill 410
sound of –
alarm 669
speaking – 418
– blast 404
– call 550, 741
– forth 531
trumpeter
musician 416
messenger 534
boaster 884
trumpet-toned 410
trumpet-tongued 404, 531
truncate 201, 241
truncated 53
truncheon
weapon 727
staff of office 747
instrument of punishment 975
trundle 284, 312
trunk *whole* 50
origin 153
paternity 166
box 191
trunk-hose 225
trunnion
support 215
projection 250
truss *tie* 43
pack, packet 72
support 215
trust
belief 484
combination 709
property 780
credit 805
hope 858
– to a broken reed 699
– to the chapter of accidents 621
trustee
consignee 758
possessor 779
treasurer 801
trustful 484
trustless 940
trustworthy
certain 474
belief 484
- *memory* 505
veracious 543
honorable 939
truth
exactness **494**
veracity 543
probity 939
arrive at the – 480*a*
in – *certainly* 474
love of – 543
of a – 535, 543
prove the – of 937
religious – 983*a*
speak the – 529, 543
in very – 543
Truth, Spirit of – 976
truthless 544
trutination 319
try *experiment* 463
adjudge 480
endeavor 675
use 677
lawsuit 969
– a case 967
– a cause 480
– conclusions
discuss 476
quarrel 713
contend 720
– one's hand 675
– one's luck 621
– one 704
– out 463
– the patience 830
– a prisoner 967
– one's temper 824
– one's utmost 686
trying 688, 704
tryst 892
trysting-place 74
tsar [*see* czar]
tu quoque 718
– argument
counter-evidence 468
confutation 479
accuse 938
tub 191
– thumper 582
– to a whale 545, 617
tuba 417
tubam trepidat, ante – 860, 862
tubby 202
tube 260
test – 144
tubercle 250
tuberculous 655
tuberosity 250
tubman 968
tubular 260
tubulated 260
tubule 260
tuck *fold* 258
dagger 727
– in *locate* 184
eat 298
insert 300
tucker 225
tuft *collection* 72
rough 256
tufted 256
tuft-hunter 836, 943
tuft-hunting 886, 933
tug *ship* 273
pull 285
effort 686
– of war 720, 722
athletic sport 840
tuition 537
tulip *variegated* 440
gaudy 882
tumble *derange* 61
destruction 162
fall 306
agitate 315
fail 732
rough and – 59
– down 665
tumbler *athlete* 159
glass 191
actor 599
buffoon 844
tumbrel 272
tumefaction 194
tumid
expanded 194
- *style* 577
tumor
expansion 194
prominence 250
tumult *disorder* 59
agitation 315
revolt 742
emotion 825
tumultuous 59, 173
tumulus 363
tun *receptacle* 191
large 192
drunkard 959
tunable 413
tund 972
tundra 344
tune 402, 415
in – 413
out of –
unmusical 414
imperfect 651
deteriorated 659
put in –
prepare 673
concord 714
to the – of
quantity 25
payment 807
price 812
– up 416
tuneful *music* 413
poetry 597
– nine 416, 597
tuneless 414
tunic 225
tunicle 999
tuning-fork 417
tunnage 192
tunnel *concave* 252
opening 260
passage 627
tup 366, 373
turban 225
turbary 267
turbid 426, 653
turbinated 248, 312
turbine 153
turbulence
violence 173
agitation 315
excitation 825
turbulent 59
Turcism 984
tureen 191
turf *lawn* 344
grass 367
fuel 388
gambling 621
races 720
race-course 728
amusement 840
turgid
expanded 194
- *style* 577
redundant 641
ostentatious 882
Turk
polygamist 903
grand – 745
'bear like the – no rival near the throne' 878
turkey-trot 840
Turkish bath 386, 652
turlupinade 842
turmoil
confusion 59
violence 173
agitation 315
turn *state* 7
crisis 134
period of time 138
change 140
tendency 176
form 240
curve 245
blunt 254
stroll 266
deviate 279
circuition 311
rotate 312
aptitude 698
affections 820
emotion 821
dance 840
nausea 867
by –s 138, 148
come in its – 138
each in its – 148
meet one at every – 641
take a favorable – 658
give one a –
aid 707
excite 824
do a good – 648, 906
ill – 907
in – 58, 138
one's luck –s 735
serve one's – 644
to a – 494
take a wrong – 732
– about 148
– to account 677, 775
– adrift 73, 297
– aside *change* 140
deviate 279
hinder 706
– one's attention from 458
– away *eject* 297
not look 442
avoid 623
dismiss 756
relinquish 782
– back 145, 283
– one's back upon
oppose 708
refuse 764
disrespect 929
contempt 930
– the brain 503
– of the cards 156
– color 821
– a corner
go round 311
succeed 731
– the corner 140, 658

umbra 421
magni nominis – 659
umbrage *shade* 424
hatred 898
take – *anger* 900
umbrageous 421
umbrella
covering 223
shade 424
protection 666
umpire
judgment 480
mediator 724
judge 967
unâ voce 488
unabashed
bold 861
vain 880
insolent 885
unabated 31
unable 158
– to say 'No' 605
unacceptable 830
unaccommodating
disagreeing 24
disagreeable 830
discourteous 895
sulky 901*a*
unaccompanied 87
unaccomplished 730
unaccountable
exceptional 83
unintelligible 519
irresponsible 927*a*
arbitrary 964
unaccustomed
unusual 83
unused 614
unskilful 699
unachievable 471
unacknowledged 489, 917
unacquainted 491
unacquired 777*a*
unadmonished 665
unadorned 576, 849
beauty – 845
unadulterated 42, 494, 652
unadventurous 864
unadvisable 647
unadvised 665, 699
unaffected
genuine 494
sincere 543
– *style* 578
obstinate 606
artless 703
insensible 823
simple 849
taste 850
unafflicted 831
unaided *weak* 160
unalarmed 861
unalienable 924
unallayed 159
unallied 10
unallowable 923
unallowed 925
unalloyed 42
– happiness 827
– truth 494
unalluring 866
unalterable 150
unaltered 13, 150
unamazed 871
unambiguous 518
unambitious 866
unamiable 907
unanimated 823
unanimity 23, 488, 714
unannexed 44
unanswerable
demonstrative 478
irresponsible 927*a*
arbitrary 964
unanswered 478
unanticipated 508
unappalled 861
unappareled 226
unapparent 526
unappeasable 173
unappetizing 398
unapplied 678
unappreciated 482
unapprehended 491
unapprehensive 861
unapprized 491
unapproachable
great 31
infinite 105
distant 196
unapproached 33
unappropriated 782
unapproved 932
unapt
incongruous 24
important 158
unskilful 699
unarmed 158
unarranged 59, 674
unarrayed 849
unascertained 475, 491
unasked 602, 766
unaspiring 866, 881
unassailable 664
unassailed 748
unassembled 73
unassisted 160, 706
– eye 441
unassociated 44
unassuming 881
unatoned 951
unattached 44
unattackable 664
unattainable 471
unattained 732
unattempted 623
unattended 87
– to 460
unattested 468
unattracted
indifferent 866
unattractive 866
unauthenticated
unproved 468
uncertain 475
error 495
unauthoritative 475
unauthorized
prohibited 761
undue 925
lawless 964
unavailing 645, 918
unavenged 918
unavoidable 474, 601
unavowed 489
unawakened 683
unaware 491, 508
take –s 674
unawed 861
unbalanced 28
unbar 750
unbearable 830
unbeaten 123
unbeauteous 846
unbecoming
incongruous 24
disreputable 874
undue 925
dishonorable 940
– a gentleman 895
unbefitting 24, 925, 940
[*see* unbecoming]
unbegotten 2
unbeguile 527, 529
unbegun 67, 674
unbelief **485**, 989
unbeloved 898
unbend
straighten 246
repose 687
– the mind 452
unbending 323
unbenevolent 907
unbenign 907
unbeseeming 851, 940
unbesought 766
unbetrayed 939
unbewailed 932
unbiassed 498, 748
unbidden 600, 742
unbigoted 498
unbind 44, 750
unblamable 946
unblamed 946
unblemished 650, 946
unblenching 861
unblended 42
unblest 735, 932
– with 777*a*
unblown 674
uncommenced 67
unblushing
proud 878
vain 880
imprudent 885
unboastful 881
unbodied 317
unboiled 674
unbolt 750
unbookish 491
unborn 2, 152
unborrowed 787, 788
unbosom oneself 529
unbought
not bought 796
honorary 815
honorable 939
unselfish 942
unbound 748, 927*a*
unbounded 105
unbrace 160, 655
unbreathed 526
unbred 895
unbribed 939, 942
unbridled
violent 173
lax 738
free 748
unbroken
entire 50
continuous 69
preserved 670
unviolated 939
unbruised 50
unbuckle 44
unburden
– one's mind 529
unburdened 705
unburied 362
unbusinesslike 699
unbuttoned 748
uncalculating 863
uncalled for
redundant 641
useless 645
not used 678
uncandid 544, 907
uncanny 846, 980
uncanonical 984
uncared for
neglected 460
indifference 866
disliked 867
hated 898
uncase 226
uncaught 748
uncaused 156
unceasing 112
uncensured 931
unceremonious 880, 895
uncertain
irregular 139
not certain 475
doubtful 485
in an – degree 32
uncertainty **475**
unchain 44, 750
unchained 748
unchallenged 488, 924
unchangeable 150, 604*a*
unchanged 16, 141
unchanging 5
uncharitable 907
unchartered 925, 964
unchaste 961
unchastised 970
unchecked 748
uncheckered 141
uncheerful 837
unchivalric 940
unchristian 984, 989
uncial 590
uncinated 244
uncircumscribed 180
uncircumspect 460
uncivil 851, 895
uncivilized 876, 895
unclaimed 748
unclassical 851
uncle *kin* 11
my –'s
pawnshop 787
unclean 653
– spirit 978, 980
uncleanness **653**
unclipped 50
unclog 705, 750
unclose 260, 750
unclothe 226
unclouded 420, 446
unclubbable 893
unclutch 790
uncoif 226
uncoil 313
uncolored
achromatic 429
true 494
uncombed 653, 851
uncombined
simple 42
incoherent 47
uncomeatable 471
uncomely 846
uncomfortable 828, 830
uncommenced 67
uncommendable
blamable 932
bad 945
guilt 947
uncommensurable 24
uncommon 31, 83, 137
uncommonly 31
uncommunicated 781
uncommunicative 528
uncompact 322
uncompassionate 914*a*
uncompelled 748
uncomplaisant 764
uncompleted
incomplete 53
unfinished 730
failure 732
uncomplying 742, 764
uncompounded 42
uncompressed 320, 322
uncompromising
conformable 82
severe 739
unconcealable 525
unconceived
uncreated 12
unintelligible 519
unconcern 823, 866
unconcocted 674
uncondemned 970
unconditional
complete 52
free 748
permission 760
consent 762
release 768*a*
unconducive 175*a*
unconfined 748
unconfirmed 475
unconformity
disagreement 24
irregularity **83**
unconfused
methodical 58
clear 518
unconfuted 478, 494
uncongealed 333
uncongenial 24, 657
unconnected
irrelative 10
disjointed 44
discontinuous 70

marriage 903
unionist 712
union-jack 550
union-pipes 417
unique
dissimilar 18
original 20
exceptional 83
alone 87
unirritating 174
unison
agreement 23
melody 413
concord 714
unit 51, 87
Unitarian 984
unite *join* 43
combine 48
assemble 72
concur 178
converge 290
party 712
one's efforts 709
– in pairs 89
– with 709
united 46, 714
unity *identity* 14
uniformity 16
whole 50
complete 52
single **87**
concord 714
– of time 120
Unity, Trinity in –
976
universal 78
– Church 983*a*
– favourite 899
universality 52
universe 318
university 542
– education 537
– extension 537
go to the – 539
unjust *wrong* 923
impious 988
unjustifiable
wrong 923
inexcusable 938
wicked 945
unjustified 923
undue 925
unkempt
unclean 753
vulgar 851
unkennel *eject* 297
disclose 529
unkind 907
–est cut of all 828
unknightly 940
unknit (44)
unknowable 519
unknowing 491
unknown
ignorant 491
latent 526
– to fame
inglorious 874
low-born 876
– quantities 491
unlabored
- *style* 578
unprepared 674
unlace (44)
unlade 297
unladylike
vulgar 851
rude 895
unlamented
hated 898
disapproved 932
unlatch 44, 750
unlawful
undue 925
illegal 964
unlearn 506
unlearned 491
unleavened 674
unless
circumstances 8
except 83
qualification 469
unlettered 491
– Muse 579
unlicensed 761
unlicked
unprepared 674
vulgar 851
clownish 876
– cub
youngster 129
shapeless 241
unmannerly 895
unlike 18
unlikely 473
unlikeness 15
unlimber 323
unlimited
great 31
infinite 105
free 748
– space 180
unliquefied 321
unlively 837, 843
unload
displaced 185
eject 297
disencumber 705
unlock *unfasten* 44
discover 480*a*
unlooked for 508
unloose
unfasten 44
liberate 750
unloved 898
unlovely 846
unlucky
inopportune 135
bad 649
unfortunate 735
in pain 830
unmade 2
unmaimed 654
unmake 145
unman
mutilate 38
render powerless
158
madden 837
frighten 860
unmanly
effeminate 374
dishonorable 940
unmanageable
unwieldy 647
perverse 704
unmanned
dejected 837
cowardly 862
unmannered 895
unmannerly 895
unmarked 460
unmarred 654, 670
unmarried 904
unmask 529
unmatched
different 15
dissimilar 18
unparalleled 20
unmeaningness 517
unmeant 517
unmeasured
infinite 105
undistinguished
465*a*
abundant 639
unmeditated 612
unmeet 925
unmellowed 674
unmelodious 414
unmelted 321
unmentionable 874
–s 225
unmentioned 526
unmerciful 914*a*
unmerited 925
unmethodical 59
unmindful
inattentive 458
neglectful 460
ungrateful 917
unmingled 42
unmissed 460
unmistakable
certain 474
intelligible 518
manifest 525
unmitigable 173
unmitigated
great 31
complete 52
violent 173
unmixed 42
unmolested 664,
831
unmoneyed 804
unmoral 823
unmourned 898
unmoved
quiescent 265
obstinate 606
insensible 823
unmusical 424
– voice 581
unmuzzled 748
unnamed 565
unnatural
exceptional 83
affected 855
spiteful 907
unnecessary
redundant 641
useless 645
inexpedient 647
unneeded 645
unneighborly 895
unnerved
powerless 158
weak 160
dejected 837
unnoted } 460
unnoticed } 874
unnumbered 105
unnurtured 674
uno saltu 113
unobeyed 742
unobjectionable
good 648
pretty good 651
innocent 946
unobnoxious 648
unobscured 420
unobservant 458
unobserved 460
unobstructed 705,
749
unobtainable 471
unobtained 777*a*
unobtrusive 881
unoccupied
vacant 187
unthinking 452
doing nothing 681
inactive 683
untenanted 893
unoffended
enduring 826
humble 879
unofficial 964
unoften 137
unopened 261
unopposed 709
unorganized 674
– matter 358
unornamental 840
unornamented
- *style* 576
simple 849
unorthodox 984
unostentatious 881
unowed 807
unowned 782
unpacific 713, 722
unpacified 713
unpack
unfasten 44
take out 297
unpaid *debt* 806
honorary 815
the great –
magistracy 967
– worker 602
unpalatable 395,
830
unparagoned
supreme 33
best 648
perfect 650
unparalleled
unimitated 20
supreme 33
exceptional 83
unpardonable 938,
945
unparliamentary
language 895,
908
unpassable 261
unpassionate 826
unpatriotic 911
unpeaceful 720, 722
unpeople
emigration 297
banishment 893
unperceived
neglected 460
unknown 491
unperformed 730
unperjured 543,
939
unperplexed 498
unpersuadable 606
unpersuaded 616
unperturbed 826
unphilosophical 499
unpierced 261
unpin (44)
unpitied 932
unpitying 914*a*
unplaced 185
unplagued 831
unpleasant 830
unpleasing 830
unpoetical 598, 703
unpolished
rough 256
inelegant 579
unprepared 674
vulgar 851, 876
rude 895
unpolite 895
unpolluted
good 648
perfect 650
unpopular 830, 867
unpopularity 898
unportioned 804
unpossessed 777*a*
unpractical 699
unprecedented 83,
137
unprejudiced 498,
748
unpremeditated
impulsive 612
undesigned 621
unprepared 674
unprepared 508,
674
unprepossessed 498
unprepossessing
846
unpresentable 851
unpretending 881
unprevented 748
unprincipled 945
unprivileged 925
unprized 483
unproclaimed 526
unproduced 2
unproductive 645
unproductiveness
169
unproficiency 699
unprofitable
unproductive 169
useless 645
inexpedient 647
bad 649
unprolific 169
unpromising 859
unprompted 612
unpronounceable
519
unpronounced 526
unpropitious
ill-timed 135
opposed 708
hopeless 859
unproportioned 24
unprosperous 735
unprotected 665
unproved 477
unprovided
scanty 640
unprepared 674
unprovoked (616)
unpublished 526
unpunctual
tardy 133
untimely 135
irregular 139
unpunished 970
unpurchased 796
unpurified 653

unpurposed 621
unpursued 624
unqualified
incomplete 52
impotent 158
certain 474
unprepared 674
inexpert 699
unentitled 925
– truth 494
unquelled 173
unquenchable
strong 159
desire 865
unquenched
violence 173
heat 382
unquestionable 474
unquestionably 488
unquestioned 474, 488
unquiet
motion 264
agitation 315
excitable 825
unravel *untie* 44
arrange 60
straighten 246
evolve 313
discover 480*a*
interpret 522
disembarrass 705
unreached 304
unread 491
unready 674
unreal
not existing 2
erroneous 495
imaginary 515
unreasonable
impossible 471
illogical 477
misjudging 481
foolish 499
exorbitant 814
unjust 923
unreclaimed 951
unrecognizable 146
unreconciled 713
unrecorded 552
unrecounted 55
unreduced 31
unrefined 851
unreflecting 458
unreformed 951
unrefreshed 688
unrefuted 478, 494
unregarded
neglected 460
unrespected 929
unregenerate 988
unregistered 552
unreined 748
unrelated 10
unrelenting 914*a*, 919
unreliable
uncertain 475
irresolute 605
dangerous 665
unrelieved 835
unremarked 460
unremembered 506
unremitting
continuous 69
continuing 110
unvarying 143
persevering 604*a*
unremoved 184
unremunerated 808
unrenewed 141
unrepealed 141
unrepeated 87, 103
unrepentant 951
unrepining 831
unreplenished 640
unrepressed 173
unreproached 946
unreproved 946
unrequited 806, 917
unresented 918
unresenting 826
unreserved
manifest 525
veracious 543
artless 703
unresisted 743
unresisting 725
unresolved 605
unrespected 929
unrest 149, 264
unrestored 688
unrestrained
capricious 608
unencumbered 705
free 748
unrestricted
undiminished 31
free 748
unretracted 535
unrevenged 918
unreversed 143
unrevoked 143
unrewarded 806, 917
unrhymed 598
unriddle 480*a*, 529
unrig 645
unrighteous 945
unrip 260
unripe
young 127
sour 397
immature 674
unrivalled 33
unroll *evolve* 313
display 525
unromantic 494
unroot 301
unruffled
calm 174
quiet 265
unaffected 823
placid 826
unruly *violent* 173
obstinate 606
disobedient 742
unsaddle 756
unsafe 665
unsaid 526
unsaleable
useless 645
selling 796
cheap 815
unsaluted 929
unsanctified 988, 989
unsanctioned 925
unsated 865
unsatisfactory
inexpedient 647
bad 649
displeasing 830
discontent 832
unsatisfied 832, 865
unsavouriness **395**
unsay *recant* 607
unscanned 460
unscathed 654
unschooled 491
unscientific 477
unscoured 653
unscriptural 984
unscrupulous 940
unseal 529
unsearched 460
unseasonable 24, 135
unseasoned 614, 674
unseat 756
unseemly
inexpedient 647
ugly 846
vulgar 851
undue 925
vicious 945
unseen
invisible 447
neglected 460
latent 526
unseldom 136
unselfish 942
unseparated 46
unserviceable 645
unsettle *derange* 61
unsettled
mutable 149
displaced 185
uncertain 475
– in one's mind 503
unsevered 50
unsex 146
unshaded 525
unshaken 159
– belief 484
unshapely 846
unshapen 241
unshared 777
unsheathe
– the sword 722
unsheltered 665
unshielded 665
unshifting 143
unship 185, 297
unshocked 823
unshorn 50
unshortened 200
unshrinking 604, 861
unsifted 460
unsightly 846
unsinged 670
unskilfulness **699**
unslaked 865
unsleeping 604*a*, 682
unsmooth 256
unsociable 893
unsocial 893
unsoiled 652
unsold 777
unsoldierlike 862
unsolicitous 866
unsolved 526
unsophisticated
simple 42
genuine 494
artless 703
unsorted 59
unsought
avoided 623
unrequested 766
unsound
illogical 477
erroneous 495
deceptive 545
imperfect 651
– mind 503
unsown 674
unsparing
abundant 639
severe 739
liberal 816
with an – hand 818
unspeakable 31, 870
unspecified 78
unspent 678
unspied 526
unspiritual 316, 989
unspoiled 648
unspotted
clean 652
beautiful 845
innocent 946
unstable 218
changeable 149
uncertain 475
irresolute 605
precarious 665
– equilibrium 149
unstaid 149
unstained
clean 652
honorable 939
unstatesmanlike 699
unsteadfast 605
unsteady
mutable 149
irresolute 605
in danger 665
unstinted 639
unstinting 816
unstirred 823, 826
unstopped
continuing 143
open 260
unstored 640
unstrained
turbid 653
relaxed 687
– meaning 516
unstrengthened 160
unstruck 823
unstrung 160
unstudied 460
unsubject 748
unsubmissive 742
unsubservient
useless 645
inexpedient 647
unsubstantial 4
weak 160
rare 322
erroneous 495
imaginary 515
unsubstantiality **4**
unsuccessful 732
unsuccessive 70
unsuitable
incongruous 24
(*inexpedient* 647)
– time 135
unsullied *clean* 652
honorable 939
(*guiltless* 946)
unsung 526
unsupplied 640
unsupported
weak 160
(*unassisted* 706)
– by evidence 468
unsuppressed 141
unsurmountable 471
unsurpassed 33
unsusceptible 823
unsuspected
belief 484
latent 526
unsuspecting
hopeful 858
unsuspicious
belief 484
artless 703
hope 858
unsustainable 495
unsweet 395
unswept 653
unswerving
straight 246
direct 278
persevering 604*a*
unsymmetric 83
unsymmetrical 59, 243
unsystematic 59
untainted *pure* 652
healthy 654
honorable 939
untalked of 526
untamed 851, 907
untarnished 939
untasted 391
untaught 491, 674
untaxed 815
unteach 538
unteachable 499, 699
untenable
powerless 158
illogical 477
undefended 725
untenanted 187, 893
unthanked 917
unthankful 917
unthawed 321, 383
unthinkable 471
unthinking
unconsidered 452
involuntary 601
unthought of 452, 460
unthreatened 664
unthrifty
unprepared 674
prodigal 818
unthrone 756
untidy 59, 653
untie 44, 750
– the knot 705
until 106
– now 118
untilled 674
untimely 135
– end 360
untinged 42
untired 689
untiring 604*a*

untitled 876
untold
countless 105
uncertain 475
latent 526
secret 528
untouched
disused 678
insensible 823
untoward
ill-timed 135
bad 649
unprosperous 735
unpleasant 830
untraced 526
untracked 526
untractable 606, 699
untrained
unaccustomed 614
unprepared 674
unskilled 699
untrammelled 705, 748
untranslatable 523
untranslated 523
untravelled 265
untreasured 640
untried *new* 123
not decided 481
untrimmed 674, 849
untrodden *new* 123
impervious 261
not used 678
untroubled 174, 721
untrue 495, 546
untrustworthy
uncertain 475
erroneous 495
danger 665
dishonorable 940
untruth 544, **546**
untunable 414
unturned 246
untutored
ignorant 491
unprepared 674
artless 703
untwine 313
untwist 313
unused
new 123
unaccustomed 614
unskilful 699
unusual 83
unusually *very* 31
unutterable 31, 519, 870
unvalued
underrated 483
undesired 866
disliked 898
unvanquished 748
unvaried
continuing 143
- *style* 575, 576
unvarnished
true 494
- *style* 576
unreserved 703
simple 849
tale 494, 543
unvarying 16, 143
unveil 525, 529
unventilated 261
unveracious 544
unversed 491
unvexed 831
unviolated 939
unvisited 893
unwakened 683
unwarlike 862
unwarmed 383
unwarned 508, 665
unwarped judgment 498
unwarrantable 923
unwarranted
illogical 477
undue 925
illegal 964
unwary 460
unwashed 653
great – 876
unwatchful 460
unwavering 604*a*
unweakened 159
unwearied
persevering 604*a*
indefatigable 682
refreshed 689
unwedded 904
unweeded garden 674
unweeting 491
unweighed 460
unwelcome 830, 893
unwell 655
unwept 831
unwholesome 657
unwieldy
large 192
heavy 319
cumbersome 647
difficult 704
ugly 846
unwilling 489
unwillingness 603
unwind *evolve* 313
unwiped 653
unwise 499
unwished 866
unwithered 159
unwitting
ignorant 491
involuntary 601
unwittingly 621
unwomanly 373
unwonted 83, 614
unworldly 939
unworn 159
unworshipped 929
unworthy
shameful 874
vicious 945
– of belief 485
– of notice 643
unwrap 246
unwrinkled 255
unwritten
latent 526
obliterated 552
spoken 582
– law 697, 963
unwrought 674
unyielding
tough 323
resolute 604
obstinate 606
resisting 719
up
aloft 206
vertical 212
effervescing 353
excited 824
the game is – 735
prices looking – 814
time – 111
– in arms
prepared 673
active 682
opposition 708
attack 716
resistance 719
warfare 722
– and at them 716
– and doing 682
– and down 314
– on end 212
– in 698
– to [*see below*]
all – with
destruction 162
failure 732
adversity 735
up to
time 106
power 157
knowing 490
skilful 698
brave 861
– the brim 52
– date 123
– one's ears 611
– one's eyes 641
– the mark
equal 27
sufficient 639
good 648
due 924
– snuff 702
– this time
time 106
past 122
Upas tree 663
upbear 215, 307
upbraid 932
upcast 307
upgrow 206
upgrowth 194, 305
upheaval 146
upheave 307
uphill
acclivity 217
ascent 305
laborious 686
difficult 704
uphoist 307
uphold
continue 143
support 215
evidence 467
aid 707
praise 931
upholder 488, 711
upholstery 633
uplands 180, 206, 344
uplift 307, 658
upon:
– my honor 535
– oath 535
– which 117, 121
upper 206
– boxes, – circle 599
– classes 875
– hand
influence 175
success 731
sway 737
– story
summit 210
intellect 450
wisdom 498
– ten thousand 875
be on one's –'s 804
uppermost 210
say what comes – 612
– in the mind
thought 451
topic 454
attention 457
– in one's thoughts
memory 505
upraise 307
uprear 307
upright
vertical 212
honest 939
uprise 305
uprising 742
uproar
disorder 59
violence 173
noise 404
uproarious 825
uproot 301
ups and downs of life 151, 735
upset *destroy* 162
invert 218
throw down 308
defeat 731
excite 824
disconcert 874
– the apple cart 732
upshot *result* 154
judgment 480
completion 729
upside down 218
upstairs 206
upstart
new 123
prosperous 734
plebeian 876
upturn 210
upwards 206
– of 33, 100
uranology 318
urban 189
urbane 894
urbis conditæ, anno – 106
urceole 998
urchin
child 129
small 193
wretch 949
imp 980
urge *violence* 173
impel 276
incite 615
hasten 684
beg 765
urgent
required 630
important 642
haste 684
request 765
urn *vase* 191
funereal 363
heater 386
cinerary – 363
usage 613, 677
usance 806
use *habit* 613
waste 638
utility 644
employ **677**
property 780
make good – of 658
in – 677
be of – to *aid* 707
benevolence 906
– one's discretion 600
– one's endeavor 675
– a right 924
– up 677
used to 613
used up
deteriorated 659
disuse 678
fatigue 688
weary 841
satiated 869
useful 644
render – 677
useless 645
user,
right of – 780
usher
guard 263
receive 296
teacher 540
servant 746
courtesy 894
wedding 903
– in *precedence* 62
begin 66
precession 280
announce 511
– into the world 161
usque ad nauseam 841
U.S.S. 726
ustulation 384
usual
general 78
ordinary 82
customary 6
usufruct 677
usurer
lender 787
merchant 7
credit 805
miser 819
usurious 819
usurp *assume* 739
seize 789
illegal 925
– authority 738
usurpation
insolence 885
usurper 737
usury 806
utensil 191, 633
uti possidetis
permanence 141
possession 777
retention 781
utilitarian 677, 910
utility 644
general –
actor 599

utilize 677
utmost 33
do one's – 686
– height 210
in one's – need 735
deserted in one's – need 893
Utopia 515, 858
utricle 191
utter *extreme* 31
distribute 73
disclose 529
publish 531
speak 580, 582
money 800
utterly 52
uttermost 31
to the – parts of the earth 180, 196
uxorious 897

V

va sans dire, cela 474, 525
vacant *void* 4
absent 187
thoughtless 452
unmeaning 517
scanty 640
– hour 685
– mind *folly* 499
vacate *displace* 185
absent 137
depart 293
resign 757
vacation 687
vaccine 366
vache 191
vacillate
changeable 149
undulate 314
waver 605
vacuity 187
vacuous
unsubstantial 4
absent 187
vacuum 187
– cleaner 653
vade mecum 527, 542
vadium 771
væ victis! *war* 722
threat 909
vagabond
wanderer 268
low person 876
rogue 949
vagabondage 266
vagary
absurdity 497
imagination 515
whim 608
antic 840
vagrant
changeable 149
roving 266
traveler 268
deviating 279
vague
unsubstantial 4
uncertain 475
unreasoning 477
unmeaning 517
obscure 519
- *language* 571
– suggestion 514
vail *panel* 228
donation 784
reward 973
vain *unreal* 2
unprofitable 645
unvalued 866
conceited 880
in – *failure* 732
labor in –
come short 304
useless 645
fail 732
take a name in – 895
– attempt 732
use – efforts 645
– expectation 509
vainglorious
haughty 878
vain 880
boasting 884
vaivode 745
valance 231
vale 252
– of years 128
valeat quantum 467
valediction 293, 894
valedictory 293
valentine 902
valet 631, 746
valet
– de chambre 746
– de place 524, 527
valetudinarian 655, 656
Valhalla 981
valiant 861
valid *confirmed* 150
powerful 157
strong 159
true 494
sufficient 639
– reasoning 476
valise 191
valley 252
– of the shadow of death 360
vallum 717
valoir, se faire – 884
valor 861
valorem, ad – 812
valuable 644, 648
value *color* 423
measure 466
estimate 480
importance 642
utility 644
goodness 648
price 812
approbation 931
of priceless – 814
set a – upon 482
– received 810
–s *painting* 556
valueless 645
valve *stop* 263
conduit 350
safety – *safety* 664
refuge 666
escape 671
vamp *change* 140
music 463
– up *improve* 658
restore 660
prepare 673
vampire 913, 980
vampirism 789, 992
van *beginning* 66
front 234
wagon 272
in the – 234
precession 280
van-courier 64
Vandal
destroyer 165
vulgar 851
commonalty 876
evil-doer 913
vandalism 851
vandyke 257
Vandyke brown 433
vane *wind* 349
indication 550
vanguard 234
vanish
unsubstantial 4
transient 111
disappear 449
vanishing 32, 193
vanity *useless* 645
conceit **880**
– bag 191
Vanity Fair 852
vanquish 731
vantage ground
superiority 33
power 157
influence 175
height 206
vapid *insipid* 391
- *style* 575
vaporization **336**
vaporous
imaginary 515
opaque 426
vapor *gas* 334
bubbles 353
fancy 515
boast 884
insolence 885
– bath 386, 652
vaporer 887
vapors
dejection 837
variable 149, 605
variance
difference 15
disagreement 24
discord 713
at – *enmity* 889
at – with 489
variant 15
variation
difference 15
diverseness **20a**
number 84
chance 140
music 415
varied 15
variegated 16*a*, 440
variegation **440**
variety
difference 15
class 75
multiformity 81
exception 83
entertainment 599
variform 81
various 15, 102
– places 182
– times 119
varlet 949
varnish
overlay 223
resin 356*a*
sophistry 477
falsehood 544
painting 556
decorate 847
excuse 937
vary *differ* 15
dissimilar 18
variation 20*a*
change 140
fluctuate 149
vascular *cells* 191
holes 260
pipes 350
vase 191
vassal 746
vassalage 749
vast *great* 31
spacious 180
large 192
– learning 490
vasty deep 341
vat 191
Vatican 995, 1000
thunders of the – 908
vaticination 511
vatum, genus irritabile – 597
vaudeville 599, 840
vault
cellar 191
curve 245
leap 309
tomb 363
store 636
– of heaven 318
vaulted 245, 252
vaulting 33, 865
vaunt 884
vaurien 949
vavasour
possessor 779
nobleman 875
V.C. 733
vection 270
Vedas 986
vedette 668
Vedidad 986
veer
change 140
deviate 279
go back 283
change intention 607
vegetability **365**
vegetable **367**
– kingdom 367
– life 386
– oil 356
– physiology 369
vegetarian 298, 953
vegetate 365
exist 1
grow 194
stagnate 265
inactive 681, 683
insensible 823
vegetation 365
vehemence
violence 173
feeling 821
emotion 825
vehement
- *language* 574
vehicle
carriage **272**
instrument 631
veil *covering* 225
shade 424
concealment 526, 527
conceal 528
ambush 530
behind the – 360
draw aside the – 529
take the – 893, 995
veiled
uncertain 475
invisible 447
concealed 528
vein *temper* 5
tendency 176
thin 203
thread 205
channel 350
humor 602
mine 636
affections 820
in the – 602
not in the – 603
veined 440
veld 344
velis et remis 274
velitation 720
velleity 600
vellicate 315
vellicating 392
vellum 590
veloce *music* 415
velocipede 272
velocity 264, **274**
angular – 244
veluti in speculum 17
velvet 255, 256
pleasure 377
on – *easy* 705
venal *price* 812
stingy 819
dishonest 940
selfish 943
venation 622
vend 796
vendee 795
vender 796
vendetta 919
vendible 796
vendition 884
vendor 796
veneer 204, 223
venenation 659
venerable *old* 124
aged 128
sage 500
respected 928
veneration
respect 928
piety 987
venereal disease 655
venery *killing* 361
hunting 622
impurity 961
venesection
ejection 297

remedy 662
Venetian blinds 351
vengeance 919
cry to heaven for – 923
with a – 31, 173
vengeful 919
veni vidi vici 731
venial 937
veniam petimusque damusque vicissim 918
venienti occurrere morbo 673
venison 394
venom 663, 907
venomous *bad* 649
poisonous 657
rude 895
maleficent 907
vent *opening* 260
egress 295
air-pipe 351
disclose 529
escape 671
sale 796
find – *egress* 295
passage 302
publish 531
escape 671
give – to 297, 529
– one's rage 900
– one's spleen 900
venter 191
ventiduct 351
ventilate
begin 66
air 338
wind 349
discuss 595
– a question 461, 476
ventilator 349, 351
ventosity 349
vent-peg
stopper 263
safety 666
escape 671
ventre
– à terre 274
danse du – 840
ventricle 191
ventriloquism 580
venture
chance 621
danger 665
try 675
courage 861
I'll – to say 535
venturesome
undertaking 677
brave 861
rash 863
venue 74, 183
Venus *woman* 374
planet 423
beauty 845
love 897
goddess 919
veracity **543**
verandah 191
verbal 562
– intercourse 582, 588
– quibble 497, 842
verbatim
imitation 19
exact 494
words 562
verbiage
unmeaning 517
words 562
diffuse 573
verbis:
totidem – 494
– ad verbera 720
verborum, copia –
diffuse 573
eloquence 582
loquacious 584
verbosity
words 562
diffuse 573
loquacity 584
verboten 761
verbum sapienti 527
verdant 367, 435
verd-antique 435
verdict
opinion 480
lawsuit 969
snatch a – 545, 702
verdigris 435
verditer 435
verdure 367, 435
verecundiam, argumentum ad – 874, 939
verecundity 879, 881
veredical 543
Verein 712
verge
tendency 176
near 197
edge 231
limit 233
direction 278
verger 996
veriest 31
verification 463, 771
verify 463
evidence 467
demonstrate 478
find out 480a
verily *truly* 494
verisimilitude 472
veritable 494
veritas, nuda – 494
vérité, palais de – 703
verity 494
verjuice 397
vermicular
convoluted 248
worm 366
vermiform 248
vermilion 434
vermin
animal 366
unclean 653
base 876
vernacular
native 188
internal 221
language 560
habitual 613
vernal 123, 125
vernier
minuteness 193
– *scale* 466
vero, vitam impendere – 535, 939
verrons, nous – 507
versatile 149
verse *division* 51
poetry 597
versed in 490
versicolor 440
versify 597
version *change* 140
special 79
interpretation 522
versus 278, 708
vert 435
vertebral 222
vertebrate 366
vertex 210
verticality **212**
verticity 312
vertigo
rotation 312
delirium 503
verve
imagination 515
vigorous language 574
energy 682
feeling 821
very 31
– best 648
– image 554
– many 102
– minute 113
– much 31
– picture 17
– small 32
– thing
identity 13
agreement 23
exact 494
– true 488
– well 831
Véry light 423
vesicle *cell* 191
covering 223
globe 249
vesicular 191, 260
vespers 126, 990
vespertine 126
vessel
receptacle 191
tube 260
ship 273
vest *place* 184
dress 225
– in *belong to* 777
give 784
Vesta 979
vesta *match* 388
vestal 960
vested *fixed* 150
legal 963
– in *located* 184
– interest
given 780
due 924
vestibule 66, 191
vestige 551
vestigia:
veteris – flammæ 505, 613
– nulla retrorsum 282, 604a
vestment 225, 999
vestry *council* 696
churchdom 995
church 1000
vesture 225
vesuvian
match 388
veteran *old* **130**
adept 700
warrior 726
veterinary art 370
veteris vestigia flammae 505, 613
veto 761
vetturino 694
vex 830, 898
vexata quaestio 704, 713
vexation 828, 830
– of spirit 828
discontent 832
resentment 900
vexatious 830
vexed question 704, 713
vi et armis
violence 173
exertion 686
compulsion 744
viâ 278, 627
viable 359
via lactea 318
viaduct 627
vial 191
vials:
– of hate 898
– of wrath 900
viands 298
viaticum
provision 637
rite 998
vibrate 314
– between two extremes 149
vibrato 415
vibratory 149
vibroscope 314
vicar *deputy* 759
clergyman 996
– of Bray 607, 886
vicarage 1000
vicariate 995
vicarious 147
vicarship 995
vice *deputy* 759
holder 781
wickedness **945**
vice versâ
reciprocal 12
contrary 14
interchange 148
vice-admiral 745
Vice-Chancellor 967
–'s Court 966
vicegerency 755
vicegerent 758, 759
vice-president 694
vice-regal 759
viceroy
governor 745
deputy 759
vicesimal 98
vicinage 197
vicinism 145
vicinity 197, 227
vicious 173, 945
render – 659
– reasoning 477
vicissitude 149
Vickers gun 727
victim *dupe* 547
defeated 732
sufferer 828
victimize *kill* 361
deceive 545
injure 649
baffle 731
victis, væ – 722, 909
victor 731
victoria
carriage 272
Victoria Cross 733
victory 731
victual *provide* 637
victuals 298
videlicet 79, 522
viduage 905
viduity 905
vie *good* 648
– with 720
vielle 417
view
sight 441
appearance 448
attend to 457
opinion 484
landscape painting 556
intention 620
bring into – 525
come into – 446
commanding – 441
in – *visible* 446
intended 420
expected 507
keep in – 457
on – 448
present to the – 448
with a – to 620
– as 484
– in a new light 658
viewer 444
viewless 447
view-point 441
vigesimal 98
vigil *care* 459
vigilance *care* 459
wisdom 498
activity 682
caution 864
vigils *worship* 990
vignette 558, 594, 847
vigor *strength* 159
energy 171
style **574**
resolution 604
health 654
activity 682
viking 792
vile *valueless* 643
bad 649
painful 830
disgraceful 874
plebeian 876
dishonorable 940
vicious 945
vilify *shame* 874
malediction 908
censure 932
detract 934
vilipend
disrespect 929

cuique – 865
voluptuary 954*a*, 962
voluptuous
pleasure 377
delightful 829
intemperate 954
impure 961
volutation 312
volute 248
vomit 297
vomitory 260, 295
voodoo 992, 994
voracious *desire* 865
glutton 957
vortex *rotation* 312
agitation 315
river 348
danger 667
vorticist 556
votary
auxiliary 711
devotee 865
vote 535, 609
– for 488
voting machine 553
votis, hoc erat in – 865
votive 768
– offering 990
vouch *assert* 535
– for 467
voucher
evidence 467
indication 550
security 771
payment 807
vouchsafe
permit 760
consent 762
ask 765
condescend 879
vow *affirmation* 535
promise 768
worship 990
take –s 995
vowel 561
vox:
– faucibus hæsit
voiceless 581
fear 860
wonder 870
– populi
assent 488
publication 531
choice 609
– et praeterea nihil
unsubstantial 4
powerless 158
unmeaning 517
vain 880
boasting 884
voyage 267
voyager 268
vraisemblance 472
vue d'oeil, à – 132, 446
Vulcan 690, 979
vulgar *inelegant* 579
low born 876
– tongue 560
vulgarian 851
vulgarity
want of refinement 851
Vulgate 985
vulgus, ignobile – 876
vulnerable 665
vulnerary 662
vulnus:
æternum servans sub pectore – 919
immedicabile – 619
vulpine 702
vulture 739, 913

W

wabble *slow* 275
oscillate 314
wad 263
wadding *lining* 224
stopper 263
soft 324
waddle 275
wade 267
– in blood 361
– through
learn 539
exertion 686
waddle 314
wafer *cement* 45
thin 203
lamina 204
waft *transfer* 270
blow 349
wafted, be – 267
wag *oscillate* 314
agitate 315
joker 844
– on *journey* 266
progression 282
wage war 722
wager 621
– of battle 722
– of law 467
wages 973
waggery *wit* 842
waggish 836, 853
waggle 314, 315
wagon 272
wagoner 268
wagonette 272
wagon-load 31
waif 618, 782
waifs and estrays 73, 268
wail 412, 839
wain 272
wainscot 211, 224
waist 203
waistcoat 225
put in a strait – 751
wait 133, 681
lie in – for 530
– for 507
– impatiently 133
– on *accompany* 88
aid 707
– to see how the wind blows 607
– upon *serve* 746
call on 894
waiter *servant* 746
– on Providence
neglect 460
inactive 683
content 831
waiting 507
be kept – 133
waiting-maid 746
waitress 746
waits 416
waive *defer* 133
not choose 609*a*
not use 678
waiwode 745
wake *sequel* 65
rear 235
funeral 363
trace 551
excite 824
amusement 840
in the – of 281
enough to – the dead 404
– the thoughts 457
– up 824
wakeful
careful 459
active 682
Walhalla 981
walk *region* 181
lane 189
move 266
business 625
way 627
conduct 692
arena 728
– one's chalks 293, 623
– the earth 250
– of life 625
–ed off one's legs 688
– off with 791
– over the course 705, 731
– in the shoes of 19
walker 268
walking gentleman 599
wall *vertical* 212
parietes 224
inclosure 232
refuge 666
obstacle 706
defence 717
prison 752
driven to the – 704
go to the –
destruction 162
die 360
fail 732
pushed to the – 601
take the – 873, 878
wooden –s 726
–eyed 442
– in 229, 751
wallah 746
wallet 191
wallop 315
wallow *low* 207
plunge 310
rotate 312
– in 377, 641
– in the mire 653
– in riches 803
– in voluptuousness 954
wallsend 388
Wall-street 799
– slang 563
waltz 415, 840
wamble
vacillate 149
oscillate 314
dislike 867
wampum 800
wan 429, 837
wand *scepter* 747
magic 993
wave a – 992
wander *move* 264
journey 266
deviate 279
delirium 503
the attention –s 458
wanderer 268
wandering
exceptional 83
– Jew 268
wane
decrease 36
age 128
contract 195
decay 659
one's star on the – 735
wax and – 140
wangle 943
want
inferiority 34
shortcoming 304
requirement 630
insufficiency 640
poverty 804
desire 865
wanted 187
wanting
incomplete 53
absent 187
imbecile 499
found –
imperfect 651
disapproval 932
guilt 947
wantless 639
wanton
unconformable 83
capricious 608
unrestrained 748
amusement 840
rash 863
impure 961
wapentake 181
war 722
at – 24, 720
at – with 708, 722
declare – 713
man of – 727
seat of 728
– correspondent 534, 593
– of words 588, 720
warble 416
war-cry *alarm* 669
defiance 715
war 722
ward *part* 51
parish 181
safety 664
asylum 666
dependent 746
restraint 751
watch and – 459, 753
– off 706, 717
war-dance 715
warden
guardian 664
master 745
deputy 759
warder
perforator 262
porter 263
guardian 664
keeper 753
wardmote 966
wardrobe 191, 225
ward-room 191
war-drum 417
wardship 664
ware
warning 668
merchandise 798
warehouse 636, 799
warfare 722
discord 713
war-horse 726
warlike 722
warlock 994
warm
violent 173
hot 382
make hot 384
red 434
orange 439
wealthy 803
ardent 821
excited 824
angry 900
irascible 901
flog 972
– bath 386
– the blood 824
– the cockles of the heart 829
– imagination 515
– man 803
– reception
repel 717
welcome 892
– up 658, 660
– work 686
warm-hearted
feeling 821
sensibility 822
friendship 888
benevolence 906
warming 384
warming-pan
locum tenens 147
heater 386
preparation 673
warmth
vigorous language 574
warn *dissuade* 616
caution 668
– off 761
warning *omen* 512
dissuasion 616
caution 668
give – *dismiss* 678
relinquish 782
– voice *alarm* 666
warp *change* 140
tend 176
contract 195
distort 243
navigate 267